**helps you learn the core concepts in psychology!**

The **free** Companion Website for this text includes *Live!Psych*—a series of interactive modules covering psychology's "core concepts." The modules include animation, simulations, audio narration, and quizzes to make learning the core concepts more fun!

Whenever you see (Live! psych) in the margin of your text, go to the Morris 12/e Companion Website at www.prenhall.com/morris and follow three easy steps to access this exciting learning tool:

STEP **1** Click on the number of the chapter you are studying.

STEP **2** Click on (Live! psych) on the left navigation bar.

STEP **3** Click on the name of the module you want to study and start interacting!

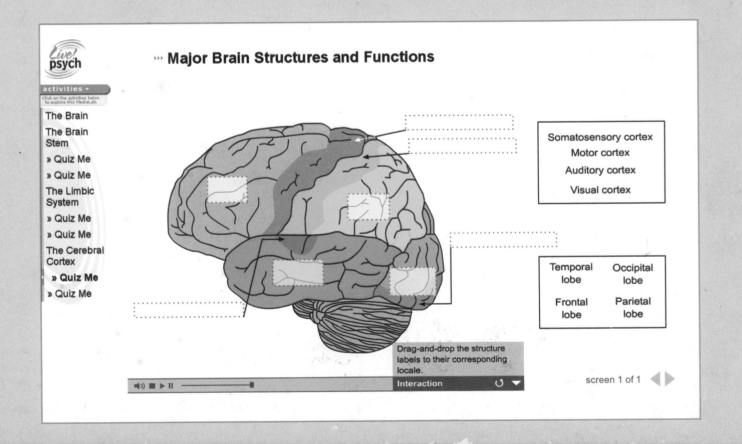

››› **Major Brain Structures and Functions**

activities ▾
Click on the activities below to explore this MediaLab.

The Brain
The Brain Stem
» Quiz Me
» Quiz Me
The Limbic System
» Quiz Me
» Quiz Me
The Cerebral Cortex
» **Quiz Me**
» Quiz Me

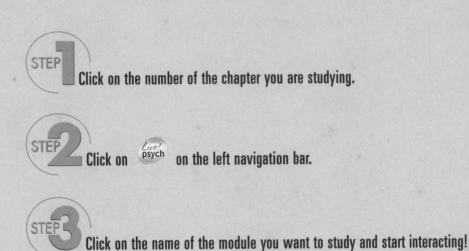

Somatosensory cortex
Motor cortex
Auditory cortex
Visual cortex

| Temporal lobe | Occipital lobe |
| Frontal lobe | Parietal lobe |

Drag-and-drop the structure labels to their corresponding locale.

Interaction

screen 1 of 1

twelfth edition

Psychology
AN INTRODUCTION

CHARLES G. MORRIS
University of Michigan

ALBERT A. MAISTO
University of North Carolina at Charlotte

PEARSON
Prentice
Hall

Upper Saddle River, New Jersey 07458

Library of Congress Cataloging-in-Publication Data

Morris, Charles G.
  Psychology : an introduction / Charles G. Morris, Albert A. Maisto.—12th ed.
    p. cm.
  Includes bibliographical references and indexes.
  ISBN 0-13-189147-2
  1. Psychology—Textbooks.   I. Maisto, Albert A. (Albert Anthony)   II. Title.

  BF121.M598 2005
  150—dc22

                                                    2004000899

Editor in Chief: Leah Jewell
Senior Acquisitions Editor: Jayme Heffler
Sponsoring Editor: Stephanie Johnson
Editorial Assistant: Jennifer M. Conklin
Senior Media Editor: David Nusspickel
Supplements Editor: Kevin Doughton
Development Editor: Carolyn Viola-John
Director of Marketing: Beth Mejia
Executive Marketing Manager: Sheryl Adams
Assistant Managing Editor (Production): Maureen Richardson
Full Service Liaison: Marianne Peters-Riordan
Production Editor: Bruce Hobart/Pine Tree Composition

Manufacturing Buyer: Tricia Kenny
Copyeditor: Amy Jolin
Creative Design Director: Leslie Osher
Interior and Cover Designer: Kathy Mystkowska
Art Production Manager: Guy Ruggiero
Electronic Artist: Mirella Signoretto
Permissions Supervisor: Ronald Fox
Text Permissions Specialist: Tracy Metivier
Image Permissions Coordinator: Craig A. Jones
Photo Researcher: Teri Stratford
Cover Photo: Jean-Francois Podevin/Theispost
Printer/Binder: Courier Companies Inc.

Credits and acknowledgments borrowed from other sources and reproduced, with permission, in this textbook appear on appropriate page within text (or on pages 669–70).

Pearson Education LTD.
Pearson Education Singapore, Pte. Ltd
Pearson Education, Canada, Ltd
Pearson Education-Japan
Pearson Education Australia PTY, Limited

Pearson Education North Asia Ltd
Pearson Educación de Mexico, S.A. de C.V.
Pearson Education Malaysia, Pte. Ltd
Pearson Education, Upper Saddle River, NJ

10 9 8 7 6 5 4 3 2 1
ISBN 0-13-189147-2 (college)
ISBN 0-13-192018-9 (school)

BRIEF CONTENTS

1	The Science of Psychology	2
2	The Biological Basis of Behavior	46
3	Sensation and Perception	92
4	States of Consciousness	144
5	Learning	184
6	Memory	224
7	Cognition and Language	258
8	Intelligence and Mental Abilities	292
9	Motivation and Emotion	328
10	Life Span Development	364
11	Personality	416
12	Stress and Health Psychology	450
13	Psychological Disorders	484
14	Therapies	526
15	Social Psychology	560
APPENDIX A	Measurement and Statistical Methods	598
APPENDIX B	Industrial/Organizational Psychology	610

CONTENTS

SPECIAL FEATURES   ix

PREFACE   xi

ACKNOWLEDGMENTS   xviii

TO THE STUDENT   xx

1 The Science of Psychology   2

WHAT IS PSYCHOLOGY?   4
The Fields of Psychology   4   •   Enduring Issues   8   •   Psychology as Science   9

THE GROWTH OF PSYCHOLOGY   13
The "New Psychology": A Science of the Mind   13   •   Redefining Psychology: The Study of Behavior   16   •   The Cognitive Revolution   18   •   New Directions   19   •   Where are the Women?   21

HUMAN DIVERSITY   24
Gender   25   •   Race and Ethnicity   27   •   Culture   28

RESEARCH METHODS IN PSYCHOLOGY   30
Naturalistic Observation   30   •   Case Studies   31   •   Surveys   31   •   Correlational Research   32   •   Experimental Research   34   •   Multimethod Research   35   The Importance of Sampling   35   •   Ethics and Psychological Research   37

CAREERS IN PSYCHOLOGY   40
Academic and Applied Psychology   41   •   Clinical Settings   41

2 The Biological Basis of Behavior   46

NEURONS: THE MESSENGERS   48
The Neural Impulse   50   •   The Synapse   51   •   Neural Plasticity and Neurogenesis   55

THE CENTRAL NERVOUS SYSTEM   58
The Organization of the Nervous System   58   •   The Brain   59   •   Hemispheric Specialization   65   •   Tools for Studying the Brain   68   •   The Spinal Cord   71

THE PERIPHERAL NERVOUS SYSTEM   73
The Somatic Nervous System   73   •   The Autonomic Nervous System   73

THE ENDOCRINE SYSTEM   76

GENES, EVOLUTION, AND BEHAVIOR   79
Genetics   79   •   Behavior Genetics   80   •   Evolutionary Psychology   84   Social Implications   87

3 Sensation and Perception   92

THE NATURE OF SENSATION   93
The Basic Process   94   •   Sensory Thresholds   95   •   Subliminal Perception   97   Extrasensory Perception   98

VISION   99
The Visual System   100   •   Color Vision   104
Theories of Color Vision   105

HEARING   108
Sound   109   •   The Ear   111   •   Theories of
Hearing   112   •   Hearing Disorders   113

THE OTHER SENSES   115
Smell   115   •   Taste   117   •   Kinesthetic and
Vestibular Senses   119   •   Sensations of Motion   120
The Skin Senses   120   •   Pain   121

PERCEPTION   124
Perceptual Organization   125   •   Perceptual
Constancies   126   •   Perceiving Distance and Depth
129   •   Perceiving Movement   133   •   Visual
Illusions   134   •   Observer Characteristics: Individual
Differences and Culture   135

4   States of Consciousness   144

CONSCIOUS EXPERIENCE   146
What Is Waking Consciousness?   146   •   Explaining
Waking Consciousness   147   •   Daydreaming and
Fantasy   148

SLEEP   149
Circadian Cycles: The Biological Clock   151   •   The
Rhythms of Sleep   152   •   Sleep Disorders   154

DREAMS   158
What Do We Dream?   159   •   Why Do We Dream?
159   •   Do We Need to Dream?   161

DRUG-ALTERED CONSCIOUSNESS   162
Substance Use, Abuse, and Dependence   163
Depressants: Alcohol, Barbiturates, and Opiates   165
Stimulants: Caffeine, Nicotine, Amphetamines, and
Cocaine   170   •   Hallucinogens and Marijuana   173
Explaining Abuse and Addiction   175

MEDITATION AND HYPNOSIS   178
Meditation   178   •   Hypnosis   179

5   Learning   184

CLASSICAL CONDITIONING   186
Elements of Classical Conditioning   186   •   Classical
Conditioning in Humans   187   •   Classical
Conditioning Is Selective   190

OPERANT CONDITIONING   193
Elements of Operant Conditioning   193   •   Types of
Reinforcement   194   •   Punishment   195

Operant Conditioning Is Selective   197   •   Superstitious Behavior   198   •   Learned Helplessness   198
Shaping Behaviorial Change Through Biofeedback   199

COMPARING CLASSICAL AND OPERANT
CONDITIONING   201
Response Acquisition   201   •   Extinction and
Spontaneous Recovery   202   •   Generalization and
Discrimination   206   •   New Learning Based on
Original Learning   207   •   Contingencies   208
Summing Up   211

COGNITIVE LEARNING   213
Latent Learning and Cognitive Maps   213   •   Insight
and Learning Sets   214   •   Learning by Observing
216   •   Cognitive Learning in Nonhumans   218

6   Memory   224

THE SENSORY REGISTERS   226
Visual and Auditory Registers   226   •   Attention   227

SHORT-TERM MEMORY   229
Capacity of STM   229   •   Encoding in STM   231
Maintaining STM   231

LONG-TERM MEMORY   232
Capacity of LTM   232   •   Encoding in LTM   232
Serial Position Effect   232   •   Maintaining LTM
233   •   Types of LTM   235

THE BIOLOGY OF MEMORY   239
How Are Memories Formed?   239   •   Where Are
Memories Stored?   240

FORGETTING   242
The Biology of Forgetting   242   •   Experience and
Forgetting   243   •   How to Reduce Forgetting   246

SPECIAL TOPICS IN MEMORY   249
Autobiographical Memory   249   •   Childhood
Amnesia   250   •   Extraordinary Memory   250
Flashbulb Memories   251   •   Eyewitness Testimony   252
Recovered Memories   253   •   Cultural Influences
on Memory   254

7   Cognition and Language   258

THE BUILDING BLOCKS OF THOUGHT   260
Language   260   •   The Structure of Language   260
Images   261   •   Concepts   262

LANGUAGE, THOUGHT, AND CULTURE   265
Language and Cognition   265   •   Is Our
Language Male-dominated?   266   •   Culture and
Cognition   267

NONHUMAN THOUGHT AND LANGUAGE   268
Animal Cognition   268   •   The Question of
Language   270

PROBLEM SOLVING   273
The Interpretation of Problems   274   •   Producing
Strategies and Evaluating Progress   275   •   Obstacles
to Solving Problems   277   •   Experience and
Expertise   280

DECISION MAKING   281
Logical Decision Making   282   •   Decision-Making
Heuristics   282   •   Framing   284   •   Decisions
Under Pressure   284   •   Explaining Our
Decisions   285

8   Intelligence and Mental Abilities   292

THEORIES OF INTELLIGENCE   295
Early Theories: Spearman, Thurstone and Cattell   295
Contemporary Theories: Sternberg, Gardner, and
Goleman   297   •   Comparing the Theories   298

INTELLIGENCE TESTS   300
The Stanford-Binet Intelligence Scale   300
The Wechsler Intelligence Scales   301   •   Group Tests
302   •   Performance and Culture-Fair Tests   303

WHAT MAKES A GOOD TEST?   304
Reliability   304   •   Validity   306   •   Criticisms
of Intelligence Tests   307

WHAT DETERMINES INTELLIGENCE?   310
Heredity   310   •   Environment   311   •   Heredity
vs. Environment: Which Is More Important?   314

MENTAL ABILITIES AND HUMAN DIVERSITY   315
Gender   315   •   Culture   316

EXTREMES OF INTELLIGENCE   319
Mental Retardation   319   •   Giftedness   320

CREATIVITY   322
Creativity and Intelligence   322   •   Creativity
Tests   323

9   Motivation and Emotion   328

PERSPECTIVES ON MOTIVATION   330
Instincts   330   •   Drive-Reduction Theory   330
Arousal Theory   330   •   Intrinsic and Extrinsic
Motivation   332

HUNGER AND THIRST   333
Biological Factors   333   •   Cultural and

Environmental Factors   335   •   Eating Disorders and
Obesity   335   •   Thirst   339

SEX   340
Sexual Motivation   340   •   Sexual Behavior   341
Sexual Orientation   342

OTHER MOTIVES   343
Exploration and Curiosity   344   •   Manipulation and
Contact   344   •   Aggression   345   •   Achievement
347   •   Affiliation   348   •   A Hierarchy of Motives
348

EMOTIONS   350
Basic Emotions   350   •   Theories of Emotion   352

NONVERBAL COMMUNICATION OF EMOTION
356
Voice Quality   356   •   Facial Expression   356
Body Language   356   •   Personal Space   357
Explicit Acts   357

GENDER, CULTURE, AND EMOTION   358
Gender and Emotion   358

10   Life Span Development   364

METHODS IN DEVELOPMENTAL PSYCHOLOGY
366

PRENATAL DEVELOPMENT   368

THE NEWBORN BABY   369
Reflexes   370   •   Temperament   370   •   Perceptual
Abilities   371

INFANCY AND CHILDHOOD   373
Physical Development   374   •   Motor Development
374   •   Cognitive Development   376   •   Moral
Development   378   •   Language Development   380
Social Development   382   •   Sex-Role
Development   388   •   Television and Children   389

ADOLESCENCE   391
Physical Changes   392   •   Cognitive Changes   394
Personality and Social Development   394   •
Forming an Identity   395   •   Some Problems of
Adolescence   397

ADULTHOOD   399
Love, Partnerships, and Parenting   399   •   The World
of Work   403   •   Cognitive Changes   404
Personality Changes   405

LATE ADULTHOOD   406
Physical Changes   407   •   Social Development   408
Cognitive Changes   409   •   Facing the End of Life
410

11 Personality   416

PSYCHODYNAMIC THEORIES   418
Sigmund Freud   419   •   Carl Jung   424   •   Alfred Adler   425   •   Karen Horney   426   •   Erik Erikson   427   •   A Psychodynamic View of Jaylene Smith   428   Evaluating Psychodynamic Theories   428

HUMANISTIC PERSONALITY THEORIES   431
Carl Rogers   431   •   A Humanistic View of Jaylene Smith   432   •   Evaluating Humanistic Theories   433

TRAIT THEORIES   433
Development of Trait Theory   433   •   The Big Five   434   •   A Trait View of Jaylene Smith   436   Evaluating Trait Theories   436

COGNITIVE–SOCIAL LEARNING THEORIES   438
Expectancies, Self-Efficacy and Locus of Control   438   A Cognitive–Social Learning View of Jaylene Smith   439   Evaluating Cognitive–Social Learning Theories   439

PERSONALITY ASSESSMENT   441
The Personal Interview   442   •   Direct Observation   442   •   Objective Tests   442   •   Projective Tests   445

12 Stress and Health Psychology   450

SOURCES OF STRESS   452
Life Changes   453   •   Everyday Hassles   453   Stress and Individual Differences   457

COPING WITH STRESS   460
Direct Coping   460   •   Defensive Coping   461   Socioeconomic and Gender Differences   462

STRESS AND HEALTH   464
The Biology of Stress   464   •   Stress and Heart Disease   466   •   Stress and the Immune System   467

STAYING HEALTHY   469
Methods to Reduce Stress   469   •   Adopt a Healthy Life Style   472

EXTREME STRESS   474
Sources of Extreme Stress   474   •   Post-traumatic Stress Disorder   476

THE WELL-ADJUSTED PERSON   479

13 Psychological Disorders   484

PERSPECTIVES ON PSYCHOLOGICAL DISORDERS   485
Historical Views of Psychological Disorders   486   Theories of the Nature, Causes, and Treatment of Psychological Disorders   487   •   Classifying Psychological Disorders   489   •   The Prevalence of Psychological Disorders   490   •   Mental Illness and the Law   491

MOOD DISORDERS   492
Depression   492   •   Mania and Bipolar Disorder   493   Causes of Mood Disorders   495   •   Suicide   496

ANXIETY DISORDERS   498
Specific Phobias   498   •   Panic Disorder   499   Other Anxiety Disorders   499   •   Causes of Anxiety Disorders   500

PSYCHOSOMATIC AND SOMATOFORM DISORDERS   501
Psychosomatic Disorders   502   •   Somatoform Disorders   502   •   Causes of Somatoform Disorders   503

DISSOCIATIVE DISORDERS   504
Dissociative Amnesia   504   •   Dissociative Identity Disorder   505   •   Depersonalization Disorder   505   Causes of Dissociative Disorders   506

SEXUAL DISORDERS   506
Sexual Dysfunction   507   •   Paraphilias   508   Gender-Identity Disorders   509

PERSONALITY DISORDERS   510
Types of Personality Disorders   511   •   Causes of Antisocial Personality Disorder   512

SCHIZOPHRENIC DISORDERS   514
Types of Schizophrenic Disorders   515   •   Causes of Schizophrenia   515

CHILDHOOD DISORDERS   518
Attention-Deficit/Hyperactivity Disorder (AD/HD)   518   Autistic Disorder   519

GENDER AND CULTURAL DIFFERENCES IN PSYCHOLOGICAL DISORDERS   520
Gender Differences   520   •   Cultural Differences   521

14 Therapies   526

INSIGHT THERAPIES   527
Psychoanalysis   527   •   Client-Centered Therapy   529   •   Gestalt Therapy   530   •   Recent Developments   532

BEHAVIOR THERAPIES   533
Using Classical Conditioning Techniques   534   Operant Conditioning   535   •   Modeling   535

COGNITIVE THERAPIES   536
Stress-Inoculation Therapy   537   •   Rational-Emotive Therapy   537   •   Beck's Cognitive Therapy   538

GROUP THERAPIES   539
Family Therapy   539   •   Couple Therapy   540
Self-Help Groups   540

EFFECTIVENESS OF PSYCHOTHERAPY   541
Does Psychotherapy Work?   542   •   Which Type of
Therapy Is Best for Which Disorder?   543

BIOLOGICAL TREATMENTS   546
Drug Therapies   546   •   Electroconvulsive Therapy
549   •   Psychosurgery   549

INSTITUTIONALIZATION AND ITS ALTERNATIVES
551
Deinstitutionalization   551   •   Alternative Forms of
Treatment   552   •   Prevention   553

GENDER AND CULTURAL DIFFERENCES IN
TREATMENTS   554
Gender Differences   554   •   Cultural Differences
555

15 Social Psychology   560

SOCIAL COGNITION   561
Impression Formation   562   •   Attribution   564
Interpersonal Attraction   566

ATTITUDES   571
The Nature of Attitudes   571   •   Prejudice and
Discrimination   572   •   Attitude Change   577

SOCIAL INFLUENCE   581
Cultural Influence   581   •   Cultural Assimilators
581   •   Conformity   582   •   Compliance   584
Obedience   584

SOCIAL ACTION   586
Deindividuation   586   •   Helping Behavior   587
Group Decision Making   590   •   Leadership   591
Organizational Behavior   593

APPENDIX A   MEASUREMENT AND STATISTICAL METHODS   598

APPENDIX B   INDUSTRIAL/ORGANIZATIONAL PSYCHOLOGY   610

GLOSSARY   619   REFERENCES   629

PHOTO CREDITS   669   NAME INDEX   671

SUBJECT INDEX   684

SPECIAL FEATURES

ENDURING ISSUES

Window on the Mind 48	Chapter 2
Neural Plasticity 55	Chapter 2
The Pendulum Swings 79	Chapter 2
Deaf Culture 114	Chapter 3
How Does Ethnicity Influence Perception? 136	Chapter 3
Do Perceptual Experiences Reflect the Outside World? 139	Chapter 3
Women and Alcohol 168	Chapter 4
Is Addiction a Physical Disease? 176	Chapter 4
Classical Conditioning and the Immune System 190	Chapter 5
The Evolutionary Basis of Fear 191	Chapter 5
What Is Punishment? 197	Chapter 5
Human Insight 215	Chapter 5
Effects of Stress on Body and Brain 234	Chapter 6
Memory and Culture 255	Chapter 6
Do We All Think Alike? 265	Chapter 7
Where Does Creativity Come From? 278	Chapter 7
Test Reliability and Changes in Intelligence 305	Chapter 8
Tracking the Future 308	Chapter 8
Not Everyone Wants to Be Special 321	Chapter 8
The Evolutionary Basis of Arousal Seeking 332	Chapter 9
The Hunger Drive 334	Chapter 9
Are Emotions Universal? 351	Chapter 9
Holding Anger In 359	Chapter 9
Different from Birth 370	Chapter 10
Sex-Typed Behavior 389	Chapter 10
The "Change of Life" 405	Chapter 10
Universal Human Archetypes 424	Chapter 11
Is Biology Destiny? 427	Chapter 11
Is Personality Inherited? 434	Chapter 11
How Stable is Personality Over Time? 437	Chapter 11
How Does Personality Interact with Environment? 439	Chapter 11
Coping Strategies 461	Chapter 12
Psychological Stress and Physical Illness 466	Chapter 12
Causes of Mental Disorders 489	Chapter 13
The Chicken or the Egg? 496	Chapter 13
What's Normal? 506	Chapter 13
Are We All Alike? 521	Chapter 13
Combining Drugs and Psychotherapy 549	Chapter 14
On Being Culture Bound 555	Chapter 14
Interpreting Behavior 564	Chapter 15
Does Discrimination Reflect Prejudice? 572	Chapter 15
Social Influence Across Cultures 583	Chapter 15

ON THE CUTTING EDGE

Prescription Privileges for Psychologists 42	Chapter 1
In Search of the Human Genome 81	Chapter 2
Engineering Smarter Mice 85	Chapter 2
Do Humans Communicate with Pheromones? 118	Chapter 3
Most of Us Need More Sleep Than We Get 150	Chapter 4
Classical Eyeblink Conditioning and Clues to Alzheimer's Disease 189	Chapter 5
Storing Emotional Experiences 237	Chapter 6
Culture and Cognition 267	Chapter 7
Biological Measures of Intelligence 302	Chapter 8
How the Brain Reads the Face 357	Chapter 9
The Evolution of Language from a Neuroscience Perspective 383	Chapter 10
The Genetic Basis of Personality Traits 437	Chapter 11
"Tend and Befriend": A Female Response to Stress? 463	Chapter 12
The Neuroscience Revolution 488	Chapter 13
Virtual Therapy 532	Chapter 14
Beauty and Privilege 567	Chapter 15

APPLYING PSYCHOLOGY

Critical Thinking—A Fringe Benefit of Studying Psychology 12	Chapter 1
Can the Brain and Nervous System Repair Themselves? 57	Chapter 2
How Do We See Objects and Shapes? 129	Chapter 3
Coping with Occasional Insomnia 157	Chapter 4
Modifying Your Own Behavior 207	Chapter 5
Improving Your Memory for Textbook Material 248	Chapter 6
Becoming a More Skillful Problem Solver 279	Chapter 7

Intervention Programs: Do They
        Work? 313   Chapter 8
The Slow (but lasting) Fix for Weight
        Gain 338   Chapter 9
Resolving Conflicts in Intimate
        Relationships 401   Chapter 10
Evaluating Your Personality 444   Chapter 11
Recognizing Depression 494   Chapter 13
How to Find Help 545   Chapter 14
Understanding Ethnic Conflict and
        Violence 575   Chapter 15

Types of Memory 236   Chapter 6
Nonhuman Cognition 270   Chapter 7
Solving Problems 280   Chapter 7

THINKING CRITICALLY

Autonomy 21   Chapter 1
The Universal Male 26   Chapter 1
Psychology and Minority Students 28   Chapter 1
Einstein's Brain 67   Chapter 2
Depression 86   Chapter 2
Media Accounts of Research 87   Chapter 2
Advertising and Subconscious Messages 97   Chapter 3
An Ancient Question 110   Chapter 3
Television, Daydreams, and Creativity 147   Chapter 4
Mental Illness and Substance Abuse 163   Chapter 4
Teenage Use of Marijuana 175   Chapter 4
Clinical Applications of Hypnosis 180   Chapter 4
Corporal Punishment 196   Chapter 5
Schedules of Reinforcement 211   Chapter 5
Media Violence and Aggressive
        Behavior 218   Chapter 5
Elaborative Rehearsal 234   Chapter 6

Multiple Intelligences 298   Chapter 8
School Testing 303   Chapter 8
The Flynn effect 314   Chapter 8
Primary Drives 330   Chapter 9
The Sex Drive 340   Chapter 9
Culture and Aggression 345   Chapter 9
Nonverbal Communication of
        Emotion 350   Chapter 9
Television's Effects 390   Chapter 10
Psychoanalysis 428   Chapter 11
Cultural Universals 436   Chapter 11
Projective Tests 445   Chapter 11
Road Rage and You 456   Chapter 12
"Genes Lie Behind Only About 30%
        of Cancers" 466   Chapter 12
Who Is Well Adjusted? 479   Chapter 12
Causation 512   Chapter 13
Genius and Mental Disorders 516   Chapter 13
AD/HD 518   Chapter 13
Survey Results 543   Chapter 14
Access to Mental Health Care 554   Chapter 14
Intimacy and the Internet 569   Chapter 15
Attitudes Toward Smoking 579   Chapter 15
Helping Someone in Distress 588   Chapter 15

PREFACE

Part of the excitement of studying psychology is the fact that our understanding changes rapidly as new research is published and old research is re-examined and re-interpreted. One measure of that change is the fact that more than 400 new references to work published in the years 2001–2003 have been added to this edition. That's one new reference for every two days since the last edition was written! And for every new reference cited in this edition, several dozen others were considered and rejected. Thus the task of capturing recent developments in psychology is an extraordinary challenge, but it is more than made up for by the excitement of discovery and the joy of accomplishment.

At the same time much remains the same in this edition. There is, of course, the wealth of knowledge that forms the foundation on which new knowledge is built. As with previous editions, we have worked hard to make the text accurate, interesting, and understandable. And we continue to focus on three unifying themes which have run throughout every edition of our text: (1) Psychology is a science that is rapidly evolving; (2) human behavior and thought are diverse, varied, and affected by culture; and (3) the study of psychology involves active thinking, questioning, and problem solving.

Psychology Is a Science

We know that our readers value Psychology: An Introduction as a book that "gets it right" and that pares down the voluminous psychological literature to present only the most important research and topics. Every edition of this text has reflected the fact that psychology is the scientific study of behavior and mental processes, and this new edition is no exception. Key topics are presented in a balanced, scientific manner, incorporating both classic studies and the most recent developments. Below is a summary of some of the significant revisions we've made for the twelfth edition.

New or Revised Content

Chapter 1 provides an updated description of the roots of psychology as well as some of the new directions the field has taken in recent years including increased emphasis on evolutionary psychology, positive psychology and diversity. New to this edition is a discussion of prescription privileges for psychologists.

Chapter 2 has been thoroughly reviewed and updated to ensure that it presents the most recent developments in the fast-changing fields of neuroscience and behavioral genetics. The artwork in the chapter, which was completely redrawn for the previous edition, has been further revised for greater clarity with the addition of special captions. The text has been updated to include the latest information on the role of the limbic system, cortical centers for language processing, advances in brain imaging techniques, the effect of hormones on cognition, the status of the Human Genome Project, and the difficulty of teasing apart the effects of heredity and environment.

In Chapter 3, Sensation and Perception, we have expanded the discussion of feature detectors, individual differences in perception of pain, and the effect of pheromones on sexual attractiveness.

Consciousness (Chapter 4) has been expanded significantly to include new material on the biological basis of circadian cycles, more detail on sleep disorders, substance abuse, the effects of alcohol, binge drinking, and sleep deprivation.

Chapter 5, Learning, begins with several new opening vignettes. As always, we use those vignettes later in the chapter to illustrate key principles. We have also added material to the discussion of classical conditioning in humans, the evolutionary basis of fear, conditioned food aversions, learned helplessness, biofeedback and cognitive learning.

In Chapter 6, Memory, we have added material on domain specific working memory, the advantages of dual coding in short term memory, explicit and implicit memory, the biology of memory, and the effect of strong emotions on memories.

In Chapter 7, Cognition and Language, much of the material on problem solving has been rewritten for greater clarity. New material has been added on linguistic determinism, animal cognition, and animal communication.

Chapter 8, Intelligence, contains updated presentations of contemporary theories of intelligence (Sternberg, Gardner, Goleman), new material on the relevance of IQ scores to academic and non-academic success, the effect of extreme malnutrition in infancy on later intelligence, the recent rise in IQ scores ("Flynn Effect"), and mental retardation.

In Chapter 9, Motivation and Emotion, we have expanded the discussion of sensation-seeking and the implications of that research for drive-reduction and arousal theories. We have included recent work on the causes of hunger and muscle dysmorphia. We have greatly expanded the discussion of obesity and weight control as well as sexual motivation and behavior. Primary emotions receive more attention as do happiness and well-being.

Chapter 10, Life Span Development, explores new research on the biological basis of temperament, the effects of different styles of parenting, the importance of peers, cross-cultural research on "storm and stress" in adolescence, adolescent self-esteem and youth violence. We have updated information on marriage, cognitive changes in adulthood and old age, menopause, the biological basis of aging, and health and well-being in later adulthood.

The chapter on Personality (Chapter 11) now includes the discussion of defense mechanisms that in previous editions was contained in Chapter 12. This is a major organizational change that allows us to put that discussion into the context of psychodynamic personality theory and also free up space in Chapter 12 for some of the exciting new work being done in health psychology. We have also updated the discussion of the Big Five trait theory (including new cross-cultural research and a self-rating scale), added new material on the biological basis of personality traits, and rewritten portions of social learning theories for greater clarity. We have also expanded the discussion of the MMPI-II and added a table summarizing the 10 clinical scales of the MMPI-II.

Chapter 12, Stress and Health Psychology, opens with first-hand accounts of the attacks on the World Trade Center which leads to an overview of the concepts of stress and adjustment. Increased attention is given to individual differences in responding to stress (including gender differences), chronic stress and the immune system, and the relationship between religious belief and well-being, A significant addition is a new section on adopting a healthy life style (diet, exercise, smoking, high-risk behaviors) as well as greater attention to post-traumatic stress disorder.

In Chapter 13 (Psychological Disorders), we have updated the data on the prevalence and incidence of disorders. The information on suicide has been updated and an entirely new discussion has been added on the contribution of neuroscience to our understanding of disorders.

Chapter 14 (Therapies) opens with new vignettes that point out the great variety of therapies. New material has been added to the discussions of behavior contracting, self-help groups, the effectiveness of therapies and the move toward eclecticism, the effectiveness of drugs (especially antidepressants), as well as virtual therapy.

Chapter 15 (Social Psychology) includes some new cross-cultural information on the self-serving bias and conformity, as well as updated information on the determinants of attraction, the role of self-persuasion in attitude change, and an entirely new discussion of gender and leadership.

Human Diversity

Over the last decade, the body of research examining issues of diversity has grown rapidly. Thus we continue to expand the consideration of diversity in this textbook, both diversity within the North American population and diversity across cultures worldwide. The twelfth edition includes lengthy discussions of aspects of gender and culture in almost every chapter. In Chapter 1 we have expanded the existing discussion of gender, race and ethnicity, and culture. In Chapter 3 we have given increased attention to individual differences in perception of pain. Chapter 7 includes new material on cross-cultural differences in language and their effect on cognition. Chapter 8 (Intelligence and Mental Abilities) is almost entirely concerned with diversity but we have added new cross-cultural information on the "Flynn Effect." Chapter 9 contains new material on gender, cultural, and environmental factors that affect human sexuality as well as gender differences in eating disorders. Chapter 10 includes an expanded discussion of adolescent "storm and stress" across cultures. Chapter 11 includes new cross-cultural material on the Big Five personality traits. Chapter 12 gives greater attention to individual differences and gender differences in responses to stress. And Chapter 15 has new cross-cultural information on the self-serving bias and conformity and a new discussion of gender differences in leadership styles and effectiveness.

Pedagogy that Encourages Active Thinking, Questioning, and Problem Solving

Throughout every edition of Psychology: An Introduction, we have kept in mind that our final audience consists primarily of college undergraduates. Having taught undergraduates for a combined total of 70 years, we realize that it is essential to make a textbook as accessible and helpful as possible. A successful course in general psychology (or, for that matter, most other disciplines) helps students develop their ability to ask questions, analyze the ideas of others, and ultimately form their own ideas. Teaching active, critical thinking has long been a major objective of the courses we teach and of this text. It remains a basic theme of the twelfth edition, which includes numerous features designed to arouse, engage, and involve students, all based on cognitive research about effective learning from textbooks. The result is that students don't just process lists of unrelated facts, but instead have a cognitive map in which they can conceptualize, better understand, and more effectively relate and recall concepts.

The chapter-opening **Overview** provides students with a road map for each chapter, and then reinforces material for students when major headings reappear. These same major headings in turn provide the structure for the end-of-chapter summary.

Questions at the beginning of each major section of the chapter stimulate interest about the material in that portion of the chapter. Examples of these intriguing, practical questions include: "Why do more car accidents take place at night than during the day?" (Chapter 3); "How many items can most people hold in short-term memory at one time?" (Chapter 6); "Do intelligence test scores predict success in later life?" Chapter 8; "Why do people usually get hungry at meal time?" (Chapter 9); "Do young children think differently from adults?" (Chapter 10); "What are the most effective ways of coping with stress?" (Chapter 12); "When does a normal fear become a phobia?" (Chapter 13); "Are first impressions of other people usually accurate?" (Chapter 15). Each question appears at the beginning of the section in which its answer can be found. Thus these questions serve as advance organizers while at the same time piquing the students' interest in the material.

NEW!   Check Your Understanding quizzes appear at the end of each major section within chapters. These brief quizzes encourage students to review some of the important material in what they have just finished reading and to test their understanding of that material before going on.

Improved!   Many of the **anatomical illustrations** have been enhanced to include "talking graphics," which provide step-by-step explanations to make sure students understand the key concepts. These are found particularly in the areas of neuroscience (chapter 2), sensation (chapter 3), and memory (chapter 6).

NEW!   Applying Psychology boxes help students understand how psychology is relevant in their own lives. For example, "Becoming a More Skillful Problem Solver" (Chapter 7); "Intervention Programs: How Much Can We Boost IQ? " (Chapter 8); "Resolving Conflicts in Intimate Relationships " (Chapter 10); "Recognizing Depression " (Chapter 13); "How to Find Help " (Chapter 14); and "Understanding Ethnic Conflict and Violence " (Chapter 15).

ON THE CUTTING EDGE

THE EVOLUTION OF LANGUAGE FROM A NEUROSCIENCE PERSPECTIVE

Steven Pinker, a cognitive neuroscientist at MIT, has put forth a provocative new theory about the evolution and nature of human language (Pinker, 1994, 1999). Drawing extensively from the fields of linguistics, evolutionary psychology, and neurolinguistics (Jenkins, 2000; Obler & Gjerlow, 1999), Pinker constructs a convincing case that language should not be viewed as a "cultural artifact"—in other words, it is not simply something we learn, like chess or badminton. Neither is it simply a set of

tax, demonstrating competence with linguis she is generally incompetent at recognizing ot symbols, such as religious symbols or traffic s The language instinct, like other instincts, evo natural selection, taking the form of an innate the brain that uses complex computational ceive, organize, and transmit information. It i this adapted circuitry, for instance, that hum dispo

On the Cutting Edge boxes were introduced in the eleventh edition to overwhelmingly favorable responses from our adopters. These boxes highlight the most current research being carried out in psychology, research that may "rock the boat" and dramatically change the way psychologists think. These boxes show students the many fascinating directions in which psychology is going, and underscore the fact that psychology as a science is still in its infancy. New Cutting Edge boxes in this edition include: "Prescription Privileges for Psychologists" (Chapter 1); "In Search of the Human Genome" (Chapter 2); "The Biological Basis of Classical Conditioning May Yield Clue to Alzheimer's Disease" (Chapter 5); "Culture and Cognition" (Chapter 7); and "The Neuroscience Revolution" (Chapter 13).

ations, special techniques s may help you to tie new rmation already in LTM. plest mnemonic techniques nd jingles that we often use tes and other facts. "Thirty ember, April, June, and enables us to recall how in a month. We are also other simple mnemonic we make up words or sen- material to be recalled. We e colors of the visible spec- nge, yellow, green, blue, et—by g their first let-

THINKING CRITICALLY

Female and Male Management Styles

A 5-year study of 2,482 managers in more than 400 organizations found that female and male coworkers say that women make better managers than men (Kass, 1999). The reason seems to be that female managers have added such traditionally "masculine" task-oriented traits as decisiveness, planning, and setting standards to such "feminine" relationship-oriented assets as communication, feedback, and empowering other employees, whereas male managers still rely on an autocratic style that emphasizes individual competition and achievement. Think about your experiences with men and women in leadership positions.

Thinking Critically boxes—Several times in each chapter, this feature holds up a magnifying glass to the topic at hand and asks students to analyze, evaluate, and form a judgment. New Thinking Critically boxes for this edition include: "Autonomy" (Chapter 1) and "Memory Research" (Chapter 6).

nections among neurons increases as does the likelihood that cells will excite one another through electrical discharges, a process known as Long-Term Potentiation (LTP).
In particular, two hormones, epinephrine and cortisol, affect long-term retention.

ENDURING ISSUES   mindbody

Effects of Stress on Body and Brain

Epinephrine secretion is part of the "fight or flight" syndrome (see Chapter 12, Stress and Health Psychology) and has the effect of arousing the organism to action. However, the effect of epinephrine and other stress relat hormones on memory is not merely the result eneral arousal parently th

We believe that an important part of active learning is for students to make connections about the material they are reading. Early in chapter 1, we introduce a set of five **Enduring Issues** that cut across and unite all subfields of psychology: person-situation; heredity-environment; stability-change; diversity-universality; and mind-body. Discussions of these Enduring Issues occur throughout the text wherever appropriate, helping students to form links to content from other chapters and showing the underlying unity of the entire field of psychology. Examples of new Enduring Issues features in this edition include "Sex-Typed Behavior" (Chapter 10); "Is Personality Inherited?" (Chapter 11); and "How Stable Is Personality Over Time?" (Chapter 11).

Within each chapter, **Summary Tables** provide concise reviews of key concepts (for example, defense mechanisms, types of memory, theories of intelligence, theories of personality, neurotransmitters, structures and functions of the brain).

Our detailed **Summaries,** organized by first- and second-level headings, including all the glossary terms highlighted in the chapter, provide excellent review opportunities at the end of each chapter.

New! Integrated Multimedia

Multimedia games might be fun, but what students really need are tools for understanding and retaining the basics. In this edition, we have enhanced the **Companion Website** to provide students with the tools to understand and master the basic concepts of introductory psychology.

Within each chapter of the Companion Website, students will find an exciting new component called *Live!Psych*, which offers highly interactive media simulations, animations, and assessments. All *Live!Psych* modules were created in consultation with psychology instructors and carefully reviewed by a board of experts to ensure accuracy and pedagogical effectiveness. Modules focus on the concepts students find most challenging, such as the major brain structures and functions; neurons and neural impulses; the structures of the human eye and ear; stages of sleep and brainwave patterns; the classical and operant conditioning processes; and many others. *Live!Psych* helps students master these difficult concepts by allowing them to see and experience them in a more interactive format than can be achieved in any textbook. All of the material on the Morris Companion Website, including the *Live!Psych* modules, can be accessed without restriction at www.prenhall.com/morris.

Supplements

It is increasingly true today that, as valuable as a good textbook is, it is still only one element of a comprehensive package. Throughout all twelve editions of this book, Prentice Hall and the authors have labored to produce not only a well-written text but also a full range of supplemental learning tools. The supplements package that accompanies the twelfth edition is the most comprehensive and useful yet.

Print and Media Supplements for Instructors

Instructor's Resource Manual   (0-13-189150-2) by Aaron Bolin, Arkansas State University. Each chapter of the manual contains a Chapter Outline; a list of Learning Objectives which correspond to the exercises in the Study Guide; Lecture Suggestions describing additional topics of interest; suggested Demonstrations and Activities such as class projects and experiments; a description of the Live!Psych activities and suggestions on how to use them in your course; and other Student Assignments including reports and out-of-class exercises. Additionally, each chapter contains a list of the multimedia resources, transparencies, and PowerPoint slides available to accompany the text, plus Handouts for use with the Demonstrations and Activities.

Test Item File (0-13-189151-0) by Gary Piggrem, DeVry Institute of Technology. Contains over 4000 multiple choice, true/false, and essay questions. To facilitate instructors in creating tests, each question is page referenced to the textbook, is described as either factual, conceptual, or applied, and is identified as being new, from the previous edition, or revised. As always, I welcome your comments, suggestions, and teaching feedback on this important ancillary. Send them directly to: Charles G. Morris, Department of Psychology, University of Michigan, Ann Arbor, MI 48109-1109.

Prentice Hall TestGen Software (0-13-189152-9) Available on one dual-platform CD-ROM, this test tenerating software provides instructors "best in class" features in an easy-to-use program. Create tests using the TestGen Wizard and easily select questions with drag-and-drop or point-and-click functionality. Add or modify test questions using the built-in Question Editor and print tests in a variety of formats. The program comes with full technical support.

PH Color Acetate Transparencies (0-13-189149-9) Designed to be used in large lecture settings, this set of over 130 full-color transparencies contains illustrations from the text as well as images from a variety of other sources. Available in acetate form, online at Psychology Central, or on the Instructor's Resource CD-ROM.

PowerPoint Slides Scores of illustrations, figures and graphs from the text have been downloaded and made accessible via the popular PowerPoint program from Microsoft. Instructors can edit or otherwise customize these images and slides and project them onto a screen while delivering lectures or clip them for Web-based learning systems. The PowerPoint slides may be accessed and downloaded from the Morris Companion Website at www.prenhall.com/morris.

Instructor's Resource Center on CD-ROM This valuable, time-saving supplement provides you with an electronic version of teaching resources all in one place so that you may customize your lecture notes and media presentations. This CD-ROM includes electronic files for the Instructor's Resource Manual and the Test Item File, PowerPoint slides, electronic versions of the artwork in the text, electronic versions of the Acetate Transparencies, and all of the animations and simulations from the *Live!Psych* modules.

Psychology Central Web Site at www.prenhall.com/psychology Password protected for instructors' use only, this site gives you online access to all of Prentice Hall's psychology supplements. You'll find a multitude of resources for teaching introductory psychology. From this site, you can download any of the key supplements available for the twelfth edition, including the following: Instructor's Resource Manual, Test Item File, PowerPoint slides, chapter graphics, and electronic versions of the Introductory Psychology Transparencies. Contact your Prentice Hall representative for the User ID and Password to access this site.

FREE On-Line Course Management with WebCT, BlackBoard, or CourseCompass Upon adoption of the text, professors interested in using on-line course management have a choice of options. Each course comes preloaded with text-specific quizzing and testing material and can be fully customized for your course. Contact your local Prentice-Hall representative or visit www.prenhall.com/demo for more information.

Video Resources for Instructors

NEW: Prentice Hall's *Lecture Launcher* Video for Introductory Psychology Adopters can receive this new videotape that includes five- to eight-minute clips covering all major topics in introductory psychology. The videos have been carefully selected from the Films for Humanities and Sciences library, and edited to provide brief and compelling video content for enhancing your lectures. Contact your local representative for a full list of video clips on this tape.

***The Brain* Video Series** Qualified adopters can select videos from this series of eight, one-hour programs that blend interviews with world-famous brain scientists and dramatic reenactments of landmark cases in medical history. Programs include The Enlightened Machine; The Two Brains; Vision and Movement; Madness; Rhythms and Drives; States of Mind; Stress and Emotion; and Learning and Memory. Contact your local representative for more details.

The *Discovering Psychology* Video Series   Qualified adopters can select videos from this series produced in association with the American Psychological Association. The series includes thirteen tapes, each containing two half-hour segments. Contact your local sales representative for a list of videos.

***ABC News* Videos for Introductory Psychology, Series III**   Qualified adopters can obtain this series consisting of segments from the *ABC Nightly News with Peter Jennings, Nightline, 20/20, Prime Time Live,* and *The Health Show.*

***Films for Humanities and Sciences* Video Library**   Qualified adopters can select videos on various topics in psychology from the extensive library of Films for the Humanities and Sciences. Contact your local sales representative for a list of videos.

Print and Media Resources for Students

Study Guide   (0-13-189148-0) by Steve Isonio, Golden West College. Each chapter contains an Overview to introduce students to the chapter; Class Notes Outline with space for students to take notes from the text and during lecture; a Learning Objectives exercise to test students' understanding of the main themes; a multiple choice Pretest and Posttest for gauging students' progress; Short Essay Questions to develop writing skills; Language Support Section for extra support in English; and Flash Cards of vocabulary terms.

***Video Classics in Psychology* CDrom**   Using the power of video to clarify key concepts in the text, this CDrom offers original footage of some of the best-known classic experiments in psychology, including Milgram's obedience study, Watson's Little Albert, Bandura's BoBo doll, Pavlov's dog, Harlow's monkey, and others. In addition, students can see interviews with renowned contributors to the field like B.F. Skinner, Carl Rogers, Erik Erickson, Carl Jung, and others. Each video is preceded by background information on the importance of that experiment or researcher to the field, and is followed by questions that connect the video to concepts presented in the text. The Video Classics CDrom can be packaged free with this text. Please contact your local representative for the package ISBN.

Companion Web Site (www.prenhall.com/morris):   Deanna Riveira has created and selected the resources on Companion Web Site to reinforce students' understanding of the concepts in the text. Students can take online quizzes and get immediate scoring and feedback, use the flashcard feature to review key terms, and much more. An exciting new addition to the website is *Live!Psych*, a series of interactive animations and demonstrations (described below). Access to the Morris Companion Web Site (www.prenhall.com/morris) is free and unrestricted to all students.

***Live!Psych* Activities on the Companion Web Site**   This series of highly interactive media simulations, animations, and activities was developed to teach the key concepts—and often the concepts students find most challenging—crucial to understanding introductory psychology. Designed to encourage students to interact with the material and to appeal to different learning styles, these *Live!Psych* activities were created in consultation with psychology instructors and carefully reviewed by a board of experts to ensure accuracy and pedagogical effectiveness. Each *Live!Psych* activity is integrated into the presentation of the text material throught the use of the *Live!Psych* icon. Chapter-specific *Live!Psych* activities can be found on the Companion Web Site at www.prenhall.com/morris. Special thanks go to Lynne Blesz Vestal, the content author, and to the members of our *Live!Psych* review board: Kim Ainsworth-Darnell (Georgia State University); Eric J. Chudler (University of Washington); Margaret Gatz (University of Southern California); Karen Hoblit (Victoria Community College); Gail Knapp (Mott Community College); John Krantz (Hanover College); Nancy Simpson (Trident Technical College); and Chuck Slem (Cal Poly-San Luis Obispo).

ResearchNavigator Research Navigator features three exclusive databases full of source material, including:

- EBSCO's ContentSelect Academic Journal Database, organized by subject. Each subject contains 50 to 100 of thw leading academic journals by keyword, topic, or multiple topics. Articles include abstract and citation information and can be cut, pasted, e-mailed, or saved for later use.

- *The New York Times* Search-by-Subject One Year Archive, organized by subject and searchable by keyword or multiple keywords. Instructors and students can view the full text of the article.

- Link Library, organized by subject, offers editorially selected "best of the Web" sites. Link Libraries are continually scanned and kept up to date, providing the most relevant and accurate links for research assignments.

To see how this resource works, take a tour at www.researchnavigator.com, or ask your local Prentice Hall representative for more details.

Supplemental Texts

Any one of these texts can be packaged with Psychology: An Introduction, 12th Edition at a reduced price:

Experiencing Psychology by Gary Brannigan (State University of New York at Plattsburgh). This activity book contains thirty-nine active learning experiences corresponding to major topics in psychology to provide students with hands-on experience in "doing" psychology.

Forty Studies That Changed Psychology, Ffith Edition, by Roger Hock (Mendocino College). Presenting the seminal research studies that have shaped modern psychological study, this supplement provides an overview of the research, its findings, and the impact these findings have had on current thinking in the discipline.

How to Think Like a Psychologist: Critical Thinking in Psychology, Second Edition, by Donald McBurney (University of Pittsburgh). This brief paperback supplementary text uses a question-answer format to explore some of the most common questions students ask about psychology.

The Psychology Major: Careers and Strategies for Success by Eric Landrum (Idaho State University), Stephen Davis (Emporia State University), and Terri Landrum (Idaho State University). This 160-page paperback provides valuable information on career options available to psychology majors, tips for improving academic performance, and a guide to the APA style of research reporting.

Acknowledgments

As always, we are indebted to the assistance we received from the people who reviewed this and prior editions. Their thoughtful comments have helped greatly to focus our attention on areas in special need of attention.

Linda Baker, Catawba Valley Community College
Erika Beck, Nevada State College
Chris Crandall, University of Kansas
Jack Culbertson, Edinboro University
Joseph A. Davis, San Diego State University
Kimberley Duff, Cerritos College
Pamela B. Hill, San Antonio College
Richard Howe, College of the Canyons
Susan K. Johnson, University of North Carolina, Charlotte
Stephen Klein, Mississippi State University
Elizabeth McPhaul-Moore, Piedmont Community College
Barbara Lane Radigan, Community College of Allegheny County
Deanna R. Riveira, College of the Canyons
Lori Rosenthal, Emerson College
Wade Rowatt, Baylor University
N. Clayton Silver, University of Nevada, Las Vegas
Emily G. Soltano, Worcester State College
David A. Wittrock, North Dakota State University
Peter Wooldridge, Durham Technical Community College

We are also immensely grateful to the talented team of professionals at Prentice Hall, all of whom made major contributions to this revision. Carolyn Viola-John, our development editor, labored long and hard to oversee the entire revision process and to keep us pointed in the right direction when we began to stray! Rochelle Diogenes, Editor-in-Chief of Development, Maureen Richardson, Assistant Managing Editor for Production, and Bruce Hobart of Pine Tree Composition helped guide this edition through the critical development and production phases. Jayme Heffler, Senior Acquisitions Editor, and Stephanie Johnson, Sponsoring Editor, helped to shape the direction of this revision. Jennifer Conklin provided essential administrative support throughout the project. Leslie Osher, Creative Design Director, and Kathy Mystkowska, Designer, produced an exciting and vibrant new design. David Nusspickel, Senior Media Editor, and Kevin Doughten, Supplements Editor, handled the important task of producing the print and media ancillaries on time and in a quality fashion. And finally, we are indebted to the Prentice Hall sales force, whose professionalism and persistence continue to impress us and our adopters.

Charles G. Morris
Albert A. Maisto

Getting the Most Out of *Psychology: An Introduction*

With 15 chapters on topics from brain physiology to social psychology, this text can appear daunting, but there are tools in it to help you master the material. For example, there is an Applying Psychology feature on page 248, Improving Your Memory for Textbook Material, that will help you to do your best in college. We urge you to read this box first, before you begin.

Study Tools

Every chapter begins with an Overview, a road map to the chapter. Read through the overview to get a sense of the structure and major topics discussed. The Think About It! questions below the overview are designed to stimulate thinking about the material in the chapter. They can help you organize your thoughts in advance. Each question also appears under the text heading for the topic discussed. Brief quizzes called "Check Your Understanding" appear at the end of each major section. Answering these questions will help you review the section you just read before going any further.

As you read, you will find key terms and definitions in the margin. Study them as you go along, rather than waiting until you have finished reading the chapter. In this way, you will be actively learning the important concepts as you go. Focus also on the Summary Tables, which organize concepts in a visual way. After you have read a chapter, read the Summary. See if you can define the key terms that appear there in boldface.

Here's how to use these tools to study efficiently.

Preview the Chapter Previewing prepares you to read information in an organized way. Properly done, it will help you read faster and comprehend better. To preview a

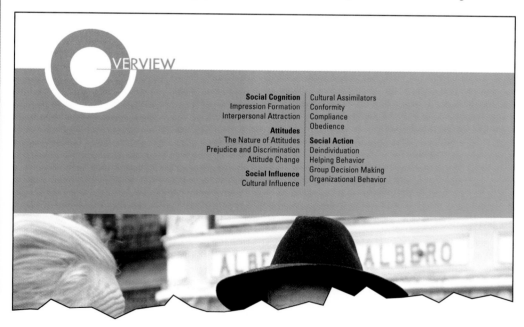

OVERVIEW

Social Cognition	Cultural Assimilators
Impression Formation	Conformity
Interpersonal Attraction	Compliance
	Obedience
Attitudes	
The Nature of Attitudes	**Social Action**
Prejudice and Discrimination	Deindividuation
Attitude Change	Helping Behavior
	Group Decision Making
Social Influence	Organizational Behavior
Cultural Influence	

chapter, read the Overview, the Think About It! questions, the key terms and definitions, and the Summary.

Ask Yourself Questions Ask yourself the Think About It! questions as you read the chapter. This technique stimulates thinking and learning, as you actively search for answers while you read. Also, take a moment to complete the "Check Your Understanding" quizzes at the end of each section, to make sure you understand the material you just read before moving on.

Use the Charts, Graphs, and Photographs In every chapter, charts, graphs, and summary tables will help you to organize information, and photographs will help you visualize concepts.

Study in Chunks Researchers have discovered that we remember the first and last things we learn far better than the material in the middle. Breaking up your studying into many short sessions creates many more beginnings and endings, and it also reduces fatigue.

Take Study Breaks Taking study breaks every 20 to 40 minutes gives your brain the time it needs to process new information. Without this processing time, the brain may lose the information quickly, long before you need to recall it for an exam. Begin with short breaks of about 5–10 minutes each, adding a longer break of about 30 minutes after a couple of hours.

Review Often One of the earliest memory researchers, Hermann Ebbinghaus, discovered that the rate of forgetting is highest during the first hour after learning new information, so it is important to review what you have studied.

CHECK YOUR UNDERSTANDING

1. Which of the following is not a form of meditation?
___ a. Sufism
___ b. TM
___ c. Zen
___ d. Astorism

2. When it first became popular in the eighteenth century, hypnosis was known as
___ a. egotism
___ b. existentialism
___ c. transcendentalism
___ d. Mesmerism

Answers: 1. d, 2. d

The Biology of Memory

Where are short-term memories stored?

Research on the biology of memory focuses mainly on the question, How and where are memories stored? Simple as the question is, it has proved enormously difficult to answer, although considerable progress has been made in the last two decades.

How Are Memories Formed?

Everything you learn is ultimately recorded in the brain in the form of changes in the size, shape, chemical functioning, and connectedness of neurons (Squire & Kandel, 1999). When we learn new things, new connections are formed in the brain; when we review or practice previously learned things, old connections are strengthened. These chemical and structural changes can continue over a period of months or years (Squire, Slater & Chace, 1975), during w... ...mber of connections among neuro... ...reases as do... ...e likeli...

Psychology
AN INTRODUCTION

OVERVIEW

What Is Psychology?
The Fields of Psychology
Enduring Issues
Psychology as Science

The Growth of Psychology
The "New Psychology":
A Science of the Mind
Redefining Psychology:
The Study of Behavior
The Cognitive Revolution

New Directions
Where Are the Women?

Human Diversity
Gender
Race and Ethnicity
Culture

Research Methods in Psychology
Naturalistic Observation
Case Studies
Surveys

Correlational Research
Experimental Research
Multimethod Research
The Importance of Sampling
Ethics and Psychological
Research

Careers in Psychology
Academic and Applied
Psychology
Clinical Settings

The Science of Psychology

1

ey Ramos graduated from Harvard University, magna cum laude, and was accepted by Harvard Medical School—against all odds. Rey grew up in the South Bronx, an urban ghetto where young males are more likely to go to jail than they are to graduate from high school, and where early, violent death is not uncommon. All anyone asked of Rey was that he stay out of trouble and stay alive. As a young boy, he was considered a problem child, out of control. In the eighth grade, Rey's principal told Rey's mother that her son was being expelled and reassigned to a program for students with learning problems.

REY: "My Mom just started crying, you know, in front of him, and I saw that. And I felt ashamed of myself."

Rey entered the ninth grade determined to turn his life around. His math teacher recognized both his change in attitude and his ability in math.

MATH TEACHER: "When he got here, I knew he wasn't joking around anymore. He knew this was it. This was where it starts new."

REY: "And I started feeling good about this one teacher who said good things about me, and that made me feel good."

Rey also excelled in science, but the high school he attended (considered one of the worst in New York City and since shut down) offered little. Rey enrolled in a special science program at a local college and graduated first in his class. It was his biology teacher who first suggested to Rey that he might be "Harvard material."

BIOLOGY TEACHER: "I was trying to push him to believe in himself and do something, because I felt he was incredible."

Rey accepted the challenge. In his Harvard application he wrote, "The four years I invest in Harvard will probably be the most important four years of my life. I will waste no time while I attend Harvard University." True to his word, Rey maintained a 3.4 grade point average, enlisted in ROTC, joined a Latino fraternity, and worked part-time. At graduation, he looked back.

REY: "My father always said you can't change anything; destiny has everything written for you. And I told him no. I rebelled against that, and I told him I was going to make my own destiny, and so far I've never heard him say that line to me again."

After graduating, Rey planned to marry Maiysha, his childhood sweetheart; to enter Harvard Medical School in the fall; and to fulfill his lifelong dream of returning to the South Bronx as a doctor.

THINKABOUTIT

You will find the answers to these questions in the chapter:

1. "Most psychologists study mental and emotional problems and work as psychotherapists." Is this statement true or false?

2. Psychology has a long past but a short history. What do you think this means?

3. Are ethnic minorities underrepresented among psychologists?

4. How do psychologists design experiments?

5. What can you do with a background in psychology or an advanced degree?

Rey Ramos's story is the American Dream. Indeed, he was chosen to represent "The American Spirit" on *NBC Nightly News* (June 13, 1997). How did Rey Ramos escape from the "mean streets" to the Ivy League and a future as a physician? What can psychology tell us about his success story? What does it say about intelligence and motivation in general, and about the many factors that shape who we become?

We begin this chapter by introducing you to the rich and varied field of psychology: the many different topics psychologists study, the enduring issues that underlie all psychological inquiry, the meaning of psychology as a science, and the many ways scientific or critical thinking can help you. Then we look at the growth of psychology, from its beginning as an obscure science of the mind to its current stature, broad scope, and current emphasis on human diversity. Next, we examine the research methods psychologists use to describe, explain, and predict behavior as well as the ethical guidelines psychologists use to balance research goals with concern for human participants and animal subjects. Finally, we look at careers in psychology.

What Is Psychology?

"Most psychologists study mental and emotional problems and work as psychotherapists." Is this statement true or false?

Answering the question "What is psychology?" is not as simple as one might think. Most contemporary psychologists would agree that **psychology** is the science of behavior and mental processes.[1] But this general definition does not capture the breadth, depth, or excitement of the field. Psychologists seek to explain how we perceive, learn, remember, solve problems, communicate, feel, and relate to other people, from birth to death, in intimate relationships and in groups. They attempt to understand, measure, and explain the nature of intelligence, motivation, and personality, as well as individual and group differences. Psychologists may focus on mental and emotional disturbances, personal and social problems, psychotherapy, or improving group morale and intergroup relations.

In the late twentieth century, psychology expanded dramatically. New research technologies, new fields of inquiry, and new approaches to studying behavior and mental processes emerged. These advances led to greater specialization within psychology, more collaboration with other sciences—and the academic equivalent of an identity crisis. As a result, psychology is continually redefining itself (Evans, 1999). Perhaps the best way to introduce psychology is to look at what topics interest psychologists.

The Fields of Psychology

Contemporary psychology is less a single, unified field than "an umbrella for a loose confederation of subdisciplines" (Evans,1999). The American Psychological Association has 53 divisions, representing the major fields of psychological inquiry, as well as specialized research and professional interests (see Table 1–1). Each of the major subfields described here has its own focus and models of behavior and mental processes.

Developmental Psychology Developmental psychologists study human mental and physical growth from the prenatal period through childhood, adolescence, adulthood, and old age. They are interested both in universal patterns of development and in cultural and individual variations. *Child psychologists* focus on infants and children. They are concerned with such issues as whether babies are born with distinct personalities and temperaments, how infants become attached to their parents and caretakers, how children acquire language and develop morals, how and when sex differences in behavior emerge, and how to evaluate changes in the meaning and importance of friendship during childhood. *Adolescent psychologists* specialize in the teenage years including how puberty, changes in relationships with peers and parents, and the search for identity can make this a difficult period for some young people. *Life-span psychologists* focus on the adult years and the different ways

---

[1]Note that we did not define psychology as the science of human behavior and mental processes. Some psychologists study the behavior of other species. And some use other animals as substitutes for human beings in experiments—a topic we will address when we consider the ethics of psychology.

Psychology The scientific study of behavior and mental processes.

Child psychologists study many facets of childhood behavior including play, relating to other children, and creativity.

individuals adjust to partnership and parenting, middle age, retirement, and eventually the prospect of death.

Neuroscience and Physiological Psychology   *Physiological psychologists* and *neuroscientists* investigate the biological basis of human behavior, thoughts, and emotions. In particular, they study the effects of both natural substances that act as chemical messengers, chiefly hormones, and synthetic chemical messengers, including psychoactive medications (such as antidepressants) and "social drugs" (such as alcohol, marijuana, or cocaine). Why do our hearts beat faster when we feel threatened, or why do our palms sweat when we're nervous? They also study how the brain and the nervous system develop, function, and sometimes malfunction. Does the brain stop growing at a certain point, or does it continue to change over some or all of the life span? Are some areas of the brain more active when people work on mathematical problems? Are others more active when people play or listen to music? *Behavioral geneticists* investigate the impact of heredity on both normal and abnormal traits and behavior. To what degree is intelligence hereditary? What about shyness? Do illnesses such as alcoholism and depression run in families? To what extent are differences in the way men and women think, act, and respond to situations rooted in biology?

Experimental Psychology   Experimental psychologists conduct research on basic psychological processes, including learning, memory, sensation, perception, cognition, motivation, and emotion. They are interested in answering such questions as: How do people remember, and what makes them forget? How do we make decisions and solve problems? Do men and women approach complex problems in different ways? Why are some people more motivated than others? Are emotions universal—that is, do people from different cultures experience the same emotions in similar situations? Or do different cultures emphasize some emotions and dismiss or disregard others?

Personality Psychology   Personality psychologists study the differences among individuals in such traits as anxiety, sociability, self-esteem, the need for achievement, and aggressiveness. Psychologists in this field attempt to determine what causes

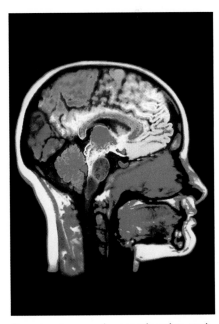

Recent advances in neuroimaging techniques enable physiological psychologists to investigate how specific regions of the brain are involved in complex behaviors and mental processes.

table ¹⁻¹ AMERICAN PSYCHOLOGICAL ASSOCIATION DIVISIONS (2003)

The two major organizations of psychologists in the United States are the American Psychological Association (APA), founded over 100 years ago, and the American Psychological Society (APS), founded in 1988. Members of both groups work in a wide variety of areas. The following list of divisions of the APA reflects the enormous diversity of the field of psychology.

Division*

1. General Psychology
2. Society for the Teaching of Psychology
3. Experimental Psychology
5. Evaluation, Measurement, and Statistics
6. Behavioral Neuroscience and Comparative Psychology
7. Developmental Psychology
8. Society for Personality and Social Psychology
9. Society for the Psychological Study of Social Issues (SPSSI)
10. Psychology and the Arts
12. Society of Clinical Psychology
13. Consulting Psychology
14. The Society for Industrial and Organizational Psychology
15. Educational Psychology
16. School Psychology
17. Counseling Psychology
18. Psychologists in Public Service
19. Military Psychology
20. Adult Development and Aging
21. Applied Experimental and Engineering Psychology
22. Rehabilitation Psychology
23. Society for Consumer Psychology
24. Theoretical and Philosophical Psychology
25. Experimental Analysis of Behavior
26. History of Psychology
27. Society for Community Research and Action
28. Psychopharmacology and Substance Abuse
29. Psychotherapy
30. Psychological Hypnosis
31. State Psychological Association Affairs
32. Humanistic Psychology
33. Mental Retardation and Developmental Disabilities
34. Population and Environmental Psychology
35. Society for the Psychology of Women
36. Psychology of Religion
37. Child, Youth, and Family Services
38. Health Psychology
39. Psychoanalysis
40. Clinical Neuropsychology
41. American Psychology—Law Society
42. Psychologists in Independent Practice
43. Family Psychology
44. Society for the Psychological Study of Lesbian, Gay, and Bisexual Issues
45. Society for the Psychological Study of Ethnic Minority Issues

table 1-1 AMERICAN PSYCHOLOGICAL
ASSOCIATION DIVISIONS (2003) (Cont.)

Division*
46. Media Psychology
47. Exercise and Sport Psychology
48. Society for the Study of Peace, Conflict, and Violence
49. Group Psychology and Group Psychotherapy
50. Addictions
51. Society for the Psychological Study of Men and Masculinity
52. International Psychology
53. Clinical Child Psychology
54. Society of Pediatric Psychology
55. American Society for the Advancement of Pharmacotherapy

* There are no divisions 4 or 11.

For information on a division, e-mail the APA at division@apa.org, or locate them on the Internet at http://www.apa.org/about/division.html.

Source: American Psychological Association (2003). Divisions of the American Psychological Association. Retrieved April 12, 2003, from the World Wide Web: http://www.apa.org/about/division.html.

some people to be moody and nervous and others to be cheerful and easygoing, and why some people are sedate and cautious whereas others are restless and impulsive. They also study whether there are consistent differences between men and women or members of different racial and cultural groups on such characteristics as sociability, anxiety, and conscientiousness. Ongoing issues for personality psychologists include: Is personality inborn and stable, or is it learned and subject to change? Do different cultures tend to produce different "personality types" (clusters of traits that usually occur together)? What is the best way to assess or measure personality?

Clinical and Counseling Psychology When asked to describe a "psychologist," many people think of a therapist who sees patients (or "clients") in his or her office, a clinic, or a hospital. This popular view is half correct. About half of all psychologists specialize in clinical or counseling psychology. *Clinical psychologists* are primarily interested in the diagnosis, cause, and treatment of psychological disorders. *Counseling psychologists* are primarily concerned with "normal" problems of adjustment that most of us face at some point, such as choosing a career or coping with marital problems. Clinical and counseling psychologists often divide their time between treating patients and conducting research on the causes of psychological disorders and the effectiveness of different types of psychotherapy and counseling.

Social Psychology Social psychologists study how people influence one another. They explore such issues as first impressions and interpersonal attraction; how attitudes are formed, maintained, or changed; prejudice and persuasion; conformity and obedience to authority; and whether people behave differently when they are part of a group or crowd than they would on their own. Although most social psychologists are researchers and theorists, not practitioners, this subfield has given rise to numerous practical applications (Hunt, 1994). The principles of social psychology are in support groups for substance abusers, cancer patients, compulsive gamblers, and other people in crisis; the treatment of family conflict through family (rather than individual) therapy; sensitivity training (aimed, for example, at reducing sexual harassment or combating racial and ethnic prejudice); the use of cooperative rather than competitive methods in classrooms; and programs to give hospital patients and elderly residents of nursing homes more control and decision-making power.

Industrial and Organizational (I/O) Psychology Industrial and organizational (I/O) psychologists are concerned with such practical issues as selecting and training personnel, improving productivity and working conditions, and the impact of computerization and automation on workers. Is it possible to determine in advance who will be an effective salesperson or airline pilot, and who will not? Do organizations tend to operate differently under female or male leadership? Research shows that work groups with high morale usually are more productive than those with low morale; are there specific strategies that managers can use to improve group morale?

This is only a sample of what interests psychologists. New specialties continue to emerge, including *rehabilitation psychology* (the study and application of psychosocial principles on behalf of persons with disabilities); *sports psychology* (the study of psychological factors that improve athletic performance, as well as the effects of exercise on psychological adjustment and general well-being); *forensic psychology* (which includes clinical work in correctional facilities, working as a consultant to trial lawyers, serving as an expert witness in jury trials, and formulating public policy on psychology and the law); *environmental psychology* (the investigation of how natural, constructed, and social surroundings influence people's thinking and behavior); *community psychology* (dedicated to theory, research, and social action at the neighborhood level); and *peace psychology* (the study of the causes and consequences of group conflict, strategies for anticipating and avoiding violent confrontations, and methods for helping victims rebuild their lives after conflicts occur).

ENDURING ISSUES

Given this broad range of careers and interests, what holds psychology together? What do psychologists who study organizations, psychological disorders, memory and cognition, behavioral genetics, or attachment in infants have in common? All psychologists share a common interest in five enduring issues that override their areas of specialization and cut to the core of what it means to be human.

PersonSituation

To what extent is behavior caused by processes that occur inside the person, such as thoughts, emotions, motives, attitudes, values, personality, and genes? In contrast, to what extent is behavior caused or triggered by factors outside the person, such as incentives, cues in the environment, and the presence of other people? Put another way, are we masters of our fate or victims of circumstances? We will encounter these questions most directly in our consideration of behavior genetics, learning, emotion and motivation, personality, and social psychology.

NatureNurture

Is the person we become a product of innate, inborn tendencies, or a reflection of experiences and upbringing? This is the famous "nature versus nurture" debate. For decades, psychologists argued about the degree of influence that heredity or genes versus environment or experience have on thought and behavior. This issue appears in our discussions of behavior genetics, intelligence, development, personality, and abnormal psychology, though it will arise elsewhere as well.

StabilityChange

Are the characteristics we develop in childhood more or less permanent and fixed, or do we change in predictable (and unpredictable) ways over the course of our lives? Is the child "father to the man"? Or can you "teach old dogs new tricks"? Is the self a cognitive construct, a "fictional character" we create to maintain a sense of inner continuity in the face of varied, sometimes unpredictable experiences? Developmental psychologists are especially interested in these questions, as are psychologists who specialize in personality, adjustment, abnormal psychology, and therapy, as well as other areas.

DiversityUniversality

To what extent is every person in certain respects (a) like all other people, (b) like some other people, (c) like no other person? (Adapted from Kluckhohn, Murray, & Schneider, 1961, p. 53.) Human diversity is a central concern for psychologists. Throughout the book we will encounter these questions: Does our understanding apply equally well to every human being? Or does it apply only to men or women, or only to particular racial or ethnic groups or only to particular cultures (especially our own)? Do we perhaps need "different psychologies" to account for the wide diversity of human behaviors?

MindBody

Finally, how are mind and body connected? Many psychologists are fascinated by the relationship between what we experience (such as thoughts and feelings) and biological processes (such as activity in the nervous system). This mind-body issue will arise most clearly in our discussions of the biological basis of behavior, sensation and perception, altered states of consciousness, emotion and motivation, adjustment/health psychology, and disorders/therapy.

These five issues have been a running theme in the history of psychology—and will be a running theme in this book. Depending on the times and the intellectual climate, one or another of these issues has assumed special prominence in the history of psychology. Depending on what subject they are studying, psychologists in one area or one school may emphasize the person or the situation, heredity or environment, stability or change, diversity or universality, or subjective experience or biological processes. While philosophers have pondered these issues for centuries, psychologists look at these topics through a scientific lens.

Throughout this book, we will highlight the importance of these issues. Several times in each chapter, we will call your attention to the way in which the topic under consideration—whether it is new discoveries about communication within the nervous system, research into how we learn, or the reason that people abuse drugs—is relevant to one of these issues. In this way, we will show the surprising unity and coherence of the diverse and exciting science of psychology.

Psychology as Science

Earlier we defined psychology as the science of behavior and mental processes. The key word in this definition is *science*. Psychologists rely on the **scientific method** when seeking to answer questions. They collect data through careful, systematic observation; attempt to explain what they have observed by developing theories; make new predictions based on those theories; and then systematically test those predictions through additional observations and experiments to determine whether they are correct. Thus, like all scientists, psychologists use the

Scientific method An approach to knowledge that relies on collecting data, generating a theory to explain the data, producing testable hypotheses based on the theory, and testing those hypotheses empirically.

Theory Systematic explanation of a phenomenon; it organizes known facts, allows us to predict new facts, and permits us to exercise a degree of control over the phenomenon.

Hypotheses Specific, testable predictions derived from a theory.

scientific method to *describe, understand, predict,* and eventually, achieve some measure of *control* over what they study. (The scientific method is not for scientists only; see *Applying Psychology: Critical Thinking—A Fringe Benefit of Studying Psychology.*)

Take, for example, the issue of males, females, and aggression. Many people believe that males are naturally more aggressive than females. Others contend that boys learn to be aggressive because our society and culture encourages—indeed requires—males to be combative, even violent. How would psychologists approach this issue? First, they would want to find out whether men and women *actually* differ in aggressive behavior. A number of research studies have addressed this question, and the evidence seems conclusive: Males are more aggressive than females, particularly when we're talking about physical aggression (Knight, Fabes, & Higgins, 1996; Wright, 1994). Perhaps girls and women make nasty remarks or yell, but boys and men are far more likely to fight. Having established that there are sex differences in physical aggression and described those differences, the next step is to explain them. A number of explanations are possible. Physiological psychologists would probably ascribe these differences to genetics or body chemistry; developmental psychologists might look to the ways a child is taught to behave "like a boy" or "like a girl"; and social psychologists might explain the differences in terms of cultural norms, which both require males to "stand up for themselves" and teach that physical aggression isn't "feminine."

Each of these explanations stands as a **theory** about the causes of sex differences in aggression; each attempts to distill a few principles from a large number of facts. And each theory allows us to make a number of new **hypotheses,** or predictions, about the phenomenon in question. If gender differences in aggression arise because males have higher levels of testosterone than females do, then we would predict that extremely violent men should have higher levels of testosterone than do men who are generally nonviolent. If sex differences in aggression stem from early training, then we would predict that there should be fewer sex

Males seem to be more physically aggressive than females. Different schools of psychology have different explanations for why this is the case.

differences in aggression in families where parents did not stress gender differences. Finally, if sex differences in aggression reflect cultural norms, then we would predict that in societies that do not prohibit girls and women from fighting, or those that consider physical aggression abnormal or improper for *both* sexes, the differences should be small.

Each of these predictions or hypotheses can be tested through research, and the results should indicate whether one theory is better than another at accounting for known facts and predicting new facts. If one or more of the theories is supported by research evidence, it should be possible to control aggressive behavior to a greater degree than was possible before. For example, if cultural norms are part of the reason for differences in aggression, then these differences should be smaller in situations where individuals do not feel that they are being evaluated in terms of their masculinity or femininity. One research team tested this hypothesis with a computer war game (Lightdale & Prentice, 1994). When the researcher introduced participants in a way that made clear who was male or female, women played less aggressively than men; when told that they were anonymous to the researchers and other participants, however, women played just as aggressively as men did.

CHECK YOUR UNDERSTANDING

1. If you choose to become a developmental psychologist, your studies will focus on
___ a. an individual's personality traits such as cheerfulness or moodiness
___ b. the biological basis of behavior
___ c. people's lifespans, from prenatal to old age
___ d. behavioral disorders

2. You design an experiment to test whether the members of Alcoholics Anonymous who volunteer to become sponsors remain sober longer than those who don't volunteer. You are most likely a
___ a. sports psychologist
___ b. personality psychologist
___ c. neuroscientist
___ d. social psychologist

3. "How do people remember?" and "What makes people forget?" are questions typically asked by a(an)
___ a. personality psychologist
___ b. experimental psychologist
___ c. organizational psychologist
___ d. forensic psychologist

4. When a psychologist uses the scientific method, she or he
___ a. collects data through careful observation
___ b. explains observations by developing theories
___ c. makes and tests predictions
___ d. all of the above

Answers: 1.c, 2.d, 3.b, 4.d

APPLYING PSYCHOLOGY

CRITICAL THINKING—A FRINGE BENEFIT OF STUDYING PSYCHOLOGY

- Gifted children are less well adjusted than other children.

- Opposites attract.

- Subliminal messages on self-help audiotapes have beneficial effects.

Do you agree with these statements? Many people answer "yes" without a moment's hesitation, on the grounds that "everybody knows that." Critical thinkers, however, question common knowledge.

What exactly is critical thinking? It is the process of examining the information we have and then, based on this inquiry, making judgments and decisions. When we think critically, we define problems, examine evidence, analyze assumptions, consider alternatives, and ultimately find reasons to support or reject an argument. To think critically, you must adopt a certain state of mind, one characterized by objectivity, caution, a willingness to challenge other people's opinions, and—perhaps most difficult of all—a willingness

"Critical thinkers question common knowledge."

to subject your own deepest beliefs to scrutiny. In other words, you must think like a scientist.

Let's apply critical thinking to the question of whether the second statement above, "Opposites attract," is correct.

1. **Define the problem or the question you are investigating.** Do opposites in fact attract each other?

2. **Collect and examine all the available evidence.** In doing so, be skeptical of people's self-reports, as they may be subjectively biased. If data conflict, try to find more evidence. Research on attraction yields no support for the idea that opposites attract, whereas many studies confirm that people of similar looks, interests, age, family background, religion, values, and attitudes seek each other.

3. **Suggest a theory or a reasonable explanation for the data.** Perhaps people who are similar often belong to the same social circles ("birds of a feather flock together"). Research suggests proximity is a big factor in attraction.

4. **Analyze assumptions.** Perhaps people believe that opposites attract because balancing different people's

Although the plots of many romantic movies and books are built on the idea that opposites attract, psychological research shows that the opposite is true.

strengths and weaknesses is a good way to form a group; they assume incorrectly that therefore it is probably a good basis for personal relationships as well. Or perhaps they believe that since they can think of cases where opposites attract, it must be generally true of personal relationships.

5. **Avoid oversimplifying.** F. Scott Fitzgerald wrote that "the test of a first-rate intelligence is the ability to hold two opposed ideas in mind at the same time." Don't assume that because similarity on some characteristics leads to attraction it will do so for all characteristics. For example, even people of similar temperaments find living together rather difficult in some ways. Living with someone who is as tense as you are may be harder than living with someone of calm temperament—your opposite.

6. **Draw conclusions carefully.** It seems safe to conclude that, in general, opposites don't attract, but be alert to the possibility that there are situations and relationships in which this general rule will not apply. Moreover, it may apply more to some cultures and societies than to others.

7. **Consider every alternative interpretation.** Although it may indeed be true that people who are similar often belong to the same social circles and that is a reason for their mutual attraction, realize that there may be other and better explanations for their attraction.

8. **Recognize the relevance of research to events and situations.** Many people, including quite a few introductory psychology students, view psychology as nothing more than common sense "dressed up" with fancy jargon. But in fact, psychology is based on data resulting from carefully designed research—data that often contradict common knowledge. Research shows that the psychology course you are taking, and those that follow, will sharpen your own critical-thinking skills (Lehman, Lempert, & Nisbett, 1988; Nisbett et al., 1987). Whenever you are trying to explain behavior, ask "What is the research evidence?" and realize that it may contradict your own experiences and common knowledge.

Throughout this book we will offer you the opportunity to develop and refine your own critical-thinking skills by asking you to evaluate research studies, reflect on what you read, and consider alternative explanations. By the way, psychological research has demonstrated that the other two statements at the beginning of this section are also false.

The Growth of Psychology

Psychology has a long past but a short history. What do you think this means?

Since the time of Plato and Aristotle, people have wondered about human behavior and mental processes. But not until the late 1800s did they begin to apply the scientific method to questions that had puzzled philosophers for centuries. Only then did psychology come into being as a formal, scientific discipline separate from philosophy, and the foundations of the "new psychology"—the science of psychology—were laid.

The "New Psychology": A Science of the Mind

The history of psychology can be divided into three main stages: the emergence of a science of the mind, the behaviorist decades, and the "cognitive revolution."

Wilhelm Wundt and Edward Bradford Titchener: Voluntarism and Structuralism   By general agreement, psychology was born in 1879, the year Wilhelm Wundt founded the first psychological laboratory at the University of Leipzig in Germany. In the public eye, a laboratory identified a field of inquiry as "science" (Benjamin, 2000). At the outset, Wundt did not attract much attention; only four students attended his first lecture. By the mid-1890s, however, his classes were filled to capacity.

Wundt set about trying to explain immediate experience and to develop ways to study it scientifically, though he also believed that some mental processes could not be studied through scientific experiments (Blumenthal, 1975). Wundt gave a central place to selective attention—the process by which we determine what we are going to attend to at any given moment. For Wundt, attention is actively controlled by intentions and motives, which gave rise to his use of the term *voluntarism* in describing his view of psychology; it is this that sets human attention apart from attention in other organisms. In turn, attention controls other psychological processes, such as perceptions, thoughts, and memories. We will examine the role of attention more closely in Chapter 4 (States of Consciousness) and Chapter 6 (Memory), but for the moment it is sufficient to note that in establishing a laboratory and insisting on measurement and experimentation, Wundt moved psychology out of the realm of philosophy into the world of science (Benjamin, 2000).

One important product of the Leipzig lab was its students, who carried the new, scientific psychology to universities in other countries, including the United States. G. Stanley Hall, who established the first American psychology laboratory at Johns Hopkins University in 1883, studied with Wundt; so did J. McK. Cattell, the first American to be called a "professor of psychology" (at the University of Pennsylvania in 1888). Yet another student, British-born Edward Bradford Titchener, went to Cornell University. Titchener's ideas in many respects differed sharply from those of his mentor (Zehr, 2000). Titchener was impressed by recent advances in chemistry and physics, achieved by analyzing complex compounds (molecules) in terms of their basic elements (atoms). Similarly, Titchener reasoned, psychologists should analyze complex experiences in terms of their simplest components. For example, when people look at a banana they immediately think, "Here is a fruit, something to eat." But this perception is based on associations with past experience; Titchener looked for the most fundamental elements, or "atoms," of thought.

Titchener broke consciousness down into three basic elements: physical sensations (what we see), feelings (such as liking or disliking bananas), and images (memories of other bananas). Even the most complex thoughts and feelings, he argued, can be reduced to these simple elements. Titchener saw psychology's role as identifying these elements and showing how they can be combined and integrated—an approach known as **structuralism**. Although the structuralist school of psychology was relatively short-lived and has had little long-term effect, the study of perception and sensation continues to be very much a part of contemporary psychology (see Chapter 3, Sensation and Perception).

William James: Functionalism One of the first academics to challenge structuralism was an American, William James (son of the transcendentalist philosopher Henry James, Sr., and brother of novelist Henry James). As a young man, James earned a degree in physiology and studied philosophy on his own, unable to decide which interested him most. In psychology he found the link between the two. In 1875, James offered a class in psychology at Harvard. He later commented that the first lecture he ever heard on the subject was his own.

James held that Titchener's "atoms of experience"—pure sensations without associations—simply do not exist in real-life experience. "No one," he wrote, "ever had a simple sensation by itself." Our minds are constantly weaving associations, revising experience, starting, stopping, and jumping back and forth in time. Perceptions, emotions, and images cannot be separated, James argued; consciousness flows in a continuous stream. James was greatly influenced by Charles Darwin's theory of evolution (see Chapter 2, The Biological Basis of Behavior). According to Darwin, both anatomy and behavior are the result of natural selection. It seemed clear to James that consciousness evolved because it performs an adaptive function. If we could not recognize a banana, we would have to figure out what it was each

Structuralism School of psychology that stressed the basic units of experience and the combinations in which they occur.

time we saw one. Mental associations allow us to benefit from previous experience. When we get up in the morning, get dressed, open the door, and walk down the street, we don't have to think about what we are doing; we act out of habit. James suggested that when we repeat something, our nervous systems are changed so that each repetition is easier than the last.

James developed a **functionalist theory** of mental processes and behavior that raised questions about learning, the complexities of mental life, the impact of experience on the brain, and humankind's place in the natural world. Many of these ideas still seem current today. Although impatient with experiments, James shared Wundt and Titchener's belief that the goal of psychology was to analyze experience. Wundt was not impressed. After reading James's *The Principles of Psychology* (1890), he commented, "It is literature, it is beautiful, but it is not psychology" (in Hunt, 1994, p. 139).

Sigmund Freud: Psychodynamic Psychology   Of all psychology's pioneers, Sigmund Freud is by far the best known—and the most controversial. A medical doctor, unlike the other figures we have introduced, Freud was fascinated by the central nervous system. He spent many years conducting research in the physiology laboratory of the University of Vienna and only reluctantly became a practicing physician. After a trip to Paris, where he studied with a neurologist who was using hypnosis to treat nervous disorders, Freud established a private practice in Vienna. His work with patients convinced him that many nervous ailments are psychological rather than physiological in origin. Freud's clinical observations led him to develop a comprehensive theory of mental life that differed radically from the views of his predecessors.

Freud held that human beings are not as rational as they imagine and that "free will," which was so important to Wundt, is largely an illusion. Rather, we are motivated by unconscious instincts and urges that are not available to the rational, conscious part of our mind. Other psychologists had referred to the unconscious in passing, as a dusty warehouse of old experiences and information we could retrieve as needed. In contrast, Freud saw the unconscious as a dynamic cauldron of primitive sexual and aggressive drives, forbidden desires, nameless fears and wishes, and traumatic childhood memories. Although repressed (or hidden from awareness), unconscious impulses press on the conscious mind and find expression in disguised or altered form, including dreams, mannerisms, slips of the tongue, and symptoms of mental illness, as well as in socially acceptable pursuits such as art and literature. To uncover the unconscious, Freud developed a technique, *psychoanalysis*, in which the patient lies on a couch, recounts dreams, and says whatever comes to mind (free association).

Freud's **psychodynamic theory** was as controversial at the turn of the century as Darwin's theory of evolution had been 25 years earlier. Many of Freud's Victorian contemporaries were shocked, not only by his emphasis on sexuality, but also by his suggestion that we are often unaware of our true motives and thus are not entirely in control of our thoughts and behavior. Conversely, members of the medical community in Vienna at that time generally held Freud's new theory in high regard, nominating him for the position of *Professor Extraordinarious* at the University of Vienna (Esterson, 2002). Freud's lectures and writings attracted considerable attention in the United States as well as in Europe; he had a profound impact on the arts and philosophy, as well as on psychology. However, Freud's theories and methods continue to inspire heated debate.

Psychodynamic theory, as expanded and revised by Freud's colleagues and successors, laid the foundation for the study of personality and psychological disorders, as we will discuss later in this book (Chapters 11, 13, and 14). His revolutionary notion of the unconscious and his portrayal of human beings as constantly at war

Functionalist theory Theory of mental life and behavior that is concerned with how an organism uses its perceptual abilities to function in its environment.

Psychodynamic theories Personality theories contending that behavior results from psychological forces that interact within the individual, often outside conscious awareness.

Sigmund Freud

Behaviorism School of psychology that studies only observable and measurable behavior.

with themselves are taken for granted today, at least in literary and artistic circles. Freud's theories were never totally accepted by mainstream psychology, however, and in recent decades his influence on clinical psychology and psychotherapy has declined (Robins, Gosling, & Craik, 1999; see also Westen, 1998a).

Redefining Psychology: The Study of Behavior

Up to the beginning of the twentieth century, psychology saw itself as the study of mental processes that may be conscious or unconscious (psychodynamic psychology), viewed as discrete units and compounds (structuralism), or as an ever-changing flow (functionalism). The primary method of collecting data was introspection or self-observation in a laboratory or on an analyst's couch. Then, a new generation of psychologists rebelled against this "soft" approach. The leader of the challenge was the American psychologist John B. Watson.

John B. Watson: Behaviorism   John B. Watson argued that the whole idea of mental life was superstition, a relic left over from the Middle Ages. In "Psychology as a Behaviorist Views It" (1913), Watson contended that you cannot see or even define consciousness any more than you can observe a soul. And if you cannot locate or measure something, it cannot be the object of scientific study. For Watson, psychology was the study of observable, measurable behavior—and nothing more.

Watson's view of psychology, known as **behaviorism,** was based on the work of the Russian physiologist Ivan Pavlov, who had won a Nobel Prize for his research on digestion. In the course of his experiments, Pavlov noticed that the dogs in his laboratory began to salivate as soon as they heard their feeder coming, even before they could see their dinner. He decided to find out whether salivation, an automatic reflex, could be shaped by learning. He began by repeatedly pairing the sound of a buzzer with the presence of food. The next step was to observe what happened when the buzzer was sounded without introducing food. This experiment clearly demonstrated what Pavlov had noticed incidentally: after repeated pairings, the dogs salivated in response to the buzzer alone. Pavlov called this simple form of training *conditioning*. Thus a new school of psychology was inspired by a casual observation followed by rigorous experiments.

Watson came to believe that all mental experiences—thinking, feeling, awareness of self—are nothing more than physiological changes in response to accumulated experiences of conditioning. An infant, he argued, is a *tabula rasa* (Latin for "blank slate") on which experience may write virtually anything:

> Give me a dozen healthy infants, well-formed, and my own specialized world to bring them up in, and I'll guarantee to take any one at random and train him to become any type of specialist I might select—doctor, lawyer, artist, merchant chief and, yes, even beggar man, and thief, regardless of his talents, penchants, tendencies, abilities, vocations, and race. (Watson, 1924, p. 104)

Watson attempted to demonstrate that all psychological phenomena—even Freud's unconscious motivations—are the result of conditioning (Rilling, 2000). In one of the most infamous experiments in psychology's history, Watson attempted to create a conditioned fear response in an 11-month-old boy. "Little Albert" was a secure, happy baby who enjoyed new places and experiences. On his first visit to Watson's laboratory, Albert was delighted by a tame, furry white rat, but he became visibly frightened when Watson banged a steel bar with a hammer just behind the infant's head. On his second visit, Watson placed the rat near Albert, and the moment the baby reached out and touched it, he banged the hammer. After half a dozen pairings, little Albert began crying the instant the rat was introduced, without any banging. Further experiments found that Alfred was frightened by anything white and furry—a rabbit, a dog, a sealskin coat, cotton wool, and Watson wearing a Santa Claus mask (Watson & Rayner, 1920). Freud labeled the transfer of emotions from one person or object to another "displacement," a neurotic response that he traced to the unconscious. Drawing on Pavlov, Watson called the same phenomenon *generalization*, a simple matter of conditioning (Rilling, 2000). As far as he was concerned, psychodynamic theory and psychoanalysis were "voodooism."

One of Watson's graduate students, Mary Cover Jones (1924), conducted the Little Albert experiment in reverse. Jones successfully reconditioned a boy to overcome a fear of rabbits (not caused by laboratory conditioning) by presenting the rabbit at a great distance and then gradually bringing it closer while the child was eating. Known as *desensitization*, similar techniques are used by many clinical psychologists today (see Chapter 14, Therapies).

In 1920, a personal scandal forced Watson to resign from his position at Johns Hopkins University. He moved to New York, where he became the resident psychologist with the J. Walter Thompson advertising agency. For some years thereafter, he continued to write popular magazine articles and books on psychology. But the task of refining behaviorism through research fell to others, mainly to B. F. Skinner.

Mary Cover Jones

B. F. Skinner: Behaviorism Revisited   B. F. Skinner became one of the leaders of the behaviorist school of psychology. Like Watson, Skinner fervently believed that the mind, or the brain and nervous system, was a "black box," invisible—and irrelevant—to scientists. Psychologists should concern themselves with what goes into the black box and what comes out, and not worry about what goes on inside (Skinner, 1938, 1987, 1989, 1990). He, too, was primarily interested in changing behavior through conditioning—and in discovering natural laws of behavior in the process.

Skinner added a new element to the behaviorist repertoire: reinforcement. He rewarded his subjects for behaving the way he wanted them to behave. For example, an animal (rats and pigeons were Skinner's favorite subjects) was put into a special cage and allowed to explore. Eventually, the animal reached up and pressed a lever or pecked at a disk on the wall, whereupon a food pellet dropped into the box. Gradually, the animal learned that pressing the bar or pecking at the disk always brought food. Why did the animal learn this? Because the animal was reinforced, or rewarded, for doing so. Skinner thus made the animal an active agent in its own training, a process he called *operant* or *instrumental conditioning*.

Conditioning is not limited to simple learning in nonhuman animals. We can only guess at the vast amount of conditioning that occurs in everyday human life. Why do we feel hungry at meal times, sleepy at bedtime, frightened by rats and snakes, or sexually aroused by a song or scent? These physical urges and private feelings are at least partly the result of conditioning, as are many more complex reactions (see Chapters 5 and 9).

Behaviorism dominated academic psychology in the United States well into the 1960s. One unintended and, at the time, largely unnoticed consequence was that psychology developed an environmental bias: virtually every aspect of human behavior was attributed to learning and experience, and investigating evolutionary influences on behavior, or studying hereditary, genetic influences on individual and groups differences, was considered taboo (Evans, 1999). Behaviorists sought to identify universal principles of learning that transcended species, culture, gender, or age. Whether a researcher conducted experiments with rats or pigeons, monkeys or human beings, infants or adults, did not matter; the same laws of learning applied.

B. F. Skinner

The Cognitive Revolution

In the 1960s, behaviorism began to loosen its grip on the field. On the one hand, research on perception, personality, child development, interpersonal relations, and other topics that behaviorists had ignored raised questions they couldn't readily explain. On the other hand, research in other fields (especially anthropology, linguistics, neurobiology, and computer science) was beginning to shed new light on the workings of the mind. Psychologists came to view behaviorism not as an all-encompassing theory or paradigm but as only one piece of the puzzle (Robins et al., 1999). They began to look *into* the black box and put more emphasis on humans (and other animals) as "sentient"—conscious, perceptive, and alert—beings; as active learners, not passive recipients of life's lessons.

The Precursors: Gestalt and Humanistic Psychology   Not all psychologists had accepted behaviorist doctrines. Two schools that paved the way for the cognitive revolution were Gestalt psychology and humanistic psychology.

During the period that behaviorism reigned supreme in American psychology, a group of psychologists in Germany was attacking structuralism from another direction. Max Wertheimer, Wolfgang Köhler, and Kurt Koffka were all interested in perception, but particularly in certain tricks that the mind plays on itself. For example, when we see a series of still pictures flashed at a constant rate (for example, movies or "moving" neon signs), why do the pictures seem to move?

Phenomena like these launched a new school of thought, **Gestalt psychology.** Roughly translated from German, *Gestalt* means "whole" or "form." When applied to perception, it refers to our tendency to see patterns, to distinguish an object from its background, to complete a picture from a few cues. Like William James, the Gestalt psychologists rejected the attempt to break down perception and thought into their elements. When we look at a tree, we see just that, a tree, not a series of isolated leaves and branches. Gestalt psychology laid the foundation for the modern study of sensation and perception (see Chapter 3) and contributed to the revival of interest in mental (or cognitive) processes.

During the same period, the American psychologist Abraham Maslow, who studied under Gestalt psychologist Max Wertheimer and anthropologist Ruth Benedict, developed a more holistic approach to psychology, in which feelings and yearnings play a key role. Maslow referred to **humanistic psychology** as the "third force"— beyond Freudian theory and behaviorism. Humanistic psychologists emphasize human potential and the importance of love, belonging, self-esteem, self-expression, peak experiences (when one becomes so involved in an activity that self-consciousness fades), and self-actualization (the spontaneity and creativity that result from focusing on problems outside of oneself and looking beyond the boundaries of social conventions). They focus on mental health and well-being, on self-understanding and self-improvement, rather than on mental illness.

Humanistic psychology has made important contributions to the study of motivation and emotions (see Chapter 9), as well as to the subfields of personality and psychotherapy (Chapters 11 and 14). But it has never been totally accepted by mainstream psychology. Because humanistic psychology is interested in questions of meaning, values, and ethics, many people—including its own members—see this school of psychology more as a cultural and spiritual movement than as a branch of science (Rabasca, 2000a). In recent years, however, positive psychologists (introduced below) have begun to reinvestigate some of the questions humanistic psychologists raised a half-century ago (Bohart & Greening, 2001).

The Rise of Cognitive Psychology   In the 1960s, psychology began to come full circle. The field returned from a period in which consciousness was considered to

Gestalt psychology School of psychology that studies how people perceive and experience objects as whole patterns.

Humanistic psychology School of psychology that emphasizes nonverbal experience and altered states of consciousness as a means of realizing one's full human potential.

be inaccessible to scientific inquiry, and psychologists began to investigate and the-orize about the mind—but now with new research methods and behaviorism's com-mitment to objective, empirical research. Even the definition of psychology changed. Psychology is still the study of human behavior, but psychologists' concept of "behavior" has been expanded to include thoughts, feelings, and states of con-sciousness.

The phrase *cognitive revolution* refers to a general shift away from a limited focus on behavior toward a broad interest in mental processes. This new focus holds for both existing and new subfields of psychology. In developmental psychology, for example, the idea that a child is a blank slate, whose development is shaped entirely by his or her environment, was replaced by a new view of babies and children as aware, competent, social beings. In this new view, children actively seek to learn about and make sense of their world. Moreover, all healthy children are "equipped" with such distinctively human characteristics as the ability to acquire language, without formal education, through exposure. Developmental psychology is only one subfield that both contributed to, and benefited from, the emergence of cogni-tive psychology.

Cognitive psychology is the study of our mental processes in the broadest sense: thinking, feeling, learning, remembering, making decisions and judgments, and so on. If the behaviorist model of learning resembled an old-fashioned tele-phone switchboard (a call or stimulus comes in, is relayed along various circuits in the brain, and an answer or response goes out), the cognitive model resembles a high-powered, modern computer. Cognitive psychologists are interested in the ways in which people "process information"—that is, how we acquire information, process or transform bits of information into programs, and use those programs to solve problems.

In contrast to behaviorists, cognitive psychologists believe that mental processes can and should be studied scientifically. Although we cannot observe memories or thoughts directly, we can observe behavior and make inferences about the kinds of cognitive processes that underlie that behavior. For example, we can read a lengthy story to people and then observe the kinds of things they remember from that story, the ways in which their recollections change over time, and the sorts of errors in recall they are prone to make. On the basis of systematic research of this kind, we can gain insight into the cognitive processes underlying human memory. Moreover, with the advent of new brain-imaging techniques (discussed in Chapter 2), cognitive psychologists have begun to address questions about the neurological mechanisms that underlie such cognitive processes as learning, memory, intelligence, and emotion, giving rise to the rapidly expanding field of cognitive neuroscience (D'Esposito, Zarahn, & Aguirre, 1999; Schacter, 1999).

In just a short time, cognitive psychology has had an enormous impact on almost every area of psychology (Sperry, 1988, 1995) and has become the most prominent school in contemporary scientific psychology (Johnson & Erneling, 1997; Robins et al., 1999).

New Directions

During much of the twentieth century, psychology was divided into competing the-oretical schools. Crossing theoretical lines was considered intellectual heresy. Today, psychologists are more flexible in considering the merits of new approaches, combining elements of different perspectives as their interests or research findings dictate, and new theories and initiatives are emerging.

Evolutionary Psychology   As the name indicates, **evolutionary psychology** focuses on the evolutionary origins of behavior patterns and mental processes,

Cognitive psychology School of psy-chology devoted to the study of mental processes in the broadest sense.

Evolutionary psychology An approach to, and subfield of, psychology that is concerned with the evolutionary origins of behaviors and mental processes, their adaptive value, and the purposes they continue to serve.

Given the vast cultural difference between the environment in which humans evolved and the environment in which we live, psychologists disagree on whether evolutionary explanations can provide valid descriptions of our behavior today.

exploring what adaptive value they have or had and what functions they serve or served in our emergence as a distinct species (DeKay & Buss, 1992; Wright, 1994). All of the theoretical views we have discussed so far seek to explain modern humans, or *Homo sapiens.* In contrast, evolutionary psychologists ask "How did human beings get to be the way we are?" They study such diverse topics as perception, language, helping others (altruism), parenting, happiness, sexual attraction and mate selection, jealousy, and violence (Bernhard & Penton-Voak, 2002; Buss, 2000a; Buss & Shackelford, 1997; Caporael, 2001). By studying such phenomena in different species, different habitats, different times, different cultures, and in males and females, evolutionary psychologists seek to understand the basic programs that guide thinking and behavior (Archer, 1996; Buss & Malamuth, 1996; Byrne, 2002; DeKay & Buss, 1992; Scarr, 1993).

Cognitive psychologists tend to see the human mind as a "general purpose" computer that requires software (experience) to process information. In contrast, many evolutionary psychologists see the mind as "hardwired," so that human beings are predisposed to think and act in certain ways (Cosmides, Tooby, & Barkow, 1992; Goode, 2000b; Siegert & Ward, 2002). Further, they contend that these fixed programs evolved hundreds of thousands of years ago when our ancestors lived as hunter-gatherers, and that the problem-solving strategies that benefited early humans may or may not be adaptive in the modern era.

Positive Psychology   Another emerging perspective is **positive psychology,** the view that psychology should devote more attention to "the good life," or the study of subjective feelings of happiness and well-being; the development of such individual traits as intimacy, integrity, leadership, altruism, and wisdom; and what kinds of families, work settings, and communities encourage individuals to flourish (Seligman & Csikszentmihalyi, 2000).

Positive psychologists argue that psychologists have learned a great deal about the origins, diagnosis, and treatment of mental illness but relatively little about the origins and nurturance of mental wellness. We have come to understand a lot about how individuals survive and endure under conditions of extreme adversity, but far less about ordinary human strengths and virtues (Sheldon & King, 2001). We know more about intelligence than about wisdom; more about conformity than about originality; and more about stress than about tranquility. There have been many studies of

Positive psychology An emerging field of psychology that focuses on positive experiences, including subjective well-being, self-determination, the relationship between positive emotions and physical health, and the factors that allow individuals, communities, and societies to flourish.

prejudice and intergroup hostility, for example, but very few about tolerance and intergroup harmony. In recent decades, psychologists have made great strides in understanding the neurology of depression, schizophrenia, and other disorders.

Today's positivists do not argue that psychologists should abandon their role as a science of healing. To the contrary, they support efforts to promote better, more widespread use of what psychologists have learned. But they argue that psychology has reached a point where building positive qualities should receive as much emphasis as repairing damage.

Multiple Perspectives As we noted earlier, contemporary psychologists are less likely than those of previous generations to advocate one theoretical perspective to the exclusion of all others (Friman, Allen, Kerwin, & Larzelere, 1993). Rather, psychologists today tend to see different perspectives as complementary, with each contributing to our understanding of human behavior.

Consider the study of aggression. Psychologists no longer limit their explanations to the behavioral view (aggressive behavior is learned as a consequence of reward and punishment) or to the Freudian perspective (aggression is an expression of unconscious hostility toward a parent). Instead, most contemporary psychologists trace aggression to a number of factors, including long-standing adaptations to the environment (evolutionary psychology) and the influences of culture, gender, and socioeconomic status on how people perceive and interpret events—"That guy is making fun of me" or "She's asking for it"—(cognitive psychology). Likewise, physiological psychologists no longer limit themselves to identifying the genetic and biochemical roots of aggression, instead they study how heredity and the environment *interact*.

Sometimes these theoretical perspectives mesh beautifully, with each one enhancing the others; at other times adherents of one approach challenge their peers, arguing for one viewpoint over all the others. But all psychologists agree that the field advances only with the addition of new evidence to support or challenge existing theories.

Where Are the Women?

As you read the brief history of modern psychology, you may have concluded that the founders of the new discipline were all men. But did psychology really have only fathers and no mothers? If there were women pioneers, why are their names and accomplishments missing from historical accounts?

In fact, psychology has profited from the contributions of women from its beginnings. Women presented papers and joined the national professional association as soon as it was formed in 1892 (Furumoto & Scarborough, 1986). In 1906, James McKeen Cattell published *American Men of Science*, which, despite its title, included a

THINKING CRITICALLY

Autonomy

The January, 2000, edition of the journal *American Psychologist* was dedicated to positive psychology. The issue included two articles on autonomy, or self-determination.

In one, the authors (Ryan & Deci, 2000) conclude that autonomy—freedom to make one's own decisions—is essential to motivation and personal growth. Without options, they argue, people become passive. In the other, the author (Schwartz, 2000) argues that too much freedom of choice is debilitating. Without strong cultural guidelines, people have no way of evaluating their choices and so are more vulnerable to depression.

- Which conclusion do you support? How did you arrive at this view? From personal experience, or from experience in other cultures?

- Play "devil's advocate" in the sense of developing arguments for the view you oppose. What does this exercise teach you?

- In the United States, we tend to assume that everyone should have freedom of choice, and we espouse this view for everyone, in every culture and society. Is our view culturally biased? What kind of research evidence would you need to determine whether your view is in fact correct?

Suggestion: In debating this question with yourself and others, we urge you the read the original articles:

Ryan, R. M., & Deci, E. L. (2000). Self-determination theory and the facilitation of intrinsic motivation, social development, and well-being. *American Psychologist, 55,* 68–78.

Schwartz. B. (2000). Self-determination: The tyranny of freedom. *American Psychologist, 55,* 79–88.

Mary Whiton Calkins
Source: Archives of the History of American Psychology—the University of Akron.

Margaret Floy Washburn

number of women, among them 22 female psychologists. Cattell rated three of these women as among the 1,000 most distinguished scientists in the country: Mary Whiton Calkins (1863–1930), Christine Ladd-Franklin (1847–1930), and Margaret Floy Washburn (1871–1939).

Often, however, female psychologists faced discrimination. Some colleges and universities did not grant degrees to women, professional journals were reluctant to publish their work, and teaching positions were often closed to them (Evans, 1999; Kite et al., 2001; Minton, 2002; O'Connell & Russo, 1990; Russo & Denmark, 1987; Stevens & Gardner, 1982). As a result, most early female psychologists found positions in therapeutic and other nonacademic settings; pursued careers in allied professions, such as child development and education, which were considered acceptable fields for women; or gained recognition by collaborating on research projects and books with their spouses (Evans, 1999).

Christine Ladd-Franklin completed the requirements for a doctorate in psychology at Harvard in the 1880s, but was not awarded a Ph.D. until 1926—more than 40 years later—when Johns Hopkins finally lifted its restrictions against granting doctoral degrees to women. Because of the prevailing prejudice against women who sought to combine a career with marriage and motherhood, she never held a permanent academic position (Furumoto & Scarborough, 1986). Nevertheless, she became one of this country's leading theorists in color vision.

Like Ladd-Franklin, Mary Whiton Calkins studied psychology at Harvard. William James described her as his brightest student. Yet she, too, was denied a degree because of her gender. Calkins went on to head the psychology department at Wellesley College, where she developed an influential theory of self-psychology and an important research technique for studying verbal learning (Furumoto, 1980). In 1905, she became the first woman to be elected president of the American Psychological Association (APA).

Margaret Floy Washburn began her studies at Columbia University, but soon transferred to Cornell University, one of the few institutions that did grant doctorates to women (Furumoto & Scarborough, 1986). She was Edward B. Titchener's first doctoral student and also the first woman in America to receive a Ph.D. in psychology. Washburn later became the head of the psychology department at Vassar College, where she remained for 34 years. Washburn wrote several influential books, including *Movement and Mental Imagery* (1916), which anticipated current research on the role of imagery in directing thought and activity. In addition, Washburn was an editor of the *American Journal of Psychology* for many years and was elected president of APA in 1921.

After World War II, the cultural climate for women began to change, albeit slowly. Coeducation became the norm, and the policy of systematically denying women graduate degrees was abandoned. Over the next two to three decades, most of the degrees and positions awarded to women were in applied psychology, and men continued to dominate academic experimental psychology. Not until the 1970s and 1980s did women win recognition for contributions in all of psychology's subfields (Pion et al., 1996).

In recent decades, the number of women who receive Ph.D.s in psychology has grown dramatically (see Figure 1–1). Today, women have begun to outnumber men in psychology. According to the most recent APA survey, women receive three-fourths of the baccalaureate degrees awarded in psychology; represent just under three-fourths of psychology graduate students; and earned two out of three doctorate degrees in psychology awarded in 1997 (APA, 2000).

The apparent absence of women from the history of psychology is only one aspect of a much bigger and more troubling concern: the relative inattention to human diversity that has characterized psychology through most of the twentieth century. Only recently have psychologists looked closely at the ways in which culture, gender, race, and ethnicity can affect virtually all aspects of human behavior. In the next section of the chapter, we will begin our examination of this important topic.

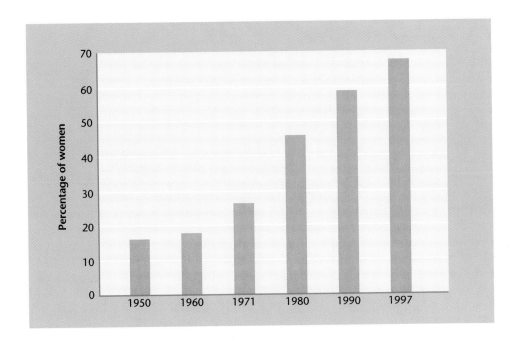

Figure 1–1
Percentage of women recipients of Ph.D.s in psychology, 1950–1997
Source: Summary Report: Doctorate Recipients from United States Universities (Selected Years). National Research Council. Figure compiled by the APA Research Office. Copyright © 2000 by the American Psychological Association. Reprinted with permission.

CHECK YOUR UNDERSTANDING

1. Psychology began in 1879 at the University of Leipzig. Who started it and used the term "voluntarism" to describe it?

___ a. Sigmund Freud

___ b. John B. Watson

___ c. Mary Whiton Calkins

___ d. Wilhelm Wundt

2. "No one ever had a simple sensation by itself," said this opponent of structuralism who defined consciousness as a continuous stream. Identify the person and his theory.

___ a. John B. Watson and behaviorist theory

___ b. William James and functionalist theory

___ c. Sigmund Freud and psychodynamic theory

___ d. Abraham Maslow and humanistic theory

3. Gestalt psychology studies

___ a. perception of objects as whole patterns

___ b. self-improvement and self-understanding

___ c. observable and measurable behavior

___ d. gender stereotypes

4. Which one of these best sums up the beginnings of cognitive psychology?

___ a. a shift toward sexuality and away from free will

___ b. a shift away from behavior to mental processes

___ c. a shift toward greater use of laboratory experiments

___ d. a shift toward conditioning in both humans and animals

Answers: 1.d, 2.b, 3.a, 4.b

Human Diversity

Are ethnic minorities underrepresented among psychologists?

For today's students—and tomorrow's citizens of the globe—understanding human diversity is essential. The reason is all around you. Our major cities are home to people from diverse backgrounds, with diverse values and goals, living side by side. But proximity does not always produce harmony; sometimes it leads to aggression, prejudice, and conflict. Understanding cultural, racial, and ethnic differences in thinking and behavior gives us the tools to reduce some of these interpersonal tensions. In the past, men and women led very different lives. Today, women in many societies are as likely as men to obtain higher education; to work full-time, pursue careers, and start businesses; and to be active in politics. And men are more likely to be more active parents and homemakers than their fathers were. Yet stereotypes about how the "typical male" looks and acts or the "accepted social roles" for females still lead to confusion and misunderstandings between the sexes. Looking at human diversity from a scientific perspective will allow you to separate fact from fiction in your daily interactions with people. Moreover, once you understand how and why groups differ in their values, behaviors, approaches to the world, thought processes, and responses to situations, you will be better able to savor the diversity around you. Finally, the more you comprehend human diversity, the more you will appreciate the many *universal* features of humanity.

In the early twentieth century, psychology was a white male profession with a distinctly American accent (Strickland, 2000). The great majority of research studies were conducted by white male professors at American universities, using white, male, American college students as subjects. This was not a conscious or deliberate decision to study just one particular group. Like other sciences and prestigious professions in Europe and North America, psychology took for granted that what was true of white, Western males would be true for other people as well. One critical history of psychology during this period was entitled *Even the Rat Was White!* (Guthrie, 1976).

Examining and overcoming past assumptions and biases has been a slow and uneven process, but a new appreciation of human diversity is taking shape (Phinney, 1996; Tucker & Herman, 2002). Psychologists have begun to question assumptions based on gender, race, and culture explicitly. Are women more likely to help a person in distress than men are? Are African Americans more vulnerable to certain types of mental illness than European Americans, or vice versa? Do the Japanese view children's ability to learn in the same way Americans do? Do homosexuals have

To understand human behavior fully, we must appreciate the rich diversity of human beings throughout the world.

different motives and emotions than heterosexuals? Research indicates that the answer to such questions often is "no."

Gender

Gender has many layers. *Male* and *female* refer to one's biological makeup, the physical and genetic facts of being one sex or the other. Some scientists use the term *sex* to refer exclusively to biological differences in anatomy, genetics, or physical functioning and **gender** to refer to the psychological and social meanings attached to being biologically male or female. Because distinguishing what is biologically produced from what is socially influenced is almost impossible, in our discussion of these issues we will use the terms *sex* and *gender* interchangeably.

In contrast, the terms *masculine* and *feminine* have distinct psychological and social meanings. "Masculine" preferences, attributes, and interests are those that are typically associated with being a male in a given society and culture, whereas "feminine" preferences, attributes, and interests are those associated with being a female. These terms are based on people's cultural notions about the sexes (and indeed, about themselves) rather than on biological facts. Whereas individuals are either biological males or females, masculinity and femininity are better viewed as a continuum, with masculinity at one extreme and femininity at the other with many overlapping traits in between.

Gender Stereotypes "Women talk too much; men are strong and silent." "Men have pals; women have confidants." "Women worry about their looks and their children; men, about their jobs and their bank accounts." "Men monopolize the TV zapper; women monopolize the bathroom mirror." The list of **gender stereotypes**—characteristics that are assumed to be typical of each sex—is endless. In general, our culture holds that men are dominant, strong, and aggressive, whereas women are accommodating, emotional, and affectionate. As a result, many boys learn to hide their emotions, to deny feelings of weakness even to themselves, and to fight, whereas many girls learn to hide their ambitions, to deny their talents

Gender The psychological and social meanings attached to being biologically male or female. Often used interchangeably with one's biological makeup or sex.

Gender stereotypes General beliefs about characteristics that are presumed to be typical of each sex.

Carol Gilligan.

Our expectations concerning gender roles often reflect traditional gender stereotypes. What were your first reactions to these photos?

Gender roles Behaviors that we expect each gender to engage in.

Feminist theory Feminist theories offer a wide variety of views on the social roles of women and men, the problems and rewards of those roles, and the prescriptions for changing them.

Sexual orientation Refers to the direction of one's sexual interest toward members of the same sex, the other sex, or both sexes.

and strengths even to themselves, and perhaps to give in. Stereotypes are rarely benign. As we will see in Chapter 10 (Life Span Development), these particular stereotypes have significant negative effects on both boys and girls.

Beyond our stereotypes about what males and females "typically" are like, we have general beliefs about **gender roles,** cultural expectations regarding acceptable behavior and activities for males and females, respectively. As a rule, cultural norms change more slowly than behavior patterns. Although most American families depend on two salaries today, the assumption that the husband should be the chief breadwinner and the wife should put her home and children first remains powerful. Working wives and mothers work a "second shift" (keeping house and caring for children) at home—as much because they feel it's their responsibility and area of expertise as because their husbands still expect them to do so (Hochschild & Machung, 1989).

The study of gender similarities and differences has become part of mainstream psychology. Psychologists in virtually every subfield conduct research to determine whether their findings apply equally to males and females, and if not, why. As we will see, **feminist theory** is not for women only.

Feminist Psychology   As the number of female psychologists has grown in recent decades, so has the concern about traditional psychological theories, research, and clinical practices (Minton, 2002). Feminist psychologists such as Carol Gilligan make three main points. First, much of the research supporting key psychological theories, such as moral development, was based on all-male samples. Measured against "universal male" standards, females often were found "lacking." Second, reports of gender differences tend to focus on the extremes, exaggerating small differences and ignoring much greater similarities (Tavris, 1992). Third, the questions psychologists ask and the topics they study reflect what they consider to be important.

Beyond research and theory, contemporary feminist psychology has begun to influence every facet of psychological practice by seeking mechanisms to empower women in the community, by advocating action to establish policies that advance equality and social justice, and by increasing women's representation in global leadership. Feminists also took the lead in urging other psychologists to recognize sexual orientation as simply another aspect of human diversity.

Sexual Orientation   The term **sexual orientation** refers to whether a person is sexually attracted to members of the opposite sex (heterosexuality), the same sex (homosexuality), or both sexes (bisexuality). Division 44 of the American Psychological Association, "Society for the Psychological Study of Lesbian, Gay, and Bisexual Issues," was founded in 1985 to promote research and education regarding sexual orientation, for psychologists as well as the general public. Psychologists have only just begun to investigate the many sensitive issues associated

THINKING CRITICALLY

The Universal Male

Studies of gender often treat males as the standard and women as the variable. For example, a researcher gave men and women a test of creativity, then asked them to explain their scores in a mock job interview (Olson, 1988). The researcher was not interested in which sex was more creative (they were equal), but in their explanations. She found that women were more likely to attribute success to luck and failure to inability, whereas men were more likely to attribute success to ability and failure to bad luck. Why do women take less credit for their achievements? The researcher concluded, "The feminine goal of appearing modest inhibits women from making self-promoting attributions in achievement situations."

- How is this researcher using the "universal male" standard?

- What would happen if you turned around the sentence in quotes and used women as the standard?

  Try filling in the blanks:

- Why do men make more _____ explanations than women do?

- The masculine goal of appearing _____ inhibits men from making more modest explanations, acknowledging the role of luck, or admitting they received help from others (Tavris, 1992, p. 28).

- What are the hidden assumptions?

- Can you think of alternative explanations for the findings?

- What would you need to know about this study to have confidence that the results apply to people generally, rather than just the people who were studied?

As psychologists study the origins of homosexuality, gay couples seek social acceptance as parents.

with this dimension of human diversity—including such topics as the origins of sexual orientation (LeVay & Hamer, 1994), brain differences between heterosexual and homosexual men (Swaab & Hoffman, 1995), and the impact of allowing gays and lesbians in the military (Jones & Koshes, 1995).

Race and Ethnicity

One of the first things we notice about a person (along with sex) is their race or ethnicity (Omi & Winant, 1994). **Race** is a biological term used to refer to a subpopulation whose members have reproduced exclusively among themselves and therefore are genetically similar and distinct from other members of the same species (Betancourt & López, 1993; Diamond, 1994; Macionis, 1993). Most people simply take for granted the idea that the human species can be divided into a number of distinct races (Asians, Africans, Caucasians, Native Americans, and so on). However, human beings have migrated, intermarried, and commingled so frequently over time that it is impossible to identify biologically separate races. To a greater or lesser degree, all humans are "racial hybrids." Moreover, the criteria people use to differentiate among different races are arbitrary. In the United States we assign people to different races primarily on the basis of skin color and facial features. In central Africa, members of the Tutsi and Hutu tribes see themselves as different races, although they are similar in skin color and facial features. In spite of these different definitions, most people continue to *believe* that racial categories are meaningful, and as a result, race shapes people's social identities, their sense of self, their experiences in their own and other societies, and even their health.

Whereas racial categories are based on physical differences, **ethnicity** is based on cultural characteristics. An ethnic group is a category of people who see themselves—and are perceived by others—as distinctive because of a common homeland and history, language, religion, or traditional cultural beliefs and social practices. For example, Hispanic Americans may be black, white, or any shade in between. What unites them is their language and culture.

Race A subpopulation of a species, defined according to an identifiable characteristic (e.g., geographic location, skin color, hair texture, genes, facial features).

Ethnicity A common cultural heritage—including religion, language, or ancestry—that is shared by a group of individuals.

Culture The tangible goods and the values, attitudes, behaviors, and beliefs that are passed from one generation to another.

By the mid-1980s, there was sufficient interest among psychologists in ethnicity that the American Psychological Association created a new division devoted to the psychological study of ethnic minority issues (Division 45). Increasing numbers of psychologists are now studying why ethnicity is so important in our country (and others) and how individuals select or create an identity and respond to ethnic stereotypes.

Racial and Ethnic Minorities in Psychology Most ethnic minorities are still underrepresented among the ranks of American psychologists. According to the APA, ethnic-minority students account for almost 25 percent of college entrants, but only 16 percent of graduates who majored in psychology, 14 percent of those who enroll in graduate school in psychology, 12 percent of those who receive master's degrees in psychology, and 9 percent of those who earn doctorates (Sleek, 1999). Why? One possibility is that when black, Hispanic, Native American, and other students look at the history of psychology or at the psychology faculties of today's universities, they find few role models; likewise, when they look at psychological research, they find little about themselves and their realities (Strickland, 2000). As recently as the 1990s, a survey of psychology journals found that less than 2 percent of the articles focused on U.S. racial and ethnic minorities (Iwamasa & Smith, 1996). Nonetheless, their small numbers have not prevented them from achieving prominence and making significant contributions to the field. For example, Kenneth Clark, a former president of the American Psychological Association, received national recognition for the important work he and his wife, Mamie Clark, did on the effects of segregation on black children (Lal, 2002). This research was cited by the Supreme Court in the *Brown v. Board of Education* decision of 1954 that outlawed segregated schools in the United States (Keppel, 2002).

Kenneth Clark's research on the effects of segregation influenced the Supreme Court to outlaw segregated schools in *Brown v. Board of Education.*

In an effort to remedy the underrepresentation of ethnic minorities, the APA's Office of Ethnic Minority Affairs is sponsoring programs to attract ethnic-minority students to psychology (Rabasca, 2000a). This initiative includes summer programs for high school students, recruitment at the high school and college levels, mentoring and other guidance programs, and a clearinghouse for college students who meet the requirements for graduate programs.

Culture

A classic definition of **culture** is a people's "design for living" (Kluckhohn, 1949). A culture provides modes of thinking, acting, and communicating; ideas about how the world works and why people behave as they do; beliefs and ideals that shape our individual dreams and desires; information about how to use and improve technology; and perhaps most important, criteria for evaluating what natural events, human actions, and life itself mean. All large, complex modern societies also include subcultures—groups whose values, attitudes, behavior, and vocabulary or accent distinguish them from the cultural mainstream. Most Americans participate in a number of subcultures as well as mainstream culture.

Many of the traits we think of as defining us as human—especially language, morals, and technology—are elements of culture. Even one's sense of self is dependent on culture and subculture (Segall, Lonner, & Berry, 1998). Thus psychology must take cultural influences into account. For example, cross-cultural research on motivation

THINKING CRITICALLY

Psychology and Minority Students

In the text, we cited Strickland's conclusion that members of minority groups are underrepresented among psychology majors and in psychology postgraduate programs because a majority of their instructors and professors are white, and because so many of the research studies they read about in introductory psychology are based on white-only participants (Strickland, 2000). Do you agree with Strickland? Why or why not?

- What other reasons might explain why whites are more likely than people of color to choose psychology as their main area of study and future career?

- How might you go about determining whether those various explanations are in fact valid? What kind of research evidence would lead you to favor one explanation over another?

Most Americans are members of a subculture as well as being members of the mainstream culture.

and emotions, personality and self-esteem, has called attention to a broad distinction between *individualistic* cultures (which value independence and personal achievement) and *collectivist* cultures (which value interdependence, fitting in, and harmonious relationships) (Kagitcibasi, 1997). Moreover, cross-cultural studies have had a significant impact on the study of gender. Anthropologist Margaret Mead's classic, *Sex and Temperament in Three Primitive Societies* (1935) is still cited by feminists and others as showing that definitions of masculinity and femininity are not biological givens, but learned, cultural constructs and therefore subject to change. Finally, in our increasingly multicultural society, psychologists will be dealing with diverse clients, research participants, and students (Hall, 1997). To prepare for this future, psychology must begin educating and training "culturally competent" professionals.

Throughout this book we will explore similarities and differences among individuals and among groups of people. For example, we will examine differences in personality characteristics, intelligence, and levels of motivation; we will look at similarities in biological functioning and developmental stages. In almost every chapter, we will examine research on males and females, members of different racial and ethnic groups, and cross-cultural studies.

CHECK YOUR UNDERSTANDING

1. The terms "masculine" and "feminine" are based on

___ a. biological facts

___ b. stereotypes

___ c. feminist psychology

___ d. cultural notions

2. If *race* is a biological term, *ethnicity* is a _____ term?

___ a. cultural

___ b. sexual

___ c. arbitrary

___ d. feminist

3. When psychologists use the term "culture," they mean the study of

___ a. the good life

___ b. ethnic minorities

___ c. designs for living

___ d. aggressive behavior

Answers: 1.d, 2.a, 3.c

Research Methods in Psychology

How do psychologists design experiments?

All sciences—psychology, sociology, economics, political science, biology, and physics—require **empirical evidence** based on careful observation and experimentation. To collect data systematically and objectively, psychologists use a variety of research methods, including naturalistic observation, case studies, surveys, correlational research, and experimental research. Each of these research strategies has advantages and disadvantages compared to the others.

Naturalistic Observation

Psychologists use **naturalistic observation** to study human or animal behavior in its natural context. One psychologist with this real-life orientation might observe behavior in a school or a factory; another might actually join a family to study the behavior of its members; still another might observe monkeys in the wild rather than in cages. The primary advantage of naturalistic observation is that the behavior observed in everyday life is likely to be more natural, spontaneous, and varied than that observed in a laboratory.

For example, naturalistic observation was used in a recent study (Hammen, Gitlin, & Altshuler, 2000) designed to understand why some patients with *bipolar disorder* (a mental disorder discussed more fully in Chapter 13, Psychological Disorders) are more likely to adjust successfully to the workplace than others. By carefully studying 52 people over a 2-year period in their natural settings, these authors found that the people who displayed the most successful work adjustment were those who also had strong supportive personal relationships with other people. Surprisingly, stressful life events did not seem to play an important role in how well these people adjusted to work. Because simulating a genuine workplace environment in a laboratory would have been extremely difficult (especially over an extended period of time), naturalistic observation provided a practical alternative to exploring this issue.

Naturalistic observation is not without its drawbacks. Psychologists using naturalistic observation have to take behavior as it comes. They cannot suddenly yell, "Freeze!" when they want to study what is going on in more detail. Nor can psychologists tell people to stop what they are doing because it is not what they are interested in researching. Moreover, simply describing one's impressions of "a day in the life" of a particular group or how different people behave in the same setting is not science. Observers must measure behavior in a systematic way, for example, by devising a form that enables them to check what people are doing at timed intervals.

The main drawback in naturalistic observation is **observer bias.** As we will see in Chapter 6 (Memory), eyewitnesses to a crime are often very unreliable sources of information. Even psychologists who are trained observers may subtly distort what they see to make it conform to what they were hoping to see. For this reason, contemporary researchers often use videotapes that can be analyzed and scored by

psych **1.1**

Empirical evidence Information derived from systematic, objective observation.

Naturalistic observation Research method involving the systematic study of animal or human behavior in natural settings rather than in the laboratory.

Observer bias Expectations or biases of the observer that might distort or influence his or her interpretation of what was actually observed.

other researchers who do not know what the study is designed to find out. Another potential problem is that psychologists may not observe or record behavior that seems to be irrelevant. Therefore, many observational studies employ a team of trained observers who pool their notes. This strategy often generates a more complete picture than one observer could draw alone.

Unlike laboratory experiments that can be repeated over and over again, each natural situation is a one-time-only occurrence. Therefore, psychologists prefer not to make general statements based on information from naturalistic studies alone. Rather, they test the information from naturalistic observation under controlled conditions in the laboratory before they apply it to situations other than the original one.

Despite these disadvantages, naturalistic observation is a valuable tool. After all, real-life behavior is what psychology is all about. Naturalistic observation often provides new ideas and suggests new theories, which can then be studied more systematically and in more detail in the laboratory. This method also helps researchers maintain perspective by reminding them of the larger world outside the lab.

Primatologist Jane Goodall has spent most of her adult life observing chimpanzees in their natural environment in Africa. Her work has yielded detailed information about the behavior of our species' nearest living relative.

Case Studies

A second research method is the **case study:** a detailed description of one (or a few) individuals. Although in some ways similar to naturalistic observation, the researcher uses a variety of methods to collect information that yields a detailed, in-depth portrait of the individual. A case study usually includes real-life observation, interviews, scores on various psychological tests, and whatever other measures the researcher considers revealing. For example, the Swiss psychologist, Jean Piaget, developed a comprehensive theory of cognitive development by carefully studying each of his three children as they grew and changed during childhood. Other researchers have tested his theory with experiments involving larger numbers of children, in our own and other cultures (see Chapter 10, Life Span Development).

Like naturalistic observation, case studies can provide valuable insights but also have significant drawbacks. Observer bias is as much a problem here as it is with naturalistic observation. Moreover, because each person is unique, we cannot confidently draw general conclusions from a single case. Nevertheless, case studies figure prominently in psychological research. For example, the famous case of Phineas Gage, who suffered severe and unusual brain damage, led researchers to identify the front portion of the brain as important for the control of emotions and the ability to plan and carry out complex tasks (see Chapter 2, The Biological Basis of Behavior). The case study of another brain-damaged patient (Milner, 1959), called "H. M.," who could remember events that preceded his injury but nothing that happened after it, prompted psychologists to suggest that we have several distinct kinds of memory (see Chapter 6, Memory).

When people are unaware that they are being watched, they behave naturally. A one-way mirror is therefore sometimes used for naturalistic observation.

Case study Intensive description and analysis of a single individual or just a few individuals.

Survey research Research technique in which questionnaires or interviews are administered to a selected group of people.

Surveys

In some respects, surveys address the shortcomings of naturalistic observation and case studies. In **survey research,** a carefully selected group of people is asked a set of predetermined questions in face-to-face interviews or in questionnaires. Perhaps the most familiar surveys are the polls taken before major elections: For months, even a

Jean Piaget based his theory of cognitive development on case studies of children.

year, before the election, we are bombarded with estimates of the percentage of people likely to vote for each candidate. But surveys are used for other purposes as well. For example, one survey found that 61 percent of the adults questioned by telephone believed that advertisers embedded subliminal messages in their ads, and 56 percent were convinced that such messages make people buy things they do not want (Lev, 1991). (There is no scientific evidence to support these beliefs.) According to a 1995 Department of Defense survey of 28,000 active-duty personnel, 78 percent of women and 38 percent of men reported one or more incidents of sexual harassment (Hay & Ellig, 1999). This survey—and others conducted more recently—indicates that sexual harassment occurs quite frequently in a wide variety of settings, often affecting both males and females (Larimer, Lydum, Anderson, & Turner, 1999).

Surveys, even those with a low response rate, can generate a great deal of interesting and useful information at relatively low cost, but to be accurate, the survey questions must be unambiguous and clear, the people surveyed must be selected with great care (see sampling, below), and they must be motivated to respond to the survey thoughtfully and carefully (Krosnick, 1999). For example, asking parents, "Do you ever use physical punishment to discipline your children?" may elicit the socially correct answer, "No." Asking "When was the last time you spanked your child?" or "In what situations do you feel it is necessary to hit your child?" is more likely to elicit honest responses, because the questions are specific and imply that most parents use physical punishment; the researcher is merely asking when and why. At the same time, survey researchers must be careful not to ask leading questions, such as, "Most Americans approve of physical punishment; do you?" Guaranteeing participants in a survey anonymity can also be important.

Naturalistic observations, case studies, and surveys can provide a rich set of raw data that *describes* behaviors, beliefs, opinions, and attitudes. But these research methods are not ideal for making predictions, explaining, or determining the causes of behavior. For these purposes, psychologists use more powerful research methods, as we will see in the next two sections.

Correlational Research

Correlational research Research technique based on the naturally occurring relationship between two or more variables.

A psychologist, under contract to the Air Force, is asked to predict which applicants for a pilot-training program will make good pilots. An excellent approach to this problem would be **correlational research.** The psychologist might select several hundred trainees, give them a variety of aptitude and personality tests, and then compare the results to their performance in training school. This approach would tell him whether some characteristic or set of characteristics is closely related to, or correlated with, eventual success as a pilot.

Suppose he finds that the most successful trainees score higher than the unsuccessful trainees on mechanical aptitude tests and that they are also cautious people who do not like to take unnecessary risks. The psychologist has discovered that there is a *correlation*, or relationship, between these traits and success as a pilot trainee: High scores on tests of mechanical aptitude and caution predict success as a pilot trainee. If these correlations are confirmed in new groups of trainees, then the psychologist could recommend with some confidence that the Air Force consider using these tests to select future trainees.

Correlational data are useful for many purposes, but they do not permit the researcher to explain cause and effect. This important distinction is often overlooked. *Correlation* means that two phenomena seem to be related: when one goes up the other goes up (or down). For example, young people with high IQ scores usually earn higher grades in school than do students with average or below-average scores. This correlation allows researchers to predict that children with high IQ scores will do well on tests and other classwork. But correlation does not identify the direction of influence. A high IQ might cause or enable a child to be a good student. But the reverse might also be true: working hard in school might cause children to score higher on IQ tests. Or a third, unidentified factor might intervene. For example, growing up in a middle-class family that places a high value on education might cause both higher IQ scores and higher school grades (see Appendix A for more on correlation).

So it is with our example. This psychologist has *described* a relationship between skill as a pilot and two other characteristics, and as a result he is able to use those relationships to *predict* with some accuracy which trainees will and will not become skilled pilots. But he has no basis for drawing conclusions about cause and effect. Does the tendency to shy away from risk taking make a trainee a good pilot? Or is it the other way around: Learning to be a skillful pilot makes people cautious? Or is there some unknown factor that causes people to be both cautious and capable of acquiring the different skills needed in the cockpit?

Despite limitations, correlational research often sheds light on important psychological phenomena. In this book you will come across many examples of correlational

Surveys can generate a great deal of useful data, but only if the questions are clear and the people surveyed are carefully selected and answer the questions honestly.

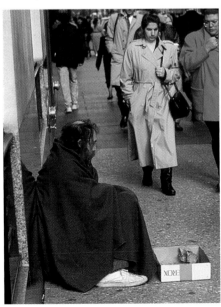

Researchers might use a correlational study to understand the conditions under which passersby are more likely to stop and help such people. The same study, undertaken in both countries, might reveal significant cross-cultural differences, or it might show that Japanese and Americans respond similarly to the homeless.

1.2

research: People who are experiencing severe stress are more prone to develop physical illnesses than people who are not; children whose parent(s) have schizophrenia are more likely to develop this disorder than are other children; and when someone needs help, the more bystanders, the less likely it is that any one of them will come forward to offer help. These interesting findings allow us to make some predictions, but psychologists want to move beyond simply making predictions. To explain the causes of psychological phenomena, psychologists most often use experimental research.

Experimental Research

A psychology instructor notices that on Monday mornings most students in her class do not remember materials as well as they do later in the week. She has discovered a correlation between the day of the week and memory for course-related material. Based on this correlation, she could predict that next Monday and every Monday after that the students in her class will not absorb material as well as on other days. But she wants to go beyond simply predicting her students' behavior; she wants to understand or explain why their memories are poorer on Mondays than on other days of the week.

Based on her own experiences and some informal interviews with students, she suspects that students stay up late on weekends and their difficulty remembering facts and ideas presented on Mondays is due to lack of sleep. This hypothesis appears to make sense, but the psychologist wants to prove that it is correct. To gather evidence that lack of sleep actually causes memory deficits, she turns to the **experimental method.**

Her first step is to select **participants,** people whom she can observe to find out whether her hypothesis is correct. She decides to use student volunteers. To keep her results from being influenced by sex differences or intelligence levels, she chooses a group made up of equal numbers of men and women, all of whom scored between 520 and 550 on the verbal section of their College Boards.

Next, she designs a memory task. She needs something that none of her participants will know in advance. If she chooses a chapter in a history book, for example, she runs the risk that some of her participants will be history buffs. Given the various possibilities, the psychologist decides to print a page of geometric shapes, each labeled with a nonsense word. Circles are "glucks," triangles, "rogs," and so on. She gives students half an hour to learn the names from this page, then takes it away and asks them to assign those same labels to geometric shapes on a new page.

The psychologist also needs to know which participants are sleep-deprived. Simply asking people whether they have slept well is not ideal: Some may say "no" so they will have an excuse for doing poorly on the test, others may say "yes" because they do not want a psychologist to think they are so unstable they cannot sleep. And two people who both say they "slept well" may not mean the same thing by that phrase. So the psychologist decides to intervene—that is, to control the situation more closely. Everyone in the experiment, she decides, will spend the night in the same dormitory. They will be kept awake until 4:00 A.M., and then they will be awakened at 7:00 A.M. sharp. She and her colleagues will patrol the halls to make sure that no one falls asleep ahead of schedule. By *manipulating* the amount of time the participants sleep, the psychologist is introducing and controlling an essential element of the experimental method: an **independent variable.** The psychologist believes that the students' ability to learn and remember labels for geometric shapes will depend on their having had a good night's sleep. Performance on the memory task (the number of correct answers) thus becomes the dependent variable. According to the hypothesis, changing the independent variable (the amount of sleep) should also change the **dependent variable** (performance on the memory task). Her prediction is that this group of participants, who get no more than three hours of sleep, should do quite poorly on the memory test.

Experimental method A research technique in which an investigator deliberately manipulates selected events or circumstances and then measures the effects of those manipulations on subsequent behavior.

Participants Individuals whose reactions or responses are observed in an experiment.

Independent variable In an experiment, the variable that is manipulated to test its effects on the other, dependent variables.

Dependent variable In an experiment, the variable that is measured to see how it is changed by manipulations in the independent variable.

At this point, the experimenter begins looking for loopholes in her experimental design. How can she be sure that poor test results mean that the participants did less well than they would have done had they had more sleep? For example, their poor performance could simply be the result of knowing that they were being closely observed. To be sure that her experiment measures only the effects of inadequate sleep, the experimenter creates two groups, containing equal numbers of males and females of the same ages and with the same College Board scores. One of the groups, the **experimental group,** will be kept awake, as described, until 4:00 A.M. That is, they will be subjected to the experimenter's manipulation of the independent variable—amount of sleep. Members of the other group, the **control group,** will be allowed to go to sleep whenever they please. If the only consistent difference between the two groups is the amount of sleep they get, the experimenter can be much more confident that if the groups differ in their test performance, the difference is due to the length of time they slept the night before.

Finally, the psychologist questions her own objectivity. Because she believes that lack of sleep inhibits students' learning and memory, she does not want to prejudice the results of her experiment; that is, she wants to avoid **experimenter bias.** So she decides to ask a neutral person, someone who does not know which participants did or did not sleep all night, to score the tests.

The experimental method is a powerful tool, but it, too, has limitations. First, many intriguing psychological variables, such as love, hatred, or grief, do not readily lend themselves to experimental manipulation. And even if it were possible to induce such strong emotions as part of a psychological experiment, this would raise serious ethical questions. In some cases, psychologists may use animals rather than humans for experiments. But some subjects, such as the emergence of language in children or the expression of emotions, cannot be studied with other species. Second, because experiments are conducted in an artificial setting, participants—whether human or nonhuman—may behave differently than they would in real life.

The Summary Table lays out the most important advantages and disadvantages of each of the research methods we have discussed. Because each method has drawbacks, psychologists often use more than one method to study a single problem.

Multimethod Research

Suppose a psychologist was interested in studying creativity. She might begin her research by giving a group of college students a creativity test that she invented to measure their capacity to discover or produce something new. Next she would compare the students' scores with their scores on intelligence tests and with their grades to see if there is a *correlation* between them. Then she would spend several weeks *observing* a college class and *interviewing* teachers, students, and parents to correlate classroom behavior and the adults' evaluations with the students' scores on the creativity test. She would go on to test some of her ideas with an *experiment* using a group of students as participants. Finally, her findings might prompt her to revise the test, or they might give the teachers and parents new insight into a particular student.

The Importance of Sampling

One obvious drawback to every form of research is that it is usually impossible, or at least impractical, to measure every single occurrence of a characteristic. No one could expect to measure the memory of every human being, to study the responses of all individuals who suffer from phobias (irrational fears), or to record the maternal behavior of all female monkeys. No matter what research method is used, whenever researchers conduct a study, they examine only a relatively small number of people or animals of the population they seek to understand. In other words, researchers almost always study a small **sample** and then use the results of that

Experimental group In a controlled experiment, the group subjected to a change in the independent variable.

Control group In a controlled experiment, the group not subjected to a change in the independent variable; used for comparison with the experimental group.

Experimenter bias Expectations by the experimenter that might influence the results of an experiment or its interpretation.

Sample Selection of cases from a larger population.

 1.3

summarytable BASIC METHODS OF RESEARCH

Research Method	Advantages	Limitations
Naturalistic Observation Behavior is observed in the environment in which it occurs naturally.	Naturalistic observation provides a great deal of firsthand behavioral information that is more likely to be accurate than reports after the fact. The participant's behavior is more natural, spontaneous, and varied than behaviors taking place in the laboratory. It is a rich source of hypotheses as well.	The presence of an observer may alter the participants' behavior; the observer's recording of the behavior may reflect a preexisting bias; and it is often unclear whether the observations can be generalized to other settings and other people.
Case Studies Behavior of one person or a few people is studied in depth.	Case studies yield a great deal of detailed descriptive information. Theare useful for forming hypotheses.	The case(s) studied may not be a representative sample. Can be time consuming and expensive. Observer bias is a potential problem.
Surveys A large number of participants are asked a standard set of questions.	Surveys enable an immense amount of data to be gathered quickly and inexpensively.	Sampling biases can skew results. Poorly constructed questions can result in answers that are ambiguous, so data are not clear. Accuracy depends on ability and willingness of participants to answer questions accurately.
Correlational Research Employs statistical methods to examine the relationship between two or more variables.	Correlational research may clarify relationships between variables that cannot be examined by other research methods. They allow prediction of behavior.	This does not permit researchers to draw conclusions regarding cause-and-effect relationships.
Experimental Research One or more variables are systematically manipulated, and the effect of that manipulation on other variables is studied.	Strict control of variables offers researchers the opportunity to draw conclusions about cause-and-effect relationships.	The artificiality of the lab setting may influence subjects' behavior; unexpected and uncontrolled variables may confound results; many variables cannot be controlled and manipulated.

limited study to generalize about larger populations. For example, the psychology instructor who studied the effect of lack of sleep on memory assumed that her results would apply to other students in her classes (past and future), as well as to students in other classes and at other colleges.

How realistic are these assumptions? How confident can researchers be that the results of research conducted on a relatively small sample of people apply to the much larger population from which the sample was drawn? Social scientists have developed several techniques to deal with sampling error. One is to select participants at random from the larger population. For example, the researcher studying pilot trainees might begin with an alphabetical list of all trainees and then select every third name or every fifth name on the list to be in his study. These participants would constitute a **random sample** from the larger group of trainees, because every trainee had an equal chance of being chosen for the study.

Random sample Sample in which each potential participant has an equal chance of being selected.

Another way to make sure that conclusions apply to the larger population is to pick a **representative sample** of the population being studied. For example, researchers looking for a representative cross-section of Americans would want to ensure that the proportion of males and females in the study matched the national proportion, that the number of participants from each state matched the national population distribution, and so on. Even with these precautions, however, unintended bias may influence psychological research. This issue has received a great deal of attention recently, particularly in relation to women and African Americans, as we discussed earlier.

Representative sample Sample carefully chosen so that the characteristics of the participants correspond closely to the characteristics of the larger population.

 1.4

Ethics and Psychological Research

Almost all psychological research involves people (often college students) or live animals. What responsibilities do psychologists have toward their human and non-human research subjects?

Ethics in Research on Humans   If your college or university has a research facility, you will probably have a chance to become a participant in a psychology experiment. Most likely, you will be offered a small sum of money or class credit to participate. But you may not learn the true purpose of the experiment until after it's over. Is this deception necessary? What if the experiment causes you discomfort? Before answering, consider the ethical debate that flared up in 1963 when Stanley Milgram published the results of several experiments he had conducted.

Milgram used ads in local newspapers to hire people to participate in a "learning experiment." When a participant arrived at the laboratory, he was met by a stern-faced researcher in a lab coat; another man in street clothes was sitting in the waiting room. The researcher explained that he was studying the effects of punishment on learning. When the two men drew slips out of the hat, the participant's slips said "teacher." The teacher watched as the "learner" was strapped into a chair and an electrode attached to his wrist. Then the teacher was taken into an adjacent room and seated at an impressive looking "shock generator" with switches from 15 to 450 volts, labeled "Slight Shock," "Very Strong Shock" up to "Danger: Severe Shock" and finally "XXX." The teacher's job was to read a list of paired words, which the learner would attempt to memorize and repeat. The teacher was instructed to

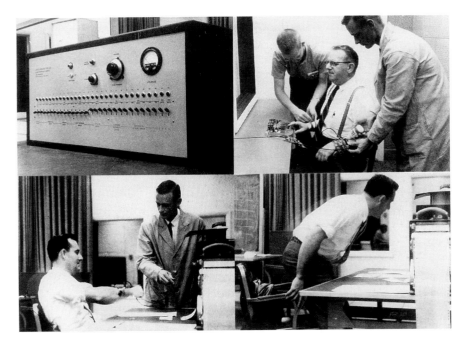

Stanley Milgram's Obedience Experiment.
(A) The shock generator used in the experiment. (B) With electrodes attached to his wrists, the learner provides answers by pressing switches that light up on an answer box. (C) The subject administers a shock to the learner. (D) The subject breaks off the experiment. Milgram's study yielded interesting results, but it also raised serious questions about the ethics of such experimentation.
Source: From the film *Obedience,* copyright 1965 by Stanley Milgram and distributed by Penn State Media Sales. Permission granted by Alexandra Milgram.

deliver a shock whenever the learner gave a wrong answer and to increase the intensity of the shock each time the learner made a mistake. At 90 volts, the learner began to grunt; at 120 volts, he shouted "Hey, this really hurts!"; at 150 volts he demanded to be released; and at 270 volts his protests became screams of agony. Beyond 330 volts, the learner appeared to pass out. If the teacher became concerned and asked to stop, the experimenter politely but firmly replied that he was expected to continue, that this experiment was being conducted in the interests of science.

In reality, Milgram was studying obedience, not learning. He wanted to find out whether ordinary people would obey orders to cause another person pain. As part of his research, Milgram (1974) described the experiment to 110 psychiatrists, college students, and middle-class adults and asked them at what point they thought participants would stop. Members of all three groups guessed that most people would refuse to continue beyond 130 volts, and no one would go beyond 300 volts. The psychiatrists estimated that only one in a thousand people would continue to the XXX shock panel. Astonishingly, 65 percent of Milgram's participants administered the highest level of shock, even though many worried aloud that the shocks might be causing the learners serious damage.

To find out what he wanted to know, Milgram had to deceive his participants. The stated purpose of the experiment—to test learning—was a lie. The "learners" were Milgram's accomplices, who had been trained to act as though they were being hurt; the machines were fake; and the learners received no shocks at all (Milgram, 1963). But, critics argued, the "teachers"—the real participants in the study—were hurt. Most not only voiced concern, but showed clear signs of stress: They sweated, bit their lips, trembled, stuttered, or in a few cases broke into uncontrollable nervous laughter. Critics also worried about the effect of the experiment on the participants' self-esteem.

Although the design of this experiment was not typical of the vast majority of psychological experiments, it sparked such a public uproar that the APA reassessed its ethical guidelines, first published in 1953 (APA, 1953). A new code of ethics on psychological experimentation was approved. The code is assessed each year and periodically revised to ensure that it adequately protects participants in research studies. In addition to outlining the ethical principles guiding research and teaching, the code spells out a set of ethical standards for psychologists who offer therapy and other professional services, such as psychological testing (see Chapter 14, Therapies).

The APA code of ethics requires that researchers obtain informed consent from participants and stipulates that:

- Participants must be informed of the nature of research in clearly understandable language.

- Informed consent must be documented.

- Risks, possible adverse effects, and limitations on confidentiality must be spelled out in advance.

- If participation is a condition of course credit, equitable alternative activities must be offered.

- Participants cannot be deceived about aspects of the research that would affect their willingness to participate, such as risks or unpleasant emotional experiences.

- Deception about the goals of the research can be used only when absolutely necessary to the integrity of the research.*

*"Ethical Principles of Psychologists and Code of Conduct." From *American Psychologist*, 1992, 47, 1597–1611.

In addition, psychological researchers are required to follow the government's Code of Federal Regulations, which includes an extensive set of regulations concerning the protection of human participants in all kinds of research. If a researcher fails to abide by these regulations, federal funding for the researcher may be terminated and the research institution where he or she works may be penalized.

Despite these formal ethical and legal guidelines, controversy still rages about the ethics of psychological research on humans. Some hold that research procedures that might be emotionally or physically distressing should be prohibited (Baumrind, 1985); others assert that the guidelines are too strict and may cripple future research (Gergen, 1973; Sears, 1994). Some believe that the APA guidelines, which state that researchers can never deceive participants ". . . about aspects of the research that would affect their willingness to participate . . . (and) can be used only when absolutely necessary to the integrity of the research . . .," are adequate to balance the rights of participants and the needs of research (Kimmel, 1998; Korn, 1998; Bröder, 1998). Others assert that deception is never justified (Ortmann & Hertwig, 1997, 1998). Still another view is that the explanations necessary to produce informed consent may foster a better understanding of the goals and methods of research (Blanck, Bellack, Rasnow, Rotheram-Borus, & Schooler, 1992). Finally, some hold that psychology, as a science, should base its ethical code on documented evidence about the effects of research procedures on participants, not on conjecture about what is "probably" a good way to conduct research (Holmes, 1976; Trice, 1986).

Ethics in Research on Nonhuman Subjects   In recent years, questions have also been raised about the ethics of using nonhuman subjects in psychological research (Herzog, 1995; Plous, 1996; Rowan & Shapiro, 1996; Shapiro, 1991). Psychologists conduct research with animals for three main reasons. The first is to study general behavior principles that apply to humans as well. Crowding mice into small cages, for example, has yielded valuable insights into the effects of overcrowding on humans. The second is for comparison. By comparing the behavior of great apes (our closest biological kin) to that of humans, psychologists gain insight into what makes humans unique and also what our ancestors might have been like (evolutionary psychology). Third, researchers use animals in experiments where it would be clearly unethical to use human participants, such as in studies involving brain lesions (cutting into the brain) or electric stimulation of parts of the brain. In fact, much of what we know about sensation, perception, drugs, emotional attachment, and the neural basis of behavior is derived from animal research (Domjan & Purdy, 1995).

At the heart of this debate is the pain and suffering that experiments can cause animals. A number of animal-rights groups, including Psychologists for the Ethical Treatment of Animals (PsyETA), are urging legislators to place stricter limits on experimentation with animals on the grounds that many such experiments are inhumane (especially when there are alternative, painless ways of studying the brain), that most are unnecessary (the point has already been made in prior research), and that the results of studies of other species do not necessarily apply to humans (Shapiro, 1991; Singer, 1998). Their opponents contend that the goals of scientific research justify the means, even though they agree that animals should be made to suffer as little as possible (Gallistel, 1981; Novak, 1991). They argue that procedures now in place, including the use of anesthesia in many experiments, are adequate.

How do psychologists themselves feel about this issue? Results of a national survey showed that the majority of psychologists support animal studies involving observation and confinement but generally disapprove of animal studies involving pain or death (Plous, 1996). The APA has addressed this issue in its ethical guidelines, noting that psychologists using animals in research must ensure "appropriate consideration of [the animal's] comfort, health, and humane treatment." Under these guidelines, animals may not be subjected to "pain, stress, or privation" when an alternative procedure is available (APA, 1992). The National Institutes of Health (NIH), which funds about 40 percent of biomedical research in the United States, has instituted more stringent policies governing animal research. A project cannot receive NIH funding unless it has been sanctioned by an animal-research committee. An attempt by Congress to require researchers to use the same safeguards for small animals (mice, rats, and birds) as they are required to use for larger animals (dogs, cats, and monkeys) failed with the passage of H.R. 2646 in May, 2002 which excludes those small animals from protection under the Animal Welfare Act.

CHECK YOUR UNDERSTANDING

1. Observer bias is the main drawback in which kind of research?

___a. surveys

___b. naturalistic observation

___c. correlational research

___d. experimental research

2. Of the many kinds of research in the field of psychology, correlational research:

___a. explains cause and effect

___b. enables predictions to be made about two or more variables

___c. gives a detailed description of one individual

___d. sets up an experiment with independent and dependent variables

3. Researchers try to head off sampling error by which method?

___a. getting a good night's sleep

___b. wording the survey questions just right

___c. repeating the survey every two years for ten years

___d. random and representative sampling

5. Animal-rights advocates believe that research on animals is ethical under which of these conditions?

___a. APA-sanctioned experiments

___b. NIH-approved experiments

___c. naturalistic observation

___d. no conditions

Answers: 1.b, 2.b, 3.d, 4.c

Careers in Psychology

What can you do with a background in psychology or an advanced degree?

Some readers may be studying psychology out of general interest; others may be considering careers in psychology. What kinds of careers are open to psychology graduates? People with bachelor's degrees in psychology may find jobs assisting psychologists in mental-health centers, vocational rehabilitation, and correctional centers. They may also work as research assistants, teach psychology in high school, or land jobs as trainees in government or business.

Community college graduates with associate's degrees in psychology are well qualified for paraprofessional positions in state hospitals, mental-health centers, and

Individuals with associate degrees and bachelor degrees in psychology are often well qualified to serve as paraprofessionals in mental health centers and other human-service settings.

other human-service settings. Job responsibilities may include screening and evaluating new patients, keeping records, and assisting in consultation sessions.

Many careers outside psychology draw on a person's knowledge of psychology without requiring postgraduate study. For example, personnel administrators deal with employee relations; vocational rehabilitation counselors help people with disabilities find employment; directors of volunteer services recruit and train volunteers; probation officers work with parolees; and day-care center supervisors oversee the care of the preschool children of working parents. Indeed, employers in areas such as business and finance seek out psychology majors because of their knowledge of the principles of human behavior and their skills in experimental design and data collection and analysis. Typical entry-level jobs include research or administrative assistants and sales or management trainees.

Academic and Applied Psychology

For those who pursue advanced degrees in psychology—a master's degree or doctorate—career opportunities span a wide range. Many doctoral psychologists join the faculties of colleges and universities. Others work in applied settings such as school, health, industrial, commercial, and educational psychology. Nearly half of doctoral psychologists are clinicians or counselors who treat people experiencing mental, emotional, or adaptation problems. Master's graduates in psychology often work as researchers, collecting and analyzing data at universities, in government, or for private companies. Students with a masters degree in Industrial/Organizational Psychology are particularly sought after by large corporations to work in personnel and human resource departments, while doctoral graduates in Industrial/Organizational Psychology are hired into management or consulting positions in industry (Murray, 2002). Others work in health, industry, and education. APA standards require that master's graduates who work in clinical, counseling, school, or testing and measurement settings be supervised by a doctoral-level psychologist.

Clinical Settings

Many students who major in psychology want to become therapists. (And at some point in their lives, others may want to consult a therapist.) What training programs qualify you, or someone you might consult, to offer therapy? To practice *psychotherapy*

ON THE CUTTING EDGE

PRESCRIPTION PRIVILEGES FOR CLINICAL PSYCHOLOGISTS

On March 2, 2002, the State of New Mexico granted prescription privileges to clinical psychologists who have appropriate training in pharmacology. This landmark legislation made New Mexico the first state where psychologists can prescribe medication for their patients. Previously only medical doctors, principally psychiatrists, could prescribe drugs for patients with mental disorders (Daw, 2002).

At a time when prescription medications have become increasingly important in the treatment of mental disorders, this change dramatically increases the range of treatment options available to psychologists. As we will see in Chapter 14 (Therapies), prescription medications are commonly used today to treat a wide range of mental disorders including depression, schizophrenia, bipolar disorder, and attention deficit disorder. Prescription medications have been shown to be particularly effective when combined with the more traditional forms of psychotherapy offered by psychologists. In addition, research has shown that when medication and psychotherapy are provided by the same professional, quality care is more cost effective than when split between two providers (Goldman, McCulloch, Cuffel, Zarin, Suarez & Burns, 1998).

To gain prescription privileges, New Mexico law requires that clinical psychologists first complete 400 hours of coursework, undergo supervised training, and pass a national exam. Afterwards, they receive a two-year license to prescribe medication under the supervision of a medical doctor. If, following the two-year period, the medical supervisor approves and an oversight board agrees, the psychologist may apply to prescribe medication independently. The prescription license will be limited to prescribing only medications used to treat mental disorders, much like dentists and optometrists are limited to prescribing medications relevant to the body parts they treat.

Though some psychiatrists and psychologists have misgivings about the change, a carefully designed study conducted by the Department of Defense has shown that psychologists with appropriate training can use prescription privileges to provide safe and high quality care to patients (see APA Practice, 2003).

Advocates of this legislation believe it may set an important precedent for other states to follow. Currently, four other states (Georgia, Illinois, Hawaii, and Tennessee) have pending legislation that would provide limited prescription privileges for psychologists, and 31 states have task forces lobbying for legislation.

you need a state license, which in most (but not all) states requires a doctorate degree. But there are important differences in training and approach among licensed practitioners as well.

- *Licensed social workers* (LSW) may have a master's degree (M.S.W.) or doctorate (D.S.W.). Social workers usually work under psychiatrists or clinical psychologists, though in some states they may be licensed to practice independently.

- *Counseling psychologists* help people to cope with situational problems. School counselors work with elementary and middle school children and their parents, high school students applying to college, and college students who are having difficulty adjusting or are seeking vocational guidance. Marriage, family, and child counselors (MFCC) work with couples and/or parents and children who have troubled relationships.

- *Clinical psychologists* assess and treat mental, emotional, and behavioral disorders, ranging from short-term crises to chronic disorders such as schizophrenia. They hold advanced degrees in psychology (a Ph.D. or Psy.D.[2])—the result of a 4- to 6-year graduate program, plus a 1-year internship in psychological assessment and psychotherapy and at least one more year of supervised practice.

[2]A Ph.D. degree requires courses in quantitative research methods and a dissertation based on original research; a Psy.D. usually is based on practical work and examinations rather than a dissertation.

- *Psychiatrists* are medical doctors (M.D.s) who, in addition to four years of medical training, have completed three years of residency training in psychiatry, most of which is spent in supervised clinical practice. Psychiatrists specialize in the diagnosis and treatment of abnormal behavior. As a rule, clinical psychologists have more training in current psychological theory and practice. Until 2002 when New Mexico granted prescription privileges to clinical psychologists, psychiatrists were the only mental health professionals who were licensed to prescribe medications (see *On the Cutting Edge: Prescription Privileges for Clinical Psychologists*).

- *Psychoanalysts* are psychiatrists or clinical psychologists who have received additional specialized training in psychoanalytic theory and practice, usually at an institute that requires them to undergo psychoanalysis before practicing. Many work in private practice, where they treat clients who choose to go into psychoanalysis, which usually means two to five sessions a week for a year or more.

The APA maintains a web site, http://www.apa.org/, which contains up-to-date information about employment opportunities, as well as a vast array of related material of interest to psychology students. A free booklet titled *Careers in Psychology* is available by calling the order department of the American Psychological Association at 1-800-374-2721.

CHECK YOUR UNDERSTANDING

1. You need a medical degree before you can become a

___a. psychiatrist

___b. psychology professor

___c. clinical psychologist

___d. school counselor

2. Psychologists work in a variety of settings including:

___a. research labs

___b. schools

___c. corporations

___d. all of the above

Answers: 1.a, 2.d

summary

What Is Psychology?

As the science of behavior and mental processes, **psychology** is an extremely broad discipline. It seeks to both describe and explain every aspect of human thought, feelings, perceptions, and actions.

The Fields of Psychology   Psychology has many major subdivisions. *Developmental psychology* is concerned with processes of growth and change over the life course, from the prenatal period through old age and death. *Neuroscience* and *physiological psychology* focus on the body's neural and chemical systems, studying how these affect thought and behavior. *Experimental psychology* investigates basic psychological processes, such as learning, memory, sensation, perception, cognition, motivation, and emotion. *Personality psychology* looks at differences among people in traits such as anxiety, aggressiveness, and self-esteem. *Clinical and counseling psychology* specializes in diagnosing and treating psychological disorders, whereas *social psychology* focuses on how people influence each other's thoughts and actions. Finally, *industrial and organizational psychology* studies problems in the workplace and other kinds of organizations.

Enduring Issues   A number of fundamental questions cut across the various subfields of psychology, unifying them with similar themes. Some fundamental questions are (1) Is behavior caused more by inner traits or by external situations? (2) How do genes and experiences interact to influence people? (3) How much do we stay the same as we develop and how much do we change? (4) In what ways do people differ in how they think and act? (5) What is the relationship between our internal experiences and our biological processes?

Psychology as Science   As a science, psychology relies on the **scientific method** to find answers to questions. This method involves careful observation and collection of data, efforts to explain observations by developing **theories** about relationships and causes, and the systematic testing of **hypotheses** (or predictions) to rule out theories that aren't valid.

The Growth of Psychology

It was not until the late 1800s that psychology emerged as a formal discipline. Over its relatively brief history a number of key people and perspectives have helped to shape its directions.

The "New Psychology": A Science of the Mind   In 1879 Wilhelm Wundt established the first psychology laboratory at the University of Leipzig in Germany. There the use of experiment and measurement marked the beginnings of psychology as a science. One of Wundt's students, Edward Titchener, established a perspective called **structuralism,** which was based on the belief that psychology's role was to identify the basic elements of experience and how they combine.

The American psychologist William James criticized structuralism, arguing that sensations cannot be separated from the mental associations that allow us to benefit from past experiences. Our rich storehouse of ideas and memories is what enables us to function in our environment, James said. His perspective became known as **functionalist theory.**

The theories of Sigmund Freud added another new dimension to psychology: the idea that much of our behavior is governed by unconscious conflicts, motives, and desires. Freud's ideas gave rise to **psychodynamic theories.**

Redefining Psychology: The Study of Behavior   John B. Watson, a spokesman for the school of thought called **behaviorism,** argued that psychology should concern itself only with observable, measurable behavior. Watson based much of his work on the conditioning experiments of Ivan Pavlov.

B. F. Skinner's beliefs were similar to Watson's, but he added the concept of reinforcement or rewards. In this way he made the learner an active agent in the learning process. Skinner's views dominated American psychology into the 1960s.

The Cognitive Revolution   According to **Gestalt psychology,** perception depends on the human tendency to see patterns, to distinguish objects from their backgrounds, and to complete pictures from a few clues. In this emphasis on wholeness the Gestalt school radically differed from structuralism.

During the same period, the American psychologist Abraham Maslow developed a more holistic approach to psychology. **Humanistic psychology** emphasizes the goal of reaching one's full potential.

Cognitive psychology is the study of mental processes in the broadest sense, focusing on how people perceive, interpret, store, and retrieve information. Unlike behaviorists, cognitive psychologists believe that mental processes can and should be studied scientifically. This view has had a far-reaching impact on psychology.

New Directions   **Evolutionary psychology** focuses on the functions and adaptive values of various human behaviors, trying to understand how they have evolved. In this way it seeks to add a new dimension to psychological research.

Positive psychology differs from most other schools of psychological thought in that it emphasizes positive feelings and traits rather than problems.

Most contemporary psychologists do not adhere to just one school of thought. They believe that different theories can often complement each other and together enrich our understandings.

Despite their contributions to the field, women psychologists often faced discrimination in the early years of the discipline. Some colleges and universities did not grant degrees to women, and many did not hire them to teach. Professional journals often refused their work. In recent decades, the number of women has grown dramatically, and women have begun to outnumber men in psychology.

Human Diversity

A rich diversity of behavior and thought exists in the human species, both among individuals and among groups. This diversity has become an important focus in psychology.

Gender   One area of research on diversity involves differences in thought and behavior between the two sexes or **genders.** Popular beliefs regarding these differences are called **gender stereotypes.** Psychologists are trying to determine the causes of gender differences—both the contribution of heredity and that of culturally learned **gender roles. Feminist theory** offers a variety of views on the social roles of women and men and feminist psychology has begun to influence every facet of psychological practice.

Sexual orientation refers to whether a person is sexually attracted to members of the opposite sex, the same sex, or both sexes.

Race and Ethnicity   **Race** is a biological term that refers to a subpopulation whose members have reproduced exclusively among themselves and therefore are genetically distinct. Because human beings have migrated and commingled so frequently over time, it is impossible to identify biologically separate races. **Ethnicity** is based on common cultural characteristics. Psychologists study why ethnicity is important and how individuals select or create an identity and respond to ethnic stereotypes. An ethnic group is a category of people who see themselves—and are perceived by as others—as distinctive common culture.

Most ethnic minorities are still underrepresented among psychologists, possibly because they find few role models and few studies of themselves. Members of minority groups have nonetheless distinguished themselves as psychologists.

Culture   **Culture** consists of all the tangible things a society produces, as well as the intangible beliefs, values, traditions, and norms of behavior its people share. In a society as large and diverse as ours is, there are many subcultural groups with their own cultural identities.

Research Methods in Psychology

All sciences require **empirical evidence** based on careful observation and experimentation. Psychologists use a variety of methods to study behavior and mental processes. Each has its own advantages and limitations.

Naturalistic Observation   Psychologists use **naturalistic observation** to study behavior in natural settings. Since there is minimal interference from the researcher, the behavior observed is likely to be more accurate, spontaneous, and varied than behavior studied in a laboratory. One potential problem with naturalistic observation is **observer bias,** the expectations or biases of the observer that might distort his or her interpretations of what was observed.

Case Studies   Researchers conducting a **case study** investigate the behavior of one person or a few persons in depth. This method can yield a great deal of detailed, descriptive information useful for forming hypotheses.

Surveys   **Survey research** generates a large amount of data quickly and inexpensively by asking a standard set of questions of a large number of people. Great care must be taken, however, in how the questions are worded.

Correlational Research   **Correlational research** is used to investigate the relation, or *correlation*, between two or more variables. Correlational research is useful for clarifying relationships between preexisting variables that can't be examined by other means.

Experimental Research   In the **experimental method** one variable (the **independent variable**) is systematically manipulated and the effects on another variable (the **dependent variable**) are studied, usually using both an **experimental group** of **participants** and a **control group** for comparison purposes. By holding all other variables constant, the researcher can draw conclusions about cause and effect. Often a neutral person is used to record data and score results, so **experimenter bias** doesn't distort the findings.

Multimethod Research   Since each research method has benefits as well as limitations, many psychologists use multiple methods to study a single problem. Together they can give much fuller answers to questions.

The Importance of Sampling   Regardless of the particular research method used, psychologists almost always study a small **sample** of participants and then generalize their results to larger populations. **Random samples,** in which participants are chosen randomly, and **representative samples,** in which participants are chosen to reflect the general characteristics of the population as a whole, are two ways of ensuring that results have broader application.

Ethics and Psychological Research   The American Psychological Association (APA) has a code of ethics for conducting research involving human or animal subjects. Still, controversy over ethical guidelines continues, with some thinking they are too strict and impede psychological research, and others thinking they are not strict enough to protect subjects from harm.

A key part of the APA code regarding research on humans is the requirement that researchers obtain informed consent from participants in their studies. Participants must be told in advance about the nature of the research and the possible risks involved. People should not feel pressured to participate if they do not want to.

Although much of what we know about certain areas of psychology has come from animal research, the practice of experimenting on animals has strong opponents. APA and federal guidelines govern the humane treatment of laboratory animals, but animal-rights advocates argue that the only ethical research on animals is naturalistic observation.

Careers in Psychology

Psychology is one of the most popular majors in colleges and universities. A background in it is useful in a wide range of fields because so many jobs involve a basic understanding of people.

Academic and Applied Psychology   Careers for those with advanced degrees in psychology include both academic and applied work. They include teaching, research, jobs in government and private business, and a number of occupations in the mental health field.

Clinical Settings   Opportunities in the mental-health field depend on one's degree of training. They include the occupations of psychiatrist; the job of clinical psychologist, which involves getting a doctoral degree; and the jobs of counseling psychologist and social worker.

key terms

Psychology	4	Gender	25	Survey research	31
Scientific method	9	Gender stereotypes	25	Correlational research	32
Theory	10	Gender roles	26	Experimental method	34
Hypotheses	10	Feminist theory	26	Participants	34
Structuralism	14	Sexual orientation	26	Independent variable	34
Functionalist theory	15	Race	27	Dependent variable	34
Psychodynamic theories	15	Ethnicity	27	Experimental group	35
Behaviorism	16	Culture	28	Control group	35
Gestalt psychology	18	Empirical evidence	30	Experimenter bias	35
Humanistic psychology	18	Naturalistic observation	30	Sample	35
Cognitive psychology	19	Observer bias	30	Random sample	36
Evolutionary psychology	19	Case study	31	Representative sample	37
Positive psychology	20				

VERVIEW

Neurons: The Messengers
The Neural Impulse
The Synapse
Neural Plasticity and
Neurogenesis

The Central Nervous System
The Organization
of the Nervous System
The Brain

Hemispheric Specialization
Tools for Studying the Brain
The Spinal Cord

The Peripheral Nervous System
The Somatic Nervous System
The Autonomic Nervous System

The Endocrine System

Genes, Evolution, and Behavior
Genetics
Behavior Genetics
Evolutionary Psychology
Social Implications

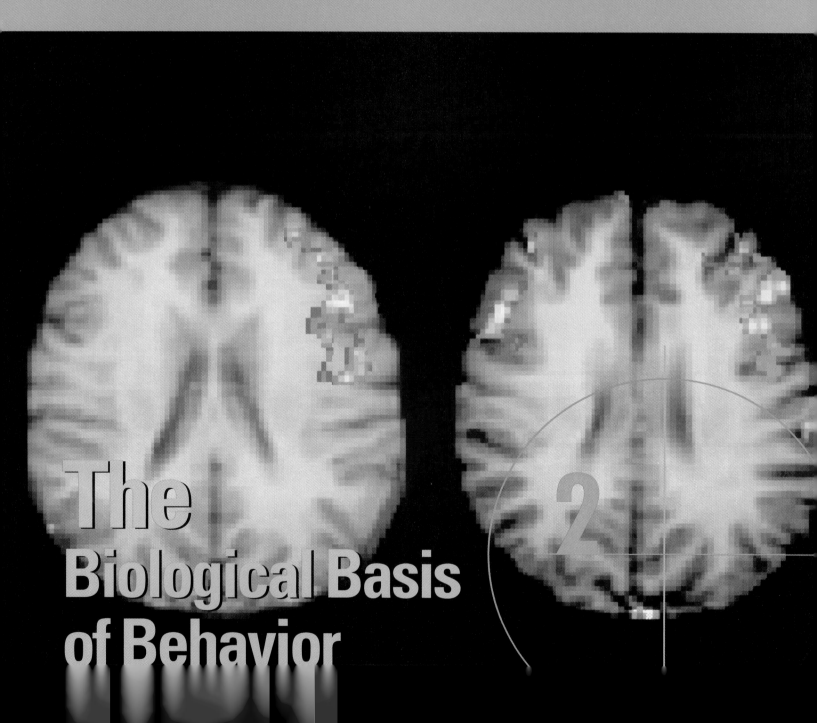

The Biological Basis of Behavior

2

hen Alex was born, the left side of his brain, which normally controls speech, was smothered by a tangle of abnormal blood vessels that left him mute, half-blind, semi-paralyzed, and prone to epileptic seizures. As Alex got older, the seizures became increasingly frequent and severe. Unable to control his epilepsy with medication, Alex's doctors recommended surgery to remove the entire left side of his brain. They were reasonably sure that this procedure would reduce Alex's seizures, but warned his parents not to expect much other improvement. At eight years of age, he was long past the age when a mute child could learn to talk.

The operation was a success; the seizures stopped. Then, ten months later, Alex stunned everyone by beginning to speak, first in single words and then in complete sentences. At age 11 he still pronounced some words incorrectly, as if he had a foreign accent; now age 23, he is fluent. To date, more than 50 epileptic children have undergone successful *hemispherectomies* (removal of the left or right half of the brain). All are expected to be able to lead normal lives.

The brain is the master control center of everything we say and do. One would think that removing half a child's brain would leave him or her severely disabled. But Alex and others have shown that just the opposite is true. Children emerge from the operation with their memory, personality, and sense of humor intact. Like Alex, some show dramatic improvement in speech, coordination, and other areas. How can this be?

First, the human brain—the product of millions of years of evolution—is an extremely complex organ. Our brains contain billions of cells, arranged in countless overlapping pathways and networks, with many backup systems—far more "mental equipment" than we need. In addition, the two hemispheres of the brain are similar though not identical, like our right and left hands. Normally, the two work together. But if the left hemisphere is removed, the right hemisphere takes over most of its functions as it did in Alex's case.

Second, the human brain demonstrates extraordinary *plasticity*, the ability to adapt to new environmental conditions. Although the brain may be the command center of our bodies, it also responds to feedback from the senses and surrounding environment, and changes as a result. One reason why children like Alex improve after a hemispherectomy is that their environment changes when their seizures stop and they no longer need antiseizure medications (powerful sedatives that make children groggy). Before the operation, the internal environment of their bodies is chaotic and their ability to respond to the external environment is dulled. After the operation, their internal environment is calmer and their awareness of the external environment enhanced. All the organs of our body—and all our behavior—depend on intricate feedback-and-control patterns. We live surrounded by objects and events, and our biological systems are geared to make adjustments that keep us in tune with our surroundings.

This chapter introduces **psychobiology,** the branch of psychology that deals with the biological bases of behavior and mental processes. Psychobiology overlaps with a much larger interdisciplinary field of study called **neuroscience,** which specifically focuses on the study of the brain and the nervous system. Many psychobiologists who study the brain's influence on behavior call themselves *neuropsychologists*.

THINKABOUTIT

You will find answers to these questions in the chapter:

1. What "language" do neurons speak?

2. Why does frontal lobe damage result in personality change?

3. Is the "fight or flight" response still useful in the modern world?

4. Why are psychologists interested in hormones?

5. Is intelligence inherited? Is alcoholism?

Psychobiology The area of psychology that focuses on the biological foundations of behavior and mental processes.

Neuroscience The study of the brain and the nervous system.

We begin our journey by looking at the basic building blocks of the brain and nervous system: nerve cells or *neurons*. Then we will explore the two major systems that integrate and coordinate our behavior, keeping us in constant touch with what is going on "out there." One is the *nervous system*, which is divided into the central nervous system (the brain and spinal cord) and the peripheral nervous system. The other is the *endocrine system*, made up of glands that secrete chemical messages into the blood. Last, we examine the influence of heredity and human evolution on behavior.

ENDURING ISSUES   mindbody

Window on the Mind

In the mind-body debate, neuropsychologists sit at the crossroad, where our sense of self intersects with advances in scientific knowledge. How does the organ we call the brain create the experience of what we call the mind? Until recently this question seemed unanswerable (Damasio, 1999, 2003). After all, the body and brain are observable, physical entities. Whether looking at how a person behaves or studying a brain scan, different observers see the same things. In contrast, the mind is a subjective entity, private and unique, and observable only to its owner. In the 1990s—called the Decade of the Brain—neuropsychologists learned more about the brain than during the entire previous history of psychology. New technology enabled researchers to identify—in a normal, living person—which areas of the brain were active during such different activities as naming an object or studying a face. A number of neuropsychologists believe that in the near future we will be able to describe and explain the mind in biological terms (Damasio, 1999, 2003).

Neurons: The Messengers

What "language" do neurons speak?

The brain of an average human being contains as many as 100 billion nerve cells, or **neurons**. Billions more neurons are found in other parts of the nervous system. Yet a single neuron holds many of the secrets of behavior and mental activity.

Neurons vary widely in size and shape, but they are all specialized to receive and transmit information. A typical neuron is shown in Figure 2–1. Like other cells, the neuron's cell body is made up of a nucleus, which contains a complete set of chromosomes and genes; cytoplasm, which keeps the cell alive; and a cell membrane, which encloses the whole cell. What makes a neuron different from other cells are the tiny fibers that extend out from the cell body, enabling a neuron to perform its special job: receiving and transmitting messages. The short fibers branching out around the cell body are **dendrites** (from the Greek word for "tree"). Their role is to pick up incoming messages from other neurons and transmit them to the cell body. The single long fiber extending from the cell body is an **axon** (from the Greek for "axle"). The axon's job is to carry outgoing messages to neighboring neurons or to a muscle or gland. Axons vary in length from 1 or 2 millimeters to 3 feet (for example, in adults, the axons that run from the brain to the base of the spinal cord or from the spinal cord to the tip of the thumb). Although a neuron has only one axon, near its end the axon splits into many terminal branches. When we talk about a **nerve (or tract)**, we are referring to a group of axons bundled together like wires in an electrical cable.

Neurons Individual cells that are the smallest units of the nervous system.

Dendrites Short fibers that branch out from the cell body and pick up incoming messages.

Axon Single long fiber extending from the cell body; it carries outgoing messages.

Nerve (or tract) Group of axons bundled together.

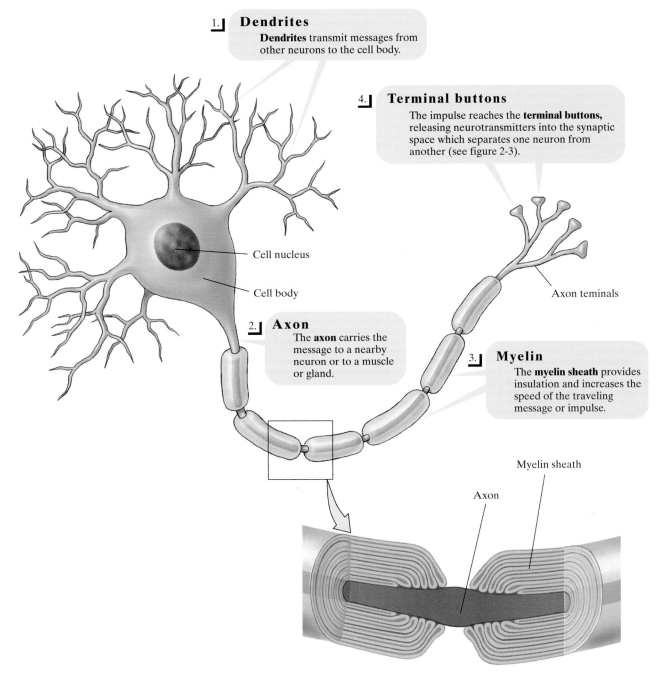

1. **Dendrites**
Dendrites transmit messages from other neurons to the cell body.

4. **Terminal buttons**
The impulse reaches the **terminal buttons,** releasing neurotransmitters into the synaptic space which separates one neuron from another (see figure 2-3).

Cell nucleus

Cell body

Axon teminals

2. **Axon**
The **axon** carries the message to a nearby neuron or to a muscle or gland.

3. **Myelin**
The **myelin sheath** provides insulation and increases the speed of the traveling message or impulse.

Myelin sheath

Axon

Figure 2–1
This typical myelinated neuron shows the cell body, dendrites, axon, myelin sheath, and terminal buttons.
Source: Adapted from *Fundamentals of Human Neuropsychology* (4/e), by Brian Kolb and Ian Q. Whishaw. Copyright © 1980, 1985, 1990, 1996 by W. H. Freeman and Company. Reprinted with permission.

The axon in Figure 2–1 is surrounded by a white, fatty covering called a **myelin sheath**. The myelin sheath is "pinched" at intervals, which makes the axon resemble a string of microscopic sausages. Not all axons have this covering, but myelinated axons are found in all parts of the body. (Because of this white covering, tissues made up primarily of myelinated axons are known as "white matter," whereas tissues made up primarily of unmyelinated axons are called "gray matter.") The myelin sheath has two functions: first, it provides insulation, so that signals from

 2.1

Myelin sheath White fatty covering found on some axons.

Sensory (or afferent) neurons Neurons that carry messages from sense organs to the spinal cord or brain.

Motor (or efferent) neurons Neurons that carry messages from the spinal cord or brain to the muscles and glands.

Interneurons (or association neurons) Neurons that carry messages from one neuron to another.

Glial cells (or glia) Cells that form the myelin sheath; they insulate and support neurons by holding them together, removing waste products, and preventing harmful substances from passing from the bloodstream into the brain.

Ions Electrically charged particles found both inside and outside the neuron.

Resting potential Electrical charge across a neuron membrane due to excess positive ions concentrated on the outside and excess negative ions on the inside.

Polarization The condition of a neuron when the inside is negatively charged relative to the outside; for example, when the neuron is at rest.

Neural impulse (or action potential) The firing of a nerve cell.

Graded potential A shift in the electrical charge in a tiny area of a neuron.

Threshold of excitation The level an impulse must exceed to cause a neuron to fire.

All-or-none law Principle that the action potential in a neuron does not vary in strength; the neuron either fires at full strength or it does not fire at all.

adjacent neurons do not interfere with each other; second, it increases the speed at which signals are transmitted.

Neurons that collect messages from sense organs and carry those messages to the spinal cord or the brain are called **sensory (or afferent) neurons**. Neurons that carry messages from the spinal cord or the brain to the muscles and glands are called **motor (or efferent) neurons**. And neurons that carry messages from one neuron to another are called **interneurons (or association neurons)**.

The nervous system also contains a vast number of **glial cells or glia** (from the Greek word meaning "glue"). Glial cells hold the neurons in place, provide nourishment and remove waste products, prevent harmful substances from passing from the bloodstream into the brain, and form the myelin sheath that insulates and protects neurons. Recent evidence suggests that glial cells may play an important role in learning and memory and thereby affect the brain's response to new experiences (Featherstone, Fleming, & Ivy, 2000; Roitbak, 1993).

The Neural Impulse

How do neurons "talk" to one another? What form do their messages take? Neurons speak in a language that all cells in the body understand: simple yes-no, on-off electrochemical impulses.

When a neuron is at rest, the membrane surrounding the cell forms a partial barrier between the fluids that are inside and outside of the neuron. Both solutions contain electrically charged particles, or **ions** (see Figure 2–2A). Because there are more negative ions inside the neuron than outside, there is a small electrical charge (called the **resting potential**) across the cell membrane. Thus, the resting neuron is said to be in a state of **polarization.** A resting or polarized neuron is like a spring that has been compressed or a guitar string that has been pulled but not released. All that is needed to generate a neuron's signal is the release of this tension.

When a small area on the cell membrane is adequately stimulated by an incoming message, pores (or channels) in the membrane at the stimulated area open, allowing a sudden inflow of positively charged sodium ions. This process is called *depolarization*; now the inside of the neuron is positively charged relative to the outside. Depolarization sets off a chain reaction. When the membrane allows sodium to enter the neuron at one point, the next point on the membrane opens. More sodium ions flow into the neuron at the second spot and depolarize this part of the neuron, and so on, along the entire length of the neuron. As a result, an electrical charge, called a **neural impulse or action potential,** travels down the axon, much like a fuse burning from one end to the other (see Figure 2–2B and 2–2C). When this happens, we say that the neuron has "fired." The speed at which neurons carry impulses varies widely, from as fast as nearly 400 feet per second on largely myelinated axons to as slow as 3 feet per second on those with no myelin.

As a rule, single impulses received from neighboring neurons do not make a neuron fire. The incoming message causes a small, temporary shift in the electrical charge, called a **graded potential,** which is transmitted along the cell membrane and may simply fade away, leaving the neuron in its normal polarized state. For a neuron to fire, graded potentials caused by impulses from many neighboring neurons—or from one other neuron firing repeatedly—must exceed a certain minimum **threshold of excitation.** Just as a light switch requires a minimum amount of pressure to be activated, an incoming message must be above the minimum threshold to make a neuron fire.

Neurons either fire or they do not, and every firing of a particular neuron produces an impulse of the same strength. This is called the **all-or-none law.** However, the neuron is likely to fire *more often* when stimulated by a strong signal. The result is rapid neural firing that communicates the message "There's a very strong stimu-

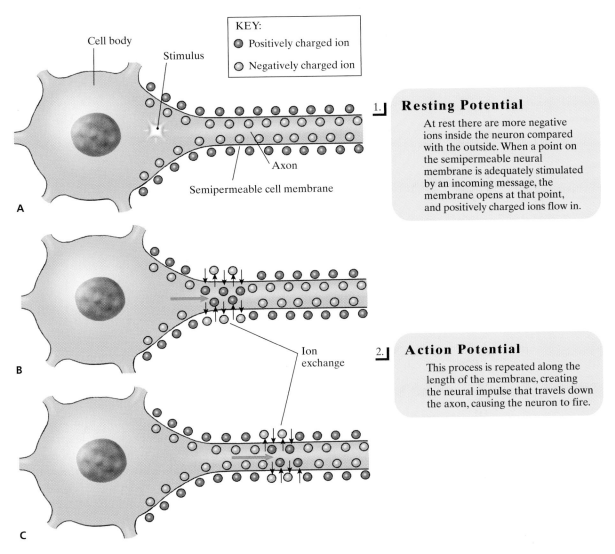

Cell body

Stimulus

Axon

Semipermeable cell membrane

A

1. **Resting Potential**

At rest there are more negative ions inside the neuron compared with the outside. When a point on the semipermeable neural membrane is adequately stimulated by an incoming message, the membrane opens at that point, and positively charged ions flow in.

B

Ion exchange

2. **Action Potential**

This process is repeated along the length of the membrane, creating the neural impulse that travels down the axon, causing the neuron to fire.

C

Figure 2–2
The neural impulse: communication within the neuron.

lus out here!" Immediately after firing, the neuron goes through an **absolute refractory period:** for about a thousandth of a second, the neuron will not fire again, no matter how strong the incoming messages may be. In the **relative refractory period,** when the cell is returning to the resting state, the neuron will fire, but only if the incoming message is considerably stronger than is normally necessary to make it fire. Finally, the neuron returns to its resting state, ready to fire again, as shown in Figure 2–3.

A single neuron may have many hundreds of dendrites, and its axon may branch out in numerous directions, so that it is in touch with hundreds or thousands of other cells at both its input end (dendrites) and its output end (axon). At any given moment, a neuron may be receiving messages from other neurons, some of which are primarily excitatory and others, primarily inhibitory. The constant interplay of excitation and inhibition determine whether the neuron is likely to fire or not.

The Synapse

Neurons are not directly connected like links in a chain. Rather, they are separated by a tiny gap, called a **synaptic space** or **synaptic cleft,** where the axon terminals of one neuron *almost* touch the dendrites or cell body of other neurons. When a

 2.2

Absolute refractory period A period after firing when a neuron will not fire again no matter how strong the incoming messages may be.

Relative refractory period A period after firing when a neuron is returning to its normal polarized state and will fire again only if the incoming message is much stronger than usual.

Synaptic space (or synaptic cleft) Tiny gap between the axon terminal of one neuron and the dendrites or cell body of the next neuron.

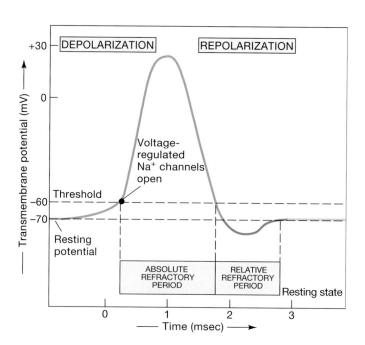

Figure 2–3
Electrical changes during the action potential.
The incoming message must be above a certain threshold to cause a neuron to fire. After it fires, the neuron is returned to its resting state. This process happens very quickly, and within a few thousandths of a second (msec) the neuron is ready to fire again.

 psych 2.3

Terminal button (or synaptic knob) Structure at the end of an axon terminal branch.

Synapse Area composed of the axon terminal of one neuron, the synaptic space, and the dendrite or cell body of the next neuron.

Synaptic vesicles Tiny sacs in a terminal button that release chemicals into the synapse.

Neurotransmitters Chemicals released by the synaptic vesicles that travel across the synaptic space and affect adjacent neurons.

Receptor site A location on a receptor neuron into which a specific neurotransmitter fits like a key into a lock.

neuron fires, an impulse travels down the axon, out through the terminal branches, into a tiny swelling called a **terminal button** or **synaptic knob.** The entire area composed of the axon terminals of one neuron, the synaptic space, and the dendrites and cell body of the next neuron is called the **synapse** (see Figure 2–4).

For the neural impulse to move on to the next neuron, it must somehow cross the synaptic space. It is tempting to imagine that the neural impulse simply leaps across the gap like an electrical spark, but in reality the transfer is made by chemicals. What actually happens is this: Most axon terminals contain a number of minute oval sacs called **synaptic vesicles** (see Figure 2–4). When the neural impulse reaches the end of the terminals, it causes these vesicles to release varying amounts of chemicals called **neurotransmitters** into the synaptic space. Each neurotransmitter has specific matching **receptor sites** on the other side of the synaptic space. Neurotransmitters fit into their corresponding receptor sites just as a key fits into a lock. This lock-and-key system ensures that neurotramsitters do not randomly stimulate other neurons, but follow orderly pathways.

Once their job is complete, neurotransmitters detach from the receptor site. In most cases, they are either reabsorbed into the axon terminals to be used again, broken down and recycled to make new neurotransmitters, or disposed of by the body as waste. The synapse is cleared and returned to its normal state.

Neurotransmitters In recent decades, psychobiologists have identified hundreds of neurotransmitters; their exact functions are still being studied (see *Summary Table: Major Neurotransmitters and Their Effects*). However, a few brain chemicals are well known.

Acetylcholine (ACh) acts where neurons meet skeletal muscles. It also appears to play a critical role in arousal, attention, memory, and motivation (Panksepp, 1986). Alzheimer's disease, which involves loss of memory and severe language problems, has been linked to degeneration of the brain cells that produce and respond to ACh (Froelich & Hoyer, 2002).

Dopamine generally affects neurons associated with voluntary movement, learning, memory, and emotions. The symptoms of Parkinson's disease—tremors, muscle spasms, and increasing muscular rigidity—have been traced to loss of the brain cells that produce dopamine (Costa et al., 2003). (Medication can reduce the symptoms of Parkinson's, sometimes for years, but to date there is no permanent cure.)

Some neurotransmitters carry specific information or instructions from specific synapses to particular regions of the brain or body (for example, "incoming sound" or telling muscles to "contract" or "relax"). However, a few have widespread effects. *Serotonin*, popularly known as "the mood molecule," is an example. Serotonin is like a master key that opens many locks—that is, it attaches to as many as a dozen receptor sites. Serotonin sets an emotional tone. For example, other neurotransmitters enable us to see clouds in the sky; serotonin affects whether we experience the day as sunny or gray. Other neurotransmitters tell our brain how much water is in a glass; serotonin affects whether we think of the glass as half empty or half full.

Another group of brain chemicals regulates the sensitivity of large numbers of synapses, in effect "turning up" or "turning down" the activity level of whole portions of the nervous system. For example, *endorphins*, chains of amino acids, appear to reduce pain by inhibiting, or "turning down," the neurons that transmit pain messages in the brain. One endorphin was found to be 48 times more potent than morphine when injected into the brain and 3 times more potent when injected into the bloodstream (S. H. Snyder, 1977).

Endorphins were discovered in the early 1970s. Researchers Candace Pert and Solomon Snyder (1973) were attempting to explain the effects of *opiates*—painkilling drugs such as morphine and heroin that are derived from the poppy plant—when they discovered that the central nervous system contained receptor sites for these substances. They reasoned that these receptor sites would not exist

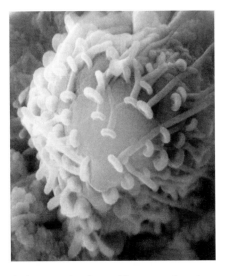

A photograph taken with a scanning electron microscope, showing the synaptic knobs at the ends of axons. Inside the knobs are the vesicles that contain neurotransmitters.

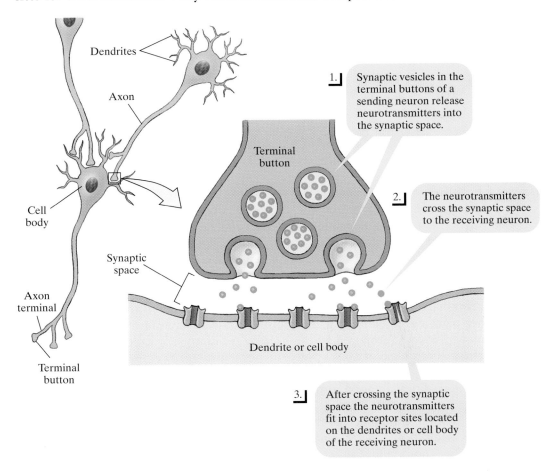

Figure 2–4
Synaptic transmission—communication between neurons.
When a neural impulse reaches the end of an axon, tiny oval sacs, called synaptic vesicles, at the end of most axons, release varying amounts of chemical substances called neurotransmitters. These substances travel across the synaptic space and affect the next neuron.

summarytable MAJOR NEUROTRANSMITTERS AND THEIR EFFECTS

Acetylcholine (ACh)	Distributed widely throughout the central nervous system, where it is involved in arousal, attention, memory, motivation, and movement. Involved in muscle action through presence at neuromuscular junctions (specialized type of synapse where neurons connect to muscle cells). Degeneration of neurons that produce ACh have been linked to Alzheimer's disease. Too much can lead to spasms and tremors; too little, to paralysis or torpor.
Dopamine	Involved in a wide variety of behaviors and emotions, including pleasure. Implicated in schizophrenia and Parkinson's disease.
Serotonin	Involved in the regulation of sleep, dreaming, mood, eating, pain, and aggressive behavior. Implicated in depression.
Norepinephrine	Affects arousal, wakefulness, learning, memory, and mood.
Endorphins	Involved in the inhibition of pain. Released during strenuous exercise. May be responsible for "runner's high."
Glutamate	Involved in long-term memory and the perception of pain.
GABA (Gamma aminobutyric acid)	A largely inhibitory neurotransmitter distributed widely throughout the central nervous system. Implicated in sleep and eating disorders. Low levels of GABA have also been linked to extreme anxiety.
Glycene	Principally responsible for inhibition in the spinal cord and lower brain centers.

unless the body produced its own natural painkillers. Not long after, researchers discovered the endorphins. Morphine and other narcotics lock into the receptors for endorphins and have the same painkilling effects. Research on endorphins has provided clues to why people become addicted to morphine, heroin, and other opiates. When a person takes one of these drugs repeatedly, the body's production of *natural* painkillers slows down. As a result, an addict needs more of the artificial drug to feel "normal."

Imbalances in neurotransmitters appear to contribute to many types of mental illness. Schizophrenia, for example, has been associated with an overabundance of, or hypersensitivity to, dopamine. An undersupply of serotonin and norepinephrine has been linked to depression and other disorders. As in the case of endorphins, the design and testing of drugs has helped neuroscientists to identify the functions of neurotransmitters.

Psychopharmacology Most psychoactive drugs and toxins (or poisons) work by either blocking or enhancing the transmission of chemicals across synapses. For example, *botulism* (produced by the bacteria in improperly canned or frozen food) prevents the release of ACh, which carries signals to the muscles. The result is paralysis and, sometimes, rapid death. *Curare*, a poison some native people of South America traditionally used to tip their arrows, instantly stuns and sometimes kills their prey or enemies. Curare blocks the ACh *receptors*—that is, it has the same effect as botulism, but acts at the other side of the synapse. Likewise, the antipsychotic medications *chlorprozamine* (trade name Thorazine) and *clozapine* prevent dopamine from binding to receptor sites; this reduction in stimulation apparently reduces schizophrenic hallucinations.

Other substances do the opposite: they enhance the activity of neurotransmitters. Some do this by increasing the release of a transmitter. For example, the poison of the black widow spider causes ACh to spew into the synapses of the nervous system. As a result, neurons fire repeatedly, causing spasms and tremors. In a slightly more

Endorphins, which are released into the brain and body during exercise, are neurotransmitters that act as natural painkillers.

complex loop, *caffeine* increases release of excitatory, arousing neurotransmitters by blocking the action of adenosine, a transmitter that inhibits the release of these substances (Nehlig, Daval, & Debry, 1992). Two or three cups of coffee contain enough caffeine to block half the adenosine receptors for several hours, producing a high state of arousal and, in some cases, anxiety and insomnia.

Other substances interfere with the removal of neurotransmitters from the synapse after they have done their job so that they continue to stimulate receptor neurons. *Cocaine*, for example, prevents dopamine from being reabsorbed. As a result, excess amounts of dopamine accumulate in the synapses, producing heightened arousal of the entire nervous system (Freeman et al., 2002).

The same processes are used by antidepressant medications that reduce the hopeless/helpless symptoms of severe depression, and by antipsychotic medications that alleviate the hallucinations of schizophrenia. We will say more about these "miracle drugs" in Chapter 13, Psychological Disorders, and Chapter 14, Therapies.

Although less publicized, research in the 1990s also led to revolutionary discoveries about the brain's potential capacity to heal itself.

> **Neural Plasticity** The ability of the brain to change in response to experience.

ENDURING ISSUES　**stability**change

Neural Plasticity

The brain is the one organ in the body that is unique to each individual. From birth, your brain has been encoding experience, developing the patterns of emotion and thought that make you who you are. At the same time, your brain is continually changing as you learn new information and skills and adjust to changing conditions. How do neurons perform this intricate balancing act, maintaining stability while adapting to change? Even more remarkably, how does the brain recover from injury (as in the example at the beginning of the chapter)? The answer lies in **neural plasticity,** the ability of the brain to be changed structurally and chemically by experience.

Neural Plasticity and Neurogenesis

In a classic series of experiments, M. R. Rosenzweig (1984) demonstrated the importance of experience to neural development in the laboratory. Rosenzweig divided rats into several groups. Members of one group were isolated in barren cages (an impoverished environment); members of the second group were raised with other rats in cages equipped with a variety of toys, and hence opportunities for exploration, manipulation, and social interaction (an enriched environment). He found that the rats raised in enriched environments had larger neurons with more synaptic connections than those raised in impoverished environments (see Figure 2–5). In more recent experiments, Rosenzweig (1996) showed that similar changes occur in rats of any age. Other researchers have found that rats raised in stimulating environments perform better on a variety of cognitive tests and develop more synapses when required to perform complex tasks (Kleim, Vij, Ballard, & Greenough, 1997). These combined results suggest that neural plasticity is a feedback loop: experience leads to changes in the brain, which, in turn, facilitate new learning, which leads to further neural change, and so on (Nelson, 1999).

Reorganization of the brain as a result of experience is not limited to rats. For example, violinists, cellists, and other string musicians spend years developing

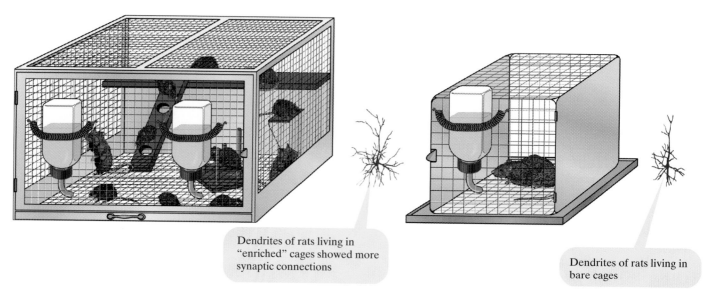

Dendrites of rats living in "enriched" cages showed more synaptic connections

Dendrites of rats living in bare cages

Figure 2–5
Brain growth and experience.
In Rosenzweig's experiment, young rats lived in two kinds of cages: "impoverished," with nothing to manipulate or explore, or "enriched," with a variety of objects. When Rosenzweig examined the rats' brains, he found that the enriched group had larger neurons with more synaptic connections (shown as dendrites in the drawing) than the rats that lived in the bare cages. Experience, then, can actually affect the structure of the brain.
Source: From "Brain changes in response to experience" by M. R. Rosenzweig, E. L. Bennett, and M. C. Diamond. Copyright © 1972, Scientific American, Inc. All rights reserved. Adapted with permission of the estate of Bunji Tagawa.

precise left-hand sensitivity and dexterity. Researchers have found that the area of the musicians' brains associated with left-hand sensation is larger than the area that represents the right hand (which string musicians use for bowing), and larger than the left-hand area in nonmusicians (Elbert, Pantev, Wienbruch, Rockstroh, & Taub, 1995). In deaf people, an area of the brain usually responsible for hearing rewires itself to read lips and sign language (Bosworth & Dobkins, 1999).

Experience also causes changes in the *strength* of communication across synapses. Stimulating the left hand of string musicians resulted in a strong increase in neural activity, but a comparatively weak response in nonmusicians (Elbert et al., 1995). Interestingly, this effect was most pronounced for musicians who began playing a string instrument before age 12. Other researchers have studied this phenomenon at the cellular level (Bliss & Collingridge, 1993; Nicoll & Malenka, 1999). When neurons in the hippocampus (a brain structure involved in forming memories in humans and other animals) are stimulated by an electrical pulse, the initial response in nearby neurons is very weak. But repeated stimulation of the same pathway causes the nearby neurons to respond vigorously, an effect that lasts weeks after the stimulation was stopped. *Long-term potentiation* (LTP), as this is called, appears to help the brain learn and store new information (Martinez, Barea-Rodriguez, & Derrick, 1998).

We have seen that experience can lead to dramatic changes in the number and complexity of synaptic connections in the brain; that is, in the connections between neurons. Might experience also produce new neurons? For many years, psychologists believed that organisms are born with all the brain cells they will ever have. New research appears to overturn this traditional view. A number of studies conducted in the 1990s showed that adult brains are capable of **neurogenesis,** the production of new brain cells. In the mid-1990s, some researchers demonstrated that human brain tissue (obtained from patients undergoing surgery for severe epilepsy) grown in a supportive environment in the laboratory produced functionally mature neurons (L. K. Altman, 1995), but most scientists at the time doubted that this occurs in real life. A

Neurogenesis The growth of new neurons.

APPLYING PSYCHOLOGY

CAN THE BRAIN AND NERVOUS SYSTEM REPAIR THEMSELVES?

After a stroke in 1993, Sylvia Elam lost most of the sensation and movement on the right side of her body (Pollack, 2000). She recognized the benefits of an operation performed in 1999 almost as soon as she reached the recovery room. When she ate lunch, she could taste the food for the first time in years. Soon she was talking without stammering, walking without a cane some of the time, and even able to drive a car. "It was absolutely beyond our wildest dreams," said her husband, Ira (p. F1).

Traditionally, injuries to the brain and spinal cord have been considered permanent; treatment was limited to stabilizing the patient to prevent further damage, treating related infections, and using rehabilitation to maximize remaining capabilities (McDonald, 1999). Some individuals with brain damage recovered over time, but they were the exception. New discoveries have changed this prognosis. Specific treatments may take years to develop, but people suffering from neurological disorders such as Parkinson's and Alzheimer's disease, as well as victims of spinal cord injuries and stroke now have hope (Barinaga, 2000a; Gage, 2000; McMillan, Robertson, & Wilson, 1999; Van Praag & Gage, 2002).

Scientists have long known that embryos contain large numbers of stem cells: undifferentiated, precursor or "precells" that, under the right conditions, can give rise to any specialized cell in the body—liver, kidney, blood, heart, or neurons (Bjornson, Rietze, Reynolds, Magli, & Vescovi, 1999). Remarkably, in tests with animals, stem cells transplanted into a brain or spinal cord spontaneously migrated to damaged areas and began to generate specialized neurons for replacement (McKay, 1997). It was as if stem cells moved through the brain, going from one neuron to the next looking for damage. If damage was found, the stem cells began to divide and produce specialized neurons appropriate for that area of the brain.

"It was as if stem cells moved through the brain, going from one neuron to the next looking for damage."

In clinical trials with human patients suffering from Parkinson's disease, fetal nerve cell transplants have improved motor control for periods of 5 to 10 years (Barinaga, 2000a). But the supply of fetal tissue is limited, and its harvest and use raise ethical questions.

The discovery of adult neurogenesis removed these ethical questions and raised new possibilities. Could adult precursor cells grown in the laboratory be transplanted into patients with neurological damage? Sylvia Elam was one of the first people to volunteer for this procedure. Not all human trials have been as successful, and Mrs. Elam suffered a second, unrelated stroke several months after her operation. Still, researchers are hopeful.

Another potential use of new research findings is to stimulate the brain's own stem cells to provide "self-repair." Once the chemicals that regulate neurogenesis are more fully understood, it may be possible to increase the amounts of these substances in areas of the central nervous system where neural growth needs to occur (Gage, 2000). Some researchers have already begun to identify substances and environmental conditions that show promise of stimulating neural regrowth (Auvergne et al., 2002; Rasika, Alvarez-Buylla, & Nottebohm, 1999). One substance in particular, inosine has been shown in rats to stimulate undamaged nerve fibers to grow new connections and restore motor functioning following strokes (Chen, Goldberg, Kolb, Lanser, & Benowitz, 2002).

To translate this discovery into treatment, scientists need to learn more about what causes (or blocks) the production of adult stem cells, and what causes their "daughter cells" to become mature, specialized neurons and to migrate to different areas of the brain (Gage, 2000; Van Praag & Gage, 2002). But a groundwork has been laid that may someday provide successful treatments for patients with damaged spinal cords and nervous system disorders like Parkinson's disease and Alzheimer's disease.

Severing the spinal cord at the neck typically causes paralysis of everything below the head because nerves connecting to the body's muscles no longer have a cable to the brain. Actor Christopher Reeve suffered this tragedy after being thrown from a horse. He and others may someday benefit from research on neurogenesis.

major breakthrough came in November 1998 when a group of American and Swedish researchers reported on autopsies of the brains of elderly patients who had died of cancer. A substance injected into their tumors to monitor how fast the tumors were growing revealed that the patients' brains had continued to produce new neurons up to the end of their lives (Eriksson et al., 1998). The discovery of lifelong neurogenesis has widespread implications for treating neurological disorders (see *Applying Psychology: Can the Brain and Nervous System Repair Themselves?*).

CHECK YOUR UNDERSTANDING

1. All of these are parts of a neuron EXCEPT a(n)

___ a. dendrite

___ b. glia

___ c. myelin sheath

___ d. axon

2. Synaptic vesicles release varying amounts of chemicals called

___ a. receptors

___ b. neurotransmitters

___ c. neurons

___ d. antidepressants

3. Experiments have shown that a more stimulating environment leads to development of more synapses. This is evidence of

___ a. neurogenesis

___ b. left-handed dexterity

___ c. epilepsy

___ d. neural plasticity

4. This "mood molecule" has been likened to a master key because it opens many locks. Name it.

___ a. endorphin

___ b. ACh

___ c. seratonin

___ d. curare

Answers: 1.b, 2.b, 3.d, 4.c

The Central Nervous System

Why does frontal lobe damage result in personality change?

The Organization of the Nervous System

Central nervous system Division of the nervous system that consists of the brain and spinal cord.

Every part of the nervous system is connected to every other part. To understand its anatomy and functions, however, it is useful to analyze the nervous system in terms of the divisions and subdivisions shown in Figure 2–6. The **central nervous system**

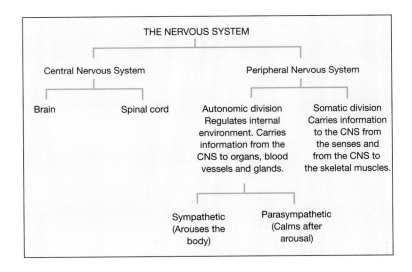

Figure 2–6
A schematic diagram of the divisions of the nervous system and their various subparts.

includes the brain and spinal cord, which together contain more than 90 percent of the body's neurons. The **peripheral nervous system** consists of nerves that connect the brain and spinal cord to every other part of the body, carrying messages back and forth between the central nervous system and the sense organs, muscles, and glands. The peripheral nervous system is subdivided into the *somatic nervous system*, which transmits information about body movements and the external environment, and the *autonomic nervous system*, which transmits information to and from the internal organs and glands. (We will discuss the endocrine system, which works hand in hand with the nervous system, later in the chapter.)

The Brain

The brain is the seat of awareness and reason, the place where learning, memory, and emotions are centered. It is the part of us that decides what to do and whether that decision was right or wrong, and it imagines how things might have turned out if we had acted differently. The spinal cord receives less attention but is no less important to understanding behavior and mental processes.

The human brain—our "crowning glory"—is the product of millions of years of evolution. As new, more complex structures were added, older structures were retained. One way to understand the brain is to look at three layers that evolved in different stages of evolution: (1) the primitive *central core*; (2) the *limbic system*, which evolved later; and (3) the *cerebral hemispheres*, which are in charge of higher mental processes (see Figure 2–7). We will use these three basic divisions to describe the parts of the brain, what they do, and how they interact to influence our behavior (see the *Summary Table: Parts of the Brain and Their Functions*).

The Central Core   At the point where the spinal cord enters the skull, it becomes the **hindbrain.** Because the hindbrain is found in even the most primitive vertebrates, it is believed to have been the earliest part of the brain to evolve. The part of the hindbrain nearest to the spinal cord is the *medulla*, a narrow structure about 1.5 inches long. The medulla controls such bodily functions as breathing, heart rate, and blood pressure. The medulla is also the point at which many of the nerves from the body cross over on their way to and from the higher brain centers; nerves from the left part of the body cross to the right side of the brain and vice versa (a topic to which we will return). Near the medulla lies the *pons*, which produces chemicals that help maintain our sleep–wake cycle (discussed in Chapter 4, States of Consciousness). Both the medulla and the pons transmit messages to the upper areas of the brain.

 2.5

Peripheral nervous system Division of the nervous system that connects the central nervous system to the rest of the body.

Hindbrain Area containing the medulla, pons, and cerebellum.

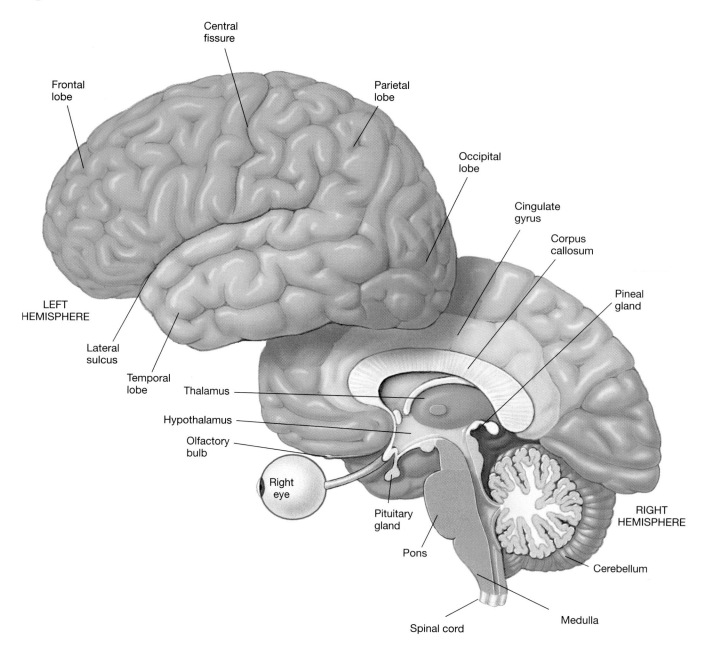

Figure 2–7
The divisions of the brain.

Cerebellum Structure in the hindbrain that controls certain reflexes and coordinates the body's movements.

Midbrain Region between the hindbrain and the forebrain; it is important for hearing and sight, and it is one of several places in the brain where pain is registered.

Thalamus Forebrain region that relays and translates incoming messages from the sense receptors, except those for smell.

At the top and back of the brain stem is a convoluted structure called the **cerebellum** (or "little brain"), which is responsible for our sense of balance and for coordinating the body's actions to ensure that movements go together in efficient sequences. Damage to the cerebellum causes severe problems in movement, such as jerky motions and stumbling.

Above the cerebellum, the brain stem widens to form the **midbrain.** The midbrain is especially important for hearing and sight. It is also one of several places in the brain where pain is registered.

More or less directly over the brain stem are the two egg-shaped structures that make up the **thalamus.** The thalamus is often described as a relay station: Almost all sensory information from the lower parts of the central nervous system passes through the thalamus on the way to higher levels of the brain. The thalamus both integrates and shapes incoming signals. Directly below the thalamus is the smaller

summarytable PARTS OF THE BRAIN AND THEIR FUNCTIONS

Central Core	Medulla	Regulates respiration, heart rate, blood pressure
	Pons	Regulates sleep–wake cycles
	Cerebellum	Regulates reflexes and balance
		Coordinates movement
	Thalamus	Major sensory relay center
		Regulates higher brain centers and peripheral nervous system
	Hypothalamus	Emotion and motivation
		Stress reactions
Limbic System	Hippocampus	Formation of new memories
	Amygdala	Governs emotions related to self-perservation
Cerebral Cortex	Occipital lobe	Receives and processes visual information
	Temporal lobe	Smell
		Hearing
		Balance and equilibrium
		Emotion and motivation
		Some language comprehension
		Complex visual processing
	Parietal lobe	Sensory projection and association areas
		Visual/spatial abilities
	Frontal lobe	Goal-directed behavior
		Concentration
		Emotional control and temperament
		Motor projection and association areas
		Coordinates messages from other lobes
		Complex problem solving
		Involved in many aspects of personality

hypothalamus, which exerts an enormous influence on many kinds of motivation. Portions of the hypothalamus govern hunger, thirst, sexual drive, and body temperature (Winn, 1995) and are directly involved in emotional behavior such as rage, terror, and pleasure.

The **reticular formation (RF)** is a netlike system of neurons that weaves through all of these structures. Its main job seems to be to send "Alert!" signals to the higher parts of the brain in response to incoming messages. The RF can be subdued, however. During sleep, the RF is turned down; anesthetics work largely by temporarily shutting this system off; and permanent damage to the RF can induce a coma.

Hypothalamus Forebrain region that governs motivation and emotional responses.

Reticular formation (RF) Network of neurons in the hindbrain, the midbrain, and part of the forebrain whose primary function is to alert and arouse the higher parts of the brain.

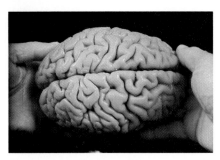

The human brain, viewed from the top. Its relatively small size belies its enormous complexity.

The Limbic System   The **limbic system** is a ring of loosely connected structures located between the central core and the cerebral hemispheres (see Figure 2–8). In evolutionary terms, the limbic system is more recent than the central core and fully developed only in mammals. Animals with primitive limbic systems, such as fish and reptiles, have limited behavioral repertoires: Their patterns of feeding, attacking, or mating are fixed. Mammals (including humans) are more flexible in their responses to the environment, suggesting that the limbic system suppresses some instinctive behavior.

The limbic system appears to play a central role in times of stress, coordinating and integrating the activity of the nervous system. One part of the limbic system, the *hippocampus*, also plays an essential role in the formation of new memories. People with severe damage to this area can still remember names, faces, and events that they embedded in memory before they were injured, but cannot remember anything new. Animals with damage in these areas fail to recognize where they have just been; as a result, they explore the same small part of their environment over and over again, as if it were constantly new to them.

The *amygdala* and the hippocampus are also involved in governing and regulating emotions (Davidson, Jackson, & Kalin, 2000; Hamann, Ely, Hoffman, & Kilts, 2002), particularly those related to self-preservation (MacLean, 1970). When portions of these structures are damaged or removed, aggressive animals become tame and docile. In contrast, stimulation of some portions of these structures causes animals to exhibit signs of fear and panic, whereas stimulation of other portions triggers unprovoked attacks. Other limbic structures heighten the experience of pleasure. Given the opportunity to press a bar that electrically stimulates portions of the septum, animals do so endlessly, ignoring food and water. Humans also experience pleasure when some areas of the septum are electrically stimulated, though apparently not as intensely (Kupfermann, 1991; Olds & Forbes, 1981). Even our ability to read the facial expressions of emotion in other people (such as smiling or frowning) are registered in the limbic system (Lange et al., 2003). We will return to the limbic system in Chapter 9, Motivation and Emotion.

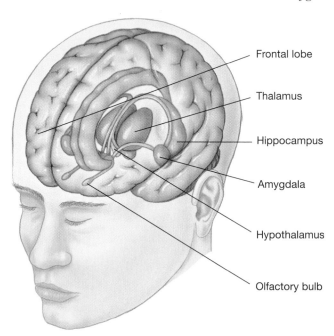

- Frontal lobe
- Thalamus
- Hippocampus
- Amygdala
- Hypothalamus
- Olfactory bulb

Figure 2–8
The limbic system.

Limbic system Ring of structures that play a role in learning and emotional behavior.

Cerebral cortex The outer surface of the two cerebral hemispheres that regulates most complex behavior.

The Cerebral Cortex   Ballooning out over and around the central core and limbic system, virtually hiding them, is the *cerebrum*. The cerebrum is divided into two hemispheres and covered by a thin layer of gray matter (unmyelinated cells) called the **cerebral cortex.** This is what most people think of first when they talk about "the brain"; it is the part of the brain that processes thought, vision, language, memory, and emotions. The cerebral cortex takes up most of the room inside the skull, accounting for about 80 percent of the weight of the human brain and containing about 70 percent of the neurons in the central nervous system.

The cerebral cortex is the most recently evolved part of the nervous system, and more highly developed in humans than in any other animal. Fish have no cerebral cortex, and reptiles and birds have only a primitive cortex. In lower mammals, such as rats, the cerebral cortex is small and relatively smooth. As one moves up the phylogenetic scale from lower to higher mammals, especially primates, the cerebral cortex becomes larger and increasingly wrinkled (an adaptation that allows more cortical tissue to fit inside the skull without, literally producing "swelled heads"). Spread out, the human cortex would cover 2 to 3 square feet and be about as thick as an uppercase letter on a typed page. But an intricate pattern of folds, hills, and valleys, called *convolutions*, enable the cerebral hemispheres to fit inside our relatively small heads. In each person, these convolutions form a pattern that is as unique as a fingerprint.

A number of landmarks on the cortex allow us to identify functional areas. The first is a deep cleft, running from front to back, that divides the brain into *right* and *left hemispheres*. As seen in Figure 2–9 each of these hemispheres can be divided into four *lobes* (described below), which are separated from one another by crevices. A *central fissure*, running sideways, roughly from ear to ear, separates the *primary somatosensory cortex*, which receives sensory messages from the entire body, from the *primary motor cortex*, which sends messages from the brain to various muscles and glands in the body. In addition, there are large areas on the cortex of all four lobes called **association areas.** Scientists generally believe that information from diverse parts of the cortex is integrated in the association areas and that these areas are the sites of such mental processes as learning, thinking, remembering, comprehending, and using language. Support for this view comes from comparing the cortex of different mammals. In rats, most of the cortex consists of sensory or motor areas; in cats, association areas are slightly larger, and in monkeys still larger; in humans, most of the cortex is devoted to association areas.

Association areas Areas of the cerebral cortex where incoming messages from the separate senses are combined into meaningful impressions and outgoing messages from the motor areas are integrated.

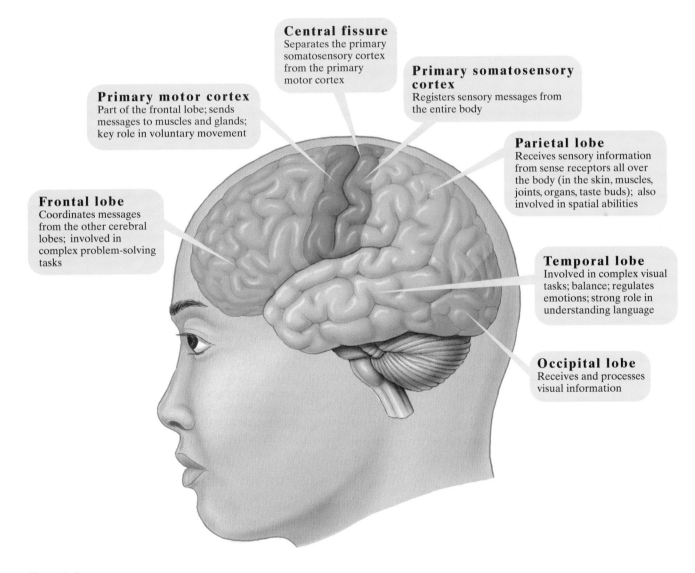

Central fissure
Separates the primary somatosensory cortex from the primary motor cortex

Primary somatosensory cortex
Registers sensory messages from the entire body

Primary motor cortex
Part of the frontal lobe; sends messages to muscles and glands; key role in voluntary movement

Parietal lobe
Receives sensory information from sense receptors all over the body (in the skin, muscles, joints, organs, taste buds); also involved in spatial abilities

Frontal lobe
Coordinates messages from the other cerebral lobes; involved in complex problem-solving tasks

Temporal lobe
Involved in complex visual tasks; balance; regulates emotions; strong role in understanding language

Occipital lobe
Receives and processes visual information

Figure 2–9
The four lobes of the cerebral cortex.
Deep fissures in the cortex separate these areas or lobes. Also shown are the primary somatosensory and motor areas.

Occipital lobe Part of the cerebral hemisphere that receives and interprets visual information.

Temporal lobe Part of the cerebral hemisphere that helps regulate hearing, balance and equilibrium, and certain emotions and motivations.

Parietal lobe Part of the cerebral cortex that receives sensory information from throughout the body.

Primary somatosensory cortex Area of the parietal lobe where messages from the sense receptors are registered.

Frontal lobe Part of the cerebral cortex that is responsible for voluntary movement; it is also important for attention, goal-directed behavior, and appropriate emotional experiences.

Primary motor cortex The section of the frontal lobe responsible for voluntary movement.

Live! psych **2.7**

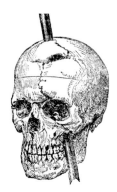

The skull of Phineas Gage, showing where the tamping iron passed through it, severely damaging his frontal lobes.

The different lobes of the cerebral hemispheres are specialized for different functions. The **occipital lobe,** located at the very back of the cerebral hemispheres, receives and processes visual information. Damage to the occipital lobe can produce blindness or visual hallucinations (Beniczky et al., 2002).

The **temporal lobe,** located in front of the occipital lobe, roughly behind the temples, plays an important role in complex visual tasks such as recognizing faces. The temporal lobe also receives and processes information from the ears, contributes to balance and equilibrium, and regulates emotions and motivations such as anxiety, pleasure, and anger. In addition, the ability to understand and comprehend language is thought to be concentrated primarily in the rear portion of the temporal lobes, though some language comprehension may also occur in the parietal and frontal lobes (Ojemann, Ojemann, Lettich, & Berger, 1989).

The **parietal lobe** sits on top of the temporal and occipital lobes and occupies the top back half of each hemisphere. This lobe receives sensory information from all over the body—from sense receptors in the skin, muscles, joints, internal organs, and taste buds. Messages from these sense receptors are registered in the **primary somatosensory cortex.** The parietal lobe also seems to oversee spatial abilities, such as the ability to follow a map or to tell someone how to get from one place to another (A. Cohen & Raffal, 1991).

The **frontal lobe,** located just behind the forehead, accounts for about half the volume of the human brain. Yet it remains the most mysterious part of the brain. The frontal lobe receives and coordinates messages from the other three lobes of the cortex and seems to keep track of previous and future movements of the body. This ability to monitor and integrate the complex tasks that are going on in the rest of the brain has led some investigators to hypothesize that the frontal lobe serves as an "executive control center" for the brain (Kimberg, D'Esposito, & Farah, 1997; Waltz et al., 1999). Recent research also indicates that the lateral prefrontal cortex (roughly above the outer edge of your eyebrows) is the portion of the brain most heavily involved in a wide range of problem-solving tasks, including answering both verbal and spatial IQ-test questions (Duncan et al., 2000). The section of the frontal lobe known as the **primary motor cortex** plays a key role in voluntary action. The frontal lobe also seems to play a key role in the behaviors we associate with personality, including motivation, persistence, affect (emotional responses), character, and even moral decision making (Greene & Haidt, 2002).

Until recently, our knowledge of the frontal lobes was based on research with nonhuman animals, whose frontal lobes are relatively undeveloped, and on studies of rare cases of people with frontal lobe damage. One famous case, involving a bizarre accident, was reported in 1848. Phineas Gage, the foreman of a railroad construction gang, made a mistake while using some blasting powder. A 4-foot long, 1/4-inch thick tamping iron tore through his cheek and severely damaged his frontal lobes. To the amazement of those who witnessed the accident, Gage remained conscious, walked part of the way to a doctor, and suffered few physical aftereffects. His memory and skills seemed to be as good as ever. However, Gage underwent major personality changes. Once a friendly, considerate fellow and steady worker, he became increasingly profane and irreverent, lost interest in work, and drifted from job to job. Gage's personality changes were so radical that, in the view of his friends, he was no longer the same man.

A century later, most neuropsychologists agree that personality change—especially loss of motivation and ability to concentrate—is the major outcome of frontal lobe damage. The frontal lobes seem to permit and anticipate goal-directed behavior and the ability to lead a mature emotional life (Rule, 2001). When adults suffer strokes or other traumas to the prefrontal cortex, their ability to make judgments is impaired. Typically, they accumulate debts, betray their spouses, abandon their friends, and/or lose their jobs. Laboratory tests show that they know the difference between right and wrong, but do not follow these rules consistently in their everyday decisions.

Much more research needs to be done before psychologists can understand how this part of the cortex contributes to such a wide and subtle range of mental activities (see *Summary Table: Parts of the Brain and Their Functions*).

Hemispheric Specialization

The cerebrum, as noted earlier, consists of two separate cerebral hemispheres. Quite literally, humans have a "right half-brain" and a "left half-brain." The primary connection between the left and the right hemispheres is a thick, ribbonlike band of nerve fibers under the cortex called the **corpus callosum** (Figure 2–10).

Under normal conditions, the left and right cerebral hemispheres are in close communication through the corpus callosum and work together as a coordinated unit (Banich, 1998; Hellige, 1993; Hoptman & Davidson, 1994; Semrud-Clikeman & Hynd, 1990). But research suggests that the cerebral hemispheres are not really equivalent (see Figure 2–10).

Corpus callosum A thick band of nerve fibers connecting the left and right cerebral cortex.

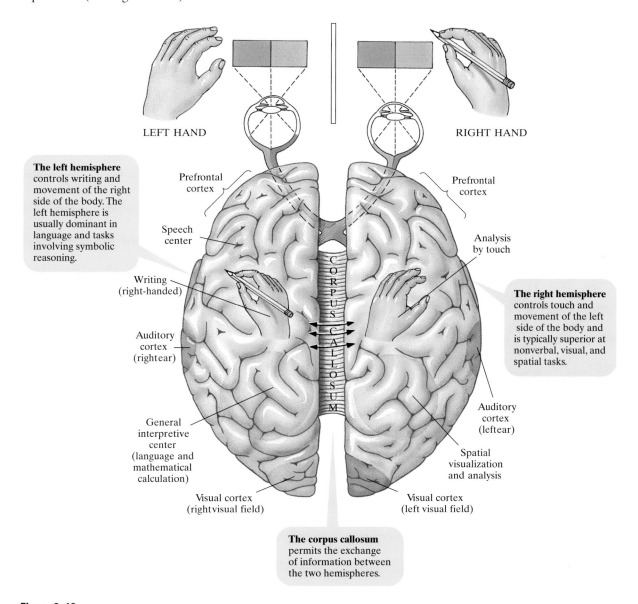

The left hemisphere controls writing and movement of the right side of the body. The left hemisphere is usually dominant in language and tasks involving symbolic reasoning.

The right hemisphere controls touch and movement of the left side of the body and is typically superior at nonverbal, visual, and spatial tasks.

The corpus callosum permits the exchange of information between the two hemispheres.

LEFT HAND   RIGHT HAND

Prefrontal cortex — Prefrontal cortex
Speech center — Analysis by touch
Writing (right-handed)
Auditory cortex (right ear)
General interpretive center (language and mathematical calculation)
Visual cortex (right visual field) — Visual cortex (left visual field)
Auditory cortex (left ear)
Spatial visualization and analysis
CORPUS CALLOSUM

Figure 2–10
The two cerebral hemispheres.
Each hemisphere specializes in processing specific types of information, as shown on the diagram.
Source: Adapted from Carol Ward © 1987, Discover Publications.

The most dramatic evidence comes from "split-brain" patients. In some cases of severe epilepsy, surgeons cut the corpus callosum to stop the spread of epileptic seizures from one hemisphere to the other. In general, this procedure is successful: The patients' seizures are reduced and sometimes eliminated. But their two hemispheres are functionally isolated; in effect, their right brain doesn't know what their left brain is doing (and vice versa). Since sensory information typically is sent to both hemispheres, in everyday life, split-brain patients function quite normally. However, a series of ingenious experiments revealed what happens when the two hemispheres cannot communicate (Sperry, 1964, 1968, 1970).

In one such experiment, split-brain patients were asked to stare at a spot on a projection screen. When pictures of various objects were projected to the *right* of that spot, they could name the objects. And, with their right hands, they could pick them out of a group of hidden objects (see Figure 2–11A). However, when pictures of objects were shown on the *left* side of the screen, something changed. Patients could pick out the objects by feeling them with their left hands, but they couldn't say what the objects were! In fact, when asked what objects they saw on the left side of the screen, split-brain patients usually said "nothing" (see Figure 2–11B).

The explanation for these unusual results is found in the way each hemisphere of the brain operates. When the corpus callosum is cut, the *left hemisphere* receives information only from the right side of the body and the right half of the visual field. As a result, it can match an object shown in the right visual field with information received by touch from the right hand, but it is unaware of (and thus unable to identify) objects shown in the left visual field or touched by the left hand. Conversely, the *right hemisphere* receives information only from the left side of the visual field and the left side of the body. Consequently, the right hemisphere can match an object shown in the left visual field with information received by touch from the left hand, but it is unaware of any objects shown in the right visual field or touched with the right hand.

But why can't the right hemisphere verbally identify an object that is shown in the left visual field? The answer is that for the great majority of people (even for

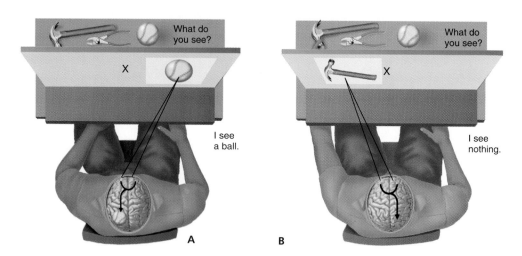

Figure 2–11

(A) When split-brain patients stare at the "X" in the center of the screen, visual information projected on the right side of the screen goes to the patient's left hemisphere, which controls language. When asked what they see, patients can reply correctly. (B) When split-brain patients stare at the "X" in the center of the screen, visual information projected on the left side of the screen goes to the patient's right hemisphere, which does not control language. When asked what they see, patients cannot name the object but can pick it out by touch with the left hand.

Source: Adapted from Carol Ward, ©1987, Discover Publications.

most left-handers), language ability is concentrated primarily in the *left* hemisphere (Hellige, 1990, 1993). As a result, when an object is in the left visual field, the nonverbal right hemisphere can see the object but can't name it. The verbal left hemisphere, in contrast, can't see an object in this location, so when asked what it sees, it answers that nothing is on the screen.

Does the left hemisphere specialize in any other tasks besides language? Some researchers think that it may also operate more analytically, logically, rationally, and sequentially than the right hemisphere does (Kingstone, Enns, Mangun, & Gazzaniga, 1995). In contrast, the right hemisphere excels at visual and spatial tasks—nonverbal imagery, including music, face recognition, and the perception of emotions (Hellige, 1990, 1993; Metcalfe, Funnell, & Gazzaniga, 1995; Semrud-Clikeman & Hynd, 1990). Put another way, the left hemisphere specializes in analyzing sequences and details, whereas the right hemisphere specializes in holistic processing (Reuter-Lorenz & Miller, 1998).

The frontal lobes of the two hemispheres may also influence temperament in distinctive ways. People whose left frontal lobe is more active than the right tend to be more cheerful, sociable, ebullient, and self-confident, whereas people with more right frontal lobe activity are more easily stressed, frightened, and upset by unpleasant things. They also tend to be more suspicious and depressed than people with predominantly left frontal lobe activity (Henriques & Davidson, 1990; Tomarken et al., 1990).

 2.8

Although such research is fascinating and fun to speculate about, it is necessary to be cautious in interpreting it. First, not everyone shows the same pattern of differences between the left and right hemispheres. In particular, the differences between the hemispheres may be greater in men than in women (Hellige, 1993; Seamon & Kenrick, 1992; Semrud-Clikeman & Hynd, 1990). Second, it is easy to oversimplify and exaggerate differences between the two sides of the brain. Split-brain research has given rise to several popular but misguided books that classify people as "right-brain" or "left-brain" thinkers. It is important to remember that under normal conditions, the right and left hemispheres are in close communication through the corpus callosum and so work together in a coordinated, integrated way (Hoptman & Davidson, 1994).

Language The notion that human language is controlled primarily by the left cerebral hemisphere was first set forth in the 1860s by a French physician named Paul Broca. Broca's ideas were modified a decade later by the scientist Karl Wernicke. Thus, it should come as no surprise that the two major language areas in the brain have traditionally been called Broca's area and Wernicke's area (see Figure 2–12).

Wernicke's area lies toward the back of the temporal lobe. This area is crucial in

THINKING CRITICALLY

Einstein's Brain

If asked to name a genius, you would be likely to say, "Albert Einstein." Einstein revolutionized our concepts of time, space, and motion—the foundations of physical reality—not once but three times in his career. Was there something special about Einstein's brain that accounts for his brilliance? The pathologist who conducted a routine autopsy at Einstein's death in 1955 reported that the great physicist's brain was within the normal range—no bigger or heavier than the average person's. But a new analysis by Canadian neuroscientists revealed distinctive characteristics (Witelson, Kigar, & Harvey, 1999). A region of Einstein's parietal lobe was 15 percent larger and more densely packed with neurons than average. Other research indicates that this region of the brain governs mathematical ability and spatial reasoning, the kind of thinking behind Einstein's major insights.

- Does this study prove that the parietal lobe was the "site" of Einstein's genius?

- If researchers examined the brains of other mathematical geniuses and found the same "abnormality," would that prove cause and effect?

Remember that case studies (a sample of one) provide clues for productive avenues of future research, but do not provide sufficient evidence for conclusions—even when they seem plausible, as this connection does. Also, correlation does not prove cause and effect. Suppose this region of the brain were found to be enlarged in a significant number of mathematical innovators. We still would not know whether this caused them to have insights (they were born that way), or the amount of thought they gave to mathematical and spatial puzzles caused the region of the brain to become enlarged, or that there is some other explanation entirely.

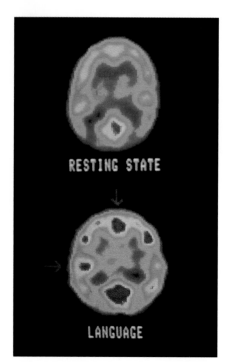

RESTING STATE

↓

LANGUAGE

PET scans of a person at rest (top) and using language (bottom). The "hot" colors (red and yellow) indicate greater brain activity. These scans show that language activity is located primarily, but not exclusively, in the brain's left hemisphere.

processing and understanding what others are saying. By contrast, Broca's area, found in the frontal lobe, is considered to be essential to our ability to talk. To over-simplify a bit, Wernicke's area seems to be important for listening, and Broca's area seems to be important for talking. Support for these distinctions comes from patients who have suffered left-hemisphere strokes and resulting brain damage. Such strokes often produce predictable language problems, called *aphasias*. If the brain damage primarily affects Broca's area, the aphasia tends to be "expressive." That is, the patients' language difficulties lie predominantly in sequencing and producing language (talking). If the damage primarily affects Wernicke's area, the aphasia tends to be "receptive," and patients generally have profound difficulties understanding language (listening). Neuroimagining studies confirm the role of Broca's and Wernicke's areas in language production and reception (Gernsbacher & Kaschak, 2003).

Tools for Studying the Brain

For centuries, our understanding of the brain depended entirely on observing patients who had suffered brain injury or from examining the brains of cadavers. Another approach (and one that is still in use) was to remove or damage the brains of nonhuman animals and study the effects. But the human cerebral cortex is far more complicated than that of any other animal. How can scientists study the living, fully functioning human brain? Contemporary neuroscientists have four basic techniques—microelectrodes, macroelectrodes, structural imaging, and functional imaging. New, more accurate techniques have appeared almost every year and are used both for diagnosis and research. (The *Summary Table: Tools for Studying the Nervous System* reviews these techniques and their uses.)

Microelectrode Techniques   *Microelectrode* recording techniques are used to study the functions of single neurons. A microelectrode is a tiny glass or quartz pipette or tube (smaller in diameter than a human hair) that is filled with a conducting liquid. When technicians place the tip of this electrode inside a neuron, they can study changes in the electrical conditions of that neuron. Microelectrode techniques have been used to understand the dynamics of action potentials, the effects of drugs or toxins on neurons, and even processes that occur in the neural membrane.

Macroelectrode Techniques   *Macroelectrode* recording techniques are used to obtain an overall picture of the activity in particular regions of the brain, which may

 2.9

Broca's area is involved in the production of speech. Damage to this region affects the ability to talk, but understanding spoken or written language is hardly affected.

Wernicke's area is involved in our understanding of spoken or written language. Damage to this region affects comprehension of language, but speech is hardly affected.

Figure 2–12
Processing of speech and language.
Broca's and Wernicke's areas, generally found only on the left side of the brain, work together, enabling us to produce and understand speech and language.

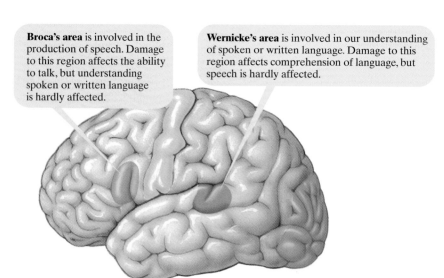

summarytable TOOLS FOR STUDYING THE NERVOUS SYSTEM

Microelectrode Techniques	Used to study the functions of individual neurons.
Macroelectrode Techniques	Used to obtain a picture of the activity in a particular region of the brain. The EEG is one such technique.
Structural Imaging	Family of techniques used to map structures in a living brain.
Computerized axial tomography (CAT or CT)	Permits three-dimensional imaging of a living human brain.
Magnetic resonance imaging (MRI)	Produces pictures of inner brain structures.
Functional Imaging Techniques	Family of techniques that can image activity in the brain as it responds to various stimuli.
EEG imaging	Measures brain activity on a millisecond-by-millisecond basis.
Magnetoencephalography (MEG)	Two procedures that are similar to EEG imaging but have greater accuracy.
Magnetic source imaging (MSI)	
Positron emission tomography (PET) scanning	Three techniques that use radioactive energy to map exact regions of brain activity.
Radioactive PET	
Single photon emission computed tomography (SPECT)	
Functional magnetic resonance imaging (fMRI)	Measures the movement of blood molecules in the brain, pinpointing specific sites and details of neuronal activity.

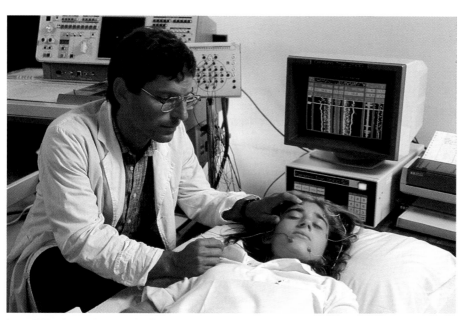

In an EEG, electrodes attached to the scalp are used to create a picture of neural activity in the brain.

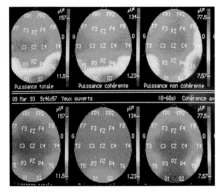

EEG imaging of one person's alpha brain waves. Red and violet colors indicate greater alpha-wave activity.

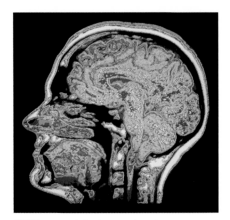

MRI image of the human head.

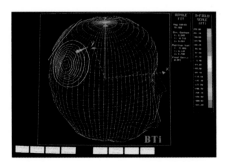

A computer printout of an MEG.

contain millions of neurons. The first such device—the *electroencephalograph* (EEG) developed by Hans Berger in 1929—is still in use today. Flat electrodes, taped to the scalp, are linked by wires to a device that translates electrical activity into lines on a moving roll of paper (or, more recently, images on a computer screen). These so-called brain waves provide an index of both the strength and rhythm of neural activity. The shape and pattern of these waves vary depending on what you happen to be doing at the time. *Alpha waves* are commonly found when you are relaxing with your eyes closed. Alphas change to higher-frequency *beta waves* when you are awake and still but your eyes are open. At the other extreme are the low-frequency *delta waves*, which occur during deepest sleep. As we will see in Chapter 4, States of Consciousness, this technique has given researchers valuable insights into changes in brain waves during sleep and dreaming.

The macroelectrode technique enables researchers to "listen" to what is going on in the brain, but it does not allow them to *look* through the skull and *see* what is happening. Some newer techniques do just that.

Structural Imaging   When researchers want to map the structures in a living human brain, they turn to two newer techniques. *Computerized axial tomography* (CAT or CT) *scanning* allows scientists to create three-dimensional images of a human brain without performing surgery. To produce a CAT scan, an X-ray photography unit rotates around the person, moving from the top of the head to the bottom; a computer then combines the resulting images. *Magnetic resonance imaging* (MRI) is even more successful at producing pictures of the inner regions of the brain, with its ridges, folds, and fissures. Here the person's head is surrounded by a magnetic field, and the brain is exposed to radio waves, which causes hydrogen atoms in the brain to release energy. The energy released by different structures in the brain generates an image that appears on a computer screen.

Recent advances in MRI technology now enable scientists to compare precise three-dimensional images obtained over extended periods. This permits tracking of progressive structural changes in the brain that accompany slow neurodegenerative disorders like Alzheimer's disease. One study for example, was able to compare the nerve tissue loss in patients with Alzheimer's disease to elderly people without the disorders. Alzheimer's patients showed an average of 5 percent loss of brain tissue compared to a 0.5 percent loss for the healthy people (Thompson et al., 2003).

Functional Imaging   In many cases, researchers are interested in more than structure; they want to look at the brain's *activity* as it actually reacts to sensory stimuli such as pain, tones, and words. This is the goal of several functional imaging methods. EEG *imaging* measures brain activity "on a millisecond-by-millisecond basis" (Fischman, 1985, p. 18). In this technique, more than two dozen electrodes are placed at important locations on the scalp. These electrodes record brain activities, which are then converted by a computer into colored images on a television screen. These images show the distribution of alpha waves, beta waves, and other activity. This technique has been extremely useful in detecting abnormal cortical activity such as that observed during an epileptic seizure.

Two related techniques, called *magnetoencephalography* (MEG) and *magnetic source imaging* (MSI), take the procedure a step further. In standard EEG, electrical signals are distorted as they pass through the skull, and their exact origin is difficult to determine. However, those same electrical signals create magnetic fields that are unaffected by bone. Both MEG and MSI measure the strength of the magnetic field and identify its source with considerable accuracy. Using these procedures, neuroscientists have begun to determine exactly which parts of the brain do most of the work in such psychological processes as memory (Gabrieli et al., 1996), language processing (Tulving et al., 1994), and reading. In turn, this research is beginning to shed new light on such disorders as amnesia and dyslexia (a reading disorder).

Another family of functional imaging techniques—*positron emission tomography* (PET) *scanning*, *radioactive* PET, and *single photon emission computed tomography* (SPECT)—uses radioactive energy to map brain activity. In all these techniques, a person first receives an injection of a radioactive substance. Brain structures that are especially active immediately after the injection absorb most of the substance. When the substance starts to decay, it releases subatomic particles. By studying where most of the particles come from, researchers can determine exactly which portions of the brain are most active. Some of the findings produced by these techniques have been surprising. For example, one study found that, in general, the brains of people with higher IQ scores are *less* active than those of people with lower IQ scores, perhaps because they process information more efficiently (Haier, 1993). Progress has also been made in locating the damaged brain region in Parkinson's disease. Other researchers have used these techniques to investigate how our memory for words and images is stored in the brain (Cabeza & Nyberg, 2000; Craik et al., 1999). These techniques also increase our knowledge of the effects of psychoactive drugs, such as antidepressants.

One of the newest and most powerful techniques for recording activity in the brain is called *functional magnetic resonance imaging* (fMRI). Functional MRI measures the movement of blood molecules (which is an index of neuron activity) in the brain, permitting neuroscientists to pinpoint specific sites and details of neuronal activity. By comparing brain activity in normal learners to brain activity in children with learning problems, researchers have begun to identify the biological origins of attention-deficit/hyperactivity disorder (ADHD) (Vaidya et al., 1998); dyslexia (Shaywitz et al., 1998); and difficulties with math (Dehane, Spelke, Stanescu, Pinel, & Tsivkin, 1999). Because fMRI enables us to collect extremely precise images rapidly, and does not require the injection of radioactive chemicals (making it less invasive), it is especially promising as a new research tool (Esposito, Zarahn, & Aguirre, 1999; Nelson et al., 2000).

By combining these various techniques, neuroscientists can simultaneously observe anatomical structures (from CAT and MRI), sites of energy use (PET, SPECT, MEG), blood and water movement (fMRI), and areas of electrical activity in the brain (EEG and ERP). As a result, scientists have begun to study, with unprecedented success, the impact of drugs on the brain, the formation of memories (Craik et al., 1999), and the sites of many other mental activities (Sarter, Berntson, & Cacioppo, 1996).

The Spinal Cord

We talk of the brain and the spinal cord as two distinct structures, but in fact, there is no clear boundary between them; at its upper end the spinal cord enlarges into the brain stem (see Figure 2–13).

The **spinal cord** is our communications superhighway, connecting the brain to most of the rest of the body. Without it, we would be literally helpless. More than 400,000 Americans are partially or fully paralyzed—about half as a result of sudden traumas to the spinal cord (most often due to car crashes, gunshot wounds, falls, or sports injuries), and half as a result of tumors, infections, and such disorders as multiple sclerosis (McDonald, 1999). When the spinal cord is severed, parts of the body are literally disconnected from the brain. These victims lose all sensations from the parts of the body that can no longer send information to higher brain areas, and they can no longer control the movements of those body parts. In some cases, spinal injuries cause problems with bowel and bladder control or low blood pressure, which makes it difficult to maintain a comfortable body temperature.

The spinal cord is made up of soft, jellylike bundles of long axons, wrapped in insulating myelin (white matter) and surrounded and protected by the vertebral bones. There are two major neural pathways in the spinal cord. One consists of

Spinal cord Complex cable of neurons that runs down the spine, connecting the brain to most of the rest of the body.

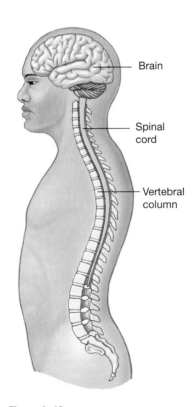

Figure 2–13
Brain and spinal cord.
Source: Human Physiology, 3rd edition by Dee Unglaub Silverthorn, Copyright © 2004 by Pearson Education, Inc., Upper Saddle River, NJ. Reprinted by permission.

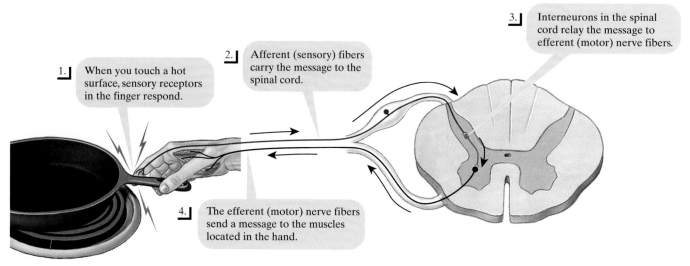

1. When you touch a hot surface, sensory receptors in the finger respond.

2. Afferent (sensory) fibers carry the message to the spinal cord.

3. Interneurons in the spinal cord relay the message to efferent (motor) nerve fibers.

4. The efferent (motor) nerve fibers send a message to the muscles located in the hand.

Figure 2–14
The spinal cord and reflex action.

motor neurons, descending from the brain, that control internal organs and muscles and help to modulate the autonomic nervous system (described later). The other consists of ascending, sensory neurons that carry information from the extremities and internal organs to the brain. In addition, the spinal cord contains neural circuits that produce reflex movements (and control some aspects of walking). These circuits do not require input from the brain: Incoming messages produce an instantaneous response that is the same every time. Most spinal reflexes are protective: They enable the body to avoid serious damage and maintain muscle tone and proper position.

To understand how the spinal cord works, consider the simple act of burning your finger on the stove. You pull your hand away without thinking, but that quick response was the last event in a series of reactions in your nervous system. First, special sensory cells pick up the message that your finger is burned. They pass this information along to *interneurons* located in the spinal cord. The interneurons, in turn, connect to motor neurons triggering a quick withdrawal of your hand (see Figure 2–14). At the same time, the message is being sent to other parts of your nervous system. Your body goes on "emergency alert": You breathe faster, your heart pounds, your entire body (including the endocrine system) mobilizes itself against the wound. Meanwhile, your brain is interpreting the messages it receives: You feel pain, you look at the burn, and you run cold water over your hand. A simple, small burn, then, triggers a complex, coordinated sequence of activities. This reaction began in the peripheral nervous system.

CHECK YOUR UNDERSTANDING

1. Breathing, heart rate and blood pressure are controlled by which part of the brain?

___ a. pons

___ b. cerebellum

___ c. medulla

___ d. thalamus

2. The region of the cerebral cortex where visual information is processed, and if damaged results in blindness is the:

___ a. temporal lobe

___ b. parietal lobe

___ c. frontal lobe

___ d. occipital lobe

3. This part of the brain's left hemisphere enables your best friend to understand what you mean when you say, "I'll take mine with milk, thanks."

___ a. Broca's area

___ b. Wernicke's area

___ c. the corpus callosum

___ d. the amygdala

4. You vigorously stir the pasta you're making, some boiling water splashes out, and you jump back to avoid being burned. This automatic reflex is controlled by

___ a. your spinal cord

___ b. your brain

___ c. your limbic system

___ d. your endorphins

Answers: 1.c, 2.d, 3.b, 4.a

The Peripheral Nervous System

Is the "fight or flight" response still useful in the modern world?

The central nervous system depends on the peripheral nervous system: The neural circuits collect information about your external environment from the sense organs and your internal environment from the body organs and glands, carry this information to the spinal cord and brain, and then transmit "instructions" from the brain and spinal cord, telling your body how to respond.

As noted earlier, the peripheral nervous system has two major divisions: the somatic and autonomic systems.

The Somatic Nervous System

The **somatic nervous system** is composed of all the *afferent*, or sensory, neurons that carry information to the central nervous system and all the *efferent*, or motor, neurons that carry messages from the central nervous system to the skeletal muscles of the body. All the things that we can sense—sights, sounds, smells, temperature, pressure, and so on—have their origins in the somatic nervous system. Likewise, all our voluntary actions—eating and drinking, reading and writing, turning on a computer, playing piano or baseball—are guided by the somatic nervous system. In later chapters, we will see how the somatic nervous system affects our experience of the world both inside and outside our bodies.

The Autonomic Nervous System

The **autonomic nervous system** comprises all the neurons that carry messages between the central nervous system and the internal organs of the body (the glands and the smooth muscles such as the heart and digestive system). The autonomic nervous system is crucial to such body functions as breathing, digestion, and circulation. But it also figures in the experience of various emotions—a fact that makes it of special interest to psychologists.

Somatic nervous system The part of the peripheral nervous system that carries messages from the senses to the central nervous system and between the central nervous system and the skeletal muscles.

Autonomic nervous system The part of the peripheral nervous system that carries messages between the central nervous system and the internal organs.

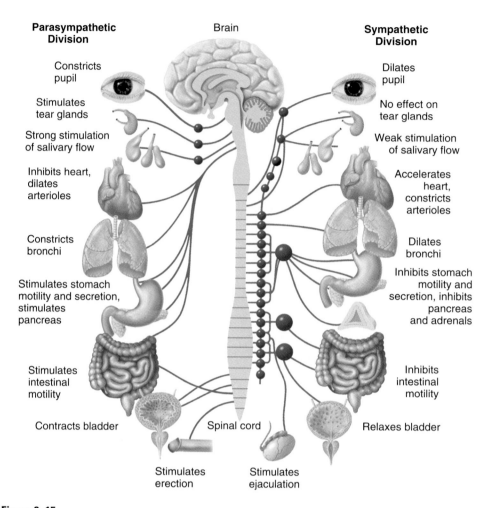

Parasympathetic Division

Constricts pupil

Stimulates tear glands

Strong stimulation of salivary flow

Inhibits heart, dilates arterioles

Constricts bronchi

Stimulates stomach motility and secretion, stimulates pancreas

Stimulates intestinal motility

Contracts bladder

Stimulates erection

Brain

Spinal cord

Stimulates ejaculation

Sympathetic Division

Dilates pupil

No effect on tear glands

Weak stimulation of salivary flow

Accelerates heart, constricts arterioles

Dilates bronchi

Inhibits stomach motility and secretion, inhibits pancreas and adrenals

Inhibits intestinal motility

Relaxes bladder

Figure 2–15

The sympathetic and parasympathetic divisions of the autonomic nervous system.

The sympathetic division generally acts to arouse the body, preparing it for "fight or flight." The parasympathetic follows with messages to relax.

Source: Adapted from *General Biology,* revised edition, 1st edition, by Willis Johnson, Richard A. Laubengayer, and Louis E. Delanney, © 1961. Reprinted with permission of Brooks/Cole, a division of Thomson Learning: www.thomsonrights.com. Fax 800 730-2215.

The autonomic nervous system consists of two branches: the *sympathetic* and *parasympathetic divisions* (see Figure 2–15). These two divisions act in almost total opposition to one another, but both branches are directly involved in controlling and integrating the actions of the glands and the smooth muscles within the body.

The nerve fibers of the **sympathetic division** are busiest when you are frightened, angry, or aroused. They carry messages that tell the body, "This is an emergency! Get ready to act now." In response, your heart pounds, you breathe faster, your pupils enlarge, and your digestion stops. The sympathetic nervous system also tells the endocrine system to start pumping chemicals into the bloodstream to strengthen these reactions (as described below). Sympathetic nerve fibers connect to every internal organ in the body, which explains why the body's reaction to sudden stress is so widespread. However, the sympathetic division can also act selectively on a single organ.

The sympathetic nervous system tends to act as a unit, rapidly mobilizing your entire body for immediate and sustained action. You see a deer bound onto the road, you brake, and avoid a collision. Rapid mobilization is clearly adaptive. But why does your heart continue to pound—and your sympathetic nervous system remain on alert—for some time after the danger is passed? Evolutionary biologists argue

Sympathetic division Branch of the autonomic nervous system; it prepares the body for quick action in an emergency.

that the autonomic nervous system evolved during a period when our distant ancestors were essentially a "prey species," smaller, weaker, slower, and less well armed than the predators that hunted them, and they needed not only to react quickly, but also to have the strength, energy, and stamina to run away or to stand and fight. Today, many situations require a quick response, but few require sustained physical action. Most of the challenges we face—getting into college, landing a job, balancing parenthood and a career—require more brains than brawn. In many situations, staying calm is more adaptive than exploding in anger. Yet we retain the "fight or flight" response as part of our evolutionary heritage (a subject we take up later in this chapter and again in Chapter 12, Stress and Health Psychology).

Although sympathetic reactions are often sustained even after danger is passed, eventually even the most intense sympathetic division reaction fades and the body calms down. This calming effect is promoted by the **parasympathetic division.** Parasympathetic nerve fibers connect to the same organs as the sympathetic nerve fibers, but cause the opposite effects. The parasympathetic division says, in effect, "Okay, the heat's off, back to normal." The heart then goes back to beating at its normal rate, the stomach muscles relax, digestion resumes, breathing slows down, and the pupils of the eyes contract. So the sympathetic division arouses the body in response to stress; then the parasympathetic division quiets down the system once danger has passed.

Traditionally, the autonomic nervous system was regarded as the "automatic" part of the body's response mechanism (hence its name). You could not, it was believed, tell your own autonomic nervous system when to speed up or slow down your heartbeat or when to stop or start your digestive processes. However, studies have shown that humans (and animals) have some control over the autonomic nervous system. For example, people can learn to moderate the severity of high blood pressure (Buist, 2002) or migraine headaches (Hermann & Blanchard, 2002), and even to regulate their own heart rate and brain waves (Monastra, Monastra, & George, 2002) through *biofeedback*, a subject we will look at more closely in Chapter 5, Learning.

When you are in a frightening situation, such as being confronted with an angry dog, the sympathetic division of the autonomic nervous system triggers a number of responses within your body. These responses give you the strength and stamina to either fight the danger or flee from it.

CHECK YOUR UNDERSTANDING

1. The somatic and autonomic nervous systems are divisions of
___ a. the central nervous system
___ b. the peripheral nervous system
___ c. the spinal cord
___ d. the reproductive system

2. Which description is *not* associated with the sympathetic nervous system?
___ a. My heart was pounding as I gave my presentation in front of the whole class.
___ b. I got so scared in the movie I could hardly catch my breath.
___ c. Going into the exam I was so jumpy I could hardly sit still.
___ d. Boy was I relieved when the exam was over and I could relax.

3. The neurons of the autonomic nervous system carry messages between the central nervous system and
___ a. the heart
___ b. the stomach
___ c. the glands
___ d. all of the above

Answers: 1.b, 2.d, 3.d

Parasympathetic division Branch of the autonomic nervous system; it calms and relaxes the body.

Endocrine glands Glands of the endocrine system that release hormones into the bloodstream.

Hormones Chemical substances released by the endocrine glands; they help regulate bodily activities.

Thyroid gland Endocrine gland located below the voice box; it produces the hormone thyroxin.

Parathyroids Four tiny glands embedded in the thyroid; they secrete parathormone.

Pineal gland A gland located roughly in the center of the brain that appears to regulate activity levels over the course of a day.

The Endocrine System

Why are psychologists interested in hormones?

The nervous system is not the only mechanism that regulates the functioning of our bodies. The endocrine system plays a key role in helping to coordinate and integrate complex psychological reactions. In fact, as we've noted throughout this chapter, the nervous system and the endocrine system work together in a constant chemical conversation. The **endocrine glands** release chemical substances called **hormones** that are carried throughout your body by the bloodstream. Hormones serve a similar function to neurotransmitters: They carry messages. Indeed, the same substance—for example, norepinephrine—may serve both as a neurotransmitter and as a hormone. A main difference between the nervous and endocrine systems is speed. A nerve impulse may travel through the body in a few hundredths of a second. Traveling through the bloodstream is a slower process: Hormones may take seconds, even minutes, to reach their goal.

Hormones interest psychologists for two reasons. First, at certain stages of development, hormones *organize* the nervous system and body tissues. At puberty, for example, hormone surges trigger the development of secondary sex characteristics, including breasts in females, a deeper voice in males, and pubic and underarm hair in both sexes. Second, hormones *activate* behaviors. They affect such things as alertness or sleepiness, excitability, sexual behavior, the ability to concentrate, aggressiveness, reactions to stress, even the desire for companionship. Hormones can also have dramatic effects on mood, emotional reactivity, the ability to learn, and the ability to resist disease. Radical changes in some hormones may also contribute to serious psychological disorders such as depression.

The locations of the endocrine glands are shown in Figure 2–16. Here we focus on those glands whose functions are best understood and that have the most impact on behavior and mental processes.

The **thyroid gland** is located just below the larynx, or voice box. It produces one primary hormone, *thyroxin*, which regulates the body's rate of metabolism and thus how alert and energetic people are and how fat or thin they tend to be. An overactive thyroid can produce a variety of symptoms: overexcitability, insomnia, reduced attention span, fatigue, agitation, acting out of character, and snap decisions, as well as reduced concentration and difficulty focusing on a task. Too little thyroxin leads to the other extreme: the desire to sleep and sleep and yet feel constantly tired. Not surprisingly, thyroid problems are often misdiagnosed as depression or simply "problems in living."

Embedded in the thyroid gland are the **parathyroids**—four tiny organs that control and balance the levels of calcium and phosphate in the body, which in turn influence levels of excitability.

The pea-sized **pineal gland** is located in the middle of the brain. It secrets the hormone *melatonin*, which helps to regulate sleep–wake cycles. Disturbances in melatonin are responsible, in part, for "jet lag." We will discuss the biological clock in greater detail in Chapter 4, States of Consciousness.

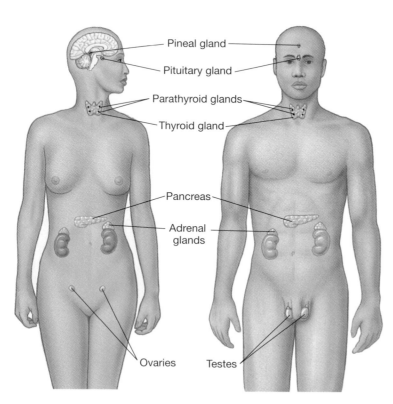

Pineal gland

Pituitary gland

Parathyroid glands

Thyroid gland

Pancreas

Adrenal glands

Ovaries   Testes

Figure 2–16
The glands of the endocrine system.

The **pancreas** lies in a curve between the stomach and the small intestine. The pancreas controls the level of sugar in the blood by secreting two regulating hormones: *insulin* and *glucagon*. These two hormones work against each other to keep the blood-sugar level properly balanced. Underproduction of insulin leads to *diabetes mellitus*, a chronic disorder characterized by too much sugar in the blood and urine; oversecretion of insulin leads to the chronic fatigue of *hypoglycemia*, a condition in which there is too little sugar in the blood.

The **pituitary gland** which is located on the underside of the brain, is connected to the hypothalamus. The pituitary produces the largest number of different hormones and thus has the widest range of effects on the body's functions. The pituitary influences blood pressure, thirst, contractions of the uterus during childbirth, milk production, sexual behavior and interest, body growth, the amount of water in the body's cells, and other functions as well. It is often called the "master gland" because of its influential role in regulating other endocrine glands.

The **gonads**—the *testes* in males and the *ovaries* in females—secrete hormones that have traditionally been classified as masculine (the *androgens*) and feminine (the *estrogens*). Both sexes produce both types of hormone, but androgens predominate in males, whereas estrogens predominate in females. These hormones play a number of important organizing roles in human development. For example, animal studies have shown that if the hormone *testosterone* is present during the third and fourth month after conception, the offspring (regardless of its sex) will develop a variety of male characteristics such as increased aggressiveness. On the other hand, the absence of testosterone during this period promotes female behaviors such as nesting (Kalat, 1988).

Testosterone has long been linked to aggressive behavior. Violence is greatest among males between 15 and 25 years of age, the years when testosterone levels are at their highest. Both male and female prisoners with high levels of testosterone are likely to have committed more violent crimes, at an earlier age, than other prisoners (Dabbs et al., 1995; Dabbs & Morris, 1990). Even in a noncriminal population, men with higher levels of testosterone "more often reported having trouble with parents, teachers, and classmates . . ." (Dabbs & Morris, 1990, p. 209).

Recent studies contradicting some of these findings suggest that the role of estrogen *and* testosterone in aggressive behavior may be more complex. Some studies point to an excess of estrogen, rather than testosterone, as the source of aggressive behavior in both males and females. Male mice that are genetically engineered to lack estrogen receptors are much less aggressive than normal male mice (Ogawa et al., 1997). In humans, men who have low levels of testosterone report feeling aggressive and irritable before they receive replacement testosterone (Angier, 1995). When testosterone levels are experimentally lowered in normal males, they feel more aggressive. Indeed, when boys and girls have delayed onset of puberty and are therapeutically treated with hormones, girls given estrogen actually become more aggressive than boys given testosterone (Angier, 1995).

Interestingly, testosterone levels also appear to differ between married and unmarried men, and between married men who have children and those who do not. Research has shown that married men have lower testosterone levels than unmarried men, and this difference is even larger for married men with children (Gray, Kahlenbert, Barrett, Lipson, & Ellison, 2002). For example, the fathers of newborns have a 33 percent lower testosterone level when compared to fathers-to-be (Berg & Wynne-Edwards, 2001). Evolutionary psychologists suggest these variations in testosterone level may be associated with a physiological response of the male body that increases the nurturing capacity of men who become fathers and husbands. Further research is necessary however to confirm this provocative hypothesis.

Testosterone and other androgens are also linked to sexual interest and behavior in adults of both sexes. Whether estrogen influences sexual behavior is still unclear.

Pancreas Organ lying between the stomach and small intestine; it secretes insulin and glucagon to regulate blood-sugar levels.

Pituitary gland Gland located on the underside of the brain; it produces the largest number of the body's hormones.

Gonads The reproductive glands, testes in males and ovaries in females.

Adrenal glands Two endocrine glands located just above the kidneys.

Most female mammals, including humans, are more sexually receptive during the ovulatory phase of their menstrual cycles, when estrogen levels are highest (Adams, Gold, & Burt, 1978). However, when the ovaries have been surgically removed, which dramatically lowers levels of estrogen, human female sexual activity and interest do not diminish significantly. Thus, researchers have concluded that estrogen does not affect sexual drive or behavior directly (Davis, 2000; Dennerstein & Burrows, 1982; Martin, Roberts, & Clayton, 1980). Interestingly, estrogen seems to boost cognitive abilities. During the ovulatory phase of their menstrual cycles, women tend to perform better on certain tests of manual dexterity, verbal skills, and perceptual speed. In addition, postmenopausal women show improvement in these tasks when they undergo estrogen replacement therapy (E. Hampson & Kimura, 1992; Kimura & Hampson, 1994). Moreover, the effects of the sex hormones on cognition may not be limited to women. Studies with elderly men have also shown that the higher their testosterone levels, the better their performance on cognitive tasks (Yaffe, Yung, Zmuda, & Cauley, 2002).

The two **adrenal glands** are located just above the kidneys. Each adrenal gland has two parts: an inner core, called the *adrenal medulla*, and an outer layer, called the *adrenal cortex*. Both the adrenal cortex and the adrenal medulla affect the body's reaction to stress. Stimulated by the autonomic nervous system, the adrenal cortex pours several hormones into the bloodstream. One, *epinephrine*, activates the sympathetic nervous system, making the heart beat faster, stopping digestion, enlarging the pupils of the eyes, sending more sugar into the bloodstream, and preparing the blood to clot fast, if necessary. Another hormone, *norepinephrine* (also a neurotransmitter) not only raises blood pressure by causing the blood vessels to become constricted, but also is carried by the bloodstream to the anterior pituitary, where it triggers the release of still more adrenocorticotropic hormone (ACTH), thus prolonging the response to stress. This is why it takes time for the body to return to normal after extreme emotional excitement. (We will see other examples of this interaction in Chapter 9, Motivation and Emotion.)

Live! psych **2.10**

◼◼◼ CHECK YOUR UNDERSTANDING

1. Which gland regulates metabolism?
___ a. pineal
___ b. pancreas
___ c. thyroid
___ d. adrenal

2. The pineal gland secretes which sleep-wake regulating hormone?
___ a. melatonin
___ b. insulin
___ c. epinephrine
___ d. estrogen

3. Called "the master gland," it produces the largest number of hormones. Which one is it?
___ a. the pituitary gland
___ b. the thyroid gland
___ c. the adrenal gland
___ d. the pineal gland

Answers: 1.c, 2.a, 3.a

Genes, Evolution, and Behavior

Is intelligence inherited? Is alcoholism?

Our brain, nervous system, and endocrine system keep us aware of what is happening outside (and inside) our bodies; enable us to use language, think, and solve problems; affect our emotions; and thus guide our behavior. To understand why they function as they do, we need to look at our genetic heritage, as individuals and as members of the human species.

Behavior genetics Study of the relationship between heredity and behavior.

Evolutionary psychology A subfield of psychology concerned with the origins of behaviors and mental processes, their adaptive value, and the purposes they continue to serve.

Genetics Study of how traits are transmitted from one generation to the next.

Genes Elements that control the transmission of traits; they are found on the chromosomes.

Chromosomes Pairs of threadlike bodies within the cell nucleus that contain the genes.

ENDURING ISSUES   **heredity**environment

The Pendulum Swings

Try asking a dozen people "Why are some individuals more intelligent than others?" The chances are, most will say, "heredity"; intelligence is inborn or innate. If you had asked the same question 25 years ago, in all probability most people would have answered that intelligence is a result of "upbringing" (parents who encouraged learning, good schools, and so on). This shift in popular opinion parallels changes in scientific thinking.

For many years, scientists were divided by the so-called *nature versus nurture* debate. Psychologists in one camp emphasized genes and heredity (or "nature"). Psychologists in the other camp emphasized the environment and experience (or "nurture"). Most contemporary psychologists view this debate as artificial: *Both* genes and environment shape human behavior. As described in our section on neural plasticity, researchers have made great strides in understanding how these two forces interact. Nonetheless, strong disagreement still exists regarding the relative influence of heredity and environment on our thoughts, abilities, personalities, and behaviors.

Two different but related fields address the influence of heredity on human behavior. **Behavior genetics** focuses on the extent to which heredity accounts for individual differences in behavior and thinking. **Evolutionary psychology** studies the evolutionary roots of behaviors and mental processes that all human beings share.

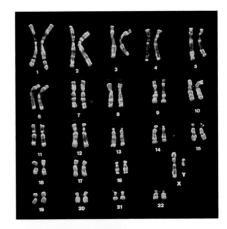

The 23 pairs of chromosomes found in every normal human cell. The two members of 22 of these pairs look exactly alike. The two members of the 23rd pair, the sex chromosomes, may or may not look alike. Females have equivalent X chromosomes, while males have one X and one Y, which look very different. Shown in the inset is the chromosome pattern that causes Down syndrome—the presence of three chromosomes number 21.

Genetics

Genetics is the study of how living things pass on traits from one generation to the next. Offspring are not carbon copies or "clones" of their parents, yet some traits reappear from generation to generation in predictable patterns. At the turn of the century, scientists named the basic units of inheritance **genes.** But they did not know what genes were or how they were transmitted.

Today we know much more about genes and how they work. Genes are carried by **chromosomes,** tiny threadlike bodies found in the nucleus of all cells. Chromosomes vary in size and shape and usually come in pairs. Each species has a constant number: Mice have 20 pairs, monkeys have 27, and peas have 7. Human beings have 23 pairs of chromosomes in every normal cell. The exceptions are sex cells, which have only half a set of chromosomes. At fertilization, the chromosomes from the father's sperm link to the chromosomes from the mother's egg, creating a new cell called a *zygote*. That single cell, and all of the billions of body cells that develop from it (except sperm and ova), contain 46 chromosomes, arranged as 23 pairs.

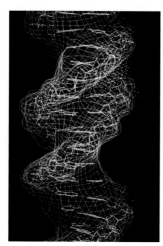

The twisted chain of the long DNA molecule contains the genetic code.

 2.11

Deoxyribonucleic acid (DNA)
Complex molecule in a double-helix configuration that is the main ingredient of chromosomes and genes and forms the code for all genetic information.

Human genome The full complement of genes within a human cell.

Dominant gene Member of a gene pair that controls the appearance of a certain trait.

Recessive gene Member of a gene pair that can control the appearance of a certain trait only if it is paired with another recessive gene.

Polygenic inheritance Process by which several genes interact to produce a certain trait; responsible for our most important traits.

The main ingredient of chromosomes is **deoxyribonucleic acid (DNA),** a complex organic molecule that looks like two chains twisted around each other in a double helix pattern. DNA is the only known molecule that can replicate or reproduce itself, which happens each time a cell divides. A gene is a small segment of DNA that carries directions for a particular trait or group of traits. Each human chromosome contains thousands of genes in fixed locations. The **human genome**, the sum total of all the genes needed to build a human being, is approximately 30,000 genes. (See *On the Cutting Edge: In Search of the Human Genome*.)

Genes, like chromosomes, occur in pairs. In some cases, such as eye color, one may be a **dominant gene** (B for brown eyes) and the other a **recessive gene** (b for blue eyes). A child who inherits the gene for blue eyes from both parents (bb) will have blue eyes. A sibling who inherits the gene for brown eyes from both parents (BB) will have brown eyes; and so will a sibling who inherits the gene for brown eyes from one parent and the gene for blue eyes from the other (Bb or bB). But her children and grandchildren may have blue eyes if this recessive gene is paired with another.

Examples of a single gene that controls a single trait are rare, however. In **polygenic inheritance,** a single gene contributes to more than one trait, while one trait depends on the actions of a number of genes. Weight, height, and skin pigmentation, and countless other characteristics are polygenic. Just as each instrument in a symphony orchestra contributes separate notes to the sound that reaches the audience, each of the genes in a polygenic system contributes separately to the total effect (McClearn et al., 1991).

Heredity need not be immediately or fully apparent. In some cases, expression of a trait is delayed until later in life. For example, many men inherit "male-pattern baldness" that does not show up until middle age. Moreover, quite often genes may predispose a person to developing a particular trait, but full expression of the characteristic depends on environmental factors. For example, people with an inherited tendency to gain weight may or may not become obese, depending on their diet, exercise program, and overall health. Put another way, genes establish a range of potential outcomes. Height (and numerous other traits) depends on the interactions of many genes with the environment. Given the same environment, a person who inherits "tall" genes will be tall, and a person who inherits "short" genes, short. But if the first person is malnourished in childhood and the second person well nourished as a child, they may be the same height as adults. On average, Americans today are taller than their grandparents and great-grandparents, whose genes they share. The reason is that they enjoyed better food as children and were less likely to contract growth-stunting childhood diseases.

So far, we have used physical characteristics as examples. Behavior geneticists apply the same principles to *psychological* characteristics.

Behavior Genetics

Behavior geneticists study the topics that interest all psychologists—perception, learning and memory, motivation and emotions, personality, and psychological disorders—but from a genetic perspective. Their goal is to identify what genes contribute to intelligence, temperament, talents, and other characteristics, as well as genetic predispositions to psychological and neurological disorders (Brunner, Nelen, Breakefield, Ropers, & Van Oost, 1993; Cunningham, 2003; D. Johnson, 1990; Loehlin, Willerman, & Horn, 1988; Plomin, 1999b; Plomin, DeFries, & McClearn, 1990; Plomin & Rende, 1991). Of course, genes do not directly cause behavior. Rather, they affect both the development and operation of the nervous system and the endocrine system, which, in turn, influence the likelihood that a certain behavior will occur under certain circumstances (Wahlsten, 1999).

ON THE CUTTING EDGE

IN SEARCH OF THE HUMAN GENOME

The term *genome* refers to the full complement of an organism's genetic material. Thus, the genome for any particular organism contains a complete blueprint for building all the structures and directing all the living processes for the lifetime of that organism. Scientists estimate the human genome is made up of about 30,000 individual genes, located on the 23 pairs of chromosomes that make up human DNA. These genes, contained within every cell of our body, distinguish us from other forms of life. Small variations in the genetic code separate humans from their closest relatives. For instance humans share 98.7 percent of their genes with chimpanzees (Olson & Varki, 2003). Surprisingly minute variations in the human genome are responsible for the individual differences we see in the world's 6 billion people. Experts believe that the average variation in the human genetic code for any two different people, such as Shakespeare or Michael Jackson, is much less than 1 percent.

As we've noted, the Human Genome Project has yielded remarkable results with great promise for preventing and treating genetic diseases. Researchers have already begun to identify specific genes that contribute to the development of disorders such as cystic fibrosis, mental retardation, and some forms of cancer.

Although rich with promise, the Human Genome Project raises many social and ethical questions. For example, will predicting the likelihood of cancer in an individual lead to discrimination from potential employers and insurers? Will the knowledge that a person has a 25 percent chance of producing a child with Parkinson's disease affect the choice of having children? How will the products of the Human Genome Project, such as medicines and diagnostic techniques, be shared by the international community, patented, and commercialized? Fortunately, committees made up of ethicists, physicians, researchers, and other concerned professionals have already begun to confront many of these issues. As our understanding of human genetic inheritance continues to grow, it will not, we hope, outpace our understanding of how to apply this knowledge in ways that are both effective and socially responsible.

In the remainder of this chapter, we will look at some of the methods used by behavior geneticists as well as some of their more interesting discoveries. We will start with methods appropriate for animal studies and then examine the techniques used to study behavior genetics in humans.

Animal Behavior Genetics Much of what we know about behavior genetics comes from studies of nonhuman animals. Mice are favorite subjects because they breed quickly and have relatively complex behavior patterns. In **strain studies,** close relatives, such as siblings, are intensively inbred over many generations to create strains of animals that are genetically similar to one another and different from other strains. When animals from different strains are raised together in the same environment, differences between them largely reflect genetic differences in the strains. This method has shown that performance on learning tasks, as well as sense of smell and susceptibility to seizures, are affected by heredity.

Selection studies are another way to assess heritability. If a trait is closely regulated by genes, when animals with the trait are interbred with one another, more of their offspring should have the trait than one would find in the general population. Heritability is measured in terms of the proportion of successive generations that have the trait.

Humans have practiced selective breeding for thousands of years to create breeds of dogs and other domesticated animals that have desirable traits. The evidence suggests that dogs resembled wolves until about 15,000 years ago, when humans began to establish permanent settlements. Using artificial selection, they bred dogs to act as herders, guards, beasts of burden, pointers, retrievers, and, of course, companions. Psychological qualities were as important as physical qualities: Guard dogs

People clearly do inherit physical traits from their parents. Whether—and to what extent—they also inherit behavioral traits remains uncertain.

Strain studies Studies of the heritability of behavioral traits using animals that have been inbred to produce strains that are genetically similar to one another.

Selection studies Studies that estimate the heritability of a trait by breeding animals with other animals that have the same trait.

Family studies Studies of heritability in humans based on the assumption that if genes influence a certain trait, close relatives should be more similar on that trait than distant relatives.

Twin studies Studies of identical and fraternal twins to determine the relative influence of heredity and environment on human behavior.

Identical twins Twins developed from a single fertilized ovum and therefore identical in genetic makeup at the time of conception.

Fraternal twins Twins developed from two separate fertilized ova and therefore different in genetic makeup.

need to be aggressive, but totally loyal to the "head of their pack," their master; herding dogs need intense concentration to control large number of animals bigger than themselves; and so on. Today, with more than 400 breeds, dogs are more variable in size and shape than any other species—with the possible exception of humans.

Human Behavior Genetics   For obvious reasons, scientists cannot conduct strain or selection studies with human beings. But there are a number of ways to study behavioral techniques indirectly.

Family studies are based on the assumption that if genes influence a trait, close relatives should share that trait more often than distant relatives because close relatives have more genes in common. For example, overall, schizophrenia occurs in only 1 to 2 percent of the general population (Robins & Regier, 1991). Siblings of people with schizophrenia are about eight times more likely, and children of schizophrenic parents about ten times more likely, to develop the disorder than someone chosen randomly from the general population. Unfortunately, because family members share not only some genes but also similar environments, family studies alone cannot clearly distinguish the effects of heredity and environment (Plomin, DeFries, & McClearn, 1990).

Identical twins develop from a single ovum and consequently start out with the same genetic material. Fraternal twins develop from two different fertilized ova and so are as different in genetic makeup as any two children of the same parents.

To obtain a clearer picture of the influences of heredity and environment, psychologists often use **twin studies. Identical twins** develop from a single fertilized ovum and are therefore identical in genetic makeup. Any differences between them must be due to environmental influences. **Fraternal twins,** however, develop from two separate fertilized egg cells and are no more similar genetically than are other brothers and sisters. If twin pairs grow up in similar environments, and if identical twins are no more alike in a particular characteristic than fraternal twins, then heredity cannot be very important for that trait.

Twin studies have provided evidence for the heritability of a number of behaviors, ranging from verbal skills (Eley, Bishop, et al., 1999), to aggressiveness (Eley, Lichenstein, & Stevenson, 1999), to mannerisms such as the strength of a handshake (Farber, 1981), to depression and anxiety (Eley & Stevenson, 1999; O'Connor, McGuire, Reiss, Hetherington, & Plomin, 1998). When one identical twin develops schizophrenia, the chances that the other twin will develop the disorder are about 50 percent. For fraternal twins, the chances are about 15 percent (Gottesman, 1991). The much higher rate exhibited by twins, particularly identical twins, suggests that heredity plays a crucial role in schizophrenia.

Similarities between twins, even identical twins, cannot automatically be attributed to genes, however; twins nearly always grow up together. Parents and others may treat them alike—or try to emphasize their differences, so that they grow up as separate individuals. In either case, the data for heritability may be skewed. To avoid this problem, researchers attempt to locate identical twins who were separated at birth or in very early childhood and then raised in different homes. A University of Minnesota team led by Thomas Bouchard followed separated twins for more than 10 years (Bouchard, 1984, 1996; Bouchard et al., 1990). They confirmed that genetics plays a major role in mental retardation, schizophrenia, depression, and intelligence. Bouchard and his colleagues have also found that complex personality traits, interests, and talents, and even the structure of brain waves are guided by genetics.

Studies of twins separated shortly after birth do have some weaknesses. For example, the environment in the uterus may be more traumatic for one twin than the other (Phelps, Davis, & Schartz, 1997). Also, since adoption agencies usually try to place twins in similar families, their environments may not be much different (Ford, 1993; Wyatt, 1993). Finally, the number of twin pairs separated at birth is fairly small, so scientists sometimes rely on other types of studies to investigate the influence of heredity.

Adoption studies focus on children who were adopted at birth and brought up by parents not genetically related to them. Adoption studies provide additional evidence for the heritability of intelligence, some forms of mental illness (Horn, 1983; Scarr & Weinberg, 1983), and in behavior thought to be solely determined by environmental influences, even smoking (Boomsma, Koopmans, Van Doornen, & Orlebeke et al., 1994; Heath & Martin, 1993; Lerman et al., 1999). One study located 47 people whose mothers had schizophrenia but who had been adopted at birth and reared by normal parents. Of these 47 people, 5 subsequently suffered from schizophrenia. In a control group of adoptees whose parents did not have schizophrenia, there was not a single case (Heston, 1966). By combining the results of *twin, adoption,* and *family* studies, psychologists have obtained an even clearer picture of the role of heredity in schizophrenia. As shown in Figure 2–17, the average risk of schizophrenia steadily increases in direct relation to the closeness of one's biological relationship to an individual with the disorder.

So far, we have been talking about the environment as if it were something *out there,* something that happens *to* people, over which they have little control. But individuals also shape their environment. The genes and predispositions individuals inherit alter that environment in several ways (Plomin, 1994; Plomin, Defries, Craig, & McGuffin, 2003; Scarr & McCartney, 1983). Parents not only pass on genes to their children but also shape their environment. For example, children whose parents read to them tend to do well in school. But parents who read with their children usually enjoy reading and read well themselves. In other words, a child's environment reinforces his or her heredity. Also, different children evoke

different responses from the people around them (as suggested in our discussion of twins). Cheerful, outgoing children elicit more positive attention from other people than do somber, shy children; as a result they tend to experience a friendlier environment, which, again, reinforces their inborn tendencies. Children and adults actively seek out environments they find comfortable and people they find compatible. For example, a shy infant—or an irritable one—responds positively to an aunt who is calm and gentle (which is rewarding for her). A bubbly, active infant responds positively to an uncle who is rough and challenging, an uncle who might terrify the other infants, and hence receives more attention from him. Thus, children growing up in what appears to be the same environment may *experience* that environment differently. Because genes and environments interact in so many intricate ways, trying to separate and isolate the effects of heredity and environment—nature and nurture—is artifical (Collins, Maccoby, Steinberg, Hetherington, & Bornstein, 2000, 2001; Plomin, 1997).

Adoption studies Research carried out on children, adopted at birth by parents not related to them, to determine the relative influence of heredity and environment on human behavior.

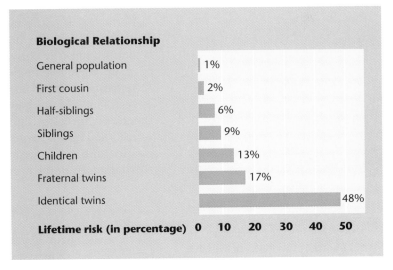

Figure 2–17
Average risk of schizophrenia among biological relatives of people with schizophrenia.
Source: Adapted from I. I. Gottesman, *Schizophrenia genesis: The origins of madness,* New York: Freeman, 1991, p. 96. Reprinted by permission of Henry Holt and Company, LLC.

Another example of gene-environment interaction can be found in studies of alcoholism. Numerous studies have shown that in males, Type I alcoholism, characterized by late onset and neurotic features is less than 40 percent heritable, whereas Type II alcoholism, characterized by early onset and high levels of antisocial behavior, is 90 percent heritable (McGue, 1999). (Interestingly, studies of women have not shown as high heritability.) East Asians, whose cultures do not promote drinking as a male pastime, have much lower rates of chronic alcoholism than Westerners, suggesting cultural influences are also important determinants of alcoholism. But further studies revealed that one-third to one-half of East Asians have low levels of an enzyme that makes people more susceptible to hangovers (nausea, dizziness, headaches)—a genetic predisposition that probably acts as a deterrent to alcohol abuse. In general, research shows that genetic factors override environmental factors in alcohol abuse. Thus, children of nonalcoholic parents adopted and reared by alcoholic parents are not at high risk. However, if the adopted child has a *sibling* who is the adoptive parents' biological child and who also abuses alcohol, the risk that the adoptive child will abuse alcohol increases. In other words, siblings—especially if they are the same sex and about the same age—may exert a stronger environmental influence than parents do.

Molecular Genetics   Until recently, behavioral geneticists could study heritability only indirectly. But new molecular genetics techniques make it possible to study, and even change, the human genetic code directly. The goal of the Human Genome Project, launched in 1990, is to map all 23 pairs of human chromosomes and to determine which genes influence which characteristics (Johnson, 1990; Plomin & Rende, 1991). In June 2000—ahead of schedule—researchers announced the first rough map of the entire human genome. Already, researchers have identified individual genes on specific chomosomes that are associated with Alzheimer's disease (Corder et al., 1993; Papassotiropoulos et al., 2002). Other specific chromosome sites for alcoholism (Uhl, Blum, Nobel, & Smith, 1993), schizophrenia, (Blouin et al., 1998; Kendler et al., 2000), suicide (Du et al., 1999), cognitive functioning (Gécz & Mulley, 2000), intelligence (Plomin et al., 1994), and even aging (Migliaccio et al., 1999) have also been identified. By using these genetic markers, researchers expect not only to prevent or reverse genetic diseases, but also to understand the role of heredity in even the most complex behaviors (Plomin & Crabbe, 2000; Plomin, Defries, Craig, & McGuffin, 2003; Plomin, DeFries, & McClearn, 1990; Wahlsten, 1999).

In the recent past, genetic engineering was confined to science fiction. No longer. Remarkably, scientists have boosted intelligence and even increased the life span of laboratory mice by changing their genes. One team of researchers created smarter mice by adding a single gene to their chromosomes (see *On the Cutting Edge: Engineering Smarter Mice*). Another team extended the life span of mice by 30 percent by removing just one gene (Migliaccio et al., 1999). Many people find the prospect of genetic engineering frightening, especially if applied to humans but also with other animals and plants. From Mary Shelley's *Frankenstein* (1818) to present-day films, the creation of new life forms has been the stuff of horror stories. Doesn't genetic engineering interrupt the normal, more or less orderly processes of evolution?

Evolutionary Psychology

Much as behavior geneticists try to explain the individual differences in human behavior, evolutionary psychologists try to explain the behavioral traits that people have in common. The key to these shared characteristics, they feel, is the process of evolution by **natural selection**, first described by Charles Darwin in *On the Origin of Species* (1859).

According to the principle of natural selection, those organisms that are best adapted to their environments are most likely to survive and reproduce. If the traits

Natural selection The mechanism proposed by Darwin in his theory of evolution, which states that organisms best adapted to their environment tend to survive, transmitting their genetic characteristics to succeeding generations, whereas organisms with less adaptive characteristics tend to vanish from the earth.

ON THE CUTTING EDGE

ENGINEERING SMARTER MICE

"Smarter mice set the stage for raising human IQs," (Maugh, 1999) the headlines read. By adding a single gene to fertilized eggs, researchers created mice that learned faster, and remembered what they learned longer, than ordinary mice (Tang et al., 1999; Tsien, 2000). Soon after the research was announced, the smart mice made the infamous Top Ten List on "The Late Show with David Letterman." The comedian suggested term paper topics for the furry geniuses, including "Our Pearl Harbor: The Day Glue Traps Were Invented" and "Outsmarting the Mousetrap: Just Take the Cheese Off Really, Really Fast."

Humor aside, this research made an important contribution to the decades-long search to understand "exactly what happens in the brain during learning and what memories are made of" (Tsien, 2000, p. 62). Fifty years earlier, Donald O. Hebb (1949) had hypothesized that memories are formed when connected neurons fire repeatedly, strengthening the synapse between them; subsequent research on long-term potentiation (LTP) supported this hypothesis (see p. 56). Still other research identified tiny pores on the receiving side of the synapse, called NMDA receptors, as central to this process. The longer NMDA receptors stay open, the stronger the synaptic connection (and by implication, the memory) becomes. With age, these molecules become less active, which might explain why young animals are usually able to learn more readily, and to remember what they have learned longer, than are adults.

The researchers implanted an extra gene for NMDA receptors in the fertilized eggs or zygotes that developed into the smarter mice. In laboratory experiments, these genetically enhanced mice remembered previously encountered objects and mazes much longer than did normal mice. Moreover, as adults, their ability to learn and remember was as good as that of juvenile mice that had not been genetically altered. In contrast, when the researchers removed, or "knocked out," this gene in other mice, their ability to learn their way around a maze and perform other tasks requiring memory was severely impaired.

Can this discovery be applied to humans? The researchers are cautious. Like humans, mice use their brains to find their way around, grasp cause and effect (as in what foods are poisonous), and generalize (if the "thing" [trap] in the kitchen snapped, so might the thing in the living room). But humans are capable of far more specialized and complex activities. Mouse "geniuses" will never be able to do differential equations or play the stock market. Rather, smart mice are better at solving the problems ordinary mice face in the wild, such as finding food and avoiding danger, whether a predator or a mousetrap. In other words, genetic engineering can improve the skills they already have, but it can't make mice think like people. Yet the identification of the NMDA receptor might someday lead to therapies that slow or reduce such disorders as Alzheimer's disease in humans.

---

that give them a survival advantage are genetically based, those same genetic characteristics are passed on to their offspring. Organisms that do not possess the adaptive traits tend to die off before they reproduce, and therefore the less-adaptive traits do not get passed along to future generations.

Natural selection therefore promotes the survival and reproduction of individuals who are genetically well adapted to their particular environment. If the environment changes or the individual moves into a new environment, the survival and reproductive value of inherited characteristics may also change, and so eventually may the frequency of genes in the population's gene pool.

As described in Chapter 1, evolutionary psychologists study the origins of behaviors and mental processes, emphasizing the adaptive or survival value of such traits. Rather than focusing on the *structural* changes in organisms, as evolutionary biologists do, evolutionary psychologists look at the role natural selection might have played in selecting for adaptive *behaviors*, especially during the long period that our ancestors lived as hunter-gatherers. They argue that just as our hands and upright posture are products of natural selection, so are our brains. As a result, our brains are "prewired" to learn some things more easily than others, to analyze problems in certain ways, and to communicate in distinctively human ways.

Evolutionary psychologists cite language as a prime example (Pinker, 1994, 1997, 2002). As we will see in Chapter 10 (Life Span Development), all normal children acquire language without explicit instruction, children in different cultures acquire language at about the same ages and in predictable stages, and the underlying structure of all human languages (nouns and verbs, subjects and objects, questions and conditional phrases, and so on) is basically the same. Taken as a whole, evolutionary psychologists argue, the evidence strongly suggests that our human brains have a built-in "program" for language. In support of this notion, scientists recently identified a specific gene, distinct to humans, that may have played the pivotal role in stimulating the emergence of language among our early ancestors (Enard et al., 2002).

Evolutionary psychologists cite mate selection as another example. In choosing a partner, males and females tend to pursue different strategies. Why? Evolutionary psychologists answer this way. Human females usually have only one child at a time; moreover, they invest more in each child—going through pregnancy, caretaking, and providing nourishment—than men do. It would seem to be most adaptive for females to look for males who will provide the best genes, resources, and long-term parental care. Males, on the other hand, are limited only by the number of prospective mates they can attract, because sperm are plentiful and quickly replaced. It may be most adaptive for males to seek to mate with as many females as they can and to compete with other males for access to females. Studies analyzing human behaviors associated with sexual selection have found that men and women do indeed take different approaches to sexuality, mate choice, and aggression, as predicted by evolutionary psychology (Buss, 1989, 2000b; Callahan, 2000). Comparing evolutionary explanations with more traditional social learning explanations of sex differences in social behavior, another researcher concluded that evolutionary psychology did a much better job of accounting for overall patterns (Archer, 1996).

Evolutionary psychologists are also interested in why natural selection has not weeded out characteristics that seem maladaptive. For example, Joe Z. Tsien (2000), one of the scientists who created smart mice (see *On the Cutting Edge: Engineering Smarter Mice*), asks, If a brain molecule is good for learning and memory, why does it become less active with age? Tsien favors an evolutionary hypothesis. Older individuals in most cases have already reproduced. Therefore, reducing their ability to compete for food and other resources increases the opportunities for younger individuals to reproduce.

Pondering another apparently maladaptive set of genes, Nesse (1998, 2000) holds that in some cases, depression is adaptive. "If I had to put my position in a nutshell," he said, "I'd say that mood exists to regulate investment strategies, so that we spend more time on things that work, and less time on things that don't work" (Nesse 1998, 2000). Nesse believes that some cases of depression are the result of neurochemical imbalances, but argues that medicating everyone who experiences depression may interfere with a normal defensive strategy that is part of our evolutionary heritage.

Evolutionary psychology is not without its critics (Siegert & Ward, 2002). First, evolutionary explanations often sound like "just so" stories: If a characteristic (such as fading memory or depression) is widespread, then it must serve some adaptive function. Second, to some extent evolutionary psychology tends to justify the status quo. The fact (or assumption) that behaviors were adaptive in the distant past does not mean that they are adaptive today. Unlike other species that react reflexively to most situations, human

THINKING CRITICALLY

Depression

We have touched on depression a number of times in this chapter: in our discussion of neuropharmacology, hormones, hemispheric specialization, behavioral genetics, and, here, evolutionary psychology. Based on what you have read:

- Is depression inherited (nature), acquired (nurture), or both?

- Are these different perspectives on depression mutually exclusive or complementary?

- Do psychologists know what causes depression?

Hints: Avoid either/or thinking, confusing correlation with cause and effect, and jumping to conclusions. Look for alternative explanations, for example, the possibility that there are different forms of depression, with different origins.

beings have the capacity to adapt flexibly to changing circumstances. Evolutionary psychologists are quick to point out that their aim is not to justify behavior patterns or to shape social policy, but to understand the origins of human behavior. They emphasize that behavior should not be viewed as justifiable or even adaptive simply because at one time it might have served an important adaptive function; "what is" should not be confused with "what should be." But this point often gets lost, particularly in popular accounts of scientific research (Pinker, 2002).

 2.12

Social Implications

Science is not simply a process that takes place in a laboratory; its influence on all of our lives is enormous. Consider, for example, intelligence testing. Most psychologists agree that heredity is a major factor in intelligence. Moreover, scores on IQ tests are a good predictor of grades in school and other measures of intelligence. However, there is considerable controversy, about whether IQ tests measure innate intelligence or cultural knowledge, and, about interpretations of group differences in IQ scores (a subject we will discuss in depth in Chapter 8, Intelligence and Mental Abilities). Yet a child may be assigned to an academic program ("normal," college-bound, or special education) on the basis of standardized test scores—a decision that affects his or her opportunities by influencing what subjects the child studies, how teachers view the child's abilities, and how the child views him- or herself. At many points in your life, such as applying to college or graduate school or applying for a job, your opportunities will depend on test scores. Do the psychologists who design these tests have a responsibility to inform social policy makers and educate the public about what such tests measure and what they do not? To speak out when they feel tests are being misused? Most psychologists would answer yes.

In recent decades, scientists have embraced a more sophisticated view of the interplay between genes and environment. But in the mass media, new discoveries often are reported in simplified, either/or sound bites ("a gene for x"). As a result, the pendulum of popular opinion seems to have swung from an environmental (or nurture) position, which holds that all individuals have significant potential, to a genetic (or nature) position, which holds that intelligence, temperament, and other qualities are inborn (de Waal, 1999).

In the past, biological views of human behavior were used to promote racist and sexist political agendas by so-called social Darwinists in late-nineteenth-century Europe, who twisted the theory of evolution to rationalize social and economic inequality as "the survival of the fittest"; by the eugenics movement in the United States in the early twentieth century, which sought to improve humanity through involuntary sterilization of thousands of people designated as "imbeciles" and otherwise socially undesirable; and in Nazi Germany, where more than 6 million Jews, Gypsies, homosexuals, and others were put to death in the name of "racial purity." The late-twentieth-century civil wars in Rwanda-Burundi and the former Yugoslavia (especially Bosnia) were also fueled, in part, by inaccurate views of heredity.

New technology could conceivably lead to new evils. Genocide and eugenics aimed to eliminate certain categories of people, but in the near future scientists could create new

THINKING CRITICALLY

Media Accounts of Research

What is wrong with this headline?

"Scientists Find Gene for Intelligence"

Robert Plomin (1998) compared genetic data on 50 children whose SAT scores were equivalent to IQ scores of 160 or higher to a control group. He found that a variant of a particular gene was twice as common in children with ultra-high IQs as in children with average IQs (scores of 100). Scientists estimate that about 50 percent of the variation in IQ scores is due to heredity. The gene had a small effect, accounting for about 2 percent of the variance among individuals, or 4 IQ points, but the researchers made an important first step in uniting biological technology with behavioral genetics.

What rules of critical thinking did this headline ignore? How would you rewrite this headline?

Hints: Consider the size of the sample, the danger of focusing on extremes, and what "heritability" means.

categories of people. Potentially, a government could create a genetic division of labor by breeding "strains" of human beings specially designed to be soldiers, perform manual labor, bear and rear children, and so on.

Modern techniques of prenatal screening now make it possible to detect many genetic defects even before a baby is born. *Chorionic villus sampling* and *amniocentesis* are two procedures for obtaining samples of cells from fetuses in order to analyze their genes. In the first, the cells are taken from membranes surrounding the fetus; in the second, the cells are harvested from the fluid in which the fetus grows. Using these procedures, genetic problems are detected in about 2 percent of pregnancies. Does the child in these cases nonetheless have a right to live? Do the parents have a right to abort the fetus? Should society protect all life no matter how imperfect it is in the eyes of some? If not, which defects are so unacceptable that abortion is justified? Most of these questions have a long history, but recent progress in behavior genetics and medicine has given them a new urgency. We are reaching the point at which we will be able to intervene in a fetus's development by replacing some of its genes with others. For which traits might this procedure be considered justified, and who has the right to make those decisions? If in tampering with genes we significantly change our society's gene pool, are future generations harmed or benefited? Such questions pose major ethical dilemmas (Barinaga, 2000a; Patenaude, Gutmacher, & Collins, 2002).

The study of behavior genetics and evolutionary psychology makes many people uneasy. Some fear that it may lead to the conclusion that who we are is written in some kind of permanent ink before we are born. Some people also fear that research in these fields could be used to undermine movements toward social equality. But far from finding human behavior to be genetically predetermined, recent work in behavior genetics shows just how important the environment is in determining which genetic predispositions come to be expressed and which do not (Rutter, 1997). In other words, we may inherit predispositions, but we do not inherit destinies. The emerging picture confirms that both heredity and environment (nature *and* nurture) together shape most significant behaviors and traits (Plomin, Defries, Craig, & McGuffin, 2003).

CHECK YOUR UNDERSTANDING

1. How many pairs of chromosomes are in human cells?

___ a. 7

___ b. 20

___ c. 27

___ d. 23

2. Name the complex molecule that contains all genetic information.

___ a. DNA

___ b. RNA

___ c. NRA

___ d. EPA

3. Twin studies have provided evidence for the heritability of

___ a. depression

___ b. schizophrenia

___ c. alcoholism

___ d. all of the above

Answers: 1.d, 2.a, 3.d

This chapter introduces **psychobiology,** which deals with the basic biological processes that are at the root of our thoughts, feelings, and actions, and **neuroscience,** the study of the brain and the nervous system. The body possesses two systems for coordinating and integrating behavior: the nervous system and the endocrine system.

Neurons: The Messengers

The billions of **neurons,** or nerve cells, that underlie all the activity of the nervous system form a communication network that coordinates all the systems of the body and enables them to function. Neurons usually receive messages from other neurons through short fibers, called **dendrites,** that pick up messages and carry them to the neuron's cell body. Neurons that carry messages from the sense organs to the brain or spinal cord are called **sensory (afferent) neurons.** Neurons that carry messages from the brain or spinal cord to the muscles and glands are called **motor (efferent) neurons.** And neurons that carry messages from one neuron to another are called **interneurons (or association neurons).** The **axon** carries outgoing messages from the cell. A group of axons bundled together makes up a **nerve.** Some axons are covered with a **myelin sheath,** made up of **glial cells.** The *myelin sheath* increases neuron efficiency and provides insulation.

The Neural Impulse   Neurons communicate through electrochemical impulses. When the neuron is at rest, or at its **resting potential,** a slightly higher concentration of negative **ions** exists inside the membrane surrounding the cell body than outside, so there is a negative electrical charge inside relative to outside. At rest, a neuron is in a state of **polarization.** When an incoming message is strong enough, the electrical charge is changed, an **action potential (neural impulse)** is generated, and the neuron is depolarized. Incoming messages cause **graded potentials,** which, when combined, may exceed the minimum **threshold of excitation** and make the neuron fire. After firing, the neuron goes through the **absolute refractory period,** when it will not fire again, and then enters the **relative refractory period,** when firing will only occur if the incoming message is much stronger than usual. However, according to the **all-or-none law,** the impulse sent by a neuron does not vary in strength.

The Synapse   The **synapse** is composed of the axon terminals of one neuron, the synaptic space, and the dendrites and cell body of the next neuron. **Neurotransmitter** molecules, released by **synaptic vesicles,** cross the tiny **synaptic space (or cleft)** between the **terminal button (or synaptic knob)** of the sending neuron and the dendrite of the receiving neuron, where they latch on to a **receptor site,** much the way a key fits into a lock. This is how they pass on their excitatory or inhibitory messages. Some of the best known neurotransmitters are acetylcholine (ACh), which plays an important role in arousal and attention; dopamine, which affects neurons associated with voluntary movement; serotonin, which sets an emotional tone; and endorphins, which reduce pain by turning down neurons that transmit pain impulses. Imbalances in neurotransmitters contribute to many types of mental illness, and many psychoactive drugs and toxins act by affecting the transmission of neurotransmitters. Examples are botulism toxin, which prevents the release of ACh; caffeine, which blocks the release of adenosine, an inhibitory neurotransmitter; and cocaine, which prevents reabsorption of dopamine, leading to heightened arousal. Antidepressant and antipsychotic medications use the same processes.

Neural Plasticity and Neurogenesis   The connections between the billions of neurons in the brain are weak at birth, but the number and complexity of synaptic connections multiplies rapidly throughout childhood. The key to this growth in complexity is experience, which can strengthen and enhance brain function. The brain has **neural plasticity,** that is, it can be physically and chemically altered by experience. It also has the capacity for **neurogenesis,** or production of new brain cells. Research with birds, adult mice, guinea pigs, and other mammals show evidence of the growth of new brain cells when animals are challenged by enriched environments, intense training, or injury. A study of adult human cancer patients showed that their brains produced new neurons. Lifelong neurogenesis has important implications for treating neurological disorders.

The Central Nervous System

The Organization of the Nervous System   The billions of neurons in the brain are connected to neurons throughout the body by trillions of synapses. The nervous system is organized into two parts: the **central nervous system,** which consists of the brain and the spinal cord, and the **peripheral nervous system,** which connects the central nervous system to the rest of the body.

The Brain   Physically, the brain has three more or less distinct areas: the central core, the limbic system, and the cerebral cortex.

The central core consists of the hindbrain, cerebellum, midbrain, thalamus and hypothalamus, and reticular formation. The **hindbrain** is found in even the most primitive vertebrates. It is made up of the medulla, a narrow structure nearest the spinal cord that controls breathing, heart rate, and blood pressure, and the pons, which produces chemicals that maintain our sleep–wake cycle. The medulla is the point at which many of the nerves from the left part of the body cross to the right side of the brain and vice versa. The **cerebellum** controls the sense of balance and coordinates the body's actions. The **midbrain,** which is above the cerebellum, is important for hearing and sight and is one of the places in which pain is registered. The **thalamus** is a relay station that integrates and shapes incoming sensory signals before transmitting them to the higher levels of the brain. The **hypothalamus** is important to motivation and emotional behavior. The **reticular formation,** which is woven through all of these structures, alerts the higher parts of the brain to incoming messages.

The **limbic system,** a ring of structures located between the central core and the cerebral hemispheres, is a more recent evolutionary development than the central core. It includes the hippocampus, which is essential to the formation of new memories, and the amygdala, which together with the hippocampus governs emotions related to self-preservation. Other portions of the limbic system heighten the experience of pleasure. In times of stress, the limbic system coordinates and integrates the nervous system's response.

The cerebrum takes up most of the room inside the skull. The outer covering of the cerebral hemispheres is known as the **cerebral cortex.** The cerebral hemispheres are what most people think of when they think of the brain. They are the most recently evolved portion of the brain, and they regulate the most complex behavior. Each cerebral hemisphere is divided into four lobes, delineated by deep fissures on the surface of the brain. The **occipital lobe** of the cortex, located at the back of the head, receives and processes visual information. The **temporal lobe,** located roughly behind the temples, helps us perform complex visual tasks, such as recognizing faces. The **parietal lobe,** which sits on top of the temporal and occipital lobes, receives sensory information from all over the body and figures in spatial abilities. Messages from these receptors are registered in the **primary somatosensory cortex.** The ability to comprehend language is concentrated in two areas in the parietal and temporal lobes. The **frontal lobe** receives and coordinates messages from the other lobes and keeps track of past and future body movement. It is primarily responsible for goal-directed behavior and is key to the ability to lead a mature emotional life. The **primary motor cortex** is responsible for voluntary movement.

Each lobe contains areas for specific motor sensory function as well as association areas. The **association areas**—areas that are free to process all kinds of information—make up most of the cerebral cortex and enable the brain to produce behaviors requiring the coordination of many brain areas.

Hemispheric Specialization

The two cerebral hemispheres are linked by the **corpus callosum,** through which they communicate and coordinate. Nevertheless, they appear to have some separate functions. The right hemisphere excels at nonverbal and spatial tasks, whereas the left hemisphere is usually more dominant in verbal tasks such as speaking and writing. The right hemisphere controls the left side of the body, and the left hemisphere controls the right side. In general terms, the ability to talk is concentrated in Broca's area, located in the left frontal lobe, and the ability to listen is concentrated in Wernicke's area, located in the left temporal lobe. In addition to language functions, the left hemisphere may operate more analytically, logically, and sequentially than the right, whereas the right hemisphere excels at visual and spatial tasks, visual images, music, and perception and expression of emotion. Not everyone shows the same pattern of differences between the two hemispheres, and in most people the right and left hemispheres work together closely.

Tools for Studying the Brain

In recent decades, science has developed increasingly sophisticated techniques for investigating the brain and nervous system. Among the most important tools are microelectrode techniques, macroelectrode techniques (EEG), structural imaging (CAT scanning, MRI), and functional imaging (EEG imaging, MEG, MSI, fMRI, and PET scanning). Scientists often combine these techniques to study brain activity in unprecedented detail.

The Spinal Cord

The **spinal cord** is a complex cable of nerves that connects the brain to most of the rest of the body. It is made up of bundles of long nerve fibers and has three basic functions: to carry motor impulses to the internal organs and muscles; to carry information from the extremities and internal organs to the brain; and to permit some reflex movements.

The Peripheral Nervous System

The second major division of the nervous system, the peripheral nervous system, carries messages to and from the central nervous system. It comprises two parts: the somatic and the autonomic nervous systems.

The Somatic Nervous System

The **somatic nervous system** is composed of the sensory (afferent) neurons that carry messages to the central nervous system and the motor (efferent) neurons that carry messages from the central nervous system to the skeletal muscles of the body.

The Autonomic Nervous System

The **autonomic nervous system** carries messages between the central nervous system and the internal organs. It has two parts: the **sympathetic** and **parasympathetic divisions.** The first acts primarily to arouse the body; the second, to relax and restore the body to normal levels of arousal. The sympathetic nervous system tends to act as a unit, rapidly mobilizing the entire body. The parasympathetic division, in contrast, tends to calm the body down more slowly, reflecting an evolutionary heritage in which stamina was an important human trait. The two divisions of the autonomic nervous system tend to work in tandem, but they can work independently or even simultaneously.

The Endocrine System

The endocrine system—the other communication system in the body—is made up of **endocrine glands** that produce **hormones,** chemical substances released into the bloodstream to guide such processes as metabolism, growth, and sexual development. Hormones are also involved in regulating emotional life. At puberty, hormones organize the entire nervous system and other body tissues. Throughout life, they activate behaviors by affecting such factors as alertness, excitability, sexual behavior, concentration, aggressiveness, and reactions to stress.

The **thyroid gland** secretes thyroxin, a hormone that can reduce concentration and lead to irritability when the thyroid is overactive, and cause drowsiness and a sluggish metabolism when the thyroid is underactive. Within the thyroid are four tiny pea-shaped organs, the **parathyroids,** that secrete parathormone to control and balance the levels of calcium and phosphate in the blood and tissue fluids. This, in turn, affects the excitability of the nervous system. The **pineal gland** secretes melatonin, which helps regulate sleep–wake cycles. The **pancreas** controls the level of sugar in the blood by secreting insulin and glucagon.

The **pituitary gland,** which is located on the underside of the brain, is connected to the hypothalamus. The pituitary produces the largest number of different hormones and thus has the widest range of effects on the body's functions. The pituitary influences blood pressure, thirst, and contractions of the uterus during childbirth, milk production, sexual behavior, and sexual interest. In addition, this complex gland plays an important role in body growth, the amount of water in the body's cells, and other functions as well. It is often called the "master gland" because of its influential role in regulating other endocrine glands.

The **gonads**—the testes in males and the ovaries in females—secrete androgens (including testosterone) and estrogens, which regulate sexual development and are linked to sexual interest and behaviors.

The two **adrenal glands** are located above the kidneys. Each has two parts: an outer covering, the adrenal cortex, and an inner core, the adrenal medulla. Both produce several important hormones, including epinephrine, which activates the sympathetic nervous system, and norepinephrine (a neurotransmitter), which raises blood pressure and triggers release of the hormone ACTH in the anterior pituitary, prolonging the body's response to stress.

Genes, Evolution, and Behavior

The related fields of **behavior genetics** and **evolutionary psychology** help psychologists explore the influence of heredity on human behavior.

Genetics   **Genetics** is the study of how living things pass on traits from one generation to the next through **genes.** The transmission of traits is referred to as heredity. Each gene is lined up on tiny threadlike bodies called **chromosomes,** which are made up predominantly of **deoxyribonucleic acid** (DNA). All the genes in all human chromosomes make up the **human genome.** Members of a gene pair can be either **dominant** or **recessive genes.** In **polygenic inheritance,** several genes interact to produce a certain trait. In some cases, expression of a trait is delayed until late in life and depends on environmental factors.

Behavior Genetics   Psychologists use a variety of methods to study the relationships between genes and various behaviors. **Strain studies** help to determine the heritability of certain traits in inbred animals; **selection studies** estimate the heritability of a trait by breeding animals with other animals that have the same trait. Through **family studies,** scientists examine genetic influences on human behavior, whereas **twin studies** probe **identical twins** who share identical genetic makeup, as opposed to **fraternal twins** who are only as genetically similar as regular siblings. **Adoption studies** are useful in determining the influence of heredity and environment on human behavior.

Genes interact with the environment in many complex ways, and it is often difficult for psychologists to determine whether a behavior results from the influence of an inherited trait or an environmental factor. The Human Genome Project has identified specific chromosome sites associated with some forms of Alzheimer's disease, some forms of alcoholism, schizophrenia, cognitive functioning, and intelligence.

Evolution   In 1859 Charles Darwin proposed the theory of natural selection to account for evolution—the idea that groups of organisms change over time. In modern terms, the theory of **natural selection** states that organisms best adapted to their environment tend to survive, transmitting their genetic characteristics to succeeding generations, whereas organisms with less adaptive characteristics tend to disappear.

Evolutionary Psychology   Evolutionary psychology analyzes human thoughts, traits, and behaviors by examining their adaptive value from an evolutionary perspective. It has proved useful in explaining many cross-cultural commonalities in human behavior. It has also proved useful in explaining language development, differing sexual strategies in men and women, and depression. Critics claim, however, that the presence of a behavior in individuals of many different cultures does not prove that it is hard-wired into the brain.

Social Implications   The study of behavior genetics and evolutionary psychology makes many people uneasy. With the development of amniocentesis and chorionic villus sampling, prospective parents can often detect genetic abnormalities in a fetus, leading to questions about the rights of a child versus those of the parents. Some fear that research in evolutionary psychology will undermine movements toward social equality by attempting to justify the adaptive value of certain forms of social injustice. Others fear that it will make people feel that genetics is destiny—that who we are is written in some kind of permanent ink before we are born.

key terms

Psychobiology	47	Neural Plasticity	55	Hormones	76
Neuroscience	47	Neurogenesis	56	Thyroid gland	76
Neurons	48	Central nervous system	58	Parathyroids	76
Dendrites	48	Peripheral nervous system	59	Pineal gland	76
Axon	48	Hindbrain	59	Pancreas	77
Nerve (or tract)	48	Cerebellum	60	Pituitary gland	77
Myelin sheath	49	Midbrain	60	Gonads	77
Sensory (or afferent) neurons	50	Thalamus	60	Adrenal glands	78
Motor (or efferent) neurons	50	Hypothalamus	61	Behavior genetics	79
Interneurons (or association neurons)	50	Reticular formation (RF)	61	Evolutionary psychology	79
Glial cells (or glia)	50	Limbic system	62	Genetics	79
Ions	50	Cerebral cortex	62	Genes	79
Polarization	50	Association areas	63	Chromosomes	79
Resting potential	50	Occipital lobe	64	Deoxyribonucleic acid (DNA)	80
Neural impulse (or action potential)	50	Temporal lobe	64	Human genome	80
Graded potentia	50	Parietal lobe	64	Dominant gene	80
Threshold of excitation	50	Primary somatosensory cortex	64	Recessive gene	80
All-or-none law	50	Frontal lobe	64	Polygenic inheritance	80
Absolute refractory period	51	Primary motor cortex	64	Strain studies	81
Relative refractory period	51	Corpus callosum	65	Selection studies	81
Synaptic space (or synaptic cleft)	51	Spinal cord	71	Family studies	82
Terminal button (or synaptic knob)	52	Somatic nervous system	73	Twin studies	82
Synapse	52	Autonomic nervous system	73	Identical twins	82
Synaptic vesicles	52	Sympathetic division	74	Fraternal twins	82
Neurotransmitters	52	Parasympathetic division	75	Adoption studies	83
Receptor site	52	Endocrine glands	76	Natural selection	84

The Nature of Sensation
The Basic Process
Sensory Thresholds
Subliminal Perception
Extrasensory Perception

Vision
The Visual System
Color Vision
Theories of Color Vision

Hearing
Sound

The Ear
Theories of Hearing
Hearing Disorders

The Other Senses
Smell
Taste
Kinesthetic and Vestibular
  Senses
Sensations of Motion
The Skin Senses
Pain

Perception
Perceptual Organization
Perceptual Constancies
Perceiving Distance and Depth
Perceiving Movement
Visual Illusions
Observer Characteristics:
  Individual Differences
  and Culture

Sensation
and Perception

3

n a rainy night, a 33-year-old mathematician took a fateful after-dinner stroll. His friends had always considered him a "gourmet's gourmet" because he had an uncanny ability to taste a dish and name all of its ingredients. One commented that he had "perfect pitch" for food. As he stepped into the street that night, a slow-moving van ran into him and he fell to the sidewalk, hitting his head. When he got out of the hospital he discovered, to his horror, that his sense of smell was gone. Because smell and taste are physiologically connected, his days as a gourmet were over.

His taste buds were working: He could tell whether food was salty, bitter, sour, or sweet. But without aromas, he could no longer experience the subtle mixtures of flavors that make food delicious and memorable. Eating became a chore.

Some years later he sued the driver of the van, claiming, first, that his enjoyment of life had been damaged beyond repair, and second, that loss of the sense of smell was life-threatening. Indeed, he had failed to notice the smell of smoke when his apartment building caught fire; he had been poisoned when he didn't realize he was eating spoiled food; and he could not detect the smell of a gas leak. He won his case. The technical term for his disorder is anosmia (from the Latin/Greek combination "without smell") (Ackerman, 1995).

We take our sense of smell for granted, like the air we breathe. And, indeed, every breath we take is scented. Without the dark aroma of fresh brewed coffee, the salty tang of the ocean breeze, the clean aroma of fresh laundry, even the atmosphere of a stable, life would be extraordinarily bland. Ask the two million Americans who suffer from smell and taste disorders. "I feel empty, in a sort of limbo," the mathematician said (Ackerman, 1995, p. 41). A woman whose sense of smell was restored compared the day she realized she could taste food again to "the moment in 'The Wizard of Oz,' when the world is transformed from black and white to Technicolor" (Ackerman, 1995, p. 42). Our sense of smell may not be as keen as that of other animals, such as dogs, yet aromas are part of our experience of life.

Sensations, which include smells, sights, sounds, tastes, balance, touch, and pain, are the raw data of experience. Our various sense organs are continuously bombarded by bits of information, all competing for attention and by themselves as meaningless as pieces of a giant jigsaw puzzle. **Perception** is the mental process of sorting, identifying, and arranging these bits into meaningful patterns. Sensation and perception are the foundation of consciousness; together, they tell us what is happening both inside and outside of our bodies.

We begin this chapter by looking at the basic principles of sensation: how we acquire information from the outside (and inside) world. We will examine the body's different sense organs to see how each converts physical energy—light or sound waves, for example—into nerve impulses. But sensation is only half the story. Our eyes register only light, dark, and color, yet we "see" a tree. Our ears pick up sound waves, yet we distinguish between a baby's cry and a Bach fugue. We explore these issues in the last section of the chapter, on perception.

The Nature of Sensation

How is light or sound converted into a message to the brain?

All of our information about the world comes to us through our senses. Each sense has its own characteristics, yet certain basic principles apply to all.

THINKABOUTIT

You will find the answers to these questions in the chapter:

1. How is light or sound converted into a message to the brain?

2. Why is vision our most important sense?

3. Is hearing loss inevitable in old age?

4. Why do humans have a weaker sense of smell than many other mammals?

5. Why do people who are lost in the desert "see" a mirage?

Sensation The experience of sensory stimulation.

Perception The process of creating meaningful patterns from raw sensory information.

Receptor cell A specialized cell that responds to a particular type of energy.

The Basic Process

The sequence of events that produces a sensation seems quite simple. First, some form of energy—light waves, sound vibrations, airborne or blood-borne chemical molecules—stimulates a **receptor cell** in one of the sense organs, such as the eye or the ear. If the stimulus is strong enough, the receptor sends a signal along the sensory nerves to the appropriate area of the cerebral cortex (see Chapter 2, Figure 2–9). The brain sits in the skull, isolated from external events, yet bombarded by electrical signals coming in over millions of nerve fibers. How does the brain distinguish between sights and sounds, sensations of touch and balance?

Receptor cells connected to neural pathways are specialized for one sense or another. In effect, sensory messages enter the brain on different channels: the hearing channel, the touch channel, the smell channel, and so on. The signals carried in the optic nerve are not "visual," nor are those in an auditory nerve audible. But they reliably produce an experience we call vision or hearing when they reach the proper areas in the brain.

Even if the signals in the optic nerve are caused by something other than light, the result is still a visual experience. For example, if you close your eyes and press gently on your eyelid, you will see a brief flash of light. Even though the stimulus is pressure, the brain interprets signals from the optic nerve as visual patterns. In the same way, both a symphonic recording and a stream of water trickling into the ear stimulate the auditory nerve, and both cause us to hear something. Johannes Müller, a nineteenth-century German physiologist, discovered this one-to-one relationship between stimulation of a specific nerve and the resulting type of sensory experience, a theory known today as the *doctrine of specific nerve energies.*

How does the brain identify variations in the *same* sensory mode, such as vision or smell? Different stimuli affect *how many* neurons fire, *which* neurons are activated or inhibited by a signal, and the *rate* at which they fire (see Chapter 2). The resulting pattern acts as a code, providing the brain with details about what kind of image or sound the senses have picked up. For instance, a very bright light might be coded as the rapid firing of a set of nerve cells, whereas a dim light would set off a much slower firing sequence. And both these signals would be transmitted on different channels and coded in a different way than a loud, piercing noise. Thus, by the time signals from receptor cells reach the brain, the simple signal—"something is going

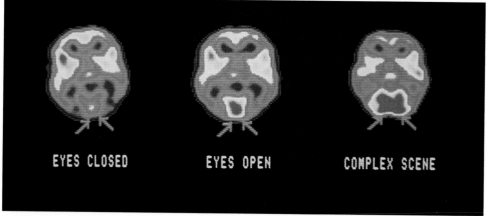

EYES CLOSED   EYES OPEN   COMPLEX SCENE

Nerve fibers from each eye cross to opposite sides of the brain, enabling the optic nerves to carry visual information to different parts of the brain. These PET scans show the level of activity in the brain as viewed from the top (green arrows point to the back of the brain). The more complex the scene, the more the visual areas of the brain (primarily the occipital lobes to the rear of both hemispheres, as shown by the green arrows) are engaged in active processing. (High levels of brain activity are shown as yellow and red; low levels of activity as green and blue.)

on"—has been transformed into a specific message that enables you to distinguish pink from purple, a slap from a tickle, a note played on a piano from the same note played on a trumpet.

Sensory Thresholds

The energy reaching a receptor must be sufficiently intense for it to have a noticeable effect. The minimum intensity of physical energy required to produce any sensation at all is called the **absolute threshold.** How much sensory stimulation is needed to produce a sensation? How loud does a sound have to be, for example, for a person to hear it? How bright does a "blip" on a radar screen have to be for the operator to see it?

To answer these kinds of questions, psychologists present a stimulus at different intensities and ask people whether they sense anything. You might expect that at a certain point people suddenly say, "Now I see the flash" or "Now I hear a sound." In fact, sensitivity to light, sound, pressure, or other stimuli varies from person to person, and even from moment to moment for the same person. For this reason, psychologists have agreed to set the absolute threshold at the point at which a person can detect the stimulus 50 percent of the time that it is presented (see Figure 3–1).

The absolute threshold for each of our senses is remarkably low. The absolute thresholds under ideal circumstances—in extremely quiet or dark or "taste-free" or "smell-free" conditions—are as follows (McBurney & Collings, 1984):

Absolute threshold The least amount of energy that can be detected as a stimulation 50 percent of the time.

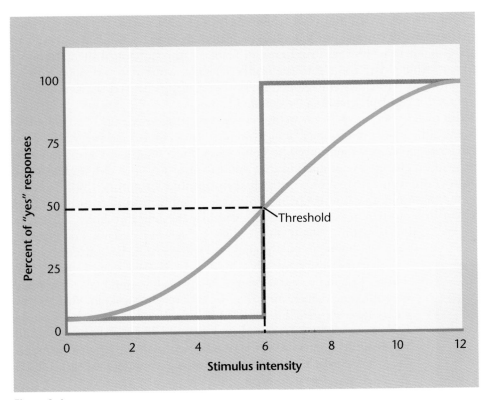

Figure 3–1
Determining a sensory threshold.
The red line represents an ideal case: at all intensities below the threshold, the person reports no sensation or no change in intensity; at all intensities above the threshold, the person reports a sensation or a change in intensity. In actual practice, however, we never come close to the ideal of the red line. The blue line shows the actual responses of a typical person. The threshold is taken as the point where the person reports a sensation or a change in intensity 50 percent of the time.

Adaptation An adjustment of the senses to the level of stimulation they are receiving.

Difference threshold or **just noticeable difference (jnd)** The smallest change in stimulation that can be detected 50 percent of the time.

Weber's law The principle that the jnd for any given sense is a constant fraction or proportion of the stimulation being judged.

- Taste: 1 gram (.0356 ounce) of table salt in 500 liters (529 quarts) of water.

- Smell: 1 drop of perfume diffused throughout a three-room apartment.

- Touch: The wing of a bee falling on your cheek from a height of 1 centimeter (.39 inch).

- Hearing: The tick of a watch from 6 meters (20 feet) in very quiet conditions.

- Vision: A candle flame seen from 50 kilometers (30 miles) on a clear, dark night.

Under normal conditions, absolute thresholds vary depending on the level and nature of ongoing sensory stimulation. For example, when you walk into a darkened movie theater, you can hardly see anything except the image on the screen. Gradually, however, your eyes become accustomed to the dark. Likewise, after you eat a bag of salty popcorn, it would take much more than 1 gram of salt in 500 liters of water for you to notice a salty taste. This phenomenon is called sensory **adaptation.** Our senses automatically adjust to the overall, average level of stimulation in a particular setting. When confronted by a great deal of stimulation, they become much less sensitive than when the overall level of stimulation is low. By the same token, when the level of stimulation drops, our sensory apparatus becomes much more sensitive than under conditions of high stimulation.

Adaptation allows our senses to be keenly attuned to environmental conditions without becoming overloaded. When you enter a hushed room, you are able to hear the faint tick of a wristwatch. But when you go out onto a busy city street at rush hour, the noise of street traffic would seem deafening, even painful, unless your ears adapted and became less sensitive to noise. Similarly, through visual adaptation, you can move from a dark room into the bright sunshine without experiencing pain or damaging your visual system (Hood, 1998). Later in this chapter we will examine various kinds of adaptation in more detail.

With each of our senses, what we notice most is change—change from no stimulation to stimulation, or change from less stimulation to more (and vice versa). How much stronger must a sound become before you notice that it has grown louder? The smallest change in stimulation that you can detect 50 percent of the time is called the **difference threshold,** or the **just noticeable difference (jnd).** Like the absolute threshold, the difference threshold varies from person to person and from moment to moment for the same person. And like absolute thresholds, difference thresholds tell us something about the flexibility of sensory systems. For example,

Adding 1 pound to this barbell would not produce a noticeable difference because 1 pound would fall below the difference threshold for this amount of weight.

adding 1 pound to a 10-pound load will certainly be noticed, suggesting that the difference threshold must be less than 1 pound. Yet adding 1 pound to a 100-pound load probably would not make much of a difference, suggesting that the difference threshold must be considerably *more* than 1 pound. How can the difference threshold be both less than and greater than 1 pound? The difference threshold varies according to the strength or intensity of the original stimulus. In other words, the greater the existing stimulus, the greater the change necessary to produce a jnd.

In the 1830s, Ernst Weber concluded that the difference threshold is a constant *fraction* or *proportion* of the specific stimulus, a theory known as **Weber's law.** The values of these fractions vary significantly for the different senses. Hearing, for example, is very sensitive: We can detect a change in sound of 0.3 percent (1/3 of 1 percent). By contrast, producing a jnd in taste requires a 20 percent (1/5) change. A change in weight of 2 percent (1/50) is necessary to produce a jnd.

Thus, adding 1 pound to a 50-pound load would produce a noticeable difference 50 percent of the time; adding 1 pound to a 100-pound load would not.

Subliminal Perception

The idea of absolute thresholds implies that certain events in the outside world occur outside our conscious awareness. Do we nonetheless register and respond to these *subliminal* (or "below threshold") messages? For decades the story has circulated that refreshment sales increased dramatically when a movie theater in New Jersey flashed subliminal messages to "Drink Coca-Cola" and "Eat Popcorn." In fact, sales of Coke and popcorn did not change. According to one survey, nearly two-thirds of Americans believe that advertisers put hidden messages and images in their advertisements to increase sales of their products (Lev, 1991).

Can people be influenced by information of which they are not consciously aware? The answer is a qualified yes. For example, in one study an experimental group was exposed to a subliminal list of words related to competition, whereas a control group was exposed to a subliminal list of neutral words. The words were flashed on a screen too rapidly for participants to identify them. But later, when they played a game, participants from the experimental group were especially competitive. In another study, one group of participants was subliminally exposed to words conveying honesty (a positive trait), and another group, to words conveying meanness (a negative trait). Then, all the participants were asked to read a neutral description of a woman and then assess the woman's personality characteristics. Members of the first group gave her more positive and honest ratings, whereas members of the second group tended to judge the woman more harshly (Erdley & D'Agostino, 1988). A review of more than 50 such studies found that subliminal presentations of "comfort" phrases tended to reduce feelings of anxiety, hostility, and threat, and to promote recall of more positive memories (Hardaway, 1991).

These studies and others like them (Arndt, Greenberg, Pyszczynski, & Solomon, 1997; Bar & Biederman, 1998; Kunst-Wilson & Zajonc, 1980; Monahan, Murphy, & Zajonc, 2000) indicate that *in a controlled laboratory setting* people can process and respond to information of which they are not consciously aware. But this does *not* mean that people automatically or mindlessly "obey" subliminal messages in advertisements, rock music, self-help tapes, or any other form. To the contrary, independent scientific studies show that hidden messages outside the laboratory have no significant effect on behavior (Beatty & Hawkins, 1989; Gable, Wilkins, Harris, & Feinberg, 1987; Greenwald, Spangenberg, Pratkanis, & Eskenazi, 1991; K. H. Smith & Rogers, 1994; T. G. Russell, Rowe, & Smouse, 1991; Underwood, 1994).

However, the mind can play tricks on itself. In another series of studies, volunteers used

THINKING CRITICALLY

Advertising and Subconscious Messages

TV ads do not contain hidden, subliminal messages, but they do attempt to make viewers associate products with idealized images and lifestyles. For example, luxury sedans are shown in front of mansions and opera houses; sports utility vehicles are shown in remote canyons. Ads also play on our senses. Visual cues (the models, the setting, the cuts from one scene to another) and auditory cues (the voice-over, musical background, sounds of nature) are the most obvious examples. But tactile cues (a car's leather interior) and kinesthetic cues (the feeling of a test drive created by placing the camera inside a moving car) are also common.

1. Analyze a series of ads for sensory content. Choose a specific category, such as ads for vacations or pain medications. What sensory cues are the advertisers using to hold your attention? to create conscious or subconscious associations? (*Hint:* Try turning off the sound to focus on visual cues; close your eyes to analyze auditory cues.)

2. What is the underlying message—that is, the associations beyond the specific information the ad conveys?

NOTE: This exercise is not designed to make you more skeptical of advertising (although this may be one outcome), but rather to make you as aware of sensory communication as advertisers are!

self-improvement tapes with subliminal messages for several weeks. About half said that the tapes worked and that they felt better about themselves, but objective tests detected no measurable change. Moreover, the reported improvement had more to do with the label on the tape than its subliminal content: About half the people who received a tape labeled "Improve Memory" said their memory had improved, even though many had actually received a tape intended to boost self-esteem; and about one-third of the people who listened to tapes labeled "Increase Self-Esteem" said their self-esteem had gone up, though many of them had actually been listening to tapes designed to improve memory (Greenwald et al., 1991).

Questions about subliminal perception inevitably lead to questions about extrasensory perception. Do some individuals have special powers of perception? Psychologists continue to debate this issue.

Extrasensory Perception

Some people claim to have an extra power of perception, one beyond those of the normal senses. This unusual power, known as *extrasensory perception*, or *ESP*, has been defined as "a response to an unknown event not presented to any known sense" (McConnell, 1969). ESP refers to a variety of phenomena, including *clairvoyance*—awareness of an unknown object or event; *telepathy*—knowledge of someone else's thoughts or feelings; and *precognition*—foreknowledge of future events. The operation of ESP and other psychic phenomena is the focus of a field of study called *parapsychology*.

Much of the research into ESP has been criticized for poor experimental design, failure to control for dishonesty, selective reporting of results, or inability to obtain replicable results (Hansel, 1969). Nevertheless, psychologists continue to explore the possibility of psychic phenomena using increasingly sophisticated procedures. For instance, Bem and Honorton (1994), using what has come to be known as the *autoganzfeld* procedure, reported encouraging results in their initial investigations of telepathy. In this procedure, a "sender," isolated in a soundproof room, concentrates on a picture or video segment randomly selected (by a computer) from a set of 80 photos or 80 videotape segments. A "receiver" is placed alone in another soundproof room. The receiver engages in deep relaxation while wearing a half Ping-Pong ball over each eye and headphones playing a hissing sound (to provide uniform visual and auditory stimulation). The receiver then tries to experience any message or image coming from the sender. The experiment concludes with a test in which a computer displays four photos or videotape segments to the receiver, who rates them for similarity to impressions or images received during the sending phase of the experiment. Although receivers did not identify all the actual photos and videos that the senders were looking at, they performed significantly better than would be expected by chance alone.

Unfortunately, recent attempts to replicate Bem and Honorton's original findings have only met with mixed success. One extensive review of 30 studies, collectively testing over 1,100 participants, concluded that no convincing evidence for psychic functioning had been demonstrated using the autoganzfeld procedure (Milton & Wiseman, 1999). However, a more recent analysis of a large number of studies provided support for ESP using the autoganzfeld procedure (Storm & Ertel, 2001). Although research *to date* has failed to demonstrate clearly the existence of ESP, some psychologists and other scientists do not rule out entirely the idea that it might be a real phenomenon. Instead, they point out that experimentation has not yet given scientific support to its existence.

All sensations occur as a result of the same basic series of events, but each of the body's sensory systems works a little differently. These individual sensory systems contain receptor cells that specialize in converting a particular kind of energy into neural signals. The threshold at which this conversion occurs varies from system to system. So do the mechanisms by which sensory data are processed and coded and sent to the brain.

CHECK YOUR UNDERSTANDING

1. Receptor cells are stimulated by

___a. pheromones

___b. energy

___c. the optic nerve

___d. neurons

2. The point at which a person can detect a stimulus 50 percent of the time is

___a. the absolute threshold

___b. the just noticeable difference

___c. the difference threshold

___d. adaption

3. The difference threshold or jnd is the smallest change in stimulation detectable

___a. 25 percent of the time

___b. 100 percent of the time

___c. 75 percent of the time

___d. 50 percent of the time

4. ESP includes all these except

___a. subliminal messages

___b. precognition

___c. telepathy

___d. clairvoyance

5. Ernst Weber's difference threshold is a(n) _____ fraction for a particular sense.

___a. variable

___b. constant

___c. diminishing

___d. increasing

Answer: 1.b, 2.a, 3.d., 4.a, 5.b

Vision

Why is vision our most important sense?

Different animal species depend more on some senses than on others. Dogs rely heavily on the sense of smell, bats on hearing, some fish on taste. For humans, vision ranks as the most important sense. Seventy percent of our body's sense receptors are located in our eyes (Ackerman, 1995). To identify objects in the environment through touch or taste, we have to be in direct contact; to smell or hear things

Cornea The transparent protective coating over the front part of the eye.

Pupil A small opening in the iris through which light enters the eye.

Iris The colored part of the eye.

Lens The transparent part of the eye inside the pupil that focuses light onto the retina.

Retina The lining of the eye containing receptor cells that are sensitive to light.

Blind spot The place on the retina where the axons of all the ganglion cells leave the eye and where there are no receptors.

Fovea The area of the retina that is the center of the visual field.

Light The small segment of the electromagnetic spectrum to which our eyes are sensitive.

Rods Receptor cells in the retina responsible for night vision and perception of brightness.

Cones Receptor cells in the retina responsible for color vision.

we can be father away. With sight we can perceive the minutest detail of objects that are close up, take in wide panoramas of open fields and distant mountains, or gaze at the stars, light years away.

The Visual System

The structure of the human eye, including the cellular path to the brain, is shown in Figure 3–2. Light enters the eye through the **cornea,** the transparent protective coating over the front of the eye. It then passes through the **pupil,** the opening in the center of the **iris,** the colored part of the eye. In very bright light, the muscles in the iris contract to make the pupil smaller, which both protects the eye and helps us see well in bright light. In dim light, the muscles relax to open the pupil wider and let in as much light as possible.

Inside the pupil, light moves through the **lens,** which focuses it onto the **retina,** the light-sensitive inner lining of the back of the eyeball. The lens changes shape to focus on objects that are closer or farther away. Normally the lens is focused on a middle distance. To focus on an object that is very close to the eyes, tiny muscles around the lens contract and make the lens rounder. To focus on something far away, the muscles work to flatten the lens. One spot on the retina, where the optic nerve leaves the eye for the brain, has no receptor cells: what we call our **blind spot.** Even when light from a small object is focused directly on the blind spot, the object will not be seen (see Figure 3–3).

On the retina, directly behind the lens, lies a depressed spot called the **fovea** (see Figure 3–4). The fovea occupies the center of the visual field, and images are in sharpest focus here. When we want to examine something in fine detail, we bring it close to the fovea.

The Receptor Cells The retina of each eye contains the *receptor cells* responsible for vision. These cells are sensitive to only a fraction of the spectrum of electromagnetic energy, which includes **light** along with other energies (see Figure 3–5).

The retina contains two kinds of receptor cells, **rods** and **cones,** named for their characteristic shapes (see Figure 3–6). The retina of each eye contains about 120 million rods and 8 million cones. Rods respond to varying degrees or intensities of light and dark, but not to colors. They are chiefly responsible for *night vision.* Cones allow us to see colors as well as light and dark. Operating chiefly in daylight, cones are less sensitive to light than rods are (MacLeod, 1978). Cones, like color film, work best in relatively bright light. The more sensitive rods, like black-and-white film, respond to much lower levels of illumination.

Cones are found mainly in the fovea, which contains no rods. The greatest density of cones is in the very center of the fovea, which is where images are projected onto the retina in sharpest focus. Rods predominate just outside the fovea. As we move outward from the fovea toward the edges of the retina, both rods and cones get sparser; almost no cones and only a few rods can be found at the extreme edges of the retina.

Both rods and cones connect to specialized neurons called **bipolar cells,** which have only one axon and one dendrite (see Figure 3–7). In the fovea, cones generally connect with only one bipolar cell—a sort of "private

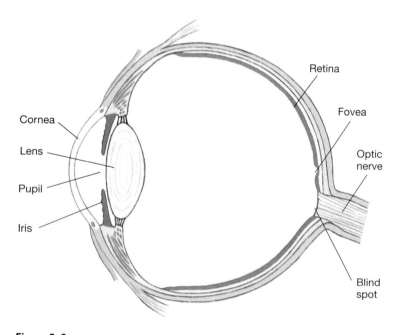

Figure 3–2
A cross-section of the human eye.
Light enters the eye through the cornea, passes through the pupil, and is focused by the lens onto the retina.
Source: Adapted from Hubel, 1963.

Figure 3–3
Finding your blind spot.
To locate your blind spot, hold the book about a foot away from your eyes. Then close your right eye, stare at the "X," and slowly move the book toward you and away from you until the red dot disappears.

line" to the optic nerve. Elsewhere, several rods and/or cones usually share a single bipolar cell. Receptor cells outside the fovea pool information, which increases sensitivity to light but cuts down on fine details in the signal that goes to the brain. As a result, peripheral vision is somewhat blurred.

The one-to-one connection between cones and bipolar cells in the fovea allows for maximum **visual acuity**—the ability to visually distinguish fine details. (*Acuity* comes from the Greek word for "sharp.") To see this for yourself, hold this book about 18 inches from your eyes and look at the "X" in the center of the line below.

This is a test to show how visualXacuity varies across the retina.

Your fovea picks up the "X" and about four letters to either side. This is the area of greatest visual acuity. Notice how your vision drops off for words and letters toward the left or right end of the line.

In the dark, however, the fovea is almost useless. To see an object we have to look to one side so that the image falls on the light-sensitive rods. When we want to examine something closely, we move it into the sunlight or under a lamp so that more cones are stimulated. For activities such as reading, sewing, and writing, the more light the better.

Adaptation   Adaptation, as described earlier, is the process by which our senses adjust to different levels of stimulation. In visual adaptation the sensitivity of rods and cones changes according to how much light is available (Hood, 1998). When you go from bright sunlight into a dimly lit theater and look for a seat, at first you see little or nothing. The reason is that both rods and cones are initially fairly insensitive to light. During the first five or ten minutes in the dark, the cones become more and more sensitive to the dim light. After about ten minutes, you will be able to see things directly in front of you; cones do not get any more sensitive after this point. But the rods continue to become more sensitive to the light for another 20 minutes or so, reaching maximum sensitivity after about 30 minutes. The process by which rods and cones become more sensitive to light in response to lowered levels of illumination is called **dark adaptation.** Even so, there is not enough energy in very dim light to stimulate the cones to respond to colors. In the dark, you see the world only in black, white, and gray.

When you move from the dark into the light, your eyes must readapt. By the time you leave a movie theater, your rods and cones have grown very sensitive. In the bright outdoor light, all the eye's neurons fire at once, almost blinding you. You squint and shield your eyes, and each iris contracts, reducing the amount of light entering your pupils and striking each retina. Within about a minute, both rods and cones are fully adapted to the light. At this point, you no longer need to squint and shield your eyes. The process by which rods and cones become less sensitive to light in response to increased levels of illumination is called **light adaptation.**

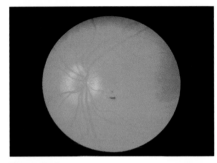

Figure 3–4
The retina.
A view of the retina through an ophthalmoscope, an instrument used to inspect blood vessels in the eye. The small dark spot is the fovea. The yellow circle marks the *blind spot,* where the optic nerve leaves the eye.

Bipolar cells Neurons that have only one axon and one dendrite; in the eye, these neurons connect the receptors on the retina to the ganglion cells.

Visual acuity The ability to distinguish fine details visually.

Dark adaptation Increased sensitivity of rods and cones in darkness.

Light adaptation Decreased sensitivity of rods and cones in bright light.

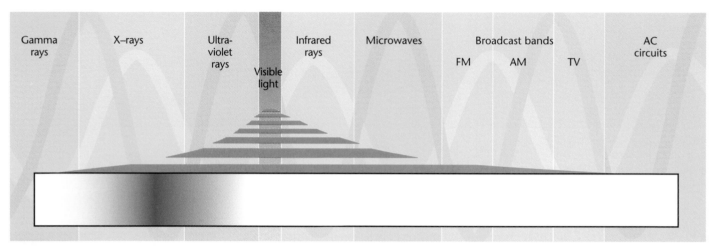

Figure 3–5
The electromagnetic spectrum.
The eye is sensitive to only a very small segment of the spectrum, known as visible light.

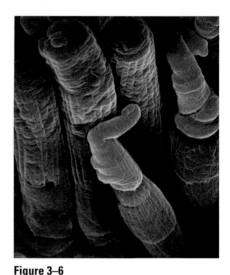

Figure 3–6
Rods and cones.
As you can see from this photomicrograph, the rods and cones are named for their shapes.

Afterimage Sense experience that occurs after a visual stimulus has been removed.

Ganglion cells Neurons that connect the bipolar cells in the eyes to the brain.

Optic nerve The bundle of axons of ganglion cells that carries neural messages from each eye to the brain.

Problems with dark adaptation are one reason more highway accidents occur at night than in the day (Leibowitz & Owens, 1977). When people drive at night, they must shift their eyes back and forth between the darkened interior of the car, the road illuminated by the headlights, and the darker areas at the side of the road. Unlike the situation in a darkened movie theater, these changing night-driving conditions do not allow for complete adaptation of either rods or cones; so neither system operates at maximum efficiency.

Visual adaptation is thus a partial, back-and-forth kind of process. The eyes adjust—from no stimulation to stimulation, from less stimulation to more, and vice versa—but they never adapt completely. This is why you sometimes experience an **afterimage,** as explained in Figure 3–8. If stimulation remained constant and the eyes adapted completely, all the receptors would gradually become totally insensitive and we would not be able to see anything at all. In the real world our eyes do not adapt completely, because light stimulation is rarely focused on the same receptor cells long enough for them to become totally insensitive. Rather, small involuntary eye movements keep the image moving slightly on the retina, so the receptor cells never have time to adapt completely.

From Eye to Brain   We don't actually "see" with our eyes; we see with our brain. Messages from the eye must make their way to the brain for sight to occur. As shown in Figure 3–7, the connections between eye and brain are quite intricate. To begin with, rods and cones are connected to bipolar cells in many different numbers and combinations. In addition, *interneurons* link receptor cells to one another and bipolar cells to one another. Eventually these bipolar cells hook up with the **ganglion cells,** leading out of the eye. The axons of the ganglion cells join to form the **optic nerve,** which carries messages from each eye to the brain.

Although each retina has more than 125 million rods and cones, the optic nerve has only about 1 million ganglion cells. The information collected by the 125 million receptor cells must be combined and reduced in some fashion to fit the mere 1 million "wires" that lead from each eye to the brain. Research indicates that most of this reduction takes place in the interconnections between the ganglion and receptor cells (Hubel & Livingstone, 1990; Livingstone & Hubel, 1988b; Kolb, 2003). To simplify, it appears that a single ganglion cell, connected to a large number of receptor cells, "summarizes and organizes" the information collected by these receptor

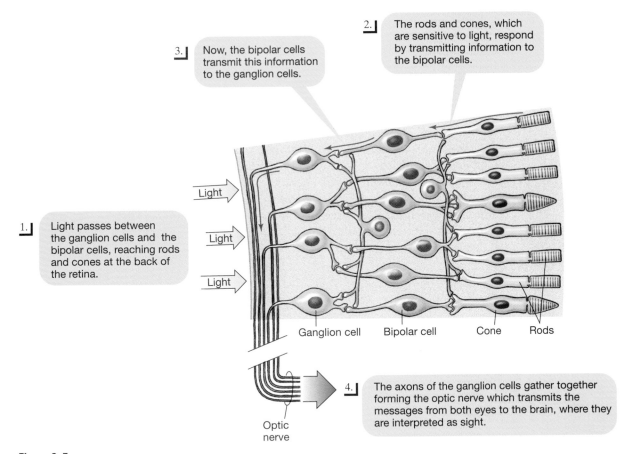

3. Now, the bipolar cells transmit this information to the ganglion cells.

2. The rods and cones, which are sensitive to light, respond by transmitting information to the bipolar cells.

1. Light passes between the ganglion cells and the bipolar cells, reaching rods and cones at the back of the retina.

Light

Light

Light

Ganglion cell   Bipolar cell   Cone   Rods

4. The axons of the ganglion cells gather together forming the optic nerve which transmits the messages from both eyes to the brain, where they are interpreted as sight.

Optic nerve

Figure 3–7
A close-up of the layers of the retina.
Light must pass between the ganglion cells and the bipolar cells to reach the rods and cones. The sensory messages then travel back out from the receptor cells via the bipolar cells, to the ganglion cells. The axons of the ganglion cells gather together to form the optic nerve, which carries the messages from both eyes to the brain (see Figure 3-2).

cells and then sends this condensed, or coded, message to the brain (Kolb, 2003). (We will say more about coding in the section on Perception, later in this chapter.)

After they leave the eyes, these fibers, which make up the optic nerves, separate, and some of them cross to the other side of the head at the **optic chiasm** (see Figure 3–9). The nerve fibers from the right side of each eye travel to the right hemisphere of the brain; those from the left side of each eye travel to the left hemisphere. Thus, as shown in Figure 3–9, visual information about any object in the *left visual field*, the area to the left of the viewer, will go to the right hemisphere (the pathway traced by the red line in Figure 3–9). Similarly, information about any object in the *right visual field*, the area to the right of the viewer, will go to the left hemisphere (the pathway traced by the blue line). (See also Figure 2–11 in Chapter 2.) The optic nerves carry their messages to different parts of the brain. Some messages reach the segment of the brain that controls the reflex movements that adjust the size of the pupil. Others find their way to the area of the brain that directs the eye muscles to change the shape of the lens. But the main destination for signals from the retina is the cerebral cortex.

How does the brain register and interpret these signals, "translating" light into visual images? In research for which they received a Nobel Prize, David H. Hubel and Torsten N. Wiesel (1959, 1979) found that certain brain cells—called **feature detectors**—are highly specialized to detect particular elements of the visual field, such as horizontal or vertical lines. Other feature-detector cells register more

 3.1

Optic chiasm The point near the base of the brain where some fibers in the optic nerve from each eye cross to the other side of the brain.

Feature detectors Specialized brain cells that only respond to particular elements in the visual field such as movement or lines of specific orientation.

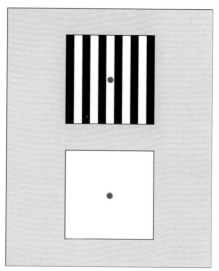

Figure 3–8
An afterimage.
First stare continuously at the center of the upper square for about 20 seconds, then look at the dot in the lower square. Within a moment, a gray-and-white afterimage should appear inside the lower square.

complex information, with some being sensitive to movement, others to depth, and still others to color. These different types of feature detectors send messages to specific, but nearby, regions of the cortex. Visual experience, then, depends on the brain's ability to combine these pieces of information into a meaningful image.

"Cortical blindness," caused by severe damage to the visual cortex, is especially puzzling. People suffering from this problem often have healthy retinas and optic nerves, but they report partial or total blindness. Yet some demonstrate an odd phenomenon called *blindsight:* They behave as if they can see forms, colors, and motion—even though they cannot see (Barbur, Harlow, & Weiskrantz, 1994; Gazzaniga, Fendrich, & Wessiner, 1994; Weiskrantz, Barbur, & Sahraie, 1995). For example, such a patient might duck if an object is thrown at her, even though she reports *not* having seen it; and she might turn her head toward a bright flashing light although she says she can't see a light. Some researchers speculate that the ability to sense light without actually "seeing" it stems from lower and older brain centers, rather than the visual cortex (Gazzaniga et al., 1994; Weiskrantz, 1995; Zeki, 1992, 1993).

Color Vision

Humans, like many—but not all—other animals see in color, at least during the day. Color vision is highly adaptive for an animal that needs to know when fruit is ripe or how to avoid poisonous plants and berries (which tend to be brightly hued), as our ancestors did.

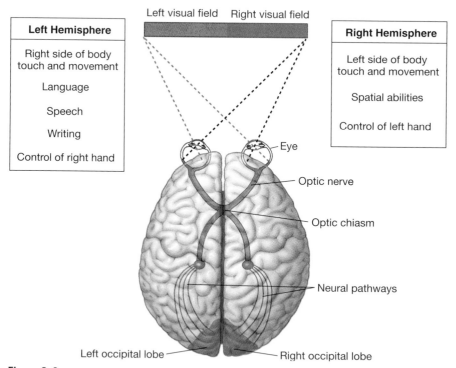

Figure 3–9
The neural connections of the visual system.
Messages about the red-colored area in the left visual field of each eye travel to the right occipital lobe; information about the blue area in the right visual field of each eye goes to the left occipital lobe. The crossover point is the *optic chiasm.*
Source: Adapted from "The Split Brain of Man," by Michael S. Gazzaniga. Copyright © 1967 by Scientific American, Inc. Adapted with permission of the estate of Eric Mose.

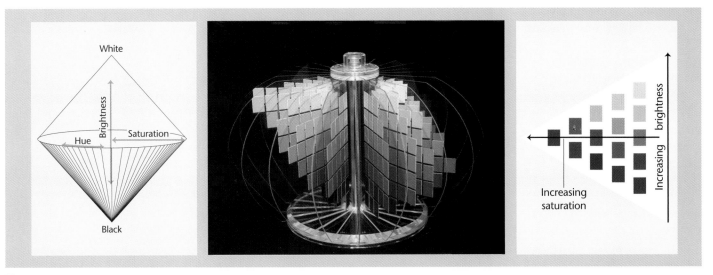

Figure 3–10
The color solid.
In the center portion of the figure, known as a color solid, the dimension of *hue* is represented around the circumference. *Saturation* ranges along the radius from the inside to the outside of the solid. *Brightness* varies along the vertical axis. The drawing (at left) illustrates this schematically. The illustration at right shows changes in saturation and brightness for the same hue.

Properties of Color   Look at the color solid (the central portion) of Figure 3–10. What do you see? Most people say they see a number of different colors: some oranges, some yellows, some reds, and so forth. Psychologists call these different colors **hues**, and to a great extent, what hues you see depend on the wavelength of the light reaching your eyes (see Figure 3–5).

Now look at the triangle of green colors on the right side of Figure 3–10. Although each color patch on the triangle is the same hue, the green color is deepest or richest toward the left side of the triangle. Psychologists refer to the vividness or richness of a hue as its **saturation**.

Finally, notice that the colors near the top of the triangle are almost white, whereas those close to the bottom are almost black. This is the dimension of **brightness,** which varies to a great extent based on the strength of the light entering your eyes. If you squint your eyes and look at the color solid, you will reduce the apparent brightness of all the colors in the solid, and many of them will appear to become black.

Hue, saturation, and brightness are three separate aspects of our experience of color. Most people can identify about 150 distinct hues (Coren, Porac, & Ward, 1984), but gradations of saturation and brightness allow us to see many variations on those hues.

Theories of Color Vision

How do our eyes identify and process color? If you look closely at a color television screen, you will see that the picture is actually made up of tiny red, green, and blue dots that blend together to give all possible hues. The same principle is at work in our own ability to see thousands of colors.

For centuries, scientists have known that they could produce all 150 basic hues by mixing together only a few lights of different colors (see Figure 3–11). Specifically, red, green, and blue lights—the primary colors for light mixtures—can be combined to create any hue. For example, red and green lights combine to give

Hue The aspect of color that corresponds to names such as red, green, and blue.

Saturation The vividness or richness of a hue.

Brightness The nearness of a color to white as opposed to black.

Additive color mixing The process of mixing lights of different wavelengths to create new hues.

Subtractive color mixing The process of mixing pigments, each of which absorbs some wavelengths of light and reflects others.

Trichromatic theory The theory of color vision that holds that all color perception derives from three different color receptors in the retina (usually red, green, and blue receptors).

Trichromats People who have normal color vision.

Color blindness Partial or total inability to perceive hues.

Dichromats People who are blind to either red-green or yellow-blue.

Monochromats People who are totally color-blind.

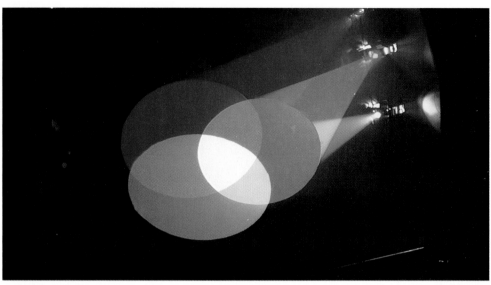

Figure 3–11
Additive color mixing.
Mixing light waves is an additive process. When red and green lights are combined, the resulting hue is yellow. Adding blue light to the other two yields white light.

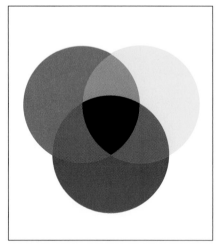

Figure 3–12
Subtractive color mixing.
The process of mixing paint pigments rather than lights is a subtractive process, because the pigments absorb some wavelengths and reflect others. A mixture of the three primary pigments (red, yellow, and blue) absorbs all wavelengths, producing black.

yellow; red and blue lights combine to make magenta. Combining red, green, and blue lights in equal intensities produces white. The process of mixing lights of different wavelengths is called **additive color mixing,** because each light adds additional wavelengths to the overall mix.

As every painter knows, mixing the three primary colors—red, yellow, and blue—in different combinations creates an almost infinite variety of hues. Color mixing with paint follows different rules than does color mixing with light. With light, different wavelengths add together, but the color of paint depends not on which wavelengths are *present*, but rather on which are *absorbed* and which are *reflected*. For example, red paint absorbs light from the blue end of the spectrum and reflects light from the red end. Since paint mixing depends on what colors are absorbed, or subtracted, the process is called **subtractive color mixing** (see Figure 3–12).

In the early nineteenth century, the German physiologist Hermann von Helmholtz proposed a theory of color vision based on additive color mixing. Helmholtz reasoned that the eye contains some cones that are sensitive to red, others that pick up green, and still others that respond most strongly to blue-violet. According to this view, color experiences come from mixing the signals from the three receptors. For example, yellow light would stimulate the red and green cones fairly strongly and the blue cones minimally, resulting in a pattern of receptor firing that would be experienced as yellow. Helmholtz's explanation of color vision is known as **trichromatic** (or three-color) **theory.**

Trichromatic theory explains how three primary colors can be combined to produce any other hue. It also accounts for some kinds of color blindness. People with normal color vision are called **trichromats.** Trichromats perceive all hues by combining the three primary colors. However, approximately 10 percent of men and 1 percent of women display some form of **color blindness. Dichromats** are blind either to red-green or blue-yellow (see Figure 3–13). Among humans, **monochromats,** who see no color at all but respond only to shades of light and dark, are extremely rare. But trichromatic theory does not adequately explain all color experiences. Why, for example, don't people with normal color vision ever see a light or a pigment that can be described as "reddish-green" or "yellowish-blue"? And what accounts for *color afterimages?* If you look at the flag in Figure 3–14 for about 30 seconds and then look at a sheet of white paper, you will see an afterimage. Where the picture is green, you will see a red afterimage; where the picture is yellow, you will see a bright blue afterimage; and where the picture is black, you will see a white afterimage.

In the later nineteenth century, Edward Hering, another German scientist, proposed an alternative theory of color vision that can explain these phenomena. Hering posited the existence of three *pairs* of color receptors: a yellow-blue pair and a red-green pair that determine the hue you see; and a black-white pair that determines the brightness of the colors you see. The yellow-blue pair can relay messages about yellow *or* blue, but not messages about yellow *and* blue light at the same time; the same is true for red-green receptors. Thus the members of each pair work in opposition to each other, which explains why we never see yellowish-blue or reddish-green. Hering's theory is now known as the **opponent-process theory.**

Opponent-process theory also explains color afterimages. While you were looking at the green stripes in the flag in Figure 3–14, the red-green receptors were sending "green" messages to your brain; but they were also adapting to the stimulation by becoming less sensitive to green light. When you later looked at the white page (made up of light from all parts of the spectrum), the red-green receptors responded vigorously to wavelengths in the red portion of the spectrum, and so you saw a red bar.

Today psychologists believe that both the trichromatic and opponent-process theories are valid, but at different stages in the visual process. We now know that the human eye usually has three kinds of cones for color (although some individuals may have four; Neitz, Neitz, & Jacobs, 1993). One set of receptors is most sensitive to violet-blue light, another set to green light, and the third set to yellow light. However, all the receptors are at least somewhat responsive to a broad range of colors. Contrary to Helmholtz's original theory, there is no "red" receptor in the retina, but the yellow cones respond to red more than the other two types of cones do. Thus, trichromatic theory corresponds fairly closely to the types of color receptors in the retina. Neurons higher up in the visual pathway appear to code color in the manner suggested by the opponent-process theory (Engel, Zhang, & Wandell, 1997). Together, trichromatic and opponent-process theory account for most color phenomena.

Color Vision in Other Species Most of us assume that color is "out there," in the environment; our eyes simply take it in. But studies of other species show, that to a great extent, color is in the eye of the beholder. Many animals—including some reptiles, fish, and insects (Neitz, Geist, & Jacobs, 1989; Rosenzweig & Leiman, 1982)—have color vision, but what colors they see varies. Humans and most other primates are trichromats; we perceive a wide range of colors. Most other mammals are dichromats—they experience the world only in reds and greens or blues and yellows (Abramov & Gordon, 1994; Jacobs, 1993). Hamsters, rats, squirrels, and other rodents are completely color-blind, or monochromats. So are owls, nocturnal birds of prey that have only rods in their eyes.

At the same time, however, other animals can see colors that we can't. Bees, for example, see ultraviolet light (Ackerman, 1995). To a bee's eyes, flowers with white petals that look drab to us flash like neon signs pointing the way to nectar. Birds, bats, and moths find red flowers irresistible, but bees pass them by. Tradition notwithstanding, bulls can't see red either; they are red-green color-blind. The matador's cape is bright red to excite the human audience, who find red arousing, perhaps especially when they expect to see blood, whether the bull's or the matador's. Given the roar of the crowd, confinement in the stadium, and the strange shape of the cape, the bull would charge no matter what the cape's color.

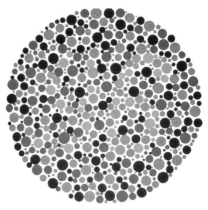

Figure 3–13
Experiencing colorblindness.
Perceiving the number 96 embedded in the mass of green circles is easy, except for people who have red-green colorblindness.
Source: Ishiharo, *Test for Color Deficiency.* Courtesy of the Isshinkai Foundation founded by Prof. Ishihara, Tokyo, Japan.

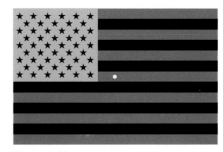

Figure 3–14
Afterimage.
Stare at the white spot in the center of the flag for about 30 seconds. Then look at a blank piece of white paper and you will see an *afterimage* in complementary colors.

Opponent-process theory Theory of color vision that holds that three sets of color receptors (yellow-blue, red-green, black-white) respond to determine the color you experience.

CHECK YOUR UNDERSTANDING

1. The spot on the retina with no receptor cells is the

___a. bright spot

___b. afterimage

___c. blind spot

___d. optic chiasm

2. Which of the following identifies the center of the visual field?

___a. fovea

___b. lens

___c. cornea

___d. retina

3. Rods and cones connect to

___a. bipolar cells

___b. the optic nerve

___c. the cerebral cortex

___d. ganglion cells

4. People who can perceive all hues are

___a. color blind

___b. monochromats

___c. trichromats

___d. dichromats

Answers: 1.c, 2.a, 3.a, 4.c

Hearing

Is hearing loss inevitable in old age?

If you had to make a choice, would you give up your sight or your hearing? Presented with this hypothetical choice, most people say they would give up hearing first. But the great teacher and activist Helen Keller, who was both blind and deaf from infancy, regretted her inability to hear more than anything else.

> I am just as deaf as I am blind. The problems of deafness are deeper and more complex, if not more important than those of blindness. Deafness is a much worse misfortune. For it means the loss of the most vital stimulus—the sound of the voice that brings language, sets thoughts astir and keeps us in the intellectual company of man. (Keller, 1948; quoted in Ackerman, 1995, pp. 191–192)

For some animals, hearing is the most acute sense. Bats, for example, are not blind (although they do not see in color). But they "see" more with their ears than with their eyes. When flying, they emit steady streams of high-pitched chirps that bounce off nearby objects. Neurons in their auditory systems extract an extraordinary amount of information from these echoes, a process known as *echolocation*. Remarkably, if a flying insect is nearby, the bat can determine exactly where it is, how far away it is, how fast it is flying, its size, characteristics of its wing beats, and its general features. Each of those coded messages goes to a different area of the bat's brain (Suga, 1990). Whales use echolocation, too. And during mating season, humpbacks and other whale species serenade females with haunting "ballads" that last from several minutes to a half hour and carry as far as 100 miles. Still, no other species use sound to *create* meanings, in music as well as language, as extensively as humans do.

Sound

The sensation we call **sound** is our brain's interpretation of the ebb and flow of air molecules pounding on our eardrums. When something in the environment moves, pressure is caused when molecules of air or fluid collide with one another and then move apart again. This pressure transmits energy at every collision, creating **sound waves.** The simplest sound wave—what we hear as a pure tone—can be pictured as a *sine* wave (see Figure 3–15). The tuning fork vibrates, causing the molecules of air first to contract and then to expand. The **frequency** of the waves is measured in cycles per second, expressed in a unit called **hertz (Hz).** Frequency primarily determines the **pitch** of the sound—how high or how low it is. The human ear responds to frequencies from about 20 Hz to 20,000 Hz. A double bass can reach down to about 50 Hz, a piano as high as 5,000 Hz.

The height of the wave represents its **amplitude,** which, together with frequency, determines the perceived *loudness* of a sound. Loudness is measured in **decibels** (see Figure 3–16). As we grow older, we lose some of our ability to hear low-intensity sounds. We can hear high-intensity sounds, however, as well as ever. This is why elderly people may ask you to speak louder, and then when you oblige by speaking *much* louder respond, "There's no need to shout!"

Musical instruments are designed to create sound waves. Unlike a tuning fork, which can produce a tone that is almost pure, instruments produce **overtones**—accompanying sound waves that are different multiples of the frequency of the basic tone. Because of physical differences in their construction, a violin and a piano that play the same note will be "in tune" but will produce different overtones. Thus, the two instruments can play the same melody, yet retain their distinctive sounds. Similarly, two vocalists may sing the same note, but because of the way their voices resonate in response to their different vocal cords and body shapes, their voices

Sound A psychological experience created by the brain in response to changes in air pressure that are received by the auditory system.

Sound waves Changes in pressure caused when molecules of air or fluid collide with one another and then move apart again.

Frequency The number of cycles per second in a wave; in sound, the primary determinant of pitch.

Hertz (Hz) Cycles per second; unit of measurement for the frequency of sound waves.

Pitch Auditory experience corresponding primarily to frequency of sound vibrations, resulting in a higher or lower tone.

Amplitude The magnitude of a wave; in sound, the primary determinant of loudness.

Decibel Unit of measurement for the loudness of sounds.

Overtones Tones that result from sound waves that are multiples of the basic tone; primary determinant of timbre.

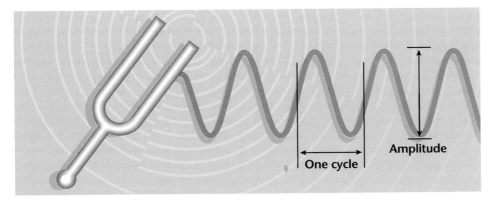

Figure 3–15
Sound waves.
As the tuning fork vibrates, it alternately compresses and expands the molecules of air, creating a *sound wave.*

Timbre The quality or texture of sound; caused by overtones.

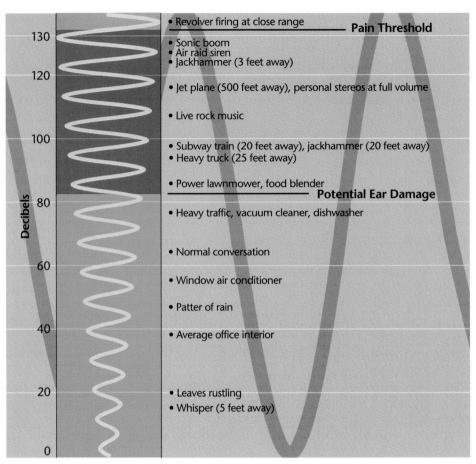

Figure 3–16
A decibel scale for several common sounds.
Prolonged exposure to sounds above 85 decibels can cause permanent damage to the ears, as can even brief exposure to sounds near the pain threshold.
Source: Adapted from Dunkle, 1982.

 psych 3.2

sound different. This complex pattern of overtones determines the **timbre,** or "texture," of a sound. Music synthesizers mimic different instruments electronically by producing not only pure tones, but also the overtones or timbre of different instruments.

Like our other senses, hearing undergoes adaptation so that it can function optimally under a wide variety of conditions. When city residents go to the country, at first they are struck by how quiet everything seems. After a day or two, however, the country starts to sound very noisy: Birds chirp, insects buzz, leaves rustle, and so on. The visitors' hearing, which had been adapted to the noise of the city, readapts to the relatively low level of sound in the country. Our sense of hearing adapts to tone as well. If you have difficulty hearing the difference between two tones, for example, listening repeatedly to only one of the tones will cause adaptation for that tone, making it much easier to detect the difference between that tone and the other.

THINKING CRITICALLY

An Ancient Question

At one time or another, everyone has debated the ancient question, "If a tree falls in the forest and no one is there, does the tree make a sound?"

• How would a psychologist answer this question? *Hints:* Think about one of the major themes of this chapter: sights, sounds, and other sensations are *psychological* experiences created by the brain in response to stimulation. Put another way, psychologists distinguish between what happens in the environment (e.g., sound waves) and what we perceive (e.g., sounds).

Prolonged exposure to loud sounds, such as those present at rock concerts, can lead to permanent hearing loss.

The Ear

Hearing begins when sound waves strike the eardrum (see Figure 3–17) and cause it to vibrate. The quivering of the eardrum prompts three tiny bones in the middle ear, the **hammer,** the **anvil,** and the **stirrup,** to hit each other in sequence and thus carry the vibrations to the inner ear. The last of these three bones, the stirrup, is attached to a membrane called the **oval window.** Vibrations of the oval window, in turn, are transmitted to the fluid inside a snail-shaped structure called the **cochlea.** The cochlea is divided lengthwise by the **basilar membrane,** which is stiff near the oval window but gradually becomes more flexible toward its other end. When the fluid in the cochlea begins to move, the basilar membrane ripples in response.

Lying on top of the basilar membrane, and moving in sync with it, is the **organ of Corti.** Here the messages from the sound waves finally reach the receptor cells for the sense of hearing: thousands of tiny hair cells that are embedded in the organ of Corti (Spoendlin & Schrott, 1989). As you can see in Figure 3–18, each hair cell is topped by a bundle of fibers. These fibers are pushed and pulled by the vibrations of the basilar membrane. The brain pools the information from thousands of these cells to perceive sounds.

Neural Connections   The sense of hearing is truly bilateral. Each ear sends messages to both cerebral hemispheres. En route to the temporal lobes, auditory messages pass through at least four lower brain centers—a much less direct route than visual messages follow. The switching station where the nerve fibers from the ears

Hammer, anvil, stirrup The three small bones in the middle ear that relay vibrations of the eardrum to the inner ear.

Oval window Membrane across the opening between the middle ear and inner ear that conducts vibrations to the cochlea.

Cochlea Part of the inner ear containing fluid that vibrates, which in turn causes the basilar membrane to vibrate.

Basilar membrane Vibrating membrane in the cochlea of the inner ear; it contains sense receptors for sound.

Organ of Corti Structure on the surface of the basilar membrane that contains the receptor cells for hearing.

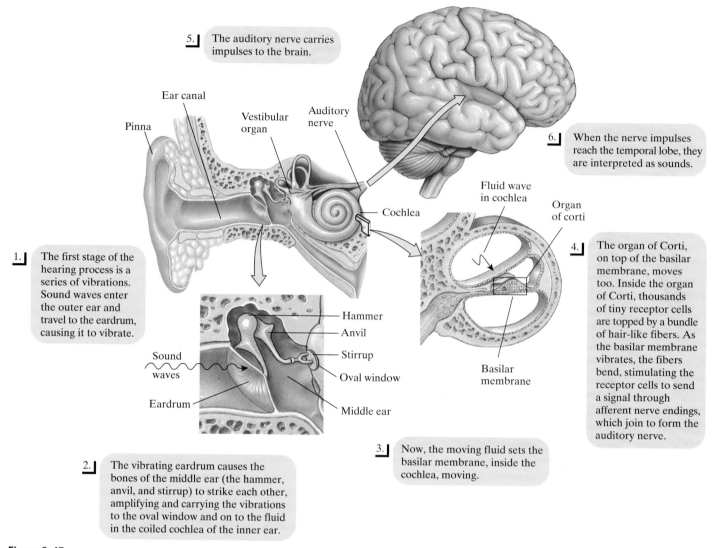

5. The auditory nerve carries impulses to the brain.

6. When the nerve impulses reach the temporal lobe, they are interpreted as sounds.

1. The first stage of the hearing process is a series of vibrations. Sound waves enter the outer ear and travel to the eardrum, causing it to vibrate.

4. The organ of Corti, on top of the basilar membrane, moves too. Inside the organ of Corti, thousands of tiny receptor cells are topped by a bundle of hair-like fibers. As the basilar membrane vibrates, the fibers bend, stimulating the receptor cells to send a signal through afferent nerve endings, which join to form the auditory nerve.

3. Now, the moving fluid sets the basilar membrane, inside the cochlea, moving.

2. The vibrating eardrum causes the bones of the middle ear (the hammer, anvil, and stirrup) to strike each other, amplifying and carrying the vibrations to the oval window and on to the fluid in the coiled cochlea of the inner ear.

Ear canal · Pinna · Vestibular organ · Auditory nerve · Cochlea · Fluid wave in cochlea · Organ of corti · Basilar membrane

Sound waves · Eardrum · Hammer · Anvil · Stirrup · Oval window · Middle ear

**Figure 3–17
How we hear.**

 psych 3.3

cross over is in the medulla, part of the hindbrain (see Figure 2–7). From the medulla, other nerve fibers carry the messages from the ears to the higher parts of the brain. The primary destinations for these auditory messages are the auditory areas in the temporal lobes of the two cerebral hemispheres. At each stage along the way, auditory information becomes more precisely coded (Feng & Ratnam, 2000).

Theories of Hearing

How are the different sound-wave patterns coded into neural messages? One aspect of sound, loudness, seems to depend on how many neurons are activated: The more cells that fire, the louder the sound seems to be. The coding of messages about pitch is more complicated. There are two basic views of pitch discrimination: place theory and frequency theory. According to **place theory,** the brain determines pitch by noting the *place* on the basilar membrane at which the message is strongest. This theory asserts that any given sound wave has a point on the basilar membrane at which vibrations are most intense. Thus, high-frequency sounds cause the greatest vibration at the stiff base of the basilar membrane; low-frequency sounds resonate most strongly at the opposite end (Zwislocki, 1981). The brain detects the location

Place theory Theory that pitch is determined by the location of greatest vibration on the basilar membrane.

of the most intense nerve-cell activity and uses this to determine the pitch of a sound.

The **frequency theory** of pitch discrimination holds that the *frequency* of vibrations of the basilar membrane as a *whole*, not just *parts* of it, is translated into an equivalent frequency of nerve impulses. Thus, if a hair bundle is pulled or pushed rapidly, its hair cells send a high-frequency message to the brain. However, because neurons cannot fire as rapidly as the frequency of the highest-pitched sound that can be heard, theorists have modified the frequency theory to include a **volley principle**. According to this view, auditory neurons can fire in sequence: One neuron fires, then a second one, then a third. By then, the first neuron has had time to recover and can fire again. In this way, several neurons together, firing in sequence, can send a more rapid series of impulses to the brain than any single neuron could send by itself.

Because neither place theory nor frequency theory alone fully explains pitch discrimination, some combination of the two is needed. Frequency theory appears to account for the ear's responses to frequencies up to about 4,000 Hz; above that, place theory provides a better explanation of what is happening.

Hearing Disorders

Because our auditory system is so subtle and complicated, hearing problems are relatively common. An estimated 28 million Americans suffer from partial or total deafness. Injury, infections, cigarette smoking, explosions, and—yes—long-term exposure to loud noise can harm the ear and cause partial or complete deafness. About 10 million Americans have irreversible hearing damage because of exposure to noise, and 30 million are exposed to damaging noise levels every day, on the job or at home. The chief culprits are leaf blowers, chain saws, snowmobiles, jet planes, and personal stereo systems (refer back to Figure 3–16) (Goldstein, 1999; Leary, 1990).

The good news is that hearing loss can be prevented or delayed in many cases. People ages 45 to 65 are most likely to experience hearing problems. With age, some decline in hearing acuity is almost inevitable, but deafness is not. Most cases of deafness in old age are the result of undetected ear infections in childhood, exposure to noise, or smoking.

For people with irreversible damage, a number of remedies are available. New digital technology has made hearing aids, which simply amplify sound, more precise by enhancing speech perception and reducing background noise. Surgery can help people with conductive hearing loss due to a stiffening of the connections between the bones (hammer, anvil, and stirrup) of the middle ear.

Implants offer hope to people who suffer from deafness due to cochlear damage (Clark, 1998). One or more platinum electrodes are inserted into the cochlea of one ear. The electrodes bypass the damaged hair cells and convey electrical signals from a miniature sound synthesizer directly to the auditory nerve. In some people who were totally deaf, these implants have produced as much as 70 percent correct word recognition (Erickson, 1990; Loeb, 1985). Not surprisingly, the younger a hearing-impaired child is when they receive cochlear implants, the more their speech recognition and language development is improved, promting many experts to recommend the surgery be performed during the first three years of life (Kileny, Zwolan, & Ashbaugh, 2001). For people who have auditory nerve damage, scientists have begun to explore new procedures that bypass the cochlea entirely—sending electrical signals directly to the brain (LeVay, 2000). Although still experimental, these procedures show promise. Other researchers are working on techniques to regenerate hair cells, through *neurogenesis* (see Chapter 2; Stone, Oesterle, & Rubel, 1998).

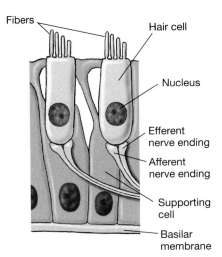

Figure 3–18
A detailed drawing of a hair cell located in the organ of Corti.
At the top of each hair cell is a bundle of fibers. If the fibers bend so much as 100 trillionths of a meter, the receptor cells transmit a sensory message to the brain.
Source: Adapted from "The Hair Cells of the Inner Ear," by A. J. Hudspeth, © 1983 by Scientific American, Inc. All rights reserved. Reprinted with permission from the estate of Bunji Tagawa.

Frequency theory Theory that pitch is determined by the frequency with which hair cells in the cochlea fire.

Volley principle Refinement of frequency theory; it suggests that receptors in the ear fire in sequence, with one group responding, then a second, then a third, and so on, so that the complete pattern of firing corresponds to the frequency of the sound wave.

Deaf Culture

Should doctors do everything possible to restore hearing in children who are born deaf or become deaf at an early age? Surprisingly perhaps, The National Association of the Deaf argues no. Many of these procedures only partially restore hearing. As a result, the association argues, children are left in limbo. On the one hand, they are denied access to sign language and to the deaf subculture; on the other, they are pushed into a hearing culture that labels them "disabled," reducing self-esteem (Bat-Chava, 1994). The association holds that sign language is a legitimate language (Emmorey, 1994) and should be recognized as such (see Chapter 7, Cognition and Language). Children who learn sign language as their native language function quite well, often better than children who struggle to understand spoken language they can barely hear.

Underlying this position is the view that deafness is *not* a disability; indeed, it can lead to a sharpening of the other senses (Clay, 1997). Rather, deafness is a variation on the common human pattern, a form of human diversity.

Far from not hearing enough sound, some people hear too much of the wrong kind of sound and suffer greatly because of it. Almost everybody has at some time heard a steady, high-pitched hum that persists even in the quietest room. This sound, which seems to come from inside the head, is called *tinnitus*, and is estimated to afflict approximately one out of every eight people to some degree (Johansson & Arlinger, 2003). In some people, it becomes unbearably loud—like the screeching of subway brakes—and does not go away (Dunkle, 1982). In most cases, tinnitus results from irritation or damage to the hair cells. Prolonged exposure to loud sound or toxins, certain medical conditions, even some antibiotics, can cause permanent damage to the hair cells. In many cases, drug therapies, implants that create "white noise" (or sound blockage), and biofeedback can provide relief.

CHECK YOUR UNDERSTANDING

1. Hertz is a measurement of _____ in sound waves.

___a. amplitude

___b. frequency

___c. decibels

___d. echolocation

2. Hearing first starts when sound waves strike the

___a. cochlea

___b. organ of Corti

___c. ear drum

___d. oval window

3. Place theory, frequency theory, and the volley principle all refer to

___a. pitch

___b. amplitude

___c. deafness

___d. loudness

Answers: 1.b; 2.c; 3.a

The Other Senses

Why do humans have a weaker sense of smell than many other mammals?

Vision and hearing dominate human consciousness; we rely primarily on these two senses to gather information about our environment. Our other senses—including smell, taste, balance, motion, pressure, temperature, and pain—are also in play, even when we are less conscious of them. We turn first to the chemical senses: smell and taste.

Smell

Of all our senses, smell is the most primitive and evocative. We find some scents alluring and others repulsive, but we rarely perceive odors as *neutral*. A mere whiff can trigger sudden, unexpected, emotionally charged memories—of a summer by the sea, a forgotten romance, or a childhood home. Part of the reason smells evoke powerful memories is anatomical. Some of the nerves in our nose are directly connected to the amygdala and the hippocampus, lower brain centers that figure prominently in emotion and memory (see Chapter 2). But evolutionary psychologists suggest a deeper reason (Azar, 1998b). Most animals use odors to distinguish between *good* and *bad*, safe and unsafe. They depend on their sense of smell to determine whether it is safe or dangerous to enter a territory, eat a specific food, or approach another animal. In humans, this function of smell appears to have shifted to our emotions, so that smell often plays a crucial role in determining our *likes* and *dislikes*.

Evolutionary theory also explains why our sense of smell is weak compared with that of other animals (Ackerman, 1995). Animals with the sharpest sense of smell generally walk on all fours with their heads close to the ground, where pungent odors lie. Pigs can smell truffles buried underground. Elephants "remember" by swishing their trunks back and forth over a trail used years before. When our ancestors left the forest for the open plains and began to walk upright, enemies and prey, edible plants, landmarks, and potential mates all became visible, and their sense of smell became less important.

Modern humans have a paltry five million receptor cells devoted to the sense of smell, compared with 220 million in a sheepdog. But our relatively small smell organs are extremely sensitive—according to one estimate, about 10,000 times more sensitive than our sense of taste (Moncrieff, 1951). Certain substances, such as decayed cabbage, lemons, and rotten eggs, can be detected in tiny amounts. Mercaptan, a foul-smelling substance added to natural gas (which is odorless and can be lethal if inhaled), can be smelled in concentrations as small as 1 part per 50 billion parts of air.

Our sense of smell undergoes adaptation, much like the other senses. Although we can discriminate among a large number of odors, we may find it difficult to identify many familiar smells (Cain, 1982; Engen, 1982). The perfume that was so pleasant to its wearer early in the evening seems to have worn off after a few hours, though others still notice it. Similarly, the aroma that enticed you into a restaurant seems to have disappeared by the time your meal begins, though it continues to draw other patrons.

Detecting Common Odors How do we detect odors? Distinguish between the citrus scents of lemon and orange and the sour smell of spoiled milk? Our sense of smell is activated by a

Certain animal species rely more on their sense of smell than humans do. This dog has been trained to use its keen sense of smell to detect bombs hidden in luggage at an airport.

Olfactory epithelium Nasal membranes containing receptor cells sensitive to odors.

Olfactory bulb The smell center in the brain.

Pheromones Chemical molecules that communicate information to other members of a species, and influence their behavior.

complex protein, called odorant binding protein (OBP), produced in a nasal gland. As we breathe, a fine mist of this protein is sprayed through a duct in the tip of the nose and binds with airborne molecules that then activate receptors located high in each nasal cavity in a patch of tissue called the **olfactory epithelium** (see Figure 3–19). The olfactory epithelium, only about half the size of a postage stamp, is packed with millions of receptor cells. The axons from these millions of receptors go directly to the **olfactory bulb,** where some recoding takes place. From the olfactory bulb, messages are routed via the olfactory tract to the temporal lobes of the brain, resulting in our awareness of the smells. But messages are also routed to the brain core, as noted above.

Odor sensitivity is related to gender. Numerous studies confirm that women generally have a better sense of smell than men do (Cain, 1982; Dalton, Doolittle, & Breslin, 2002). Age also makes a difference: Generally, the ability to smell is sharpest during the early adult years (ages 20 to 40) (Doty, 1989; Doty et al., 1984; Schiffman, 1997). Of the people tested by Doty and his colleagues, one-quarter of those over the age of 65 and half of those over the age of 80 had completely lost their ability to smell. *Anosmia*, the complete loss of smell described in the opening of this chapter, can be devastating.

Communicating with Pheromones   Many animals use chemicals as a means of communication. Invisible, sometimes odorless molecules called **pheromones** secreted by glands or in urine can have powerful effects on other animals' behavior.

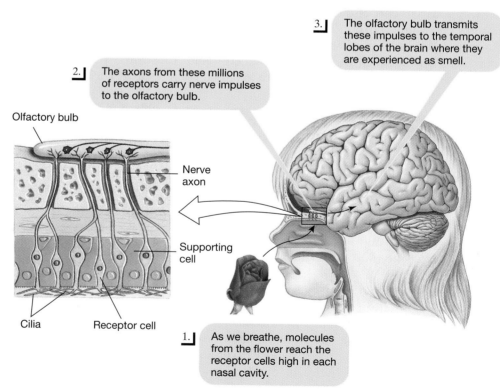

3. The olfactory bulb transmits these impulses to the temporal lobes of the brain where they are experienced as smell.

2. The axons from these millions of receptors carry nerve impulses to the olfactory bulb.

Olfactory bulb

Nerve axon

Supporting cell

Cilia   Receptor cell

1. As we breathe, molecules from the flower reach the receptor cells high in each nasal cavity.

Figure 3–19
The human olfactory system.
The sense of smell is triggered when odor molecules in the air reach the olfactory receptors located inside the top of the nose. Inhaling and exhaling odor molecules from food does much to give food its flavorful "taste."
Source: From *Human Anatomy and Physiology* by Anthony J. Gaudin and Kenneth C. Jones. Copyright © 1989. Reprinted with permission.

Pheromones stimulate receptors in the **vomeronasal organ (VNO),** located in the roof of the nasal cavity. The VNO sends messages to a second olfactory bulb specially designed to interpret pheromonal communications (Bartoshuk & Beauchamp, 1994; Wysocki & Meredith, 1987). Stimulation of the VNO also activates the hypothalamus and amygdala—two areas of the brain known to be involved in reproductive and defensive behaviors, although the precise pathways are not yet fully understood (Keverne, 1999; Stern & Marx, 1999).

Pheromones also provide information about another animal's identity. By sniffing another member of their species—or the scent marks they leave behind—animals can learn what the other animals ate last, how dominant they are, whether they are healthy, male or female, and, in the case of females, sexually receptive. Pheromones also indicate whether another animal is under stress, aggressive and likely to attack, or fearful and likely to flee. One study found that hamsters can identify members of their own family using smell, even when they have been separated from them at birth and raised with unrelated hamsters (Mateo & Johnston, 2000). They seem to avoid aggressive or sexual contact with family members, adaptive behavior that protects individuals who share many of their genes and prevents inbreeding.

Humans, like other mammals, have a VNO (Takami, Getchell, Chen, Monti-Bloch, & Berliner, 1993). For decades scientists dismissed this as a nonfunctional relic of our evolutionary past. But new research suggests that humans might have an active VNO and that we secrete and detect pheromones (Benson, 2002; Thorne, Neave, Scholey, Moss, & Fink, 2002; also see Doty, 2001). (see *On the Cutting Edge: Do Humans Communicate with Pheromones?*).

Taste

Human beings are *omnivores* (meaning we eat everything). Although tastes vary widely from culture to culture, there is hardly anything on earth that some group, somewhere, hasn't declared "delicious." As babies, we prefer bland foods and sweets. As we get older, however, we seem to crave novelty: pickles, mustard, and even ice cream (so cold it almost burns the tongue) are acquired tastes.

To understand taste, we must first distinguish it from *flavor*. The flavor of food arises from a complex combination of taste and smell (as illustrated at the beginning of the chapter). If you hold your nose when you eat, most of the food's flavor disappears, though you still recognize the basic taste qualities: *sweet, sour, salty,* and *bitter.* In other words, you get the taste, but not the flavor. Recently, investigators have found evidence for at least one additional taste—*umami,* which accounts for our sensitivity to monosodium glutamate (MSG) and related proteins (Chaudhari, Landin, & Roper, 2000; Smith & Margolskee, 2001). The receptor cells for the sense of taste are housed in the **taste buds,** most of which are found on the tip, sides, and back of the tongue. An adult has about 10,000 taste buds (Bartoshuk, 1993). The number of taste buds decreases with age, a fact that may partly explains why older people often lose interest in food.

The taste buds are embedded in the tongue's **papillae,** bumps that you can see if you look at your tongue in the mirror. Each taste bud contains a cluster of taste receptors or taste cells (see Figure 3–20), which die and are replaced about every seven days. The chemical substances in the foods we eat dissolve in saliva and fall into the crevices between the papillae of the tongue, where they come into contact with the taste receptors. The chemical interaction between food substances and the taste cells causes adjacent neurons to fire, sending a nerve impulse to the parietal lobe of the brain and to the limbic system. This happens very quickly: People can accurately identify a taste within one-tenth of a second after something salty or sweet has touched the tongue (Cain, 1981). The same nerves also conduct

Vomeronasal organ (VNO) Location of receptors for pheromones in the roof of the nasal cavity.

Taste buds Structures on the tongue that contain the receptor cells for taste.

Papillae Small bumps on the tongue that contain taste buds.

ON THE CUTTING EDGE

DO HUMANS COMMUNICATE WITH PHEROMONES?

Thirty years ago, as an undergraduate at Wellesley College, future psychologist Barbara McClintock noticed that the women in her dormitory had remarkably similar menstrual cycles (McClintock, 1971). In other social animals, this pattern is adaptive. "When you see others successfully rearing young," McClintock says, "it means it's a good time for you too" (in Kluger, 1998). Numerous studies involving both humans and nonhumans have demonstrated that menstrual synchronicity and duration are affected by some kind of pheromone communication (McClintock, 1978, 1999; Preti, Cutler, Garcia, Huggins, & Lawley, 1986).

Do pheromones play a role in sexual attraction and mate selection? Some research suggests that women may use pheromones to select genetically appropriate mates. In one study, female volunteers were asked to smell T-shirts previously worn by males and to rate the smells for pleasantness and sexiness (Wedeking, Seebeck, Bettens, & Paepke, 1995). The participants were then sorted into categories based on characteristics of their immune systems. Interestingly, females preferred T-shirts worn by men who had immune systems most different from their own. Offspring of parents with different immune systems will possess a broader immune response (and thus be more likely to survive) than will offspring of parents with similar immune systems (Mirsky, 1995). Thus, evolution might favor females who are most attracted to males with very different immune systems. In a parallel development, researchers in New Mexico and Sweden have reported that, particularly at their most fertile time of month, women prefer T-shirts worn by the fittest-looking men (Berreby, 1998).

In another series of studies, researchers have shown that when males are exposed to a natural female pheromone their general mood is elevated, and their ratings of the *sexual attractiveness* of females described in an experimental vignette are enhanced. Similarly, when females are exposed to a natural male pheromone, their general mood is also elevated as are their ratings of male *sexual attractiveness* (Scholey, Bosworth, & Dimitrakaki, 1999; Thorne, Neave, Scholey, Moss, & Fink, 2002; Thorne, Scholey, & Neave, 2000). Consistent with these findings are the results of neuroimaging studies that have shown that different areas of male and female brains become active when men and woman are exposed to the smell of testosterone and estrogen (Savic, Berglund, Gulyas, & Roland, 2001).

Additional evidence that humans communicate with smells is derived from studies showing that people who are closely related can often identify their family members using scent. For example, mothers can identify their newborns by smell after only a few hours of contact (Porter, Cernich, & McLaughlin, 1983). In turn, newborn infants can discriminate between their mothers' body odors and the odors of other mothers (Schaal, 1986), and they will even turn their heads toward the scent of a perfume that has been worn by their mothers while ignoring a different perfume (Schleidt & Genzel, 1990). Moreover, human fetuses appear to be sensitive to the smells of their unique prenatal environment—displaying a positive preference for the odor of their particular amniotic fluid months later as newborns (Schaal, Marlier, & Soussignan, 1998). Scent recognition may even bind families throughout life: Adults can recognize clothing worn by their relatives, even after they have been separated for several years (Porter, Balogh, Cernoch, & Franchi, 1986).

Other psychologists are not fully convinced that human beings "follow their noses." They point out that samples in many of these studies have been small, and the procedure (the ubiquitous sweaty T-shirts) may have led women to focus more on smell than they do in real life. Moreover, studies that do not find any correlation between immune system and sexual attraction or mate selection have been largely ignored (e.g., Cutler, Friedmann, & McCoy, 1998; Berreby, 1998; Quadagno, 1987). Some psychologists accept the evidence that people do respond to pheromones, but argue the real question is *how much* they affect our behavior. Would the women who preferred certain T-shirts be attracted to the wearers if they saw their photographs and had an opportunity to meet and talk with them in person? Would pheromones override visual and auditory cues? Surely there is more to human mate selection, mothering, and kinship than chemicals.

Critics notwithstanding, McClintock and others are investigating clinical applications. Pheromone treatments to control ovulation might help couples having difficulty conceiving a child or serve as a noninvasive form of birth control. Mood-altering pheromones might one day help to relieve depression and stress. Pheromones might even regulate prostate activity in men and be used to reduce the risk of cancer. But these possibilities lie in the future.

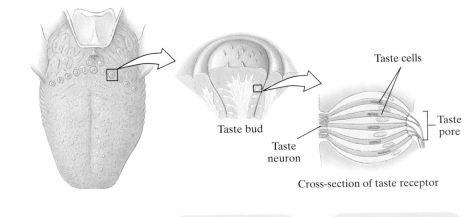

Taste cells

Taste bud

Taste pore

Taste neuron

Cross-section of taste receptor

1. The taste buds are embedded in small lumps on the tongue called papillae.

2. When we eat, chemicals in the food dissolve in saliva and come into contact with the taste cells (receptors) within the taste buds.

3. Now, adjacent neurons fire, sending nerve impulses to the brain's parietal lobe, where the messages are perceived as taste.

Figure 3–20
The structure of a taste bud.
The sensory receptors for taste are found primarily on the tongue. Taste cells can detect only sweet, sour, salty, and bitter qualities. All other tastes result from different combinations of these taste sensations.

information about chewing, swallowing, and the texture and temperature of food. Recent studies have shown that temperature also stimulates our sensation of taste: Warmth is sometimes interpreted as sweet or bitter and cold as salty or sour (Cruz & Green, 2000).

Taste, like the other senses, displays adaptation. Thus when you eat salted peanuts, the saltiness is quite strong at first, but gradually becomes less noticeable. Furthermore, exposure to one quality of taste can modify other taste sensations—after brushing your teeth in the morning, for instance, you may notice that your orange juice has lost its sweetness.

Kinesthetic and Vestibular Senses

Most of us can imagine, to some degree, what it's like to be blind or deaf; we've been in situations where we couldn't see or couldn't hear. A bad cold deprives us of our senses of taste and smell. But what is it like to lose all sense of balance; to be able to move yet not know what our body is doing? The book *Pride and a Daily Marathon Runner* (Cole, 1995) describes Ian Waterman's life after he lost these senses due to a rare viral infection. Waterman had to monitor everything he did—walking across a room, sitting down, climbing stairs, picking up an object, eating or drinking—with his eyes alone. If the lights suddenly went out, he collapsed in a heap and could not get up. Similarly, when aircraft pilots lose visual references to the world outside and have to fly using only the instruments in the cockpit, they frequently find that their feelings of motion and orientation are quite wrong. Thus, a large part of learning to fly on instruments involves learning to disregard sensory experiences and to rely totally on the aircraft's instruments. John F. Kennedy, Jr., who was not rated to fly on instruments, may have lost visual references in the haze over the Atlantic and failed to rely totally on his instruments in the moments prior to his fatal accident.

The **kinesthetic senses** provide information about the speed and direction of our movement in space. More specifically, they relay information on muscle movement, changes in posture, and strain on muscles and joints. Specialized nerve endings, called **stretch receptors,** are attached to muscle fibers, and different nerve endings, known as **Golgi tendon organs,** are attached to the tendons, which connect muscle to bones. Together, these receptors provide constant feedback from the stretching and contraction of individual muscles. This information travels via the

Kinesthetic senses Senses of muscle movement, posture, and strain on muscles and joints.

Stretch receptors Receptors that sense muscle stretch and contraction.

Golgi tendon organs Receptors that sense movement of the tendons, which connect muscle to bone.

This Olympic gymnast is utilizing information provided by both her kinesthetic and her vestibular senses. Her kinesthetic senses are relaying messages pertaining to muscle strain and movements; her vestibular senses supply feedback about her body position in space.

spinal cord to the cortex of the parietal lobes, the same area that perceives the sense of touch.

The **vestibular senses** give us clues about our orientation or position in space (Leigh, 1994), telling us which way is up and which way is down. Birds and fish rely on these senses to determine in which direction they are heading when they cannot see well. Like hearing, the vestibular senses originate in the inner ear. Movement of fluid in the *semicircular canals* of the inner ear relays messages about the speed and direction of body rotation; movement of fluid in two **vestibular sacs** gives us information about movement forward and backward, up and down.

The nerve impulses from both vestibular organs travel to the brain along the auditory nerve, but their ultimate destinations in the brain are still something of a mystery. Certain messages from the vestibular system go to the cerebellum, which controls many of the reflexes involved in coordinated movement. Others reach the areas that regulate the internal body organs, and some find their way to the parietal lobe of the cerebral cortex for analysis and response.

Sensations of Motion

Perhaps we are most acutely aware of our vestibular senses when we experience *motion sickness*. Certain kinds of motion, such as riding in ships, cars, airplanes, even on camels and elephants, trigger strong reactions in some people (Stern & Koch, 1996). Two-thirds of astronauts experience motion sickness during their first flights, as a result of zero gravity conditions (Davis, Vanderploeg, Santy, Jennings, & Stewart, 1988). According to one theory, motion sickness stems from discrepancies between visual information and vestibular sensations (Stern & Koch, 1996); in other words, our eyes and our body sense are sending our brain contradictory information. The same thing occurs when we watch an automobile chase scene that was filmed from inside a moving car: Our eyes tell our brain that we are moving, but the organs in our inner ear insist that we are sitting still. The following are some techniques for avoiding motion sickness:

- Avoid reading while traveling in a car, boat, or plane.
- Never sit in a seat that faces backward.
- Try to sit in a front seat and look out at distant objects. This allows your eyes to experience the same motion that is detected by your body and vestibular sense.
- Open a window. This may help stimulate skin receptors, providing you with another sense of motion.
- If necessary, a physician can recommend motion sickness medications. However, it is usually better to allow your vestibular system to adapt to the motion by providing consistent input from other senses.

The Skin Senses

Of all our senses, touch may be the most comforting. By touching and being touched by others, we bridge, at least momentarily, our isolation and give and receive tenderness and care. In most societies hellos and goodbyes are accompanied by touch—shaking hands, brushing lips against cheeks, or hugging; in almost every culture, lovers express their affection by kissing, holding hands, and caressing.

Touch plays a crucial role in human development. Some years ago, premature babies were placed in "isolettes," fed intravenously, and touched as little as possible, on the grounds that they were too fragile for contact. But numerous studies found that premature babies who were massaged gently gained weight more quickly than did premature infants left untouched; were more responsive to human faces and

Vestibular senses The senses of equilibrium and body position in space.

Vestibular sacs Sacs in the inner ear that sense gravitation and forward, backward, and vertical movement.

rattles; were released from the hospital sooner; and, at eight months, performed better on tests of mental and motor ability (e.g., Field, 1986). Similar effects are seen in other species (Levine, Johanson, & Gonzales, 1985).

Our skin is actually our largest sense organ. A person 6 feet tall has about 21 square feet of skin. In addition to protecting us from the environment, holding in body fluids, and regulating our internal temperature, the skin is a sense organ with numerous nerve receptors distributed in varying concentrations throughout its surface. The nerve fibers from all these receptors travel to the brain by two routes. Some information goes through the medulla and the thalamus and from there to the sensory cortex in the parietal lobe of the brain—which is presumably where our experiences of touch arise. Other information goes through the thalamus and then on to the reticular formation, which, as we saw in the previous chapter, is responsible for arousing the nervous system or quieting it down.

Skin receptors give rise to the sensations of pressure, temperature, and pain, but the relationship between these receptors and our sensory experiences is a subtle one. Researchers believe that our brains draw on complex information about the patterns of activity received from many different receptors to detect and discriminate among skin sensations (Craig & Rollman, 1999). For example, we have cold fibers that speed their firing rate as the skin cools down and slow down their firing when the skin heats up. Conversely, we have warm fibers that accelerate their firing rate when the skin gets warm and slow down when the skin cools. The brain may use the combined information from these two sets of fibers as the basis for determining skin temperature. If both sets are activated at once, the brain usually reads their combined pattern of firings as "hot" (Craig & Bushnell, 1994). Thus, you might sometimes think that you are touching something hot when you are really touching something warm and something cool at the same time. This phenomenon is known as *paradoxical heat* (see Figure 3–21).

Skin senses are also influenced by our expectations. For example, when someone else tickles us, we become unexpectedly sensitive and excited; but tickling ourselves does not have the same effect (Blakemore, Wolpert, & Frith, 1998). The reason seems to be that the cerebellum *anticipates* the consequences of specific sensory experiences and can effectively cancel some out (in effect saying, "It's just me, don't get excited").

The skin senses are remarkably sensitive: Skin displacement of as little as .00004 inch can result in a sensation of pressure. Moreover, various parts of the body differ greatly in their sensitivity to pressure: Your face and fingertips are extremely sensitive, whereas your legs, feet, and back are much less so (Weinstein, 1968). The remarkable sensitivity in our fingertips makes possible Braille touch reading, which requires identifying patterns of tiny raised dots.

Like other senses, the receptors on our skin undergo sensory adaptation. When you first sit in a hot bath, the temperature may be barely tolerable, but in a few minutes, you adapt to the heat, just as your eyes adapt to darkness. Similarly, when you put on clothes that are a bit tight, you may feel uncomfortable at first but not even notice it later on. How soon this adaptation occurs, or whether it occurs at all, appears to depend on how large an area of the skin is being stimulated and the intensity of the pressure (Geldard, 1972): The larger the area and the more intense the pressure, the longer it takes for us to adapt.

Pain

Pain serves as a *warning signal*, telling us that we have been injured or that something is wrong. It demands our attention and urges us to act (Eccleston & Crombez, 1999). Pain also tells us that our body is fighting back and informs the body's defenses when they may be reacting too much and signals them to stop (Keefe & France, 1999; Strausbaugh et al., 1999).

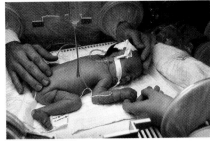

The human response to touch may sometimes be therapeutic. Gentle massage tends to calm agitated premature babies, and by regularly massaging them their growth rate can be increased. These findings substantiate the common belief that touch is among our most comforting senses.

Warm water   Cold water

Figure 3–21
Paradoxical heat.
Touching a warm pipe and a cold pipe at the same time causes two sets of skin receptors to signal at once to the brain. The brain reads their combined pattern of firings as "hot," a phenomenon known as *paradoxical heat.*

Gate control theory The theory that a "neurological gate" in the spinal cord controls the transmission of pain messages to the brain.

Biopsychosocial theory The theory that the interaction of biological, psychological, and cultural factors influence the intensity and duration of pain.

The sensation of pain, as unwelcome as it is familiar, is extraordinarily complex. One might assume a direct relationship between damage to the body and pain. But in some cases physical injury is not accompanied by pain (Manfredi et al., 1981). For example, a young Canadian girl reported feeling nothing when she inadvertently bit off part of her tongue and suffered third-degree burns as a result of kneeling on a hot radiator (Baxter & Olszewski, 1960; McMurray, 1950).

In other cases people feel pain even though they have not been injured or long after the injury has healed. One of the most perplexing examples of this is the *phantom limb phenomenon* (Sherman, 1996). When people undergo amputation of an arm or leg, they often continue to feel that the limb is still there. It may itch, tickle, or cramp; they may even forget that it is gone and try to move it. Often the missing limb is also a source of considerable pain. Phantom limb pain occurs in about 85 percent of amputees. Fortunately, the pain often subsides with time as the brain slowly reorganizes the neurons associated with the amputated limb (Flor, Elbert, Knecht, Weinbruch, & Pantev, 1995),which is another example of neuronal plasticity (see Chapter 2).

One might also assume that we sense pain when specific pain receptors are stimulated. In fact, scientists have had difficulty locating pain receptors at all. The most likely candidate is the simple free nerve ending, which also contributes to our sense of touch or pressure. New research suggests that injuries stimulate the release of chemicals that convert free nerve endings from touch and pressure sensors into pain sensors (Dubner & Gold, 1998).

Individual Differences Individuals vary widely in both their pain threshold (the amount of stimulation required to feel pain) and pain tolerance (the amount of pain with which they are able to cope). Most people do experience pain, but the degree to which they suffer from the same injury or illness is surprisingly variable. There is no absolute correspondence between the perception of pain and the amount of tissue damage sustained (Irwin & Whitehead, 1991; Piotrowski, 1998; Schiffman, 1982).

How do psychologists explain varying sensitivities to pain? One widely accepted view is **gate control theory,** which suggests that a "neurological gate" in the spinal cord controls the transmission of pain impulses to the brain (Melzack & Wall, 1965; Wall & Melzack, 1996). If the gate is open, we experience more pain than we do if it is closed. Whether the gate is closed or open depends on the interaction or competition between two different types of sensory nerve fibers: large fibers that tend to "close the gate" when they are stimulated, thus preventing pain impulses from reaching the brain; and small fibers that "open the gate," allowing pain messages to get through to the brain. Gate control theory suggests that individual differences are due to the numbers of small fibers or large fibers that a person has, or varying levels of control exerted on the gate mechanism from higher brain areas. Heredity may also be a factor. Some people appear to have faulty neurological gates, causing them to experience more or less pain, because they have too many or too few *receptor sites* at the synapses that control the gates (Uhl, Sora, & Wang, 1999).

A number of psychologists think gate control theory oversimplifies the complex experience we call "pain." **Biopsychosocial theory** holds that pain is a dynamic process that involves biological mechanisms (underlying injury or disease), psychological mechanisms (thoughts, beliefs, and emotions), and social mechanisms (family, work, and sociocultural environments) (Keefe & France, 1999). This theory holds that *all* pain results from the interaction of these three variables.

Biologically, individual differences in the intensity and duration of pain often depend on past experience. Pain alters pathways in the nervous system. As a result, the nerves in the spinal cord become hypersensitive. For example, suppose you break a bone in your foot and do not do anything about it until it's so painful you can't walk; even after the break heals, a mild blow to your foot may be painful. Early administration of pain-killing medications (before surgery, for example) can prevent the formation of hypersensitive neural pathways for pain.

Pain is an assault on our psyche as well as our body, heightening our sense of vulnerability. Beliefs about pain can affect our experience of it. Hospital patients who were told that a medical procedure was not painful actually reported experiencing less pain than people who had not been given that information (DiMatteo & Friedman, 1982). Motivation also has an impact. Athletes injured during a game often feel no pain until the excitement of competition has passed. One researcher found that only 25 percent of soldiers wounded during battle requested pain medication, whereas more than 80 percent of surgical patients asked for painkillers for comparable "wounds" (Beecher, 1972).

Glowing coals smolder under the feet of these participants in an annual ritual at Mt. Takao, Japan. How do they do it? Is it mind over matter—the human ability to sometimes "turn off" pain sensations? The secret in this case may actually lie more in the coals than in the men. Because wood is a poor conductor of heat, walking over wood coals quickly may not be that painful after all.

Personality factors also come into play. Some people make an active effort to cope with pain: Confident that they can overcome pain, they avoid negative feelings ("I'll get better"), engage in activities that divert their attention from pain, and refuse to let pain interfere with their normal activities. Others suffering from the same injuries or disorders are overwhelmed: They feel "victimized," that their pain is beyond their control and is ruling their life, and that no one understands. Recent studies indicate that believing that one can cope may actually cause higher brain centers to reduce or block pain signals (Wall & Melzack, 1996).

Genetics also appears to account for some of the individual differences in the perception of pain. Recently, scientists identified a small variation in a specific gene which seems to account for at least some of the reason why different people experience different amounts of pain. Not surprisingly, this gene produces an enzyme involved in the production of endorphins in the brain, which as we saw in see Chapter 2, are implicated in regulating pain and mood (Zubieta et al., 2003).

Alternative Approaches   Increasingly, Americans are turning to so-called alternative medicine to treat intractable pain. Acupuncture and hypnosis are two of the most popular. Are people who use these approaches fooling themselves? Many studies have shown that if you give pain sufferers a chemically inert pill, or *placebo*, but tell them that it is an effective pain reducer, they often report some relief. No doubt many home remedies and secret cures rely on the **placebo effect.** Placebos work, at least in part, by promoting the release of endorphins, the body's own painkillers. When patients are given drugs that block the effects of endorphins, placebos are far less effective (Coren, Ward, & Enns, 1994; He, 1987).

Other pain-management techniques apparently have nothing to do with endorphins. A recent study of 241 patients undergoing surgery found that those who used self-hypnosis needed less pain medication, had more stable vital signs, and left the operating room sooner than did members of a control group (Lang et al., 2000). Other participants in this study used concentration exercises, such as those used in the Lamaze birth technique. Although they reported more pain than the hypnotized subjects, they also used less pain medication (which was controlled by the patients) and recovered more quickly. Interestingly, hypnosis and concentration techniques are just as effective when endorphin blockers are administered, indicating that there may be a second pain-control system that works independently of the brain's chemical painkillers (Akil & Watson, 1980; Mayer & Watkins, 1984). Further research is needed before we will know whether this hypothesis is valid.

Placebo effect Pain relief that occurs when a person believes a pill or procedure will reduce pain. The actual cause of the relief seems to come from endorphins.

■■■■ CHECK YOUR UNDERSTANDING

1. Specialized smell sensors are located in the

___a. organ of Corti

___b. papillae

___c. olfactory bulb

___d. olfactory epithelium

2. Umami belongs to which sense?

___a. taste

___b. smell

___c. touch

___d. pain

3. Muscle movement information is provided by our

___a. vestibular senses

___b. skin receptors

___c. kinesthetic senses

___d. pain receptors

4. This sense is responsible for motion sickness.

___a. smell

___b. pain

___c. kinesthetic

___d. vestibular

5. Gate control theory refers to

___a. pain

___b. visual perception

___c. pheromones

___d. deaf culture

Answers: 1.d; 2.a; 3.c; 4.d; 5. a

■■■

Perception

Why do people who are lost in the desert "see" a mirage?

Our senses bring us raw data about the environment; unless we interpret this information, the world would be nothing more than "a booming, buzzing confusion," as William James (1890) put it. The eye records patterns of light and dark, but it does not "see" a bird flittering from branch to branch. The eardrum vibrates in a particular fashion, but it does not "hear" a symphony. Deciphering *meaningful* patterns in the jumble of sensory information is *perception*.

Perception takes place in the brain. Using sensory information as raw material, the brain creates perceptual experiences that go beyond what we sense directly. The close-up of Signac's painting, *Saint-Tropez, in a thunderstorm*, corresponds to sensation: mere "blips" of color (see Figure 3–22). Viewed as a whole, however, these

Figure 3–22
Closeup of a pointillist painting (left) and the entire painting (right).
Source: Signac, Paul (1863–1935). *Saint-Tropez, in a thunderstorm.* Musee de l'Annonciade, St. Tropez, France. Reunion des Musees Nationaux/Art Resource, NY.

dots become a picture—a graphic illustration of how perception transforms mere sensations into a meaningful whole.

Perceptual Organization

Early in this century, a group of German psychologists, calling themselves *Gestalt psychologists,* set out to discover the basic principles of perception. The German word *Gestalt* has no exact English equivalent, but essentially it means "whole," "form," or "pattern." Gestalt psychologists believed that the brain creates a coherent perceptual experience that is more than simply the sum of the available sensory information, and that it does so in predictable ways.

One important facet of perception is distinguishing **figures** from the **ground** against which they appear. A colorfully upholstered chair stands out from the bare walls of a room. A marble statue is perceived as a whole figure separate from the wall behind it. The figure-ground distinction pertains to all our senses, not just vision. We can distinguish a violin solo against the ground of a symphony orchestra, a single voice amid cocktail party chatter, and the smell of roses in a florist's shop. In each case, we perceive some objects as "figures" and other sensory information as "background."

Sometimes, however, there are not enough cues. Figure 3–23, which shows a spotted dog investigating shadowy surroundings, illustrates the problem. It is difficult to distinguish the dog because it has few visible contours and therefore seems to have no more form than the background. In real life, this would not be a problem: You would distinguish the black-and-white dog by its movements, as well as by contrast to an unmoving, multicolored background. Nature provides many examples of camouflage—visual traits that make animals (the figure) fade into the background (see Figure 3–24). A zebra's gaudy stripes may seem like the antithesis of camouflage. But when they sense a predator, zebras move as a group, creating a swirl of white and black that makes it difficult for a predator to pick out one individual as "dinner."

Sometimes a figure with clear contours can be perceived in two very different ways because it is unclear which part of the stimulus is the figure and which the ground. Examples of such reversible figures are shown in Figures 3–25 and 3–26, as well as in

Figure Entity perceived to stand apart from the background.

Ground Background against which a figure appears.

Figure 3–23
Random dots or something more?
This pattern does not give us enough cues to allow us to easily distinguish the figure of the Dalmatian dog from the ground behind it.
Source: Adapted from Gregory, 1978.

Figure 3–24
Camouflage.
Predators may have difficulty seeing the figure of the walking stick against the background of its natural environment.

It's not what it looks like.

the cartoon below. At first glance, you perceive figures against a specific background, but as you stare at the illustrations, you will discover that the figures and the ground reverse, making for two very different perceptions of the same illustration. The artwork or stimulus hasn't changed, but your perception has changed (Adelson, 2002; Vecera, Vogel, & Woodman, 2002).

Figure 3–27 illustrates other important principles of perceptual organization. In each case, perception "leaps" beyond the available sensory information. As creatures searching for meaning, we tend to "fill in the blanks," to group various objects together, to see whole objects and hear meaningful sounds rather than just random bits and pieces of raw sensory data (see *Applying Psychology: How Do We See Objects and Shapes?*).

Some psychologists believe that just as frogs have "bug detector" cells, humans and other higher animals must have neural structures sensitive to the complex patterns that these species must perceive in order to survive. Through evolution, we may be prewired to perceive many of the complex shapes and movements that appear in our natural environment. For example, newborns, given the choice, will spend significantly more time gazing at sketches of human faces than at other types of patterns or figures (see Chapter 10, Life Span Development). Yet we could not possibly be born with an innate grasp of all the different objects that we encounter; learning and experience clearly play an important part in the way we organize perception (Ashissar, 1999; Fagiolini & Hensch, 2000; Goldstein, 1999; Quinn, Bhatt, Brush, Grimes, & Sharpnack, 2002; Sengpiel, Stawinski, & Bonhoeffer, 1999). Nowhere is this clearer than in *perceptual constancies*, which we examine next.

Perceptual Constancies

When anthropologist Colin Turnbull (1961) studied the Mbuti pygmies of Zaire, most had never left the dense Ituri rain forest and had rarely encountered objects that were more than a few feet away. On one occasion, Turnbull took a pygmy guide

Figure 3–25
The reversible figure and ground in this M. C. Escher woodcut cause us to see first black devils and then white angels in each of the rings.
Source: M. C. Escher's "Circle Limit IV" © 2003 Cordon Art B.V., Baarn, Holland. All rights reserved.

Figure 3–26
Figure-ground relationship . . . How do you perceive this figure?
Do you see a vase or the silhouettes of a man and a woman? Both interpretations are possible, but not at the same time. Reversible figures like this work because it is unclear which part of the stimulus is the figure and which is the neutral ground against which the figure is perceived.

named Kenge on a trip onto the African plains. When Kenge looked across the plain and saw a distant herd of buffalo, he asked what kind of insects they were. He refused to believe that the tiny black spots he saw were buffalo. As he and Turnbull drove toward the herd, Kenge believed that magic was making the animals grow larger. Because he had no experience of distant objects, he could not perceive the buffalo as having constant size.

Perceptual constancy refers to the tendency to perceive objects as relatively stable and unchanging despite changing sensory information. Once we have formed a stable perception of an object, we can recognize it from almost any position, at almost any distance, under almost any illumination. A white house looks like a white house by day or by night and from any angle. We see it as the same house. The sensory information may change as illumination and perspective change, but the object is perceived as constant. Without this ability, we would find the world very confusing (as Kenge did).

We tend to perceive familiar objects at their true size regardless of the size of the image that they cast on the retina. As Figure 3–28 shows, the farther away an object is from the lens of the eye, the smaller the retinal image it casts. We might guess that a woman some distance away is 5 feet 4 inches tall when she is really 5 feet 8 inches, but hardly anyone would perceive her as being 3 feet tall, no matter how far away she is. We know from experience that adults are seldom that short. **Size constancy** depends partly on experience—information about the relative sizes of objects stored in memory—and partly on distance cues.

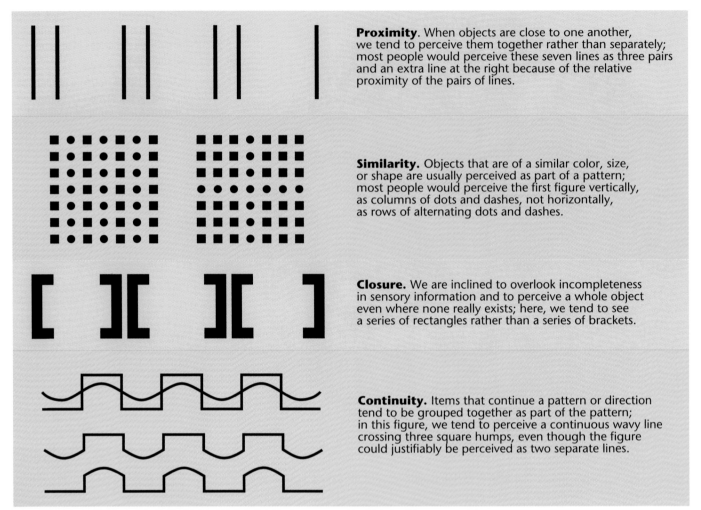

Proximity. When objects are close to one another, we tend to perceive them together rather than separately; most people would perceive these seven lines as three pairs and an extra line at the right because of the relative proximity of the pairs of lines.

Similarity. Objects that are of a similar color, size, or shape are usually perceived as part of a pattern; most people would perceive the first figure vertically, as columns of dots and dashes, not horizontally, as rows of alternating dots and dashes.

Closure. We are inclined to overlook incompleteness in sensory information and to perceive a whole object even where none really exists; here, we tend to see a series of rectangles rather than a series of brackets.

Continuity. Items that continue a pattern or direction tend to be grouped together as part of the pattern; in this figure, we tend to perceive a continuous wavy line crossing three square humps, even though the figure could justifiably be perceived as two separate lines.

Figure 3–27
Gestalt principles of perceptual organization.

Shape constancy A tendency to see an object as the same shape no matter what angle it is viewed from.

Color constancy An inclination to perceive familiar objects as retaining their color despite changes in sensory information.

Familiar objects also tend to be seen as having a constant shape, even though the retinal images they cast change as they are viewed from different angles (this is called **shape constancy**). A dinner plate is perceived as a circle even when it is tilted and the retinal image is oval. A rectangular door will project a rectangular image on the retina only when it is viewed directly from the front. From any other angle, it casts a trapezoidal image on the retina, but it is not perceived as having suddenly become a trapezoidal door (see Figure 3–29).

Similarly, we tend to perceive familiar objects as keeping their colors, regardless of information that reaches the eye. If you own a red automobile, you will see it as red whether it is on a brightly lit street or in a dark garage, where the low light may send your eye a message that it is closer to brown or black than red. But **color constancy** does not always hold true. When objects are unfamiliar or there are no customary color cues to guide us, color constancy may be distorted—as when you buy a pair of pants in a brightly lit store, only to discover that in ordinary daylight they are not the shade you thought they were.

Perceptual constancy, based on memory and experience, also influences how we see human faces and figures. Look at Figure 3–30. If you see former President Clinton and Vice President Gore, look again! Actually, Clinton's face has been superimposed over Gore's. Because we focus on the perceptual cues of head shape, hair style, and context (the microphones and the president are standing in front of

APPLYING PSYCHOLOGY

HOW DO WE SEE OBJECTS AND SHAPES?

Stop reading for a moment, and just look at your open psychology text. Almost without thinking, you see a book. Regardless of the angle from which you look at it, whether it is open or closed, the lighting in the room, or how close it is to you, you still perceive a book. You can close your eyes and come up with fairly clear images of a book viewed from different perspectives. How are we able to transform raw sensory data into complex, meaningful perceptions?

Psychologists assume that perception begins with some real-world object with real-world properties "out there." Psychologists call that object, along with its important perceptual properties, the *distal stimulus.* We never experience the distal stimulus directly, however. Energy from it (or in the case of our chemical senses, molecules from it) must activate our sensory system. We call the information that reaches our sensory receptors the *proximal stimulus.* Although the distal stimulus and the proximal stimulus are never the same thing, our perception of the distal stimulus is usually very accurate. So, as we view the book on the desk, how does the pattern on the retina (the proximal

> *"Somehow we take the very basic information provided by detector cells and use it to create coherent perceptual experiences."*

stimulus) become an integrated perception of the book (the distal stimulus)—one that captures all the important aspects of "bookness"?

The discovery of detector cells (Hubel & Wiesel, 1959, 1979), described in the text, was a first step closer to answering this question. But these detector cells provide only fundamental information about lines, positions, angles, motion, and so on. Somehow we take the very basic information provided by detector cells and use it to create coherent perceptual experiences.

To date, no theory explains exactly how we transform meaningless raw sensory information into complex meaningful perceptions, but psychologists have advanced a number of theories to explain how this process might work. Some theorist argue that the image on the retina is literally decomposed into its fundamental properties, such as color, curves, positions, and motion, and is then reassembled in the brain (Treisman, 1986; Treisman, Cavanagh, Fischer, Ramachandran, & Von der Heydt, 1990). Other theorists propose that multiple, specialized subsystems figure in object perception (Kosslyn, 1980, 1987). For example, one subsystem might recognize the *kind* or *category* of the thing we see, while another subsystem might provide information about its spatial position or spatial relationships. *Computational neuroscience* offers an entirely different approach to form perception. Theorists in this area hold that visual perception emerges from the brain's complex mathematical analysis of patterns of light and dark areas, edges, ends of segments, and positions (Marr, 1982). Through sophisticated high-speed calculations, this analysis produces a finished visual image (see also Kosslyn, 1994).

No one can say with certainty which of these approaches sheds the most light on form perception. No doubt researchers employing some of the latest brain-imaging techniques (described in Chapter 2) will do an even better job of explaining our perception of forms (e.g., Dae-Shik, Duong, & Seong-Gi, 2000; Fagiolini & Hensch, 2000; Sengpiel, Stawinski, & Bonhoeffer, 1999; Ulf, 1999).

the vice president, as protocol requires) we perceive the more likely image of the president and vice president standing together (Sinha, 1996).

 3.4

Perceiving Distance and Depth

The ability to judge distance and depth is critically important if an organism is to move freely in its environment. For example, honeybees must judge the distance to a source of food if they are to communicate a source of pollen accurately to their companions. And research has shown they use distance and direction cues to do this (Collett, 2000; Srinivasan, Zhang, Altwein, & Tautz, 2000).

People, too, must constantly judge the distance between themselves and other objects. When you walk through a room, your perception of distance helps you avoid bumping into the furniture. If you reach out to pick up a pencil, you automatically judge how far to extend your arms. As a matter of course, you also assess the depth of objects—how much total space they occupy. This is a far more remarkable

Figure 3–28
The relationship between distance and the size of the retinal image.
Object A and object B are the same size, but A, being much closer to the eye, casts a much larger image on the retina.

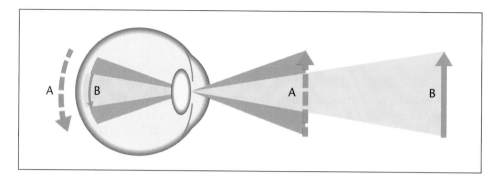

process than most people realize, because the image of the world on the retina is essentially flat or two-dimensional, yet we perceive the world as three-dimensional! To do that, we use various subtle cues to determine the distance, depth, and shape of objects. Some of these cues depend on visual messages that one eye alone can transmit; these are called **monocular cues.** Others, known as **binocular cues,** require the use of both eyes. Binocular vision allows us to make more accurate judgments about distance and depth, particularly when objects are relatively close. But monocular cues alone are often all we need to judge distance and depth quite accurately.

Monocular Cues   Distant objects have a hazy appearance and a somewhat blurred outline, a phenomenon known as **aerial perspective.** On a clear day, mountains often seem to be much closer than on a hazy day, when their outlines become indistinct. An object that is close also seems to have a rough or detailed texture (this distance cue is called **texture gradient**). As distance increases, the texture becomes finer and finer, until it cannot be distinguished clearly, if at all. A man standing on a pebbly beach, for example, can distinguish among the gray stones and gravel in front of his feet. As he looks down the beach, however, the stones appear to become smaller and finer until eventually he cannot make out individual stones at all. **Linear perspective** refers to the fact that, as all art students know, two parallel lines that extend into the distance appear to come together at some point on the horizon.

People traveling on buses or trains often notice that the tree or telephone poles close to the road or the railroad track seem to flash past the windows quickly,

Monocular cues Visual cues requiring the use of one eye.

Binocular cues Visual cues requiring the use of both eyes.

Aerial perspective Monocular cue to distance and depth based on the fact that more distant objects are likely to appear hazy and blurred.

Texture gradient Monocular cue to distance and depth based on the fact that objects seen at greater distances appear to be smoother and less textured.

Linear perspective Monocular cue to distance and depth based on the fact that two parallel lines seem to come together at the horizon.

Figure 3–29
Examples of shape constancy.
Even though the image of the door on the retina changes greatly as the door opens, we still perceive the door as being rectangular.
Source: From *Foundations of Psychology* by E. G. Boring, H. S. Langfeld, H. P. Weld (1976). Reprinted by permission of John Wiley & Sons.

whereas buildings and other objects farther away seem to move slowly. These differences in the speeds at which images travel across the retina as you move give you an important cue to distance and depth. You can observe the same effect if you stand still and move your head from side to side as you focus your gaze on something in the middle distance: Objects close to you seem to move in the direction opposite from the way in which your head is moving, whereas objects far away seem to move in the same direction as your head. This phenomenon is known as **motion parallax.** Superposition and two other important monocular distance cues, elevation and shadowing, are shown in Figure 3–31.

Binocular Cues   Many animals, such as horses, deer, and fish, rely entirely on monocular cues to perceive distance and depth. Although they have two eyes, their two visual fields do not overlap because their eyes are located on the sides of the head rather than in front. The higher primates (monkeys, apes, and humans), as well as predators (lions, tigers, and wolves), have a distinct advantage. Both of their eyes are set in the front of the head, so that the visual fields overlap. **Stereoscopic vision,** the result of combining the two retinal images, makes the perception of depth and distance more accurate.

Because our eyes are set approximately $2\frac{1}{2}$ inches apart, each one has a slightly different view of things. The difference between the two images that the eyes receive is known as **retinal disparity.** The left eye receives more information about the left side of an object, and the right eye receives more information about the right side. To test this, close one eye and line up a finger with some vertical line, such as the edge of a door. Then open that eye and close the other one. Your finger will appear to have moved a great distance. When you look at the finger with both eyes, however, the two different images become one.

An important binocular cue to distance comes from the muscles that control the **convergence** of the eyes. When we look at objects that are fairly close to us, our eyes tend to converge—to turn slightly inward toward each other. The sensations from the muscles that control the movement of the eyes thus provide another cue to distance. If the object is very close, such as at the end of the nose, the eyes cannot

**Figure 3–30
Look again!**
Context, hair style, and head shape lead us to believe that this is a picture of former President Clinton and Vice President Gore when, in reality, Clinton's face is superimposed over the face of Vice President Gore.

Note how the nearby pebbles on this beach appear larger and clearer than the distant ones.

Motion parallax Monocular distance cue in which objects closer than the point of visual focus seem to move in the direction opposite to the viewer's moving head, and objects beyond the focus point appear to move in the same direction as the viewer's head.

Stereoscopic vision Combination of two retinal images to give a three-dimensional perceptual experience.

Retinal disparity Binocular distance cue based on the difference between the images cast on the two retinas when both eyes are focused on the same object.

Convergence A visual depth cue that comes from muscles controlling eye movement as the eyes turn inward to view a nearby stimulus.

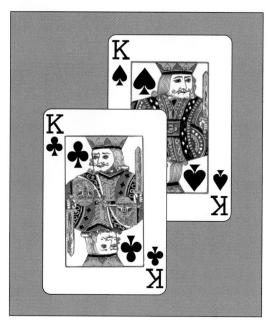

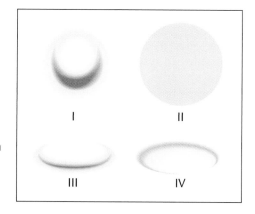

Figure 3–31
Monocular distance cues.
(A) *Superposition.* Because the king of clubs appears to have been superimposed on the king of spades, we perceive it to be closer to us.
(B) *Elevation.* Because of the higher elevation and the suggestion of depth provided by the road, the tree on the right is perceived as being more distant and about the same size as the tree at the lower left. Actually, it is appreciably smaller, as you can see if you measure the heights of the two drawings.
(C) *Shadowing.* Shadowing on the outer edges of a spherical object, such as a ball or globe, gives it a three-dimensional quality (I). Without shadowing (II), it might be perceived as a flat disk. Shadowing can also affect our perception of the direction of depth. In the absence of other cues, we tend to assume overhead lighting, so figure (III) appears to be a bump because its top edge is lit, whereas (IV) appears to be a dent. If you turn the book upside down, the direction of depth is reversed.

converge, and two separate images are perceived. If the object is more than a few yards (meters) away, the sight lines of the eyes are more or less parallel, and there is no convergence.

Stereoscopic vision no doubt played an important role in primate evolution. Our tree-dwelling primate ancestors traveled through the treetops by leaping or swinging from one tree to another—a risky form of locomotion that required them to judge precisely the distance to the next branch or vine and whether it would support their weight. One slip, and there was little chance that the individual's genes would be passed on to future generations.

 3.5

Locating Sounds Just as we use monocular and binocular cues to determine visual depth and distance, we draw on **monaural** (single-ear) and **binaural** (two-ear) **cues** to locate the source of sounds (see Figure 3–32). In one monaural cue, loud sounds are perceived as closer than faint sounds, with changes in loudness translating into changes in distance. Binaural cues work on the principle that because sounds off to one side of the head reach one ear slightly ahead of the other (in the range of a thousandth of a second), the time difference between sound waves reaching the two ears registers in the brain and helps us to make accurate judgments of location (Hudspeth, 1997). Sound signals arriving from a source off to one side are also slightly louder in the ear nearest to the source. In effect, our head blocks the sound from one side, muting the intensity of the sound in the opposite ear.

Monaural cue Cue to sound location that requires just one ear.

Binaural cue Cue to sound location that involves both ears working together.

This relative difference in loudness enables the brain to locate the sound source and to judge its distance. Sound engineers often place microphones at many different locations in a recording studio. On playback, the speakers or headphones project sounds at slightly different instants, recreating the sound patterns that you would pick up if you were listening to a live performance.

Most of us rely so heavily on visual cues that we seldom pay much attention to the rich array of auditory information available in the world around us. People who are blind attend more closely to sounds than do people who are not blind (Arias, Curet, Moyano, Joekes, & Blanch, 1993). They can figure out where obstacles lie in their paths by listening to the echoes from a cane, their own footsteps, and their own voices.

Perceiving Movement

The perception of movement involves both visual information from the retina and messages from the muscles around the eyes as they follow an object. On occasion, our perceptual processes play tricks on us, and we think we perceive movement when the objects we are looking at are, in fact, stationary. For this reason, psychologists distinguish between real and apparent movement.

Real movement refers to the physical displacement of an object from one position to another. The perception of real movement depends only in part on the movement of images across the retina of the eye. If you stand still and move your head to look around you, the images of all the objects in the room will pass across your retina. Yet you will probably perceive all the objects as stationary. Even if you hold your head still and move only your eyes, the images will continue to pass across your retina. But the messages from the eye muscles seem to counteract those from the retina, so the objects in the room will be perceived as motionless.

The perception of real movement seems to be determined less by images moving across the retina than by how the position of objects changes in relation to a background that is perceived as stationary. When you perceive a car moving along a

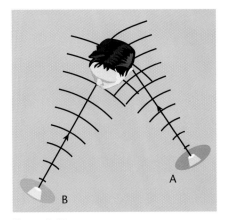

Figure 3–32
Cues used in sound localization.
Sound waves coming from source (B) will reach both ears simultaneously. A sound wave from source (A) reaches the left ear first, where it is also louder. The head casts a "shadow" over the other ear, thus reducing the intensity of the delayed sound in that ear.
Source: From *Foundations of Psychology* by E. G. Boring, H. S. Langfeld, H. P. Weld (1976). Reprinted by permission of John Wiley & Sons.

During a stereo recording session, microphones are generally placed at many different locations. On playback, the speakers or headphones project sounds picked up by the microphones at different instants, mimicking what would occur if you were hearing a live performance.

When we look at an electronic marquee such as this one, we see motion, even though the sign consists of stationary lights that are flashed on and off.

street, for example, you see the street, the buildings, and the sidewalk as a stationary background and the car as a moving object.

Apparent movement is an illusion that occurs when we perceive movement in objects that are actually standing still. One form of apparent movement is referred to as the **autokinetic illusion**—the perceived motion created by a single stationary object. If you stand in a room that is absolutely dark except for one tiny spot of light and stare at the light for a few seconds, you will begin to see the light drift. In the darkened room, your eyes have no visible framework; there are no cues telling you that the light is really stationary. The slight movements of the eye muscles, which go unnoticed most of the time, make the light appear to move.

The illusion of **stroboscopic motion** is created by a rapid series of still images. The best illustration is a motion picture—which is not in motion at all. The film consists of a series of still pictures showing people and objects in slightly different positions. When the separate images are projected sequentially onto a screen at a specific rate of speed, the people and objects seem to be moving because of the rapid change from one still picture to the next.

The **phi phenomenon** occurs as a result of stroboscopic motion. When a light is flashed on at a certain point in a darkened room, then flashed off, and a second light is flashed on a split second later at a point a short distance away, most people will perceive these two separate lights as a single spot of light moving from one point to another. This causes us to see motion in neon signs or theater marquees, where words appear to move from one side to the other as different combinations of stationary lights are flashed on and off.

Another "real-world" movement illusion is induced movement. When you are sitting in a stationary train and the train next to you begins to move forward, you seem to be moving backward. Because you have no reference point by which to tell if you are standing still, you are confused as to which train is actually moving. However, if you look at the ground, you can establish an unambiguous frame of reference and make the situation clear to yourself.

Visual Illusions

Visual illusions graphically demonstrate the ways in which we use a variety of sensory cues to create perceptual experiences that may (or may not) correspond to what is out there in the real world. By understanding how we are fooled into "seeing" something that isn't there, psychologists can gain insight into the ways that perceptual processes work in the everyday world and under normal circumstances.

Perceptual illusions typically occur because the stimulus contains misleading cues that distort the perceived size or orientation of common objects, giving rise to inaccurate or impossible perceptions (Shimamura & Prinzmetal, 1999). The illusions in Figure 3–33 result from false and misleading depth cues. For example, in Figure 3–33E, the top line is perceived as shorter than the bottom, when, in reality, both lines are the same length. In Figure 3–33F, both monsters cast the same-size image on the retina in our eyes, but the depth cues in the tunnel suggest that we are looking at a three-dimensional scene and that therefore the top monster is much farther away. In the real world, experience tells us that objects appear smaller when they are far away. Therefore, we "correct" for the apparent distance and actually perceive the top monster as larger. We do this despite other cues to the contrary: We know that the image is actually two-dimensional, but we still respond to it as if it were three-dimensional.

Autokinetic illusion The perception that a stationary object is actually moving.

Stroboscopic motion Apparent movement that results from flashing a series of still pictures in rapid succession, as in a motion picture.

Phi phenomenon Apparent movement caused by flashing lights in sequence, as on theater marquees.

Perceptual illusion Illusion due to misleading cues in stimuli that give rise to inaccurate or impossible perceptions.

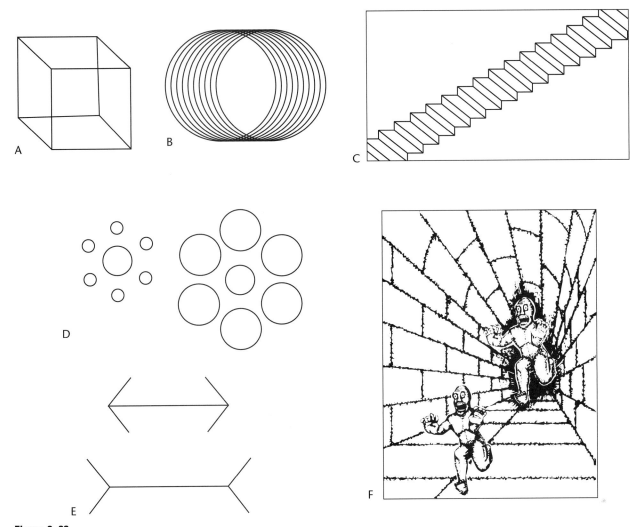

Figure 3–33
Reversible figures and misleading depth cues.
A, B, and C are examples of reversible figures—drawings that we can perceive two different ways, but not at the same time. D, E, and F show how, through the use of misleading *depth cues,* we misjudge the size of objects. The middle circles in D are exactly the same size, as are the lines in E and the monsters in F.

Three-dimensional movies also work on the principle that the brain can be deceived into seeing three dimensions if slightly different images are presented to the left and right eyes (working on the principle of retinal disparity). Artists also rely on many of these perceptual phenomena both to represent reality accurately and to distort it deliberately. All of us know that a painting or a photograph is flat and two-dimensional; yet we are easily and delightfully "seduced" by an artist's use of the principles we have described. Figure 3–34 illustrates how an artist can use distance cues not only to give realistic depth to a picture but also to create perceptual experiences that don't correspond to anything in the real world.

psych 3.6

Observer Characteristics: Individual Differences and Culture

In exploring these various principles, we have noted that perceptual experiences usually go far beyond the available sensory information. Indeed, our perceptual experiences rarely, if ever, correspond exactly to the information that we receive

Figure 3–34
Perceptual illusion.
How has the artist, M. C. Escher, manipulated distance cues to create the perceptual illusion of water traveling uphill?
Source: M. C. Escher's "Waterfall." © 2003 Cordon Art B.V., Baarn, Holland. All rights reserved.

through our senses. *Perception* is a combination of information from our senses, past experience, and the wiring of our brains.

ENDURING ISSUES   **diversity**universality

How Does Ethnicity Influence Perception?

All normal human beings have the same sense organs and perceptual capacity. Yet our individuality—our motivations, values, expectations, cognitive style, and cultural preconceptions—influences what we perceive. We focus on individual differences in this section. But as you read, think about the degree to which people's sensory and perceptual experiences differ depending on their race, culture, or gender.

Motivation   Our desires and needs shape our perceptions. People in need are more likely to perceive something that they think will satisfy that need. The best-known example of this, at least in fiction, is a *mirage:* people lost in the desert have visual fantasies of an oasis over the next dune. Research has found that when people have not eaten for some time (16 hours seems to be a cutoff point), they perceive vague images as being related to food (McClelland & Atkinson, 1948; Sanford, 1937).

Values   In an experiment that revealed how strongly perceptions can be affected by a person's values, nursery-school children were shown a poker chip. Each child was asked to compare the size of the chip to the size of an adjustable circle of light until the child said the chip and the circle of light were the same size. The children were then taken to a vending machine with a crank that, when turned, provided candy in exchange for a poker chip. Thus, the children were taught to value the poker chips more highly than they had before. After the children had been rewarded with candy for the poker chips, they were again asked to compare the size of the chips to a circle of light. This time, the chips seemed larger to the children (Lambert, Solomon, & Watson, 1949).

Expectations   Preconceptions about what we are supposed to perceive may also influence perception by causing us to *delete, insert, transpose,* or otherwise *modify* what we see (Lachman, 1996). Lachman (1984) demonstrated this by asking people to copy a group of stimuli similar to the following one:

PARIS

IN THE

THE SPRING

When the expressions were flashed briefly on a screen, the vast majority of subjects tended to omit the extra words and to report seeing more familiar (and more normal) expressions, such as PARIS IN THE SPRING. This phenomenon of *perceptual familiarization* or *perceptual generalization* reflects a strong tendency to see what we expect to see even if our expectation conflicts with external reality. In other words, "I'll see it when I believe it!"

Cognitive Style   As we mature, we develop a cognitive style—a personal way of dealing with the environment—and this also affects how we see the world. Some psychologists distinguish between two general approaches that people use in perceiving the world: *field dependence* and *field independence* (Witkin, Dyk, Faterson, Goodenough, & Karp, 1962). People who are *field dependent* tend to perceive the environment as a whole and do not clearly delineate in their minds the shape, color, size, or other qualities of individual items. If field-dependent people are asked to draw a human figure, they generally draw it so that it blends into the background. By contrast, people who are *field independent* are more likely to perceive the elements of the environment as separate and distinct from one another and to draw each element as standing out from the background.

Cognitive styles can also be viewed from the perspective of "levelers" and "sharpeners"—those who level out the distinctions among objects and those who magnify

If your livelihood depended on the health and productivity of these cattle, as that of the Masai does, you would perceive many important details about each individual. However, most Western people probably just see cows.

them. To investigate the differences between these two cognitive styles, G. S. Klein (1951) showed people sets of squares of varying sizes and asked them to estimate the size of each one. The "levelers" failed to perceive any differences in the size of the squares; the "sharpeners," however, picked up the differences in the size of the squares and made their size estimates accordingly.

Experience and Culture   Cultural background also influences people's perceptions. The language people speak affects the ways in which they perceive their surroundings (see Chapter 7, Cognition and Language). Cultural differences in people's experiences can also determine how they use perceptual cues. For example, East African Masai, who depend on herding for their living, tend to perceive individual differences in what others perceive as a herd of virtually identical animals. Because the Masai live with cattle day and night, they are quick to pick up signs that an individual cow is sick or that the herd senses a nearby lion. Professional dog breeders see championship qualities in a pup that, to the uninitiated, is barely distinguishable from its littermates. And wine experts can distinguish subtle differences in the flavor of different vintages that most of us could not detect.

Personality   A number of researchers have shown that our individual personalities influence our perceptions (for a review of the research, see Greenwald, 1992). For example, normal college students were compared to depressed or moderately anorexic students in terms of their ability to identify words related to depression and food (von Hippel, Hawkins, & Narayan, 1994). All the words in this study were flashed on a screen very quickly (generally for less than one-tenth of a second). In general, anorexic people were faster at identifying the words that referred to foods they commonly thought about than they were at identifying words for foods they rarely thought about. Similarly, depressed students were faster at identifying adjectives describing personality traits they commonly thought about (such as *quiet*, *withdrawn*, *hesitant*, and *timid*) than they were at identifying adjectives relating to traits they rarely thought about (such as *extrovert*, *lively*, and *bold*). These findings suggest that not only personality, but possibly the presence of a personality disorder, may influence perception.

personsituation

Do Perceptual Experiences Reflect the Outside World?

After reading this chapter, have your ideas changed about the relative importance of processes that occur inside the individual (thoughts, emotions, motives, attitudes, values, personalities) as opposed to objects and events in the real world? If someone were to ask you whether perceptual experiences match more closely the image on the retina or the outside world, what would you say? What examples would you select from the chapter to make your point most effectively?

CHECK YOUR UNDERSTANDING

1. A white house looks white both night and day. This is an example of

___a. binocularity

___b. texture gradient

___c. perceptual constancy

___d. autokinetic illusion

2. What is the result of stroboscopic motion?

___a. autokinetic illusion

___b. phi phenomenon

___c. aerial perspective

___d. linear perspective

3. The figure-ground distinction was first described by

___a. Gestalt psychologists

___b. Ernst Weber

___c. Ian Waterman

___d. William James

4. Perception is likely to be influenced by

___a. cognitive style

___b. personality

___c. culture

___d. all of the above

Answers: 1.c; 2.b; 3.a; 4.d

This chapter examines sensation and perception, the processes that enable us to gather and understand information from numerous sources. **Sensation** refers to the raw sensory data from the senses of sight, hearing, smell, taste, balance, touch, and pain. **Perception** is the process of creating meaningful patterns from that raw sensory data.

The Nature of Sensation

The Basic Process

In all sensory processes, some form of energy stimulates a **receptor cell** in one of the sense organs. The receptor cell converts that energy into a neural signal, which is further coded as it travels along sensory nerves. By the time it reaches the brain, the message is quite precise.

Sensory Thresholds

The energy reaching a receptor must be sufficiently intense to produce a noticeable effect. The least amount of energy needed to generate any sensation at all in a person 50 percent of the time is called the **absolute threshold.** The **difference threshold** or the **just noticeable difference (jnd)** is the smallest change in stimulation that is detectable 50 percent of the time. Generally speaking, the stronger the stimulation, the bigger the change must be to be sensed. According to **Weber's law,** the jnd for a given sense is a constant fraction of the original stimulus. In most cases, our senses adjust to the level of stimulation they are experiencing, a process known as **adaptation.**

Subliminal Perception

Subliminal messages are messages that fall below the threshold of conscious perception and are therefore assumed to be perceived subconsciously. Some studies have indicated that, in a controlled laboratory setting, people can be influenced briefly by sensory messages that are outside their conscious awareness. No scientific studies support the claims, however, that subliminal messages in advertising influence consumer choices or that subliminal phrases in self-help tapes significantly change a person's behavior.

Extrasensory Perception

Extrasensory perception (ESP) refers to "a response to an unknown event not presented to any known sense." ESP includes clairvoyance, telepathy, and precognition. Most psychologists do not dismiss ESP entirely, but point out that carefully controlled experiments have not yet verified its existence.

Vision

Unlike most animals, humans rely most heavily on their sense of vision to perceive the world.

The Visual System

In the process leading to vision, **light** enters the eye through the **cornea,** then passes through the **pupil** (in the center of the **iris**) and the **lens,** which focuses it onto the **retina.** The lens changes its shape to allow light to be focused sharply on the retina. One spot on the retina, called the **blind spot,** has no receptor cells. Directly behind the lens and on the retina is a depressed spot called the **fovea,** which lies at the center of the visual field.

The retina of each eye contains the two kinds of receptor cells responsible for vision: rods and cones. **Rods,** chiefly responsible for night vision, respond to varying degrees of light and dark but not to color. **Cones** respond to light and dark as well as to color, and operate mainly in daytime. Only cones are present in the fovea.

Rods and cones connect to nerve cells, called **bipolar cells,** leading to the brain. In the fovea, a single cone generally connects with one bipolar cell. Rods, on the other hand, share bipolar cells. The one-to-one connection between cones and bipolar cells in the fovea allows for maximum **visual acuity,** the ability to distinguish fine details. Vision is thus sharpest whenever the image of an object falls directly on the fovea.

The sensitivity of rods and cones changes according to the amount of available light. **Light adaptation** helps our eyes adjust to bright light; **dark adaptation** allows us to see, at least partially, in darkness. An **afterimage** can appear until the retina adapts after a visual stimulus has been removed.

Neural messages originating in the retina must eventually reach the brain for a visual sensation to occur. The bipolar cells connect to **ganglion cells,** whose axons converge to form the **optic nerve** that carries messages to the brain. The place on the retina where the axons of the ganglion cells join to leave the eye is the blind spot.

At the base of the brain is the **optic chiasm,** where some of the optic nerve fibers cross to the other side of the brain.

Feature detectors, cells that are highly specialized to respond to particular elements of vision, such as movement or horizontal or vertical lines, allow the brain to register and interpret visual signals.

Color Vision

The human vision system allows us to see an extensive range of colors. Hue, saturation, and brightness are three separate aspects of our experience of color. **Hue** refers to colors (red, green, blue, etc.), **saturation** indicates the vividness or richness of the hues, and **brightness** signals the intensity of the hues. Humans can distinguish only about 150 hues but, through gradations of saturation and brightness, we can perceive many variations on those hues.

Theories of Color Vision

Theories of color vision attempt to explain how the cones, which number only about 150,000 in the fovea, are able to distinguish so many different colors. One clue lies in color mixing: **Additive color mixing** is the process of mixing only a few lights of different wavelengths to create many new colors; **subtractive color mixing** refers to mixing a few pigments to come up with a whole palette of new colors.

Based on the principles of additive color mixing, the **trichromatic theory** of color vision holds that the eye contains three kinds of color receptors that are most responsive to either red, green, or blue light. By combining signals from these three basic receptors, the brain can detect any color and even subtle differences among nearly identical colors. This theory accounts for some kinds of **color blindness.** People referred to as **dichromats** have a deficiency in either red-green or blue-yellow vision; **monochromats** see no color at all. People with normal color vision are referred to as **trichromats.** By contrast, the **opponent-process theory** maintains that receptors are specialized to respond to either member of the three basic color pairs: red-green, yellow-blue, and black-white (dark and light).

Drawing on elements of the two theories, current knowledge holds that while there are three kinds of receptors for colors in the retina (for violet-blue, green, and yellow light), the messages they transmit are coded by other neurons in the visual system into opponent-process form.

Hearing

Sound   **Sounds** we hear are psychological experiences created by the brain in response to stimulation. The physical stimuli for the sense of hearing are **sound waves,** which produce vibration in the eardrum. **Frequency** is the number of cycles per second in a wave, expressed in a unit called **hertz.** Frequency is the primary determinant of **pitch**—how high or low the tone seems to be. **Amplitude** is the magnitude of a wave; it largely determines the loudness of a sound. Loudness is measured in **decibels.** The complex pattern of **overtones** determines the **timbre** of a sound.

The Ear   Hearing begins when sound waves strike the eardrum and cause it to vibrate. This vibration, in turn, makes three bones in the middle ear—the **hammer,** the **anvil,** and the **stirrup**—vibrate in sequence. These vibrations are magnified in their passage through the middle ear deep into the inner ear via the **oval window,** a membrane attached to the stirrup. In the inner ear, the vibrations cause the fluid inside the **cochlea** to vibrate, pushing the **basilar membrane** and the organ of Corti up and down.

Inside the **organ of Corti** are tiny hair cells that act as sensory receptors for hearing. Stimulation of these receptors produces auditory signals that are transmitted to brain through the auditory nerve. The brain pools the information from thousands of these cells to create the perception of sounds.

Theories of Hearing   There are two basic views that explain how different sound-wave patterns are coded into neural messages. **Place theory** states that the brain determines pitch by noting the place on the basilar membrane where the message is strongest. **Frequency theory** holds that the frequency of vibrations of the basilar membrane as a whole is translated into an equivalent frequency of nerve impulses. Neurons, however, cannot fire as rapidly as the frequency of the highest-pitched sound. This suggests a **volley principle,** whereby nerve cells fire in sequence to send a rapid series of impulses to the brain. Because neither theory fully explains pitch discrimination, some combination of the two is needed.

Hearing Disorders   Although hearing problems are common, they can often be prevented by detection and treatment of ear infections, reduced exposure to noise, and not smoking.

The Other Senses

Smell   The sense of smell is activated by substances carried by airborne molecules into the nasal cavities, where the substances activate highly specialized receptors for smell, located in the **olfactory epithelium.** From there messages are carried directly to the **olfactory bulb** in the brain, where they are sent to the brain's temporal lobe, resulting in our awareness of smells. **Pheromones** are sensed by receptors in the **vomeronasal organ (VNO),** which sends messages to a specialized olfactory bulb.

Pheromones, chemicals used by animals for communication, stimulate receptors in the VNO. Primer pheromones cause changes in the receiving animal's endocrine system. Releaser pheromones trigger specific behaviors. Humans may have an active VNO and may secrete and detect pheromones.

Taste   The receptor cells for the sense of taste are housed in the **taste buds** on the tongue, which, in turn, are found in the **papillae,** the small bumps on the surface of the tongue. Each taste bud contains a cluster of taste receptors, or taste cells, that cause their adjacent neurons to fire when they become activated by the chemical substances in food, sending a nerve impulse to the brain.

We experience five primary tastes: sweet, sour, salty, bitter, and umami (a response to MSG and related proteins). All other tastes derive from combinations of these. Flavor is a complex blend of taste and smell.

Kinesthetic and Vestibular Senses   The **kinesthetic senses** relay specific information about muscle movement, changes in posture, and strain on muscles and joints. They rely on feedback from two sets of specialized nerve endings: **stretch receptors,** which are attached to muscle fibers, and **Golgi tendon organs,** which are attached to the tendons.

The **vestibular senses** control equilibrium and create an awareness of body position. The receptors for these senses are located in the inner ear. The sensation of body rotation stems from the three semicircular canals of the inner ear. The sensation of gravitation and movement forward and backward, as well as up and down, arises in the two **vestibular sacs** that lie between the semicircular canals and the cochlea.

Sensations of Motion   The vestibular organs are also responsible for motion sickness, which triggers strong reactions in some people. Motion sickness may be caused by discrepancies between visual information and vestibular sensation.

The Skin Senses   The skin is the largest sense organ, with numerous nerve receptors distributed in varying concentrations throughout its surface. Skin receptors give rise to what are known as the cutaneous sensations of pressure, temperature, and pain. Research has not established a simple connection between the various types of receptors and these separate sensations, because the brain uses complex information about the patterns of activity on many different receptors to detect and discriminate among skin sensations.

Pain   People have varying degrees of sensitivity to pain. The most commonly accepted explanation of pain is the **gate control theory,** which holds that a "neurological gate" in the spinal cord controls the transmission of pain impulses to the brain. **Biopsychosocial theory** holds that pain is a dynamic process that involves biological, psychological, and social mechanisms. Pain involves a feedback loop and can be intensified by anxiety or fear or lightened by positive beliefs. Studies of pain relief suggest the existence of the **placebo effect,** which occurs when a pain sufferer feels relief from pain when given a chemically neutral pill but told that it is an effective pain reliever.

Perception

There are several ways in which the brain interprets the complex flow of information from the various senses and creates perceptual experiences that go far beyond what is sensed directly.

Perceptual Organization   One important way our perceptual processes work is through distinguishing **figures** from the **ground** against which they appear. The figure-ground distinction, first noted by Gestalt psychologists, pertains to all our senses, not just vision. For instance, a violin solo stands out against the "ground" of a symphony orchestra. When we use sensory information to create perceptions, we fill in the missing information, group various objects together, see whole objects, and hear meaningful sounds.

Perceptual Constancies   **Perceptual constancy** is our tendency to perceive objects as unchanging in the face of changes in sensory stimulation. Once we have formed a stable perception of an object, we can recognize it from almost any angle. Thus, **size, shape,** and **color constancies** help us understand and relate to the world better. Memory and experience play an important part in perceptual constancy, compensating for confusing stimuli.

Perceiving Distance and Depth   We can perceive distance and depth through **monocular cues,** from one eye, or **binocular cues,** which depend on the interaction of both eyes.

Superposition is a monocular distance cue in which one object, by partly blocking a second, appears closer. **Linear perspective** is another monocular cue to distance and depth based on the fact that two parallel lines seem to come together at the horizon. Other monocular cues include **aerial perspective, texture gradient,** and **motion parallax.**

With binocular cues, the **stereoscopic vision** derived from combining the two retinal images makes perceptions of depth and distance clearer. **Retinal disparity** accounts for the different images each eye receives. **Convergence** is another binocular cue. Humans, apes, and some predatory animals with the ability to use binocular cues have a distinct advantage over animals whose vision is limited to monocular cues.

Sounds, too, add to our sense of space. **Monaural cues,** such as loudness and distance, require only one ear. On the other hand, **binaural cues,** such as discrepancies in the arrival time of sound waves and their volume, help us to locate the source of a sound. Binaural cues depend on the collaboration of both ears.

Perceiving Movement   Perception of movement is a complicated process involving both the visual messages from the retina and messages from the muscles around the eyes as they shift to follow a moving object. At times our perceptual processes trick us into believing that an object is moving when, in fact, it is stationary. Thus, there is a difference between real movement and apparent movement.

Autokinetic illusion, the perceived motion created by a single stationary object, **stroboscopic motion,** resulting from the flashing of a series of still pictures in rapid succession, and the **phi phenomenon,** which occurs when lights flashed in sequence are perceived as moving, are all examples of apparent movement. Another movement illusion is induced movement.

Visual Illusions   Visual illusions occur when we use a variety of sensory cues to create perceptual experiences that do not actually exist. **Perceptual illusions** depend primarily on our own perceptual processes and occur because the stimulus contains misleading cues.

Observer Characteristics: Individual Differences and Culture   In addition to past experience and learning, several personal factors color our perception. For example, our familiarity with a symbol or object affects our expectation of how the object should look, even if we observe subtle changes in its appearance. Our perceptions are also influenced by our individual ways of dealing with the environment and by our cultural background, values, motivation, personality, and cognitive style.

key terms

Sensation	93	Cones	100	Color blindness	106
Perception	93	Bipolar cells	101	Dichromats	106
Receptor cell	94	Visual acuity	101	Monochromats	106
Absolute threshold	95	Dark adaptation	101	Opponent-process theory	107
Adaptation	96	Light adaptation	101	Sound	109
Difference threshold or just noticeable		Afterimage	102	Sound waves	109
difference (jnd)	96	Ganglion cells	102	Frequency	109
Weber's law	96	Optic nerve	102	Hertz (Hz)	109
Cornea	100	Optic chiasm	103	Pitch	109
Pupil	100	Feature detectors	103	Amplitude	109
Iris	100	Hue	105	Decibel	109
Lens	100	Saturation	105	Overtones	109
Retina	100	Brightness	105	Timbre	110
Blind spot	100	Additive color mixing	106	Hammer, anvil, stirrup	111
Fovea	100	Subtractive color mixing	106	Oval window	111
Light	100	Trichromatic theory	106	Cochlea	111
Rods	100	Trichromats	106	Basilar membrane	111

Organ of Corti	111	Vestibular senses	120	Aerial perspective	130
Place theory	112	Vestibular sacs	120	Texture gradient	130
Frequency theory	113	Gate control theory	122	Linear perspective	130
Volley principle	113	Biopsychosocial theory	122	Motion parallax	131
Olfactory epithelium	116	Placebo effect	123	Stereoscopic vision	131
Olfactory bulb	116	Figure	125	Retinal disparity	131
Pheromones	116	Ground	125	Convergence	131
Vomeronasal organ (VNO)	117	Perceptual constancy	127	Monaural cue	132
Taste buds	117	Size constancy	127	Binaural cue	132
Papillae	117	Shape constancy	128	Autokinetic illusion	134
Kinesthetic senses	119	Color constancy	128	Stroboscopic motion	134
Stretch receptors	119	Monocular cues	130	Phi phenomenon	134
Golgi tendon organs	119	Binocular cues	130	Perceptual illusion	134

OVERVIEW

Conscious Experience
What Is Waking Consciousness?
Explaining Waking
Consciousness
Daydreaming and Fantasy

Sleep
Circadian Cycles: The Biological
Clock
The Rhythms of Sleep
Sleep Disorders

Dreams
What Do We Dream?
Why Do We Dream?
Do We Need to Dream?

Drug-Altered Consciousness
Substance Use, Abuse,
and Dependence
Depressants: Alcohol,
Barbiturates, and Opiates

Stimulants: Caffeine, Nicotine,
Amphetamines, and Cocaine
Hallucinogens and Marijuana
Explaining Abuse and Addiction

Meditation and Hypnosis
Meditation
Hypnosis

4

States of Consciousness

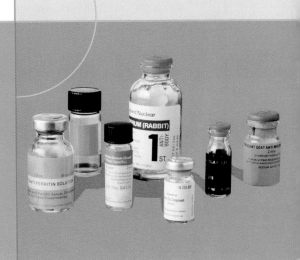

n August 18, 1993, a military cargo plane crashed into the ground just a quarter mile short of the runway at Guantanamo Bay, Cuba. All three crew members were seriously injured; the DC-8 freighter they were flying was destroyed by the impact and subsequent fire. Visibility was good and the plane was on course until the very last minute. What caused the crash? After an extensive review, the National Transportation Safety Board concluded that the accident was the result not of mechanical failure or pilot error but of "pilot fatigue."

This was the first (and only) time an aviation accident has been officially attributed to pilot fatigue. But the problem is more common than most of us recognize. According to NASA and federal aviation experts, one in seven pilots nods off in the cockpit. The problem is most acute on overnight international trips. Off the record, many pilots admit to suddenly waking up and not knowing where they are. This isn't dangerous if the copilot is awake. But flight attendants report going into the cabin and finding both pilots snoozing, which is why they regularly knock on the door and offer the crew refreshments. In one case, a cargo plane missed the Los Angeles airport and flew out over the Pacific for nearly an hour before air controllers were able to rouse the sleeping pilots and bring them back. Even when pilots remain awake, they may be too groggy to react efficiently in an emergency, which is what happened at Guantanamo Bay. Estimates are that pilot fatigue contributes to as many as one-third of aviation accidents.

Ironically, the technological advances that have made it possible to safely fly larger planes greater distances contribute to pilot fatigue. Today's jetliners virtually fly themselves. Once a plane reaches cruising altitude and the autopilot turns on, pilots face long hours with little to do. Boredom and inactivity trigger daydreaming and drowsiness. A psychologist who studies pilot fatigue warns, "If we ignore this, it's going to get worse and worse" (Merzer, 1998, p. 4).

Sleep and wakefulness are both states of **consciousness.** In everyday conversation, we use the word *consciousness* to describe being alert. Psychologists define consciousness more broadly, as our awareness of various mental processes. On any given day, we engage in a great variety of cognitive activities—concentrating, making decisions, planning, remembering, daydreaming, reflecting, sleeping, and dreaming are but a few. Those cognitive activities vary in the extent to which we are aware of our mental processes. They fall into two broad groups. **Waking consciousness** includes all the thoughts, feelings, and perceptions that occur when we are awake and reasonably alert. Waking consciousness is usually action- or plan-oriented and tuned in to the external environment. **Altered states of consciousness** differ from our normal waking consciousness in that we're detached, in varying degrees, from our external environment. Some altered states—such as sleep, daydreaming, and dreaming—occur routinely, even spontaneously. Others are induced by mind-altering drugs, such as alcohol; others by meditation and hypnosis.

In this chapter we introduce the varieties of human consciousness, beginning with waking consciousness. Next we look at how psychologists study and attempt to explain a natural state of altered consciousness, sleep, and dreams. Then we turn to the ways in which people *seek* altered states of consciousness. We begin with psychoactive drugs, from caffeine to crack, with special attention to alcohol abuse. What do these drugs do to people? What do they do for people? Last, we consider meditation and hypnosis from a scientific perspective.

THINKABOUTIT

You will find the answers to these questions in the chapter:

1. Why do people daydream?
2. Why do we need to sleep?
3. What can you learn from your dreams?
4. How is today's drug problem different from the drug use in other societies and times?
5. Can hypnosis help you overcome a problem, such as smoking or overeating?

Consciousness Our awareness of various cognitive processes, such as sleeping, dreaming, concentrating, and making decisions.

Waking consciousness Mental state that encompasses the thoughts, feelings, and perceptions that occur when we are awake and reasonably alert.

Altered state of consciousness Mental state that differs noticeably from normal waking consciousness.

Although you can easily focus on one absorbing conversation while surrounded by a number of other conversations, your attention is likely to shift if you hear someone nearby say your name or make reference to something that interests you.

Conscious Experience

Why do people daydream?

For centuries, philosophers, theologians, artists, and, most recently, scientists have tried to grasp the elusive nature of consciousness. In the words of William James, "Its meaning we know so long as no one asks us to define it" (1890, p. 225). Like the proverbial fish that doesn't know it's swimming in water, we take consciousness for granted—until we are removed from our natural element.

What Is Waking Consciousness?

Most of us equate waking consciousness with awareness: whatever in our environment we are noticing and responding to right now. Awareness is indeed part of consciousness, but only a part. At any given moment, we are exposed to an enormous variety of stimuli from the outside world, all sorts of internal sensations (such as heat and cold, touch, pressure, pain, equilibrium) as well as an array of thoughts, memories, emotions, and needs. We select only what seems most important at the moment and then filter out everything else. Thus, even when we are fully awake and alert, we are aware of only a small portion of what is available in waking consciousness. But our brain continues to process information outside our immediate awareness and will shift our attention to things that may be especially important. For example, if you are in a noisy, crowded room and you're involved in a conversation, you ignore the dozens of other conversations going on around you. When someone nearby mentions your name, however, your attention quickly shifts. Even though you were focused on one conversation, your brain was attending to and processing other information in waking consciousness but outside of your immediate awareness.

Explaining Waking Consciousness

The founders of psychology viewed the primary concern of their new science to be the study of consciousness (or, in the case of Freud, the unconscious) through introspection and analysis. In the early twentieth century, however, behaviorists and others rejected both consciousness as a topic and introspection as a method, in favor of the study of directly observable, measurable behavior (as described in Chapter 1, The Science of Psychology). Watson, one of the founders of behaviorism, declared, "I believe that we can write a psychology and never use the terms consciousness, mental states, mind . . ." (1913). Beginning in the 1960s, however, interest in altered states of consciousness, the rise of cognitive psychology, advances in psychobiology (especially neuroscience), and general dissatisfaction with the narrow confines of behaviorism led to a renewed interest in consciousness.

The Stream of Consciousness, Revisited   William James characterized consciousness as a kaleidoscope that transforms internal and external information into a coherent and continuous stream—a description that has withstood the test of time. Recently, scientists have begun to explore the neurological mechanisms that weave bits and pieces of sensation and perception into the dynamic process we call "consciousness." For example, one theory holds that individual pieces of information received from the various sensory modes are first forwarded to specific areas on the cerebral cortex, where they are analyzed and processed as the elements of our perceptual experience (see Chapter 3, Sensation and Perception). At the same time, the thalamus, deep in the center of the brain, is "sweeping or scanning" all these centers at a rate of 40 times per second (Contreras et al., 1996; Llinás, 1996; Pedroarena & Llinás, 1997). Each sweep results in a single image or "moment of consciousness." According to this theory, then, consciousness represents a dialogue between the thalamus and the cerebral cortex (Baars, 1998).

"The Tip-of-the-Iceberg," Reanalyzed   Another common view is that consciousness is only a small peak emerging from a mass of unconscious mental representations and activities that lie below the surface. No one did more to popularize this image than Sigmund Freud (see Chapter 1). We will draw on Freud's views when we explore dreaming and hypnosis later in this chapter (and in Chapter 11, Personality, and Chapter 13, Psychological Disorders). Many contemporary psychologists reject the idea that people are driven by unconscious urges. They prefer to use the term *nonconscious* to describe sensations and perceptions, thoughts and feelings, and memories and goals to which we are not paying attention at the moment, as well as automatic actions and reactions to which we rarely give much thought.

Consciousness and Adaptation   In the past, some thinkers have viewed consciousness as an inconsequential by-product of activity in the brain and nervous system. In contrast, many of today's psychologists view consciousness as highly adaptive. For

THINKING CRITICALLY

Television, Daydreams, and Creativity

A review of studies of the impact of TV on children's imaginations (Valkenburg & van der Voort, 1994) concluded that watching television increases spontaneous daydreaming (defined as a shift of attention from the here and now to imaginary thoughts and images) but decreases creative imagination (defined as the capacity to generate many different novel or unusual ideas).

What explains this paradoxical finding? Which of the following hypotheses do you think fits the authors' finding? Why?

Hypothesis 1: TV inhibits imagination by providing stereotyped characters and ready-made plots. As a result, children become "consumers" of other people's fantasies rather than the producers of their own fantasies. Instead of daydreaming, they "replay" TV shows in their minds.

Hypothesis 2: TV is essentially neutral. It provides children with a rich storehouse of images and plots for daydreams and fantasies, but whether children use these resources creatively depends on individual differences. To simplify, TV stimulates the imaginations of naturally creative children, but encourages mental passivity in less creative children.

Hypothesis 3: The rapid pace of TV shows leaves little time to reflect on what is happening (or process this information), an essential element of creative imagination. Thus TV may foster free-form daydreaming but inhibit constructive imagination.

Daydreams Apparently effortless shifts in attention away from the here-and-now into a private world of make-believe.

example, Pinker (1997) holds that human survival depends upon our ability to get along with the group. Hence it is to our advantage to be able to look at ourselves from the outside, to try to imagine how others see us, to replay and evaluate mental tapes of our own behavior, and to figure out how we can get the most out of the group. In this view, natural selection favored *self*-consciousness, which became vital to human nature.

Daydreaming and Fantasy

In James Thurber's classic short story, "The Secret Life of Walter Mitty" (1942), the meek, painfully shy central character spends much of his time weaving elaborate fantasies in which he stars as a bold, dashing adventurer. Few people live in their imaginations to the extent Walter Mitty does but everyone has **daydreams:** apparently effortless, spontaneous shifts in attention away from the here and now into a private world of make-believe.

The urge to daydream seems to come in waves, surging about every 90 minutes and peaking between noon and 2 P.M. (Ford-Mitchell, 1997). According to some estimates, the average person spends almost half of his or her waking hours fantasizing, though this varies from person to person and situation to situation. Typically, we daydream when we would rather be somewhere else or be doing something else, so daydreaming is a momentary escape.

Are daydreams random paths your mind travels? Not at all. Studies show that most daydreams are variations on a central theme: thoughts and images of unfulfilled goals and wishes, accompanied by emotions arising from an appraisal of where we are now compared to where we want to be (Baars & McGovern, 1994). Some people imagine pleasant, playful, entertaining scenarios, uncomplicated by guilt or worry. By contrast, people who are extremely achievement-oriented tend to experience recurring themes of frustration, guilt, fear of failure, and hostility, reflecting the self-doubt and competitive envy that accompanies great ambition. While most daydreaming is quite normal, it is considered maladaptive when it involves extensive fantasizing, replacing human interaction and interfering with vocational or academic success (Somer, 2002).

Does daydreaming serve any useful function? Some psychologists view daydreaming as nothing more than a retreat from the real world, especially when that world is not meeting our needs. Other psychologists stress the positive value of daydreaming and fantasy. Daydreams may provide a refreshing break from a stressful day and serve to remind us of neglected personal needs. Freudian theorists tend to view daydreams as a harmless way of working through hostile feelings or satisfying guilty desires. Cognitive psychologists emphasize that daydreaming can build problem-solving and interpersonal skills, as well as encourage creativity. Moreover, daydreaming helps people endure difficult situations: Prisoners of war have used fantasies to survive torture and deprivation. Daydreaming and fantasy, then, may provide welcome relief from unpleasant reality and reduce internal tension and external aggression.

▬▬▬▬   CHECK YOUR UNDERSTANDING

1. Decision-making, problem solving, awareness, and reasoning are all examples of

___ a. waking consciousness

___ b. altered states of consciousness

___ c. divergent thought

___ d. arcadian cycles

2. Shifting attention away from the here and now into a private world of make-believe is characteristic of

___ a. dreams

___ b. daydreams

___ c. night terrors

___ d. nightmares

Answers: 1.a, 2.b

Sleep

Why do we need to sleep?

Human beings spend about one-third of their lives in the altered state of consciousness known as sleep: a natural state of rest characterized by a reduction in voluntary body movement and decreased awareness of the surroundings. No one who has tried to stay awake longer than 20 hours at a time could doubt the necessity of sleep. Some people claim they never sleep, but when observed under laboratory conditions, they actually sleep soundly without being aware of it. When people are sleep-deprived, they crave sleep just as strongly as they would food or water after a period of deprivation (see *On the Cutting Edge: Most of Us Need More Sleep Than We Get*). Merely resting doesn't satisfy us.

Humans are not alone in their need for sleep: All birds and mammals sleep, and although scientists are not sure about reptiles, frogs, fish, and even insects go into "rest states" similar to sleep. Indeed, *Drosophila* fruit flies, a favorite subject for genetic studies because they reproduce rapidly, are remarkably like us: They are active during the day and somnolent at night; when deprived of sleep they need long naps to recover: and caffeine keeps them awake, whereas antihistamines make them drowsy (Shaw, Cirelli, Greenspan, & Tononi, 2000).

How long organisms sleep, where, in what positions, and other details vary from species to species. In general, large animals sleep less than small animals, perhaps because eating enough to support their size requires more time awake. Elephants get by on about four hours sleep, and giraffes on only two hours. In contrast, bats, armadillos, and opossums sleep more than 18 hours a day. Lions, who consume enough from a single kill to keep going for a day or two, sleep for 16 hours at a time. House cats have inherited this tendency, though they spend more time in light sleep (eyes closed but in a upright posture with ears alert) than in deep sleep (muscles relaxed, almost oblivious to their surroundings).

Dolphins and other aquatic mammals actually sleep on the move: Paddling with one flipper and periodically surfacing to breathe, they sleep with only one hemisphere of their brain at a time (Netting, 1999). Birds are also half-brain sleepers, but apparently for a different reason: to keep one eye open for predators. Other organisms, such as fish, usually find a protected place and rest for just minutes at a time by slowing their metabolism down. Brightly colored reef fish can even "turn down" their colors when they rest to reduce the risk of being seen by predators.

Nobody knows exactly why we need to sleep. Evolutionary psychologists see sleep as an adaptive mechanism that evolved to allow organisms to conserve and restore energy (Tobler, 1997). Researchers have shown that people use less energy when they are asleep than when they are awake (Madsen, 1993). Another theory is that some vital substance in the nervous system is resynthesized during sleep. But what that substance might be is still a mystery (Tobler, 1997), although a recent

ON THE CUTTING EDGE

MOST OF US NEED MORE SLEEP THAN WE GET

Inadequate sleep has become a "national epidemic" in the United States. Between one-third and one-half of all adults regularly fail to get enough sleep, and the problem is getting worse: Americans were sleeping an average of eight to twelve hours a night in the 1950s, but by 1990 they were down to only seven hours a night. In the 1980s, more than one-quarter of American adults said they felt unrested in the morning (Bliwise, 1996). The problems associated with inadequate sleep are not just isolated among adults. Recent estimates indicate that high school and college students average only about six hours of sleep a night, with 30 percent of high school students reporting they fall asleep in class about once a week (Acebo & Carskadon, 2002; Maas, 1998). Lack of sleep among adolescents has also been implicated as a contributing factor to the high rate of automobile accidents among young people (Carskadon, 2002).

Extensive research shows that losing an hour or two of sleep every night, week after week, month after month, makes it more difficult for people to pay attention (especially to monotonous tasks) and to remember things (Johnsen, Laberg, Eid, & Hugdahl, 2002). Reaction time slows down, behavior becomes unpredictable, logical reasoning is impaired, and accidents and errors in judgment increase, while productivity and the ability to make decisions decline (Babkoff, Caspy, Mikulincer, & Sing, 1991; Blagrove & Akehurst, 2000, 2001; Webb & Levy, 1984). These findings have important implications.

For example, experts estimate that sleep loss is a contributing factor in 200,000 to 400,000 automobile accidents each year, resulting in approximately 1,500 deaths. Research suggests that driving while sleepy is just as dangerous as driving while drunk (Powell et al., 2001).

Sleep deprivation may also routinely affect the performance of those in high-risk positions, such as pilots, as we saw in the opening of this chapter. Hospital staff and nuclear-power-plant operators, who often have to make critical decisions on short notice, are also at risk. A dramatic example of the effects of sleep deprivation on the ability to cope is the 1979 accident at the nuclear power plant at Three Mile Island, Pennsylvania, in which human error transformed a minor mishap into a major nuclear disaster.

Awareness of the relationship between sleep deprivation and accidents has led to changes in the working patterns of people whose jobs can have life-and-death consequences. Several states have shortened the shifts of hospital residents to prevent errors caused by sleep deprivation. Similarly, the FAA has restricted the number of hours a pilot can fly without having time off to sleep.

Unfortunately, people do not always know when they are not getting enough sleep. In one recent study by the National Transportation Safety Board, most truck drivers who were involved in accidents that clearly resulted from their falling asleep at the wheel claimed they felt rested at the time. In a laboratory study, one group of healthy college students who were getting seven to eight hours of

(cont.)

sleep a night showed no apparent signs of sleep deprivation. Yet 20 percent of them fell asleep immediately when
they were put into a dark room, a symptom of chronic
sleep loss. Another group went to bed 60 to 90 minutes
earlier than their normal bedtime for a period of time.
These students reported that they felt much more vigorous and alert—indeed, they performed significantly better
on tests of psychological and mental acuity (Carskadon &
Dement, 1982).

According to well-known sleep researcher Dr. William
Dement, one way to reduce your sleep debt is to take short
naps. Unfortunately, while in many cultures mid-afternoon is
seen as siesta time, we often reach for a cup of coffee to keep
us going. Studies have shown that even a short 20-minute
nap can moderately increase alertness, reduce irritability, and
improve efficiency, while one-hour naps show more marked
increases in performance (Mednick et al., 2002).

study suggests that the naturally occurring chemical adenosine may be involved
(Porkka-Heiskanen et al., 1997). In this study, cats kept awake an abnormally long
time were found to have elevated levels of adenosine in their brains during wakefulness. When the cats were finally permitted to sleep, the adenosine levels dropped.
To determine whether the adenosine buildup actually caused the sleepiness, the
investigators injected adenosine into well-rested cats. These cats immediately
became sleepy and began to exhibit the EEG patterns typical of drowsiness. Exactly
why a high level of adenosine appears to trigger sleepiness is not known, but additional research along this line may soon provide us with a better understanding of
the neurological processes underlying the need for sleep (Lindberg, 2002; Strecker
et al., 2002).

Circadian Cycles: The Biological Clock

Like many other biological functions, sleep and waking follow a daily, or *circadian*,
cycle (from the Latin expression *circa diem*, meaning "about a day") (Moore-Ede,
Czeisler, & Richardson, 1983a & b). **Circadian rhythms** are an ancient and fundamental adaptation to the 24-hour solar cycle of light and dark, found not only in
humans and other animals but also in plants and even one-celled organisms (Moore,
1999). The human *biological clock* is largely governed by a tiny cluster of neurons in
the lower region of the hypothalamus known as the **suprachiasmatic nucleus
(SCN)** (Novak & Albers, 2002). Interestingly, the SCN receives information about
the daily light and dark cycles directly from the eye by way of a specially dedicated
neuropathway originating in the retina (Zisapel, 2001).

In response to the light dark cycles detected by the eye, the SCN secretes specific
neurotransmitters to regions of the brain like the reticular formation and hypothalamus that in turn control our body's temperature, metabolism, blood pressure, hormone levels, and hunger, which vary predictably through the course of the day. For
example, the level of the hormone epinephrine (which causes the body to go on
alert) reaches a peak in the late morning hours and then steadily declines until
around midnight, when it suddenly drops to a very low level and remains there until
morning. By contrast, levels of melatonin (which promotes sleep) surge at night and
drop off during the day. Animal studies have shown that the SCN even responds to
seasonal variations in the length of the day (Sumova, Sladek, Jac, & Illnervoa, 2002)
in turn regulating the production of various hormones and behaviors such as mating
that are linked to seasonal changes in many species.

The biological clock is self-sustaining and continues to function, at least for short
periods of time, in the absence of external cues to the cycle of day and night. For

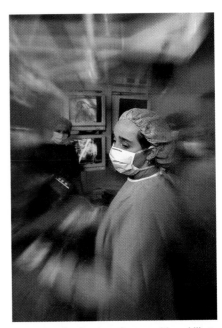

Sleep deprivation impairs cognitive skills to
a greater extent than many people realize.
When deprived of sleep we react more
slowly, have more trouble focusing attention, and are more prone to making errors in
judgment. Emergency room doctors often
lose sleep because of the unpredictable
and demanding nature of their work. This
can be a serious problem when they are
called on to make critical decisions quickly.

Circadian rhythm a regular biological
rhythm with approximately a 24 hour
period.

Suprachiasmatic nucleus (SCN) A
cluster of neurons in the hypothalamus
that receives input from the retina regarding light and dark cycles and is involved in
regulating the biological clock.

example, Czeisler, Duffy, and Shanahan (1999) studied 24 people who volunteered to live in an artificial environment for three weeks. The only time cues participants had were a weak cycle of light and dark set at 28 hours and a bedtime signal. Even in this misleading environment, their body temperatures, hormone levels, and other biological processes showed that their bodies continued to function according to their own internal 24-hour cycle.

Under normal environmental conditions, however, our body clocks reset themselves to match prevailing cycles of light and dark. Since light inhibits the production of melatonin, our sleep–wake cycles change as the days grow longer or shorter with the seasons (Lavie, 2001). The hypothalamus does not distinguish between natural and artificial light, however. Thus, exposure to bright light after dark—in our homes, offices, and other locations—suppresses our natural response to changes in the light cycle (Wehr, Giesen, Moul, Turner, & Schwartz, 1995). Even artificial changes in the level of melatonin have an effect on circadian rhythms. For example, a small dose of melatonin taken in the morning (the time when the hormone is usually tapering off) sets back or slows down the biological clock (Liu et al., 1997). Taken in the evening, melatonin speeds up the biological clock, making the person fall asleep earlier than usual (Lewy, 1992). Applying this knowledge, melatonin has been successfully used as an aide to persons with blindness, who sometimes are unable to sense dark-light cycles, causing insomnia or daytime sleepiness. Carefully timed doses of melatonin seems to "reset" the biological clocks for such people, enabling them to sleep better at night and remain alert during the day (Sack, Brandes, Kendall, & Lewy, 2000).

Disrupted Circadian Rhythms: Desynchronization   We rarely notice circadian rhythms until they are disturbed. Jet lag is a familiar example. Travelers who cross several time zones in one day often feel "out of sorts" for several days. The reason for jet lag is not so much lack of sleep as *desynchronization*. Sleep and wake cycles adapt quickly, but hormones, body temperature, and digestive cycles change more slowly. As a result, bodily functions are out of synch. Likewise, shift workers often lose weight and suffer from irritability, insomnia, and extreme drowsiness for some time after changing to a new shift (Richardson, Miner, & Czeisler, 1989–1990). People can adapt to night work fairly quickly, but night and day shifts are often assigned on a rotating basis, so the workers' bodies do not have time to resynchronize. Pilots who work variable shifts and cross and recross time zones are especially vulnerable. These disruptions of the biological clock pose a threat to safety of pilots or workers operating dangerous equipment and in some instances lead to ecological disasters: The Alaskan oil spill from the *Exxon Valdez* and the Union Carbide chemical accident in Bhopal, India, both occurred during the night shift.

The Rhythms of Sleep

Over the years researchers have accumulated a large body of observations about what happens in our bodies and brains during sleep. In a typical study, researchers recruit volunteers who spend one or more nights in a "sleep lab." Volunteers sleep comfortably as their brain waves, eye movements, muscle tension, and other physiological functions are monitored. Data from such studies show that although there are significant individual differences in sleep behavior, almost everyone goes through the same stages of sleep, each marked by characteristic patterns of brain waves, muscular activity, blood pressure, and body temperature (Anch et al., 1988; Carlson, 2000). Figure 4–1 illustrates the electrical activity related to the brain, heart, and facial muscles at each stage.

"Going to sleep" means losing awareness and failing to respond to a stimulus that would produce a response in the waking state. As measured by an EEG, brain waves

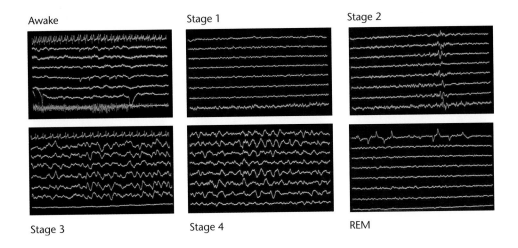

Awake   Stage 1   Stage 2

Stage 3   Stage 4   REM

Figure 4–1
Waves of sleep.
This series of printouts illustrates electrical activity in the brain, heart, and facial muscles during the various stages of sleep. Note the characteristic delta waves that begin to appear during Stage 3 and become more pronounced during Stage 4.

during this "twilight" state are characterized by irregular, low-voltage *alpha waves*. This brain-wave pattern mirrors the sense of relaxed wakefulness that we experience while lying on a beach or when resting after a big meal.

After this initial twilight phase, the sleeper enters *Stage 1* of sleep. Stage 1 brain waves are tight and of very low amplitude (height), resembling those recorded when a person is alert or excited. But, in contrast to normal waking consciousness, Stage 1 of the sleep cycle is marked by a slowing of the pulse, muscle relaxation, and side-to-side rolling movements of the eyes—the last being the most reliable indication of this first stage of sleep (Dement, 1974). Stage 1 usually lasts only a few moments. The sleeper is easily aroused at this stage and, once awake, may be unaware of having slept at all.

Stages 2 and *3* are characterized by progressively deeper sleep. During Stage 2, short rhythmic bursts of activity called *sleep spindles* periodically appear. In Stage 3, *delta waves*—slow waves with very high peaks—begin to emerge. During these stages, the sleeper is hard to awaken and does not respond to stimuli such as noises or lights. Heart rate, blood pressure, and temperature continue to drop.

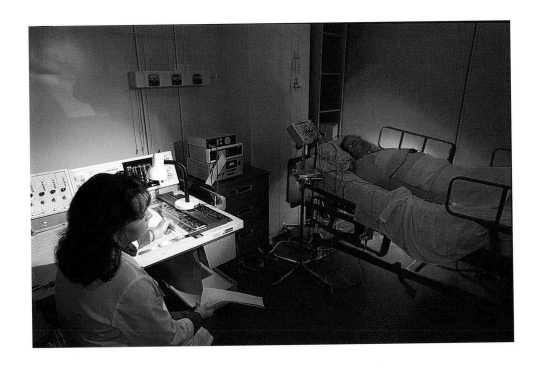

Sleep researchers monitor volunteers' brain waves, muscle tension, and other physiological changes during sleep.

REM (paradoxical) sleep Sleep stage characterized by rapid eye movements and increased dreaming.

Non-REM (NREM) sleep Non-rapid-eye-movement stages of sleep that alternate with REM stages during the sleep cycle.

In *Stage 4* sleep, the brain emits *very* slow delta waves. Heart rate, breathing rate, blood pressure, and body temperature are as low as they will get during the night. In young adults, delta sleep occurs in 15- to 20-minute segments—interspersed with lighter sleep—mostly during the first half of the night. Delta sleep time lessens with age but continues to be the first sleep to be made up after sleep has been lost.

About an hour after falling asleep, the sleeper begins to ascend from Stage 4 sleep to Stage 3, Stage 2, and back to Stage 1—a process that takes about 40 minutes. The brain waves return to the low-amplitude, saw-toothed shape characteristic of Stage 1 sleep and waking alertness. Heart rate and blood pressure also increase, yet the muscles are more relaxed than at any other point in the sleep cycle, and the person is very difficult to awaken. The eyes move rapidly under closed eyelids. This **rapid eye movement (REM) sleep** stage is distinguished from all other stages of sleep (called **non-REM** or **NREM**) that precede and follow it.

REM sleep is also called **paradoxical sleep,** because although measures of physiological functions closely resemble those recorded during waking consciousness, the person in this stage appears to be deeply asleep and is incapable of moving; the body's voluntary muscles are essentially paralyzed. Some research suggests that REM sleep is also the stage when most dreaming occurs, though dreams take place during NREM sleep as well (Stickgold, Rittenhouse, & Hobson, 1994). The first Stage 1-REM period lasts about ten minutes and is followed by Stages 2, 3, and 4 of NREM sleep. This sequence of sleep stages repeats itself all night, averaging 90 minutes from Stage 1-REM to Stage 4 and back again. Normally, a night's sleep consists of four to five sleep cycles of this sort. But the pattern of sleep changes as the night progresses. At first Stages 3 and 4 dominate; but as time passes, the Stage 1-REM periods gradually become longer and Stages 3 and 4 become shorter, eventually disappearing altogether. Over the course of a night, then, about 45 to 50 percent of the sleeper's time is spent in Stage 2, whereas REM sleep takes up another 20 to 25 percent of the total.

Sleep requirements and patterns vary considerably from person to person, though. Sleep patterns also change with age (Sadeh, Raviv, & Gruber, 2000) (see Figure 4–2). Infants sleep much longer than adults—13 to 16 hours during the first year—and much more of their sleep is REM sleep (see Figure 4–3).

Live! psych **4.1**

Figure 4–2
A night's sleep across the life span.
Sleep patterns change from childhood to young adulthood to old age. The red areas represent REM sleep, the stage of sleep that varies most dramatically across age groups.
Source: Anthony Kales, M.D., et al, "Medical Progress Sleep Disorders: Recent Findings in the Diagnosis and Treatment of Disturbed Sleep," *The New England Journal of Medicine,* 290, p. 487. Copyright © 1974 Massachusetts Medical Society. All rights reserved. Adapted with permission.

Sleep Disorders

The scientific study of typical sleep patterns has yielded insights into sleep disorders, including sleepwalking and night terrors, insomnia, apnea, and narcolepsy.

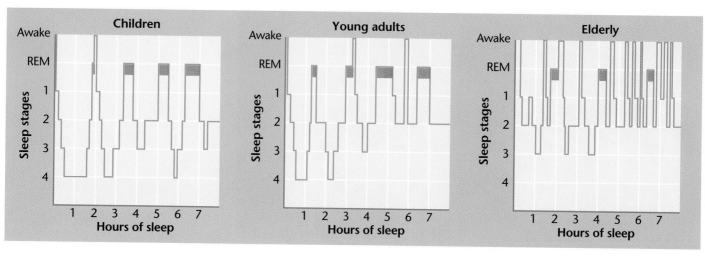

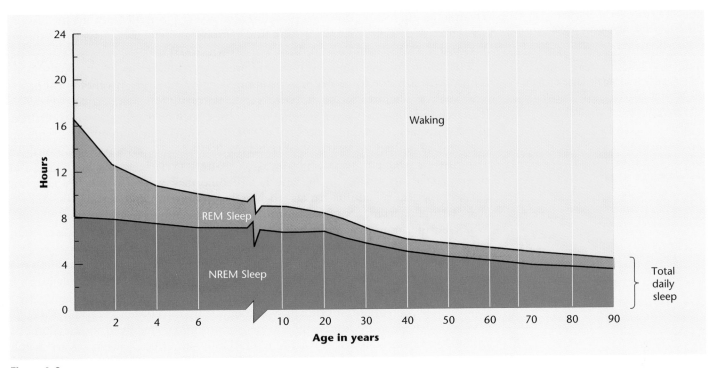

Figure 4–3
Changes in REM and NREM sleep.
The amount of REM sleep people need declines sharply during the first few years of life. Newborns spend about 8 hours, or almost half of their total sleep time in REM sleep, whereas older children and adults spend just 1 to 2 hours or about 20 to 25 percent of their total sleep time in REM sleep.
Source: Adapted with permission from Science, 152, p. 604. Copyright © 1966 by the American Association for the Advancement of Science. URL: http://www.sciencemag.org

Sleeptalking, Sleepwalking, and Night Terrors *Sleeptalking* and *sleepwalking* usually occur during Stage 4. Both are more common among children than adults: About 20 percent of children have at least one episode of either sleepwalking or sleeptalking. Boys are more likely to walk in their sleep than girls. Contrary to popular belief, waking a sleepwalker is not dangerous, but because sleepwalking commonly takes place during a very deep stage of sleep, waking a sleepwalker is not easy (Hobson, 1994).

Some people also experience sleep terrors, or night terrors, a form of nocturnal fright that makes them suddenly sit up in bed, often screaming out in fear. **Night terrors** occur during Stages 3 or 4 of NREM sleep, and are altogether different from **nightmares** (Zadra & Donderi, 2000). People generally cannot be awakened from night terrors, will push away anyone trying to comfort them, and cannot recall them the next morning. They also occur more often if the person is very tired. Nightmares, which awaken people during REM sleep are frightening dreams that can be recalled.

Although nightmares and night terrors are more common in children, adults can have them during times of stress (Muris, Merchelbach, Gadet, & Moulaert, 2000). Neither nightmares nor night terrors alone indicate psychological problems. Anxious people have no more nightmares than other people do. People whose nightmares stem from a traumatic experience, however, may be plagued by terrifying nighttime episodes for years.

Insomnia, Apnea, and Narcolepsy **Insomnia,** the inability to fall or remain asleep, afflicts as many as 35 million Americans. Most episodes of insomnia grow out of stressful events and are temporary (see *Applying Psychology: Coping with Occasional Insomnia).* But for some sufferers, insomnia is a persistent disruption.

Night terrors Frightening, often terrifying dreams that occur during NREM sleep from which a person is difficult to awaken and doesn't remember the content.

Nightmares Frightening dreams that occur during REM sleep and are remembered.

Insomnia Sleep disorder characterized by difficulty in falling asleep or remaining asleep throughout the night.

Apnea Sleep disorder characterized by breathing difficulty during the night and feelings of exhaustion during the day.

Narcolepsy Hereditary sleep disorder characterized by sudden nodding off during the day and sudden loss of muscle tone following moments of emotional excitement.

Treatments can create problems as well. Some prescription medications for insomnia can cause anxiety, memory loss, hallucinations, and violent behavior (Gathchel & Oordt, 2003; Morin, Bastien, Brink, & Brown, 2003).

The causes of insomnia vary for different individuals (Lichstein, Wilson, & Johnson, 2000). For some people, insomnia is part of a larger psychological problem, such as depression, so its cure requires treating the underlying disorder. Research indicates that interpersonal difficulties, such as loneliness can contribute to difficulty sleeping (Cacioppo et al., 2002). For others, insomnia results from an overaroused biological system. A physical predisposition to insomnia may combine with distress over chronic sleeplessness to create a cycle in which biological and emotional factors reinforce one another. People may worry so much about not sleeping that their bedtime rituals, such as brushing teeth and getting dressed for bed, "become harbingers of frustration, rather than stimuli for relaxation" (Hauri, 1982). Furthermore, bad sleep habits—such as varying bedtimes—and distracting sleep settings may aggravate or even cause insomnia.

Neurophysiological researchers looking to treat insomnia have been probing the mechanisms that enable us to switch between periods of wakefulness and sleep. One recent investigation using rats identified a specific area of the hypothalamus that appears to play an important role in switching the brain between sleep and wakefulness and vice versa by inhibiting the neurotransmitters involved in wakefulness, arousal, and consciousness throughout the brain—in effect, causing us to switch from wakefulness to sleep (Sherin et al., 1996). More research along this line may ultimately lead to a safe and effective treatment for insomnia.

Another sleep disorder, **apnea,** affects 10 to 12 million Americans. This condition, which is often inherited (Kadotani et al., 2001), is associated with breathing difficulties and snoring at night. In severe cases, the victim actually stops breathing after falling asleep (Vgontzas & Kales, 1999). When the level of carbon dioxide in the blood rises to a certain point, apnea sufferers are spurred to a state of arousal just short of waking consciousness. Because this may happen hundreds of times a night, apnea patients typically feel exhausted and fall asleep repeatedly the next day. They may also complain of depression, sexual dysfunction, difficulty concentrating, and headaches. Sleep apnea also has been shown to be related to hyperactivity, conduct disorders, and aggressiveness among children and adolescents (Chervin, Killion, Archbold, & Ruzicka, 2003).

People suffering from insomnia or apnea may envy those who have no trouble sleeping, but too much sleep also has serious repercussions. **Narcolepsy** is a hereditary disorder whose victims nod off without warning in the middle of a conversation or other alert activity. People with narcolepsy often experience a sudden loss of muscle tone when they express any sort of emotion. A joke, anger, sexual stimulation—all bring on the muscle paralysis associated with deep sleep. Suddenly, without warning, they collapse. Another symptom of the disorder is immediate entry into REM sleep, which produces frightening hallucinations that are, in fact, dreams the person is experiencing while still partly awake. Narcolepsy is believed to arise from a defect in the central nervous system (Bassetti & Aldrich, 1996).

At any given time, at least 40 million Americans suffer from chronic, long-term sleep disorders and 20 million other Americans occasionally experience sleep problems. This is of more than passing interest since there is a link between sleep and a large number of diseases, including asthma and stroke. (National Institute of Neurological Disorders and Stroke, 2003). A recent study of 72,000 female nurses found that women who sleep either too much (more than 9 hours), or too little (less than 5 hours) have an increased risk for heart disease. While the authors of this study could not determine exactly why this relationship was present, they suggested the tendency to sleep too much or too little might be indicative of underlying medical conditions (Ayas et al., 2003).

APPLYING PSYCHOLOGY

COPING WITH OCCASIONAL INSOMNIA

Sleep is sometimes elusive. The ancient Greeks believed that sleep was a gift of the god *Morpheus,* who granted or refused it to mortals. Like most people, you probably have had at least a few nights when you found it difficult to fall asleep. Episodes of even temporary or occasional insomnia can impair your ability to function during the day. So what can you do if you suddenly find yourself going through a period when you are unable to get a good night's sleep? Here are some tips that may help:

- Maintain regular bedtime hours; don't sleep late on weekends.

- Establish a regular bedtime routine that you follow each night before retiring, such as a warm bath, followed by a little reading or writing a letter.

- Abstain from drugs, including alcohol, caffeine, and nicotine, as well as the routine use of sleeping pills. Tryptophan, a substance that promotes sleep, may be taken as a sleep aid in the form of warm milk, confirming a folk remedy for sleeplessness.

- Adjust the temperature of the room if it is too cold or too warm.

- Avoid foods that may cause sleeplessness, such as chocolate.

"Episodes of even temporary or occasional insomnia can impair your ability to function during the day."

- Establish a regular exercise program during the day, but never exercise within several hours of bedtime.

- Avoid anxious thoughts while in bed. Set aside regular times during the day—well before bedtime—to mull over your worries. This technique may be supplemented by relaxation training, using such methods as biofeedback, self-hypnosis, or meditation (Gathchel & Oordt, 2003; Morin et al., 1994).

- Don't fight insomnia when it occurs. The old saying "If I can't sleep, I mop the kitchen floor" makes sense to sleep researchers, who counsel their clients to get out of bed and engage in an activity for an hour or so until they feel sleepy again.

Sleep quiz: Are you getting enough sleep? Test yourself.

According to surveys, millions of American's simply don't get enough sleep. The problem is particularly acute among adolescents and young adults, who feel pressured to work, be successful in school, and remain socially active. At the end of the day, something has to give, and all too often, it is sleep. Ironically, not getting enough sleep often interferes with the very activities that keep us awake, reducing one's effectiveness at work, school and in interpersonal relationships. Take the following sleep quiz and see if you need more sleep.

Answer yes or no to the following questions.

__Do you often fall asleep while watching TV?

__Is it common for you to fall asleep after large meals or while relaxing after dinner?

__Do you often fall asleep or fear nodding off during boring lectures, tedious activities, or in warm rooms?

__Do you need an alarm clock to wake up in the morning?

__Do you often press the snooze button on your alarm clock to get more sleep?

__Do you struggle to get out of bed in the morning?

__Do you often feel tired, irritable or stressed out during the day?

__Do you have trouble concentrating or remembering?

__Are you easily distracted or feel slow while performing tasks that require thinking, problem solving, or creativity?

__Do you sometimes feel drowsy or fear nodding off while driving?

__Do you need a nap to help you get through the day?

According to sleep researcher James Mass, if you answered yes to three or more of these questions you may need more sleep than you are getting.

Source: Adapted from: Maas, J. B. (1999). *Power sleep: The revolutionary program that prepares your mind for peak performance.* New York: Harper Collins.

CHECK YOUR UNDERSTANDING

1. The human biological clock is governed by neurons in the
___ a. pituitary gland
___ b. frontal cortex
___ c. occipital lobe
___ d. hypothalamus

2. Relaxed wakefulness and falling asleep are characterized by what kind of brain waves?
___ a. alpha waves
___ b. sleep spindles
___ c. delta waves
___ d. omega waves

3. During REM sleep, what usually occurs?
___ a. vivid dreaming
___ b. sleep walking
___ c. apnea
___ d. narcolepsy

4. Match the sleep disorder with its definition.

___ night terrors	a. sudden nodding off during the day
___ apnea	b. frightening dreams from which a person usually cannot be awakened
___ insomnia	c. difficulty breathing during the night and daytime exhaustion
___ narcolepsy	d. difficulty remaining asleep

Answers: 1.d, 2.a, 3.a, 4. Night terrors, b; apnea, c; insomnia, d; narcolepsy, a

Dreams

What can you learn from your dreams?

Every culture attributes meaning to dreams. Some people believe that dreams contain messages from their gods; some, that dreams predict the future; others, that dreams are real experiences of a spirit world that is inaccessible to waking consciousness.

Psychologists define **dreams** as visual and auditory experiences that our minds create during sleep. The average person has four or five vivid dreams a night, accounting for about two hours of the total time spent sleeping, most often during REM sleep. Less striking dreamlike experiences that resemble normal wakeful consciousness are reported about 50 percent of the time during NREM sleep.

Most dreams last about as long as the events would in real life; they do not flash on your mental screen just before waking, as was once believed. Generally, dreams consist of a sequential story or a series of stories. Stimuli, both external (such as a train whistle or a low-flying airplane) and internal (say, hunger pangs), may modify an ongoing dream, but they do not initiate dreams. Often dreams are so vivid that it is difficult to distinguish them from reality.

Dreams Vivid visual and auditory experiences that occur primarily during REM periods of sleep.

What Do We Dream?

Individuals vary widely in what they dream about, the feelings associated with their dreams, and how often they remember dreams. Nevertheless, some patterns stand out. Dream content is related to where you are in your sleep cycle, what you've been doing before you sleep, your gender, your age, and even your socioeconomic status. For example, although the dreams of men and women have become more similar over the last several decades, men more often dream about weapons, unfamiliar characters, male characters, aggressive interactions, and failure outcomes, whereas women are more likely to dream about being the victims of aggression (Bursik, 1998; Domhoff, 1996; Kolchakian & Hill, 2002).

Dream content also varies by age (Foulkes, 1999). Very young children (ages 2 to 5) tend to have brief dreams, many of which involve animals, but the images are usually unrelated to one another and there is seldom any emotion, narrative, or story line. It is not until the child is 7 to 9 years old that most dreams take on a narrative, sequential form. Feelings and emotions also make their appearance in dreams in the years between 7 and 9, and children more often appear as a character in their own dreams at that age. Between ages 9 and 15, dreams become more adultlike: Narratives follow well-developed story lines, other people play important roles, and there are many verbal exchanges, in addition to motor activity (Anch et al., 1988).

Finally, cross-cultural studies have shown that people from different cultures report dream content consistent with the unique cultural patterns inherent in their respective cultures (Domhoff, 1996).

Why Do We Dream?

Psychologists have long been fascinated by dream activity and the contents of dreams, and a number of explanations have been proposed.

Dreams as Unconscious Wishes   Sigmund Freud (1900), the first modern theorist to investigate this topic, called dreams the "royal road to the unconscious." Believing that dreams represent wishes that have not been fulfilled in reality, he asserted that people's dreams reflect the hidden motives that guide their behavior. Freud distinguished between the *manifest*, or surface, *content* of dreams and their *latent content*—the hidden, unconscious thoughts or desires that he believed were expressed indirectly through dreams.

The fanciful images of Marc Chagall's paintings capture the quality of many of our dreams. Is a dream of an entwined man and woman floating high above a city symbolic of some subconscious sexual desire, as Freud would have suggested? Or is it just an illogical image caused by random brain cell activity during sleep? As yet psychologists have no conclusive answer. Perhaps both views have merit.
Source: Marc Chagall (Russian, 1887–1985), "Above the City." Tretyakov Gallery, Moscow, Russia. SuperStock, Inc./© Artists Rights Society (ARS), New York.

According to Freud, people permit themselves to express primitive desires that are relatively free of moral controls in their dreams. For example, someone who is not consciously aware of hostile feelings toward a sister may dream about murdering her. But, even in a dream, such hostile feelings may be censored and transformed into a symbolic form. The desire to do away with one's sister (the dream's latent content) may be recast into the dream image of seeing her off at a train "terminal" (the dream's manifest content). Freud believed that this process of censorship and symbolic transformation accounts for the highly illogical nature of many dreams. Deciphering the disguised meanings of dreams is one of the principal tasks of psychoanalysts (Hill et al., 2000; Mazzoni, Lombardo, Malvagia, & Loftus, 1999).

Dreams and Information Processing   Another explanation for dreaming holds that in our dreams we reprocess information gathered during the day as a way of strengthening the memory of information crucial to survival (Carpenter, 2001; Winson, 1990). In support of this view, research has demonstrated that both humans and nonhumans spend more time in REM sleep after learning difficult material; furthermore, interfering with REM sleep immediately after learning severely disrupts the memory for the newly learned material (Smith, 1985; Smith & Kelly, 1988; Smith & Lapp, 1986). Brain-imaging studies have also found that the specific area of the brain most active while learning new material is also active during subsequent REM sleep (Maquet et al., 2000).

A variation on this view holds that people often solve problems or have flashes of insight—the "aha! experience"—during dreams. Anecdotes about creative dreams by famous inventors and artists support this idea. For example, Beethoven and Mozart are said to have heard symphonies in their dreams; the author Robert Louis Stevenson claimed that the idea for his novel *Dr. Jekyll and Mr. Hyde* came to him in a dream.

Other psychologists see dreams as a form of emotional processing where emotionally significant events are integrated with previous experiences (Farthing, 1992). For example, children's first experience of a carnival or amusement park is usually a blend of terror and excitement. Later in life, whenever they have experiences that are exciting but also somewhat frightening, carnival rides or images may dominate their dreams. Some psychologists (Cartwright, 1996) have suggested that we work through problems in our dreams—indeed, that dreams are part of the healing process after a divorce, death of a loved one, or other emotional crises. It remains unclear whether these breakthroughs are more the result of foresight or hindsight than of dreams themselves (Domhoff, 1996).

Dreams and Neural Activity   Alan Hobson (1988) stunned other dream researchers when he proposed that dreams are simply the result of neurons misfiring and are, in themselves, meaningless. According to Hobson's *activation-synthesis theory*, neurons in the pons which is a part of the brain stem (see Chapter 2) fire at random during REM sleep. Although the resulting neural signals are gibberish, higher brain centers strive to make sense of them, weaving the irrational and impossible stories we call dreams.

New research, using advanced brain-imaging techniques, provides a somewhat different picture. Braun and his colleagues (1998) found that the limbic system, which is involved with emotions, motivations, and memories, is "wildly" active during dreams, so, to a lesser extent, are the visual and auditory areas of the forebrain that process sensory information. However, areas of the forebrain involved in working memory, attention, logic, and self-monitoring are relatively inactive during dreams. This could explain the highly emotional texture of dreams, as well as bizarre imagery, and the loss of critical insight, logic, and self-reflection. This uncensored mixture of desires, fears, and memories comes very close to the psychoanalytic concept of unconscious wishes, suggesting that Freud may have come closer to the meaning of dreams than many contemporary psychologists have acknowledged.

Dreams and Waking Life   Still another theory maintains that dreams are an extension of the conscious concerns of daily life in altered (but not disguised) form (Domhoff, 1996). Research has shown that what people dream about is generally similar to what they think about and do while awake. For example, an athlete may dream about past, future, or imagined competitions; a parent who's having problems with a child may dream about childhood confrontations with his or her own parents. Dream content also appears to be relatively "consistent" for most individuals, displaying similar themes across years and even decades (Domhoff, 1996). Moreover, many of our dreams seem realistic and coherent while they are occurring and even after we are awake (Squire & Domhoff, 1998).

Do We Need to Dream?

Freud suggested that dreams serve as a psychic safety valve. If his theory is correct, depriving people of the opportunity to dream should significantly affect their waking lives, and to some extent research has supported this idea.

In early experiments designed to study the effects of dream deprivation, people were awakened just as they entered REM sleep. (Early investigators targeted the REM period because it was believed at the time that dreams occurred almost exclusively during REM sleep.) The participants in these experiments became anxious, testy, and hungry. They had difficulty concentrating and even hallucinated during their waking hours. All of these ill effects vanished as soon as the people experienced REM sleep again (Dement, 1965; May & Kline, 1987).

In addition, when the people deprived of REM sleep were finally allowed to sleep undisturbed, the amount of REM sleep they displayed nearly doubled—a phenomenon called *REM rebound*.

Unfortunately, because these early researchers did not control for the dreaming that takes place outside of the REM period, it is difficult for us to know whether the changes they observed were due simply to the loss of sleep or to the decrease in REM-stage dreaming.

CHECK YOUR UNDERSTANDING

1. The average person has how many dreams in a night?

___ a. one or two

___ b. four or five

___ c. six or seven

___ d. ten or more

2. Freud named the unconscious desires expressed through dreams the

___ a. manifest content

___ b. latent period

___ c. latent content

___ d. stream of consciousness

Psychoactive drugs Chemical substances that change moods and perceptions.

3. Which adjective does NOT describe a person deprived of REM sleep?

___ a. hungry

___ b. alert

___ c. testy

___ d. anxious

Answers: 1.b, 2.c, 3.b

Drug-Altered Consciousness

How is today's drug problem different from the drug use in other societies and times?

In nearly every known culture throughout history, people have sought ways to alter waking consciousness, most often through the use of **psychoactive drugs**—chemical substances that change people's moods, perceptions, mental functioning, or behavior. In fact, many of the drugs available today, legally or illegally, have been used for thousands of years. For example, marijuana is mentioned in the herbal recipe book of a Chinese emperor, dating from 2737 B.C. Natives of the Andes Mountains in South America chew leaves of the coca plant (which contain cocaine) as a stimulant—a custom dating back at least to the Inca Empire of the fifteenth century. In the nineteenth century, Europeans began adding coca to wine, tea, and lozenges (Platt, 1997). In the United States, *laudanum*—opium dissolved in alcohol—was the main ingredient in numerous over-the-counter (or patent) medicines. Following this trend, in 1886 an Atlanta pharmacist combined crushed coca leaves from the Andes, caffeine-rich cola nuts from West Africa, cane sugar syrup, and carbonated water in a patent medicine he called "Coca-Cola."

Nicotine and alcohol are also psychoactive drugs with a long history of usage. In 1492, Christopher Columbus discovered not only America but also tobacco, which Native Americans used for religious and medicinal purposes. Columbus, other explorers, and their crews brought the plant—and the habit—back to Spain;

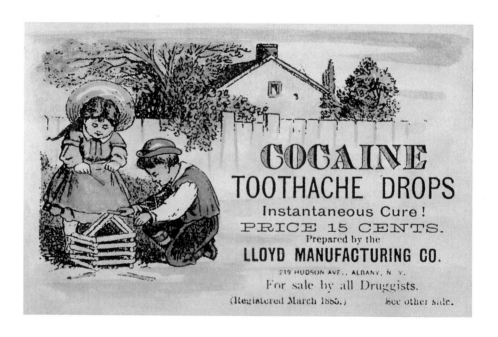

An 1885 American Advertisement for Cocaine Toothache Drops, obviously intended for young children as well as adults. The addition of cocaine to everyday products, including Coca-Cola, was quite common in the nineteenth century.

smoking for pleasure gradually spread throughout Europe. As for alcohol, archaeological evidence suggests that Late Stone Age groups began producing mead (fermented honey, flavored with sap or fruit) about 10,000 years ago. The Egyptians and Babylonians, Greeks and Romans, viewed wine as a "gift from the gods." Wine is frequently praised in the Bible—and drinking water is hardly mentioned.

Is today's "drug problem" different from the drug use in other societies and times? In many ways, the answer is yes. First, motives for using psychoactive drugs have changed. In most cultures, psychoactive substances have been used as part of religious rituals, as medicines and tonics, as nutrient beverages, or as culturally approved stimulants (much as we drink coffee). In contrast, the use of alcohol and other drugs in our society today is primarily *recreational*. For the most part, people use psychoactive drugs to relax, have fun with friends (and strangers), or get high either in settings specifically designed for recreation and inebriation or privately in their homes. Whether social or solitary, the use of psychoactive substances today is largely divorced from religious and family traditions.

Second, the drugs themselves have changed. Today's psychoactive substances often are stronger than those used in other cultures and times. For most of Western history, wine (12 percent alcohol) was often diluted with water. Hard liquor (40 to 75 percent alcohol) only appeared in the tenth century A.D. And the heroin available on the streets today is stronger and more addictive that that available in the 1930s and 1940s.

Third, new, synthetic drugs appear regularly, with unpredictable consequences. In the1990s, the National Institute for Drug Abuse created a new category, "Club Drugs," for increasingly popular psychoactive substances manufactured in small laboratories or even home kitchens (from recipes available on the Internet). Because the source, psychoactive ingredients, and possible contaminants are unknown, the symptoms, toxicity, and short- or long-term consequences are also unknown—making these drugs especially dangerous. The fact that they are often consumed with alcohol multiplies the risks.

Finally, scientists and the public know more than in the past about the negative effects of some psychoactive drugs yet those drugs continue to be used widely. Cigarettes are an obvious example. The Surgeon General's Report issued in 1964 confirmed a direct link between smoking and heart disease, as well as lung cancer. Subsequent research establishing that cigarettes are harmful not only to smokers but also to people around them (second-hand smoke) and to their unborn babies (Ness et al., 1999). Nonetheless, tens of millions of Americans still smoke, and millions of others use drugs they know to be harmful.

Substance Use, Abuse, and Dependence

If we define drugs broadly, as we did earlier, to include caffeine, tobacco, and alcohol, then most people throughout the world use some type of drug on a regular basis. The majority of these people use such drugs in moderation and do not suffer ill effects. But for many, substance use escalates into **substance abuse**—a pattern of drug use that diminishes one's ability to fulfill responsibilities at home, at work, or at school—that

Substance abuse A pattern of drug use that diminishes the ability to fulfill responsibilities at home or at work or school, that results in repeated use of a drug in dangerous situations, or that leads to legal difficulties related to drug use.

THINKING CRITICALLY

Mental Illness and Substance Abuse

The relationship between substance abuse and mental illness is called *comorbidity*. The question is, which comes first? Or are both problems the result of some other factor(s)? Does substance abuse lead to psychological disorders, for example, by triggering panic attacks, episodes of depression, and in some cases symptoms of severe disorder (psychosis)? Or do people who suffer from persistent emotional problems, such as social phobia, generalized anxiety, or posttraumatic stress, use psychoactive drugs in an attempt to medicate themselves? Or does something else entirely predispose people to both mental illness and substance abuse?

1. Which explanation do you think is most plausible? Why do you think so?

2. What kind of research evidence would convince you that your position is correct?

3. What kind of research evidence would convince you that your position is incorrect and that another explanation is better?

Substance dependence A pattern of compulsive drug taking that results in tolerance, withdrawal symptoms, or other specific symptoms for at least a year.

Tolerance Phenomenon whereby higher doses of a drug are required to produce its original effects or to prevent withdrawal symptoms.

Withdrawal symptoms Unpleasant physical or psychological effects that follow the discontinuance of a dependence-producing substance.

results in repeated use of a drug in dangerous situations, or that leads to legal difficulties related to drug use. For example, people whose drinking causes ill health and problems within their families or on their job are abusing alcohol (D. Smith, 2001).

The reasons for this self-destructive behavior are not entirely clear, but some encouraging leads are beginning to emerge. For example, one researcher found that the "addicted brain" is qualitatively different from the nonaddicted brain in a variety of ways, including metabolism and responsiveness to environmental cues (Leshner, 1996). Other investigators have focused on the role played by neurotransmitters in the addictive process, noting that addictive drugs cause dopamine levels in the brain to increase (Glassman & Koob, 1996). Also, numerous studies have shown that people who are dependent on or addicted to alcohol or other drugs—including nicotine—have a higher rate of mental illness than the general population (e.g., Merikangas et al., 1996; Pomerleau, 1997). The reverse is also true: People suffering from psychological problems are more likely to abuse alcohol and other substances (Flynn et al., 1995). Whatever the reasons, substance abuse is America's leading health problem (Martin, 2001).

The ongoing abuse of many drugs, including alcohol, may lead to compulsive use of the substance, or **substance dependence,** also known as *addiction* (see Table 4–1). Although not everyone who abuses a psychoactive substance develops dependence, dependence usually follows a period of abuse. Dependence often leads to **tolerance** whereby higher doses of the drug are required to produce its original effects or to prevent **withdrawal symptoms** (the unpleasant physical or psychological effects following discontinued use of the substance).

In analyzing drugs and drug use, it is convenient to group psychoactive substances into three categories: *depressants, stimulants,* and *hallucinogens* (see *Summary Table: Drugs: Characteristics and Effects*). (We will look at a fourth category of psychoactive drugs, medications used in the treatment of mental illness, in Chapter 14, Therapies.) These categories are not rigid (the same drug may have multiple effects

table 4-1   SIGNS OF SUBSTANCE DEPENDENCE

The most recent clinical definition of dependence (American Psychiatric Association, 1994; also see Anthony & Helzer, 2002) describes a broad pattern of drug-related behaviors characterized by at least three of the following seven symptoms over a 12-month period:

1. Developing tolerance: needing increasing amounts of the substance to gain the desired effect or experiencing a diminished effect when using the same amount of the substance. For example, the person might have to drink an entire six-pack to get the same effect formerly experienced after drinking just one or two beers.
2. Experiencing withdrawal symptoms—physical and psychological problems that occur if the person tries to stop using the substance. Withdrawal symptoms range from anxiety and nausea to convulsions and hallucinations.
3. Using the substance for a longer period or in greater quantities than intended.
4. Having a persistent desire or making repeated efforts to cut back on the use of the substance.
5. Devoting a great deal of time to obtaining or using the substance.
6. Giving up or reducing social, occupational, or recreational activities as a result of drug use.
7. Continuing to use the substance even in the face of ongoing or recurring physical or psychological problems likely to be caused or made worse by the use of the substance.

summarytable DRUGS: CHARACTERISTICS AND EFFECTS

	Typical Effects	Effects of Overdose	Tolerance/Dependence
Depressants			
Alcohol	Biphasic; tension-reduction "high," followed by depressed physical and psychological functioning.	Disorientation, loss of consciousness, death at extremely high blood-alcohol levels.	Tolerance; physical and psychological dependence; withdrawal symptoms.
Barbiturates Tranquilizers	Depressed reflexes and impaired motor functioning, tension reduction.	Shallow respiration, clammy skin, dilated pupils, weak and rapid pulse, coma, possible death.	Tolerance; high psychological and physical dependence on barbiturates, low to moderate physical dependence on such tranquilizers as Valium, although high psychological dependence; withdrawal symptoms.
Opiates	Euphoria, drowsiness, "rush" of pleasure, little impairment of psychological functions.	Slow shallow breathing, clammy skin, nausea, vomiting, pinpoint pupils, convulsions, coma, possible death.	High tolerance; physical and psychological dependence; severe withdrawal symptoms.
Stimulants			
Amphetamines Cocaine Caffeine Nicotine	Increased alertness, excitation, euphoria, increased pulse rate and blood pressure, sleeplessness.	For amphetamines and cocaine: agitation and, with chronic high doses, hallucinations (e.g., "cocaine bugs"), paranoid delusions, convulsions, death. For caffeine and nicotine: restlessness, insomnia, rambling thoughts, heart arrhythmia, possible circulatory failure. For nicotine: increased blood pressure.	For amphetamines, cocaine and nicotine: tolerance, psychological and physical dependence. For caffeine: physical and psychological dependence; withdrawal symptoms.
Hallucinogens			
LSD	Illusions, hallucinations, distortions in time perception, loss of contact with reality.	Psychotic reactions.	No physical dependence for LSD; degree of psychological dependence unknown for LSD.
Marijuana	Euphoria, relaxed inhibitions, increased appetite, possible disorientation.	Fatigue, disoriented behavior, possible psychosis.	Psychological dependence.

or different effects on different users), but this division helps organize our knowledge about drugs.

Depressants: Alcohol, Barbiturates, and Opiates

Depressants are chemicals that retard behavior and thinking by either speeding up or slowing down nerve impulses. Generally speaking, alcohol, barbiturates, and the opiates have depressant effects. People take depressants to reduce tension, to forget their troubles, or to relieve feelings of inadequacy, loneliness, or boredom.

Depressants Chemicals that slow down behavior or cognitive processes.

Alcohol Depressant that is the intoxicating ingredient in whiskey, beer, wine, and other fermented or distilled liquors.

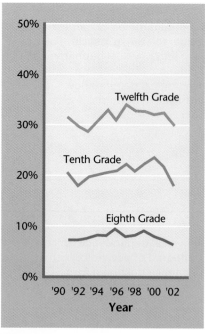

Figure 4–4

Teenage Use of Alcohol (% Drunk in Past 30 Days)

A national survey found that use of alcohol by American teenagers has begun to diminish slightly after 1999. Thirty percent of 12th graders reported getting drunk during the past 30 days in 2002, down from approximately 32 percent in 2001.

Source: Johnston, L D., O'Malley, P.M., & Bachman, J. G. (2003). Monitoring the future national survey results on adolescent drug use: Overview of key findings, 2002 (NIH Publication No. 03-5374). Bethesda, MD: National Institute on Drug Abuse. Reprinted with permission from Monitoring the Future © 2002.

Alcohol The most frequently used psychoactive drug in Western societies is **alcohol.** Many Americans see nothing wrong with moderate social drinking. Most physicians agree, with qualifications: For healthy adults, there is little harm in having one or two glasses of wine, cans of beer, or shots of liquor a day—unless the person is pregnant, taking prescription or over-the-counter medications, working with potentially dangerous equipment, or planning to drive or go for a boat ride. Indeed, moderate drinking may reduce the risk of cardiovascular disease for both men and women.

But in spite of, or perhaps because of, the fact that it is legal and socially approved, alcohol is America's number one drug problem. At least 14 million Americans have problems with drinking, including more than 8 million alcoholics who are addicted to alcohol. Three times as many men as women are problem drinkers. For both sexes, alcohol abuse and addiction is highest in the 18- to 29-year-old age group. After rising in the 1990s, alcohlol use by American teenagers has diminished slightly (see Figure 4–4).

Alcohol is a highly addictive drug with potentially devastating long-term effects. Heavy, chronic drinking can harm virtually every organ in the body, beginning with the brain. Chronic and excessive alcohol use is associated with impairments in perceptual-motor skills, visual-spatial processing, problem solving, and abstract reasoning (Nixon, 1999). Alcohol is the leading cause of liver disease and kidney damage; is a major factor in cardiovascular disease; increases the risk of certain cancers; and can lead to sexual dysfunction and infertility. Alcohol is particularly damaging to the nervous system during the teenage years. Areas of the brain that are not fully developed until age twenty-one are especially susceptible to damage from high levels of alcohol intoxication (Ballie, 2001). Approximately 100,000 Americans die each year as a result of using alcohol with other drugs or from alcohol-related problems, making it the third leading cause of preventable mortality, after tobacco and diet/activity patterns (Van Natta, Malin, Bertolucci, & Kaelbert, 1985).

The social costs of abusing alcohol are also high. Alcohol is involved in a substantial proportion of violent and accidental deaths, including suicides, which makes it the leading contributor (after AIDS) to death among young people. Alcohol is implicated in more than two-thirds of all fatal automobile accidents, two-thirds of all murders, two-thirds of all spouse beatings, and more than half of all cases of violent child abuse. Moreover, the use of alcohol during pregnancy has been linked to a variety of birth defects, the most notable being fetal alcohol syndrome (see Chapter 10, Life Span Development).

All told, alcohol abuse costs society more than $150 billion a year through lost productivity, crime, accidents, and medical treatment (Steele & Josephs, 1990; National Institute on Drug Abuse, 1999). In addition, there is the untold cost in psychological trauma suffered by the nearly 30 million children of alcohol abusers.

What makes alcohol so powerful? Physiologically, alcohol first affects the frontal lobes of the brain (Adams & Johnson-Greene, 1995), which figure prominently in inhibitions, impulse control, reasoning, and judgment. As consumption continues, alcohol impairs functions of the cerebellum, the center of motor control and balance (Johnson-Greene et al., 1997). Eventually, alcohol consumption affects the spinal cord and medulla, which regulate such involuntary functions as breathing, body temperature, and heart rate. A blood-alcohol level of 0.25 percent or more may cause this part of the nervous system to shut down and severely impairs functioning; slightly higher levels can cause death from alcohol poisoning (see Table 4–2).

The psychological effects of alcohol depend not only on the individual, the social setting, and cultural attitudes but also on how much a person consumes and how fast (see Table 4–2). Even in moderate quantities, alcohol affects perception, motor processes, memory, and judgment. It diminishes visual acuity, depth perception,

table 4-2 THE BEHAVIORAL EFFECTS OF BLOOD-ALCOHOL LEVELS

Levels of Alcohol in the Blood	Behavioral Effects
0.05%	Feels good; less alert
0.10%	Slower to react; less cautious
0.15%	Reaction time much slower
0.20%	Sensory-motor abilities suppressed
0.25%	Staggering (motor abilities severely impaired); perception is limited as well
0.30%	Semistupor
0.35%	Level for anesthesia; death is possible
0.40%	Death is likely (usually as a result of respiratory failure)

Source: Data from *Drugs, Society, and Human Behavior* (3 ed.) by Oakey Ray, 1983, St. Louis: The C. V. Mosby Co.

Since ancient times people have recognized the problems associated with alcohol abuse. Excessive drinking and public drunkenness have been widely frowned on in many cultures. In this etching, Gin Lane, by the eigteenth-century English artist William Hogarth, a baby slips carelessly from the arms of a drunken mother.
Source: William Hogarth (1697–1765), *Gin Lane.* The Metropolitan Museum of Art, Harris Brisbane Dick Fund, 1932.

perception of the differences between bright lights and colors and spatial-cognitive functioning—all clearly necessary for driving a car safely (Matthews, Best, White, Vandergriff, & Simson, 1996). Prolonged drinking impairs overall retrieval of memories and may also cause *blackouts*, which make drinkers unable to remember anything that occurred while they were drinking.

The term *alcohol myopia* (Herzog, 1999; Steele & Josephs, 1990) refers to the alcohol-induced shortsightedness that makes drinkers oblivious to many behavioral cues in the environment and less able to make sense of those cues they do perceive, which leads to poor judgments (Nixon, 1999). For example, dozens of studies demonstrate that alcohol is correlated with increases in aggression, hostility, violence, and abusive behavior (Bushman, 1993; Bushman & Cooper, 1990; Ito, Miller, & Pollock, 1996). Thus intoxication makes people less aware of and less concerned

Statistics show that alcohol use is a major cause of car accidents.

about the negative consequences of their actions. The same principle applies to potential victims. A recent study demonstrated that when women are intoxicated, their ability to accurately evaluate a dangerous situation with a potential male aggressor is diminished, so that their risk of being sexually assaulted increases (Testa, Livingston, & Collins, 2000). Alcoholic myopia also explains why people who are intoxicated are more likely to engage in unprotected sex than if they were sober (MacDonald, Fong, Zanna, & Martineau, 2000; MacDonald, MacDonald, Zanna, & Fong, 2000).

ENDURING ISSUES   **diversity**universality

Women and Alcohol

Women are especially vulnerable to the effects of alcohol (National Institute on Alcohol Abuse and Alcoholism, 2000c). Because women generally weigh less than men, the same dose of alcohol has a stronger effect on the average woman than on the average man (York & Welte, 1994). In addition, most women have lower levels of the stomach enzyme that regulates alcohol metabolism. The less of this enzyme in the stomach, the greater the amount of alcohol that passes into the bloodstream and spreads through the body. (This is why drinking on an empty stomach has more pronounced effects than drinking with meals [Frezza et al., 1990].) As a rough measure, one drink is likely to have the same effects on a woman as two drinks have on a man.

As a depressant, alcohol calms the nervous system, much like a general anesthetic (McKim, 1997). Thus, people consume alcohol to relax or to enhance their mood (Steele & Josephs, 1990). Paradoxically, alcohol is often experienced subjectively as a stimulant because it inhibits centers in the brain that govern critical judgment and impulsive behavior. Alcohol makes people feel more courageous, less inhibited, more spontaneous, and more entertaining (Steele & Josephs, 1990).

The good news is that since 1977, overall consumption of alcohol has dropped by 17 percent—and consumption of hard liquor, by almost 40 percent (Knapp, 1999). Alcohol-related traffic deaths, while still too common, are also declining (see Figure 4–5). The alarming news is that drinking in high school (and earlier) is still common: More than 50 percent of high school seniors say they get drunk. And binge drinking has become a dangerous "tradition" on college campuses.

Binge Drinking on College Campuses One of the few places today where drunkenness is tolerated, and often expected, is the American college campus. National surveys of 140 colleges and universities, conducted in 1993 and again in 1997 and 1999, found that almost half of college students engage in "binge drinking," defined as five or more drinks in a row for men, four or more drinks for women (Wechsher, Dowdall, Davenport, & DeJong, 2000). The extent of binge drinking at different schools ranged from 1 percent to 70 percent, indicating that the campus environment is an important influence on drinking patterns.

About half of binge drinkers—one in five students overall—had gone on binges three or more times during the two weeks before the survey and been intoxicated three or more times over the past month. Most of these students cited getting drunk as their main reason for drinking. Regardless of how much they drank, very few (less than 1 percent) considered themselves "problem drinkers."

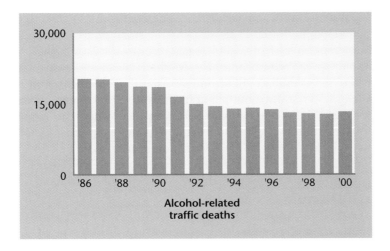

Figure 4–5
Alcohol-related traffic deaths.
Alcohol-related traffic deaths have generally declined since the 1980's although the total number for the most recent year, 13,050 in 2000, is still tragically high.

It is not surprising that frequent binge drinkers had more problems, and more serious problems, than other students. Many had missed classes, fallen behind in schoolwork, engaged in unplanned—and unprotected—sex, gotten in trouble with campus police, engaged in vandalism, or been hurt or injured. Bingers were more likely than other students to have used other drugs, especially cigarettes and marijuana. They were 10 times more likely to have driven a car after drinking and more than 15 times more likely to have ridden with a driver who was drunk or high.

The effects of binge drinking are not limited to students who participate. At schools with high binge rates, a majority of students report that they have been unable to study or sleep because of binge drinking. Many sober students have cared for drunken friends, endured drunken insults, and fended off unwanted sexual advances. Yet most are reluctant to report these problems to campus or other authorities.

Researchers emphasize that the majority of students at four-year institutions—56 percent nationally—abstain or drink in moderation, a strong foundation for change. Nevertheless, binge drinking is an extremely serious problem that not only interferes with education but also carries a high risk of disease, injury, and death.

Barbiturates   **Barbiturates,** which are commonly known as "downers," include such medications as Amytal, Nembutal, and Seconal. Discovered about a century ago, this class of depressants was first prescribed for its sedative and anticonvulsant qualities. But in the 1950s, after researchers recognized that barbiturates had potentially deadly effects—particularly in combination with alcohol—their use declined, though they are still sometimes prescribed to treat insomnia, anxiety, epilepsy, arthritis, and bed-wetting (Reinisch & Sanders, 1982). Though the barbiturates phenobarbital, Amytal, Nembutal, and Seconal are often prescribed to help people sleep, they actually disrupt the body's natural sleep patterns and cause dependence when used for long periods. Frequently prescribed for elderly people, who tend to take them chronically along with other medications, barbiturates may produce confusion and anxiety and other significant side effects (Celis, 1994).

The general effects of barbiturates are strikingly similar to those of alcohol: Taken on an empty stomach, a small dose causes light-headedness, silliness, and poor motor coordination (McKim, 1997), whereas larger doses may bring on slurred speech, loss of inhibition, and increases in aggression (Aston, 1972). When taken during pregnancy, barbiturates, like alcohol, produce such birth defects as cleft palates and malformations of the heart, skeleton, and central nervous system disorders (Wilder & Bruni, 1981).

Barbiturates Potentially deadly depressants, first used for their sedative and anticonvulsant properties, now used only to treat such conditions as epilepsy and arthritis.

Opiates Drugs, such as opium and heroin, derived from the opium poppy, that dull the senses and induce feelings of euphoria, well-being, and relaxation. Synthetic drugs resembling opium derivatives are also classified as opiates.

Stimulants Drugs, including amphetamines and cocaine, that stimulate the sympathetic nervous system and produce feelings of optimism and boundless energy.

Opiates   Psychoactive substances derived from, or resembling, the seedpod of the opium poppy, **opiates** have a long history of use—though not always abuse. A Sumerian tablet from 4,000 B.C. refers to the "joy plant." Originating in Turkey, opium spread west around the Mediterranean and east through India into China, where it was used in pill or liquid form in folk medicines for thousands of years. But changes in the way opium and its derivative, morphine, were used opened the door to abuse. In the mid-seventeenth century, when the emperor of China banned tobacco and the Chinese began to smoke opium, addiction quickly followed. During the American Civil War, physicians used a new invention, the hypodermic needle, to administer morphine, a much-needed painkiller for soldiers. In this form, morphine was far more addictive than smoking opium. Heroin—introduced in 1898 as a cure for morphine addiction—created an even stronger dependency. When the non-medicinal distribution of opiates was banned early in the twentieth century, a black market for heroin developed. In the public mind, the heroin addict became synonymous with the "dope fiend," the embodiment of social evil.

Heroin and other opiates resemble endorphins, the natural painkillers produced by the body, and occupy many of the same nerve-receptor sites (see Chapter 2, The Biological Basis of Behavior). Heroin users report a surge of euphoria soon after taking the drug, followed by a period of "nodding off" and clouded mental functioning. Regular use leads to tolerance which in turn may lead to physical dependence. In advanced stages of addiction, heroin becomes primarily a painkiller to stave off withdrawal symptoms. These symptoms, which may begin within hours of the last dose, include profuse sweating; alternating hot flashes and chills with goose bumps resembling the texture of a plucked turkey (hence the term *cold turkey*); severe cramps, vomiting, and diarrhea; and convulsive shaking and kicking (as in "kicking the habit").

Heroin abuse is associated with serious health conditions, including fatal overdose, spontaneous abortion, collapsed veins, pulmonary problems, and infectious diseases, especially HIV/AIDS and hepatitis as a result of sharing needles (Bourgois, 1999). The mortality rate of heroin users is almost 15 times higher than that of nonusers (Inciardi & Harrison, 1998). No longer solely an inner-city problem, its use is growing in suburbs and among young people and women, who often inhale or smoke heroin in the mistaken belief that it is not dangerous in this form (Kantrowitz, Rosenberg, Rogers, Beachy, & Holmes, 1993; National Institute on Drug Abuse, 2000c).

Stimulants: Caffeine, Nicotine, Amphetamines, and Cocaine

The drugs classified as stimulants range from mild, widely used substances (such as the caffeine in coffee) to the most dangerous and addictive substances known (amphetamines, cocaine, and not least of all nicotine). What all **stimulants** have in common is that they excite the central nervous system, temporarily increasing mental alertness and reducing physical fatigue. In effect, stimulants put the mind and body on alert by artificially stimulating the *fight-or-flight* response (see Chapter 12, Stress and Health Psychology).

Caffeine   Caffeine occurs naturally in coffee, tea, cocoa, and chocolate, and often is added to cola drinks and over-the-counter medications (see Figure 4–6). Probably the most widely used and socially acceptable stimulant, caffeine gives coffee and cola drinkers a "boost" (partly by slightly increasing heart rate). Although relatively benign, caffeine can become addictive. Heavy users may experience withdrawal symptoms (fatigue, headaches, and difficulty concentrating). Excessive use can lead to insomnia, gastrointestinal problems, and elevated blood pressure.

Nineteenth-century immigrants to the United States are shown gambling and smoking opium pipes at a clubhouse in New York's Chinatown. Problems associated with abuse of this drug led to it being banned for non-medical use early in the twentieth century.

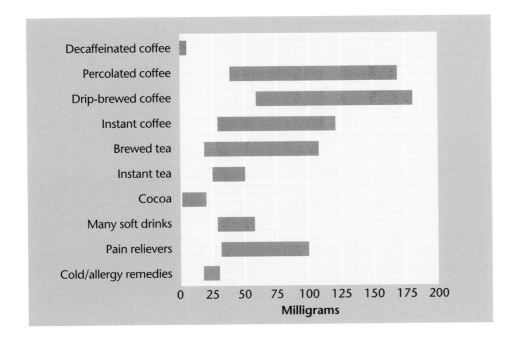

Figure 4–6
The amount of caffeine in some common preparations.
Caffeine occurs in varying amounts in coffee, tea, soft drinks, and many nonprescription medications. Americans consume about 200 mg of caffeine each day.
Source: New York Times, August 7, 1991. Copyright © 1991 by the New York Times. Reprinted with permission.

Caffeine suppresses naturally occurring sedatives, and so may interfere with prescribed medications such as tranquilizers. But caffeine may also have positive effects. One team of medical researchers found that the incidence of Parkinson's disease is lower in men who drink more than three cups of coffee per day (Ross et al., 2000).

Nicotine   Nicotine, the addictive ingredient in tobacco, is probably the most dangerous and addictive stimulant in use today. Recent studies have found that the neurochemical properties of nicotine are similar to those of cocaine, amphetamines, and morphine (Glassman & Koob, 1996; Pontieri, Tanda, Orzi, & DiChiara, 1996). When smoked, nicotine tends to arrive at the brain all at once following each puff—a rush similar to the "high" experienced by heroin users. The smoker's heart rate increases and blood vessels constrict, causing dull skin and cold hands and accelerating the process of wrinkling and aging (Daniell, 1971). Nicotine affects levels of several neurotransmitters, including norepinephrine, dopamine, and serotonin, and depending on the time, the amount smoked, and other factors, may have sedating or stimulating effects. Symptoms of withdrawal from nicotine include nervousness, difficulty concentrating, both insomnia and drowsiness, headaches, irritability, and intense craving, which continue for weeks and may recur months or even years after a smoker has quit (Brandon, 1994). Despite well-known health risks and strong social pressures, millions of Americans continue to smoke, either for the pleasure of the combined stimulant/sedative effects, or to prevent cravings and withdrawal symptoms. Particularly worrisome, the number of teenagers who start smoking each year has hardly changed. Youth aged 12 to 17 who smoke are about 12 times more likely to use illicit drugs, and sixteen times more likely to drink heavily, than their nonsmoking peers and have an increased risk of depression (National Household Survey on Drug Abuse, 1998; D. Smith, 2001).

Amphetamines   Amphetamines are powerful synthetic stimulants, first marketed in the 1930s as a nasal spray to relieve symptoms of asthma. At the chemical level, **amphetamines** resemble epinephrine, a hormone that stimulates the sympathetic nervous system (see Chapter 2, The Biological Basis of Behavior). During World War II, the military routinely gave soldiers amphetamines in pill form to relieve

Amphetamines Stimulant drugs that initially produce "rushes" of euphoria often followed by sudden "crashes" and, sometimes, severe depression.

Cocaine Drug derived from the coca plant that, while producing a sense of euphoria by stimulating the sympathetic nervous system, also leads to anxiety, depression, and addictive cravings.

fatigue. After the war, the demand for "pep pills" grew among night workers, truck drivers, students, and athletes. Because amphetamines tend to suppress the appetite, they were widely prescribed as "diet pills."

Amphetamines not only increase alertness but also produce feelings of competence and well-being. People who inject them intravenously report a "rush" of euphoria. After the drug's effects wear off, however, users may "crash" into a state of exhaustion and depression (Gunne & Anggard, 1972). As a result, amphetamines are habit-forming: Users may come to believe that they cannot function without them. Some develop tolerance. High doses can cause sweating, tremors, heart palpitations, anxiety, and insomnia—which may lead people to take barbiturates or drugs to counteract these effects. Excessive use may cause personality changes, including paranoia, homicidal and suicidal thoughts, and aggressive, violent behavior (Leccese, 1991). Chronic users may develop amphetamine psychosis, which resembles paranoid schizophrenia and is characterized by delusions, hallucinations, and paranoia. The label "dope fiend" more accurately describes the behavior of amphetamine addicts than that of heroin addicts!

Methamphetamine—known on the street as "speed" and "fire," or in a crystal, smokable form as "ice," "crystal," and "crank"—is easily produced in clandestine laboratories from ingredients available over the counter. An increasingly popular variation, *Ecstasy* (methylenedioxymethamphetamine or MDMA), acts as both a stimulant and an hallucinogen. The name *Ecstasy* reflects the users' belief that the drug makes people love and trust one another, puts them in touch with their own emotions, and heightens sexual pleasure. Short-term physical effects include involuntary teeth clenching (which is why users often wear baby pacifiers around their neck or suck lollipops), faintness, and chills or sweating. Even short-term recreational use of MDMA may have long-term harmful consequences, affecting sleep, mood, appetite, and impulsiveness by damaging the neuroconnections between lower brain centers and the cortex (Kish, Furukawa, Ang, Vorce, & Kalasinsky, 2000; McCann, Slate, & Ricaurte, 1996; McCann, Szabo, Scheffel, Dannals, & Ricaurte, 1998). Moreover, the use of Ecstasy during pregnancy has been associated with birth defects (McElhatton, Bateman, Evan, Pughe, & Thomas, 1999). One recent study also found that the recreational use of Ecstasy may lead to a decrease in intelligence test scores (Gouzoulis-Mayfrank et al., 2000). Animal research going back more than 20 years shows that high doses of methamphetamine damage the axon terminals of dopamine- and serotonin-containing neurons, perhaps permanently (National Institute on Drug Abuse, 2000b; Ricaurte, Yuan, Hatzidimitriou, Cord, McCann, 2002). Increased public awareness of the dangers associated with ecstasy explains in large part the recent and sharp decline in its usage (Johnston, O'Malley, & Bachman, 2003). Figure 4–7 illustrates the drop in teenage use of this drug. The only legitimate medical uses for amphetamines are to treat narcolepsy and attention deficit disorder (paradoxically, amphetamines have a calming effect on hyperactive children).

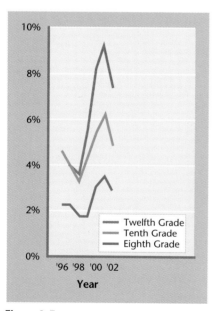

Figure 4–7
Teenage Use of Ecstasy in Past Year
Teenage use of ecstasy has dropped sharply in recent years after rising steadily after 1998.
Source: Johnston, L D., O'Malley, P. M., & Bachman, J. G. (2003). Monitoring the future national survey results on adolescent drug use: Overview of key findings, 2002 (NIH Publication No. 03-5374). Bethesda, MD: National Institute on Drug Abuse. Reprinted with permission from Monitoring the Future © 2002.

Cocaine First isolated from cocoa leaves in 1885, **cocaine** came to be used widely as a topical anesthetic for minor surgery (and still is, for example, in the dental anesthetic Novocain). Around the turn of the century, many physicians believed cocaine was beneficial as a general stimulant, as well as a cure for excessive use of alcohol and morphine addiction. Among the more famous cocaine users was Sigmund Freud. When he discovered how addictive cocaine was, Freud campaigned against it, as did many of his contemporaries, and ingesting the drug fell into disrepute.

Cocaine made a comeback in the 1970s in such unlikely places as Wall Street, among investment bankers who found that the drug not only made them high but also allowed them to wheel and deal around the clock with little sleep (Califano, 1999). In the white powdered form that is snorted (street names "coke" and "snow"), it became a status drug, the amphetamine of the wealthy. In the 1980s, a cheaper, smokable, crystallized form known as "crack" (made from the by-products of cocaine extraction) appeared in inner-city neighborhoods. Crack reaches the brain in less than 10 seconds, producing a high that lasts from 5 to 20 minutes, followed by a swift and equally intense depression. Users report that crack leads to almost instantaneous addiction. Addiction to powdered cocaine, which has longer effects, is not inevitable but likely. Babies born to women addicted to crack and cocaine often are premature or low-birth-weight, may have withdrawal symptoms, and enter school with subtle deficits in intelligence and language skills (Inciardi, Surratt, & Saum, 1997).

On the biochemical level, cocaine blocks the reabsorption of the neurotransmitter dopamine, which is associated with awareness, motivation, and, most significantly, pleasure (Swan, 1998). From an evolutionary perspective, dopamine rewards such survival-related activities as eating, drinking, and engaging in sex. Excess dopamine intensifies and prolongs feelings of pleasure—hence the cocaine user's feelings of euphoria. Normally, dopamine is reabsorbed, which leads to feelings of satiety or satisfaction; dopamine reabsorption tells the body, "That's enough." But cocaine short-circuits this feeling of satisfaction, in effect telling the body, "more!" In addition, cocaine damages the brain cells that produce dopamine, thus increasing the amount of cocaine needed to get the same high in the future (Little, Krowlewski, Zhang, & Cassin, 2003).

Hallucinogens and Marijuana

The hallucinogens include lysergic acid diethylamide (LSD, also known as "acid"), mescaline, peyote, and psilocybin. Even in very small doses, these drugs can cause striking perceptual experiences that resemble hallucinations, hence the term *hallucinogen*. Marijuana is sometimes included in this group, although its effects are normally less powerful. In large enough doses, many other drugs bring on hallucinatory or delusional experiences, mimicking those that occur in severe mental illnesses; hallucinogens do so in small doses, usually without toxic effects.

Hallucinogens   **Hallucinogens** are natural or synthetic drugs that cause shifts in perception of the outside world or, in some cases, experience of imaginary landscapes, settings, and beings that may seem more real than the outside world. How many cultural groups have used hallucinogens is not known. Historians believe that Native Americans have used mescaline, a psychedelic substance found in the mushroom-shaped tops or "buttons" of peyote cactus, for at least 8,000 years.

By contrast, the story of **lysergic acid diethylamide (LSD),** the drug that triggered the current interest in the hallucinogens, begins in the twentieth century. In 1943, an American pharmacologist synthesized LSD, and after ingesting it, he reported experiencing "an uninterrupted stream of fantastic pictures and extraordinary shapes with an intense, kaleidoscopic play of colors." His report led others to experiment with LSD as an artificial form of psychosis, a painkiller for terminal cancer patients, and a cure for alcoholism in the 1950s (Ashley, 1975). LSD came to public attention in the 1960s, when Harvard psychologist Timothy Leary, after trying the related hallucinogen psilocybin, began spreading the "Turn On, Tune In, Drop Out" gospel of the hippie movement. Use

Hallucinogens Any of a number of drugs, such as LSD and mescaline, that distort visual and auditory perception.

Lysergic acid diethylamide (LSD) Hallucinogenic or "psychedelic" drug that produces hallucinations and delusions similar to those occurring in a psychotic state.

These Native American women in Mexico are grinding dry peyote that will be mixed with water and drunk during an upcoming festival. Many Native American peoples have traditionally included peyote in their religious ceremonies.

Marijuana A mild hallucinogen that produces a "high" often characterized by feelings of euphoria, a sense of well-being, and swings in mood from gaiety to relaxation; may also cause feelings of anxiety and paranoia.

of LSD and marijuana (see below) declined steadily in the 1970s, but became popular once again in the 1990s, especially with high school and college students (Janofsky, 1994).

About an hour after ingesting LSD, people begin to experience an intensification of sensory perception, loss of control over their thoughts and emotions, and feelings of depersonalization and detachment, as if they were watching themselves from a distance. Some LSD users say things never looked or sounded or smelled so beautiful; others have terrifying, nightmarish visions. Some experience a sense of extraordinary mental lucidity; others become so confused they fear they are losing their minds. The effects of LSD are highly variable, even for the same person on different occasions.

"Bad trips," or unpleasant experiences, may be set off by a change in dosage or an alteration in setting or mood. During a bad trip, the user may not realize that the experiences are being caused by the drug, and panic. *Flashbacks*, or recurrences of hallucinations, may occur weeks after ingesting LSD. Other consequences of frequent use may include memory loss, paranoia, panic attacks, nightmares, and aggression (Gold, 1994; Seligmann, 1992).

Unlike depressants and stimulants, LSD and the other hallucinogens do not appear to produce withdrawal effects. If LSD is taken repeatedly, tolerance builds up rapidly: After a few days no amount of the drug will produce its usual effects, until use is suspended for about a week (McKim, 1997). This acts as a built-in deterrent to continuous use, which helps explain why LSD is generally taken episodically rather than habitually. After a time, users seem to get tired of the experience and decrease or discontinue their use of the drug, at least for a period of time.

Marijuana   Marijuana is a mixture of dried, shredded flowers and leaves of the hemp plant *Cannabis sativa* (which is also a source of fiber for rope and fabrics). Unlike LSD, marijuana usage has a long history. In China, cannabis has been cultivated for at least 5,000 years. The ancient Greeks knew about its psychoactive effects, and it has been used as an intoxicant in India for centuries. But only in the twentieth century did marijuana become popular in the United States. Today marijuana is the most frequently used illegal drug in the United States, and the fourth most popular drug among students, after alcohol, caffeine, and nicotine (Treaster, 1994). Figure 4–8 shows the increase in marijuana use by adolescents in recent years.

Although the active ingredient in marijuana, *tetrahydrocannabinol* (THC), shares some chemical properties with hallucinogens like LSD, it is far less potent. Marijuana smokers report feelings of relaxation; heightened enjoyment of food, music, and sex; a loss of awareness of time; and on occasion, dreamlike experiences. As with LSD, experiences are varied. Many users experience a sense of well-being, and some feel euphoric, but others become suspicious, anxious, and depressed.

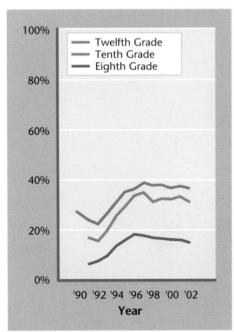

Figure 4–8
Teenage Use of Marijuana in Past Year
A national survey found that use of marijuana by American teenagers has leveled off in recent years after rising steadily in the 1990s.
Source: Johnston, L D., O'Malley, P.M., & Bachman, J. G. (2003). Monitoring the future national survey results on adolescent drug use: Overview of key findings, 2002 (NIH Publication No. 03-5374). Bethesda, MD: National Institute on Drug Abuse. Reprinted with permission of Monitoring the Future © 2002.

Marijuana has direct physiological effects, including dilation of the blood vessels in the eyes, making the eyes appear bloodshot; a dry mouth and coughing (because it is generally smoked); increased thirst and hunger; and mild muscular weakness, often in the form of drooping eyelids (Donatelle & Davis, 1993). The major physiological dangers of marijuana are potential respiratory and cardiovascular damage, including triggering heart attacks (Mittleman, 2000; Sridhar, Ruab, & Weatherby, 1994). Among the drug's psychological effects is a distortion of time, which has been confirmed under experimental conditions (Chait & Pierri, 1992): Feelings that minutes occur in slow motion, or that hours flash by in seconds, are common. In addition, marijuana may produce alterations in short-term memory and attention.

While under the influence of marijuana, people often lose the ability to remember and coordinate information, a phenomenon known as *temporal disintegration*. For instance, someone who is "high" on marijuana may forget what he or she was talking about in mid-sentence. Such memory lapses may trigger anxiety and panic (Hollister, 1986; Leccese, 1991). While high, marijuana users have shortened attention spans and delayed reactions, which contribute to concerns about their ability to drive a car or to study or work effectively (Chait & Pierri, 1992; National Institute on Drug Abuse, 1998).

Is marijuana a "dangerous drug"? This question is the subject of much debate in scientific circles as well as public forums. On the one hand are those who hold that marijuana can be psychologically if not physiologically addictive; that frequent, long-term use has a negative impact on learning and motivation; and that legal prohibitions against marijuana should be continued. The evidence for cognitive or psychological damage is mixed. One study of college students showed that critical skills related to attention, memory, and learning are impaired among people who use marijuana heavily, even after discontinuing its use for at least 24 hours (National Institute on Drug Abuse, 2000a). On the other hand are those who maintain that marijuana is less harmful than the legal drugs, alcohol and nicotine. They argue that the criminalization of marijuana forces people to buy unregulated *cannabis* from illegal sources, which means that they might smoke "pot" contaminated with more harmful substances. Moreover, some evidence indicates that marijuana can relieve some of the unpleasant side effects of chemotherapy and reduce suffering among terminal cancer patients. For instance scientists have recently begun to model new drugs based on the psychoactive ingredient in marijuana (THC) that mimics these positive medical effects (Kathuria et al., 2003; Piomelli, 2001). In short, the jury is still out, and the debate over marijuana is likely to continue (Stein, 2002).

 4.2

Explaining Abuse and Addiction

Some people drink socially and never develop a problem with alcohol, whereas others become dependent or addicted. Some experiment with crack, which is known to be almost instantly addictive, or use "club drugs," which are known to be dangerous, whereas others "just say no." Each year, millions of Americans stop smoking cigarettes. Given the known hazards of smoking, why do a significant number of them relapse after months, even years of not smoking?

The causes of substance abuse and dependence are complex, the result of a combination of biological, psychological, social, and cultural factors that varies from person to person, as well as what psychoactive drug or drugs they use (Finn, Sharkansky, Brandt, & Turcotte, 2000; Zucker & Gomberg, 1990). There is no "one-size-fits-all" explanation. But psychologists have identified a number of factors that, especially in combination, make it more likely a person will abuse drugs.

Biological Factors Are some individuals biologically vulnerable to drug abuse because

THINKING CRITICALLY

Teenage Use of Marijuana

According to the National Institute on Drug Abuse (2000a): Longitudinal research on marijuana use among young people below college age indicates those who used marijuana have lower achievement than the nonusers, more acceptance of deviant behavior, more delinquent behavior and aggression, greater rebelliousness, poorer relationships with parents, and more associations with delinquent and drug-using friends.

1. Write down as many possible explanations for the relationship between using marijuana and other behaviors mentioned as you can think of—the more, the better.

2. Now decide which of these explanations you consider most likely and why. How might you go about determining whether those explanations are, in fact, correct?

3. Examine the assumptions underlying your decisions, or exchange your list with classmates and evaluate each other's assumptions.

of hereditary factors? There is evidence of a genetic basis for alcohol abuse. People whose biological parents have alcohol-abuse problems are more likely to abuse alcohol—even if they are adopted and raised by people who do not abuse alcohol. Identical twins are far more likely to have similar drinking patterns than are fraternal twins (Gordis, 1996; McGue, 1993). Twin studies also suggest that the tendency to start smoking and the ability to quit smoking may, at least to some extent, have a hereditary basis (Lerman et al., 1999). In addition, a recent study found that identical twins were more likely than fraternal twins to report similar experiences with marijuana, suggesting that genes might play a role in their sensations (National Institute on Drug Abuse, 2000a).

Psychologists have not reached consensus on the exact role heredity plays in a predisposition for alcoholism (or abuse of other substances). Some psychologists point to hereditary differences in levels of the stomach enzyme mentioned earlier, deducing that people born with higher levels of the enzyme have to drink more alcohol to achieve the same psychological effects as those with lower levels of the enzyme. People also appear to differ genetically in their tolerance for alcohol in the blood and in the ways they react to alcohol, although the specific genetic mechanism that may put people at risk for developing alcoholism has not been identified (Bolos et al., 1990; Gordis, 1996).

Is addiction then a disease, like diabetes or high blood pressure? Alcoholics Anonymous (AA), the oldest and probably most successful self-help organization in this country, has long endorsed this view. According to the *disease model*, alcoholism is not a moral issue but a medical one, and alcohol abuse is not a sign of character flaws but a symptom of a physiological condition. Further, AA holds that accepting the disease model is an essential part of treatment. Problem drinkers must acknowledge that they are alcoholics publicly, in anonymous group meetings with others who share their problem. If they stop drinking, they must develop an identity as a *recovering* alcoholic (because alcoholism cannot be cured) and continue to attend AA or other support groups throughout their life.

ENDURING ISSUES   **mind**body

Is Addiction a Physical Disease?

The disease model has been applied to many addictions. For example, a new organization called *Nicotine Anonymous*, dedicated to helping smokers quit, now operates over 450 active groups nationwide (Lichtenstein, 1999). To some degree, the disease model has become part of conventional wisdom: Many Americans view substance abuse as a biological problem, often the result of "bad" genes, that requires medical treatment. Many health professionals share this viewpoint. Miller and Brown (1997) point out that clinical psychologists tend to view substance abuse as a medical problem, beyond their area of expertise, and to either refer clients to substance abuse programs or to focus on the consequences of substance abuse, rather than on abuse itself.

Not all psychologists agree, however. Problems with alcohol are better described as a continuum, ranging from mild to severe dependence with many stages in between. The either/or view tends to discourage people from seeking help until their problems have become severe and are more difficult to overcome, and to stigmatize people who go through cycles of sobriety and relapse as weak and contemptible, emphasizing their setbacks rather than their success. It may be best to consider addiction to have a physical basis but important psychological, social, and cultural implications as well.

Psychological, Social, and Cultural Factors   Whether a person uses a psychoactive drug, and what effects that drug has, also depend on the person's expectations, the social setting, and cultural beliefs and values. Sometimes, simply expecting that a drug will yield a particular effect is enough to produce that effect (Jensen & Karoly, 1991; Kirsch, 1999; Mitchell, Laurent, & de Wit, 1996). In some laboratory studies, participants are told that the researcher is studying the effects of, say, marijuana or caffeine, and that they will be given controlled amounts of the drug. In fact, some are given **placebos** (marijuana from which the active ingredient has been removed, or decaffeinated coffee). Frequently, these participants act as though they had actually ingested marijuana or caffeine! Whether placebos would have the same effect in a more natural setting, when people did not think they were participating in a study or being observed by a scientist, is unknown. But there is ample evidence that expectations influence drug-related behavior.

The setting in which drugs are taken is another important determinant of their effects. Every year thousands of hospital patients are given opiate-based painkillers before and after surgery. They may have experiences that a heroin or cocaine user would label as a "high," but they are more likely to consider them confusing than pleasant. Few become addicted or experience withdrawal symptoms. In this setting, psychoactive substances are clearly defined as medicine, dosage is supervised by physicians, and patients take them to get well, not to get high. In contrast, at teenage raves, college beer parties, and all-night clubs, people drink specifically to get drunk and take other drugs to get high. But even in these settings, some individuals participate without using or abusing drugs, and motives for using drugs vary. A person who drinks or smokes marijuana because he thinks he *needs* a drug to overcome social inhibitions and be accepted is more likely to slip into abuse than someone who uses the same substances in the same amounts because he wants to have more fun.

The family setting in which a child grows up also shapes attitudes and beliefs about drugs. For example, children whose parents do not use alcohol tend to abstain or to drink only moderately; to a lesser extent, children whose parents abuse alcohol tend to drink heavily (Chassin, Pitts, DeLucia, & Todd, 1999; Gordis, 1996; Harburg, DiFranceisco, Webster, Gleiberman, & Schork, 1990; Harburg, Gleiberman, DiFranceisco, Schork, & Weissfeld, 1990). A recent study suggests that such children are most likely to abuse alcohol if their family tolerates deviance in general or encourages excitement and pleasure seeking (Finn et al., 2000). Moreover, adolescents who have been physically assaulted or sexually abused in their homes are at increased risk for drug abuse (Kilpatrick et al., 2000). Parents are not the only family influence; some research indicates that siblings' and peers' attitudes and behavior have as much or more impact on young people than parents do (Ary, Duncan, Duncan, & Hops, 1999; Harris, 1998).

Culture also plays a significant role in determining drug use and drug experiences. In some cultures, such as Muslim societies or Mormon communities in the United States, alcohol is strictly forbidden; expectations regarding drinking are almost uniformly negative; and alcohol abuse isn't an issue. In other cultures, it is traditional to drink wine at family meals and gatherings. Children are introduced to alcohol (often watered wine) at an early age and have ample opportunity to observe moderate, social drinking—and ridicule of drunkenness. Alcohol doesn't have the appeal of a "forbidden pleasure," and alcoholism is generally confined to individuals who are alienated from their families and culture. From this perspective, today's drug problem may be in part a reflection of mainstream American cultural norms. To an extent, the use of chemical substances to alter consciousness has become an accepted part of everyday life in the United States (Bernstein & Lennard, 1973; South, 1999). The general message is, "Got a problem? Take a pill." Every year, Americans spend billions of dollars on prescription and over-the-counter

Placebo Chemically inactive substance used for comparison with active drugs in experiments on the effects of drugs.

medications. Every time we turn on the radio or TV, open a magazine, or go on the Internet, we see ads for over-the-counter and, increasingly, prescription medications that promise to cure everything from arthritis pain to baldness to impotence. In this sense then, the person who takes amphetamines or cocaine and one who is "hooked" on vitamins may be acting on the same cultural belief: Drugs will make you feel better.

CHECK YOUR UNDERSTANDING

1. Alcohol is a(n)

___ a. depressant

___ b. stimulant

___ c. hallucinogen

___ d. opiate

2. Today's number one drug problem is

___ a. marijuana

___ b. Ecstasy

___ c. alcohol

___ d. tobacco

3. Which one of the following is a variety of methamphetamine?

___ a. cocaine

___ b. Ecstasy

___ c. LSD

___ d. psilocybin

Answers: 1.a, 2.c, 3.b

Meditation and Hypnosis

Can hypnosis help you overcome a problem, such as smoking or overeating?

At one time Western scientists viewed meditation and hypnosis with great skepticism. However, research has shown that both techniques can produce alterations in consciousness that can be measured through such sophisticated methods as brain imaging.

Meditation

Meditation Any of the various methods of concentration, reflection, or focusing of thoughts undertaken to suppress the activity of the sympathetic nervous system.

For centuries, people have used various forms of **meditation** to experience an alteration in consciousness (Benson, 1975). Each form of meditation focuses the meditator's attention in a slightly different way. *Zen meditation* concentrates on respiration, for example, whereas *Sufism* relies on frenzied dancing and prayer (Schwartz, 1974). In *transcendental meditation (TM)*, practitioners intone a *mantra*, which is a sound, specially selected for each person, to keep all other images and problems at bay and allow the meditator to relax more deeply (Deikman, 1973; Schwartz, 1974).

In all its diverse forms, meditation suppresses the activity of the sympathetic nervous system, the part of the nervous system that prepares the body for strenuous activity during an emergency (see Chapter 2). Meditation also lowers the rate of metabolism, reduces heart and respiratory rates, and decreases blood lactate, a chemical linked to stress. Alpha brain waves (which accompany relaxed wakefulness) increase noticeably during meditation.

Meditation has been used to treat certain medical problems, especially so-called functional complaints (those for which no physical cause can be found). For example, stress often leads to muscle tension and, sometimes, to pressure on nerves—and pain. In other cases, pain leads to muscle tension, which makes the pain worse. Relaxation techniques such as meditation may bring relief (Blanchard et al., 1990). Several studies have also found that people stopped using drugs after taking up meditation (Alexander, Robinson, & Rainforth, 1994).

Besides physiological benefits, people who regularly practice some form of meditation report emotional and even spiritual gains, including increased sensory awareness and a sense of timelessness, well-being, and being at peace with oneself and the universe (Hameroff, Kaszniak, & Scott, 1996; Lantz, Buchalter, & McBee, 1997).

Meditation can help relieve anxiety and promote peace of mind and a sense of well-being.

Hypnosis

In mid-eighteenth-century Europe, Anton Mesmer, a Viennese physician, fascinated audiences by putting patients into trances to cure their illnesses. Hence the term *mesmerism* was first used to describe the phenomenon now known as **hypnosis** (*Hypnos* was the Greek god of sleep). Mesmerism was initially discredited by a French commission chaired by Benjamin Franklin; but in the nineteenth century, some respectable physicians revived interest in hypnosis when they discovered it could be used to treat certain forms of mental illness. Even today, disagreement persists about how to define hypnosis and even about whether it is a valid altered state of consciousness.

One of the reasons for the controversy is that, from a behavioral standpoint, there is no simple definition of what it means to be hypnotized (Kihlström, 1998; Kirsch & Lynn, 1998; Kirsch & Braffman, 2001; Woody & Sadler, 1998). Different individuals believed to have undergone hypnosis describe their experiences in strikingly different ways. The following quotations (Farthing, 1992, p. 349) from hypnotized people illustrate some of these disparities:

"I felt as if I were 'inside' myself; none of my body was touching anything. . . ."

"I was very much aware of the split in my consciousness. One part of me was analytic and listening to you (the hypnotist). The other part was feeling the things that the analytic part decided I should have."

Hypnotic Suggestions   Individuals also vary in their susceptibility to hypnosis. Several studies have shown that while susceptibility to hypnosis *is not* related to personal characteristics such as trust, gullibility, submissiveness, and social compliance, hypnotic suggestibility *is* related to the ability of an individual to become absorbed in reading, music, and daydreaming (see Nash, 2001). One measure of susceptibility is whether people respond to *hypnotic suggestion*. Some people who are told they cannot move their arms or that their pain has vanished do, in fact, experience paralysis or anesthesia; if told they are hearing a certain piece of music or are unable to hear anything, they may hallucinate or become deaf temporarily (Montgomery, DuHamel, & Redd, 2000). When hypnotized subjects are told, "You will remember nothing that happened under hypnosis until I tell you," some people do experience amnesia. But, contrary to rumors, hypnotic suggestion cannot force a person to do something foolish and embarrassing—or dangerous—against their will.

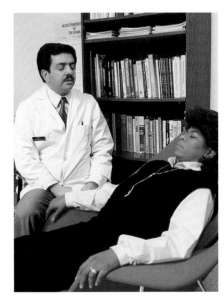

Although hypnosis is often applied in clinical situations, psychologists disagree about whether it is really an altered state of consciousness.

Hypnosis Trancelike state in which a person responds readily to suggestions.

Another measure of the success of hypnosis is whether people respond to *posthypnotic commands*. For example, under hypnosis, a person suffering from back pain may be instructed that when he feels a twinge, he will imagine that he is floating on a cloud and his body is weightless, and the pain will stop—a technique also called "imaging." A runner may be told that when she pulls on her ear, she will block out the noise of the crowd and the runners on either side of her to heighten her concentration—a form of *self-hypnosis*. As the last example suggests, hypnosis has become increasingly popular among professional athletes and their weekend counterparts (Liggett, 2000).

ENDURING ISSUES   **mind**body

Clinical Applications of Hypnosis

Because hypnotic susceptibility varies significantly from one person to another (Gfeller, 1994), its value in clinical and therapeutic settings is difficult to assess. Nevertheless, hypnosis is used in a variety of medical and counseling situations (Rhue, Lynn, & Kirsch, 1993). Some research indicates that the use of hypnosis enhances the effectiveness of traditional forms of psychotherapy (Kirsch, Montgomery, & Sapirstein, 1995), but psychologists by no means agree on this issue. Hypnosis has been shown to be effective in controlling certain types of physical pain (Patterson & Ptacek, 1997; Nash, 2001). Dentists have used it as an anesthetic for years. Hypnosis has also been used to alleviate pain in children with leukemia who have to undergo repeated bone-marrow biopsies: Those who are able to imagine themselves living temporarily in a world outside their bodies can learn to tolerate this extremely painful procedure quite well (Hilgard, Hilgard, & Kaufmann, 1983).

Can hypnosis make someone change or eliminate bad habits? In some cases, posthypnotic commands temporarily diminish a person's desire to smoke or overeat (Green & Lynn, 2000; Griffiths & Channon-Little, 1995). But even certified hypnotists agree that this treatment is effective only if people are motivated to change their behavior. Hypnosis may shore up their will, but so might joining a support group, such as Nicotine Anonymous or Weight Watchers.

CHECK YOUR UNDERSTANDING

1. Which of the following is not a form of meditation?

___ a. Sufism

___ b. TM

___ c. Zen

___ d. Astorism

2. When it first became popular in the eighteenth century, hypnosis was known as

___ a. egotism

___ b. existentialism

___ c. transcendentalism

___ d. Mesmerism

Answers: 1.d, 2.d

Conscious Experience

What is Waking Consciousness?

Consciousness is our awareness of various cognitive processes that operate in our daily lives: making decisions, remembering, daydreaming, concentrating, reflecting, sleeping, and dreaming, among others. Psychologists divide consciousness into two broad areas: **waking consciousness,** which includes the thoughts, feelings, and perceptions that arise when we are awake and reasonably alert; and **altered states of consciousness,** during which our mental state differs noticeably from normal waking consciousness.

To make sense of our complex environment, we choose what to absorb from the myriad happenings around us and filter out the rest. This applies to both external stimuli such as sounds, sights, and smells, and internal sensations such as heat, cold, pressure, and pain. Even our thoughts, memories, emotions, and needs are subjected to this selective process. We also perform familiar tasks, such as signing our names, without deliberate attention. Many psychologists believe that important mental processes go on outside of normal waking consciousness, perhaps as a form of automatic processing.

Explaining Consciousness

Consciousness has been explained as a stream of information resulting from the activity of the thalamus, which analyzes and interprets individual pieces of data received from the various sensory modes. Another view is that consciousness represents only a small portion of the activity of the brain, most of which occurs at an unconscious level. In this view, only thoughts to which we are paying attention at a given moment are conscious. A third explanation holds that consciousness is an evolutionary adaptation to the fact that humans are slow and weak compared with other animals. Consciousness enables humans to make use of their intelligence, cultural knowledge, and social organizations.

Daydreaming and Fantasy

Daydreaming occurs without effort, often when we seek to briefly escape the demands of the real world. Some psychologists see no positive or practical value in daydreaming. Others contend that **daydreams** and fantasies allow us to express and deal with hidden desires without guilt or anxiety. Still others believe that daydreams build cognitive and creative skills that help us survive difficult situations—that they serve as a useful substitute for reality or a beneficial way of relieving tension. Finally there are those who view daydreaming as a mechanism for processing the vast array of information we take in during the day, enabling us to retrieve thoughts put aside for later review and to transform them into new and more useful forms.

Sleep

Circadian Cycles: The Biological Clock

Like many other biological functions, sleep and waking follow a daily, or *circadian*, cycle. **Circadian rhythm** is a regular biological rhythm with approximately a 24 hour period. The human *biological clock* is largely governed by a tiny cluster of neurons in the lower region of the hypothalamus known as the **suprachiasmatic nucleus (SCN)** that receives input from the retina regarding light and dark cycles and is involved in regulating the biological clock. The SCN secretes specific neurotransmitters to regions of the brain that in turn control our body's temperature, metabolism, blood pressure, hormone levels, and hunger, which vary through the course of the day. People who work night shifts or travel through several times zones often experience a disruption of circadian rhythms: *desynchronization* where body functions are out of synch.

The Rhythms of Sleep

Research into sleep patterns shows that normal sleep consists of several stages. Following the initial "twilight" state, which is characterized by irregular, low-voltage alpha waves and a state of relaxed wakefulness, the sleeper enters Stage 1 of sleep. This stage, which is marked by a slowing of the pulse, muscle relaxation, and side-to-side rolling movements of the eyes, lasts only a few moments. The sleeper is easily awakened from Stage 1 sleep.

Stages 2 and 3 are characterized by progressively deeper sleep. In these stages, the sleeper is hard to awaken and does not respond to noise or light. Heart rate, blood pressure, and temperature continue to drop.

During Stage 4 sleep, when the brain emits very slow delta waves, heart and breathing rates, blood pressure, and body temperature are as low as they will get during the night. About an hour after first falling asleep, the sleeper begins to ascend through the stages back to Stage 1—a process that takes about 40 minutes. At this stage in the sleep cycle, heart rate, and blood pressure increase, the muscles become more relaxed than at any other time in the cycle, and the eyes move rapidly under closed eyelids. It is this rapid eye movement (REM) that gives this stage of sleep its name.

REM sleep is also called **paradoxical sleep** because while brain activity and other physiological symptoms resemble those recorded during waking consciousness, the sleeper appears to be deeply asleep and is incapable of moving because of paralysis of the body's voluntary muscles. **Non-REM,** or **NREM sleep,** refers to the non-rapid-eye-movement stages of sleep that alternate with REM stages during the sleep cycle.

Sleep Disorders

Sleep disorders include sleeptalking, sleepwalking, night terrors, insomnia, apnea, and narcolepsy. Most episodes of *sleeptalking* and *sleepwalking* occur during delta sleep. Unlike **nightmares, night terrors,** which are more common among children than adults, prove difficult to be awakened from and are rarely remembered the next morning. **Insomnia** is characterized by difficulty in falling asleep or remaining asleep throughout the night. **Apnea** is marked by breathing difficulties during the night and feelings of exhaustion during the day. **Narcolepsy** is a hereditary sleep disorder characterized by sudden nodding off during the day and sudden loss of muscle tone following moments of emotional excitement.

Dreams

What Do We Dream?

Dreams are visual or auditory experiences that occur primarily during REM periods of sleep. Less vivid experiences that resemble conscious thinking tend to occur during

NREM sleep. One theory to explain why REM dreams are so vivid cites the level of brain arousal during REM sleep. The brain's activity closely resembles that of normal waking consciousness, but because of its relative insensitivity to outside sensory input, it draws on nothing but internal images from memory.

Very young children tend to have brief dreams involving animals; narrative, storylike dreams appear between the ages of 5 and 9. In adults' dreams, narratives follow well-developed story lines and other people play important roles. Men more often dream about weapons and aggressive interactions, whereas women are more likely to dream about being the victims of aggression.

Why Do We Dream?   Several theories have been developed to explain the nature and content of dreams. According to Freud, dreams have two kinds of contents: manifest (the surface content of the dream itself) and latent (the disguised, unconscious meaning of the dream). One recent hypothesis suggests that dreams arise out of the mind's reprocessing of information absorbed during the day—information that is important to the survival of the organism. Thus, dreaming strengthens our memories of important information. Another proposal is that dreams are the result of neurons firing at random, sending signals that higher brain centers attempt to weave into a coherent story. Still another theory is that dreams are an extension of the conscious concerns of daily life.

Do We Need to Dream?   If people are deprived of REM sleep, they often become anxious, irritable, and testy, and, when they are permitted to have REM sleep again, the amount of REM they experience almost doubles—an effect referred to as REM rebound. It is not clear whether this indicates that we actually need to dream.

Drug-Altered Consciousness

Substance Use, Abuse, and Dependence   Some altered states of consciousness are induced with the help of **psychoactive drugs**—substances that change people's moods, perceptions, mental functioning, or behavior. It is important to distinguish between substance use and substance abuse. Substance use may be essential for medical reasons and it may also be culturally approved and valued. By contrast, **substance abuse** is a pattern of drug use that diminishes the person's ability to fulfill responsibilities at home or at work or school, that results in repeated use of a drug in dangerous situations, or that leads to legal difficulties related to drug use.

Continued abuse over time can lead to **substance dependence,** a pattern of compulsive drug taking that is much more serious than substance abuse. It is often marked by **tolerance,** the need to take higher doses of a drug to produce its original effects or to prevent withdrawal symptoms. **Withdrawal symptoms** are the unpleasant physical or psychological effects that follow discontinuance of the psychoactive substance.

Depressants: Alcohol, Barbiturates, and Opiates   Consciousness-altering drugs are grouped into three broad categories: depressants, stimulants, and hallucinogens. **Depressants** are chemicals that slow down behavior or cognitive processes. **Alcohol,** a depressant, is the intoxicating ingredient in whiskey, beer, wine, and other fermented or distilled liquors. It is responsible for tens of thousands of deaths each year and contributes to a great deal of crime and domestic violence. Its dangers notwithstanding, alcohol continues to be a popular drug because of its short-term effects. As a depressant, it calms down the nervous system working like a general anesthetic. It is often experienced subjectively as a stimulant because it inhibits centers in the brain that govern critical judgment and impulsive behavior.

Barbiturates are potentially deadly depressants. They were first used for their sedative and anticonvulsant properties, but today their use is limited to the treatment of such conditions as epilepsy and arthritis.

The **opiates** are highly addictive drugs such as opium, morphine, and heroin that dull the senses and induce feelings of euphoria, well-being, and relaxation. Morphine and heroin are derivatives of opium.

Stimulants: Caffeine, Nicotine, Amphetamines, and Cocaine   **Stimulants** are drugs such as caffeine, nicotine, amphetamines, and cocaine that stimulate the sympathetic nervous system and produce feelings of optimism and boundless energy, making the potential for their abuse significant.

Caffeine occurs naturally in coffee, tea, and cocoa; nicotine occurs naturally only in tobacco. Caffeine is considered to be a benign drug, but in large doses it can cause anxiety, insomnia, and other unpleasant conditions. Although nicotine is a stimulant, it acts like a depressant when taken in large doses.

Amphetamines are stimulants that initially produce "rushes" of euphoria often followed by sudden "crashes" and, sometimes, depression. **Cocaine** brings on a sense of euphoria by stimulating the sympathetic nervous system, but it can also cause anxiety, depression, and addictive cravings. Its crystalline form—crack—is highly addictive.

Hallucinogens and Marijuana   **Hallucinogens** are any of a number of drugs, such as LSD, psilocybin, and mescaline, that distort visual and auditory perception.

Many of the hallucinogens occur naturally in mushrooms or other fungi. In these forms, they share an ancient history with other consciousness-altering drugs of natural origin. By contrast, **lysergic acid diethylamide (LSD)** is an artificial hallucinogen, synthesized in the laboratory, that produces hallucinations and delusions similar to those that occur in a psychotic state.

Marijuana is a mild hallucinogen that is capable of producing feelings of euphoria, a sense of well-being, and swings in mood from gaiety to relaxation to paranoia. Currently, marijuana is the fourth most popular drug among students, following alcohol, caffeine, and nicotine. Though similar to hallucinogens in certain respects, marijuana is far less potent and its effects on consciousness are far less profound.

Explaining Abuse and Addiction   Several factors make it more likely that a person will abuse drugs. They include a possible genetic predisposition, the person's expectations, the social setting, and cultural beliefs and values. In the laboratory setting some participants given **placebos**—marijuana from which the active ingredient had been removed or decaffeinated coffee—act as if they had ingested marijuana or caffeine.

Meditation and Hypnosis

Meditation   **Meditation** refers to any of several methods of concentration, reflection, or focusing of thoughts intended to suppress the activity of the sympathetic nervous system. Meditation not only lowers the rate of metabolism but also reduces heart and respiratory rates. Brain activity during meditation resembles that experienced during relaxed wakefulness, and the accompanying decrease in blood lactate reduces stress.

Hypnosis　**Hypnosis** is a trancelike state in which the person responds readily to suggestions. One measure of susceptibility is whether people respond to *hypnotic suggestion*. Hypnosis has several practical applications; for instance, it eases the pain of certain medical conditions and can help people stop smoking and break other habits.

key terms

Consciousness	145	Apnea	156	Opiates	170
Waking consciousness	145	Narcolepsy	156	Stimulants	170
Altered state of consciousness	145	Dreams	158	Amphetamines	171
Daydreams	148	Psychoactive drugs	162	Cocaine	172
Circadian rhythm	151	Substance abuse	163	Hallucinogens	173
Suprachiasmatic nucleus (SCN)	151	Substance dependence	164	Lysergic acid diethylamide (LSD)	173
REM (paradoxical) sleep	154	Tolerance	164	Marijuana	174
Non-REM (NREM) sleep	154	Withdrawal symptoms	164	Placebo	177
Night terrors	155	Depressants	165	Meditation	178
Nightmares	155	Alcohol	166	Hypnosis	179
Insomnia	155	Barbiturates	169		

OVERVIEW

Classical Conditioning
Elements of Classical
Conditioning
Classical Conditioning in Humans
Classical Conditioning Is
Selective

Operant Conditioning
Elements of Operant Conditioning
Types of Reinforcement
Punishment
Operant Conditioning Is Selective
Superstitious Behavior

Learned Helplessness
Shaping Behaviorial Change
Through Biofeedback

**Comparing Classical and
Operant Conditioning**
Response Acquisition
Extinction and Spontaneous
Recovery
Generalization and Discrimination
New Learning Based on Original
Learning

Contingencies
Summing Up

Cognitive Learning
Latent Learning and Cognitive
Maps
Insight and Learning Sets
Learning by Observing
Cognitive Learning in Nonhumans

Learning

5

As unlikely as it may seem, the following situations have something in common: .

- On completion of a training course at the National Zoo, the star students demonstrate their newly acquired behaviors: Junior, a young orangutan, cleans up his cage for the chance to blow a whistle; a pair of 18-inch-long lizards jump 2 feet in the air to snatch insects from the tip of a forceps; a chinchilla weighs itself by hopping into a basket on top of a scale; and Peela the tiger retrieves a floating keg from the moat in his exhibition area.

- Jason, an 11-year-old boy, diagnosed with *attention deficit disorder* has difficulty paying attention and concentrating in school. Using a technique known as *neurofeedback*, Jason has learned to monitor and control his brain waves, which has increased his ability to concentrate and pay attention to his studies, which in turn has lead to an improvement in his grades.

- While driving along a congested boulevard, a middle-aged man glances at a park bench and, for a moment, his heart pounds as he experiences a warm feeling throughout his body. At first, he can't understand why passing this spot has evoked such a strong emotion. Then he remembers: It was the meeting place he once shared with his high school sweetheart over 20 years ago.

- Maria has chosen a complex piece for her piano recital. Several months ago, when the piece was new to her, she had to follow the sheet music closely, and she made numerous mistakes. But at the recital, she plays the same piece flawlessly from memory.

Although these situations occurred outside the confines of a school classroom, all are examples of **learning.** Most people equate learning with studying, but psychologists define it more broadly, as the process by which experience or practice results in a relatively permanent change in behavior or potential behavior. This definition certainly encompasses academic learning, but it covers many other forms of learning as well: learning to turn off lights when we leave a room, learning which way to put the key into the front door lock, learning how to avoid falling down on skis, learning how to dance.

In this chapter, we will explore several different kinds of learning. We will begin with a basic form of learning known as conditioning. **Conditioning** is a general term—used for animals as well as for human beings—that refers to the acquisition of fairly specific patterns of behavior in the presence of well-defined stimuli. For example, conditioning has occurred if a dog always runs to fetch her leash when her owner changes into running shoes. The dog has learned to associate a particular stimulus—her owner putting on her shoes—with a particular activity—going for a walk. In fact, all four examples of learning with which we opened this chapter illustrate conditioning of one sort or another. Although the examples we have used to introduce conditioning may seem simplistic or unimportant, conditioning is essential to our ability to survive in and adapt to a changing world (Hergenhahn & Olson, 1993).

After exploring conditioning, we will probe more complex forms of learning that are not tied to the immediate environment. Grouped under the heading of *cognitive learning* because they depend on thinking and reasoning processes, these include insight and observational learning, or vicarious learning. When, after pondering a math problem or similar puzzle, you suddenly see the solution in its complete form,

THINKABOUTIT

You will find the answers to these questions in the chapter:

1. How did Pavlov's discovery of classical conditioning help to shed light on learning?

2. Why is it easy to teach a dog to come when it is called, but difficult to teach it not to chase rabbits?

3. What behavioral principles enable an animal trainer to teach a tiger to jump through a flaming hoop?

4. Do children learn to behave violently by observing adults?

Learning The process by which experience or practice results in a relatively permanent change in behavior or potential behavior.

Conditioning The acquisition of specific patterns of behavior in the presence of well-defined stimuli.

Classical (or Pavlovian) conditioning The type of learning in which a response naturally elicited by one stimulus comes to be elicited by a different, formerly neutral stimulus.

Unconditioned stimulus (US) A stimulus that invariably causes an organism to respond in a specific way.

Unconditioned response (UR) A response that takes place in an organism whenever an unconditioned stimulus occurs.

Conditioned stimulus (CS) An originally neutral stimulus that is paired with an unconditioned stimulus and eventually produces the desired response in an organism when presented alone.

Conditioned response (CR) After conditioning, the response an organism produces when only a conditioned stimulus is presented.

you are experiencing insight. When you imitate the steps of professional dancers you saw last night on television, you are demonstrating observational learning. Like conditioning, cognitive learning is one of our survival strategies. Through cognitive processes, we learn which events are safe and which are dangerous without having to experience those events directly. Cognitive learning also gives us access to the wisdom of people who lived hundreds of years ago, and it will give people living hundreds of years from now some insight into our experiences and way of life.

Our discussion begins with *classical conditioning*. This simple kind of learning serves as a convenient starting point for examining what learning is and how it can be observed.

Classical Conditioning

How did Pavlov's discovery of classical conditioning help to shed light on learning?

Ivan Pavlov (1849–1936), a Russian physiologist who was studying digestive processes, discovered classical conditioning almost by accident. Because animals salivate when food is placed in their mouths, Pavlov inserted tubes into the salivary glands of dogs to measure how much saliva they produced when they were given food. He noticed, however, that the dogs salivated before the food was in their mouths: The mere sight of food made them drool. In fact, they even drooled at the sound of the experimenter's footsteps. This aroused Pavlov's curiosity. What was making the dogs salivate even before they had the food in their mouths? How had they learned to salivate in response to the sound of the experimenter's approach?

To answer these questions, Pavlov set out to teach the dogs to salivate when food was not present. He devised an experiment in which he sounded a bell just before the food was brought into the room. A ringing bell does not usually make a dog's mouth water but, after hearing the bell many times just before getting fed, Pavlov's dogs began to salivate as soon as the bell rang. It was as if they had learned that the bell signaled the appearance of food, and their mouths watered on cue even if no food followed. The dogs had been conditioned to salivate in response to a new stimulus—the bell—that would not normally have prompted that response (Pavlov, 1927). Figure 5–1, shows one of Pavlov's procedures in which the bell has been replaced by a touch to the dog's leg just before food is given.

Elements of Classical Conditioning

Generally speaking, **classical (or Pavlovian) conditioning** involves pairing an *involuntary* response (for example, salivation) that is usually evoked by one stimulus with a different, formerly neutral stimulus (such as a bell or a touch on the leg). Pavlov's experiment illustrates the four basic elements of classical conditioning. The first is an **unconditioned stimulus (US)**, such as food, which invariably prompts a certain reaction—salivation, in this case. That reaction—the **unconditioned response (UR)**—is the second element and always results from the unconditioned stimulus: Whenever the dog is given food (US), its mouth waters (UR). The third element is the neutral stimulus—the ringing bell—which is called the **conditioned stimulus (CS).** At first, the conditioned stimulus is said to be "neutral" with respect to the desired response (salivation), because dogs do not salivate at the sound of a bell unless they have been conditioned to react in this way by repeatedly presenting the CS and US together. Frequent pairing of the CS and US produces the fourth element in the classical conditioning process: the **conditioned response (CR).** The conditioned response is the behavior that the animal has learned in response to the conditioned stimulus. Usually, the unconditioned response and the conditioned

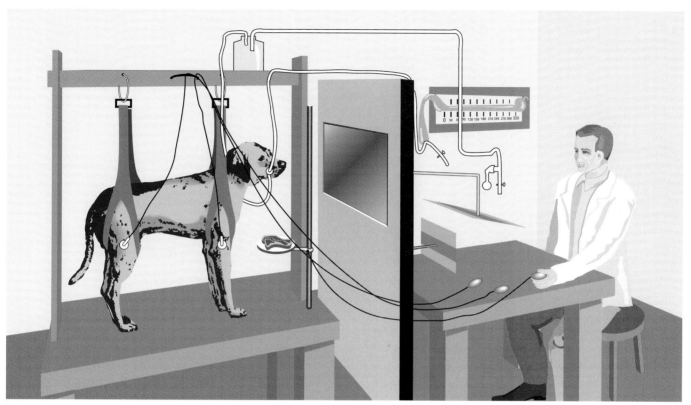

Figure 5–1
Pavlov's apparatus for classically conditioning a dog to salivate.
The experimenter sits behind a one-way mirror and controls the presentation of the conditioned stimulus (touch applied to the leg) and the unconditioned stimulus (food). A tube runs from the dog's salivary glands to a vial, where the drops of saliva are collected as a way of measuring the strength of the dog's response.

response are slightly different versions of the same response—salivation, in our example (see Figure 5–2).

You may have conditioned your own pet the same way that Pavlov trained his dogs. For instance, your cat may begin to purr when she hears the sound of a can being opened in the kitchen. The taste and smell of food are unconditioned stimuli (USs) that cause, among other responses, purring (the UR). Based on experience, your cat associates the sound of the can opener (the CS) with the food; over time, the CS by itself causes your cat to purr even before food is presented (the CR).

Changes in behavior brought about by classical conditioning are not limited to dogs and cats. Classical conditioning plays a significant role in the lives of almost all living things (Krasne & Glanzman, 1995). Moreover, this seemingly simple paradigm has yielded an enormous amount of information about how learning takes place. For example, recently psychologists have probed the biological basis of classical conditioning in an effort to understand Alzheimer's disease (see *On the Cutting Edge: Classical Eyeblink Conditioning and Clues to Alzheimer's Disease*).

 5.1

Classical Conditioning in Humans

You might wonder what Pavlov's dogs and reflexive responses have to do with human learning. Quite simply, human beings also learn behaviors through classical conditioning. Consider, for example, the positive thoughts and feelings that we associate with the smell of freshly baked bread or cake. We are not born with these reactions. They are learned through classical conditioning. Similarly, you might become tense or anxious when you hear the kind of music that always precedes a

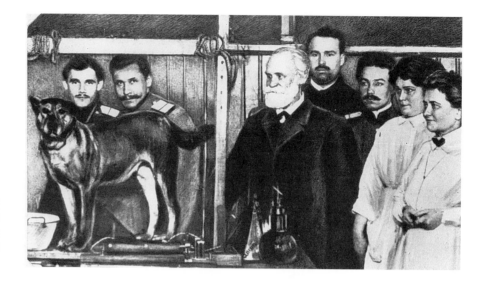

The formal study of classical conditioning can be traced to Ivan Pavlov's experiments with dogs. Here Pavlov, the bearded man in the center, looks fondly at one of his dogs while surrounded by his assistants.

frightening or startling scene in a scary film, because you have come to identify this style of music with such scenes. Or think for a moment about phobias—irrational fears of particular things, activities, or situations, such as cats, spiders, or snakes, or high places (acrophobia), closed places (claustrophobia), or busy public places (agoraphobia).

To see how phobias can develop through classical conditioning, consider a classic experiment conducted by John Watson and Rosalie Rayner (Watson & Rayner, 1920). In this famous study, an 11-month-old boy, named "Little Albert," was taught to fear a harmless laboratory rat. The experimenters started by showing Albert a white rat. At first the child displayed no apparent fear of the rodent. The infant crawled toward the rat and tried to play with it. But every time he approached the rat, the experimenters made a loud noise by striking a steel bar. Because nearly all children are afraid of loud noises, Albert's natural reaction was fear. After just a few of these experiences, Albert would cry whenever he saw the rat and quickly withdraw from it in fear. This is a simple case of classical conditioning. An unconditioned stimulus—the loud noise—caused the unconditioned response of fear. Next, the loud noise was associated several times with the rat (CS). Soon the rat alone caused Albert to behave as if he were afraid (CR).

Several years later, psychologist Mary Cover Jones demonstrated a method by which children's fears can be unlearned by means of classical conditioning (Jones, 1924). Her subject was a 3-year-old boy named Peter who, like Albert, had a fear of white rats. Jones paired the sight of a rat with a pleasant experience—eating candy. While Peter sat alone in a room, a caged white rat was brought in and placed far enough away so that the youngster would not be frightened. At this point, Peter was given plenty of candy to eat. On each successive day of the experiment, the cage was moved closer and was followed by the presentation of candy until, eventually, Peter showed no fear of the rat. In this case, eating candy (US) elicited a

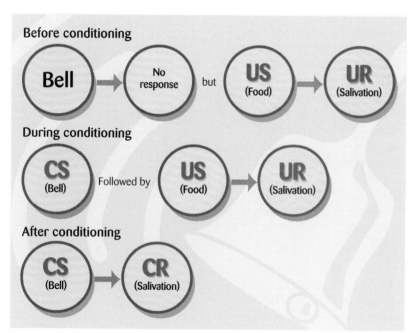

Figure 5–2
A paradigm of the classical conditioning process.

ON THE CUTTING EDGE

CLASSICAL EYEBLINK CONDITIONING AND CLUES TO ALZHEIMER'S DISEASE

As we will see in Chapter 6 (Memory), one of the most interesting problems in memory research is how the brain encodes memory. By the early 1980s, researchers had determined that the cerebellum was crucial to classical eyeblink conditioning, but they didn't know exactly how the learning takes place.

Through studies involving electrophysiological recordings, Steinmetz (1998) was able to pin down the learning to the activity of specific groups of neurons in the cerebellum. Steinmetz found that the CS and the US travel via different pathways in the brain stem.

The airpuff US travels from the eye to the brain stem, and from there the impulse goes to the cerebellum. For the CS, Steinmetz used a tone. He found that this signal was directed to a different area of the brain stem and from there to a different portion of the cerebellum. Steinmetz has shown that a third portion of the cerebellum, the *interpositus nucleus,* receives input from both the CS and US, and it is here that the learning takes place.

Steinmetz's studies of eyeblink conditioning strongly suggest that the cerebellum demonstrates neural plasticity (see Chapter 2, The Biological Basis of Behavior) and

that it is the place where the conditioned response is encoded. Following an extensive review of several studies of eyeblink conditioning, Green and Woodruff-Pak (2000) point out that the hippocampus is also actively involved in eyeblink conditioning, citing evidence that damage to the hippocampus impairs the classical conditioning response. Thus, the "simple" response that we call eyeblink classical conditioning is actually learned in at least two different parts of the brain.

Because degeneration of the hippocampus is a major factor in Alzheimer's Disease (see Chapter 6: Memory, and Chapter 10: Life Span Development), researchers have recently begun to consider if eye-blink conditioning, which requires adequate hippocampal functioning, may be used as a diagnostic tool for detecting the onset of Alzheimer's disease (Woodruff-Pak, 2001a)., Studies have shown that damage to the hippocampus leads to a slower acquisition of the eyeblink response (Woodruff-Pak, 2001b; Woodruff-Pak, Green, Heifets, & Pak, 2002). If these results are confirmed, knowledge of the biological basis of eyeblink conditioning may point the way to a better understanding of how to diagnose and ultimately treat Alzheimer's patients.

Desensitization therapy is based on the belief that we can overcome fears by learning to remain calm in the face of increasingly fear-arousing situations. Here people being desensitized for a fear of heights are able to swing high above the ground without panicking.

pleasant response (UR). By pairing the candy with the sight of the rat (CS), Jones was able to teach Peter to respond with pleasure (CR) when the rat appeared.

Many years later, psychiatrist Joseph Wolpe (1915–1997) adapted Jones's method to the treatment of certain kinds of anxiety (Wolpe, 1973, 1982). Wolpe reasoned that because irrational fears and anxieties are learned or conditioned, they could also be unlearned through conditioning. He noted that people cannot be both fearful and relaxed at the same time; therefore, if people could be taught to relax in fearful or anxious situations, their anxiety should disappear. His **desensitization therapy** works by teaching a person to associate relaxation with a stimulus that is causing unnecessary or irrational fear or anxiety. We will examine desensitization therapy in greater detail in Chapter 14 (Therapies), but for now, let's just note that it is one way in which classical conditioning can be used to change human behavior. Wolpe himself (Wolpe & Plaud, 1997) said ". . . Pavlovian conditioning represents far more than a systematic basic learning paradigm. It is also an essential theoretical foundation for the theory and practice of behavior therapy" (p. 966).

ENDURING ISSUES   mindbody

Classical Conditioning and the Immune System

In another example of classical conditioning in humans, researchers have devised a novel way to treat a group of diseases, called *autoimmune disorders*, which cause the immune system to attack healthy organs or tissues. Although powerful drugs can be used to suppress the immune system and thus reduce the impact of the autoimmune disorder, they may produce nausea and headaches and may also damage organs such as the pancreas and liver, so they must be administered sparingly. The challenge, then, is to find a treatment that will suppress the immune system without damaging vital organs. Several researchers discovered that, through classical conditioning techniques, they could use formerly neutral stimuli either to elevate or to suppress the activity of the immune system (Ader & Cohen, 1975; Hollis, 1997; Markovic, Dimitrijevic, & Jankovic, 1993). Here's how it works: The researchers use immune-suppressing drugs as USs and pair them with a specific CS, such as a distinctive smell or taste. After only a few pairings of the drug (US) with the smell or taste (CS), the CS alone suppresses the immune system (the CR) without any dangerous side effects! While the use of classical conditioning to treat autoimmune disorders shows promise, additional research is still necessary to validate its effectiveness and evaluate its potential application as a therapy (Miller & Cohen, 2001).

Classical Conditioning Is Selective

If people can develop phobias when objects are linked with frightening or anxiety-arousing stimuli, why don't people have phobias about almost everything? As M. E. P. Seligman notes, "Only rarely, if ever, do we have pajama phobias, grass phobias, electric-outlet phobias, hammer phobias, even though these things are likely to be associated with trauma in our world" (1971, p. 455). Why should this be?

To Seligman, the answer lies in *preparedness* and *contrapreparedness*. Some stimuli serve readily as CSs for certain kinds of responses (preparedness), and other stimuli do not (contrapreparedness). All the common objects of phobias—heights, snakes, cats, the dark, and so on—are "related to the survival of the human species through the long course of evolution" (Seligman, 1971, p. 455). Thus, humans may be

Desensitization therapy A conditioning technique designed to gradually reduce anxiety about a particular object or situation.

prepared to develop fear responses and phobias about these things, but we are very unlikely to acquire phobias about flowers.

The Evolutionary Basis of Fear

To what extent does our evolutionary heritage condition our fears, and to what extent are fears the result of our experiences? Recent studies suggest that the two work in tandem (Mineka & Oehman, 2002). For example, some stimuli unrelated to human survival through evolution, but which we have learned to associate with danger, can serve as CSs for fear responses. Pictures of handguns and butcher knives, for example, are as effective as pictures of snakes and spiders in conditioning fear in some people (Lovibond, Siddle, & Bond, 1993). These studies suggest that preparedness may be the result of learning rather than evolution. Other studies have shown that people who do not suffer from phobias can rather quickly unlearn fear responses to spiders and snakes if those stimuli appear repeatedly without painful or threatening USs (Honeybourne, Matchett, & Davey, 1993). Thus even if humans are prepared to fear these things, that fear can be overcome through conditioning. In other words, our evolutionary history and our personal learning histories interact to increase or decrease the likelihood that certain kinds of conditioning will occur.

Preparedness also underlies **conditioned food (or taste) aversion,** a learned association between the taste of a certain food and a feeling of nausea and revulsion. Animals rarely require more than one occasion of being poisoned to learn not to eat a particular food. John Garcia discovered this phenomenon by accident in the midst of experiments on the effects of exposure to radiation (Garcia, Kimeldorf, Hunt, & Davies, 1956). Exposing rats in a special chamber to high doses of radiation that made them sick, Garcia noticed that the rats were drinking less and less water when in the radiation chamber, although they drank normally in their "home" cages. Garcia realized that the water bottles in the radiation chamber were plastic, perhaps giving the water a different taste from the water contained in glass bottles in the home cages. He theorized that the taste of the water from the plastic bottles had served as a conditioned stimulus (CS) that the rats associated with radiation (US); as a result of this conditioning, the plastic-tasting water by itself made the rats feel ill (CR).

Conditioned food aversion is puzzling. Classical conditioning generally requires many presentations of the CS and US with a short interval between the appearance of the two. But conditioned food aversion can take place after only one bad experience; moreover, the interval between eating the food (the US) and falling ill (the UR) can be quite long—up to 12 hours among rats (Braveman & Bornstein, 1985; Brooks, Bowker, Anderson, & Palmatier, 2003; Chester, Lumeng, Li, & Grahame, 2003).

Why do taste-illness combinations produce such rapid and long-lasting learning? Garcia traces the answer to evolution: Rapid learning of taste-illness combinations increases animals' chances of survival. Rats, for example, are scavengers: They will nibble at almost anything, so they are quite likely to come into contact with potentially toxic foods. It makes sense that over thousands of generations rats would have evolved a nervous system that is especially good at remembering taste-illness combinations (Garcia & Keolling, 1966).

Conditioned food (or taste) aversion Conditioned avoidance of certain foods even if there is only one pairing of conditioned and unconditioned stimuli.

A bird's nervous system is adapted to remember sight-illness combinations, such as the distinctive color of a certain berry and subsequent food poisoning. In mammals it is generally taste-illness combinations that are quickly and powerfully learned.

Birds, however, depend on vision to find and identify their food; it follows that birds should have evolved a nervous system that is especially good at remembering sight-illness combinations—and this turns out to be the case. In one study, both rats and quail were fed water that was flavored with salt, colored blue, and contaminated with a chemical that would make both animals ill. Later they were offered a choice between water just colored blue and water just flavored with salt. The rats chose the blue water and avoided the salty water; the quails did just the reverse. The rats seemed to have associated the salty flavor cues with their illness, whereas the birds associated the blue visual cue with their illness (Wilcoxon, Dragoin, & Kral, 1971). In other words, each species seems to have been prepared or preprogrammed for certain types of learning that are critical to its own survival.

Humans also develop food aversions based on a variety of cues, including taste, appearance, and smell (Logue, Ophir, & Strauss, 1981). In fact, the conditioned aversion response is so ingrained that even when we know a particular food did not make us sick, we still tend to form an aversion to the food we ate before we became ill. For example, one psychologist described a dinner party at which he and several other guests all picked up an intestinal virus that left many of them with an aversion to tarragon chicken (the main dish) or any food with tarragon flavor (Mazur, 1994). Even though they knew that the tarragon chicken was not the source of their illness, they were unable to overcome the powerful conditioned response. Similarly, patients undergoing treatment for cancer frequently develop taste aversions. Because the drugs used in chemotherapy can cause nausea, patients commonly develop strong taste aversions for foods eaten both before and after injections of these chemicals, even though they know that the foods do not bring on their nausea (Jacobsen, Bovbjerg, Schwartz, & Andrykowski, 1994).

CHECK YOUR UNDERSTANDING

1. Predictable behavior that occurs in response to well-defined stimuli is the simplest type of learning. It is called

___ a. operant conditioning

___ b. cognitive learning

___ c. classical conditioning

___ d. observational learning

2. Pavlovian conditioning involves pairing a (an) _____ response with a (an) _____ stimulus.

___ a. involuntary/neutral

___ b. neutral/involuntary

___ c. involuntary/involuntary

___ d. neutral/neutral

3. Your cat comes running when she hears you open a kitchen cabinet door. The sound of the cabinet is a (an)

___ a. US

___ b. CS

___ c. CR

___ d. UR

4. Conditioned food aversion requires how many bad experiences?

___ a. 10

___ b. 100

___ c. 1

Operant Conditioning

Why is it easy to teach a dog to come when it is called, but difficult to teach it not to chase rabbits?

Classical conditioning is concerned with involuntary behavior that invariably follows a particular event, but most of our behavior is *voluntary* rather than triggered by outside events. Dogs learn to sit or heel on command. Children learn to pick up their toys either to avoid punishment or to gain some reward from their parents. We learn to put money into machines and pull on levers or push buttons to obtain soft drinks, food, entertainment, or a chance to win money. These and similar actions can be classified as **operant behavior.** They are learned behaviors that are designed to operate on the environment to gain a reward or avoid a punishment; they are not automatic reflexes caused by biologically important stimuli. This kind of learning is called **operant** or **instrumental conditioning.** We now turn to the basic principles of operant conditioning.

Elements of Operant Conditioning

Around the turn of the twentieth century, while Pavlov was busy with his dogs, Edward Lee Thorndike (1874–1949), an American psychologist and educator, was using a simple wooden cage to determine how cats learn (Thorndike, 1898). Thorndike placed a hungry cat in the close quarters of the "puzzle box," with food just outside the cage where the cat could see and smell it (see Figure 5–3). To get to the food, the cat had to figure out how to open the latch on the cage door. In the beginning, it took the cats quite a while to discover how to open the door. But each time a cat was put back into the puzzle box, it took less time to open the door, until the cat eventually could escape from the box in almost no time.

Thorndike's experiments illustrate two factors that are essential in operant or instrumental conditioning. The first is the *operant response*. Operant conditioning occurs when one response, called the *operant response*, operates on the environment to produce specific consequences. By pawing at the latch (the operant response) the cats were able to open the door.

The second essential element in operant conditioning is the *consequence* that follows the behavior. By opening the door, Thorndike's cats gained either freedom or a piece of fish for escaping from their constraining puzzle boxes. Similarly, a dog may get a biscuit for sitting on command; and a child may receive praise or a chance to play a computer game for helping to clear the table. Consequences like these, which *increase* the likelihood that the operant behavior will be repeated, are called **reinforcers.** By contrast, consequences that *decrease* the chances that an operant behavior will be repeated are called **punishers.** Imagine what might happen if

Operant behavior Behavior designed to operate on the environment in a way that will gain something desired or avoid something unpleasant.

Operant or instrumental conditioning The type of learning in which behaviors are emitted (in the presence of specific stimuli) to earn rewards or avoid punishments.

Reinforcer A stimulus that follows a behavior and increases the likelihood that the behavior will be repeated.

Punisher A stimulus that follows a behavior and decreases the likelihood that the behavior will be repeated.

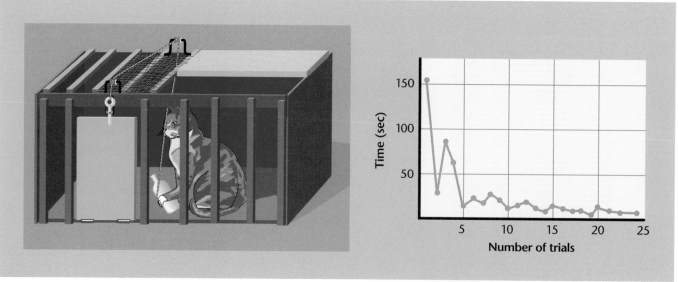

Figure 5–3
A cat in a Thorndike "puzzle box."
The cat can escape and be rewarded with food by tripping the bolt on the door. As the graph shows, Thorndike's cats learned to make the necessary response more rapidly over time.

Thorndike's cats had been greeted by a large, snarling dog when they escaped from their puzzle boxes, or a dog that sits on command is scolded for doing so, or a child who has helped to clear the table is sent to sit in a "time-out" corner.

Thorndike's understanding of the importance of reinforcement is reflected in his **law of effect:** Behavior that brings about a satisfying effect (reinforcement) is likely to be performed again, whereas behavior that brings about a negative effect (punishment) is likely to be suppressed. Contemporary psychologists often refer to the *principle of reinforcement* rather than the law of effect, but the two terms refer to the same phenomenon.

Types of Reinforcement

Positive and Negative Reinforcement   Psychologists distinguish among several kinds of reinforcers. **Positive reinforcers,** such as food or pleasant music, add something rewarding to a situation. By contrast, **negative reinforcers** subtract something unpleasant from a situation by removing a noxious or unpleasant stimulus. You might find it helpful to use the plus symbol (+) to refer to a positive (+) reinforcer that *adds* (+) something rewarding to the environment and the minus sign (−) to refer to a negative (−) reinforcer that *subtracts* (−) something negative or unpleasant from the environment. Animals will learn to press bars and open doors not only to obtain food and water (positive reinforcement) but also to escape from electric shocks or loud noises (negative reinforcement).

Both positive and negative reinforcement result in the learning of new behaviors or the strengthening of existing behaviors. Remember, in everyday conversation when we say that we have "reinforced" something, we mean we have strengthened it. "Reinforced concrete" is strengthened by the addition of steel rods or steel mesh; generals "send reinforcements" to strengthen a military force; people "reinforce" their arguments by marshaling facts that strengthen them. Similarly, in operant conditioning, all reinforcements—whether positive or negative—strengthen behavior. For example, a child might practice the piano to receive praise (positive rein-

Law of effect Thorndike's theory that behavior consistently rewarded will be "stamped in" as learned behavior, and behavior that brings about discomfort will be "stamped out" (also known as the principle of reinforcement).

Positive reinforcer Any event whose presence increases the likelihood that ongoing behavior will recur.

Negative reinforcer Any event whose reduction or termination increases the likelihood that ongoing behavior will recur.

forcement) or to escape from doing tedious homework for a while (negative reinforcement), but in either case the end result is a higher incidence of piano playing.

Some researchers have suggested that in the classroom, linking rewards to learning might actually reduce natural motivation and creativity (Tagano, Moran, & Sawyers, 1991). Most of the evidence, however, confirms the positive effects of rewards. In fact, one extensive analysis of more than 100 studies revealed that when used appropriately, rewards do not compromise intrinsic motivation or creativity (Eisenberger & Cameron, 1996). To the contrary, when applied properly, rewards may promote creativity. Rewarding highly creative behavior on one task often enhances subsequent creativity on other tasks (Eisenberger & Rhoades, 2001).

Punishment

So far, we have focused on the way reinforcers affect behavior. But behavior can also be controlled by **punishment.** For most of us, receiving a fine for speeding or littering reduces the likelihood that we will speed or litter in the future. Being rudely turned down when we ask someone for a favor makes it less likely that we will ask that person for a favor again. In both these cases, the unpleasant aftereffect reduces the likelihood that we will repeat that behavior. Be sure you understand the difference between punishment and negative reinforcement: Reinforcement of whatever kind *strengthens* (reinforces) behavior; negative reinforcement strengthens behavior by removing something unpleasant from the environment. By contrast, punishment adds something unpleasant to the environment, and as a result it tends to *weaken* behavior.

Although the examples listed above suggest that punishment works, we can all think of situations in which punishment clearly does not work. Some children continue to misbehave even after they have been punished repeatedly for that misbehavior. The family dog may sleep on the couch at night despite being punished for this behavior every morning. And some criminals continue to commit crimes when facing both threatened and real punishment. So an important question comes to mind: Under what conditions does punishment work? (Gershoff, 2002).

Punishment Any event whose presence decreases the likelihood that ongoing behavior will recur.

A punishment is any consequence that decreases the chances that a particular behavior will be repeated. This man being carried to the pillory in colonial New England will probably think twice before repeating whatever misdeed he committed, because public humiliation is a powerful form of punishment.

For punishment to be effective, it must be imposed properly. First, punishment should be *swift*. Children who misbehave should be punished right away so they know that what they have done is wrong. Punishment should also be *sufficient* without being cruel. If a parent merely warned a child not to bully other children, the effect might be less pronounced than if the warning were accompanied by the threat of being "grounded" for a day. Effective punishment should be certain: parents should try to punish children each and every time they misbehave. And punishment should be consistent: the common practice of making the punishment for each successive misdeed more severe than the last is not as effective as maintaining a constant level of punishment.

The proper application of punishment can change behavior quickly, which is critical in certain cases. A child who likes to play in the street or who enjoys poking things into electric outlets must be stopped quickly and, in these instances, punishment may be the best course of action. But even in situations like these, punishment has significant drawbacks (Gershoff, 2002; Skinner, 1953). First, punishment only suppresses behavior: It doesn't teach a more desirable behavior. If the punisher or the threat of punishment is removed, the negative behavior is likely to recur. Drivers who are speeding on a highway generally slow down when they see a radar-equipped police car on the side of the road, because the police car introduces the threat of punishment. But as soon as the threat is past, they tend to speed up again. Thus, punishment rarely works when long-term changes in behavior are sought (Pogarsky & Piquero, 2003).

Second, punishment often stirs up unpleasant emotions that can impede learning. For example, when children are learning to read and a teacher or parent scolds them every time they mispronounce a word, they are likely to become frightened and confused. As a result they may mispronounce more words and get scolded more often. In time, they may become so overwhelmed with fear that they do not want to read at all. Moreover, studies have shown that children who frequently experience corporal punishment have a higher incidence of depression, antisocial behavior, and increased difficulty relating to their peers (Matta, 2002).

Third, punishment may convey the notion that inflicting pain on others is justified, thereby inadvertently teaching undesirable aggressive behavior (Gershoff, 2002). In laboratory studies, monkeys that are punished tend to attack other monkeys; likewise, pigeons other pigeons, and so on (B. Schwartz, 1989). Finally, punishment often makes people angry, and angry people frequently become more aggressive and hostile.

If punishment must be used to suppress undesirable behavior, it should be terminated when more desirable behavior occurs (to negatively reinforce that behavior). Positive reinforcement (praise, rewards) should also be used to strengthen the desired behavior. This approach is more productive than punishment alone, because it teaches an alternative behavior to replace the actions that prompted the punishment. Positive reinforcement also makes the learning environment less threatening overall.

As a method for controlling behavior, punishment is one of the least pleasant options, because it is often ineffective and can have negative side effects. Most of us would prefer to avoid using punishment at all, relying instead on the threat of punish-

THINKING CRITICALLY

Corporal Punishment

Many school systems still use some form of corporal punishment, such as paddling, for students who misbehave. The justification is that it is an effective method of changing undesirable behavior, it develops a sense of personal responsibility, it teaches self-discipline, and it helps develop moral character.

Based on what you now know about operant conditioning,

1. under what circumstances (if any) should corporal punishment be used in schools?

2. what factors, besides the student's immediate actions, should adults consider before using corporal punishment?

3. what unintended consequences might arise from the use of corporal punishment?

ment when behavior is getting out of control. If the threat of punishment induces a change to more desirable behavior, punishment need not be imposed at all. Psychologists call this **avoidance training.**

Avoidance training with animals in a laboratory usually includes some sort of warning devices, such as a light or a buzzer. For example, an animal might be placed in a box with a wire floor that can deliver a mild shock. The animal must learn to press a bar in the box after hearing the buzzer, but before the shock starts, to prevent the shock from occurring. At first this usually happens accidentally. But once the animal discovers that pressing the bar prevents the shock, it will run to the bar whenever it hears the buzzer, thus avoiding the shock altogether.

We, too, derive lessons from avoidance training, as when we learn to carry an umbrella when it looks like rain or not to touch a hot iron. But sometimes avoidance learning outlives its usefulness. Children taught not to go into deep water may avoid deep water even after they have learned how to swim. In other cases, avoidance behavior may persist long after the fear has been removed. So while fear is essential for learning the avoidance response, it is not always necessary for *sustaining* the learned response.

Avoidance training Learning a desirable behavior to prevent the occurrence of something unpleasant such as punishment.

 5.3

ENDURING ISSUES   **diversity**universality

What Is Punishment?

We do not know whether a particular entity is reinforcing or punishing until we see whether it increases or decreases the occurrence of a response. We might assume that candy, for example, is a reinforcer for children, but some children don't like candy. We might also assume that having to work alone rather than in a group of peers would be punishing, but some children prefer to work alone. Teachers must understand the children in their classes as individuals before they decide how to reward or punish them. Similarly, what is reinforcing for men may not be reinforcing for women, and what is reinforcing to people in one culture might not have the same effect for people in other cultures.

In addition, an event or object might not be consistently rewarding or punishing over time. So even if candy is initially reinforcing for some children, if they eat large amounts of it, it can become neutral or even punishing. We must therefore be very careful in labeling items or events as reinforcers or punishers.

Operant Conditioning Is Selective

In our discussion of preparedness in classical conditioning, we saw that some stimuli serve readily as CSs for certain kinds of responses, whereas other stimuli do not. Classical conditioning is more likely to occur when a natural fit exists between the stimulus and the response—for example, a fear response to snakes or an aversive response to an unpleasant odor. Similarly, in operant conditioning, some behaviors are easier to train than others. In general, the behaviors that are easiest to condition are those that animals typically would perform in the training situation. For example, Shettleworth (1975) used food pellets to teach food-deprived hamsters to spend more time doing a variety of things: washing their faces, digging, scent marking, scratching, rearing up on their hind legs, and scraping a wall with their paws. The hamsters quickly learned to spend much more time rearing up on their hind legs, scraping walls, and digging, but there was only a slight increase in the amount of time they spent washing their faces, scratching, and scent marking. The first three

A chicken can easily be trained to "dance," like this one shown hopping from one foot to the other, but it is hard to teach a chicken to lie down and roll over. This illustrates the importance of preparedness in operant conditioning: Learning is less likely for any behavior that an animal isn't likely to perform naturally.

behaviors are responses that hamsters typically make when they are hungry, whereas the last three behaviors usually occur less often when a hamster is hungry. Thus, learning was most successful for those responses that are most likely to occur naturally in the training situation. These cases illustrate the remarkable differences among species concerning which behaviors they can learn and the circumstances under which learning will occur. These species' differences put significant constraints on both classical and operant conditioning.

Superstitious Behavior

Whenever something we do is followed closely by a reinforcer, we will tend to repeat the action—even if the reinforcement is not produced directly by what we have done. For example, if the first time you put a coin in a slot machine, you are rewarded by a payoff, you will be more likely to continue to feed the machine. In an experiment by American psychologist B. F. Skinner (1948), a pigeon was placed in a cage that contained only a food hopper. There was nothing the bird could do directly to get food, but at random intervals Skinner dropped a few grains of food into the hopper. He found that the pigeon began to repeat whatever it had been doing just before it was given food: standing on one foot, hopping around, or strutting around with its neck stretched out. None of these actions had anything to do with getting the food—it was pure coincidence that the food appeared when the bird was standing on one foot, for example, but that action would usually be repeated. Skinner labeled the bird's behavior *superstitious.*

Humans can learn superstitions in the same way (Aeschleman, Rosen, & Williams, 2003). If we happen to be wearing a particular piece of jewelry or a certain pair of socks when something good happens to us, we may come to believe that these incidental factors caused the positive incident, or reinforcement. We may even develop elaborate explanations for accidental or randomly occurring reinforcements.

Learned Helplessness

In the preceding section, we saw that the random delivery of reinforcements (beyond an organism's control) may result in superstitious behavior. But what happens if an animal experiences random exposure to painful or aversive stimuli over which it has no control? In a classic two-part experiment by Seligman and Maier (1967) (see Figure 5–4), two groups of dogs were placed in an experimental chamber that delivered an identical series of electric shocks to their feet at random intervals. The dogs in the control group could turn off (or escape) the shock by pushing a panel with their noses. The dogs in the experimental group, however, could not turn off the shock—they were, in effect, helpless.

In the second part of the experiment, both the experimental and control animals were placed in a different situation: both groups could escape shock by jumping over a hurdle. The dogs in the control group quickly learned to avoid the shock by jumping over the hurdle when a warning light came on. However, the dogs which had previously experienced unavoidable shocks failed to learn either to avoid the shock (jumping in response to the warning light) or to escape the shock (jumping after the shock started). In fact, many of the animals that had previously experienced inescapable shocks also became less active, experienced a loss of appetite, and displayed many of the symptoms associated with depression in humans. This failure to avoid or escape from an unpleasant or aversive stimulus that occurs as a result of previous exposure to unavoidable painful stimuli is referred to as **learned helplessness.**

Seligman and his colleagues have since conducted numerous experiments in learned helplessness and have produced similar results in both animals and humans (Maier & Seligman, 1976; Peterson, Maier, & Seligman, 1993b; Overmier, 2002).

Learned helplessness Failure to take steps to avoid or escape from an unpleasant or aversive stimulus that occurs as a result of previous exposure to unavoidable painful stimuli.

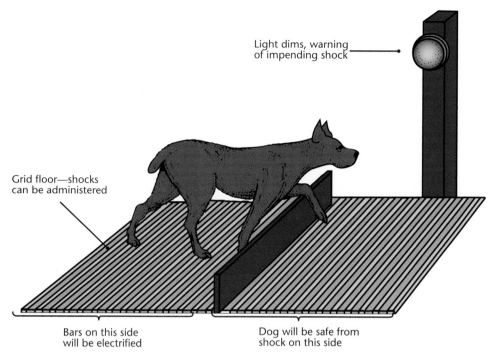

Light dims, warning of impending shock

Grid floor—shocks can be administered

Bars on this side will be electrified

Dog will be safe from shock on this side

Figure 5–4
Learned helplessness.
Dogs who had previously been able to avoid being shocked quickly learned to avoid shocks by jumping over a hurdle when a warning light came on. Other dogs, who had not been able to avoid the original series of shocks, did not learn to jump the hurdle in response to the light.

For example, when faced with a series of unsolvable problems, most college students not only eventually give up but many of them make only half-hearted attempts to solve new problems, even when the new problems are easily solvable. In fact, even if they succeed at solving new problems, they have difficulty recognizing that their behavior had anything to do with their success. Similarly, children raised in an abusive family, where punishment is unrelated to a child's behavior, often develop feelings of powerlessness. Such children, even when placed in relatively normal environments outside their home, often appear listless, passive, and indifferent. They make little attempt to either seek rewards or avoid discomfort. In recent years, researchers have begun to explore the neurological mechanisms that underlie learned helplessness (Hammack, 2002; Minor & Hunter, 2002; Saade, Balleine, & Minor, 2003) and to devise effective therapies to help people overcome it (Cemalcilar, Canbeyli, & Sunar, 2003; Flannery, 2002).

Shaping Behavioral Change through Biofeedback

Patrick, an 8-year-old third grader, was diagnosed with *attention deficit disorder (ADD)*. He was unable to attend to what was going on around him, restless, and unable to concentrate. An EEG showed increased numbers of slow brain waves. After a course of 40 training sessions, using special computer equipment that allowed Patrick to *monitor* his brain-wave activities, he learned how to produce more of the fast waves that are associated with being calm and alert. As a result, Patrick became much more "clued in" to what was going on around him and much less likely to become frustrated when things didn't go his way (Fitzgerald, 1999; Fuchs, Birbaumer, Lutzenberger, Gruzelier, & Kaiser, 2003; Rossiter, 2002).

When operant conditioning is used to control certain biological functions, such as blood pressure, skin temperature (Violani & Lombardo, 2003) or heart rate, it is

Biofeedback A technique that uses monitoring devices to provide precise information about internal physiological processes, such as heart rate or blood pressure, to teach people to gain voluntary control over these functions.

Neurofeedback A biofeedback technique that monitors brain waves using an EEG to teach people to gain voluntary control over their brain wave activity.

referred to as **biofeedback.** Instruments are used to measure particular biological responses—muscle contractions, blood pressure, heart rate, brain waves. Variations in the strength of the response are reflected in the form of a light, a tone, or some other signal. By using the signal—the tone or light—the person can learn to control the response through shaping. For example, Patrick learned to control his brain waves by controlling the movement of a Superman icon on a computer screen. When biofeedback is used to monitor and control brain waves, as in Patrick's case, it is referred to as **neurofeedback** (Fultz, 2002; Vernon et al., 2003).

Biofeedback and neurofeedback have become well-established treatments for a number of medical problems, including migraine headaches (Kropp, Siniatchkin, & Gerber, 2002; Walcutt, 2001), hypertension (Rau, Buehrer, & Weitkunat, 2003), asthma, irritable bowel conditions and peptic ulcers (Jorge, Habr, & Wexner, 2003). Biofeedback has also been used by athletes, musicians, and other performers to control the anxiety that can interfere with their performance. Marathon runners use it to help overcome the tight shoulders and shallow breathing that can prevent them from finishing races. Biofeedback has even been used in space: NASA has used biofeedback as part of a program to reduce the motion sickness astronauts experience at zero gravity.

Biofeedback treatment does have some drawbacks. Learning the technique takes considerable time, effort, patience, and discipline. But it gives patients control of their treatment, a major advantage over other treatment options and it has achieved impressive results in alleviating certain medical problems (Olton & Noonberg, 1980).

CHECK YOUR UNDERSTANDING

1. Any event whose *presence* increases the likelihood that ongoing behavior will recur is called

___ a. positive reinforcement

___ b. negative reinforcement

___ c. punishment

___ d. a generalized stimulus

2. Which of the following is not an example of operant behavior?

___ a. a rat pressing a bar after receiving food for this behavior

___ b. a rat pressing a bar to avoid a shock for this behavior

___ c. a child studying in order to get a teacher's approval

___ d. eye blinking after a flash of light

3. When people and animals cannot avoid unpleasant situations, they are most likely to display

___ a. superstitious behavior

___ b. learned helplessness

___ c. avoidance behavior

___ d. higher-order conditioning

4. Controlling blood pressure by means of operant conditioning is known as

___ a. biofeedback

___ b. higher-order conditioning

___ c. classical conditioning

___ d. stimulus generalization

Answers: 1.a, 2.d, 3.b, 4.a

Comparing Classical and Operant Conditioning

What behavioral principles enable an animal trainer to teach a tiger to jump through a flaming hoop?

Despite the clear differences between classical and operant conditioning, the two forms of learning are alike in a number of ways. We look first at how responses are acquired.

Response Acquisition

Classical Conditioning Except for conditioned food aversions, classical conditioning requires repeated pairing of the CS and US. Each pairing builds on the learner's previous experience. Psychologists refer to this "building phase" of learning as **response acquisition;** each pairing of the US and CS is called a *trial*. Learning does not increase indefinitely or by an equal amount on each successive trial (see Figure 5–5). At first, the likelihood or strength of the conditioned response increases significantly each time the conditioned stimulus and the unconditioned stimulus are paired. But learning eventually reaches a point of diminishing returns: The amount of each increase gradually becomes smaller until, finally, no further learning occurs, and the likelihood or strength of the CR remains constant despite further pairings of the US and CS.

Barry Schwartz (1989) has pointed out that the cumulative nature of most classical conditioning works to our benefit. Lots of different environmental stimuli are present when we experience pain, for example, yet most of those stimuli are irrelevant to the pain. If conditioning occurred on the basis of single events, then these irrelevant stimuli would all generate some type of CR, and we would soon become overwhelmed by the amount of learning—most of it inappropriate or unnecessary—that would take place. Because a number of pairings are usually required to produce a CR, however, in most cases only the relevant cues consistently produce this reaction.

We have seen that, up to a point, the more often the US and CS are paired, the stronger the learning. It turns out that the spacing of trials—that is, the time between one pairing and the next—is at least as important as their number. If the trials follow one another rapidly, or if they are very far apart, the subject may need many trials to achieve the expected response strength. If the trials are spaced evenly—neither too far apart nor too close together—learning will occur after fewer trials. Also the CS and US must rarely, if ever, occur alone (not paired). Pairing the CS and US on only some of the learning trials and presenting them separately on other trials is called **intermittent pairing,** a procedure that reduces both the rate of learning and the final level of learning achieved.

Operant Conditioning Response acquisition in operant conditioning is somewhat more difficult than in classical conditioning. In classical conditioning, the US invariably elicits the UR, which is the behavior we want to link to the CS. But in operant conditioning, the behavior we want to teach is usually voluntary and is not inevitably triggered by outside events. As a result, ensuring that the behavior occurs at all often poses a significant challenge. Sometimes you simply have to wait for the subject to hit

Response acquisition The "building phase" of conditioning during which the likelihood or strength of the desired response increases.

Intermittent pairing Pairing the conditioned stimulus and the unconditioned stimulus on only a portion of the learning trials.

psych 5.4

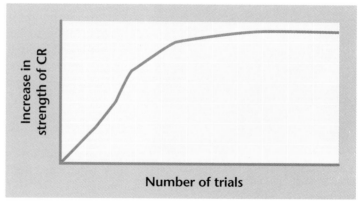

Figure 5–5
Response acquisition.
At first, each pairing of the US and CS increases the strength of the response. After a number of trials, learning begins to level off, and eventually it reaches a point of diminishing returns.

Skinner box A box often used in operant conditioning of animals, which limits the available response and thus increases the likelihood that the desired response will occur.

Shaping Reinforcing successive approximations to a desired behavior.

Figure 5–6
A rat in a Skinner box.
By pressing the bar, the rat releases food pellets into the box, which reinforces its bar-pressing behavior.

How does an animal trainer get a tiger to jump through a flaming hoop so that behavior can be rewarded? The answer is usually through shaping. The trainer reinforces closer and closer approximations of the desired response, until eventually the tiger leaps through the hoop on command.

on the correct response. In the case of Thorndike's cats, Thorndike simply waited for them to trip the latch to open the cage and then reinforced that behavior. Similarly, if parents wait long enough, most babies on their own will eventually make a sound like "mama" in the course of their babbling. Then they can reinforce the baby with smiles and hugs to increase the likelihood that the baby will say "mama" again in the future. (Because "ma" is among the easiest syllables for babies to pronounce, the word for "mother" sounds something like "mama" in many human languages, not just in English.)

Waiting for the correct response to occur spontaneously can be a slow and tedious process, however. If you were an animal tamer for a circus, imagine how long you would have to wait for a tiger to decide to jump through a flaming hoop so that you could reinforce that behavior! There are several ways to speed up the process and make it more likely that the desired response will occur so that it can then be reinforced. One possibility is to increase motivation: An alert and motivated child is more likely to perform some desired behavior than is a passive, unmotivated child.

Another way to speed up the process of operant learning is to reduce or eliminate the opportunities for making irrelevant responses, thereby boosting the chances that the correct response will occur. Many researchers interested in operant conditioning make extensive use of the **Skinner box,** a device named after B. F. Skinner, who pioneered the study of operant conditioning. A Skinner box for rats is small, with solid walls. It is relatively bare except for a bar with a cup underneath it (see Figure 5–6). In this simple environment, it doesn't take long for an active, hungry rat to happen to step on the bar, thereby releasing food pellets into the cup, which reinforces the rat's bar-pressing behavior.

Yet another way to speed up response acquisition during operant conditioning is to reinforce *successive approximations* to the desired response. This approach is called **shaping.** In a Skinner box, for example, we might first reward a rat for turning toward the response bar. Once the rat has learned this behavior, we might withhold reinforcement until the rat moves toward the bar. Later, we might reward it only for sniffing the bar or touching it with its nose or paw, and so on. In this way, by reinforcing successive approximations to the desired behavior, we gradually shape the bar-pressing response without waiting passively for the response to occur on its own.

The circus is a wonderful place to see the results of shaping. To teach a tiger to jump through a flaming hoop, the trainer might first reinforce the animal for simply jumping up on a certain pedestal. After that behavior has been learned, the tiger might be reinforced only for leaping from that pedestal to another. Next, the tiger might be required to jump through a hoop between the pedestals to gain its reward. Finally, the hoop might be set on fire and the tiger required to leap through the burning hoop to be rewarded. In much the same way, a speech therapist might reward a child with a lisp for closer and closer approximations of the correct sound of "s". To learn about how you can use operant conditioning to modify your own behavior see *Applying Psychology: Modifying Your Own Behavior.*

Extinction and Spontaneous Recovery

We have seen how classical and operant conditioning result in the acquisition of new behaviors. But how long does such learning last, and, once lost, can it be recovered?

Classical Conditioning   Let's go back to Pavlov's dogs, which had learned to salivate upon hearing a bell. What would you predict happened over time when the dogs heard the bell (CS) but no food (US) appeared? The answer is that the conditioned response to the bell—the amount of salivation—gradually decreased until eventually it stopped altogether: The dogs no longer salivated when they heard the bell. This process is called **extinction.** If the sound of a can being opened or a cupboard door opening (CS) is no longer associated with the sight or smell of food (US), your cat may no longer purr (CR) when it hears the CS. If scary music in films (CS) is not associated with frightening events on screen (US), you will eventually stop becoming tense and anxious (CR) when you hear that kind of music. These are all examples of extinction of classically conditioned responses.

Once a conditioned response has been extinguished, is the learning gone forever? Pavlov trained his dogs to salivate when they heard a bell, then extinguished the learning. A few days later, the same dogs were again taken to the laboratory. As soon as they heard the bell, their mouths began to water. The response that had been learned and then extinguished reappeared on its own, with no retraining. This phenomenon is known as **spontaneous recovery.** The dogs' response was only about half as strong as it had been before extinction, but the fact that the response occurred at all indicated that the original learning was not completely lost during extinction (see Figure 5–7). Similarly, if your cat is away for a while and then returns home, it may run to the kitchen and start purring the first few times it hears cans or cupboard doors being opened. And if you stop going to the movies for some time, you may find, the next time you go, that scary music once again makes you tense or anxious. In both cases, responses that were once extinguished have returned spontaneously after the passage of time. Note, however, that responses that reappear during spontaneous recovery do not return at full strength, and generally they extinguish again very quickly.

How can extinguished behavior disappear, then reappear again at some later time? According to Mark Bouton (1993, 1994; 2002), extinction does not erase conditioned responses. Rather, extinction occurs because *new* learning during extinction interferes with the previously learned response. That is, stimuli that were paired with conditioned responses come to elicit responses different from, and sometimes incompatible with, those original conditioned responses. A buzzer paired with electric shock initially means "Pain is coming!" and comes to elicit a number of responses—changes in heart rate and blood pressure, for example—that accompany painful stimulation. During extinction, the association between the buzzer and pain disappears, and the buzzer therefore elicits another set of responses, which may be entirely different from the originally learned responses. In fact, these new responses may even antagonize or oppose those original responses. For example, if one response during training was an increased heart rate, but the new response during extinction is a decreased heart rate, the two clearly cannot happen at the same time. The result is *interference*, and spontaneous recovery consists of overcoming this interference.

According to Bouton, one way we overcome this interference is through what he terms the *renewal effect.* Imagine that you are conditioned in one setting (for example, a dim and dark laboratory), and then your conditioned response is extinguished in a very different setting (for example, a bright and cheerful room). Even with total extinction in the new setting, if you return to the original laboratory room, your conditioned response will immediately return. This occurs because the new, interfering responses learned during extinction are associated with stimuli in the new setting and not with stimuli in the original lab room. The originally learned stimulus-response connections, then, are still intact.

Operant Conditioning   Extinction and spontaneous recovery also occur in operant conditioning. In operant conditioning, extinction happens as a result of withholding reinforcement. Yet withholding reinforcement does not usually lead to an immediate decrease in the frequency of the response; in fact, when reinforcement is first discontinued, there is often a brief increase in responding before the strength

Shaping can also be used for some types of human learning. A diver's movements are developed and perfected through a series of successive approximations.

Extinction A decrease in the strength or frequency of a learned response because of failure to continue pairing the US and CS (classical conditioning) or withholding of reinforcement (operant conditioning).

Spontaneous recovery The reappearance of an extinguished response after the passage of time, without further training.

APPLYING PSYCHOLOGY

MODIFYING YOUR OWN BEHAVIOR

Can you modify your own undesirable behaviors by using operant conditioning techniques? Yes, but first you must observe your own actions, think about their implications, and plan a strategy of intervention.

Begin by *identifying the behavior you want to acquire:* This is called the "target" behavior. You will be more successful if you focus on acquiring a new behavior rather than on eliminating an existing one. For example, instead of setting a target of being less shy, you might define the target behavior as becoming more outgoing or more sociable. Other possible target behaviors might include behaving more assertively, studying more, and getting along better with your roommates. In each case, you have spotlighted the behavior that you want to acquire rather than the behavior that you want to eliminate.

The next step is *defining the target behavior precisely:* What exactly do you mean by "assertive" or "sociable"? Imagine situations in which the target behavior could be performed. Then describe in writing the way in which you now respond to these situations. For example, if you would like to become more outgoing and sociable, you might write, "When I am sitting in a lecture hall, waiting for class to begin, I don't talk to the people around me." Next, write down how you would rather act in that situation: "In a lecture hall before class, I want to talk to at least one other person. I might ask the person sitting next to me how he or she likes the class or the professor, or simply comment on some aspect of the course."

"You will be more successful if you focus on acquiring a new behavior rather than on eliminating an existing one."

The third step is *monitoring your present behavior:* You may do so by keeping a daily log of activities related to the target behavior. This will establish your current "base rate" and give you something concrete against which to gauge improvements. At the same time, try to figure out whether your present, undesirable behavior is being reinforced in some way. For example, if you find yourself unable to study, record what you do instead (Get a snack? Watch television?) and determine whether you are inadvertently rewarding your failure to study.

The next step—the basic principle of self-modification—is *providing yourself with a positive reinforcer that is contingent on specific improvements in the target behavior:* You may be able to use the same reinforcer that now maintains your undesirable behavior, or you may want to pick a new reinforcer. For example, if you want to increase the amount of time you spend studying, you might reward yourself with a token for each 30 minutes of study. Then, if your favorite pastime is watching movies, you might charge yourself three tokens for an hour of television, whereas the privilege of going to a movie might cost six.

Remember that the new, more desirable behavior need not be learned all at once. You can use shaping or successive approximations to change your behavior gradually. A person who wants to become more sociable might start by giving rewards just for sitting next to another person in a classroom rather than picking an isolated seat. The person could then work up to rewarding increasingly sociable behaviors, such as first saying hello to another person, then striking up a conversation.

If you would like to try a program of self-improvement, a book by David Watson and Roland Tharp, *Self-Directed Behavior: Self-Modification for Personal Adjustment* (1997), is a good place to start. It contains step-by-step instructions and exercises that provide a useful guide.

or frequency of the response declines. The behavior itself also changes at the start of extinction: It becomes more variable and often more forceful. For instance, if you put coins in a vending machine and it fails to deliver the goods, you may pull the lever more violently or slam your fist against the glass panel. If the vending machine still fails to produce the item for which you paid, your attempts to get it to work will decrease, and you will finally stop trying altogether.

Just as in classical conditioning, however, extinction does not erase a response forever. Spontaneous recovery may occur if a period of time passes after initial extinction. And once again, both extinction and spontaneous recovery may be understood in terms of interference from new behaviors. If a rat is no longer reinforced for pressing a lever, it will start to engage in other behaviors—turning away from the lever, biting at the corners of the operant chamber, attempting to escape,

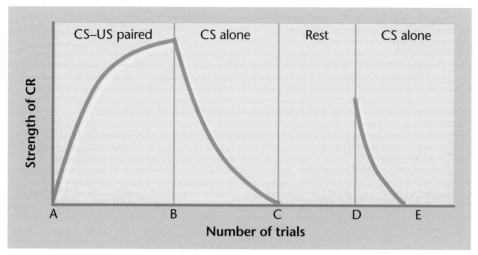

Figure 5–7
Response acquisition and extinction in classical conditioning.
From point A to point B, the conditioned stimulus and the unconditioned stimulus were paired, and learning increased steadily. From B to C, however, the conditioned stimulus was presented alone. By point C, the response had been extinguished. After a rest period from C to D, spontaneous recovery occurred—the learned response reappeared at about half the strength that it had at point B. When the conditioned stimulus was again presented alone, the response extinguished rapidly (point E).

and so on—and these new behaviors will interfere with the operant response of lever pressing, causing extinction. Spontaneous recovery is a brief victory of original training over these interfering responses.

How easy is it to extinguish behaviors learned through operant conditioning? The stronger the original learning, the longer it takes to stop the action from being performed. Also, the greater the variety of settings in which learning takes place, the

When reinforcement has been frequent, a learned behavior tends to be retained even after reinforcement is reduced. A dog "shaking hands" is an excellent example. Many previous rewards for this response tend to keep the dog offering people its paw even when no reward follows.

Discrimination is an important part of learning, as any wild mushroom fancier knows. A dog or a human who can't distinguish between an edible mushroom and a poisonous one is at a real disadvantage in the hunt for this food.

harder it is to extinguish it. Complex behavior is also much more difficult to extinguish than simple behavior. Responses that are reinforced only occasionally during acquisition usually resist extinction more strongly than responses that are reinforced every time they occur. And finally, behaviors learned through punishment rather than reinforcement are especially hard to extinguish.

Generalization and Discrimination

We have seen the kinds of circumstances that make us more likely to acquire or to extinguish conditioned responses. What kinds of situations make us more likely to generalize a learned response to a new situation?

Classical Conditioning   Recall the case of Little Albert and his conditioned fear of white rats. When the experimenters later showed Albert a white rabbit, Albert cried and tried to crawl away, even though he had not been taught to fear rabbits. Similarly, Pavlov noticed that after his dogs had been conditioned to salivate when they heard a bell, their mouths would often water when they heard a buzzer or the ticking of a metronome, even though they had not been taught to salivate to buzzers or ticking sounds. Often in classical conditioning we see that a response learned to one CS also occurs in the presence of other, similar objects or situations.

Reacting to a stimulus that is similar to the one to which you have learned to respond is called **stimulus generalization.** In Pavlov's case, the conditioned response generalized from the ringing of a bell to other unusual noises in the testing room. Albert's learned fear of white, furry rats generalized not only to white, furry rabbits but also to all kinds of white, furry objects—he came to fear cotton balls, a fur coat, and even a white-bearded Santa Claus mask.

Stimulus generalization is not inevitable in classical conditioning. In a process called **stimulus discrimination,** we can train animals and people not to generalize but rather to make a learned response only to a single specific object or event. If we present several similar objects, only one of which is followed by the unconditioned stimulus, the subject will learn over time to respond only to that stimulus and to inhibit the response in the presence of all other stimuli. If Albert has been presented with a rat and a rabbit and cotton balls and other white, furry objects, but the loud noise (US) had occurred only when the rat appeared, he would have learned to discriminate the white rat from the other objects, and the fear response would not have generalized as it did.

Learning to discriminate is essential in everyday life. As we noted earlier, most children fear loud noises. Because thunder by itself cannot harm a child, it would be helpful if children learned not to be afraid every time they heard it. Similarly, not all mushrooms are poisonous, and not all strangers are unfriendly. Thus, discrimination is crucial to learning.

Operant Conditioning   Stimulus generalization can also occur in operant conditioning. For example, a baby who is hugged and kissed for saying "mama" when he sees his mother may begin to call everyone "mama"—males and females alike. Although the person whom the baby sees—the stimulus—changes, he responds with the same word. In the same way, the skills you learn when playing tennis may be generalized to badminton, Ping-Pong, and squash.

We often encounter situations in which the same stimulus triggers responses that are different from, but similar to, the one that was taught. In operant conditioning, this process is called **response generalization.** For example, the baby who calls everyone "mama" may also call his mother "gaga" or "baba"—the learning has generalized to other sounds that are similar to the correct response, "mama." Note that in classical conditioning, response generalization does not occur. If a dog is taught

Stimulus generalization The transfer of a learned response to different but similar stimuli.

Stimulus discrimination Learning to respond to only one stimulus and to inhibit the response to all other stimuli.

Response generalization Giving a response that is somewhat different from the response originally learned to that stimulus.

to salivate when it hears a high-pitched tone, it will salivate less when it hears a low-pitched tone, but the response is still salivation.

Discrimination in operant conditioning is accomplished by reinforcing *only* the specific, desired response, and then *only* in the presence of specific stimuli. For example, babies can learn to say "mama" only for their own mothers if they are reinforced for using "mama" correctly and not reinforced when they use the term for other people. In the same way, if they are reinforced only when they say "mama" and not when they say "gaga" or "baba," they will learn that those responses are not appropriate.

New Learning Based on Original Learning

Learning would be severely limited if learned responses were elicited, or emitted, only in the presence of the specific stimuli that are present during training. We have already seen how learning can be expanded to different situations. Here, we see how original learning can be the basis for new learning. In classical conditioning, an existing conditioned stimulus can be paired with a new stimulus to produce a new conditioned reponse. This is called **higher-order conditioning.** Similarly, in operant conditioning, objects that have no intrinsic value can nevertheless become reinforcers because of their association with other, more basic reinforcers. These learned reinforcers are called *secondary reinforcers.*

Higher-Order Conditioning in Classical Conditioning Pavlov demonstrated higher-order conditioning with his dogs. After Pavlov's dogs had learned to salivate when they heard a bell, Pavlov was able to use the bell (without food) to teach the dogs to salivate at the sight of a black square. Instead of showing them the square and following it with food, he showed them the square and followed it with the bell until the dogs learned to salivate when they saw the square. In effect, the bell served as a substitute unconditioned stimulus and the black square became a new conditioned stimulus. This is an example of higher-order conditioning, not because it is more complex or because it incorporates any new principles, but simply because it is conditioning based on previous conditioning.

Higher-order conditioning is difficult to achieve because it races against extinction. The original US, the foundation of the original conditioning, is no longer presented along with the CS and, as we saw earlier, that is precisely the way to extinguish a classically conditioned response. During higher-order conditioning, Pavlov's dogs were exposed to the square and the bell, but no food was presented. In fact, the square became a signal that the bell would *not* be followed by food, so the dogs soon stopped salivating to the square/bell pairing. For higher-order conditioning to succeed, then, the US has to be reintroduced occasionally: Food must be given to the dogs once in a while at the sound of the bell, so that they will continue to salivate when they hear the bell.

Secondary Reinforcers in Operant Conditioning Classical conditioning and operant conditioning can act in concert. Specifically, we can use classical conditioning principles to explain why operant learning, particularly human operant learning, is not restricted to food reinforcers and painful punishers.

Some reinforcers, such as food, water, and sex, are intrinsically rewarding in and of themselves. These are called **primary reinforcers.** No prior learning is required to make them reinforcing. Other reinforcers have no intrinsic value, but they acquire value or a sense of reward through association with primary reinforcers. These are called **secondary reinforcers,** not because they are less important, but because prior learning or conditioning is required before they will function as reinforcers.

Higher-order conditioning
Conditioning based on previous learning; the conditioned stimulus serves as an unconditioned stimulus for further training.

Primary reinforcer A reinforcer that is rewarding in itself, such as food, water, and sex.

Secondary reinforcer A reinforcer whose value is acquired through association with other primary or secondary reinforcers.

Contingency A reliable "if-then" relationship between two events such as a CS and a US.

Blocking A process whereby prior conditioning prevents conditioning to a second stimulus even when the two stimuli are presented simultaneously.

Much like conditioned stimuli, secondary reinforcers acquire reinforcing properties because they have been paired with primary reinforcers. In humans, money is one of the best examples of a secondary reinforcer. Although money is just paper or metal, through its association with food, clothing, and other primary reinforcers, it becomes a powerful secondary reinforcer. And through the principles of higher-order conditioning, stimuli paired with a secondary reinforcer can acquire reinforcing properties. Checks and credit cards, for example, are one step removed from money, but can also be highly reinforcing.

Contingencies

Classical Conditioning Pavlov's analysis of classical conditioning emphasized that the CS and US must occur close together in time for classical conditioning to take place. More recent research, however, has shown that the CS must also precede and provide predictive information about the US. Robert Rescorla (1966, 1967, 1988) refers to this *informative* relationship between CS and US as a **contingency.**

Imagine an experiment in which animals are exposed to a tone (CS) and a mild electrical shock (US). One group always hears the tone a fraction of a second *before* it experiences the shock. Another group sometimes hears the tone just before the shock, sometimes hears the tone a fraction of a second *after* the shock, and on still other occasions the tone and shock occur simultaneously. You would expect animals in the first group to show a fear response when they hear the tone alone. You might also expect the second group also to show a startle or fear response, because the US and CS always occurred closely together in time. In fact, however, the second group will show little, if any, conditioning. This is because the first group has learned a contingency between the tone and the shock. For them, the tone *always* precedes the shock, the tone always means that a shock is coming. Not surprisingly, the animals learn to fear the sound of the tone. For the second group, however, the tone says little or nothing about the shock: Sometimes it means that a shock is coming, sometimes it means that the shock is here, and sometimes it means that the shock is over and "the coast is clear." Because the meaning of the tone is ambiguous for this second group, there is little or no conditioning of a fear response.

Although scientists once believed that conditioning was impossible if the CS followed the US, Rescorla's work demonstrates that this is not the case. Imagine a situation in which the tone (the CS) always follows the shock (the US), a so-called *backward conditioning* experiment. After many conditioning trials, we play the tone alone. It's true that we will not see a conditioned startle or fear response; after all, the tone does not predict that a shock is about to occur. But that does not mean that no conditioning has occurred. In fact, the tone predicts that the shock is all over and will not occur again for some time. Thus, the tone comes to produce a conditioned relaxation response rather than a fear response!

The idea that a CS must provide information about the US for conditioning to occur was confirmed by psychologist Leon Kamin in 1969. Kamin first conditioned a rat to fear a noise (CS) that was followed by a brief shock (US). Then, he added a second CS—a light—along with the noise. Contrary to what you might expect, the rats did not learn to fear the light even though it was regularly followed by a shock. Kamin concluded that the original learning had a **blocking** effect on new learning. Once the rats learned that noise signaled the onset of shock, adding yet another cue (a light) provided no new information about the likelihood of shock, so no new learning took place. According to Kamin, then, classical conditioning occurs only when a CS tells the learner something *new* or *additional* about the likelihood that the US will be forthcoming.

Operant Conditioning Contingencies also figure prominently in operant conditioning. Seldom, either in life or in the laboratory, are we rewarded every time we do something. And this is just as well. Experiments demonstrate that *partial* or *intermittent reinforcement* results in behavior that persists longer than behavior learned by *continuous reinforcement*. When they receive only occasional reinforcement, learners typically continue to respond apparently in hopes that they will eventually gain the desired reward. Vending machines and slot machines illustrate the effects of continuous and partial reinforcement on extinction. Each time you put the correct change into a vending machine, you get something such as food in return (reinforcement); if a vending machine is broken and you receive nothing for your coins, you are unlikely to drop additional coins into it! By contrast, casino slot machines pay off only occasionally; therefore, you might continue putting coins into a slot machine for a long time, even though you are not receiving anything in return.

Schedules of Reinforcement Whenever partial reinforcement is given, the rule for determining when and how often reinforcers will be delivered is called the **schedule of reinforcement.** Schedules are either *fixed* or *variable*, and may be based on either the number of correct responses or the elapsed time between correct responses. The most common reinforcement schedules are fixed-interval and variable-interval schedules, which are based on time, and fixed-ratio and variable-ratio schedules, which are based on the number of correct responses. Table 5–1 describes some everyday examples of reinforcement schedules. Figure 5–8 illustrates a response pattern that typically results from each type of reinforcement schedule.

On a **fixed-interval schedule,** learners are reinforced for the first correct response only after a certain time has passed following the previous correct response; that is, they have to wait for a set period before they can be reinforced again. With fixed-interval schedules, performance tends to fall off immediately after each reinforcement and then to pick up again as the time for the next reinforcement draws near. For example, when exams are given at fixed intervals—such as midterms and finals—students tend to increase the intensity of their studying just before an exam and then decrease it sharply right after the exam until shortly before the next one (see Figure 5–8).

A **variable-interval schedule** reinforces correct responses after varying lengths of time following the last reinforcement. One reinforcement might be given after 6 minutes, the next after 4 minutes, the next after 5 minutes, the next after 3 minutes. Subjects learn to give a slow, steady pattern of responses, being careful not to be so slow as to miss all the rewards. Thus, if several exams are given during a semester at unpredictable intervals, students have to keep studying at a steady rate all the time, because on any given day there might be an exam.

On a **fixed-ratio schedule,** a certain number of correct responses must occur before reinforcement is provided. This results in a high response rate because making many responses in a short time yields more rewards. Being paid on a piecework basis is an example of a fixed-ratio schedule. Farmworkers might get $3 for every 10 baskets of cherries they pick. The more they pick, the more money they make. Under a fixed-ratio schedule, a brief pause after reinforcement is followed by a rapid and steady response rate until the next reinforcement.

On a **variable-ratio schedule,** the number of correct responses necessary to gain reinforcement is not constant. The casino slot machine is a good example of a variable-ratio schedule: It may pay off, but you have no idea when. And because there is always a chance of hitting the jackpot, the temptation to keep playing is great. Learners on a variable-ratio schedule tend not to pause after reinforcement

---

Schedule of reinforcement In operant conditioning, the rule for determining when and how often reinforcers will be delivered.

Fixed-interval schedule A reinforcement schedule in which the correct response is reinforced after a fixed length of time since the last reinforcement.

Variable-interval schedule A reinforcement schedule in which the correct response is reinforced after varying lengths of time following the last reinforcement.

Fixed-ratio schedule A reinforcement schedule in which the correct response is reinforced after a fixed number of correct responses.

Variable-ratio schedule A reinforcement schedule in which a varying number of correct responses must occur before reinforcement is presented.

table 5-1 EXAMPLES OF REINFORCEMENT IN EVERYDAY LIFE

Continuous reinforcement
(reinforcement every time the response is made)

Putting money in the parking meter to avoid a ticket.

Putting coins in a vending machine to get candy or soda.

Fixed-ratio schedule
(reinforcement after a fixed number of responses)

Being paid on a piecework basis—in the garment industry, workers may be paid a fee per 100 dresses sewn.

Taking a multi-item test. This is an example of negative reinforcement—as soon as you finish those items on the test, you can leave!

Variable-ratio schedule
(reinforcement after a varying number of responses)

Playing a slot machine—the machine is programmed to pay off after a certain number of responses have been made, but that number keeps changing. This type of schedule creates a steady rate of responding, because players know if they play long enough, they will win.

Sales commissions—you have to talk to many customers before you make a sale, and you never know whether the next one will buy. Again, the number of sales calls you make, not how much time passes, will determine when you are reinforced by a sale. And the number of sales calls will vary.

Fixed-interval schedule
(reinforcement after a fixed amount of time has passed)

You have an exam coming up, and as time goes by, and you haven't studied, you have to make up for it all by a certain time, and that means cramming.

Picking up a salary check, which occurs every week or every two weeks.

Variable-internal schedule
(reinforcement of first response after varying amounts of time)

Surprise quizzes in a course cause a steady rate of studying because you never know when they'll occur, and so you have to be prepared all the time.

Watching a football game, waiting for a touchdown. It could happen anytime—if you leave the room, you may miss it, so you have to keep watching continuously.

Source: From F. J. Landy, 1987, *Psychology: The Science of People*, Second Edition (Prentice Hall), p. 212. Adapted by permission.

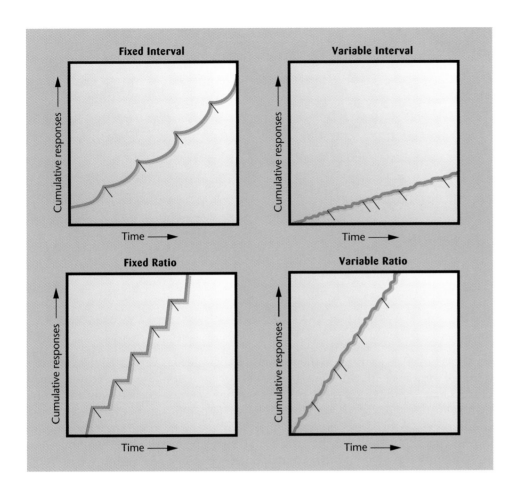

Figure 5–8

Response patterns to schedules of reinforcement.

On a fixed-interval schedule, as the time for reinforcement approaches, the number of responses increases, and the slope becomes steeper. A variable-ratio schedule produces a high rate of response with little or no pause after each reinforcement. The fixed-ratio schedule is characterized by a high rate of response and a pause after each reinforcement. On a variable-interval schedule, the response rate is moderate and relatively constant. Notice that each tick mark on the graph represents one reinforcement.

and have a high rate of response over a long period of time. Because they never know when reinforcement may come, they keep on trying. Similarly, salespeople working on commission know that every attempt will not produce a sale, but it is certain that the more customers they approach, the more sales they will make.

Summing Up

Classical and operant conditioning both focus on building associations between stimuli and responses. Both are subject to extinction and spontaneous recovery as well as to generalization and discrimination. The main difference between the two is that in classical conditioning, the learner is passive and the desired behavior is usually involuntary, whereas in operant conditioning, the learner is active and the desired behavior is usually voluntary.

However, some psychologists play down these differences, suggesting that classical and operant conditioning are simply two different ways of bringing about the same kind of learning. For example, in operant conditioning, once the operant response

THINKING CRITICALLY

Schedules of Reinforcement

Think about how you could apply the principles of behavioral learning to

1. Design the ideal slot machine, one that would keep people playing over and over again, even though they won very little money.

2. Design a reward system for a fifth-grade class that would result in both effort at schoolwork and good behavior.

3. Design an ideal lottery or mail-in contest.

4. Design an ideal payment system for salespeople (you may include both salary and commission).

For each type of reward system, think about what the reinforcers should be, what contingencies are operating, and what behaviors you want to elicit. Also think about how you would demonstrate to a skeptic that your procedures have actually resulted in a change in the desired direction.

The slot machine is a classic example of a variable-ratio schedule of reinforcement. The machine eventually pays off, but always after a variable number of plays. Because people keep hoping that the next play will be rewarded, they maintain a high rate of response over a long period of time.

becomes linked to a stimulus, the response looks and acts very much like an unconditioned response. If you have been reinforced repeatedly for stepping on the brake when a traffic light turns red, the red light comes to elicit braking behavior, just as an unconditioned stimulus elicits an unconditioned response in classical conditioning. Moreover, classical conditioning can be used to shape voluntary movements (P. L. Brown & Jenkins, 1968; Vossel & Rossman, 1986), and operant conditioning can be used to shape involuntary responses as we will see in the next section of the chapter.

CHECK YOUR UNDERSTANDING

1. To extinguish classical conditioning, break the association between which of the following pairs?

___a. US and UR

___b. CS and US

___c. US and CR

2. Identify the following schedules of reinforcement as fixed interval (FI), variable interval (VI), fixed ratio (FR) and variable ratio (VR).

___a. Reinforcement comes on the first correct response after two minutes from the last correct response.

___b. Reinforcement comes on every sixth correct response.

___c. Reinforcement comes after four correct responses, than after six more, than after five more.

___d. Reinforcement comes after varying lengths of time following the last correct response.

3. The process by which a learned response to a specific stimulus comes to be associated with a different but similar stimulus is called

___a. extinction

___b. classical conditioning

___c. stimulus generalization

___d. response generalization

4. What is it called when prior conditioning prevents conditioning to a second stimulus, even when the two are presented simultaneously?

___a. partial reinforcement

___b. blocking

___c. backward conditioning

___d. extinction

Cognitive learning Learning that depends on mental processes that are not directly observable.

Latent learning Learning that is not immediately reflected in a behavior change.

Cognitive map A learned mental image of a spatial environment that may be called on to solve problems when stimuli in the environment change.

Cognitive Learning

Do children learn to behave violently by observing adults?

Classical and operant conditioning both depend on direct experience and stimulus control. Some psychologists insist that because the elements of these types of learning can be *observed* and *measured*, they are the only legitimate kinds of learning to study scientifically. Other psychologists, however, point to the importance of mental activities such as attention, expectation, thinking, and remembering as crucial to the process of learning. We learn how to find our way around a building or neighborhood, we learn what to expect from a given situation, we learn abstract concepts, and we can even learn about situations that we have never experienced firsthand. These kinds of **cognitive learning** are impossible to observe and measure directly, but they can be *inferred* from behavior; thus, they too are legitimate subjects for scientific inquiry. In fact, much of the recent research in the area of learning concerns cognitive learning: What goes on *inside* us when we learn.

Latent Learning and Cognitive Maps

Interest in cognitive learning actually began shortly after the earliest work in both classical and operant conditioning. Edward Chace Tolman, one of the pioneers in the study of cognitive learning, argued that we do not need to show our learning in order for learning to have occurred. Tolman called learning that is not apparent because it is not yet demonstrated **latent learning.**

Tolman demonstrated the process of latent learning in a famous experiment with C.H. Honzik in 1930. Two groups of hungry rats were placed in a maze and required to find their way from a start box to an end box. The first group found food pellets (a reward) in the end box; the second group found nothing there. According to the principles of operant conditioning, the first group would learn the maze better than the second group—which was, indeed, what happened. But when Tolman took some of the rats from the second, unreinforced group and gave them food at the goal box, almost immediately they started running the maze as well as the rats in the first group (see Figure 5–9). He explained these dramatic findings by noting that the unrewarded rats had actually learned a great deal about the maze as they wandered around inside it but their learning was *latent*—stored internally in some way but not yet reflected in their behavior. When they were given a good reason (a food reward) to run the maze quickly, they put their latent learning to use.

In response to Tolman's theory of latent learning, Thorndike proposed an experiment to test whether a rat could learn to run a maze and store an image or **cognitive map** of the maze without experiencing the maze firsthand. He envisioned researchers carrying each rat through the maze in a

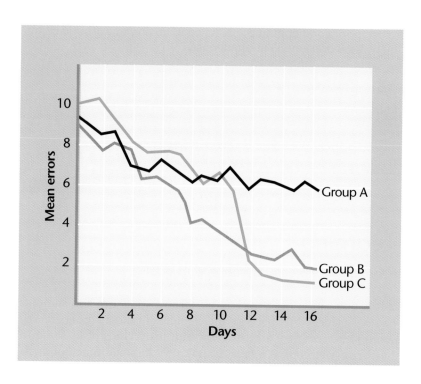

Figure 5–9
Graph showing the results of the Tolman and Honzik study.
Group A never received a food reward; Group B was rewarded each day. Group C was not rewarded until the eleventh day, but note the significant change in the rats' behavior on Day 12. The results suggest that Group C had been learning all along, although this learning was not reflected in their performance until they were rewarded with food for demonstrating the desired behaviors.
Source: From Tolman and Honzik, 1930.

small container and then rewarding the rat at the end of each trail as if it had run the maze itself. He predicted that the rat would show little or no evidence of learning compared to rats that had learned the same maze on their own through trial and error. Neither he nor Tolman ever conducted the experiment.

Two decades later, however, researchers at the University of Kansas picked up on Thorndike's idea (McNamara, Long, & Wike, 1956). But instead of taking the passive rats through the "correct" path in a simple maze, they carried each passenger rat over the same path that a free-running partner rat had taken on the same trail. Contrary to Thorndike's prediction, the passenger rats learned the maze just as well as their active counterparts. In a second version of the experiment, the experimenters covered windows and masked the lights in the room so that the passenger rats would have only the directional cues to orient them to the maze. Under these conditions, the passenger rats seemed not to have learned to run the maze at all.

The first experiment seems to confirm Tolman's view of latent learning of cognitive maps. The second experiment suggests that rats use information from their surroundings as an important part of their cognitive maps. More recent research confirms that animals demonstrate a great deal more flexibility when it comes to solving problems and making choices than can be explained by simple conditioning (Domjan, 1987). Thus, even in rats, learning involves more than a change in observable behavior. It also appears to involve changes in unobservable mental processes that may (or may not) be reflected at some future time in the subject's behavior.

Insight and Learning Sets

Another phenomenon that highlights the importance of cognitive processing in learning is **insight,** the sudden "coming together" of the elements of a situation so that the most efficient path is instantly clear or the solution to a problem suddenly strikes the learner. In this case, learning does not progress slowly and gradually on a smooth curve as a result of practice but suddenly shoots up from unsuccessful trial and error to instant success.

Insight Learning that occurs rapidly as a result of understanding all the elements of a problem.

During World War I, the German Gestalt psychologist Wolfgang Köhler conducted a series of experiments on insightful learning. He placed a chimpanzee in a cage with a banana on the ground just outside the cage, but not within reach. When the animal realized that it couldn't reach the banana by stretching out its arms, it initially reacted with frustration. After a while, the chimp started looking at what was in the cage, including a stick left there by the experimenters. Sometimes quite suddenly, the chimp would grab the stick, poke it through the bars of the cage, and drag the banana within reach. The same kind of sudden insight occurred when the banana was hung from the roof of the cage, just out of the chimp's grasp. This time, inside the cage were some boxes, which the chimp quickly learned to move to the spot under the banana and stack up high enough so it could climb up to snatch the food.

Köhler's experiments with chimpanzees illustrate learning through insight. In this photo one of the chimps has arranged a stack of boxes to reach bananas hanging from the ceiling. Insights gained in this problem-solving situation may transfer to similar ones.

ENDURING ISSUES   **stability**change

Human Insight

Insightful learning is particularly important in humans, who must learn not only where to obtain food and how to escape from predators but also such complex ethical and cultural ideas as the value of hard work, helping others, overcoming addictions, or dealing with a life crisis. In Chapter 7 (Cognition and Language), we will explore the role of insight in creative problem solving. As we will see, there are times when all other problem-solving techniques fail to produce a solution; in such cases, it is not unusual for the solution to suddenly "pop up" in a moment of insight (Novick & Sherman, 2003). Moreover, to the extent that people gain insight into their own behavior, they should be capable of changing significantly over the course of their lives (Bornstein & Masling, 1998). Indeed, as we will see in Chapter 14 (Therapies), the common goal of the various insight therapies, such as psychoanalysis, is to give people a better awareness and understanding of their feelings, motivations, and actions in the hope that this will lead to better adjustment (Pine, 1998).

Are the complex cognitive processes that produce insight limited to higher animals such as apes and humans? In a classic 1984 study, four Harvard University psychologists presented the banana-and-box problem to a small group of pigeons to see if they, too, were capable of insight learning (R. Epstein, Kirshnit, Lanza, & Rubin, 1984). Because moving boxes around is not as natural a behavior for pigeons as it is for chimps, the researchers first conditioned the pigeons, through standard shaping procedures, to push a box toward a particular target—a green spot on the wall of the training cage. On separate occasions, the pigeons were also taught to climb onto a box that was stuck to the floor and to peck at a small picture of a banana to receive a food reward. The question then was: Could the pigeons put the two new behaviors together to solve the problem of the banana and the box? When the pigeons were presented with an out-of-reach hanging picture of a banana and with a box, Epstein and his coworkers reported that each pigeon initially showed confusion and, just like Köhler's chimps, looked for a while from the hanging picture to the box. Then, fairly suddenly, each pigeon began to push the box toward the picture, stopping now and then to sight the picture and to check the direction in which to push the box. When the box was underneath the picture of the banana, each of the pigeons then climbed on top and pecked at the picture to receive its reward.

Previous learning can also be used to speed up new learning, a process demonstrated clearly in a series of studies by Harry Harlow with rhesus monkeys (Harlow,

Learning set The ability to become increasingly more effective in solving problems as more problems are solved.

Social learning theory A view of learning that emphasizes the ability to learn by observing a model or receiving instructions, without firsthand experience by the learner.

Observational (or vicarious) learning Learning by observing other people's behavior.

1949). Harlow presented each monkey with two boxes—say, a round green box on the left side of a tray and a square red box on the right side. A morsel of food was put under one of the boxes. The monkey was permitted to lift just one box; if it chose the correct box, it got the food. On the next trial, the food was put under the same box (which had been moved to a new position), and the monkey again got to choose just one box. Each monkey had six trials to figure out which box covered the food no matter where that box was located. Then the monkeys were given a new set of choices—say, between a blue triangular box and an orange pentagonal one—and another six trials, and so on with other shapes and colors of boxes.

How long did it take for the monkeys to figure out that in any set of six trials, food was always under the same box? Initially, the monkeys chose boxes randomly, by trial and error; sometimes they would find food, but just as often they would not. However, after a while their behavior changed: In just one or two trials, they would find the correct box, which they chose consistently thereafter until the experimenter supplied new boxes. They seemed to have learned the underlying principle—"food is always under the same box"—and they used that learning to solve almost instantly each new set of choices presented by the experimenter.

Harlow concluded that the monkeys had "learned how to learn"; in other words, that they had established **learning sets.** With practice, they became more effective at solving a problem, so that, within the limited range of choices available, they discovered how to tell which box would give them what they wanted. By extension, Köhler's chimps could be said to have established learning sets for various ways of obtaining food that was just out of reach. When presented with the familiar problem of reaching the banana, the chimps simply called up the appropriate learning sets and solved the problem. Epstein's pigeons, however, first had to be taught the appropriate learning sets, and then they, too, were able to solve the problem. In all these cases, the animals seemed to have learned more than just specific behaviors— they apparently learned how to learn. Whether this means that animals can think is an issue that is still being studied and debated. We will explore the question of cognitive learning in animals later in this chapter; then, in Chapter 7 (Cognition and Language), we will look more closely at the question of whether animals can think.

Learning by Observing

We have seen how cognitive psychologists came to challenge the idea that most or all human learning stems from conditioning. Another group of psychologists, *social learning theorists,* also challenged this idea. **Social learning theory** focuses on the extent to which we learn not just from firsthand experience, the kind of learning explained by classical and operant conditioning, but also from watching what happens to other people or by hearing about something. In fact, we can learn new behaviors without ever actually performing them or being reinforced for them. For example, the first time you drive a car, you tend to drive carefully because you have been told to do so, you have been warned about driving carelessly, you have watched people drive carefully, and you've seen what happens when people drive carelessly. In other words, you learned a great deal about driving before you ever got behind the wheel of a car.

This kind of **observational** (or **vicarious**) **learning** is quite common (Blackmore, 1999). But we do not imitate everything that other people do. Social learning theory accounts for this in several ways (Bandura, 1977, 1986). First, you must not only see but also *pay attention* to what the model does; this is more likely if the model commands attention (as does a famous or attractive person or an expert). Second, you must *remember* what the model did. Third, you have to convert what you learned into action: You may learn a great deal from watching a model but have no particular reason to display what you have learned as behavior. This distinction

In observational or vicarious learning, we learn by watching a model perform a particular action and then trying to imitate that action correctly. Some actions would be very difficult to master without observational learning.

between *learning* and *performance* is crucial to social learning theorists: They stress that learning can occur without any change in outward or overt behavior. Finally, the extent to which we display behaviors that have been learned through observation can be affected by **vicarious reinforcement** and **vicarious punishment.** That is, our willingness to perform acts that we learn by observation depends in part on what happens to the people we are watching. So, when children watching TV or movies see people using drugs or behaving violently, we have cause for concern about whether the plot punishes the actors for their behavior.

The foremost proponent of social learning theory is Albert Bandura, who refers to his learning theory as a *social cognitive theory* (Bandura, 1986). In a classic experiment, Bandura (1965) demonstrated that people can learn a behavior without being reinforced for doing so and that learning a behavior and performing it are not the same thing. Three groups of nursery-school children watched a film in which an adult model walked up to an adult-size plastic doll and ordered it to move out of the way. When the doll failed to obey, the model became aggressive, pushing the doll on its side, punching it in the nose, hitting it with a rubber mallet, kicking it around the room, and throwing rubber balls at it.

The film ended differently for children in each of the three groups, however. Children in the *model-rewarded condition* saw the model showered with candies, soft drinks, and praise by a second adult—an example of vicarious reinforcement. Those in the *model-punished condition* witnessed the second adult shaking a finger at the model, scolding, and spanking him—an example of vicarious punishment. Youngsters in the *no-consequences condition* saw a version of the film that ended with the scene of aggression—no second adult appeared, so there were no consequences for the model.

Immediately after seeing the film, the children were individually escorted into another room where they found a doll, rubber balls, a mallet, and many other toys. As a child played alone for ten minutes, observers recorded the youngster's behavior from behind a one-way mirror. Every time a child spontaneously repeated any of the aggressive acts seen in the film, that child was coded as *performing* the behavior. After ten minutes, an experimenter entered the room and offered the child treats in return for imitating or repeating things the model had done or said to the doll. Bandura used the number of successfully imitated behaviors as a measure of how much the child had *learned* by watching the model (see Figure 5–10).

Analysis of the data revealed that (1) children who had observed the model being rewarded were especially likely to perform the model's behavior spontaneously; but (2) children in all three groups had learned to imitate the model's behavior equally well, and quite accurately at that (see Figure 5–11).

The children in this study learned aggressive behavior without being reinforced for it and without seeing the model reinforced for it. Seeing a model reinforced or punished simply provides useful information about what is likely to happen to us if we imitate the model. By drawing attention to the importance of modeling, social learning theory also points out how *not* to teach something unintentionally. For example, suppose you want to teach a child not to hit other children. You might think that slapping the child as punishment would change the behavior. But social learning theory maintains that slapping the child only demonstrates that hitting is an effective means of getting one's way. You and the child would both be better off if your actions reflected a less aggressive way of dealing with other people (Bandura, 1973, 1977).

Bandura and more recently others (Efklides, Niemivirta, & Yamauchi, 2002; Ommundsen, 2003) stress that human beings are also capable of setting performance standards for themselves and then rewarding (or punishing) themselves for achieving or failing to achieve those standards as a way to regulate their own behavior (see *Applying Psychology: Modifying Your Own Behavior,* on page 204). Thus,

Vicarious reinforcement and vicarious punishment Reinforcement or punishment experienced by models that affects the willingness of others to perform the behaviors they learned by observing those models.

 5.5

Figure 5–10
Bandura's experiment in learned aggressive behavior.
After watching an adult behave aggressively toward an inflated doll, the children in Bandura's study imitated many of the aggressive acts of the adult model.

human beings use the powers of sight as well as insight, hindsight, and foresight to interpret their own experiences and those of others (Bandura, 1962).

Cognitive Learning in Nonhumans

We have seen that contemporary approaches to conditioning emphasize that conditioned stimuli, reinforcers, and punishers provide *information* about the environment. Classical and operant conditioning are not viewed as purely mechanical processes that can proceed without at least some cognitive activity. Moreover, animals are capable of latent learning, learning cognitive maps, and insight, all of which involve cognitive processes. Thus, because all animals can be conditioned, we might reasonably conclude that all animals are capable of at least minimal cognitive processing of information. Do nonhuman animals also exhibit other evidence of cognitive learning? The answer seems to be a qualified yes.

For example, rats that watch other rats try a novel or unfamiliar food without negative consequences show an increased tendency to eat the new food (Galef, 1993). In a different experiment, one group of rats watched another group experience extinction; as a result, the observer rats themselves extinguished faster than if they had not watched the model rats (Heyes, Jaldow, & Dawson,

Media Violence and Aggressive Behavior

In 2000, Congress held hearings on the subject of violent movies and TV programs, claiming that such media provided bad examples to young people. Comstock and Scharrer (1999) concluded that "TV violence frightens some children and excites others, but its foremost effect is to increase aggressive behavior that sometimes spills over into seriously harmful antisocial behavior."

1. If Comstock and Scharrer were present, what questions would you ask them to decide whether to have confidence in their conclusions?

2. Do you agree or disagree with their conclusions? Why, or why not? What research evidence would be required to change your opinion?

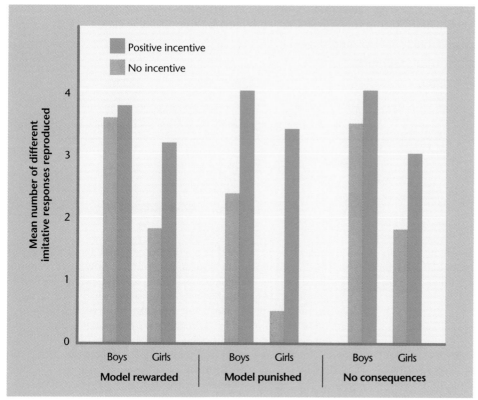

Figure 5–11
As the graph shows, even though all the children in Bandura's study of imitative aggression learned the model's behavior, they performed differently depending on whether the model they saw was rewarded or punished.

Source: Albert Bandura, *Journal of Personality and Social Psychology* 1965, 1, 589–595, Fig. 1. Copyright © 1965 by the American Psychological Association. Reprinted by permission.

1993). Apparently, the observer rats learned something about the absence of reward simply by seeing what happened to the other rats. These surprising results, along with reports that animals as diverse as chickens and octopi learn by watching others, further support the notion that nonhuman animals do indeed learn in ways that reflect the cognitive theory of learning. In Chapter 7 (Cognition and Language) we will revisit this topic, examining in more detail some of the intriguing new procedures scientists have used to explore the cognitive abilities of other animals (e.g., Boysen & Himes, 1999).

CHECK YOUR UNDERSTANDING

1. Match the following terms with the appropriate definitions.

___ latent learning   a. new, suddenly occurring idea to solve a problem

___ insight   b. learning by watching a model

___ observational learning   c. learning that has not been demonstrated in behavior

2. An ape examines a problem and the tools available for solving it. Suddenly the animal leaps up and executes a successful solution. This is an example of

___a. trial-and-error learning

___b. classical conditioning

___c. operant conditioning

___d. insight

3. According to social learning theorists, we can learn new behaviors without ever actually performing them or being reinforced for them. This is called

___a. observational learning

___b. vicarious learning

___c. a and b

s u m m a r y

This chapter concentrates on **learning,** the process by which experience or practice produces a relatively permanent change in behavior or potential behavior. The basic form of learning is known as **conditioning.**

Classical Conditioning

In **classical** (or **Pavlovian**) **conditioning,** a response naturally elicited by one stimulus comes to be elicited by a different, formerly neutral stimulus. Russian psychologist Ivan Pavlov hit upon classical (or Pavlovian) conditioning almost by accident when studying digestive processes. He trained a dog to salivate at the sound of a bell by presenting the sound just before food was brought into the room. Eventually, the dog began to salivate at the sound of the bell alone.

Elements of Classical Conditioning Classical conditioning involves pairing a response naturally caused by one stimulus with another, previously neutral stimulus. There are four basic elements to this transfer: The **unconditioned stimulus (US),** often food, invariably causes an organism to respond in a specific way. The **unconditioned response (UR)** is the reaction (such as salivation) that always results from the unconditioned stimulus. The **conditioned stimulus (CS)** is a stimulus (such as a bell) that does not initially bring about the desired response; over the course of conditioning, however, the CS comes to produce the desired response when presented alone. Finally, the **conditioned response (CR)** is the behavior that the organism learns to exhibit in the presence of a conditioned stimulus.

Classical Conditioning in Humans Humans also learn to associate certain sights or sounds with other stimuli. John Watson and Rosalie Rayner conditioned a little boy, Albert, to fear white rats by making a loud, frightening noise every time the boy was shown a rat. Using much the same principle, Mary Cover Jones developed a method for unlearning fears: She paired the sight of a caged rat, at gradually decreasing distances, with a child's pleasant experience of eating candy. This method evolved into **desensitization therapy,** a conditioning technique designed to gradually reduce anxiety about a particular object or situation. Recently, scientists have discovered that the immune system may respond to classical conditioning techniques, thus allowing doctors to use fewer drugs in treating certain disorders.

Classical Conditioning Is Selective Some kinds of conditioning are accomplished very easily, whereas other kinds may never occur.

Research demonstrating that we develop phobias about snakes and spiders, for example, but almost never about flowers or cooking utensils illustrates Seligman's principles of *preparedness* and *contrapreparedness*, respectively. The ease with which we develop **conditioned food** (or **taste**) **aversions** also illustrates learning preparedness. Conditioned food aversions are exceptions to the general rules about classical conditioning. Animals can learn to avoid poisonous food even if there is a lengthy interval between eating the food and becoming ill. In many cases, only one pairing of conditioned and unconditioned stimuli is necessary for learning to take place.

Operant Conditioning

Classical conditioning focuses on a behavior that invariably follows a particular event, whereas **operant** (or **instrumental**) **conditioning** concerns the learning of behavior that operates on the environment: The person or animal behaves in a particular way to gain something desired or avoid something unpleasant. This behavior is initially emitted rather than elicited—you wave your hand to flag down a taxi, dogs beg at the dinner table to get food. Such actions are called **operant behaviors.**

Elements of Operant Conditioning Psychologist Edward Lee Thorndike, the first researcher to study operant behavior systematically, used a "puzzle box" to determine how cats learn. His work still stands as a landmark in our understanding of the effects of both **reinforcers** and **punishers.** In operant conditioning, reinforcement (such as food) is used to increase the probability that a particular response will occur in the future. To decrease the probability that a particular response will recur, punishers (such as scolding) are used. Thorndike proposed the **law of effect,** which states that behavior that is consistently rewarded will become "stamped in" as learned behavior and behavior that is consistently punished will be "stamped out."

Types of Reinforcement There are several kinds of reinforcers; all of them strengthen behavior just as steel rods reinforce or strengthen concrete.

The presence of **positive reinforcers** (such as food) adds to or increases the likelihood that a behavior will recur. **Negative reinforcers** (such as terminating electric shocks) also increase the likelihood that a behavior will recur, but they do so by reducing or eliminating something unpleasant from the environment.

Punishment   Although all reinforcers (both positive and negative) *increase* the likelihood that a behavior will occur again, **punishment** is any event whose presence *decreases* the likelihood that ongoing behavior will recur. Reinforcement always *strengthens* behavior; punishment *weakens* it. **Avoidance training** involves learning a desirable behavior that prevents an unpleasant condition, such as punishment, from occurring.

Operant Conditioning Is Selective   Studies have revealed that in operant conditioning the behaviors that are easiest to condition are those that animals typically would perform in the training situation. These behaviors vary from species to species and put significant constraints on both classical and operant conditioning.

Superstitious Behavior   When something we do is followed closely by a reinforcer, we tend to repeat that behavior, even if it was not actually responsible for producing the reinforcement. Such behaviors are called *superstitious*. Nonhumans as well as humans exhibit superstitious behaviors.

Learned Helplessness   The failure to avoid or escape from an unpleasant or aversive stimulus that occurs as a result of previous exposure to unavoidable painful stimuli is referred to as **learned helplessness.** Learned helplessness, which has been demonstrated in both animals and humans, is associated with many of the symptoms characteristic of depression.

Shaping Behavioral Change Through Biofeedback   When operant conditioning is used to control certain biological functions, such as blood pressure, skin temperature, or heart rate, it is referred to as **biofeedback. Neurofeedback** is biofeedback used to monitor and control brain waves. Biofeedback and neurofeedback are used to treat a number of medical problems, giving patients control of their treatment.

Comparing Classical and Operant Conditioning

A number of phenomena characterize both classical conditioning and operant conditioning, and there are several terms and concepts common to both kinds of learning.

Response Acquisition   In classical conditioning, responses occur naturally and automatically in the presence of the unconditioned stimulus. During the phase of the learning process called **response acquisition,** these naturally occurring responses are attached to the conditioned stimulus by pairing that stimulus with the unconditioned stimulus. **Intermittent pairing** reduces both the rate of learning and the final level of learning achieved.

In operant conditioning, response acquisition refers to the phase of the learning process in which desired responses are followed by reinforcers. A **Skinner box** is often used to limit the range of available responses and thus increase the likelihood that the desired response will occur. To speed up this process and make the occurrence of a desired response more likely, motivation may be increased by letting the animal become hungry; the number of potential responses may also be reduced by restricting the animal's environment.

For behaviors outside the laboratory, which cannot be controlled so conveniently, the process of **shaping** is often useful: Reinforcement is given for successive approximations to the desired

behavior. However, there are differences among species in what behaviors can be learned and the circumstances under which learning will take hold.

Extinction and Spontaneous Recovery   If the unconditioned stimulus and the conditioned stimulus are no longer paired, **extinction** occurs, meaning the strength and/or frequency of the learned response diminishes. When Pavlov's dogs received no food after repeatedly hearing the bell, they ceased to salivate at the sound of the bell. However, after a while, this extinguished response may reappear without retraining in a process called **spontaneous recovery.** Extinction is complete when the subject no longer produces the conditioned response.

Extinction occurs in operant conditioning when reinforcement is withheld. However, the ease with which a behavior is extinguished varies according to several factors: the strength of the original learning, the variety of settings in which learning takes place, and the schedule of reinforcement used during conditioning. Especially hard to extinguish is behavior learned through punishment rather than reinforcement.

Generalization and Discrimination   In classical conditioning, situations or stimuli may resemble each other enough that the learners will react to one the way they have learned to react to the other through a process called **stimulus generalization.** On the other hand, the process of **stimulus discrimination** enables learners to perceive differences among stimuli so that not all loud sounds, for example, provoke fear.

Just as in classical conditioning, responses learned through operant conditioning can generalize from one stimulus to other, similar stimuli. **Response generalization** occurs when the same stimulus leads to different but similar responses. Discrimination in operant conditioning is taught by reinforcing a response only in the presence of certain stimuli.

New Learning Based on Original Learning   In both classical and operant conditioning, original learning serves as a building block for new learning.

Higher-order conditioning in classical conditioning uses an earlier conditioned stimulus as an unconditioned stimulus for further training. For example, Pavlov used the bell to condition his dogs to salivate at the sight of a black square. This sort of conditioning is difficult to achieve because of extinction: Unless the first unconditioned stimulus is presented occasionally, the initial conditioned response will be extinguished.

In operant conditioning, neutral stimuli can become reinforcers by being paired or associated with other reinforcers. A **primary reinforcer** is one that, like food and water, is rewarding in and of itself. A **secondary reinforcer** is one whose value is learned through its association with primary reinforcers or with other secondary reinforcers. Money is an example of a secondary reinforcer—in and of itself, it is not rewarding; it is valuable only for what it can buy.

Contingencies   The "if-then" relationship between conditioned stimuli and unconditioned stimuli in classical conditioning or between responses and reinforcers (or punishers) in operant conditioning is called a **contingency.**

Robert Rescorla has demonstrated that classical conditioning requires more than merely presenting an unconditioned stimulus and a conditioned stimulus together in time. His work shows that for conditioning to occur, a conditioned stimulus must provide information about the unconditioned stimulus—that is, there must be a CS–US contingency. **Blocking** can occur when prior conditioning prevents conditioning to a second stimulus, even when the two stimuli are presented simultaneously.

In operant conditioning, response contingencies are usually referred to as **schedules of reinforcement.** *Partial reinforcement*—in which rewards are given for some correct responses but not for every one—results in behavior that persists longer than that learned by continuous reinforcement. Whenever partial reinforcement is given, the rule for determining when and how often reinforcers will be delivered is the schedule of reinforcement. Schedules are either *fixed* or *variable*, and may be based on either the number of correct responses or the elapsed time between correct responses.

A **fixed-interval schedule** provides reinforcement of the first correct response after a fixed, unchanging period of time. A **variable-interval schedule** reinforces the learner for the first correct response that occurs after various periods of time, so the subject never knows exactly when a reward is going to be delivered. In a **fixed-ratio schedule,** behavior is rewarded each time a fixed number of correct responses is given; in a **variable-ratio schedule,** reinforcement follows a varying number of correct responses.

Summing Up Despite their differences, classical and operant conditioning share many similarities; both involve associations between stimuli and responses; both are subject to extinction and spontaneous recovery as well as generalization and discrimination. In fact, many psychologists now question whether classical and operant conditioning are not simply two ways of bringing about the same kind of learning.

Cognitive Learning

Both human and nonhuman animals also demonstrate **cognitive learning,** learning that is not tied to immediate experience by stimuli and reinforcers.

Latent Learning and Cognitive Maps Early experiments by Tolman and other psychologists demonstrated that learning takes place even before the subject reaches the goal and occurs whether or not the learner is reinforced. Tolman proposed the concept of **latent learning,** which maintains that subjects store up knowledge even if this knowledge is not reflected in their current behavior because it is not elicited by reinforcers. Later research suggested that latent learning is stored as a mental image, or **cognitive map.** When the proper time comes, the learner calls up this map and puts it to use.

Insight and Learning Sets One phenomenon that highlights the importance of cognitive processing in learning is **insight,** in which learning seems to occur in a "flash." Through insight learning, human and some nonhuman animals suddenly discover whole patterns of behavior or solutions to problems. **Learning sets** refer to the increasing effectiveness at problem solving that comes about as more problems are solved.

Learning by Observing **Social learning theory** argues that we learn not just from firsthand experience, but also from watching others or by hearing about something. Albert Bandura contends that **observational** (or **vicarious**) **learning** accounts for many aspects of human learning. His highly influential theory of learning holds that although reinforcement is unrelated to learning itself, reinforcement may influence whether learned behavior is actually displayed. Such observational learning stresses the importance of models in our lives. To imitate a model's behavior, we must (1) pay attention to what the model does; (2) remember what the model did; and (3) convert what we learned from the model into action. The extent to which we display behaviors that have been learned through observation can be affected by **vicarious reinforcement** and **vicarious punishment.** Social cognitive theory emphasizes that learning a behavior from observing others does not necessarily lead to performing that behavior. We are more likely to imitate behaviors we have seen rewarded.

Cognitive Learning in Nonhumans Research has demonstrated that nonhuman animals can be classically conditioned, that they can be taught to perform whole patterns of operant behaviors, and that they are capable of latent learning. All this evidence lends support to the argument that nonhuman animals use cognitive processing in learning.

key terms

Conditioning	185	Operant behavior	193	Intermittent pairing	202
Learning	185	Negative reinforcer	194	Spontaneous recovery	203
Conditioned response (CR)	186	Positive reinforcer	194	Extinction	203
Conditioned stimulus (CS)	186	Law of effect	194	Response generalization	206
Unconditioned response (UR)	186	Punishment	195	Stimulus discrimination	206
Unconditioned stimulus (US)	186	Avoidance training	197	Stimulus generalization	206
Classical (or Pavlovian) conditioning	186	Learned helplessness	198	Secondary reinforcer	207
Desensitization therapy	190	Neurofeedback	200	Primary reinforcer	207
Conditioned food (or taste) aversion	191	Biofeedback	200	Higher-order conditioning	207
Punisher	193	Response acquisition	201	Blocking	208
Reinforcer	193	Shaping	202	Contingency	208
Operant or instrumental conditioning	193	Skinner box	202	Variable-ratio schedule	209

Fixed-ratio schedule	209	Latent learning	213	Learning set	216
Variable-interval schedule	209	Cognitive learning	213	Vicarious reinforcement and vicarious punishment	217
Fixed-interval schedule	209	Insight	214		
Schedule of reinforcement	209	Observational (or vicarious) learning	216		
Cognitive map	213	Social learning theory	216		

OVERVIEW

The Sensory Registers
Visual and Auditory Registers
Attention

Short-Term Memory
Capacity of STM
Encoding in STM
Maintaining STM

Long-Term Memory
Capacity of LTM
Encoding in LTM
Serial Position Effect

Maintaining LTM
Types of LTM

The Biology of Memory
How Are Memories Formed?
Where Are Memories Stored?

Forgetting
The Biology of Forgetting
Experience and Forgetting
How to Reduce Forgetting

Special Topics in Memory
Autobiographical Memory
Childhood Amnesia
Extraordinary Memory
Flashbulb Memories
Eyewitness Testimony
Recovered Memories
Cultural Influences on Memory

Memory

6

The world-renowned conductor Arturo Toscanini memorized every single note written for every instrument in some 250 symphonies and all the music and lyrics for more than 100 operas. Once, when he could not locate a score of Joachim Raff's Quartet No. 5, he sat down and reproduced it entirely from memory—even though he had not seen or played the score for decades. When a copy of the quartet turned up, people were astonished to discover that with the exception of a single note, Toscanini had reproduced it perfectly (Neisser, 1982).

- A waiter named John Conrad routinely handled parties of six to eight people in a busy Colorado restaurant, remembering every order from soup to salad dressing, without writing them down. He once waited on a party of 19, serving 19 complete dinners to his customers without a single error (Singular, 1982).

- Before being stricken with a viral illness, a 29-year-old woman known as MZ told researchers she could remember "the exact day of the week of future or past events of almost anything that touched my life . . . all personal telephone numbers . . . colors of interiors and what people wore . . . pieces of music . . . recalling a picture, as a painting in a museum, was like standing in the museum looking at it again" (Klatzky, 1980).

Accounts of people with extraordinary memories raise many questions about the nature of **memory** itself (Wilding & Valentine, 1997): Why are some people so much better at remembering things than others? Are they simply born with this ability, or could any of us learn to remember as much as they do? And why is it that remembering may sometimes be so simple (think how effortlessly baseball fans remember the batting averages of their favorite players) and other times so difficult (as when we grope for answers on an exam)? Why do we find it so hard to remember something that happened only a few months back, yet we can recall in vivid detail some other event that happened 10, 20, even 30 years ago? Just how does memory work, and what makes it fail?

Among the first to seek scientific answers to these questions was the nineteenth-century German psychologist Hermann Ebbinghaus. Using himself as a subject, Ebbinghaus composed lists of "nonsense syllables," meaningless combinations of letters, such as PIB, WOL, or TEB. He memorized lists of 13 nonsense syllables each. Then, after varying amounts of time, he relearned each list of syllables. He found that the longer he waited after first learning a list, the longer it took to learn the list again. Most of the information was lost in the first few hours. Ebbinghaus's contributions dominated memory research for many years.

Today many psychologists find it useful to think about memory as a series of steps in which we process information, much like a computer stores and retrieves data (Massaro & Cowan, 1993). Together, these steps form what is known as the **information-processing model** of memory. In this chapter, you will find terms like *encoding*, *storage*, and *retrieval* convenient ways of comparing human memory to computers. But we will also consider the social, emotional, and biological factors that make us human and that also distinguish our memories from those of computers.

Far more information bombards our senses than we can possibly process, so the first stage of information processing involves selecting some of this material to think about and remember. Therefore, we turn first to the sensory registers and to attention, the process that allows us to select incoming information for further processing.

THINKABOUTIT

You will find the answers to these questions in the chapter:

1. What is a sensory register, and how many do we have?

2. How many items can most people hold in short-term memory at one time?

3. How do implicit memories differ from explicit ones?

4. Where are short-term memories stored?

5. How does learning contribute to forgetting?

6. How accurate is eyewitness testimony?

Memory The ability to remember the things that we have experienced, imagined, and learned.

Information-processing model A computerlike model used to describe the way humans encode, store, and retrieve information.

225

Sensory registers Entry points for raw information from the senses.

The Sensory Registers

What is a sensory register, and how many do we have?

Look slowly around the room. Each glance—which may last for only a fraction of a second—takes in an enormous amount of visual information, including colors, shapes, textures, relative brightness, and shadows. At the same time, you pick up sounds, smells, and other kinds of sensory data. All this raw information flows from your senses into what are known as **sensory registers.** These registers are like waiting rooms in which information enters and stays for only a short time. Whether we remember any of this information depends on which operations we perform on it, as you will see throughout this chapter. Although all our senses have registers, the visual and auditory registers have been studied most extensively, and therefore we focus on them.

Visual and Auditory Registers

Although the sensory registers have virtually unlimited capacity (Cowan, 1988), information disappears from them quite rapidly (Rainer & Miller, 2002). To understand how much visual information we take in, and how quickly it is lost, bring a digital camera into a darkened room and take a picture using a flash. During the split second that the room is lit up by the flash, your visual register will absorb a surprising amount of information about the room and its contents. Try to hold on to that visual image, or *icon*, as long as you can. You will find that it fades rapidly; in a few seconds it is gone. Then compare your remembered image of the room with what you actually saw at the time, as captured in the picture. You will notice that your visual register took in far more information than you were able to retain for even a few seconds.

A clever set of experiments by George Sperling (1960) clearly demonstrates the speed with which information disappears from the visual register. Sperling flashed groups of letters, arranged in rows, on a screen for just a fraction of a second. When the letters were gone, he sounded a tone to tell his participants which row of letters to recall: A high-pitched tone indicated that they should try to remember the top row of letters, a medium tone signaled them to recall the middle row, and a low tone meant they should recall the bottom row. Sperling found that if he sounded the tone immediately after the letters were flashed, his participants could usually recall three

If you were to walk into this room, your eyes and your other sense organs would pick up many impressions of what is to be found here. How much of this information would you remember later?

or four of the letters in any of the three rows; that is, they seemed to retain at least nine of the original twelve letters in their visual registers. But if he waited for even one second before sounding the tone, his participants were able to recall only one or two letters from any single row. In just one second, then, all but four or five of the original set of twelve letters had vanished from their visual registers.

Visual information may disappear from the visual register even more rapidly than Sperling thought (Cowan, 1988). In everyday life, new visual information keeps coming into the register, and this new information replaces the old information almost immediately, a process often called *masking*. This is just as well, because otherwise the visual information would simply pile up in the sensory register and get hopelessly scrambled. Under normal viewing conditions, visual information is erased from the sensory register in about a quarter of a second as it is replaced by new information.

Auditory information fades more slowly than visual information. The auditory equivalent of the icon, the *echo*, tends to last for several seconds, which, given the nature of speech, is certainly fortunate for us. Otherwise, "*You* did it!" would be indistinguishable from "You *did* it!" because we would be unable to remember the emphasis on the first word by the time we registered the last word.

Attention

If information disappears from the sensory registers so rapidly, how do we remember *anything* for more than a second or two? One way is that we select some of the incoming information for further processing by means of **attention** (see Figure 6–1). Attention is the process of *selectively* looking, listening, smelling, tasting, and feeling (Egeth & Lamy, 2003). At the same time, we give meaning to the information that is coming in. Look at the page in front of you. You will see a series of black lines on a white page. Until you recognize these lines as letters and words, they are just meaningless marks. For you to make sense of this jumble of data, you process the information in the sensory registers for meaning.

How do we select what we are going to pay attention to at any given moment, and how do we give that information meaning? Donald Broadbent (1958) suggested that a filtering process at the entrance to the nervous system allows only those

Attention The selection of some incoming information for further processing.

 6.1

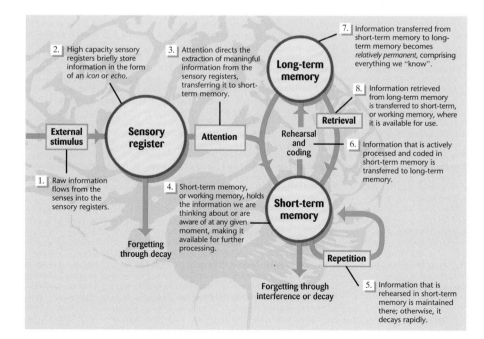

Figure 6–1
The sequence of information processing.

These children are working attentively in spite of the activity going on around them. If their teacher calls them to line up for recess, however, their attention will be quickly diverted from their work.

stimuli that meet certain requirements to pass through. Those stimuli that get through the filter are compared with what we already know, so that we can recognize them and figure out what they mean. If you and a friend are sitting in a restaurant talking, you filter out all other conversations taking place around you. As we discussed in Chapter 3, this practice is known as the *cocktail-party phenomenon* (Cherry, 1966; Conway, Cowan, & Bunting, 2001; Wood & Cowan, 1995). According to Broadbent, although you might be able to describe certain characteristics of those other conversations, such as whether the people speaking were men or women and whether their voices were loud or soft, you normally would not be able to recount what was being discussed, even at neighboring tables. Because you filtered out those other conversations, processing of that information did not proceed far enough for you to understand the meaning of what you heard.

Now suppose that during your restaurant conversation, someone at a neighboring table mentions your name. In all likelihood your attention would shift to that conversation. The filter that had screened out neighboring conversations has suddenly "let through" your name. Why? Anne Treisman (1960, 1964) modified Broadbent's filter theory to account for such phenomena. She contended that the filter is not a simple on-off switch but rather a variable control, like the volume control on a radio, that can "turn down" unwanted signals without rejecting them entirely. According to this view, we may be paying attention to only some incoming information, but we monitor the other signals at a low volume. In this way, we can shift our attention if we pick up something particularly meaningful. This automatic processing works even when we are asleep: Parents often wake up immediately when they hear the baby crying, but sleep through other, louder noises.

To summarize, we consciously attend to very little of the information in our sensory registers; instead, we select some information and process those signals further as we work to recognize and understand them. However, even unattended information receives at least some initial processing, so that we can shift our attention to focus on any element of our surroundings that strikes us as potentially meaningful.

 6.2

What happens to the information that we do attend to? It enters our short-term memory.

CHECK YOUR UNDERSTANDING

1. Raw information from the senses stops here first before it is further processed or disappears.

___ a. amygdala

___ b. sensory registers

___ c. cortex

2. Auditory information fades from the sensory registers more slowly than information from which other sense?

___ a. taste

___ b. touch

___ c. sight

3. _____ is the process of selectively looking, listening, tasting, and feeling while giving meaning to that information.

___ a. partial report

___ b. attention

___ c. filtering

Answers: 1.b, 2.c, 3.b

Short-Term Memory

How many items can most people hold in short-term memory at one time?

Short-term memory (STM) holds the information we are thinking about or are aware of at any given moment (Stern, 1985). It was originally called primary memory by William James (1890; Waugh & Norman, 1960). When you listen to a conversation or a piece of music, when you watch a ballet or a tennis tournament, when you become aware of a leg cramp or a headache—in all these cases, you are using STM both to hold on to and to think about new information coming in from the sensory registers. STM therefore has two primary tasks: to store new information briefly and to work on that information. STM is sometimes called *working memory* to emphasize the active or working component of this memory system (Baddeley & Hitch, 1994; Nairne, 2003).

Capacity of STM

The arcade fanatic absorbed in a video game is oblivious to the outside world. Chess masters at tournaments demand complete silence while they ponder their next move. You shut yourself in a quiet room to study for final exams. As these examples illustrate, STM can handle only so much information at any given moment. Research suggests that STM can hold about as much information as can be repeated or rehearsed in 1.5 to 2 seconds (Baddeley, 1986, 2002).

To get a better idea of the limits of STM, read the first row of letters in the following list just once. Then close your eyes and try to remember the letters in the correct sequence. Repeat this procedure for each subsequent row:

1. C X W
2. M N K T Y
3. R P J H B Z S
4. G B M P V Q F J D
5. E G Q W J P B R H K A

Like most people, you probably found rows 1 and 2 fairly easy, row 3 a bit harder, row 4 extremely difficult, and row 5 impossible to remember after just one reading. This gives you an idea of the limited capacity of STM.

Because of the limitations of short-term memory, a person who is intent on playing an arcade game will shut out all outside distractions.

Short-term memory (STM) Working memory; briefly stores and processes selected information from the sensory registers.

"Hold on a second, Bob. I'm putting you on a stickie."

But the limits of STM depend, in part, on the material involved. Try reading through the following set of 12 letters just once and see whether you can repeat them: TJYFAVMCFKIB. How many letters were you able to recall? In all likelihood, not all 12. But what if you had been asked to remember the following 12 letters instead: TV FBI JFK YMCA. Could you do it? Almost certainly the answer is yes. These are the same 12 letters as before, but here they are grouped into four separate meaningful "words." Organizing information so that it fits into meaningful units is called **chunking** (Gobet et al., 2001). The 12 letters have been chunked into four meaningful elements that STM can readily handle—they can be repeated in less than two seconds.

Here's another example of chunking. Try to remember this list of numbers:

106619451812

Remembering 12 separate digits is usually very difficult, but try chunking the list into three groups of four:

1066 1945 1812

For those who take an interest in military history, these three chunks will be much easier to remember than 12 unrelated digits.

By chunking words into sentences or sentence fragments, we can process an even greater amount of information in STM (Baddeley, 1994; Carter, Hardy & Hardy, 2001). For example, suppose you want to remember the following list of words: *tree, song, hat, sparrow, box, lilac, cat.* One strategy would be to cluster as many of them as possible into phrases or sentences: "The sparrow in the tree sings a song"; "a lilac hat in the box"; "the cat in the hat." But isn't there a limit to this strategy? Would five sentences be as easy to remember for a short time as five single words? Simon (1974) found that as the size of any individual chunk increases, the number of chunks that can be held in STM declines. Thus, STM can easily handle five unrelated letters or words simultaneously, but five unrelated sentences are much harder to remember.

Keep in mind that short-term memory usually has more than one task to perform at once (Baddeley & Hitch, 1994). During the brief time you spent memorizing the rows of letters on page 229, you probably gave them your full attention. But normally, you have to attend to new information while you work on whatever is already present in your short-term memory. Competition between these two tasks for the limited workspace in STM often means that neither task will be done as well as it could be. Try counting backward from 100 while trying to learn the rows of letters in our earlier example. What happens?

Now turn on some music and try to learn the rows of letters. You'll find that the music doesn't interfere much, if at all, with learning the letters. Interestingly, when two memory tasks are presented in different sensory modalities (for instance visual and auditory), they are less likely to interfere with each other than if they are in the same modality (Cocchini, Logie, Sala, MacPherson, & Baddeley, 2002). This suggests the existence *domain specific* working memory systems that can operate at the same time with very little interference.

Chunking The grouping of information into meaningful units for easier handling by short-term memory.

Encoding in STM

We encode verbal information for storage in STM *phonologically*—that is, according to how it sounds. This is so even if we see the word, letter, or number on a page rather than hear it spoken (Baddeley, 1986; Pollatasek, Rayner, & Lee, 2000). We know this because numerous experiments have shown that when people try to retrieve material from STM, they generally mix up items that sound alike (Sperling, 1960). A list of words such as *mad, man, mat, cap* is harder for most people to recall accurately than is a list such as *pit, day, cow, bar* (Baddeley, 1986).

But not all material in short-term memory is stored phonologically. At least some material is stored in visual form, and other information is retained based on its meaning (Cowan, 1988; Matlin, 1989). For example, we don't have to convert visual data such as maps, diagrams, and paintings into sound before we can think about them. Moreover, research has shown that memory for images is generally better than memory for words because we often store images both phonologically and as images, while words are usually only stored phonologically (Pavio, 1986). The *dual coding* of images accounts for why it is sometimes helpful to form a mental picture of something you are trying to learn (Sadoski & Pavio, 2001).

Maintaining STM

As we have said, short-term memories are fleeting, generally lasting a matter of seconds. However, we can hold information in STM for longer periods through **rote rehearsal**, also called *maintenance rehearsal* (Greene, 1987). Rote rehearsal consists of repeating information over and over, silently or out loud. Although this may not be the most efficient way to remember something permanently, it can be quite effective for a short time.

Rote rehearsal Retaining information in memory simply by repeating it over and over.

▰▰ CHECK YOUR UNDERSTANDING

1. What a person is thinking about at any given moment is called

___ a. episodic memory

___ b. elaborative rehearsal

___ c. emotional memory

___ d. short-term memory

2. Grouping items into meaningful and manageable units is known as

___ a. chunking

___ b. encoding

___ c. rote rehearsal

3. How are strings of letters and numbers encoded in short-term memory?

___ a. visually

___ b. phonologically

___ c. by elaborative rehearsal

4. Short term memory is sometimes called:

___ a. 1 minute memory

___ b. 2 minute memory

___ c. secondary memory

___ d. working memory

Answers: 1.d, 2.a, 3.b, 4.d

Long-term memory (LTM) The portion of memory that is more or less permanent, corresponding to everything we "know."

Serial position effect The finding that when asked to recall a list of unrelated items, performance is better for the items at the beginning and end of the list.

Long-Term Memory

How do implicit memories differ from explicit ones?

Everything that we learn is stored in **long-term memory (LTM):** the words to a popular song; the results of the last election; the meaning of *justice;* how to roller skate or draw a face; and what you are supposed to be doing tomorrow at 4 P.M.

Capacity of LTM

We have seen that short-term memory can hold only a few items, normally only for a matter of seconds unless it is maintained through rote rehearsal, but long-term memory can store a vast amount of information for many years. In one study, for example, adults who had graduated from high school more than 40 years earlier were still able to recognize the names of 75 percent of their classmates (Bahrick, Bahrick, & Wittlinger, 1974). And some people are able to remember their high school Spanish after 50 years, even if they have had little opportunity to practice it (Bahrick, 1984).

Encoding in LTM

Can you picture the shape of Florida? Do you know what a trumpet sounds like? Can you imagine the smell of a rose or the taste of coffee? When you answer the telephone, can you sometimes identify the caller immediately, just from the sound of the voice? Your ability to do most of these things means that at least some long-term memories are coded in terms of nonverbal images: shapes, sounds, smells, tastes, and so on (Cowan, 1988).

Yet most of the information in LTM seems to be encoded in terms of meaning. If material is especially familiar (the words of the national anthem, say, or the opening of the Gettysburg Address), you may have stored it verbatim in LTM, and you can often retrieve it word for word when you need it. Generally speaking, however, we do not use verbatim storage in LTM. If someone tells you a long, rambling story, complete with flashbacks, you may listen to every word, but you certainly will not try to remember the story verbatim. Instead, you will extract the main points of the story and try to remember those. Even simple sentences are usually encoded in terms of their meaning. Thus, when people are asked to remember that "Tom called John," they often find it impossible to remember later whether they were told "Tom called John" or "John was called by Tom." They usually remember the meaning of the message but not the exact words (Bourne, Dominowski, Loftus, & Healy, 1986).

Serial Position Effect

When given a list of items to remember (such as a list of grocery items), people tend to do better at recalling the first items (*primacy effect*) and the last items (*recency effect*) in the list. They also tend to do poorest of all on the items in the middle of the list (see Figure 6–2).

The explanation for this **serial position effect** resides in understanding how short- and long-term memory work together. The recency effect occurs because the last items that were presented are still contained in STM, and thus are available for recall. The primacy effect, on the other hand, reflects the opportunity to rehearse the first few items in the list—increasing their likelihood of being transferred to LTM.

Poor performance on the items in the middle of the list occurs because they were presented too long ago to still be in STM, and because so many items were presented before and after them that required attention that there was little opportunity for rehearsal. The serial position effect has been shown to occur under a wide

psych 6.3

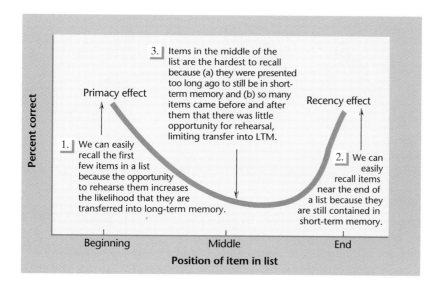

Figure 6–2
The serial position effect.
The serial position effect demonstrates how short- and long-term memory work together.

variety of conditions and situations (Neath, 1993; Suhr, 2002). A version of the serial position effect has even been demonstrated in monkeys (Wright, 1998).

Maintaining LTM

Rote Rehearsal   Rote rehearsal, the principal tool for holding information in STM, is also useful for holding information in LTM. The old saying, practice makes perfect, has some merit. Millions of students have learned the alphabet and multiplication tables by doggedly repeating letters and numbers. Rote rehearsal is probably the standard method of storing away largely meaningless material, such as phone numbers, Social Security numbers, security codes, computer passwords, birth dates, and people's names. Repetition is also important in mastering a wide variety of skills, from playing a piece of Mozart on the piano to doing a back flip on the balance beam. Mastering a skill means achieving *automaticity*, and automaticity is achieved only through long, hard, repetitive practice.

But while rote rehearsal is useful, laboratory experiments have shown that simply repeating something over and over does not always improve recall. It turns out that it is not so much the amount of rehearsal that increases memory, but rather the type of rehearsal (Craik & Watkins, 1973). Specifically, repetition without any intention to learn generally has little effect on subsequent recall (Greene, 1987; van-Hoff & Golden, 2002). You can probably prove this to yourself: Stop here and draw from memory the front side of a U.S. penny. Now look at Figure 6–3 and pick the illustration that most closely matches your memory of a penny. For most people, these tasks are surprisingly difficult: Despite seeing thousands of pennies, most people cannot accurately draw one, or even pick one out from among other, similar objects (Nickerson & Adams, 1979).

Elaborative Rehearsal   As we have seen, repetition with the intent to learn is sometimes useful in storing meaningless information in LTM. But with meaningful material, an even more effective procedure is **elaborative rehearsal** (Craik & Lockhart, 1972; Craik, 2002; Postman, 1975): the act of relating new information to something that we already know. Through elaborative rehearsal, you extract the meaning of the new information and then link it to as much of the material already in LTM as possible. For instance, suppose that you had to remember that the French word *poire* means "pear." You are already familiar with *pear*; both as a word and as a fruit. *Poire*, however, means nothing to you. To remember what it means,

Elaborative rehearsal The linking of new information in short-term memory to familiar material stored in long-term memory.

Schema (plural: schemata) A set of beliefs or expectations about something that is based on past experience.

Figure 6–3
A penny for your thoughts.
Which of these accurately illustrates a real U.S. penny? The answer is on page 235.

 6.4

you connect it to *pear*, either by telling yourself that "*pear* and *poire* both begin with *p*," or by associating *poire* with the familiar taste and image of a *pear*. The more links or associations you can make, the more likely you are to remember the new information later, just as it is easier to find a book in the library if it is cataloged under many headings rather than just one or two.

Schemata   A variation on the idea of elaborative rehearsal is the concept of **schema** (plural: **schemata**). A schema is a mental representation of an event, object, situation, person, process, or relationship that is stored in memory and that leads you to expect your experience to be organized in certain ways. For example, a class lecture schema might include a large room, seating arranged in rows, a space in the front of the room where the professor or lecturer will stand, a podium or lectern, a chalkboard, a screen, and other characteristics common to your experience of attending lectures. You enter, sit down, open your notebook, and expect the professor or lecturer to come in and address the class from the front of the room.

Schemata such as this one provide a framework into which incoming information is fitted. For example, if you enter a restaurant and see that there are no servers, that people are placing their orders at a long counter and then seating themselves, you might reasonably conclude that this is a "fast-food restaurant." Later in the day when a friend asks you where you had lunch, you might recall that it was "at a fast-food place." Schemata can also influence the amount of attention you pay to a given event, and thus your memory for that event. If you attend a lecture on environmental pollution, you will probably pay more attention than if you simply overhear a conversation on the same topic in the cafeteria. Going to a lecture on a topic primes us to approach the situation as a learning experience—to attend carefully to what is said, and to attempt to remember the information (possibly for a test) after leaving. Overhearing a conversation on the same topic would cause us to approach the situation in a much more casual way. Indeed, we would probably be astonished if someone said, "Now summarize the main points of that conversation!"

In conclusion, long-term memory offers a vast storage space for information that we can retrieve in a variety of ways. Its capacity is immense, and material stored there may endure, more or less intact, for decades. By comparison, short-term memory has a sharply limited capacity; information may

THINKING CRITICALLY

Elaborative Rehearsal

Elaborative rehearsal requires that you relate new material to information already stored in LTM. Sometimes, this requires thinking abstractly, visually, or conceptually about the things you want to remember. How would you use elaborative rehearsal to store the following information?

1. In Japanese, the word for difficult is muzukashii.

2. The 'p' in pterodactyl is silent.

3. The square root of *pi* is approximately 1.772.

Now try to develop an elaborative rehearsal strategy for something you are trying to learn, say in this or another class you are taking. Did using an elaborative rehearsal strategy increase your ability to recall the material? What types of elaborative rehearsal strategies did you devise? Which ones seem to work best for you? Why do you think that was the case?

disappear from STM as a result of decay or simply because the storage space is full. The sensory registers can take in an enormous volume of less permanent information, but they have no ability to process memories. Together, these three stages of memory—the sensory registers, STM, and LTM—comprise the information-processing view of memory (see Table 6–1).

(The accurate illustration of a penny in Figure 6–3 is the third from the left.)

Types of LTM

The information stored in LTM can take many forms. However, most long-term memories can be classified into one of several types. Although the classification system remains somewhat controversial, as we shall later see, there is reason to believe that each of these kinds of memories has its own distinct structures in the brain.

Episodic memories (Tulving, 1985) are memories for events experienced in a specific time and place. These are *personal* memories, not historical facts. If you can recall what you ate for dinner last night, what presents you got at your sixth birthday party, or reading the Sunday comics with your parents when you were little, then you are calling up episodic memories. We can think of episodic memory as a diary or daily journal that lets you "go back in time" (Wheeler, Stuss, & Tulving, 1997).

Semantic memories are facts and concepts not linked to a particular time. Semantic memory is like a dictionary or encyclopedia, filled with facts and concepts, such as the meaning of the word *semantic*, the name of the inventor of the light bulb, where the Empire State Building can be found, the value of 2 times 7, and who George Washington was.

Procedural memories are motor skills and habits (Johnson, 2003). They are not memories *about* skills and habits; they *are* the skills and habits. Procedural memories have to do with knowing *how*: how to ride a bicycle, swim, play a violin, type a letter, make coffee, write your name, comb your hair, walk across a room, or slam on a car's brakes.

Episodic memory The portion of long-term memory that stores personally experienced events.

Semantic memory The portion of long-term memory that stores general facts and information.

Procedural memory The portion of long-term memory that stores information relating to skills, habits, and other perceptual-motor tasks.

Information in LTM is highly organized and cross-referenced, like a cataloging system in a library. The more carefully we organize information, the more likely we will be to retrieve it later.

table 6-1   MEMORY AS AN INFORMATION-PROCESSING SYSTEM

System	Means by Which Information Is Encoded	Storage Organization	Storage Duration	Means by Which Information Is Retrieved	Factors in Forgetting
Sensory Register	Visual and auditory registers	None	From less than one second to only a few seconds	Reconsideration of registered information	Decay or masking
Short-Term Memory	Visual and phonological representation	None	Usually 15 to 20 seconds	Rote or maintenance rehearsal	Interference or decay
Long-Term Memory	Comprehension of meaning, elaborative rehearsal	Logical frameworks, such as hierarchies or categories	Perhaps for an entire lifetime	Retrieval cues linked to organized information	Retrieval failure or interference

Emotional memory Learned emotional responses to various stimuli.

Explicit memory Memory for information that we can readily express in words and are aware of having; these memories can be intentionally retrieved from memory.

Implicit memory Memory for information that we cannot readily express in words and may not be aware of having; these memories cannot be intentionally retrieved from memory.

Emotional memories are learned emotional responses to various stimuli: all of our loves and hates, our rational and irrational fears, our feelings of disgust and anxiety. If you are afraid of flying insects, become enraged at the sight of a Nazi flag, or are ashamed of something you did, you have emotional memories.

When we think of memory, we most often think of things we can deliberately call to mind. This typically includes episodic or semantic memories. These two kinds of memories are sometimes called *declarative memory* because we can declare (put into words) what we know (Squire, Knowlton, & Musen, 1993). For example, perhaps you know not only that Albany is the capitol of New York but also that you visited Albany once as a child, and you can state (declare) this knowledge precisely. But not all memories are like this. Many of the things we know cannot be described easily in words, and we cannot readily "bring them to mind." Procedural and emotional memories are like that. You may be a highly skilled golfer, for example, but be unable to describe precisely what you know about swinging a golf club. If someone asks you how you know the right amount of force to apply for a six-foot putt on a level and "fast" green, you will probably end up saying "I just know" or "You just have to practice." You may know that you are terrified of snakes, but that declarative knowledge is distinct from the fearful reaction you have when you see a snake.

Explicit and Implicit Memory   Because of these differences among long-term memories, psychologists distinguish between things we are aware that we know and can readily describe such as episodic and semantic memories (**explicit memory**) and things we are not aware that we know and cannot easily describe such as procedural and emotional memories (**implicit memory**).

Serious interest in the distinction between explicit and implicit memory began as a result of experiments with people who had suffered brain damage that, it was thought, prevented them from forming new long-term memories. Brenda Milner (Milner, Corkin, & Teuber, 1968) studied the now famous case of patient H. M., a young man who had a portion of his brain removed in order to control severe epileptic seizures. The surgery greatly reduced the frequency and severity of seizures, but it left behind a new problem: H. M. apparently could not form new memories. He could meet someone again and again, and each time it was as if he were meeting the person for the first time. He could read the same magazine day after day and not recall ever having seen it before. Old memories were intact: He could remember things that he had learned long before the operation, but he could not learn anything new. Or so it seemed!

One day Milner asked H. M. to trace the outline of a star while looking in a mirror. This simple task is surprisingly difficult, but with practice most people show steady progress. Surprisingly, so did H. M. Each day he got better and better at tracing the star, just as a person with an undamaged brain would do—yet each day he had no recollection of ever having attempted the task. H. M.'s performance demonstrated that he could still learn a skill but have no memory of having done so (see Table 6–2 for a summary of implicit and explicit memory; see also *On the Cutting Edge: Storing Emotional Experiences*).

Looking into a bakery window, perhaps smelling the aromas of the cakes inside, may trigger episodic memories associated with those sights and smells, formed many years ago.

THINKING CRITICALLY

Types of Memory

Experts disagree about how many different kinds of memory there are. Recently, some psychologists have suggested that the classification of memories into different types is artificial and merely confuses matters. They suggest that we should consider memory a unitary thing. What arguments can you come up with to support the practice of making distinctions among different kinds of memory?

table 6-2   TYPES OF MEMORIES

Explicit		Implicit	
Semantic	**Episodic**	**Procedural**	**Emotional**
Memories of facts and concepts	Memories of personally experienced events	Motor skills and habits	Learned emotional reactions
Example: recalling that Albany is the capital of New York	Example: recalling a trip to Albany	Example: ice skating	Example: feeling disgust at the sight of a rat

Priming   Research on a phenomenon called *priming* also demonstrates the distinction between explicit and implicit memory. For example, you might be shown a list of words including the word *tour* without being asked to remember any of the words. Later on you might be shown a list of word fragments, including _ou_, and asked to fill in the blanks to make a word. In these circumstances, you are far more likely to write *tour* than you are *four, pour,* or *sour,* all of which are just as acceptable as *tour.* Even though you weren't asked to remember the word *tour,* simply being exposed to it primes you to write it.

Interestingly, people with amnesia do as well on priming tasks as do people with normal memory. For example, one study (Warrington & Weiskrantz, 1970) gave several people with amnesia a list of words to remember. When these patients were asked to recall the words or pick them out of longer lists, they performed poorly, as one might expect. But when the experimenters showed the patients fragments of the

ON THE CUTTING EDGE

STORING EMOTIONAL EXPERIENCES

Research on implicit memory shows that we can store emotional experiences, such as physical and psychological trauma, and that those memories may affect our behavior years later even though we have no conscious recollection of the experiences (Bower & Sivers, 1998; Kihlström, 1999; Spinhoven, Nijenhuis, & Van Dyck, 1999; Westen, 1998a, 1998b). In some cases emotional memories are so overwhelming and painful, such as those resulting from war, abuse, or acts of terrorism, they can lead to a mental disorder called *posttraumatic stress disorder* PTSD (Cardena, Butler, & Spiegel, 2003) (discussed in more detail in Chapter 12: *Stress and Health Psychology*). People with PTSD experience intense anxiety and flashbacks where they sometimes relive the traumatic event in a nightmare or state of panic. Other people with PTSD exhibit depression or difficulty concentrating, and may not be able to pinpoint the precise cause of their discomfort. Sometimes a cue as subtle as an odor, which was present during the initial trauma, triggers a flashback (Vermetten & Bremner, 2003).

PTSD and other strong emotional memories that affect behavior without conscious awareness, seem at first to give credence to Freud's notion of the unconscious mind—

that we have repressed memories for traumatic incidents though those memories are still affecting our behavior. But the implicit memory research suggests instead that people can store the emotional experience separately from the episodic aspects of the experience. Thus, we may feel anxiety about flying because of a traumatic plane ride in early childhood, yet we many not remember the experience that gave rise to that anxiety. Memory of the event is out of reach, not because (as Freud thought) it has been repressed, but because the episodic and emotional components of the experience were stored separately.

Research into the biological basis of memory also lends support to this explanation. Studies have shown that under conditions of extreme stress the hippocampus (the brain structure principally involved in the storage of episodic memories) may dysfunction causing the details of the traumatic event to be poorly stored in memory (Layton & Krikorian, 2002). In contrast, the amygdala (the brain structure principally involved in the storage of emotional memories) often becomes overactive when stressed, enhancing the emotional memory of a trauma (Elzinga & Bremner, 2002).

Tip-of-the-tongue phenomenon
Knowing a word, but not being able to immediately recall it.

words and asked them to guess what the word might be or to say the first thing that popped into their heads, they produced just as many of the words on the list as did people not suffering from amnesia. In other words, the amnesia victims had perfectly good implicit memories for words that they did not explicitly know they had heard!

The Tip-of-the-Tongue Phenomenon Everyone has had the experience of knowing a word but not quite being able to recall it. This is called the **tip-of-the-tongue phenomenon** or **TOT** (Brown & McNeil, 1966; Hamberger & Seidel, 2003; Schwartz, 2002). Although everyone experiences TOTs, these experiences become more frequent during stressful situations and as people get older (White & Abrams, 2002). Moreover, other words—usually with a sound or meaning similar to the word you are seeking—occur to you while you are in the TOT state and these words interfere with and sabotage your attempt to recall the desired word. The harder you try, the worse the TOT state gets. The best way to recall a blocked word, then, is to stop trying to recall it! Most of the time, the word you were searching for will pop into your head, minutes or even hours after you stopped consciously searching for it (Schwartz, 2002). (If you want to experience TOT yourself, try naming Snow White's seven dwarfs.)

The distinction between explicit and implicit memories means that some knowledge is literally unconscious. Moreover, as we shall soon see, explicit and implicit memories also seem to involve different neural structures and pathways. However, memories typically work together. When we remember going to a Chinese restaurant, we recall not only when and where we ate and who we were with (episodic memory), but also the nature of the food we ate (semantic memory), the skills we learned such as eating with chopsticks (procedural memory), and the embarrassment we felt when we spilled the tea (emotional memory). When we recall events, we typically do not experience these kinds of memories as distinct and separate; rather they are integrally connected, just as the original experiences were. Whether we will continue to remember the experiences accurately in the future depends to a large extent on what happens in our brain.

CHECK YOUR UNDERSTANDING

1. Match the following terms with the appropriate definitions.

___ primacy effect	a. tendency to remember well items at the end of a long list
___ recency effect	b. tendency to remember well items at the beginning of a long list
___ serial position effect	c. describes our relatively weaker memory for items in the middle of a long list

2. Learning information through repetition is a process called

___ a. rote rehearsal

___ b. elaborative rehearsal

___ c. schema

3. Match the following terms with the appropriate definitions.

___ procedural memories	a. memories specific to one's own experiences
___ episodic memories	b. memories of general facts and concepts
___ emotional memories	c. memories of motor skills and habits
___ semantic memories	d. fear, love, and hate, for example, associated with specific events

4. We know and can readily describe which type of memories?

___ a. explicit

___ b. implicit

___ c. emotional

Answers: 1. primacy effect—b; recency effect—a; serial position effect—c, 2. a, 3. procedural memories—c; episodic memories—a; emotional memories—d; semantic memories—b, 4. a

The Biology of Memory

Where are short-term memories stored?

Research on the biology of memory focuses mainly on the question, How and where are memories stored? Simple as the question is, it has proved enormously difficult to answer, although considerable progress has been made in the last two decades.

How Are Memories Formed?

Everything you learn is ultimately recorded in the brain in the form of changes in the size, shape, chemical functioning, and connectedness of neurons (Squire & Kandel, 1999). When we learn new things, new connections are formed in the brain; when we review or practice previously learned things, old connections are strengthened. These chemical and structural changes can continue over a period of months or years (Squire, Slater & Chace, 1975), during which the number of connections among neurons increases as does the likelihood that cells will excite one another through electrical discharges, a process known as **Long-Term Potentiation (LTP).**

While learning takes place in the brain, it is also influenced by events occurring elsewhere in the body. In particular, two hormones, epinephrine and cortisol, affect long-term retention. A number of studies with rats, monkeys, and humans have shown, for example, that epinephrine can enhance the recall of exposure to stimuli associated with unpleasant experiences, such as exposure to shock (McGaugh, 1990).

ENDURING ISSUES   **mind**body

Effects of Stress on Body and Brain

Epinephrine secretion is part of the "fight or flight" syndrome (see Chapter 12, Stress and Health Psychology) and has the effect of arousing the organism to action. However, the effect of epinephrine and other stress related hormones on memory is not merely the result of general arousal. Apparently these hormones indirectly act on specific brain centers, such as the hippocampus and the amygdala, that are critical for memory formation (Vermetten & Bremner, 2002). In one experiment, McGaugh (1983) gave rats epinephrine following Pavlovian fear conditioning and discovered that this enhanced recall. Increased blood levels of epinephrine probably also explain improved performance in humans under conditions of

Long-Term Potentiation (LTP) A long-lasting change in the structure or function of a synapse that increases the efficiency of neural transmission, and is thought to be related to how information is stored by neurons.

mild stress (see Ledoux, 1994). Extreme stress, however, undermines both learning and later recall (Luine, Villegas, Martinez, & McEwen, 1994). If you are studying for an exam, then, a little anxiety will probably improve your performance, but a high level of anxiety will work against you.

Where Are Memories Stored?

Where in the brain does learning occur? Is there one place where all memories can be found, or is each kind of memory stored in its own special location? It has been known for a long time that the brain has specialized areas for vision and hearing (see Chapter 3, Sensation and Perception), so it seems logical that one part of the brain might be set aside for memory.

Hoping to locate the specific site of memory, Lashley (1950) systematically removed various parts of rats' brains after they had learned a task. Although losing part of the brain weakened memories, it didn't remove them completely. In fact, performance had less to do with the area of the brain removed than with the amount of tissue involved: The more of the brain Lashley removed, the less the rats remembered. Lashley was forced to conclude that memories are stored throughout the brain.

Although all memories are not stored in one place (Brewer, Zhao, Desmond, Glover, & Gabriel, 1998), this does not mean that memories are randomly distributed throughout the brain. In fact, research has provided ample evidence that different parts of the brain are specialized for the storage of certain memories (Rolls, 2000). Short-term memories, for example, seem to be located primarily in the prefrontal cortex and temporal lobe (Fuster, 1997; Rainer & Miller, 2002; Rao, Rainer, & Miller, 1997; Rolls, Tovee, & Panzeri, 1999; Szatkowska, Grabowska, & Szymanska, 2001; see Figure 6–4). Long-term semantic memories seem to be located primarily in the frontal and temporal lobes of the cortex which, interestingly, also seem to play a prominent role in consciousness and awareness (see Figure 6–4). Research shows increased activity in a particular area of the left temporal lobe, for example, when people are asked to recall the names of people. A nearby area shows increased activity when they are asked to recall the names of animals, and another neighboring area becomes active when they are asked to recall the names of tools (Damasio, Grabowski, Tranel, Hichawa, & Damasio, 1996) (see Figure 6–5). Destruction of these areas of the cortex (through head injury, surgery, stroke, or disease) results in selective memory loss (e.g., Damasio et al., 1996; Semenza & Zettin, 1989). Some patients may be unable to recall the name of a tool although they can describe how to use it, while others may be unable to recall the name of an old friend or their spouse.

Episodic memories also find their home in the frontal and temporal lobes (Nyberg et al., 2003; Wheeler, Stuss, & Tulving, 1997). But some evidence shows that episodic and semantic memories involve different portions of these brain structures. Wood and colleagues (1980) compared blood flow in the brain as people worked on two different kinds of tasks (blood flow to an area is associated with activity in that area). Some people performed a task involving episodic memory; others performed a task involving semantic memory. The researchers found that the two kinds of tasks resulted in increased blood flow to somewhat different areas of the brain.

Procedural memories appear to be located primarily in the cerebellum (an area required for balance and motor coordination) and in the motor cortex (see Figure 6–4; Gabrieli, 1998). When people perform a task that requires them to follow a rotating object with a hand-held stylus, activity in their motor cortex increases (Grafton et al., 1992).

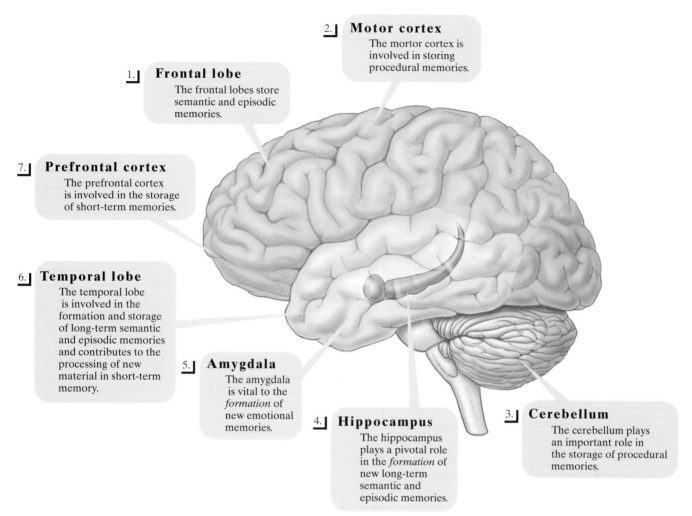

2. **Motor cortex**
The mortor cortex is involved in storing procedural memories.

1. **Frontal lobe**
The frontal lobes store semantic and episodic memories.

7. **Prefrontal cortex**
The prefrontal cortex is involved in the storage of short-term memories.

6. **Temporal lobe**
The temporal lobe is involved in the formation and storage of long-term semantic and episodic memories and contributes to the processing of new material in short-term memory.

5. **Amygdala**
The amygdala is vital to the *formation* of new emotional memories.

4. **Hippocampus**
The hippocampus plays a pivotal role in the *formation* of new long-term semantic and episodic memories.

3. **Cerebellum**
The cerebellum plays an important role in the storage of procedural memories.

Figure 6–4
The biological basis of memory.
Many different parts of the brain are specialized for the storage of memories.

Subcortical structures also play a role in long-term memory. For example, the hippocampus has been implicated in the functioning of episodic memory (Rolls, 2000), as well as being involved in the ability to remember spatial relationships (Cassaday & Rawlins, 1997; Eichenbaum, 1997; Jackson, Kesner, & Amann, 1998; Robertson, Rolls, & Georges-Francois, 1998; Rolls, 1996). Emotional memories are dependent on the amygdala (Cahill & McGaugh, 1998; Vazdarjanova & McGaugh, 1999), a structure that lies near the hippocampus. The amygdala seems to play a role in emotional memory that is similar to the role the hippocampus plays

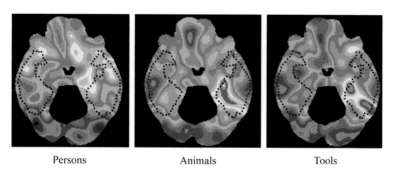

Persons   Animals   Tools

Figure 6–5
PET scanning shows increased activity in different areas of the brain when people are asked to recall the names of people, animals, and tools.
Source: Damasio, H., Grabowski, T. J., Tranel, D., Hichwa, R.D., & Damasio, A. R. A neural basis for lexical retrieval. *Nature,* 380, 499–505, 1996. Department of Neurology and Image Analysis Facility, University of Iowa. Reprinted by permission from Nature, copyright 1996 Macmillan Publishers Ltd.

in episodic, semantic, and procedural memory (Pare, Collins, & Guillaume, 2002). For example, damage to the amygdala reduces the ability to recall new emotional experiences, but it does not prevent the recall of emotional events that occurred prior to the damage though they are often remembered as neutral facts, devoid of emotional content. This may explain why people with amygdala damage are sometimes unable to "read" facial expressions, even though they recognize the person's face (Young, Hellawell, Wan de Wal, & Johnson, 1996).

Clearly, psychologists have a long way to go before they will fully understand the biology of memory, but progress is being made in this fascinating area. As we will see in the next section, another problem that is beginning to succumb to scientific analysis is, Why do we forget?

CHECK YOUR UNDERSTANDING

1. Match the following types of memories to the location in the brain where they appear to be formed and/or stored.

___ short-term memories   a. frontal and temporal lobes

___ long-term semantic and   b. cerebellum and motor cortex
episodic memories

___ procedural memories   c. amygdala

___ emotional memories   d. prefrontal cortex and temporal lobe

2. Two hormones, epinephrine and cortisol, affect which kind of memory retention?

___ a. short-term

___ b. long-term

3. Which of the following acts as memory's storage facility in the human body?

___ a. sensory registers

___ b. spinal cord

___ c. cerebral cortex

Answers: 1. short-term memories—d; long-term semantic and episodic memories—a; procedural memories—b; emotional memories—c, 2.b, 3.c

Forgetting

How does learning contribute to forgetting?

Forgetting is a very commonplace phenomenon, familiar to one and all. But why should we forget? Why do memories, once formed, not remain forever in the brain? Part of the answer has to do with the biology of memory, and another part has to do with the experiences we have before and after learning.

The Biology of Forgetting

According to the **decay theory,** memories deteriorate because of the passage of time. Most of the evidence supporting decay theory comes from experiments known as *distractor studies.* For example, in one experiment, participants learned a sequence of letters, such as PSQ. Then they were given a three-digit number, such

Decay theory A theory that argues that the passage of time causes forgetting.

as 167, and asked to count backwards by threes: 167, 164, 161, and so on, for up to 18 seconds (Peterson & Peterson, 1959). At the end of that period, they were asked to recall the three letters. The results of this test astonished the experimenters. The participants showed a rapid decline in their ability to remember the letters. Because the researchers assumed that counting backwards would not interfere with remembering, they could only account for the forgotten letters by noting that they had simply faded from short-term memory in a matter of seconds. Decay, then, seems to be at least partly responsible for forgetting in short-term memory.

Brain damage caused by accidents, surgery, poor diet, or disease is the most likely cause of severe memory loss. Damage to the hippocampus profoundly affects long-term memory formation. Studies of elderly people who are having trouble remembering new material, for instance, show that the hippocampus is smaller than normal (Golomb et al., 1994). Brain scans also reveal a diminished hippocampus in people suffering from *Alzheimer's disease*, a neurological disorder that causes severe memory loss (Bennett & Knopman, 1994; see Chapter 10, Life Span Development, for more information about Alzheimer's disease). Chronic alcoholism can lead to a form of amnesia called *Korsakoff's syndrome* caused by a vitamin deficiency in the poor diet typically eaten by people who abuse alcohol (Baddeley, 1987). Head injuries often result in **retrograde amnesia,** a condition in which people cannot remember what happened to them shortly before their injury. It is thought that in such instances, forgetting occurs because memories are not fully "anchored" in the brain. The problem is analogous to something every computer user has experienced: A momentary power outage results in the loss of information that has not been saved to the hard drive.

Neurotransmitters also play a role in forgetting. One in particular, acetylcholine, seems to be significant (Hasselmo & Bower, 1993; Hasselmo, Schnell, & Barkai, 1995; McIntyre, Marriott, & Gold, 2003). In one group of studies, rats developed memory problems after researchers destroyed acetylcholine-producing cells in their brains (Fibiger, Murray, & Phillips, 1983). Alzheimer's sufferers commonly have below-normal levels of acetylcholine in their brains, and autopsies show that many of the acetylcholine-producing neurons in their brain have been extensively damaged (Coyle, 1987). Indeed, some research with animals and humans suggests that drugs and surgical procedures that increase acetylcholine levels may alleviate some age-related memory deficits (Li & Low, 1997; Parnetti, Senin, & Mecocci, 1997; D. E. Smith, Roberts, Gage, & Tuszynski, 1999). The precise role of neurotransmitters in the memory process is complex, however, and evidence suggests that other neurotransmitters are involved as well (DeZazzo & Tully, 1995). The problem of forgetting is further complicated by the effects of experience, as we will now see.

Experience and Forgetting

Often, forgetting is simply due to inadequate learning. When you forget where you put your car keys, it is usually because you did not attend to the act of placing the car keys. If you can't find your car, most of the time you didn't take notice of where you parked the car in the first place.

Other times forgetting occurs because, although we attended to the matter to be recalled, we did not rehearse the material adequately. Merely "going through the motions" of rehearsal may do little good. Prolonged, intense practice with the intention of learning results in less forgetting than a few, desultory repetitions. Elaborative rehearsal can also help make new memories more durable. When you park your car in space G–47, you will be more likely to remember its location if you think, "G–47. My uncle *George* is about *47* years old." The bottom line is that we cannot expect to remember information for long if we have not learned it well in the first place.

Retrograde amnesia The inability to recall events preceding an accident or injury, but without loss of earlier memory.

Retroactive interference The process by which new information interferes with information already in memory.

Proactive interference The process by which information already in memory interferes with new information.

Interference Learning itself can cause forgetting because learning one thing can interfere with remembering another. Information gets mixed up with, or pushed aside by, other information and thus becomes harder to remember. Such forgetting is said to be due to interference. There are two kinds of interference (see Figure 6–6).

In one kind of interference, new material interferes with remembering information already in long-term memory; this is known as **retroactive interference.** Retroactive interference is often studied by means of *paired associate* learning. First a person learns a list of word pairs, such as *happy–apple;* when presented with *happy,* the person is expected to say *apple.* After this list is learned, the person learns a different list, including *happy-pencil;* when presented with *happy,* the person is to say *pencil.* After learning the second list, the person is tested for memory of the first list; as before, the task is to say *apple* in response to *happy.* The typical finding is that learning the second list interferes with the ability to recall the first (Thune & Underwood, 1943). Retroactive interference is an everyday occurrence. Once you learn a new telephone number, for example, you may find it difficult to recall your old number, even though you used that old number for years.

In the second kind of interference, old material in memory interferes with new material being learned; this is called **proactive interference.** These experiments proceed as above but this time the participants are tested for their memory of the *second* list they learned. Typically, they do less well than people who learned only the second list. Thus, learning the first list interferes with later learning. Like retroactive interference, proactive interference is an everyday phenomenon. Suppose you always park your car in the lot behind the building where you work. Then one day your parking space is moved to a lot across the street. It will take you longer to remember the new parking space than it would have if you had not been previously parking behind the building. Learning to look for your car behind the building interferes with your new memory that you are now parking across the street.

The most important factor in determining the degree of interference is the similarity of the competing items. In paired associate learning, for example, items such as *happy–apple* and *happy–pear* are more likely to interfere with one another

Figure 6–6
Diagram of experiments measuring retroactive and proactive interference.
In retroactive interference, the experimental group usually does not perform as well on tests of recall as those in the control group, who experience no retroactive interference from a list of words in Step 2. In proactive interference, people in the experimental group suffer the effects of proactive interference from the list in Step 1; when asked to recall the list from Step 2, they perform less well than those in the control group.

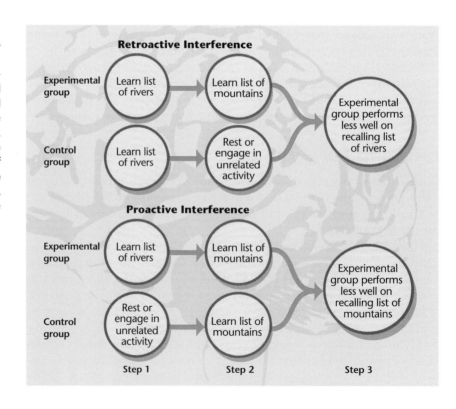

(retroactively or proactively) than *happy–oak* and *happy–train*, as shown in the following experiment (Bower & Mann, 1992). Participants learned two lists of 21 letters each. The first list was SOJFNUGPAHWMSELICBQTA, and the second was YADILOHSREKNABYHTLAEW. Then the participants were asked to recall the first list. Retroactive interference occurred because the second list consisted of a sequence of letters very similar to first list and thus interfered with it. But when some of the participants were told that the second list spells WEALTHY BANKERS HOLIDAY backwards, interference dropped significantly. This information made the second list very different from the first, so there was less interference. The more dissimilar something is from other things you have already learned, the less likely it will be to mingle and interfere with other material in memory.

 6.5

Situational Factors   Situational factors can also contribute to forgetting. In one experiment, a group of people was given a list of 40 adjectives and asked to write down the opposite of each word (Schab, 1990). The experimenter informed them that the next day he would ask them to recall the words they had written. The smell of chocolate permeated the air surrounding one group of students while they were writing their list of words. The next day, adding a chocolate smell to the air significantly increased the number of words these students recalled from the previous day. The smell of chocolate became an effective "contextual cue" or "hint" that helped them recall the correct words. Although this may seem odd, it happens all the time: Whenever we try to commit something to memory, we are also unintentionally picking up facts about the context in which the learning is taking place. Those facts become useful retrieval cues when we later try to retrieve the corresponding information from LTM.

When environmental cues that were present during learning are absent during recall, the effort to remember is often less successful. This phenomenon, called *cue-dependent forgetting*, has been demonstrated in a wide variety of situations. For instance, scuba divers recalled a list of words better if learned underwater and recalled underwater, than if learned underwater and recalled on the beach (Godden & Baddeley, 1975). Similar context effects have been demonstrated with background music (Balch & Lewis, 1996; de-l'Etoile, 2002), odors (Herz, 1997), and even classrooms (Smith, Glenberg, & Bjork, 1978). The police make use of contextual cues when they take witnesses back to the scene of a crime in the hope of improving their recall of crucial details.

State-Dependent Memory   In addition to being influenced by environmental cues, our ability to accurately recall information is affected by *internal* cues. This phenomenon is known as *state-dependent memory*. State-dependent memory refers to the intriguing finding that people who learn material in a particular physiological state tend to recall that material better if they return to the same state they were in during learning. For example, one study showed that people who learned material while under the influence of marijuana later recalled more of the material under the influence of marijuana than not (J. E. Eich, Weingartner, Stillman, & Gillin, 1975). State-dependent memory has also been demonstrated in research using other drugs such as caffeine (Keleman & Creeley, 2003). However, these studies *do not* show that being in a drug-induced state improves memory; on the contrary, being in an intoxicated state greatly reduces the overall effectiveness of memory. State-dependent memory research simply shows that the physiological state during learning can act as a cue during recall. The best results, however, occur when the person is sober and alert during both learning and recall.

The Reconstructive Process   Forgetting also occurs because of what is called the "reconstructive" nature of remembering. Earlier we talked about how schemata are used in storing information in long-term memory. Bartlett proposed that people also use schemata to "reconstruct" memories (Bartlett, 1932; Schacter, Norman, & Koutstaal, 1998). When an experience doesn't fit our view of the world or ourselves, we tend, unconsciously, to adjust it or to blot it out of memory altogether (Bremner & Marmar, 1998). In other words, people unknowingly "rewrite" past events to fit their expectations, their current image or their desired image of themselves, and their past decisions (Lyubomirsky & Ross, 1999; Mather, Shafir, & Johnson, 2000).

How to Reduce Forgetting

At a party, you're embarrassed when a familiar-looking person comes over and hugs you, but you can't remember her name. You're describing a movie you've just seen, but you can't recall its title. After returning from the grocery store, you realize that you've forgotten to buy two of the things on your list.

Has your memory always been bad, or is it deteriorating? Many people worry that their memory is not what it used to be. Studies of memory show that most people, even those who are older, have better memories than they realize. The following steps can be taken to improve recall:

1. **Develop motivation.** Without a strong desire to learn or remember something, you probably won't. But if you find a way to keep yourself alert and stimulated, you will have an easier time learning and remembering things.

2. **Practice memory skills.** To stay sharp, memory skills, like all skills, must be practiced and used. Memory experts recommend exercises such as crossword puzzles, acrostics, anagrams, Scrabble, Monopoly, Trivial Pursuit, and bridge. Or you might learn Japanese, join a chess club, or make a point of discussing current events regularly with friends.

3. **Be confident in your ability to remember.** Self-doubt often leads to anxiety, which, in turn, interferes with the ability to retrieve information from memory. Relaxation exercises, experts agree, may substantially boost your ability to retrieve information from memory. Also, if you're convinced that you won't remember something, you probably won't. For example, people who are sure they won't remember the parts of the nervous system for a psychology test will undoubtedly have more difficulty mastering this material than people who adopt a more positive attitude toward the task.

4. **Minimize distractions.** Although some people can study for an exam and listen to the radio simultaneously, most people find that outside distractions interfere with both learning and remembering. If you are being distracted, look for a quiet, even secluded, setting before attempting to commit something to memory.

5. **Stay focused.** Paying close attention to details, focusing on your surroundings, emotions, and other elements associated with an event, will help you remember it clearly.

6. **Make connections between new material and other information already stored in your long-term memory.** One key to improving memory lies in organizing and encoding material more effectively when it first enters LTM. Discuss things you want to remember with other people. Think about or write down ways in which the new information is related to things you already know. The more links you forge between new information and old information already in LTM, the more likely you are to remember the new material.

In some situations, special techniques called **mnemonics** may help you to tie new material to information already in LTM. Some of the simplest mnemonic techniques are the rhymes and jingles that we often use to remember dates and other facts. "Thirty days hath September, April, June, and November . . ." enables us to recall how many days are in a month. We are also familiar with other simple

Mnemonics Techniques that make material easier to remember.

mnemonic devices in which we make up words or sentences out of the material to be recalled. We can remember the colors of the visible spectrum—red, orange, yellow, green, blue, indigo, and violet—by using their first letters to form the name ROY G. BIV. In remembering the musical notes, the spaces in the treble clef form the word FACE, and the lines in the treble clef may be remembered by the phrase "Every Good Boy Does Fine." In addition, several studies have shown that when you can relate a mnemonic to *personal information*, such as your hobbies or interests, you are even more likely to be able to recall it later (Symons & Johnson, 1997). Whenever you can devise a mnemonic to help you remember something, do so.

 6.6

7. **Use mental imagery.** Imagery works wonders as an aid to recalling information from memory. Whenever possible, form mental pictures of the items, people, words, or activities you want to remember. For example, to remember that someone's last name is Glass, you might imagine her holding a glass or looking through a glass. If you want to remember that a friend lives on Manchester Street, you might imagine a Tarzan-like *man* (with your friend's face) beating his *chest*. If you have a sequence of stops to make, picture yourself leaving each place and heading for the next. Greek and Roman orators used a similar mnemonic technique to memorize long speeches. They would visit a large house or temple and walk through the rooms in a specific order, noting where particular objects were placed in each room. When the orators had memorized the plan of the building and its contents, they would imagine going through the rooms, placing images of the material to be remembered at different spots in the rooms. To retrieve the material in the proper sequence during the speech, the orators would imagine themselves going through the rooms in order and, by association, would recall each point of their speech as they came to each object in each room.

8. **Use retrieval cues.** The more retrieval cues you have, the more likely it is that you will remember something. One way to establish automatic retrieval cues is to create routines and structure. For example, when you come in the door, put your house and car keys in the same place every time. Then when you ask yourself, "Where did I put my keys?" the fact that you have a special place for the keys serves as a retrieval cue. Sometimes something that is clearly not routine or structured can serve as a retrieval cue. For example, if you want to remember to do something before you go to bed, leave an unusual item on your bed (perhaps a shoe or a sock); when it's time to go to bed, you'll see the unusual object, and that should help remind you of what you wanted to do.

Similarly, if you are having difficulty remembering something, you might find it useful to return to the setting where you last used that information. That way the cues present when you used that information will be available and may help you remember. If you can't do that, try to recreate the setting vividly in your mind in as much detail as possible, including the thoughts and feelings you were having at the time. This may provide enough contextual cues to pry the information from you.

9. **Rely on more than memory alone.** Human memory is less than perfect, so it's wise to make use of other tools. Write down the things you need to remember, and then post a note or list of those things somewhere obvious, such as on your bulletin board or refrigerator door. Put all the dates you want to remember on a calendar, and then put the calendar in a conspicuous place. If you witness an accident, immediately write down everything you saw and heard in as much detail as you can; then use your written account to refresh your memory periodically.

10. **Be aware that your own personal schemata may distort your recall of events.** As noted earlier, people sometimes unknowingly "rewrite" past events to fit their current image or their desired image of themselves and their past decisions. Being on guard against such distortions may help you avoid them.

APPLYING PSYCHOLOGY

IMPROVING YOUR MEMORY FOR TEXTBOOK MATERIAL

You can use all the principles discussed in this chapter to help you remember material from textbooks in most of your courses. The key to storing new material in long-term memory is making associations between that material and information that is already in LTM. If you simply passively reread the chapter over and over, you are not likely to store, retain, or retrieve information effectively (McDaniel, Waddill, & Shakesby, 1996; Wilke, 2001). Highlighting or underlining passages makes for a slight improvement, if only because you are at least thinking about which material is most important.

A more effective technique is to prepare an outline of the chapter before reading it so that you have associations and links ready to be made when you actually read the material. Some textbooks (including this one) provide you with a ready-made outline at the beginning of the chapter, but creating one yourself forces you to start thinking about the content of the chapter and how one section relates to another. Then, as you read, write comments under the headings of your outline. Your personal summary will not only help you remember material as you are reading the chapter, but will be useful when you are reviewing the material for a test.

Another memory-enhancing technique is to rehearse the material as you read the chapter. You might write in the margin of the text as you go along, recording your reactions, questions, ideas about how the new material may relate to other material, thoughts about how you might apply what you are learning in your own life, and so on. Try to relate the new material to all sorts of things you already know, expressing this relationship in your own words. You can also work with a friend, taking turns challenging each other with questions that draw on material from different sections or paragraphs. However you go about it, integrating and elaborating on the textual material forces you to process it and to form new associations among the pieces of information that you are storing.

"If you simply passively reread the chapter over and over, you are not likely to store, retain, or retrieve information effectively."

Elaborative rehearsal offers two distinct benefits: It ties the new material to information already in memory, and it generates a multitude of retrieval cues to help you recall the material when you need it. Even after you feel well prepared, continued rehearsal may improve your retention. In fact, studies have shown that if you *overlearn* a subject in school, such as a foreign language or a part in a school play, you may be able to remember much of it for the rest of your life (Bahrick, 1984; Bahrick & Hall, 1991; Noice & Noice, 2002).

A more ambitious, and even more effective, system for studying is known by the letters of its five stages: SQRRR (or SQ3R, for short):

1. **Survey.** Before you even start to read, look quickly at the chapter outline, the headings of the various sections in the chapter, and the chapter summary. This gives you an overview of what you will be reading, and helps you organize and integrate the material as you go along.

2. **Question.** Before you start to read, translate each heading in the chapter into questions about the text to follow. Before reading this chapter, for example, you might have recast the heading "Short-Term Memory" on page 233 into questions such as "Why is it called 'short-term'?" "Is there another type of memory that lasts longer?" "What good is memory if it's only short-term?" "Why do memories fade?"

3. **Read.** Now read the first section in the chapter, looking for answers to the questions you have posed. If you discover major points not directly related to your questions, either revise your old questions to encompass the new material or make up new questions.

4. **Recite.** Once you finish reading a section, close the book, and recite from memory the answers to your questions and any other major points that you can remember. You can also jot down your answers in outline form or recite them to someone else. Then open the book and check to make sure that you have covered all the key points raised in the section. Repeat steps 3 and 4 for each section of the chapter.

5. **Review.** After reading through the whole chapter, review your notes, and then recite or say mentally your questions and answers from memory. Relate the material to other ideas, to experiences in your own life, or to familiar things. Try to think of particularly good examples or illustrations of key points or concepts in the chapter. Get involved.

The SQ3R method forces you to react—to enter into a dialogue with the text. This interaction makes the material more interesting and meaningful and improves your chances of recalling it. It also organizes the material and relates it to what you already know. This method certainly takes longer than simply reading a chapter does, but you will save time later on when studying for exams.

To learn more about study skills, visit our web site at www.prenhall.com/morris.

Finally, while you're working to improve your memory, keep in mind that forgetting is not always a bad thing. Most of us have many experiences we would like very much to forget, and forgetting them might be a blessing. A study of children whose home life had been so troubled that they had been placed for a time in a child guidance clinic found that changing or "rewriting" their memories of early childhood made a difficult, disadvantaged life less of a liability. For example, when these children were interviewed 30 years later, those who incorrectly recalled their childhood as fairly normal were also the ones who had been able to develop a basically stable, conventional life of their own (Robins et al., 1985). Forgetting is sometimes a blessing, rather than a curse. (For more on improving memory, see *Applying Psychology: Improving Your Memory for Textbook Material.*)

CHECK YOUR UNDERSTANDING

1. Memories deteriorate because of the passage of time according to which theory?

___ a. Korsakoff's syndrome

___ b. decay

___ c. brain damage

___ d. interference

2. Mnemonics are memory

___ a. aids

___ b. blockers

___ c. disrupters

3. The smell of chocolate helped students remember information they had learned previously because it was in the air at the time of the original learning. The previous sentence describes a

___ a. situational factor

___ b. hint

___ c. contextual cue

___ d. all of the above

Answers: 1.b, 2.a, 3.d

Special Topics in Memory

How accurate is eyewitness testimony?

Autobiographical Memory

Autobiographical memory refers to our recollection of events that happened in our life and when those events took place (Koriat, Goldsmith, & Pansky, 2000); as such, it is a form of episodic memory. Autobiographical memories are of fundamental importance. Indeed, Conway (1996) contends that "autobiographical memory is central to self, to identity, to emotional experience, and to all those attributes that define an individual" (p. 295).

Research confirms that, in general, more recent life events are easier to recall than earlier ones (Crovitz & Schiffman, 1974). But one review of the research shows that people over 50 years of age are more likely than younger people to recall events

Older people are likely to think about the people and events in their young adulthood, when they made the choices that shaped their lives.

from relatively early in life (Holland & Rabbitt, 1990). Because we typically make the most pivotal life choices (such as those concerning marriage and career) in late adolescence and young adulthood, and the outcomes of these choices shape the rest of our lives, it makes sense for us to focus on this period when we look back to summarize and evaluate our lives (Mackavey, Malley, & Stewart, 1991).

You might like to explore your own earliest memories. You and a friend should each make up a list of 20 nouns, such as *table*, *robin*, and *Brussels sprouts*, that can be easily pictured, and then switch lists and write down the earliest personal memory that comes to mind for each of the *other* person's words. Try to date each memory as accurately as possible. Did you have more memories for recent events than for events early in your life? Did you have any memories for events in the first three or four years of your life?

Childhood Amnesia

Research shows that our earliest personal memories tend to date back to between three and four years of age (Eacott, 1999; Kihlström & Harackiewicz, 1982; Newcombe et al., 2000). People rarely recall events that occurred before they were two years old. This phenomenon is sometimes called **childhood amnesia** or *infantile amnesia*.

Exactly why people have difficulty remembering events from their first years of life is not well understood, although several explanations have been advanced (Eacott, 1999; Newcombe, Drummey, Fox, Lie, & Ottinger-Alberts, 2000; Wang, 2003; Wheeler et al., 1997). One hypothesis holds that childhood amnesia is a result of the child's brain not being fully developed at birth. Jacobs and Nadel (1997) point out that the hippocampus, which is so important in the formation of episodic and semantic memories, is not fully formed until about age two. Another theory suggests that childhood amnesia occurs because the very young do not possess a clear sense of self (Wheeler et al., 1997). Without a sense of one's self, very young children find it difficult to organize and integrate their experiences into a coherent autobiographical memory scheme. Still other theorists contend that childhood memories are lost because young children do not possess the language skills necessary to strengthen and consolidate early experiences (Hudson & Sheffield, 1998).

Extraordinary Memory

As you saw at the beginning of this chapter, some people are able to perform truly amazing feats of memory. From time to time, the newspaper will carry a report of a person with a "photographic memory." Such people can apparently create unusually sharp and detailed visual images of something they have seen—a picture, a scene, a page of text. This phenomenon, called **eidetic imagery,** enables people to see the features of an image in minute detail, sometimes even to recite an entire page of a book they read only once.

One study screened 500 elementary schoolchildren before finding 20 with eidetic imagery (Haber, 1969). The children were told to scan a picture for 30 seconds, moving their eyes to see all its various parts. The picture was then removed, and the children were told to look at a blank easel and report what they saw in an eidetic image. They needed at least three to five seconds of scanning to produce an image, even when the picture was familiar. In addition, the quality of eidetic imagery seemed to vary from child to child. One girl in this study could move and reverse images and

Childhood amnesia The difficulty adults have remembering experiences from their first two years of life.

Eidetic imagery The ability to reproduce unusually sharp and detailed images of something one has seen.

recall them several weeks later. Three children could produce eidetic images of three-dimensional objects, and some could superimpose an eidetic image of one picture onto another and form a new picture. Interestingly, the children with eidetic imagery performed no better than their noneidetic classmates on other tests of memory.

One of the most famous documented cases of extraordinary memory comes from the work of the distinguished psychologist Alexander Luria (Luria & Solotaroff, 1987). For over 20 years, Luria studied a Russian newspaper reporter named Shereshevskii ("S"). In *The Mind of a Mnemonist* (1968), Luria described how "S" could recall masses of senseless trivia as well as detailed mathematical formulas and complex arrays of numbers. He could easily repeat lists of up to 70 words or numbers after having heard or seen them only once.

"S" and other people with exceptional memories were not born with a special gift for remembering things. Rather, they have carefully developed memory techniques using certain principles. For example, Luria discovered that when "S" studied long lists of words, he would form a graphic image for every item. When reading a long and random list of words, for example, "S" might visualize a well-known street, specifically associating each word with some object along the way. When asked to recite the lists of words, he would take an imaginary walk down that street, recalling each object and the word associated with it. By organizing his data in a way that was meaningful to him, he could more easily link it to existing material in his long-term memory. In turn, this connection provided him with many more retrieval cues than he would have had for isolated, meaningless facts.

Developing an exceptional memory takes time and effort (Ericsson & Charness, 1994, Wilding & Valentine, 1997). **Mnemonists** (pronounced nee-MON-ists), people who are highly skilled at using memory techniques, frequently have compelling reasons for developing their memories. "S" used his memory skills to his advantage as a newspaper reporter. As we will see in the next chapter, chess masters also sometimes display astonishing recall of meaningful chessboard configurations (Bédard & Chi, 1992; Haberlandt, 1997). For example, some master chess players are able to recall the position of every single piece on the board after only a 5-second exposure to a particular pattern. Yet when these same masters view a totally random and meaningless array of chess pieces, their recall is no better than yours or mine (Ericsson & Chase, 1982).

In view of research data such as these, one memory researcher concluded:

> One of the most interesting things we've found is that just trying to remember things does not insure that your memory will improve. It's the active decision to get better and the number of hours you push yourself to improve that makes the difference. Motivation is much more important than innate ability. (Singular, 1982, p. 59)

Flashbulb Memories

Where were you and what were you doing when you first learned of the terrorist attacks on the World Trade Center on September 11, 2001? Most people can describe exactly where they were and what they were doing at that moment. This is an example of a **flashbulb memory,** the experience of remembering vividly a certain event and the incidents surrounding it even after a long time has passed. We often remember events that are shocking or otherwise highly significant in this way (Davidson & Glisky, 2002). The death of a close relative, a birth, a graduation, or

People who develop exceptional memories usually have a strong need or desire to do so. Successful actors, like James Earl Jones, pictured here as Othello, must memorize parts in sometimes long and complicated scripts. What kinds of cues and mnemonic devices might they use to help them remember their lines?

Mnemonist Someone with highly developed memory skills.

Flashbulb memory A vivid memory of a certain event and the incidents surrounding it even after a long time has passed.

Millions of people will forever have a vivid flashbulb memory of planes flying into the twin towers of the World Trade Center in New York City on September 11, 2001.

wedding day may all elicit flashbulb memories. So can dramatic events in which we were not personally involved, such as the attacks on the World Trade Center.

Researchers have developed several theories about how people form such memories (Finkenauer et al., 1998). According to the "now print" theory, a mechanism starts up in the brain when something especially significant, shocking, or noteworthy is at hand. The entire event is captured and then "printed," much like a photograph. The "print" is then stored, like a photograph in an album, for long periods, perhaps for a lifetime. It is periodically strengthened, because such an important event is bound to be remembered and discussed many times throughout the years.

The "now print" theory implies, among other things, that flashbulb memories are accurate, that they form at the time of an event, and that we remember them better because of their highly emotional content. All these implications have come under criticism. First, flashbulb memories are certainly not always accurate. Although this is a difficult contention to test, let's consider just one case. Psychologist Ulric Neisser vividly recalled what he was doing on the day in 1941 when the Japanese bombed Pearl Harbor. He clearly remembered that he was listening to a professional baseball game on the radio, which was interrupted by the shocking announcement. But professional baseball is not played in December, when the attack took place, so this sharp flashbulb memory was simply incorrect (Neisser, 1982).

Even if an event is registered accurately, it may undergo periodic revision, just like other long-term memories. We are bound to discuss and rethink a major event many times, and we probably also hear a great deal of additional information about that event in the weeks and months after it occurs. As a result, the flashbulb memory may undergo reconstruction and become less accurate over the years until it sometimes bears little or no resemblance to what actually occurred. For instance, one study asked college students how they first heard about the O.J. Simpson trial verdict. The researchers found that the recollections they initially reported just three days after the verdict had changed markedly after a year had passed. In addition, inaccuracies and distortions continued to increase when the students were questioned again three years after the event (Schmolck, Buffalo, & Squire, 2000).

Eyewitness Testimony

"I know what I saw!" When an eyewitness to a crime gives evidence in court, that testimony often overwhelms evidence to the contrary. Faced with conflicting or ambiguous testimony, jurors tend to put their faith in people who saw an event with their own eyes. However, there is now compelling evidence that this faith in eyewitnesses is often misplaced (Brodsky, 1999; Wells & Olsen, 2003).

In several classic studies, Loftus and Palmer (1974) showed people a film depicting a traffic accident. Some of the people were asked, "About how fast were the cars going when they hit each other?" Other people were asked the same question, but with the words *smashed into, collided with, bumped into,* and *contacted* in place of *hit*. The researchers discovered that people's reports of the cars' speed depended on which word was inserted in the question. Those asked about cars that "smashed into" each other reported that the cars were going faster than those who were asked about cars that "contacted" each other. In another experiment, people were shown a film of a collision and then asked either "How fast were the cars going when they hit each other?" or "How fast were the cars going when they smashed into each other?" One week later, they were asked some additional questions about the accident they had seen on film the week before. One of the questions was "Did you see any broken glass?" More of the participants who had been asked about cars that had "smashed into" each other reported that they had seen broken glass than did participants who had been asked the speed of cars that "hit" each other.

Why do eyewitnesses make such mistakes? Some research suggests that the problem may be *source error:* People are sometimes unable to tell the difference between what they witnessed and what they merely heard about or imagined (Garry & Polaschek, 2000; Lindsay & Johnson, 1989; Reyna & Titcomb, 1997; Taylor, Pham, Rivkin, & Armor, 1998). This is especially true for young children (Shapiro, 2002). We all know what it is like to imagine an event in a particularly vivid way and then later have difficulty remembering whether the event really happened or we simply imagined it. Indeed, studies have shown that imagining an event sometimes makes people believe it actually happened (Garry & Polaschek, 2000; Henkel, Franklin, & Johnson, 2000).

Similarly, if you hear information about an event you witnessed, you might later confuse your memory of that information with your memory of the original event. The impact of subsequent information seems to be particularly strong when it is repeated several times (Zaragoza & Mitchell, 1996), as is often the case with extensive media coverage, or when it comes from an authority figure such as a police officer (Roper & Shewan, 2002). Based on this research, many psychologists (Lindsay, 1993; Zaragoza, Lane, Ackil, & Chambers, 1997) contend that if people paid more attention to the source of their memories, eyewitness accounts would be more reliable.

Father Bernard Pagano (right) was identified as an armed robber by seven eyewitnesses and was nearly convicted for crimes actually committed by the man on the left.

Whatever the reason for eyewitness errors, there is good evidence that such mistakes can send innocent people to jail (Kassin, Tubb, Hosch, & Memon, 2001). A study of over 1,000 cases in which innocent people were convicted of crimes concludes that errors made by eyewitnesses were the single most persuasive element leading to false conviction (Wells, 1993). Increasingly, courts are recognizing the limits of eyewitness testimony. For example, judges instruct juries to be skeptical about eyewitness testimony and to evaluate it critically.

Recovered Memories

In recent years a controversy has raged, both within the academic community and in society at large, about the validity of *recovered memories* (McNally, 2003). The idea is that it is possible for people to experience an event, then lose all memory of it, and then later recall it, often in the course of psychotherapy or while under hypnosis. Often, the recovered memories concern physical or sexual abuse during childhood. No one denies the reality of childhood abuse, or the damage that such experiences cause. But are the recovered memories real? Did the remembered abuse really occur? The answer is by no means obvious. There is ample evidence that people can be induced to "remember" events that never happened (Smith et al., 2003). For example, Loftus and her colleagues (Loftus, Coan, & Pickrell, 1996; Loftus & Pickrell, 1995) conducted experiments in which adults were asked to recall events that a close relative had supposedly mentioned. Three events had actually occurred, the other had not. Twenty-five percent of the participants eventually "remembered" the fictitious event.

Other research confirms that it is relatively easy to implant memories of an experience merely by asking about it. The more times people are asked about the event, the more likely they are to "remember" it. Sometimes these memories become quite real to the participant. In one experiment (Hyman, Husband, & Billings, 1995), 25 percent of adults "remembered" fictitious events by the third time they were interviewed about them. One of the fictitious events involved knocking over a punch bowl onto the parents of the bride at a wedding reception. At the first interview, one participant said that she had no recollection whatsoever of the event; by the second interview she "remembered" that the reception was outdoors and that she knocked over the bowl while running around. Some people even "remembered" details about the event, such as what people looked like and what they wore. Yet the researchers documented that

As the result of testimony from Eileen Franklin, based on repressed memory, her father was found guilty of murder. The validity of repressed memory, especially in investigating crimes, remains controversial. Can you think of a test to tell whether a recovered memory is accurate or not?

Look carefully at these cows and try to notice significant distinguishing characteristics of each animal. Is this task difficult for you? It probably is, unless you have been working closely with cattle all your life, as these two people have.

these events never occurred. Other research shows that people can even become convinced that they remember experiences from infancy that never happened (Spanos, 1996; Spanos, Burgess, Burgess, Samuels, & Blois, 1997).

Yet there is reason to believe that not all recovered memories are merely the product of suggestion. There are numerous case studies of people who have lived through traumatic experiences, including natural disasters, accidents, combat, assault, and rape, who then apparently forgot these events for many years, and who later remembered them (Arrigo & Pezdek, 1997). For example, Wilbur J. Scott, a sociologist, claimed to remember nothing of his tour of duty in Vietnam during 1968–1969, but during a divorce in 1983 he discovered his medals and souvenirs from Vietnam and the memories came back to him (Arrigo & Pezdek, 1997).

What is needed is a reliable way of separating real memories from false ones, but so far no such test is available. The sincerity and conviction of the person who "remembers" long-forgotten childhood abuse is no indication of the reality of that abuse. We are left with the conclusion that recovered memories are not, in themselves, sufficiently trustworthy to justify criminal convictions. There must also be corroborative evidence. For, as Loftus (1997) has noted, without corroboration there is no way even the most experienced examiner can separate real memories from false ones.

Cultural Influences on Memory

Does culture have an effect on memory? Research evidence indicates that it does indeed (Confino & Fritzsche, 2002; Mistry & Rogoff, 1994). For example, in many Western cultures, being able to recite a long list of words or numbers, to repeat the details of a scene, and to provide many facts and statistics about historical events are all signs of a "good memory." In fact, such tasks are often used to test people's memory abilities. But these kinds of memory tasks reflect the type of learning, memorization, and categorization skills taught in Western schools and considered important in Western culture. Members of other cultures often perform poorly on such memory tests because the exercises seem odd or foreign to them.

In contrast, consider the memory skills of a person living in a society where a rich oral tradition passes cultural information on from one generation to the next. This individual may be able to recite the deeds of the culture's heroes in verse or rattle off the lines of descent of families, larger lineage groups, and elders. Or perhaps the individual has a storehouse of knowledge about the migration of animals or the life cycles of plants—information that helps people to obtain food and know when to harvest crops. An oral tradition of epic poetry (D'Azevedo, 1982), detailed recollection of the workings of nature, and the ability to recite long genealogies (Bateson, 1982) all demonstrate impressive memory skills that are to a great extent dependent on a person's culture.

ENDURING ISSUES   **diversity**universality

Memory and Culture

Frederic Bartlett, whose work on memory was discussed earlier in this chapter, anticipated the intertwining of memory and culture long ago. Bartlett (1932) related a tale of a Swazi cowherd who had a prodigious memory for facts and figures about cattle. The cowherd could recite, with virtually no error, the selling price, type of cattle bought, and circumstances of the sale for purchases dating back several years. These skills are not surprising when you know that in Swazi culture the care and keeping of cattle are very important in daily life, and many cultural practices focus on the economic and social importance of cattle. In contrast, Bartlett reported, Swazi children did no better than his young European subjects in recalling a 25-word message. Stripped of its cultural significance, their memory performance was not exceptional.

CHECK YOUR UNDERSTANDING

1. Older adults are more likely than younger adults to remember events that occurred during which time period?

___ a. childhood

___ b. late adolescence

___ c. early adulthood

2. What phenomenon enables people to create detailed visual images of things they have seen?

___ a. mnemonics

___ b. flashbulb memory

___ c. eidetic imagery

3. It is relatively easy to implant memories for events that never happened.

___ a. True

___ b. False

s u m m a r y

Scientific research on **memory** began with Ebbinghaus's experiments in the 19th century. Today the **information-processing model** of memory describes how information is encoded, stored, and retrieved from memory.

The Sensory Registers

Sensory registers are the entry points for raw information from all the senses. If we do not process this information further, it disappears.

Visual and Auditory Registers As new visual information enters the registers, old information (the icon, or visual image) is "masked" almost immediately and disappears. Otherwise, the registers would overload as visual information piled up and became scrambled. Auditory information fades more slowly; the echo may last for several seconds.

Attention From the mass of incoming information, we select elements for further processing. In this process, called **attention,** we also give meaning to the information.

Short-Term Memory

Information that we attend to enters **short-term memory (STM),** also called primary memory and working memory. STM contains everything that we are thinking about or are aware of at any instant. STM not only briefly stores information but also processes that information further.

Capacity of STM STM has its limits. Researchers have found that STM can hold only as much information as can be repeated or rehearsed in 1.5 to 2 seconds, which is usually 5 to 10 separate bits of information. We can process more information by grouping it into larger meaningful units, a process called **chunking.**

Encoding in STM Information can be encoded for storage in STM phonologically (according to the way it sounds), in visual form, or in terms of its meaning. Researchers conclude that STM has a greater capacity for material encoded visually than for information encoded phonologically.

Maintaining STM Through **rote rehearsal,** or maintenance rehearsal, we retain information in STM for a minute or two by repeating it over and over again. However, rote memorization does not promote long-term memory.

Long-Term Memory

Long-term memory (LTM) is more or less permanent and stores everything we "know."

Capacity of LTM Long-term memory can store a vast amount of information for many years.

Encoding in LTM Most of the information in LTM seems to be encoded in terms of meaning.

Serial Position Effect Short- and long-term memory work together to explain the **serial position effect,** the fact that when given a list of items to remember, people tend to recall the first and last items in the list.

Maintaining LTM Rote rehearsal is useful for holding information in LTM, particularly meaningless material such as phone numbers. Through **elaborative rehearsal,** we extract the meaning of information and link it to as much material that is already in LTM as possible. Elaborative rehearsal processes new data in a deeper and more meaningful way than simple rote repetition. The way in which we encode material for storage in LTM affects the ease with which we can retrieve it later on.

A **schema** is a mental representation of an object or event that is stored in memory. Schemata provide a framework into which incoming information is fitted. They may prompt the formation of stereotypes and the drawing of inferences.

Types of LTM **Episodic memories** are memories for events experienced in a specific time and place. **Semantic memories** are facts and concepts not linked to a particular time. **Procedural memories** are motor skills and habits. **Emotional memories** are learned emotional responses to various stimuli.

Explicit memory refers to memories we are aware of, including episodic and semantic memories. **Implicit memory** refers to memories for information that either was not intentionally committed to LTM or is retrieved unintentionally from LTM, including procedural and emotional memories. This distinction is illustrated by research on priming, which finds that people are more likely to complete fragments with items seen earlier than with other, equally plausible items.

The Biology of Memory

How Are Memories Formed? Memories consist of changes in the synaptic connections among neural cells. The process by which these changes occur is often very slow.

Where Are Memories Stored? There is no one place where all memories are stored, but research has shown that different parts of the brain are specialized for the storage of memories. Short-term memories seem to be located primarily in the prefrontal cortex and temporal lobe. Long-term memories seem to involve both subcortical and cortical structures. Semantic and episodic memories seem to be located primarily in the frontal and temporal lobes of the cortex, and procedural memories appear to be located primarily in the cerebellum. Emotional memories are dependent on the amygdala.

Forgetting

The Biology of Forgetting According to the **decay theory,** memories deteriorate because of the passage of time. Severe memory loss can be traced to brain damage caused by accidents, surgery, poor diet, or disease. Head injuries can cause **retrograde amnesia,** the inability of people to remember what happened shortly before their accident. Some studies have focused on the role of the hippocampus in long-term memory formation. Other research has emphasized the role of neurotransmitters, especially acetylcholine, in the memory process.

Experience and Forgetting
To the extent that information is apparently lost from LTM, researchers attribute the cause to inadequate learning or to interference from competing information. Interference may come from two directions: In **retroactive interference,** new information interferes with old information already in LTM; **proactive interference** refers to the process by which old information already in LTM interferes with new information.

When environmental cues that were present during learning are absent during recall, cue-dependent forgetting may occur. The ability to recall information is also affected by one's physiological state when the material was learned; this is known as state-dependent memory.

Sometimes we "reconstruct" memories for social or personal self-defense.

How to Reduce Forgetting
A number of steps can be taken to improve recall: Develop motivation. Practice memory skills. Be confident in your ability to remember. Minimize distractions. Stay focused. Make connections between new material and other information already stored in your long-term memory, using such techniques as **mnemonics.** Use mental imagery. Use retrieval cues. Rely on more than memory alone. Be aware that your own personal schemata may distort your recall of events.

Special Topics in Memory

Autobiographical Memory
Autobiographical memory refers to our recollection of events that happened in our life and when those events took place.

Childhood Amnesia
People generally cannot remember events that occurred prior to age two. This phenomenon, known as **childhood amnesia,** is not well understood.

Extraordinary Memory
People with exceptional memories have carefully developed memory techniques. Mnemonists are individuals who are highly skilled at using those techniques. A phenomenon called **eidetic imagery** enables some people to see features of an image in minute detail.

Flashbulb Memories
Years after a dramatic or significant event occurs, people often have vivid memories of that event as well as the incidents surrounding it. These memories are known as **flashbulb memories.** According to the "now print" theory, the event triggers a mechanism in the brain that captures the memory, prints it like a photograph, and stores it for a long time. Recent research has challenged the assumptions that flashbulb memories are accurate and stable.

Eyewitness Testimony
Jurors tend to put their faith in witnesses who saw an event with their own eyes. However, some evidence suggests that eyewitnesses sometimes are unable to tell the difference between what they witnessed and what they merely heard about or imagined.

Recovered Memories
There are many cases of people who experience a traumatic event, lose all memory of it, but then later recall it. Such **recovered memories** are highly controversial, since research shows that people can be induced to "remember" events that never happened. So far there is no way to distinguish real recovered memories from false ones.

Cultural Influences on Memory
Cultural values and practices influence what kinds of things we remember and how easily we recall them.

key terms

Memory	225	Schema (plural: schemata)	234	Retrograde amnesia	243
Information-processing model	225	Episodic memory	235	Retroactive interference	244
Sensory registers	226	Semantic memory	235	Proactive interference	244
Attention	227	Procedural memory	235	Mnemonics	246
Short-term memory (STM)	229	Emotional memory	236	Childhood amnesia	250
Chunking	230	Explicit memory	236	Eidetic imagery	250
Rote rehearsal	231	Implicit memory	236	Mnemonist	251
Long-term memory (LTM)	232	Tip-of-the-tongue phenomenon	238	Flashbulb memory	251
Serial position effect	232	Long-Term Potentiation (LTP)	239		
Elaborative rehearsal	233	Decay theory	242		

The Building Blocks of Thought
Language
The Structure of Language
Images
Concepts

Language, Thought, and Culture
Language and Cognition
Is Our Language Male-
Dominated?
Culture and Cognition

**Nonhuman Thought
and Language**
Animal Cognition
The Question of Language

Problem Solving
The Interpretation of Problems
Producing Strategies and
Evaluating Progress
Obstacles to Solving Problems
Experience and Expertise

Decision Making
Logical Decision Making
Decision-Making Heuristics
Framing
Decisions Under Pressure
Explaining Our Decisions

**Answers to Problems
in the Chapter**

OVERVIEW

Cognition
and Language

7

At the Braefield School for the Deaf, I met Joseph, a boy of eleven who had just entered school for the first time—an eleven-year-old with no language whatever. He had been born deaf, but this had not been realized until he was in his fourth year. His failure to talk, or understand speech, at the normal age was put down to "retardation," then to "autism," and these diagnoses had clung to him. When his deafness finally became apparent he was seen as "deaf and dumb," dumb not only literally, but metaphorically, and there was never any attempt to teach him language.

Joseph longed to communicate, but could not. Neither speaking nor writing nor signing was available to him, only gestures and pantomimes, and a marked ability to draw. What has happened to him? I kept asking myself. What is going on inside, how has he come to such a pass? He looked alive and animated, but profoundly baffled: His eyes were attracted to speaking mouths and signing hands—they darted to our mouths and hands, inquisitively, uncomprehendingly, and, it seemed to me, yearningly. He perceived that something was "going on" between us, but he could not comprehend what it was—he had, as yet, almost no idea of symbolic communication, of what it was to have a symbolic currency, to exchange meaning. . . .

Joseph was unable, for example, to communicate how he had spent the weekend. . . . It was not only language that was missing: there was not, it was evident, a clear sense of the past, of "a day ago" as distinct from "a year ago." There was a strange lack of historical sense, the feeling of a life that lacked autobiographical and historical dimension, . . . a life that only existed in the moment, in the present. . . .

Joseph saw, distinguished, categorized, used; he had no problems with perceptual categorization or generalization, but he could not, it seemed, go much beyond this, hold abstract ideas in mind, reflect, play, plan. He seemed completely literal—unable to juggle images or hypotheses or possibilities, unable to enter an imaginative or figurative realm. And yet, one still felt, he was of normal intelligence, despite the manifest limitations of intellectual functioning. It was not that he lacked a mind, but that he was not using his mind fully . . . (Sacks, 2000, pp. 32–34)

As Sacks suggests, language and thought are intertwined. We find it difficult to imagine one without the other, and we consider both part of what it means to be human. Joseph seemed to have no sense of the past, and was unable to imagine or hypothesize. Reviewing the past, contemplating the future, and thinking about possibilities are key elements of human **cognition,** by which psychologists mean all the processes whereby we acquire and use information. We have already considered several cognitive processes, including perception, learning, and memory. In later chapters, we examine cognition's crucial relation to intelligence, coping and adjustment, abnormal behavior, and interpersonal relations. In this chapter, our main focus will be on a family of cognitive processes known as "directed thinking," or how we "use our heads"—and, to a significant degree, language—to solve problems and make decisions.

We begin this chapter by looking at the building blocks of thought—at how we use language, imagery, and concepts to give structure and meaning to our experiences. We then consider whether language and cognition are unique to human beings. Last we turn to problem solving and decision making, focusing on common strategies for dealing with life's puzzles.

THINKABOUTIT

You will find the answers to these questions in the chapter:

1. When we think, are we simply talking to ourselves?

2. Does the language you speak affect what you can think about?

3. Can scientists learn what is on an animal's mind?

4. Sometimes we are totally stumped by a problem or puzzle. When we learn the answer, it seems so obvious we can't believe we didn't see it right away. Why?

5. People spend considerable time wondering about "what might have been" if only they had made a different decision. Is this time well spent?

Cognition The processes whereby we acquire and use knowledge.

Language A flexible system of communication that uses sounds, rules, gestures, or symbols to convey information.

Phonemes The basic sound units of a language that indicate changes in meaning.

Morphemes The smallest meaningful units of speech, such as simple words, prefixes, and suffixes.

Grammar The language rules that determine how sounds and words can be combined and used to communicate meaning within a language.

Syntax The rules for arranging words into grammatical phrases and sentences.

The Building Blocks of Thought

When we think, are we simply talking to ourselves?

The phone rings, and it's your friend Sherryl. "I was just thinking about you!" you exclaim. What exactly do you mean when you say you were *thinking* about her? You may have been talking silently to yourself about her as you unpacked a bag of groceries, thoughts such as "I want to call Sherryl tonight" or "I wish I could be more like her." An image of her might have crossed your mind—probably her face, but perhaps also the sound of her voice. You may have been comparing Sherryl to another friend, using various concepts or categories such as *woman, kind, funny, strong, caring, dynamic, gentle.* Language, images, and concepts are the main building blocks of thought.

Language

Human **language** is a flexible system of symbols that enables us to communicate our ideas, thoughts, and feelings. Unlike nonhuman communication, human language is *semantic*, or meaningful: We can exchange detailed information about all kinds of objects and events, feelings, and ideas. We can tell others not only, "Watch out!" but also *why*. Human language is also characterized by *displacement:* it frees us from the here-and-now so we can communicate over time and space to people who have never been to the place or had the experience we are describing. Faced with a problem, we can contemplate alternative solutions, estimate their consequences, and weigh the costs and benefits of different actions in our head before we actually do anything. In short, language allows us to conduct mental experiments: *If . . . then.* Finally, human language is *productive:* we can combine sounds to make new words, arrange words into phrases, and string phrases into sentences—the possibilities are almost infinite.

The Structure of Language

Sound and Meaning Spoken language is based on universal sound units called **phonemes** that indicate changed meaning. There are about 45 phonemes in English, and as many as 85 in some languages (Bourne, Dominowski, Loftus, & Healy, 1986). In English, /z/ and /s/ are phonemes: The sounds *z* and *s* have no inherent meaning, but phonemes can be grouped together to form words, or parts of words. The word *zip* has a different meaning from the word *sip*. **Morphemes,** meaningful combinations of phonemes, are the smallest units of meaning in a language. This term can be applied to whole words (*red, calm,* or *hot*) or to parts of words that carry meaning. The suffix *-ed* signifies "in the past" (as in *walked* or *liked* or *cared*). The prefix *pre-* reflects the idea of "before" (as in *preview* or *predetermined*). We can use the same sounds (phonemes) to produce different words (morphemes): For example, the phonemes *e, n,* and *d* produce the morphemes *end, den,* and *Ned.* And we can combine morphemes to make up complex words that represent quite complex ideas, such as *pre-exist-ing, un-excell-ed,* and *psycho-logy.*

Grammar In turn, words can be joined into even more complex thoughts. Just as there are rules for combining phonemes and morphemes, there are also rules for structuring sentences and their meaning. These rules are what linguists call **grammar.** The two major components of grammar are *syntax* and *semantics.* **Syntax** is the system of rules that governs how we combine words to form meaningful phrases and sentences. For example, in English and many other languages, the meaning of a sentence is often determined by *word order:* "Sally hit the car" means one thing; "The car hit Sally" means something quite different; and "Hit Sally car the" is meaningless.

Semantics describes how we assign meaning to morphemes, words, phrases, and sentences—in other words, the content of language. The linguist Noam Chomsky (1957) greatly influenced psychologists' understanding of syntax and semantics (Chomsky, Place, & Schoneberger, 2000). When we are thinking about something—say, the ocean—our ideas usually consist of phrases and sentences, such as "The ocean is unusually calm tonight." Sentences have both a **surface structure**—the particular words and phrases—and a **deep structure**—the underlying meaning. The same deep structure can be conveyed by various different surface structures:

The ocean is unusually calm tonight.

Tonight the ocean is particularly calm.

Compared to most nights, tonight the ocean is calm.

Syntax and semantics enable speakers and listeners to perform what Chomsky calls *transformations* between the surface and the deep structure. According to Chomsky, when you want to communicate an idea, you start with a thought, then choose words and phrases that will express the idea, and finally produce the speech sounds that make up those words and phrases. Speaking requires *top-down processing*, and you can see from the left arrow in Figure 7–1 that the movement is indeed from top to bottom. When you want to understand a sentence, your task is reversed. You must start with speech sounds and work your way up to the meaning of those sounds. This is called *bottom-up processing*, as shown by the right arrow in Figure 7–1.

Words, phrases, and sentences are among the building blocks of thought. Images are another, as we will see in the next portion of the chapter.

Images

Think for a moment about Abraham Lincoln. Your thoughts of Lincoln may include such phrases as "wrote the Gettysburg Address," "president during the Civil War," and "assassinated by John Wilkes Booth." But you probably also have mental

Semantics The criteria for assigning meaning to the morphemes in a language.

Surface structure The particular words and phrases used to make up a sentence.

Deep structure The underlying meaning of a sentence.

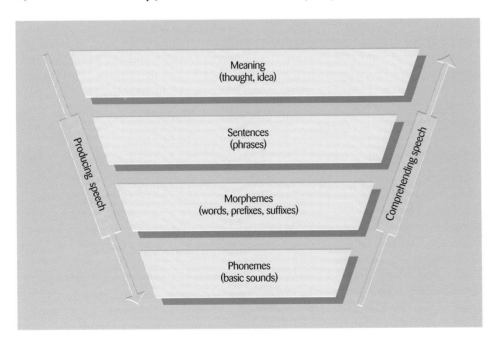

Figure 7–1
The direction of movement in speech production and comprehension.
Producing a sentence involves movement from thoughts and ideas to basic sounds; comprehending a sentence requires movement from basic sounds back to the underlying thoughts and ideas.

We can use visual and auditory images to think about things, such as this famous "I Have A Dream" speech by Martin Luther King, Jr. delivered at the Lincoln Memorial in Washington DC on August 28, 1963.

images of Lincoln: his bearded face, his lanky body, or perhaps a log cabin. **Images,** or *nonverbal* (visual, auditory, olfactory) mental representations, can be exceptionally powerful. We can visualize the Statue of Liberty or people we know; we can smell Thanksgiving dinner; we can hear Martin Luther King, Jr., saying "I have a dream!" In short, we can think about things using images. Albert Einstein relied heavily on his powers of visualization to understand phenomena that he later described in complex mathematical formulas. Einstein believed that his skill in visualizing abstract concepts led to his extraordinary insights (Miller, 1992; Shepard, 1978). Although few can match Einstein's brilliance, we all use imagery to think about and solve problems.

Not only do we visualize things in order to think about them, but we can also manipulate these mental images (Stylianou, 2002). Shepard and Metzler (1971) presented people with pairs of geometrical patterns (see Figure 7–2). In some cases, the two pictures were of the same pattern rotated to provide different views (see Figures 7–2A and 7–2B). In other cases, the two pictures were of different patterns (see Figure 7–2C). People were asked to determine whether each pair of patterns was the same or different. The researchers discovered that people invariably rotated the image of one pattern in their minds until they could see both patterns from the same perspective. Then they tried to see whether the mental image of one pattern matched the other pattern. Subsequent studies have supported these findings (e.g., Kosslyn & Sussman, 1995).

Concepts

Concepts are mental categories for classifying specific people, things, or events (Komatsu, 1992). *Dogs, books,* and *cars* are all concepts that let us categorize objects in the world around us. *Fast, strong,* and *interesting* are also concepts that can classify things, events, or people. Concepts provide a way of grouping or categorizing experiences so that encounters with something new need not be a surprise. We know, to some extent, what to think, and do not have to create a new word for every new experience. Instead, we draw on concepts that we have already formed, and we place the new object or event into the appropriate categories. In the process, we may modify some of our concepts to better match our experience. Consider, for example, the concept of *professor.* No doubt you had some concept of *professor* before you attended any college classes. After you took your first college courses and actually met some

Image A nonverbal mental representation of a sensory experience.

Concept A mental category for classifying objects, people, or experiences.

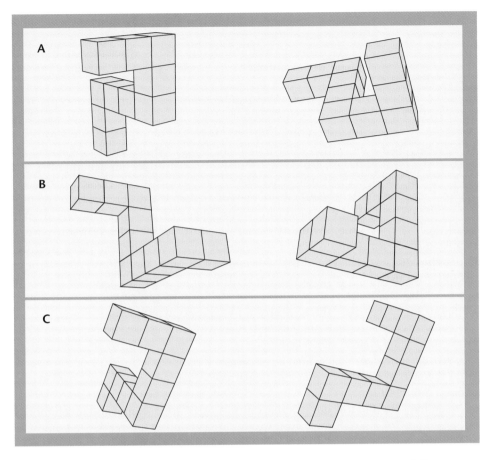

Figure 7–2
Examples of the pairs of geometrical patterns used in Shepard and Metzler's (1971) experiment.
The researchers found that participants first rotated an image of one pattern in their minds until they could see both patterns from the same perspective. They then matched the mental images of the pairs of patterns to decide whether they were the same (A and B) or different (C).

professors, your concept probably changed. Your concept will become fuller as you add new information about professors based on your experiences at college. In the future, because you have formed a concept of *professor*, you will not have to respond to each new professor as a totally new experience.

Equally important, concepts can be organized in hierarchies, with the narrowest, most specific category at the bottom and the most general at the top (Reed, 1996). For example, *collie* is a subset of the category *dog*, and *dog* is a subset of the category

When you think about the concept *bird,* you don't think about every different kind of bird you know, nor do you imagine a list of features that all birds share (wings, feathers, beak, two feet, egg-laying). Instead you think of a prototype of a "typical" bird, which probably looks like this bluebird. A penguin doesn't match this prototype very well, but you can still tell it is a bird by its degree of category membership.

"Well, you don't look like an experimental psychologist to me."

animal. Likewise, *maple* is a subset of the category *tree,* and *tree* is a subset of the category *plant.* The hierarchical nature of concepts helps us to think about things efficiently and how they relate to one another.

Prototypes   We may be tempted to think of concepts as simple and clear-cut. But many concepts are neither simple nor unambiguous, they are "fuzzy." They overlap one another and are often poorly defined. For example, most people can tell a mouse from a rat, but few can produce an accurate list of the critical differences between mice and rats (Rosch, 1973, 1978, 1998, 2002). If we cannot explain the difference between mouse and rat, how can we use these *fuzzy concepts* in our thinking? One possibility is that we construct a model, or **prototype,** of a representative mouse and one of a representative rat; we then use those prototypes in our thinking. Rosch argued that our concept of bird, for example, does not consist only of a list of key attributes such as "feathers," "wings," "two feet," and "lives in trees." Instead, most of us also have a model bird, or prototype, in mind—such as a bluebird or a sparrow—that captures for us the essence of *bird.*

When we encounter new animals or drawings of animals, we compare them to these prototypes using what Rosch called *degree of category membership* to determine whether they are, in fact, mice or rats. That is, we decide what is most probable or most sensible given the facts at hand. For example, a sparrow and a mouse both have two eyes. But unlike a mouse the sparrow has wings and feathers, only two legs, and no whiskers, all of which indicate that it is quite unlike our prototype for a mouse and much more like our prototype for a bird. Similarly, if we were to encounter a three-legged mouse with no whiskers, we would in all likelihood still recognize it as a mouse.

We have seen that language, images, and concepts form important building blocks for thought. To what extent do they shape the kinds of things people can think about and the ways they think about them? And to what extent do people who speak different languages and come from different cultures think differently? In the next section of the chapter we will explore those issues.

CHECK YOUR UNDERSTANDING

1. Language and concepts are two of the three most important building blocks of thought. What is the third?

___a. prototypes

___b. displacement

___c. images

2. Meaningful sentences are constructed according to the rules of _____?

___a. grammar

___b. semantics

___c. category membership

3. Universal sound units found in every language are called

___a. morphemes

___b. phonemes

___c. transformations

Prototype According to Rosch, a mental model containing the most typical features of a concept.

Answers: 1.c, 2.a, 3.b

Language, Thought, and Culture

Does the language you speak affect what you can think about?

ENDURING ISSUES   **diversity**universality

Do We All Think Alike?

For at least 100 years, a fundamental assumption in psychology as well as philosophy was that the basic processes of human cognition are universal. It was accepted that cultural differences affect what people think about—thus Masai elders in the Serengeti count their wealth in heads of cattle whereas Wall Street bankers measure theirs in stocks and bonds. But habits of thought—the ways people process information—were assumed to be the same everywhere. The tendency to categorize objects and experiences, the ability to reason logically, and the desire to understand situations in terms of cause and effect were thought to be part of human nature, whatever the cultural setting (Goode, 2000a). In this section, we will examine the validity of these viewpoints.

Language and Cognition

We have seen that language is closely tied to the expression and understanding of thoughts. Because our language determines not only the words we use but also the way in which we combine those words into sentences, can language also determine what we can think about? Some theorists believe that it does indeed. Recall that in Chapter 6, Memory, we noted that language affects long-term memory. As Lindsay and Norman (1977) point out, "memory for single perceptual experiences is directly related to the ease with which language can communicate that experience" (p. 483). In a study of this effect, participants looked at color patches and assigned each one a name (Brown & Lenneberg, 1954). Colors that were quickly and easily named (such as blue) were remembered more easily than were those that took longer to name and were given less common labels (such as sky blue or pale blue).

If language affects our ability to store and retrieve information, it should also affect our ability to think about things. Benjamin Whorf (1956) was an early spokesperson for this position which is called **linguistic determinism.** Whorf noted, for example, that the Hopi, a Native American people of the southwestern United States, have only two nouns for everything that flies. One noun refers to birds; the other is used for everything else, whether airplanes, kites, or dragonflies. Thus, according to linguistic determinism, the Hopi would interpret all flying things in terms of either of these two nouns—something in the air would be either a bird or a nonbird.

Linguistic determinism has intuitive appeal, but when it is tested in the field a rather different picture emerges. For example, cultures vary in the number of colors their language identifies. Nonetheless, people can perceive color distinctions for which their language has no words. The Dani, a people who live in the highlands of New Guinea, use only two color terms, which correspond roughly to "light" and "dark," and have no words for geometric shapes. Nonetheless, they remember basic colors such as red, green, and yellow. In addition, the Dani, and people from other cultures with limited color naming terminology, judge the similarity of colors much as English-speaking people do (Heider & Oliver, 1972; Roberson, Davies, & Jules, 2000; Rosch, 1973). Thus, people from different cultures with very different

Linguistic determinism The idea that patterns of thinking are determined by the specific language one speaks.

The Dani of New Guinea can perceive and remember the many colors of their world just as readily as you can, even though their language has only two color terms—"light" and "dark."

languages think about some things, such as color, in very similar ways, even if their language contains no words for those things. Language may indeed influence thought, but it doesn't seem to restrict thought to the extent that some linguistic determinists believed.

Moreover, experience and thought actually influence language. For example, English-speaking skiers, realizing that different textures of snow can affect their downhill run, have coined such differentiated words for snow as *powder, corn,* and *ice.* The growth of personal computers and the Internet has inspired a vocabulary of its own, such as *hard drive, RAM, gigabytes, software, online,* and *CD-ROM.* In short, people create new words when they need them—experience shapes language. If the Hopi had been subjected to air raids, they would probably have created words to distinguish a butterfly from a bomber!

Psychologists and linguists have not dismissed linguistic determinism altogether, but rather have softened it. Clearly, language, thought, and culture are intertwined (Matsumoto, 1996). People create words to capture important aspects of their experiences, and to some extent words shape how people think and what they think about. But people also can think about things for which they have no words. Experience shapes language, and language, in turn, affects subsequent experience.

Is Our Language Male-Dominated?

The English language has traditionally used masculine terms such as "man" and "he" to refer to all people, female as well as male. Does this affect the way that English speakers think? Several studies suggest that it does indeed. Hyde (1984a) asked children to complete stories after she gave them a first line such as, "When a kid goes to school, _____ often feels excited on the first day." When Hyde filled in the blank with "he," the children nearly always composed stories about boys. When she used "he or she" in the blank, a third of the children made up stories about girls.

In another study, Hyde (1984b) discovered that the use of "he" or "she" to describe a factory worker who made "wudges" (imaginary plastic parts for video games) affected how children thought male and female wudgemakers would perform their jobs. Those children who heard wudgemakers described by the masculine pronoun "he" rated women wudgemakers poorly; children who heard wudgemakers identified by the pronoun "she" judged female wudgemakers most positively; and the ratings of children who heard gender-neutral descriptions of wudgemakers fell in between those of the two other groups. All the groups of children, however, viewed male wudgemakers equally positively.

More recent research has focused on the unconscious, automatic nature of gender stereotyping and language (Greenwald & Banaji, 1995). In an experiment that required men and women to respond rapidly to gender-neutral and gender-specific pronouns, both sexes responded more quickly to stimuli that contained traditional gender stereotypes (e.g., nurse/she) than to stimuli that contained nontraditional gender stereotypes (e.g., nurse/he). This occurred even among participants who were explicitly opposed to gender stereotyping (Banaji & Hardin, 1996).

From research such as this, it appears that referring to doctors, college professors, bankers, and executives by the generic "he" may contribute to the gender stereotyping of these respected occupations as appropriate for men but not for women. In contrast, referring to secretaries and housekeepers as "she" may reinforce the stereotype that those occupations are appropriate occupations for women, not men (Christie, 2003).

Culture and Cognition

All known cultures use categories to help form concepts, but what information gets included in a given category, and how the categories are shaped by experience, can differ substantially from one culture to another (Rogoff & Chavajay, 1995). Cross-cultural psychologist David Matsumoto provides an amusing example of how cultural differences can affect perception, cognition, and behavior:

> We have probably all seen imported, handmade, brass pitchers of various designs and sizes. Once, after dinner with a Persian friend at an American's home, we all gathered in the living room. After a moment, our Persian friend turned red, giggled, and looked embarrassed, but didn't say anything. When the host left the room a few minutes later, the Persian pointed out a large ornate brass pitcher with a long spout that was sitting on a coffee table as a decoration. It had been made in the Middle East where toilet paper is scarce and people clean themselves after going to the bathroom by using such pitchers to pour water on themselves. So what was a prized decoration to our host was an embarrassment to my friend. (Matsumoto, 1995, p. 52)

As this example illustrates, two people perceiving the same object may assign it to very different categories!

Anthropologists and other Westerners who have spent time in Asia often say that Eastern and Western cultures are worlds apart—that people in these cultures not

ON THE CUTTING EDGE

CULTURE AND COGNITION

Richard Nisbett and his colleagues conducted a series of rigorous, controlled experiments to determine whether subjective impressions about the ways Easterners and Westerners think are valid. Their comparisons of American to Japanese, Chinese, and Korean cognitive styles indicate that this is a case in which stereotypes are largely accurate. In one experiment (Nisbett, Peng, Choi, & Norenzayan, 2001), American and Japanese students were shown an underwater scene and asked to describe what they saw. Most Japanese participants described the scene as a whole, beginning with the background; most American participants described the biggest, brightest, fastest fish. (In psychological terms, the Japanese were "field dependent" and the Americans, "field independent"; see Chapter 3, Sensation and Perception).

This different attitude toward contexts carried over into social perceptions. In group decision-making situations, Chinese students generally preferred compromise to conflict; their American counterparts were more likely to focus on differences of opinion and to hold out until one side won or the other lost. Similarly, when presented with examples of interpersonal conflict—for example, between a mother and daughter—American students typically sided with one or the other and made comments such as "The mother is too controlling" or "The daughter is out of control." Chinese students often saw merits on both sides and came to such conclusions as, "Both the mother and daughter have failed to understand each other." Many Americans were bothered by this tendency to see both sides of a story and irritated by such Chinese proverbs as "Too modest is half boastful."

The researchers also found evidence of different styles of reasoning. Participants were presented with logical sequences such as this syllogism: "All animals with fur hibernate. Rabbits have fur. Therefore rabbits hibernate." Americans were more likely to accept an argument on logical grounds (if the first two premises are correct, the conclusion must be true); Asians more often rejected abstract, logical reasoning in favor of concrete or empirical knowledge (in this case, the fact that all animals with fur do not hibernate).

Nisbett and his colleagues conclude that these studies reflect fundamental, qualitative differences in how Easterners and Westerners, Orientals and Occidentals, perceive and think about the world. They also emphasize that these differences are cultural, not genetic, in origin because the cognitive approach of Asian Americans born in the United States is indistinguishable from that of European Americans (Peng & Nisbett, 1999; Nisbett et al., 2001; Nisbett & Norenzayan, 2002).

only think *about* different things but also differ in *how* they think. The impression is that Easterners think "holistically": They pay more attention to contexts and relationships than to individuals, put more faith in knowledge acquired through experience than in abstract reasoning, and are more comfortable with contradictions. In contrast, Westerners are seen as more "analytical": They view actors and objects as independent of context, rely more on formal logic, and are uncomfortable with inconsistencies. Some recent research has confirmed these and other cultural differences in ways of thinking (see *On the Cutting Edge: Culture and Cognition*).

CHECK YOUR UNDERSTANDING

1. Benjamin Whorf championed the idea that patterns of thinking are determined by

___a. a person's grasp of correct grammar

___b. the language a person speaks

___c. a person's grasp of semantics

2. Psychologists and linguists have softened the theory of linguistic determinism by suggesting that _____ also has an effect on language.

___a. culture

___b. experience

___c. a and b

___d. none of the above

Answers: 1.b, 2.c

Nonhuman Thought and Language

Can scientists learn what is on an animal's mind?

Can animals think? Ask people who live with pets, and they almost certainly will answer yes—and follow with stories about a cat who jumped out of a car miles from home yet found the way back, a dog that saved its owner's life, and other amazing feats. Ask someone who does not live with, or particularly like, pets and you may well get a sarcastic reply: "Does a bullfrog have wings?" Ask psychologists, and their most likely response will be a thoughtful pause, and then, "That's a difficult question."

In evaluating research on nonhuman animals, scientists seek to avoid *anthropomorphism*—the all-too-human tendency to attribute human characteristics to other animals (Mitchell, Thompson, & Miles, 1997). Yet they are also conscious of the opposite tendency, *anthropocentrism*—the equally human tendency to view our own species as unique, overlooking our own evolutionary heritage as well as abilities in other species (Fouts, 1997). Questions about animal intelligence are probably as old as human intelligence, but only recently have psychologists developed scientific techniques for learning how other animals use their brains and identifying the similarities and differences between human and nonhuman thought (Boysen & Himes, 1999).

Animal Cognition

Numerous studies indicate that other animals have some humanlike cognitive capacities. Parrots, for example, are known to be exceptionally good vocal mimics. Every schoolchild knows the expression "Polly wanna cracker?" But do parrots know what they are saying? According to Irene Pepperberg (2000, 2002) Alex, an African gray parrot, does. Pepperberg, who has worked with Alex for more than two decades, reports that he can count to six; identify more than 50 different objects; and classify objects according to color, shape, material, and relative size. For example, if given a tray full of different colored objects, Alex can accurately count the number of blue blocks or green wool balls without being distracted by the other objects on the tray. He recognizes that the same object (a green triangle) can have several different attributes (a rudimentary form of abstract thought), correctly answering the questions "What shape?" and "What color?" When asked "What color is corn?" Alex answers, "Yellow" even when no corn is present. Based on her studies, Professor Pepperberg believes that Alex is demonstrating more than simple mimicry in these behaviors. Indeed she argues that his actions reflect reasoning, choice, and to some extent thinking.

Researchers have also taught dolphins to respond to requests—in the form of human hand and arm gestures or computer-generated whistles—to bring a Frisbee to a surfboard on the *right* or the *left* (Herman, Richards, & Wolz, 1984; Rumbaugh, 1990) and to select which of two objects is identical to a sample object—the basis of the concepts *same* and *different* (Harley, Roitblat, & Nachtigall, 1996; Roitblat, Penner, & Nachtigall, 1990). Recent studies have shown that rhesus monkeys can learn the concept of numeration (the capacity to use numbers) and serialization (the ability to place objects in a specific order based on a concept) (Brannon & Terrace, 1998; Terrace, Son, & Brannon, 2003). In short, it appears that humans are not totally unique in their ability to form concepts.

The great apes—chimpanzees, gorillas, and orangutans—are of special interest in studies of nonhuman cognition (and language). Apes are our closest kin: We share 97 to 99 percent of our genes with them (which means we are more closely related to them than a lion is to a tiger, or a zebra is to a horse). We also have many characteristics in common. If any other animal thinks like we do, great apes are the most likely candidates. In fact, apes have demonstrated sophisticated problem-solving skills. For example, in Chapter 5 (Learning) we saw that chimpanzees figured out various ways to retrieve a bunch of bananas out of their reach. In more recent studies, chimpanzees provided with computer keyboards have learned to use symbols to make and respond to complex requests (Premack, 1971, 1976), to identify and categorize objects (especially food), to place objects in order (Kawai & Matsuzawa, 2000), and even to solve analogies similar to those found on college entrance tests, such as *"Symbol A is to symbol B as symbol C is to what symbol?"* (Cook, 1993).

But do the chimps and dolphins and parrots know what they know? In other words, do nonhuman animals have a *sense of self* (Blumberg & Wasserman, 1995)? George Gallup (1985, 1998) at the Tulane University primate research center noticed that after a few days' exposure, chimpanzees began using a mirror to make faces and to examine and groom parts of their body that they had never seen before. To test whether the animals actually understood that they were looking at themselves, he anesthetized the chimpanzees and painted a bright red mark above their eyebrow ridge and on the top of one ear. If, the first time they looked at the mirror after awakening, they reached up and touched the red marks, presumably they recognized themselves.

The mirror test has been used by hundreds of researchers, with many other animals, for three decades. Only two nonhuman species consistently show signs of self-awareness, even after extended exposure to mirrors—chimpanzees and orangutans (Boysen & Himes, 1999; Gallup, 1985; Vauclair, 1996). For that matter, even human infants do not demonstrate mirror-recognition until they reach 18 to 24 months of age.

If chimpanzees possess self-awareness, do they understand that others have information, thoughts, and emotions that may be different from their own?

Only humans, chimpanzees, and orangutans consistently pass the mirror test of self-recognition.

Signs Stereotyped communications about an animal's current state.

Telegraphic speech An early speech stage of one- and two-year-olds that omits words that are not essential to the meaning of a phrase.

Observational studies suggest they do have at least a limited sense of other-awareness (de Waal, 1989; Goodall, 1971; Menzel, 1974; Savage-Rumbaugh & Fields, 2000). One measure of other-awareness is deception. For example, if a chimpanzee discovers a hidden store of food and another chimpanzee happens along, the first may begin idly grooming himself. Presumably, the first chimpanzee recognizes that the second (a) is equally interested in food and (b) will interpret the behavior as meaning there is nothing interesting nearby. Both in the wild and in captive colonies, chimpanzees frequently practice deception in matters of food, receptive females, and power or dominance.

The Question of Language

In one way or another, all animals communicate. Birds do it, bees do it, whales and chimpanzees do it (to paraphrase Cole Porter's song). The forms of animal communications vary widely. Honeybees enact an intricate waggle dance that tells their hive mates exactly where to find pollen (von Frisch, 1974), and the quality of the pollen at that location (Waddington, Nelson, & Page, 1998). Humpback whales perform haunting solos, ranging from deep basso rumblings to high soprano squeaks and continuing for as long as a half hour. In the wild, chimpanzees communicate by means of some three dozen vocalizations plus an array of gestures, postures, and facial expressions. The technical term for such messages is **signs,** general or global statements about the animal's *current* state.

To be sure, human beings also use signs. We utter exclamations—such as "Help! or "Yippee"—that are not much different from a chimpanzee's *waaaa* (for danger) or *hoot* (for excitement) and use body language to supplement or substitute for words. But fixed, stereotyped signals are a far cry from language. The distinguishing features of language, as described earlier, are *meaningfulness* (or semantics), *displacement* (communication about objects and events not present in the here and now), and *productivity* (the ability to produce and understand new and unique expressions). Using these criteria, as far as we know, no other species has its own language.

Early attempts to teach chimpanzees to speak (Hayes & Hayes, 1951; Kellogg, 1968) met with little success, for the (now) obvious reason that chimpanzees do not have the vocal equipment to produce speechlike sounds. Then R. A. Gardner and B. Gardner attempted to teach American Sign Language (ASL) to a chimpanzee named Washoe whom they acquired as an infant (1969, 1975, 1977). The Gardners raised Washoe as if she were a deaf child, communicating with her (and other humans in her presence) only by signing. They used modeling and shaping to teach her gestures, rewarding her for correct responses. Washoe learned 38 signs by age 2, 85 by age 4, and 160 by age 5. She combined one-word signs into simple two-word sentences (such as "more milk") similar to the **telegraphic speech** of 1- and 2-year-old human toddlers. Also like small children, Washoe generalized signs (such as "open") to a variety of objects and situations (containers, bottles, and even the door to outside). Moreover, she invented sign combinations for new situations (simple productivity), such as "water bird" the first time she saw a swan and "black bug" the first time she encountered another chimpanzee (Fouts, 1973)!

Research with the other great apes has found similar capabilities. Francine Patterson (Bonvillian & Patterson, 1997; Patterson, 1978, 1980, 1981) reared Koko, a lowland gorilla much like Washoe, and has worked with her for two decades. By age 5, Koko had a working vocabulary of 500 signs—about the same level as a 5-year-old deaf child who uses sign language, though

THINKING CRITICALLY

Nonhuman Cognition

1. Based on what you have read in this chapter, do you believe that nonhuman animals can think and use language? Why do you think so? What kind of evidence would cause you to change your mind?

2. What can we learn about ourselves by studying these processes in other species?

Chimpanzees, our closest living relative, use a wide repertoire of gestures, facial expressions, and vocalizations to communicate.

far lower than a hearing, speaking child's vocabulary of 1,000 to 5,000 words (Patterson & Cohn, 1990). Now in her mid-20s, Koko reportedly signs about her own and her companions' emotions, such as happy, sad, or angry. Most interesting, Koko refers to the past and the future (displacement). Using signs *before* and *later*, *yesterday* and *tomorrow* appropriately, she mourned the death of her pet kitten and expressed a desire to become a mother.

Critics have been quick to point out potential flaws in these sign language studies. Gestures are subject to varied interpretations: Skeptics argue that these researchers were reading meaning and intentions into simple gestures. Moreover, as we will see in Chapter 10 (Life Span Development), human children learn language effortlessly and swiftly without deliberate, explicit adult instruction. In contrast, these apes required intensive training and constant reinforcement to develop very limited language skills (Limber, 1977). One of the most outspoken critics, Herbert Terrace (1979, 1985), attempted to teach sign language to "Nim Chimpsky" (respectfully named for the cognitive linguist Noam Chomsky, who proposed a specifically human language acquisition device), and concluded that the apes' accomplishments reflected simple operant conditioning, not linguistic aptitude. Terrace argued that apes do not understand syntax—the rules for combining words in meaningful orders, so that "Nim eat banana" means something quite different from "Banana eat Nim." The result, as Terrace put it, was "word salad" (Savage-Rumbaugh & Lewin, 1994, p. 131). Noam Chomsky emphatically agrees (Johnson, 1995).

To reduce the ambiguity of hand signs, other researchers began using computer keyboards to teach and record communications with apes (Rumbaugh, 1977; Rumbaugh & Savage-Rumbaugh, 1978; Rumbaugh, von Glaserfeld, Warner, Pisani, & Gill, 1974); to document behavior with and without humans on camera; to use double-blind procedures; and also to study another ape species, bonobos (formerly called "pygmy chimpanzees"). Most impressive—and surprising—was a bonobo named Kanzi (Savage-Rumbaugh & Lewin, 1994). When brought to the Language Research Center near Atlanta, Kanzi was adopted by an older female who was unable (or unwilling) to use a keyboard. Some months later, the researchers discovered that Kanzi, who accompanied his mother to lessons, was learning keyboard

Chimps and Symbols
Sue Savage-Rumbaugh and her colleagues at the Yerkes Primate Center and Georgia State University have studied the basic question of whether chimps understand symbols. Their research suggests that the answer is yes.

symbols and spoken English on his own, *without formal training*, much as children do. Sue Savage-Rumbaugh decided to continue this naturalistic education through social interaction, expanding his horizons with walks around the Center's grounds. Kanzi understands spoken English and more than 200 keyboard symbols. He responds to vocal and keyboard requests that he has not heard before (such as, "Put the key in the refrigerator"), and uses the keyboard to make requests, comment on his surroundings, state his intentions, and—sometimes—to indicate what he is thinking about.

Washoe, now in her thirties, lives with four other chimpanzees at the Chimpanzee and Human Communications Institute in Washington state. Her caretakers, Roger and Deborah Fouts, who communicate only in sign language in the compound, report that the chimpanzees use signs to communicate with each other (even when they are alone, as recorded by hidden cameras) as well as with humans. Washoe's adopted son, Loulis, learned signs not from human trainers (who did not sign in his presence) but from the other chimpanzees. What do they sign about? The usual stuff: "Wanna play?" is most common among young males. With Loulis, Washoe has more motherly concerns, especially discipline and comfort. This possible anthropomorphism aside, Loulis is the only ape to learn signs exclusively from other apes.

The studies of Kanzi and Loulis answer one criticism—that apes learn signs only through intensive training and to win favor and obtain rewards from human trainers. But the second criticism—that even if apes can learn to use signs and symbols, they do not grasp the deep structure (or underlying rules) of language—is far from resolved (Blumberg & Wasserman, 1995). At most, apes have reached the linguistic level of a 2- to 2-1/2-year-old child. Not surprisingly, critics see this as evidence of severe limitations, whereas their trainers (and others) see this as an extraordinary accomplishment.

Ultimately, research on nonhuman language raises as many questions as it answers. Are humans and great apes separated by an unbridgeable divide, or are the differences between us a matter of degree? If, as many scientists believe, humans and great apes are descended from a common ancestor—and if, as some scientists conclude, great apes have at least a rudimentary capacity for symbolic communication—why didn't they develop a language of their own? Equally significant, why did we?

So far, we have been talking about *what* humans and nonhumans think about. As we will see in the next section, cognitive psychologists are equally interested in *how* people use thinking to solve problems and make decisions.

CHECK YOUR UNDERSTANDING

1. Chimpanzees and orangutans are the only two nonhuman species to consistently show

___a. self-awareness

___b. problem-solving ability

___c. numeration comprehension

2. Humans use language to communicate. What is the nonhuman animal equivalent of language?

___a. grunts

___b. squeaks

___c. signs

Answers: 1.a, 2.c

Figure 7–3

Problem Solving

Sometimes we are totally stumped by a problem or puzzle. When we learn the answer, it seems so obvious we can't believe we didn't see it right away. Why?

Our minds do not passively record information from the environment just as it is presented to the senses; rather, they actively select and interpret sensory data. Typically, we transform and reorganize external data so that they fit our existing mental framework (including our concepts, images, and language); sometimes, however, we need to modify our mental structures to accommodate new data and new ways of thinking. Nowhere is the transformational nature of cognition more apparent than in problem solving.

Let's begin with some problems.

1.   Problem 1. You have three measuring spoons (Figure 7–3). One is filled with 8 teaspoons of salt; the other two are empty but have a capacity of 2 teaspoons each. Divide the salt among the spoons so that only 4 teaspoons of salt remain in the largest spoon.

2.   Problem 2. You have a 5-minute hourglass and a 9-minute hourglass (Figure 7–4), How can you use them to time a 14-minute barbecue? (Adapted from Sternberg, 1986)

Most people find these easy to solve. But now consider more elaborate versions of the same three problems:

5 min.   9 min.

Figure 7–4

Problem representation The first step in solving a problem: defining the problem.

Figure 7–5

Figure 7–6

1. **Problem 3**. You have three measuring spoons (Figure 7–5). One (spoon A) is filled with 8 teaspoons of salt. The second and third spoons are both empty; the second spoon (spoon B) can hold 5 teaspoons, and the third (spoon C) can hold 3 teaspoons. Divide the salt among the spoons so that spoon A and spoon B each have exactly 4 teaspoons of salt and spoon C is empty.

2. **Problem 4**. You have a 5-minute hourglass and a 9-minute hourglass (Figure 7–4). How can you use them to time a 13-minute barbecue? (Adapted from Sternberg, 1986)

Most people find the last two problems much more difficult than the first two. (The answers to these and other numbered problems appear at the end of the chapter.) Why? The answer lies in interpretation, strategy, and evaluation. Problems 1 and 2 are considered trivial because it's so easy to interpret what is called for, the strategies for solving them are simple, and you can effortlessly verify that each step you take moves you closer to a solution. Problems 3 and 4, in contrast, require some thought to interpret what is called for, the strategies for solving them are not immediately apparent, and it is harder to evaluate whether any given step has actually made progress toward your goal. These three aspects of problem solving—interpretation, strategy, and evaluation—provide a useful framework for investigating this topic.

The Interpretation of Problems

The first step in solving a problem is called *problem representation:* interpreting or defining the problem. For example, if your business is losing money, you might define the problem as deciphering how to cut costs. But by defining the problem so narrowly, you have ruled out other options. A better representation of the problem would be to figure out ways to boost profits—by cutting costs, by increasing income, or both. To see the importance of problem representation, consider these two problems.

1. **Problem 5**. You have four pieces of chain, each of which is made up of three links (Figure 7–6). All links are closed at the beginning of the problem. It costs two cents to open a link and three cents to close a link. How can you join all 12 links together into a single, continuous circle without paying more than 15 cents?

2. **Problem 6**. Arrange six kitchen matches into four equilateral triangles (Figure 7–7). Each side of every triangle must be only one match in length.

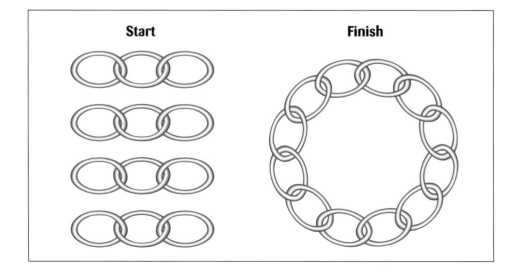

These two problems are difficult because people tend to represent them in ways that impede solutions. For example, in Problem 5, most people assume that the best way to proceed is to open and close the end links on the pieces of chain. As long as they persist with this "conceptual block," they will be unable to solve the problem. If the problem is represented differently, the solution is almost immediately obvious. Similarly, for the kitchen match problem, most people assume that they can work only in two dimensions—that is, that the triangles must lie flat on a surface— or that one match cannot serve as the side of two triangles. When the problem is represented differently, the solution becomes much easier. (The solutions to both of these problems appear at the end of this chapter.)

If you have successfully interpreted Problems 5 and 6, give number 7 a try:

Figure 7–7
The six-match problem
Arrange the six matches so that they form four equilateral triangles. The solution is given in Figure 7–11.

1. **Problem 7.** A monk wishes to get to a retreat at the top of a mountain. He starts climbing the mountain at sunrise and arrives at the top at sunset of the same day. During his ascent, he travels at various speeds and stops often to rest. He spends the night engaged in meditation and starts his descent at sunrise, following the same narrow path that he used to climb the mountain. As before, he travels at various speeds and stops often to rest. Because he takes great care not to trip and fall on the way down, the descent takes as long as the ascent, and he does not arrive at the bottom until sunset. Prove that there is one place on the path that the monk passes at exactly the same time of day on the ascent and on the descent.

This problem is extremely difficult to solve if it is represented verbally or mathematically. It is considerably easier to solve if it is represented visually, as you can see from the explanation that appears at the end of this chapter.

Another aspect of successfully representing a problem is deciding which category the problem belongs to. Properly categorizing a problem can provide clues about how to solve it. In fact, once a problem has been properly categorized, its solution may be very easy. Quite often, people who seem to have a knack for solving problems are actually just very skilled at categorizing them in effective ways. Star chess players, for example, can readily categorize a game situation by comparing it with various standard situations stored in their long-term memories. This strategy helps them interpret the current pattern of chess pieces with greater speed and precision than the novice chess player can. Similarly, a seasoned football coach may quickly call for a particular play because the coach has interpreted a situation on the field in terms of familiar categories. Gaining expertise in any field, from football to physics, consists primarily of increasing your ability to represent and categorize problems so that they can be solved quickly and effectively (Haberlandt, 1997).

Producing Strategies and Evaluating Progress

Once you have properly interpreted a problem, the next steps needed are selecting a solution strategy and evaluating progress toward your goal. A solution strategy can be anything from simple trial and error, to information retrieval based on similar problems, to a set of step-by-step procedures guaranteed to work (called an algorithm), to rule-of-thumb approaches known as heuristics.

Trial and Error   Trial and error is a strategy that works best when there are only limited choices. For example, if you have only three or four keys to choose from, trial and error is the best way to find out which one unlocks your friend's garage door. In most cases, however, trial and error wastes time because there are so many different options to test. It is better to eliminate unproductive approaches and to zero in on an approach that will work. Let's consider some alternative strategies.

Algorithm A step-by-step method of problem solving that guarantees a correct solution.

Heuristics Rules of thumb that help in simplifying and solving problems, although they do not guarantee a correct solution.

Hill climbing A heuristic problem-solving strategy in which each step moves you progressively closer to the final goal.

Subgoals Intermediate, more manageable goals used in one heuristic strategy to make it easier to reach the final goal.

 7.1

Information Retrieval   One approach is to retrieve from long-term memory information about how such a problem was solved in the past. Information retrieval is an especially important option when a solution is needed quickly. For example, pilots simply memorize the slowest speed at which a particular airplane can fly before it stalls.

Algorithms   More complex problems require more complex strategies. An **algorithm** is a problem-solving method that guarantees a solution if it is appropriate for the problem and is properly carried out. For example, to calculate the product of 323 and 546, we multiply the numbers according to the rules of multiplication (the algorithm). If we do it accurately, we are guaranteed to get the right answer. Similarly, to convert temperatures from Fahrenheit to Celsius, we use the algorithm C = 5/9 (F − 32).

Heuristics   Because we don't have algorithms for every kind of problem, we often turn to **heuristics,** or rules of thumb. Heuristics do not guarantee a solution, but they may bring it within reach. Part of problem solving is to decide which heuristic is most appropriate for a given problem (Bourne et al., 1986).

A very simple heuristic is **hill climbing:** We try to move continually closer to our goal without going backward. At each step, we evaluate how far "up the hill" we have come, how far we still have to go, and precisely what the next step should be. On a multiple-choice test, for example, one useful hill-climbing strategy is first to eliminate the alternatives that are obviously incorrect. In trying to balance a budget, each reduction in expenses brings you closer to the goal and leaves you with a smaller deficit.

Another problem-solving heuristic is to create **subgoals.** By setting subgoals, we break a problem into smaller, more manageable pieces, each of which is easier to solve than the problem as a whole (Reed, 1996). Consider the problem of the Hobbits and the Orcs:

1.   **Problem 8**. Three Hobbits and three Orcs are on the bank of a river. They all want to get to the other side, but their boat will carry only two creatures at a time. Moreover, if at any time the Orcs outnumber the Hobbits, the Orcs will attack the Hobbits. How can all the creatures get across the river without danger to the Hobbits?

The solution to this problem may be found by thinking of it in terms of a series of subgoals. What has to be done to get just one or two creatures across the river safely, temporarily leaving aside the main goal of getting everyone across? We could first send two of the Orcs across and have one of them return. That gets one Orc across the river. Now we can think about the next trip. It's clear that we can't then send a single Hobbit across with an Orc, because the Hobbit would be outnumbered as soon as the boat landed. Therefore, we have to send either two Hobbits or two Orcs. By working on the problem in this fashion—concentrating on subgoals—we can eventually get everyone across.

Once you have solved Problem 8, you might want to try Problem 9, which is considerably more difficult (the answers to both problems are at the end of the chapter):

1.   **Problem 9**. This problem is identical to Problem 8, except that there are five Hobbits and five Orcs, and the boat can carry only three creatures at a time.

Subgoals are often helpful in solving a variety of everyday problems. For example, a student whose goal is to write a term paper might set subgoals by breaking the project into a series of separate tasks: choosing a topic, doing research and taking notes, preparing an outline, writing the first draft, editing, rewriting, and so on. Even the subgoals can sometimes be broken down into separate tasks: Writing the first draft of the paper might break down into the subgoals of writing the introduction, describing the position to be taken, supporting the position with evidence, drawing conclusions, writing a summary, and writing a bibliography. Subgoals make problem solving more manageable because they free us from the burden of having to "get to the other side of the river" all at once. Although the overall purpose of setting subgoals is still to reach the ultimate goal, this tactic allows us to set our sights on closer, more manageable objectives.

One of the most frequently used heuristics, called **means-end analysis,** combines hill climbing and subgoals. Like hill climbing, means-end analysis involves analyzing the difference between the current situation and the desired end, and then doing something to reduce that difference. But in contrast to hill climbing—which does not permit detours away from the final goal in order to solve the problem— means-end analysis takes into account the entire problem situation. It formulates subgoals in such a way as to allow us temporarily to take a step that appears to be backward in order to reach our goal in the end. One example is the pitcher's strategy in a baseball game when confronted with the best batter in the league. The pitcher might opt to walk this batter intentionally even though doing so moves away from the major subgoal of keeping runners off base. Intentional walking might enable the pitcher to keep a run from scoring and so contribute to the ultimate goal of winning the game. This flexibility in thinking is a major benefit of means-end analysis.

But means-end analysis also poses the danger of straying so far from the end goal that the goal disappears altogether. One way of avoiding this situation is to use the heuristic of **working backward** (Bourne et al., 1986). With this strategy, the search for a solution begins at the goal and works backward toward the "givens." Working backward is often used when the goal has more information than the givens and when the operations involved can work in two directions. For example, if you wanted to spend exactly $100 on clothing, it would be difficult to reach that goal simply by buying some items and hoping that they totaled exactly $100. A better strategy would be to buy one item, subtract its cost from $100 to determine how much money you have left, then purchase another item, subtract its cost, and so on, until you have spent $100.

Obstacles to Solving Problems

In everyday life, many factors can either help or hinder problem solving. One factor is a person's level of motivation, or emotional arousal. Generally, we must generate a certain surge of excitement to motivate ourselves to solve a problem, yet too much arousal can hamper our ability to find a solution (see Chapter 9, Motivation and Emotion).

Another factor that can either help or hinder problem solving is **mental set**— our tendency to perceive and to approach problems in certain ways. Set determines which information we tend to retrieve from memory to help us find a solution. Set can be helpful if we have learned operations that we can apply to the present situation. Much of our formal education involves learning sets and ways to solve problems (that is, learning heuristics and algorithms). But sets can also create obstacles, especially when a novel approach is needed. The most successful problem solvers have many different sets to choose from and can judge when to change sets or when to abandon them entirely. Great ideas and inventions come out of such flexibility.

One type of set that can seriously hinder problem solving is called **functional fixedness.** Consider Figure 7–8. Do you see a way to mount the candle on the wall? If not, you are probably stymied by functional fixedness. The more you use an object in only one way, the harder it is to see new uses for it, because you have "assigned" the object to a fixed function. To some extent, part of the learning process is to assign correct functions to objects—this is how we form concepts. But we need to be open to seeing that an object can be used for an entirely different function. (The solution to this problem appears at the end of the chapter.) (See *Applying Psychology: Becoming a More Skillful Problem Solver* for techniques that will improve your problem-solving skills.)

Means-end analysis A heuristic strategy that aims to reduce the discrepancy between the current situation and the desired goal at a number of intermediate points.

Working backward A heuristic strategy in which one works backward from the desired goal to the given conditions.

Mental set The tendency to perceive and approach problems in certain ways.

Functional fixedness The tendency to perceive only a limited number of uses for an object, thus interfering with the process of problem solving.

 7.2

 7.3

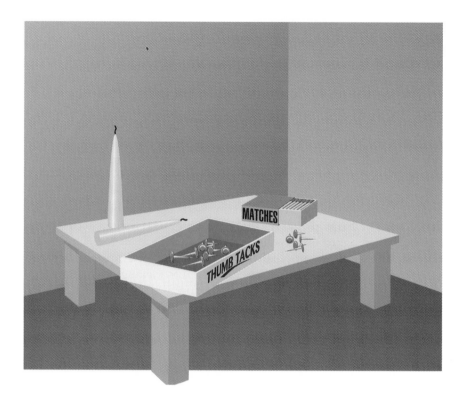

Figure 7–8
To test the effects of functional fixedness, participants might be given the items shown on the table and asked to mount a candle on the wall. See Figure 7–13 for a solution.

The Guggenheim Museum in Bilbao, Spain, is a feat of creative problem solving. The architect, Frank Gehry, gave the outside a dramatic shimmering effect by using a skin of titanium. The originality of the design is further heightened by its unusual juxtaposition of shapes. Divergent thinking underlies creative ideas like these.

Because creative problem solving requires thinking up original ideas, deliberate strategies don't always help. Solutions to many problems rely on insight (Novick & Sherman, 2003), often a seemingly arbitrary flash "out of the blue." (See Chapter 5, Learning.) But you can't always sit back and wait for a flash of insight to solve a problem. When you need a quick solution, you can do some things that encourage creative answers. Sometimes we get so enmeshed in the details of a problem that we lose sight of the obvious. If we stop thinking about the problem for a while, we may return to it from a new angle (H. G. Murray & Denny, 1969). Then we may be able to redefine the problem, circumventing an unproductive mind-set.

The value of looking for new ways to represent a difficult problem cannot be overstressed. Ask yourself, "What is the real problem here? Can the problem be interpreted in other ways?" Also be open to potential solutions that at first seem unproductive. The solution may turn out to be more effective, or it may suggest related solutions that will work. This is the rationale behind the technique called **brainstorming:** generating a lot of ideas before you review and evaluate them.

Finally, people often become more creative when exposed to creative peers and teachers (Amabile, 1983). Although some creative people work well alone, many others are stimulated by working in teams with other creative people.

ENDURING ISSUES   **person**situation

Brainstorming A problem-solving strategy in which an individual or a group produces numerous ideas and evaluates them only after all ideas have been collected.

Where Does Creativity Come From?

It is tempting to think that creativity arises from within the individual—that some people are simply more creative than others. And some evidence suggests that this

APPLYING PSYCHOLOGY

BECOMING A MORE SKILLFUL PROBLEM SOLVER

Even the best problem solvers occasionally get stumped, but by applying the principles described in this chapter, you can do some things that will help you find a solution. These tactics encourage you to discard unproductive approaches and find strategies that are more effective.

1. **Eliminate poor choices.** When we are surer of what won't work than what will, the *tactic of elimination* can be very helpful. First, list all the possible solutions you can think of, and then discard all the solutions that seem to lead in the wrong direction. Now examine the list more closely. Some solutions seem to be ineffective but on closer examination may turn out to be good.

"Many problems require some original thinking."

2. **Visualize a solution.** Sometimes people who are stumped by a problem can find a solution by using a basic building block of thought: visual images. *Visualizing* often involves diagramming courses of action. For example, in the Hobbit and Orc problem, draw a picture of the river, and show the Hobbits and Orcs at each stage of the solution as they are ferried across. Drawing a diagram can help you grasp what a problem calls for. You also can visualize mentally.

3. **Develop expertise.** People get stumped on problems because they lack the knowledge to find a quick solution. Experts not only know more about a particular subject but also organize their information in larger "chunks" that are extensively interconnected, much like a cross-referencing system in a library.

4. **Think flexibly.** Striving to be more flexible and creative is an excellent tactic for becoming a better problem solver. Many problems require some original thinking. For example, how many unusual uses can you think of for a brick? Problems that have no single correct solution and that require a flexible, inventive approach call for *divergent thinking*—or thinking that involves generating many different possible answers. In contrast, *convergent thinking* is thinking that narrows its focus in a particular direction, assuming that there is only one solution, or at most a limited number of right solutions. You should not be surprised to learn that many business and engineering schools stress divergent thinking skills to encourage more creative problem solving.

view is correct, as we will see in the next chapter. But there is also some intriguing evidence that creative solutions come from posing creative problems—in other words, that creative problems "draw out" creative responses from people who otherwise would not be particularly creative. Hackman and Morris (1975) gave small groups a variety of tasks. Some groups were asked to discuss issues, come to a consensus, and write down their position. For example:

Come to an agreement as to what your group feels is the best meaning of the word *intellectual*, and write a paragraph or two summing up your ideas.

Other groups were asked to solve problems, such as:

In recent years the increasing population of the United States has resulted in overcrowded classrooms. Write a proposal, about a paragraph long, outlining a program to resolve this problem. Be specific.

Still others were asked to be creative. This last group were posed such tasks as:

METHALAGALOGIMUS. The task for your group is to write a story involving in some way the word above. This story should be as original and creative as possible. It must contain a title, a beginning, a middle, and an end.

Independent judges rated the creativity of each group's work on a seven-point scale. The groups that received problems to solve averaged 2.49; the groups that discussed issues averaged 2.72; the group that received the creative tasks averaged 4.76. In other words, the task itself had a profound effect on creativity: Groups that received creative tasks were far more likely than other groups to come up with a creative result, even though the members of those groups were no more or less creative than the members of the other groups.

Experience and Expertise

Numerous studies have found qualitative differences in the way experts and beginners approach and solve problems. We have already seen that experts, when presented with a problem in their field, are likely to recognize it as belonging to a familiar set of problems they have solved before and thus solve it much more quickly than beginners. Research also shows that experts think in larger units, or "chunks," that include many pieces of information, algorithms, and heuristics and that are so welded together that they require no further thought (see discussion of chunking in Chapter 6, Memory.) These chunks are extensively interconnected, much like a cross-referencing system in a library (Bédard & Chi, 1992). Beginners work through a problem one step at a time. Chunking enables experts to approach a problem with many more potentially relevant ideas than a novice would. It also reduces the mental time and energy required to process basic data, allowing an expert to devote more attention to selecting problem-solving strategies, monitoring their effectiveness, and carrying out other higher-level activities. Given the same problem, experts take fewer but much larger steps than novices.

Chess masters are the classic example of chunking (Huffman, Mathews, & Gagne, 2001). When shown a board for five seconds and asked to recreate the positions a few minutes later, grand masters and masters rarely make a mistake; other players (including experts) get more positions wrong than right. The reason is not that chess masters have "better visual memory"; when shown a board with positions that would never occur in an actual game, they perform as poorly as novices. Their expertise is based on their conceptual grasp of chess, not memory of visual patterns (Waters, Gobet, & Leyden, 2002). The most important difference between chess masters and novices is not that the masters can conceive a greater number of moves; rather, the chess masters recognize the significance of various board positions that have little or no meaning to novices (Bédard & Chi, 1992). Recognizing a situation as familiar, in turn, enables them to generate a good next move more quickly (Klein, Wolf, Militello, & Zsambok, 1995).

Chunking plays a role in the development of any skill. The novice typist pecks slowly and laboriously, one letter at a time; skilled typists know the entire keyboard, common groups of letters, words, and even phrases so well that they don't even look at the keyboard. Making a turn, a beginning driver struggles to coordinate slowing down, clicking the turn signal, turning the wheel, and stepping on the gas: Each step requires conscious attention. The experienced driver performs such operations with hardly a thought. One way to understand the power of chunking is to try teaching a child or other beginner how to ride a bicycle or perform long division. You've learned the entire procedure so well that it requires effort to remember—much less explain—what operations are required!

Expertise has limits, however. Under some circumstances, it may even become a hindrance (Bédard & Chi, 1992; Wiley, 1998). For example, expertise in one area (e.g., medicine) often does not transfer very well to another domain (e.g., interpersonal skills). Moreover, an expert may become so accustomed to handling problems a certain way that a novice performs better when a novel or creative response is required.

THINKING CRITICALLY

Solving Problems

Think for a moment of the last time you were confronted with a difficult problem.

1. What types of thinking or reasoning did you use to deal with that problem?

2. Having read this portion of the chapter, would you respond differently if you were faced with a similar problem? If so, what would you do differently?

3. You are headed for Mount Rushmore, and you can see it from a distance. You have no map. What is the best problem-solving strategy you can use to get there, and why?

CHECK YOUR UNDERSTANDING

1. Match the problem-solving strategy with the appropriate definition.

___ algorithm

___ heuristic

___ hill climbing

___ means-end analysis

___ working backward

___ subgoal creation

a. rule-of-thumb approach

b. each step moves you closer to a solution

c. step-by-step method

d. moving from the goal to the starting point

e. reducing the discrepancy between the situation and the goal at a number of intermediate points

f. breaking down the problem to smaller, more manageable steps

2. The first step in solving a problem is called

___ a. trial and error

___ b. problem representation

___ c. information retrieval

3. Mental set can _____ problem solving.

___ a. help

___ b. hinder

___ c. a and b

___ d. none of the above

4. What minimizes the effect of mental sets?

___ a. brainstorming

___ b. heuristics

___ c. trial and error

Answers: 1. algorithm—c; heuristic—a; hill climbing—b; means-end analysis—e; working backward—d; subgoal creation—f, 2.b, 3.c, 4.a

The ability quickly to recognize and respond to the situation on a basketball court, as well as to visualize complex new plays, are just two of the factors that give expert basketball players an edge over beginners.

Decision Making

People spend considerable time wondering about "what might have been" if only they had made a different decision. Is this time well spent?

Decision making is a special kind of problem solving in which we already know all the possible solutions or choices. The task is not to come up with new solutions, but rather to identify the best available one or the choice that comes closest to meeting your needs and goals. Decisions range from trivial matters, such as what to wear or where to have dinner, to such major decisions as where to go to college or whether to buy a house, to matters of life and death. Individuals may know exactly what they want or have only a vague idea; they may have hundreds of choices or only two. They may have a great deal of information at their disposal or very little; they may arrive at a decision quickly or become mired in indecision. Whereas some problems have one solution and you know whether you have answered correctly or not, decisions are more often based on probabilities. You cannot predict the outcome of one or another decision, and often have no clear way to measure whether a decision was the right one. How do you make decisions in the face of these uncertainties?

Right now, this child has to think about every aspect of riding a bike—how to keep her balance, when to start and stop pedaling, when to turn the handlebars. Before long, however, she will develop expertise that will enable her to perform this skill automatically and effortlessly.

Compensatory model A rational decision-making model in which choices are systematically evaluated on various criteria.

Representativeness A heuristic by which a new situation is judged on the basis of its resemblance to a stereotypical model.

Logical Decision Making

You want to buy a car and, after shopping around, have identified a number of possible choices within your budget. How do you make a decision? The logical way to proceed is to decide on a set of criteria (factors that are most important); rate each of the available choices according to these criteria; and then add up the pros and cons to see how well each choice matches your criteria. Each choice will probably have attractive features that offset or compensate for unattractive features; thus, this approach is called the **compensatory model** of decision making.

Table 7–1 illustrates one of the most useful compensatory models, applied to the car decision. The buyer has three criteria, which are weighted in terms of importance: price (not weighted heavily), gas mileage, and service record (both weighted more heavily). Each car is then rated from 1 (poor) to 5 (excellent) on each of the criteria. You can see that Car 1 has an excellent price (5) but relatively poor gas mileage (2) and service record (1); Car 2 has a less desirable price but fairly good mileage and service record. Each rating is then multiplied by the weight for that criterion (e.g., for Car 1, the price rating of 5 is multiplied by the weight of 4, and the result is put in parentheses next to the rating). Then ratings are added to give a total for each car. Clearly Car 2 is the better choice: It has a less desirable price, but that is offset by the fact that its mileage and service record are better, and these two criteria are more important than price to this particular buyer.

Using a table like this one allows individuals to evaluate a large number of choices on a large number of criteria. If the criteria are weighted properly and the choices rated correctly, the alternative with the highest total score is the most rational choice, given the information available. Does this mean that most day-to-day decision making is rational? Not necessarily. In many instances we don't have all of the relevant information; it's impossible to quantify the pros and cons; the decisions are equally attractive (or unattractive); and the consequences of one or another decision are a matter of probabilities, not certainties. In short, many if not most everyday decisions involve a high degree of ambiguity (Mellers, Schwartz, & Cooke, 1998). In such cases, we must often rely on heuristics.

Decision-Making Heuristics

Research has identified a number of common heuristics that people use to make decisions. We use these because, for the most part, they have worked in the past and because they simplify decision making, even though they may lead to less-than-optimal decisions.

We use the **representativeness** heuristic whenever we make a decision on the basis of certain information that matches our model of the typical member of a category. For example, if every time you went shopping you bought the least expensive items, and if all of these items turned out to be poorly made, you might eventually decide not to buy anything that seems typical of the category "very cheap." A good illustration of representativeness is a study conducted by Tversky and Kahneman

table 7-1   COMPENSATORY DECISION TABLE FOR PURCHASING A NEW CAR

	Price (weight = 4)	Gas Mileage (weight = 8)	Service Record (weight = 10)	Weighted Total
Car 1	5(20)	2(16)	1(10)	(46)
Car 2	1(4)	4(32)	4(40)	(76)
Ratings:	5 = Excellent	1 = Poor		

(1973) in which students at a particular university were asked to choose whether a student who was described as "neat and tidy," "dull and mechanical," and a "poor writer" was a computer science major or a humanities major. More than 95 percent chose computer science as the student's major. Even after they were told that more than 80 percent of the students at their school were majoring in humanities, the estimates remained virtually unchanged. Thus, although representativeness enables us to make decisions quickly, it will also lead us to make mistakes in some situations.

Another common heuristic is **availability.** In the absence of full and accurate information, we often base decisions on whatever information is most readily available to memory, even though this information may not be accurate. In one experiment, for example, the participants were asked whether the letter *r* appears more frequently as the first or third letter in English words (Tversky & Kahneman, 1973). Most guessed that *r* was usually the first letter; in fact, the opposite is true. The participants answered the question by trying to think of words that begin with *r* (red, round, right) and words in which it is the third letter (car, strong, dare, bird). Because it's much easier to remember words beginning with *r*, participants assumed that words beginning with *r* are more common.

A familiar example of the availability heuristic is the so-called *subway effect* (Gilovich, 1991). It seems to be a law of nature that if you are waiting at a subway station, one train after another will come along headed in the opposite direction from the direction you want to go. Similarly, if you need a taxi in a hurry, inevitably an unusually long string of occupied or off-duty taxis will pass by. The problem here is that once a subway train or a taxi does come along, we leave the scene, so we never get to see the opposite situation: several subway trains going in our direction before one comes the other way, or a long string of empty taxis. As a result, we tend to assume that those situations seldom or never occur and make our decisions accordingly.

Another heuristic, closely related to availability, is **confirmation bias**—the tendency to notice and remember evidence that supports our beliefs and to ignore evidence that contradicts them (Myers, 1996). For example, individuals who believe that AIDS is something that happens to "other people" (homosexual men and intravenous drug-users, not middle-class heterosexuals) are more likely to remember articles about rates of HIV infection in these groups or in third-world countries than articles about AIDS cases among people like themselves (Fischhoff & Downs, 1997). Convinced that HIV is not something that they, personally, need to worry about, they ignore evidence to the contrary.

A related phenomenon is our tendency to see *connections* or *patterns of cause and effect* where none exist (Kahneman & Tversky, 1996; Rottenstreich & Tversky, 1997). For example, some historians still report that President William Henry Harrison caught a case of fatal pneumonia on the day of his inaugural speech because he delivered it in a freezing rain. In fact a virus, not exposure to inclement weather, causes pneumonia. Many people still believe that chocolate causes acne to flare up in susceptible teenagers, yet this myth was disproved almost half a century ago; acne is a bacterial infection, although the tendency to get acne has a strong genetic component (Kolata, 1996a). Many parents strongly believe that sugar may cause hyperactivity in children—despite research evidence to the contrary. The list of commonsense beliefs that persist in the face of contrary evidence is long.

Nonetheless, for the most part people are reasonably satisfied with the decisions they make in the real world (Kleinmuntz, 1991). In part, this is so because decisions often can be revised if an initial choice does not work out as expected. Moreover, many real-world decisions don't have to be ideal, as long as the results are acceptable. A financial investment that returns a 15 percent profit in one year is still an excellent investment, even if another investment might have returned 20 percent or 25 percent. However, some decisions have serious consequences, and they must be made quickly without all the facts. In the next section we will see how people go about making decisions in those difficult situations.

Availability A heuristic by which a judgment or decision is based on information that is most easily retrieved from memory.

Confirmation bias The tendency to look for evidence in support of a belief and to ignore evidence that would disprove a belief.

If you believe that most elderly people suffer declining health and cognitive abilities, you are likely to ignore evidence showing how active and mentally capable they can be. At the same time, you are apt to focus on evidence that confirms your existing stereotypes. Decisions about specific elderly people that are based on these skewed perceptions illustrate the representativeness heuristic.

Framing The perspective or phrasing of information that is used to make a decision.

Framing

One way in which a decision may be intentionally or unintentially swayed is by how the information provided to make the decision is presented or *framed*. Psychologists use the term **framing** to refer to the perspective or phrasing of information that is used to make a decision. Numerous studies have shown that subtle changes in the way information is presented can dramatically affect the final decision (Detweiler, Bedell, Salovey, Pronin, & Rothman, 1999; Jones, Sinclair, & Courneya, 2003; LeBoeuf & Shafir, 2003; Wolsko, Park, Judd, & Wittenbrink, 2000). A classic study by McNeil, Pauker, Sox, and Tversky (1982) illustrates how framing may influence a medical decision. In this study, experimental participants were asked to choose between surgery and radiation therapy to treat lung cancer. However, the framing of information provided to make this choice was manipulated. In the *survival frame*, the participants were given the statistical outcomes of both procedures in the form of survival statistics and were told that of 100 people who had surgery 90 survived the surgery, 68 were alive a year following surgery, and 34 were alive 5 years after the surgery. With regard to radiation therapy, participants were told that of 100 people receiving radiation therapy, everyone survived the therapy, 77 of the 100 were alive at the end of one year, and 22 of the 100 were alive at the end of 5 years. In the *mortality frame*, the participants were given the same information, although this time it was presented (or framed) in the form of the mortality statistics associated with each procedure. Thus, the participants were told that of the 100 people who had surgery, 10 died during the procedure, 32 died by the end of the first year, and 66 had died by the end of 5 years. With regard to radiation, the mortality frame informed the participants that of 100 people who had radiation therapy none had died during the treatment, 23 had died by the end of the first year, and 78 had died by the end of 5 years.

Interestingly, while the actual number of deaths and survivors associated with each procedure was identical in both the survival and mortality frames, the percentage of participants who chose one procedure over another varied dramatically depending on how the information was framed. Of the participants who were in the survival frame group, only 18 percent chose radiation therapy, whereas 44 percent of the participants in the mortality frame group chose radiation therapy. Generally speaking, then, surgery was viewed as a more attractive option compared to radiation when the participants were read the survival frame compared to the mortality frame. Probably most surprising was that this framing effect was found even when 424 experienced physicians with a specialty in radiology served as the experimental participants!

Decisions Under Pressure

Individuals do not always have the luxury of contemplating different perspectives or the time to think about alternatives, weigh them against each other, and then decide which best fits the situation. At times, individuals have to make immediate, potentially life-or-death, decisions that cannot be reversed later. Such is often the case with police officers, military commanders, and nurses on intensive care units.

In a series of field studies, psychologist Gary Klein (1997) observed how firefighters make decisions in situations that nearly always are dangerous. On one occasion, a fire ground commander pulled his team out of a burning house just minutes before the floor collapsed. When first questioned, the commander couldn't say why he ordered the evacuation. There were no clear signs of imminent danger. On further questioning, however, he realized that the situation had seemed strange to him; the fire wasn't behaving like other fires he had seen before. So he decided to pull out and regroup. His decision was based on experience, not careful analysis.

In other professions, the potential for disaster is constant but actual emergencies are rare. For example, Spettle and Liebert (1986) studied decision making among operators at nuclear power plants. They found that the stress of an emergency situation causes decision making to deteriorate, sometimes leading to panic. In March

1979, during the worst nuclear accident in U.S. history, one of two reactors at the Three Mile Island power plant near Harrisburg, Pennsylvania, came perilously close to a meltdown. During the crisis, so many alarms in the power plant's control center were sounding and blinking that operators actually turned them off.

Spettle and Liebert suggest that training under simulated emergency conditions can prepare people to use efficient and effective decision-making strategies not only in those particular types of emergency, but also in unanticipated situations where quick and accurate decisions are crucial. Preparatory training is also central to the Outward Bound program. This program was originally developed because British sailors whose boats were torpedoed panicked and died when calm decision making would have ensured their survival. The Outward Bound program puts people in a variety of stressful wilderness situations in the belief that they will learn effective decision-making strategies that can be transferred to a wide variety of everyday situations.

The stress caused by an emergency situation can cause decision making to deteriorate. In March 1979, during the worst nuclear accident in U.S. history, one of two reactors at the Three Mile Island power plant came close to a meltdown.

Explaining Our Decisions

Whether a choice is exceptionally good, extraordinarily foolish, or somewhere in between, most people ruminate over their decisions after the fact. Retrospective thinking takes different forms. The term **hindsight bias** refers to the tendency to view outcomes as inevitable and predictable *after* we know the outcome, and to believe that we could have predicted what happened, or perhaps that we did (Azar, 1999b; Fischoff, 1975; Pohl, Schwarz, Sczesny, & Stahlberg, 2003). For example, physicians remember being more confident about their diagnoses when they learn they were correct than they were at the time of the actual diagnoses. An investor buys a stock on a hunch: If it goes up, she is convinced that she "knew it all along"; if the stock goes down, she is equally convinced that she knew it was a mistake. The phrase "Monday morning quarterback" describes fans who, having watched a football game on Sunday, insist the next day that if *they* had been making the calls, their team would have won.

According to an old saying, "hindsight is always 20:20." Psychologists have long viewed the hindsight bias as a cognitive flaw—a self-serving mechanism, conscious or unconscious, that restores our faith in our own judgment (see Louie, Curren, & Harich, 2000). A team of researchers in Berlin, however, argues that the hindsight bias serves a useful function (Hoffrage, Hertwig, & Gigerenzer, 2000). "Correcting" memory is a quick and efficient way to replace misinformation or faulty assumptions, so that our future decisions and judgments will be closer to the mark. In a sense, hindsight functions like the "find and replace" function in a word processing program, eliminating extra, time-consuming keystrokes and mental effort.

In addition to hindsight, at times everyone imagines alternatives to reality and mentally plays out the consequences. "What if I had gone to a large university instead of a small college?" "What if I had majored in acting instead of computer science?" "What if I were a great tennis player?" "What if I had asked for her/his phone number?" Psychologists refer to such musings on alternative realities and things that never happened as **counterfactual thinking**—they are counter to the facts (Roese, 1997; Segura, & McCloy, 2003; Walchle & Landman, 2003). Counterfactual thinking often takes the form of "If only" constructions, in which we mentally revise the events or actions that led to a particular outcome: "If only I had studied harder"; "If only I had taken that job"; "If only I had driven straight home." More directed than daydreams, counterfactual thoughts typically deal with causes and consequences.

Theoretically, the question "What if . . . ?" has no limits. Most of us have far-fetched thoughts from time to time: "What if I had lived in ancient Egypt?" "What if aliens invaded earth?" But research shows that counterfactual thinking usually centers around a small number of themes: reversing a course of events that led to a negative experience; explaining atypical or abnormal events by assigning responsibility to someone or something; and regaining a sense of personal control (Roese, 1997). For example, suppose it's a bright sunny day, you decide to drive home by

Hindsight bias The tendency to view outcomes as inevitable and predictable after we know the outcome.

Counterfactual thinking Thinking about alternative realities and things that never happened.

way of a longer but more scenic route, and you have a car accident. A common response is the thought, "If only I had taken my usual route, this wouldn't have happened" (Mandel & Lehman, 1996). Accidents are, by definition, unpredictable. Yet most people feel more comfortable with the idea that there was a reason for the accident; that it didn't just happen, even if this means blaming themselves.

Like physical pain, negative counterfactual thinking tells us that something is wrong and prompts us to think about why and perhaps make better decisions in the future. But it can also lead to distortions. Obsessive "If only" thinking may promote feelings of shame, guilt, and regret. It is common for the families and friends of accident victims to have endless "If only" thoughts that exact a high psychological price: "If only I hadn't delayed him by talking about . . .", "If only I hadn't insisted that he drive back tonight," "If only I'd made a different plane reservation for her" and so on.

The many strategies we use to make decisions—and to rethink decisions—emphasize one of the defining features of human beings: We are a storytelling species.

CHECK YOUR UNDERSTANDING

1. Match each decision-making heuristic with the appropriate definition.

___ representativeness heuristic

a. making judgments on the basis of whatever information can be most readily retrieved from memory

___ availability heuristic

b. attending to evidence that supports your existing beliefs and ignoring other evidence

___ confirmation bias

c. making decisions on the basis of information that matches your model of what is "typical" of a certain category

2. The way that information needed in decision making is presented is called

___a. cause and effect

___b. framing

___c. availability

3. Which type of thinking is often phrased "What if . . .?"

___a. counterfactual

___b. hindsight bias

___c. mortality frame

4. What model of decision making involves selecting a set of criteria, rating each one and adding up the ratings?

___a. framing

___b. heuristic

___c. compensatory

Answers: 1. representativeness heuristic—c; availability heuristic—a; confirmation bias—b, 2. b, 3. a, 4. c

Answers to Problems in the Chapter

1.   Problem 1. Fill each of the smaller spoons with salt from the larger spoon. That will require four teaspoons of salt, leaving exactly four teaspoons of salt in the larger spoon.

2. **Problem 2.** Turn the 5-minute hourglass over; when it runs out, turn over the 9-minute hourglass. When it, too, runs out, 14 minutes have passed.

3. **Problem 3.** As shown in Figure 7–9, fill spoon C with salt from spoon A (now A has 5 teaspoons of salt and C has 3). Pour the salt from spoon C into spoon B (now A has 5 teaspoons of salt and B has 3). Again fill spoon C with salt from spoon A (leaving A with only 2 teaspoons of salt, while B and C each have 3). Fill spoon B with salt from spoon C (this leaves 1 teaspoon of salt in spoon C while B has 5 teaspoons and A has only 2). Pour all the salt from spoon B into spoon A (now A has 7 teaspoons of salt and C has 1). Pour all the salt from spoon C into spoon B, and then fill spoon C from spoon A (this leaves 4 teaspoons of salt in A, 1 teaspoon in B, and 3 teaspoons in C). Finally, pour all the salt from spoon C into spoon B (this leaves 4 teaspoons of salt in spoons A and B, which is the solution).

4. **Problem 4.** Start both hourglasses. When the 5-minute hourglass runs out, turn it over to start it again. When the 9-minute hourglass runs out, turn over the 5-minute hourglass. Because there is 1 minute left in the 5-minute hourglass when you turn it over, it will run for only 4 minutes. Those 4 minutes, together with the original 9 minutes, give the required 13 minutes for the barbecue.

5. **Problem 5.** Take one of the short pieces of chain shown in Figure 7–10 and open all three links (this costs six cents). Use those three links to connect the remaining three pieces of chain (closing the three links costs nine cents).

6. **Problem 6.** Join the matches to form a pyramid as shown in Figure 7–11.

7. **Problem 7.** One way to solve this problem is to draw a diagram of the ascent and the descent, as shown in Figure 7–12. From this drawing, you can see that indeed there is a point that the monk passes at exactly the same time on both days. Another way to approach this problem is to imagine that there are two monks on the mountain; one starts ascending at 7 A.M. and the other starts descending at 7 A.M. on the same day. Clearly, sometime during the day the monks must meet somewhere along the route.

8. **Problem 8.** This problem has four possible solutions, one of which is shown in Figure 7–14 (the other three solutions differ only slightly from this one).

9. **Problem 9.** This problem has 15 possible solutions, of which this is one: One Hobbit and one Orc cross the river in the boat; the Orc remains on the opposite side while the Hobbit rows back. Next, three Orcs cross the river; two of those Orcs remain on the other side (making a total of three Orcs on the opposite bank) while one Orc rows back. Now three Hobbits cross the river; two stay on the opposite

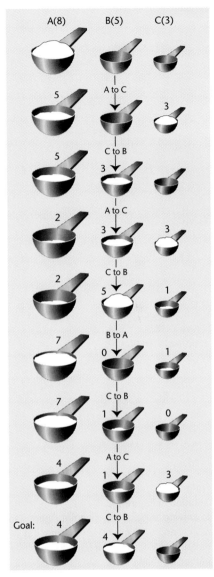

Figure 7–9
Solution to Problem 3.

Figure 7–10
Solution to Problem 5.
Step 1: Cut one piece of chain into three open links.
Step 2: Use three links to join three remaining pieces of chain.

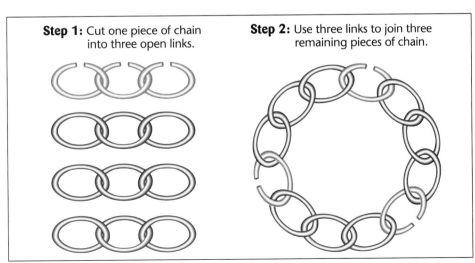

Step 1: Cut one piece of chain into three open links. **Step 2:** Use three links to join three remaining pieces of chain.

Figure 7–11
Solution to Problem 6.

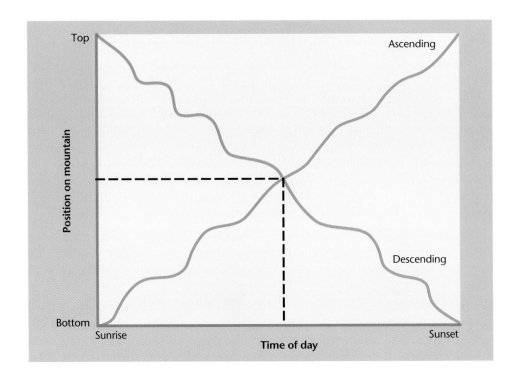

Figure 7–12
Solution to Problem 7.

side with two Orcs while one Hobbit and one Orc row the boat back. Again, three Hobbits row across the river, at which point all five Hobbits are on the opposite bank with only two Orcs. One of the Orcs then rows back and forth across the river twice to transport the remaining Orcs to the opposite side.

Figure 7–13
Solution to Figure 7–8.
In solving the problem given in Figure 7–8, many people have trouble realizing that the box of tacks can also be used as a candle-holder, as shown here.

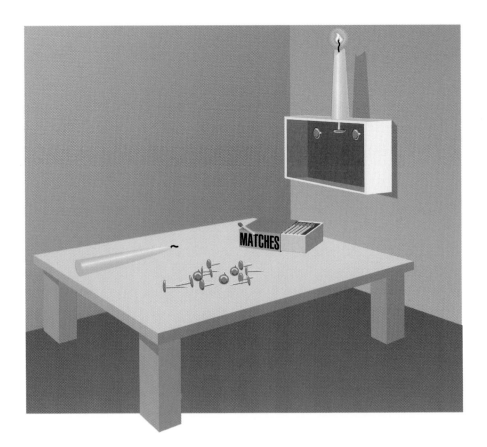

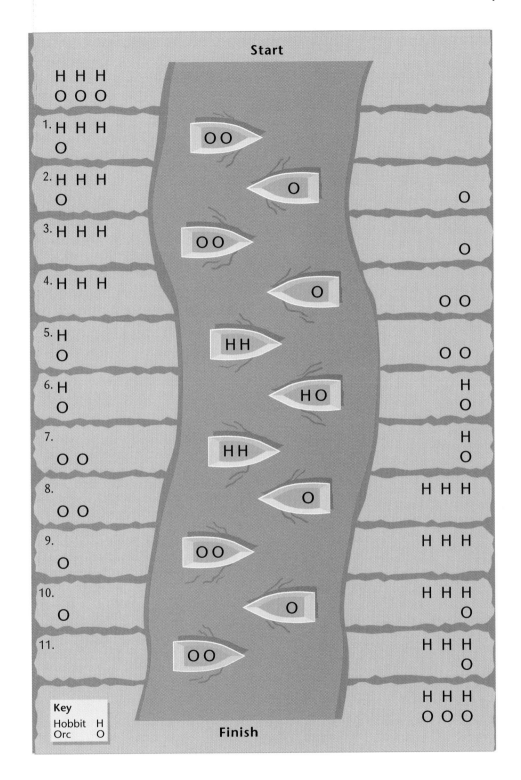

Figure 7–14
Solution to Problem 8.

summary

The term **cognition** refers to all the processes whereby we acquire and use information. These include thinking and language.

The Building Blocks of Thought

The main building blocks of thought are language, images, and concepts.

Language

Language is a flexible system of symbols that enables us to communicate our ideas, thoughts, and feelings. Human language differs from nonhuman communication in that it is semantic, or meaningful. It is also characterized by displacement (it is not limited to the here-and-now) and productivity (it can produce new words, phrases, and sentences).

The Structure of Language

Spoken language is based on universal sound units called **phonemes** that indicate changed meaning. Phonemes are combined to form **morphemes**, the smallest units of meaning in a language, such as words or parts of words, prefixes, and suffixes.

The rules for structuring sentences and their meaning are called **grammar**. Syntax and semantics are the two major components of grammar. **Syntax** is the system of rules that governs how we combine words to form meaningful phrases and sentences. **Semantics** describes how we assign meaning to morphemes, words, phrases, and sentences.

Sentences have both a **surface structure** (particular words and phrases) and a **deep structure** (the underlying meaning). Speaking requires *top-down processing* in which we move from the underlying idea or thought (deep structure) to the words and phrases that express the idea (surface structure). Understanding speech requires *bottom-up processing*, which requires moving from specific words and phrases to their underlying meaning.

Images

An **image** is a nonverbal mental representation. Images allow us to think in nonverbal ways. We not only visualize things in order to think about them but also manipulate these mental images.

Concepts

A **concept** is a mental category for classifying people, things, or events. Concepts provide a way of categorizing experiences so that encounters with something new need not be a surprise. They can be organized in hierarchies, with the most specific category at the bottom and the most general at the top.

Many concepts are "fuzzy," lacking clear-cut boundaries. Therefore, we often use **prototypes**, mental models of the most typical examples of a concept, to classify new objects.

Language, Thought, and Culture

Language and Cognition

Language is closely tied to the expression and understanding of thought. According to Benjamin Whorf, patterns of thinking are determined by the language one speaks, a process called **linguistic determinism**. Some critics of this theory maintain that people from cultures with different languages think about some things in similar ways, even if their language contains no words for those things. Others point out that people create new words when they need them.

Is Our Language Male-Dominated?

Some evidence indicates that the use of "man" and "he" to refer to all people affects the way that English speakers think. Referring to doctors, college professors, bankers, and executives by the generic "he" may contribute to the gender stereotyping of these respected occupations as appropriate for men but not for women. In contrast, referring to secretaries and housekeepers as "she" may reinforce the stereotype that those occupations are appropriate occupations for women, not men.

Culture and Cognition

All known cultures use categories to form concepts. What information is included in a given category, and how categories are shaped by experience, vary from culture to culture. For example, recent research confirms that people from Eastern cultures tend to think holistically, whereas Westerners tend to think analytically.

Nonhuman Thought and Language

Animal Cognition

Research indicates that some animals have some humanlike cognitive capacities, such as the ability to form concepts and to reason. Apes have demonstrated sophisticated problem-solving skills. However, only chimpanzees and orangutans consistently show signs of self-awareness and perhaps a limited sense of other-awareness.

The Question of Language

Nonhuman animals communicate primarily through **signs**: general or global statements about the animal's current state. No other species has its own language, but chimpanzees have been taught to use American Sign Language. Similar to young children, chimpanzees have been observed using two-word combinations called **telegraphic speech** during early language acquisition. Nonetheless, the extent to which animals have the ability to acquire and use true language is still not clear. For example, apes do not demonstrate a syntactical use of language—the ability that allows humans to understand and create complex sentences.

Problem Solving

Typically, we transform external data to fit our existing mental framework, but sometimes we need to modify our mental structures to accommodate new data. This is most apparent in problem solving.

The Interpretation of Problems

Problem representation—defining or interpreting the problem—is the first step in problem solving. The importance of problem representation is shown by the fact that a problem represented or categorized in one way may be difficult or impossible to solve, while the same problem represented differently may be solved easily.

Producing Strategies and Evaluating Progress

When there are only a limited number of solutions to a problem, trial and error may be the best way to find the correct one. At other times, a problem may be solved simply by retrieving information. But more complex problems require more complex problem solving strategies. An **algorithm** is a problem-solving method that guarantees a solution if it fits the problem and is carried out correctly. Solving a mathematical problem by use of a formula is an example of the use of an algorithm. **Heuristics** are rules of thumb that help simplify problems, though they do not guarantee a solution. **Hill climbing** is a heuristic in which each step moves the problem solver closer to the final goal. Another heuristic is the creation of **subgoals**—intermediate, more manageable goals that may make it easier to reach the final goal. **Means-end analysis,** a heuristic that combines hill climbing and subgoals, aims to reduce the discrepancy between the current situation and the desired goal at a number of intermediate points. **Working backward** involves working from the desired goal back to the given conditions.

Obstacles to Solving Problems
A factor that can help or hinder problem solving is **mental set,** a tendency to perceive and approach problems in certain ways. Sets enable us to draw on past experience to solve a present problem, but a strong set can also interfere with the ability to use novel approaches to solving a problem. One set that can seriously hamper problem solving is **functional fixedness,** the tendency to assign a fixed function to something we learn to use in a particular way. One way to reduce the effect of mental sets is to stop thinking about the problem for a while and then return to it from a new angle; by redefining the problem, it may be possible to get around the unproductive mind-set. Another way to minimize mental sets is the technique of **brainstorming** in which an individual or group collects numerous ideas and evaluates them only after all possible ideas have been collected. In this way, no potential solution is rejected prematurely.

Experience and Expertise
Expertise in a field increases a person's ability to interpret a particular problem. Experts not only know more about their subject but also think in larger units that include many interconnected pieces of information, algorithms, and heuristics. Expertise in a field is an asset in solving problems because experts do not need the elaborate preparations required of a beginner. However, an expert may become so accustomed to handling problems a certain way that a novice performs better when a novel or creative response is required.

Decision Making

Unlike other kinds of problem solving, decision making starts off with knowledge of all the possible solutions or choices.

Logical Decision Making
A logical approach is to select a set of criteria, rate each of the choices on those criteria, and add up the ratings to see how well each choice matches the criteria. This is called the **compensatory model** of decision making. Although it allows a person to evaluate a large number of alternatives on a large number of criteria and to identify the optimal choice from among those alternatives, it does not work well for many day-to-day decisions where we do not have all of the relevant information, where it is impossible to quantify pros and cons, where the alternatives are equally attractive or unattractive, or where the consequences of some decisions are uncertain. In those cases, decisions are most often made on the basis of heuristics.

Decision-Making Heuristics
When we lack complete or accurate information about one or more alternatives, we may end up judging a new situation in terms of its resemblance to a more familiar model—the **representativeness** heuristic. Another common heuristic is **availability,** in which we base a judgment or decision on information that is most readily available to memory, whether or not that information is accurate. Another faulty heuristic, **confirmation bias,** involves the tendency to notice and remember evidence that supports our beliefs and to ignore evidence that does not support them. A related phenomenon is the tendency to see connections or patterns of cause and effect where none exist.

In the real world, the use of faulty heuristics does not always spell disaster. This is partly because such decisions are often not final, and partly because we often do not need to make an absolutely perfect decision so long as the results are satisfactory.

Framing
The term **framing** refers to the perspective or phrasing of information that is used to make a decision. Subtle changes in the way information is presented can dramatically affect the final decision even though the underlying facts remain unchanged.

Decisions Under Pressure
The stress of an emergency situation may cause decision making to deteriorate. Training under simulated emergency conditions can prepare people to make better decisions under such conditions.

Explaining Our Decisions
Most people ruminate over their decisions after the fact. The term **hindsight bias** refers to the tendency to view outcomes as inevitable and predictable after they are known. **Counterfactual thinking** refers to thinking about alternative realities that are counter to the facts ("What if. . . .?" or "If only. . . .") as a way of mentally reversing a course of events that led to a negative experience, explaining atypical or abnormal events by assigning responsibility to someone or something, or regaining a sense of personal control.

key terms

Cognition	259	Prototype	264	Mental set	277
Language	260	Linguistic determinism	265	Functional fixedness	277
Phonemes	260	Signs	270	Brainstorming	278
Morphemes	260	Telegraphic speech	270	Compensatory model	282
Grammar	260	Problem representation	274	Representativeness	282
Syntax	260	Algorithm	276	Availability	283
Semantics	261	Heuristics	276	Confirmation bias	283
Surface structure	261	Hill climbing	276	Framing	284
Deep structure	261	Subgoals	276	Hindsight bias	285
Image	262	Means-end analysis	277	Counterfactual thinking	285
Concept	262	Working backward	277		

OVERVIEW

Theories of Intelligence
Early Theories: Spearman,
Thurstone, and Cattell
Contemporary Theories:
Sternberg, Gardner, and Goleman
Comparing the Theories

Intelligence Tests
The Stanford-Binet Intelligence
Scale
The Wechsler Intelligence Scales
Group Tests
Performance and Culture-Fair Tests

What Makes a Good Test?
Reliability
Validity
Criticisms of Intelligence Tests

What Determines Intelligence?
Heredity
Environment
Heredity vs. Environment: Which
Is More Important?

**Mental Abilities and Human
Diversity**
Gender
Culture

Extremes of Intelligence
Mental Retardation
Giftedness

Creativity
Creativity and Intelligence
Creativity Tests

Intelligence and Mental Abilities

8

n many societies, one of the nicest things you can say to a person is "You're smart." In those same societies, one of the most insulting things you can say is "You're stupid." Intelligence is so basic to our view of human nature that any characterization of another person that neglects to mention his or her level of intelligence is considered incomplete. Intelligence affects our success in school, the kind of work we do, the kinds of recreation we enjoy, and even our choice of friends.

Because of its importance in our society, intelligence has been one of the key concepts studied by psychologists almost since psychology emerged as a science. Yet after a hundred years of study, psychologists are still struggling to understand this complex and elusive concept. In reading this chapter, you may come to appreciate the difficulty of their task. Toward that end, we begin by asking you to struggle with some questions intended to measure intelligence:

1. Describe the difference between *laziness* and *idleness*.
2. Which direction would you have to face so your right hand would be facing the north?
3. What does *obliterate* mean?
4. In what way are an *hour* and a *week* alike?
5. Choose the set of words that, when inserted in the sentence, best fits in with the meaning of the sentence as a whole: *From the first, the islanders, despite an outward _____, did what they could to _____ the ruthless occupying power.*
   (a) harmony . . . assist (b) enmity . . . embarrass (c) rebellion . . . foil (d) resistance . . . destroy (e) acquiescence . . . thwart
6. Choose the lettered block that best completes the pattern in the figure below.

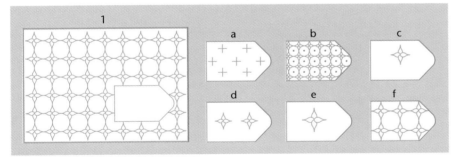

Figure 8–1

7. The opposite of *hate* is:
   (a) enemy (b) fear (c) love (d) friend (e) joy
8. If three pencils cost 25 cents, how many pencils can be bought for 75 cents?
9. Choose the word that is most nearly opposite in meaning to the word in capital letters:
   SCHISM: (a) majority (b) union (c) uniformity (d) conference (e) construction
10. Select the item that completes the following series of four figures:

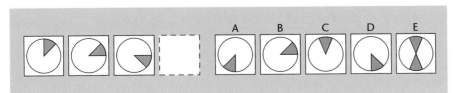

Figure 8–2

THINKABOUTIT

You will find the answers to these questions in the chapter:

1. How do contemporary concepts of intelligence differ from earlier concepts?

2. What kind of intelligence tests are in use today?

3. Do intelligence test scores predict success in later life?

4. What do adoption studies reveal about the sources of intelligence?

5. Are males naturally better than females at mathematics?

6. Is giftedness more than just a high IQ?

7. What is the relationship between creativity and intelligence?

11. Select the lettered pair that best expresses a relationship similar to that expressed in the original pair: CRUTCH : LOCOMOTION: (a) paddle: canoe (b) hero: worship (c) horse: carriage (d) spectacles: vision (e) statement: contention

12. The first three figures are alike in some way. Find the figure at the right that goes with the first three.

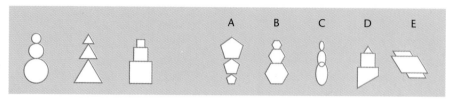

Figure 8–3

13. Decide how the first two figures are related to each other. Then find the one figure at the right that goes with the third figure in the same way that the second figure goes with the first.

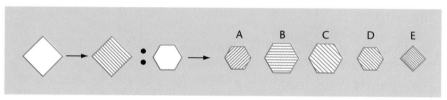

Figure 8–4

14. For each figure, decide whether it can be completely covered by using some or all of the given pieces without overlapping any.

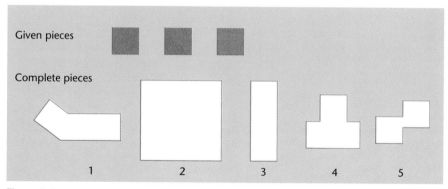

Figure 8–5

These questions are drawn from various intelligence tests designed to measure general mental abilities (the answers appear near the end of the chapter). What do such tests actually tell us? Do they reflect all the abilities that make up intelligence? And what exactly *is* intelligence? How is it related to creativity? Do intelligence tests measure all the aspects of intelligence needed for success in school? Do such tests predict your success on the job or in your personal life?

Before we explore the answers to these questions, let's consider the way psychologists use the words *intelligence*, *ability*, and *aptitude*. This is not a simple matter, because psychologists have not always used these words consistently. The distinction between abilities and aptitudes is the most straightforward. An *ability* refers to a skill that people actually have and for which they need no additional training. An *aptitude* is a *potential* ability. For example, someone may have an aptitude for playing the violin but not yet possess the ability to play the instrument. If a test is designed to *predict* an individual's future achievement in a specific area, it is usually called an aptitude test (Anastasi & Urbina, 1997). **Intelligence** refers to a person's general intellectual ability; thus intelligence tests are usually designed to test general mental ability. People who do well on **intelligence tests** are also likely to do well in school. Therefore, we should not be surprised to discover that scholastic aptitude tests and intelligence tests often ask similar types of questions.

What specific mental abilities should be considered signs of intelligence? On this point, there is considerable disagreement among psychologists. As Sternberg and Kaufman (1998) point out, ". . . the answer depends on whom you ask, and (it) . . . differs widely across disciplines, time, and places" (p. 48). Before reading further, write down some behaviors that *you* believe reflect intelligence. How are they different from behaviors that reflect a lack of intelligence?

Robert Sternberg and his associates (Sternberg, 1982; Sternberg, Conway, Ketron, & Bernstein, 1981) discovered that people with no training in psychology generally think of intelligence as a mix of practical problem-solving ability, verbal ability, and social competence. Practical problem-solving ability includes using logic, connecting ideas, and viewing a problem in its entirety. Verbal ability encompasses using and understanding both written and spoken language in well-developed ways. Social competence refers to interacting well with others—being open-minded about different kinds of people and showing interest in a variety of topics. When Sternberg and his colleagues asked psychologists who specialize in the area of intelligence for their ideas about intelligence, they generally agreed that it includes verbal and problem-solving abilities, but they did not agree that it includes social competence. Instead, they said that practical intelligence is an important component of overall intelligence (see Table 8–1). In addition, many experts now list creativity and the ability to adapt to the environment as crucial components of intelligence (Snyderman & Rothman, 1987).

Compare your own description of intelligent behaviors with those listed in Table 8–1. Was your description closer to that of the laypersons or the experts? Which of the characteristics of intelligence do you think are most important? Why do you think so?

In the next section, we will look more closely at the ways in which psychologists think about intelligence, and then we will see how those formal theories of intelligence affect the content of intelligence tests.

Theories of Intelligence

How do contemporary concepts of intelligence differ from earlier concepts?

For more than a century, psychologists have pondered and argued about what constitutes general intelligence—or even if the notion of intelligence has any validity at all. In particular, they have wrestled with the question of whether intelligence is a singular, general aptitude or ability or whether it is composed of many separate and distinct aptitudes or abilities (see Lubinski, 2000).

Early Theories: Spearman, Thurstone, and Cattell

Charles Spearman, an early twentieth-century British psychologist, maintained that intelligence is quite general—a kind of well, or spring, of mental energy that flows through every action. Spearman noted that people who are bright in one area are

Intelligence A general term referring to the ability or abilities involved in learning and adaptive behavior.

Intelligence tests Tests designed to measure a person's general mental abilities.

table 8-1   SOME CHARACTERISTICS OF INTELLIGENCE AS SEEN BY LAYPERSONS AND EXPERTS

Laypersons	Experts
Practical problem-solving ability: reasons logically, makes connections among ideas, can see all sides of a problem, keeps an open mind, responds thoughtfully to the ideas of others, is good at sizing up situations, interprets information accurately, makes good decisions, goes to original source for basic information, has good source of ideas, perceives implied assumptions, deals with problems in a resourceful way.	*Problem-solving ability:* makes good decisions, displays common sense, shows objectivity, is good at solving problems, plans ahead, has good intuition, gets to the heart of problems, appreciates truth, considers the results of actions, approaches problems thoughtfully.
Verbal ability: speaks articulately, converses well, is knowledgeable about a particular field, studies hard, reads widely, writes without difficulty, has a good vocabulary, tries new things.	*Verbal intelligence:* has a good vocabulary, reads with high comprehension, is intellectually curious, sees all sides of a problem, learns rapidly, shows alertness, thinks deeply, shows creativity, converses easily on a wide range of subjects, reads widely, sees connections among ideas.
Social competence: accepts others as they are, admits mistakes, shows interest in the world at large, arrives on time for appointments, has social conscience, thinks before speaking and acting, shows curiosity, avoids snap judgments, makes fair judgments, assesses the relevance of information to the problem at hand, is sensitive to others, is frank and honest with self and others, shows interest in the immediate environment.	*Practical intelligence:* sizes up situations well, determines how best to achieve goals, shows awareness of world around him or her, shows interest in the world at large, uses self-knowledge of own motives to select the tasks that will best accomplish own goals.

Source: Sternberg, 1982; Wagner & Sternberg, 1986.

often bright in other areas as well. The intelligent person understands things quickly, makes sound decisions, carries on interesting conversations, and tends to behave intelligently in a variety of situations. Although it's true that each of us is quicker in some areas than in others, Spearman saw these differences simply as ways in which the same underlying general intelligence reveals itself.

The American psychologist L. L. Thurstone disagreed with Spearman. Thurstone (1938) argued that intelligence comprises seven distinct mental abilities: spatial ability, perceptual speed, numerical ability, verbal meaning, memory, word fluency, and reasoning. Unlike Spearman, he believed that these abilities are relatively independent of one another. Thus, a person with exceptional spatial ability might lack word fluency. For Thurstone, these seven primary mental abilities, taken together, make up general intelligence.

In contrast to Thurstone, psychologist R. B. Cattell (1971) identified just two clusters of mental abilities. The first cluster—what Cattell called *crystallized intelligence*—includes abilities such as reasoning and verbal and numerical skills. Because these are the kinds of abilities stressed in school, Cattell believed that crystallized intelligence is greatly affected by experience, especially formal education. The second cluster of abilities makes up what Cattell called *fluid intelligence*—skills such as spatial and visual imagery, the ability to notice visual details, and rote memory. Education and other kinds of experience are thought to have little effect on fluid intelligence (Beauducel, Brocke, & Liepmann, 2001).

Contemporary Theories: Sternberg, Gardner, and Goleman

Sternberg's Triarchic Theory   More recently, Robert Sternberg (1986, 2002) has proposed a **triarchic theory of intelligence.** Sternberg argues that human intelligence encompasses a broad variety of skills. Among them are skills that influence our effectiveness in many areas of life. These, says Sternberg, are just as important as the more limited skills assessed by traditional intelligence tests. As the name implies, the theory suggests that there are three basic kinds of intelligence. **Analytical intelligence** refers to the mental processes emphasized by most theories of intelligence, such as the ability to learn how to do things, acquire new knowledge, solve problems, and carry out tasks effectively. According to Sternberg, most intelligence tests assess analytical intelligence. **Creative intelligence** is the ability to adjust to new tasks, use new concepts, combine information in novel ways, respond effectively in new situations, gain insight, and adapt creatively. People who score high in **practical intelligence** are very good at finding solutions to practical and personal problems. They make the most of their talents by seeking out situations that match their skills, shaping those situations so they can make optimal use of their skills, and knowing when to change situations to better fit their talents. Sternberg points out that while practical intelligence is not taught in school, it is sometimes more important than analytical intelligence because it enables people to get along successfully in the world.

Gardner's Theory of Multiple Intelligences   Another influential theory of intelligence is the **theory of multiple intelligences** advanced by Howard Gardner and his associates at Harvard (Gardner, 1983a, 1993, 1999). Gardner, like Thurstone, believes that intelligence is made up of several distinct abilities, each of which is relatively independent of the others. Precisely how many separate intelligences might exist is difficult to determine, but Gardner lists eight: *logical-mathematical, linguistic, spatial, musical, bodily-kinesthetic, interpersonal, intrapersonal,* and *naturalistic.* The first four are self-explanatory. Kinesthetic intelligence is the ability to manipulate one's body in space; a skilled athlete shows high levels of this kind of intelligence. People who are extraordinarily talented at understanding and communicating with others, such as exceptional teachers and parents, have strong interpersonal intelligence. Intrapersonal intelligence reflects the ancient adage "Know thyself." People who understand themselves and who use this knowledge effectively to attain their goals would rank high in intrapersonal intelligence. Finally, naturalistic intelligence reflects an individual's ability to understand, relate to and interact with the world of nature.

Gardner's approach has become quite influential, largely because he emphasizes the unique abilities that each person possesses. Gardner also notes that the different forms of intelligence often have different values placed on them by different cultures. For example, Native American culture places a much higher value on naturalistic intelligence than does contemporary mainstream American culture. Because we have unique patterns of strengths and weaknesses in separate abilities, Gardner believes that education should be designed to suit the profile of abilities demonstrated by each child.

Goleman's Theory of Emotional Intelligence   Recently, psychologist Daniel Goleman (1997) has proposed a new theory of **emotional intelligence,** which refers to how effectively people perceive and understand their own emotions and the emotions of others and can manage their emotional behavior. Goleman was puzzled about the fact that people with high IQ scores sometimes fail in life,

Triarchic theory of intelligence
Sternberg's theory that intelligence involves mental skills (analytical aspect), insight and creative adaptability (creative aspect), and environmental responsiveness (practical aspect).

Analytical intelligence According to Sternberg, the ability to acquire new knowledge and solve problems effectively.

Creative intelligence Sternberg's term for the ability to adapt creatively in new situations, to use insight.

Practical intelligence According to Sternberg, the ability to select contexts in which you can excel, to shape the environment to fit your strengths and to solve practical problems.

Theory of multiple intelligences Howard Gardner's theory that there is not one intelligence, but rather many intelligences, each of which is relatively independent of the others.

Emotional intelligence According to Goleman, a form of intelligence that refers to how effectively people perceive and understand their own emotions and the emotions of others, and can manage their emotional behavior.

Author Toni Morrison, whose vivid, compelling prose has been likened to poetry, possesses an abundance of what Howard Gardner calls linguistic intelligence. In recognition of her exceptional talent, she was awarded a Nobel Prize in literature.

whereas those with more modest intellectual skills prosper. He contends that one of the reasons IQ tests sometimes fail to predict success accurately is that they do not take into account an individual's emotional competence. According to Goleman, even "The brightest among us can flounder on the shoals of unbridled passions and unruly impulses; people with high IQ scores can be stunningly poor pilots of their private lives" (Goleman, 1997, p. 34).

Five traits are generally recognized as contributing to one's emotional intelligence (Goleman, 1997; Goleman, Boyatzis, & McKee, 2002):

1. **Knowing one's own emotions.** The ability to monitor and recognize our own feelings is of central importance to self-awareness and all other dimensions of emotional intelligence.

2. **Managing one's emotions.** The ability to control impulses; to cope effectively with sadness, depression, and minor setbacks; as well as to control how long emotions last.

3. **Using emotions to motivate oneself.** The capacity to marshal emotions toward achieving personal goals.

4. **Recognizing the emotions of other people.** The ability to read subtle, nonverbal cues that reveal what other people really want and need.

5. **Managing relationships.** The ability accurately to acknowledge and *display* one's own emotions as well as being sensitive to the emotions of others.

Because the concept of emotional intelligence is relatively new, researchers have only begun to evaluate its measurement (Salovey, Mayer, Caruso, & Lopes, 2003; Sotres, Velasquez, & Cruz, 2002) and its scientific merit (Matthews, Zeidner, & Roberts, 2002). Nevertheless, some studies have shown promising results. For example, Mayer and Gehr (1996) found that the ability of people to identify emotions accurately in other people correlates with SAT scores. And, as you might expect, the ability to manage and regulate one's emotions in the workplace also appears to be important (Grandey, 2000).

Other investigators, however, remain more skeptical. In a series of three studies aimed at identifying the unique nature of emotional intelligence, Davies, Stankov and Roberts (1998) concluded that emotional intelligence may not represent a new concept at all. Instead, they argue that emotional intelligence is no different than traits that are already assessed by more traditional measures of intelligence and personality. More research is obviously needed before we can gain a full understanding of the scientific validity and usefulness of this intriguing and potentially important new theory of intelligence (Mayer, 1999).

Comparing the Theories

How do these formal theories of intelligence compare with each other? Spearman had the simplest view: He believed that

THINKING CRITICALLY

Multiple Intelligences

Gardner's theory clearly includes abilities not normally included under the heading of intelligence.

1. We earlier defined intelligence as general intellectual or mental ability. Do you agree that all of Gardner's facets of intelligence fit that definition? Should some be excluded? Or should the definition of intelligence perhaps be modified to include them? What might such a modified definition look like?

2. Some people have excellent "color sense"—they seem to know which colors go well together. Should this ability be included as one aspect of intelligence? What about rhyming ability?

3. In answering the first two questions, what criteria did you use for deciding which abilities to include as aspects of intelligence and which to exclude? Do other people share your viewpoint, or do their criteria differ? How might you go about deciding which viewpoints have most merit?

table 8-2 GARDNER'S, STERNBERG'S, AND GOLEMAN'S THEORIES OF INTELLIGENCE

Gardner's Multiple Intelligences	Sternberg's Triarchic Intelligences	Goleman's Emotional Intelligence
Logical-Mathematical Linguistic	Analytical	
Spatial Musical Body-Kinesthetic	Creative	
Interpersonal	Practical	Recognizing emotions in others and managing relationships
Intrapersonal		Knowing, managing, and motivating yourself with emotions

This highly detailed pen-and-ink drawing was made by an autistic prodigy, Stephen Wiltshire, at age 16.
Source: St. Basil's Cathedral, pen & ink © Stephen Wiltshire, from *Floating Cities* (M. Joseph, 1991).

people had different amounts of the "mental energy" he called general intelligence. Thurstone and Cattell attempted to identify the structure of mental abilities in more detail. The two most influential contemporary theorists are Sternberg and Gardner. Their theories both emphasize practical abilities, but the two theories differ in some basic ways. Sternberg has shown great ingenuity in designing mental tests to measure and validate different aspects of intelligence (Sternberg, 1993; Sternberg, Castejon, Prieto, Hautamaeki, & Grigorenko, 2001) as well as in proposing educational interventions to help students develop their intelligence (Keane & Shaughnessy, 2002; Sternberg, 1997a). Gardner, by contrast, has relied more on anecdotal evidence about the development of a specific intelligence in a particular person. It is entirely possible that future work will lead to a synthesis of these two approaches (Gardner, 1993). Finally, Goleman has added a new dimension (emotion) to the concept of intelligence; whether and how emotional intelligence can be integrated with other views of intelligence remains to be seen (see Table 8–2).

Formal theories of intelligence shape the content of intelligence tests and other measures of mental abilities. These tests are used to help evaluate the abilities of millions of people. We look now at how these tests are developed and administered, whether they accurately measure intelligence, and how they should be used.

CHECK YOUR UNDERSTANDING

1. Match each of the following with the correct concept of intelligence.

___ Spearman	a. intelligence encompasses seven relatively independent mental abilities
___ Thurstone	b. proposed a triarchic theory of intelligence
___ Cattell	c. intelligence is general
___ Sternberg	d. specified two clusters of mental ability
___ Gardner	e. intelligence is ability to recognize one's own and other's emotions
___ Goleman	f. advanced a theory of multiple intelligences

2. Logical-mathematical, linguistic, spatial, musical, bodily-kinesthetic, interpersonal, intrapersonal and naturalistic are the components of intelligence according to which influential theorist?

___ a. Spearman

___ b. Goleman

___ c. Gardner

3. Match each of the following with the definition specified by Robert Sternberg in his triarchic theory of intelligence.

___ analytical intelligence   a. ability to solve personal problems

___ creative intelligence   b. ability to adjust to new tasks

___ practical intelligence   c. ability to learn new things

Answers: 1. Spearman—c; Thurstone—a; Cattell—d; Sternberg—b; Gardner—f; Goleman—e, 2, c, 3. analytical—c; creative—b; practical—a

Intelligence Tests

What kind of intelligence tests are in use today?

The Stanford-Binet Intelligence Scale

The first intelligence test was designed for the French public school system by Alfred Binet, director of the psychological laboratory at the Sorbonne, and his colleague, Theodore Simon. Binet and Simon developed a number of questions and tested them on schoolchildren in Paris to identify those who might have difficulty in school.

The first **Binet-Simon Scale** was issued in 1905. It consisted of 30 tests arranged in order of increasing difficulty. With each child, the examiner started with the easiest tests and worked down the list until the child could no longer answer correctly. By 1908, enough children had been tested to predict how the average child would perform at each age level. From these scores Binet developed the concept of *mental age:* A child who scores as well as an average 4-year-old has a mental age of 4; a child who scores as well as an average 12-year-old has a mental age of 12; and so on.

During the decade following the debut of the Binet-Simon Scale, numerous Binet adaptations were issued. The best known of these was the **Stanford-Binet Intelligence Scale,** prepared at Stanford University by L. M. Terman and published in 1916. Terman introduced the now-famous term **intelligence quotient, or IQ,** to establish a numerical value of intelligence, setting the score of 100 for a person of average intelligence. Terman arrived at a person's IQ by determining his or her mental age, dividing the mental age by the person's chronological age, and then multiplying by 100. Thus, a 5-year-old with a mental age of 6 has an IQ of 120; a 12-year-old with a mental age of 10 has an IQ of 83. Figure 8–1 shows an approximate distribution of IQ scores in the population.

The Stanford-Binet has been revised several times since 1916 (Caruso, 2001). The current version of the Stanford-Binet Intelligence Scale, comprising 15 different subtests, is designed to measure four kinds of mental abilities that are almost universally considered to be components of intelligence: *verbal reasoning, abstract/visual reasoning, quantitative reasoning,* and *short-term memory.* Scores on these subtests are used to estimate overall intelligence (Sattler, 2002). Test items vary according to the person's age. For example, a 3-year-old might be asked to

Binet-Simon Scale The first test of intelligence, developed for testing children.

Stanford-Binet Intelligence Scale Terman's adaptation of the Binet-Simon Scale.

Intelligence quotient (IQ) A numerical value given to intelligence that is determined from the scores on an intelligence test; the average IQ is arbitrarily set at 100.

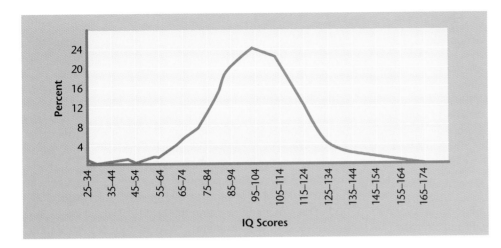

Figure 8–1
The approximate distribution of IQ test scores in the population.
Compare this figure to a normal curve, as shown in the Appendix (Figure A–3). Note the slight bulge at the lower end of the distribution, which some interpret as a sign of biologically based mental retardation. There is also a slight excess of people in the range of 70–90, and a slight deficit of people in the range of 90–120, compared with what a normal distribution would predict. Finally, there are more people in the 130+ range (4.3 percent) than the normal distribution would predict (2.3 percent).

describe the purpose of a cup and to name objects such as a chair and a key. A 6-year-old might be asked to define words such as *orange* and *envelope* and to complete a sentence such as "An inch is short; a mile is _____." A 12-year-old might be asked to define *skill* and *juggler* and to complete the sentence: "The streams are dry _____ there has been little rain" (Cronbach, 1990). Questions 1 and 2 at the opening of this chapter were drawn from an early version of the Stanford-Binet.

The Stanford-Binet test is given individually by a trained examiner and resembles an interview.

Testing usually begins with an item that is just below the expected mental age of the subject. If the person fails that item, he or she is then tested at the next lower level until he or she is successful. This level is then established as the subject's *basal age.* Once the basal age is determined, the examiner continues testing at higher and higher levels until the person misses a certain number of items in a row when the test stops. The examiner determines the subject's mental age by adding to the basal age credits for each test item above that age level. Although the Stanford-Binet is used with older people, it is best suited for children, adolescents, and very young adults.

The Wechsler Intelligence Scales

The most commonly used individual test of intelligence for adults is the **Wechsler Adult Intelligence Scale–Third Edition (WAIS–III).** The first version of the WAIS, was developed in 1939 by David Wechsler, a psychologist at Bellevue Hospital in New York City. He developed the test mainly because he wanted an instrument that would be more suitable for adults than the Stanford-Binet. In addition, whereas the Stanford-Binet emphasizes verbal skills, Wechsler felt that adult intelligence consists more in the ability to handle life situations than in solving verbal and abstract problems.

The WAIS–III is divided into two parts. One part stresses verbal skills, the other performance skills. The verbal scale includes tests of information ("Who wrote Paradise Lost?"), simple arithmetic ("Sam had three pieces of candy, and Joe gave him four more. How many pieces of candy did Sam have then?"), and comprehension ("What should you do if you see someone forget a book on a bus?"). All of these tests require a verbal response. The performance scale measures routine nonverbal tasks such as finding the missing part, copying patterns; and arranging three to five pictures so that they tell a story. Questions 3 and 4 at the start of this chapter resemble questions on the WAIS–III.

The content of the WAIS–III is somewhat more sophisticated than that of the Stanford-Binet, but Wechsler's chief innovation was in scoring: His test offers separate verbal and performance scores as well as an overall IQ. Second, on some items, points can be earned depending on the complexity of the answer given. This

The Wechsler Intelligence Scales, developed by David Wechsler, are individual intelligence tests administered to one person at a time. There are versions of the Wechsler Scales for both adults and children. Here a child is being asked to copy a pattern using blocks.

Wechsler Adult Intelligence Scale–Third Edition (WAIS–III) An individual intelligence test developed especially for adults; it yields verbal, performance, and full scale IQ scores.

ON THE CUTTING EDGE

BIOLOGICAL MEASURES OF INTELLIGENCE

All of the intelligence tests we describe in the text are psychological measures. Numerous efforts have been made to assess intelligence through biological measures (Haier, 2003; Stelmack, Knott, & Beauchamp, 2003; Vernon, 1993, 2000). Beginning early in the twentieth century, attempts were made to correlate brain size with intelligence. The correlations were very weak but always positive, suggesting that brain size and intelligence are related in some way. Other researchers have found correlations between intelligence and "evoked potentials," the electrical response of brain cells to stimulation (Stelmack et al., 2003). These correlations are somewhat higher than for brain size, but are still very modest. A similar approach measures the speed at which impulses travel along nerves, but these measures are not consistently related to IQ.

More recently, researchers have studied glucose metabolism, or how much energy the brain uses when solving a problem (Haier, 2003). The results suggest that people who are more intelligent focus their brain resources, using smaller regions of the brain that are essential to solving the problem. As a result, they use less glucose when performing an intellectual task (Neubauer, 2000). Does this suggest that the brains of more intelligent people work more efficiently? We do not know, and to date, no biological measure of intelligence has been found that approaches, much less surpasses, the accuracy of psychological tests.

---

unique scoring system gives credit for the reflective qualities that we expect to find in intelligent adults. Third, on some questions, both speed and accuracy affect the score.

Wechsler also developed a similar intelligence test for use with school-aged children. Like the WAIS–III, the **Wechsler Intelligence Scale for Children–Third Edition (WISC–III)** yields separate verbal and performance scores as well as an overall IQ score.

Group Tests

The Stanford-Binet, the WAIS–III, and the WISC–III are individual tests. The examiner takes the person to an isolated room and spends from 30 to 90 minutes administering the test. The examiner may then take another hour or so to score the test according to detailed instructions in the manual. It is a time-consuming, costly operation. Moreover, the examiner's behavior may greatly influence the score.

For these reasons, test makers have devised **group tests.** These are written tests of mental abilities that a single examiner can administer to a large group of people at the same time. Instead of sitting across the table from a person who asks you questions, you receive a test booklet that contains questions for you to answer within a certain amount of time. Questions 5 through 14 at the start of this chapter are drawn from group intelligence tests.

Group tests have some distinct advantages over individualized tests. They eliminate bias on the part of the examiner. Answer sheets can be scored quickly and objectively. And because more people can be tested in this way, norms are easier to establish. But group tests also have some distinct disadvantages. The examiner is less likely to notice whether a person is tired, ill, or confused by the directions. People who are not used to being tested tend to do less well on group tests than on individual tests. Finally, emotionally disturbed children and children with learning disabilities often do better on individual tests than on group tests (Anastasi & Urbina, 1997).

Wechsler Intelligence Scale for Children–Third Edition (WISC–III) An individual intelligence test developed especially for school-aged children; it yields verbal, performance, and full scale IQ scores.

Group tests Intelligence tests administered by one examiner to many people at one time.

Performance and Culture-Fair Tests

The intelligence tests we have discussed thus far share one limitation: To perform well, people must be able to read, speak, and understand English. In an effort to get around that problem, psychologists have devised performance tests and culture-fair tests of intelligence.

Performance tests consist of problems that minimize or eliminate the use of words. One of the earliest performance tests, the *Seguin Form Board*, was devised in 1866 to test people with mental retardation. The form board is essentially a puzzle. The examiner removes specifically designed cutouts, stacks them in a predetermined order, and asks the person to replace them as quickly as possible. A more recent performance test, the *Porteus Maze*, consists of a series of increasingly difficult printed mazes. Subjects trace their way through the maze without lifting the pencil from the paper. Such tests require the test taker to pay close attention to a task for an extended period and to continuously plan ahead in order to make the correct choices that solve the maze.

One of the most effective tests used for very young children is the *Bayley Scales of Infant Development*, now in its second edition (Bayley–II) (Bayley, 1993). The Bayley Scales are used to evaluate the developmental abilities of children from 1 month to 3 1/2 years of age. The Bayley–II has three scales: One scale tests perception, memory, and the beginning of verbal communication; a second measures sitting, standing, walking, and manual dexterity; the third is designed to assess emotional, social, and personality development. The Bayley Scales can detect early signs of sensory and neurological deficits, emotional difficulties, and troubles in a child's home environment (Maisto & German, 1986; Niccols & Latchman, 2002).

Culture-fair tests are designed to measure the intelligence of people who are outside the culture in which the test was devised. Like performance tests, culture-fair tests minimize or eliminate the use of language. Culture-fair tests also try to downplay skills and values—such as the need for speed—that vary from culture to culture. An example of this is the *Goodenough-Harris Drawing Test*. People are asked to draw the best picture of a person that they can. Drawings are scored for proportions, correct and complete representation of the parts of the body, detail in clothing, and so on. They are not rated on artistic talent.

Cattell's *Culture-Fair Intelligence Test* combines some questions that demand verbal comprehension and specific cultural knowledge with questions that are not tied to North American culture. By comparing scores on the two kinds of questions, cultural factors can be isolated from general intelligence. An example of a culture-fair item from the Cattell test is question 10 at the beginning of this chapter.

Another culture-fair test is the *Progressive Matrices* (question 6 at the start of this chapter). This test consists of 60 designs, each with a section removed. The task is to find, from among 6 to 8 patterns, the one that matches the missing section. The test involves various logical relationships, requires discrimination, and can be given to one person or to a group.

Moreover, some research suggests that another way to avoid the cultural bias inherent with most standardized intelligence

Performance tests Intelligence tests that minimize the use of language.

Culture-fair tests Intelligence tests designed to reduce cultural bias by minimizing skills and values that vary from one culture to another.

THINKING CRITICALLY

School Testing

If you are like most students, you have taken a number of intelligence tests and academic achievement tests in school.

Some people complain that American students are tested excessively—that many hours of instructional time are spent taking tests from which the student learns nothing. What do you think about this?

1. Were you overtested as a student?

2. How often should intelligence tests be given in school? Every year? Every five years? Never?

3. How would you justify the inclusion (or elimination) of intelligence testing in schools?

4. As a result of testing, have you obtained information that was useful to you in school or in life?

The Bayley Scales are a performance test used to assess the development of very young children. Such performance tests are essential to gauge developmental progress when children are too young to answer questions.

tests is by using a tester with appropriate training and expertise in a given culture who can often adjust a standardized test for use in another culture (Greenfield, 1997).

CHECK YOUR UNDERSTANDING

1. After determining a person's mental age, dividing it by her chronological age, and multiplying by 100, what will you know?

___ a. her fluid intelligence quotient

___ b. her emotional intelligence quotient

___ c. her IQ

2. The individual IQ test most often given to adults is

___ a. WISC–III

___ b. Stanford-Binet

___ c. WAIS–III

3. Which test is given individually by a trained examiner?

___ a. WISC–III

___ b. Stanford-Binet

___ c. WAIS–III

___ d. all the above

Answers: 1. c, 2. c, 3. b

What Makes a Good Test?

Do intelligence test scores predict success in later life?

All the tests we have looked at so far claim to measure a broad range of mental abilities, or "intelligence." How can we tell whether they really do measure what they claim to be measuring? And how do we determine whether one test is better than another? Psychologists address these questions by referring to a test's reliability and validity. As you read the following sections, keep in mind that the issues of reliability and validity apply equally to all psychological tests, not just to tests of mental abilities.

Reliability

By **reliability** psychologists mean the dependability and consistency of the scores yielded by a given test. If your alarm clock is set for 8:15 A.M. and goes off at that time every morning, it is reliable. But if it is set for 8:15 and rings at 8:00 one morning and 8:40 the next, you cannot depend on it; it is unreliable. Similarly, if you score 110 on an intelligence test one week and 60 on the same or an equivalent test a week later, something is wrong.

How do we know whether a test is reliable? The simplest way is to give the test to a group of people and then, after a short time, give the same people the same test again. If they obtain similar scores each time, the test is said to have high test-retest reliability. For example, Table 8–3 shows the IQ scores of eight people tested one

Reliability Ability of a test to produce consistent and stable scores.

year apart using the same test. Although the scores did change slightly, none changed by more than six points.

This way of determining reliability poses a serious problem, however: If the same test is used on both occasions, people might not only remember their answers from the first testing and repeat them the second time around but also give correct answers to items that they missed the first time around. To avoid this *practice effect,* alternate forms of the test are often used. In this method, two equivalent tests are designed to measure the same ability. If people get similar scores on both forms, the tests are considered to be highly reliable. One way to create alternate forms is to split a single test into two parts—for example, to assign odd-numbered items to one test and even-numbered items to the other. If scores on the two halves agree, the test is said to have **split-half reliability.** Most intelligence tests do, in fact, have alternate equivalent forms.

table 8-3 IQ SCORES ON THE SAME TEST GIVEN ONE YEAR APART

Person	First Testing	Second Testing
A	130	127
B	123	127
C	121	119
D	116	122
E	109	108
F	107	112
G	95	93
H	89	94

ENDURING ISSUES   **stability**change

Test Reliability and Changes in Intelligence

If a person takes an intelligence test on Monday and obtains an IQ score of 90, and then retakes the test on Tuesday and scores 130, clearly something is amiss. But what? Is the test at fault, or do the differences in scores accurately reflect changes in performance?

People vary from moment to moment and day to day. Changes in health and motivation can affect test results even with the most reliable tests. And although IQ scores tend to be remarkably stable after the age of five or six, intellectual ability does sometimes change dramatically—for better or worse. One person's mental ability may decline substantially after a mild head injury; another person's scores on intelligence tests may rise after years of diligent intellectual study. Also, recent evidence indicates that intelligence, as measured by performance tasks, declines steadily throughout adulthood, beginning around age 20 (Park, 1998; Park, Cherry, Smith, & Frieske, 1997). A test that yields the same IQ scores for these individuals would appear to be reliable, but it would not reflect real changes in ability.

Since scores on even the best tests vary somewhat from one day to another, many testing services now report a person's score along with a range of scores that allows for variations. For example, a score of 110 might be reported with a range of 104–116. This implies that the true score is most likely within a few points of 110, but almost certainly does not fall lower than 104 or higher than 116.

These methods of testing reliability can be very effective. But is there some way of being more precise than simply calling a test "very reliable" or "fairly reliable"? Psychologists express reliability in terms of **correlation coefficients,** which measure the relationship between two sets of scores (see Appendix A for a discussion of correlation coefficients). If test scores on one occasion are absolutely consistent with those on another occasion, the correlation coefficient is 1.0. If there is no relationship between the scores, the correlation coefficient is zero. In Table 8–3, where there is a very close, but not perfect, relationship between the two sets of scores, the correlation coefficient is .96.

How reliable are intelligence tests? In general, people's scores in intelligence tests are quite stable (see Meyer et al., 2001). Reliability coefficients on most tests

Split-half reliability A method of determining test reliability by dividing the test into two parts and checking the agreement of scores on both parts.

Correlation coefficients Statistical measures of the degree of association between two variables.

are around .90, which is about as stable as the scores in Table 8–3. Performance and culture-fair tests are somewhat less reliable.

We turn now to another question. Do intelligence tests really measure intelligence? We know that intelligence test scores are fairly consistent from day to day, but how do we know that the consistency is due to intelligence and not to something else? When psychologists ask these questions, they are concerned with test validity.

Validity

Validity refers to a test's ability to measure what it has been designed to measure. How can we determine whether a given test actually measures what it claims to measure?

Content Validity   One measure of validity is known as **content validity**—the extent to which the test items represent the knowledge or skills being measured. If all of the questions on an algebra test concerned behavior genetics, the test would lack validity. To have content validity, then, an intelligence test must assess the full range of mental abilities that constitute intelligence.

Do the results of IQ tests truly reflect the kinds of mental abilities that they set out to assess? The answer is somewhat mixed. Most people would agree that the content of the Stanford-Binet reflects at least part of what we commonly consider "intelligence," so we can conclude that the Stanford-Binet has some content validity. But because of its heavy emphasis on verbal skills, the test may not adequately sample all aspects of intelligence equally well. The WAIS–III and WISC–III appear to cover many of the primary abilities that Thurstone included under the heading of "intelligence" and that Cattell grouped under the headings of "fluid" and "crystallized" intelligence. Thus, the WAIS–III and WISC–III also appear to have reasonable content validity as intelligence tests. Most group intelligence tests, such as those from which questions 5 through 14 at the beginning of this chapter were taken, also seem to measure many of the mental abilities that make up intelligence. Yet intelligence tests do not measure every type of mental ability. Some tests focus on skills that other tests leave out, and each intelligence test emphasizes certain abilities more than others. Thus, no intelligence has perfect content validity.

Criterion-Related Validity   Another way of measuring a test's validity is to determine the extent to which it correlates with other accepted measures of what is being tested. This is called **criterion-related validity.** Think of two rulers, one that measures in inches and one that measures in centimeters. The measurements obtained by one ruler should correspond with those obtained by the other, because both rulers measure the same thing—length. Similarly, two different measures of intelligence should be correlated with each other if indeed they are both measuring intelligence.

In fact, various intelligence tests do correlate well with one another despite the differences in their content: People who score high on one test tend to score high on the others. Again, we can use the correlation coefficient to describe the strength of the relationship. The Stanford-Binet and WISC correlate around .80. The Progressive Matrices and the Porteus Maze Test correlate .40 to .80 with other intelligence tests. The Goodenough-Harris Drawing Test correlates about .50 or higher with other tests. Thus, despite their differences in surface content, most intelligence tests do seem to be measuring similar things.

However, the fact that intelligence tests tend to correlate with one another is not sufficient evidence of their validity, for it is conceivable that the tests could be measuring the same things but that these things do not constitute intelligence. To demonstrate that the tests are valid, we need an independent measure of intelligence

Validity Ability of a test to measure what it has been designed to measure.

Content validity Refers to a test's having an adequate sample of questions measuring the skills or knowledge it is supposed to measure.

Criterion-related validity Validity of a test as measured by a comparison of the test score and independent measures of what the test is designed to measure.

against which to compare intelligence test scores. The independent measure most commonly used for this purpose is academic achievement (Anastasi & Urbina, 1997). The underlying idea is that individual differences in school grades must reflect individual differences in intelligence, at least to some extent. Therefore, students with good grades should get high scores on the Stanford-Binet and other intelligence tests, and students with poor grades should do less well on such tests. And in fact they do. Even the strongest critics agree that intelligence tests are strongly correlated with school grades (Aiken, 1988). Correlations between grades and intelligence tests typically range between .50 and .75 (Parker, Hanson, & Hunsley, 1988). Evidence on the various performance and culture-fair tests suggests that these tests do not predict school grades as well as other intelligence tests do (Blum, 1979).

Summing Up We know that intelligence tests are quite reliable since scores on these tests are consistent from one testing session to another. These tests also seem to assess many of the qualities that psychologists define as components of intelligence; thus, they have generally good content validity. And intelligence test scores agree with one another and with other indicators of intelligence, such as school grades, which provides evidence of their criterion-related validity. Nonetheless, in recent decades, intelligence tests have come under severe criticism.

Criticisms of Intelligence Tests

Test Content and Score One major criticism of IQ tests concerns their content. Many critics believe that intelligence tests assess only a very narrow set of skills: passive verbal understanding; the ability to follow instructions; common sense; and scholastic aptitude (Ginsberg, 1972; Sattler, 1992). For example, one critic observes, "Intelligence tests measure how quickly people can solve relatively unimportant problems making as few errors as possible, rather than measuring how people grapple with relatively important problems, making as many productive errors as necessary with no time factor" (Blum, 1979, p. 83).

A related criticism is that if there is one thing that all intelligence tests measure, it is the ability to take tests. This would explain why people who do well on one IQ test also tend to do well on others. And it would also explain why intelligence test scores correlate so closely with school performance since academic grades also depend heavily on test scores. However, recent reviews of the evidence demonstrate that both school grades and intelligence tests are good predictors of occupational success (Barret & Depinet, 1991). This suggests that test scores (on IQ tests and classroom tests) do not merely reflect test-taking ability. Thus, this particular criticism of intelligence tests may have to be reconsidered.

Still other critics maintain that the content and administration of IQ tests discriminate against minorities. As we have seen, most IQ tests require considerable mastery of standard English, which biases the tests in favor of middle- and upper-class white people. Moreover, white middle-class examiners may not be familiar with the speech patterns of lower-income black children or children from homes where English is not the primary language, a complication that may hamper good test performance (Greenfield, 1997; Sattler, 1992). In addition, certain questions may have very different meanings for children of different social classes. The Stanford-Binet, for instance, asks, "What are you supposed to do if a child younger than you hits you?" The "correct" answer is, "Walk away." But for a child who lives in an environment where survival depends on being tough, the "correct" answer might be, "Hit him back." This answer, however, receives zero credit.

Even presumably culture-fair tests may accentuate the very cultural differences that they were designed to minimize, to the detriment of test takers (Linn, 1982).

Some people argue that intelligence tests largely measure test-taking skills, not a person's underlying mental capabilities. Others contend that the content of these tests and the ways they are administered discriminate against minorities.

For example, when given a picture of a head with the mouth missing, one group of Asian American children responded by saying that the body was missing, thus receiving no credit. To them, the absence of a body under the head was more remarkable than the absence of the mouth (Ortar, 1963).

Although some investigators believe that the most widely used and thoroughly studied tests are not biased against minorities (Bersoff, 1981; Damas, 2002; Herrnstein & Murray, 1994), not everyone agrees (Helms, 1992). The issue of whether tests are unfair to minorities will be with us for some time. If intelligence tests were used only for obscure research purposes, their results would not matter much, but because they are used for so many significant purposes, it is critical that we understand their strengths and their weaknesses.

Use of Intelligence Tests   Recall that Alfred Binet developed the first IQ test to help the French public school system identify students who needed to be put in special classes. In fact, Binet believed that courses of "mental orthopedics" could be used to help those with low IQ scores. But the practice of using IQ tests to put a person into a "track" or "slot" in school may backfire. To the extent that children get low scores on IQ tests because of test bias, language handicap, or their own lack of interest in test taking, the administrative decision to label these children as "slow" or "retarded" and put them into special classes apart from "normal" students can have a disastrous effect—one that may get worse, not better, with time.

ENDURING ISSUES   **person**situation

Tracking the Future

Tracking, the practice of assigning students who "test low" to special classes for slow learners, can work to the student's disadvantage if the test results do not reflect the student's true abilities. However, the opposite mistake may sometimes work to the student's advantage: A student of mediocre ability who is identified early on as above average may receive special attention, encouragement, and tutoring that would otherwise have been considered "wasted effort" on the part of teachers. Thus, intelligence test scores can set up a self-fulfilling prophecy, so that students defined as slow become slow, and those defined as quick become quick (Dahlström, 1993). In this way, intelligence tests may not only predict achievement but also help determine it.

Although intelligence tests are useful for predicting academic performance, they do not measure other variables that affect academic achievement—motivation, emotion, and attitudes, for example. Yet in many instances, these characteristics may have more to do with an individual's success and effectiveness than IQ does. Let's look briefly at the relationship between intelligence test scores and success.

IQ and Success   Despite their limitations, IQ tests do a good job of predicting future school performance. People with high IQ scores tend to enter high-status occupations: Physicians and lawyers tend to have higher IQ scores than truck drivers and janitors. However, the relationship between IQ scores and later job status can be explained in various ways. People with higher IQ test scores tend to do better in school, stay in school longer and earn advanced degrees, which, in turn, open the door to higher-status jobs. Moreover, children from wealthy families are more likely to have the money needed for graduate school and advanced occupational training. They also tend to have helpful family connections. Perhaps most important, they grow up in environments that encourage academic success and reward good performance on tests (Blum, 1979; Ceci & Williams, 1997).

Although research confirms that people with high IQ scores are more successful in school and tend to get higher-status jobs, are these people also more likely to succeed in their careers? In a classic paper, David C. McClelland (1973) of Harvard University argued that IQ scores and grades in college have very little to do with later occupational success. His review of the research evidence seemed to indicate that when education and social class are held constant, on a wide range of jobs people with high IQ scores do not perform better than people with lower IQ scores. However, a subsequent survey of the relevant research contradicts McClelland's conclusion. Barret and Depinet (1991) found considerable evidence that grades and results on tests of intellectual ability *do* predict occupational success. They concluded that "test results were not an artifact of social status, nor were they unfair to minorities" (p. 1021). Similarly, Ree and Earles (1992) presented evidence that measures of general intelligence are excellent predictors of job performance. They concluded that "if an employer were to use only intelligence tests and select the highest-scoring applicant for each job, training results would be predicted well regardless of the job, and overall performance from the employees selected would be maximized" (p. 88).

In this section, we have reviewed several criticisms that have been leveled at IQ tests and their use. But not all critics of intelligence tests want to see them eliminated. Many simply want to make IQ tests more useful. For example, Jane Mercer has developed a *System of Multicultural Pluralistic Assessment (SOMPA)*, designed for children between the ages of 5 and 11. SOMPA involves collecting a wide range of data on a child, including information about health and socioeconomic status, that provides a context within which IQ test scores can be interpreted. SOMPA takes into account both the dominant school culture and the child's family background, and then adjusts the child's score (based on the Wechsler Scales) accordingly (Rice, 1979). And, as we have seen, Sternberg, Gardner, and Goleman are developing new intelligence test items that will tap a much broader set of skills that may underlie intelligence.

CHECK YOUR UNDERSTANDING

1. Which of the following makes a good test?

____ a. high visibility

____ b. high validity

____ c. high reliability

____ d. b and c

2. Psychologists express a test's reliability in terms of

____ a. correlation coefficients

____ b. factor analyses

____ c. a and b

3. Most of the criticism of intelligence tests has focused on

____ a. scoring methodology

____ b. examiner bias

____ c. test-taking anxiety

____ d. test content

Answers: 1. d, 2. a, 3. d

What Determines Intelligence?

What do adoption studies reveal about the sources of intelligence?

Heredity

Robert C. Tryon (1901–1967) of the University of California, Berkeley, was a pioneer in behavior genetics. More than 50 years ago, he began investigating whether the ability to run mazes could be bred into rats. Tryon isolated eligible pairs of "maze-bright" rats in one pen and "maze-dull" rats in another. The animals were left free to breed. The brightest offspring of the bright rats were then identified and allowed to breed, as were the dullest offspring of the dull rats. This procedure was repeated for each succeeding generation. Within a few generations, the difference between the two groups was astounding: The maze-dull rats made many more mistakes learning a maze than their bright counterparts (Tryon, 1940). Thus, Tryon demonstrated that a specific ability can be passed down from one generation of rats to another.

Obviously, selective breeding of humans is unethical. However, as we saw in Chapter 2, The Biological Basis of Behavior, scientists can use studies of identical twins to measure the effects of heredity in humans. Twin studies of intelligence begin by comparing the IQ scores of identical twins who have been raised together. As Figure 8–2 shows, the correlation between their IQ scores is very high. But these twins grow up in very similar environments: They share parents, home, teachers, vacations, and probably friends and clothes, too. These common experiences could explain their similar IQ scores. To check this possibility, researchers have tested identical twins who were separated early in life—generally before they were six months old—and raised in different families. As Figure 8–2 shows, even when

Figure 8–2
Correlations of IQ scores of family members.
Identical twins who grow up in the same household have IQ scores that are almost identical to each other. Even when they are reared apart, their scores are highly correlated.
Source: Adapted from "Genetics and Intelligence: A Review," by L. Erlenmeyer-Kimling and L. F. Jarvik 1963, *Science, 142*, pp. 1477–1479. Reprinted with permission from "Genetics and intelligence: A review" by Erlenmeyer-Kimling and L. F. Jarvik 1963, *Science, 142*, pp. 1477–79. Copyright 1963 American Association for the Advancement of Science and the author. URL: http://www.sciencemag.org

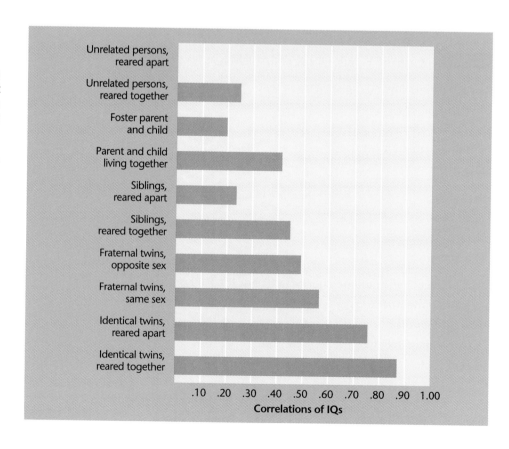

identical twins are raised in different families, they tend to have very similar test scores; in fact, the similarity is much greater than that between siblings who grow up in the *same* environment.

These findings make a strong case for the heritability of intelligence. However, twin studies do not constitute "final proof" of this assertion because finding identical twins who were separated at birth is very difficult; therefore, relatively few such pairs have been studied. Assessing the influence of heredity given such a small sample of subjects is extremely difficult (Loehlin, 1989). Also, adoption agencies try to match natural and adoptive parents. If twins are born to educated middle-class parents, the adopted children will most likely be placed with educated middle-class adoptive parents. Thus, twins reared apart will often share somewhat similar environments. Finally, even if twins grow up in radically different environments, they lived for nine very critical months inside the same mother: Their prenatal experiences were virtually identical. It is difficult to determine the extent to which these shared experiences might contribute to similar IQ scores. Therefore, closely correlated IQ scores of identical twins could, conceivably, have as much to do with shared environments as with shared genes.

But other evidence favors genetics. Adopted children have been found to have IQ scores that are more similar to those of their *biological* mothers than to those of the mothers who are raising them (Loehlin, Horn, & Willerman, 1997). Researcher John Loehlin finds these results particularly interesting because "[they] reflect genetic resemblance in the absence of shared environment: These birth mothers had no contact with their children after the first few days of life . . ." (Loehlin et al., 1997, p. 113).

What, then, is the case for the influence of the environment? We turn now to that question.

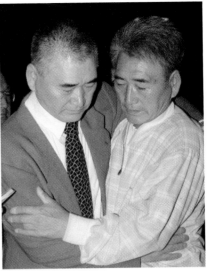

Kim In Hyong (left) and his twin brother Kim Won Hyong were separated during childhood. Despite being reared by different families and spending more than 40 years apart, their IQ test scores should be quite similar.

Environment

Probably no psychologist denies that genes play a role in determining intelligence, but many believe that genes merely provide a base or starting point. Each of us inherits a certain body build from our parents, but our actual weight is greatly determined by what we eat and how much we exercise. Similarly, although we inherit certain mental capacities, the development of those inherited intellectual abilities depends on what we see around us as infants, how our parents respond to our first attempts to talk, the schools we attend, the books we read, the television programs we watch—even what we eat.

For example, extreme malnutrition during infancy can lower IQ scores. Severely undernourished children in South Africa had IQ scores that averaged 20 points lower than the IQ scores of similar children with adequate diets (Stock & Smythe, 1963). Subsequent research in Great Britain (Benton & Roberts, 1988) and in California (Schoenthaler, Amos, Eysenck, Peritz, & Yudkin, 1991) has suggested that the addition of vitamin supplements to the diet of young children can increase IQ test scores, possibly even among children who are not malnourished. Recent studies have even demonstrated that infants who were breastfed for up to 9 months after birth generally score slightly higher on adult intelligence tests than those that were not breastfed (Mortensen, Michaelsen, Sanders, & Reinisch, 2002). However, these findings are still controversial. Nutrition has an impact on children before birth as well: A number of studies show that prenatal nutrition affects intelligence test scores (Hack et al., 1991). In one study of pregnant women who were economically deprived, half were given a dietary supplement, and half were given placebos. When given intelligence tests between the ages of 3 and 4, the children of the mothers who had taken the supplement scored significantly higher than the children given placebos (Harrell, Woodyard, & Gates, 1955).

Compared with women who eat poor diets during pregnancy, those who eat nutritious ones tend to have larger, healthier newborns who go on to become preschoolers with higher IQ scores than peers who were not well nourished prenatally.

Individual differences in intelligence can be partly explained by differences in environmental stimulation and encouragement. The specific forms of stimulation given vary from culture to culture. Because our culture assigns importance to developing academic skills, the stimulation of reading and exploring information in books can give children an IQ edge over those who are not so encouraged.

Further evidence for the importance of environment comes from follow-up experiments using Tryon's maze-bright and maze-dull rats. Psychologists raised one group of mixed bright and dull rats in absolutely plain surroundings and another mixed group in a stimulating environment that contained toys, an activity wheel, and a ladder. When the rats were grown, they were tested on Tryon's mazes. The experimenters discovered that there was no longer much difference between genetically bright and dull rats: In the restricted environment, the inherited abilities of the bright rats apparently failed to develop, and all the rats acted like maze-dull rats. In the stimulating environment, the genetically maze-dull rats apparently made up through experience what they lacked in heredity and, as a result, all the rats in this environment acted like maze-bright rats (Cooper & Zubek, 1958). In subsequent experiments, Rosenzweig and Bennett (1976) confirmed that enriched environments improved rats' ability to learn.

Quite by chance, psychologist H. M. Skeels found evidence in the 1930s that IQ scores among children also depend on environmental stimulation. While investigating orphanages for the state of Iowa, Skeels noticed that the wards where the children lived were overcrowded and that the few adults charged with caring for the children had almost no time to play with them, talk to them, or read them stories. Many of these children were classified as "subnormal" in intelligence. Skeels followed the cases of two girls who, after 18 months in an orphanage, were sent to a ward for women with severe retardation. Originally, the girls' IQ scores were in the range of retardation, but after a year on the adult ward their IQ scores had risen to normal (Skeels, 1938). He repeated the experiment by placing 13 slow children as houseguests in adult wards (Skeels, 1942). Within 18 months, the mean IQ of these children had risen from 64 to 92 (within the normal range). These dramatic improvements apparently occurred because the children had had someone (even someone of below-normal intelligence) to play with them, to read to them, to cheer them when they took their first steps, and to encourage them to talk. During the same period, the mean IQ of a group of children who had been left in orphanages dropped from 86 to 61. Thirty years later, Skeels found that all 13 of the children raised on adult wards were self-supporting, their occupations ranging from waiting on tables to real-estate sales. Of the contrasting group, half were unemployed, four were still in institutions, and all those who had jobs were dishwashers (Skeels, 1966).

A study conducted in France by Capron and Duyme (1989) also provides strong support for the influence of the environment on intelligence. Half the children in this study had been born to parents of high socioeconomic status (SES), and half had been born to parents of low SES. Half the children born to high-SES parents were adopted and raised by parents of similar status, and half were adopted and raised by low-SES parents. Similarly, half the children born to low-SES parents were adopted and raised by high-SES parents, and half were adopted and raised by other low-SES parents. The results showed that the socioeconomic status of the adoptive parents had an effect on their adopted children's IQ scores. Regardless of the socioeconomic status of the child's biological parents, those children adopted by high-SES parents had higher IQ scores than did those children adopted by low-SES parents. Why? High-SES families tend to provide children with better nutrition, more interaction with their parents, and a more educational environment, particularly use of language (Hart & Risley, 1995). These results are consistent with

APPLYING PSYCHOLOGY

INTERVENTION PROGRAMS—DO THEY WORK?

Launched in 1961, the purpose of the Milwaukee Project was to learn whether intervening in a child's family life could offset the negative effects of cultural and socioeconomic deprivation on intelligence test scores. Rick Heber and his associates at the University of Wisconsin Infant Center worked with 40 poor pregnant women in the Milwaukee area (Garber & Heber, 1982; Heber, Garber, Harrington, & Hoffman, 1972). On average, the women initially scored less than 75 on the Wechsler intelligence scales. They were then split into two groups. One group was given job training and sent to school. As they found jobs, they were also instructed in child care, household management, and personal relationships. The other group received no special education or job training and served as a control group.

After all 40 women had their babies, the research team began to concentrate on the children. Starting when they were three months old and continuing for the next six years, the children of the mothers who were being given special training spent the better part of each day in an infant education center, where they received nourishing meals and participated in an educational program that included a wide range of educational toys. They were cared for by paraprofessionals who behaved like nonworking mothers in affluent families. The other group of children, those in the control group, had no access to the education center. All the children were periodically tested for IQ. The children in the experimental group, whose mothers received special train-

> *"Evidence suggests that the involvement of parents in the Head Start program has been crucial to its success."*

ing and who themselves had access to the education center, achieved an average IQ of 126—51 points higher than their mothers' average scores. By contrast, the children in the control group had an average IQ of 94.

The nation's largest intervention program, Head Start, began in 1965 and today provides comprehensive services for nearly a million children lasting at least a half a day for up to two years (Kassebaum, 1994; Ripple, Gilliam, Chanana, & Zigler, 1999). Head Start focuses on preschoolers between the ages of three and five who live in low-income families. It has two key goals: to provide the children with some educational and social skills before they get to school and to provide information about nutrition and health to the children and their families. Head Start involves parents in all its aspects, from daily activities to administration of the program itself, because evidence suggests that the involvement of parents in the Head Start program has been crucial to its success (Cronan, Walen, & Cruz, 1994; Mendez & Martha, 2001).

Several studies evaluating the long-term effects of Head Start concluded that the program had improved children's cognitive abilities (Barnett, 1998; Brown & Grotberg, 1981; Zigler, 1998). Today, however, some experts are concerned that these improvements may not be lasting. For example, some evidence suggests that boosts in IQ tend to be modest or short term. Nevertheless, there seems to be no question that children leaving Head Start are in a better position to profit from schooling than they would be otherwise (Zigler & Styfco, 1994). Even social skills and the ability to make friends in school appear to be positively affected by participation in Head Start (Vaughn et al., 2000). Researchers who followed Head Start graduates until age 27 found several benefits, including higher academic achievement. The Head Start graduates tended to stay in school longer, were more likely to graduate from college and had a lower level of delinquency. Thus, even if the mental ability gains due to Head Start are not long lasting, the program still seems to provide long-term, practical benefits (Schweinhart, Barnes, & Weikart, 1993; Zigler & Styfco, 2001; Zigler, 2003).

Overall, the effectiveness of early intervention appears to depend on the quality of the particular program (Collins, 1993; Ramey, 1999; Zigler & Muenchow, 1992; Zigler & Styfco, 1993). Intervention programs that have clearly defined goals; that explicitly teach basic skills, such as counting, naming colors, and writing the alphabet; and that take into account the broad context of human development, including health care and other social services, achieve the

Although researchers debate whether Head Start produces significant and lasting boosts in IQ, it does have many school-related benefits for those who participate in it.

biggest and most durable gains. Also, interventions that begin in the preschool years and include a high degree of parental involvement (to ensure continuity after the official program ends) are generally more successful (Zigler, Finn-Stevenson, & Hall, 2002).

research that shows the detrimental effects of poverty on intellectual development (McLoyd, 1998). In *Applying Psychology: Intervention Programs—Do They Work?* we look at the results of several studies aimed at enhancing the environments of children from lower-SES families.

Heredity vs. Environment: Which Is More Important?

Both heredity and environment have important effects on mental abilities. Is one of those factors more important than the other? As Turkheimer (1991) observes, the question of whether mental abilities are determined primarily by nature (genes) or nurture (environment) is almost as old as psychology itself, and it is still being hotly debated (e.g., Herrnstein & Murray, 1994; Sternberg, 2003). The answer to the heredity/environment debate may depend on whose IQs you are comparing. A useful way to think about heredity, environment, and intelligence comes from plants (Turkheimer, 1991). Suppose you take groups of the same type of plant. You grow one group in enriched soil and the other in poor soil. The enriched group will grow to be higher and stronger than the nonenriched group; the difference between the two groups in this case is due entirely to differences in their environment. However, *within* each group of plants, differences among individual plants are likely to be due primarily to genetics, because all plants in the same group share essentially the same environment. Nevertheless, the height and strength of any single plant will reflect both heredity and environment. Similarly, group differences in IQ test scores might be due to environmental factors, differences *within* racial groups could be due primarily to genetics, and the IQ test score of particular individuals would therefore reflect the effects of both heredity and environment.

An interesting side note to this debate is the fact that IQ scores have *gone up* in the population as a whole (Humphreys, 1992; Jensen, 1992; Neisser et al., 1996; Neisser, 1998; Resing & Nijland, 2002). Because James Flynn (Flynn, 1984, 1987) of the University of Otago in New Zealand was the first to report this finding, it is often called the *Flynn Effect*. In his original research, Professor Flynn gathered evidence showing that between 1932 and 1978 intelligence test scores rose about three points per decade. More recently, by pulling together data from five nations (Britain, Netherlands, Israel, Norway, and Belgium) Flynn (1999) has shown that the average increase in IQ may be as high as six points per decade. Consistent with this result is a finding by Flieller (1999) that children today between the ages of 10 and 15 years old display significant cognitive advancement compared with children of the same age tested 20 and 30 years ago. And, as Neisser (1998) points out, accompanying this general increase in IQ scores is a decrease in the difference in intelligence scores between blacks and whites.

Although this finding has many possible explanations, none of them seem to account entirely for the magnitude of the effect

THINKING CRITICALLY

The Flynn Effect

Flynn and others have found that IQ scores are rising, but what does this really mean? As Flynn (1999) points out, it is hard to see how genes could account for so rapid an increase in IQ. Clearly, some aspect of the environment must account for most or all of the increase in IQ scores.

1. Of the possible explanations mentioned in the text, which seem to you to be most likely? Why? How might you go about determining whether one explanation is better than another?

2. How long do you think intelligence test scores have been rising? How long do you think the trend will continue? Are your thoughts on these two questions related to your thoughts about the first question?

3. Could the increase in scores result from biological changes, such as improvements in diet or less exposure to lead and other toxins?

4. Does a rise in IQ test scores necessarily mean that there has been a comparable increase in intelligence?

5. Because an environmental explanation for the increase in IQ test scores is most likely, does that provide support for the notion that intelligence can be improved through education? What are the implications of the Flynn Effect for intervention programs such as Head Start?

(Flynn, 1999: Rowe & Rodgers, 2002). Are people getting smarter, or are they simply getting better at taking tests? Are environmental factors, such as improved nutrition and health care, responsible for this trend (Lynn, 1989)? Is it possible that the sheer complexity of the modern world is responsible for this trend (Schooler, 1998)? Might the proliferation of televisions, computers, and video games be contributing to the rise in IQ scores (Greenfield, 1998; Neisser, 1998)? While no definitive answers to these questions have been found, continued research on the Flynn Effect will undoubtedly shed more light on our understanding of the nature of intelligence and the factors that influence its development.

CHECK YOUR UNDERSTANDING

1. The discovery that a specific ability can be passed down from one generation of rats to another is credited to

___ a. H.M. Skeels

___ b. Robert C. Tryon

___ c. Alfred Binet

___ d. Daniel Goleman

2. What factor helps foster the ability to learn?

___ a. enriched environment

___ b. better prenatal nutrition

___ c. better post-natal nutrition

___ d. all of the above

3. Which of the following is the correct definition of the *Flynn Effect?* In recent years:

___ a. IQ scores have remained steady in the population as a whole.

___ b. IQ scores have declined in the population as a whole.

___ c. IQ scores have increased in the population as a whole.

Answers: 1. b, 2. d, 3. c

Mental Abilities and Human Diversity

Are males naturally better than females at mathematics?

Are there differences in mental abilities between males and females or among people from different cultures? Many people assume, for example, that males are naturally better at mathematics and that females excel in verbal skills. Others believe that the sexes are basically alike in mental abilities. Similarly, how do we account for the superior academic performance by students from certain countries and certain cultural backgrounds? Research offers some interesting insights into these controversial issues.

Gender

In 1974 psychologists Eleanor Maccoby and Carol Jacklin published a review of psychological research on gender differences. They found no differences at all between males and females in most of the studies they examined. However, a few differences did appear in cognitive abilities: Girls tended to display greater verbal ability and boys tended to exhibit stronger spatial and mathematical abilities. Largely as a result of this research, gender differences in verbal, spatial, and mathematical abilities became so widely accepted that they were often cited as one of the established facts of psychological research (Hyde, Fennema, & Lamon, 1990; Hyde & Linn, 1988).

Yet a closer examination of the research literature, including more recent work, indicates that gender differences in math and verbal ability may be virtually nonexistent. Janet Shibley Hyde and her colleagues analyzed 165 research studies, involving more than a million people, in which gender differences in verbal ability were examined. They concluded that "there are no gender differences in verbal ability, at least at this time, in American culture, in the standard ways that verbal ability has been measured" (Hyde & Linn, 1988, p. 62). In a similar analysis of studies examining mathematical ability, Hyde and her colleagues concluded that "females outperformed males by only a negligible amount. . . . Females are superior in computation, there are no gender differences in understanding of mathematical concepts, and gender differences favoring males do not emerge until the high school years" (Hyde et al., 1990, pp. 139, 151).

Males apparently do have an advantage over females in *spatial ability*, however (Choi & Silverman, 2003; Halpern, 1992, 1997; Voyer, Voyer, & Bryden, 1995). Spatial tasks include mentally rotating an object and estimating horizontal and vertical dimensions (see the figures at the beginning of the chapter). These skills are particularly useful in solving certain engineering, architecture, and geometry problems. They are also handy in deciding how to arrange furniture in your new apartment or how to fit all those suitcases into the trunk of your car!

Men also differ from women in another way: They are much more likely than women to fall at the extremes of the intelligence range (Brody, 2000; Halpern, 1997). In one review of several large studies, Hedges and Nowell (1995) found that males accounted for seven out of eight people with extremely high IQ scores. These authors also reported that males represented an almost equally large proportion of the IQ scores within the range of mental retardation.

What should we conclude from these findings? First, the differences between males and females appear to be restricted to specific cognitive skills (Stumpf & Stanley, 1998). Scores on tests such as the Stanford-Binet or the WAIS reveal no

Research shows that there are only negligible differences between men and women in mathematical ability.

gender differences in general intelligence (Halpern, 1992). Second, gender differences in specific cognitive abilities typically are small and in some cases appear to be diminishing—even when studied cross-culturally (Skaalvik & Rankin, 1994). Finally, we do not know whether the origins of the differences that do exist are a result of biological or cultural factors (Hyde & Mezulis, 2002).

Culture

Many U.S. educators, policymakers, and parents are concerned that American students are falling behind students in other countries. Is this concern valid? And if it is, does it reflect an underlying difference in intelligence across cultures?

In a series of comprehensive studies, a team of researchers led by Harold Stevenson investigated differences in academic performance among members of various cultures (Stevenson, 1992, 1993; Stevenson, Chen, & Lee, 1993). In 1980, he and his colleagues began their research by examining the performance of first- and fifth-grade children in American, Chinese, and Japanese elementary schools (Stevenson, Lee, & Stigler, 1986). At that time, the American students at both grade levels lagged far behind the other two countries in mathematics and came in second in reading. A decade later, when the study was repeated with a new group of fifth-graders, the researchers discovered that the American students fared even worse than they had earlier. In 1990, the research team also studied the original first-graders from all three cultures, now in the eleventh grade. The result? The American students retained their low standing in mathematics compared with the Asian students.

Having established that the performance of the children from these three cultures was, in fact, different, the next question was why. One explanation advanced by Stevenson's team suggested that cultural attitudes toward ability and effort might, in part, be responsible. To test this hypothesis, Stevenson and his colleagues (1993) asked students, their parents, and their teachers in all three countries whether they thought effort or ability had a greater impact on academic performance. From first through eleventh grade, American students disagreed with the statement that "everyone in my class has about the same natural ability in math." In other words, the Americans thought that "studying hard" has little to do with performance. Their responses appear to reflect a belief that mathematical skill is primarily a function of innate ability. American mothers expressed a similar view. Moreover, 41 percent of the American eleventh-grade teachers thought "innate intelligence" is the most important factor in mathematics performance. By contrast, Asian students, parents, and teachers believed that effort and "studying hard" determined success in math.

Asians and Americans clearly hold different opinions concerning the origins of academic performance, and these culturally influenced views of the relative importance of effort and innate ability may have a profound effect on the way children and their parents approach the task of learning. Students who believe that learning is based on natural ability will see little value in working hard to learn a difficult subject but, students who believe that academic success comes from studying are more likely to work hard. Indeed, even the brightest students will not get far without making an effort. Although many Americans no doubt believe in the value of effort and hard work, our widespread perception of innate ability as the key to academic success may be affecting the performance of U.S. students (Stevenson, Lee, & Mu, 2000).

But there is also evidence that the nature of the educational system in the three cultures may play a crucial role. First, when the eleventh-grade American, Japanese, and Chinese schoolchildren were tested on general information that they could have learned outside of school, all three groups earned nearly identical scores. This suggests that American students are just as competent as their Asian counterparts at learning information that does not originate in the school curriculum. Second, when the students' mothers were polled, 79 percent of the American mothers thought the schools were doing a "good" or "excellent" job of educating their children. Asian mothers were more critical of their schools' performance. Third, American mothers and students were generally satisfied with students' academic performance, even though it was comparatively low.

Stevenson (1992, 1993) has proposed that the structure of the school day and the role of the teacher might also contribute to cultural differences in student performance. Asian students spend more time in school each day than American students do. However, much of this additional time is taken up by longer lunch periods, more frequent recesses, and almost universal participation in after-school clubs and activities. During the typical American school day, students have a single recess and a short lunch, then tend to leave soon after the last class ends. In Stevenson's view, the diversity of activities in Asian schools contributes to students' liking and wanting to attend school each day and, therefore, indirectly contributes to academic achievement. Moreover, teachers in Asian schools typically are better trained in educational methods, have more time to spend with students, and are required to do fewer course preparations than American teachers. As a result, Chinese and Japanese teachers have more time, energy, and skills to work closely and actively with their pupils.

In short, while Stevenson's research confirms the existence of significant differences in student performance across various cultures, the evidence suggests that these differences reflect cultural attitudes toward the importance of ability and effort and the differing nature of the school systems, not an underlying difference in intelligence across the cultures.

We have been discussing various factors that influence intelligence and achievement. But we have focused only on people within the "normal" range of intellectual functioning. We look next at the extremes of the intellectual continuum.

CHECK YOUR UNDERSTANDING

1. A look at the current literature shows that gender differences in math and verbal ability

___ a. have declined recently

___ b. have increased recently

___ c. are virtually nonexistent

2. On the whole, which of the following groups is most likely to display superior spatial ability and to fall into the extremes of the intelligence range?

___ a. men

___ b. women

___ c. middle-class men and women

3. Differences in academic performance between Asian and American students can be attributed to

___ a. cultural attitudes

___ b. greater innate ability

___ c. education systems

___ d. a and c

Answers: 1. c, 2. a, 3. d

Extremes of Intelligence

Is giftedness more than just a high IQ?

Mental retardation Condition of significantly subaverage intelligence combined with deficiencies in adaptive behavior.

The average score on intelligence tests is 100. Nearly 70 percent of the population have IQ scores between 85 and 115, and all but 5 percent have IQ scores that fall between 70 and 130. In this section, we will focus on individuals who score at the two extremes of intelligence—people with mental retardation and those who are intellectually gifted.

Mental Retardation

Mental retardation encompasses a vast array of mental deficits with a wide variety of causes, treatments, and outcomes. The American Psychiatric Association (1994) defines mental retardation as "significantly subaverage general intellectual functioning . . . that is accompanied by significant limitations in adaptive functioning" (p. 39); in addition, the condition must appear before the individual is 21 years old. This definition makes several important points. First, people with mental retardation are well below normal in intelligence (see Table 8–4). But a low IQ is not in itself sufficient for diagnosing mental retardation. The term *mental retardation* also implies an inability to perform at least some of the ordinary tasks of daily living (Wielkiewicz & Calvert, 1989). A person who is able to live independently, for example, is not considered to have mental retardation however low his or her IQ may be.

Moreover, people with mental retardation sometimes display exceptional skills in areas other than general intelligence. Probably the most dramatic and intriguing examples involve *savant performance* (Boelte, Uhlig, & Poustka, 2002). Some people with mental retardation (or other mental handicaps) exhibit remarkable abilities in highly specialized areas, such as numerical computation, memory, art, or music (Miller, 1999; O'Connor & Hermelin, 1987). Savant performances include mentally calculating large numbers almost instantly; determining the day of the week for any date over many centuries; and playing back a long musical composition after hearing it played only once.

table 8-4   MENTAL RETARDATION

Level of Retardation	IQ Range	Attainable Skill Level
Mild	Low 50s–70s	The individual may be able to function adequately in society. He or she can learn academic skills comparable to those of a sixth-grader and can be minimally self-supporting, although requiring special help at times of unusual stress.
Moderate	Mid 30s–low 50s	These people profit from vocational training and may be able to travel alone. They can learn on a second-grade level and perform skilled work in a sheltered workshop if provided with supervision and guidance.
Severe	Low 20s–mid 30s	Such people do not learn to talk or to practice basic hygiene until after age six. Although they cannot learn vocational skills, simple tasks can be carried out with supervision.
Profound	Below 20 or 25	Constant care is needed. Usually, people in this group have a diagnosed neurological disorder.

Source: Based on APA, DSM-IV, 1994.

Down syndrome is a common biological cause of mental retardation, affecting 1 in 600 newborns. The prognosis for Down syndrome children today is much better than it was in the past. With adequate support, many children with the affliction can participate in regular classrooms and other childhood activities.

Causes What causes mental retardation, and what can be done to overcome it? In most cases, the causes are simply not known (Beirne-Smith, Patton, & Ittenbach, 1994). This is especially true of mild retardation, which accounts for nearly 90 percent of all cases. Where causes can be identified, most often they stem from a wide variety of genetic, environmental, social, nutritional, and other risk factors (Baumeister & Baumeister, 2000).

About 25 percent of cases, especially the more severe forms of retardation, appear to involve genetic or biological disorders. More than 100 single genetic traits that can result in mental retardation have been identified (Plomin, 1997). One such cause is the genetically based disease *phenylketonuria*, or *PKU*. In people suffering from PKU, the liver fails to produce an enzyme necessary for early brain development. PKU occurs in about 1 out of 25,000 people (Minton & Schneider, 1980). Fortunately, early dietary intervention—which involves removing *phenylalanine* from the diet—can prevent the symptoms of mental retardation from developing. Another cause of severe mental retardation is chromosomal abnormality. For example, babies with *Down syndrome* are born with defects on part of chromosome 21 (see the photo on page 79). Down syndrome is named for the nineteenth-century British physician Langdon Down, who first described the symptoms. It is marked by moderate to severe mental retardation and also by a characteristic pattern of physical deformities, including skinfolds on the hands, feet, and eyelids.

Another common type of mental retardation is *fragile X syndrome* (Hagerman & Hagerman, 2002). This disorder, which affects about 1 in every 1,250 males and 1 in every 2,500 females, is hereditary (Plomin, 1997): A defect in a single gene on the X chromosome is passed on from one generation to the next (Hoffman, 1991). Since boys have only one X chromosome while girls have two, boys are more likely to be severely affected by this defective gene. While most boys with fragile X have mental retardation, most girls with fragile X do not experience significant intellectual impairment.

Although little can be done to reverse the biological conditions that cause many cases of severe mental retardation, the effects of retardation can be moderated through education and training (Ramey, Ramey, & Lanzi, 2001). For people with no physical impairment but with a history of social and educational deprivation, education and social contact may have a dramatic impact. Today the majority of students with mental retardation are educated in local school systems through a process called *mainstreaming*, which helps these students to socialize with their nondisabled peers (Lipsky & Gartner, 1996; Schroeder, Schroeder, & Landesman, 1987). The principle of mainstreaming, also known as *inclusion* (Kavale, 2002), has also been applied to programs for adults with mental retardation, by taking them out of large, impersonal institutions and placing them in smaller community homes that offer a greater opportunity for normal life experiences and personal growth (Anderson, Prouty, & Lakin, 1999; Conroy, 1996; Landesman & Butterfield, 1987; Maisto & Hughes, 1995; Stancliffe, 1997).

Giftedness

At the other extreme of the intelligence scale are "the gifted"—those with exceptional mental abilities as measured by scores on intelligence tests. As with mental retardation, the causes of **giftedness** are not fully understood (Winner, 2000).

The first and now-classic study of giftedness was begun by Lewis Terman and his colleagues in the early 1920s. Terman (1925) conducted the first major research study in which giftedness was defined in terms of academic talent and measured by an IQ in the top two percent of the population. Most current definitions of giftedness have moved away from simply equating it with a high IQ, broadening it to include such things as creativity and motivation (Csikszentmihalyi, Rathunde, & Whalen, 1993; Robinson & Clinkenbeard, 1998; Subotnik & Arnold, 1994).

Giftedness Refers to superior IQ combined with demonstrated or potential ability in such areas as academic aptitude, creativity, and leadership.

Renzulli (1978), for instance, proposed thinking of gifted-ness as the interaction of above-average general ability, exceptional creativity, and high levels of commitment. Sternberg and Davidson (1985) defined giftedness as especially effective use of what we earlier called the ana-lytical aspects of intelligence: planning, allocating resources, acquiring new knowledge, and carrying out tasks effectively.

People have used various criteria to identify gifted stu-dents, including scores on intelligence tests, teacher rec-ommendations, and achievement test results. School systems generally use diagnostic testing, interviews, and evaluation of academic and creative work (Sattler, 1992). These selection methods can identify students with a broad range of talent, but they can miss students with spe-cific abilities, such as a talent for mathematics or music. This is important because research suggests that most gifted individuals display special abilities in only a few areas. "Globally" gifted people are rare (Achter, Lubinski, & Benbow, 1996; Lubinski & Benbow, 2000; Winner, 1998, 2000).

A common view of the gifted is that they have poor social skills and are emotionally maladjusted. However, research does not support this stereotype (Robinson & Clinkenbeard, 1998). Indeed, one review (Janos & Robinson, 1985) concluded that "Being intellectually gifted, at least at moderate levels of ability, is clearly an asset in terms of psychosocial adjustment in most situa-tions" (p. 181). Nevertheless, children who are exceptionally gifted sometimes do experience difficulty "fitting in" with their peers.

Because gifted children sometimes become bored and socially isolated in regular classrooms, some experts recommend that they be offered special programs (Olzewski-Kubilius, 2003; Winner, 1997). But not everyone supports this idea. Some ask, "Who is to say what kinds of talents qualify a student for special treat-ment: math, science, music, art, poetry, logic, chess?" Other critics are concerned that gifted minority students will not be identified as gifted, and so not benefit from the program (Baldwin, 1985), although special tests have been devised to meet this concern (Bruch, 1971; Mercer & Lewis, 1978). Others complain that singling out certain students as gifted is elitist: It puts these students on the fast track, leaving others behind. Finally, although there are many gifted programs, there is little hard evidence that gifted students benefit from them (Reis, 1989).

Definitions of giftedness have recently broadened beyond high scores on IQ tests. These young people at the Moscow School of Music, for exam-ple, have demonstrated exceptional musical abilities. They are consid-ered gifted in their own country, as they would be in ours.

ENDURING ISSUES   **diversity**universality

Not Everyone Wants to Be Special

Special classes for the gifted would seem to be something the gifted themselves would want, but this is not always the case. Special classes, and even more, special schools, can separate gifted students from their friends and neighbors. And stereo-types about the gifted may mean that, once identified as gifted, the student is less likely to be invited to participate in certain school activities, such as dances, plays, and sports. Gifted students also sometimes object to being set apart, labeled "brains," and pressured to perform beyond the ordinary. Many gifted students wel-come the opportunities offered by special programs, but not all do.

Any discussion of giftedness inevitably leads to the topic of creativity. The two topics are, indeed, closely related, as we shall see in the next section.

CHECK YOUR UNDERSTANDING

1. The IQ scores of what percentage of the population fall between 85 and 115?

___ a. nearly 50 percent

___ b. nearly 60 percent

___ c. nearly 70 percent

___ d. nearly 80 percent

2. A mistaken but common view of the gifted is that they are

___ a. socially inept

___ b. often bored

___ c. emotionally maladjusted

___ d. a and c

3. Some known causes of mental retardation include

___ a. PKU

___ b. Down syndrome

___ c. fragile-X syndrome

___ d. all the above

Answers: 1. c, 2. d, 3. d

Creativity

What is the relationship between creativity and intelligence?

Creativity is the ability to produce novel and socially valued ideas or objects. The ideas and objects may range from philosophy to painting, from music to mousetraps so long as they are novel and socially valued (Mumford & Gustafson, 1988; Sternberg, 1996, 2001). The effort to understand creativity began with an attempt to identify the relationship between creativity and intelligence.

Creativity and Intelligence

Some researchers believe that creativity is simply one aspect of intelligence. For example, the study by Sternberg and his associates (1981), mentioned earlier in the chapter, found that experts on intelligence generally placed creativity under the heading of verbal intelligence (see Table 8–1). Sternberg also includes creativity and insight as important elements in the creative component of human intelligence.

Although some psychologists believe that creativity is one aspect of intelligence (Szobiova, 2001), most IQ tests do not measure creativity, and many researchers in the area of cognitive abilities would argue that intelligence and creativity are not the same thing. What, then, is the relationship between intelligence and creativity? For instance, are people who score high on IQ tests likely to be more creative than those who score low?

Creativity The ability to produce novel and socially valued ideas or objects.

Early studies typically found little or no relationship between creativity and intelligence (e.g., Getzels & Jackson, 1962; Wing, 1969). Critics pointed out, however, that these early studies examined only bright students. The average IQ of the students tested by Getzels and Jackson, for example, was 132. Perhaps creativity and intelligence are linked until IQ reaches a certain level, or threshold, after which there is little or no relationship between them. This is called the *threshold theory* and there is considerable evidence to support it. One study found that intelligence and creativity correlated .88 for people with IQ scores below 90, .69 for those with IQ scores ranging from 90 to 110, −.30 for those with IQ scores between 110 and 130, and −.09 for those with IQ scores above 130. In other words, intelligence was important up to an IQ of 110, but above this threshold there was little or no relationship between IQ and creativity. Other studies have borne out these findings (Barron, 1963; Yamamoto & Chimbidis, 1966). All of these studies relied heavily on tests of creativity, but other studies of people who have demonstrated outstanding creativity in their lives also support the threshold theory. These studies (e.g., Bachtold & Werner, 1973; Barron, 1963; Cattell, 1971; Helson, 1971) show that creative people tend to be highly intelligent; that is, highly creative artists, writers, scientists, and mathematicians tend, as a group, to score high on intelligence tests. But for individuals in this special group, there is little relationship between IQ scores and levels of creative achievement, just as the threshold theory would predict. Thus, a certain level of intelligence appears to be a necessary, but not sufficient, condition for creative work (Amabile, 1983).

The highly imaginative costuming and staging of the Broadway musical *The Lion King* is one example of creativity: the ability to produce novel and socially valued ideas. Is a person who is extremely creative also more intelligent than most other people? Researchers are still exploring the relationship between creativity and intelligence. But it seems as if a certain threshold level of intelligence is needed for high creativity to develop.

Interestingly, creative people are often *perceived* as being more intelligent than less creative people who have equivalent IQ scores. Perhaps some characteristic that creative people share—possibly "effectiveness" or some quality of social competence—conveys the impression of intelligence even though it is not measured by intelligence tests (Barron & Harrington, 1981).

Creativity Tests

Measuring creativity poses special problems (Naglieri & Kaufman, 2001). Because creativity involves original responses to situations, it is difficult to measure with questions that can be answered true or false, a or b. More open-ended items are often better: Instead of asking for one predetermined answer to a problem, the test taker is asked to think of as many answers as possible. Scores are based on the number and originality of the person's answers.

In one such test, the *Torrance Test of Creative Thinking*, people are asked to explain what is happening in a picture, how the scene came about, and what its consequences are likely to be. The *Christensen-Guilford Test* asks people to list as many words containing a given letter as possible; to name things belonging to a particular category—such as liquids that will burn; and to write four-word sentences beginning with the letters RDLS—"Rainy days look sad, Red dogs like soup, Renaissance dramas lack symmetry," and so on.

One of the most widely used creativity tests, S. A. Mednick's (1962) *Remote Associates Test (RAT)*, asks people to give a single verbal response that relates to a set of three apparently unrelated words. For example, the three stimulus words might be *poke, go,* and *molasses.* A desirable response—although not the only possible one—relates them through the word *slow: slowpoke, go slow, slow as molasses.* Arriving at such responses is not easy, especially because the stimulus words have no apparent connection to one another.

The newer *Wallach and Kogan Creative Battery* focuses on having the person form associative elements into new combinations that meet specific requirements. Children are asked to "name all the round things you can think of," and to find similarities between objects such as a potato and a carrot. Although people who do not have high IQ scores can score well on the Wallach and Kogan test, the Torrance test seems to require a reasonably high IQ for adequate performance. Current tests of creativity do not show a high degree of criterion-related validity (Feldhusen & Goh, 1995), so measurements derived from them must be interpreted with caution.

CHECK YOUR UNDERSTANDING

1. The ability to produce unique ideas and objects is termed

___ a. emotional intelligence

___ b. creativity

___ c. tacit knowledge

___ d. verbal ability

2. Indicate whether the following sentences are true (T) or false (F).

___ a. New tests developed to measure creativity are nearly always valid.

___ b. Highly intelligent people are almost always highly creative.

___ c. Creativity demands a minimum level of intelligence.

___ d. Most intelligence tests do not measure creativity.

Answers: 1. b, 2. a—F; b—F; c—T; d—T

Answers to Chapter Opening Questions

1. Idleness generally means the state of being inactive, not busy, unoccupied; laziness generally means an unwillingness or reluctance to work. Laziness is one possible cause of idleness, but not the only cause.

2. If you face west, your right hand will be toward the north.

3. Obliterate means to erase or destroy something completely, without a trace.

4. Both an hour and a week are measures of time.

5. Alternative (e) makes the most sense. The phrase "despite an outward" implies that the words in the blanks should form a contrast of some sort. Acquiescence (agreeing, consenting without protest) certainly contrasts with thwarting (opposing, hindering, obstructing).

6. Alternative (f) is the correct pattern.

7. The opposite of hate is love (c).

8. 75 cents will buy nine pencils.

9. Union (b) is most nearly opposite in meaning to schism. Union means a uniting or joining of several parts into a whole; schism means a splitting apart or dividing of something that was previously united.

10. Alternative (d) is correct. Each sector starts where the previous sector left off and extends 45 degrees clockwise around the circle.

11. Alternative (d) is correct. A crutch is used to help someone who has difficulty with locomotion; spectacles are used to help someone who has difficulty with vision.

12. Alternative (b) is correct. In each case, the figure is made up of three shapes that are identical except for their size; the largest shape goes on the bottom and the smallest on top, with no overlapping between the shapes.

13. Alternative (d) is correct. The second figure is the same shape and size but with diagonal cross-hatching from upper left to lower right.

14. Figures 3, 4, and 5 can all be completely covered by using some or all of the given pieces.

summary

This chapter examines **intelligence,** or general intellectual ability, whether actual or potential, which is measured by **intelligence tests.**

Considerable disagreement exists over what specific mental abilities should be considered signs of intelligence. In the early 1980s, Sternberg and his associates discovered that both experts and nonexperts described an intelligent person as someone with practical problem-solving ability and verbal ability, but laypersons included social competence in their concepts of intelligence. Many experts now list creativity and the ability to adapt to the environment as crucial components of intelligence.

Theories of Intelligence

Intelligence theorists fall into two categories. In one group are those who argue for a "general intelligence," a single, general aptitude or ability. In the other are those who believe that intelligence is composed of many separate and distinct aptitudes or abilities.

Early Theories: Spearman, Thurstone, and Cattell   Spearman believed that intelligence is general: People who are bright in one area are bright in other areas as well. Thurstone disagreed: He believed that intelligence encompasses seven mental abilities that are relatively independent of one another.

In contrast, Cattell divided mental abilities into two clusters. The first is crystallized intelligence, or abilities such as reasoning and the verbal and numerical skills that are stressed in school. The second is fluid intelligence, or skills such as spatial and visual imagery, the ability to notice visual details, and rote memory.

Contemporary Theories: Sternberg, Gardner, and Goleman   In the mid-1980s, Yale psychologist Robert Sternberg proposed a **triarchic theory of intelligence** that includes a much broader range of skills and abilities. According to this theory, there are three basic kinds of intelligence: **analytical intelligence,** the mental processes emphasized by most theories of intelligence, such as the ability to acquire new knowledge and carry out tasks efficiently; **creative intelligence,** the ability to adjust to new tasks, use new concepts, gain insight, and adapt creatively; and **practical intelligence,** which is seen in people who are good at capitalizing on their strengths and compensating for their weaknesses.

Howard Gardner has proposed a **theory of multiple intelligences,** which asserts that intelligence is made up of eight distinct abilities *logical-mathematical, linguistic, spatial, musical, bodily-kinesthetic, interpersonal, intrapersonal, and naturalistic*—each of which is relatively independent of the others.

Daniel Goleman's theory of **emotional intelligence** refers to how effectively people perceive and understand their own emotions and those of others and can manage their emotional behavior.

Comparing the Theories   Spearman's view of general intelligence is the simplest of the formal theories of intelligence. Thurstone and Cattell attempted to identify the structure of mental abilities in more detail. Sternberg and Gardner's theories both emphasize practical abilities. Goleman broadens the concept of intelligence considerably by emphasizing the ways in which people perceive and manage emotions.

Intelligence Tests

The Stanford-Binet Intelligence Scale   The **Binet-Simon Scale,** the first test of intelligence, was developed in France by Alfred Binet and Theodore Simon for testing children. Originally issued in 1905, it consisted of 30 tests arranged in order of increasing difficulty. From the average scores of children, Binet developed the concept of mental age.

The best-known Binet adaptation, created by Stanford University's L. M. Terman in 1916, is the **Stanford-Binet Intelligence Scale.** Terman introduced the term **intelligence quotient (IQ),** which is a numerical value given to scores on an intelligence test (a score of 100 corresponds to average intelligence).

The Stanford-Binet is designed to measure skills in four areas: verbal reasoning, abstract/visual reasoning, quantitative reasoning, and short-term memory.

The Wechsler Intelligence Scales   The **Wechsler Adult Intelligence Scale–Third Edition (WAIS–III)** was developed by David Wechsler especially for adults. The test measures both verbal and performance abilities. Wechsler also created the **Wechsler Intelligence Scale for Children–Third Edition (WISC–III),** which is meant to be used with school–aged children. It measures verbal and performance abilities separately, though it also yields an overall IQ.

Group Tests   **Group tests** are administered by one examiner to many people at one time. Group tests are most commonly used by schools. The California Test of Mental Maturity (CTMM) and the SAT are group tests.

Group tests aim to overcome the problems of time and expense associated with individual tests and to eliminate bias on the part of the examiner. However, in a group setting the examiner is less likely to notice whether an individual test taker is tired, ill, or confused by the directions. Emotionally disturbed children and people who have less experience taking tests usually do better on individual tests than on group tests.

Performance and Culture-Fair Tests   Some intelligence tests may discriminate against members of certain cultural or ethnic groups. **Performance tests** are intelligence tests that do not involve language, so they can be useful for testing people who lack a strong command of English. The Seguin Form Board, the Porteus Maze, and the Bayley Scales of Infant Development are performance tests.

Culture-fair tests are designed to eliminate cultural bias by minimizing skills and values that vary from one culture to another. The Goodenough-Harris Drawing Test, Cattell's Culture-Fair Intelligence Test, and the Progressive Matrices are examples of culture-fair tests.

What Makes a Good Test?

Psychologists use reliability and validity as measures of a test's quality, and for purposes of comparing different tests.

Reliability   **Reliability** is the ability of a test to produce dependable and consistent scores. The simplest way to determine a test's reliability is to give the test to a group and then, after a short time, give it again to the same group. If the group scores the same each time, the test is reliable. The problem with this way of determining reliability is that the group may have remembered the answers from the first testing. One method of eliminating this *practice effect* is to use alternative forms of the test and check the consistency of people's scores on both forms. If the scores agree, the test is said to have **split-half reliability.** Psychologists express reliability in terms of **correlation coefficients,** which measure the relationship between two sets of scores. The reliability of intelligence tests is about .90; that is, scores remain fairly stable across repeated testing.

Validity   **Validity** is the ability of a test to measure what it has been designed to measure. **Content validity** exists if a test contains an adequate sample of questions relating to the skills or knowledge it is supposed to measure. In general, most intelligence tests assess many of the abilities considered to be components of intelligence: planning, memory, language comprehension, and writing. However, a single test may not cover all the areas of intelligence, and tests differ in their emphasis on the abilities they do measure.

Criterion-related validity refers to the relationship between test scores and independent measures of whatever the test is designed to measure. In the case of intelligence, the most common independent measure is academic achievement. Despite their differences in surface content, most intelligence tests are good predictors of academic success. Based on this criterion, these tests seem to have adequate criterion-related validity.

Criticisms of Intelligence Tests   Much of the criticism of intelligence tests has focused on their content. Critics point out that most intelligence tests are concerned with only a narrow set of skills and may, in fact, measure nothing more than the ability to take tests. Critics also maintain that the content and administration of IQ tests are shaped by the values of Western middle-class society and that, as a result, they may discriminate against minorities. IQ tests are also criticized because the results are often used to label some students as slow learners. Finally, IQ tests do not offer information on motivation, emotion, attitudes, and other similar factors that may have a strong bearing on a person's success in school and in life.

Other critics hold that intelligence is far too complex to be precisely measured by tests. IQ tests are also criticized for neglecting to account for social influences on a person's performance. According to recent reviews of the evidence, intelligence tests are good predictors of success on the job.

What Determines Intelligence?

Heredity   Historically, research on the determinants of intelligence has focused on identical twins—some reared together, others reared apart in separate households. The correlation between the IQ scores of all identical twins is usually very high, indicating that their identical genetic inheritance is a more powerful determinant of intelligence than their experiences. But critics of this research make several strong points: (1) It is difficult to find identical twins who have been separated at birth, so that there are only a few such studies; (2) identical twins tend to be placed in households similar in socioeconomic background to those of their biological parents; and (3) even twins separated at birth have had nearly identical prenatal experiences.

Environment   Considerable evidence suggests that environment is a factor in the development of superior intellectual ability. Even though certain mental abilities are inherited, without the necessary stimulation a child's intelligence will not develop. This finding is important because lower-income families don't have access to the kinds of resources that other families do. Significantly, when they are placed in more stimulating environments, economically deprived children show an improvement in their level of intelligence. For example, lower-income children raised in middle-class homes display significant gains in IQ compared with their counterparts growing up in low-income households. Finally, intervention programs can significantly increase intelligence.

Heredity vs. Environment: Which Is More Important?   Accounting for group differences in IQ poses a vexing problem in psychology. Group differences in IQ test scores might be due to environmental factors, differences *within* racial groups could be due primarily to genetics, and the IQ test score of particular individuals would therefore reflect the effects of both heredity and environment.

Mental Abilities and Human Diversity

Gender   Overall, women and men do not differ significantly in general intelligence as measured by scores on standardized tests. Women may show a slight advantage in mathematical computation skills and men a slight advantage in spatial ability.

Culture   Differences in academic performance between American and Asian students are found from first grade through high school in mathematics and reading. Extensive research by Stevenson suggests that at least some of these differences may be related to cultural attitudes toward ability and effort, as well as to the nature of the educational system in different cultures.

Extremes of Intelligence

The IQ scores of nearly 70 percent of the general population fall between 85 and 115, and all but 5 percent of the population have IQ scores between 70 and 130. Individuals with mental retardation and those who are gifted score at the two extremes of intelligence.

Mental Retardation   **Mental retardation** is defined as significantly subaverage general intellectual functioning that is accompanied by significant limitations in adaptive functioning. The condition includes a range of mental deficits with a wide variety of causes, treatments, and outcomes. Varying degrees of mental retardation range from mild to profound. In addition to having a low IQ, to be considered mentally retarded, a person must lack skills essential for independent daily living.

In most cases, the causes of mental retardation are not known. Where causes can be identified, the majority of cases involve a variety of environmental, social, nutritional, and other risk factors.

About 25 percent of mental retardation cases can be traced to genetic or biological causes, including PKU, Down syndrome, and fragile-X syndrome.

Giftedness   **Giftedness** refers to superior IQ combined with exceptional creativity and high levels of commitment. The recent movement to identify gifted children in schools has come under criticism, as have the assumptions underlying notions of giftedness. Critics say, among other things, that gifted people may not be a distinct group superior to the general population in all areas, but rather people who excel only in some areas.

Creativity

Creativity and Intelligence   **Creativity**—the ability to produce novel and socially valued ideas or objects—is regarded by some psychologists as one aspect of intelligence. But there is some disagreement about the link between creativity and intelligence. The threshold theory of the relation between intelligence and creativity states that although creativity requires a certain amount of intelligence, once intelligence rises above the threshold level, creativity and intelligence are related only moderately, if at all.

Creativity Tests   Because creativity involves original responses to situations, it is helpful to measure it with tests composed of open-ended questions. Mednick's Remote Associates Test (RAT) and the Wallach and Kogan Creative Battery are two examples of creativity tests.

key terms

Intelligence	295	Stanford-Binet Intelligence Scale	300	Reliability	304
Intelligence tests	295	Intelligence quotient (IQ)	300	Split-half reliability	305
Triarchic theory of intelligence	297	Wechsler Adult Intelligence Scale–Third		Correlation coefficients	305
Analytical intelligence	297	Edition (WAIS–III)	301	Validity	306
Creative intelligence	297	Wechsler Intelligence Scale for Children–		Content validity	306
Practical intelligence	297	Third Edition (WISC–III)	302	Criterion-related validity	306
Theory of multiple intelligences	297	Group tests	302	Mental retardation	319
Emotional intelligence	297	Performance tests	303	Giftedness	320
Binet-Simon Scale	300	Culture-fair tests	303	Creativity	322

OVERVIEW

Perspectives on Motivation
Instincts
Drive-Reduction Theory
Arousal Theory
Intrinsic and Extrinsic Motivation

Hunger and Thirst
Biological Factors
Cultural and Environmental Factors
Eating Disorders and Obesity
Thirst

Sex
Sexual Motivation

Sexual Behavior
Sexual Orientation

Other Motives
Exploration and Curiosity
Manipulation and Contact
Aggression
Achievement
Affiliation
A Hierarchy of Motives

Emotions
Basic Emotions
Theories of Emotion

**Nonverbal Communication
of Emotion**
Voice Quality
Facial Expression
Body Language
Personal Space
Explicit Acts

Gender, Culture, and Emotion
Gender and Emotion
Culture and Emotion

Motivation
and Emotion

9

lassic detective stories are usually studies of motivation and emotion. At the beginning, all we know is that a murder has been committed: After eating dinner with her family, sweet old Amanda Jones collapses and dies of strychnine poisoning. "Now, why would anyone do a thing like that?" everybody wonders. The police ask the same question, in different terms: "Who had a motive for killing Miss Jones?" In a good mystery, the answer is: "Practically everybody."

There is, for example, the younger sister—although she is 75 years old, she still bristles when she thinks of that tragic day 50 years ago when Amanda stole her sweetheart. And there is the next-door neighbor, who was heard to say that if Miss Jones's poodle trampled his peonies one more time there would be consequences. Then there is the spendthrift nephew who stands to inherit a fortune from the deceased. Finally, the parlor maid has a guilty secret that Miss Jones knew and had threatened to reveal. All four suspects were in the house on the night of the murder, had access to the poison (which was used to kill rats in the basement), and had strong feelings about Amanda Jones. All of them had a motive for killing her.

In this story, motivation and emotion are so closely intertwined that drawing distinctions between them is difficult. However, psychologists do try to separate them. A **motive** is a specific need or desire that arouses the organism and directs its behavior toward a goal. All motives are triggered by some kind of stimulus: a bodily condition, such as low levels of blood sugar or dehydration; a cue in the environment, such as a "Sale" sign; or a feeling, such as loneliness, guilt, or anger. When a stimulus induces goal-directed behavior, we say it has motivated the person.

Emotion refers to the experience of feelings such as fear, joy, surprise, and anger. Like motives, emotions also activate and affect behavior, but it is more difficult to predict the kind of behavior that a particular emotion will prompt. If a man is hungry, we can be reasonably sure that he will seek food. If, however, this same man experiences a feeling of joy or surprise, we cannot know with certainty how he will act.

The important thing to remember about both motives and emotions is that they push us to take some kind of action—from an act as drastic as murder to a habit as mundane as drumming our fingers on a table when we are nervous. Motivation occurs whether or not we are aware of it. We do not need to think about feeling hungry to make a beeline for the refrigerator or to focus on our need for achievement before we study for an exam. Similarly, we do not have to recognize consciously that we are afraid before we step back from a growling dog or to know that we are angry before raising our voice at someone. Moreover, the same motivation or emotion may produce different behaviors in different people. Ambition might motivate one person to go to law school and another to join a crime ring. Feeling sad might lead one person to cry alone and another to seek out a friend. On the other hand, the same behavior might arise from different motives or emotions. You may go to a movie because you are happy, bored, or lonely. In short, the workings of motives and emotions are very complex.

In this chapter, we will first look at some specific motives that play important roles in human behavior. Then we will turn our attention to emotions and the various ways they are expressed. We begin our discussion of motivation with a few general concepts.

THINKABOUTIT

You will find the answers to these questions in the chapter:

1. Why have psychologists moved away from instincts in explaining human behavior?

2. Why do people usually get hungry at mealtime?

3. What are the arguments for and against a biological explanation of sexual orientation?

4. Why might evolution have produced people with a strong need for affiliation?

5. How many basic emotions are there?

6. What is the most obvious indicator of emotion?

7. Are men less emotional than women?

Motive Specific need or desire, such as hunger, thirst, or achievement, that prompts goal-directed behavior.

Emotion Feeling, such as fear, joy, or surprise, that underlies behavior.

Instinct Inborn, inflexible, goal-directed behavior that is characteristic of an entire species.

Drive State of tension or arousal that motivates behavior.

Drive-reduction theory Theory that motivated behavior is aimed at reducing a state of bodily tension or arousal and returning the organism to homeostasis.

Homeostasis State of balance and stability in which the organism functions effectively.

Primary drive An unlearned drive, such as hunger, that is based on a physiological state.

Secondary drive A learned drive, such as ambition, that is not based on a physiological state.

Salmon swimming upstream to spawn provide an example of instinctive behavior. All salmon innately engage in this behavior without having to learn it from other salmon. Psychologists question whether human behavior can be explained in terms of instincts.

Perspectives on Motivation

Why have psychologists moved away from instincts in explaining human behavior?

Instincts

Early in the twentieth century psychologists were inclined to attribute behavior to **instincts**—specific, inborn behavior patterns characteristic of an entire species. Instincts motivate salmon to swim upstream to spawn and spiders to spin webs. Similarly, instincts were thought to account for much of human behavior. But by the 1920s, instinct theory began to fall out of favor as an explanation of human behavior for three reasons: (1) Most important human behavior is learned; (2) human behavior is rarely rigid, inflexible, unchanging, and found throughout the species, as is the case with instincts; and (3) ascribing every conceivable human behavior to a corresponding instinct explains nothing (calling a person's propensity to be alone an "antisocial instinct," for example, merely names the behavior without pinpointing its origins). So, after World War I, psychologists started looking for more credible explanations of human behavior.

Drive-Reduction Theory

An alternative view of motivation holds that bodily needs (such as the need for food or the need for water) create a state of tension or arousal called a **drive** (such as hunger or thirst). According to **drive-reduction theory,** motivated behavior is an attempt to reduce this unpleasant state of tension in the body and to return the body to a state of **homeostasis,** or balance. When we are hungry, we look for food to reduce the hunger drive. When we are tired, we find a place to rest. When we are thirsty, we find something to drink. In each of these cases, behavior is directed toward reducing a state of bodily tension or arousal.

According to drive-reduction theory, drives can generally be divided into two categories. **Primary drives** are unlearned, are found in all animals (including humans), and motivate behavior that is vital to the survival of the individual or species. Primary drives include hunger, thirst, and sex.

Not all motivation stems from the need to reduce or satisfy primary drives, however. Humans, in particular, are also motivated by **secondary drives,** drives that are acquired through learning. For instance, no one is born with a drive to acquire great wealth, yet many people are motivated by money. Other secondary drives include getting good grades in school and achieving career success.

Arousal Theory

Drive-reduction theory is appealing, but it cannot explain all instances of behavior. It implies, for example, that, if able, people would spend as much time as possible at rest. They would seek food when hungry, water when thirsty, and so on, but once the active drives were satisfied, they would do little. They would literally have no motivation. Yet this is obviously not the case. People work, play, chat with one another, and do all manner of things for which there is no known biological deficiency that they are striving to fulfill.

Some psychologists suggest that motivation might have more to do with arousal or

THINKING CRITICALLY

Primary Drives

Primary drives (hunger, thirst, sex) are, by definition, unlearned. But learning clearly affects how these drives are expressed. We learn how and what to eat and drink, and how to pursue a relationship with another person. Given this information, design an experiment to determine what aspects of a given drive, say hunger, are learned and which are not.

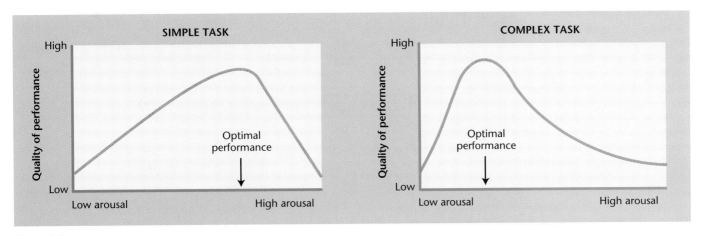

Figure 9–1
The Yerkes-Dodson law.
A certain amount of arousal is needed to perform most tasks, but a very high level of arousal interferes with the performance of complicated activities. That is, the level of arousal that can be tolerated is higher for a simple task than for a complex one.
Source: After Hebb, 1955.

state of alertness. The level of arousal at any given moment falls along a continuum from extreme alertness to sleep. **Arousal theory** suggests that each individual has an optimum level of arousal that varies from one situation to another and over the course of the day. According to the theory, behavior is motivated by the desire to maintain the optimum level of arousal for a given moment. Sometimes behavior seems to be motivated by a desire to reduce the state of arousal. For example, when you are sleepy, you are likely to turn off the television and turn off the light. Other times behavior appears to be motivated by a desire to increase the state of arousal. For example, when you are bored, you may turn on the television, take a walk, or call a friend.

Not surprisingly, an individual's arousal level affects how well he or she performs in different situations. However, there is no single answer to what is the best level of arousal necessary to perform all tasks. The **Yerkes-Dodson law** puts it this way: The more complex the task, the lower the level of arousal that can be tolerated without interfering with performance. Thus, higher levels of arousal are optimal when one is required to perform simple tasks, and relatively lower levels of arousal are best when performing complex tasks (see Figure 9–1).

Arousal theory has some advantages over drive-reduction theory, but neither one can readily account for some kinds of behavior. For example, many people today participate in activities that are stimulating in the extreme: rock climbing, skydiving, bungee jumping, and hang gliding. Such thrill-seeking activities do not seem to be drive-reducing nor is it clear that they done in pursuit of an optimal level of arousal. Zuckerman (1979, 1994; 2000; 2002) accounts for such activities by suggesting that *sensation seeking* is itself a basic motivation, at least some aspects of which are inherited. In general, high-sensation seekers, compared to low sensation seekers, are more likely to:

- Prefer dangerous sports like skydiving, bungee jumping, and mountain climbing;

- Choose vocations that involve an element of risk and excitement like firefighting, rescue work, or a career in emergency medicine;

- Smoke, drink heavily, and use illicit drugs (D'Silva, Grant-Harrington, Palmgreen, Donohew & Pugzles-Lorch, 2001).

- Engage in unsafe driving, (high sensation seekers also report being more likely to fall asleep at the wheel than low sensation seekers on a monotonous straight highway) (Thiffault & Bergeron, 2003);

Thrill-seeking behaviors cannot be explained by drive-reduction theory, because thrill seekers are trying to increase arousal, not reduce it. Everyone sometimes seeks to increase arousal, but thrill seekers seem to desire higher levels of arousal than most people do.

Arousal theory Theory of motivation that propose organisms seek an optimal level of arousal.

Yerkes-Dodson law States that there is an optimal level of arousal for the best performance of any task; the more complex the task, the lower the level of arousal that can be tolerated before performance deteriorates.

- Have more sexual partners and engage in more varied sexual activities;
- Be classified in school as delinquent or hyperactive (though not more aggressive) (Ang & Woo, 2003)

The Evolutionary Basis of Arousal Seeking

Some evolutionary theorists argue that the drive to seek high arousal states may have an evolutionary basis. For example, Cosmides and Tooby (2000) propose that risk-taking behavior may have played an important adaptive role for our ancestors by providing them with opportunities for limited exposure to potentially dangerous situations, and giving them a chance to develop successful strategies to deal with such dangers. Thus, early humans who took risks were potentially better equipped to cope with danger and turmoil in their environment than those who did not—making them more likely to survive and reproduce. This might help explain why some people today seek out high-risk activities such as skydiving, extreme skiing, and mountain climbing.

Still other theorists note that events outside the organism are also important in motivation. For example, bakery aromas may prompt us to eat, even if we have just finished a satisfying meal; a sample copy of a new magazine, a demonstration of a new product, or a store window display may lead us to buy something we would not have otherwise bought. In other words, objects in the environment—called **incentives**—can also motivate behavior (Bolles, 1972; Rescorla & Solomon, 1967). We need not be aware of incentives for them to affect our behavior. A person may buy something without being aware that the purchase was triggered by an advertisement in the newspaper or a magazine. Similarly, we may enter a restaurant without being aware that the aroma of food from the restaurant caused us to do so.

Intrinsic and Extrinsic Motivation

Some psychologists further distinguish between intrinsic and extrinsic motivation. **Intrinsic motivation** refers to motivation provided by an activity itself. Play is a good example. Children typically climb trees, finger paint, and play games for no other reason than the fun they get from the activity itself. In the same way, many adults solve crossword puzzles, play golf, and tinker in a workshop largely for the enjoyment they get from the activity. **Extrinsic motivation** refers to motivation that derives from the consequences of an activity. For example, a child may do chores not because he enjoys them but because doing so earns an allowance, and an adult who hates golf may play a round with a client because doing so may help close a sale.

Whether behavior is intrinsically or extrinsically motivated can have important consequences. For example, if parents offer a reward to their young daughter for writing to her grandparents, the likelihood of her writing to them when rewards are no longer available may actually decrease. One recent analysis of some 128 studies that examined the effect of extrinsic rewards on the behavior of children, adolescents, and adults found that when extrinsic rewards are offered for a behavior, intrinsic motivation and sense of personal responsibility for that behavior are likely to decrease, at least for a short time (Deci, Koestner, & Ryan, 1999, 2001).

Incentive External stimulus that prompts goal-directed behavior.

Intrinsic motivation A desire to perform a behavior that stems from the behavior performed.

Extrinsic motivation A desire to perform a behavior to obtain an external reward or avoid punishment.

However, unexpected (as opposed to contractual) rewards do not necessarily reduce intrinsic motivation, and positive feedback (including praise) may actually increase intrinsic motivation (Chance, 1992; Deci et al., 1999).

We have reviewed some basic concepts about motivation. With these concepts in mind, we now turn our attention to specific motives. We will begin with hunger. From there we will turn to sexual behavior, which is responsive to both internal states and external incentives. We then examine several motives, such as curiosity and manipulation, that depend heavily on external environmental cues. Finally, we describe several additional motives that figure prominently in human social relationships.

▬▬▬▬ CHECK YOUR UNDERSTANDING

1. All motives are triggered by some kind of

___a. emotion

___b. drive

___c. stimulus

___d. arousal

2. Match the following terms with the appropriate definition.

___ drive	a. external stimulus that prompts goal-directed behavior
___ drive reduction	b. state of balance in which the organism functions effectively
___ homeostasis	c. theory that motivated behavior aims to reduce tension
___ incentive	d. tension or arousal that motivates behavior
___ intrinsic motivation	e. behavior performed for an external reward or to avoid punishment
___ extrinsic motivation	f. motivation derived from the behavior itself

Answers: 1. c, 2. drive—d; drive reduction—c; homeostasis—b; incentive—a; intrinsic motivation—f; extrinsic motivation—e

▬▬▬

Hunger and Thirst

Why do people usually get hungry at mealtime?

When you are hungry, you eat. If you don't eat, your need for food will continue to increase but your hunger will come and go. You will probably be hungriest around mealtimes and less hungry at other times. The psychological state of hunger, then, is not the same as the biological need for food, although that need often sets the psychological state in motion.

Biological Factors

Early research established the importance of the hypothalamus as the brain center involved in hunger and eating. Initially, researchers identified two regions in the hypothalamus as controlling our experience of hunger and satiety (satiety means being full to satisfaction). One of these centers, the *lateral hypothalamus*, appeared to act as the feeding center, because when stimulated, animals began to eat, but when it was destroyed the animals stopped eating to the point of starvation. The

We do not know the precise role that the brain plays in hunger, but after lesions were made in the hypothalamus of this rat, it ate so much that its body weight tripled.

ventromedial hypothalamus, in contrast, was thought to be the satiety center, because when it was stimulated animals ceased eating, but when it was destroyed animals ate to the point of extreme obesity. The hypothalamus seemed to be a kind of "switch" that turned eating on or off, at least in rats.

However, more recent studies have challenged this simple "on-off" explanation for the control of eating by showing that a number of other areas of the brain are also involved (Winn, 1995). For instance, a third center in the hypothalamus called the *paraventricular nucleus* appears to influence the drive to eat specific foods. Studies have also shown that regions of the cerebral cortex and spinal cord play an important role in regulating food intake. Moreover, the connections among brain centers that control hunger are now known to be considerably more complex than were once thought (Blundell & Halford, 1998; Flier & Maratos-Flier, 1998; Lin, Umahara, York, & Bray, 1998; Woods, Seeley, Porte, & Schwartz, 1998).

How do these various areas of the brain know when to stimulate hunger? It turns out that the brain monitors the blood levels of *glucose* (a simple sugar used by the body for energy), fats, carbohydrates and insulin. Changes in the blood levels of these substances signal the need for food (Seeley & Schwartz, 1997). The presence of a particular hormone leptin also influences our desire to eat (Chua et al., 1996; Holtkamp et al., 2003; Leroy et al., 1996; Ravussin et al., 1997; Vaisse et al., 1996). Fat cells within our body produce leptin, which travels in the bloodstream and is sensed by the hypothalamus. High levels of leptin signal the brain to reduce appetite, or to increase the rate at which fat is burned. Research with mice suggests that a defective gene may fail to regulate the level of leptin in the brain and at least be partly responsible for obesity. Replacing this hormone in obese animals results in a rapid loss of body fat. Because leptin also appears to be involved in the human response to hunger (Ravussin et al., 1997, Holtkamp, et al., 2003), this finding may someday lead to safe and effective treatments for obesity in humans (Wauters et al., 2001).

The brain also monitors the amount and kind of food that you have eaten. Receptors in the stomach sense not only how much food the stomach is holding but also how many calories that food contains. Signals from these receptors travel to the brain. When food enters the small intestine, a hormone is released into the bloodstream and carried to the brain, where it serves as an additional source of information about the body's nutritional needs (Albus, 1989; Takaki, Nagai, Takaki, & Yanaihara, 1990).

But, as we noted earlier, a biological need for food does not always result in hunger. The sensation of hunger is the product not only of things going on in the body, but also of things going on outside the body. The smell of a cake baking in the oven, for example, may trigger the desire to eat whether the body needs fuel or not. Sometimes just looking at the clock and realizing that it is dinnertime can make us feel hungry. One intriguing line of research suggests that such external cues set off internal biological processes that mimic those associated with the need for food. For example, Rodin (1985) found that the mere sight, smell, or thought of food causes an increase in insulin production, which, in turn, lowers glucose levels in the body's cells, mirroring the body's response to a physical need for food. Thus, the aroma from a nearby restaurant may serve as more than an incentive to eat; it may actually trigger an apparent need for food.

ENDURING ISSUES   **diversity**universality

The Hunger Drive

The hunger drive is tied to emotions in complex ways. Some people head for the refrigerator whenever they are depressed, bored, anxious, or angry. Others lose all interest in food at these times and complain that they are "too upset to eat." One student studying for an important exam spends as much time eating as reading; another student studying for the same exam lives on coffee until the exam is over. Under emotionally arousing conditions, what one person craves may turn another person's stomach.

Social influences also affect our motivation to eat. Say you are at an important business lunch where you need to impress a prospective client. You may not feel very hungry, even though this lunch is taking place an hour past your usual lunchtime. Conversely, social situations may prompt you to eat even when you are not hungry. Imagine that on a day when you have slept late and eaten a large breakfast, you visit your grandparents. When you arrive, you discover, much to your dismay, that a wonderful home-cooked meal is being served in a few minutes. Although you are not at all hungry, you may decide to eat merely out of courtesy toward your grandparents.

Anorexia nervosa A serious eating disorder that is associated with an intense fear of weight gain and a distorted body image.

Cultural and Environmental Factors

How you respond when you are hungry will vary according to your experiences with food, which are mostly governed by learning and social conditioning. The majority of Americans eat three meals a day at regular intervals. A typical American family eats breakfast at 7 A.M., lunch around noon, and dinner about 6 P.M. But in Europe, people often have dinner much later in the evening. Italians, for example, rarely eat dinner before 9 P.M. Numerous studies with both humans and animals have shown that regularly eating at particular times during the day leads to the release at those times of the hormones and neurotransmitters that cause hunger (see Woods, Schwartz, Baskin, & Seeley, 2000). In other words, we get hungry around noon partly because the body "learns" that if it's noon, it's time to eat.

Culture also influences what we choose to eat and how much. Although most Americans will not eat horsemeat, it is very popular in several European countries. Some preindustrial peoples traditionally ate insect larvae, the thought of which would disgust most Americans. Yet many Americans consume pork, which violates both Islamic and Jewish dietary laws (Scupin, 1995). The environment influences what animals eat as well. Rats and chimpanzees both prefer to consume foods that they have seen eaten by other members of their species. In addition, a study with rats suggests that how hungry an animal is when it first tastes a food also influences how much it will prefer to eat that food later on, even when it is not hungry (Harris, Gorissen, Bailey, & Westbrook, 2000). So although hunger is basically a biological drive, it is not merely an internal state that we satisfy when our body tells us to. Hunger is the product of the complex interaction of both environmental and biological forces.

How and when you satisfy hunger and thirst depends on social, psychological, environmental, and cultural influences as well as on physiological needs. For example, the Japanese tea ceremony is concerned more with restoring inner harmony than with satisfying thirst. Do you think the office worker in the top photo is drinking coffee because she is thirsty?

Eating Disorders and Obesity

Anorexia Nervosa and Bulimia Nervosa   "When people told me I looked like someone from Auschwitz [the Nazi concentration camp], I thought that was the highest compliment anyone could give me." This confession comes from a young woman who as a teenager suffered from a serious eating disorder known as **anorexia nervosa.** She was 18 years old, 5 feet 3 inches tall, and weighed 68 pounds. This young woman was lucky. She managed to overcome the disorder and has since maintained normal body weight. Others are less fortunate, The world-class gymnast Christy Henrich succumbed to the disease, weighing just 61 pounds at her death (Pace, 1994).

People with anorexia nervosa perceive themselves as overweight and strive to lose weight, usually by severely limiting their intake of food. Even after they

Bulimia nervosa An eating disorder characterized by binges of eating followed by self-induced vomiting.

become very thin, they constantly worry about weight gain. The following four symptoms are used in the diagnosis of anorexia nervosa (APA, 1994):

1. Intense fear of becoming obese, which does not diminish as weight loss progresses.

2. Disturbance of body image (for example, claiming to "feel fat" even when emaciated).

3. Refusal to maintain body weight at or above a minimal normal weight for age and height.

4. In females, the absence of at least three consecutive menstrual cycles.

Approximately 1 percent of all adolescents suffer from anorexia nervosa; about 90 percent of these are white upper- or middle-class females (Rosenvinge, Borgen, & Boerresen, 1999). Generally, people suffering from anorexia enjoy an otherwise normal childhood and adolescence. They are usually successful students and cooperative, well-behaved children. They have an intense interest in food but view eating with disgust. They also have a very distorted view of their own body (Grant, Kim, & Eckert, 2002), although this characteristic is less prevalent among African-American woman with this disorder (White, Kohlmaier, Varnado, & Williamson, 2003).

Anorexia is frequently compounded by another eating disorder known as **bulimia nervosa** (Fairburn & Wilson, 1993; O'Brien, & Vincent, 2003). The following criteria are used for the diagnosis of bulimia nervosa (APA, 1994):

1. Recurrent episodes of binge eating (rapid consumption of a large amount of food, usually in less than two hours).

2. Recurrent inappropriate behaviors to try to prevent weight gain, such as self-induced vomiting.

3. The binge eating and compensatory behaviors must occur at least twice a week for three months.

4. Body shape and weight excessively influence the person's self-image.

5. The above behaviors occur at least sometimes in the absence of anorexia.

Approximately 1 to 2 percent of all adolescent females suffer from bulimia nervosa (Gotesdam & Agras, 1995). The binge-eating behavior usually begins at about age 18, when adolescents are facing the challenge of new life situations. Not surprisingly, residence on a college campus is associated with a higher incidence of bulimia (Squire, 1983). The socioeconomic group at high risk for bulimia—again, primarily upper-middle- and upper-class women—is highly represented on college campuses.

Although anorexia and bulimia are apparently much more prevalent among females than males (S. Turnbull, Ward, Treasure, Jick, & Derby, 1996), many more men are affected by these disorders than was once suspected (Al Dawi et al., 2002; Tanofsky, Wilfley, Spurrell, Welch, & Brownell, 1997). For example, in a 1992 survey of people who had graduated from Harvard University in 1982, reported cases of eating disorders had dropped by half for women over the decade but had doubled for men (Seligman, Rogers, & Annin, 1994). Interestingly, a related phenomenon called *muscle dysmorphia* appears to be on the increase among young men (Pope, 2000). Muscle dysmorphia is an obsessive concern with one's muscle size. Men with muscle dysmorphia, many of whom are well-muscled, are distressed at their perceived puniness, and spend an inordinate amount of time fretting over their diet and exercising to increase their muscle mass (Leit, Gray, & Pope, 2002).

Because studies of eating disorders have focused almost entirely on females, we know very little about what might predispose an adolescent male to develop such a disorder. Among adolescent women, several factors appear likely (Brooks-Gunn, 1993). The media promote the idea that a woman must be thin to be attractive (Crandall, 1994). How often have you seen a fashion magazine cover feature a well-proportioned woman of normal weight for her height? Perhaps because of this emphasis on weight, American women are prone to overestimate their body size (Bruch, 1980; Fallon & Rozin, 1985). One study found that over 95 percent of the female participants believed they were about one-fourth larger than they actually were in the waist, thighs, and hips (Thompson & Thompson, 1986).

Psychological factors also contribute to the risk of eating disorders (Walters & Kendler, 1995). An individual with an obsessive-compulsive disorder (see Chapter 13, Psychological Disorders) who feels personally ineffective and depends on others fits the portrait of an adolescent with an eating disorder (Phelps & Bajorek, 1991). Women with bulimia commonly have low self-esteem, are hypersensitive to social interactions (Steiger, Gauvin, Jabalpurwala, Seguin, & Stotland, 1999), and have experienced some form of clinical depression prior to the development of the eating disorder (Klingenspor, 1994; Wade, Bulik, Neale, & Kendler, 2000). Feelings of vulnerability and helplessness apparently dispose people to adopt inappropriate ways of controlling the world around them.

Anorexia and bulimia are notoriously hard to treat, and there is considerable disagreement on the most effective approach to therapy (BenTovim, 2003; Fairburn, Cooper, & Shafran, 2003). In fact, some psychologists doubt that we can ever eliminate eating disorders in a culture bombarded with the message that "thin is in." Regrettably, in many developing countries such as Taiwan, Singapore, and China, where dieting is becoming a fad, eating disorders, once little known, are now becoming a serious problem (Hsu, 1996; Lee, Chan, & Hsu, 2003).

Obesity According to the U.S. Surgeon General, obesity is the most pressing health problem in America today (Johnson, 2003). Obesity has increased by more than 50 percent during the last decade; with more than two-thirds of Americans being either overweight or obese. Even more disturbing, the rate of obesity among young people has more than tripled since 1980, with over nine million overweight adolescents in America today (see Figure 9–2). This problem is particularly serious since children and adolescents who are overweight are more likely to grow up to become overweight adults who are at an increased risk for serious diseases like hypertension, cardiovascular disease, diabetes, and sleep apnea (Nishimura, Nishimura, Hattori, Hattori, Yonekura, & Suzuki, 2003).

These two young South Korean women embody the dictum that "thin is in."

Figure 9–2
Rising obesity among American youth.
The number of overweight children and adolescents has increased sharply in recent years. From 1980 to 2000, the percentage of adolescents who are overweight has tripled. This trend is particularly disturbing since overweight children and adolescents are likely to become overweight adults, placing them at increased risk for cardiovascular disease, hypertension, and diabetes.
Source: CDC/NCHS, NHES and NHANES.

NOTES: Excludes pregnant women starting with 1971–74. Pregnancy status not available for 1963–65 and 1966–70. Data for 1963–65 are for children 6–11 years of age; data for 1966–70 are for adolescents 12–17 years of age, not 12–19 years.

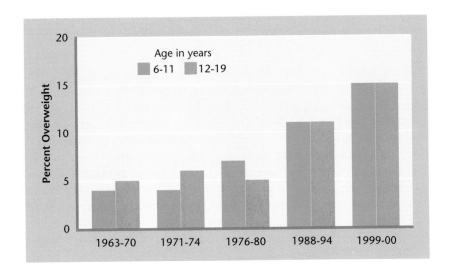

APPLYING PSYCHOLOGY

THE SLOW (BUT LASTING) FIX FOR WEIGHT GAIN

The study of hunger and eating has led to some interesting insights into the problem of weight control. It appears that our bodies are genetically "set" to maintain a certain weight (Bennett & Gurin, 1982). Thus, according to this *set point theory,* if you consume more calories than you need for that weight, your metabolic rate will go up, and you will feel an increase in energy that will prompt you to be more active, thereby burning more calories. If you eat fewer calories than you need for your weight, your metabolic rate will go down, and you will feel tired and become less active, thereby burning fewer calories. This mechanism was no doubt helpful during the thousands of years that our species lived literally hand-to-mouth, but it is less helpful where food is abundant, as in modern industrialized nations.

"People want quick fixes, so they often go overboard on dieting or exercise, sometimes with disastrous consequences."

An implication of our current understanding of hunger and weight regulation is that a successful weight-control program must be long-term and must work with, rather than against, the body's normal tendency to maintain weight. It should be undertaken only after consultation with a doctor. Based on studies of the hunger drive and the relationship between eating and body weight, here is our formula for weight control:

1. First, check with your doctor before you start. People want quick fixes, so they often go overboard on dieting or exercise, sometimes with disastrous consequences. Make sure your weight loss program will be safe.

2. Increase your body's metabolism through regular exercise. The most effective metabolism raiser is 20–30 minutes of moderate activity several times a week.

Only about 200–300 calories are burned off during each exercise session (Craighead, 1990), but the exercise increases the resting metabolic rate. This means that you burn more calories when not exercising. Thus, exercise is an important part of a weight reduction program (Wadden et al., 1997).

3. Modify your diet. A moderate reduction in calories is beneficial. Also reduce your consumption of fats (particularly saturated fats) and sugars. Sugars trigger an increase in the body's level of insulin, and high levels of fat and insulin in the blood stimulate hunger.

4. Reduce external cues that encourage you to eat undesirable foods. The mere sight or smell of food can increase the amount of insulin in the body, thus triggering hunger. Many people find that if they do their grocery shopping on a full stomach, it is easier to resist the temptation to buy junk foods.

5. Set realistic goals. Focus at least as much on preventing weight gain as on losing weight. If you must lose weight, try to shed just one pound a week for two or three months, then concentrate on maintaining that new, lower weight for several months before moving on to further weight loss.

6. Reward yourself—in ways unrelated to food—for small improvements. Use some of the behavior-modification techniques described in Chapter 5: Reward yourself not only for each pound of weight lost but also for each day or week that you maintain that weight loss. And remember, the only way you can keep the weight off is by continuing to adhere to a reasonable diet and exercise plan (Abdel, 2003; McGuire, Wing, Klem, Lang, & Hill, 1999).

To learn more about weight control visit our website at www.prenhall.com/morris.

Many factors contribute to overeating and obesity (Fairburn & Brownell, 2002). Some people inherit a tendency to be overweight (Bulik, Sullivan, & Kendler, 2003; Yanovski & Yanovski, 2002). Children born to two obese parents are seven times more likely to become obese than children born to parents of normal weight. A more sedentary lifestyle, where children are more likely to watch television and play video games than play tag or dodge ball, contributes to the problem. Abundant opportunities and encouragement to overeat in American culture are also factors. Portion size has increased in recent years, as has the constant availability of food from vending machines and fast food restaurants. In contrast to anorexia nervosa and bulimia nervosa, obesity is more prevalent among poor black women than among white women with higher incomes (White, Kohlmaier, Varnado, & Williamson, 2003).

Adding to the medical difficulties that accompany obesity, overweight people often face ridicule and discrimination resulting in significant economic, social, and educational loss (Waite, 1995). Despite federal laws prohibiting employment bias against people who are overweight, studies have shown they are nevertheless discriminated against in school and in the work place. For example, in one study overweight women reported feelings of lowered self-confidence and being victimized in school and in the work place because of their weight (Rothblum, Brand, Miller, & Oetjen, 1990). In another study, obese male lawyers were found to earn less than male lawyers of normal weight (Saporta & Halpern, 2002). Thus, it is not surprising that men and woman who are overweight are more likely to be plagued by feelings of lowered self-esteem and helplessness (Johnson, 2002). Even children who are overweight, display increased rates of behavior problems including aggression, lack of discipline, immaturity, anxiety, and depression when compared to their normal weight peers (Yang & Chen, 2001).

With all of the problems associated with being overweight, it is not surprising that so many people are constantly trying to lose weight. While there are no quick fixes to weight loss, see *Applying Psychology: The Slow (but Lasting) Fix for Weight Gain*, for some suggestions on how to lose weight and keep it off.

Thirst

Like hunger, thirst is stimulated by both internal and external cues. Internally, thirst is controlled by two regulators that interact and complement each other. One monitors the level of fluids inside the cells of the body, prompting activation of the thirst drive when the cells become dehydrated. The other thirst regulator monitors the amount of fluid outside the cells. When the level of extracellular fluid drops, less blood flows to the kidneys, which, in turn, releases a substance into the bloodstream that triggers the thirst drive (Epstein, Fitzsimmons, & Simmons, 1969).

Just as we become hungry in response to external cues, research with rats has shown that the experience of thirst is also affected by environmental factors (W. G. Hall, Arnold, & Myers, 2000; Rowland, 2002). We sometimes get thirsty when we see a TV commercial featuring people savoring tall, cool drinks in a lush, tropical setting. Seasonal customs and weather conditions also affect our thirst-quenching habits: Ice-cold lemonade is a summer staple, whereas hot chocolate warms cold winter nights.

CHECK YOUR UNDERSTANDING

1. Identify which of the following stimulate hunger.

___a. the hormone leptin

___b. glucose in the blood

___c. the smell of a baking cake

___d. all the above

2. Match the following terms with the appropriate definition.

___hypothalamus	a. intense fear of weight gain and distorted body image
___anorexia nervosa	b. portion of the brain that contains a hunger and satiety center
___bulimia nervosa	c. binge eating followed by self-induced vomiting

Answers: 1. d, 2. hypothalamus—b; anorexia nervosa—a; bulimia nervosa—c

Testosterone The primary male sex hormone.

Sex

What are the arguments for and against a biological explanation of sexual orientation?

Sex is the primary drive that motivates reproductive behavior. Like the other primary drives, it can be turned on and off by biological conditions in the body and by environmental cues. But it differs from them in one important way: Hunger and thirst are vital to the survival of the individual, but sex is vital only to the survival of the species.

Sexual Motivation

Among lower animals, sexual activity is largely controlled by hormones and is tied to the female's reproductive cycle. Thus it was reasonable to assume that fluctuations in the level of hormones such as **testosterone**—the male sex hormone—determined the human sex drive as well. Today, however, we realize that hormonal influences on human sexual behavior are considerably more complex. Unlike lower animals, humans are capable of sexual arousal at any time. And while testosterone plays a role in early sexual development (such as the onset of puberty), the differentiation of male and female sex organs, and to some extent characteristic patterns of adult sexual behavior (Kalat, 1988), moment-to-moment fluctuations in testosterone levels are not necessarily linked to sex drive. In fact, adult males who have been castrated (resulting in a significant decrease in testosterone levels) often report little decrease in sex drive (Persky, 1983).

The brain exerts a powerful influence on the sex drive, too. In particular, the limbic system, located deep within the brain, is involved in sexual excitement (see Chapter 2, Biological Basis of Behavior). When experimenters implanted electrodes into the limbic system of male monkeys, they located three areas that, when stimulated, caused erections (Hyde, 1982). Two people who had electrodes placed in their limbic systems for therapeutic reasons reported sexual pleasure when the electrodes were electrically stimulated (Heath, 1972).

Finally, like other primary drives, the sex drive is affected by external stimuli. For example, many animals secrete substances called *pheromones* that promote sexual readiness in potential partners (see Chapter 3, Sensation and Perception). Some indirect evidence suggests that humans, too, secrete pheromones, in the sweat glands of the armpits and in the genitals and that they may influence human sexual attraction (Thornhill & Gangestad, 1999; Wedeking, Seebeck, Bettens, & Paepke, 1995). But humans are susceptible to a much wider variety of external, sexual stimulants than are other animals. The sight of one's lover, the smell of perfume or aftershave lotion—both of these can stimulate sexual excitement. Soft lights and music often have an aphrodisiac effect. One person may be unmoved by an explicit pornographic movie but aroused by a romantic love story, whereas another may respond in just the opposite way. The human sexual response is also affected by social experience, sexual experience, nutrition, emotions—particularly feelings about one's sex partner—and age. In fact, just thinking about or having fantasies about sex can lead to sexual arousal in humans (Laan, Everaerd, van Berlo, & Rijs, 1995; Leitenberg & Henning, 1995). Ideas about what is moral, appropriate, and pleasurable also influence our sexual behavior.

THINKING CRITICALLY

The Sex Drive

The sex drive is said to have no survival value for the individual; its only value is the survival of the species. Suppose that humans were capable of reproducing, but no longer had a sex drive. How would life be different? In answering that question, would it help to collect data on people alive today who, for one reason or another, have lost their sex drive? Are there ways in which information from such people might *not* be useful to you?

Men and women tend to be sexually aroused in different ways. In general, men are more aroused by visual cues, whereas women respond more to touch (Schulz, 1984). A man may be aroused to erection simply by watching his partner undress, but a woman may need to have her body caressed to achieve the same state of arousal. In addition, although descriptions or scenes of sexual activity are arousing to both men and women (Koukounas & Over, 1997; Laan, Everaerd, & Evers, 1995), the rate of arousal in women is slow compared with the instantaneous response that often occurs in males (Christensen, 1986). The focus of interest also differs for males and females: Men tend to favor viewing close-ups of sexual acts, whereas women respond more to style, setting, and mood. When it comes to thinking about sex, more than half of men say that they think about sex every day or several times a day, whereas only 19 percent of women report thinking about sex so often (Lewin, 1994b).

Finally, culture guides our views of sexual attractiveness. Culture and experience may influence the extent to which we find particular articles of clothing or body shapes sexually arousing. In some cultures, most men prefer women with very large breasts, but in other cultures small delicate breasts are preferred. Among some African cultures, elongated earlobes are considered very attractive. In our own culture, what we find attractive often depends on the styles of the time.

Do his elongated ear lobes and other bodily adornments enhance this young man's sexual attractiveness? It all depends on your cultural point of view. In the Samburu society of Kenya in which he lives, these particular adornments are considered highly attractive.

Sexual Behavior

The biology of sexual behavior is better understood than that of the sex drive itself. Sex researchers William Masters and Virginia Johnson long ago identified a *sexual response cycle* that consists of four phases: *excitement*, *plateau*, *orgasm*, and *resolution* (Masters & Johnson, 1966). In the *excitement phase*, the genitals become engorged with blood. In the male, this causes erection of the penis; in the female it causes erection of the clitoris and nipples. This engorgement of the sexual organs continues into the *plateau phase*, in which sexual tension levels off. During this phase, breathing becomes more rapid and genital secretions and muscle tension increase. During *orgasm*, the male ejaculates and the woman's uterus contracts rhythmically, and both men and women experience some loss of muscle control. The *resolution phase* is one of relaxation in which muscle tension decreases and the engorged genitals return to normal. Heart rate, breathing, and blood pressure also return to normal. Figure 9–3 displays the pattern of sexual responses for males and females.

Regarding sexual activity, contrary to media portrayals in publications such as *Playboy* or TV shows such as *Sex in the City*, which depict Americans as oversexed and unwilling to commit to long-term relationships, research indicates that most people are far more conservative in their sex lives. One carefully designed study (Michael, Gagnon, Laumann, & Kolata, 1994) of 3,480 randomly selected people between the ages of 18 and 59 revealed the following patterns in the sexual activity of American men and women:

- About one-third of those sampled had sex twice a week or more, one-third a few times a month, and the remaining third a few times a year or not at all.

- The overwhelming majority of respondents did not engage in kinky sex. Instead, vaginal intercourse was the preferred form of sex for over 90 percent of those sampled. Interestingly, watching their partner undress was ranked second and oral sex third.

- Married couples reported having sex more often, and being more satisfied with their sex lives, than did unmarried persons.

- The average duration of sexual intercourse reported by most people was roughly 15 minutes.

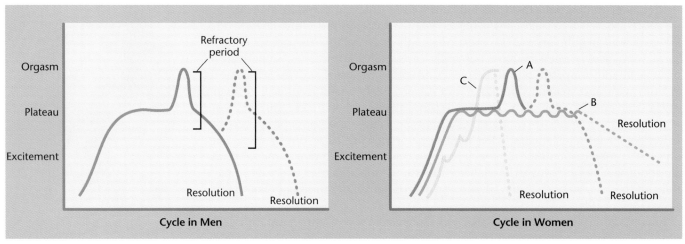

Figure 9–3
The sexual response cycle in males and females.
As the illustration shows, males typically go through one complete response cycle and are then capable of becoming excited again after a refractory period. Females have three characteristic patterns: one similar to the male cycle (A); one that includes a lengthy plateau phase with no orgasm (B); and a rapid cycle including several increases and decreases of excitement (C).
Source: Adapted from Masters & Johnson, 1966. Reprinted by permission of The Masters and Johnson Institute.

- The median number of partners over the lifetime for males was six and for females two. (Seventeen percent of men and three percent of women reported having sex with over 20 partners)

- About 25 percent of men and 15 percent of women had committed adultery.

Sexual Orientation

As noted in Chapter 1 (The Science of Psychology), *sexual orientation* refers to the direction of an individual's sexual interest. People with a *heterosexual orientation* are sexually attracted to members of the opposite sex; those with a *homosexual orientation* are sexually attracted to members of their own sex; and *bisexuals* are attracted to members of both sexes. Early surveys (Kinsey, Pomeroy, & Martin, 1948; Kinsey, Pomeroy, Martin, & Gebhard, 1953) estimated that approximately 10 percent of the population was homosexual. More recent statistics, however, indicate that only about 2.8 percent of males and 1.4 percent of females have a homosexual orientation (Laumann, Gagnon, Michaels, & Michaels, 1994; Sell, Wells, & Wypij, 1995).

Interestingly, among other animals, homosexual activity seems to occur with some degree of regularity. For instance, among bonobos, or pygmy chimpanzees, about 50 percent of all observed sexual activity is between members of the same sex. Even male giraffes commonly entwine their necks until both become sexually stimulated. And, among some birds, such as greylag geese, homosexual unions have been observed to last up to 15 years (Bagemihl, 2000).

Why people display different sexual orientations, and in particular homosexuality, has been argued for decades in the form of the classic nature-versus-nurture debate. Those on the nature side hold that sexual orientation has its roots in biology and is primarily influenced by genetics. They point out that homosexual men and women generally know before puberty that they are "different" and often remain "in the closet" regarding their sexual orientation for fear of recrimination. They cite evidence from family and twin studies that show a higher incidence of homosexuality in families with other gay men and a higher rate of homosexuality among men with a homosexual twin, even when the twins were raised separately (LeVay & Hamer, 1994). Moreover, they contend if homosexuality were the result of early

Homosexual activity is common among animals. For example, male giraffes often engage in extreme necking, entwining, and rubbing, and becoming sexually aroused as they do.

learning and socialization, children raised by gay or lesbian parents would be more likely to become homosexual. Research however, has clearly demonstrated that this is not the case (Patterson, 2000). The nature position also derives some support from studies suggesting differences between the brains of homosexual and heterosexual men (Allen & Gorski, 1992; LeVay, 1991; Swaab & Hoffman, 1995).

On the nurture side are those who hold that sexual orientation is primarily a learned behavior, influenced by early experience and largely under voluntary control. They criticize research supporting the biological position as methodologically flawed—sometimes confusing what causes homosexuality with what results from homosexuality (Byne, 1994). They contend that early socialization determines sexual orientation. Moreover, they find support for their position from cross-cultural studies that show sexual orientations occurring at different frequencies in various cultures.

To date, neither the biological nor the socialization theory has provided a completely satisfactory explanation for the origin of sexual orientation. As with most complex behaviors, a more likely explanation probably involves a combination of these two positions (Garnets, 2002; Kelley & Dawson, 1994).

CHECK YOUR UNDERSTANDING

1. Match the following terms with the appropriate definition.

___heterosexual orientation   a. the male sex hormone

___pheromones   b. sexual attraction to members of one's own sex

___homosexual orientation   c. the direction of a person's sexual interest

___the limbic system   d. sexual attraction to members of the opposite sex

___sexual orientation   e. scents that may cause sexual attraction

___testosterone   f. brain center involved in sexual excitement

2. What is the first phase Masters and Johnson identified in the sexual response cycle?

___a. plateau

___b. orgasm

___c. excitement

___d. resolution

Answers: 1. heterosexual orientation—d; pheromones—e; homosexual orientation—b; the limbic system—f; sexual orientation—c; testosterone—a; 2. c

Other Motives

Why might evolution have produced people with a strong need for affiliation?

In our discussion so far, we have moved from motives that heavily depend on biological needs (hunger and thirst) to a motive that, in humans, at least, is considerably more sensitive to external cues—sex. Next, we will consider motives that are even more responsive to environmental stimuli. These motives, called **stimulus motives,** include *curiosity, exploration, manipulation,* and *contact;* they push us to investigate, and often to change, our environment.

Stimulus motive Unlearned motive, such as curiosity or contact, that prompts us to explore or change the world around us.

Exploration and Curiosity

Where does that road go? What is in that dark little shop? How does a television set work? Answering these questions has no obvious benefit: You do not expect the road to take you anywhere you need to go or the shop to contain anything you really want. Nor are you about to start a TV repair service. You just want to know. Exploration and curiosity are motives sparked by the new and unknown and directed toward no more specific goal than "finding out." They are not unique to humans. The family dog will run around a new house, sniffing and checking things out, before it settles down to eat its dinner. Even rats, when given a choice, will opt to explore an unknown maze rather than run through a familiar one. But although curiosity is not uniquely human, it is perhaps particularly characteristic of humans.

Psychologists disagree about the nature and causes of curiosity (Loewenstein, 1994). William James viewed it as an emotion; Freud considered it a socially acceptable expression of the sex drive. Others have seen it as a response to the unexpected and as evidence of a human need to find meaning in life. We might assume that curiosity is a key component of intelligence, but studies attempting to establish a positive correlation between the two have been inconclusive. However, curiosity has been linked to creativity (Kashdan & Fincham, 2002).

Curiosity can also vary according to our familiarity with events and circumstances. As we continually explore and learn from our environment, we raise our threshold for the new and complex, and in turn our explorations and our curiosity become much more ambitious. In this respect, curiosity is linked to cognition. A gap in our understanding may stimulate our curiosity. But as our curiosity is satisfied and the unfamiliar becomes familiar, we tend to become bored. This, in turn, prompts us to explore our surroundings further (Loewenstein, 1994).

Manipulation and Contact

Why do you suppose that museums have *Do Not Touch* signs everywhere? It is because the staff knows from experience that the urge to touch is almost irresistible. Unlike curiosity and exploration, manipulation focuses on a specific object that must be touched, handled, played with, and felt before we are satisfied. Manipulation is a motive limited to primates, which have agile fingers and toes. In contrast, the need for *contact* is more universal than the need for manipulation and it is not limited to touching with the fingers—it may involve the whole body.

In a classic series of experiments, Harry Harlow demonstrated how important the need for contact is (Harlow, 1958; Harlow & Zimmerman, 1959). Newborn baby monkeys were separated from their mothers and given two "surrogate mothers." Both surrogate mothers were the same shape, but one was made of wire mesh and had no soft surfaces. The other was cuddly—layered with foam rubber and covered with terry cloth. Both surrogate mothers were warmed by means of an electric light placed inside them, but only the wire-mesh mother was equipped with a nursing bottle. Thus, the wire-mesh mother fulfilled two physiological needs for the infant monkeys: the need for food and the need for warmth. But baby monkeys most often gravitated to the terry-cloth mother, which did not provide food: When they were frightened, they would run and cling to it as they would to a real mother. Because both surrogate mothers were warm, the researchers concluded that the need for closeness goes deeper than a need for mere warmth. The importance of contact has also been demonstrated with premature infants. Low-birthweight babies who are held and massaged gain weight faster and are calmer than those who are seldom touched (Field, 1986).

An infant monkey with Harlow's surrogate "mothers"—one made of bare wire, the other covered with soft terry cloth. The baby monkey clings to the terry-cloth mother, even though the wire mother is heated and dispenses food. Apparently, there is contact comfort in the cuddly terry cloth that the bare wire mother can't provide.

Aggression

Where people are concerned, the term **aggression** encompasses all behavior that is intended to inflict physical or psychological harm on others. Intent is a key element of aggression (R. Beck, 1983). Accidentally hitting a pedestrian with your car is not an act of aggression, but deliberately running down a person is.

Judging from the statistics (which often reflect underreporting of certain types of crimes), aggression is disturbingly common in this country. According to the *FBI's Uniform Crime Reports*, there were over 1.4 million violent crimes in the United States in 2001, including 16,000 murders, 90,000 forcible rapes, 422,000 robberies, and 906,000 aggravated assaults. Family life also has a violent underside: One-quarter of families experience some form of violence. Some 3 to 4 million women are battered by their partners each year; more than 25 percent of these battered women seek medical attention for their injuries. In addition, over 900,000 cases of child abuse were reported in 2001, with more than 1,300 children dying as a result of the abuse. Children young than one year of age accounted for 41 percent of the fatalities (National Clearing House on Child Abuse and Neglect, 2003).

Why are people aggressive? Freud considered aggression an innate drive, similar to hunger and thirst, that builds up until it is released. In his view, one important function of society is to channel the aggressive drive into constructive and socially acceptable avenues, such as sports, debating, and other forms of competition. If Freud's analysis is correct, then expressing aggression should reduce the aggressive drive. Research shows, however, that under some circumstances at least venting one's anger is more likely to increase than to reduce future aggression (Bushman, Baumeister, & Stack, 1999).

According to another view, aggression is a vestige of our evolutionary past (Buss & Shackelford, 1997) that is triggered by pain or frustration (Lorenz, 1968). Some evidence shows that pain can indeed prompt aggressive behavior. In one experiment, for example, a pair of rats received electric shocks through the grid floor of their cage; they immediately attacked each other. As the frequency and intensity of the shocks increased, so did the fighting (Ulrich & Azrin, 1962).

Frustration also plays a role in aggression. In one experiment, researchers told people they could earn money by soliciting charitable donations over the telephone (Kulik & Brown, 1979). Some participants were told that previous callers had been quite successful in eliciting pledges; others were led to expect only scant success. Each group was given a list of prospective donors, all of whom were confederates of the experimenters and had instructions to refuse to pledge any money. The researchers assumed that people who expected to have an easy time would experience more frustration than those who anticipated difficulty. The results showed that the more frustrated group tended to argue with uncooperative respondents and even slam down the phone. They expressed considerably more frustration than the other group.

However, frustration does not always produce aggression. In fact, individuals have very different responses to frustration: Some seek help and support, others withdraw from the source of frustration, and some choose to escape into drugs or alcohol. Frustration seems to generate aggression only in people who have learned to be aggressive as a means of coping with unpleasant situations (Bandura, 1973).

How, then, do we learn to be aggressive? As we saw in Chapter 5, one way this hap-

Aggression Behavior aimed at doing harm to others; also the motive to behave aggressively.

THINKING CRITICALLY

Culture and Aggression

The United States has one of the highest standards of living in the world and sends a greater proportion of its young people to college than most industrialized nations. Yet we have a very high incidence of violent crime.

1. Why do you think Americans are so violent? Can you design a research study to test your ideas?

2. How might the problem of widespread violence be reduced? What kind of evidence would be required to show that your ideas in fact work?

Some psychologists believe that aggression is largely a learned behavior. Professional athletes in contact sports often serve as models of aggressive behavior.

pens is by observing aggressive models. Recall that children who viewed aggressive behavior *learned* aggressive behavior, regardless of whether the aggressive model was rewarded or punished. The same results were obtained in a study in which children were shown films of aggressive behavior. Those children who saw the aggressive model being punished were less aggressive than those who saw the aggressive model rewarded, but both groups of children were more aggressive than those who saw no aggressive model at all. These data are consistent with research showing that exposure to cinematic violence of any sort causes a small to moderate increase in aggressive behavior among children and adolescents (Wood, Wong, & Chachere, 1991). So, simply seeing an aggressive model seems to increase aggression among children, even if the model is punished; it also makes little difference whether the model is live or shown on film (e.g., C. A. Anderson, 1997). Not surprisingly, children who grow up in violent homes are particularly likely to behave aggressively toward others (Feldman et al., 1995, Onyskiw, 2000).

Aggression and Culture Cultures vary in how they handle aggression (Moghaddam, Taylor, & Wright, 1993; Smith & Bond, 1994; Triandis, 1994). For example, cultures as diverse as the Semai of the Malaysian rain forest, the Tahitian Islanders of the Pacific, the Zuni and Blackfoot nations in North America, the Pygmies of Africa, and the residents of Japan and the Scandinavian nations place a premium on resolving conflicts peacefully. They tend to withdraw from confrontations rather than risk open conflict. In contrast, cultures such as the Yanomanö of South America, the Truk Islanders of Micronesia, and the Simbu of New Guinea encourage aggressive behavior among their members, particularly the males. Actually, we need not travel to exotic, faraway lands to find such diversity. Within the United States, subcultures such as Quakers, the Amish, the Mennonites, and the Hutterites have traditionally valued nonviolence and peaceful coexistence. This contrasts markedly with attitudes and practices in the larger American culture.

Cultural differences in aggressiveness are reflected in statistics on violent crimes. The United States struggles with violent crime rates that are shockingly high compared with those of other nations. The murder rate in Norway, for example, is less than 1 per 100,000 people; in England and Wales it is 1.5 per 100,000 and in France it is 1.6. In contrast, in the United States, the 2001 murder rate was 5.6 per 100,000 people. The United States also reports higher rates of rape and vandalism.

These striking cultural differences in aggressive behavior suggest that aggression is very much influenced by the learning that takes place within a particular cultural context and by cultural norms and values. In fact, most relatively nonaggressive cultures are *collectivist* societies that emphasize the good of the group over the desires of the individual. Members of collectivist societies are more likely to seek compromise or to withdraw from a threatening interaction because of their concern for maintaining group harmony. In contrast, most relatively aggressive cultures are *individualist* societies whose members are more likely to follow the adage "Stand up for yourself."

Gender and Aggression Across cultures and at every age, males are more likely than females to behave aggressively. In particular, men are more likely than women to murder, to use force to achieve their goals, and to prefer aggressive sports such as hockey, football, and boxing. Two meta-analyses that reviewed more than 100 studies of aggression concluded that males are more aggressive than females both verbally (taunts, insults, threats) and, in particular, physically (hitting, kicking, fighting) (Eagly & Steffen, 1986; Hyde, 1984b). These gender differences tend to be greater in natural settings than in controlled laboratory settings (Hyde, 1984b), and appear to be remarkably stable (Knight, Fabes, & Higgins, 1996). Indeed, even historical data that goes back to sixteenth-century Europe shows that males committed more than three times as many violent crimes as females (see Ellis & Coontz, 1990).

Is the gender difference in aggression biological or social in origin? The answer is not simple. On the one hand, as we saw in Chapter 2 (The Biological Basis of Behavior), low levels of testosterone and high levels of estrogen in both males and females are associated with aggressiveness and irritability. Moreover, exposure to high levels of testosterone during prenatal development is associated with increased aggressiveness (Reinisch, Ziemba-Davis, & Sanders, 1991). Other research suggests that human aggression has its roots in evolution and can be traced to defensive behaviors characteristic of our ancestors (Buss & Shackelford, 1997).

At the same time, our society clearly tolerates and even encourages greater aggressiveness in boys than in girls (Sommers-Flanagan, Sommers-Flanagan, & Davis, 1993). For example, we are more likely to give boys toy guns and to reward them for behaving aggressively; girls are more likely than boys to be taught to feel guilty for behaving aggressively or to expect parental disapproval for their aggressive behavior (Perry, Perry, & Weiss, 1989).

The most accurate conclusion is that both biological and social factors contribute to gender differences in aggressive behavior. Like most of the complex behaviors we have reviewed, aggression undoubtedly depends on the interaction of nature and nurture (Geen, 1998).

Achievement

Climbing Mount Everest, sending rockets into space, making the dean's list, rising to the top of a giant corporation—all these actions may have mixed underlying motives. But in all of them there is a desire to excel, "to overcome obstacles, to exercise power, to strive to do something difficult as well and as quickly as possible" (Murray, 1938, pp. 80–81). It is this desire for achievement for its own sake that leads psychologists to suggest there is a separate **achievement motive.**

Using a self-report questionnaire called the Work and Family Orientation (WOFO) scale to study achievement motivation, some researchers discovered three separate but interrelated aspects of achievement-oriented behavior: *work orientation*, the desire to work hard and do a good job; *mastery*, the preference for difficult or challenging feats, with an emphasis on improving one's past performance; and *competitiveness*, the enjoyment of pitting one's skills against those of other people (Helmreich & Spence, 1978).

How do individual differences in the three aspects of achievement motivation relate to people's attainment of goals? Surprisingly, having a high degree of competitiveness may actually interfere with achievement. In one study, students' grade-point averages (GPAs) were compared to their WOFO scores. As you might expect, students who scored low in work, mastery, and competitiveness had lower GPAs. But students who scored high in all three areas did not have the highest GPAs. It turned out that the students with the highest grades were those who had high work and mastery scores but low competitiveness scores. The counterproductive effect of competitiveness curbs achievement in other groups of people as well, including business people, elementary-school students, and scientists. What accounts for this phenomenon? No one knows for sure, but some researchers speculate that highly competitive people alienate the very people who would otherwise help them achieve their goals; others suggest that preoccupation with winning distracts them from taking the actions necessary to attain their goals.

From psychological tests and personal histories, psychologists have developed a profile of people with a high level of achievement motivation. These people are fast learners. They relish the opportunity to develop new strategies for unique and challenging tasks, whereas people with a low need for achievement rarely deviate from methods that worked for them in the past. Driven less by the desire for fame or fortune than by the need to live up to a high, self-imposed standard of performance

Achievement motive The need to excel, to overcome obstacles.

High achievement is partly a matter of great commitment and effort. Just as this student keeps working late into the night, so those who excel in any field are willing to work hard for success. The desire to excel not for tangible rewards but for the pleasure of being "one of the best" is called achievement motivation.

Affiliation motive The need to be with others.

(Carr, Borkowski, & Maxwell, 1991), people with a high level of achievement motivation are self-confident, willingly take on responsibility, and do not readily bow to outside social pressures. Although they are energetic and allow few things to stand in the way of their goals, they are also apt to be tense and to suffer from stress-related ailments, such as headaches. They may also feel like impostors even—or especially—when they achieve their goals.

Affiliation

Generally, people have a need for affiliation—to be with other people. If they are isolated from social contact for a long time, they may become anxious. Why do human beings seek one another out?

For one thing, the **affiliation motive** is aroused when people feel threatened. Cues that signal danger, such as illness or catastrophe, appear to increase our desire to be with others (Rofe, 1984). *Esprit de corps*—the feeling of being part of a sympathetic group—is critical among troops going into a battle, just as a football coach's pregame pep talk fuels team spirit. Both are designed to make people feel they are working for a common cause or against a common foe.

Fear and anxiety may also be closely tied to the affiliation motive. When rats, monkeys, or humans are placed in anxiety-producing situations, the presence of a member of the same species who remains calm will reduce the fear of the anxious ones. Patients with critical illnesses tend to prefer being with healthy people rather than with other seriously ill patients or by themselves (Rofe, Hoffman, & Lewin, 1985). In the same way, if you are nervous on a plane during a bumpy flight, you may strike up a conversation with the calm-looking woman sitting next to you, especially if the agitation of the plane does not seem to be worrying her.

Based on these facts, some theorists have argued that our need for affiliation has an evolutionary basis (see Ainsworth, 1989; Baumeister & Leary, 1995; Buss, 1990, 1991). In this view the formation and maintenance of social bonds provided our ancestors with both survival and reproductive benefits. Social groups can share resources such as food and shelter, provide opportunities for reproduction, and assist in the care for offspring. Children who chose to stay with adults were probably more likely to survive, and ultimately reproduce, than those who wandered away from their groups. Thus, it is understandable that people in general tend to seek out other people.

In any given case, affiliation behavior (like most behavior) usually stems from a subtle interplay of biological and environmental factors. Whether you strike up a conversation with the person sitting next to you on a bumpy airplane flight depends on how friendly you normally are, what is considered proper behavior in your culture, as well as on how scared you feel at the moment, how calm your neighbor appears to be, and how turbulent the flight is.

A Hierarchy of Motives

You have probably noticed that our narrative has gradually moved from primitive motives, shared by all animals, to motives that are more sophisticated, complex, and specifically human. A number of years ago, Abraham Maslow (1954), a humanistic psychologist, arranged motives in such a hierarchy, from lower to higher. The lower motives spring from bodily needs that must be satisfied. As we move higher in Maslow's hierarchy of needs, the motives have more subtle origins: the desire to live as comfortably as possible, to deal as well as we can with other human beings, and to make the best possible impression on others. Maslow believed that the highest motive in the hierarchy is self-actualization—the drive to realize one's full potential. Maslow's hierarchy of motives is illustrated in Figure 9–4.

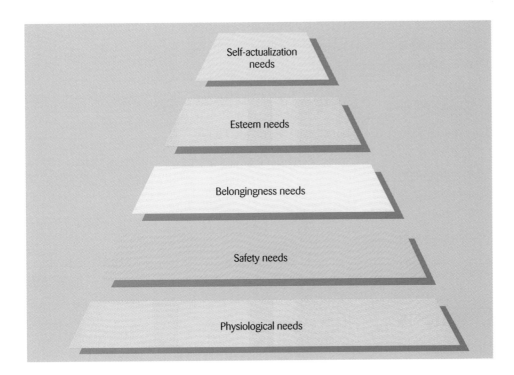

Figure 9–4
A pyramid representing Maslow's hierarchy of needs.
From bottom to top, the stages correspond to how fundamental the motive is for survival and how early it appears in both the evolution of the species and the development of the individual. According to Maslow, the more basic needs must largely be satisfied before higher motives can emerge.
Source: After Maslow, 1954.

According to Maslow's theory, higher motives emerge only after the more basic ones have been largely satisfied: A person who is starving doesn't care what people think of her table manners.

Maslow's model offers an appealing way to organize a wide range of motives into a coherent structure. But recent research challenges the universality of his views. Maslow based his hierarchical model on observations of historical figures, famous living individuals, and even friends whom he admired greatly. However, the majority of these people were white males living in Western society. In many simpler societies people often live on the very edge of survival, yet they form strong and meaningful social ties and possess a firm sense of self-esteem (Neher, 1991). In fact, difficulty in meeting basic needs can actually foster the satisfaction of higher needs: A couple struggling financially to raise a family may grow closer as a result of the experience. In our discussion of development during adolescence and early adulthood (Chapter 10, Life Span Development), we will examine some research indicating that males must have a firm sense of their own identity (and thus a degree of self-esteem) before they can successfully establish the kinds of close relationships with others that satisfy the need for belonging. As a result of such research findings, many psychologists now view Maslow's model with a measure of skepticism although it continues to be a convenient way to think of the wide range of human motives.

CHECK YOUR UNDERSTANDING

1. Stimulus motives include such things as

___a. thirst

___b. manipulation

___c. curiosity

___d. b and c

2. What is the kind of behavior that intentionally inflicts harm on others?

___a. aggressive

___b. competitive

___c. collective

___d. manipulative

3. Fear and anxiety are most closely associated with

___a. affiliation

___b. aggression

___c. curiosity

___d. achievement

Answers: 1.d, 2.a, 3.a

Emotions

How many basic emotions are there?

Just as motives may both arouse and direct our behavior, so, too, do emotions. "She shouted for joy," we say, or "I was so angry I could have strangled him."

Ancient Greek rationalists thought emotions, if not held in check, would wreak havoc on higher mental abilities such as rational thought and decision making. In the past, psychologists, too, often viewed emotions as a "base instinct"—a vestige of our evolutionary heritage that needed to be repressed.

More recently, however, scientists have begun to see emotions in a more positive light. Today they are thought of as essential to survival and a major source of personal enrichment (National Advisory Mental Health Council, 1995). Emotions are linked to variations in immune function and, thereby, to disease (Lazarus, 1993; O'Leary, 1990; see Chapter 12, Stress and Health Psychology). As we saw in Chapter 8 (Intelligence and Mental Abilities), emotions may also play an important role in determining how successful we are (Goleman, 1997; Goleman, Boyatzis, & McKee, 2002). It is clear, then, that if we would understand human behavior, we must understand emotions. Unfortunately, that is easier said than done. As you will soon see, even identifying how many emotions there are is difficult.

Basic Emotions

Many people have attempted to identify and describe the basic emotions experienced by humans (Ekman, 1992; Plutchik, 1980; also see Cornelius, 1996). Some years ago, Robert Plutchik (1980), for example, proposed that there are eight basic emotions: *fear, surprise, sadness, disgust, anger, anticipation, joy,* and *acceptance*. Each of these emotions helps us adjust to the demands of our environment, although in different ways. Fear, for example, underlies flight, which helps protect animals from their enemies; anger propels animals to attack or destroy.

Emotions adjacent to each other on Plutchik's emotion "circle" (see Figure 9–5) are more alike than those situated opposite each other or that are farther away from each other. Surprise is more closely related

THINKING CRITICALLY

Nonverbal Communication of Emotion

Some people are clearly better than others at reading and sending emotional messages. The question is, why? How might you determine:

1. if differences in these skills are learned or inherited?

2. the kinds of learning experiences that produce high skills?

3. whether it is possible to teach the skills?

to fear than to anger; joy and acceptance are more similar to each other than either is to disgust. Moreover, according to Plutchik's model, different emotions may combine to produce an even wider and richer spectrum of experience. Occurring together, anticipation and joy, for example, yield optimism; joy and acceptance fuse into love; surprise and sadness make for disappointment.

Within any of Plutchik's eight categories, emotions vary in intensity, represented by the vertical dimensions of the model in Figure 9–6. At the top of the figure lie rage, vigilance, ecstasy, adoration, terror, amazement, grief, and loathing—the most intense forms of his eight basic emotions. As we move toward the bottom, each emotion becomes less intense, and the distinctions among the emotions become less sharp. Anger, for example, is less intense than rage, and annoyance is even less intense than anger. But all three emotions—annoyance, anger, and rage—are closely related.

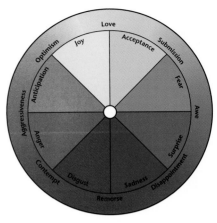

Figure 9–5
Plutchik's eight basic categories of emotion.
Source: Plutchik, 1980.

ENDURING ISSUES   diversityuniversality

Are Emotions Universal?

Some scientists challenge Plutchik's model, noting that it may apply only to the emotional experience of English-speaking people. Anthropologists report enormous differences in the ways that other cultures view and categorize emotions. Some languages, in fact, do not even have a word for "emotion" (Russell, 1991). Languages also differ in the number of words they have to name emotions. English includes over 2,000 words to describe emotional experiences, but Taiwanese Chinese has only 750 such descriptive words. One tribal language has only seven words that could be translated into categories of emotion. Some cultures lack words for "anxiety" or "depression" or "guilt." Samoans have one word encompassing love, sympathy, pity, and liking—all distinct emotions in our own culture (Russell, 1991).

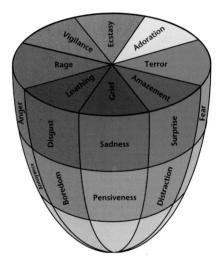

Figure 9–6
Plutchik's three-dimensional model of the eight basic emotions.
Source: Plutchik, 1980.

Because of the differences in emotions from one culture to another, the tendency now is to distinguish between primary and secondary emotions. Most researchers use four criteria to identify primary emotions (see Plutchick, 1994): The emotion must (1) be evident in all cultures; (2) contribute to survival; (3) be associated with a distinct facial expression; and (4) be evident in nonhuman primates (see Figure 9–7). As yet no consensus exists about what emotions qualify as primary, but the number is small, very likely no more than a dozen. They include, at a minimum, fear, anger, and pleasure, but may also include sadness, disgust, surprise, and perhaps a few others.

Secondary emotions are those that are found in only some cultures. There are many more secondary emotions than primary emotions, but there is, again, no consensus about what those emotions are or how many they number.

Recent attempts to identify primary emotions have generally used cross-cultural methodologies (Ekman et al., 1987; Izard, 1994). For example, one group of researchers asked participants from ten countries to interpret photographs depicting various facial expressions of emotions (Ekman et al., 1987). The percentage of participants from each country who correctly identified the emotions ranged from 60 to 98 percent (see Figure 9–8). The researchers used this and other evidence to argue for the existence of six primary emotions—*happiness, surprise, sadness, fear, disgust,* and *anger* (see also Cornelius, 1996). You might note that love is not included in this list. Although Ekman did not find a universally recognized facial expression for love, many psychologists nevertheless hold that love is a primary emotion (Hendrick & Hendrick, 2003). Its outward expression, however, may owe much to the stereotypes promoted by a culture's media (Fehr, 1994). In one study in which American college students were asked to display a facial expression for love, the participants mimicked

psych 9.1

Figure 9–7
Display of anger in animal and human.
Compare the facial expressions. The human face is that of a Kabuki player who is simulating anger. Note how the actor bares his teeth, copying the mandrill's display of emotion.

James-Lange theory States that stimuli cause physiological changes in our bodies, and emotions result from those physiological changes.

the conventional "Hollywood" prototypes such as sighing deeply, gazing skyward, and holding their hand over their heart (see Cornelius, 1996).

Happiness and Well-Being You may be struck by how many negative emotions are included in the lists of primary emotions above. Fear, anger, sadness, and disgust certainly stand out. But if you recall from Chapter 1, a relatively new perspective called *positive psychology* has emerged in recent years that concerns itself with understanding one of our most postive emotions: happiness (Seligman, 2003). For psychologists, happiness is just one aspect of *subjective well-being* (SWB). In addition to happiness, SWB includes having more positive than negative emotions and having feelings of overall life satisfaction.

To understand the roots of happiness and feelings of well-being, researchers looked first at external events and the demographic characteristics of happy people. But after decades of research, and despite what "common sense" might suggest, they found that external events and demographic characteristics have very little influence on SWB (DeNeve & Cooper, 1998; Diener, Suh, Lucas, & Smith, 1999; also see Myers, 2000). More specifically, they found no correlation between age, gender, or intelligence and happiness (DeNeve & Cooper, 1998; Diener & Suh, 1998; Diener et al., 1999). Researchers did find that people who are married, wealthy, well educated, and in good health tend to be happier than others, but the difference is often small (Breetvelt & Van Dam, 1991; Brickman, Coates, & Janoff-Bulman, 1978; Diener et al., 1999).

If these variables don't have a major effect on happiness, then what *does?* Increasingly, researchers are coming to believe that the keys to happiness are the goals people have, their ability to adapt to conditions around them, and their personalities (Diener, 2000; Seligman, 2003). Consistent with this view is the fact that personality is a strong and consistent predictor of well-being over a period of years (Diener et al., 1999). Also people who are happy in one area of their lives (such as at work) tend to be happy in other areas as well. Thus, researchers believe that stable personality factors predispose people to feel happy or unhappy in a wide range of situations, though current life events may significantly influence happiness at any given moment. Specifically, DeNeve and Cooper (1998) found that happy people and those reporting more positive than negative emotions tend to be enthusiastic, accommodating, understanding, flexible, gregarious, energetic, confident, optimistic, and affectionate.

Techniques for adapting and coping also seem to contribute to happiness (Diener, 2000). Many people who suffer severe injuries or who are imprisoned for long periods of time report that within a relatively short time following these episodes, they regain their normal levels of happiness. Most people who lose life partners take longer to return to normal, but many do so eventually (Loewenstein & Frederick, 1998). We don't yet know exactly how adaptation contributes to happiness. It may be that most people simply "get used to" unpleasant situations, it may be that they change the way they *perceive* the new situation, it may be that they restructure their lives to fit the changed conditions, or the explanation may lie elsewhere entirely. But adaptive techniques could help to explain the relative stability of happiness and feelings of well-being over time.

Theories of Emotion

Early Theories of Emotion: James-Lange and Cannon-Bard The American psychologist William James formulated the first modern theory of emotion in the 1880s (James, 1884); at almost the same time, a Danish psychologist, Carl Lange, reached the same conclusions. According to the **James-Lange theory,** stimuli in the environment cause physiological changes in our bodies that we interpret as emotions. If you are hiking in the woods one day, for example, and suddenly find yourself face to face with a grizzly bear, your body will respond in predictable ways: Your heart will beat faster, your pupils will enlarge, your breathing will become

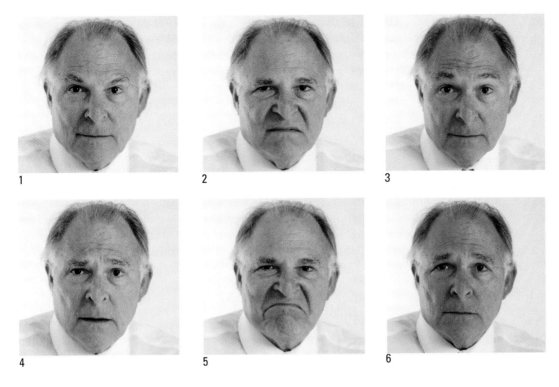

Figure 9–8
Name That Face

Dr. Paul Ekman believes that facial expressions are distinct, predictable and easy to read for someone who has studied them. His research involved breaking the expressions down into their specific muscular components and developing programs to help train people to become more accurate observers of the feelings that flit briefly across others' faces.

Here he demonstrates eight emotional states. How many of them can you match to the pictures? The answers are below.

A. Fear
B. Neutral (no emotion)
C. Sadness
D. Anger
E. Surprise
F. Disgust

Source: © 2003 by the *New York Times.* Reprinted with permission.

Answers: 1. B (Neutral) 2. F (Disgust) 3. E (Surprise) 4. A (Fear) 5. D (Anger) 6. C (Sadness)

faster and more shallow, and you will perspire more heavily. The emotion of fear, said James and Lange, is simply the awareness of these physiological changes. In James's words, the "object-simply-apprehended" becomes the "object-emotionally-felt." All of this, of course, happens almost instantaneously and in an automatic way.

If these physiological changes alone *cause* specific emotions, we should be able to pinpoint different bodily changes for each emotion. And, indeed, some evidence shows that the physiological changes associated with fear and anxiety are somewhat different from those that accompany anger and aggression (McGeer & McGeer, 1980). Similarly, fear and anger appear to be distinguishable from happiness by subtle changes in heart rate acceleration (Levenson, 1992). Moreover, to some extent different emotions are associated with different brain areas. Positive emotions are accompanied by an increase in the electrical activity on the left side of the brain, whereas negative emotions result in more activity on the right side (Davidson, 1992).

Unfortunately, the James-Lange theory does have problems. As we saw in Chapter 2 (The Biological Basis of Behavior), sensory information about bodily changes flows to the brain through the spinal cord. If bodily changes are the source of emotions, then people with severe spinal cord injuries should experience fewer and less intense emotions. Research, however, has demonstrated that this is not so (Chwalisz, Diener, & Gallagher, 1988). Moreover, most emotions are accompanied by quite similar physiological changes. Thus, bodily changes do not cause specific emotions and may not even be necessary for emotional experience.

An alternative theory of emotions, the **Cannon-Bard theory,** dating back nearly 70 years, holds that the processing of emotions and bodily responses occur simultaneously, not one after another. Thus, when you see the bear, you feel afraid *and* your heart races—neither of these precedes the other nor is one dependent on the other.

Cognitive Theories of Emotion   Cognitive psychologists have modified Cannon-Bard's theory by contending that our perception of situations is absolutely essential to our emotional experience (Ellsworth, 2002; Lazarus, 1982, 1991a, 1991b, 1991c).

Cannon-Bard theory States that the experience of emotion occurs simultaneously with biological changes.

Cognitive theory States that emotional experience depends on one's perception or judgment of the situation one is in.

According to the **cognitive theory** of emotion, the situation gives us clues as to how we should interpret our state of arousal. One of the first theories of emotion that took into account cognitive processes was advanced by Stanley Schachter and Jerome Singer (1962, 2001). According to Schachter and Singer's *Two-Factor Theory of Emotion*, when we see a bear, there are indeed bodily changes; but we then use information about the situation to tell us how to respond to those changes. Only when we *cognitively* recognize that we are in danger do we experience those bodily changes as fear. (See Figure 9–9 for a comparison of these three theories of emotion.)

In an early test of the cognitive theory of emotion, people were shown a violent, stress-inducing film that aroused strong emotional responses (Spiesman, 1965). But the researcher was able to manipulate people's emotional responses to the film by varying the sound track. Those who heard a sound track that narrated what was happening in the film responded with more emotion than those who saw the film with no accompanying narration. But those who heard a sound track that described the events in a detached and clinical way and those who heard a sound track that glossed over, denied, or spoke in glowing terms about what was depicted experienced much less emotion than either of the first two groups. These results show that our emotional responses are directly and sharply affected by how we interpret a situation, or how it is interpreted for us.

Challenges to Cognitive Theory   Although cognitive theories of emotion make a great deal of sense, some critics reject the idea that feelings always stem from cognitions. Quoting the poet e. e. cummings, Zajonc (pronounced *ZY-unz*) argues that "feelings come first." Zajonc (1980) notes that we have the ability to respond instantaneously to the situations in which we find ourselves, without taking time to interpret and evaluate those situations. Zajonc (1984) believes that we invent explanations to label feelings: Cognition thus comes after emotion.

Another direct challenge to the cognitive theory claims that emotions can be experienced without the intervention of cognition (Izard, 1971). According to this view, a situation such as separation or pain provokes a unique pattern of unlearned facial movements and body postures that may be completely independent of conscious thought (Trotter, 1983). When information about our facial expressions and posture reaches the brain, we automatically experience the corresponding emotion. According to Carroll Izard, then, the James-Lange theory was essentially right in suggesting that emotional experience arises from bodily reactions. But Izard's theory stresses facial expression and body posture as crucial to the experience of emotion, whereas the James-Lange theory emphasized muscles, skin, and internal organs.

The effects of *sensorimotor* feedback from facial and postural movement as a cause of emotion have been well documented. For example, when information about our facial expressions and posture reaches the brain, we automatically experience the corresponding emotion (Soussignan, 2002). Tomkins (1962) speculated that certain facial expressions initiate neural programs that produce emotional experiences. There may be valuable advice in the 1960s refrain, "put on a happy face!" Specific facial movements may create a change in blood flow to the brain resulting in changes in cerebral brain temperature and, presumably, neurochemical processes that mediate feeling states (Zajonc, Murphy, & Inglehart, 1989).

CHECK YOUR UNDERSTANDING

1. Match the following theories with the appropriate description.

___ Cannon-Bard   a. emotions and bodily responses are simultaneous

___ cognitive theory   b. emotions result from physiological changes caused by stimuli

___ James-Lange   c. emotional experience depends on perception of the specific situation

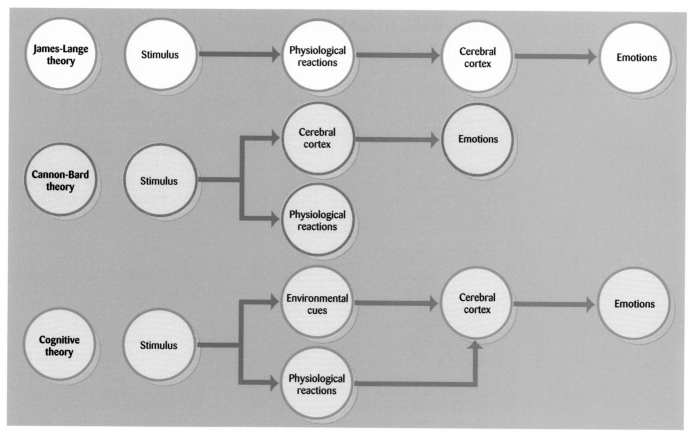

Figure 9–9
The three major theories of emotion.
According to the *James-Lange* theory, the body first responds physiologically to a stimulus, and then the cerebral cortex determines which emotion is being experienced. The *Cannon-Bard* theory holds that impulses are sent simultaneously to the cerebral cortex and the peripheral nervous system; thus, the response to the stimulus and the processing of the emotion are experienced at the same time, but independently. *Cognitive theorists* assert that the cerebral cortex interprets physiological changes in the light of information about the situation to determine which emotions we feel.

2. According to Robert Plutchik, the richness of human emotional experience is due to the fact that each of the eight basic emotions varies in _____.

___a. saturation

___b. heritability

___c. intensity

___d. cognition

3. Izard's theory of emotion stresses

___a. cognition

___b. expressive behavior

___c. environmental cues

Answers: 1. Cannon-Bard—a; cognitive theory—c; James-Lange—b; 2.c, 3.b

Nonverbal Communication of Emotion

What is the most obvious indicator of emotion?

Sometimes you are vaguely aware that a person makes you feel uncomfortable. When pressed to be more precise, you might say: "You never know what she is thinking." But you do not mean that you never know her opinion of a film or what she thought about the last election. It would probably be more accurate to say that you do not know what she is *feeling*. Almost all of us conceal our emotions to some extent, but usually people can tell what we are feeling. Although emotions can often be expressed in words, much of the time we communicate our feelings nonverbally. We do this through, among other things, voice quality, facial expression, body language, personal space, and explicit acts.

Voice Quality

If your roommate is washing the dishes and says acidly, "I hope you're enjoying your novel," the literal meaning of his words is quite clear, but you probably know very well that he is not expressing a concern about your reading pleasure. He is really saying, "I am furious that you are not helping to clean up after dinner." Other emotions can be expressed through voice quality as well. When Mae West, a once-famous film star and master of sexual innuendo, asked, "Why don't you come up and see me sometime?" her voice oozed sensuality. Similarly, if you receive a phone call from someone who has had very good or very bad news, you will probably know how she feels before she has told you what happened. In the same way, we can literally hear fear in a person's voice, as we do when we listen to a nervous student give an oral report. Much of the information we convey is not contained in the words we use, but in the way those words are expressed.

Facial Expression

Facial expressions are perhaps the most obvious emotional indicators. We can tell a good deal about a person's emotional state by observing whether that person is laughing, crying, smiling, or frowning. Many facial expressions are innate, not learned (Ekman, 1994; Goldsmith, 2002). Children who are born deaf and blind use the same facial expressions as other children do to express the same emotions. Charles Darwin first advanced the idea that most animals share a common pattern of muscular facial movements. For example, dogs, tigers, and humans all bare their teeth in rage. Darwin also observed that expressive behaviors serve a basic biological as well as social function. Darwin's notion that emotions have an evolutionary history and can be traced across cultures as part of our biological heritage laid the groundwork for many modern investigations of emotional expression (Izard, 1992, 1994; see Figure 9–10). Today, psychologists who take an evolutionary approach believe facial expressions served an adaptive function, enabling our ancestors to compete successfully for status, to win mates, and to defend themselves (Ekman, 1992; Tooby & Cosmides, 1990).

Body Language

Body language is another way we communicate messages nonverbally. When we are relaxed, we tend to stretch back into a chair; when we are tense, we sit more stiffly with our feet together. Slumping and straightness of the back supply clues about which emotion someone is feeling. Beier (1974) videotaped people acting out six emotions: anger, fear, seductiveness, indifference, happiness, and sadness. Surprisingly, most people could communicate only two out of the six emotions. Indeed, one young woman

ON THE CUTTING EDGE

HOW THE BRAIN READS THE FACE

It is known that activity in brain circuits involving the amygdala is critical for the release of emotions (Schafe & LeDoux, 2002). The amygdala may also be critical for our ability to correctly interpret facial expressions. Adolphs and colleagues (1994) reported the remarkable case of a 30-year-old woman (S. M.) with a rare disease that caused nearly complete destruction of the amygdala. Although S. M. could correctly identify photographs of familiar faces with 100 percent accuracy, and easily learned to recognize new faces, she had great difficulty recognizing fear and discriminating between different emotions, such as happiness and surprise. Other research also has shown that people with amygdala damage have trouble "reading faces" (Adolphs, Tranel, & Damasio, 1998). Indeed, some researchers have suggested that abnormalities in the brain circuits associated with the amygdala can, in some cases, make it difficult for people to perceive threat accurately and that, in turn, can lead to unprovoked violence and aggression (Davidson, Putnam, & Larson, 2000).

appeared angry no matter which emotion she tried to project; another was invariably thought to be seductive.

Personal Space

The distance that people maintain between themselves and others is called *personal space*. This distance varies depending on the nature of the activity and the emotions felt. If someone stands closer to you than is customary, it may indicate either anger or affection; if farther away than usual, it may indicate fear or dislike. The normal conversing distance between people varies from culture to culture: Two Swedes conversing would ordinarily stand much farther apart than would two Arabs or Greeks.

Explicit Acts

Explicit acts, of course, can also serve as nonverbal clues to emotions. When we receive a telephone call at 2 A.M., we expect that the caller has something urgent to say. A slammed door may tell us that the person who just left the room is angry. If friends drop in for a visit and you invite them into your living room, you are probably less at ease with them than with friends who generally sit down with you at the kitchen table. Gestures, such as a slap on the back or an embrace, can also indicate feelings. Whether people shake your hand briefly or for a long time, firmly or limply, tells you something about how they feel about you.

You can see from this discussion that nonverbal communication of emotions is important. However, a word of caution is needed here. Although nonverbal behavior may offer a clue to a person's feelings, it is not an *infallible* clue. Laughing and crying sound alike, for example, and we bare our teeth in smiles as well as in snarls. Crying may signify sorrow, joy, anger, nostalgia—or that you are slicing an onion. Moreover, as with verbal reports, people sometimes "say" things nonverbally that they do not mean. We all have done something thoughtlessly—turned our backs, frowned when thinking about something else, laughed at the wrong time—that has given offense because these acts were interpreted as an expression of an emotion that we were not, in fact, feeling.

Also, many of us overestimate our ability to interpret nonverbal cues. In one study of several hundred "professional lie catchers," including members of the Secret Service, government lie detector experts, judges, police officers, and psychiatrists, every group

Figure 9–10
People throughout the world use the "brow-raise" greeting when a friend approaches.
Source: Eibl-Eibesfeldt, 1972. Copyright © 1972 by Holt, Rinehart & Winston. Reprinted with permission.

When having a conversation, most Arabs stand closer to one another than most Americans do. In our society, two men would not usually stand as close together as these two Arabs unless they were very aggressively arguing with each other (a baseball player heatedly arguing with an umpire, for example).

except the psychiatrists rated themselves above average in their ability to tell whether another person was lying. In fact, only one group, the Secret Service agents, managed to identify the liars at a better-than-chance rate (Ekman & O'Sullivan, 1991). Similar results have been obtained with other groups of people (e.g., DePaulo & Pfeifer, 1986).

CHECK YOUR UNDERSTANDING

1. Which of the following is a nonverbal cue to emotion?

___a. swearing under your breath

___b. explicit act

___c. body language

___d. b and c

2. According to research, which of the following are able to identify liars at a better-than-chance level?

___a. psychiatrists

___b. government lie detector experts

___c. Secret Service agents

___d. all the above

3. Crying is an example of a(n) _____ emotional cue.

___a. ambiguous

___b. infallible

___c. cognitive

Answers: 1.d, 2.c, 3.a

Gender, Culture, and Emotion

Are men less emotional than women?

Gender and Emotion

Experience tells us that males and females differ considerably in how they express emotion and the emotions they choose to express. For example, men are often said to be less emotional than women. But do men feel less emotion, or are they simply less likely to express the emotions they feel? And are there some emotions that men are more likely to express than women?

Research sheds some light on these issues. In one study, when men and women saw depictions of people in distress, the men showed little emotion but the women expressed feelings of concern for those in distress (Eisenberg & Lennon, 1983). However, physiological measures of emotional arousal (such as heart rate and blood pressure) showed that the men in the study were actually just as affected as the women were. The men simply inhibited the expression of their emotions, whereas the women were more open about their feelings. Emotions such as sympathy, sadness, empathy, and distress are often considered "unmanly," and boys are trained from an early age to suppress those emotions in public (O'Leary & Smith, 1988). The fact that men are less likely than women to seek help in dealing with emotional issues (Komiya, Good, & Sherrod, 2000) is probably a result of this early training.

In addition, women tend to have stronger emotional reactions to self-generated thoughts and memories (Carter, 1998; see Figure 9–11).

Men and women are also likely to react with very different emotions to the same situation. For example, in one study participants responded to hypothetical situations in which they were betrayed or criticized by another person (Brody, 1985). Males usually said that they would feel angry; females were likely to report that they would feel hurt, sad, or disappointed.

When men get angry, they generally turn their anger outward, against other people and against the situation in which they find themselves. Women, as a rule, are more likely to see themselves as the source of the problem and turn their anger inward, against themselves. Given these gender-specific reactions, it is not surprising that men are four times more likely than women to become violent in the face of life crises, whereas women are much more likely than men to become depressed.

Men, in general, often have less skill than women at decoding the emotional expressions of others. One reason may be that men aren't usually the primary caregivers of children who are too young to speak, and so they get less practice "reading" emotion in the face and body. As traditional sex roles in our society change and fathers take a larger role in the care of very young children, many men may become more attuned to the subtleties of emotional expression.

ENDURING ISSUES   mindbody

Holding Anger In

Women who frequently feel anger and hostility may be at a serious health risk if they don't allow themselves to express their anger (Julius, Harburg, Cottington, & Johnson, 1986). Tracking a group of women over 18 years, the study found that those who scored high on hostility were three times more likely to die during the course of the study than those who scored low. However, this higher level of risk applied only to participants who said they got angry in many situations but did not vent their anger. Other participants who reported frequent bouts of anger, which they expressed, were in the same low-risk group as those who said they rarely or never felt angry.

Research indicates that men and women also differ in their ability to interpret nonverbal cues of emotion. A meta-analysis of studies in this area (Hall, 1984) concluded that women are more skilled than men at decoding the facial expressions, body cues, and tones of voice of others. Several explanations could account for these gender differences (McClure, 2000; Taylor, Peplau, & Sears, 1994). One is that because many women are the primary caregivers for preverbal infants, they need to become more attuned than men to the subtleties of emotional expressions. Some psychologists have even suggested that this skill may be genetically programmed into females. Consistent with this evolutionary perspective, research has shown that male and female infants do express and self-regulate emotions differently (Weinberg, Tronick, Cohn, & Olson, 1999).

Another explanation of gender differences is based on the relative power of women and men. Because women historically have occupied less powerful positions in society, they may have felt the need to become acutely attuned to the emotional displays of others, particularly those in more powerful positions (namely, men). This idea is supported by evidence that, regardless of gender, followers are more sensitive to the emotions of leaders than vice versa (Snodgrass, 1992).

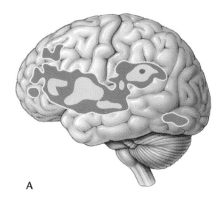

A

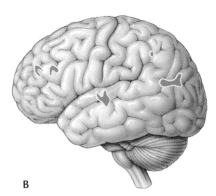

B

Figure 9–11
Emotion and brain activity in men and women.
When asked to think of something sad, women (A) generate more activity in their emotional brains than men (B).
Source: Carter, R. 1998, p. 100. *Mapping the Mind.* Berkeley: University of California Press, p. 100. Reprinted by permission of Moonrunner Design Ltd., Dorset, UK. Shading added.

The fact that men are more likely than women to hold positions of power may affect emotional experience in other ways as well. In the types of jobs traditionally held by women, workers are often called on to regulate, manage, or otherwise alter their emotional expression. Sociologist Arlie Hochschild (1983) described this process as *emotional labor*. In a study of flight attendants, the majority of whom were women, Hochschild found clear guidelines regarding which emotions were to be displayed, to whom, by whom, and how often. Most of the flight attendants felt they were being robbed of genuine emotional experiences on the job: ". . . [I]n the flight attendant's work, smiling is separated from its usual function, which is to express a personal feeling, and attached to another one—expressing a company feeling" (p. 127). Hochschild also noted that jobs that are high in emotional labor—such as secretaries, registered nurses, cashiers, social workers, and bank tellers—tend to be filled by women.

Culture and Emotion

Emotional experiences across cultures are similar in certain ways and very different in others. The death of a loved one, for example, is sure to produce feelings of grief and sadness in all cultures. Similarly, being unexpectedly attacked will produce fear and surprise in anyone. In contrast, the feelings experienced after a job promotion are likely to differ depending on one's cultural values and the meaning one attaches to personal success. If you perceive your work as an individual effort, you will no doubt feel proud, happy, and perhaps boastful when you are promoted. If, however, you see your success as reflecting the efforts of your group, you will still be happy, but you will probably be more reluctant to take credit for the success.

For psychologists, the key issue is how cultures help shape emotional experiences. One defining element is whether a culture is individualist or collectivist, a distinction we mentioned earlier. For example, the English language has many terms for self-focused emotions (anger, sadness), whereas the Japanese language has many terms for other-focused emotions (sympathy, empathy) (Markus & Kitayama, 1991). This difference parallels the predominantly individualist orientation of most English-speaking cultures and the collectivist orientation of Japanese culture. The emotions of people in collectivist cultures also tend to be shorter in duration than those of individualists (Markus & Kitayama, 1991). American college students, for example, reported experiencing emotions that lasted longer, were more intense, and were accompanied by more bodily symptoms than emotions reported by Japanese students (Matsumoto, Kudoh, Scherer, & Wallbott, 1988). Matsumoto and his colleagues suggest that, in general, "collective cultures will foster emotional displays of their members that maintain and facilitate group cohesion, harmony, or cooperation to a greater degree than individualistic cultures" (p. 132).

In contrast to emotional experiences, the ways in which emotions are expressed seem to be more constant from one culture to another. As we saw earlier in the chapter, Ekman and his colleagues have concluded from cross-cultural studies that at least six emotions are accompanied by universal facial expressions: happiness, sadness, anger, surprise, fear, and disgust. Carroll Izard (1980) conducted similar studies in England, Germany, Switzerland, France, Sweden, Greece, and Japan with similar results. Regardless of culture, people tended to agree on which emotions others were expressing facially. However, the participants in these studies were all members of developed countries that likely had been exposed to one another through movies, magazines, and tourism. Thus, they might simply have become familiar with the facial expressions seen in other cultures.

Stronger evidence for the universal expression of some emotions was made possible by the discovery of several contemporary cultures that had been totally isolated from Western culture for most of their existence. Members of the Fore and the Dani cultures of New Guinea, for example, had their first contact with anthropologists only a few years before Ekman's research took place. If members of these cultures gave the same interpretation of facial expressions and produced the same expressions on their own faces as people in Western cultures, there would be much stronger evidence for the universality of facial expressions of emotion. Ekman and his colleagues (Ekman & Friesen, 1971; Ekman, Sorenson, & Friesen, 1969) presented members of the Fore culture with three photographs of people from outside their culture and asked them to point to the picture that represented how they would feel in a certain situation. For example, if a participant was told "Your child has died and you feel very sad," he or she would have the opportunity to choose which of the three pictures most closely corresponded to sadness. The results indicated very high rates of agreement on facial expressions of emotions. Moreover, when photographs of the Fore and Dani posing the primary emotions were shown to college students in the United States, the same high agreement was found (Ekman & Friesen, 1975).

If facial expressions of primary emotions are fairly constant from one culture to another, why are people so often confused about the emotions being expressed by people in other cultures? The answer lies in a principle called **display rules** (Ekman & Friesen, 1975). Display rules refer to the circumstances under which it is appropriate for people to show emotion. Display rules differ substantially from culture to culture (Matsumoto & Kupperbusch, 2001). In a study of Japanese and American college students (Ekman, Friesen, & Ellsworth, 1972), the participants watched graphic films of surgical procedures, either by themselves or in the presence of an experimenter. The students' facial expressions were secretly videotaped as they viewed the films. The results showed that when the students were by themselves, both the Japanese and the Americans showed facial expressions of disgust, as expected. But when the participants watched the film in the presence of an experimenter, the two groups displayed different responses. American students continued to show disgust on their faces, but the Japanese students showed facial expressions that were more neutral, even somewhat pleasant.

Why the sudden switch? The answer lies in the different display rules of the two cultures. The Japanese norm says "Don't display strong negative emotion in the presence of a respected elder" (in this case, the experimenter). Americans typically don't honor this display rule; hence, they expressed their true emotions whether they were alone or with someone else. To interpret what others are feeling, we need to understand both the universal expression of emotions and the particular rules operating in a culture.

Display rules Culture-specific rules that govern how, when, and why expressions of emotion are appropriate.

CHECK YOUR UNDERSTANDING

1. _____ rules refer to the circumstances under which it is appropriate to show emotion.

___a. display

___b. inhibition

___c. anger

___d. nonverbal

2. When men get angry, they generally turn their anger

___a. against themselves

___b. against institutions

___c. against other people

Answers: 1.a, 2. c

Motivation and emotion help guide our behavior. A **motive** is a specific need or desire that arouses the organism and directs its behavior toward a goal. **Emotion** is the experience of feelings such as fear, joy, surprise, and anger, which also activates and affects behavior.

Perspectives on Motivation

Instincts   At the turn of the twentieth century, psychologists believed that motivated behavior was caused by **instincts**—specific, inborn behavior patterns characteristic of an entire species.

Drive-Reduction Theory   **Drive-reduction theory** viewed motivated behavior as an attempt to reduce an unpleasant state of tension or arousal (a **drive**) and return the body to a state of **homeostasis,** or balance. **Primary drives** are unlearned and motivate behavior that is vital to survival. **Secondary drives** are acquired through learning.

Arousal Theory   Today scientists assert that an organism seeks to maintain an optimum state of arousal. **Arousal theory** suggests that each individual has an optimum level of arousal that varies from one situation to another and over the course of the day. The best level of arousal necessary to perform all tasks, however, is not known. The **Yerkes-Dodson law** states that the more complex the task, the lower the level of arousal that can be tolerated without interfering with performance. Objects in the environment, called **incentives,** also motivate behavior.

Intrinsic and Extrinsic Motivation   Motivation can be intrinsic (rewards provided by an activity itself) or extrinsic (rewards obtained as a consequence of the activity).

Hunger and Thirst

Biological Factors   Hunger is primarily regulated by two regions in the hypothalamus: the feeding center, which stimulates eating, and the satiety center, which reduces the feeling of hunger. A third center in the hypothalamus appears to influence the drive to eat specific foods. Changes in the level of the simple sugar glucose in the blood signal the need for food. Receptors in the stomach and a hormone released by the small intestine also send signals to the brain.

Cultural and Environmental Factors   How a person responds when hungry will vary according to his or her experiences with food, which are mostly governed by learning and social conditioning. Culture also influences what we choose to eat and how much.

Eating Disorders and Obesity   **Anorexia nervosa** is a serious eating disorder associated with an intense fear of weight gain and a distorted body image. Another eating disorder, **bulimia nervosa,** is characterized by binge eating followed by self-induced vomiting. Eating disorders are notoriously difficult to treat, especially in a culture obsessed with dieting. Many factors including heredity, more sedentary life styles, availability of fast food, and portion size have contributed to the rise of overeating and obesity in America. In addition to the serious medical risks associated with obesity, overweight people often have lowered self-confidence, and are victimized and discriminated against in school and in the workplace.

Thirst   Thirst parallels hunger in that both internal and external cues can trigger the thirst drive. Dehydration both inside and outside the cells prompts activation of the thirst drive; so do external stimuli such as weather conditions.

Sex

Sex is a primary drive that motivates reproductive behavior, which is vital to the survival of the species.

Sexual Motivation   Biological factors have a complex effect on sexual response. The male sex hormone—**testosterone**—influences early sexual development, the differentiation of male and female sex organs, and to some extent characteristic patterns of adult sexual behavior. The brain, in particular, the limbic system is involved in sexual excitement. It is also possible that scents, called pheromones, secreted by one sex promote sexual readiness in potential partners. Humans are susceptible to a wide variety of external stimuli such as sight and smell. The human sexual response is affected by social experience, sexual experience, nutrition, emotions, and age. Culture guides people's views of sexual attractiveness.

Sexual Behavior   The *sexual response cycle* in humans progresses through four phases: excitement, plateau, orgasm (climax), and resolution. Research indicates that most people are far more conservative in their sexual life than media portrayals of sexual behavior indicate.

Sexual Orientation   *Sexual orientation* refers to the direction of an individual's sexual interest—heterosexuals are sexually attracted to members of the opposite sex and homosexuals to members of their own sex. As with most complex behaviors, the origins of sexual orientation appear to involve both biological and environmental factors.

Other Motives

Stimulus motives depend more on environmental stimuli than on internal states.

Exploration and Curiosity   Exploration and curiosity are motives activated by the unfamiliar and are directed toward the goal of "finding out." Psychologists disagree on the nature and causes of curiosity, but it has been linked to creativity.

Manipulation and Contact   Humans and other primates have a strong urge to manipulate objects. The need for contact is another important stimulus motive. Although manipulation requires active "hands-on" exploration, contact may be passive.

Aggression   Any behavior that is intended to inflict physical or psychological harm on others is an act of **aggression.** Freud saw aggression as an innate drive that must be channeled into constructive and socially acceptable avenues. Another view is that aggression is triggered by pain or frustration. Many contemporary psychologists believe aggression is a learned response, modeled after the aggressive behavior of others.

Cultural differences in aggressiveness are reflected in statistics on violent crimes. Individualist cultures, which value personal independence, tend to be high in crime, whereas collectivist cultures, which emphasize interdependence and group cohesion, tend to be lower. Research has also linked the dimension of individualism/collectivism to how various cultures interpret aggressive behavior.

Across cultures and at every age, males are more likely than females to behave aggressively both verbally and physically. Both biological and social factors appear to contribute to these gender differences.

Achievement   The **achievement motive,** a learned social motive, underlies the desire to excel, to overcome obstacles, and to strive to do something difficult as well and as quickly as possible. The need for achievement, which varies among individuals, has been measured using the Work and Family Orientation scale, a questionnaire that measures work orientation, mastery, and competitiveness. It has been found that a high degree of competitiveness may actually interfere with achievement.

Affiliation   The **affiliation motive,** the need to be with other people, is especially pronounced when people feel threatened. But we may also choose to get together with others to obtain positive feedback or to alleviate anxiety. Our need for affiliation may have an evolutionary basis stemming from the survival value associated with maintaining social bonds.

A Hierarchy of Motives   Abraham Maslow suggested that the various motives can be arranged in a hierarchy. The lower motives spring from bodily needs that must be satisfied for survival; higher motives such as self-actualization, the drive to realize one's full potential, do not emerge until the more basic motives have largely been satisfied. Recent research challenges this view by indicating that in some societies difficulty in meeting lower needs can actually foster the satisfaction of higher needs.

Emotions

Emotions, like motives, both arouse and direct our behavior.

Basic Emotions   Robert Plutchik's classification system for emotions uses a "circle" to position eight basic categories of emotions that motivate various kinds of adaptive behavior. However, not all cultures view or categorize emotions this way. Because of these differences, psychologists distinguish between primary emotions, which are shared by people everywhere, and secondary emotions, which are found in some cultures but not in all.

A cross-cultural analysis of emotional expression has led Paul Ekman and his colleagues to argue for the universality of at least six emotions—happiness, surprise, sadness, fear, disgust, and anger. Many psychologists also add love to this list of basic emotions.

Positive psychology concerns itself with understanding one of our most positive emotions: happiness. Happiness is just one aspect of *subjective well-being.* To understand the roots of happiness and feelings of well-being, researchers looked first at external events and the demographic characteristics of happy people.

Theories of Emotion   According to the **James-Lange theory,** environmental stimuli bring on physiological changes in our bodies that we interpret as emotions. The **Cannon-Bard theory** states that the processing of emotions and bodily responses occurs simultaneously rather than one after the other. The **cognitive theory** of emotion holds that the situation that we are in when we are aroused—the overall environment—gives us clues that help us interpret this general state of arousal. According to recent research, facial expression may influence emotions apart from cognition.

Izard proposes four highly interactive activators of emotion: neural, sensorimotor, motivational, and cognitive.

Nonverbal Communication of Emotion

Voice Quality   Much of the information we convey is contained not in the words we use but in the way they are expressed.

Facial Expression   Facial expressions are the most obvious emotional indicators. Certain inborn or universal facial expressions serve an adaptive function.

Body Language   Body language—our posture, the way we move, our preferred personal distance from others when talking to them—also expresses emotion.

Personal Space   Personal space—the distance people maintain between themselves and others—varies according to the emotions felt.

Explicit Acts   Explicit acts, such as slamming a door, are another clue to someone's emotional state. People vary in their sensitivity to nonverbal cues.

Gender, Culture, and Emotion

Gender and Emotion   When confronted with a person in distress, women are more likely than men to express emotion about the situation, even though the levels of physiological arousal for the two sexes are the same. In some stressful situations men and women label what they are feeling differently. Women also tend to be better at decoding emotional expression and tend to regulate their own expression more than men.

Culture and Emotion   The individualism/collectivism dimension helps to explain the diversity across cultures in the experience of emotions. Members of collectivist cultures, for example, tend to have many terms for other-focused emotions, have emotions of shorter duration, and promote emotional displays that are designed to maintain group cohesion.

Facial expressions of emotions appear to have a universal quality: The face shows a similar expression for a given emotion regardless of the cultural background of the expressor. This is known as the universalist position. In contrast, the culture-learning view suggests that facial expressions of emotion are learned within a particular culture.

Overlaying the universal expression of emotion are **display rules,** which govern the circumstances under which it is appropriate to show emotion. These do tend to differ from culture to culture.

key terms

Emotion	329	Yerkes-Dodson law	331
Motive	329	Arousal theory	331
Homeostasis	330	Extrinsic motivation	332
Secondary drive	330	Intrinsic motivation	332
Primary drive	330	Incentive	332
Drive-reduction theory	330	Anorexia nervosa	335
Drive	330	Bulimia nervosa	336
Instinct	330	Testosterone	340

Stimulus motive	343
Aggression	345
Achievement motive	347
Affiliation motive	348
James-Lange theory	352
Cannon-Bard theory	353
Cognitive theory	354
Display rules	361

OVERVIEW

Methods in Developmental Psychology
Prenatal Development
The Newborn Baby
Reflexes
Temperament
Perceptual Abilities
Infancy and Childhood
Physical Development
Motor Development
Cognitive Development

Moral Development
Language Development
Social Development
Sex-Role Development
Television and Children

Adolescence
Physical Changes
Cognitive Changes
Personality and Social Development
Forming an Identity
Some Problems of Adolescence

Adulthood
Love, Partnerships, and Parenting
The World of Work
Cognitive Changes
Personality Changes

Late Adulthood
Physical Changes
Social Development
Cognitive Changes
Facing the End of Life

Life Span Development

10

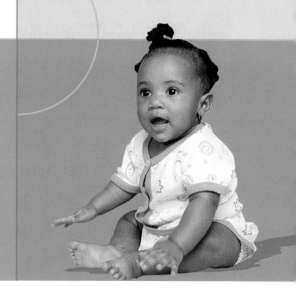

ay's was a very unusual childhood. Born the fourth of five children in a very wealthy family, she grew up in palatial houses tended by large staffs of servants. Yet oddly enough, she had no sense of being wealthy. Money was never talked about in her home, and she and her brother and sisters were never showered with expensive toys. From her earliest days she saw herself as shy, passive, and lacking self-assurance, dowdy and never quite "measuring up." She envied her second sister's rebellious nature, but didn't have the courage to be rebellious herself. Her mother did nothing to nurture greater self-confidence. She set such high expectations for her children that reaching those heights seemed an impossible goal. The man Kay married was brilliant, witty, charming, and extremely successful. He dominated all the decisions in their family life. He was the creative thinker, she the implementer. He was the provider of excitement and zest, she the dutiful follower. And yet, after quietly suffering her husband's bouts of heavy drinking, his unpredictable anger, his long struggle with manic depression, and his eventual violent suicide, she went on to take over the family business and become the talented and powerful head of a highly influential newspaper. This poor little rich girl so burdened with self-doubts was Katharine Graham (1917–2001), former publisher of *The Washington Post*. In her eighties, she won a Pulitzer Prize in 1997 for her autobiography (Graham, 1997).

The study of how people change from birth to old age is called **developmental psychology.** Because virtually everything about a person changes over the life span, developmental psychology includes all the other topics that psychologists study, such as thinking, language, intelligence, emotions, and social behavior. But developmental psychologists focus only on a certain aspect of these topics: how and why changes in them occur as people grow older.

In trying to understand both the "what" and the "why" of human development, psychologists focus on three of the enduring issues we introduced in Chapter 1. One is the theme of individual characteristics versus shared human traits. Although there are many common patterns to human development, each person's development is also in some ways unique. Katharine Graham's life illustrates this well. Like so many other women, she progressed through the stages of childhood, adolescence, and adulthood; she married, had children, worked at a job, and eventually became a grandmother. These are all common developmental milestones. Yet in other ways, Katharine Graham's development was not like everyone else's. Not every woman is born into such a wealthy family, feels the shyness and insecurity that she did, has to cope with the early death of a husband, or achieves such heights in the business world. This combination of shared and distinctive elements is characteristic of all human development. We all take essentially the same developmental journey, but each of us travels somewhat different roads and experiences events in different ways.

A second theme that developmental psychologists stress is stability versus change. Human development is characterized by both major life transitions *and* continuities with the past. Again, Katharine Graham's life is an excellent example. The death of her husband and her takeover of his job at the family-owned *Post* was certainly a major turning point in her development. She went from being the dutiful, subordinate wife to becoming the accomplished head of a major American newspaper. And yet with all the changes this transition brought, she still had ties to the person she had been before. Self-doubts about her job performance plagued her endlessly, even at the pinnacle of her success. She would lie awake at night reliving

THINKABOUTIT

You will find the answers to these questions in the chapter:

1. How do psychologists study developmental changes?

2. What factors can affect children before birth?

3. What can newborn babies do?

4. Do young children think differently from adults?

5. What are the developmental challenges of adolescence?

6. How does personality change during adulthood?

7. Is late adulthood a period of decline?

Developmental psychology The study of the changes that occur in people from birth through old age.

365

Shy and insecure as a child, Katherine (Meyer) Graham rose to the top of her profession and became one of America's most influential and admired people.

how she handled situations, wondering how she might have done better. The little girl fearful of never being "good enough" still lingered on inside her.

Finally, the issue of heredity versus environment is central to developmental psychology. Human development can be explained by a combination of biological forces and environmental experiences. These two constantly interact to shape how people grow. What made Katharine Graham into the person she became? She herself has said that she lacked the "proper instincts" to be self-assured and daring, that what she was to some extent stemmed from her inherited makeup. And yet she also recognizes the crucial importance of environment. How different might she have been had she been born into a different family, married a different husband, or chosen a different life's work? People, she writes, are "molded by the way they spend their days." This is an important concept in developmental psychology.

You will meet these three major issues often in this chapter as we journey through the human life course. We begin with human development in its earliest moments—when the individual eventually to be born is just a single cell floating in the darkness of the mother's uterus. This starts the stage of prenatal development.

Methods in Developmental Psychology

How do psychologists study developmental changes?

Developmental psychologists use the same research methods that psychologists in other areas use: naturalistic observations, correlational studies, and experiments (see Chapter 1, the Science of Psychology). However, because developmental psychologists are interested in processes of change over time, they use these methods in three special types of studies: cross-sectional, longitudinal, and biographical.

In a **cross-sectional study,** researchers examine developmental change by observing or testing people of different ages at the same point in time. For example, they might study the development of logical thought by testing groups of 6-year-olds, 9-year-olds, and 12-year-olds, and then looking for differences among the age groups. Or, if they are interested in cognitive changes during adulthood, they might study 40-year-olds, 60-year-olds, and 80-year-olds. The problem with cross-sectional studies is that they do not distinguish age differences from *cohort differences.* A **cohort** is a group of people born during the same period of history; all Americans born in 1940, for example, form a cohort. Cohort differences are differences between individuals stemming from the fact that they were born and grew up at different historical times. If we found that 40-year-olds were able to solve harder math problems than 80-year-olds, we wouldn't know whether this result was due to the difference in their ages or to cohort differences. After all, the 80-year-olds grew up in an era when educational opportunities were more limited and there were no calculators or computers.

Cross-sectional study A method of studying developmental changes by comparing people of different ages at about the same time.

Cohort A group of people born during the same period in historical time.

A **longitudinal study** examines developmental changes by testing the same people two or more times, as they grow older. Thus, researchers who are interested in the development of logical thought might begin their study testing a group of 6-year-olds, wait 3 years and test the same children again at age 9, then wait another 3 years to test them again at age 12. Longitudinal studies have problems, too. They do not distinguish age differences from differences that arise from improved assessment or measurement tools. For example, researchers retesting a cohort at age 9 might have access to a more sensitive measure of logical thought than they did when they tested that cohort at age 6. So if significant improvements turned up over this 3-year period, it wouldn't be clear to what extent they reflected the advance in age or the more sensitive measuring tool. Another problem is that carrying out a longitudinal study takes considerable time, even if the researchers are interested only in development during childhood. If they are studying changes that take place over the course of adulthood, a longitudinal study could require 50 years or more.

To avoid the huge expense of such a long study, researchers have devised a third way of studying adulthood: the **biographical** or **retrospective study.** Whereas a longitudinal study might start with some 20-year-olds and follow them as they grow older, a biographical approach might start with some 70-year-olds and pursue their lives backward. That is, the researchers would try to reconstruct their participants' past by interviewing them and by consulting various other sources, much as a biographer does when writing someone's life. Biographical data are less trustworthy than either longitudinal or cross-sectional data, however, because people's recollections of the past are not always accurate.

Each of these three kinds of studies has both advantages and disadvantages, which are summarized in Table 10–1. You will come across examples of all three methods in this chapter.

Longitudinal study A method of studying developmental changes by evaluating the same people at different points in their lives.

Biographical (or retrospective) study A method of studying developmental changes by reconstructing people's past through interviews and inferring the effects of past events on current behaviors.

table 10-1 ADVANTAGES AND DISADVANTAGES OF DIFFERENT TYPES OF DEVELOPMENTAL RESEARCH METHODS

Method	Advantages	Disadvantages
Cross-Sectional	• Inexpensive • Takes relatively little time to complete • Avoids high attrition rate (dropout of participants from study)	• Different age groups are not necessarily very much alike • Differences across age groups may be due to cohort differences rather than age
Longitudinal	• Generates detailed information about individuals • Allows for the study of developmental change in great detail • Eliminates differences due to different cohorts	• Expensive and time consuming • Potential for high attrition rate—participants may drop out over a long period of time • Differences over time may be due to differences in assessment tools rather than age
Biographical or Retrospective	• Generates rich detail about one individual's life • Allows for in-depth study of one individual	• Individual's recall often untrustworthy • Can be very time consuming and expensive

Prenatal development Development from conception to birth.

Embryo A developing human between 2 weeks and 3 months after conception.

Fetus A developing human between 3 months after conception and birth.

Placenta The organ by which an embryo or fetus is attached to its mother's uterus and that nourishes it during prenatal development.

Teratogens Toxic substances such as alcohol or nicotine that cross the placenta and may result in birth defects.

Critical period A time when certain internal and external influences have a major effect on development; at other periods, the same influences will have little or no effect.

CHECK YOUR UNDERSTANDING

In a _____ study the researcher studies a group of subjects two or more times as they grow older.

___a. cross-sectional

___b. retrospective

___c. longitudinal

Answer: c

Prenatal Development

What factors can affect children before birth?

During the earliest period of **prenatal development**—the stage of development from conception to birth—the fertilized egg divides, embarking on the process that will transform it, in just nine months, from a one-celled organism into a complex human being. The dividing cells form a hollow ball, which implants itself in the wall of the uterus. Two weeks after conception, the cells begin to specialize: Some will form the baby's internal organs, others will form muscles and bones, and still others will form the skin and the nervous system. No longer an undifferentiated mass of cells, the developing organism is now called an **embryo.**

The embryo stage ends three months after conception, when the *fetal stage* begins. At this point, although it is only one inch long, the **fetus** roughly resembles a human being, with arms and legs, a large head, and a heart that has begun to beat. Although it can already move various parts of its body, another month is likely to pass before the mother feels those movements.

An organ called the **placenta** nourishes the embryo and the fetus. Within the placenta, the mother's blood vessels transmit nutritive substances to the embryo or fetus and carry waste products away from it. Although the mother's blood never actually mingles with that of her unborn child, toxic agents that she eats, drinks, or inhales (known as **teratogens**) are capable of crossing the placenta and compromising the baby's development (Roy, Seidler, & Slotkin, 2002; Wass, Simmons, Thomas, & Riley, 2002). Diseases can also cross the placenta and infect the fetus, often with disastrous results.

Many potentially harmful substances have a **critical period** when they are most likely to have a major effect on the fetus. At other times, the same substance may have no effect at all. For example, if a woman contracts rubella during the first three months of pregnancy, the effects can range from death of the fetus to a child who is born deaf. However, rubella contracted during the final three months of pregnancy is unlikely to cause severe damage to the fetus because the critical period for the formation of major body parts has passed.

Pregnancy is most likely to have a favorable outcome when the mother gets good nutrition and good medical care, and when she avoids exposure to substances that could be harmful to her baby, including alcohol and nicotine. Alcohol is the drug most often abused by pregnant women, and with devastating consequences (Riley et al., 2003). Pregnant women

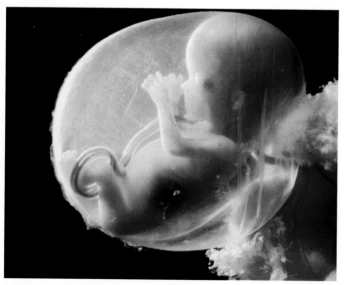

At four months, the fetus is two to four inches long and has a conspicuously human appearance.

who consume large amounts of alcohol risk giving birth to a child with **fetal alcohol syndrome (FAS),** a condition characterized by facial deformities, heart defects, stunted growth, and cognitive impairments (Mattson, Riley, Gramling, Delis, & Jones, 1998; Shaffer, 1999). Even small amounts of alcohol can cause neurological problems (Hunt, Streissguth, Kerr, & Olson, 1995; Shriver & Piersel, 1994). This is why doctors recommend that pregnant women and those who are trying to become pregnant abstain from drinking alcohol altogether.

Pregnant women are also wise not to smoke. Smoking restricts the oxygen supply to the fetus, slows its breathing, and speeds up its heartbeat. These changes are associated with a significantly increased risk of miscarriage (Ness et al., 1999). In this country alone, smoking may cause over 100,000 miscarriages a year. Babies of mothers who smoke are also more apt to suffer low birth weight, which puts the child at risk for other developmental problems (DiFranza & Lew, 1995).

Increased psychological stress, and how it is coped with during pregnancy also appears to be related to the health of a newborn. For instance, one study (Rini, Dunkel-Schetter, Wadhwa, & Sandman, 1999) found that the risks of prematurity and low birth weight were higher in mothers with low self-esteem who felt pessimistic, stressed, and anxious during pregnancy.

Differences in access to good nutrition and health care help explain why the infant death rate in this country is over twice as high for African Americans as it is for whites (see Figure 10–1; Singh & Yu, 1995). A much higher percentage of African Americans live in poverty, and it is much harder for the poor to eat a healthy diet and see a doctor regularly during pregnancy (Roussy, 2000; Aved, Irwin, Cummings, & Findeisen, 1993).

Figure 10–1
Mortality rates for white and African American infants.
Source: National Center for Health Statistics, 1995 (through 1990); BlackHealthCare.com, 2000 (for 1991–1996); Centers for Disease Control (for 2000).

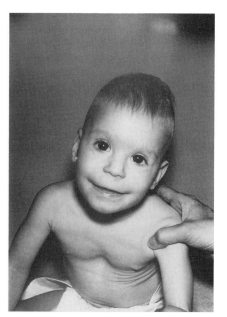

Children born with fetal alcohol syndrome often exhibit facial deformities, heart defects, stunted growth, and cognitive impairments that can last throughout life. The syndrome is entirely preventable but not curable.

| | | | CHECK YOUR UNDERSTANDING |

Match the following terms with the appropriate definition.

___ fetus   a. substances that cross the placenta, causing birth defects

___ prenatal development   b. times at which major damage can be done to the fetus

___teratogens   c. the fertilized egg, two weeks after conception

___embryo   d. the developing organism, after three months

___critical periods   e. the period from conception to birth

___placenta   f. the organ that nourishes the fetus

Answers: fetus—d; prenatal development—e; teratogens—a; embryo—c; critical periods—b; placenta—f

The Newborn Baby

What can newborn babies do?

Research has disproved the old idea that **neonates,** or newborn babies, do nothing but eat, sleep, and cry, while remaining oblivious to the world. True, newborns can sleep up to 20 hours a day, but when awake they are much more aware and competent than they may seem at first glance.

Fetal alcohol syndrome (FAS) A disorder that occurs in children of women who drink alcohol during pregnancy that is characterized by facial deformities, heart defects, stunted growth, and cognitive impairments.

Neonates Newborn babies.

Rooting reflex The reflex that causes a newborn baby to turn its head toward something that touches its cheek and to grope around with its mouth.

Sucking reflex The newborn baby's tendency to suck on objects placed in the mouth.

Swallowing reflex The reflex that enables the newborn baby to swallow liquids without choking.

Grasping reflex The reflex that causes newborn babies to close their fists around anything that is put in their hands.

Stepping reflex The reflex that causes newborn babies to make little stepping motions if they are held upright with their feet just touching a surface.

Temperament Characteristic patterns of emotional reactions and emotional self-regulation.

Reflexes

For one thing, newborns come equipped with a number of useful reflexes. Many of these reflexes, such as those that control breathing, are essential to life outside the uterus. Some enable babies to nurse. The baby's tendency to turn his or her head toward anything that touches the cheek is called the **rooting reflex.** The rooting reflex is very useful in helping the baby find the mother's nipple. The **sucking reflex** is the tendency to suck on anything that enters the mouth, and the **swallowing reflex** enables them to swallow milk and other liquids without choking.

Other reflexes have purposes that are less obvious. The **grasping reflex** is the tendency to cling vigorously to an adult's finger or to any object placed in their hands. The **stepping reflex** refers to the fact that very young babies take what looks like walking steps if they are held upright with their feet just touching a flat surface. These two reflexes normally disappear after two or three months, reemerging later as voluntary grasping (at around five months of age) and real walking (at the end of the first year).

Very young babies are also capable of a surprisingly complex kind of behavior: imitating the facial expressions of adults. If an adult opens his or her mouth or sticks out his or her tongue, newborn babies often respond by opening their mouths or sticking out their tongues (McCall, 1979; Meltzoff & Moore, 1989). The behavior disappears after a few weeks, and then reemerges in a more complex form many months later (Bjorklund, 1989; Wyrwicka, 1988).

Almost all newborns respond to the human face, the human voice, and the human touch. This improves their chances of survival. After all, babies are totally dependent on the people who take care of them, so it is essential that their social relationships get off to a good start. From the very beginning, they have a means of communicating their needs to those they live with: They can cry. And very soon—in only about six weeks—they have an even better method of communication, one that serves as a thank you to the people who are working so hard to keep them happy: They can smile.

Temperament

We may be tempted to talk about babies as if they are all the same, but babies display individual differences in **temperament** (Gartstein & Rothbart, 2003; Goldsmith & Harman, 1994). Some cry much more than others; some are much more active. Some babies love to be cuddled; others seem to wriggle uncomfortably when held. Some are highly reactive to stimuli around them, whereas others are quite placid no matter what they see or hear.

ENDURING ISSUES **diversity**universality

Different from Birth

In a classic study of infant temperament, Alexander Thomas and Stella Chess (1977) identified three types of babies: "easy," "difficult," and "slow-to-warm-up."

- "Easy" babies are good-natured and adaptable, easy to care for and please.

- "Difficult" babies are moody and intense, reacting to new people and new situations both negatively and strongly.

- "Slow-to-warm-up" babies are relatively inactive and slow to respond to new things, and when they do react, their reactions are mild.

To these three types, Jerome Kagan and his associates (Kagan, Reznick, Snidman, Gibbons, & Johnson, 1988; Kagan & Snidman, 1991) have added a fourth: the "shy child." Shy children are timid and inhibited, fearful of anything new or strange. Their nervous systems react to stimuli in a characteristically hypersensitive way (Kagan, 1994). Kagan and his colleagues have speculated that such differences may be due in large part to the effects of different gene pools and genetic predispositions (Kagan, Arcus, & Snidman, 1993). Additional evidence to support the notion that temperament is largely biologically based and stable comes from neuroimaging studies showing that the amygdala of shy infants overreacts (compared to less shy and inhibited infants) when they are presented with a novel stimulus or situation (Schwartz et al., 2003b). Moreover, longitudinal research that examined the amygdalar response to novel stimuli in adolescents who had been shy and inhibited during their infancy revealed that they too displayed a hyperactive amygdala during their adolescent years. Furthermore, this research also found that these previously shy and inhibited infants had largely grown up to become shy and inhibited teenagers (Schwartz, Christopher, Shin, Kagan, & Rauch, 2003).

If they are raised in a compatible environment, easy, uninhibited babies will most likely grow to be outgoing children and adults.

Some evidence suggests, however, that differences in temperament may be due to prenatal influences (Azar, 1997b; DiPietro, Hodgson, Costigan, & Johnson, 1996). In particular, maternal stress produces reliable changes in heartbeat and movement in the fetus, and these, in turn, are correlated with temperament in the child (Huizink et al., 2002). Regardless of what initially causes a baby's temperament, it often remains quite stable over time (Rothbart, Derryberry, & Hershey, 2000). In one study that asked mothers to describe their children's temperaments, characteristics such as degree of irritability, flexibility, and persistence were all relatively stable from infancy through age 8 (Pedlow, Sanson, Prior, & Oberklaid, 1993). Other studies have found that fussy or difficult infants are likely to become "problem children" who are aggressive and have difficulties in school (Guérin, 1994; Patterson & Bank, 1989; Persson-Blennow & McNeil, 1988). A longitudinal study of shy children and some of their less inhibited peers showed that most shy infants continue to be relatively shy and inhibited in middle childhood, just as most uninhibited infants remained relatively outgoing and bold (Kagan & Snidman, 1991).

A combination of biological and environmental factors generally contributes to this stability in behavior. For instance, if a newborn has an innate predisposition to cry often and react negatively to things, the parents may find themselves tired, frustrated, and often angry. These reactions in the parents may serve to reinforce the baby's difficult behaviors, and so they tend to endure. Even if children are born with a particular temperament, then, they need not have that temperament for life. Each child's predispositions interact with his or her experiences, and how the child turns out is the result of that interaction (Kagan, 1989, 1994; Kagan, Snidman, & Arcus, 1992; Maccoby, 2000).

Perceptual Abilities

Newborns can see, hear, and understand far more than previous generations gave them credit for. Their senses work fairly well at birth and rapidly improve to near-adult levels. Neonates begin to absorb and process information from the outside world as soon as they enter it—or, in some cases, even before.

Vision Unlike puppies and kittens, human babies are born with their eyes open and functioning, even though the world looks a bit fuzzy to them at first. They see most clearly when faces or objects are only eight to ten inches away from them. Visual acuity (the clarity of vision) improves rapidly, however, and so does the ability to focus on objects at different distances. By six or eight months of age, babies can see almost as well as the average college student, though their visual system takes another three or four years to develop fully (Maurer & Maurer, 1988).

Even very young babies already have visual preferences. They would rather look at a new picture or pattern than one they have seen many times before. If given a choice between two pictures or patterns, both of which are new to them, they generally prefer the one with the clearer contrasts and more simple patterns. As babies get older and their vision improves, they prefer more and more complex patterns, perhaps reflecting their need for an increasingly complex environment (Acredolo & Hake, 1982; Fantz, Fagan, & Miranda, 1975; Slater, 2000).

In general, infants find human faces and voices particularly interesting (see Flavell, 1999). They not only like to look at another person's face, but also will follow the other person's gaze. Hood, Willen, and Driver (1998) presented a photograph of a human face on a video monitor. Sometimes the adult depicted looked straight ahead, sometimes to the left or right. The researchers found that infants as young as three months noticed the direction of the adult's gaze and shifted their gaze accordingly. Newborns also prefer to look at their own mother rather than at a stranger (Walton, Bower, & Bower, 1992). Because they see the mother so often, they acquire sets of different images of her. This visual familiarity makes the mother the preferred person in their environment (Walton & Bower, 1993).

Live! psych 10.1

Depth Perception Although researchers have been unable to find evidence of depth perception in babies younger than 4 months (Aslin & Smith, 1988), the ability to see the world in three dimensions is well developed by the time a baby learns to crawl, between 6 and 12 months of age. This was demonstrated in a classic experiment using a device called a *visual cliff* (Walk & Gibson, 1961). Researchers divided a table into three parts. The center was a solid runway, raised above the rest of the table by about an inch. On one side of this runway was a solid surface decorated in a checkerboard pattern and covered with a sheet of clear glass. The other side was also covered with a thick sheet of clear glass, but on this side—the visual cliff—the checkerboard surface was not directly under the glass, but 40 inches below it. An infant of crawling age was placed on the center runway, and the mother stood on one side or the other, encouraging the baby to crawl toward her across the glass. All of the 6- to 14-month-old infants tested refused to crawl across the visual cliff, even though they were perfectly willing to cross the "shallow" side of the table. When the "deep" side separated the baby from the mother, some of the infants cried; others peered down at the surface below the glass or patted the glass with their hands. Their behaviors clearly showed that they could perceive depth.

But what about younger babies? Because most infants younger than six months cannot crawl, they cannot be tested in the standard way using the visual cliff. In one study, they were simply placed facedown on the two sides of the table, and their pulse rates were measured in both positions. When the infants were moved from the shallow to the deep side, their heart rates slowed down, a reaction typical of both infants and adults who stop to orient themselves in new situations (Campos, Langer, & Krowitz, 1970). Thus, although they did not yet show apprehension toward the cliff, babies younger than six months did seem to realize that something was different about the deep side. Apparently, the emergence of apprehension toward heights depends on experience with self-produced movement, such as crawling (Bertenthal, Campos, & Kermoian, 1994).

When placed on a visual cliff, babies of crawling age (about 6 to 14 months) will not cross the deep side, even to reach their mothers. This classic experiment tells us that by the time they can crawl, babies can also perceive depth.

Other Senses Even before babies are born their ears are in working order. Fetuses in the uterus can hear sounds and will startle at a sudden, loud noise in the mother's environment. After birth, babies show signs that they remember sounds they heard in the womb.

Babies also are born with the ability to tell the direction of a sound. They show this by turning their heads toward the source of a sound (Muir, 1985.) By four months, they can even locate the source of a sound in the dark, where there are no visual cues (Hillier, Hewitt, & Morrongiello, 1992).

Infants are particularly tuned in to the sounds of human speech. One-month-olds can distinguish among similar speech sounds such as "pa-pa-pa" and "ba-ba-ba" (Eimas & Tartter, 1979). In some ways, young infants are even better at distinguishing speech sounds than are older children and adults. As children grow older, they often lose their ability to hear the difference between two very similar speech sounds that are not distinguished in their native language (Werker & Desjardins, 1995). For example, young Japanese infants have no trouble hearing the difference between "ra" and "la," sounds that are not distinguished in the Japanese language. By the time they are one year old, however, Japanese infants can no longer tell these two sounds apart (Werker, 1989).

With regard to taste and smell, newborns have clear-cut likes and dislikes. They like sweet flavors, a preference that persists through childhood. Babies only a few hours old will show pleasure at the taste of sweetened water but will screw up their faces in disgust at the taste of lemon juice (Steiner, 1979).

As infants grow older, their perceptions of the world become keener and more meaningful. Two factors are important in this development. One is physical maturation of the sense organs and the nervous system; the other is gaining experience in the world.

CHECK YOUR UNDERSTANDING

1. Two reflexes normally disappear after two to three months. They are

___a. sucking and swallowing

___b. grasping and rooting

___c. stepping and grasping

___d. stepping and rooting

2. Temperament differences in babies are attributable to

___a. biological factors

___b. maternal emotions during pregnancy

___c. parental reactions to an infant's crying after a baby's birth

___d. all of the above

3. Newborns prefer looking at what kind of patterns?

___a. colorful ones

___b. moving ones

___c. contrasting ones

Answers: 1.c, 2.d, 3.c

Infancy and Childhood

Do young children think differently from adults?

During the first dozen or so years of life, a helpless baby becomes a competent member of society. Many important kinds of developments occur during these early years. Here we discuss physical and motor changes as well as cognitive and social ones.

Developmental norms Ages by which an average child achieves various developmental milestones.

Physical Development

In the first year of life, the average baby grows 10 inches and gains 15 pounds. By 4 months, birth weight has doubled, and by the first birthday, birth weight has tripled. During the second year, physical growth slows considerably. Rapid increases in height and weight will not occur again until early adolescence.

An infant's growth does not occur in the smooth, continuous fashion depicted in growth charts. Rather, growth takes place in fits and starts (Lampl, Veidhuis, & Johnson, 1992). When babies are measured daily over their first 21 months, most show no growth 90 percent of the time, but when they do grow, they do so rapidly—sometimes startlingly so. Incredible though it may sound, some children gain as much as 1 inch in height overnight!

Marked changes in body proportions accompany changes in a baby's size. During the first 2 years after birth, children have heads that are large relative to their bodies as the brain undergoes rapid growth. A child's brain reaches three-quarters of its adult size by about the age of 2, at which point head growth slows down and the body does most of the growing. Head growth is virtually complete by age 10, but the body continues to grow for several more years (see Figure 10–2).

Motor Development

Motor development refers to the acquisition of skills involving movement, such as grasping, crawling, and walking. The *average ages* at which such skills are achieved are called **developmental norms.** By about 9 months, for example, the average infant can stand up while holding onto something. Crawling occurs, on average, at 10 months, and walking at about 1 year. However, some normal infants develop much faster than average, whereas others develop more slowly. A baby who is 3 or 4 months behind schedule may be perfectly normal, and one who is 3 or 4 months ahead is not necessarily destined to become a star athlete. To some extent, parents can accelerate the acquisition of motor skills in children by providing them with ample training, encouragement, and practice. Differences in these factors seem to account for most of the cross-cultural differences in the average age at which children reach certain milestones in motor development (Hopkins & Westra, 1989, 1990).

Much early motor development consists of substituting voluntary actions for reflexes (Clark, 1994). The newborn grasping and stepping reflexes, for instance, give way to voluntary grasping and walking in the older baby. Motor development proceeds in a *proximodistal* fashion—that is, from nearest the center of the body (proximal) to farthest from the center (distal). For example, the infant initially has much greater control over gross arm movements than over movements of the fin-

Figure 10–2
Body proportions at various ages.
Young children are top heavy: They have large heads and small bodies. As they get older, the body and legs become longer, and the head is proportionately smaller.
Source: Adapted from Bayley, Nancy, *Individual Patterns of Development*, 27, 45–74. Copyright © 1956 by the Society for Research in Child Development. Reprinted with permission of the Society for Research and Child Development.

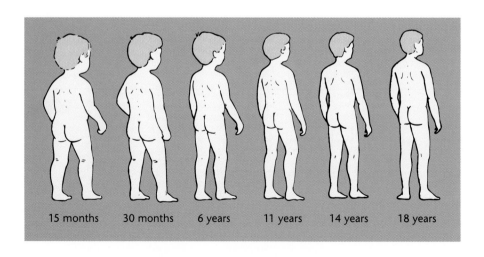

15 months   30 months   6 years   11 years   14 years   18 years

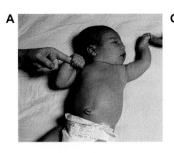

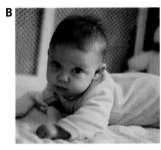

The normal sequence of motor development. (A) Neonates will cling to an adult's finger or to any other object placed in their hands. (B) At about 2 months, babies can lift their heads and shoulders. (C) They can sit up by themselves at about 6 1/2 months. (D) At about 9 months, they can stand (while holding on to something). (E) Crawling begins, on average, at 10 months. (F) Walking begins at around 1 year.

gers. Babies start batting at nearby objects as early as 1 month, but they cannot reach accurately until they are about 4 months old. It takes them another month or two before they are consistently successful in grasping objects they reach for (von Hofsten & Fazel-Zandy, 1984). At first, they grasp with the whole hand, but by the end of the first year, they can pick up a tiny object with the thumb and forefinger.

Maturation refers to biological processes that unfold as a person grows older and contribute to orderly sequences of developmental changes, such as the progression from crawling to toddling to walking. Psychologists used to believe that maturation of the central nervous system largely accounted for many of the changes in early motor skills—that environment and experience played only a minor part in their emergence. But in recent years this view has been changing (Thelen, 1994, 1995). Many researchers now see early motor development as arising from a combination of factors both within and outside the child. The child plays an active part in the process by exploring, discovering, and selecting solutions to the demands of new tasks. A baby who is learning to crawl, for example, must figure out how to position the body with belly off the ground and coordinate arm and leg movements to maintain balance while managing to proceed forward (Bertenthal et al., 1994). What doesn't work must be discarded or adapted; what does work must be remembered and called on for future use. This is a far cry from seeing the baby as one day starting to crawl simply because he or she has reached the point of maturational "readiness."

As coordination improves, children learn to run, skip, and climb. At 3 and 4, they begin to use their hands for increasingly complex tasks, learning how to put on mittens and shoes, then grappling with buttons, zippers, shoelaces, and pencils. Gradually, through a combination of practice and the physical maturation of the body and the brain, they acquire increasingly complex motor abilities, such as bike riding, rollerblading, and swimming. By the age of about 11 some begin to be highly skilled at such tasks (Clark, 1994).

Maturation An automatic biological unfolding of development in an organism as a function of the passage of time.

Sensory-motor stage In Piaget's theory, the stage of cognitive development between birth and 2 years of age in which the individual develops object permanence and acquires the ability to form mental representations.

Object permanence The concept that things continue to exist even when they are out of sight.

Mental representations Mental images or symbols (such as words) used to think about or remember an object, a person, or an event.

By uncovering the hidden toy, this baby is demonstrating object permanence.

Cognitive Development

The most influential theorist in the area of cognitive development was the Swiss psychologist Jean Piaget (1896–1980). Piaget observed and studied children, including his own three. He watched them play games, solve problems, and perform everyday tasks, and he asked them questions and devised tests to learn how they thought. As a result of his observations, Piaget believed that cognitive development is a way of adapting to the environment. In Piaget's view, children are intrinsically motivated to explore and understand things. As they do so, according to Piaget they progress through four basic stages of cognitive development. These are outlined in the Summary Table.

Sensory-Motor Stage (Birth to 2 Years)   According to Piaget, babies spend the first 2 years of life in the **sensory-motor stage** of development. They start out by simply applying the skills they are born with—primarily sucking and grasping—to a broad range of activities. Young babies delight in taking things into their mouths—their mother's breast, their own thumb, or anything else within reach. Similarly, young babies will grasp a rattle reflexively. When they eventually realize that the noise comes from the rattle, they begin to shake everything they can get hold of in an effort to reproduce the sound. Eventually, they distinguish between things that make noise and things that do not. In this way, infants begin to organize their experiences, fitting them into rudimentary categories such as "suckable" and "not suckable," "noise making" and "not noise making."

Another important outcome of the sensory-motor stage, according to Piaget, is the development of **object permanence,** an awareness that objects continue to exist even when out of sight. For a newborn child, objects that disappear simply cease to exist—"out of sight, out of mind." But as children gain experience with the world, they develop a sense of object permanence. By the time they are 18 to 24 months old, they can even imagine the movement of an object that they do not actually see move. This last skill depends on the ability to form **mental representations** of objects and to manipulate those representations in their heads. This is a major achievement of the late sensory-motor stage.

By the end of the sensory-motor stage, toddlers have also developed a capacity for self-recognition—that is, they are able to recognize the child in the mirror as

summarytable PIAGET'S STAGES OF COGNITIVE DEVELOPMENT

Stage	Approximate Age	Key Features
Sensory-motor	0–2 years	Object permanence
		Mental representations
Preoperational	2–7 years	Representational thought
		Fantasy play
		Symbolic gestures
		Egocentrism
Concrete-operational	7–11 years	Conservation
		Complex classification
Formal-operational	Adolescence–adulthood	Abstract and hypothetical thought

"myself." In one famous study, mothers put a dab of red paint on their child's nose while pretending to wipe the child's face. Then each child was placed in front of a mirror. Babies under 1 year of age stared in fascination at the red-nosed baby in the mirror; some of them even reached out to touch the nose's reflection. But babies between 21 and 24 months reached up and touched their own reddened noses, thereby showing that they knew the red-nosed baby in the mirror was "me" (Brooks-Gunn & Lewis, 1984).

Preoperational Stage (2 to 7 Years)   When children enter the **preoperational stage** of cognitive development, their thought is still tightly bound to their physical and perceptual experiences. But their increasing ability to use mental representations lays the groundwork for the development of language, for engaging in *fantasy play* (a cardboard box becomes a castle) and for using *symbolic gestures* (slashing the air with an imaginary sword to slay an imaginary dragon).

In Piaget's famous experiment, the child has to judge which glass holds more liquid: the tall, thin one or the short, wide one. Although both glasses hold the same amount, children in the preoperational stage say that the taller glass holds more, because they focus their attention on only one thing—the height of the column of liquid.

Although children this age have made advances over sensory-motor thought, in many ways they don't yet think like older children and adults. For example, preschool children are **egocentric.** They have difficulty seeing things from another person's point of view or putting themselves in someone else's place. Children this age are also easily misled by appearances (Flavell, 1986). They tend to concentrate on the most outstanding aspect of a display or event, ignoring everything else. In a famous experiment, Piaget showed preoperational children two identical glasses, filled to the same level with juice (see photo). The children were asked which glass held more juice, and they replied (correctly) that both had the same amount. Then Piaget poured the juice from one glass into a taller, narrower glass. Again the children were asked which glass held more juice. They looked at the two glasses, saw that the level of the juice in the tall, narrow one was much higher, and replied that the narrow glass had more. According to Piaget, children at this stage cannot consider the past (Piaget simply poured all the juice from one container into another) or the future (if he poured it back again, the levels of juice would be identical). Nor can they consider a container's height and width at the same time. Thus, they can't understand how an increase in one dimension (height) might be offset by a decrease in another dimension (width).

Concrete Operations (7 to 11 Years)   During the **concrete-operational stage,** children become more flexible in their thinking. They learn to consider more than one dimension of a problem at a time and to look at a situation from someone else's viewpoint. This is the age at which they become able to grasp **principles of conservation,** such as the idea that the volume of a liquid stays the same regardless of the size and shape of the container into which it is poured. Other related conservation concepts have to do with number, length, area, and mass. All involve an understanding that basic amounts remain constant despite superficial changes in appearance, which can always be reversed.

Another accomplishment of this stage is the ability to grasp complex classification schemes such as those involving superordinate and subordinate classes. For instance, if you show a preschooler four toy dogs and two toy cats and ask whether there are more dogs present or more animals, the child will almost always answer "more dogs." It is not until age 7 or 8 that children are able to think about objects as being simultaneously members of two classes, one more inclusive than the other.

Preoperational stage In Piaget's theory, the stage of cognitive development between 2 and 7 years of age in which the individual becomes able to use mental representations and language to describe, remember, and reason about the world, though only in an egocentric fashion.

Egocentric Describes the inability to see things from another's point of view.

Concrete-operational stage In Piaget's theory, the stage of cognitive development between 7 and 11 years of age in which the individual can attend to more than one thing at a time and understand someone else's point of view, though thinking is limited to concrete matters.

Principle of conservation The concept that the quantity of a substance is not altered by reversible changes in its appearance.

Formal-operational stage In Piaget's theory, the stage of cognitive development between 11 and 15 years of age in which the individual becomes capable of abstract thought.

Yet even well into the elementary school years children's thinking is still very much stuck in the "here and now." Often, they are unable to solve problems without concrete reference points that they can handle or imagine handling.

Formal Operations (11 to 15 Years)   This limitation is overcome in the **formal-operational stage** of cognitive development, often reached during adolescence. Youngsters at this stage can think in abstract terms. They can formulate hypotheses, test them mentally, and accept or reject them according to the outcome of these mental experiments. Therefore, they are capable of going beyond the here and now to understand things in terms of cause and effect, to consider possibilities as well as realities, and to develop and use general rules, principles, and theories.

Criticisms of Piaget's Theory   Piaget's work has produced a great deal of controversy. Many question his assumption that there are distinct stages in cognitive development that always progress in an orderly, sequential way, and that a child must pass through one stage before entering the next (Brainerd, 1978; Siegel, 1993). Some see cognitive development as a more gradual process, resulting from the slow acquisition of experience and practice rather than the abrupt emergence of distinctly higher levels of ability (Paris & Weissberg, 1986).

Piaget's theory has also sparked criticism for assuming that young infants understand very little about the world, such as the permanence of objects in it (see Gopnik, Meltzoff, & Kuhl, 1999; Meltzoff & Gopnik, 1997). When young babies are allowed to reveal their understanding of object permanence without being required to conduct a search for a missing object, they often seem to know perfectly well that objects continue to exist when hidden by other objects (Baillargeon, 1994). They also show other quite sophisticated knowledge of the world that Piaget thought they lacked, such as a rudimentary grasp of numbers (Wynn, 1995). At older ages, too, milestone cognitive achievements seem to be reached much sooner than Piaget believed (Gopnik, 1996).

Other critics have argued that Piaget underplayed the importance of social interaction in cognitive development. For instance, the influential Russian psychologist Lev Vygotsky contended that people who are more advanced in their thinking provide opportunities for cognitive growth for children they interact with (Vygotsky, 1979). These learning experiences greatly depend on a society's culture, another factor that Piaget ignored (Daehler, 1994).

 10.2

Finally, although Piaget's theory gives a schematic road map of cognitive development, the interests and experiences of a particular child may influence the development of cognitive abilities in ways not accounted for in the theory. Piaget's theory, in other words, does not adequately address human diversity.

Moral Development

One of the important changes in thinking that occurs during childhood and adolescence is the development of moral reasoning. Lawrence Kohlberg (1979, 1981) studied this kind of development by telling his participants stories that illustrate complex moral issues. The "Heinz dilemma" is the best known of these stories:

> In Europe, a woman was near death from cancer. One drug might save her, a form of radium that a druggist in the same town had recently discovered. The druggist was charging $2,000, ten times what the drug cost him to make. The sick woman's husband, Heinz, went to everyone he knew to borrow the money, but he could only get together about half of what it cost. He told the druggist that his wife was dying and asked him to sell it cheaper or let him pay later. But the druggist said, "No." The husband got desperate and broke into the man's store to steal the drug for his wife. (Kohlberg, 1969, p. 379)

The children and adolescents who heard this story were asked, "Should the husband have done that? Why?"

On the basis of his participants' replies to these questions (particularly the second one, "Why?"), Kohlberg theorized that moral reasoning develops in stages, much like Piaget's account of cognitive development.

- *Preconventional level* Preadolescent children are at what Kohlberg called the pre-conventional level of moral reasoning: They tend to interpret behavior in terms of its concrete consequences. Younger children at this level base their judgments of "right" and "wrong" behavior on whether it is rewarded or punished. Somewhat older children, still at this level, guide their moral choices on the basis of what satisfies needs, particularly their own.

- *Conventional level* With the arrival of adolescence and the shift to formal-operational thought, the stage is set for progression to the second level of moral reasoning, the conventional level. At this level, the adolescent at first defines right behavior as that which pleases or helps others and is approved by them. Around mid-adolescence, there is a further shift toward considering various abstract social virtues, such as being a "good citizen" and respecting authority. Both forms of conventional moral reasoning require an ability to think about such abstract values as "duty" and "social order," to consider the intentions that lie behind behavior, and to put oneself in the "other person's shoes."

- *Postconventional level* The third level of moral reasoning, the postconventional level, requires a still more abstract form of thought. This level is marked by an emphasis on abstract principles such as justice, liberty, and equality. Personal and strongly felt moral standards become the guideposts for deciding what is right and wrong. Whether these decisions correspond to the rules and laws of a particular society at a particular time is irrelevant. For the first time, people may become aware of discrepancies between what they judge to be moral and what society has determined to be legal.

Kohlberg's views have been criticized on several counts. First, research indicates that many people in our society, adults as well as adolescents, never progress beyond the conventional level of moral reasoning (Conger & Petersen, 1991). Does this mean that these people are morally "underdeveloped," as Kohlberg's theory implies?

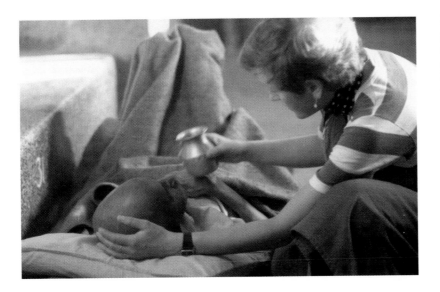

What influences the development of compassionate behavior? Researchers in moral development want to understand why people make the moral choices they do. This young woman has volunteered to work in the Mother Teresa Home for the Dying in India.

Babbling A baby's vocalizations, consisting of repetition of consonant-vowel combinations.

Second, Kohlberg's theory does not take account of cultural differences in moral values (Nucci, 2002). Kohlberg put considerations of "justice" at the highest level of moral reasoning. In Nepal, however, researchers discovered that a group of adolescent Buddhist monks placed the highest moral value on alleviating suffering and showing compassion, concepts that have no place in Kohlberg's scheme of moral development (Huebner, Garrod, & Snarey, 1990).

Third, Kohlberg's theory has been criticized as sexist. Kohlberg found that boys usually scored higher than girls on his test of moral development. According to Carol Gilligan (1982, 1992), this was because boys are more inclined to base their moral judgments on the abstract concept of justice, whereas girls tend to base theirs more on the criteria of caring about other people and the importance of maintaining personal relationships. In Gilligan's view, there is no valid reason to assume that one of these perspectives is morally superior to the other. Although subsequent research has found that gender differences in moral thinking tend to diminish in adulthood (L. D. Cohn, 1991), concerns about gender bias in Kohlberg's theory still remain.

More recent research on moral development has moved in the direction of broadening Kohlberg's focus on changes in moral reasoning. These researchers are interested in the factors that influence moral choices in everyday life, and the extent to which those choices are actually put into action. In other words, they want to understand moral behavior as much as moral thinking (Power, 1994).

Language Development

The development of language follows a predictable pattern. At about 2 months of age, an infant begins to *coo* (a nondescript word for nondescript sounds). In another month or two, the infant enters the **babbling** stage and starts to repeat sounds such as *da* or even meaningless sounds that developmental psychologists refer to as "grunts"; these sounds are the building blocks for later language development (Dill, 1994). A few months later, the infant may string together the same sound, as in *dadadada*. Finally, the baby will form combinations of different sounds, as in *dabamaga* (Ferguson & Macken, 1983).

Even deaf babies with deaf parents who communicate with sign language engage in a form of babbling (Pettito & Marentette, 1991). Like hearing infants, these babies begin to babble before they are 10 months old—but they babble with their hands! Just as hearing infants utter sounds over and over, deaf babies make repetitive movements of their hands, like those of sign language.

Gradually, an infant's babbling takes on certain features of adult language. At about age 4 to 6 months, the infant's vocalizations begin to show signs of *intonation*, the rising and lowering of pitch that allows adults to distinguish, for example, between questions ("You're tired?") and statements ("You're tired."). Also around this time babies learn the basic sounds of their native language and can distinguish them from the sounds of other languages (Cheour et al., 1998). By 6 months, they may recognize commonly used words, such as their own names (Kuhl, Williams, & Lacerda, 1992; Mandel, Jusczyk, & Pisoni, 1995) and the words *mommy* and *daddy* (Tincoff & Jusczyk, 1999).

By around their first birthday, babies begin to use intonation to indicate commands and questions (Greenfield & Smith, 1976). At about the same age, they show signs of understanding what is said to them, and they begin not only to imitate what others say but also to use sounds to get attention. Vocalization also becomes more and more communicative and socially directed. Parents facilitate this process by speaking to their babies in what is called *motherese*. This "mother talk" is spoken slowly, and uses simple sentences, a higher-pitched voice, repetition, and exaggerated intonations—all of which engage babies' attention and help them to distinguish the sounds of their language (Hampson & Nelson, 1993).

The culmination of all this preparation is the utterance of the first word, usually *dada*, at about 12 months. During the next 6 to 8 months, children build a vocabulary of one-word sentences called **holophrases:** "Up!"; "Out!"; "More!" At first, they use these words to describe their own behavior, but later they use the words to describe the actions of others (Huttenlocher, Smiley, & Charney, 1983). Children may also use compound words such as *awgone* [all gone]. To these holophrases they add words used to address people—*Bye-bye* is a favorite—and a few exclamations, such as *Ouch!*

In the second year of life, the overwhelming passion of children is naming. With little or no prompting, they will name virtually everything

From 12 to 24 months babies typically point at and name, although not always correctly, whatever object interests them.

they see, though not always correctly! Children at this age are fascinated by objects. If they don't know the name of an object, they will simply invent one or use another word that is almost right. Feedback from parents ("No, that's not a dog, it's a cow") enhances vocabulary and helps children understand what names can and cannot be assigned to classes of things ("dog" is not used for big four-legged animals that live on farms and moo rather than bark).

During the third year of life, children begin to form two- and three-word sentences such as "See daddy," "Baby cry," "My ball," and "Dog go woof-woof." Recordings of mother-child conversations show that children from 24 to 36 months old noticeably omit auxiliary verbs and verb endings ([Can] "I have that?"; "I [am] eat[ing] it up"), as well as prepositions and articles ("It [is] time [for] Sarah [to] take [a] nap") (Bloom, 1970). Apparently, children this age seize on the most important parts of speech, those that contain the most meaning.

After 3 years of age, children begin to fill in their sentences ("Nick school" becomes "Nick goes to school"), and language production increases dramatically. Children start to use the past tense as well as the present. Sometimes they *overregularize* the past tense, by applying the regular form when an irregular one is called for (saying "goed" instead of "went," for example). Such mistakes are signs that the child has implicitly grasped the basic rules of language (Marcus, 1996). Preschoolers also ask more questions and learn to employ "Why?" effectively (sometimes monotonously so). By the age of 5 or 6, most children have a vocabulary of over 2,500 words and can construct sentences of 6 to 8 words. This increase in the number of words a child uses when communicating is only one aspect of mastering language. Complexity of sentence structure (the use of subordinate clauses, for example) is another good indicator of a child's level of language development.

Theories of Language Development Children readily pick up the vocabulary of their native language, as well as the complex rules for putting words together into sentences. Psychologists have wondered what explains this rapid acquisition of language. How do children learn to speak so well so quickly?

There are two very different theories about how language develops. B. F. Skinner (1957) believed that parents and other people listen to the infant's cooing and babbling and reinforce those sounds that most resemble adult speech. If the infant says something that sounds like *mama*, mommy reinforces this behavior with smiles and attention. As children get older, the things they say must sound more and more like

Holophrases One-word sentences commonly used by children under 2 years of age.

Language acquisition device A hypothetical neural mechanism for acquiring language that is presumed to be "wired into" all humans.

adult speech in order to be reinforced. Children who call the wrong person "mama" are less likely to be smiled at; they are praised only when they use the word appropriately. Skinner believed that an understanding of grammar, word construction, and so on are acquired in much the same way.

Most psychologists and linguists now believe that learning alone cannot explain the speed, accuracy, and originality with which children learn to use language (Chomsky, 1986; Jenkins, 2000; Pinker, 1994, 1999). Noam Chomsky (1965, 1986) has been the most influential critic of the notion that children must be *taught* language. Instead, he argues that children are born with a **language acquisition device,** an internal mechanism that is "wired into" the human brain, facilitating language learning and making it universal (Kuhn, Williams, & Lacerda, 1992). This language acquisition device enables children to understand the basic rules of grammar, to make sense of what they hear, and to form their own sentences. It is as though they have an internal "map" of language: All the child has to do is to fill in the blanks with information supplied by the environment. An American child fills in the blanks with English words, a Mexican child with Spanish words, and so on. A more recent theory advanced by Steven Pinker (1994, 1999) holds that, to a large extent, evolutionary forces may have shaped language, providing humans with what he calls a *language instinct* (see *On the Cutting Edge: The Evolution of Language from a Neuroscience Perspective*).

But the environment must do more for children than provide words to fill in the blanks in their internal map of language. Without the social stimulus of people to talk to, children are slow to pick up words and grammatical rules. Babies reared in institutions, without smiling adults around to reward their efforts, babble like other children but take much longer to begin talking than children reared in families (Brown, 1958). The greater attention paid to first-born children may explain why these children tend to be more advanced in their language development than those born later (Jones & Adamson, 1987).

Bilingualism and the Development of a Second Language   Listening to a bilingual child switch from one language to another is fascinating. Moreover, investigating how children learn a second language improves our understanding of how language in general develops. Modern technology has even allowed us to explore the brain organization associated with speaking two languages. In one such study (Kim, Relkin, Lee, & Hirsch, 1997), MRI scans showed that people who acquired a second language in infancy have a single Broca's area in the brain, an area that is specialized for producing speech; this area of the brain serves both languages. But interestingly, among those who became bilingual in adolescence, the brain has two Broca's areas, one dedicated to each language (Kim, Relkin, Lee, & Hirsch, 1997). Apparently, when people learn a second language beginning about age 11, the skills needed to generate its sounds and actively use its grammar are separate from those needed to speak a first language. This may help explain why learning a second language in adolescence or adulthood is often such a struggle.

Social Development

Learning to interact with others is an important aspect of development in childhood. Early in life, children's most important relationships are with their parents and other caregivers. But by the time they are 3, their important relationships have usually expanded to include siblings, playmates, and other children and adults outside the family. Their social world expands further when they start school. As we will see, social development involves both ongoing relationships and new or changing ones.

ON THE CUTTING EDGE

THE EVOLUTION OF LANGUAGE FROM A NEUROSCIENCE PERSPECTIVE

Steven Pinker, a cognitive neuroscientist at MIT, has put forth a provocative new theory about the evolution and nature of human language (Pinker, 1994, 1999, 2002). Drawing extensively from the fields of linguistics, evolutionary psychology, and neurolinguistics, Pinker constructs a convincing case that language should not be viewed as a "cultural artifact"—in other words, it is not simply something we learn, like chess or badminton. Neither is it simply a set of symbols linked to universal grammar or language structures, as some linguists have proposed (Chomsky, 1986). Instead, Pinker argues that language is "a distinct piece of the biological makeup of our brains." He contends, ". . . people know how to talk in more or less the sense that spiders know how to spin webs." Just as a spider spins a web without any special education or aptitude, language develops spontaneously in a child, without formal education or conscious awareness of its underlying complexity. Following Darwin, he describes language as an "instinct to acquire an art," much like song learning in birds.

According to Pinker, the language instinct is a biological adaptation designed for communication. Breaking from the tradition of linguists such as Whorf, who saw thought as dependent on language, or Chomsky, who saw language as dependent on thought, Pinker conceptualizes language as a distinct and independent cognitive ability that he calls the *language instinct.* From an evolutionary perspective, Pinker argues that the language centers in the brain, including Broca's and Wernicke's areas, have evolved what he terms *adapted computational modules* that specialize in processing linguistic information. These language modules evolved to perform a specific task, just as the visual area of the occipital lobe evolved specialized cells that respond to specific features of the visual world (see Chapter 2, The Biological Basis of Behavior).

As evidence for this view, Pinker points out that even in newborns, the language centers of the brain display a unique sensitivity to speech sounds (Stromswold, 1995). Moreover, Pinker sees these adapted language modules as independent of other forms of symbolic processing. Although the average 3-year-old has a good grasp of syntax, demonstrating competence with linguistic symbols, she is generally incompetent at recognizing other types of symbols, such as religious symbols or traffic signs.

The language instinct, like other instincts, evolved through natural selection, taking the form of an innate circuitry in the brain that uses complex computational rules to perceive, organize, and transmit information. It is because of this adapted circuitry, for instance, that humans are predisposed to attach meaning to words, a process that cognitive neuroscientists recognize as exceedingly complex (Miller, 1999). This circuitry also guides the language acquisition process.

To some extent, the innate language circuitry is revealed in the pattern of errors young children make, such as saying *goed* instead of *went* or *builded* instead of *built* (Pinker, 1999). Obviously, children do not learn these incorrect forms by imitating adults' speech. They use them because they are overapplying a grammatical rule that is built into the circuitry of their brains—in this case, the rule that tells English speakers to form the past tense by adding the suffix "ed" to a verb. Pinker's research reveals that not only English speakers, but speakers of many other languages, go through a similar stage of *overregularization* as they master grammatical rules (Pinker, 1999).

Their adapted language circuitry also enables children to attend to minor but important differences in the pronunciation of words, such as *talk* and *talks,* when they listen to adult speech (Pinker, 1999). This is important because only by focusing on the relevant aspects of speech could a child ever master the grammatical rules of a language. Recent research with Tamarin monkeys suggests that attending to certain properties of speech may be a characteristic of other primates as well (Ramus, Hauser, Miller, Morris, & Mehler, 2000).

While Pinker's evolutionary position is intriguing, not everyone agrees with it (Karmiloff-Smith, 2002; MacWhinney, 1999; Sampson, 1999). Critics are quick to point out that research has not yet identified any of the specific neural circuits or adapted computational modules that Pinker describes. Also, other theories, based more on learning than on instinct, can just as easily explain many aspects of human language. Quite possibly, advances in neuroimaging (see Chapter 2, The Biological Basis of Behavior) or behavior genetics (Enard et al., 2002) will soon shed more light on this debate by providing a clearer picture of exactly how the brain processes linguistic information.

Soon after hatching, ducklings will follow the first moving object they see. In this photograph, the imprinted object was ethologist Konrad Lorenz.

Parent-Child Relationships in Infancy: Development of Attachment   Young animals of many species follow their mothers around because of **imprinting.** Shortly after they are born or hatched, they form a strong bond to the first moving object they see. In nature, this object is normally the mother, the first source of nurturance and protection. But in laboratory experiments, certain species of animals, such as geese, have been hatched in incubators and have imprinted on decoys, mechanical toys, and even human beings (Hoffman & DePaulo, 1977; Lorenz, 1935). These goslings faithfully follow their human "mother," showing no interest whatever in adult females of their own species.

Human newborns do not imprint on first-seen moving objects, but they do gradually form an **attachment,** or emotional bond, to the people who take care of them (regardless of the caregiver's gender). This attachment is built on many hours of interaction during which baby and parent come to form a close relationship. Signs of attachment are evident by the age of 6 months or even earlier. The baby will react with smiles and coos at the caregiver's appearance and with whimpers and doleful looks when the caregiver goes away. At around 7 months, attachment behavior becomes more intense. The infant will reach out to be picked up by the caregiver, and will cling to the caregiver, especially when tired, frightened, or hurt. The baby will also begin to be wary of strangers, sometimes reacting with loud wails at even the friendliest approach by an unfamiliar person. If separated from the caregiver even for a few minutes in an unfamiliar place, the baby will usually become quite upset.

Ideally, infants learn in the first year of life that mother and other primary caregivers can be counted on to be there when needed. Psychologist Erik Erikson (1902–1994) called this the development of *basic trust* (see Chapter 11, Table 11–1). If babies' needs are generally met, they develop faith in other people and also in themselves. They see the world as a secure, dependable place and have optimism about the future. In contrast, babies whose needs are not usually met, perhaps because of an unresponsive or often absent caregiver, grow to be fearful and overly anxious about their own security. Erikson referred to these two possible outcomes as *trust versus mistrust.*

As infants develop basic trust, they are freed from preoccupation with the availability of the caregiver. They come to discover that there are other things of interest in the world. Cautiously at first, then more boldly, they venture away from the caregiver to investigate objects and other people around them. This exploration is a first indication of children's developing **autonomy,** or a sense of independence. Autonomy and attachment may seem to be opposites, but they are actually closely related. The child who has formed a secure attachment to a caregiver can explore the environment without fear. Such a child knows that the caregiver will be there when really needed, and so the caregiver serves as a "secure base" from which to venture forth (Ainsworth, 1977).

Children who are insecurely attached to their mothers are less likely to explore an unfamiliar environment, even when their mother is present. Moreover, if left in a strange place, most young children will cry and refuse to be comforted, but the insecurely attached child is more likely to continue crying even after the mother returns, either pushing her away angrily or ignoring her altogether. In contrast, a securely attached 12-month-old is more likely to rush to the returning mother for a hug and words of reassurance and then happily begin to play again (Ainsworth, Blehar, Waters, & Wall, 1978).

The importance of secure attachment early in life is evident for many years afterward. Studies of children from 1 through 6 years of age have shown that those who

Imprinting The tendency in certain species to follow the first moving thing (usually its mother) it sees after it is born or hatched.

Attachment Emotional bond that develops in the first year of life that makes human babies cling to their caregivers for safety and comfort.

Autonomy Sense of independence; a desire not to be controlled by others.

formed a secure attachment to their mothers by the age of 12 months later tended to be more at ease with other children, more interested in exploring new toys, and more enthusiastic and persistent when presented with new tasks (Harris & Liebert, 1991).

At about 2 years of age, children begin to assert their growing independence, becoming very negative when interfered with by parents. They refuse everything: getting dressed ("No!"), going to sleep ("No!"), using the potty ("No!"). The usual outcome of these first declarations of independence is that the parents begin to discipline the child. Children are told they have to eat and go to bed at a particular time, they must not pull the cat's tail or kick their sister, and they must respect other people's rights. The conflict between the parents' need for peace and order and the child's desire for autonomy often creates difficulties. But it is an essential first step in **socialization,** the process by which children learn the behaviors and attitudes appropriate to their family and their culture.

Erikson viewed independence at this age as a healthy sign. He called this stage one of *autonomy versus shame and doubt.* If a toddler fails to acquire a sense of independence and separateness from others, self-doubt may take root. The child may begin to question his or her own ability to act effectively in the world. If parents and other adults belittle a toddler's efforts, the child may also begin to feel ashamed. Fortunately, most young children and their parents avoid these negative outcomes. They negotiate their relationship in ways that allow a reasonable amount of independence for the child, while still respecting adherence to social rules and values. In this way, the needs for both autonomy and socialization are met.

Parent-Child Relationships in Childhood   As children grow older, their social world expands. They play with siblings and friends, they go off to nursery school or day care, and they eventually enter kindergarten. Erikson saw the stage between ages 3 and 6 as one of growing initiative, surrounded by a potential for guilt (*initiative versus guilt*). Children this age become increasingly involved in independent efforts to accomplish goals—making plans, undertaking projects, mastering new skills—from bike riding to table setting to drawing, painting, and writing simple words. Parental encouragement of these initiatives leads to a sense of joy in taking on new tasks. But if children are repeatedly criticized and scolded for things they do wrong, they may develop strong feelings of unworthiness, resentment, and guilt. In Erikson's view, avoiding these negative feelings is the major challenge of this stage.

The relationship between parental behavior and children's outlook and behavior has been the subject of extensive research. For example, Diana Baumrind (1972, 1991, 1996) identified four basic parenting styles:

- *Authoritarian* parents, who control their children's behavior rigidly and insist on unquestioning obedience. Authoritarian parents are likely to produce children who generally have poor communication skills, are moody, withdrawn, and distrustful.

- *Permissive-indifferent* parents exert too little control, failing to set limits on their children's behavior. They are also neglectful and inattentive, providing little emotional support to their children. The children of permissive-indifferent parents tend to be overly dependent and lacking in social skills and self-control.

- *Permissive-indulgent* parents are very attentive and supportive of their children, but fail to set appropriate limits on their behavior. The children of permissive-indulgent parents tend to be immature, disrespectful, impulsive, and out of control.

Socialization Process by which children learn the behaviors and attitudes appropriate to their family and culture.

According to Erik Erikson, children between the ages of 3 and 6 take the initiative to try to master new skills.

Solitary play A child engaged in a recreational activity alone; the earliest form of play.

Parallel play Two children playing side by side at similar activities but paying little or no attention to each other; the earliest kind of social interaction between toddlers.

- *Authoritative* parents, according to Baumrind, represent the most successful parenting style. Authoritative parents provide firm structure and guidance without being overly controlling. They listen to their children's opinions and give explanations for their decisions, but it is clear that they are the ones who make and enforce the rules. Parents who use this approach are most likely to have children who are self-reliant and socially responsible.

Although there are many studies such as Baumrind's that show a relationship between parent behavior and child development, it is important to be cautious when drawing conclusions about cause and effect from these data. First, parents do not determine the parent-child relationship on their own: Children also affect it (Collins, Maccoby, Steinberg, Hetherington, & Bornstein, 2000). Parents do not act the same way toward every child in the family (even though they may try to), because each child is a different individual. A thoughtful, responsible child is more likely to elicit authoritative parenting, whereas an impulsive child who is difficult to reason with is more likely to elicit an authoritarian style. For instance, children with conduct disorders meet with controlling responses from a great many adults, even from those who do not behave toward their own children in a controlling way (O'Leary, 1995). Thus, children influence the behavior of their caregivers at the same time that the caregivers are influencing them.

Second, there is a great deal of research that indicates that the importance of parents may be overestimated. An extreme version of this position is described in a controversial book titled *The Nurture Assumption*, by Judith Rich Harris (1998). Harris contends that parents have little influence on their child's personality (except for their genetic contribution). Instead, she argues that peers are the key factor in shaping adult personality. In the next section of the chapter we will examine peer influences on development and then return to an evaluation of Harris's position.

Relationships with Other Children   At a very early age, infants begin to show an interest in other children, but the social skills required to play with them develop only gradually (Pellegrini & Galda, 1994). Children first play alone; this is called **solitary play.** Then between 1 1/2 and 2, they begin to engage in **parallel play**—that is, they play side by side, doing the same or similar things, but not interacting

At around age 3 or 3 1/2, children engage in cooperative play that requires interaction.

much with each other. By age 3 or 3 1/2, they are engaging in **cooperative play,** including games that involve group imagination such as "playing house" (Eckerman, Davis, & Didow, 1989).

Among the first peers that most children encounter are their siblings. The quality of sibling relationships can have a major impact, especially on how children learn to relate to other peers. Sibling relations are usually most compatible when other relationships within the family are good, including between husband and wife and between parents and children (Brody, 1985). Siblings also influence one another indirectly, simply by their order of birth. In general, first-born children tend to be more anxious and fearful of physical injury, but also more intellectually able and more achievement oriented than their later-born siblings. Among boys, first-borns also tend to be more creative. These differences probably have to do with the extra attention (both negative and positive) that parents tend to give their first-born children (Eisenman, 1994).

Peer influences outside the family increase greatly when children start school. Now they are under a great deal of pressure to be part of a **peer group** of friends. In peer groups children learn many valuable things, such as how to engage in cooperative activities aimed at collective goals and how to negotiate the social roles of leader and follower (Rubin, Coplan, Chen, & McKinnon, 1994). As children get older, they develop a deeper understanding of the meaning of friendship (Rubin et al., 1994). For preschoolers, a friend is simply "someone I play with," but around age 7 children begin to realize that friends "do things" for one another. At this still egocentric age, however, friends are defined largely as people who "do things for me." Later, at about age 9, children come to understand that friendship is a two-way street and that, while friends do things for us, we are also expected to do things for them. During these early years, friendships often come and go at dizzying speed; they endure only as long as needs are being met. It is not until late childhood or early adolescence that friendship is viewed as a stable and continuing social relationship requiring mutual support, trust, and confidence (Selman, 1981).

Successfully making friends is one of the tasks that Erikson saw as centrally important to children between the ages of 7 and 11, the stage of *industry versus inferiority*. At this age, children must master many increasingly difficult skills, social interaction with peers being only one of them. Others have to do with mastering academic skills at school, meeting growing responsibilities placed on them at home, and learning to do various tasks that they will need as independent-living adults. In Erikson's view, if children become stifled in their efforts to prepare themselves for the adult world, they may conclude that they are inadequate or inferior and lose faith in their power to become self-sufficient. Those whose industry is rewarded develop a sense of competence and self-assurance.

We have seen that peers can have a significant effect on development. Does it follow, as Harris argued in *The Nurture Assumption*, that parents matter very little (see preceding section)? Harris argues that children logically are more likely to imitate the behaviors of their peers, because peers are their future collaborators and are responsible for creating the culture in which they ultimately will live. To support her position, she cites studies showing that the best predictor of an adolescent becoming a smoker is whether or not her peers smoke, not the smoking habits of her parents. Most psychologists reject such an extreme position (Collins, Maccoby, Steinberg, Hetherington, & Bornstein, 2000; Maccoby, 2000; Parke & O'Neil, 1999; Williams, 1999). For example, they point to studies showing that parents can significantly affect a child's personality even in the face of strong peer influence by monitoring and by buffering the negative effects of peers (Ary, Duncan, Duncan, & Hops, 1999; Voydanoff & Donnelly, 1999). Moreover, most developmental psychologists believe that peer influence is just one example of a much broader class of environmental factors called the **nonshared environment** (Plomin, 1999a;

Cooperative play Two or more children engaged in play that requires interaction.

Peer group A network of same-aged friends and acquaintances who give one another emotional and social support.

Nonshared environment The unique aspects of the environment that are experienced differently by siblings even though they are reared in the same family.

Turkheimer & Waldron, 2000). Even children who grow up in the same home, with the same parents, nonetheless are likely to have very different day-to-day human relationships, and this nonshared environment can have a significant effect on their development. "The message is not that family experiences are unimportant," concludes one review of the research. Rather, the crucial environmental influences that shape personality development are "specific to each child, rather than general to an entire family" (Plomin & Rende, 1991, p. 180).

Children in Dual-Career Families   Most dual-career families must entrust their young children to the care of someone else for a sizable percentage of the children's waking hours. In America over half of the children between birth and third grade spend some time being regularly cared for by persons other than their parents (America's Children: Key National Indicators of Well-Being, 2000). Is it a good idea to leave infants and very young children with substitute caregivers?

Some research shows clear benefits for the children of mothers who work, even if the children are still very young (Greenstein, 1993). For example, the children of employed mothers tend to be more independent and self-confident and to have less stereotyped views of males and females (Harris & Liebert, 1991). Moreover, children of working mothers who are placed in a quality day care, even at very early ages, are no more likely to develop behavior problems or have problems with their self-esteem than children reared at home (Harvey, 1999). Nonetheless, there has been concern that being entrusted to caregivers outside the immediate family may interfere with the development of secure attachments and put children at greater risk for emotional maladjustment (Barglow, Vaughn, & Molitor, 1987; Belsky & Rovine, 1988). But according to the findings of one large-scale longitudinal study (NICHD, 1997), placing a baby in full-time day care even in the first few months of life doesn't in itself undermine attachment. Working parents and their babies still have ample opportunity to engage in the daily give-and-take of positive feelings on which secure attachments are built. When a mother provides generally insensitive and unresponsive care, however, her baby is even *more* likely to develop an insecure attachment to her if the child also experiences extensive day care, especially poor-quality care or changing day-care arrangements. One conclusion, then, is that *quality of care counts* (Brobert, Wessels, Lamb, & Hwang, 1997; Scarr, 1999). A secure, affectionate, stimulating environment is likely to produce children who are healthy, outgoing, and ready to learn, just as an environment that encourages fears and doubts is likely to stunt development.

Sex-Role Development

By about age 3, both boys and girls have developed a **gender identity**—that is, a little girl knows that she is a girl, and a little boy knows that he is a boy. At this point, however, children have little understanding of what that means. A 3-year-old boy might think that he could grow up to be a mommy, or that if you put a dress on him and a bow in his hair, he will turn into a girl. By the age of 4 or 5, most children know that gender depends on what kind of genitals a person has (Bem, 1989). They have acquired **gender constancy,** the realization that gender cannot be changed.

At quite a young age children also start to acquire **gender-role awareness,** a knowledge of what behaviors are expected of males and of females in their society (Lewin, 1996). As a result, they develop **gender stereotypes,** or oversimplified beliefs about what the "typical" male and female are like (Sinnott, 1994). Girls are supposed to be clean, neat, and careful, whereas boys are supposed to like rough, noisy, physical play; women are kind, caring, and emotional, whereas men are strong, dominant, and aggressive. There is much consistency across cultures

Gender identity A little girl's knowledge that she is a girl, and a little boy's knowledge that he is a boy.

Gender constancy The realization that gender does not change with age.

Gender-role awareness Knowledge of what behavior is appropriate for each gender.

Gender stereotypes General beliefs about characteristics that men and women are presumed to have.

regarding the gender stereotypes children develop (Williams & Best, 1990b). This is partly because gender roles tend to be similar in many different cultures, and gender stereotypes tend to "match" the tasks thought appropriate for the sexes.

At the same time that children acquire gender-role awareness and gender stereotypes, they also develop their own **sex-typed behavior.** Although the behavioral differences between boys and girls are minimal in infancy, quite major differences tend to develop as children grow older (Prior, Smart, Sanson, & Oberklaid, 1993): Girls tend to play with dolls, and boys tend to play with trucks; girls put on pretty clothes and fuss with their hair, and boys run around and wrestle with each other. Boys also become more active and physically aggressive, and tend to play in larger groups. Girls talk more, shove less, and tend to interact in pairs. If aggression is displayed among girls, it is more likely to take the form of spiteful words and threats of social isolation (Zuger, 1998).

By school age, boys and girls tend to play by the rules of sex-typed behavior. Typically, girls play nonaggressive games, such as hopscotch, in pairs or small groups, whereas boys prefer more active group games.

ENDURING ISSUES   **heredity**environment

Sex-Typed Behavior

Because some signs of sex-typed behavior appear fairly early in development (even before the age of 3), Eleanor Maccoby, a specialist in this area, believes that they are at least partly biological in origin. In addition to the influence of genes, some evidence suggests that prenatal exposure to hormones plays a part (Collaer & Hines, 1995). But Maccoby thinks that such biologically based differences are small at first and later become exaggerated because of the different kinds of socialization experienced by boys and girls. In particular, she suggests that much gender-typical behavior is the product of children playing with others of their sex (Maccoby, 1998). Undoubtedly, popular culture—especially as portrayed on television—also influences the norms of gender-appropriate behavior that develop in children's peer groups. And parents, too, can sometimes add input, especially during critical transitions in the child's life when parents feel it is important to behave in more sex-stereotyped ways (Fagot, 1994). The end result is substantial sex-typed behavior by middle childhood. Research on this topic continues, but the growing consensus is that both biology and experience contribute to gender differences in behavior (Collaer & Hines, 1995; Collins, Maccoby, Steinberg, Hetherington, & Bornstein, 2000).

Television and Children

American children spend more time watching television than they do engaging in any other activity besides sleeping (Huston, Watkins, & Kunkel, 1989). Not surprisingly, psychologists, educators, and parents are very concerned about the

Sex-typed behavior Socially prescribed ways of behaving that differ for boys and girls.

Studies confirm that watching television is associated with aggressive behavior in children, but only if the content of the shows is violent.

influence TV may have on children. Indeed, the American Academy of Pediatrics (1999) goes so far as to say that children under the age of 2 should not watch television at all, and older children should not have television sets in their bedrooms.

One concern is the violence that pervades much TV entertainment. Children who watch 2 hours of TV daily (well below our national average) will see about 8,000 murders and 100,000 other acts of violence by the time they leave elementary school (Kunkel et al., 1996). Even Saturday morning cartoons average more than 20 acts of violence per hour (Seppa, 1997). Does witnessing this violence make children more aggressive, and if so, does TV violence account, at least in part, for the rapid rise in violent crime among adolescents?

Scientific answers concerning the effects of TV violence are still uncertain, because the causal links aren't clear. There is convincing evidence that children who frequently watch TV violence are more aggressive than other children (Eron, 1982; Singer & Singer, 1983), and that their aggressive behavior is more likely to persist into adulthood (Huesmann, Moise, Podolski, & Eron, 2003). Nevertheless these findings might simply mean that children who are prone to aggression are also drawn to violent shows (Aluja-Fabregat & Torrubia-Beltri, 1998). Perhaps the best evidence that watching TV violence can encourage violent behavior comes from a study that compared rates of violence in three similar towns, one of which did not have television until 1973 (Will, 1993). Two years after television was introduced into that remote community, the rate of physical aggression soared by 45 percent for both boys and girls, whereas it did not change in the two other towns that already had television.

On the other hand, there is evidence that children can learn worthwhile things from watching television (Anderson, 1998; Wright et al., 1999). In one long-term study, the TV viewing habits of 5-year-olds was monitored and recorded by parents and electronic devices. Years later an examination of the high school records of these same children found that the more time they had spent viewing such educational programs as *Sesame Street* and *Mr. Rogers' Neighborhood* the higher their high school grades were. In contrast, children who watched a lot of noneducational and violent programming at the age of 5 had comparatively lower high school grades than their peers (Anderson, Huston, Wright, & Collins, 1998). However, like the studies of violence on TV, these data are correlational and leave open the question of cause and effect. Somewhat stronger evidence comes from a study in which 12- to 18-month-old babies learned new words by hearing them used on a TV show, making TV a kind of "talking picture book" for them (Lemish & Rice, 1986). In addition, the content of some children's shows has been shown to promote good health and nutrition (Calvert & Cocking, 1992).

To summarize, television can be a significant influence on children's development. It presents both "good" and "bad" models for them to copy, and it provides vast amounts of information. In the end, whether television's influence is positive or negative appears to depend not only on what children watch and how much they watch, but also on the child who is watching.

THINKING CRITICALLY

Television's Effects

Unless you are a rare exception, you watched a great deal of television when you were growing up. Consider the effects this may have had on you:

1. Do you think you would be very different now if there had been no television in your home when you were growing up? If so, in what ways do you think you would be different?

2. What kinds of things did you miss out on as a result of TV viewing? How would you have spent your time differently had you not had a TV to watch?

3. Will your own children (or future children) be better off if there is no TV in the house? How might you go about determining whether in fact this is so?

██████ ███ CHECK YOUR UNDERSTANDING

1. Match each of Piaget's stages of cognitive development with the appropriate description.

___ sensory-motor stage

___ preoperational stage

___ concrete-operational stage

___ formal-operational stage

a. the ability to use representational thought expands

b. the ability to think abstractly emerges

c. the ability to consider two dimensions at once and to classify things emerges

d. awareness of object permanence emerges

2. Indicate the order in which language developments emerge.

___ holophrases

___ babbling

___ overregularization of verbs

___ two- and three-word sentences

a. first

b. second

c. third

d. fourth

3. Match Lawrence Kohlberg's moral stages to the appropriate definition.

___ preconventional

___ conventional

___ postconventional

a. right and wrong as a function of what others think

b. behavior based on a system of values and justice

c. right and wrong as a function of physical consequences

4. A child's desire for autonomy, which clashes with the parents' need for peace and order, is the first step in

___a. imprinting

___b. gender-role awareness

___c. socialization

___d. attachment

5. By about what age does a child develop gender identity?

___a. 2

___b. 3

___c. 4

___d. 5

Answers: 1. sensory-motor stage—d; preoperational stage—a; concrete operations—c; formal operations—b, 2. holophrases—b; babbling—a; overregularization of verbs—d; two- and three-word sentences—c, 3. preconventional—c; conventional—a; postconventional—a; 4. b, c; 5. b

██ ████

Adolescence

What are the developmental challenges of adolescence?

Adolescence is the period of life between roughly age 10 and 20 when a person is transformed from a child into an adult. This involves not just the physical changes of a maturing body, but also many cognitive and social-emotional changes.

Growth spurt A rapid increase in height and weight that occurs during adolescence.

Puberty The onset of sexual maturation, with accompanying physical development.

Menarche First menstrual period.

Physical Changes

A series of dramatic physical milestones ushers in adolescence. The most obvious is the **growth spurt,** a rapid increase in height and weight that begins, on average, at about age 10 1/2 in girls and 12 1/2 in boys, and reaches its peak at age 12 in girls and 14 in boys. The typical adolescent attains his or her adult height about 6 years after the start of the growth spurt (Tanner, 1978). Changes also occur in body shape, in the size of oil glands in the skin (which can contribute to acne) and in sweat glands. The heart, lungs, and digestive system also expand.

Teenagers are acutely aware of the changes taking place in their bodies. Many become anxious about whether they are the "right" shape or size and obsessively compare themselves with the models and actors they see on television and in magazines. Because few adolescents can match these ideals, it is not surprising that when young adolescents are asked what they most dislike about themselves, physical appearance is mentioned more often than anything else (Conger & Petersen, 1991). These concerns can lead to serious eating disorders, as we saw in Chapter 9, Motivation and Emotion.

Sexual Development The visible signs of **puberty**—the onset of sexual maturation—occur in a different sequence for boys and girls. In boys, the initial sign is growth of the testes, which starts, on average, at around 11 1/2, about a year before the beginning of the growth spurt in height. Along with the growth spurt comes enlargement of the penis. Development of pubic hair takes a little longer, and development of facial hair longer still. Deepening of the voice is one of the last noticeable changes of male maturation.

In females, the beginning of the growth spurt is typically the first sign of approaching puberty. Shortly thereafter, the breasts begin to develop; some pubic hair appears at around the same time. **Menarche,** the first menstrual period, occurs about a year or so later—between 12 1/2 and 13 for the average American girl (Powers, Hauser, & Kilner, 1989). The timing of menarche is affected by health and nutrition, with heavier girls maturing earlier than thinner ones. Smoking and drinking alcohol also are associated with early menarche (Danielle, Rose, Viken, & Kaprio, 2000).

The onset of menstruation does not necessarily mean that a girl is biologically capable of becoming a mother. It is uncommon (though not unheard of) for a girl to become pregnant during her first few menstrual cycles. Female fertility increases gradually during the first year after menarche. The same is true of male fertility. Boys achieve their first ejaculation at an average age of 13 1/2, often during sleep. But first ejaculations contain relatively few sperm (Tanner, 1978). Nevertheless, adolescents are capable of producing babies long before they are mature enough to take care of them.

Psychologists used to believe that the beginnings of sexual attraction and desire in young people coincided with the physical changes of puberty, but recent research is changing this view. Hundreds of case histories that researchers have collected tend to put the first stirrings of sexual interest in the fourth and fifth grade, before the onset of puberty. The cause may be increases in an adrenal sex hormone that begin at age 6 and reach a critical level around age 10 (McClintock & Herdt, 1996). Other pubertal hormones may also begin their rise much earlier than we formerly knew (Marano, 1997). If so, the onset of the obvious physical changes that we now call puberty may actually be more of an ending to a process than a beginning.

As the students in this middle-school group show, the age at which adolescents reach sexual maturity varies widely. Differences can lead to problems for teenagers of both sexes.

Early and Late Developers   Individuals differ greatly in the age at which they go through the changes of puberty. Some 12-year-old girls and 14-year-old boys still look like children, whereas others their age already look like young women and men. Among boys, early maturing has psychological advantages. Boys who mature earlier do better in sports and in social activities and receive greater respect from their peers (Conger & Petersen, 1991). For girls, early maturation appears to be a mixed blessing. A girl who matures early may be admired by other girls but is likely to be subjected to embarrassing treatment as a sex object by boys (Clausen, 1975).

Adolescent Sexual Activity   The achievement of the capacity to reproduce is probably the single most important development in adolescence. But sexuality is a confusing issue for adolescents in our society. Fifty years ago, young people were expected to postpone expressing their sexual needs until they were responsible, married adults. Since then, major changes have occurred in sexual customs. Three-fourths of all males and more than half of all females between the ages of 15 and 19 have had intercourse; the average age for first intercourse is 16 for boys and 17 for girls (Stodghill, 1998).

Boys and girls tend to view their early sexual behavior in significantly different ways (Lewin, 1994a). Fewer high school girls than boys report feeling good about their sexual experiences (46 percent versus 65 percent). Similarly, more girls than boys said they should have waited until they were older before having sex (65 percent compared with 48 percent).

Teenage Pregnancy and Childbearing   Since the late 1950s, the rate of childbearing has declined dramatically among women aged 15 to 19, from 96 per 1,000 in 1957 to 49 per 1,000 in 2000. The trend is widespread, affecting all races and ethnic groups and women in every state in the union. The teen pregnancy rate (which includes pregnancies ending in abortion and miscarriage as well as live births) has also declined. The news is not all good, however. The United States still has the highest teen birth rate in the industrialized world. It is, for example, more than 7 times the rate in France, 12 times the rate in Japan, and more than double the rate in Canada. One reason for our higher teen birth rate may be the relative ignorance of the most basic facts concerning reproduction among our young people. In countries such as Norway, Sweden, and the Netherlands, which have extensive programs of sex education, teenage pregnancy rates are much lower (Hechtman, 1989). Another explanation for some unwanted teenage pregnancies may be the adolescent tendency to believe that "nothing bad will happen to me." This sense of invulnerability, in the absence of effective sex education, may blind some teenagers to the possibility of becoming a parent (Quadrel, Prouadrel, Fischoff, & Davis, 1993).

Whatever the causes of teenage pregnancy and teen childbearing, its consequences can be devastating particularly if the mother is unmarried, if she has no parental support, or if she is living in poverty. She is less likely to graduate from high school, less likely to improve her economic status, and less likely to get married and stay married than a girl who postpones childbearing (see Coley & Chase-Lansdale, 1998). Babies are also apt to suffer when born to teen mothers. They are more likely to be of low birth weight, which is associated with learning disabilities and later problems in school, childhood illnesses, and neurological problems (Furstenberg, Brooks-Gunn, & Chase-Lansdale, 1989; Moore, Morrison, & Greene, 1997). In addition, children of teenage mothers are more likely to be neglected and abused than are children of older mothers (Coley & Chase-Lansdale, 1998; Goerge & Lee, 1997). The decline in teen births is, then, an important step forward, even though it is clear that there is considerable room for improvement.

Imaginary audience Elkind's term for adolescents' delusion that they are constantly being observed by others.

Personal fable Elkind's term for adolescents' delusion that they are unique, very important, and invulnerable.

Cognitive Changes

Just as bodies mature during adolescence, so do patterns of thought. As we saw earlier, Piaget (1969) believed that for many people adolescence marks the beginning of formal-operational thought which in turn allows adolescents to understand and manipulate abstract concepts, speculate about alternative possibilities, and reason in hypothetical terms. However, not all adolescents reach the stage of formal operations, and many of those who do fail to apply formal-operational thinking to the everyday problems they face (Flavell, Miller, & Miller, 2002). Younger adolescents especially are unlikely to be objective about matters concerning themselves and have not yet achieved a deep understanding of the difficulties involved in moral judgments.

Moreover, in those who do achieve formal-operational thinking, this advance has its hazards, among them overconfidence in new mental abilities and a tendency to place too much importance on one's own thoughts. Some adolescents also fail to realize that not everyone thinks the way they do and that other people may hold different views (Harris & Liebert, 1991). Piaget called these tendencies the "egocentrism of formal operations" (Piaget, 1967).

David Elkind (1968, 1969) used Piaget's notion of adolescent egocentrism to account for two fallacies of thought he noticed in this age group. The first is the **imaginary audience**—the tendency of teenagers to feel they are constantly being observed by others, that people are always judging them on their appearance and behavior. This feeling of being perpetually "onstage" may be the source of much self-consciousness, concern about personal appearance, and showing off in adolescence.

The other fallacy of adolescent thinking is the **personal fable**—adolescents' unrealistic sense of their own uniqueness. For instance, a teenager might feel that others couldn't possibly understand the love they feel toward a boyfriend or girlfriend because that love is so unique and special. This view is related to the feeling of invulnerability we mentioned earlier. Many teenagers believe they are so different from other people that they won't be touched by the negative things that happen to others. This feeling of invulnerability is consistent with the reckless risk taking among people in this age group (Arnett, 1991).

Personality and Social Development

Adolescents are eager to establish independence from their parents, but at the same time they fear the responsibilities of adulthood. They have many important tasks ahead of them and many important decisions to make. Particularly in a technologically advanced society like ours, this period of development is bound to involve some stress. But exactly how stressful is adolescence for most teenagers?

How "Stormy and Stressful" Is Adolescence? Early this century many people saw adolescence as a time of great instability and strong emotions. For example, G. Stanley Hall (1904), one of the first developmental psychologists, portrayed adolescence as a period of "storm and stress," fraught with suffering, passion, and rebellion against adult authority. Recent research, however, suggests that the "storm and stress" view greatly exaggerates the experiences of most teenagers (Arnett, 1999). The great majority of adolescents do not describe their lives as filled with turmoil and chaos (Eccles et al., 1993). Most adolescents manage to keep stress in check, experience little disruption in their everyday lives, and generally develop more positively than is commonly believed (Bronfenbrenner, 1986; Galambos & Leadbeater, 2002). For instance, a cross-cultural study that sampled adolescents from ten countries including the United States, found that over 75 percent of them had healthy self-images, were generally happy, and valued the time they spent at school and at work (Offer, Ostrov, Howard, & Atkinson 1988).

Still, adolescence is inevitably accompanied by some stress related to school, family, and peers, and this stress can at times be difficult to manage (Crystal et al., 1994). But individuals differ in their ability to cope with even the worst conditions. Some young people are particularly *resilient* and able to overcome great odds, partly because of a strong belief in their own ability to make things better (Werner, 1995). In contrast, those whose prior development has been stressful are likely to experience greater stress during adolescence. Thus, the degree of struggle growing up that any given adolescent faces is due to an interaction of developmental challenges on the one hand and factors that promote resilience on the other (Compas, Hinden, & Gerhardt, 1995).

Forming an Identity

To make the transition from dependence on parents to dependence on oneself, the adolescent must develop a stable sense of self. This process is called **identity formation,** a term derived from Erik Erikson's theory, which sees the major challenge of this stage of life as *identity versus role confusion* (Erikson, 1968). The overwhelming question for the young person becomes "Who am I?" In Erikson's view, the answer comes by integrating a number of different roles—say, talented math student, athlete, and artist or political liberal and aspiring architect—into a coherent whole that "fits" comfortably. Failure to form this coherent sense of identity leads to confusion about roles.

James Marcia (1980) believes that finding an identity requires a period of intense self-exploration called an **identity crisis.** He recognizes four possible outcomes of this process. One is *identity achievement*. Adolescents who have reached this status have passed through the identity crisis and succeeded in making personal choices about their beliefs and goals. They are comfortable with those choices because the choices are their own. In contrast are adolescents who have taken the path of *identity foreclosure*. They have prematurely settled on an identity that others provided for them. They have become what those others want them to be without ever going through an identity crisis. Other adolescents are in *moratorium* regarding the choice of an identity. They are in the process of actively exploring various role options, but they have not yet committed to any of them. Finally, there are teens who are experiencing *identity diffusion*. They avoid considering role options in any conscious way. Many are dissatisfied with this condition, but are unable to start a search to "find themselves." Some resort to escapist activities such as drug or alcohol abuse (Adams & Gullota, 1983). Of course, any given adolescent's identity status can change over time as the person matures or even regresses.

Relationships with Peers   For most adolescents, the peer group provides a network of social and emotional support that helps enable both the movement toward greater independence from adults and the search for personal identity. But peer relationships change during the adolescent years. Friendship groups in early adolescence tend to be small unisex groups, called **cliques,** of three to nine members. Especially among girls, these unisex friendships increasingly deepen and become more mutually self-disclosing as the teens develop the cognitive abilities to better understand themselves and one another (Holmbeck, 1994). Then, in mid-adolescence, unisex cliques generally break down and give way to mixed-sex groups. These, in turn, are usually replaced by groups consisting of couples. Between the ages of 16 and 19, most adolescents settle into more stable dating patterns. No longer group oriented, and more confident of their sexual maturity, they begin to gain competence at longer-term relationships. Some even decide to get married while still in their teens. But these early marriages have a very high failure rate compared with marriages between people in their 20s or 30s (Cavanaugh, 1990).

Identity formation Erikson's term for the development of a stable sense of self necessary to make the transition from dependence on others to dependence on oneself.

Identity crisis A period of intense self-examination and decision making; part of the process of identity formation.

Cliques Groups of adolescents with similar interests and strong mutual attachment.

Peer groups help adolescents develop identities apart from family influences. Cliques are small groups of friends that offer closeness but can also exert significant control over adolescents' lives.

Relationships with Parents   While they are still searching for their own identity, striving toward independence, and learning to think through the long-term consequences of their actions, adolescents require guidance and structure from adults, especially from their parents. But being the parent of an adolescent is far from easy. In their struggle for independence, adolescents question everything and test every rule. Unlike young children who believe their parents know everything and are all-powerful and good, adolescents are all too aware of their parents' shortcomings. It takes many years for adolescents to see their mothers and fathers as real people with their own needs and strengths as well as weaknesses (Smollar & Youniss, 1989). In fact, many young adults are surprised that their parents have gotten so much smarter in the last 7 or 8 years!

"Is everything all right, Jeffrey? You never call me 'dude' anymore."

The low point of parent-child relationships generally occurs in early adolescence, when the physical changes of puberty are occurring. Then the warmth of the parent-child relationship ebbs and conflict rises. Warm and caring relationships with adults outside the home, such as those at school or at a supervised community center, are valuable to adolescents during this period (Eccles et al., 1993). However, conflicts with parents tend to be over minor issues and are usually not intense (Holmbeck, 1994). In only a small minority of families does the relationship between parents and children markedly deteriorate in adolescence (Paikoff & Brooks-Gunn, 1991).

Some Problems of Adolescence

Adolescence is a time when certain kinds of developmental problems are apt to arise, especially problems that have to do with self-perceptions, feelings about the self, and negative emotions in general.

Declines in Self-Esteem   We saw earlier that adolescents are especially likely to be dissatisfied with their appearance. Satisfaction with one's appearance tends to be tied to satisfaction with oneself. Thus, adolescents who are least satisfied with their physical appearance tend also to have low self-esteem (Adams & Gullota, 1983; Altabe & Thompson, 1994). Since adolescent girls are especially likely to be dissatisfied with their appearance, and since perceived attractiveness and self-esteem are more closely related for females than for males (Allgood-Merten, Lewinsohn, & Hops, 1990), it is no surprise that adolescent girls have significantly lower self-esteem than adolescent boys for whom there is little or no decline in self-esteem during adolescence (Kling, Hyde, Showers, & Buswell, 1999).

Depression and Suicide   The rate of suicide among adolescents has increased more than 600 percent since 1950, though there are signs that since the mid-1990s it has begun to decrease at least among males. Suicide is the third leading cause of death among adolescents, after accidents and homicides (Centers for Disease Control and Prevention, 1999; Hoyert, Kochanek, & Murphy, 1999). Although successful suicide is much more common in males than in females, twice as many females *attempt* suicide (National Adolescent Health Information Center, 2003).

Research shows that suicidal behavior in adolescents (including thinking about suicide as well as actually attempting it) is often linked to other psychological problems, such as depression, drug abuse, and disruptive behaviors (see Table 10–2)

table 10-2   MENTAL DISORDERS IN OLDER ADOLESCENTS WHO ATTEMPT SUICIDE

Disorder	Males		Females	
	% of Attempters	% of Nonattempters	% of Attempters	% of Nonattempters
Major depression	65	10	56	21
Alcohol abuse	19	4	14	4
Drug abuse	29	6	13	5
Disruptive behaviors	32	9	12	4
Adjustment disorder	7	5	10	7
Anxiety disorder	10	6	19	11

Source: Adapted from "Suicidal attempts among older adolescents: Prevalence and co-occurrence with psychiatric disorders" by J. A. Andrews and P. M. Lewinsohn, 1992, *Journal of the American Academy of Child and Adolescent Psychiatry, 31*, pp. 655–662. Copyright © 1992. Reprinted with permission.

(Andrews & Lewinsohn, 1992; Studer, 2000), though it is not related to risk taking behaviors (Stanton, Spirito, Donaldson, & Doergers, 2003). One study of more than 1,700 adolescents revealed that a set of related factors put an adolescent at higher-than-average risk for attempting suicide. Among these are being female, thinking about suicide, having a mental disorder (such as depression), and having a poorly educated father who is absent from the home. A history of physical or sexual abuse and poor family communication skills are also associated with suicide and suicide attempts. Although these data allow us to identify people at risk, it is hard to tell which higher-than-average risk adolescents will actually attempt suicide. For example, depression in and of itself rarely leads to suicide: Although 3 percent of adolescents suffer severe depression at any one time, the suicide rate among adolescents is only .01 percent (Connelly, Johnston, Brown, Mackay, & Blackstock, 1993). Apparently, a combination of depression and other risk factors makes suicide more likely, but exactly which factors are most important and what kinds of intervention might reduce adolescent suicides are still unclear (Wagner, 1997).

Youth Violence   In April 1999 two boys, one 17 and the other 18, opened fire on their classmates at Columbine High School in Littleton, Colorado. Armed with two sawed-off shotguns, a semi-automatic rifle, and a semi-automatic pistol, they killed 13 fellow students and a teacher and wounded 23 others before killing themselves. Fortunately, 30 bombs filled with shrapnel and planted throughout the school were found and defused before they exploded. One of the shooters arrived at school that day wearing a favorite shirt that read "SERIAL KILLER."

In the days after the shootings, people throughout the country expressed their shock and outrage and offered different theories as to the reasons for the tragedy. But well before these shootings took place, surveys had repeatedly shown that violence and crime are the issues of greatest concern to most Americans. And, despite an overall decrease in criminal activities in the 1990s, juvenile crime continues to rise (Pellegrini, Roundtree, Camagna, & Queirolo, 2000), as does violence directed toward children.

Are there any warning signs that might alert family and friends to potential violence? Indeed there are. Lack of connection, masking emotions, withdrawal (being habitually secretive and antisocial), silence, rage, increased lying, trouble with friends, hypervigilance, cruelty toward other children and animals—these factors should all be a cause for concern. This is especially true if they are exhibited by a boy who comes from a family with a history of criminal violence, who has been abused, who belongs to a gang, who abuses drugs or alcohol, who has previously been arrested, or who has experienced problems at school (Leschied & Cummings, 2002).

CHECK YOUR UNDERSTANDING

1. The most obvious physical milestone in adolescence is

_____a. acne

_____b. a growth spurt

_____c. expansion of the heart, lung, and digestive system

2. Elkind's name for the pattern of adolescent thought characterized by a sense of invulnerability is

_____a. the imaginary audience

_____b. the personal fable

3. Match each status regarding identity formation with the appropriate definition.

_____ identity achievement

_____ identity foreclosure

_____identity moratorium

_____identity diffusion

a. prematurely settling on an identity that others provide

b. success in making personal choices about beliefs and goals

c. avoiding consideration of role options

d. exploring role options but not yet committing to any

Answers: 1. b, 2. b, 3. identity achievement—b; identity foreclosure—a; identity moratorium—d; identity diffusion—c

Adulthood

How does personality change during adulthood?

Compared with adolescent development, development during adulthood is much less predictable, much more a function of the individual's decisions, circumstances, and even luck. In adulthood, as distinct from childhood and adolescence, developmental milestones do not occur at particular ages. Still, certain experiences and changes take place sooner or later in nearly everyone's life and nearly every adult tries to fulfill certain needs, including nurturing partnerships and satisfying work.

Love, Partnerships, and Parenting

Nearly all adults form a long-term, loving partnership with another adult at some point in their lives. This can happen at any stage in the life course, but it is especially common in young adulthood. According to Erik Erikson, the major challenge of young adulthood is *intimacy versus isolation*. Failure to form an intimate partnership with someone else can cause a young adult to feel painfully lonely and incomplete.

Forming Partnerships   Almost 90 percent of Americans eventually get married (U.S. Bureau of the Census, 2002a), but those who marry are waiting longer to do so. For example, in 1970, the median age of an American women marrying for the first time was 20.8 years; this increased to 25.3 years by 2002. Similarly, for American men, the median age for first marriages was 23.2 years in 1970, increasing to 26.9 years by 2002 (U.S. Bureau of the Census, 2002b). This postponement of marriage is even greater among African Americans than among whites (Balaguer & Markman, 1994).

Although heterosexual marriage is still the statistical norm in our society, other types of partnerships are increasingly meeting the needs of a diverse population. Long-term cohabiting relationships are one example. Contrary to popular belief, the greatest recent increase in cohabiting couples is not among the very young, but rather among people over age 35 (Steinhauer, 1997). Among elderly widows and widowers, cohabitation is increasingly seen as a way of enjoying a life together without financial complications and tax penalties.

Homosexual couples are another example of intimate partnerships outside the tradition of heterosexual marriage. Studies show that most gays and lesbians seek the same loving, committed, and meaningful partnerships as most heterosexuals do (Peplau & Cochran, 1990). Moreover, successful relationships among them have

Most people marry someone of similar race, religion, education, and social background. The couple shown here are marrying in an Eastern Orthodox wedding ceremony.

the same characteristics as successful relationships in the heterosexual world: high levels of mutual trust, respect, and appreciation; shared decision making; good communication; and good skills at resolving conflicts (Birchler & Fals-Stewart, 1994; Edwards, 1996; Kurdek, 1991, 1992; Laird, 2003).

Forming and maintaining any kind of close relationship is important to living a long and happy life. In one 6-year study of men aged 24 to 60, those who had good social support networks outlived those who lacked such support (Kaplan & Novorr, 1994). People who didn't join social organizations were twice as likely to die during the same period as those who did join such groups. And those who were dissatisfied with the quality of their interpersonal relationships were twice as likely to die as those who were satisfied with them. (See *Applying Psychology: Resolving Conflicts in Intimate Relationships.*)

Parenthood For most parents, loving and being loved by their children is an unparalleled source of fulfillment. However, the birth of the first child is also a major turning point in a couple's relationship, one that requires many adjustments. Romance and fun often give way to duty and obligations. Young children demand a lot of time and energy, which may leave parents with little time or energy for each other. New parents in particular may worry about the mixed emotions they sometimes feel toward their baby. Parenthood may also heighten conflicts between pursuit of careers and responsibilities at home. This is especially likely among women who have had an active career outside the home.

Given the demands of child rearing, it isn't surprising that marital satisfaction tends to decline after the arrival of the first child (Ruble, Fleming, Hackel, & Stangor, 1988; see Figure 10–3). But once children leave home, many parents experience renewed satisfaction in their relationship as a couple. Rather than lamenting over their "empty nests," many women breathe a sigh of relief (Rovner, 1990), expe-

APPLYING PSYCHOLOGY

RESOLVING CONFLICTS IN INTIMATE RELATIONSHIPS

Even the closest, most loving couples have disagreements. People, after all, are different. They have different desires, approaches, and priorities—and different points of view. For those reasons, conflict is inevitable in every intimate relationship. But conflict does not necessarily mean destructive forms of fighting. Conflict can be resolved in constructive ways that don't tear a couple apart. Constructive fighting can actually bring people closer together in search of mutually satisfactory solutions.

Psychologists who have studied intimate relationships often suggest a number of steps that lead to constructive conflict resolution:

1. **Carefully choose the time and place for an argument.** People who start airing a grievance at some inappropriate time shouldn't be surprised when the outcome is unsatisfactory. Try not to begin a major disagreement while your partner is in the middle of completing some important task or is ready to fall asleep after a long, tiring day. Bring up the subject when there is ample time to discuss it fully.

2. **Be a good listener.** Don't go on the defensive as soon as your partner brings up a concern or complaint. Listen carefully without interrupting. Try to understand what your partner is saying from his or her point of view. Listening calmly, without anger, will help to get the discussion off to a good start. Don't let your body give nonverbal cues that contradict good listening. For instance, don't continue to do chores or watch television while your partner is speaking. Don't shrug your shoulders or roll your eyes as if discounting your partner's view.

3. **Give feedback regarding your understanding of the other person's grievance.** Restate what your partner has told you in your own words. Ask questions about anything you're not sure of. For instance, if a wife says she is fed up with the amount of time her husband spends watching sports on television, he might respond by saying, "I know you don't like me watching sports a lot, but do you expect me to stop entirely?" Such feedback helps to clarify and avoid misunderstandings.

4. **Be candid. Level with your partner about your feelings.** Say what you really think. If you are angry, don't make your partner guess your feelings by giving the silent treatment or showing anger in indirect ways. Of course, being candid does not mean being tactless or hurtful. Don't engage in name calling, sarcasm, mockery, or insults. Such tactics are counterproductive.

5. **Use "I" rather than "you" statements.** For instance, if you're angry with your partner for being late, say, "I've been really worried and upset for the last hour" rather than "You're a whole hour late! Why couldn't you get here on time?" "You" statements sound like accusations and tend to put people on the defensive. "I" statements sound more like efforts to communicate feelings in nonjudgmental ways.

6. **Focus on behavior, not on the person.** For example, focus on your partner's lateness as a problem, don't accuse your partner of being thoughtless and self-centered. People respond defensively to broadside attacks on their character. Such attacks threaten their self-esteem.

7. **Don't overstate the frequency of a problem or overgeneralize about it.** Don't tell your partner that he's always late or that she's exactly like her mother. Such exaggerations are annoying and tend to lead discussions away from legitimate complaints.

8. **Focus on a limited number of specific issues.** Don't overwhelm your partner with a barrage of grievances. Stick to current concerns of high priority. Don't get distracted by trivial matters that waste emotional energy. Don't dredge up a long list of complaints from the past.

9. **Don't find scapegoats for every grievance against you.** We all tend to explain away our shortcomings by blaming them on circumstances or sometimes on other people. Resist the temptation to offer excuses designed to get you "off the hook." Take responsibility for your actions and encourage your partner to do the same.

10. **Suggest specific, relevant changes to solve a problem.** Both participants in the conflict should propose at least one possible solution. A proposed solution should be reasonable and take into account the other person's viewpoint as well as your own.

11. **Be open to compromise.** Settling disputes successfully often involves negotiation. Both people must be willing to give in a little. Don't back your partner into a corner by giving an ultimatum: "Do what I want or else!" Partners need to be willing to change themselves to some extent in response to each other's feelings. This willingness is the essence of being in an intimate relationship. Being loved by your partner doesn't necessarily mean being accepted exactly as you are.

12. **Don't think in terms of winner and loser.** A competitive approach to conflict resolution is unfortunate in intimate relationships. If one partner is repeatedly the winner and the other repeatedly the loser, their relationship inevitably suffers. Strive for solutions that are satisfactory to both parties. Think of each other as allies attacking a mutual problem. In this way, your relationship will become stronger.

Most homosexuals seek the same loving, committed, and meaningful partnerships as most heterosexuals do.

riencing an increase in positive mood and well-being (Dennerstein, Dudley, & Guthrie, 2002). For the first time in years, the husband and wife can be alone together and enjoy one another's company (Orbuch, Houser, Mero, & Webster, 1996).

Ending a Relationship Intimate relationships frequently break up. Although this is true for all types of couples—married and unmarried, heterosexual and homosexual—most of the research on ending relationships has focused on married, heterosexual couples. The U.S. divorce rate has risen substantially since the 1960s, as it has in many other developed nations (Lewin, 1995). Although the divorce rate appears to have stabilized, almost half of American marriages eventually end in divorce (U.S. Bureau of the Census (2002a).

Figure 10–3
Marital satisfaction.
This graph shows when married people are most and least content with their marriage, on a scale of 1 (very unhappy) to 7 (very happy).
Source: American Sociological Association; adapted from *USA Today,* August 12, 1997, p. D1.

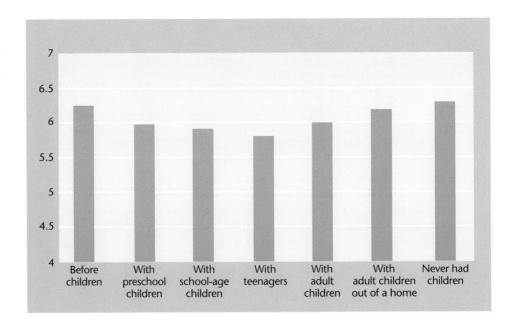

Rarely is the decision to separate a mutual one. Most often, one partner takes the initiative in ending the relationship after a long period of slowly increasing unhappiness. Making the decision does not necessarily bring relief. In the short term, it often brings turmoil, animosity, and apprehension. However, in the longer term, most divorced adults report that the divorce was a positive step that eventually resulted in greater personal contentment and healthier psychological functioning, although a substantial minority seem to suffer long-term negative effects (Kelly, 1982; Stack, 1994).

Divorce can have serious and far-reaching effects on children—especially on their school performance, self-esteem, gender-role development, emotional adjustment, relationships with others, and attitudes toward marriage (Barber & Eccles, 1992; Collins, Maccoby, Steinberg, Hetherington, & Bornstein, 2000; Forgatch & DeGarmo, 1999; Vaughn, 1993). And children who have been involved in multiple divorces are placed at an even greater risk (Kurdek, Fine, & Sinclair, 1995). Children adapt more successfully to divorce when they have good support systems, when the divorcing parents maintain a good relationship, and when sufficient financial resources are made available to them. The effects of divorce also vary with the children themselves: Those who have easygoing temperaments and who were generally well behaved before the divorce usually have an easier time adjusting (Davies & Cummings, 1994; Hetherington, Bridges, & Insabella, 1998; Miller, Kliewer, & Burkeman, 1993).

The divorce rate in the United States has risen dramatically since the 1960s. Divorce can have serious and far-reaching effects on both the couple and the couple's children.

The World of Work

For many young people, the period from the late teens through the early twenties is crucial because it sets the stage for much of adult life. The educational achievements and training obtained during these transitional years often establishes the foundation that will shape the income and occupational status for the remainder of adult life (Arnett, 2000).

Three or four generations ago, choosing a career was not an issue for most young adults. Men followed in their fathers' footsteps or took whatever apprenticeships were available in their communities. Most women were occupied in child care, housework, and helping with the family farm or business, or they pursued such "female" careers as secretarial work, nursing, and teaching. Today career choices are far more numerous for both men and women, but on average, women get paid 30 percent less than men for doing the same work, and they are less likely than men to advance to managerial and executive positions (Valian, 1998; see Figure 10–4). Women hold 53 percent of the professional jobs in the United States, for example, but mostly in the less-well-paid fields, such as education. Only 28 percent of the professional jobs that paid over $40,000 in 1998 were held by women (Doyle, 2000). In the last 50 years, the number of married women in the paid labor force has increased dramatically: 71 percent of married women with school-aged children and 60 percent of women with children under 6 now have jobs outside the home (Gilbert, 1994; Harris & Liebert, 1991). This increasing role of women as economic providers is a worldwide trend (Elloy & Mackie, 2002).

Balancing the demands of career and family is a problem in many families, especially for women. Even when the wife has a full-time job outside the home, she is likely to end up doing far more than half of the housework and child care. She is also likely to be aware of this imbalance and to resent it (Benin & Agostinelli, 1988). True equality—the hopeful goal of the dual-career movement—has yet to be achieved (Viers & Prouty, 2001).

Despite the pressures associated with the double shift, most women report increases in self-esteem when they have a paid job (Baruch & Barnett, 1986). They also tend to experience less anxiety and depression than childless working women

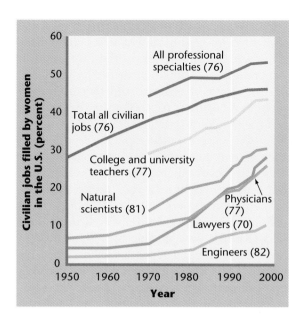

Figure 10–4
Percentage of selected jobs filled by women in the United States, 1950–2000.
This graph shows the percentage of each job filled by women. The figures in parentheses indicate women's earnings as a percentage of men's in the given field.
Source: Scientific American, April 2000, p. 30; data from U.S. Bureau of the Census and Bureau of Labor Statistics. © 2000 Rodger Doyle. Reprinted with permission.

do (Barnett, 1994). The vast majority say they would continue to work even if they didn't need the money (Schwartz, 1994). Those women most apt to feel stressed by a double shift are those who do not find satisfaction in their various roles (Barnett, 1994).

Cognitive Changes

Only recently have researchers begun to explore the ways in which adult thinking differs from that of an adolescent. Nonetheless, a few conclusions have begun to emerge from the research literature. Although adolescents are able to test alternatives and to arrive at what they see as the "correct" solution to a problem, adults gradually come to realize that there isn't a single correct solution to every problem—there may, in fact, be no correct solution, or there may be several. Adolescents rely on authorities to tell them what is "true," but adults realize that "truth" often varies according to the situation and one's viewpoint. Adults are also more practical: They know that a solution to a problem must be realistic as well as reasonable (Cavanaugh, 1990). No doubt these changes in adult thinking derive from greater experience of the world. Dealing with the kinds of complex problems that arise in adult life requires moving away from the literal, formal, and somewhat rigid thinking of adolescence and young adulthood (Labouvie-Vief, 1986).

Most of the measurable cognitive changes that do take place during adulthood do not simply involve a rise or fall in general ability. Instead, for most people some cognitive skills, such as vocabulary and verbal memory increase steadily through the sixth decade of life. While other cognitive skills, such as reasoning and spatial orientation generally peak during the 40s, falling off only slightly with increasing age. The ability to perform mathematical computations, and perceptual speed, however show the largest declines with age. Interestingly, perceptual speed (which involves the ability to make quick and accurate visual discriminations) begins to decline as early as 25, while the ability to perform mathematical computations does not begin to decline until approximately 40 years of age (Schaie, 1983, 1996; Schaie & Willis, 2001; Willis & Schaie, 1999).

Just as physical exercise is necessary for optimal physical development, so mental exercise is necessary for optimal cognitive development. For example, adults who received training in spatial orientation skills improved their performance by 40 percent. Thus, although some decline in cognitive skills is inevitable as people age, these declines can be minimized if people stay mentally active (Schaie, 1994).

Personality Changes

Psychological health generally increases in adulthood compared to adolescence. And those adolescents with greater psychological health tend to improve even further in adulthood (Jones & Meredith, 2000). Both men and women tend to become less self-centered and develop better coping skills with age (Neugarten, 1977). Also, people in their middle years feel an increasing commitment to and responsibility for others, develop new ways of adapting, and are more comfortable in interpersonal relationships (Vaillant, 1977). Such findings suggest that the majority of people are successfully meeting what Erik Erikson saw as the major challenge of middle adulthood: *generativity versus stagnation*. Generativity refers to the ability to continue being productive and creative, especially in ways that guide and encourage future generations. For those who fail to achieve this state, life becomes a drab and meaningless routine, and the person feels stagnant and bored.

Feelings of boredom and stagnation in middle adulthood may be part of what is called a **midlife crisis.** The person in midlife crisis feels painfully unfulfilled, ready for a radical, abrupt shift in career, personal relationships, or lifestyle. Research shows, however, that the midlife crisis is not typical; most people do not make sudden dramatic changes in their lives in mid-adulthood (Martino, 1995). For example, one large scale study found that the majority of middle aged adults reported lower levels of anxiety and worry than young adults, and generally felt positively about their lives. Despite describing themselves as being in poor physical condition, most people in midlife have few serious illnesses. In fact, only about 10 percent reported experiencing a midlife crisis (Brim, 1999). Daniel Levinson, who studied personality development in men and women throughout adulthood (Levinson, 1978, 1986, 1987), preferred the term **midlife transition** for the period when people tend to take stock of their lives. Many of the men and women in his studies, confronted with the first signs of aging, began to think about the finite nature of life. They realized that they may never accomplish all that they had hoped to do, and they questioned the value of some of the things they had accomplished so far, wondering how meaningful they were. As a result, some gradually reset their life priorities, establishing new goals based on their new insights.

ENDURING ISSUES   **stability**change

The "Change of Life"

A decline in the function of the reproductive organs occurs during middle age. In women, the amount of estrogen (the principal female hormone) produced by the ovaries drops sharply at around age 45, although the exact age varies considerably from woman to woman. Breasts, genital tissues, and the uterus begin to shrink, and menstrual periods become irregular and then cease altogether at around age 50. The cessation of menstruation is called **menopause.**

The hormonal changes that accompany menopause often cause certain physical symptoms; the most noticeable are "hot flashes." In some women, menopause also leads to a serious thinning of the bones, making them more vulnerable to fractures. While both of these symptoms can be prevented by hormone replacement therapy (a pill or a skin patch that must be prescribed by a physician), recent studies have shown that taking hormones to reduce the symptoms of menopause may also place woman at a higher risk for heart disease and breast cancer (Rymer, Wilson &

Midlife crisis A time when adults discover they no longer feel fulfilled in their jobs or personal lives and attempt to make a decisive shift in career or lifestyle.

Midlife transition According to Levinson, a process whereby adults assess the past and formulate new goals for the future.

Menopause The time in a woman's life when menstruation ceases.

Ballard, 2003). Since the severity of menopausal symptoms vary from woman to woman, as do the risk factors associated with breast cancer and heart disease it is important for women to approach hormone therapy carefully under the careful supervision of a physician.

Experts disagree about whether a "male menopause" exists. Men never experience as severe a drop in testosterone (the principal male hormone) as women do in estrogen. Instead, studies have found a more gradual decline—perhaps 30 to 40 percent—in testosterone in men between 48 and 70 (Angier, 1992; Crooks & Bauer, 2002). Recent evidence also confirms the common belief that with increasing age, male fertility slowly decreases as well (Ford et al., 2000). In any case, there is much disagreement about whether older men should be treated with hormones, as menopausal women commonly are. Some are concerned that hormone therapy could increase men's risk of prostate cancer and heart disease.

CHECK YOUR UNDERSTANDING

1. Compared with adolescent development, development during adulthood is

___a. more predictable

___b. less predictable

2. The greatest recent increase in cohabiting adults is among

___a. the very young

___b. people over 35

3. Among women who work, anxiety and depression are highest if

___a. they have children

___b. they are childless

Answers: 1. b, 2. b, 3. b

Late Adulthood

Is late adulthood a period of decline?

Older adults constitute the fastest-growing segments of the U.S. population. Indeed, during this century, the percentage of Americans over 65 has more than tripled, and those over 85 now represent the fastest-growing segment of the population (APA's Task Force on Diversity, 1998). In the 2000 census, 35 million Americans were over age 65; by the year 2030, it is expected that there will be more than 70 million in this age group. This dramatic rise stems from the aging of the large baby boom generation, coupled with increases in life expectancy due primarily to better health care and nutrition (Downs, 1994; see Figure 10–5).

However, a sizable gender gap exists in life expectancy. The average woman today enjoys a life span that is 7 years longer than that of the average male. The reasons for this gender gap are still unclear, but likely factors include differences in hormones, exposure to stress, health-related behaviors, and genetic makeup.

There is also a gap in life expectancy between whites and African Americans in this country. The average white American child is likely to live to age 76, whereas the average African American child is apt to live only to age 71. This difference seems to stem largely from disparities in socioeconomic well-being.

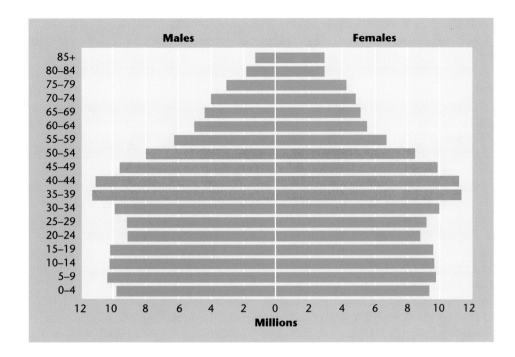

Figure 10–5
Population age structure, 1999.
The U.S. population will continue to age over the next several decades, as the huge baby boom generation moves through the population.
Source: U.S. Census Bureau. Available online at http://www.census.gov/population/www.dbna/db-aging-toc.html.

Because older adults are becoming an increasingly visible part of American society, it is important to understand their development. Unfortunately, our views of older adults are often heavily colored by myths. For example, many people believe that most older adults are lonely, poor, and troubled by ill health. Even health-care professionals sometimes assume that it is natural for elderly people to feel ill. As a result, symptoms that would indicate a treatable medical problem in younger people are taken as inevitable signs of decay in the elderly and frequently go untreated. The false belief that "senility" is inevitable in old age is another damaging myth, as is the belief that most older adults are helpless and dependent on their families for care and financial support. All the research on late adulthood contradicts these stereotypes. Increasingly, people age 65 and over are healthy, productive, and able (Cutler, 2001; Kolata, 1996b; Manton & Gu, 2001).

Physical Changes

Nevertheless, aging does bring with it some inevitable physical deterioration. Beginning in middle adulthood and continuing through late adulthood, physical appearance and the functioning of every organ change. The hair thins and turns white or gray. The skin wrinkles. Bones become more fragile. Muscles lose power, and joints stiffen or wear out. Circulation slows, blood pressure rises, and because the lungs hold less oxygen, the older adult has less energy. Body shape and posture change, and the reproductive organs atrophy. Difficulties in falling asleep and staying asleep become more common, and reaction times are slower. Vision, hearing, and the sense of smell all become less acute (Cavanaugh, 1990; Whitbourne, 1998). Most people are at first unaware of these changes, because they occur gradually. But the decline eventually becomes undeniable.

Curiously, we do not yet know why physical aging happens (DiGiovanna, 1994). One theory is that genes may program our cells eventually to deteriorate and die. According to this theory, the aging process is inherited, directing the body to age and deteriorate just as maturation shapes early growth and development. The role that inheritance plays in aging is supported by a recent finding of a gene that appears to be related to exceptional longevity (Puca et al., 2001). Another theory

Late adulthood can be a successful and productive time of life. Pianist Eubie Blake, for example, continued to perform well into his 90s.

Although physical changes are inevitable during late adulthood, how people respond to these changes has a major effect on their quality of life.

holds that *telomeres*, special structures located on the tips of the chromosomes that protect the chromosomes during replication, become shorter with each replication. After about 100 replications, the telomeres have been so significantly reduced in size that cells are no longer capable of precise replication. One of the more recent and widely accepted theories of aging, the *free radical theory*, holds that unstable oxygen molecules collect within cells over time causing them to age (De la Fuente, 2002). In this theory, the unstable oxygen molecules ricochet around within cells and damage DNA and the other cellular components. This damage may lead to the wide variety of disorders that accompany aging, including arthritis, cancer, and cognitive decline (Berr, 2002; Knight, 2000; Leborgne, Maziere, & Andrejak, 2002).

Whatever the ultimate explanation for physical decline, many factors affect the physical well-being of older adults, and some are things they can control: particularly diet, exercise, health care, smoking, drug use, and overexposure to sun (Levenson & Aldwin, 1994). Attitudes and interests also matter. People who have a continuing sense of usefulness, who maintain old ties, investigate new ideas, and take up new activities, and who feel in control of their lives have the lowest rates of disease and the highest survival rates (Butler & Lewis, 1982; Caspi & Elder, 1986). Indeed, a survey of 2,724 people ranging in age from 25 to 74 years found that older adults reported experiencing more positive emotions during the past month than younger adults did (Mroczek & Kolarz, 1998). So there's a good deal of truth in the saying "You're only as old as you feel." In fact, psychologists are starting to use functional or psychological age, instead of chronological age, to predict an older adult's adaptability to life's demands.

Social Development

Far from being weak and dependent, most men and women over 65 live autonomous lives apart from their children and outside of nursing homes, and most are very satisfied with their lifestyles. In one survey of people 65 years and older, more than half reported being just as happy as when they were younger. Three-quarters said they were involved in activities that were as interesting to them as any they had engaged in during their younger years (Birren, 1983). Moreover, those that remain physically and mentally active, travel, exercise, and attend meetings, are more likely to report being happier and more satisfied with their lives than those that stay at home (George, 2001). Political interest certainly does not decline with age: Almost 90 percent of older adults are registered to vote, and two-thirds vote regularly—the greatest percentage turnout of any age group.

Still, gradual social changes do take place in late adulthood. In general older people interact with fewer people and perform fewer social roles. Behavior becomes less influenced by social rules and expectations than it was earlier in life. And finally, most older people step back and assesses life, and realize there is a limit to the capacity for social involvement, and learn to live comfortably with those restrictions. This process does not necessarily entail a psychological "disengagement" from the social world, as some researchers have contended. Instead, older people may simply be making sensible choices that suit their more limited time frames and physical capabilities (Carstensen, 1995).

Retirement   Another major change that most people experience in late adulthood is retiring from paid employment. People's reactions to retirement differ greatly, partly because society has no clear idea of what retirees are supposed to do. Should they sit in rocking chairs and watch life go by, or should they play golf, become foster grandparents, and study Greek? The advantage to this lack of clear social expectations is that older adults have the flexibility to structure their retirement as they please. Interestingly, men and women often go about this differently. Men generally see retirement as a time to slow down and do less, whereas women often view it as a

"Then it's moved and seconded that the compulsory retirement age be advanced to ninety-five."

time to learn new things and explore new possibilities (Helgesen, 1998). This can cause obvious problems for retired couples (also see Moen, Kim, & Hofmeister, 2001).

Of course, the nature and quality of retired life depend in part on financial status. If retirement means a major decline in a person's standard of living, that person will be less eager to retire and will lead a more limited life after retirement. Another factor in people's attitudes toward retirement is their feelings about work. People who are fulfilled by their jobs are usually less interested in retiring than people whose jobs are unrewarding (Atchley, 1982). Similarly, people who have very ambitious, hard-driving personalities tend to want to stay at work longer than those who are more relaxed. The feeling of being forced to retire before you are ready can be a source of real stress. In general, involuntary retirees suffer more depression, ill health, and poor adjustment than do people who choose to retire.

Sexual Behavior   A common misconception about the aged is that they have outlived their sexuality. This myth reflects our stereotypes. To the extent that we see the elderly as physically unattractive and frail, we find it difficult to believe that they are sexually active. True, older people respond more slowly and are less sexually active than younger people, but the majority of older adults can enjoy sex and have orgasms. One survey revealed that 37 percent of married people over 60 have sex at least once a week, 20 percent have sex outdoors, and 17 percent swim in the nude (Woodward & Springen, 1992). Another study of people ages 65 to 97 found that about half the men still viewed sex as important, and slightly over half of those in committed relationships were satisfied with the quality of their sex lives (Clements, 1996).

Cognitive Changes

Healthy people who remain intellectually active maintain a high level of mental functioning in old age (Schaie, 1984; Shimamura, Berry, Mangels, Rusting, & Jurica, 1995). Far from the common myth that the brain cells of elderly people are rapidly dying off, the brain of the average person shrinks only about 10 percent in size between the ages of 20 and 70 (Goleman, 1996). This means that, for a sizable number of older adults, cognitive abilities remain largely intact. For instance, interviews with men in their 70s, who were part of a long-running longitudinal study of "gifted children," found that those who had remained mentally active and healthy showed no noticeable declines in intellect or vocabulary (Shneidman, 1989). True, the aging mind works a little more slowly (Birren & Fisher, 1995; Salthouse, 1991), and certain types of memories are a little more difficult to store and retrieve (Craik, 1994), but these changes are not serious enough to interfere with the ability to enjoy an active, independent life. Moreover, older adults who stay mentally active, especially through work related activities, generally experience significantly less cognitive decline than those who do not (Bosma, vanBoxtel, Ponds, Houx, & Jolles, 2003). Training, and practice on cognitive tasks can also help reduce the decline in cognitive performance in later adulthood (Guenther, Schaefer, Holzner, & Kemmler, 2003; Saczynski, Willis, & Schaie, 2002; Willis & Schaie, 1986).

Alzheimer's Disease   Unfortunately, some people in late adulthood are not functioning so well. They forget the names of their children or are unable to find their way home from the store. Some even fail to recognize their life-long partners. These people are not suffering from the normal consequences of aging, but rather are victims of **Alzheimer's disease,** named for the German neurologist Alois Alzheimer. For many years, Alzheimer's disease was considered rare, and it was diagnosed only in people under 60 who developed symptoms of memory loss and confusion. But now Alzheimer's is recognized as a common disorder in older people

Alzheimer's disease A neurological disorder, most commonly found in late adulthood, characterized by progressive losses in memory and cognition and changes in personality.

Because people with Alzheimer's disease suffer memory loss, signs are often used to remind them to perform ordinary activities.

who used to be called "senile." According to current estimates, about 10 percent of adults over 65 and nearly half of adults over 85 suffer from Alzheimer's disease (Bennett & Knopman, 1994). Alzheimer's usually begins with minor memory losses, such as difficulty in recalling words and names or in remembering where one put something. As it progresses—and this may take anywhere from 2 to 20 years—personality changes are also likely. First, people may become emotionally withdrawn or flat. Later, they may suffer from delusions, such as thinking that relatives are stealing from them. These people become confused and may not know where they are or what time of day it is. Eventually, they lose the ability to speak, to care for themselves, and to recognize family members. If they do not die of other causes, Alzheimer's will eventually prove fatal (Wolfson et al., 2001).

At present there is no known cure for Alzheimer's, but breakthroughs in research are occurring so fast that a drug to slow the progress of the disorder or even a vaccine to prevent it may be developed in the near future (Henry, 1996; Novak, 1999; Pennisi, 1999).

Facing the End of Life

Fear of death is seldom a central concern for people in later adulthood. In fact, such fear seems to be a greater problem in young adulthood or in middle age, when the first awareness of mortality coincides with a greater interest in living (Kimmel, 1974). One study of attitudes toward death found that 19 percent of young adults were afraid of dying, compared with less than 2 percent of people over age 65 (Rogers, 1980). But the elderly do have some major fears associated with dying. They fear the pain, indignity, and depersonalization they might experience during a terminal illness, as well as the possibility of dying alone. They also worry about burdening their relatives with the expenses of their hospitalization or nursing care. An elder person's relatives have their own fears about dying, and these fears, combined with the psychological pain of watching a loved one die, sometimes makes them distance themselves just at the time when an elder person most needs comfort and compassion (Kübler-Ross, 1975).

Stages of Dying Psychiatrist Elisabeth Kübler-Ross (1969) interviewed more than 200 dying people of all ages to try to understand the psychological aspects of dying. From these interviews, she described a sequence of five stages that she believed people pass through as they react to their own impending death.

1. Denial: The person denies the diagnosis, refuses to believe that death is approaching, insists that an error has been made, and seeks other, more acceptable opinions or alternatives.

2. Anger: The person now accepts the reality of the situation, but expresses envy and resentment toward those who will live to fulfill a plan or dream. The question becomes "Why me?" Anger may be directed at the doctor or randomly in all directions. The patience and understanding of other people are particularly important at this stage.

3. Bargaining: The person desperately tries to buy time, negotiating with doctors, family members, clergy, and God in a healthy attempt to cope with the realization of death.

4. Depression: As bargaining fails and time is running out, the person may succumb to depression, lamenting failures and mistakes that can no longer be corrected.

5. Acceptance: Tired and weak, the person at last enters a state of "quiet expectation," submitting to fate.

According to Kübler-Ross, Americans have a greater problem coping with death than people in some other cultures. She observes that while some cultures are *death affirming*, American culture is *death denying*: "We are reluctant to reveal our age; we spend fortunes to hide our wrinkles; we prefer to send our old people to nursing homes" (1975, p. 28). We also shelter children from knowledge of death and dying. By trying to protect them from these unpleasant realities, however, we may actually make them more fearful of death.

Some observers have found fault with Kübler-Ross's model of dying. Most of the criticisms have focused on her methodology. She studied only a relatively small sample of people and provided little information about how they were selected and how often they were interviewed. Also, all her patients were suffering from cancer. Does her model apply as well to people dying from other causes? Finally, some critics question the universality of her model. Death itself is universal, but reactions to dying may differ greatly from one culture to another.

Despite these legitimate questions, there is nearly universal agreement that Kübler-Ross deserves credit for pioneering the study of the transitions people undergo during the dying process. She was the first to investigate an area long considered taboo, and her research has made dying a more "understandable" experience, perhaps one that is easier to deal with.

Widowhood   The death of one's spouse may be the most severe challenge people face during late adulthood. Especially if it was unexpected, people respond to such a loss with initial disbelief, followed by numbness. Only later is the full impact of the loss felt, and that can be severe. The incidence of depression rises significantly following the death of a spouse (Norris & Murrell, 1990). Moreover, a long-term study of several thousand widowers 55 years of age and older revealed that nearly 5 percent of them died in the 6-month period following their wife's death, a figure that is well above the expected death rate for men that age. Thereafter, the mortality rate of these men fell gradually to a more normal level (Butler & Lewis, 1982).

Perhaps because they are not as used to taking care of themselves, men seem to suffer more than women from the loss of a mate. But because women have a longer life expectancy, there are many more widows than widowers. Thus, men have a better chance of remarrying. More than half the women over 65 are widowed, and half of them will live another 15 years without remarrying. For somewhat different reasons, then, the burden of widowhood is heavy for both men and women (Feinson, 1986).

CHECK YOUR UNDERSTANDING

1. Match the following stages of dying with the appropriate definition.

_____ denial	a. person submits to fate
_____ anger	b. person expresses resentment toward others
_____ bargaining	c. person refuses to believe that death is approaching
_____ depression	d. person may lament mistakes
_____ acceptance	e. person tries to buy time

2. On average, women live how many years longer than men?

_____a. 5
_____b. 6
_____c. 7
_____d. 10

s u m m a r y

This chapter deals with **developmental psychology,** the study of the changes that occur in people from birth through old age.

Methods in Developmental Psychology

To examine changes that take place over time, developmental psychologists use three different methods. In **cross-sectional studies,** researchers test groups of people of different ages. In **longitudinal studies,** researchers test the same people—usually a **cohort,** or group of people born during the same historical period—as they grow older. For studying adulthood, researchers sometimes use **biographical** or **retrospective studies,** in which people's lives are examined backward through interviews. Each of these methods has certain advantages and disadvantages.

Prenatal Development

The period from conception to birth is called **prenatal development.** Two weeks after conception, the fertilized egg has become an **embryo;** 3 months after conception, the developing organism is called a **fetus.** The fetus is nourished by an organ called the **placenta.** Disease-producing organisms and substances the mother eats, drinks, or inhales can pass through the placenta and, at **critical periods,** do major harm to the fetus. Those substances that cross the placenta and cause birth defects are called **teratogens.** Pregnant women who consume large amounts of alcohol may give birth to a child with **fetal alcohol syndrome (FAS).**

The Newborn Baby

Reflexes **Neonates** (newborn babies) come equipped with a number of reflexes, such as those that help them breathe and nurse. The **rooting reflex** causes a newborn, when touched on the cheek, to turn its head in that direction and grope around with its mouth. The **sucking reflex** causes the newborn to suck on anything that is placed in its mouth, and the **swallowing reflex** enables it to swallow liquids without choking. The **grasping reflex** causes a newborn to close its fist around anything that is put in its hand. The **stepping reflex** causes the newborn to make little stepping motions if held upright with its feet just touching a surface.

Temperament Babies are born with personalities that differ in **temperament.** Temperament often remains quite stable over time.

Perceptual Abilities Infants can see as soon as they are born. Vision is fuzzy at first, but visual acuity improves rapidly. Newborns prefer patterns with clear contrasts, so they like looking at black-and-white patterns better than at colored ones. As they grow older they prefer more complex patterns. They also prefer to look at their mother rather than a stranger. A classic experiment using a device called the visual cliff showed that infants of crawling age can perceive depth.

Fetuses can hear sounds in the uterus, and newborns can tell the direction of a sound. Infants can distinguish between some speech sounds that are indistinguishable to an adult. Infants also have clear-cut preferences in taste and smell.

Infancy and Childhood

Physical Development Growth of the body is most rapid during the first year, when it can occur in startling spurts. It then slows down until early adolescence. During the prenatal period and the first 2 years of life, the head grows rapidly. The body does most of the growing from then on.

Motor Development Motor development refers to the acquisition of abilities such as grasping and walking. **Developmental norms** indicate the ages at which the average child achieves certain developmental milestones. During early motor development, the reflexes of the newborn give way to voluntary action. **Maturation**—the biological processes that unfold as we grow older—interacts with environmental factors in promoting developmental changes in our early motor skills.

Cognitive Development Cognitive development refers to changes in the way children think about the world. The Swiss psychologist Jean Piaget saw cognitive development as a way of adapting to the environment and theorized that it proceeds in a series of distinct stages.

During the **sensory-motor stage** (birth to age 2), infants develop **object permanence,** the concept that things continue to exist even when they are out of sight. At birth, there is no sign of object permanence, but the concept is fully developed by 18 to 24 months, when the child acquires the ability to form **mental representations**—mental images or symbols (such as words) used in thinking and remembering. The development of self-recognition also occurs during the sensory-motor stage.

In the **preoperational stage** (ages 2 through 7), children are able to use mental representations and language assumes an important role in describing, remembering, and reasoning about the world. But preoperational thought is **egocentric:** Children of this age are unable to see things from another person's point of view. They are also easily misled by appearances and tend to focus on the most striking aspect of an object or event.

Children in the **concrete-operational stage** (7 to 11) can pay attention to more than one thing at a time and are able to understand someone else's point of view. They grasp the **principles of conservation**—that basic amounts remain constant despite changes in appearance—and they can understand classification schemes.

When they enter the **formal-operational stage** (between 11 and 15), adolescents can think in abstract terms and test their ideas internally, using logic. Thus, they can grasp theoretical cause-and-effect relationships and consider possibilities as well as realities.

Piaget's theory has been criticized for the content of the stages as well as for his assumption that all children proceed through the stages in the same order. Critics also fault Piaget for not taking human diversity into consideration.

Moral Development Like Piaget, Lawrence Kohlberg developed a stage theory, although his involves moral development. Kohlberg's stages—preconventional, conventional, and postconventional—hinge on the different ways the developing child views morality. The preconventional child sees doing right and wrong as a function of physical consequences; the conventional child sees it as a function of what others think; and the postconventional individual sees right behavior as based on a system of values and justice.

Language Development Language begins with cooing and progresses to **babbling,** the repetition of speechlike sounds. The first word is usually uttered at about 12 months; at the same age, infants show signs of understanding what is said to them. In the next 6 to 8 months, children build a vocabulary of one-word sentences, called **holophrases.** Between 2 and 3, children begin to put words together into simple sentences, though they leave out unimportant parts of speech such as auxiliary verbs. Between 3 and 4, children fill out their sentences and are able to use past and present tenses. By 5 or 6, most children have a vocabulary of over 2,500 words and can create sentences of 6 to 8 words.

There are two different theories of language development. Skinner proposed that parents listen to their infant's babbling and reinforce (reward) the infant for making sounds that most resemble adult speech. Chomsky, on the other hand, maintained that children are born with a **language acquisition device,** an innate mechanism that enables them to understand the rules of grammar, make sense of the speech they hear, and form intelligible sentences themselves. Most researchers agree with Chomsky's view, but the work of Hart and Risley shows that parental use of language is critically important.

The critical period hypothesis postulates that there is a critical time for the acquisition of language. If language is not acquired during that time, it will be very difficult for the child to master it later.

Social Development A baby duck or goose follows its mother because of a phenomenon called **imprinting,** a primitive form of bonding. Bonding in humans is a more complex emotional process called **attachment.** The first attachment is likely to be to the infant's primary caregiver, usually the mother. It develops during the first year of life, usually along with a wariness of strangers.

Infants who are securely attached to their mothers are better able to develop **autonomy,** a sense of independence. Children who are insecurely attached to others are less likely to explore an unfamiliar environment.

At about 2 years of age, the child's desire for autonomy clashes with the parents' need for peace and order. These conflicts are a necessary first step in **socialization,** the process by which children learn the behaviors and attitudes appropriate to their family and culture. Parenting style affects children's behavior and self-image. The most successful parenting style is authoritative, in which parents provide firm guidance but are willing to listen to the child's opinions. However, parents do not act the same way toward every child in the family because children are different from each other and elicit different parental responses. The **nonshared environment** refers to the unique aspects of the environment that are experienced differently by siblings even though they are reared in the same family.

The earliest kind of play is **solitary play**—children engaging in some activity all by themselves. The earliest kind of social interaction is **parallel play,** in which two toddlers play side by side at the same activity but largely ignore each other. By 3 or 3 1/2, they are engaging in **cooperative play** involving group imagination. As children get older, they develop a deeper understanding of the meaning of friendship and come under the influence of a **peer group.**

Sex-Role Development By age 3, a child has developed a **gender identity,** a girl's knowledge that she is a girl and a boy's knowledge that he is a boy. But children that age have little idea of what it means. By 4 or 5, most children develop **gender constancy,** the realization that gender depends on what kind of genitals one has and cannot be changed.

Gender-role awareness—the knowledge of what behavior is appropriate for each gender—develops as children interact with their society. As a result they develop **gender stereotypes,** oversimplified beliefs about "typical" males and females. From an early age, children show **sex-typed behavior**—behavior that is typical of females (for example, playing with dolls) or of males (for example, playing with trucks).

Television and Children American children spend more time watching television than engaging in any other activity except sleeping. If TV viewing involves constant exposure to scenes of violence, the evidence suggests that children become more aggressive in their behavior. The most convincing theoretical argument linking violent behavior with TV watching is based on social learning theory. Viewing behaviors on television that are violent and characters who are reinforced for such violence leads children to imitate that behavior. Some evidence suggests that TV can be an effective teaching tool.

Adolescence

Adolescence is the period of life when the individual is transformed from a child to an adult between age 10 and 20.

Physical Changes The **growth spurt** is a rapid increase in height and weight that begins, on the average, at about age 10 1/2 in girls and 12 1/2 in boys, and reaches its peak at age 12 in girls and 14 in boys. Growth is essentially complete about 6 years after the start of the growth spurt. During this period, changes occur in body shape and proportions as well as in size.

Signs of **puberty**—the onset of sexual maturation—begin around 11 1/2 in boys. In girls, the growth spurt typically precedes the approaching puberty. **Menarche,** the first menstrual period, occurs between 12 1/2 and 13 for the average American girl. But individuals vary widely in when they go through puberty.

Although the rate of births to teenagers has decreased recently, the United States still has the highest teen birth rate in the industrialized world. The consequences of unmarried teenage childbearing can be serious.

Cognitive Changes The cognitive abilities of adolescents undergo an important transition to formal-operational thought, allowing them to manipulate abstract concepts, reason hypothetically, and speculate about alternatives. These new mental abilities often make them overconfident and overimpressed with their own importance. Elkind described two patterns of thought characteristic of this age: the **imaginary audience,** which makes teenagers feel they are constantly being watched and judged; and the **personal fable,** which gives young people the sense that they are unique and invulnerable and encourages them to take needless risks.

Personality and Social Development The classical view of adolescence as a period of "storm and stress" fraught with conflict, anxiety, and tension is not borne out in most teenagers' lives, although there is inevitably some stress to handle.

Forming an Identity **Identity formation** is the process by which a person develops a stable sense of self. According to Marcia, identity formation takes place during an intense period of self-exploration called an **identity crisis.**

Most adolescents rely on a peer group for social and emotional support, often rigidly conforming to the values of their friends. From small unisex **cliques** in early adolescence, friendship groups change to mixed-sex groups in which short-lived romantic interests are common. Later stable dating patterns emerge.

Parent-child relationships are difficult during adolescence. Teenagers become aware of their parents' faults and question every parental role. Conflicts are most common during early adolescence, though only in a minority of families does the parent-child relationship show a severe deterioration.

Some Problems of Adolescence   Dissatisfaction with one's body image and one's academic performance can lower an adolescent's self-esteem. A sizable number of adolescents thinks about committing suicide; a much smaller proportion attempt it. Depression, drug abuse, and disruptive behaviors are linked to suicidal thoughts.

Adulthood

Unlike childhood and adolescence, adulthood is not marked by clear, predictable milestones. Still, there are certain experiences and changes that nearly everyone goes through and certain needs that nearly everyone tries to fulfill.

Love, Partnerships, and Parenting   Almost every adult forms a long-term loving partnership with at least one other adult at some point during his or her life. More than 90 percent of all Americans eventually get married, although they are waiting longer to do so. Most people select a marriage or cohabitation partner of similar race, religion, education, and background. Heterosexual marriage is the norm, but other relationships include long-term cohabitation and homosexual partnerships.

Parenthood entails new responsibilities and adjustments. It often heightens conflicts between career and domestic concerns. Once children leave home, parents often renew their relationship as a couple.

Almost half of American marriages end in divorce, which has far-reaching effects on children's school performance, self-esteem, emotional adjustment, and other aspects of their development.

The World of Work   The educational achievements and training obtained during the late teens and early twenties set the stage for the world of work. Today both men and women have numerous career choices, although women are more likely to experience discrimination at work. The emergence of the dual-career family has brought with it the need to balance the demands of career and family and to find quality child care.

Cognitive Changes   An adult's thinking is more flexible and practical than an adolescent's. Whereas adolescents search for the one "correct" solution to a problem, adults realize that there may be several "right" solutions or none at all.

One model of cognitive change maintains that cognitive exercises can minimize the inevitable decline in cognitive functioning as people age.

Personality Changes   Adults become less self-centered and develop better coping skills with age. Some people may experience a **midlife crisis,** when they feel unfulfilled and ready for a decisive shift in career or lifestyle. More commonly, people go through a **midlife transition,** a period of taking stock of one's life and formulating new goals.

Middle adulthood also brings a decline in the functioning of the reproductive organs. Women go through **menopause,** the cessation of menstruation accompanied by a sharp drop in estrogen.

Late Adulthood

Older adults are the fastest-growing segment of the U.S. population. Our stereotypes of "elderly" people are contradicted by research showing that people 65 and older are increasingly healthy, productive, and able.

Physical Changes   The physical changes of late adulthood affect outward appearance and the functioning of every organ. Although aging is inevitable, heredity and lifestyle play a role in the timing of this process.

Social Development   Most older adults have an independent and satisfactory lifestyle and engage in social activities that interest them. But they gradually go through a process of disengagement and life assessment and accept necessary limitations on their social involvement.

People's reactions to leaving the world of paid employment differ, depending on their financial status and their feelings about work.

Sexual responses are slower in older adults, but most recent information indicates that people continue to enjoy sex.

Cognitive Changes   Cognitive abilities remain largely intact for a sizable number of older adults. Older adults who engage in intellectually stimulating activities remain mentally alert.

Old people who used to be called "senile" are now recognized as having a specific disorder called **Alzheimer's disease,** which causes progressive losses in memory and cognition and changes in personality. However, it is important to distinguish Alzheimer's disease from other causes of mental impairment that may be treatable.

Facing the End of Life   Elderly people fear death less than younger people. What they do fear are the pain, indignity, depersonalization, and loneliness associated with a terminal illness. They also worry about being a financial burden to their families.

Kübler-Ross described a sequence of five stages that people go through when they are dying: denial, anger, bargaining, depression, and acceptance.

Widowhood may be the most severe challenge people face as older adults. Loss of a spouse may bring on depression. Men seem to suffer more from loss of a mate but have a better chance of remarrying.

key terms

Developmental psychology	365	Maturation	375	Nonshared environment	387
Cross-sectional study	366	Sensory-motor stage	376	Gender identity	388
Cohort	366	Object permanence	376	Gender constancy	388
Longitudinal study	367	Mental representations	376	Gender-role awareness	388
Biographical (or retrospective) study	367	Preoperational stage	377	Gender stereotypes	388
Prenatal development	368	Egocentric	377	Sex-typed behavior	389
Embryo	368	Concrete-operational stage	377	Growth spurt	392
Fetus	368	Principle of conservation	377	Puberty	392
Placenta	368	Formal-operational stage	378	Menarche	392
Teratogens	368	Babbling	380	Imaginary audience	394
Critical period	368	Holophrases	381	Personal fable	394
Fetal alcohol syndrome (FAS)	369	Language acquisition device	382	Identity formation	395
Neonates	369	Imprinting	384	Identity crisis	395
Rooting reflex	370	Attachment	384	Cliques	395
Sucking reflex	370	Autonomy	384	Midlife crisis	405
Swallowing reflex	370	Socialization	385	Midlife transition	405
Grasping reflex	370	Solitary play	386	Menopause	405
Stepping reflex	370	Parallel play	386	Alzheimer's disease	409
Temperament	370	Cooperative play	387		
Developmental norms	374	Peer group	387		

OVERVIEW

Psychodynamic Theories
Sigmund Freud
Carl Jung
Alfred Adler
Karen Horney
Erik Erikson
A Psychodynamic View of
Jaylene Smith
Evaluating Psychodynamic Theories

Humanistic Personality Theories
Carl Rogers
A Humanistic View of Jaylene Smith

Evaluating Humanistic Theories
Trait Theories
Development of Trait Theory
The Big Five
A Trait View of Jaylene Smith
Evaluating Trait Theories

**Cognitive–Social Learning
Theories**
Expectancies, Self-Efficacy,
and Locus of Control

A Cognitive–Social Learning View
of Jaylene Smith
Evaluating Cognitive–Social
Learning Theories

Personality Assessment
The Personal Interview
Direct Observation
Objective Tests
Projective Tests

Personality

11

The Case of Jaylene Smith   Thirty-year-old Jaylene Smith is a talented physician who visits a psychologist because she is troubled by certain aspects of her social life. Acquaintances describe Jay in glowing terms—highly motivated, intelligent, attractive, and charming. But Jay feels terribly insecure and anxious. When asked by a psychologist to pick out some self-descriptive adjectives, she selected "introverted," "shy," "inadequate," and "unhappy."

Jay was the firstborn in a family of two boys and one girl. Her father is a quiet and gentle medical researcher. His work often allowed him to study at home, so he had extensive contact with his children when they were young. He loved all his children but clearly favored Jay. His ambitions and goals for her were extremely high, and as she matured, he responded to her every need and demand almost immediately and with full conviction. Their relationship remains as close today as it was during Jay's childhood.

Jay's mother worked long hours away from home as a store manager and consequently saw her children primarily at night and on an occasional free weekend. When she came home, Mrs. Smith was tired and had little energy for "nonessential" interactions with her children. She had always been career oriented, but she experienced considerable conflict and frustration trying to reconcile her roles as mother, housekeeper, and financial provider. Mrs. Smith was usually amiable toward all her children but tended to argue more with Jay, until the bickering subsided when Jay was about 6 or 7 years of age. Today their relationship is cordial but lacks the closeness apparent between Jay and Dr. Smith. Interactions between Dr. and Mrs. Smith were sometimes marred by stormy outbursts over seemingly trivial matters. These episodes were always followed by periods of mutual silence lasting for days.

Jay was very jealous of her first brother, born when she was 2 years old. Her parents recall that Jay sometimes staged temper tantrums when the new infant demanded and received a lot of attention (especially from Mrs. Smith). The temper tantrums intensified when Jay's second brother was born, just one year later. As time went on, the brothers formed an alliance to try to undermine Jay's supreme position with their father. Jay only became closer to her father, and her relationships with her brothers were marked by greater-than-average jealousy and rivalry from early childhood to the present.

Throughout elementary, junior high, and high school, Jay was popular and did well academically. Early on she decided on a career in medicine. Yet off and on between the ages of 8 and 17, she had strong feelings of loneliness, depression, insecurity, and confusion—feelings common enough during this age period, but stronger than in most youngsters and very distressing to Jay.

Jay's college days were a period of great personal growth, but several unsuccessful romantic involvements caused her much pain. The failure to achieve a stable and long-lasting relationship persisted after college and troubled Jay greatly. Although even-tempered in most circumstances, Jay often had an explosive fit of anger that ended each important romantic relationship she had. "What is wrong with me?" she would ask herself. "Why do I find it impossible to maintain a serious relationship for any length of time?"

In medical school, her conflicts crept into her consciousness periodically: "I don't deserve to be a doctor"; "I won't pass my exams"; "Who am I, and what do I want from life?"

How can we describe and understand Jaylene Smith's personality? How did she become who she is? Why does she feel insecure and uncertain despite her obvious

THINKABOUTIT

You will find the answers to these questions in the chapter:

1. How great a role does the unconscious play in personality?

2. To what extent do people strive toward positive growth?

3. What is the key focus of trait theories?

4. How do personal and situational factors combine to shape behavior?

5. How do psychologists test personality?

Personality An individual's unique pattern of thoughts, feelings, and behaviors that persists over time and across situations.

Psychodynamic theories Personality theories contending that behavior results from psychological forces that interact within the individual, often outside conscious awareness.

success? Why do her friends see her as charming and attractive, though she describes herself as introverted and inadequate? These are the kinds of questions that personality psychologists are likely to ask about Jay—and the kinds of questions we will try to answer in this chapter.

Psychologists typically define **personality** as an individual's unique pattern of thoughts, feelings, and behaviors that persists over time and across situations. Notice that this definition has two important parts. First, personality refers to *unique differences*—those aspects that distinguish a person from everyone else. Second, the definition asserts that personality persists through time and across situations—that is, personality is relatively *stable* and *enduring*. Perhaps you have had the chance to view yourself at various ages in home movies or videos. At each age some of the same characteristics are evident—maybe you are a natural performer, always showing off for the camera, or it could be you are a director type, telling the camera operator what to do at 4 years of age as well as at 14. We expect people's personalities to be relatively consistent from day to day and from one situation to another; in fact, when that is not so, we generally suspect that something is wrong with the person.

Psychologists approach the study of personality in a number of ways. Some try to identify the most important characteristics of personality. Others seek to understand why personalities differ. Among the latter group, some psychologists identify the family as the most important factor in the development of the individual's personality, whereas others emphasize environmental influences outside the family, and still others see personality as the result of how we learn to think about ourselves and our experiences. In this chapter, we will explore these various approaches by examining some representative theories each approach has produced. We will also see how each theoretical paradigm sheds light on the personality of Jaylene Smith. Finally, we evaluate the strengths and weaknesses of each approach to understanding personality.

Psychodynamic Theories

How great a role does the unconscious play in personality?

Psychodynamic theories see behavior as the product of psychological forces within the individual, often outside conscious awareness. Freud drew on the physics of his day to coin the term *psychodynamics*: As thermodynamics is the study of heat and mechanical energy and how one may be transformed into the other, psychodynamics is the study of psychic energy and how it is transformed and expressed in behavior. Although psychodynamic theorists disagree about the exact nature of this psychic energy and how it affects behavior, the following five propositions are central to all psychodynamic theories and have withstood the tests of time (Westen, 1998a):

1. Much of mental life is unconscious, and as a result, people may behave in ways that they themselves do not understand.

2. Mental processes such as emotions, motivations, and thoughts operate in parallel, which may lead to conflicting feelings.

3. Not only do stable personality patterns begin to form in childhood, but early experiences strongly affect personality development.

4. Our mental representations of ourselves, of others, and of our relationships tend to guide our interactions with other people.

5. The development of personality involves learning to regulate sexual and aggressive feelings as well as becoming socially interdependent rather than dependent.

Sigmund Freud

To this day, Sigmund Freud (1856–1939) is the best known and most influential of the psychodynamic theorists. As we saw in Chapter 1, Freud created an entirely new perspective on the study of human behavior. Up to his time, psychology had focused on consciousness—that is, on those thoughts and feelings of which we are aware. Freud, however, stressed the **unconscious**—all the ideas, thoughts, and feelings of which we are not normally aware. Freud's ideas form the basis of **psychoanalysis,** a term that refers to both his theory of personality and to the form of therapy that he invented.

According to Freud, human behavior is based on three kinds of unconscious instincts, or drives. Some instincts are aggressive and destructive. Others, such as hunger, thirst, and self-preservation are necessary to the survival of the individual. Finally, there is the desire for pleasure which Freud believed is the most critical factor in the development of personality.

How Personality Is Structured Freud theorized that personality is formed around three structures: the *id*, the *ego*, and the *superego*. The **id** is the only structure present at birth and is completely unconscious (see Figure 11–1). In Freud's view, the id consists of all the unconscious urges and desires that continually seek expression. It operates according to the **pleasure principle**—that is, it tries to obtain immediate pleasure and to avoid pain. As soon as an instinct arises, the id seeks to gratify it. Because the id is not in contact with the real world, however, it has only two ways of obtaining gratification. One is by reflex actions, such as coughing, which relieve unpleasant sensations at once. Another is through fantasy, or what Freud referred to as *wish fulfillment*: A person forms a mental image of an object or situation that partially satisfies the instinct and relieves the uncomfortable feeling.

Unconscious In Freud's theory, all the ideas, thoughts, and feelings of which we are not and normally cannot become aware.

Psychoanalysis The theory of personality Freud developed as well as the form of therapy he invented.

Id In Freud's theory of personality, the collection of unconscious urges and desires that continually seek expression.

Pleasure principle According to Freud, the way in which the id seeks immediate gratification of an instinct.

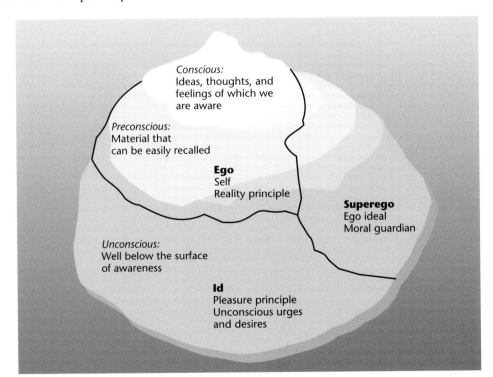

Figure 11–1
The structural relationship formed by the id, ego, and superego.
Freud's conception of personality is often depicted as an iceberg to illustrate how the vast workings of the mind occur beneath its surface. Notice that the ego is partly conscious, partly unconscious, and partly preconscious; it derives knowledge of the external world through the senses. The superego also works at all three levels. But the id is an entirely unconscious structure.
Source: Adapted from *New Introductory Lectures on Psychoanalysis* by Sigmund Freud, 1933, New York: Carlton House.

Ego Freud's term for the part of the personality that mediates between environmental demands (reality), conscience (superego), and instinctual needs (id); now often used as a synonym for "self."

Reality principle According to Freud, the way in which the ego seeks to satisfy instinctual demands safely and effectively in the real world.

Superego According to Freud, the social and parental standards the individual has internalized; the conscience and the ego ideal.

Ego ideal The part of the superego that consists of standards of what one would like to be.

Defense mechanisms Self-deceptive techniques for reducing anxiety and guilt, including denial, repression, projection, identification, regression, intellectualization, reaction formation, displacement, and sublimation.

Denial Refusal to acknowledge a painful or threatening reality.

Wish fulfillment occurs most often in dreams and daydreams, but it may take other forms. For instance, if someone enrages you and you spend the next half hour imagining all the brilliant things you might say or do to get even, you are engaging in a form of wish fulfillment.

Mental images of this kind provide fleeting relief, but they cannot fully satisfy most needs. Just thinking about being with someone you love is a poor substitute for actually being with that person and does not bring as much pleasure. Therefore, the id by itself is not very effective at gratifying instincts. It must link up with reality if it is to do a better job of satisfying needs. The id's link to reality is the ego.

Freud conceived of the **ego** as the psychic mechanism that controls all thinking and reasoning activities. The ego operates partly consciously, partly *preconsciously*, and partly unconsciously. ("Preconscious" refers to material that is not currently in awareness but can easily be recalled.) The ego learns about the external world through the senses and sees to the satisfaction of the id's drives in the external word. But instead of acting on the pleasure principle, the ego operates by the **reality principle:** By means of intelligent reasoning, the ego tries to delay satisfying the id's desires until it can do so safely and successfully. For example, if you are thirsty, your ego will attempt to determine how best to obtain something to quench your thirst effectively and safely.

A personality that consisted only of ego and id would be completely selfish. It would behave effectively but unsociably. Fully adult behavior is governed not only by reality but also by morality—that is, by the individual's conscience, or the moral standards the individual develops through interaction with parents and society. Freud called this moral watchdog the **superego.**

The superego is not present at birth. In fact, young children are amoral and do whatever is pleasurable. As we mature, however, we assimilate, or adopt as our own, the judgments of our parents about what is "good" and "bad." In time, the external restraint applied by our parents gives way to our own internal self-restraint. The superego, eventually acting as conscience, takes over the task of observing and guiding the ego, just as the parents once observed and guided the child. Like the ego, it works at the conscious, preconscious, and unconscious levels.

According to Freud, the superego also compares the ego's actions with an **ego ideal** of perfection and then rewards or punishes the ego accordingly. Unfortunately, the superego is sometimes too harsh in its judgments. An artist dominated by such a punishing superego, for example, may realize the impossibility of ever equaling Rembrandt and give up painting in despair.

Defense Mechanisms Ideally, our id, ego, and superego work in harmony, the ego satisfying the demands of the id in a reasonable, moral manner approved by the superego. However, in Freud's view, when the ego is unable to control impulses from the id in a way that is acceptable to the superego, it experiences *anxiety*, manifested as intense feelings of uneasiness, apprehension, or worry. To reduce the discomfort caused by the anxiety, the ego may resort to using a variety of **defense mechanisms** to keep the unacceptable impulses of the id from reaching consciousness. While Freud believed that these self-deceptive mechanisms are entirely unconscious, not all psychologists agree. Often, we are aware that we are putting something out of mind or otherwise deceiving ourselves. For example, all of us have blown up at one person when we *knew* we were really angry at someone else. Whether defense mechanisms operate consciously or unconsciously, they do provide a means of coping with stress that might otherwise be unbearable.

Denial Denial is the refusal to acknowledge a painful or threatening reality. As we saw in Chapter 10 (Life Span Development), denial is often the first reaction of a person who is faced with their own impending death. By temporarily denying

summarytable DEFENSE MECHANISMS

Denial	Refusing to acknowledge a painful or threatening reality: Ray, who is told that he has terminal cancer, believes instead that he simply has bronchitis.
Repression	Excluding uncomfortable thoughts from consciousness: Lisa, who was once caught shoplifting when she was in high school, has no recollection of the embarrassing event.
Projection	Attributing one's own repressed motives, feelings, or wishes to others: Marilyn is unfairly passed over for a promotion; she denies that she is angry about this, but is certain that her supervisor is angry with her.
Identification	Taking on the characteristics of someone else to avoid feeling incompetent: Anthony, uncertain of his own attractiveness, takes on the dress and mannerisms of a popular teacher.
Regression	Reverting to childlike behavior and defenses: Angry because his plan to reorganize his division has been rejected, Bob throws a tantrum.
Intellectualization	Thinking abstractly about stressful problems as a way of detaching oneself from them: After learning that she has not been asked to a classmate's costume party, Tina coolly discusses the ways in which social cliques form and how they serve to regulate and control school life.
Reaction formation	Expression of exaggerated ideas and emotions that are the opposite of one's repressed beliefs or feelings: At work, Michael loudly professes that he would never take advantage of a rival employee, though his behavior indicates quite the opposite.
Displacement	Shifting repressed motives from an original object to a substitute object: Angry at his instructor's unreasonable request that he rewrite his term paper, but afraid to confront his instructor, Nelson comes home and yells at his housemates for telling him what to do.
Sublimation	Redirecting repressed motives and feelings into more socially acceptable channels: The child of parents who never paid attention to him, Bill is running for public office.

reality, the person may be better equipped to avoid emotions that would otherwise be overwhelming.

Repression   The most common mechanism for blocking out painful feelings and memories is **repression**: Individuals exclude painful thoughts and feelings from consciousness without realizing that they are doing so. Soldiers who break down in the field often block out the memory of the experiences that led to their collapse. Repression may indicate that the person is struggling against impulses (such as aggression) that conflict with values. For example, most of us were taught in childhood that violence and aggression are wrong. This conflict between our feelings and our values can create stress, and one way of coping defensively with that stress is to repress our feelings, to block out completely any awareness of our underlying anger and hostility.

Denial and repression are the most basic defense mechanisms. In denial, we block out situations we can't cope with; in repression, we block out unacceptable impulses or thoughts. These psychic strategies form the bases for several other defensive ways of coping.

Projection   If a problem cannot be denied or completely repressed, we may distort its nature so that we can handle it more easily. One example of this is **projection**: attributing our own repressed motives, ideas, or feelings to others. In other words, we "project" feelings that we do not want to acknowledge as our own onto someone else. A corporate executive who feels guilty about the way he rose to power may project his own ruthless ambition onto his colleagues. He is simply

Repression Excluding uncomfortable thoughts, feelings, and desires from consciousness.

Projection Attributing one's own repressed motives, feelings, or wishes to others.

Identification Taking on the characteristics of someone else to avoid feeling incompetent.

Regression Reverting to childlike behavior and defenses.

Intellectualization Thinking abstractly about stressful problems as a way of detaching oneself from them.

Reaction formation Expression of exaggerated ideas and emotions that are the opposite of one's repressed beliefs or feelings.

Displacement Shifting repressed motives and emotions from an original object to a substitute object.

Sublimation Redirecting repressed motives and feelings into more socially acceptable channels.

doing his job, he believes, while his associates are all crassly ambitious and consumed with power.

Identification   The reverse of projection is **identification:** *taking on* the characteristics of someone else so that we can vicariously share in that person's triumphs. A parent with unfulfilled career ambitions may share emotionally in a son's or daughter's professional success. When the child is promoted, the parent may feel personally triumphant. Identification is often used as a form of self-defense in situations where a person feels utterly helpless, for example, in a hostage situation. To survive, victims sometimes seek to please their captors, and may identify with them as a way of defensively coping with unbearable and inescapable stress. This is called the "Stockholm Syndrome," (Cassidy, 2002) after four Swedes who were held captive in a bank vault for nearly a week but, on release, defended their captors.

Regression   People under severe stress may revert to childlike behavior through a process called **regression.** Why do people regress? Some psychologists say that it is because an adult cannot stand feeling helpless. Children, on the other hand, feel helpless and dependent every day, so becoming more childlike can make total dependency or helplessness more bearable. For example, adults may cry or throw temper tantrums when their arguments fail and expect those around them to react sympathetically, as their parents did when they were children.

Intellectualization   **Intellectualization** involves detaching ourselves from our feelings about our problems by analyzing them logically and objectively, almost as if they concerned other people. Parents who start out intending to discuss their child's difficulties with a teacher, but instead talk to her about educational philosophy, may be intellectualizing a very upsetting situation. They appear to be dealing with their problems, but in fact they are not because they have cut themselves off from their disturbing emotions.

Reaction Formation   **Reaction formation** refers to expressing ideas and emotions that are the exact opposite of what the person is actually thinking or feeling. Exaggeration is the clue to this behavior: Someone who extravagantly praises a rival may be covering up jealousy over the opponent's success. Reaction formation may be a way of unconsciously convincing oneself that one's motives are pure. The man who feels ambivalent about being a father may devote a disproportionate amount of time to his children in an attempt to prove to himself that he is a good father.

Displacement   **Displacement** involves the redirection of repressed motives and emotions from their original objects to substitute objects. The woman who has always wanted to be a mother may feel inadequate when she learns that she cannot have children. As a result, she may become extremely attached to a pet or to a niece or nephew. Perhaps the most familiar example of displacement is the person who must smile and agree with a difficult boss, then comes home and "blows up" at family members for no reason.

Sublimation   **Sublimation** refers to transforming repressed motives or feelings into more socially acceptable forms. Aggressiveness, for instance, might be channeled into competitiveness in business or sports. A strong and persistent desire for attention might be transformed into an interest in acting or politics. Freud believed that sublimation is not only necessary but desirable. People who can transform their sexual and aggressive drives into more socially acceptable forms are clearly better off, for they are able to at least partially gratify instinctual drives with relatively little anxiety and guilt. Moreover, society benefits from the energy and effort such people channel into the arts, literature, science, and other socially useful activities.

Is a person who uses a defense mechanism immature, unstable, or on the edge of a "breakdown"? Not necessarily. As Coleman, Glaros, and Morris (1987) point out, defenses are "essential for softening failure, alleviating tension and anxiety, repairing emotional hurt, and maintaining our feelings of adequacy and worth" (p. 190). In the short run, especially if there are few other options, using defense mechanisms may reduce anxiety and thus allow for the highest possible level of adaptation (Cramer, 2000). Over the long run, however, the overuse of the defense mechanisms can hinder successful adjustment. Defense mechanisms are maladaptive when they interfere with a person's ability to deal directly with a problem or create more problems than they solve.

How Personality Develops   Freud's theory of personality development focuses on the way in which we satisfy the sexual instinct during the course of life. Freud called the energy generated by the sexual instinct **libido.** As infants mature, their libido becomes focused on different sensitive parts of the body each of which provides some pleasure. During the first 18 months of life, the dominant source of sensual pleasure is the mouth. At about 18 months, sensuality shifts to the anus; and at about age 3, it shifts again, this time to the genitals. According to Freud, children's experiences at each of these stages stamp their personality with tendencies that endure into adulthood. If a child is deprived of pleasure (or allowed too much gratification) from the part of the body that dominates a certain stage, some sexual energy may remain permanently tied to that part of the body, instead of moving on in normal sequence to give the individual a fully integrated personality. This is called **fixation,** and as we shall see, Freud believed that it leads to immature forms of sexuality and to certain characteristic personality traits. Let's look more closely at the psychosexual stages that Freud identified and their presumed relationship to personality development.

In the **oral stage** (birth to 18 months), infants, who depend completely on other people to satisfy their needs, experience pleasure by sucking and swallowing; when their baby teeth come in, they obtain pleasure from chewing and biting. According to Freud, infants who receive too much oral gratification at this stage grow into overly optimistic, gullible and dependent adults; those who receive too little may turn into pessimistic, sarcastic, argumentative and hostile people later in life.

During the **anal stage** (roughly 18 months to 3 1/2 years) the primary source of sexual pleasure shifts from the mouth to the anus. Just about the time children begin to derive pleasure from holding in and excreting feces, toilet training takes place, and they must learn to regulate this new pleasure. In Freud's view, if parents are too strict in toilet training, some children throw temper tantrums and may live in self-destructive ways as adults. Others become obstinate, stingy, and excessively orderly.

When children reach the **phallic stage** (after age 3), they discover their genitals and develop a marked attachment to the parent of the opposite sex while becoming jealous of the same-sex parent. Freud called this the **Oedipus complex,** after the character in Greek mythology who killed his father and married his mother. Girls go through a corresponding **Electra complex,** involving possessive love for their fathers and jealousy toward their mothers. Most children eventually resolve these conflicts by identifying with the parent of the same sex. However, Freud contended that fixation at this stage leads to vanity and egotism in adult life, with men boasting of their sexual prowess and treating women with contempt, and women becoming flirtatious and promiscuous. Phallic fixation may also prompt feelings of low self-esteem, shyness, and worthlessness.

At the end of the phallic period, Freud believed, children lose interest in sexual behavior and enter a **latency period.** During this period, which begins around the age of 5 or 6 and lasts until age 12 or 13, boys play with boys, girls play with girls, and neither sex takes much interest in the other.

Libido According to Freud, the energy generated by the sexual instinct.

Fixation According to Freud, a partial or complete halt at some point in the individual's psychosexual development.

Oral stage First stage in Freud's theory of personality development, in which the infant's erotic feelings center on the mouth, lips, and tongue.

Anal stage Second stage in Freud's theory of personality development, in which a child's erotic feelings center on the anus and on elimination.

Phallic stage Third stage in Freud's theory of personality development, in which erotic feelings center on the genitals.

Oedipus complex and Electra complex According to Freud, a child's sexual attachment to the parent of the opposite sex and jealousy toward the parent of the same sex; generally occurs in the phallic stage.

Latency period In Freud's theory of personality, a period in which the child appears to have no interest in the other sex; occurs after the phallic stage.

Freud believed that during the oral stage, when babies are dependent on others to fulfill their needs, they derive pleasure from the mouth, lips, and tongue.

Genital stage In Freud's theory of personality development, the final stage of normal adult sexual development, which is usually marked by mature sexuality.

Personal unconscious In Jung's theory of personality, one of the two levels of the unconscious; it contains the individual's repressed thoughts, forgotten experiences, and undeveloped ideas.

Collective unconscious In Jung's theory of personality, the level of the unconscious that is inherited and common to all members of a species.

Archetypes In Jung's theory of personality, thought forms common to all human beings, stored in the collective unconscious.

At puberty, the individual enters the last psychosexual stage, which Freud called the **genital stage.** At this time, sexual impulses reawaken. In lovemaking, the adolescent and the adult are able to satisfy unfulfilled desires from infancy and childhood. Ideally, immediate gratification of these desires yields to mature sexuality, in which postponed gratification, a sense of responsibility, and caring for others all play a part.

Freud is certainly not without his critics. Feminists have assailed Freud's male-centered, phallic view of personality development, especially because he also hypothesized that all little girls feel inferior because they do not have a penis. Many people now see penis envy as much less central to female personality development than Freud thought it was (Dahl, 1996; Gelman, 1990). In fact, the whole notion that male and female personality development proceeds along similar lines is being challenged. For example, if the developmental tasks facing boys and girls are quite different, then the unique developmental tasks encountered by girls may leave them with important skills and abilities that Freud overlooked or minimized.

Moreover, Freud's beliefs, particularly his emphasis on sexuality, were not completely endorsed even by members of his own psychoanalytic school. Carl Jung and Alfred Adler, two early associates of Freud, eventually broke with him and formulated their own psychodynamic theories of personality. Jung accepted Freud's stress on unconscious motivation but expanded the scope of the unconscious well beyond the selfish satisfactions of the id. Adler believed that human beings have positive—and conscious—goals that guide their behavior. Other psychodynamic theorists put greater emphasis on the ego and its attempts to gain mastery over the world. These neo-Freudians, principally Karen Horney and Erik Erikson, also focused more on the influence of social interaction on personality.

Carl Jung

Carl Jung's (1875–1961) *analytic psychology* embraced many of Freud's tenets; however, his beliefs differed from Freud's in many novel ways. Jung contended that libido, or psychic energy, represents *all* the life forces, not just the sexual ones. Both Freud and Jung emphasized the role of the unconscious in determining human behavior. But where Freud viewed the id as a "cauldron of seething excitations" that the ego has to control, Jung saw the unconscious as the ego's source of strength and vitality. He also believed that the unconscious consists of the personal unconscious and the collective unconscious. Within the realm of the **personal unconscious** fall our repressed thoughts, forgotten experiences, and undeveloped ideas, which may rise to consciousness if an incident or sensation triggers their recall.

According to Carl Jung, the image of a motherlike figure with protective, embracing arms is an archtype that stems from the important, nurturing role of women throughout human history. This thought form is depicted here in a Bulgarian clay figure of a goddess that dates back some six or seven thousand years.

ENDURING ISSUES ° **diversity**universality

Universal Human Archetypes

The **collective unconscious,** Jung's most original concept, comprises the memories and behavior patterns that are inherited from past generations and therefore are shared by all humans. Just as the human body is the product of millions of years of evolution, so too, according to Jung, is the human mind. Over millennia it has developed "thought forms," or collective memories, of experiences that people have had in common since prehistoric times. He called these thought forms **archetypes.** Archetypes appear in our thoughts as typical mental images, or mythical representations. Because all people have mothers, for example, the archetype of "mother" is universally associated with the image of one's own mother, with Mother Earth, and with a protective presence. The archetype of "hero" may enter one's thoughts as a tribal chieftain, Joshua at the battle of Jericho, or Nelson Mandela, depending on one's particular moment in history.

Jung felt that specific archetypes play special roles in shaping personality. The **persona** (an archetype whose meaning stems from the Latin word for "mask") is the element of our personality that we project to other people—a shell that grows around our inner self. For some people, the public self so predominates that they lose touch with their inner feelings, leading to personality maladjustments.

Two other important archetypes are anima and animus. Jung saw men and women as each having aspects of both sexes in their personalities. The **anima** is the female archetype as it is expressed in a man; the **animus** is the male archetype as expressed in the female personality. Thus, Jung considered aggressive behavior in females and nurturant behavior in males to be manifestations of the animus and the anima, respectively.

Jung also divided people into two general attitude types—introverts and extroverts. **Extroverts** turn their attention to the external world. They take an active interest in other people and in the events going on around them. **Introverts** are more caught up in their own private worlds. They tend to be unsociable and lack confidence in dealing with other people. Everyone, Jung felt, possesses some aspects of both attitude types, but one is usually dominant.

Jung further divided people into **rational individuals,** who regulate their actions by thinking and feeling, and **irrational individuals,** who base their actions on perceptions, whether through the senses (sensation) or through unconscious processes (intuition). Most people exhibit all four psychological functions: thinking, feeling, sensing, and intuiting. Jung felt, however, that one or more of these functions is usually dominant. Thus, the thinking person is rational and logical and decides on the basis of facts. The feeling person is sensitive to his or her surroundings, acts tactfully, and has a balanced sense of values. The sensing type relies primarily on surface perceptions and rarely uses imagination or deeper understanding. And the intuitive type sees beyond obvious solutions and facts to consider future possibilities.

While Freud emphasized the primacy of the sexual instincts, Jung stressed people's rational and spiritual qualities. And while Freud considered development to be shaped in childhood, Jung thought that psychic development only comes to fruition during middle age. Jung also contended that a person moves constantly toward self-realization—toward blending all parts of the personality into a harmonious whole. Both because Jung broke with Freud and because of the symbolism and mysticism that characterize his theories, many psychologists have somewhat neglected Jung's ideas (Neher, 1996). Recently, however, his concept of archetypes has been "rediscovered" by those interested in the power of myth (Ellens, 2002; Goode, 1992; Nuttall, 2002).

Alfred Adler

Alfred Adler (1870–1937) disagreed sharply with Freud's concept of the conflict between selfish id and the morality-based superego. To Adler, people possess innate positive motives and strive for personal and social perfection. Early in his career Adler believed that personality develops through the individual's attempt to overcome physical weaknesses, an effort he called **compensation.** Later on, Adler modified and broadened his views, contending that people seek to overcome *feelings* of inferiority that may or may not have a basis in reality. He thought such feelings often spark positive development and personal growth. Still, some people become so fixated on their feelings of inferiority that they become paralyzed and develop what Adler called an **inferiority complex.**

Persona According to Jung, our public self, the mask we put on to represent ourselves to others.

Anima According to Jung, the female archetype as it is expressed in the male personality.

Animus According to Jung, the male archetype as it is expressed in the female personality.

Extrovert According to Jung, a person who usually focuses on social life and the external world instead of on his or her internal experience.

Introvert According to Jung, a person who usually focuses on his or her own thoughts and feelings.

Rational individuals According to Jung, people who regulate their actions by the psychological functions of thinking and feeling.

Irrational individuals According to Jung, people who base their actions on perceptions, either through the senses (sensation) or through unconscious processes (intuition).

Compensation According to Adler, the person's effort to overcome imagined or real personal weaknesses.

Inferiority complex In Adler's theory, the fixation on feelings of personal inferiority that results in emotional and social paralysis.

"I'm only a <u>good</u> dane."

Source: The Cartoon Bank © 2000. Mike Twohy from cartoonbank.com. All rights reserved

Karen Horney, a psychotherapist during the first half of the 20th century, disagreed with Freud's emphasis on sexual instincts. She considered environmental and social factors, especially the relationships we have as children, to be the most important influences on personality.

Anxiety In Horney's theory, the individual's reaction to real or imagined threats.

Neurotic trends Horney's term for irrational strategies for coping with emotional problems and minimizing anxiety.

Still later in his life, Adler again shifted his theoretical emphasis in a more positive direction when he concluded that strivings for superiority and perfection were more important to personality development than overcoming feelings of inferiority. He suggested that people strive both for personal perfection and for the perfection of the society to which they belong, setting important goals for themselves that guide their behavior. These personal goals need not be realistically attainable; what is important is that a person acts as if they are. Although all people strive for individual and social perfection, each individual develops a particular set of directions and beliefs that become his or her *style of life*. Adler believed that this style of life emerges by age 4 or 5.

Unlike Freud, Adler believed that people have the capacity to master their own fate. The emphasis Adler placed on positive, socially constructive goals and on striving for perfection is in marked contrast to Freud's pessimistic vision of the selfish person locked into eternal conflict with society. Adler reintroduced into psychology the idea, which Freud had deleted, that a person's voluntary effort toward personally positive and socially beneficial goals is an important part of human personality and development. Because of this, Adler has been hailed by many psychologists as the father of humanistic psychology (Cain, 2002), a topic we will explore in greater depth later in this chapter.

Karen Horney

Karen Horney (1885–1952), another psychodynamic personality theorist greatly indebted to Freud, nevertheless took issue with some of his most prominent ideas, especially his analysis of women and his emphasis on sexual instincts. Based on her experience as a practicing therapist in Germany and the United States, Horney concluded that environmental and social factors are the most important influences in shaping personality, and among these, the most pivotal are the human relationships we experience as children.

In Horney's view, Freud overemphasized the sex drive, leading him to present a distorted picture of human relationships. Although Horney believed that sexuality does figure in the development of personality, she thought that nonsexual factors, such as the need for a sense of basic security and the response to real or imagined threats, play an even larger role. For example, all people share the need to feel loved and nurtured by their parents, regardless of any sexual feelings they might have about them. Conversely, parents' protective feelings toward their children emerge not only from biological forces but also from the value society places on the nurturance of children.

Horney viewed **anxiety**—an individual's reaction to real or imagined dangers—as a powerful motivating force. Whereas Freud believed that anxiety usually emerges from sexual conflicts, Horney stressed that feelings of anxiety also originate in a variety of nonsexual contexts. In childhood, anxiety arises because children depend on adults for their very survival. Insecure about receiving continued nurturance and protection, children develop inner protections, or defenses, that provide both satisfaction and security. They experience more anxiety when those defenses are threatened.

Anxious adults, according to Horney (1937), adopt one of three coping strategies, or **neurotic trends**, that help them deal with emotional problems and ensure safety, albeit at the expense of personal independence: moving toward people (submission), moving against people (aggression), and moving away from people (detachment). Each person's characteristic reliance on one or another of these strategies is reflected in his or her patterns of behavior, or *personality type*. A compliant type is an individual who has an overriding need to give in or submit to others and feels safe only when receiving their protection and guidance. This is neurotic, according to Horney, because the resultant friendliness is superficial and masks feelings of aggression and anxiety. In contrast, the aggressive type masks his or her submissive feelings and relates to others in a hostile and domineering manner. The aggressive type, however, is also hiding basic feelings of insecurity and anxiety. Finally, the detached type copes with basic anxiety by withdrawing from other people. This person seems to be saying, "If I withdraw, nothing can hurt me."

Well-adjusted people also experience anxiety and may use one or more of these coping strategies in moderation, but because their childhood environment enabled them to satisfy their basic emotional needs, they were able to develop without becoming trapped in neurotic lifestyles.

ENDURING ISSUES   **stability**change

Is Biology Destiny?

Horney's conviction that cultural forces are far more important than biological forces had a profound effect on her views of human development. For example, she believed that adults can continue to develop and change throughout life. Because biology is not destiny, adults can come to understand the source of their basic anxiety and try to eliminate neurotic anxiety. Horney's belief, shared by other psychodynamic thinkers, in the possibility of change through self-understanding also relates to the mind–body question. Psychodynamic therapies, which involve delving into past experiences and hidden motives, rely on the premise that destructive thought patterns and behaviors can change through mental effort only.

Horney also opened the way to a more constructive and optimistic understanding of male and female personality. She emphasized that culture and not anatomy determines many of the characteristics that differentiate women from men, and pointed out that those cultural forces can be changed. For example, to the extent that women feel dissatisfied with their gender or men are overly aggressive, the explanation is likely to be found in their social status and social roles, not in their anatomy, and social status and social roles can be changed. Indeed, she was a forerunner of contemporary thinkers, in particular feminist theorists, who believe that we can change culture and society and, in the process, transform human relationships (Gilman, 2001).

Erik Erikson

Erik Erikson (1902–1994) studied with Freud in Vienna. Another psychodynamic theorist who took a socially oriented view of personality development, Erikson agreed with much of Freud's thinking on sexual development and the influence of libidinal needs on personality. The quality of parent-child relationships was also important for Erikson, because the family constitutes the child's first brush with society. He believed that parents can discipline children in a way that makes them feel loved or hated. The key is that children should feel their own needs and desires are compatible with those of society as embodied in their family. Only if children feel competent and valuable, in their own eyes and in society's, will they develop a secure sense of identity. In this way Erikson shifted the focus of Freud's personality theory to ego development. Recent studies of Erikson's concepts of identity, intimacy, and generativity have reaffirmed the importance of these central ideas to personality development (Bradley, 1997; Marcia, 1994; Orlofsky, 1993).

Erik Erikson, another psychodynamic theorist, also stressed the importance of parent-child relationships on how personality is shaped. His eight-stage theory of personality development is still influential today.

Industry versus inferiority. A child's challenge during the school years is to begin acquiring the skills needed for a fulfilling adulthood. Success during these years builds confidence to face the future; continued failure or discouragement can fill a child with self-doubt.

In the last chapter we examined how some aspects of Erikson's theory have been incorporated in the contemporary view of human development. A brief description of Erikson's eight stages of personality development appear in Table 11–1. The first five of the eight stages correspond to Freud's stages of personality development. According to Erikson, success at each stage depends on the person's adjustments in previous stages.

A Psychodynamic View of Jaylene Smith

According to Freud, personality characteristics such as insecurity, introversion, and feelings of inadequacy and worthlessness often arise from fixation at the phallic stage of development. Thus, had Freud been Jaylene's therapist, he would probably have concluded that Jay has not yet effectively resolved her Electra complex. Working from this premise, he would have hypothesized that Jay's relationship with her father was either very distant and unsatisfying or unusually close and gratifying. We know, of course, that it was the latter.

In all likelihood, Freud would also have asserted that at around age 5 or 6, Jay had become aware that she could not actually marry her father and do away with her mother, as he would say she wished to do. This might account for the fact that fights between Jay and her mother subsided when Jay was about 6 or 7 years of age. Moreover, we know that shortly thereafter, Jay began to experience "strong feelings of loneliness, depression, insecurity, and confusion." Clearly, something important happened in Jay's life when she was 6 or 7.

Finally, the continued coolness of Jay's relationship with her mother and the unusual closeness with her father would probably have confirmed Freud's suspicion that Jay has still not satisfactorily resolved her Electra complex. Freud would have predicted that Jay would have problems making the progression to mature sexual relationships with other men. Jay, of course, is very much aware that she has problems relating to men, at least when these relationships get "serious."

And what does Erikson's theory tell us about Jaylene Smith's personality? Recall that for Erikson, one's success in dealing with later developmental crises depends on how effectively one has resolved earlier crises. Because Jay is having great difficulty in dealing with intimacy (Stage 6), he would have suggested that she is still struggling with problems from earlier developmental stages. Erikson would have looked for the source of these problems in the quality of Jay's earlier relationships. We know that her mother subtly communicated her own frustration and dissatisfaction to her children and spent little time on "nonessential" interactions with them. These feelings and behavior patterns would not have instilled in a child the kind of basic trust and sense of security that Erikson believed were essential to the first stage of development. In addition, her relationship with her mother and brothers continued to be less than fully satisfactory. It is not surprising, then, that Jay had some difficulty working through subsequent developmental crises. Although she developed a close and caring relationship with her father, Jay was surely aware that his affection partly depended on her fulfilling the dreams, ambitions, and goals he had for her.

THINKING CRITICALLY

Psychoanalysis

Freud's original theory was based on case studies of his patients, and the literature on psychoanalysis consists mainly of case studies—descriptions of individual cases of psychopathology, probable causes, and their treatment. Today, however, psychological science depends increasingly on experimental evidence and biological explanations for mental phenomena. Review the five basic concepts of psychodynamic theory described by Westen and think about what kinds of evidence might convince you that they are indeed correct. What evidence would lead you to conclude that they are not in fact correct?

Evaluating Psychodynamic Theories

Freud's emphasis on the fact that we are not always, or even often, aware of the real causes of our behavior has fundamentally changed the way people view themselves and others. Freud's ideas have also had a lasting impact on history, literature, and the arts. Yet Freud was

table 11-1   ERIKSON'S EIGHT STAGES OF LIFE

Age	Psychosocial Stage	Characteristics
Infancy (to 1 year)	Trust versus mistrust	Infants come to trust that their parents will meet their needs. If needs are met, they come to trust environment and themselves; if not, mistrust and fear develop.
Early childhood (1–3)	Autonomy versus shame and doubt	Children gain increasing autonomy. They learn to walk, hold onto things, and control themselves. If they repeatedly fail to master these skills, self-doubt may take root. If their efforts are belittled by adults, shame and a lasting sense of inferiority may develop.
Childhood (3–6)	Initiative versus guilt	Children undertake new projects, make plans, and conquer new challenges. Parental encouragement for these initiatives leads to a sense of joy in exercising initiative and tackling new challenges. If children are scolded for these initiatives, strong feelings of guilt, unworthiness, and resentment may take hold.
Later childhood (6–12)	Industry versus inferiority	Children learn the skills needed to become well-rounded adults, including personal care, productive work, and independent social living. If children are stifled in their efforts to become competent and industrious, they may conclude that they are inadequate and lose faith in their power to become self-sufficient.
Adolescence (12–19)	Identity versus role confusion	The critical problem at this stage is to find one's identity by integrating a number of roles—student, sister or brother, friend, and so on—into a coherent pattern that gives the young person a sense of inner continuity or identity. Failure to forge an identity leads to role confusion and despair.
Young adulthood (19–40)	Intimacy versus isolation	The question of intimacy is the critical issue at this stage. To love someone else, young adults must feel secure in their identities, be trusting, and autonomous. Failure at intimacy brings a painful sense of loneliness and the feeling of incompleteness.
Adulthood (40–65)	Generativity versus stagnation	People who have successfully negotiated the six earlier stages are likely to find meaning and joy in all the major activities of life—career, family, community participation. The challenge is to remain productive and creative in all aspects of one's life. For others, who do not expand their concerns, life becomes a dull routine.
Maturity (65+)	Integrity versus despair	This stage is an opportunity to attain full selfhood—an acceptance of one's life, a sense that it is complete and satisfactory. People who have gained full maturity by resolving the earlier conflicts possess the integrity to face death with a minimum of fear. For others, this is a period of despair at the loss of former roles and regret at lost opportunities.

Source: Adapted from *Childhood and Society* by Erik H. Erikson. Copyright 1950, © 1963 by W. W. Norton & Company, Inc., renewed © 1978, 1991 by Erik H. Erikson. Used by permission of W. W. Norton & Company, Inc. and the Hogarth Press.

a product of his time and place. Critics of his theories have pointed out that he was apparently unable to imagine a connection between his female patients' sense of inferiority and their subordinate position in society. In addition, when patients allegedly told him of sexual abuse they had endured at the hands of family members, Freud initially took these stories at face value but later reversed himself and saw them as fantasies, supporting his theory of the Oedipus and Electra complexes.

Freud's reversal has been challenged on two fronts. First, given our heightened awareness of the high rates of sexual abuse of children, some critics claim that the stories were probably true, and Freud's about-face amounted to caving in to the social disapproval of his hypotheses regarding childhood sexuality (Masson, 1984). More disturbingly, there is growing evidence that Freud's patients may never have actually reported instances of sexual abuse to him; rather, it appears that Freud may have *inferred* sexual abuse in their childhoods from their adult symptoms (Esterson, 1993, 1998; Schatzman, 1992).

Psychodynamic views have also been criticized because they are based largely on retrospective (backward-looking) accounts of individuals who have sought treatment rather than on research with individuals who have not sought treatment. Yet it is often difficult to translate psychodynamic personality theories into hypotheses that can be tested experimentally (Cloninger, 1993).

Still, Freud's theory has received limited confirmation from research. Orally fixated people also seem to depend heavily on others, as Freud predicted (Fisher & Greenberg, 1985). In addition, some research indicates that a few characteristics of anally fixated people do tend to appear together; for instance, individuals who are stingy are indeed also likely to be neat (Fisher & Greenberg, 1985). Moreover, research confirms an association between specific personality types in childhood and later development of psychological problems. For example, in a longitudinal study, children who were described as inhibited at age 3 were more likely than a control group to be depressed at age 21 (Caspi, Moffitt, Newman, & Silva, 1996). Similarly, research that uses stimuli designed to activate or "trigger" particular unconscious processes lends some support to Freud's theory (Cloninger, 1993). The effectiveness of psychoanalysis as a therapy has also been cited as evidence in support of Freud's theories. Still, as we shall see in Chapter 14, Therapies, psychoanalysis does not seem to be any more or less effective than therapies based on other theories (Stiles, Shapiro, & Elliott, 1986).

Erikson's theory of stages of identity has also prompted a good deal of research, particularly the concept of identity resolution. It has been found that people who successfully handled the crises of the first four stages were, in fact, more likely to achieve a stable source of identity in the fifth stage (Waterman, Beubel, & Waterman, 1970). Research has also shown that forging a strong identity is necessary for achieving intimacy. College men who were the least isolated socially were also those with the clearest sense of self (Orlofsky, Marcia, & Lesser, 1973). In a follow-up study of the same group of college men, identity continued to be related to intimacy (Marcia, 1976). Yet another study found the same connection between identity and intimacy for both sexes. Men and women both believe that a positive sense of identity is crucial to achieving satisfactory relationships (Orlofsky, 1978).

Freud's theories have clearly expanded our understanding of personality, or they would not still be so vigorously debated today, more than 100 years after he proposed them. Whatever their merit as science, psychodynamic theories attempt to explain the root causes of all human behavior. The sheer magnitude of this undertaking helps to account for their lasting attractiveness.

CHECK YOUR UNDERSTANDING

1. Match the Freudian *concept* with the appropriate definition.

___ unconscious   a. energy that comes from the sexual instinct

___ superego   b. mediator between reality, the superego, and the id

___ id   c. unconscious urges seeking expression

___ ego   d. ideas and feelings of which we are normally not aware

___ libido   e. moral guardian of the ego

2. Match the Jungian concept with the appropriate definition.

___ persona   a. typical mental image or mythical representation

___ collective unconscious   b. memories and behavior patterns inherited from past generations

___ archetype   c. aspect of the personality by which one is known to other people

3. Match each stage of childhood with its major challenge, according to Erik Erikson's theory.

___ infancy   a. industry versus inferiority

___ toddlerhood   b. trust versus mistrust

___ preschool years   c. autonomy versus shame and doubt

___ elementary school years   d. initiative versus guilt

Answers: 1. unconscious—d; superego—e; id—c; ego—b; libido—a. 2. persona—c; collective unconscious—b; archetype—a. 3. infancy—b; toddlerhood—c; preschool years—d; elementary school years—a

Humanistic Personality Theories

To what extent do people strive toward positive growth?

Psychodynamic theorists generally believe that personality grows out of the resolution of unconscious conflicts and developmental crises. However, as we noted earlier, although Alfred Adler began as a psychodynamic theorist, later in his life he arrived at a very different view of human nature that focused on positive growth and a striving for personal perfection. For these reasons, Adler is sometimes called the first humanistic personality theorist.

Humanistic personality theory emphasizes that we are positively motivated and progress toward higher levels of functioning—in other words, that there is more to human existence than dealing with hidden conflicts. Humanistic psychologists believe that life is a process of opening ourselves to the world around us and experiencing joy in living. Humanists stress people's potential for growth and change as well as the ways they subjectively experience their lives right now, rather than dwelling on how they felt or acted in the past. This approach holds all of us personally responsible for our lives. Finally, humanists also believe that given reasonable life conditions, people will develop in desirable directions (Cloninger, 1993). Adler's concept of striving for perfection laid the groundwork for later humanistic personality theorists such as Abraham Maslow and Carl Rogers. We discussed Maslow's theory of the hierarchy of needs leading to self-actualization in Chapter 9, Motivation and Emotion. We now turn to Rogers's theory of self-actualization.

Carl Rogers

One of the most prominent humanistic theorists, Carl Rogers (1902–1987), contended that men and women develop their personalities in the service of positive

Humanistic personality theory Any personality theory that asserts the fundamental goodness of people and their striving toward higher levels of functioning.

Actualizing tendency According to Rogers, the drive of every organism to fulfill its biological potential and become what it is inherently capable of becoming.

Self-actualizing tendency According to Rogers, the drive of human beings to fulfill their self-concepts, or the images they have of themselves.

Fully functioning person According to Rogers, an individual whose self-concept closely resembles his or her inborn capacities or potentials.

Unconditional positive regard In Rogers's theory, the full acceptance and love of another person regardless of our behavior.

Conditional positive regard In Rogers's theory, acceptance and love that are dependent on behaving in certain ways and fulfilling certain conditions.

goals. According to Rogers, every organism is born with certain innate capacities, capabilities, or potentialities—"a sort of genetic blueprint, to which substance is added as life progresses" (Maddi, 1989, p. 102). The goal of life is to fulfill this genetic blueprint, to become the best of whatever each of us is inherently capable of becoming. Rogers called this biological push toward fulfillment the **actualizing tendency.** Although Rogers maintained that the actualizing tendency characterizes all organisms—plants, animals, and humans—he noted that human beings also form images of themselves, or *self-concepts.* Just as we try to fulfill our inborn biological potential, so, too, we attempt to fulfill our self-concept, our conscious sense of who we are and what we want to do with our lives. Rogers called this striving the **self-actualizing tendency.** If you think of yourself as "intelligent" and "athletic," for example, you will strive to live up to those images of yourself.

When our self-concept is closely matched with our inborn capacities, we are likely to become what Rogers called a **fully functioning person.** Such people are self-directed: They decide for themselves what it is they wish to do and to become, even though their choices may not always be sound ones. They are not unduly swayed by other people's expectations for them. Fully functioning people are also open to experience—to their own feelings as well as to the world and other people around them—and thus find themselves "increasingly willing to be, with greater accuracy and depth, that self which [they] most truly [are]" (Rogers, 1961, pp. 175–176).

According to Rogers, people tend to become more fully functioning if they are brought up with **unconditional positive regard,** or the experience of being treated with warmth, respect, acceptance, and love regardless of their own feelings, attitudes, and behaviors. But often parents and other adults offer children what Rogers called **conditional positive regard:** They value and accept only certain aspects of the child. The acceptance, warmth, and love the child receives from others then depends on the child's behaving in certain ways and fulfilling certain conditions. The condition may be expressed explicitly, such as "Daddy won't love you if . . ." or "Mommy doesn't love girls who. . . ." But it may also come through subtly, as in such statements as "That's a nice idea, but wouldn't you rather do . . .?" Not surprisingly, one response to conditional positive regard is a tendency to change your self-concept to include those things that you "ought to be," to become more like the person you are expected to be to win the caregiver's love. In the process, your self-concept comes to resemble your inborn capacity less and less, and your life deviates from the genetic blueprint.

When people lose sight of their inborn potential, according to Rogers they become constricted, rigid, and defensive. They feel threatened and anxious and experience considerable discomfort and uneasiness. Because their lives are directed toward what other people want and value, they are unlikely to experience much real satisfaction in life. At some point, they may realize that they don't really know who they are or what they want.

A Humanistic View of Jaylene Smith

Humanistic personality theory would focus on the discrepancy between Jay's self-concept and her inborn capacities. For example, Rogers would point out that Jay is intelligent and achievement-oriented but nevertheless feels that she doesn't "deserve to be a doctor," worries about whether she will ever be "truly happy," and remembers that when she was 13, she never was able to be herself and really express her feelings, even with a good friend. Her unhappiness, fearfulness, loneliness, insecurity, and other dissatisfactions similarly stem from Jay's inability to become what she "most truly is." Rogers would suspect that other people in Jay's life made acceptance and love conditional on her living up to their ideas of what she should become. We know

This young woman's work painting houses for the poor suggests that she sees herself as kind and caring and is striving to reflect that image in her actions. In Rogers's view she would be on the way to becoming a self-actualized person.

that for most of her life, Jay's father was her primary source of positive regard. Very possibly he conditioned his love for Jay on her living up to his goals for her.

Evaluating Humanistic Theories

The central tenet of most humanistic personality theories—that the overriding purpose of the human condition is to realize one's potential—is difficult if not impossible to verify scientifically. The resulting lack of scientific evidence and rigor is one of the major criticisms of these theories. In addition, some critics claim that humanistic theories present an overly optimistic view of human beings and fail to take into account the evil in human nature. Others contend that the humanistic view fosters self-centeredness and narcissism and reflects Western values of individual achievement rather than universal human potential.

Nonetheless, Maslow and, especially, Rogers did attempt to test some aspects of their theories scientifically. For example, Rogers studied the discrepancy between the way people perceived themselves and the way they ideally wanted to be. He presented people with statements such as "I often feel resentful" and "I feel relaxed and nothing really bothers me." They were asked to sort the statements into several piles indicating how well the statements described their real selves. Then they were asked to sort them again, this time according to how well they described their *ideal* selves. In this way, Rogers discovered that people whose real selves differed considerably from their ideal selves were more likely to be unhappy and dissatisfied.

CHECK YOUR UNDERSTANDING

1. Humanistic personality theory says human behavior is

___a. driven primarily by unconscious conflicts

___b. genetically predetermined

___c. positively motivated and directed toward higher levels of functioning

2. The phrase associated with humanist theorist Carl Rogers is

___a. self-actualizing tendency

___b. neurotic trends

___c. trust versus mistrust

Answers: 1. c, 2. a

Trait Theories

What is the key focus of trait theories?

Development of Trait Theory

The personality theories we have examined all emphasize the importance of early-childhood experiences in personality development. Other personality theorists take a different approach. They focus on the present, describing the ways in which already-developed adult personalities differ from one another. These *trait theorists*, as they are known, assert that people differ according to the degree to which they possess certain **personality traits**, such as dependency, anxiety, aggressiveness, and sociability.

Personality traits Dimensions or characteristics on or in which people differ in distinctive ways.

Factor analysis A statistical technique that identifies groups of related objects; used by Cattell to identify trait clusters.

Big Five Five traits or basic dimensions currently thought to be of central importance in describing personality.

We infer a trait from how a person behaves. If someone consistently throws parties, goes to great lengths to make friends, and travels in groups, we might safely conclude that this person possesses a high degree of sociability. Our language has many words that describe personality traits. Gordon Allport, along with his colleague H. S. Odbert (1936), went through the dictionary and found nearly 18,000 words that might refer to personality traits.

ENDURING ISSUES   **heredity**environment

Is Personality Inherited?

For Allport, traits—or "dispositions," as he called them—are literally encoded in the nervous system as structures that guide consistent behavior across a wide variety of situations. Allport also believed that while traits describe behaviors that are common to many people, each individual personality comprises a unique constellation of traits. While few psychologists today would deny the influence of the environment in shaping personality, recent evidence substantiating the importance of genetic factors to the development of specific personality traits supports Allport's hunch that at least some personality traits are encoded biologically (Krueger & Markon, 2002).

Only about 2,800 of the words on Allport and Odbert's list concern the kinds of stable or enduring characteristics that most psychologists would call personality traits, and when synonyms and near-synonyms are removed, the number of possible personality traits drops to around 200—which is still a formidable list. Psychologist Raymond Cattell (1965), using a statistical technique called **factor analysis,** found that those 200 traits tend to cluster in groups. Thus, a person who is described as persevering or determined is also likely to be thought of as responsible, ordered, attentive, and stable and probably would not be described as frivolous, neglectful, and changeable. On the basis of extensive research, Cattell originally concluded that just 16 traits account for the complexity of human personality; later he suggested that it might be necessary to add another 7 traits to the list (Cattell & Kline, 1977).

Other theorists thought that Cattell used too many traits to describe personality. For example, Eysenck (1976) argued that personality could be reduced to just three basic dimensions: *emotional stability, introversion–extroversion,* and *psychoticism.* According to Eysenck, *emotional stability* refers to how well people control their emotions; *introversion–extroversion* refers to the degree that a person is inwardly or outwardly oriented; and *psychoticism* describes people characterized by insensitivity and uncooperativeness at one end and warmth, tenderness, and helpfulness at the other end.

The Big Five

Contemporary trait theorists have boiled personality traits down to five basic dimensions: *extroversion, agreeableness, conscientiousness, emotional stability,* and *culture* (see Table 11–2; Botwin & Buss, 1989; Goldberg, 1993; Tupes & Christal, 1961; Wiggins, 1996). There is a growing consensus today that these **Big Five** personality dimensions, also known as the *five-factor model,* capture the most salient dimensions of human personality (Funder, 1991; McCrae & Costa, 1996; Wiggins, 1996), although there is some disagreement about whether the fifth dimension should be called "culture" or "openness to experience" (McCrae & Costa, 1985, 1987, 1989) or "intellect" (Digman & Takemoto-Chock, 1981; Peabody & Goldberg, 1989). Recently, each of the Big Five traits has been shown to have at least six *facets,* or components, as shown in Table 11–2 (Jang, Livesey, McCrae, Angleitner, & Riemann, 1998). The 30 identified facets are not an exhaustive listing of all aspects of personality; rather, they represent a broad sample of important traits (Costa & McCrae, 1992, 1995).

One survey of the literature found that the Big Five dimensions of personality may have some important real-world applications—particularly as they relate to employment decisions (Hogan, Hogan, & Roberts, 1996). For example, one study (Ones, Viswesvaran, & Schmidt, 1993) found that the dimensions of conscientiousness and emotional stability were reliable predictors of job performance in a wide variety of occupational settings. In addition, research has shown that absenteeism in the workplace is related to the conscientiousness, extraversion, and neuroticism scales (Conte & Jacobs, 2003). Thus, the Big Five dimensions of personality show promise as reliable predictors of job performance, especially when other criteria such as technical skills and experience are also considered (Hogan et al., 1996).

Are the Big Five Personality Traits Universal? Most studies of the Big Five have been conducted in the United States. Would the same five personality dimensions be evident in other cultures? The answer appears to be yes. Costa and McCrae (1992) developed a test to measure the Big Five personality dimensions that has since been translated into numerous languages, including German, Portuguese, Hebrew, Chinese, Korean, and Japanese. McCrae and Costa (1997) then compared the results from the various tests. The Big Five personality dimensions were clearly evident. As the authors noted, "The structure found in American volunteers was replicated in Japanese undergraduates and Israeli job applicants. A model of personality rooted in English-language trait adjectives could be meaningfully applied not only in a closely related language like German but also in such utterly distinct languages as Chinese and Korean" (p. 514). Other researchers have found the same thing using quite different techniques (deRaad & Szirmak, 1994; Salgado, Moscoso, & Lado, 2003; Williams, Satterwhite, & Saiz, 1998).

Surprisingly, many of these same personality traits apparently exist in a number of species besides humans. Gosling & John (1999) found that the Big Five, with the two added factors of dominance and activity, could be used to rate and describe

According to trait theorists, this woman would probably rate high on the traits of cheerfulness, extroversion, friendliness, and sociability. Trait theorists seek to identify sets of human characteristics on the basis of which personality can be assessed.

table 11-2 THE "BIG FIVE" DIMENSIONS OF PERSONALITY

Traits	Facets
Extroversion	warmth, gregariousness, assertiveness, activity, excitement-seeking, positive emotions
Agreeableness	trust, straightforwardness, altruism, compliance, modesty, tender-mindedness
Conscientiousness/Dependability	competence, order, dutifulness, achievement-striving, self-discipline, deliberation
Emotional Stability	anxiety, hostility, depression, self-consciousness, impulsiveness, vulnerability
Culture/Intellect/Openness	fantasy, aesthetics, feelings, actions, ideas, values

Source: Adapted from Jang, K. L., Livesley, W. J., McCrae, R. R., Angleitner, A., & Riemann, R. (1998). Heritability of facet-level traits in a cross-cultural twin sample: Support for a hierarchical model of personality. *Journal of Personality and Social Psychology, 74*, 1556–1665. Table 3, p. 1560. Copyright © 1998 by the American Psychological Association. Adapted with permission.

PETER WAS A BORN WORRIER ...

I HOPE THIS GUY KNOWS WHAT HE'S DOING.

Source: Drawing by Chas. Addams; © 1984 The New Yorker Magazine, Inc.

personality characteristics in species including gorillas, chimpanzees, rhesus and vervet monkeys, hyenas, dogs, cats, and pigs!

These data clearly suggest that there is some kind of common genetic basis for the Big Five personality traits that cuts across cultures and species (see *On the Cutting Edge: The Genetic Basis of Personality Traits?*).

A Trait View of Jaylene Smith

A psychologist working from the trait perspective would infer certain traits from Jay's behavior. When we observe that Jay chose at an early age to become a doctor, did well academically year after year, and graduated first in her medical-school class, it seems reasonable to infer a trait of determination or persistence to account for her behavior. Similarly, we might reasonably conclude from her description that she also has traits of sincerity, motivation, and intelligence, as well as insecurity, introversion, shyness, and anxiety. These relatively few traits account for a great deal of Jay's behavior, and they also provide a thumbnail sketch of "what Jay is like."

Evaluating Trait Theories

Traits are the language that we commonly use to describe other people (e.g., as shy or insecure or arrogant). Thus, the trait view of personality has considerable commonsense appeal. Moreover, although psychologists disagree as to the exact number of traits, it is easier to scientifically study personality traits than to study such things as self-actualization and unconscious motives. But trait theories have several shortcomings (Eysenck, 1993; Kroger & Wood, 1993).

First, they are primarily descriptive: They seek to delineate the basic dimensions of personality but generally do not try to explain causes (Funder, 1991). For example, the trait view of Jaylene Smith tells us little about why she is the way she is. Thus, the five-factor theory of personality helps us much the way north-south and east-west axes do in mapmaking (Goldberg, 1993, cited in Ozer & Reise, 1994)—that is, it helps us to locate personality more precisely. But like a point on a map, it gives us no information about what kind of terrain is there and how it got to be that way.

Second, traits are identified through factor analyses of individual differences in large populations (Cervone & Shoda, 1999). The traits therefore represent statistical properties of populations, not of individuals. But can the Big Five model adequately describe the qualities of an individual? In fact, two recent studies have found that the five-factor model does not appear to describe the psychological properties of individuals (Borkenau & Ostendorf, 1998; Fleeson, 1998). Although the researchers found that individuals reported coherent and meaningful dispositions over time, these tendencies did not match the traits on the five-factor model.

In addition, some critics argue that the dangers in reducing the diversity and complexity of human nature to just a few traits are greater than the usefulness that traits offer in terms of description and classification (Mischel & Shoda, 1995). Psychologists also disagree about the number of traits

THINKING CRITICALLY

Cultural Universals

Is it fair to conclude that the Big Five are in fact universal traits? To answer this question, think about the following questions:

- What types of cultures have so far been studied? What do all of these cultures have in common? What types of cultures have not been studied?

- How would researchers determine whether the Big Five traits are in fact the most important ones in the cultures they have studied? Might other, equally important, traits not be measured? Did the researchers explore what personality traits are important in various cultures or simply confirm that people in a variety of cultures recognize the Big Five traits?

- What do we have to know in order to say that something is universal?

ON THE CUTTING EDGE

THE GENETIC BASIS OF PERSONALITY TRAITS

Recent evidence shows that not only the Big Five but also many of their individual facets are strongly influenced by heredity (Livesley, Jang, & Vernon, 2003). Although some early theorists (Eysenck, 1947) suggested that physiological mechanisms underlie basic personality traits, only recently has solid evidence from twin studies begun to support this idea (Eaves, Heath, Neale, Hewitt, & Martin, 1993; Heath, Cloninger, & Martin, 1994; Jang, Livesley, McCrae, Angleitner, & Riemann, 1998; Plomin, 1994).

Behavior genetic studies rely strongly on twin studies to tease apart the relative contribution of heredity and environment. For example, Jang and colleagues (1998, 2002) analyzed facet-level scores of almost 1,000 sets of twins from Germany and Canada. Their results indicated that genetic effects accounted for a substantial portion of the differences between people's scores on 26 of the 30 facet scales. In addition, the genetic and environmental influences were similar for the Canadian and German samples. In other words, genes seem to affect personality, and they seem to do so to the same extent in at least two different cultures.

Other investigators have had similar results. In a twin study, researchers found that the Big Five dimensions are all substantially *heritable,* and to an equal degree (Loehlin, McCrae, Costa, & John, 1998). Another group found the following estimates of heritability for the Big Five traits: neuroticism, 41 percent; extraversion, 53 percent; openness, 61 percent; agreeableness, 41 percent; and conscientiousness, 44 percent (Jang, Livesley, & Vernon, 1996).

Researchers have also confirmed that genetic factors play a significant role in shaping abnormal and dysfunctional personality traits. In one study comparing 128 pairs of identical and fraternal twins on both normal and abnormal personality traits, the influence of genetic factors was found to slightly outweigh the influence of the environment. In addition, the pattern of genetic and environmental influence was similar for both the abnormal and the normal personality traits (Markon, Krueger, Bouchard, & Gottesman, 2002). Other studies have confirmed that genetic factors also contribute to the personality traits that predispose individuals toward alcohol abuse (Mustanski, Viken, Kaprio, & Rose, 2003), eating disorders (Klump, McGue & Iacono, 2002), depression, marijuana dependence and antisocial personality disorder (Fu et al, 2002).

What are the implications of these findings? There are several, although it is important to keep in mind that saying a particular trait such as extraversion has a genetic component does *not* mean that researchers have found a *gene* for extraversion. Nor are they likely to, because genes represent a code for specific proteins, not complex personality traits. It does mean, however, that the Big Five traits and their facets may be hardwired into the human species rather than being cultural artifacts. It also most likely means that complex traits such as extraversion are influenced by many different genes, not just one. That would explain why individual traits are normally distributed throughout the population, such as the physical traits of eye color or hair type, instead of forming distinct types. Many genes—perhaps thousands of them—surely work in combination to account for such complex traits. Though the precise role that genes play in personality is still far from clear, most psychologists would agree that biological factors contribute significantly to the development of most personality traits (Livesley et al., 2003).

sufficient to capture the complexity of human personality (Almagor, Tellegen, & Waller, 1995; Eysenck, 1992; Lubinski, 2000; Mershon & Gorsuch, 1988).

 11.1

ENDURING ISSUES **stability**change

How Stable Is Personality Over Time?

Some psychologists question whether traits describe and predict behavior very well over time. Are "agreeable" people at age 20 still agreeable at age 60? As we saw in Chapter 10, Life Span Development, numerous research studies have shown that temperament remains quite stable over time. Similarly, the Big Five dimensions of personality show considerable stability during early childhood and appear to be "essentially fixed by age 30" (McCrae & Costa, 1994, p. 173). Though to some extent adults can vary their behavior to fit the situations in which they find themselves, in general it seems that when it comes to personality traits, "You can't teach old dogs new tricks."

■■ CHECK YOUR UNDERSTANDING

1. Trait theorists concentrate on

___a. biology

___b. criminality

___c. personality

2. Eysenck argued that personality could be reduced to three basic dimensions: emotional stability, introversion–extroversion, and

___a. sincerity

___b. agreeableness

___c. psychoticism

3. The Big Five refers to

___a. the number of universal personality traits

___b. the number of biologically determined behaviors

___c. factor analysis of 200 traits

Answers: 1. c, 2. c, 3. a

■■

Cognitive–Social Learning Theories

How do personal and situational factors combine to shape behavior?

In contrast to trait theories of personality, **cognitive–social learning theories** hold that people internally organize their expectancies and values to guide their own behavior. This set of personal standards is unique to each one of us, growing out of our own life history. Our behavior is the product of the interaction of cognitions (how we think about a situation and how we view our behavior in that situation), learning and past experiences (including reinforcement, punishment, and modeling), and the immediate environment.

Expectancies, Self-Efficacy, and Locus of Control

Albert Bandura (1977, 1986, 1997) asserts that people evaluate a situation according to certain internal **expectancies,** such as personal preferences, and this evaluation affects their behavior. Environmental feedback that follows the actual behavior, in turn, influences future expectancies. In this way, expectancies guide behavior in a given situation, and the results of the behavior in that situation shape expectancies in future situations. In turn, expectancies lead people to conduct themselves according to unique **performance standards,** individually determined measures of excellence by which they judge their behavior. Those who succeed in meeting their own internal performance standards develop an attitude that Bandura calls **self-efficacy** (Bandura & Locke, 2003). For example, two young women trying a video game for the first time may experience the situation quite differently, even if their scores are

Cognitive–social learning theories Personality theories that view behavior as the product of the interaction of cognitions, learning and past experiences, and the immediate environment.

Expectancies In Bandura's view, what a person anticipates in a situation or as a result of behaving in certain ways.

Performance standards In Bandura's theory, standards that people develop to rate the adequacy of their own behavior in a variety of situations.

Self-efficacy According to Bandura, the expectancy that one's efforts will be successful.

similarly low. One with a high sense of self-efficacy may find the experience fun and be eager to gain the skills necessary to go on to the next level of games, whereas the other with a lower sense of self-efficacy may be disheartened by getting a low score, assume she will never be any good at video games, and never play again. Similarly, a person with high self-efficacy who interprets math problems as opportunities to succeed will approach the math SAT with a different expectancy than someone who sees math problems as opportunities to fail.

Note that in our example the two young women approach the experience with different expectancies. To Julian Rotter (1954), **locus of control** is a prevalent expectancy, or cognitive strategy, by which people evaluate situations. People with an *internal locus* of control are convinced they can control their own fate. They believe that through hard work, skill, and training, they can find reinforcements and avoid punishments. People with an *external locus* of control do not believe they control their fate. Instead, they are convinced that chance, luck, and the behavior of others determine their destiny and that they are helpless to change the course of their lives.

Both Bandura and Rotter, two of the leading cognitive-social learning theorists, have tried to combine personal variables (such as expectancies) with situational variables in an effort to understand the complexities of human behavior. Both theorists believe that expectancies become part of a person's *explanatory style*, which, in turn, greatly influences behavior. Explanatory style, for example, separates optimists from pessimists. It is what causes two beginners who get the same score on a video game to respond so differently.

General expectancies or explanatory styles such as optimism or pessimism can have a significant effect on behavior. Some research shows that children as young as 8 years old have already developed a habitual explanatory style. In one study, third-graders were asked to read descriptions of 12 good and 12 bad events and then come up with reasons the events happened. Their scores reflected their degree of pessimism or optimism. Pessimists tended to believe that negative events were due to personal characteristics they could not change; optimists viewed negative events as unfortunate incidents they could remedy. Children with a more pessimistic style were found to be more prone to depression and to do worse on achievement tests (Nolen-Hoeksema, Girgus, & Seligman, 1986).

In a now-famous study, researchers tracked 99 students from the Harvard graduation classes of 1939 to 1944. The men were interviewed about their experiences and underwent physical checkups every 5 years. When researchers analyzed the men's interviews for signs of pessimism or optimism, they found that the explanatory style demonstrated in those interviews predicted the state of an individual's health decades later. Those men who were optimists at age 25 tended to be healthier at age 65, whereas the health of the pessimists had begun to deteriorate at about age 45 (Peterson, Vaillant, & Seligman, 1988). Although the reasons for these findings are not yet clear, a separate investigation that used a checklist about health habits found that the pessimists in this study were less careful about their health than were optimists. They tended to smoke and drink more and reported twice as many colds and visits to doctors.

Locus of control According to Rotter, an expectancy about whether reinforcement is under internal or external control.

ENDURING ISSUES **person**situation

How Does Personality Interact with Environment?

We have seen that trait theorists tend to believe that behavior is relatively consistent across situations. "Agreeable" people tend to be agreeable in most situations all the time. In contrast, cognitive social learning theorists view personality as the

An individual's behavior often appears quite consistent across both time and situations. We are not surprised when the child who spent hours studying his shell collection becomes a doctor who thoughtfully ponders sets of x-rays. But how consistent is behavior really? Some psychologists believe that the consistencies we perceive may be as much the result of our own selective attention as of reality.

relatively stable cognitive processes that underlie behavior, which is a product of the person and the situation: At any time, our actions are influenced by the people around us, by the way we think we are supposed to behave in a given situation. According to this latter view, although underlying personality is relatively stable, behavior is likely to be more inconsistent than consistent from one situation to another.

If behavior is relatively inconsistent across situations, why does it *appear* to be more consistent than it actually is? One explanation is that since we see a person only in those situations that tend to elicit the same behavior, we tend to assume that they are consistent across a wide range of situations. Moreover, there is considerable evidence that people need to find consistency and stability even in the face of inconsistency and unpredictability. We therefore see consistency in the behavior of others even when there is none (Hayden & Mischel, 1976; Mischel, 2003; Mischel & Shoda, 1998).

A Cognitive–Social Learning View of Jaylene Smith

Jaylene may have learned to be shy and introverted because she was rewarded for spending much time by herself studying. Her father probably encouraged her devotion to her studies; certainly, she earned the respect of her teachers. Moreover, long hours of studying helped her avoid the somewhat uncomfortable feelings that she experienced when she was around other people for long periods.

Reinforcement may have shaped other facets of Jay's personality as well. No doubt her father and her teachers reinforced her self-discipline and her need to achieve academically. Even her aggression toward men may have been learned in childhood as a successful coping mechanism. If her hostility put an end to her brothers' taunts and was also rewarded by her father's affection, she may have learned to react with aggression to perceived threats from males in general.

In addition, at least some aspects of Jaylene's personality were formed by watching her parents and brothers and learning subtle lessons from these family interactions. Her aggressive behavior with boyfriends, for example, may have grown out of seeing her parents fight. As a young child, she may have observed that some people deal with conflict by means of outbursts. Moreover, as Bandura's concept of self-efficacy would predict, Jay surely noticed that her father enjoyed both his family life and his career as a medical researcher, whereas her mother's two jobs as homemaker and store manager left her somewhat frustrated and overtired. This contrast may have contributed to Jay's own interest in medicine and to her mixed feelings about establishing a close relationship that might lead to marriage.

Evaluating Cognitive–Social Learning Theories

Cognitive–social learning theories of personality seem to have great potential. They put mental processes back at the center of personality and focus on conscious behavior and experience. We can define and scientifically study the key concepts of these theories, such as self-efficacy and locus of control, which is not true of the key concepts of psychodynamic and humanistic theories. Moreover, cognitive–social learning theories help explain why people behave inconsistently, an area in which trait approaches fall short. Cognitive–social learning theories of personality have also spawned useful therapies that help people recognize and change a negative sense of self-efficacy or explanatory styles. In particular, as we will see in Chapter 14 (Therapies), these therapies have helped people overcome depression. Cognitive social learning theory has also been embraced by management theorists because of its practical implications for work performance. Many studies, conducted over more than 20 years, have shown a positive correlation between self-efficacy and performance in workplaces, schools, and clinical settings.

However, it is still too early to say how well cognitive–social learning theories account for the complexity of human personality. Some critics point out that the benefit of hindsight allows us to explain any behavior as the product of certain cognitions, but that doesn't mean those cognitions were the *causes*—or at least the sole causes—of the behavior.

Just as there is great diversity in the way psychologists view personality, psychologists also disagree on the best way to measure or assess personality, the topic we turn to next.

CHECK YOUR UNDERSTANDING

1. Match the following terms with the appropriate definition.

___ internal locus of control   a. separates optimists from pessimists

___ external locus of control   b. degree to which we believe we can meet our goals

___ explanatory style   c. belief that luck controls destiny

___ self-efficacy   d. belief that people control their own fate

2. Albert Bandura believes that people evaluate a situation according to

___a. internal expectancies

___b. environmental feedback

___c. future expectancies

3. Expectancies and locus of control have proved useful in predicting

___a. health

___b. depression

___c. both a and b

Answers: 1. internal locus of control—d; external locus of control—c; explanatory style—a; self-efficacy—b, 2. a, 3. c

Personality Assessment

How do psychologists test personality?

In some ways, testing personality is much like testing intelligence: We are trying to measure something intangible and invisible (see Chapter 8, Intelligence and Mental Abilities). And in both cases, a "good test" is one that is both *reliable* and *valid*: It gives dependable and consistent results, and it measures what it claims to measure. Also such factors as fatigue, the desire to impress the examiner, and the fear of being tested can affect a person's test performance. But there are some special difficulties in measuring personality. Personality, as you know, reflects *characteristic* behavior. In assessing personality, then, we are not interested in someone's *best* behavior. We are interested in *typical* behavior—how a person usually behaves in most situations. And in many cases, we must rely upon self-report which, as we will see, brings its own problems.

In the intricate task of measuring personality, psychologists use four basic tools: the personal interview; direct observation of behavior; objective tests; and projective tests. The tools most closely associated with each of the major theories of personality are shown in the Summary Table.

summarytable THEORIES OF PERSONALITY

Theory	Roots of Personality	Methods of Assessing
Psychodynamic	Unconscious thoughts, feelings, motives, and conflicts; repressed problems from early childhood.	Projective tests, personal interviews.
Humanistic	A drive toward personal growth and higher levels of functioning.	Objective tests and personal interviews.
Trait	Relatively permanent dispositions within the individual that cause the person to think, feel, and act in characteristic ways.	Objective tests.
Social Learning	Determined by past reinforcement and punishment as well as by observing what happens to other people.	Interviews, objective tests, observations.

The Personal Interview

An interview is a conversation with a purpose: to obtain information from the person being interviewed. Some interviews are *unstructured*—that is, the interviewer asks the client questions about any material that comes up and asks follow-up questions whenever appropriate. But when conducting systematic research on personality, investigators more often rely on the *structured* interview. Here the order and content of the questions are fixed and the interviewer adheres to the set format. Although less personal, this kind of interview allows the interviewer to obtain comparable information from everyone interviewed. They also are more effective at drawing out information about sensitive topics that might not come up spontaneously in an unstructured interview.

Direct Observation

Another way to find out how a person usually behaves is to *observe* that person's actions in everyday situations over a long period. Behaviorists and social learning theorists prefer this method of assessing personality because it allows them to see how situations influence behavior and to note the range of behaviors the person is capable of exhibiting. Because most people are self-conscious when they suspect they are being watched, observation works best with young children. But this technique can be used successfully with people of almost any age and in many settings—a company cafeteria, an assembly line, wherever people work or socialize together.

Ideally, the unbiased accounts of observers paint an accurate picture of behavior, but an observer runs the risk of misinterpreting the true meaning of an act. For example, the observer may think that children are being hostile when they are merely protecting themselves from the class bully. An expensive and time-consuming method of research, direct observation may also yield faulty results if, as noted earlier, the presence of the observer affects people's behavior.

Objective Tests

To avoid depending on the skills of an interviewer or the interpretive abilities of an observer in assessing personality, psychologists devised **objective tests,** or personality inventories. Generally, these are written tests that are administered and scored according to a standard procedure. The tests are usually constructed so that the person merely chooses a "yes" or "no" response or selects one answer among many

Objective tests Personality tests that are administered and scored in a standard way.

choices. Objective tests are the most widely used tools for assessing personality, but they have two serious drawbacks. First, they rely entirely on self-report. If people do not know themselves well, or cannot be entirely objective about themselves, or want to paint a particular picture of themselves, self-report questionnaire results have limited usefulness (Funder, 1991). In fact, some research indicates that peers who know you well often do a better job characterizing you than you do yourself (Funder, 1995). Second, if people have taken other personality questionnaires, their familiarity with the test format may affect their responses to the present questionnaire. This is a particular problem on college campuses, where students are likely to participate in many research studies that rely on personality inventories (Council, 1993). (See *Applying Psychology: Evaluating Your Personality.*)

Because of their interest in accurately measuring personality traits, trait theorists favor objective tests. Cattell, for example, developed a 374-question personality test called the **Sixteen Personality Factor Questionnaire.** Not surprisingly, the 16PF (as it is usually called) provides scores on each of the 16 traits originally identified by Cattell. The 16PF has proved useful in studies aimed at understanding the role personality factors play in cancer (Nair, Deb, & Mandal, 1993), heart disease (Pruneti, L'Abbate, & Steptoe, 1993), alcoholism (Rodriguez, 1994), and war-related stress (Poikolainen, 1993).

More recently, objective tests such as the **NEO-PI-R** have been developed to assess the Big Five personality traits described earlier in this chapter (Costa & McCrae, 1992, 1995). The NEO-PI-R yields scores for each facet as well as each of the Big Five traits. It consists of 240 questions, each answered on a 5-point scale. For each question, the person indicates to what degree he or she disagrees with the statement made. The primary use of the test is to assess the personality of a normal adult, although recent studies suggest it may also prove useful in some clinical settings (Sanderson & Clarkin, 2002).

The most widely used and thoroughly researched objective personality test is the **Minnesota Multiphasic Personality Inventory (MMPI-2)** (Dorfman & Leonard, 2001). The MMPI was originally developed as an aid in diagnosing psychiatric disorders (Hathaway & McKinley, 1942). To accommodate social changes over the last 50 years, the MMPI was revised and updated in the 1980s. The person taking the test is asked to answer "true," "false," or "cannot say" to such questions as "Once in a while I put off until tomorrow what I ought to do today," "At times I feel like swearing," and "There are persons who are trying to steal my thoughts and ideas." There are two versions of the test: The full-length, adult form of the MMPI-2 has 704 items, and the adolescent form has 654 items. Both include 550 items from the original MMPI to ensure that clinical information from the new test does not differ too much from that on the original. Table 11–3 shows the 10 clinical scales that are assessed by the MMPI-2.

Some of the items on the MMPI-2 repeat very similar thoughts in different words: For example, "I tire easily" and "I feel weak all over much of the time." This redundancy provides a check on the possibility of false or inconsistent answers. The test also includes several scales that check the validity of the responses. For example, if a person answers too many items "cannot say," the test is considered invalid. Another example is the L, or lie, scale which uses 15 items scattered throughout the test such as "I do not always tell the truth" and "I gossip a little at times." Most of us would have to admit that our answers to these two questions would be "true." People who mark these and many other similar items "false" are probably consciously or unconsciously distorting the truth to present themselves in a more favorable light. The MMPI's ability to detect the truthfulness of an individual's responses makes it particularly useful in legal settings where examinees may benefit from portraying themselves as insane or suffering from a mental disorder (Lees-Haley, Iverson, Lange, Fox, & Allen, 2002).

Sixteen Personality Factor Questionnaire Objective personality test created by Cattell that provides scores on the 16 traits he identified.

NEO-PI-R An objective personality test designed to assess the Big Five personality traits.

Minnesota Multiphasic Personality Inventory (MMPI-2) The most widely used objective personality test, originally intended for psychiatric diagnosis.

444   **Chapter 11** • Personality

APPLYING PSYCHOLOGY

EVALUATING YOUR PERSONALITY

The following scales provide a way for you to assess your own personality on the Big Five personality traits, the extent to which others agree with your assessment, the extent to which your behavior is consistent across a range of situations, and the extent to which your personality has been stable over time. The adjectives correspond to the six facets for each of the Big Five traits (see Table 11–2).

For each of the adjectives, indicate the extent to which you think it applies to you. Write your answers on a separate sheet of paper, then ask others to do the same and compare their answers to your own. Friends, close relatives, and others who know you well are likely to provide the most useful information. You also might try to get ratings from people who see you in different situations—perhaps some people who see you only in class, some who see you only in informal social situations, and others who have known you for a very long time in a wide variety of situations. That will give you an opportunity to see the extent to which different situations cause you to behave in different ways which in turn could lead others, who see you only in those situations, to conclude that your *personality* is different than perhaps it really is.

You might also fill out the form, or have others fill it out, as you were in the past, and compare that to how you are today. It would be interesting to speculate on the reasons for any significant changes over time.

Use the following scale to rate yourself on each adjective:

1. Almost never true of me
2. Seldom true of me
3. Sometimes true of me
4. Often true of me
5. Almost always true of me

Extroversion

Outgoing	1	2	3	4	5
Sociable	1	2	3	4	5
Forceful	1	2	3	4	5
Energetic	1	2	3	4	5
Adventurous	1	2	3	4	5
Enthusiastic	1	2	3	4	5

Agreeableness

Forgiving	1	2	3	4	5
Not demanding	1	2	3	4	5
Warm	1	2	3	4	5
Not stubborn	1	2	3	4	5
Modest	1	2	3	4	5
Sympathetic	1	2	3	4	5

Conscientiousness

Efficient	1	2	3	4	5
Organized	1	2	3	4	5
Responsible	1	2	3	4	5
Thorough	1	2	3	4	5
Self-disciplined	1	2	3	4	5
Deliberate	1	2	3	4	5

Emotional Stability

Tense	1	2	3	4	5
Irritable	1	2	3	4	5
Depressed	1	2	3	4	5
Self-conscious	1	2	3	4	5
Moody	1	2	3	4	5
Not self-confident	1	2	3	4	5

Openness

Curious	1	2	3	4	5
Imaginative	1	2	3	4	5
Artistic	1	2	3	4	5
Wide interests	1	2	3	4	5
Excitable	1	2	3	4	5
Unconventional	1	2	3	4	5

table 11-3   THE 10 CLINICAL SCALES OF THE MMPI-2

Clinical Scale	Symbol	Description
Hypochondriasis	**Hs**	Excessive concern with physical health and bodily function, somatic complaints, chronic weakness
Depression	**D**	Unhappiness, loss of energy, pessimism, lack of self-confidence, hopelessness, feeling of futility
Hysteria	**Hy**	Reacts to stress with physical symptoms such as blindness; paralysis lacks insights about motives and feelings
Psychopathic Deviation	**Pd**	Disregard for rules, laws, ethics, and moral conduct; impulsiveness, rebellious toward authority figures, may engage in lying, stealing and cheating
Masculinity-Femininity	**Mf**	Adherence to nontraditional gender traits, or rejection of the typical gender role
Paranoia	**Pa**	Suspiciousness, particularly in the area of interpersonal relations, guarded, moralistic, and rigid; overly responsive to criticism
Psychasthenia	**Pt**	Obsessiveness and compulsiveness, unreasonable fears, anxious, tense, and high-strung
Schizophrenia	**Sc**	Detachment from reality, often accompanied by hallucinations, delusions, and bizarre thought processes; often confused, disorganized
Hypomania	**Ma**	Elevated mood, accelerated speech, flight of ideas, overactivity, energetic, and talkative
Social Introversion	**Si**	Shy, insecure, and uncomfortable in social situations; timid, reserved, often described by others as cold and distant

By analyzing people's answers on the MMPI, researchers have extracted a number of personality scales from this test such as masculinity–femininity, depression, and hypochondriasis. These elements make the MMPI useful as a tool for differentiating among psychiatric populations (Anastasi & Urbina, 1997) and, to a lesser extent, to differentiate among more normal personality dimensions, such as extroversion–introversion and assertiveness.

Projective Tests

Psychodynamic theorists, who believe that people are often unaware of the determinants of their behavior, put very little faith in objective personality tests that rely on self-reports. Instead, they prefer to use **projective tests** of personality. Most projective tests consist of simple ambiguous stimuli that can elicit an unlimited number of responses. People may be shown some essentially meaningless material or a vague picture and be asked to explain what the material means to them. Or they may be given a sentence fragment, such as "When I see myself in the mirror, I . . ." and be asked to complete the statement. They get no clues regarding the "best way" to interpret the material or complete the sentence.

Projective tests have several advantages for testing personality. Because these tests are flexible and can even be treated as games or puzzles, people can take them in a relaxed atmosphere, without the tension and self-consciousness that sometimes accompany objective, self-report tests. Often, the person being examined doesn't even know the true purpose of the test, so responses are less likely to be faked. Some psychologists believe that the projective test can uncover

Projective tests Personality tests, such as the Rorschach inkblot test, consisting of ambiguous or unstructured material.

THINKING CRITICALLY

Projective Tests

Critics of projective tests say that it is the clinician whose personality is actually revealed by the tests, because the clinician's report is itself an interpretation of an ambiguous stimulus (the client's verbal response).

1. Do you agree or disagree? Why?

2. How might this potential source of error be reduced?

3. What are the real or potential advantages to using projective tests?

Rorschach test A projective test composed of ambiguous inkblots; the way people interpret the blots is thought to reveal aspects of their personality.

Thematic Apperception Test (TAT) A projective test composed of ambiguous pictures about which a person is asked to write a complete story.

unconscious thoughts and fantasies, such as latent sexual or family problems. In any event, the accuracy and usefulness of projective tests depend largely on the skill of the examiner in eliciting and interpreting responses.

The **Rorschach test** is the best known and one of the most frequently used projective personality tests (Ball, Archer, & Imhof, 1994; C. E. Watkins, Campbell, Nieberding, & Hallmark, 1995). It is named for Hermann Rorschach, a Swiss psychiatrist who in 1921 published the results of his research on interpreting inkblots as a key to personality (see Figure 11–2). Each inkblot design is printed on a separate card and is unique in form, color, shading, and white space. People are asked to specify what they see in each blot. Test instructions are minimal so people's responses will be completely their own. After interpreting all the blots, the person goes over the cards again with the examiner and explains which part of each blot prompted each response. There are different methods of interpreting a person's responses to the blots on the Rorschach test, and some produce more valid results than others (Exner, 1996; Masling, 2002; Viglione & Taylor, 2003; Weiner, 1996, 1997). A recent analysis of several studies concluded that the MMPI-2 is more valid than the Rorschach (Garb, Florio, & Grove, 1998).

Somewhat more demanding is the **Thematic Apperception Test (TAT),** developed at Harvard by H. A. Murray and his associates. It consists of 20 cards picturing one or more human figures in deliberately ambiguous situations (see Figure 11–3; Morgan, 2002). A person is shown the cards one by one and asked to write a complete story about each picture, including what led up to the scene depicted, what the characters are doing at that moment, what their thoughts and feelings are, and what the outcome will be.

Although various scoring systems have been devised for the TAT (Hibbard, Farmer, Wells, Difillipo, & Barry, 1994), examiners usually interpret the stories in the light of their personal knowledge of the storyteller. One key in evaluating the TAT is whether the person identifies with the hero or heroine of the story or with one of the minor characters. Then the examiner determines what the attitudes and feelings of the character reveal about the storyteller. The examiner also assesses each story for content, language, originality, organization, and consistency. Certain themes, such as the need for affection, repeated failure, or parental domination, may recur in several plots.

Both the Rorschach and the TAT may open up a conversation between a clinician and a person who is reluctant or unable to talk about personal problems. Both may also provide useful information about motives, events, or feelings of which the person is unaware. However, because projective tests are often not administered in a standard fashion, their validity and reliability have been called into question (Dawes, 1994; Wierzbicki, 1993). As a result, their use has declined since the 1970s. Still, when interpreted by a skilled examiner, these tests can offer useful insight into a person's attitudes and feelings.

CHECK YOUR UNDERSTANDING

1. The Sixteen Personality Factor Questionnaire, the NEO-PI-R, and the Minnesota Multiphasic Personality Inventory are examples of what kind of tests?

___ a. projective

___ b. personal interview

___ c. objective

2. An example of an "inkblot test" is the _____ Test, which is one kind of _____ test.

___ a. Rorschach, projective

___ b. Rorschach, objective

___ c. Thematic Apperception, projective

Figure 11–2
Inkblots used in the Rorschach projective test.

Figure 11–3
A sample item from the Thematic Apperception Test (TAT).
In the photo on the right the person is making up a story to explain the scene in the painting shown to the left. The examiner then interprets and evaluates the person's story for what it reveals about her personality.
Source: Reprinted by permission of the publisher from *Thematic Apperception Test* by Henry A. Murray, Cambridge, MA: Harvard University Press, Copyright © 1943 by the President and Fellows of Harvard College, © 1977 by Henry A. Murray.

3. Match the following tests with the appropriate definition.

___ objective tests

___ MMPI

___ projective tests

   a. personality tests administered and scored in a standard way

   b. personality tests using ambiguous pictures

   c. the most widely used personality test

Answers: 1.c, 2.a, 3. objective tests—a; MMPI—c; projective tests—b.

summary

Personality is a person's unique pattern of thoughts, feelings, and behaviors that persists over time and across situations.

Psychodynamic Theories

Psychodynamic theories of personality consider behavior to be the result of psychological dynamics within the individual. Often, these processes go on outside of awareness.

Sigmund Freud   For Freud, the founder of **psychoanalysis,** our personality is rooted in the dynamics of our **unconscious**—all the ideas, thoughts, and feelings of which we are normally unaware. Freud identified sexual and aggressive instincts as the primary unconscious drives that determine human behavior.

According to Freud, personality is made of three structures. The **id,** the only personality structure present at birth, operates in the unconscious according to the **pleasure principle,** meaning it tries to obtain immediate pleasure and avoid pain. The **ego,** the id's link to the real world, controls all conscious thinking and reasoning activities and operates according to the **reality principle.** It tries to delay satisfying the id's desires until it can do so safely and effectively in the real world. The **superego** acts as the person's moral guardian or conscience and helps the person function in society. It also compares the ego's actions with an **ego ideal** of perfection.

In Freud's view, when the ego is unable to control impulses from the id in a way that is acceptable to the superego, it experiences *anxiety*

and may resort to using **defense mechanisms** to reduce the discomfort caused by the anxiety. Such self-deceptive techniques for reducing anxiety include **denial,** the refusal to acknowledge a painful or threatening reality; **repression,** excluding uncomfortable thoughts from consciousness; **projection,** attributing one's own repressed motives or feelings on others; **identification,** taking on the characteristics of someone else to avoid feeling incompetent; **regression,** reverting to childlike behavior and defenses; **intellectualization,** detaching oneself from stressful problems by thinking about them abstractly; **reaction formation,** expressing exaggerated ideas or emotions that are the opposite of ones repressed beliefs or feelings; **displacement,** shifting repressed motives and emotions from an original object to a substitute; and **sublimation,** redirecting repressed motives and feelings into more socially acceptable channels.

Freud called energy generated by the sexual instinct **libido.** As an infant matures, his or her libido becomes focused on different sensitive parts of the body. A **fixation** occurs if a child is deprived of pleasure or allowed too much pleasure from the part of the body that dominates one of the five developmental stages—**oral, anal, phallic, latency,** and **genital**—and some sexual energy may remain permanently tied to that part of the body. Strong attachment to the parent of the opposite sex and jealousy of the parent of the same sex—which develops during the phallic stage—is called the **Oedipus** or **Electra complex.**

Carl Jung   Carl Jung believed that the unconscious consists of two distinct components: the **personal unconscious,** which contains an individual's repressed thoughts, forgotten experiences, and undeveloped ideas; and the **collective unconscious,** a subterranean river of memories and behavior patterns flowing to us from previous generations.

Over the millennia, the human mind has developed certain thought forms, called **archetypes,** which give rise to mental images or mythological representations. The **persona,** one of the many archetypes Jung described, is that part of our personality by which we are known to other people, like a mask we put on to go out in public. Two other important archetypes are the **anima,** the expression of female traits in a man, and the **animus,** the expression of male traits in a woman.

Jung also believed that people generally exhibit one of two attitudes toward the world: **Extroverts** are interested in other people and the world at large, whereas **introverts** are more concerned with their own private worlds. Jung further divided people into **rational individuals,** who regulate their behavior by thinking and feeling, and **irrational individuals,** who base their actions on perceptions.

Alfred Adler Adler believed that people possess innate positive motives and strive toward personal and social perfection. He originally proposed that the main shaper of personality is **compensation,** the individual's attempt to overcome actual physical weakness. He later modified his theory to stress the importance of feelings of inferiority. When people become so fixated on their feelings of inferiority that they become paralyzed by them, they are said to have an **inferiority complex.** Later still, Adler concluded that strivings for superiority and perfection, both in one's own life and in the society in which one lives, are crucial to personality development.

Karen Horney For Horney, a person's reaction to real or imagined dangers or threats, which she defined as **anxiety,** is a stronger motivating force than the sexual drive, or libido. She believed that there are several **neurotic trends** or strategies that people use to cope with emotional problems, and that these strategies are reflected in personality type: the compliant type of personality, whose strategy is to move toward others (submission); the aggressive type of personality, whose strategy is to move against others (aggression); and the detached type, whose strategy is to move away from others (detachment). Horney emphasized that culture and not anatomy determines many of the personality traits that differentiate women from men.

Erik Erikson For Erikson, the quality of the parent-child relationship affects the development of the personality in that it helps determine whether the child feels competent and valuable and is able to form a secure sense of identity. Erikson believed that the personality develops over a lifetime. He outlined eight life stages—trust versus mistrust, autonomy versus shame and doubt, initiative versus guilt, industry versus inferiority, identity versus role confusion, intimacy versus isolation, generativity versus stagnation, and integrity versus despair. Success in each stage depends on whether adjustments in previous stages were successful.

Evaluating Psychodynamic Theories Psychodynamic theories have had a profound impact on the way we view ourselves and others as well as on the arts. However, some of Freud's theories have been criticized as unscientific and culture-bound, especially penis envy in women and the Oedipus and Electra complexes. Some experimental evidence supports the existence of the unconscious, but this research does not show a clear link between unconscious processes and personality. As a therapy, psychoanalysis has been shown to be beneficial in some cases, but no more so than other therapies.

Humanistic Personality Theories

Adler's notion of the individual's perpetual striving for perfection laid the groundwork for **humanistic personality theory.**

Carl Rogers For Rogers, people develop their personalities in the service of positive goals. The biological push to become whatever it is that we are capable of becoming is called the **actualizing tendency.** In addition to trying to realize our biological potential, we attempt to fulfill our conscious sense of who we are, which Rogers called the **self-actualizing tendency.** A **fully functioning person** is someone whose self-concept closely matches his or her inborn capabilities. Fully functioning people were usually raised with **unconditional positive regard,** or the experience of being valued by other people regardless of their emotions, attitudes, and behaviors. Often, children are brought up with **conditional positive regard**— that is, with parents and others who accept and value only certain aspects of their individuality. These people tend to deviate from their inborn capacities to construct a personality more in line with how other people see them.

Evaluating Humanistic Theories Humanistic theories of personality suffer from a lack of scientific evidence. In addition, they are criticized as taking too rosy a view of human nature and as promoting a view of the self that fosters self-centeredness. However, research on humanist therapies, particularly Rogers's client-centered therapy, has shown that they do promote self-acceptance.

Trait Theories

Trait theorists insist that each person possesses a unique constellation of fundamental **personality traits.**

Psychologists disagree about the number of different personality traits. Gordon Allport argued that possibly several thousand words could be used to describe human personality traits. Raymond Cattell identified 16 basic traits using a statistical technique called **factor analysis.** Eysenck argued that personality could be reduced to three basic dimensions: emotional stability, introversion–extroversion, and psychoticism.

The Big Five Recently, considerable research has focused on the importance of five basic personality traits. Included in the **Big Five** are extroversion, agreeableness, conscientiousness, emotional stability, and culture or openness. The Big Five traits appear to be universal across cultures, and some evidence suggests they may have, in part, a physiological basis.

Evaluating Trait Theories Trait theories are primarily descriptive. They provide a way of classifying personalities, but they do not explain why a person's personality is what it is. But trait theories do have the advantage of being rather easy to test experimentally, and research does support the value of the five-factor model in pinpointing personality.

Cognitive–Social Learning Theories

Expectancies, Self-Efficacy, and Locus of Control **Cognitive–social learning theories** view behavior as the product of the interaction of cognitions, learning and past experiences, and the immediate environment. Albert Bandura suggests that certain internal **expectancies** determine how a person evaluates a situation and that this evaluation has an effect on the person's behavior. Expectancies lead people to conduct themselves according to unique **performance standards,** individually determined measures of excellence by which they judge their behavior. Those who succeed in meeting their own internal performance standards develop an attitude that Bandura calls **self-efficacy. Locus of control** is one prominent expectancy. People with an internal locus of control believe they can control their own fate through their actions, whereas people with an external locus of control believe their fate rests with chance and the behavior of others.

Evaluating Cognitive–Social Learning Theories Cognitive–social learning theories avoid the narrowness of trait and behavioral theories, as well as the reliance on case studies and anecdotal evidence that weakens psychodynamic and humanistic theories. Expectancies and locus of control can be tested scientifically, and they have proved to be useful concepts for predicting health and depression. However, such correlations do not provide evidence for causes of behavior.

Personality Assessment

Psychologists use four different methods to assess personality: the personal interview, direct observation of behavior, objective tests, and projective tests.

The Personal Interview There are two types of personal interviews. During an unstructured interview, the interviewer asks questions about any material that comes up during the course of the conversation as well as follow-up questions where appropriate. In a structured interview, the order and the content of the questions are fixed and the interviewer does not deviate from the format.

Observation Behavioral and social learning theorists prefer the technique of direct observation of a person over time to determine the environmental influence on that person's behavior. This method of personality assessment doesn't rely on self-reports, and it gives a good idea of the range of a person's behaviors, but it is expensive and time consuming and open to misinterpretation.

Objective Tests **Objective tests** of personality, such as the **Sixteen Personality Factor Questionnaire,** the **NEO-PI-R,** and the **Minnesota Multiphasic Personality Inventory (MMPI),** are given and scored according to standardized procedures. These tests are inexpensive to use and easy to score, but rely on people's self-report of their own behavior.

Projective Tests Psychodynamic theorists are more likely to use **projective tests,** which consist of ambiguous stimuli that can draw out an unlimited number of responses and are thought to tap the unconscious. The **Rorschach test** has 10 inkblots that the person interprets. The **Thematic Apperception Test (TAT)** asks people to make up stories about 20 pictures.

key terms

Personality	418	Oral stage	423	Self-actualizing tendency	432
Psychodynamic theories	418	Anal stage	423	Fully functioning person	432
Unconscious	419	Phallic stage	423	Unconditional positive regard	432
Psychoanalysis	419	Oedipus complex and Electra complex	423	Conditional positive regard	432
Id	419	Latency period	423	Personality traits	433
Pleasure principle	419	Genital stage	424	Factor analysis	434
Ego	420	Personal unconscious	424	Big Five	434
Reality principle	420	Collective unconscious	424	Cognitive–social learning theories	438
Superego	420	Archetypes	424	Expectancies	438
Ego ideal	420	Persona	425	Performance standards	438
Defense mechanisms	420	Anima	425	Self-efficacy	438
Denial	420	Animus	425	Locus of control	439
Repression	421	Extrovert	425	Objective tests	442
Projection	421	Introvert	425	Sixteen Personality Factor	
Identification	422	Rational individuals	425	Questionnaire	443
Regression	422	Irrational individuals	425	NEO-PI-R	443
Intellectualization	422	Compensation	425	Minnesota Multiphasic Personality	
Reaction formation	422	Inferiority complex	425	Inventory (MMPI-2)	443
Displacement	422	Anxiety	426	Projective tests	445
Sublimation	422	Neurotic trends	426	Rorschach test	446
Libido	423	Humanistic personality theory	431	Thematic Apperception Test (TAT)	446
Fixation	423	Actualizing tendency	432		

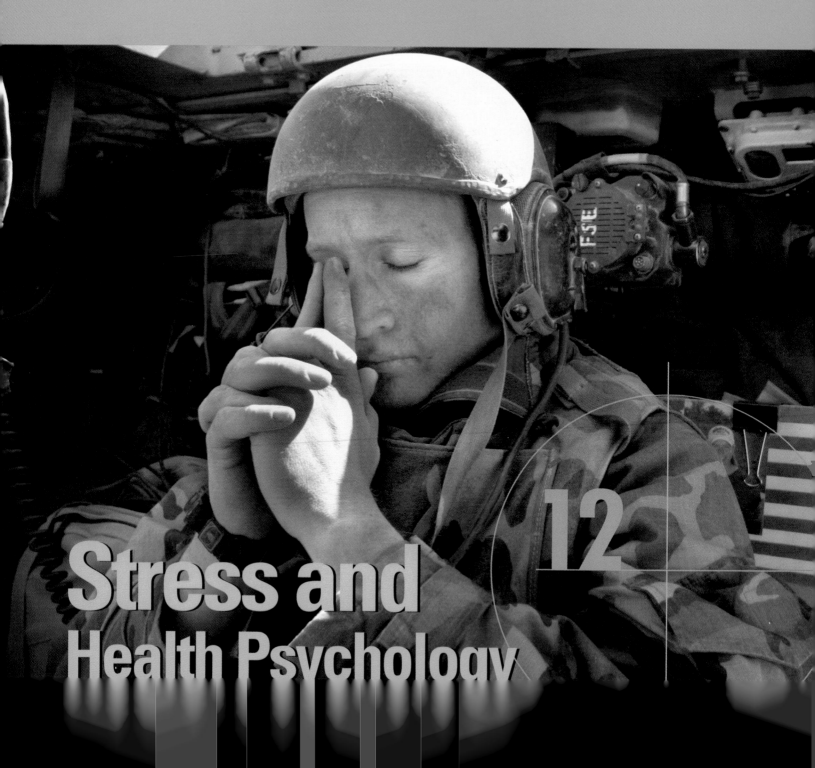

OVERVIEW

Sources of Stress
Life Changes
Everyday Hassles
Stress and Individual Differences

Coping with Stress
Direct Coping
Defensive Coping

Socioeconomic and Gender
Differences

Stress and Health
The Biology of Stress
Stress and Heart Disease
Stress and the Immune System

Staying Healthy
Methods of Reducing Stress
Adopt a Healthy Life Style

Extreme Stress
Sources of Extreme Stress
Post-Traumatic Stress Disorder

The Well-Adjusted Person

Stress and Health Psychology

12

t about 15 minutes to 9, Anne Prosser, 29, rode the elevator to the 90th floor of Tower 1 [of the World Trade Center] where her global banking office was. As the doors opened, she heard what seemed like an explosion. She didn't know it, but the first plane had just hit several floors above her. 'I got thrown to the ground before I got to our suite,' she said. 'I crawled inside. Not everybody was at work.' She said she tried to leave but there was so much debris in the air she couldn't breathe. Rescuers finally steered her to a stairway. . . [10:05 AM]. Ten or so blocks north of the towers, the smoke had been outrun, and it began to dissipate into the air. People stopped, turned and looked downtown. As the air cleared, an unthinkable site presented itself: empty space where a 110-story tower had been. People gasped. They trembled. They sobbed. 'It can't be,' an elderly woman said. 'It just can't be. Where did it go? Oh, lord, where did it go?' Many of the onlookers stayed put, frozen in horror. Slowly, the next thought crept into their consciousness: The other tower would come down too. . . . [10:28 AM] People started walking briskly north until the premonition became real—another horrifying eruption, as one floor after another seemed to detonate. Another giant cloud, soot, smoke streaming through the avenues. Again, people ran. Many of them stopped at Canal Street and watched the smoke dissolve. People cried at what they saw: a crystalline sky with nothing in it. 'Oh my God,' Tim Lingenfelder said, 'there's nothing there.' That was when he lost it and began to cry. People stood, numb, transfixed by what had to be a mirage. 'All that was left of the buildings was the steel girders in like a triangular sail shape,' said Ross Milanytch. 'The dust was about an inch and a half thick on the ground.' Onlookers gathered in clumps and tried to understand. People with cars opened the doors and turned on the radios, and knots of people leaned close to hear what was happening. The news came of the plane at the Pentagon and the plane in Pittsburgh. 'It's like Pearl Harbor,' said a middle-aged man at a small parking lot on Canal Street. 'It's Pearl Harbor. It's war.' 'It's sickos,' someone else said. 'Sickos.' 'This is America,' a man said. 'How can it happen in America? How?'" (Kleinfield, 2001. Copyright © 2001 by the New York Times Co. Reprinted with permission.) (http://www.nytimes.com/2001/09/12/nyregion/12REAC.html)

Nightmares/Day Terrors A 40-year-old cancer survivor received bone-marrow transplants to treat his leukemia. Three years later, tests found no evidence that the leukemia had returned. Yet he had flashbacks of receiving radiation treatment whenever he heard the sound of a generator. Colors that reminded him of the hospital triggered nausea, sweating, and chills. He often woke in the middle of the night, not knowing whether he was at home or in the hospital. He forbade his family to bring a Christmas tree into the house because the scent reminded him of the pine-scented lotion he used while undergoing treatment. Like some other cancer survivors, he was diagnosed with post-traumatic stress disorder—a diagnosis usually applied to soldiers, hostages, and others who have lived through extreme and unusual experiences. (Adapted from Rabasca, 1999a, p. 28)

The unemployed ghetto resident: "There's nothing out there. What they're doing, they're selling drugs, they're working here and there, they're living off of different women, you know, off each other. . . . You got men out there that are trying to survive and get educated, but the ones in my community, the ones that I see, education's the farthest thing from [their minds]. . . . They hear all this stuff on TV, and

THINKABOUTIT

You will find the answers to these questions in the chapter:

1. Stress is always a response to negative events in our lives. True or false?

2. What are the most effective ways of coping with stress?

3. Does stress cause disease? Can a positive attitude cure or slow the progress of cancer?

4. How does a healthy life style help us control stress?

5. What is post-traumatic stress disorder? What kinds of events are most likely to trigger it?

6. How do psychologists define a well-adjusted person?

Stress A state of psychological tension or strain.

Adjustment Any effort to cope with stress.

Health psychology A subfield of psychology concerned with the relationship between psychological factors and physical health and illness.

Stressors The events or circumstances that trigger stress.

they just don't have any hope for the future." (Harry, 1995; in Johnson, Levine, & Doolittle, 1999, p. 58)

What do the witnesses to terrorism, the recovered cancer patient, and the unemployed ghetto resident share? The common denominator in their stories is stress. When people feel threatened physically or psychologically, when they wonder if they can cope with the demands of their environment, when their heart pounds and their stomach feels queasy, they are experiencing stress. In this context, the term **stress** refers to psychological tension or strain—the uncomfortable emotional and bodily responses to stressful situations. **Adjustment** is any attempt—successful or not—to cope with stress, to balance our needs against the demands of the environment, to weigh our desires against realistic possibilities, and to manage as well as we can.

This chapter begins by looking at the common, everyday sources of stress in our lives, and why some individuals seem particularly vulnerable to stress and others are stress-hardy and resilient. Next we look at how people cope with stress, which strategies are most effective, and whether a person's income and gender affect how he or she handles stress. In the section that follows we examine the biological model of stress and the ways in which psychological factors such as stress influence wellness and illness (**health psychology**). Next we examine what you can do to stay healthy by reducing stress and developing a healthy lifestyle. Finally we look at extreme stress and its aftereffects and what psychologists mean when they say a person is well-adjusted.

Sources of Stress

Stress is always a response to negative events in our lives. True or false?

Stressors are the events or circumstances that trigger stress. Stressors vary in intensity and duration—from the mild, short-lived aggravation of misplacing keys or eyeglasses to the prolonged tragedy of caring for a parent who has Alzheimer's disease. Moreover, the same event—say, a chemistry exam—may be a stressor for one person but not for another. Some people are acutely sensitive to threats of failure or humiliation; others are frightened by specific experiences or objects. But quarrels with friends, pressure at work, conflicts at home, public embarrassment, and personal rebukes are stressors for nearly everyone.

Even in inherently stressful situations, when our life or our future is at risk, the time of greatest stress is not necessarily the time of greatest danger. Typically, we experience the most stress when we're anticipating the danger. Parachutists, for example, report feeling most afraid as the time for the jump approaches. Once they are in line and cannot turn back, they calm down. By the time they reach the most dangerous part of the jump—in free fall and waiting for their chutes to open—their fears have subsided (Epstein, 1962). Similarly, the tension and quarrels leading up to a decision to divorce, and negotiating child custody and property settlements, can be more stressful than the divorce itself. Indeed, the official divorce decree may come as a relief.

Stress is not limited to life-and-death situations or even to unpleasant experiences. Even happy occasions may be stressors because they require us to change or adapt in order to meet our needs (Morris, 1990). For example, a wedding is stressful as well as exciting because most weddings are very complicated affairs to arrange, and marriage marks a profound change in many relationships. Being promoted is gratifying—but it demands that we relate to new people in new ways, learn new skills, and perhaps dress differently, travel more, or work longer hours.

Here we will look at stressors that virtually everyone encounters over the course of their life. (Later in the chapter we will look at extreme stress.)

Life Changes

All of the stressors we have considered so far involve change. Most people seek order, continuity, and predictability in their lives. Therefore, they experience change—whether good or bad—as stressful. In general, the more adjustments an event requires, the more stressful it will be. By the same token, when people must cope with a large number of changes in a relatively short time, stress mounts.

The classic instrument for measuring the amount of stress a person is experiencing as a result of "life changes" is the Social Readjustment Rating Scale (SRRS) devised by T. H. Holmes and R. H. Rahe (1967). The scale consists of several dozen events that are assigned a point value based on the amount of adjustment they require. To determine the amount of stress a person experienced during a given period, one simply adds up the stress ratings of all the changes with which he or she had to cope.

Although intuitively appealing, some of the items on the SRRS deal with events that are only appropriate for adults (e.g., death of a spouse, retirement, change in work responsibilities). Also, the SRRS assumes that everyone will experience the same amount of stress when confronted with a particular stressor. Thus it fails to take into account the meaning of events for different people. For instance, the amount of stress associated with pregnancy will be very different for a couple who planned to have a child and an unwed teenager who became pregnant by accident (Oltmanns & Emery, 1998). Nevertheless, the SRRS is still widely used with some success (Scully, Tosi, & Banning, 2000), and with modification, appears to have some cross-cultural applications (Yahiro, Inoue, & Nozawa, 1993).

Renner and Mackin (1998, 2002) devised a similar measure of stress that is intended for college students. Their College Life Stress Inventory (Table 12–1) includes such potentially stressful events as "finals week," writing a major term paper, talking in front of class, difficulties with a roommate, and starting a new semester. Two-thirds of the students tested by Renner and Mackin had scores between 800 and 1,700, but scores ranged from a low of 182 to a high of 2,571.

Everyday Hassles

Many of the items on the SRRS and the College Life Stress Inventory concern stress that arises from fairly dramatic, relatively infrequent events. However, many psychologists have pointed out that much stress is generated by "hassles," life's petty annoyances, irritations, and frustrations (Chang & Sanna, 2003; Ruffin, 1993; Safdar & Lay, 2003; Whisman & Kwon, 1993). Such seemingly minor matters as a broken zipper, waiting in long lines, or a petty argument with a friend take their toll. Lazarus believes that big events matter so much because they trigger numerous little hassles that eventually overwhelm us with stress. "It is not the large dramatic events that make the difference," notes Lazarus, "but what happens day in and day out, whether provoked by major events or not" (1981, p. 62). Both major and minor events are stressful in large part because they lead to feelings of pressure, frustration, and conflict.

Pressure Pressure occurs when we feel forced to speed up, intensify, or shift direction in our behavior, or when we feel compelled to meet a higher standard of performance (Morris, 1990). Pressure on the job is a familiar example. In recent years, many companies have adopted a policy of *lean production* (sometimes called "downsizing"): maintaining the same or higher levels of production with fewer workers. As a result, workers who remain on the job are required to take on additional responsibilities

All major life changes involve a certain amount of stress. This is partly because major life changes typically bring strong emotion, and even joy and elation can arouse the body and begin to take a toll on its resources. Major life events can also be stressful because any new experience requires some adjustment.

Pressure A feeling that one must speed up, intensify, or change the direction of one's behavior or live up to a higher standard of performance.

table 12-1 COLLEGE LIFE STRESS INVENTORY

Copy the "stress rating" number into the last column for any item that has happened to you in the last year, then add these.

Event	Stress Ratings	Your Items	Event	Stress Ratings	Your Items
Being raped	100		Lack of sleep	69	
Finding out that you are HIV-positive	100		Change in housing situation (hassles, moves)	69	
Being accused of rape	98		Competing or performing in public	69	
Death of a close friend	97		Getting in a physical fight	66	
Death of a close family member	96		Difficulties with a roommate	66	
Contracting a sexually transmitted disease (other than AIDS)	94		Job changes (applying, new job, work hassles)	65	
Concerns about being pregnant	91		Declaring a major or concerns about future plans	65	
Finals week	90		A class you hate	62	
Concerns about your partner being pregnant	90		Drinking or use of drugs	61	
Oversleeping for an exam	89		Confrontations with professors	60	
Flunking a class	89		Starting a new semester	58	
Having a boyfriend or girlfriend cheat on you	85		Going on a first date	57	
Ending a steady dating relationship	85		Registration	55	
Serious illness in a close friend or family member	85		Maintaining a steady dating relationship	55	
Financial difficulties	84		Commuting to campus or work, or both	54	
Writing a major term paper	83		Peer pressures	53	
Being caught cheating on a test	83		Being away from home for the first time	53	
Drunk driving	82		Getting sick	52	
Sense of overload in school or work	82		Concerns about your appearance	52	
Two exams in one day	80		Getting straight A's	51	
Cheating on your boyfriend or girlfriend	77		A difficult class that you love	48	
Getting married	76		Making new friends; getting along with friends	47	
Negative consequences of drinking or drug use	75		Fraternity or sorority rush	47	
Depression or crisis in your best friend	73		Falling asleep in class	40	
Difficulties with parents	73		Attending an athletic event (e.g., football game)	20	
Talking in front of a class	72		Total		

Source: Renner, M. J., & Mackin, R. S. (1998). A Life Stress Instrument for Classroom Use. *Teaching of Psychology*, 25(1), p. 47. Reprinted by permission of Lawrence Erlbaum Associates, Inc.

and tasks with less assistance. Not surprisingly, they are likely to report increased stress and depression, as well as lower job satisfaction (Kaminski, 1999).

In our private lives, trying to live up to social and cultural norms about what we *should* be doing, as well as our family and friends' expectations, also adds pressure to meeting our personal needs. Perhaps the most consistent and relentless of these demands are that we compete, that we adapt to the rapid rate of change in our society, and that we live up to what our family and friends expect of us. Competitive forces affect nearly all relationships in American life. We compete for grades, for popularity, for sexual and marital partners, and for jobs. We are taught to see failure as shameful. Hence the pressure to win can be intense. The pressures of economic hardship are another source of stress. In fact, as we shall see later in this chapter, stressful events of the same severity often have a more harmful impact on the emotional lives of people of lower socioeconomic status.

Frustration **Frustration** occurs when a person is prevented from reaching a goal because something or someone stands in the way. A high school student with great SATs and a high average does not get into the Ivy League school, a woman does not receive a promotion on the grounds that she does not have manufacturing experience; a scientist's budget is cut just when he or she feels close to a breakthrough; a frequent flier who constantly faces flight delays and cancellations—all of these people are likely to experience frustration.

In addition to these major sources of frustration, there are countless minor frustrations that can add up to cause significant stress. Morris (1990) identified five sources of frustration that are especially common in American life. *Delays* are annoying because our culture puts great stock in the value of time. *Lack of resources* is frustrating to those Americans who cannot afford the new cars or lavish vacations that the mass media tout as every citizen's due. *Losses,* such as the end of a love affair or a cherished friendship, cause frustration because they often make us feel helpless, unimportant, or worthless. *Failure* generates intense frustration—and accompanying guilt—in our competitive society. Our culture holds that success or failure depend on individual talent and effort—not luck, good fortune, or simply being in the right place at the right time. We imagine that if we had done things differently, we might have succeeded; thus, we usually feel personally responsible for our setbacks and tend to assume that others blame us for not trying harder or being smarter. *Discrimination* also frustrates us: Being denied opportunities or recognition simply because of one's sex, age, religion, or skin color diminishes people's faith in their future and perhaps in themselves.

As our highways have become more congested, incidents of aggressive driving—popularly known as "road rage"—have become more common and more dangerous. One survey found that 9 in 10 drivers had been threatened by speeding, tailgating, failure to yield right of way, lane changes without signaling, weaving, cutting in, and rude, provocative gestures and comments during the previous year. Psychologist Leon James (James & Nahl, 2000) has studied driving patterns for more than a decade. James views road rage as a behavioral syndrome that is rooted in exaggerated forms of cultural norms, especially our annoyance with delays and winner-take-all view of competition. What surprised James is how many aggressive drivers are "ordinary people," with no history of violence, and how many considered themselves to be victims of inconsiderate drivers.

Conflict Of all life's troubles, **conflict** is probably the most common. A boy does not want to go to his aunt's for dinner, but neither does he want to listen to his parents complain if

Frustration The feeling that occurs when a person is prevented from reaching a goal.

Conflict Simultaneous existence of incompatible demands, opportunities, needs, or goals.

Approach/approach conflict
According to Lewin, the result of simultaneous attraction to two appealing possibilities, neither of which has any negative qualities.

Avoidance/avoidance conflict
According to Lewin, the result of facing a choice between two undesirable possibilities, neither of which has any positive qualities.

Approach/avoidance conflict
According to Lewin, the result of being simultaneously attracted to and repelled by the same goal.

he stays home. A student finds that both the required courses she wanted to take this semester are given at the same hours on the same days. A voter supports one candidate's foreign policy, but the opposing candidate's domestic agenda. A couple is planning their vacation: One wants to go to Florida and relax on the beach, the other wants to go to New York to visit museums and go to the theater.

In the 1930s, Kurt Lewin described conflict in terms of two opposing tendencies: approach and avoidance. When something attracts us, we want to approach it; when something frightens us, we try to avoid it. Lewin (1935) showed how different combinations of these tendencies create three basic types of conflict: approach/approach conflict, avoidance/avoidance conflict, and approach/avoidance conflict.

Approach/approach conflict occurs when a person is simultaneously attracted to two appealing goals. A student who has been accepted at two equally desirable colleges or universities, a job-seeker who is offered two equally exciting and high-paying positions, or a person who finds two equally attractive apartments, neither of which has any significant drawbacks, are examples. The stress in approach/approach conflict arises from the fact that in choosing one desirable option, we must give up the other.

The reverse of this dilemma is **avoidance/avoidance conflict,** in which a person is confronted with two undesirable or threatening possibilities, neither of which has any positive features. The popular way of expressing this dilemma is being "caught between a rock and a hard place." When faced with an avoidance/avoidance conflict, people usually try to escape the situation altogether. If escape is impossible, they try to select the least threatening option, or "the lesser of two evils." Most often people vacillate between choosing one threat or the other, like a baseball runner caught in a rundown between first and second base. The player starts to run toward second, then realizes that he will be tagged and turns around, only to realize that he will be tagged on first if he tries to go back there. In no-exit situations like this, people may simply wait for events to resolve their conflict for them.

In **approach/avoidance conflict,** a person is both attracted to and repelled by the same goal. The most common form of conflict, this too is often difficult to resolve. According to Lewin, the closer we come to a goal with good and bad features, the stronger grow our desires both to approach and to avoid, but the tendency to avoid increases more rapidly than the tendency to approach. In an approach/avoidance conflict, therefore, we approach the goal until we reach the point at which the tendency to approach equals the tendency to avoid the goal. Afraid to go any closer, we stop and vacillate, making no choice at all, until the situation changes. A familiar example is a couple whose only quarrel is that one wants to get married, but the other is unsure. The second person wants to continue the relationship (approach), but is wary of making a life-long commitment (avoidance). In real life, we are often faced simultaneously with two or more goals, each of which is less than

THINKING CRITICALLY

Road Rage and You

One of the techniques Professor James uses in his research on aggressive driving is to ask people to tape record their experiences and feelings (a technique called "self-witnessing") when they are driving in traffic. At first he was shocked by how often ordinarily polite, considerate people became intolerant and antisocial when they got behind the wheel—what he calls a "Jekyll and Hyde effect."

- Try tape recording your thoughts as you drive (and be honest); ask several friends to do the same. Do you find the "Jekyll and Hyde effect" James documented?

There are three main theories of road rage. Which of the following do you find most convincing? Why? How might you go about determining which theory has the most merit?

- *The crowding hypothesis:* More cars→more traffic→more frustration→more stress→more anger→more hostility→more violence.

- *The cultural hypothesis:* Americans learn aggressive and dangerous driving patterns as children, by watching their parents and other adults behind the wheel, and by viewing risky driving in movies and television commercials.

- *The displacement hypothesis:* People are more likely to lose their tempers while driving if they have suffered recent blows to their self-esteem, and seek to recoup their sense of worth by winning battles on the road.

ideal but each of which also has enough positive features to attract us. The existence of multiple goals increases our stress, for the conflict inherent in each goal is multiplied by the conflict of choosing from among the various goals.

Lewin's types of conflict are outlined in the Summary Table.

Stress and Individual Differences

Why do some people find it easy to cope with major life stressors whereas others find it hard to deal with even minor problems? Much depends on how people appraise a potentially stressful event. According to Shelley Taylor, people evaluate changes, first, in terms of whether they have a lot or a little at stake (*primary appraisal*), and second, in terms of whether they believe they have the personal skills, knowledge, and experience, as well as social resources (people to whom they can turn for advice and encouragement) to cope with the event (*secondary appraisal*) (see Figure 12–1) (S. E. Taylor, 1986). According to this view, if an event is seen as harmful, threatening or challenging (primary appraisal) and if the person believes that he or she does not have the necessary skills and resources to cope with the event (secondary appraisal) then stress is likely to be high. Conversely, if an event is seen as being an opportunity and the person believes that he or she has the skills and resources to respond to it, then stress is likely to be low; the event is likely to be perceived as an opportunity for mastery or gain and be greeted with eagerness, excitement, and confidence (Folkman & Moskovitz, 2000). Cognitive therapists hold that faulty appraisal of situations is often the source of psychological distress, and that reappraisal is often the cure (see Chapter 14, Therapies).

Other researchers emphasize an individual's overall appraisal of life and general attitude toward events, especially *optimism* versus *pessimism* (Peterson, 2000). The classic expression of the difference is that, presented with the same circumstances, an optimist sees the glass as half full; a pessimist sees the glass as half empty. Optimists tend to appraise events as challenges rather than threats; to remain hopeful when the odds are not in their favor; to focus on what they can do to improve a situation, rather than ruminating about what they can't change; and to take pleasure and pride in what they do accomplish, rather than dwelling on failures. Pessimists are the opposite.

Optimism and pessimism have, in turn, been related to *locus of control* (see Chapter 11, Personality). Individuals who have an internal locus of control tend to believe that their circumstances are largely a result of their own decisions and actions and hence appraise situations as challenges (Ryan & Deci, 2000). Individuals who have an external locus of control tend to see themselves as victims of circumstance, doubt their ability to defend themselves or to improve their situation, and are more likely to appraise events negatively, as threats.

Hardiness and Resilience Suzanne Kobasa (1979) identified a trait that she called *hardiness* in people who tolerate stress exceptionally well or seem to thrive on it. Stress-hardy people are open to change. Rather than viewing loss of a job as a

A classic example of avoidance/avoidance conflict is a baseball player caught between two bases. Running in either direction is an undesirable option to be avoided.

summarytable TYPES OF CONFLICT

Type of Conflict	Nature of Conflict
Approach/Approach	The person is attracted to two incompatible goals at the same time.
Avoidance/Avoidance	Repelled by two undesirable alternatives at the same time, the person is inclined to try to escape, but often other factors prevent such an escape.
Approach/Avoidance	The person is both repelled by, and attracted to, the same goal.

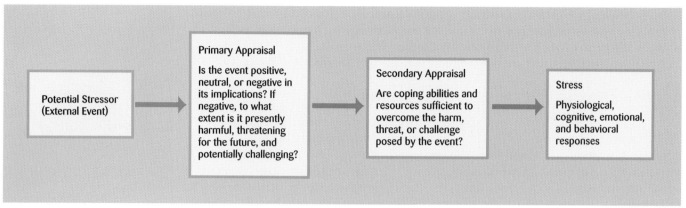

Figure 12–1
Appraising stress.
Whether a particular life event becomes a major stressor has a great deal to do with how the individual appraises that event.
Source: Shelley E. Taylor (1986). *Health Psychology.* New York: Random House, p. 149. Copyright © 1986. Reprinted with permission.

Resilient children are able to become competent, caring adults, even if they grow up in very difficult circumstances. These children in a low-income neighborhood of Chicago probably experience more stress in their lives than their middle- and upper-class peers.

catastrophe, they define the situation as an opportunity to begin a new career. They are internally rather than extrinsically motivated, deeply committed to their work, and immerse themselves in meaningful activities. Finally, stress-hardy people experience difficult demands from the environment as challenging rather than intimidating. Kobasa's study suggested that, to a significant degree, people's response to stress depends on whether they believe they have some control over events or whether they feel helpless. Psychologically hardy individuals feel they control their own destinies and are confident about being able to cope with change (see also Kessler, Price, & Wortman, 1985; Taylor, 2003). Conversely, individuals who have little confidence that they can master new situations and exercise control over events feel powerless and apathetic (Peterson, Maier, & Seligman, 1993b). (Recall our discussion of learned helplessness in Chapter 5, Learning.) Even when change offers new opportunities for taking charge of their situation, they remain passive.

Other psychologists are interested in *resilience*: the ability to "bounce back," recovering one's self-confidence, good spirits, and hopeful attitude, after extreme or prolonged stress (Beasley, Thompson, & Davidson, 2003). In particular, psychologists want to understand why some children who grow up in adverse circumstances (such as extreme poverty, dangerous neighborhoods, abusive parents, and/or exposure to drugs and alcohol) become well-adjusted adults, whereas others remain troubled—and frequently get into trouble—throughout their lives (Feinauer, Hilton, & Callahan, 2003).

One team of researchers identified 240 high-risk children in Hawaii who had experienced stress at birth, poverty, and family conflict, and followed their development for 40 years (Werner, 1996). Two-thirds of the children became involved in crime or developed psychological problems, but one-third became confident, competent, caring adults. The resilient members of this sample tended to be affectionate and outgoing from birth, which attracted other people to them. They had interests and talents (intellectual, artistic, athletic) that helped them make friends, develop a sense of purpose, and gain self-esteem. Equally important, they had warm, supportive relationships with at least one adult other than their parents who viewed them as special and important. Compared to their troubled peers—and to a control group of children who grew up in secure environments—the resilient children grew into adults with the highest percentage of stable marriages and lowest proportions of unemployment, divorce, and serious health problems. Another study of adolescents whose parents suffer from depression (Brown, cited in Huang, 1998) found that the most resilient teenagers had a strong relationship with an outside adult and a hobby at which they excelled, both of which gave them a sense of value. Taken together, these studies suggest that two ways to foster resilience in high-risk children are mentor programs (such as Big Brother/Sister, which teams an adult volunteer with a needy child) and after-school programs that offer a range of activities (also see Clauss & Caroline, 2003).

Self-imposed Stress   At the opposite extreme from hardy and resilient people are those who create problems for themselves quite apart from stressful events in their environment. As a result they frequently experience anxiety or other symptoms of stress in the absence of external stressors. Albert Ellis pointed out that such people typically have irrational, self-defeating beliefs that add unnecessarily to the normal stresses of living (Ellis & Harper, 1975). One example is the belief, "It is essential to be loved or approved by almost everyone for everything I do." For people who hold this belief, any sign of disapproval will be a source of considerable stress. Another impossible belief is, "I must be competent, adequate, and successful at everything I do." Such people take the slightest sign of failure or inadequacy as evidence that they are worthless human beings. Still another is the belief, "It is disastrous if everything doesn't go the way I would like." When things don't go their way, such people feel upset, miserable, and unhappy. As we will see in the next chapter, Aaron Beck (1984, 2002) believes that many cases of depression arise from self-defeating thoughts such as these.

CHECK YOUR UNDERSTANDING

1. A job promotion or wedding is an experience some find stressful because it requires

___ a. change

___ b. conflict

___ c. confrontation

2. Match each type of conflict with the appropriate definition.

___ approach/approach   a. choosing between two undesired yet unavoidable
                             alternatives

___ avoidance/avoidance   b. attracted to and repelled by the same goal

___ approach/avoidance   c. attracted to two goals at once

3. Delays, lack of resources, losses, failure, and discrimination are examples of

___ a. goals

___ b. frustrations

___ c. conflicts

4. Pressure can derive from

___ a. competition

___ b. a shift in direction such as downsizing

___ c. a promotion

___ d. all of the above

Answers: 1.a, 2. approach/approach—c; avoidance/avoidance—a; approach/avoidance—b, 3.b, 4.d

Cope Make cognitive and behavioral efforts to manage psychological stress.

Confrontation Acknowledging a stressful situation directly and attempting to find a solution to the problem or attain the difficult goal.

Compromise Deciding on a more realistic solution or goal when an ideal solution or goal is not practical.

Coping with Stress

What are the most effective ways of coping with stress?

Whatever its source, stress requires that we **cope**: that is, make cognitive and behavioral efforts to manage psychological stress (Lazarus, 1993). Psychologists distinguish between two general types of coping: direct coping and defensive coping. *Direct coping* refers to intentional efforts to change an uncomfortable situation. Direct coping tends to be problem-oriented and to focus on the immediate issue. When our needs or desires are frustrated, for example, we may attempt to remove the obstacles between ourselves and our goals, or we may withdraw. Similarly, when we are threatened, we may try to eliminate the source of the threat, either by attacking it or by escaping from it. In contrast, *defensive coping* refers to various forms of self-deception that provide a means of protecting our self-esteem and reducing stress (Cramer, 2000). For example, people may convince themselves that they are not really threatened or that they do not really want something they cannot get. Defensive coping tends to be emotion-oriented and to focus on our state of mind.

Direct Coping

When we are threatened, frustrated, or in conflict, we have three basic choices for coping directly: *confrontation*, *compromise*, or *withdrawal*. We can meet a situation head-on and intensify our efforts to get what we want (confrontation). We can give up some of what we want and perhaps persuade others to give up part of what they want (compromise). Or we can admit defeat and stop fighting (withdrawal).

Take the case of a woman who has worked hard at her job for years but is not promoted. She learns that the reason is her stated unwillingness to move temporarily from the company's main office to a branch office in another part of the country to acquire more experience. Her unwillingness to move stands between her and her goal of advancing in her career. She has several choices.

Confrontation   Acknowledging to oneself that there is a problem for which a solution must be found, attacking the problem head-on, and pushing resolutely toward one's goals is called **confrontation.** The hallmark of the "confrontational style" is making intense efforts to cope with stress and to accomplish one's aims (Morris, 1990). This may involve learning skills, enlisting other people's help, or just trying harder. Or it may require steps to change either oneself or the situation. The woman whom we have described above might decide that if she wants very much to move up in the company, she will have to agree to relocate. Or she might try to change the situation itself in one of several ways. She could challenge the assumption that working at the branch office would give her the kind of experience her supervisor thinks she needs. She could also try to persuade her boss that she is ready to handle a better job in the main office.

Confrontation may also include expressions of anger. Anger may be effective, especially if we really have been treated unfairly and if we express our anger with restraint instead of exploding in rage. A national magazine once reported an amusing, and effective, example of controlled anger in response to an annoying little hassle. As a motorist came to an intersection, he had to stop for a frail old lady crossing the street. The driver of the car behind him honked his horn impatiently, whereupon the first driver shut off his engine, removed the key, walked back to the other car, and handed the key to the second driver. "Here," he said, "you run over her. I can't do it. She reminds me of my grandmother."

Compromise   One of the most common, and effective, ways of coping directly with conflict or frustration is **compromise.** We often recognize that we cannot have everything we want and that we cannot expect others to do just what we would like them to do. In such cases, we may decide to settle for less than we originally sought. The woman denied a job promotion may agree to take a less desirable position that doesn't require branch office experience, or she may strike a bargain to go to the branch office for a shorter time.

Withdrawal　In some circumstances, the most effective way of coping with stress is **withdrawal** from the situation. A person at an amusement park who is overcome by anxiety just looking at a roller coaster may simply move on to a less threatening ride. The woman whose promotion depends on temporarily relocating might quit her job and join another company. A college freshman who feels he doesn't fit in at the college he chose—he hasn't made friends, the courses are not what he expected, the campus is too isolated—may transfer to another school.

We often disparage withdrawal as a refusal to face problems. But sometimes withdrawal is a positive and realistic response, such as when we realize that our adversary is more powerful than we are, or that there is no way we can effectively change ourselves, alter the situation, or reach a compromise, and that any form of aggression would be self-destructive. For example, if a driver with road rage confronts you, it is better to defuse the situation and withdraw.

Perhaps the greatest danger of coping by withdrawal is that we will come to avoid all similar situations. Someone who grew extremely anxious looking at the roller coaster may refuse to go to any amusement or theme park again, and begin avoiding any type of potentially risky activity. The woman who did not want to relocate to her company's branch office may quit her job without even looking for a new one. The student may drop out of college altogether. In such cases, coping by withdrawal becomes maladaptive avoidance. Moreover, people who have given up on a situation can miss out on an effective solution. In short, withdrawal, in whatever form, is a mixed blessing. Although it can be an effective method of coping, it has built-in dangers. The same can be true of defensive coping.

Withdrawal Avoiding a situation when other forms of coping are not practical.

Defensive Coping

So far, we have focused on stress that arises from recognizable sources, but at times, we either cannot identify or cannot deal directly with the source of our stress. For example, you return to a parking lot to discover that someone has damaged your new car and then left the scene. Or a trip you have planned for months is delayed by an airline strike. Other problems are too emotionally threatening to be faced directly. Perhaps you find out that someone close to you is seriously ill. Or you learn that after four years of hard work you have not been admitted to medical school and may have to abandon your plan to become a doctor.

In such situations, many people automatically adopt defense mechanisms as a way of coping. (See the discussion of defense mechanisms in Chapter 11, Personality.) What is important to remember is that while defense mechanisms such as denial, repression, and projection do reduce stress associated with frustration, conflict, and anxiety, it comes at the cost of *self-deception*. Thus, in the short run, especially if there are few other options available, using defense mechanisms may reduce our level of stress. Over the long run, however, using defense mechanisms can hinder successful adjustment, by distorting reality and interfering with a person's ability to deal directly with a problem.

ENDURING ISSUES　　**person**situation

Coping Strategies

Individuals use various coping strategies in different combinations and in different ways to deal with stressful events. It is tempting to conclude that styles of coping, like personality, reside within the individual. Yet a good deal of research indicates that how much stress people encounter, and how they cope, depends to a significant degree on the situation; on their physical, social, economic, and cultural environment (S. E. Taylor & Repetti, 1997).

Socioeconomic and Gender Differences

Consider the impact of socioeconomic status on stress and coping. In poor neighborhoods, even the basic aspects of daily living are stressful. Housing is often substandard and crowded; there are fewer stores, offering lower quality goods; crime and unemployment rates are likely to be high; and schools have lower teacher-student ratios, higher staff turnover, and more part-time teachers. In short, poor people have to deal with more stress than people who are financially better off (N. Adler et al., 1994; S. Cohen & Williamson, 1988; Evans & English, 2002). Moreover, some data indicate that people in low-income groups cope less effectively with stress and that, as a result, stressful events have a harsher impact on their emotional lives. Psychologists have offered several possible explanations for these data (Evans & English, 2002). People in lower socioeconomic classes often have fewer resources for coping with hardship and stress. Low-income people also have fewer people to turn to and fewer community resources to draw on for support during stressful times. In addition, people living in poverty may believe to a greater extent than other people that external factors are responsible for what happens to them and that they have little personal control over their lives. Finally, some evidence suggests that members of low-income groups are more likely to have low self-esteem and to doubt their ability to master difficult situations. All these factors help explain why stress often takes a greater toll on people in lower socioeconomic classes.

Are there gender differences in coping with stress? At present, the answer seems to be "yes," at least under some circumstances. One study of victims of Hurricane Andrew found that although women reported experiencing more stress than men, men and women turned out to be affected equally when stress was measured physiologically (Adler, 1993b). In another study of 300 dual-earner couples, women and men felt equally stressed by the state of their marriage, their jobs, and how well their children were doing. However, the women in this study experienced greater stress than men when problems developed in long-term relationships, largely because they were more committed to their personal and professional relationships than the men were (Barnett, Brennan, & Marshall, 1994). Women and men also appear to respond differently to the stress caused by an automobile accident, with woman experiencing more stress both immediately after the accident and several months later (Bryant & Harvey, 2003). Some research indicates that when faced with equally stressful situations, men and women generally use quite similar coping strategies (Porter & Stone, 1995). Other research suggests that in at least some circumstances, men and women may use rather different coping strategies (Bellman, Forster, Still, & Cooper, 2003; Ptacek, Smith, & Dodge, 1994; see also Anshel, Porter, & Quek, 1998; Narayanan, Shanker, & Spector, 1999). For example, one recent study (Nolen-Hoeksema, 1999) found that when men are down or depressed, they are more likely than women to turn to alcohol; when women are blue, sad, or mad, they are more likely to ruminate about the problem, revisiting negative emotions and the events that led up to them in their minds (see *On the Cutting Edge: "Tend and Befriend": A Female Response to Stress?*)

ON THE CUTTING EDGE

"TEND AND BEFRIEND": A FEMALE RESPONSE TO STRESS?

Imagine that two families are walking down a dark street and notice that a suspicious stranger is following them. Both the mothers and the fathers in this group are likely to experience the same symptoms of stress. But do they react in the same way? Or do the men turn to confront the stranger while the women gather the youngsters together and reassure their children and each other that everything will be all right? A recent study suggests that females and males—across species—respond to stress in different ways (S. E. Taylor et al., 2000).

When a student casually mentioned that most studies of stress in animals were carried out with male rats, psychologist Shelley E. Taylor and her colleagues reviewed several hundred previous studies of stress in rodents, monkeys, and humans. In studies of humans, only 17 percent of the subjects were female. The researchers also found that females didn't fit the standard pattern. Rather, danger evokes a "*tend-and-befriend*" response in females, who tend their young and seek contact and support from others, especially other females. For example, women coming home from a bad day at work spend time with their children or call a friend; men tend to withdraw or get into arguments. This might also help to explain why females are less likely than males to be physically aggressive.

The tend-and-befriend response may be linked to the hormone oxytocin, which is also produced during childbirth and nursing and linked to maternal behavior and social affiliation. Research shows that oxytocin makes rats and humans calmer, more social, and less fearful. Under stress, both males and females secrete oxytocin, but the male hormone testosterone seems to reduce its effect, whereas the female hormone estrogen amplifies it. These hormonal differences might explain why men have higher rates of stress-related health problems than women do, and why the "classic" symptoms of heart attack—such as pain radiating down the arm—are more common in men than women experiencing heart attacks, who are more likely to experience shortness of breath (Goode, 2000c).

Dr. Taylor and her colleagues explain sex differences in response to stress in evolutionary terms. Long ago, when our ancestors were hunter/gatherers who did not build permanent villages, predators—perhaps including human competitors—were a constant danger. Under those environmental conditions, it was adaptive for men to confront danger (by fighting) or to divert an enemy (by fleeing) while women guarded the children. Taylor argues that this adaptation became "hardwired" and remains with us today. Other psychologists (Eagly & Wood, 1999; Pitman, 2003) are quick to point out that the difference could just as likely be the result of learning and cultural conditioning. As Pavlov demonstrated, physiological responses (whether salivation or hormone production) can be altered through conditioning (see Chapter 5, Learning). So, does an inborn physiological response to stress cause females to seek and provide comfort? Or does a culturally conditioned seek-and-provide-comfort response stimulate physiological changes?

For her part, Taylor thinks the most important message of this research is that people respond to stress in different ways. Most studies of stress looked at lone male subjects. Perhaps in group situations males, too, have a tend-and-befriend response to stress. Proving or disproving this hypothesis will require additional research.

CHECK YOUR UNDERSTANDING

1. People generally adjust to stress in two ways, through direct coping and

___ a. confrontation

___ b. defensive coping

___ c. compromise

___ d. withdrawal

2. Denial, repression, and projection are examples of

___ a. stressors

___ b. direct coping

___ c. defense mechanisms

3. People from low income groups generally cope _____ with stress than people from high-income groups.

___ a. equally well

___ b. more effectively

___ c. less effectively

Stress and Health

Does stress cause disease? Can a positive attitude cure or slow the progress of cancer?

"We know that 50 percent of deaths are directly related to human behaviors, and yet we spend too little time doing research and implementing programs related to them," said David Satcher, U.S. Surgeon General (Satcher, 1999, p. 16). Physicians and psychologists agree that stress management is an essential part of programs to prevent disease and promote health.

The Biology of Stress

To understand how our body responds to stress, examine how we react to danger. Suppose you are walking alone down an unfamiliar street late at night when you notice a suspicious stranger is following you. Suddenly, your heart begins to pound, your respiration increases, and you develop a queasy feeling in your stomach. What is happening to you? The hypothalamus, a center deep in your brain is reacting to your perception of danger by organizing a generalized response that affects several organs throughout your body (Figure 12–2). Almost immediately, the hypothalamus stimulates the sympathetic branch of the autonomic nervous system and the adrenal glands to release stress hormones such as *adrenaline* and *norepinephrine* into the blood—leading to increases in heart rate, blood pressure, respiration, and perspiration. Other organs respond, such as the liver, which increases the available sugar in the blood for extra energy, and the bone marrow, which increases the white blood cell count to combat infection. Conversely, the rate of some bodily functions is decreased, such as the rate of digestion, which is obviously of less importance when we are facing imminent danger—and which, by the way, accounts for the queasy feeling in the stomach.

psych 12.1

The noted physiologist Walter Cannon (1929) first described the basic elements of this sequence of events as a *fight or flight response*, because it appeared that its primary purpose was to prepare an animal to respond to external threats by either attacking or fleeing from them. Cannon also observed that this physiological mobilization took the same form, regardless of the nature of the threat. For instance, the fight or flight response can be triggered by physical trauma, fear, emotional arousal, or simply by having a *really* bad incident happen at work or school. The adaptive significance of the fight or flight response in people was obvious to Cannon, in that it ensured the survival of early humans when faced with danger.

Extending Cannon's theory of the fight or flight response, the Canadian physiologist Hans Selye (1907–1982) held that we react to physical and psychological stressors in three stages he collectively called the **general adaptation syndrome (GAS)** (Selye, 1956, 1976). These three stages are alarm reaction, resistance, and exhaustion.

Stage 1, *alarm reaction*, is the first response to stress. It begins when the body recognizes that it must fend off some physical or psychological danger. Emotions run

General adaptation syndrome (GAS) According to Selye, the three stages the body passes through as it adapts to stress: alarm reaction, resistance, and exhaustion.

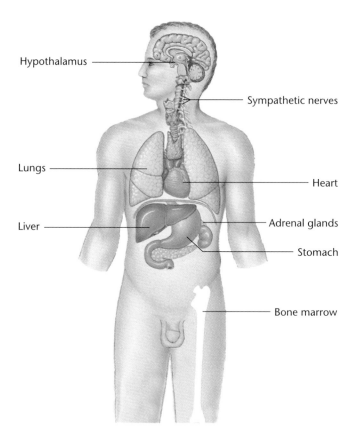

Hypothalamus

Sympathetic nerves

Lungs

Heart

Liver

Adrenal glands

Stomach

Bone marrow

Figure 12–2
The physiological response to stress.
When the body is confronted with a stress-ful situation, the hypothalamus stimulates the sympathetic nervous system and the adrenal glands to release stress hor-mones. Other organs, such as the liver and the bone marrow, also respond.

high. Activity of the sympathetic nervous system is increased, resulting in the release of hormones from the adrenal gland. We become more sensitive and alert, our respiration and heartbeat quicken, our muscles tense, and we experience other physiological changes as well. All these changes help us to mobilize our coping resources to deal with the threat. At the alarm stage we might use either direct or defensive coping strategies. If neither of these approaches reduces the stress, we eventually enter the second stage of adaptation.

During Stage 2, *resistance*, physical symptoms and other signs of strain appear as we struggle against increasing psychological disorganization. We intensify our use of both direct and defensive coping techniques. If we succeed in reducing the stress, we return to a more normal state. But if the stress is extreme or prolonged, we may turn in desperation to inappropriate coping techniques and cling to them rigidly, despite the evidence that they are not working. When that happens, we begin to deplete our physical and emotional resources, and signs of psychic and physical wear and tear become even more apparent.

In Stage 3, *exhaustion*, we draw on increasingly ineffective defense mechanisms in a desperate attempt to bring the stress under control. Some people lose touch with real-ity and show signs of emotional disorder or mental illness at this stage. Others show signs of "burnout," including inability to concentrate, irritability, procrastination, and a cynical belief that nothing is worthwhile (Freudenberger, 1983; Maslach & Leiter, 1997). Physical symptoms such as skin or stomach problems may erupt, and some vic-tims of burnout turn to alcohol or drugs to cope with the stress-induced exhaustion. In other words, the physiological reactions that prepared us to cope effectively in the alarm and resistance phases weaken us in the long run. If the stress continues, the per-son may suffer irreparable physical or psychological damage or even death.

At the time, Selye's theory that prolonged psychological stress can make us sick was highly controversial. Today the idea that psychological stress contributes to

psych 12.2

physical illness has become part of common wisdom (in this case, backed by years of research). Still, many questions remain. For example, some psychologists have questioned the idea that "fight or flight" is a universal response to danger, arguing that women respond to threats differently.

ENDURING ISSUES   **mindbody**

Psychological Stress and Physical Illness

How exactly does psychological stress lead to or influence physical illness? There are at least two routes. First, when people experience stress, their hearts, lungs, nervous systems, and other physiological systems are forced to work harder. The human body is not designed to work in high gear and be exposed to the powerful biological changes that accompany alarm and mobilization for long periods. When stress is protracted, people are more likely to experience some kind of physical disorder. Second, stress has a powerful negative effect on the body's immune system, and prolonged stress can undermine the body's ability to defend itself from disease. Indirectly, stress may lead to unhealthy behavior (such as smoking, drinking, overeating or skipping meals, and not getting enough exercise or sleep), as well as avoiding medical checkups and tests or skipping medications and other recommended treatments.

THINKING CRITICALLY

"Genes Lie Behind Only About 30% of Cancers Studied"*

S top, look away from this book, and repeat what you just read. Was your first impression that genes cause one-third of cancers? The headline is worded so that your eyes might register: **Genes Lie Behind 30% of Cancers**. Given the emphasis on genes in media reports of science, your mind-set may lead to selective perception of genetic causes. Now consider the scientific study behind this headline.

According to a report in the *New England Journal of Medicine*, researchers have concluded that the chances of developing cancer are largely determined by lifestyle, not inheritance (Lichtenstein et al., 2000). In one of the largest studies of its kind, researchers analyzed longitudinal data on 44,788 pairs of Scandinavian twins born between 1870 and 1958. The data revealed that 10,803 of these individuals developed cancers. The researchers found that even when one identical twin developed cancer, the chances that the other twin got the same cancer was very low. In contrast to what you may have believed from the newspaper headline, the authors concluded "that the overwhelming contributor to the causation of cancer in the populations of twins that we studied was the environment" (p. 80).

- How much confidence do you have in this report? Why?

- If this report is correct, what can you do to reduce the risk that you will develop cancer?

- Should someone with a family history of cancer ignore his or her heredity? Ask a doctor whether to have periodic tests so that, if they inherited a predisposition toward developing cancer, the cancer will be detected early? Undergo genetic tests, if and when these are available?

*Headline from the *Los Angeles Times,* July 11, 2000, p. 1A.

Stress and Heart Disease

Stress is a major contributing factor in the development of coronary heart disease (CHD), the leading cause of death and disability in the United States (McGinnis, 1994). Heredity influences our risk of developing CHD, but even among identical twins, the incidence of CHD is closely linked to attitudes toward work, problems in the home, and the amount of leisure time available (Kringlen, 1981; also see O'Callahan, Andrews, & Krantz, 2003). Frequent or chronic stress can damage the heart and blood vessels (Heinz et al., 2003). For example, the stress hormone cortisol increases blood pressure (which weakens the walls of blood vessels), can trigger arrhythmias (erratic heartbeats that may lead to sudden death), and increases cholesterol levels (which causes a plaque buildup and, over time, arteriosclerosis or "hardening" of the arteries).

In addition to the amount of stress, the way in which individuals respond to stress is a predictor of heart disease. In the 1950s, cardiologists Meyer Friedman and Ray Rosenman identified a behavior pattern they called *Type A personality:* people who respond to life events with impatience, hostility, competitiveness, urgency, and constant striving (Friedman & Rosenman, 1959). They devised a structured interview to distinguish Type A people from more easygoing Type B people. The interview not only assesses people's own accounts of their achievement and striving, but also attempts to provoke interviewees because Friedman and Rosenman were convinced that Type A behavior was most likely to surface in stressful situations.

A number of studies have shown that the Friedman and Rosenman structured interview not only does an excellent job of identifying people with Type A behavior, but also predicts CHD (Booth-Kewley & Friedman, 1987; Carmona, Sanz, & Marin, 2002; T. Q. Miller, Turner, Tindale, Posavac, & Dugoni, 1991). Most Type A people do not develop cardiovascular disorders. However, a study of men who had no signs of cardiovascular disorders when given a personality interview found that, 8½ years later, Type A personalities were twice as likely as Type B personalities to have developed cardiovascular disorders (Rosenman et al., 1975). A more recent study found that when Type A personalities were being evaluated, subjected to harassment or criticism, or playing video games, their heart rate and blood pressure were much higher than those of Type B personalities under the same circumstances (Lyness, 1993).

Current research indicates that some aspects of Type A behavior are more toxic than others—especially *chronic anger and hostility*, which do indeed predict heart disease (T. Q. Miller et al., 1996; Williams, 2001). A recent 6-year study followed 13,000 people who appeared free of heart disease when the study began (J. C. Williams et al., 2000). Those who scored high on an anger scale were 2.5 times more likely to have heart attacks or sudden cardiac deaths during the next 6 years than their calmer peers. In other words, impatience and ambition may not be damaging, but constant annoyance is. Not surprisingly, Friedman and his colleagues (1996) have reported some success in reducing the incidence of CHD through the use of counseling designed to diminish hostility in patients with Type A behavior.

Surprisingly, evidence that *depression* is associated with heart disease and premature death is also mounting (McCabe, Schneiderman, Field, & Wellens, 2000; Rugulies, 2002; Schwartzman & Glaus, 2000). People suffering from clinical depression feel sad and lethargic—the opposite of a Type A personality. It turns out that although they may appear to have given up, their bodies are in a constant state of fight or flight arousal and, as we have seen, long-term exposure to stress hormones damages the heart and blood vessels.

Chronic stress, especially when it results in anger and hostility, is associated with an increased incidence of coronary heart disease.

Stress and the Immune System

Scientists have long suspected that stress also affects the functioning of the immune system. Recall that the immune system is strongly affected by hormones and signals from the brain. The function of the immune system is to defend the body against invading substances, or *antigens*, such as bacteria, viruses and other microbes, and tumors. It does so primarily with the help of white blood cells called lymphocytes. To the extent that stress disrupts the functioning of the immune system, it can impair health (S. Cohen & Herbert, 1996). The relatively new field of **psychoneuroimmunology (PNI)** studies the interaction between stress on the one hand and immune, endocrine, and nervous system activity on the other (Azar, 1999a; Stowell, McGuire, Robles, Glaser, & Kiecolt-Glaser, 2003).

What is more common than a cold? We are exposed to cold viruses all the time, but usually our immune system fights them off. To the extent that stress disrupts the functioning of the immune system, it can impair health. In a recent study (S. Cohen et al., 1998), 256 healthy participants were given a battery of tests, including a life-stresses interview, a health-practices questionnaire, and immunological and endocrine assessments. Then they were exposed to one of five cold viruses or to saline (the control group), quarantined for 5 days, and tested daily to see if they had contracted a cold. Cohen found that severe but short-term stress (lasting 1 month or less) was not linked to getting a bug. But people who had suffered severe *chronic*

Psychoneuroimmunology (PNI) A field that studies the interaction between stress on the one hand and immune, endocrine, and nervous system activity on the other.

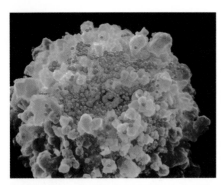

A T-lymphocyte blood cell infected with HIV, the virus that causes AIDS. HIV particles can be seen budding on the cell's lumpy membrane. Eventually, the HIV will cripple the cell, making it ineffective in combating the microorganisms that cause diseases.

stress (lasting 1 month or longer) were more than twice as likely to catch a cold as people who did not have stressors. The *type* of stress also predicted who got sick. Participants who had serious problems in close relationships or had been underemployed or unemployed were 2.5 to 3 times more like to catch a cold than those without these problems. Chronic stress, such as caring for an elderly parent, living in poverty, depression (Kiecolt-Glaser & Glaser, 2002; Oltmanns & Emery, 1998), or even the stress associated with college exams (O'Leary, 1990) have been linked to suppressed functioning of the immune system (Irwin, 2002).

Psychoneuroimmunologists have also established a possible relationship between stress and cancer (Herberman, 2002). Stress does not cause cancer, but it apparently impairs the immune system so that cancerous cells are better able to establish themselves and spread throughout the body. Animal research has demonstrated this connection between stress and cancer. For example, one study used mice known to be vulnerable to cancer (Riley, 1981). The mice were kept in a crowded, noisy, high-stress environment for 400 days. By the end of this period, 92 percent had developed cancer. By contrast, only 7 percent of a comparable group of mice kept in quiet, low-stress conditions developed cancer. (The low-stress environment only delayed the onset of cancer, however; after 600 days the incidence of tumors in both groups was similar.) Current animal research is focused on finding the exact cellular mechanisms that link stress to cancer (e.g., Herberman, 2002; Quan et al., 1999).

Establishing a direct link between stress and cancer in humans is more difficult. For obvious reasons, researchers cannot conduct similar experiments with human participants. Several new cancer drugs work by boosting the immune system, but this does not necessarily mean that damage to the immune system makes people more vulnerable to cancer (Azar, 1999b). Some early research showed a correlation between stress and incidence of cancer (McKenna, Zevon, Corn, & Rounds, 1999; O'Leary, 1990), however more recent research has not confirmed these findings (Maunsell, Brisson, Mondor, Verreault, & Deschenes, 2001). Thus the jury is still out on whether stress contributes to cancer in humans.

Apart from shedding light on the role of stress in cancer, many medical practitioners agree that psychologists can also play a vital role in improving the quality of life for cancer patients (McGuire, 1999; Rabasca, 1999a). For example, faced with the diagnosis of late-stage breast cancer, women understandably experience high levels of depression and mental stress. Many physicians now routinely recommend that their breast cancer patients attend group therapy sessions, which are effective in reducing depression, mental stress, hostility, insomnia, and the perception of pain (Giese-Davis et al., 2002; Goodwin et al., 2001; Kissane et al., 1997; Quesnel, 2003; Spiegel, 1995). However, despite some initial reports that breast cancer patients who attended group therapy session actually had an increased survival rate (Spiegel & Moore, 1997), more recent investigations have not supported this claim (Edelman, Lemon, Bell, & Kidman, 1999; Goodwin et al., 2001).

 12.3

CHECK YOUR UNDERSTANDING

1. Match the following terms with the appropriate definition.

___ alarm reaction   a. signs of psychic and physical wear and tear begin to show

___ resistance   b. body recognizes that it must fend off danger

___ exhaustion   c. "burnout" can occur here

2. Walking by yourself down a street late at night makes your heart beat fast. This is an example of

___ a. fight or flight

___ b. your hypothalamus being stimulated

___ c. a and b

3. People who suffer severe chronic stress are _____ to catch a cold as people who did not have stressors.

___ a. equally likely

___ b. less likely

___ c. more than twice as likely

4. _____ is the study of the interaction between stress on the one hand and immune, endocrine, and nervous system activity on the other.

___ a. Immunology

___ b. PNI (psychoneuroimmunology)

___ c. Biology

Answers: 1. alarm reaction—b; resistance—a; exhaustion—c, 2.c, 3.c, 4.b

Staying Healthy

How does a healthy life style help us control stress?

Methods of Reducing Stress

Scientists do not have a simple explanation for the common cold, much less cancer. But they do have advice on how to reduce stress and stay healthy.

Calm Down　Stress may be part of life, but there are proven ways to reduce the negative impact of stress on your body and your health. *Exercise* is one. Running, walking, biking, swimming, or whatever aerobic exercise you enjoy doing regularly lowers your resting heart rate and blood pressure, so that your body does not react as strongly to stress and recovers more quickly. Moreover, numerous studies show that people who exercise regularly and are physically fit have higher self-esteem than those who do not; are less likely to feel anxious, depressed, or irritable; and have fewer aches and pains, as well as fewer colds (Biddle, 2000; Sonstroem, 1997).

　　Relaxation training is another stress buster. A number of studies indicate that relaxation techniques lower stress (Pothier, 2002) and improve immune functioning (Andersen, Kiecolt-Glaser, & Glaser, 1994). Relaxation is more than flopping on the couch with the TV zapper, however. Healthful physical relaxation requires lying quietly and alternately tensing and relaxing every voluntary muscle in your body—from your head to your toes—in part to learn how to recognize muscle tension, in part to learn how to relax your body. Breathing exercises can have the same effect: if you are tense, deep, rhythmic breathing is difficult, but learning to do so relieves bodily tension. (See also Chapter 4, States of Consciousness, for a discussion of meditation, and Chapter 5, Learning, for a discussion of biofeedback, both of which can be useful in relaxing and reducing stress.)

Reach Out　A strong network of friends and family who provide *social support* can help to maintain good health (Uchino, Cacioppo, & Kiecolt-Glaser, 1996). One review of the literature concluded that the positive relationship between social support and health is on a

Because it benefits your cardiovascular system, regular aerobic exercise helps your body react less strongly to stress as well as recover more quickly when inevitable stress arises.

par with the negative relationship of health to such well-established risk factors as physical inactivity, smoking, and high blood pressure (House, Landis, & Umberson, 1988). Exactly why the presence of a strong social support system is related to health is not fully understood. Some researchers contend that social support may directly affect our response to stress and health by producing physiological changes in endocrine, cardiac, and immune functioning (Uchino et al., 1996).

Whatever the underlying mechanism, most people can remember times when other people made a difference in their lives by giving them good advice (informational support), helping them to feel better about themselves (emotional support), providing assistance with chores and responsibilities or financial help (tangible support), or simply by "hanging out" with them (belonging support) (Uchino, Uno, & Holt-Lunstad, 1999; R. B. Williams et al., 1992). However, not all relationships are alike. Knowing a lot of people or having a partner may or may not be a stress buffer; what matters are the characteristics of one's friends and partners and the quality of the relationships (Hartup & Stevens, 1999). For example, studies have found that married couples who argue in a hostile way—criticizing, belittling, and insulting one another—had suppressed immune function compared to couples who interacted in more constructive ways—listening to one another's points of view, seeking common ground and compromise, and using humor to break up tension (Hobfoll, Cameron, Chapman, & Gallagher, 1996; Kiecolt-Glaser, Malarkey, Chee, Newton, & Cacioppo, 1993; Kiecolt-Glaser, Bane, Glaser, & Malarkey, 2003).

Religion and Altruism   Health psychologists are also investigating the role religion may play in reducing stress and bolstering health (Rabin & Koenig, 2002; Siegel, Anderman, & Schrimshaw, 2001; Smith, 2000). For example, research has found that elderly people who pray or attend religious services regularly enjoy better health and markedly lower rates of depression than those who do not (Koenig, 1997; Koenig et al., 1997). Other studies have shown that having a religious commitment may also help to moderate high blood pressure and hypertension (Levin & Vanderpool, 1989).

Exactly why there is an association between health and religion is unclear. One explanation however, holds that religion provides people with a system of social support that includes caring friends and opportunities for close personal interactions. As described above, a strong network of social support can reduce stress in a variety of ways, and in turn, reduced stress is associated with better health (Uchino et al., 1996, 1999). However, it is equally likely that people who enjoy good health are more likely to pray and attend religious services (Sloan, Bagiella, & Powell, 1999).

Altruism—reaching out and giving to others because this brings *you* pleasure—is one of the more effective ways to reduce stress (Vaillant, 2000). Caring for others tends to take our minds off our own problems, to make us realize that there are others who are worse off than we are, and to foster the feeling that we're involved in something larger than our own small slice of life (Folkman, Chesney, & Christopher-Richards, 1994). Interestingly, altruism is a component of most religions, suggesting that altruism and religious commitment may have something in common that helps to reduce stress. Altruism may also channel loss, grief, or anger into constructive action. An example is Mothers Against Drunk Driving (MADD), an organization founded by a mother whose son was killed by a drunken driver.

Learn to Cope Effectively   How you appraise events in your environment—and how you appraise your ability to cope with potentially unsettling, unpredictable events—can minimize or maximize stress and its impact on health.

Proactive coping is the psychological term for anticipating stressful events and taking advance steps to avoid them or to minimize their impact (Aspinwall & Taylor, 1997). Proactive coping does not mean "expect the worst"; constant vigilance actually increases stress and may damage health. Rather, proactive coping means (as in

Altruistic behavior, such as demonstrating for a cause, can help channel personal feelings of grief into constructive action.

the Boy Scout motto) "Be prepared." This may include accumulating resources (time, money, social support, and information), recognizing potential stress in advance, and making realistic plans. For example, a recent widower anticipates that his first Christmas without his late wife will be lonely and makes plans to spend the holidays with friends. A woman who is moving to a new city knows the transition may be stressful. She finds out as much as she can about her new location before she moves—whether her friends have friends there, where she can participate in activities she enjoys (such as taking classes in drawing or karate), places and groups or organizations where she might meet people who share her interests (a house of worship, the best jazz clubs, the local animal shelter), and so on.

In many cases you cannot change or escape stressful circumstances, but you can change the way you think about things. *Positive reappraisal* helps people to make the best of a tense or painful situation. A low grade can been seen as a warning sign, not a catastrophe; a job you hate provides information on what you really want in your career; instead of brooding about a nasty remark from your sister, ask what does this tell you about *her*? Positive reappraisal does not require you to become a "Pollyanna" (the heroine of a novel who was optimistic to the point of being ridiculous). Rather it requires finding new meaning in a situation, a perspective or insight you had overlooked. After his partner died, one HIV caregiver told researchers, "What his death did was snap a certain value into my behavior, which is, 'Listen, you don't know how long you've got. You've just lost another one. Spend more time with the people who mean something to you'" (S. E. Taylor, Kemeny, Reed, Bower, & Gruenwald, 2000, p. 105).

One of the most effective, stress-relieving forms of reappraisal is *humor*. As Shakespeare so aptly put it in *The Winter's Tale*: "A merry heart goes all the day/ Your sad tires in a mile" (*Act IV, Scene 3*). And journalist Norman Cousins (1981) attributed his recovery from a life-threatening disease to regular "doses" of laughter. Watching classic comic films, he believed, reduced both his pain and the inflammation in his tissues. He wrote:

> What was significant about the laughter . . . was not just the fact that it provides internal exercise for a person flat on his or her back—a form of jogging for the innards—but that it creates a mood in which the other positive emotions can be put to work, too. In short it helps make it possible for good things to happen. (pp. 145–146)

Health psychologists agree (e.g., Salovey, Rothman, Detweiler, & Steward, 2000; Vaillant, 2000): A healthy body and a sense of humor go hand-in-hand.

Coping with Stress at College. It is two weeks before finals and you have two papers to write and four exams to study for. You are very worried. You are not alone. To help students cope with the pressures of finals week, and indeed, the stress that many students feel throughout the semester, many colleges and universities are offering stress-reduction workshops, aerobics classes, and counseling. At the University of California at Los Angeles, students are taught to visualize themselves calmly answering difficult test questions. Even if you do not attend a special program for reducing stress, you can teach yourself techniques to help cope with the pressures of college life.

1. Plan ahead. Do not procrastinate. Get things done well before deadlines. Start working on large projects well in advance.

2. Prioritize. Make a list of everything you have to do right down to doing the laundry, then star the highest priority tasks, the ones that really have to be done first (a looming deadline) or those that will take a long time. Focus on the high priority tasks, crossing them off as they are done, and adjust the priorities so that the most critical tasks are always starred.

3. Exercise. Do whatever activity you enjoy.

4. Listen to your favorite music, watch a TV show, or go to a movie as a study break.

5. Talk to other people.

6. Meditate or use other relaxation techniques. See the paperback *The Relaxation Response* (Benson & Klipper, 2000).

Adopt A Healthy Life Style

While learning how to avoid and cope with stress is important, the positive psychology movement has prompted many health psychologists to explore other ways to promote good health by adopting a healthier life style. Developing healthy habits like eating a well-balanced diet, getting regular exercise, not smoking and avoiding high-risk behaviors are all important to maintaining health (Friedman, 2002).

Diet A good diet of nutritious foods is important because it provides the energy necessary to sustain a vigorous lifestyle while promoting healthy growth and development. Although there is some disagreement about what *exactly* constitutes a well-balanced diet, the consensus among reputable scientists would agree that it should:

- include a variety of foods,
- contain at least five portions of fruits and vegetables a day,
- be derived primarily from plant sources, including plenty of whole grains, and
- be supplemented with modest portions of fish and lean meats for protein.

Thus, most experts advise eating a wide variety of fruits, vegetables, nuts, whole grain breads, and cereals, accompanied by small portions of fish and lean meats. Conversely, eating excessive amounts of fatty meats, deep-fried foods, dairy products that are high in cholesterol, like whole milk and butter, and foods that are high in artificial sugars like soda and candy (which are often lacking in vitamins and minerals) is generally considered unhealthy (Friedman, 2002).

Several studies have documented that eating a well-balanced diet, similar to the one described above, can help improve the quality of life, increase longevity, and reduce the risk of heart disease, cancer, and stroke (Trichopoulou, Costacou, Bamia, & Trichopoulos, 2003). Unfortunately, many Americans simply eat too much fast food (such as hamburgers, French fries, and soda) and snack foods (such as potato

Regular exercise is an important part of a healthy life style.

chips and candy) which are high in saturated fats and sugar and are often deficient in vitamins and minerals. As a result, despite the abundant availability of nutritious foods in America, poor eating habits are, in part, responsible for the comparatively high levels of heart disease, cancer, and stroke seen in the United States.

The problem however, is not just with the quality of food consumed in America. As we discussed in Chapter 9 (*Motivation and Emotion*), many Americans simply eat too much, resulting in obesity, while others develop eating disorders like anorexia nervosa that can put their lives at risk from eating too little.

Exercise   The importance of regular aerobic exercise (such as jogging, brisk walking or swimming) for maintaining a healthy body has been well established. In addition, health psychologists have shown that regular aerobic exercise can also help people cope better with stress, feel less depressed, more vigorous and have more energy. One study for example, randomly divided mildly depressed college woman into three groups. One group participated in regular aerobic exercise, one group received relaxation therapy, and the last group (a control group) received no treatment at all. After ten weeks, the mildly depressed women in the aerobic activity group reported a marked decrease in their depression when compared to the no treatment group. The relaxation group also showed benefits from relaxation therapy, but they were not as significant as the group that had engaged in the regular aerobic exercise program (McCann & Holmes, 1984). Numerous other studies have also demonstrated a link between regular exercise, reduced stress, increased self-confidence, and improved sleep quality (Gandhi, Depauw, Dolny, & Freson, 2002; Rice, 1997; see also Weinberg & Gould, 1999).

Quit Smoking   While fewer Americans smoke today than in the past, and over half of those who did smoke have quit, cigarette smoking still poses a serious health threat to the millions of people who continue to smoke (Millis, 1998). Smoking is linked to chronic lung disease, heart disease, and cancer. In addition, smoking can reduce the quality of life by decreasing lung efficiency. This decrease in lung efficiency is why most smokers will never be able to run a marathon, or participate in a vigorous exercise program.

Interestingly, the tendency to start smoking occurs almost exclusively during the adolescent years. Almost no one over the age of twenty-one takes up the habit for first time, but teenagers who seriously experiment with cigarettes or have friends who smoke are more likely start smoking than those who do not (Choi, Pierce, Gilpin, Farkas, & Berry, 1997). For these reasons, health psychologists realize that initiatives aimed at preventing smoking should primarily focus their efforts on young people.

Most adults who smoke want to quit, but their addiction to nicotine (discussed in Chapter 4) makes quitting very difficult. Fortunately, several alternative methods to help people quit smoking have been developed in recent years. For instance, prescription antidepressant medications such as *Zyban, Wellbutrin,* and *Effexor,* which work at the neurotransmitter level, have proved useful in helping people stop smoking. Nicotine substitutes, usually in the form of chewing gum, patches, or inhalers have also produced encouraging results. Many people who are attempting to quit also find that modifying the environment that they have come to associate with smoking is important. For instance, because people often smoke in bars, or during coffee breaks, changing routines to avoid the cues that have come to be associated with lighting up can also help. And then, of course there is "cold turkey," where people simply decide to stop smoking and then do so without any external support or change in their lifestyle. Regardless of how one manages to quite smoking, studies have shown that quitting will generally add years to your life, so doing whatever it takes to stop is worth it.

Avoid High Risk Behaviors   Every day we make dozens of small, seemingly insignificant choices that can potentially impact our health and well-being. For instance, choosing to wear a seat belt every time you ride in a car, though small, is one of the more significant things you can do to reduce the risk of injury and early death. Similarly, not engaging in unprotected sex reduces your chances of contracting sexually transmitted diseases, including AIDS.

To this end, health psychologists, working with public agencies, are designing intervention programs to help people make safer choices in their everyday lives. For example, John Jemmott and his colleagues (Jemmott, Jemmott, Fong, & McCaffree, 2002) studied the impact of a *safe-sex* program that stressed the importance of condom use and other safe-sex practices on a sample of 496 high-risk inner city African-American adolescents. Six months after the program began, a follow-up evaluation of the participants revealed that they reported a lower incidence of high-risk sexual behavior, including unprotected intercourse, than did adolescents who did not participate in the program. Research like this underscores the important role that health psychologists can play in helping people learn to avoid risky behavior and improve the quality of their life.

CHECK YOUR UNDERSTANDING

1. Anticipating stressful events is an example of

___ a. proactive coping

___ b. positive reappraisal

___ c. altruism

2. Exercise, meditation, and humor _____

___ a. lower heart rate and blood pressure

___ b. increase incidence of colds

___ c. reduce stress

___ d. a and c

3. Your sister remarks that your clothes look "dated." Your reaction is to wonder what this says about her. You are practicing

___ a. proactive coping

___ b. positive reappraisal

___ c. altruism

4. Adopting a healthy life style includes eating a well-balanced diet and

___ a. avoiding stress

___ b. not smoking

___ c. exercising regularly

___ d. all of the above

Answers: 1.a, 2.d, 3.b, 4.d

Extreme Stress

What is post-traumatic stress disorder? What kinds of events are most likely to trigger it?

Sources of Extreme Stress

Extreme stress has a variety of sources, ranging from unemployment to wartime combat, from violent natural disaster to rape. Extreme stress marks a radical departure from everyday life, such that a person cannot carry on as before and, in some cases, never fully recovers. What are some major stressors? What effect do they have on people? How do people cope?

Unemployment and Underemployment   Joblessness is a major source of stress. When the jobless rate rises, so do first admissions to psychiatric hospitals, infant mortality, deaths from heart disease, alcohol-related diseases, and suicide (Almgren, Guest, Immerwahr, & Spittel, 2002; Brenner, 1973, 1979; Rayman & Bluestone, 1982). "Things just fell apart," one worker said after both he and his wife lost their jobs. People usually react to the stress of unemployment in several stages (Powell & Driscoll, 1973). First comes a period of relaxation and relief, in which they take a vacation of sorts, confident they will find another job. Stage 2, marked by continued optimism, is a time of concentrated job hunting. In Stage 3, a period of vacillation and doubt, jobless people become moody, their relationships with family and friends deteriorate, and they scarcely bother to look for work. By Stage 4, a period of malaise and cynicism, they have simply given up. Although these effects are not universal, they are quite common. Moreover, there are indications that joblessness may not so much create new psychological difficulties as bring previously hidden ones to the surface. Studies have shown that death rates go up and psychiatric symptoms worsen not just during periods of unemployment but also during short, rapid upturns in the economy (Brenner, 1979; Eyer, 1977; Hart, 1985; Hutschemaekers & van de Vijver, 1989). These findings lend support to the point we discussed earlier that change, whether good or bad, causes stress.

Divorce and Separation   As Coleman and colleagues (1987) observe, "the deterioration or ending of an intimate relationship is one of the more potent of stressors and one of the more frequent reasons why people seek psychotherapy" (p. 155). After a breakup, both partners often feel they have failed at one of life's most important endeavors. Strong emotional ties frequently continue to bind the pair. For married couples, if only one spouse wants to end the marriage, the one initiating the divorce may feel sadness and guilt at hurting a once-loved partner, and the rejected spouse may vacillate between anger, humiliation, and self-recrimination over his or her role in the failure. Even if the decision to separate was mutual, ambivalent feelings of love and hate can make life upsetting and turbulent. Adults are not the only ones who are stressed by divorce. A national survey of the impact of divorce on children (Cherlin, 1992) found that a majority suffer intense emotional stress at the time of divorce; although most recover within a year or two (especially if the custodial parent establishes a stable home and their parents do not fight about child rearing), a minority experience long-term problems (see also Wallerstein, Blakeslee, & Lewis, 2000.)

Bereavement   For decades it was widely held that following the death of a loved one, people go through a necessary period of intense grief during which they work through their loss and, about a year later, pick up and go on with their lives. But Wortman and others have challenged this view on the basis of their own research and reviews of the literature on loss (C. G. Davis, Wortman, Lehman, & Silver, 2000; Wortman & Silver, 1989).

According to Wortman, the first myth about bereavement is that people should be intensely distressed when a loved one dies, which suggests that people who are not devastated are behaving abnormally, perhaps pathologically. Often, however, people have prepared for the loss, said their goodbyes, and feel little remorse or regret; indeed, they may be relieved that their loved one is no longer suffering. The second myth—that people need to work through their grief—may lead family, friends, and even physicians to consciously or unconsciously encourage the bereaved to feel or act distraught. Moreover, physicians may deny those mourners who are deeply disturbed needed antianxiety or antidepressant medication "for their own good." The third myth holds that people who find meaning in the death, who come to a spiritual or

Divorce is a major source of extreme stress in people's lives—one that over half of newly married American couples will one day face. Divorce is stressful not only to the partners involved but also to their children, who may suffer a variety of emotional problems as a result.

existential understanding of why it happened, cope better than those who do not. In reality, people who do *not* seek greater understanding are the best adjusted and least depressed. The fourth myth—that people should recover from a loss within a year or so—is perhaps the most damaging. Parents trying to cope with the death of an infant and adults whose spouse or child died suddenly in a vehicle accident continue to experience painful memories and wrestle with depression years later. But because they have not recovered "on schedule," members of their social network may become unsympathetic. Hence, the people who need support most may hide their feelings because they do not want to make other people uncomfortable and fail to seek treatment because they, too, believe they should recover on their own.

Not all psychologists agree with this "new" view of bereavement. But most agree that research on loss must take into account individual (and group or cultural) differences, as well as variations in the circumstances surrounding a loss (Bonanno & Kaltman, 1999; Harvey & Miller, 1998).

Catastrophes   Catastrophes include floods, earthquakes, violent storms, fires, and plane crashes. Psychological reactions to all these stressful events have much in common. At first, in the *shock stage*, "the victim is stunned, dazed, and apathetic," and sometimes even "stuporous, disoriented, and amnesic for the traumatic event." Then, in the *suggestible stage*, victims are passive and quite ready to do whatever rescuers tell them to do. In the third phase, the *recovery stage*, victims regain emotional balance, but anxiety often persists, and they may need to recount their experiences over and over again (Morris, 1990). Some investigators report that in later stages survivors may feel irrationally guilty because they lived while others died.

Combat and Other Threatening Personal Attacks   Wartime experiences often cause soldiers intense and disabling combat stress that persists long after they have left the battlefield. Similar reactions—including bursting into rage over harmless remarks, sleep disturbances, cringing at sudden loud noises, psychological confusion, uncontrollable crying, and silently staring into space for long periods—are also frequently seen in survivors of serious accidents, especially children, and of violent crimes such as rapes and muggings. Figure 12–3 shows the traumatic effects of war on the civilian population, based on composite statistics obtained after recent civil wars (Mollica, 2000). Rates of clinical depression and post-traumatic stress disorder are around 50 percent, whereas rates of even 10 percent would be considered high in a normal community.

Post-Traumatic Stress Disorder

Post-traumatic stress disorder (PTSD) Psychological disorder characterized by episodes of anxiety, sleeplessness, and nightmares resulting from some disturbing event in the past.

Severely stressful events can cause a psychological disorder known as **post-traumatic stress disorder (PTSD).** Dramatic nightmares in which the victim reexperiences the terrifying event exactly as it happened are common. So are daytime flashbacks, in which the victim relives the trauma. Often, victims of PTSD withdraw from social life and from job and family responsibilities. Post-traumatic stress disorder can set in immediately after a traumatic event or within a short time. But sometimes, months or years may go by in which the victim seems to have recovered from the experience, and then, without warning, psychological symptoms reappear, then may disappear only to recur repeatedly (Kessler, Sonega, Bromet, Hughes, & Nelson, 1995). Exposure to events reminiscent of the original trauma intensifies symptoms of PTSD (Moyers, 1996).

The experiences of soldiers who fought in the Gulf War (Benotsch et al., 2000), the Korean War and, especially, the Vietnam War heightened interest in PTSD. More than one-third of men involved in heavy combat in Vietnam showed severe symptoms of this disorder. Even some veterans of the relatively short Gulf war in 1991 experienced PTSD. Many veterans of World War II, old men now, still have nightmares from which they awake sweating and shaking. The memories of combat continue to torment them after more than half a century (Gelman, 1994). Recently, therapists have begun to observe a new phenomenon: Veterans who seemed to be healthy and well adjusted throughout their postwar lives suddenly develop symptoms of PTSD when they retire and enter their "golden years" (Sleek, 1998).

Soldiers are not the only victims of war. Indeed, during the twentieth century civilian deaths outnumbered military deaths in most wars. Yet only in the last decade, especially following the tragedy of the September 11th attacks, have medical researchers begun to investigate the psychological and physiological effects of war and terrorism on civilian survivors (Gurwitch, Sitterle, Young, & Pfefferbaum, 2002; Mollica, 2000). Following the terrorists attacks of September 11, 2001 on New York and Washington, for example, many people who showed no outward signs of physical injury, experienced a large emotional toll. For some, this took the form of shock and denial, while for others it resulted in physical symptoms like headaches, nausea, and chest pains. Still others found that shortly after the tragedy, their interpersonal relationships became strained as they withdrew and isolated themselves from their usual social contacts. For many, sleep and eating patterns were also disrupted. While no one person's reaction was exactly the same as another, the affects of the trauma were evident among the thousands who witnessed this event.

A devastating trauma like those suffered in wartime can trigger post-traumatic stress disorder in its victims. Survivors may suffer terrifying nightmares and vivid daytime flashbacks.

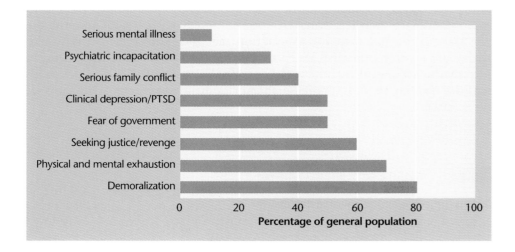

Percentage of general population

Figure 12–3
Mental trauma in societies at war.
In societies that have undergone the stress of war, nearly everyone suffers some psychological reaction, ranging from serious mental illness to feelings of demoralization. Rates of clinical depression are as high as 50 percent.
Source: Mollica, R. F. (2000, June). Invisible wounds. *Scientific American*, p. 54. Figure by Laurie Grace. Reprinted by permission of Laurie Grace.

Refugees of wars and conflicts often experience post-traumatic stress disorder. A research team who interviewed 993 refugees of the "killing fields" of Cambodia in 1975 recorded 15,000 traumatic events, including kidnapping, imprisonment, torture, and rape; 68 percent had symptoms of acute clinical depression, and 37 percent had symptoms of PTSD. Perhaps two out of three survivors of torture and beatings suffer permanent brain damage as a result. Lasting social disabilities are also common. A study of Bosnian refugees living in Croatia in 1996 found that one out of four was unable to work, to care for his or her family, or to participate in other social activities. A small percentage of survivors of mass violence suffer serious mental illness, but a majority suffer less severe but long-lasting problems, including exhaustion, hatred, and pervasive mistrust (Figure 12–3).

Whether in war zones or in countries at peace, women may be more vulnerable than men to trauma. According to one estimate (Rabasca, 1999b), women are twice as likely as men to develop PTSD. They are more likely to experience sexual and physical abuse in their homes, beginning in childhood and continuing into adulthood—in contrast to men who tend to develop PTSD as adults in response to combat or criminal victimization (Wood, Foy, Goguen, Pynoos, & James, 2002). One-third to one-half of women being treated for substance abuse suffer from PTSD.

Yet not everyone who is exposed to severely stressful events such as heavy combat or childhood sexual abuse develops PTSD. Individual characteristics including gender, personality, a family history of mental disorders, substance abuse among relatives, and even preexisting neurological disorders appear to predispose some people to PTSD more than others (Curle & Williams, 1996; Friedman, Schnurr, & McDonagh-Coyle, 1994; Gurvits, Gilbertson, Lasko, Orr, & Pittman, 1997).

Interestingly, some psychologists have found that following a significant trauma, a few particularly stable individuals experience a *positive* form of personal growth called *posttraumatic growth* (Calhoun & Tedeschi, 2001). In the rare instances where posttraumatic growth occurs, it appears to emerge largely from an individual's struggle to reconcile their loss through religious or existential understanding. When it does occur, posttraumatic growth is more likely to be seen in young adults than in older people (Powell, Rosner, Butollo, Tedeschi, & Calhoun, 2003).

Recovery from post-traumatic stress disorder is strongly related to the amount of emotional support survivors receive from family, friends, and community. Treatment consists of helping those who have experienced severe trauma to come to terms with their terrifying memories. Immediate treatment near the site of the trauma coupled with the expectation that the individual will return to everyday life is often effective. Reliving the traumatic event in a safe setting is also crucial to successful treatment (Jaycox, Zoellner, & Foa, 2002). This helps desensitize people to the traumatic memories haunting them (Oltmanns & Emery, 2001).

CHECK YOUR UNDERSTANDING

1. Underemployment and divorce can cause

___a. Type A behavior

___b. post-traumatic stress disorder

___c. extreme stress

2. People who are not intensely distressed when a loved one dies are behaving abnormally. This is

___a. a proven concept

___b. positive reappraisal

___c. a myth

3. Posttraumatic growth, though rare, can emerge through

___a. religious understanding

___b. existential understanding

___c. a and b

4. Recovery from PTSD is strongly related to

___a. a good social support system

___b. remarriage

___c. Type B personality

Answers: 1.c., 2.c., 3.c., 4.a

The Well-Adjusted Person

How do psychologists define a well-adjusted person?

What constitutes good adjustment? There is no single answer to that question. Some psychologists think that it means the ability to live according to social norms. Everyone has hostile and selfish wishes; everyone dreams impossible dreams. According to this view, people who learn to control their forbidden impulses and to limit their goals to those society allows are, by this definition, well adjusted. A woman who grows up in a small town, attends her state university, becomes a teacher, gets married, and settles into a peaceful family life might be considered well adjusted: She is living by the predominant values of her community.

Other psychologists disagree strongly with this conformist viewpoint. Barron (1963) argued that "refusal to adjust . . . is very often the mark of a healthy character." Society is not always right. If we accept its standards blindly, we renounce the right to make independent judgments. According to Barron, well-adjusted people enjoy the difficulties and ambiguities of life; they do not sidestep them through unthinking conformity. They accept challenges and are willing to endure the pain and confusion these challenges may bring. Barron has asserted that flexibility, spontaneity, and creativity, rather than simply fitting in, are signs of healthy adjustment.

Still other psychologists maintain that well-adjusted people have learned to balance conformity and nonconformity, self-control and spontaneity—to adapt flexibly as situations change. They can let themselves go at

THINKING CRITICALLY

Who Is Well Adjusted?

Write down the names of three individuals whom you consider well adjusted. Take some time before you answer. Include one person whom you know only distantly, perhaps someone you read about.

• What personal qualities set these individuals apart?

• Describe an action or situation that impressed you.

• What do these people have in common? What are their individual distinctions?

times, but can control themselves in situations where acting on impulse would run counter to their interests or better judgments. They can change themselves at society's urging, but they also work to change society when this strikes them as the better course. Such people know their strengths and admit their weaknesses, and this realistic assessment underlies an approach to life that is in harmony with their inner selves. They do not feel they must act against their values to be successful. Their self-trust enables them to face conflicts and threats without excessive anxiety and, perhaps more important, lets them risk their feelings and self-esteem in intimate relationships.

Psychologists may also evaluate adjustment by using specific criteria, such as the following (Morris, 1990), to judge an action:

1. *Does the action realistically meet the demands of the situation, or does it simply postpone resolving the problem?* Various forms of escapism—drugs, alcohol, and even endless fantasizing through books, movies, and television—may divert us from our pain, but they do not address the causes of our difficulties. Too great a reliance on escapism never makes for effective adjustment to a stressful situation.

2. *Does the action meet the individual's needs?* Often, we act to reduce external pressures by shortchanging our personal needs. An aspiring actress may abandon her own career goals to further the goals of her spouse. In the short run, she reduces external pressure, but she may be frustrated and disappointed for the rest of her life. A solution that creates such inner conflict is not an effective adjustment.

3. *Is the action compatible with the well-being of others?* Some people satisfy their needs in ways that hurt others. A young executive who ruthlessly uses people and manipulates coworkers may "get ahead" through such actions. But even if he does succeed in becoming vice president of his company, he may find himself without friends and may fear that his superiors will treat him as he does his subordinates. Ultimately, this situation can become extremely stressful and frustrating. Good adjustment takes into consideration both individual needs and the well-being of others.

For Abraham Maslow, whose humanistic views of personality and hierarchy of needs we discussed in Chapters 9 and 11, people who are well adjusted seek to "actualize" themselves. That is, they live in a way that enhances their own growth and fulfillment, not to please other people or to win social approval. Well-adjusted individuals, says Maslow (1954), perceive people and events realistically and can accept uncertainty and ambiguity. Though often quite conventional in behavior, they do not think conventionally; rather, they are creative and spontaneous thinkers. At the same time, self-actualizing people set goals for themselves and work, often independently, to achieve them.

Self-actualizing people also tend to form deep, close relationships with a few chosen individuals and are generally indifferent to such characteristics as sex, birth, race, color, and religion in responding to other people. Maslow also noted that people with a sense of humor that is broad and philosophical rather than pointed and hostile stand the best chance of adjusting to stress and achieving the most they can.

There are many standards for judging whether a person is well adjusted. A person deemed well adjusted by one standard may not be judged so by other criteria. The same holds true when we try to specify what behaviors are "abnormal"—the topic of the next chapter.

▨▨▨▨   CHECK YOUR UNDERSTANDING

The well-adjusted person has learned to balance

___a. conformity and nonconformity

___b. self-control and spontaneity

___c. flexibility and structure

___d. all of the above

Answer: d

summary

Stress is psychological tension or strain. We experience stress when we feel threatened physically or psychologically. **Adjustment** refers to any attempt we make to cope with a stressful situation, balancing our needs against the demands of the environment and the realistic possibilities available to us. How we adjust to the stresses in our lives affects our health; prolonged or severe stress can contribute to physical and psychological disorders. **Health psychology** is a subfield of psychology concerned with the relationship between psychological factors and physical health.

Sources of Stress

Stressors are the events or circumstances that trigger stress. Some life-and-death situations, such as war and natural disasters, are inherently stressful. Even events that are usually viewed as positive, such as a wedding or a job promotion, may be stressful because they require change or adaptation.

Life Changes   Because most people seek order, continuity, and predictability in their lives, any event that involves change will be experienced as stressful. The Social Readjustment Rating Scale (SRRS) developed by Holmes and Rahe measures how much stress a person has undergone in any given period by assigning point values to a series of life-changing events.

Everyday Hassles   Much stress comes from hassles, defined as petty annoyances, irritations, and frustrations. Major events often trigger the little hassles that give rise to stress.

Pressure also contributes to stress. **Pressure** can derive from both internal and external forces; in either case, we feel forced to intensify our efforts or to perform at higher levels.

Frustration occurs when someone or something stands between us and our goal. Five basic sources of frustration are delays, lack of resources, losses, failure, and discrimination.

Conflict arises when we are faced with two or more incompatible demands, opportunities, needs, or goals. Kurt Lewin analyzed conflict in terms of approach and avoidance, and showed how these tendencies combine to characterize three basic types of conflict. Someone who is simultaneously attracted to two incompatible goals experiences an **approach/approach conflict,** in which the person must either make a choice between the two goals or opportunities or

modify them so as to take some advantage of both goals. The reverse of this problem is **avoidance/avoidance conflict,** in which a person confronts two undesirable or threatening possibilities. People usually try to escape this kind of conflict or vacillate between the two possibilities. Also difficult to resolve is an **approach/avoidance conflict,** in which a person is both attracted to and repelled by the same goal or opportunity. People in this dilemma eventually reach a point where the tendency to approach equals the tendency to avoid and they vacillate until they finally make a decision or until the situation changes.

Stress and Individual Differences   Some people perceive a particular situation as stressful, whereas others are able to take the same situation in stride. Stress-resistant people may share a trait called hardiness—a tendency to experience difficult demands as challenging rather than threatening. Those who feel they have some control over an event are far less susceptible to stress than those who feel powerless in the same situation.

Sometimes people subject themselves to stress by internalizing a set of irrational, self-defeating beliefs that add unnecessarily to the normal stresses of living.

Coping with Stress

Stress requires that we **cope,** that we make cognitive and behavioral efforts to manage psychological stress. People generally adjust to stress in one of two ways: Direct coping describes any action people take to change an uncomfortable situation; defensive coping denotes the various ways people convince themselves—through a form of self-deception—that they are not really threatened or do not really want something they cannot get.

Direct Coping   When we cope directly with a particular threat or conflict, we do it in one of three ways: **confrontation, compromise,** or **withdrawal.** Confronting a stressful situation may lead us to learn new skills, enlist other people's aid, try harder to reach our goal, or express anger. Compromise usually resolves a conflict by forcing us to settle for less than we originally sought. Sometimes the most effective way of coping with a stressful situation is to distance oneself from it, but the danger of withdrawal is that it may become a maladaptive habit.

Defensive Coping   When a stressful situation arises and little can be done to deal with it directly, people often turn to defense mechanisms as a way of coping. Defense mechanisms are ways of deceiving ourselves, consciously or unconsciously, about the causes of stressful events, thus reducing conflict, frustration, pressure, and anxiety. In the short run, using defense mechanisms may reduce our level of stress, but over the long run, using defense mechanisms can interfere with a person's ability to deal directly with a problem.

Socioeconomic and Gender Differences   People living in poverty tend to experience greater stress than other people, primarily because the environments in which they live are generally more threatening and they have fewer resources to draw upon in coping with that stress. As a result, they experience more health problems than do people in better financial circumstances. Contrary to popular belief, women and men seem to be equally affected by stress, although women are more likely than men to experience stress when their marriage or other long-term relationships are deeply troubled. This appears to be a sign of greater commitment to the relationship rather than an indication of greater vulnerability to stress.

Stress and Health

The Biology of Stress   Physiologist Hans Selye identified three stages of reacting to physical and psychological stress that he called the **general adaptation syndrome (GAS).** In Stage 1, alarm reaction, the body recognizes that it must fight off some physical or psychological danger and acts accordingly. If neither direct nor defensive coping mechanisms succeed in reducing the stress, we move to Stage 2 of adaptation. During this resistance stage, physical symptoms of strain appear as we intensify our efforts to cope both directly and defensively. If these attempts to regain psychological equilibrium fail, psychological disorganization rages out of control until exhaustion, Stage 3, is reached. In this phase, we use increasingly ineffective defense mechanisms to bring the stress under control. Some people lose touch with reality, and others show signs of "burnout."

Stress and Heart Disease   Stress is known to be an important factor in the development of coronary heart disease (CHD). The Type A behavior pattern, a set of characteristics that includes hostility, urgency, competitiveness, and striving, has been linked to a greater likelihood of CHD. Current research indicates that some aspects of type A behavior—especially chronic anger and hostility—are more closely related to heart disease than other aspects.

Stress and the Immune System   Studies in **psychoneuroimmunology** have shown that stress can suppress the functioning of the immune system, increasing one's susceptibility to the common cold as well as to cancer in situations of prolonged exposure

to stress. Stress-reduction techniques can help cancer patients cope.

Staying Healthy

Methods of Reducing Stress   Exercise can reduce the negative impact of stress, as can relaxation training. People with strong social support systems enjoy better health. Some evidence suggests that social support may directly affect immune system functioning. It may be that people with high levels of social support more frequently engage in healthier behaviors, such as better diets and more physical exercise.

Other ways of minimizing stress include proactive coping—anticipating stressful events and taking advance steps to avoid them or minimize their impact—and positive reappraisal, or making the best of a tense or painful situation, particularly by using humor.

Adopt a Healthy Life Style   The positive psychology movement has prompted many health psychologists to explore other ways to promote good health by adopting a healthier life style. Developing healthy habits like eating a well-balanced diet, getting regular exercise, not smoking and avoiding high-risk behaviors are all important to maintaining health.

Extreme Stress

Sources of Extreme Stress   Extreme stress derives from a number of sources, including unemployment, divorce and separation, bereavement, catastrophes, and combat or other threatening personal attacks.

Post-traumatic Stress Disorder   Extreme trauma may result in **post-traumatic stress disorder (PTSD),** a disabling psychological disorder whose symptoms include anxiety, sleeplessness, and nightmares. Combat veterans, civilians who experience the trauma of war or terror, and refugees from war and unrest are especially vulnerable to PTSD.

The Well-Adjusted Person

What constitutes good adjustment? Some psychologists believe that well-adjusted people live according to social norms, having learned to control socially forbidden impulses and limit their goals to those that society allows. Barron, on the other hand, argues that the refusal to adjust to social norms is the mark of a healthy character. He suggests that well-adjusted people accept and enjoy challenges because they are confident of their ability to deal with problems in a realistic and mature way. Still other psychologists believe that well-adjusted people are those who have learned to balance conformity and nonconformity, self-control and spontaneity. Finally, some psychologists use specific criteria to evaluate a person's ability to adjust, such as how well the adjustment solves the problem and satisfies both personal needs and the needs of others.

key terms

Stress	452	Conflict	455	Compromise	460
Adjustment	452	Approach/approach conflict	456	Withdrawal	461
Health psychology	452	Avoidance/avoidance conflict	456	General adaptation syndrome (GAS)	464
Stressors	452	Approach/avoidance conflict	456	Psychoneuroimmunology (PNI)	467
Pressure	453	Cope	460	Post-traumatic stress disorder (PTSD)	476
Frustration	455	Confrontation	460		

OVERVIEW

Perspectives on Psychological Disorders
Historical Views of Psychological Disorders
Theories of the Nature, Causes, and Treatment of Psychological Disorders
Classifying Psychological Disorders
The Prevalence of Psychological Disorders
Mental Illness and the Law
Mood Disorders
Depression
Mania and Bipolar Disorder
Causes of Mood Disorders
Suicide
Anxiety Disorders
Specific Phobias

Panic Disorder
Other Anxiety Disorders
Causes of Anxiety Disorders
Psychosomatic and Somatoform Disorders
Psychosomatic Disorders
Somatoform Disorders
Causes of Somatoform Disorders
Dissociative Disorders
Dissociative Amnesia
Dissociative Identity Disorder
Depersonalization Disorder
Causes of Dissociative Disorders
Sexual Disorders
Sexual Dysfunction
Paraphilias

Gender-Identity Disorders
Personality Disorders
Types of Personality Disorders
Causes of Antisocial Personality Disorder
Schizophrenic Disorders
Types of Schizophrenic Disorders
Causes of Schizophrenia
Childhood Disorders
Attention-Deficit/Hyperactivity Disorder (AD/HD)
Autistic Disorder
Gender and Cultural Differences in Psychological Disorders
Gender Differences
Cultural Differences

Psychological Disorders

13

hen does behavior become abnormal? The answer to this question is more complicated than it may seem. There is no doubt that the man on the street corner claiming to be Jesus Christ or the woman insisting that aliens from outer space are trying to kill her is behaving abnormally. But what about the following people:

- A male college student is popular with women and enjoys partying. His grades have always been fairly good, but recently he is having difficulty concentrating on anything but having a good time.
- A 10-year-old child has a mild developmental delay in fine-motor coordination that makes his handwriting immature compared to his classmates. Although his reading, calculating, and reasoning abilities are all normal or advanced, his handwriting makes him feel so self-conscious that he stops trying to get good grades and withdraws socially from other children.
- A highly successful female lawyer is unmarried and, although she has many relationships with men, is unwilling to make a commitment. She feels driven to become a partner in her firm before the age of 28 (she is 27 now). Recently, she has occasionally found herself drinking to excess.

Unlike physical diseases, the presence or absence of mental illness cannot be determined objectively. Diagnosing an emotional disorder is a judgment call, and judgments can differ. Which, if any, of these three people do you think is experiencing a psychological disorder? What criteria did you use in reaching your decision?

Perspectives on Psychological Disorders

What causes psychological disorders?

Society, the individual, and the mental health professional use different standards to judge normal and abnormal behavior. Society's main standard is whether behavior conforms to the existing social order; the individual's primary criterion is his or her own sense of well-being; and the mental health professional looks chiefly at personality characteristics as well as *personal discomfort* (the person's experience of inner distress) and *life functioning* (the person's success in meeting societal expectations for performance in work or school and in social relationships). Table 13–1 presents the three distinct views of mental health.

Look again at the three cases at the start of the chapter. The popular college student apparently feels happy, and the female lawyer is unlikely to think of herself as having a psychological problem. Although their actions appear to be abnormal from the perspective of society, from their own perspectives, neither suffers from the sort of personal discomfort that can define abnormal behavior. The opposite is true of the child with handwriting problems. Perhaps society would judge his behavior as odd or unusual, but society is not likely to view him as "abnormal." His behavior does not violate any essential social rules, and he is functioning adequately. Yet he is experiencing much personal discomfort. From his own perspective, something is wrong.

Although individual and societal perspectives are in conflict in these cases, a mental health professional would have little difficulty deciding that all three people are displaying abnormal behavior. Mental health professionals define *abnormal behavior* as either maladaptive life functioning or serious personal discomfort or

THINKABOUTIT

You will find the answers to these questions in the chapter:

1. What causes psychological disorders?

2. What are some early signs of the development of depression?

3. When does a normal fear become a phobia?

4. Can psychological factors cause real physical illnesses?

5. Most patients with multiple personalities experienced childhood abuse. True or false?

6. What is considered to be abnormal sexual behavior?

7. How do "personality disorders" differ from other psychological disorders?

8. Does schizophrenia refer to "split personality."

9. What are the differences between men and women in psychological disorders?

table 13-1   PERSPECTIVES ON PSYCHOLOGICAL DISORDERS

	Standards/Values	Measures
Society	Orderly world in which people assume responsibility for their assigned social roles (e.g., breadwinner, parent), conform to prevailing mores, and meet situational requirements.	Observations of behavior, extent to which a person fulfills society's expectations and measures up to prevailing standards.
Individual	Happiness, gratification of needs.	Subjective perceptions of self-esteem, acceptance, and well-being.
Mental-health professional	Sound personality structure characterized by growth, development, autonomy, environmental mastery, ability to cope with stress, adaptation.	Clinical judgment, aided by behavioral observations and psychological tests of such variables as self-concept, sense of identity, balance of psychic forces, unified outlook on life, resistance to stress, self-regulation, ability to cope with reality, absence of mental and behavioral symptoms, adequacy in love, work, and play, adequacy in interpersonal relationships.

Source: Adapted from Strupp & Hadley. *American Psychologist*, 1977, 32, 187–196. Table 1, p. 190. Copyright © 1977 by the American Psychological Association. Reprinted with permission.

both. But now imagine that the cases were slightly different. What if the college student's grades were not suffering? What if the child was not embarrassed but simply preferred being a "loner"? What if the lawyer did not have a drinking problem? In the absence of maladaptive life functioning or serious personal discomfort, a mental health professional would conclude that none of the three people is displaying abnormal behavior.

Historical Views of Psychological Disorders

No one knows for sure what was considered abnormal behavior thousands of years ago. However, we can hazard a general description: Mysterious actions were attributed to supernatural powers, and madness was a sign that spirits had possessed a person. Sometimes people who were "possessed" were seen as sacred and their visions considered messages from the gods. At other times, their behavior indicated the presence of evil spirits and their affliction was considered dangerous to the community. It is likely that this *supernatural view* of abnormal behavior dominated all early societies.

The roots of a more *naturalistic view* of abnormal behavior can be traced to ancient Greece. The Greek physician Hippocrates (c. 460–c. 377 B.C.), for example, maintained that madness was like any other sickness—a natural event arising from natural causes. Hippocrates's naturalistic approach had a lasting positive influence: It encouraged a systematic search to uncover the causes of mental illness, and it implied that disturbed people should be treated with the care and sympathy offered to people suffering from physical ailments.

Abnormal? Probably not. In the context of a sports event, fans often behave in ways that they ordinarily would not. Psychologists have developed criteria, such as personal discomfort and inadequate life functioning, to help define abnormal behavior.

During the Middle Ages, Europeans reverted to the supernatural view of abnormal behavior (although more naturalistic accounts were kept alive in Arab cultures). Psychological disorders were often viewed as the work of demons; the emotionally disturbed person was thought to be a witch or possessed by the devil. Exorcisms, ranging from the mild to the hair-raising, were performed, and many people endured horrifying tortures. Some unfortunates were burned at the stake.

By the late Middle Ages, public and private asylums where emotionally disturbed people could be confined were being established. The move away from viewing the mentally ill as witches and demon-possessed was a significant advance. But although these institutions were founded with good intentions, most were little more than prisons. In the worst cases, inmates were chained down and deprived of food, light, or air to "cure" them.

The year 1793 was a turning point in the history of the treatment of the mentally ill. In that year, Philippe Pinel (1745–1826) became director of the Bicêtre Hospital in Paris. Under his direction, the hospital was drastically reorganized: Patients were released from their chains and allowed to move about the hospital grounds, rooms were made more comfortable and sanitary, and dubious and violent medical treatments were abandoned (Harris, 2003). Pinel's reforms were soon followed by similar efforts in England and, somewhat later, in America.

The most notable American reformer in this area was Dorothea Dix (1802–1887), a schoolteacher from Boston who led a nationwide campaign for humane treatment of mentally ill people. Under her influence, the few existing asylums in the United States were gradually turned into hospitals, and many new institutions were built. Sadly, these hospitals often failed to offer the humane treatment Dix had campaigned for, and *deinstitutionalization*—the movement of mental patients out of large hospitals—became a major goal of mental health care in the last half of the twentieth century.

Biological model View that psychological disorders have a biochemical or physiological basis.

Medieval Exorcism

Theories of the Nature, Causes, and Treatment of Psychological Disorders

The basic reason for the failed, and sometimes abusive, treatment of mentally disturbed people throughout history has been the lack of understanding of the nature, causes, and treatment of psychological disorders. Although our knowledge is still inadequate, important advances in understanding these disorders can be traced to the late nineteenth and early twentieth centuries. Three influential but conflicting models emerged during this time: the biological model, the psychoanalytic model, and the cognitive-behavioral model.

The Biological Model The **biological model** holds that psychological disorders are caused by physiological malfunctions—of the nervous systems or the endocrine glands, for example—and that heredity often plays a significant role. As we shall see, there is growing evidence in support of the biological model of mental illness. Moreover, advances in the new interdisciplinary field of *neuroscience* leave little doubt that our understanding of the role of biological factors in mental illness will continue to expand. (See *On the Cutting Edge: The Neuroscience Revolution* to learn more.)

Dorothea Dix was a nineteenth-century reformer who led a nationwide campaign for the humane treatment of mentally ill people.

ON THE CUTTING EDGE

THE NEUROSCIENCE REVOLUTION

The new interdisciplinary field of neuroscience has begun to provide exciting new insights into the nature and causes of psychological disorders. This emerging field brings together research from such diverse disciplines as psychobiology, neurology, neurochemistry, neuroendocrinology, psychiatry, psychology, neurosurgery, neuroimaging, and neuropharmacology. Throughout this book, and particularly in Chapter 2 (The Biological Basis of Behavior), we have pointed out how specific aspects of human behavior, thought, and emotion can now be linked with the brain processes that govern them. In this chapter too we will explore how current advances in neuroscience have increased our understanding of psychological disorders.

For instance, new techniques in neuroimaging have enabled researchers to pinpoint specific regions of the brain that are involved in disorders such as schizophrenia (Chance, Esiri, & Timothy, 2003; Yotsutsuji et al., 2003) and antisocial personality (Anderson, Bechara, Damasio, Tranel, & Damasio, 1999). Neurochemists, by unraveling the complex chemical interactions that take place at the synapse, have spawned advances in neuropharmacology that have led to the development of promising new drugs for the treatment of mental illness (see Chapter 14, Therapies). Moreover, as we have seen, many of these advances are also linked to the field of behavior genetics,

which is continually increasing our understanding of the role that specific genes play in the development of complex disorders such as schizophrenia (Geber et al., 2003; Hashimoto et al., 2003; Williams et al., 1999) and autism (Lamb, Moore, Bailey, & Monaco, 2000; Nurmi et al., 2003).

While recent breakthroughs in the field of neuroscience are indeed remarkable, no neuroimaging technique developed to date can provide a clear and definitive differentiation between different mental disorders (Sarason & Sarason, 1999; Callicott, 2003). And while an increasing number of medications are available to help alleviate the symptoms of some mental disorders, most drugs can only control abnormal behavior, not cure it. There is also some concern that advances in identifying the underlying neurological structures and mechanisms associated with mental illnesses may interfere with the recognition of equally important psychological causes of abnormal behavior (Widiger & Sankis, 2000). Indeed, it has even been suggested that neurophysiological explanations of mental illness are somehow more scientific and are thus preferred over psychodynamic explanations (Andreasen, 1997). As neuroscientists continue to explore the complex neurological processes that are involved in human behavior, our understanding of psychological disorders will no doubt increase.

The Psychoanalytic Model Freud and his followers developed the **psychoanalytic model** at the end of the nineteenth and the beginning of the twentieth century (see Chapter 11, Personality). According to this model, behavior disorders are symbolic expressions of unconscious internal conflicts, which generally can be traced to the early years of life. The psychoanalytic model argues that people must become aware that the source of their problems lies in their childhood and infancy before they can resolve those problems effectively.

The Cognitive-Behavioral Model A third model of psychological disorders grew out of psychological research on learning and cognition during the twentieth century. The **cognitive-behavioral model** suggests that psychological disorders, like all behavior, are the result of learning. The cognitive-behavioral model stresses both internal and external learning processes in the development and treatment of psychological disorders. For example, a bright student who considers himself academically inferior to his classmates and who believes that he doesn't have the ability to perform well on a test does not study with much care or confidence. Naturally, he performs poorly, and his poor test score both punishes his minimal efforts and confirms his belief that he is academically inferior.

The Diathesis-Stress Model and Systems Theory The three major competing theories have each shed some light on certain types of abnormality, and each may

Psychoanalytic model View that psychological disorders result from unconscious internal conflicts.

Cognitive-behavioral model View that psychological disorders result from learning maladaptive ways of thinking and behaving.

continue to do so. However, the most exciting recent developments in abnormal psychology integrate the various theoretical models to discover specific causes and specific treatments for different mental disorders.

The **diathesis-stress model** is one promising approach to integration (Fowles, 1992; Rende & Plomin, 1992; Walker & Diforio, 1997). This model suggests that a biological *predisposition*, or **diathesis,** must combine with some kind of stressful circumstance before the predisposition to a mental disorder shows up as behavior (Rosenthal, 1970). According to this model, some people are biologically prone to developing a particular disorder under stress, whereas others are not.

The **systems approach** is an even more promising method of integrating evidence on such behavior (Oltmanns & Emery, 2001). This approach examines how biological, psychological, and social risk factors combine to produce psychological disorders; for this reason, it is also known as the *biopsychosocial model*. According to this model, emotional problems are "lifestyle diseases" that, much like heart disease and many other physical illnesses, are caused by a combination of biological risks, psychological stresses, and societal pressures and expectations. In this chapter, we will follow the systems approach in examining the causes of and treatments for psychological disorders.

Diathesis-stress model View that people biologically predisposed to a mental disorder (those with a certain diathesis) will tend to exhibit that disorder when particularly affected by stress.

Diathesis Biological predisposition.

Systems approach View that biological, psychological, and social risk factors combine to produce psychological disorders. Also known as the biopsychosocial model of psychological disorders.

ENDURING ISSUES   mindbody

Causes of Mental Disorders

Throughout this chapter, as we discuss what is known about the causes of psychological disorders, you will see that biological and psychological factors are intimately connected. For example, you will see that there is strong evidence for a genetic component in some personality disorders as well as in schizophrenia. However, not everyone who inherits these factors develops a personality disorder or becomes schizophrenic. Our current state of knowledge allows us to pinpoint certain causative factors for certain conditions, but it does not allow us to completely differentiate biological and psychological factors.

Classifying Psychological Disorders

For nearly 40 years, the American Psychiatric Association (APA) has issued a manual describing and classifying the various kinds of psychological disorders. This publication, the *Diagnostic and Statistical Manual of Mental Disorders (DSM)*, has been revised four times. The fourth edition, text revision *DSM-IV-RT* (American Psychiatric Association, 2000), was coordinated with the tenth edition of the World Health Organization's *International Classification of Diseases.*

The *DSM-IV-RT* is intended to provide a complete list of mental disorders, with each category painstakingly defined in terms of significant behavior patterns so that diagnoses based on it will be reliable (see Table 13–2). As we saw in Chapter 8, Intelligence and Mental Abilities, *reliability* means repeatability, and for the *DSM* the most important test of reliability is whether different mental health professionals arrive at the same diagnosis for the same individual. Although the manual provides careful descriptions of symptoms of different disorders to bolster consistent diagnosis, it is generally silent on cause and treatment. The *DSM* has gained increasing acceptance because its detailed criteria for diagnosing mental disorders have made diagnosis much more reliable (Nathan & Langenbucher, 1999). Today it is the most widely used classification of psychological disorders.

table 13-2   DIAGNOSTIC CATEGORIES OF DSM-IV-RT

Category	Example
Disorders Usually First Diagnosed in Infancy, Childhood, or Adolescence	Mental retardation, learning disorders, autistic disorder, attention-deficit/hyperactivity disorder.
Delirium, Dementia, and Amnestic and Other Cognitive Disorders	Delirium, dementia of the Alzheimer's type, amnestic disorder.
Mental Disorders Due to a General Medical Condition	Psychotic disorder due to epilepsy.
Substance-Related Disorders	Alcohol dependence, cocaine dependence, nicotine dependence.
Schizophrenia and Other Psychotic Disorders	Schizophrenia, schizoaffective disorder, delusional disorder.
Mood Disorders	Major depressive disorder, dysthymic disorder, bipolar disorder.
Anxiety Disorders	Panic disorder with agoraphobia, social phobia, obsessive-compulsive disorder, post-traumatic stress disorder, generalized anxiety disorder.
Somatoform Disorders	Somatization disorder, conversion disorder, hypochondriasis.
Factitious Disorders	Factitious disorder with predominantly physical signs and symptoms.
Dissociative Disorders	Dissociative amnesia, dissociative fugue, dissociative identity disorder, depersonalization disorder.
Sexual and Gender-Identity Disorders	Hypoactive sexual desire disorder, male erectile disorder, female orgasmic disorder, vaginismus.
Eating Disorders	Anorexia nervosa, bulimia nervosa.
Sleep Disorders	Primary insomnia, narcolepsy, sleep terror disorder.
Impulse-Control Disorders	Kleptomania, pyromania, pathological gambling.
Adjustment Disorders	Adjustment disorder with depressed mood, adjustment disorder with conduct disturbance.
Personality Disorders	Antisocial personality disorder, borderline personality disorder, narcissistic personality disorder, dependent personality disorder.

Still, the *DSM* has its critics. Some charge that the manual is too medically oriented and that it includes too many behaviors that have nothing to do with mental illness (Sarbin, 1997). For instance, *premenstrual dysphoric disorder*, described as an increase in sadness, tension, and irritability that occurs in the week before a woman begins to menstruate, has been denounced as a sexist attempt to label as "illness" what may actually be a normal psychological reaction to significant biological changes (Adler, 1990).

Some of the controversies surrounding the *DSM* reflect political concerns, whereas others reflect legitimate scientific disagreements about the nature of psychological disorders. These controversies aside, our understanding of the nature, causes, and treatment of some forms of psychological disorders continues to grow.

Throughout this chapter, we will look at a variety of psychological disorders from the integrative systems perspective. As you read, you may occasionally feel an uncomfortable twinge of recognition. This is only natural and nothing to worry about. Much abnormal behavior is simply normal behavior greatly exaggerated or displayed in inappropriate situations.

The Prevalence of Psychological Disorders

How common are psychological disorders in the United States? Are they increasing or decreasing over time? Are some population groups more prone to these disorders than others? These questions are of interest to psychologists and public-health experts, who are concerned with both the prevalence and the incidence of mental health problems. *Prevalence* refers to the frequency with which a given disorder occurs at a given time. If there were 100 cases of depression in a population of 1,000, the prevalence of depression would be 10 percent. The *incidence* of a disorder refers to the number of new cases that arise in a given period. In a population of 1,000, if there were 10 new cases of depression in a year, the incidence rate would be 1 percent per year.

The American Psychiatric Association funded an ambitious and wide-ranging study of the prevalence of psychological disorders, which involved interviewing more than 20,000 people around the country. The results were surprising: 14.9 percent of the population was found to be experiencing a clinically significant mental disorder, and 6 percent a significant substance abuse disorder (Narrow, Rae, Robins, & Regier, 2001). The most common mental disorders were anxiety disorders, followed by phobias and mood disorders. Schizophrenia, a severe mental disorder that often involves hospitalization, was found to afflict 1 percent of the population, or over 2 million people. Substance abuse problems were found in 6 percent of the population, with abuse of alcohol being three times more prevalent than abuse of all other drugs combined. Perhaps in future years epidemiologists—scientists who study the distribution of health problems—will determine whether our 15 percent prevalence figure for mental disorders is typical of the rest of the world.

Mental Illness and the Law

Particularly horrifying crimes—assassinations of public figures, mass murders, and serial murders, for instance—have often been attributed to mental disturbance, because it seems to many people that anyone who could commit such crimes must be "crazy." But to the legal system, this presents a problem: If a person is truly "crazy," are we justified in holding him or her responsible for criminal acts? The legal answer to this question is a qualified yes. A mentally ill person is responsible for his or her crimes unless he or she is determined to be *insane*. What's the difference between being "mentally ill" and being "insane"? **Insanity** is a legal term, not a psychological one. It is typically applied to defendants who, when they committed the offense with which they are charged, were so mentally disturbed that they either lacked substantial capacity to appreciate the criminality of their actions (know right from wrong) or to conform to the requirements of the law (control their behavior).

When a defendant is suspected of being mentally disturbed or legally insane, another important question must be answered before that person is brought to trial: Is the person able to understand the charges against him or her and to participate in a defense in court? This issue is known as *competency* to stand trial. The person is examined by a court-appointed expert and, if found to be incompetent, is sent to a mental institution, often for an indefinite period. If judged to be competent, the person is required to stand trial.

At this point the defendant may decide to plead not guilty by reason of insanity. When a defendant enters an insanity plea, the court system relies heavily on the testimony of forensic psychologists and psychiatrists to determine the mental state of the defendant at the time of the crime. Because most such trials feature well-credentialed experts testifying both for the defense and for the prosecution, the jury is often perplexed about which side to believe. Furthermore, there is much cynicism about "hired-gun" professionals, who receive large fees to appear in court and argue that a defendant is or is not sane. The public, skeptical about professional jargon, often feels that psychological testimony allows dangerous criminals to "get off." Actually, those who successfully plead insanity often are confined longer in mental hospitals than they would have been in prison if

Insanity Legal term for mentally disturbed people who are not considered responsible for their criminal actions.

convicted of their crimes. Therefore, the insanity plea is not an easy way out of responsibility for a crime.

CHECK YOUR UNDERSTANDING

1. Match the following model of abnormal behavior with the appropriate description.

___ biological model   a. Abnormal behaviors result from unconscious internal conflicts.

___ psychoanalytic model   b. Abnormal behavior is the product of biological, psychological, and social-risk factors.

___ biopsychosocial model   c. Abnormal behavior is the result of learning and can be unlearned.

___ cognitive-behavior model   d. Abnormal behaviors have a biochemical, physical or a physiological basis.

2. The DSM-IV-RT is a classification system for mental disorders developed by the

___ a. American Psychiatric Association

___ b. American Psychological Association

___ c. National Institutes for Mental Health

3. At any given time, what percentage of Americans suffers from mental disorders?

___ a. 5 percent   d. 20 percent

___ b. 10 percent

___ c. 15 percent

Answers: biological model—d; psychoanalytic model—a; biopsychosocial model—b; cognitive-behavior model—c, 2.a, 3.c

Mood Disorders

What are some early signs of the development of depression?

As their name suggests, **mood disorders** are characterized by disturbances in *mood* or prolonged emotional state, sometimes referred to as *affect*. Most people have a wide emotional range—that is, they are capable of being happy or sad, animated or quiet, cheerful or discouraged, overjoyed or miserable, depending on the circumstances. In some people with mood disorders, this range is greatly restricted. They seem stuck at one or the other end of the emotional spectrum—either consistently excited and euphoric or consistently sad—whatever the circumstances of their lives. Other people with a mood disorder alternate between the extremes of euphoria and sadness.

Depression

The most common mood disorder is **depression**, a state in which a person feels overwhelmed with sadness, loses interest in activities, and displays other symptoms such as excessive guilt or feelings of worthlessness. People suffering from depression are unable to experience pleasure from activities they once enjoyed. They are tired and apathetic, sometimes to the point of being unable to make the simplest everyday decisions. They may feel as if they have failed utterly in life, and they tend to blame themselves for their problems. Seriously depressed people often have insomnia and lose interest in food and sex. They may have trouble thinking or concentrating—even to the extent of finding it difficult to read a newspaper. In fact, some research indicates that difficulty concentrating and subtle changes in

Mood disorders Disturbances in mood or prolonged emotional state.

Depression A mood disorder characterized by overwhelming feelings of sadness, lack of interest in activities, and perhaps excessive guilt or feelings of worthlessness.

short-term memory are sometimes the first signs of the onset of depression (Williams et al., 2000). In very serious cases, depressed people may be plagued by suicidal thoughts or may even attempt suicide (Cicchetti & Toth, 1998).

It is important to distinguish between *clinical depression* and the "normal" kind of depression that all people experience from time to time. It is entirely normal to become sad when a loved one has died, when you've come to the end of a romantic relationship, when you have problems on the job or at school—even when the weather's bad or you don't have a date for Saturday night. Most psychologically healthy people also get "the blues" occasionally for no apparent reason. It has even been suggested that depression may in some cases be an adaptive response, one that helped our ancestors survive periods of hardship (Nesse, 2000). But in all of these instances, the mood disturbance is either a normal reaction to a "real-world" problem (for example, grief) or passes quickly. Only when depression is serious, lasting, and well beyond the typical reaction to a stressful life event is it classified as a mood disorder (APA, 2000). (See *Applying Psychology: Recognizing Depression.*)

The *DSM-IV-RT* distinguishes between two forms of depression. *Major depressive disorder* is an episode of intense sadness that may last for several months; in contrast, *dysthymia* involves less intense sadness (and related symptoms) but persists with little relief for a period of 2 years or more. Some depressions can become so intense that people become **psychotic**—that is, they lose touch with reality. For example, consider the case of a 50-year-old depressed widow who was transferred to a medical center from a community mental health center. This woman believed that her neighbors were against her, that they had poisoned her coffee, and that they had bewitched her to punish her for her wickedness (Spitzer, Skodal, Gibbon, & Williams, 1981).

Children and adolescents can also suffer from depression. In very young children, depression is sometimes difficult to diagnose because the symptoms are usually different than those seen in adults. For instance, in infants or toddlers, depression may be manifest as a "failure to thrive" or gain weight, or as a delay in speech or motor development. In school-age children, depression may be manifested as antisocial behavior, excessive worrying, sleep disturbances, or unwarranted fatigue.

A disorder that is often mistaken for depression sometimes occurs following a head injury, as may result from an automobile accident or a sudden jolt. The symptoms, which may include fatigue, headache, loss of sex drive, apathy, and feelings of helplessness, generally last for only a few days, although they can persist for a couple of months. When such symptoms arise following a sudden trauma to the brain, they are more likely to be diagnosed as *mild traumatic brain injury (MTBI)* than depression (Rabasca, 1999b Rapoport, McCullagh, Streiner, & Feinstein, 2003).

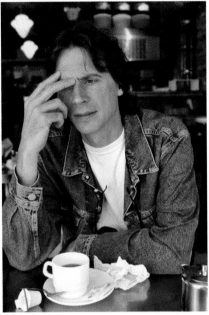

Most people feel unhappy and low now and then, but depression goes much deeper than mere unhappiness. Clinically depressed people lose interest in the things that usually give them pleasure. Typically, they feel overwhelmed by sadness, loss, and guilt.

Mania and Bipolar Disorder

Another mood disorder, less common than depression, is **mania,** a state in which the person becomes euphoric or "high," extremely active, excessively talkative, and easily distracted. People suffering from mania may become *grandiose*—that is, their self-esteem is greatly inflated. They typically have unlimited hopes and schemes but little interest in actually carrying them out. People in a manic state sometimes become aggressive and hostile toward others as their self-confidence grows. At the extreme, people going through a manic episode may become wild, incomprehensible, or violent until they collapse from exhaustion.

Manic episodes rarely appear by themselves; rather, they usually alternate with depression. Such a mood disorder, in which both mania and depression are present, is known as **bipolar disorder.** In bipolar disorder, periods of mania and depression alternate (each lasting from a few days to a few months), sometimes with periods of

Psychotic Marked by defective or lost contact with reality.

Mania A mood disorder characterized by euphoric states, extreme physical activity, excessive talkativeness, distractedness, and sometimes grandiosity.

Bipolar disorder A mood disorder in which periods of mania and depression alternate, sometimes with periods of normal mood intervening.

APPLYING PSYCHOLOGY

RECOGNIZING DEPRESSION

Almost everyone from time to time feels depressed. Failing a major exam, breaking up with a boyfriend or girlfriend, even leaving home and friends to attend college can all produce a temporary state of "the blues." More significant life events can have an even greater impact: the loss of one's job or of a loved one can produce a sense of hopelessness about the future that feels very much like a slide into depression.

The preceding instances would typically be considered "normal" reactions to negative life events. But at what point do these normal responses cross the line into clinical depression? How do clinicians determine whether the hopelessness and despair being expressed by a person constitute a major depressive episode or just a period of sadness that will eventually pass?

The DSM-VI-RT provides the framework for making this distinction. First, clinical depression is characterized by depressed mood, by the loss of interest and pleasure in usual activities, or both. Clinicians also look for some significant impairment or distress in social, occupational, or other important areas of functioning. People suffering from depression not only feel sad or empty but also have significant problems in carrying on a normal lifestyle.

Doctors look, too, for other explanations of the symptoms: Could they be due to substance abuse or the side effects of medication that the person is taking? Could they be the result of a medical condition, such as hypothyroidism (the inability of the thyroid gland to produce an adequate amount of its hormones)? Could the symptoms be better interpreted as an intense grief reaction?

"People suffering from depression ... have significant problems in carrying on a normal lifestyle."

If the symptoms do not seem to be explained by the preceding causes, how do clinicians make a diagnosis of depression? The DSM-IV-RT notes that at least five of the following symptoms, including at least one of the first two, must be present:

1. **Depressed mood:** Does the person feel sad or empty for most of the day, almost every day, or do others observe these symptoms?

2. **Loss of interest in pleasure:** Has the person lost interest in performing normal activities, such as working or going to social events? Does the person seem to be "just going through the motions" of daily life without deriving any pleasure from them?

3. **Significant weight loss or gain:** Has the person gained or lost more than 5 percent of body weight in a month? Has the person lost interest in eating or complain that food has lost its taste?

4. **Sleep disturbances:** Is the person having trouble sleeping? Or, conversely, is the person sleeping too much?

5. **Disturbances in motor activities:** Do others notice a change in the person's activity level? Does the person just "sit around," or does the behavior reflect agitation or unusual restlessness?

6. **Fatigue:** Does the person complain of being constantly tired and having no energy?

7. **Feelings of worthlessness or excessive guilt:** Does the person express feelings such as "you'd be better off without me around" or "I'm evil and I ruin everything for everybody I love"?

8. **Inability to concentrate:** Does the person complain of memory problems ("I just can't remember anything anymore") or the inability to focus attention on simple tasks, such as reading a newspaper?

9. **Recurrent thoughts of death:** Does the person talk about committing suicide or express the wish that he or she were dead?

When these symptoms are present and are not due to other medical conditions, a diagnosis of major depression is typically the result, and appropriate treatment can be prescribed. As you will learn in Chapter 14: Therapies, appropriate diagnosis is the first step in the effective treatment of psychological disorders.

Source: Diagnostic and Statistical Manual of Mental Disorders, Fourth Edition, Text Revision. Washington, DC, American Psychiatric Association, 2000. Reprinted with permission from the *Diagnostic and Statistical Manual of Mental Disorders, Fourth Edition.* Copyright 1994 American Psychiatric Association.

normal mood intervening. Occasionally, bipolar disorder is seen in a mild form: The person has alternating moods of unrealistically high spirits followed by moderate depression. Research suggests that bipolar disorder differs in several ways from unipolar depression. Bipolar disorder is much less common and, unlike depression, it is equally prevalent in men and women. Bipolar disorder also seems to have a stronger biological component than depression: It is more strongly linked to heredity and is most often treated by drugs (Gershon, 1990; Maj, 2003).

Causes of Mood Disorders

Some people insist that mood disorders are caused solely by nature or by nurture. You may have heard, for example, that depression results from "a chemical imbalance in the brain" or "unresolved grief." However, consistent with the biopsychosocial model, most psychologists now believe that mood disorders result from a combination of risk factors. Although we can identify many of the causative factors, we still do not yet know exactly how they interact to cause a mood disorder.

Biological Factors   There is consistent evidence that genetic factors play an important role in the development of depression (Mineka, Watson, & Clark, 1998), particularly, as we have noted, in bipolar disorder (Badner, 2003; Katz & McGuffin, 1993). The strongest evidence comes from studies of twins. If one identical twin is clinically depressed, the other twin (who is genetically identical) is more likely to be clinically depressed also. Among fraternal twins (who share only about half their genes), if one twin is clinically depressed, the likelihood is much less that the second twin will also be clinically depressed (McGuffin, Katz, Watkins, & Rutherford, 1996).

But just what is it that some people seem to inherit that predisposes them to a mood disorder? Some promising research has linked mood disorders to certain chemical imbalances within the brain—principally to high and low levels of certain neurotransmitters, the chemicals involved in the transmission of nerve impulses from one cell to another (Kato, 2001).

Biological research on mood disorders is promising. In fact, as we shall see in the next chapter, several medications have been found to be effective in treating mood disorders. Still, there is no firm evidence linking high or low levels of neurotransmitters to an increased genetic risk for mood disorders. In fact, the so-called chemical imbalance in the brain associated with depression could be caused by stressful life events. Biology affects psychological experience, but psychological experience also alters biological functioning.

Psychological Factors   Although a number of psychological factors are thought to play a role in causing severe depression, in recent years research has focused on the contribution of maladaptive **cognitive distortions.** According to Aaron Beck (1967, 1976, 1984, 2002), during childhood and adolescence some people undergo such wrenching experiences as the loss of a parent, severe difficulties in gaining parental or social approval, or humiliating criticism from teachers and other adults. One response to such experience is to develop a negative self-concept—a feeling of incompetence or unworthiness that has little to do with reality but that is maintained by a distorted and illogical interpretation of real events. When a new situation arises that resembles the situation under which the self-concept was learned, these same feelings of worthlessness and incompetence may be activated, resulting in depression.

Considerable research supports Beck's view of depression (Alloy, Abramson, Whitehouse, Hogan, Tashman, Steinberg, Rose, & Donovan, 1999; Alloy, Abramson, & Francis, 1999). For instance, Lauren Alloy and her colleagues have

Cognitive distortions An illogical and maladaptive response to early negative life events that leads to feelings of incompetence and unworthiness that are reactivated whenever a new situation arises that resembles the original events.

found that college students with negative cognitive styles are at considerably higher risk of developing depression than are students with more positive cognitive styles. When compared to people who are not depressed, depressed people also seem to perceive and recall information in more negative terms (Roth & Rehm, 1980; Watkins, Vache, Verney, Mathews, & Muller, 1996). Critics of Beck's theories have pointed out that such negative responses may be the *result* of depression instead of the cause (Hammen, 1985). However, prospective studies, which analyze people's cognitive styles when they are not depressed and then monitor the same group of people over time, suggest that cognitive style has predictive value (Alloy, Abramson, & Francis, 1999; Kwon & Oei, 2003). As we shall see in the next chapter, therapy based on Beck's theories has proved quite successful in the treatment of depression.

Social Factors   Many social factors have been linked with mood disorders, particularly difficulties in interpersonal relationships. Freud viewed depression as resulting from excessive and irrational grief over a real or "symbolic" loss. Freud's view of how "unresolved grief" is transformed into depression is complex and not supported by current evidence (Crook & Eliot, 1980). However, the analogy he drew between grief and depression has been fruitfully noted by other theorists, and there is considerable research linking depression with troubled close relationships (Monroe & Simons, 1991). In fact, some theorists have suggested that the link between depression and troubled relationships explains the fact that depression is two to three times more prevalent in women than in men (Culbertson, 1997; Weissman & Olfson, 1995), since women tend to be more relationship-oriented than men are in our society (Gilligan, 1982). Yet not every person who experiences a troubled relationship becomes depressed. As the systems approach would predict, it appears that a genetic predisposition or cognitive distortion is necessary before a distressing close relationship or other significant life stressor will result in a mood disorder.

ENDURING ISSUES   **person**situation

The Chicken or the Egg?

It is sometimes difficult to tease apart the relative contribution of the person's biological or cognitive tendencies and the social situation. People with certain depression-prone genetic or cognitive tendencies may be more likely than others to encounter stressful life events by virtue of their personality and behavior. For example, studies show that depressed people tend to evoke anxiety and even hostility in others, partly because they require more emotional support than people feel comfortable giving. As a result, people tend to avoid those who are depressed, and this shunning can intensify the depression. In short, depression-prone and depressed people may become trapped in a vicious circle that is at least partly of their own creation (Coyne & Whiffen, 1995).

Suicide

More than 29,000 people in the United States commit suicide each year making it the 11th leading cause of death. Indeed, suicides outnumber homicides by 5 to 3 in the United States, and more than twice as many people die of suicide than of HIV/AIDS (NIMH, 2000). More women than men attempt suicide, but more men actually succeed at it, partly because men more often choose violent and lethal means, such as guns.

Although the largest number of suicides occurs among older white males, since the 1960s the rates of suicide attempts have been rising among adolescents and young adults (see Figure 13–1). In fact, adolescents account for 12 percent of all suicide attempts in this country, and suicide is the third leading cause of death in that age group (Centers for Disease Control and Prevention, 1999; Hoyert, Kochanek, & Murphy, 1999). As yet, no convincing explanation has been offered for the increase, though the stresses of leaving home, meeting the demands of college or career, and surviving loneliness or broken romantic attachments seem to be particularly great at this time. External problems such as unemployment, the financial costs of attending college, and the dread that one's future is threatened by economic decline may also add to people's personal problems. Still, suicidal behavior is more common among adolescents who have psychological problems.

There are several dangerous myths concerning suicide.

Myth: Someone who talks about committing suicide will never do it.

Fact: Most people who kill themselves have talked about it. Such comments should always be taken seriously.

Myth: Someone who has tried suicide and failed is not serious about it.

Fact: Any suicide attempt means that the person is deeply troubled and needs help immediately. A suicidal person will try again, picking a more deadly method the second or third time around.

Myth: Only people who are life's losers—those who have failed in their careers and in their personal lives—commit suicide.

Fact: Many people who kill themselves have prestigious jobs, conventional families, and a good income. Physicians, for example, have a suicide rate several times higher than that for the general population; in this case the tendency to commit suicide may be related to their work stresses.

People considering suicide are overwhelmed with hopelessness. They feel that things cannot get better and see no way out of their difficulties. This is depression in the extreme, and it is not a state of mind that someone can easily be talked out of. It does little good to tell a suicidal person that things aren't really so bad; the person will only take this as further evidence that no one understands his or her suffering. But most suicidal people do want help, however much they may despair of

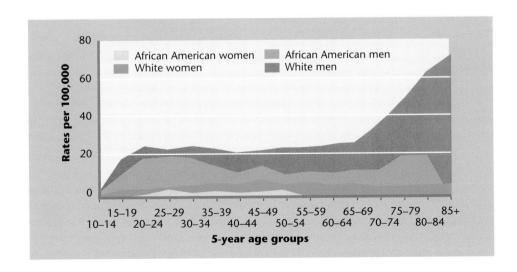

Figure 13–1
Gender and race differences in the suicide rate across the life span.
White males, who commit the highest number of suicides at all ages, show a sharp rise in the rate of suicide after age 65. In contrast, the suicide rate for African American females, which is the lowest of that for any group, remains relatively stable throughout the life span.
Source: Suicide and Life-Threatening Behavior, by Moscicki, E. K. Copyright 1995 by Guilford Pubns Inc. Reproduced with permission of Guilford Pubns Inc in the format Textbook via Copyright Clearance Center.

obtaining it. If a friend or family member seems at all suicidal, getting professional help is urgent. A local community mental health center is a good starting place. Calling one of the national suicide hot lines (see telephone numbers listed in Chapter 14, Therapies) can be helpful as well.

CHECK YOUR UNDERSTANDING

1. If a person feels overwhelmed with sadness, loses interest in activities, and displays feelings of worthlessness, he is most likely

___ a. anxious

___ b. depressed

___ c. manic

2. If a person is extremely active, excessively talkative, and easily distractible, she may be

___ a. manic

___ b. depressed

___ c. obsessive-compulsive

3. Mood disorders are a result of

___ a. biological factors

___ b. psychological factors

___ c. social factors

___ d. all of the above

Answers: 1.b, 2.a, 3.d

Anxiety Disorders

When does a normal fear become a phobia?

Although all of us are afraid from time to time, we usually know why we are fearful: Our fear is caused by something appropriate and identifiable, and it passes with time. But in the case of **anxiety disorders,** either the person does not know why he or she is afraid, or the anxiety is inappropriate to the circumstances. In either case, the person's fear and anxiety don't seem to make sense. The main types of anxiety disorders that we will consider are *specific phobias, panic disorder, generalized anxiety disorder,* and *obsessive-compulsive disorder.*

Specific Phobias

Anxiety disorders Disorders in which anxiety is a characteristic feature or the avoidance of anxiety seems to motivate abnormal behavior.

Specific phobia Anxiety disorder characterized by intense, paralyzing fear of something.

A national survey has found that anxiety disorders are more common than any other form of mental disorder (Kessler et al., 1994). Anxiety disorders can be subdivided into more specific diagnostic categories. One familiar subtype of anxiety disorder is **specific phobia.** A specific phobia is an intense, paralyzing fear of something that perhaps should be feared, but the fear is excessive and unreasonable. In fact, the fear in a specific phobia is so great that it leads the person to avoid routine or adaptive activities, and thus interferes with life functioning. For example, it is not inappropriate to be a bit fearful as an airplane takes off or lands, but it is inappropriate to be so afraid of flying that you refuse to get on or even go near an airplane—particularly if your career demands frequent travel. Other common phobias focus on animals, heights, closed places, blood, needles, or injury. Some fear of all these objects or situations is normal and common, but excessive, intense, paralyzing fear is a sign of specific phobia. Estimates indicate that about 1 in 10 people in the United States suffer from at least one specific phobia.

Another important subtype of phobia is **social phobia**, which refers to excessive, inappropriate fears connected with social situations or performances in front of other people. Intense fear of public speaking is a common form of social phobia. In other cases, simply talking with people or eating in public causes such severe anxiety that the phobic person will go to great lengths to avoid these situations. As with specific phobias, it is normal to experience some mild fear or uncertainty in many social situations. These fears are only considered to be social phobias when they are excessive enough to interfere significantly with life functioning.

Agoraphobia is a much more debilitating type of anxiety disorder than social phobias. *Agoraphobia* is a term formed from Greek and Latin words that literally means "fear of the marketplace," but the disorder typically involves multiple, intense fears, such as the fear of being in public places from which escape might be difficult, of being in crowds, of being alone, of traveling in an automobile, or of going through tunnels or over bridges. The common element in all these situations seems to be a great dread of being separated from sources of security.

A phobia causes paralyzing fear in a situation that most people find nonthreatening. Pictured is Dr. Carol Zimmerman with a patient in therapy for acrophobia (fear of heights).

Panic Disorder

Another type of anxiety disorder is **panic disorder,** a problem characterized by recurrent panic attacks. A *panic attack* is a sudden, unpredictable, and overwhelming experience of intense fear or terror without any reasonable cause. During a panic attack, a person may have feelings of impending doom, chest pain, dizziness or fainting, sweating, difficulty breathing, and a fear of losing control or dying. A panic attack usually lasts only a few minutes, but such attacks may recur for no apparent reason.

Panic attacks not only cause tremendous fear while they are happening but also leave the sufferer with a dread of having another panic attack that can persist for days or even weeks. This dread can be so overwhelming that it leads to the development of agoraphobia: In their efforts to prevent a recurrence, some people avoid any circumstance that might cause anxiety and cling to people or situations that help keep them calm. In other words, their agoraphobia develops out of their attempt to avoid further panic attacks.

Other Anxiety Disorders

The various phobias and panic attacks have a specific source of anxiety, such as fear of heights, fear of social situations, or fear of being in crowds. In contrast, **generalized anxiety disorder** is defined by prolonged vague but intense fears that are not attached to any particular object or circumstance. Generalized anxiety disorder perhaps comes closest to the everyday meaning attached to the term *neurotic*. Its symptoms include inability to relax, constantly feeling restless or keyed up, muscle tension, rapid heart beat or pounding heart, apprehensiveness about the future, hypervigilance (constant alertness to potential threats), and sleeping difficulties.

Social phobia An anxiety disorder characterized by excessive, inappropriate fears connected with social situations or performances in front of other people.

Agoraphobia An anxiety disorder that involves multiple, intense fear of crowds, public places, and other situations that require separation from a source of security such as the home.

Panic disorder An anxiety disorder characterized by recurrent panic attacks in which the person suddenly experiences intense fear or terror without any reasonable cause.

Generalized anxiety disorder An anxiety disorder characterized by prolonged vague but intense fears that are not attached to any particular object or circumstance.

Extreme stress can cause acute stress disorder. The soldier at left has just learned that his close friend was killed by friendly fire during the Gulf War.

Considerable research indicates that generalized anxiety disorder and major depressive disorder may share a common genetic basis, although the specific genetic factors that account for this relationship remain unclear (Mineka, Watson, & Clark, 1998).

A very different form of anxiety disorder is **obsessive-compulsive disorder, or OCD.** *Obsessions* are involuntary thoughts or ideas that keep recurring despite the person's attempts to stop them, and *compulsions* are repetitive, ritualistic behaviors that a person feels compelled to perform. Obsessive thoughts are often of a horrible and frightening nature. One person, for example, reported that "when she thought of her boyfriend she wished he were dead; when her mother went down the stairs, she 'wished she'd fall and break her neck'; when her sister spoke of going to the beach with her infant daughter [she] 'hoped that they would both drown'" (Carson & Butcher, 1992, p. 190). Truly compulsive behaviors may be equally dismaying to the person who feels driven to perform them. They often take the form of washing or cleaning, as if the compulsive behavior were the person's attempt to "wash away" the contaminating thoughts. Another common type of compulsion is checking: repeatedly performing some kind of behavior to make sure that something was or was not done in a certain way. For example, a person might feel compelled to check dozens of times whether the doors are locked before going to bed.

Anyone can experience mild obsessions or compulsions at times. Most of us have occasionally been unable to get a particular song lyric out of our head or have felt that we had to walk so as to avoid stepping on cracks in the sidewalk. But in OCD, the obsessive thoughts and compulsive behavior are of a more serious nature. For example, a man who checks his watch every 5 minutes when his wife is late coming home is merely being normally anxious. But a man who feels that he must go through his house every hour checking every clock for accuracy, even though he knows there is no reason to do so, is showing signs of an obsessive-compulsive disorder.

Because people who experience obsessions and compulsions often do not seem particularly anxious, you may wonder why this disorder is considered an anxiety disorder. The answer is that if such people try to stop their irrational behavior, or if someone else tries to stop them, they experience severe anxiety. In other words, the obsessive-compulsive behavior seems to keep anxiety at bay.

Finally, two types of anxiety disorders are clearly caused by some specific highly stressful event. Some people who have lived through a fire, flood, tornado, or airplane crash experience repeated episodes of fear and terror after the event itself is over. If the anxious reaction occurs soon after the event, the diagnosis is *acute stress disorder.* If it takes place long after the event is over, the diagnosis is likely to be *posttraumatic stress disorder,* which we discussed in the previous chapter (Oltmanns & Emery, 2001).

Causes of Anxiety Disorders

A starting point in considering the cause of anxiety disorders is to recall our discussion of phobias in Chapter 5, Learning. We noted that phobias are often learned after only one fearful event and are extremely difficult to shed. We also saw that there is a relatively limited and predictable range of phobic objects: Even though people are more likely to be injured in an automobile accident than by a snake or spider bite, snake and spider phobias are far more common than car phobias. Some theorists, therefore, believe phobias are *prepared responses*—that is, responses that evolution has made us biologically predisposed to acquire through learning so that we seem to be "hardwired" to associate certain stimuli with intense fears (Marks & Nesse, 1994; Nesse, 2000; Öhman, 1996).

From a cognitive perspective, people who feel they are not in control of stressful events in their lives are more likely to experience anxiety than those who believe

Obsessive-compulsive disorder (OCD) An anxiety disorder in which a person feels driven to think disturbing thoughts and/or to perform senseless rituals.

they have control over such events. As one real-life example of this, African Americans who live in high-crime areas have a higher incidence of anxiety disorders than other Americans (Neal & Turner, 1991). In the same situation, though, some people develop unrealistic fears and others do not. Why?

Psychologists working from the biological perspective point to heredity, arguing that a predisposition to anxiety disorders may be inherited (Eysenck, 1970; Sarason & Sarason, 1987). In fact, some evidence suggests that anxiety disorders tend to run in families (Kendler, Neale, Kessler, Heath, & Eaves, 1992; Torgersen, 1983; Weissman, 1993), and have a higher concordance rate among identical twins compared to fraternal twins (Skre, Onstad, Torgersen, & Lygren, 1993).

Finally, any comprehensive model of anxiety must account for what would seem to be the vital role of internal psychological conflicts. From the Freudian perspective, unacceptable impulses or thoughts (usually sexual or aggressive in nature) can threaten to overwhelm the ego and break through into full consciousness. The Freudian defense mechanisms protect the conscious mind against such threats, but at a cost in anxiety.

CHECK YOUR UNDERSTANDING

1. Match the following terms with the appropriate description.

___ specific phobia	a. great dread of being separated from sources of security
___ social phobia	b. an unreasonable, paralyzing fear of something
___ agoraphobia	c. a sudden, unpredictable, and overwhelming experience of intense fear or terror without any reasonable cause
___ panic attack	d. feeling driven to think disturbing thoughts or to perform meaningless rituals
___ generalized anxiety disorder	e. excessive, inappropriate fears connected with social situations or performances in front of other people
___ obsessive-compulsive disorder	f. prolonged vague but intense fears not attached to any particular object or circumstance

2. Phobias are often learned after only one fearful event and are _____ to shed.

___a. easy

___b. hard

___c. impossible

Answers: 1. specific phobia—b; social phobia—e; agoraphobia—a; panic attack—c; generalized anxiety disorder—f; obsessive-compulsive disorder—d, 2.b

Psychosomatic and Somatoform Disorders

Can psychological factors cause real physical illnesses?

To many people, the term *psychosomatic* implies that a condition is not "real," that it exists "only in your head." In fact, **psychosomatic disorders** are *real* physical illnesses that appear to have a psychological cause. The term *psychosomatic* perfectly captures the interplay of psyche (mind) and soma (body) that characterizes these disorders. In contrast, **somatoform disorders** are characterized by physical

Psychosomatic disorders Disorders in which there is real physical illness that is largely caused by psychological factors such as stress and anxiety.

Somatoform disorders Disorders in which there is an apparent physical illness for which there is no organic basis.

Somatization disorder A somatoform disorder characterized by recurrent vague somatic complaints without a physical cause.

Conversion disorders Somatoform disorders in which a dramatic specific disability has no physical cause but instead seems related to psychological problems.

symptoms without any identifiable physical cause. Despite reassurances to the contrary from physicians, people suffering from somatoform disorders *believe* they are physically ill and describe symptoms that correspond to physical illnesses, yet there is no evidence of physical illness. Their problem is somatic (physical) in appearance only, as indicated by the term *somatoform* (somatic in form or appearance).

Psychosomatic Disorders

Tension headaches are an example of a psychosomatic disorder. They are caused by muscle contractions brought on by stress. The headache is real, but it is called "psychosomatic" because psychological factors (such as stress and anxiety) appear to play an important role in causing the symptoms. People suffering from tension headaches are often taught relaxation techniques that relieve stress and reduce muscle tension.

Scientists used to believe that psychological factors contributed to the development of some physical illnesses, principally headaches, allergies, asthma, and high blood pressure, but not others, such as infectious diseases. Today modern medicine leans toward the idea that *all* physical ailments are to some extent "psychosomatic"—in the sense that stress, anxiety, and various states of emotional arousal alter body chemistry, the functioning of bodily organs, and the body's immune system (which is vital in fighting infections). As we saw in the previous chapter, we now recognize that stress and psychological strains can also alter *health behavior*, which includes positive actions such as eating a balanced diet and exercising as well as such negative activities as cigarette smoking and excessive alcohol consumption. As we noted earlier in the chapter, both physical and mental illnesses are now conceptualized as "lifestyle diseases" that are caused by a combination of biological, psychological, and social factors.

Somatoform Disorders

People who suffer from somatoform disorders do not consciously seek to mislead others about their physical condition. The symptoms are real to them; they are not faked or under voluntary control (APA, 2000). For example, in one kind of somatoform disorder, **somatization disorder,** the person experiences vague, recurring physical symptoms for which medical attention has been sought repeatedly but no organic cause found. Common complaints are back pains, dizziness, partial paralysis, abdominal pains, and sometimes anxiety and depression. The following case is typical:

> An elderly woman complained of headaches and periods of weakness that lasted for over six months. Her condition had been evaluated by doctors numerous times; she was taking several prescription medications, and she had actually undergone 30 operations for a variety of complaints. She was thin, but examination showed her to be within normal limits in terms of physical health (except for numerous surgical scars). Her medical history spanned half a century, and there can be little doubt that she suffered from somatization disorder. (Quill, 1985)

Another form of somatoform disorder involves complaints of far more bizarre symptoms, such as paralysis, blindness, deafness, seizures, loss of feeling, or false pregnancy. Sufferers from such **conversion disorders** have intact, healthy muscles and nerves, yet their symptoms are very real. For example, a person with such a "paralyzed" limb has no feeling in it, even if stuck with a pin. Sometimes it is easy to determine that there is no organic cause for the symptoms of a conversion disorder because the symptoms are anatomically impossible. Take *glove anesthesia*, which is a lack of feeling in the hand from the wrist down. There is no way that damage to the nerves running into the hand could cause such a localized pattern of anesthesia.

Psychologists also look for evidence that the "illness" resolves a difficult conflict or relieves the patient of the need to confront a difficult situation. For example, a housewife reported serious attacks of dizziness, nausea, and visual disturbances that came on in the late afternoon and cleared up at about 8:00 P.M. After ruling out any physical cause for her problems, a therapist discovered that she was married to an extremely tyrannical man who, shortly after coming home from work in the evening, habitually abused her verbally, criticizing her housekeeping, the meal she had prepared, and so on. Her psychological distress was unconsciously converted to physical symptoms that served to remove her from this painful situation (Spitzer et al., 1981).

Yet another somatoform disorder is **hypochondriasis.** Here, the person interprets some small symptom—perhaps a cough, bruise, or perspiration—as a sign of a serious disease. Although the symptom may actually exist, there is no evidence that the serious illness does. Nevertheless, repeated assurances of this sort have little effect, and the person is likely to visit one doctor after another in search of a medical authority who will share his or her conviction.

Body dysmorphic disorder, or imagined ugliness, is a recently diagnosed and poorly understood type of somatoform disorder. Cases of body dysmorphic disorder can be very striking. One man, for example, felt that people stared at his "pointed ears" and "large nostrils" so much that he eventually could not face going to work—so he quit his job. Clearly people who become that preoccupied with their appearance cannot lead a normal life. Ironically, most people who suffer body dysmorphic disorder are not ugly. They may be average looking or even attractive, but they are unable to evaluate their looks realistically. When they look in the mirror, all they seem to see is their "defect"—greatly magnified.

Causes of Somatoform Disorders

Somatoform disorders (especially conversion disorders) present a challenge for psychological theorists. They seem to involve some kind of unconscious processes. Freud concluded that the physical symptoms were often related to traumatic experiences buried in a patient's past: A woman who years earlier saw her mother physically abused by her father suddenly loses her sight; a man who was punished for masturbating later loses the use of his hand. By unconsciously developing a handicap, Freud theorized, people accomplish two things. First, they prevent themselves from acting out forbidden desires or repeating forbidden behavior; Freud called this the *primary gain* of the symptom. Second, the symptoms often allow the person to avoid an unpleasant activity, person, or situation; Freud called this *secondary gain*.

Cognitive behavioral theories of somatoform disorders focus on Freud's idea of secondary gain—that is, they look for ways in which the symptomatic behavior is being rewarded. For example, a person may have learned in the past that aches, pains, and so on can be used to avoid unpleasant situations. (Timely headaches and stomachaches have "solved" a lot of problems over the years.) Later in life, this person may use somatic symptoms to avoid facing unpleasant or stressful situations. Moreover, people who are ill often enjoy a good deal of attention, support, and care, which is indirectly rewarding.

Now we turn to the biological perspective. Research has shown that at least some diagnosed somatoform disorders actually were real physical illnesses that were overlooked or misdiagnosed. For example, one set of follow-up studies indicated that some cases of "conversion disorder" eventually proved to be undiagnosed neurological problems such as epilepsy or multiple sclerosis (Shalev & Munitz, 1986). Still, most cases of conversion disorder cannot be explained by current medical science. These cases pose as much of a theoretical challenge today as they did when conversion disorders captured Freud's attention over a century ago.

Hypochondriasis A somatoform disorder in which a person interprets insignificant symptoms as signs of serious illness in the absence of any organic evidence of such illness.

Body dysmorphic disorder A somatoform disorder in which a person becomes so preoccupied with his or her imagined ugliness that normal life is impossible.

▬▬▬▬ CHECK YOUR UNDERSTANDING

1. Match the following terms with the appropriate description.

___somatoform disorder
   a. the person's interpretation of some small symptom as a sign of a serious disease

___body dysmorphic disorder
   b. recurring physical symptoms for which no organic cause is found

___conversion disorders
   c. imagined ugliness

___hypochondriasis
   d. condition in which sufferers have healthy muscles and nerves, yet their symptoms of paralysis, blindness, deafness, seizures, loss of feeling, or pregnancy are real

2. Freud called developing symptoms that allow a person to avoid an unpleasant activity

___a. a primary gain

___b. a secondary gain

___c. neither a primary nor secondary gain

Answers: 1. somatoform disorder—b; body dysmorphic disorder—c; conversion disorders—d; hypochondriasis—a, 2.b

Dissociative Disorders

Most patients with multiple personalities experienced childhood abuse. True or false?

Dissociative disorders are among the most puzzling forms of mental disorders, both to the observer and to the sufferer. *Dissociation* means that part of an individual's personality is separated, or dissociated, from the rest, and for some reason the person cannot reassemble the pieces. It usually involves memory loss and a complete—though generally temporary—change in identity. Rarely, several distinct personalities may be present in one person.

Dissociative Amnesia

Loss of memory without an organic cause may be a reaction to intolerable experiences. People often block out an event or a period of their lives that has been extremely stressful. During World War II, some hospitalized soldiers could not recall their names, where they lived, where they were born, or how they came to be in battle. But war and its horrors are not the only causes of **dissociative amnesia.** The man who betrays a friend to complete a business deal or the woman who has been raped may also forget—selectively—what has happened. Sometimes an amnesia victim leaves home and assumes an entirely new identity, although this phenomenon, known as **dissociative fugue,** is highly unusual.

Total amnesia, in which people forget everything, is quite rare, despite its popularity in novels and films. In one unusual case of fugue, the police picked up a 42-year-old man after he became involved in a fight with a customer at the diner where he worked. The man reported that he had no memory of his life before drifting into that town a few weeks earlier. Eventually, the authorities discovered that he matched the description of a missing person who had wandered from his home 200 miles away. Just before he disappeared, he had been passed over for promotion at work and had had a violent argument with his teenage son (Spitzer et al., 1981).

Dissociative disorders Disorders in which some aspect of the personality seems separated from the rest.

Dissociative amnesia A dissociative disorder characterized by loss of memory for past events without organic cause.

Dissociative fugue A dissociative disorder that involves flight from home and the assumption of a new identity, with amnesia for past identity and events.

Dissociative Identity Disorder

Even more bizarre than amnesia is **dissociative identity disorder**—commonly known as *multiple personality*—in which a person has several distinct personalities that emerge at different times. This dramatic disorder, which has been the subject of popular fiction and films, is thought by most psychologists to be extremely rare—although in recent years the number of cases appears to be increasing (Eich, Macaulay, Loewenstein, & Dihle, 1997). In the true multiple personality, the various personalities are distinct people, with their own names, identities, memories, mannerisms, speaking voices, and even IQs. Sometimes the personalities are so separate that they don't know they inhabit a body with other "people"; at other times, the personalities do know of the existence of other "people" and will even make disparaging remarks about them. Consider the case of Maud and Sara K., two personalities that coexisted in one woman:

> In general demeanor, Maud was quite different from Sara. She walked with a swinging, bouncing gait contrasted to Sara's sedate one. While Sara was depressed, Maud was ebullient and happy. . . . Insofar as she could Maud dressed differently from Sara. . . . Sara used no make-up. Maud used a lot of rouge and lipstick, [and] painted her fingernails and toenails deep red. . . . Sara was a mature, intelligent individual. Her mental age was 19.2 years, IQ, 128. A psychometric done on Maud showed a mental age of 6.6, IQ, 43. (Carson, Butcher, & Coleman, 1988, p. 206)

This case is typical in that the personalities contrasted sharply with each other. It is as if the two (and sometimes more) personalities represent different aspects of a single person—one the more socially acceptable, "nice" side of the person, the other the darker, more uninhibited or "evil" side.

The origins of dissociative identity disorder have long puzzled researchers and clinicians. One common suggestion is that it develops as a response to childhood abuse. The child learns to cope with abuse by a process of dissociation—by assigning the abuse, in effect, to "someone else," that is, to a personality who is not conscious most of the time (Putnam, Guroff, Silberman, Barban, & Post, 1986). The fact that one or more of the multiple personalities in almost every case is a child (even when the patient is an adult) seems to support this idea, and clinicians report a history of child abuse in over three-quarters of their cases of dissociative identity disorder (Ross, Norton, & Wozney, 1989).

Other clinicians suggest that dissociative identity disorder is not a real disorder at all but an elaborate kind of role playing—feigned in the beginning, and then perhaps genuinely believed in by the patient (Lilienfeld & Lynn, 2003; Mersky, 1992; Rieber, 1998). However, some intriguing biological data show that in at least some patients with dissociative identity disorder, the various personalities have different blood pressure readings, different responses to medication, different allergies, different vision problems (necessitating several pairs of glasses, one for each personality), and different handedness—all of which would be difficult to feign. Each personality may also exhibit distinctly different brain-wave patterns (Putnam, 1984).

Depersonalization Disorder

A far less dramatic (and much more common) dissociative disorder is **depersonalization disorder.** Its essential feature is that the person suddenly feels changed or different in a strange way. Some people feel they have left their bodies, others that their actions have suddenly become mechanical or dreamlike. A sense of losing control over one's own behavior is common, and it is not unusual to imagine changes in one's environment. This kind of feeling is especially common during adolescence and young adulthood, when our sense of ourselves and our interactions with others changes rapidly. Only when the sense of depersonalization becomes a

When she was found by a Florida park ranger, Jane Doe was suffering from amnesia. She could not recall her name, her past, or how to read and write. She never regained her memory of the past.

Dissociative identity disorder A dissociative disorder in which a person has several distinct personalities that emerge at different times.

Depersonalization disorder A dissociative disorder whose essential feature is that the person suddenly feels changed or different in a strange way.

long-term or chronic problem or when the alienation impairs normal social functioning can this be classified as a dissociative disorder (APA, 2000).

Causes of Dissociative Disorders

Dissociative disorders, like conversion disorders, seem to involve some kind of unconscious processes. The loss of memory is real in amnesia, fugue, and in many cases of multiple personality disorder as well. The patient often lacks awareness of the memory loss, and memory impairments usually cannot be overcome despite the patient's desire and effort to do so. Biological factors may also play a role in some cases. We know that dissociation and amnesia result from some physical processes: Memory impairments are commonly associated with aging and disorders such as Alzheimer's disease, and dissociative experiences are a common consequence of the ingestion of some drugs such as LSD. Trauma is a psychological factor that is of obvious importance in the onset of amnesia and fugue; it also appears to play a role in the development of dissociative identity disorder (Oltmanns & Emery, 2001). Nonetheless, we must admit that all these observations are only early leads in the fascinating mystery of what causes dissociative disorders.

CHECK YOUR UNDERSTANDING

1. Match the following terms with the appropriate description.

___ dissociative amnesia

    a. loss of memory without an organic cause, possibly in reaction to intolerable experiences

___ dissociative fugue

    b. state in which the person feels suddenly changed or different in a strange way that becomes a long-term or chronic problem

___ dissociative identity disorder

    c. a highly unusual amnesia in which the victim leaves home and assumes an entirely new identity

___ depersonalization disorder

    d. commonly known as multiple personality, a person has several different personalities that suddenly emerge at different times.

2. Researchers in their discussion of _____ cite child abuse and role-playing.

___a. dissociative amnesia

___b. dissociative identity disorder

___c. depersonalization disorder

Answers: 1. dissociative amnesia—a; dissociative fugue—c; dissociative identity disorder—d; depersonalization disorder—b, 2.b

Sexual Disorders

What is considered to be abnormal sexual behavior?

ENDURING ISSUES **diversity**universality

What's Normal?

Ideas about what is normal and abnormal in sexual behavior vary with the times, the individual, and, sometimes, the culture. Alfred Kinsey and his associates showed years ago (1948, 1953) that many Americans enjoy a variety of sexual activities, some of which were, and still are, forbidden by law. We know that there are a number of sexual universals that all people share, regardless of culture (D. E. Brown, 1991). These include great interest in sex, sexual attractiveness based on signs of health, avoidance of incest, and sexual relations carried out in private. So in spite of the wide variation in courtship and marriage customs and other sexual practices, some things remain universally human—and some are universally shunned. Throughout the late twentieth century, as psychologists became more aware of the diversity of "normal" sexual behaviors, they increasingly narrowed their definition of abnormal sexual behavior. Today the *DSM-IV-RT* recognizes only three main types of sexual disorders: sexual dysfunction, paraphilias, and gender-identity disorders. We will discuss each of these in turn.

Sexual Dysfunction

Sexual dysfunction is the loss or impairment of the ordinary physical responses of sexual function (see Figure 13–2). In men, this may take the form of **erectile disorder** or **erectile dysfunction (ED),** the inability to achieve or keep an erection. In women, it often takes the form of **female sexual arousal disorder,** the inability to become sexually excited or to reach orgasm. (These conditions were once called "impotence" and "frigidity," respectively, but professionals in the field have rejected these terms as negative and judgmental.) Occasional problems with achieving or maintaining an erection in men or with lubrication or reaching orgasm in women are common. Only when the problem is frequent or constant, and when enjoyment of sexual relationships becomes impaired, should it be considered serious.

Studies have shown that the incidence of ED is quite high, even among otherwise healthy men. One survey found, for example, that nearly 10 percent of 40- to 70-year-old men had complete ED, 25 percent moderate ED, and 17 percent minimal ED. Less than half the men in this age group reported having no ED (Lamberg, 1998). Fortunately, the medication *sildenafil citrate*, known popularly as *Viagra*, has been shown to be extremely effective in treating many men who have ED, regardless of whether the disorder has an organic or a psychological origin (Dinsmore et al., 1999; Goldstein et al., 1998; Marks, Duda, Dorey, Macairan, & Santos, 1999; also see Meston & Frohlich, 2000). Research has even demonstrated the effectiveness of Viagra in helping men with spinal cord injury regain a normal sex life (Derry et al., 1998).

Although Viagra appears to help most male patients overcome ED, it is of little value unless a man is first sexually aroused. Unfortunately, some men and women find it difficult or impossible to experience any desire for sexual activity to begin with. **Sexual desire disorders** involve a lack of interest in sex or perhaps an active distaste for it. Low sexual desire is more common among women than among men and plays a role in perhaps 40 percent of all sexual dysfunctions (Southern & Gayle, 1982). The extent and causes of this disorder in men or women is difficult to analyze, because some people simply have a low motivation for sexual activity; scant interest in sex is normal for them and does not necessarily reflect any sexual disorder (Beck, 1995). Others report no anxiety about or aversion to sex but exhibit physiological indicators of inhibited desire (Wincze, Hoon, & Hoon, 1978). This fact has led some researchers to conclude that the disorder is sometimes caused by a physical abnormality. In those people who report feeling neutral about sex or having an aversion to it, investigators suggest that the problem may have originated in earlier traumatic experiences or unfulfilling relationships.

Other people are able to experience sexual desire and maintain arousal but are unable to reach **orgasm,** the peaking of sexual pleasure and the release of sexual tension. These people are said to experience **orgasmic disorders.** Male orgasmic disorder—the inability to ejaculate even when fully aroused—is rare but seems to be becoming increasingly common as more men find it desirable to practice the delay

Sexual dysfunction Loss or impairment of the ordinary physical responses of sexual function.

Erectile disorder or erectile dysfunction (ED) The inability of a man to achieve or maintain an erection.

Female sexual arousal disorder The inability of a woman to become sexually aroused or to reach orgasm.

Sexual desire disorders Disorders in which the person lacks sexual interest or has an active distaste for sex.

Orgasm Peaking of sexual pleasure and release of sexual tension.

Orgasmic disorders Inability to reach orgasm in a person able to experience sexual desire and maintain arousal.

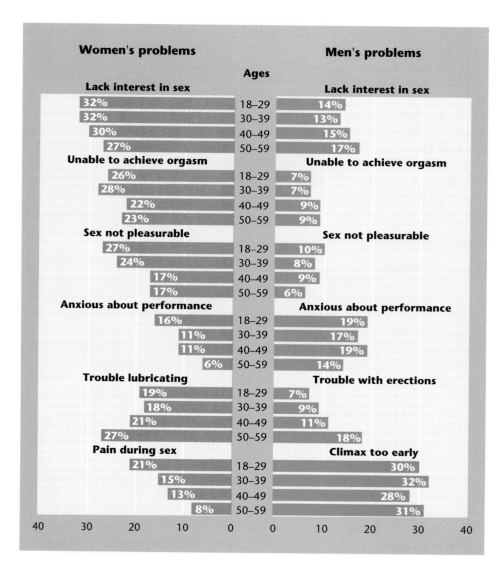

Figure 13–2
Sexual dysfunction in the United States.
This illustration shows the incidence of the most common types of sexual dysfunction in men and women, by age group.
Source: USA Today, May 18, 1999, p. 7D. Data from the National Health and Social Life Survey, published in the *Journal of the American Medical Association,* February 1999. Copyright 1999, *USA Today.* Reprinted with permission.

of orgasm (Rosen & Rosen, 1981). Masters and Johnson (1970) attributed male orgasmic disorder primarily to such psychological factors as traumatic experiences. The problem also seems to be a side effect of some medications, such as certain antidepressants. This difficulty is considerably more common among women than among men (see Figure 13–2).

Among the other problems that can occur during the sexual response cycle are **premature ejaculation,** a fairly common disorder that the *DSM-IV-RT* defines as the male's inability to inhibit orgasm as long as desired, and **vaginismus,** involuntary muscle spasms in the outer part of a woman's vagina during sexual excitement that make intercourse impossible. Again, the occasional experience of such problems is common; the *DSM-IV-RT* considers them dysfunctions only if they are "persistent and recurrent."

Paraphilias

A second group of sexual disorders, known as **paraphilias,** involves the use of unconventional sex objects or situations to obtain sexual arousal. Most people have unconventional sexual fantasies at some time, and this kind of fantasizing can be a healthy stimulant of normal sexual enjoyment. However, the repeated use of a non-human object—a shoe, for instance, or underwear—as the preferred or exclusive

Premature ejaculation Inability of man to inhibit orgasm as long as desired.

Vaginismus Involuntary muscle spasms in the outer part of the vagina that make intercourse impossible.

Paraphilias Sexual disorders in which unconventional objects or situations cause sexual arousal.

method of achieving sexual excitement is considered a sexual disorder known as **fetishism**. Fetishes are typically articles of women's clothing, or items made out of rubber or leather (Junginger, 1997; Mason, 1997). People with fetishisms are almost always male, and the fetish frequently begins during adolescence. At least one theorist has suggested that fetishes derive from unusual learning experiences: As their sexual drive develops during adolescence, some boys learn to associate arousal with inanimate objects, perhaps as a result of early sexual exploration while masturbating or because of difficulties in social relationships (Bertolini, 2001; Wilson, 1987).

Other unconventional patterns of sexual behavior are **voyeurism,** watching other people have sex or spying on people who are nude; achieving arousal by **exhibitionism,** the exposure of one's genitals in inappropriate situations, such as to strangers; **frotteurism,** achieving sexual arousal by touching or rubbing against a nonconsenting person in situations like a crowded subway car; and **transvestic fetishism,** wearing clothes of the opposite sex for sexual excitement and gratification. **Sexual sadism** ties sexual pleasure to aggression. To attain sexual gratification, sadists humiliate or physically harm sex partners. **Sexual masochism** is the inability to enjoy sex without accompanying emotional or physical pain. Sexual sadists and masochists sometimes engage in mutually consenting sex, but at times sadistic acts are inflicted on unconsenting partners.

One of the most serious paraphilias is **pedophilia,** which is technically defined as "recurrent, intense sexually arousing fantasies, sexual urges, or behaviors involving sexual activity with a prepubescent child" (APA, 1994, p. 528). Child sexual abuse has been found to be shockingly common in the United States. Moreover, evidence indicates that in most cases the person who commits the abuse is someone close to the child, not a stranger. According to one survey, 5 percent of adult women living in the San Francisco area reported that they had been forced into oral, anal, or genital intercourse by their father, stepfather, or brother during their childhood years (Russell, 1986). Other studies suggest that the frequency of sexual abuse of both male and female children is much higher than this (Finkelhor, Hotaling, Lewis, & Smith, 1990).

Pedophiles are almost invariably men under the age of 40 (Barbaree & Seto, 1997). Although there is no single cause of pedophilia, some of the most common explanations are: Pedophiles cannot adjust to the sexual role of an adult male and have been interested exclusively in children as sex objects since adolescence; they turn to children as sexual objects in response to stress in adult relationships in which they feel inadequate; they have records of unstable social adjustment and generally commit sexual offenses against children in response to a temporary aggressive mood. Studies also indicate that the majority of pedophiles have histories of sexual frustration and failure, tend to perceive themselves as immature, and are dependent, unassertive, lonely, and insecure (Cohen & Galynker, 2002).

Gender-Identity Disorders

Gender-identity disorders involve the desire to become—or the insistence that one really is—a member of the other biological sex. Some little boys, for example, want to be girls instead. They may reject boys' clothing, desire to wear their sisters' clothes, and play only with girls and with toys that are considered "girls' toys." In these cases, the diagnosis is **gender-identity disorder in children.** The same is true for girls who wear boys' clothing and play only with boys and "boys' toys." In all these cases, the children are uncomfortable with being a male or a female and are unwilling to accept themselves as such.

Most gender-identity disorders begin in childhood, and although many children with the disorder eventually develop normal gender identities, others carry the disorder into adult life. *Sexual reassignment surgery* (Hage, 1995) is one possible (and

Fetishism A paraphilia in which a non-human object is the preferred or exclusive method of achieving sexual excitement.

Voyeurism Desire to watch others having sexual relations or to spy on nude people.

Exhibitionism Compulsion to expose one's genitals in public to achieve sexual arousal.

Frotteurism Compulsion to achieve sexual arousal by touching or rubbing against a nonconsenting person in public situations.

Transvestic fetishism Wearing the clothes of the opposite sex to achieve sexual gratification.

Sexual sadism Obtaining sexual gratification from humiliating or physically harming a sex partner.

Sexual masochism Inability to enjoy sex without accompanying emotional or physical pain.

Pedophilia Desire to have sexual relations with children as the preferred or exclusive method of achieving sexual excitement.

Gender-identity disorders Disorders that involve the desire to become, or the insistence that one really is, a member of the other biological sex.

Gender-identity disorder in children Rejection of one's biological gender in childhood, along with the clothing and behavior society considers appropriate to that gender.

controversial) option for adults with gender-identity disorder: Surgical procedures, accompanied by hormonal treatments, are used to remove sex organs and create reasonable facsimiles of the organs of the opposite sex. Generally, people who have undergone sexual reassignment surgery are satisfied with the outcome. In addition, evidence from psychological tests indicate they experience reduced levels of anxiety and depression following the surgery (Bodlund & Kullgren, 1996).

The causes of gender-identity disorders are not known. Both animal research and the fact that these disorders are often apparent from early childhood suggest that biological factors are major contributors. In fact, some biologists believe that human gender identity exists along a continuum and that two sexes are not adequate to encompass human sexuality. As evidence, they cite the many babies born each year with ambiguous genitalia or whose genitalia do not match their chromosomal sex (Fausto-Sterling, 1993, 2000a, 2000b). However, family dynamics and learning experiences may also be contributing factors.

CHECK YOUR UNDERSTANDING

1. A paraphilia is

___a. a form of sexual dysfunction.

___b. a sexual attraction to unconventional objects.

___c. a type of sex reassignment surgery.

2. Erectile disorders in men and sexual arousal disorders in women are examples of

___a. sexual dysfunctions.

___b. paraphilias.

___c. gender identity disorders.

3. Biologists point to babies born with ambiguous genitalia as evidence

___a. that two sexes are not adequate to encompass human sexuality.

___b. of pedophilia.

___c. of sexual dysfunction.

Answers: 1.b, 2.a, 3.a

Personality Disorders

How do "personality disorders" differ from other psychological disorders?

In Chapter 11, Personality, we saw that personality is the individual's unique and enduring pattern of thoughts, feelings, and behavior. We also saw that, despite having certain characteristic views of the world and ways of doing things, people normally can adjust their behavior to fit the needs of different situations. But some people, starting at some point early in life, develop inflexible and maladaptive ways of thinking and behaving that are so exaggerated and rigid that they cause serious distress to themselves or problems to others. People with such **personality disorders** range from harmless eccentrics to cold-blooded killers. A personality disorder may also coexist with one of the other problems already discussed in this chapter; that is, someone with a personality disorder may also become depressed, develop sexual problems, and so on.

Personality disorders Disorders in which inflexible and maladaptive ways of thinking and behaving learned early in life cause distress to the person and/or conflicts with others.

Types of Personality Disorders

One group of personality disorders is characterized by odd or eccentric behavior. For example, people who exhibit **schizoid personality disorder** lack the ability or desire to form social relationships and have no warm or tender feelings for others. Such loners cannot express their feelings and are perceived by others as cold, distant, and unfeeling. Moreover, they often appear vague, absentminded, indecisive, or "in a fog." Because their withdrawal is so complete, persons with schizoid personality disorder seldom marry and may have trouble holding jobs that require them to work with or relate to others (APA, 2000).

People with **paranoid personality disorder** also exhibit odd behavior. They are suspicious and mistrustful even when there is no reason to be, and they are hypersensitive to any possible threat or trick. They refuse to accept blame or criticism even when it is deserved. They are guarded, secretive, devious, scheming, and argumentative, although they often see themselves as rational and objective.

Another cluster of personality disorders is characterized by anxious or fearful behavior. Among these are dependent personality disorder and avoidant personality disorder. People with **dependent personality disorder** are unable to make decisions on their own or to do things independently. They rely on parents, a spouse, friends, or others to make the major choices in their lives and usually are extremely unhappy being alone. Their underlying fear seems to be that they will be rejected or abandoned by important people in their lives. In **avoidant personality disorder,** the person is timid, anxious, and fearful of rejection. Not surprisingly, this social anxiety leads to isolation, but unlike the schizoid type, the person with avoidant personality disorder *wants* to have close relationships with other people.

Another cluster of personality disorders is characterized by dramatic, emotional, or erratic behavior. For example, people with **narcissistic personality disorder** display a grandiose sense of self-importance and a preoccupation with fantasies of unlimited success. (The word *narcissism* comes from a character in Greek mythology named Narcissus who fell in love with his own reflection in a pool and pined away because he could not reach the beautiful face he saw before him.) Such people believe they are extraordinary, need constant attention and admiration, display a sense of entitlement, and tend to exploit others. They are given to envy and arrogance and lack the ability to really care for anyone else (APA, 2000).

Psychologists know relatively little about the causes of most personality disorders, but some are better understood than others. One such is **borderline personality disorder,** which is characterized by marked instability—in self-image, mood, and interpersonal relationships. People with this personality disorder tend to act impulsively and often in self-destructive ways. They feel uncomfortable being alone, and they often manipulate their self-destructive impulses in an effort to control or solidify their personal relationships. Such self-destructive behavior includes promiscuity, drug and alcohol abuse, and threats of suicide (Gunderson, 1984, 1994).

Borderline personality disorder is both common and serious. The available evidence indicates that although it runs in families, genetics do not seem to play an important role in its development (Oltmanns & Emery, 2001). Instead, studies of people with borderline personality disorder point to the influence of dysfunctional relationships with their parents, including a pervasive lack of supervision, frequent exposure to domestic violence, and physical and sexual abuse (Guzder, Paris, Zelkowitz, & Marchessault, 1996). Moreover, it is often accompanied by mild forms of brain dysfunction (such as attention-deficit disorder), schizophrenic-like conditions, and mood disorders, which has led some psychologists to question whether borderline personality disorder should be considered a separate and distinguishable category of personality disorder (Akiskal, 1994; Tyrer, 1994). On the other hand,

Schizoid personality disorder
Personality disorder in which a person is withdrawn and lacks feelings for others.

Paranoid personality disorder
Personality disorder in which the person is inappropriately suspicious and mistrustful of others.

Dependent personality disorder
Personality disorder in which the person is unable to make choices and decisions independently and cannot tolerate being alone.

Avoidant personality disorder
Personality disorder in which the person's fears of rejection by others leads to social isolation.

Narcissistic personality disorder
Personality disorder in which the person has an exaggerated sense of self-importance and needs constant admiration.

Borderline personality disorder
Personality disorder characterized by marked instability in self-image, mood, and interpersonal relationships.

Antisocial personality disorder
Personality disorder that involves a pattern of violent, criminal, or unethical and exploitative behavior and an inability to feel affection for others.

People with antisocial personality disorder will lie, cheat, or kill without regret. Ted Bundy, shown here, was a serial killer who expressed no remorse for murdering as many as 50 women.

family studies show that relatives of people diagnosed as borderline individuals are much more likely to be treated for borderline disorder than for other types of personality disorders. This finding supports the position that borderline disorder is a legitimate category of personality disorder.

One of the most widely studied personality disorders is **antisocial personality disorder.** People who exhibit this disorder lie, steal, cheat, and show little or no sense of responsibility, although they often seem intelligent and charming on first acquaintance. The "con man" exemplifies many of the features of the antisocial personality, as does the person who compulsively cheats business partners because he or she knows their weak points. Antisocial personalities rarely show the slightest trace of anxiety or guilt about their behavior. Indeed, they are likely to blame society or their victims for the antisocial actions that they themselves commit.

Approximately 3 percent of American men and less than 1 percent of American women suffer from antisocial personality disorder. Not surprisingly, the prevalence of the disorder is high among prison inmates. One study categorized 50 percent of the populations of two prisons as having antisocial personalities (Hare, 1983). Not all people with antisocial personality disorder are convicted criminals, however. Many skillfully and successfully manipulate others for their own gain while steering clear of the criminal justice system.

Causes of Antisocial Personality Disorder

Because of the consequences for society, the causes of antisocial personality disorders have been studied much more extensively than the causes of other personality disorders. Antisocial personality disorder seems to result from a combination of biological predisposition, adverse psychological experiences, and an unhealthy social environment (Moffitt, 1993). Some findings suggest that heredity is a risk factor for the later development of antisocial behavior (Fu et al., 2002; Lyons et al., 1995). Impulsive violence and aggression have also been linked with abnormal levels of certain neurotransmitters (Virkkunen, 1983). Evidence suggests that in some people with antisocial personalities the autonomic nervous system is less responsive to stress (Patrick, 1994). Thus, they are more likely to engage in thrill-seeking behaviors, which can be harmful to themselves or others. In addition, because they respond less emotionally to stressful situations, punishment is less effective for them than for other people (Hare, 1993).

Another intriguing explanation for the cause of antisocial personality disorder is that it arises as a consequence of damage to the prefrontal region of the brain during infancy. One case study reported that two infants who had experienced damage to the prefrontal cortex prior to 16 months of age had defective social and moral reasoning and displayed no empathy as adults. Although these patients' cognitive abilities were not impaired, both appeared insensitive to the future consequences of their decisions. As adults, both patients were also compulsive liars and thieves and never expressed guilt or remorse for their actions (Anderson, Bechara, Damasio, Tranel, & Damasio, 1999).

Some psychologists feel that emotional deprivation in early childhood predisposes people to antisocial personality disorder. The child for whom no one cares, say

THINKING CRITICALLY

Causation

We have offered a number of different theories about the cause of antisocial personality disorder, all supported by research. Think about each of these theories and try to answer the following questions:

- To what extent do the different perspectives conflict? To what extent do they support one another?

- What kind of evidence—what kinds of research studies—is offered in support of each theory?

- Which theory would be most useful from a clinical, or treatment, point of view? Which would be most likely to spawn further research?

- Why do different theoretical perspectives exist?

psychologists, cares for no one. The child whose problems no one identifies with can identify with no one else's problems. Respect for others is the basis of our social code, but if you cannot see things from the other person's perspective, rules about what you can and cannot do will seem nothing more than an assertion of adult power to be defied as soon as possible.

Family influences may also prevent the normal learning of rules of conduct in the preschool and school years. Theorists reason that a child who has been rejected by one or both parents is not likely to develop appropriate social behavior. They also point out the high incidence of antisocial behavior in people with an antisocial parent and suggest that antisocial behavior may be partly learned and partly inherited from parents. Once serious misbehavior begins in childhood, there is an almost predictable progression: The child's conduct will result in rejection by peers and failure in school, followed by affiliation with other children who have behavior problems. By late childhood or adolescence, the deviant patterns that will later show up as a full-blown antisocial personality disorder are well established (Hill, 2003; Patterson, DeBaryshe, & Ramsey, 1989).

Cognitive theorists emphasize that in addition to the failure to learn rules and develop self-control, moral development may be arrested among children who are emotionally rejected and inadequately disciplined (Soyguet & Tuerkcapar, 2001). For example, between the ages of about 7 and 11, all children are apt to respond to unjust treatment by behaving unjustly toward someone else who is vulnerable. At about age 13, when they are better able to reason in abstract terms, most children begin to think more in terms of fairness than vindictiveness. This seems to be especially true if new cognitive skills and moral concepts are reinforced by parents and peers (Berkowitz & Gibbs, 1983).

CHECK YOUR UNDERSTANDING

1. Lifelong patterns of relatively "normal" but rigid and maladaptive behaviors are called

___a. schizophrenia

___b. personality disorders

___c. anxiety disorders

2. Match the following personality disorders with the appropriate description.

___schizoid personality disorder	a. shows instability in self-image, mood, and relationships
___paranoid personality disorder	b. is fearful and timid
___dependent personality disorder	c. is mistrustful even when there is no reason
___avoidant personality disorder	d. shows little sense of responsibility
___narcissistic personality disorder	e. exhibits extreme dramatic behavior and self-centeredness
___borderline personality disorder	f. lacks the ability to form social relationships
___antisocial personality disorder	g. is unable to make own decisions

Answers: 1.b. 2. schizoid personality disorder—f; paranoid personality disorder—c; dependent personality disorder—g; avoidant personality disorder—b; narcissistic personality disorder—e; borderline personality disorder—a; antisocial personality disorder—d

Schizophrenic disorders Severe disorders in which there are disturbances of thoughts, communications, and emotions, including delusions and hallucinations.

Hallucinations Sensory experiences in the absence of external stimulation.

Delusions False beliefs about reality that have no basis in fact.

Schizophrenic Disorders

Does schizophrenia refer to "split personality"?

A common misconception is that schizophrenia means split personality. This is not the case at all. As we have already seen, split personality (or multiple personality) is actually a dissociative identity disorder. The misunderstanding begins with the root *schizo*, which comes from the Greek verb meaning "to split." But what is split in schizophrenia is not so much personality as the connections among thoughts.

Schizophrenic disorders are severe conditions marked by disordered thoughts and communications, inappropriate emotions, and bizarre behavior that lasts for months, even years. People with schizophrenia are out of touch with reality, which is to say they are psychotic. Many also suffer from **hallucinations,** false sensory perceptions that usually take the form of hearing voices that are not really there. (Visual, tactile, or olfactory hallucinations are more likely to result from substance abuse or organic brain damage than from schizophrenia.) They also frequently have **delusions**—false beliefs about reality with no factual basis—that distort their relationships with their surroundings and with other people. Typically, these delusions are paranoid: People with schizophrenia believe that someone is out to harm them. They may think that a doctor wishes to kill them or that they are receiving radio messages from aliens invading from outer space. They often regard their own bodies—as well as the outside world—as hostile and alien. These distorted thoughts sometimes lead to self-destructive behaviors, increasing the risk of suicide (McGuire, 2000).

Because their world is utterly different from the one most people live in, people with schizophrenia usually cannot live anything like a normal life unless they are successfully treated with medication (see Chapter 14, Therapies). Often, they are unable to communicate with others, for when they speak, their words are incoherent. The following case illustrates some of the characteristic features of schizophrenia:

> For many years [a 35-year-old widow] has heard voices, which insult her and cast suspicion on her chastity. . . . The voices are very distinct, and in her opinion, they must be carried by a telescope or a machine from her home. Her thoughts are dictated to her; she is obliged to think them, and hears them repeated after her. She . . . has all kinds of uncomfortable sensations in her body, to which something

A young person suffering from schizophrenia painted this picture of the monsters he claimed to see in his room.

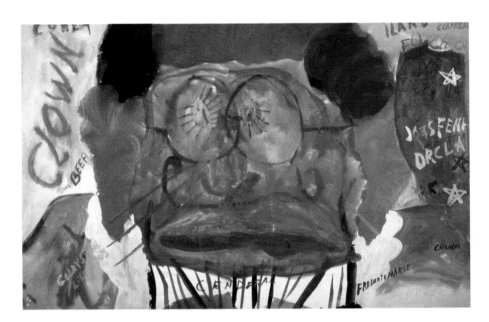

is "done." In particular, her "mother parts" are turned inside out, and people send a pain through her back, lay ice-water on her heart, squeeze her neck, injure her spine, and violate her. There are also hallucinations of sight—black figures and the altered appearance of people—but these are far less frequent. . . . (Spitzer et al., 1981, pp. 308–309)

There are actually several kinds of schizophrenic disorders, which have different characteristic symptoms.

Types of Schizophrenic Disorders

Disorganized schizophrenia includes some of the more bizarre symptoms of schizophrenia, such as giggling, grimacing, and frantic gesturing. People suffering from disorganized schizophrenia show a childish disregard for social conventions and may urinate or defecate at inappropriate times. They are active but aimless, and they are often given to incoherent conversations.

The primary feature of **catatonic schizophrenia** is a severe disturbance of motor activity. People with this disorder alternate between a *catatonic* state, in which they remain immobile, mute, and impassive, and an extremely active state, in which they become excessively excited, talking and shouting continuously. They may behave in a robotlike fashion when ordered to move, and some have even let doctors mold their arms and legs into strange and uncomfortable positions that they then manage to maintain for hours.

Paranoid schizophrenia is marked by extreme suspiciousness and complex delusions. People with paranoid schizophrenia may believe themselves to be Napoleon or the Virgin Mary, or they may insist that Russian spies with laser guns are constantly on their trail because they have learned some great secret. Because they are less likely to be incoherent or to look or act "crazy," these people can appear more "normal" than people with other schizophrenic disorders if their delusions are compatible with everyday life. However, they may become hostile or aggressive toward anyone who questions their thinking or tries to contradict their delusions. Note that this disorder is far more severe than paranoid personality disorder, which does not involve bizarre delusions or loss of touch with reality.

Finally, **undifferentiated schizophrenia** is the classification developed for people who have several of the characteristic symptoms of schizophrenia, such as delusions, hallucinations, or incoherence, yet who do not show the typical symptoms of any other subtype of the disorder.

Causes of Schizophrenia

Schizophrenia is a very serious disorder, and considerable research has been directed at trying to discover its causes. As we saw in Chapter 2, The Biological Basis of Behavior, a wide range of studies clearly show that schizophrenia has a genetic component (Gottesman, 1991). People with schizophrenia are more likely than other people to have children with schizophrenia, even when those children have lived with adoptive parents since early in life. And if one identical twin suffers from schizophrenia, the chances are about 50 percent that the other twin will also develop schizophrenia; but if a fraternal twin has schizophrenia, the chances are only about 15 percent that the other twin will also develop schizophrenia (see Figure 2–19).

These studies indicate that a biological predisposition to schizophrenia may be inherited. Recent research suggests that part of the problem may involve the faulty regulation of *dopamine* in the central nervous system, resulting in excessive accumulations of this neurotransmitter in critical regions of the brain (Koh et al., 2003). Drugs that alleviate schizophrenic symptoms also decrease the amount of dopamine in the brain and block dopamine receptors. On the other hand, amphetamines raise the amount of

Disorganized schizophrenia
Schizophrenic disorder in which bizarre and childlike behaviors are common.

Catatonic schizophrenia
Schizophrenic disorder in which disturbed motor behavior is prominent.

Paranoid schizophrenia
Schizophrenic disorder marked by extreme suspiciousness and complex, bizarre delusions.

Undifferentiated schizophrenia
Schizophrenic disorder in which there are clear schizophrenic symptoms that don't meet the criteria for another subtype of the disorder.

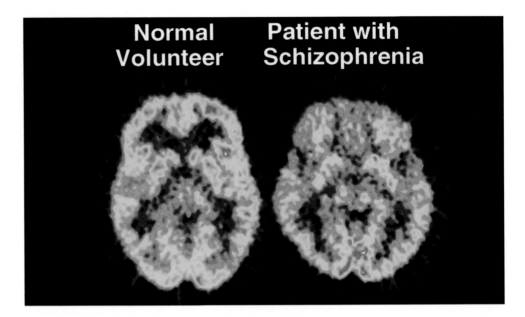

Normal Volunteer   Patient with Schizophrenia

PET scan of the brain of a patient with schizophrenia and the brain of a normal volunteer. Neuroimaging techniques often reveal important differences between the brains of patients with schizophrenia and normal volunteers. Still, neuroimaging does not provide a decisive diagnostic test for schizophrenia.

dopamine in the brain, aggravate schizophrenic symptoms, and, if taken in excess, lead to what is called *amphetamine psychosis*, which is very similar to schizophrenia.

Other research suggests that pathology in various structures of the brain plays a role in the onset of schizophrenia (van Elst & Trimble, 2003; Weinberger, 1997). For example, patients with schizophrenia have been shown to have enlarged *ventricles*, which are chambers in the brain that are filled with cerebrospinal fluid (Torrey, Bowler, Taylor, & Gottesman, 1994; Yotsutsuji et al., 2003). Because the largest ventricles are commonly seen in *chronic* or long-term cases of schizophrenia, researchers theorize that the ventricles may enlarge over the course of the illness as the neurons around these cavities degenerate (Zipursky, Lambe, Kapur, & Mikulis, 1998).

Other studies have focused on what appears to be an abnormal pattern of connections between cortical cells in patients with schizophrenia. Because these cortical connections are largely established during the prenatal period, this finding suggests that the onset of schizophrenia, which generally takes place in adulthood, may be traceable to some form of early prenatal disturbance (Wolf & Weinberger, 1996). Still, scientists have found only *average* differences in brain structure and chemistry between people with schizophrenia and healthy people (Noga, Bartley, Jones, Torrey, & Weinberger, 1996). In fact, studies of identical twins in which only one twin suffers from schizophrenia have sometimes found more evidence of brain abnormalities in the *well* twin than in the sick twin.

This finding brings us back to the research on genetics and schizophrenia. Although this point is often overlooked, studies of identical twins can also be used to identify the importance of *environment* in causing schizophrenia. How? Remember, half of the identical twins of people with schizophrenia do *not* develop schizophrenia themselves. Because identical twins are genetically identical, this means that this severe and puzzling disorder cannot be caused by genetic factors alone. Environmental factors—ranging from disturbed family relations to taking drugs to biological

THINKING CRITICALLY

Genius and Mental Disorders

Jean-Jacques Rousseau allegedly was paranoid. Mozart composed his Requiem while under the delusion that he was being poisoned. Van Gogh cut off his ear and sent it to a prostitute. Schopenhauer, Chopin, and John Stuart Mill were depressed. Robert Burns and Lord Byron apparently were alcoholics. Virginia Woolf suffered from bipolar disorder through her entire adult life.

- Do you think that creative people in general are more likely than others to suffer from psychological problems? What leads you to believe as you do?

- What evidence would you need to have in order to answer this question in a scientific way?

damage at any age, even before birth—must also figure in determining whether a person will develop schizophrenia.

Some psychologists regard family relationships as an important factor in the development of schizophrenia. The evidence regarding this position is mixed. Recent research has discovered that patients with schizophrenia whose families display high levels of negative *expressed emotion* are rehospitalized at twice the average rate for people with this disorder (Kavanagh, 1992). Moreover, treatments designed to reduce negative expressed emotion in the families of people with schizophrenia have reduced the rates of rehospitalization. Though it is still not clear how—or if—family variables such as expressed emotion combine with biological predispositions to cause some people to develop schizophrenia, research in this area continues (Subotnik, Goldstein, Nuechterlein, Woo, & Mintz, 2002).

A number of studies have demonstrated a relationship between social class and schizophrenia (Neale & Oltmanns, 1980). The prevalence of schizophrenia is decidedly higher in the lower social classes. One theory holds that lower-class socioeconomic environments—which offer little education, opportunity, or reward and put considerable stress on individuals—are a cause of schizophrenia. Another theory speculates that the symptoms of schizophrenia cause people to drift downward into the lower socioeconomic classes. There appears to be some truth to both theories.

Although they obviously differ greatly in emphasis, the various explanations for schizophrenic disorders are not mutually exclusive. Although genetic factors are universally acknowledged, many theorists believe that it takes a combination of biological, psychological, and social factors to produce schizophrenia (Gottesman, 1991). According to the systems model, genetic factors predispose some people to schizophrenia, and family interaction and life stress activate the predisposition.

CHECK YOUR UNDERSTANDING

1. Match the following terms with the appropriate description.

___ disorganized schizophrenia   a. is marked by extreme suspiciousness and complex delusions

___ catatonic schizophrenia   b. has bizarre symptoms that may include giggling, grimacing, frantic gesturing, and a childish disregard for social conventions

___ paranoid schizophrenia   c. is marked by a severe disturbance of motor activity

___ undifferentiated schizophrenia   d. is found in people who have several characteristic symptoms of schizophrenia but do not show the typical symptoms of any other subtype

2. If one identical twin suffers from schizophrenia, the chances are about _____ that the other twin will develop schizophrenia.

___a. 15 percent

___b. 50 percent

___c. 100 percent

3. If one fraternal twin has schizophrenia, the chances are about _____ that the other twin will develop it.

___a. 15 percent

___b. 50 percent

___c. 100 percent

Answers: 1. disorganized schizophrenia—b; catatonic schizophrenia—c; paranoid schizophrenia—a; undifferentiated schizophrenia—d, 2.b, 3.a

Attention-deficit/hyperactivity disorder (AD/HD) A childhood disorder characterized by inattention, impulsiveness, and hyperactivity.

Psychostimulants Drugs that increase ability to focus attention in children with AD/HD.

Childhood Disorders

Children can suffer from many of the conditions we have been discussing—depression and anxiety disorders, for example—but other disorders are either characteristic of children or are first evident in childhood. The *DSM-IV-RT* contains a long list of "disorders usually first diagnosed in infancy, childhood, or adolescence." Two of these disorders are attention-deficit/hyperactivity disorder and autistic disorder.

Attention-Deficit/Hyperactivity Disorder (AD/HD)

Attention-deficit/hyperactivity disorder was once known simply as *hyperactivity*. The new name reflects the fact that children with the disorder typically lack the ability to focus their attention in the sustained way that other children do. Instead, they are easily distracted, often fidgety and impulsive, and almost constantly in motion. Many theorists believe that this disorder—which affects nearly 5 percent of all school-aged children and is much more common in boys than girls—is present at birth but becomes a serious problem only after the child starts school. The classroom setting demands that children sit quietly, pay attention as instructed, follow directions, and inhibit urges to yell and run around; the child with AD/HD simply cannot conform to these demands.

Although the causes of AD/HD are not fully understood, most theorists believe that biological factors such as anomalies in the central nervous system or heredity are important in its development. Consistent with this idea, researchers have identified small but significant differences in the structure and functioning of the brains of children with AD/HD (Filipek et al., 1997; Vaidya et al., 1998). Family interaction and other social experiences may be more important in preventing the disorder than in causing it. That is, some exceptionally competent parents as well as patient, tolerant teachers may be successful in teaching "difficult" children to conform their behavior to the rather stringent demands of schooling. Some psychologists train the parents of AD/HD children in these management skills, but the most frequent treatment for these children is a type of drug known as a **psychostimulant**. Psychostimulants do not work by "slowing down" hyperactive children; rather, they appear to increase the children's ability to focus their attention. This enables them to attend to the task at hand, which decreases their hyperactivity (Barkley, 1990). Unfortunately, psychostimulants often produce only short-term benefits.

The use of psychostimulants to treat AD/HD does have its critics, however. Panksepp (1998) argues that these drugs simply reduce a child's natural biological tendencies to engage in rough and tumble play, and that drugs should not be used to inhibit such *natural* activities. Instead, Panksepp believes that if schools provided children with more spaces and opportunities to express their vigorous playfulness, they may see a decrease in the incidence of AD/HD.

THINKING CRITICALLY

AD/HD

When AD/HD was first conceptualized at the turn of the twentieth century, the estimated prevalence was not more than 1 percent. As of 1995, prevalence in the United States was at least 5 percent and rising (Armstrong, 1995; Panksepp, 1998). What do you think accounts for this dramatic rise? Is it a true change in incidence, perhaps resulting from environmental or biological changes that affect children's functioning? Or is it an artifact of changing social expectations of children?

- In the United States, incidence is estimated at more than 5 percent of children, but in Britain, the estimate is less than 1 percent (Jacobson, 1999). What do you think could account for this difference? What research evidence would you need in order to know whether your theory is correct?

- Researchers claim that play and physical activity are basic needs of young mammals, similar to the need for food and fluids (Panksepp, Siviy, & Normansell, 1984; Vanderschuren, Niesink, & Van Ree, 1997). Could what we call AD/HD be a normal variation of this need? In other words, is it possible that many children diagnosed with AD/HD merely have an increased need for play? How might you go about collecting evidence to determine if your view is correct?

Autistic Disorder

A very different, and profoundly serious, disorder that is first evident in childhood is **autistic disorder.** Autism is present in about one in 500 children (Filipek et al., 2000) and affects three to four times as many boys as girls (Rodier, 2000). Autistic children are usually identified as such in the first few years of life. They fail to form normal attachments to parents, remaining distant and seemingly withdrawn into their own separate worlds. As infants, they may even show distress at being picked up or held. As they grow older, they often do not develop speech, or they develop a peculiar speech pattern called *echolalia*, in which they repeat the words said to them. Autistic children typically show strange motor behavior, such as repeating body movements endlessly or walking constantly on tiptoe. Their play is not like that of normal children. They are not at all social and may use toys in odd ways, such as constantly spinning the wheels on a toy truck or tearing paper into strips. Autistic children often appear to have mental retardation, but it is hard to test their mental ability because they are frequently nonverbal. This disorder lasts into the adulthood in the great majority of cases.

The precise cause of autism is unknown, although most theorists believe that it results almost entirely from biological conditions. Some causes of mental retardation, such as fragile X syndrome (see Chapter 8, Intelligence and Mental Abilities), also seem to increase the risk of autistic disorder. Recent evidence suggests that autism may result from faulty development of brain stem structures during the early prenatal period (Rodier, 2000). Considerable evidence indicates that genetics also plays a strong role in causing this disorder (Bailey et al., 1995; Cook et al., 1998; Lamb, Moore, Bailey, & Monaco, 2000; Rodier, 2000).

Autistic disorder A childhood disorder characterized by a lack of social instincts and strange motor behavior.

In the classroom children with AD/HD have more difficulty than other children sitting still, paying attention, and following instructions.

CHECK YOUR UNDERSTANDING

1. Failure to form normal attachments to parents, lack of social instincts, and strange motor behavior are characteristic of

___a. disorganized schizophrenia

___b. AD/HD

___c. autistic disorder

___d. borderline personality disorder

2. Easily distracted, often fidgety and impulsive, and almost constantly in motion describe children who have

___a. disorganized schizophrenia

___b. AD/HD

___c. autistic disorder

___d. borderline personality disorder

Answers: 1.c, 2.b

Gender and Cultural Differences in Psychological Disorders

What are the differences between men and women in psychological disorders?

Gender Differences

For the most part, men and women are similar with respect to mental disorders, but differences do exist. Many studies have concluded that women have a higher rate of psychological disorders than men do, but this is an oversimplification (see Culbertson, 1997; Lerman, 1996; Hartung & Widiger, 1998). We do know that more women than men are *treated* for mental disorders. Indeed, as one expert observed, "Women have always been the main consumers of psychotherapy from Freud's era onward" (Williams, 1987, p. 465). But this cannot be taken to mean that more women than men have mental disorders, for in our society, it is much more acceptable for women to discuss their emotional difficulties and to seek professional help openly. It may be that mental disorders are equally common among men—or even more common—but that men do not so readily show up in therapists' offices and therefore are not counted in the studies (for further discussion see Lerman, 1996).

Moreover, those mental disorders for which there seems to be a strong biological component, such as bipolar disorder and schizophrenia, are distributed fairly equally between the sexes. Differences tend to be found for those disorders *without* a strong biological component—that is, disorders in which learning and experience play a more important role. For example, men are more likely than women to suffer from substance abuse and antisocial personality disorder. Women, on the other hand, are more likely to suffer from depression, agoraphobia, simple phobia, obsessive-compulsive disorder, and somatization disorder (Basow, 1986; Douglas, Moffitt, Dar, McGee, & Silva, 1995; Russo, 1990). These tendencies, coupled with the fact that gender differences observed in the United States are not always seen in other cultures (Culbertson, 1997), suggest that socialization plays a part in developing a disorder: When men display abnormal behavior, it is more likely to take the forms of drinking too much and acting aggressively; when women display abnormal behavior, they are more likely to become fearful, passive, hopeless, and "sick" (Basow, 1986).

One commonly reported difference between the sexes concerns marital status. Men who are separated or divorced or who have never married have a higher incidence of mental disorders than do either women of the same marital status or married men. But married women have higher rates than married men. What accounts for the apparent fact that marriage is psychologically less beneficial for women than for men?

Here, too, socialization appears to play a role. For women, marriage, family relationships, and child rearing are likely to be more stressful than they are for men (Basow, 1986). For men, marriage and family provide a haven; for women, they are a demanding job. In addition, women are more likely than men to be the victims of incest, rape, and marital battering. As one researcher has commented, "for women, the U.S. family is a violent institution" (Koss, 1990).

For some married women, employment outside the home seems to provide the kind of psychological benefits that marriage apparently provides for many men. However, these benefits are likely to be realized only if the woman freely chooses to work, has a satisfying job, receives support from family and friends, and is able to set up stable child-care arrangements (Basow, 1986; Hoffman, 1989). For women who enter the workforce because they have to rather than because they want to, whose work is routine or demeaning, or who are responsible for all domestic duties as well as their outside jobs, economic pressures and the stress of performing two demanding roles can be additional risk factors for psychological disorder.

We saw in Chapter 12 that the effects of stress are greater to the extent that a person feels alienated, powerless, and helpless. Alienation, powerlessness, and helplessness are more prevalent in women than in men. They are especially common factors among minority women, so it is not surprising that the prevalence of psychological disorders is greater among these women than among other women (Russo & Sobel, 1981). And alienation, powerlessness, and helplessness play an especially important role in anxiety disorders and depression—precisely those disorders experienced most often by women (Kessler et al., 1994). A 1990 report by a task force of the American Psychological Association noted that the rate of depression among women is twice that of men and ascribed that difference to the more negative and stressful aspects of women's lives, including lower incomes and the experiences of bias and physical and sexual abuse (APA, 1990).

In summary, women do seem to have higher rates of anxiety disorders and depression than men do, and they are more likely than men to seek professional help for their problems. However, greater stress, due in part to socialization and lower status rather than psychological weakness, apparently accounts for this statistic. Marriage and family life, associated with lower rates of mental disorders among men, introduce additional stress into the lives of women, particularly young women (25 to 45), and in some instances this added stress translates into a psychological disorder.

ENDURING ISSUES   **diversity**universality

Are We All Alike?

The frequency and nature of some psychological disorders vary significantly among the world's different cultures (López & Guarnaccia, 2000). This suggests that many disorders have a strong cultural component, or that diagnosis is somehow related to culture. On the other hand, disorders that are known to have a strong genetic component generally display a more uniform distribution across different cultures.

Cultural Differences

As the U.S. population becomes more diverse, it is increasingly important for mental health professionals to be aware of cultural differences if they are to understand and diagnose disorders among people of various cultural groups. Many disorders occur only in particular cultural groups. For example, *ataque de nervios*—literally translated as "attack of nerves"—is a culturally specific phenomenon that is seen predominately among Latinos. The symptoms of *ataque de nervios* generally include the feeling of being out of control, which may be accompanied by fainting spells, trembling, uncontrollable screaming and crying, and, in some cases, verbal or physical aggressiveness. Afterwards, many patients display amnesia of the attack, and quickly return to normal functioning. Another example, called *taijin kyofusho* (roughly translated as "fear of people"), involves a morbid fear that one's body or actions may be offensive to others. *Taijin kyofusho* is rarely seen outside of Japan. Other cross-cultural investigations have found differences in the course of schizophrenia and in the way childhood psychological disorders are manifest between different cultures (López & Guarnaccia, 2000; Weisz, McCarty, Eastman, Chaiyasit, & Suwanlert, 1997).

For some psychological disorders, the prevalence among males and females also differs markedly among countries. For instance, in the United States and most developed nations, females generally display a markedly higher incidence of depression than males. But in many underdeveloped countries of the world, such as Iran, Uganda, or Nigeria, very little or no gender difference in the incidence of depression is found (Culbertson, 1997).

Prevalence of childhood disorders also differs markedly by culture. Of course, it is adults—parents, teachers, counselors—who decide whether a child is suffering from a psychological disorder, and those decisions are likely to be influenced by cultural expectations. For example, in a series of cross-cultural studies, Thai children were more likely to be referred to mental health clinics for internalizing problems, such as anxiety and depression, compared to U.S. children, who were more likely to be referred for externalizing problems, such as aggressive behavior (Weisz, McCarty, Eastman, Chaiyasit, & Suwanlert, 1997).

CHECK YOUR UNDERSTANDING

1. Of the two genders, which one undergoes more treatment for mental disorders?

_____a. men

_____b. women

_____c. neither; both spend equal amounts of time in therapy

2. Married women have _____ incidences of mental disorder than married men.

_____a. higher

_____b. lower

_____c. the same

Answers: 1.b, 2.a

summary

Perspectives on Psychological Disorders

Whether an individual suffers from an emotional disorder is, at least in part, a subjective judgment. Mental health professionals define abnormal behavior as either maladaptive life functioning or serious personal discomfort or both.

Historical Views of Psychological Disorders   In early societies mysterious actions were often attributed to supernatural powers. The roots of a more naturalistic view of psychological disorders can be traced to Hippocrates, who maintained that madness was like any other sickness—a natural event arising from natural causes. This approach to mental illness fell into disfavor in the Middle Ages, and it was not until the nineteenth century that it again received systematic scientific attention.

Theories of the Nature, Causes, and Treatment of Psychological Disorders   Three influential, conflicting models of psycholog-ical disorders emerged during the late 1800s and early 1900s: the biological, psychoanalytic, and cognitive-behavioral models. The **biological model** states that psychological disorders have a physiological basis. The **psychoanalytic model** developed by Freud, states that psychological disorders are a symbolic expression of unconscious mental conflicts that generally can be traced to early childhood or infancy. The **cognitive-behavioral model** states that psychological disorders are the result of learning maladaptive ways of behaving and proposes that what has been learned can be unlearned. Cognitive-behavioral therapists therefore strive to modify both dysfunctional behavior and inaccurate cognitive processes in their patients. The model has been criticized for its extreme emphasis on environmental causes and treatments.

The most promising recent development in abnormal psychology is the integration of the major approaches. The **diathesis-stress model**, for example, states that psychological disorders develop when a **diathesis** (biological predisposition to the disorder) is set off by a stressful circumstance. The **systems approach** (also known as the *biopsychosocial approach to psychological disorders*) states that biological, psychological, and social risk factors combine to produce psychological disorders. According to this model, emotional problems are "lifestyle diseases" that are caused by a combination of biological risks, psychological stresses, and societal pressures and expectations.

Classifying Psychological Disorders For nearly 40 years, the American Psychiatric Association has published an official manual describing and classifying the various kinds of psychological disorders. This publication, the *Diagnostic and Statistical Manual of Mental Disorders (DSM)*, has gone through four editions. The current version, known as the *DSM-IV-RT,* provides careful descriptions of symptoms of different disorders, but includes little on causes and treatments.

The Prevalence of Psychological Disorders The *prevalence* of a disorder refers to the frequency of the disorder at a given time. The *incidence* of a disorder refers to the number of new cases that arise in a given period of time. Approximately 15 percent of Americans suffer from mental disorders at any given time.

Mental Illness and the Law A mentally ill person is responsible for his or her crimes unless he or she is determined to be insane. **Insanity** is a legal term referring to an individual who is not considered responsible for their criminal actions as a result of a mental illness.

Mood Disorders

Mood disorders are characterized by disturbances in mood or prolonged emotional state.

Depression The most common mood disorder is **depression,** a state in which a person feels overwhelmed with sadness, loses interest in activities, and displays other symptoms such as excessive guilt or feelings of worthlessness. The *DSM-IV-RT* distinguishes between two forms of depression. *Major depressive disorder* is an episode of intense sadness that may last for several months; in contrast, *dysthymia* involves less intense sadness but persists with little relief for a period of two years or more. Some depressions become so intense that people become **psychotic**—that is, lose contact with reality.

Mania and Bipolar Disorder Another, less common mood disorder is mania. People suffering from **mania** become euphoric ("high"), extremely active, excessively talkative, and easily distractible. Manic episodes rarely appear by themselves; rather, they usually alternate with depression. Such a mood disorder, in which both mania and depression are alternately present, sometimes interrupted by periods of normal mood, is known as **bipolar disorder.**

Causes of Mood Disorders Most psychologists believe that mood disorders result from a combination of biological, psychological, and social factors. Biological factors seem to play an important role in the development of depression and, especially, bipolar disorder. But just as biology affects psychological experience, so does psychological experience alter biological functioning. **Cognitive distortions,** illogical and maladaptive responses to early negative life events, can lead to feelings of incompetence that are reactivated whenever a new situation arises that resembles the original events. This psychological factor has been found to operate in many de-

pressed people, though it is uncertain whether the cognitive distortions cause the depression or are caused by it. Finally, social factors such as troubled relationships have been linked with mood disorders.

Suicide Suicide is the 11th leading cause of death in the United States. Although the largest number of suicides occurs among older white males, adolescents account for 12 percents of all suicide attempts. People considering suicide are overwhelmed with hopelessness. Suicide is depression in the extreme, and getting professional help is urgent.

Anxiety Disorders

In **anxiety disorders,** a person's anxiety is inappropriate to the circumstances.

Specific Phobias Anxiety disorders have been subdivided into many specific diagnostic categories. One familiar subtype is **specific phobia,** an intense, paralyzing fear of something that it is unreasonable to fear so excessively. Another subtype is **social phobia**—excessive, inappropriate fears connected with social situations or performances in front of other people. **Agoraphobia** is a less common and much more debilitating type of anxiety disorder that involves multiple, intense fears such as the fear of being alone or of being in public places or other situations that require separation from a source of security.

Panic Disorder **Panic disorder** is characterized by recurrent *panic attacks*, which are sudden, unpredictable, and overwhelming experiences of intense fear or terror without any reasonable cause.

Other Anxiety Disorders **Generalized anxiety disorder** is defined by prolonged vague but intense fears that are not attached to any particular object or circumstance. **Obsessive-compulsive disorder** involves either involuntary thoughts that keep recurring despite the person's attempt to stop them or compulsive rituals that a person feels compelled to perform. Two other types of anxiety disorder are caused by highly stressful events. If the anxious reaction occurs soon after the event, the diagnosis is *acute stress disorder;* if it occurs long after the event is over, the diagnosis is *post-traumatic stress disorder.*

Causes of Anxiety Disorders Some theorists believe phobias are prepared responses that evolution has made us biologically predisposed to acquire. Cognitive psychologists have suggested that people who believe they have no control over stressful events in their lives are more likely to suffer from anxiety. Psychologists with a biological perspective propose that a predisposition to anxiety disorders may be inherited because these types of disorders tend to run in families. Psychoanalytic theorists have focused on internal psychological conflicts as the source of anxiety disorders.

Psychosomatic and Somatoform Disorders

Psychosomatic Disorders **Psychosomatic disorders** are illnesses that have a valid physical basis but are largely caused by psychological factors such as stress and anxiety. In fact, many physicians now recognize that nearly every physical disease can be linked to psychological stress in the sense that such stress can negatively affect body chemistry, organ functioning, and the immune system.

Somatoform Disorders **Somatoform disorders** are characterized by physical symptoms without any identifiable physical cause. **Somatization disorder** is defined by vague, recurring, physical symptoms (such as back pains, dizziness, and abdominal pains) for which medical attention has been sought repeatedly but no organic cause found. Sufferers from **conversion disorders** have a dramatic specific disability for which there is no physical cause. In **hypochondriasis,** the person interprets some small symptom as a sign of a serious disease. **Body dysmorphic disorder,** or imagined ugliness, is a type of somatoform disorder characterized by extreme dissatisfaction with some part of one's appearance.

Causes of Somatoform Disorders Freud concluded that somatoform disorders were related to traumatic experiences in a patient's past. Cognitive behavioral therapists look for ways in which the symptomatic behavior is being rewarded. In some cases, diagnosed somatoform disorders were real physical illnesses that were overlooked or misdiagnosed.

Dissociative Disorders

In **dissociative disorders,** some part of an individual's personality or memory is separated from the rest.

Dissociative Amnesia **Dissociative amnesia** involves the loss of at least some significant aspects of memory. When an amnesia victim leaves home and assumes an entirely new identity, the disorder is known as **dissociative fugue.**

Dissociative Identity Disorder In **dissociative identity disorder**—commonly known as multiple personality—a person has several distinct personalities that emerge at different times.

Depersonalization Disorder In **depersonalization disorder,** the person suddenly feels changed or different in a strange way.

Causes of Dissociative Disorders Dissociative disorders seem to involve unconscious processes, and biological factors may also play a role in some cases.

Sexual Disorders

The *DSM-IV-RT* recognizes three main types of sexual disorders: sexual dysfunction, paraphilias, and gender-identity disorders.

Sexual Dysfunction **Sexual dysfunction** is the loss or impairment of the ability to function effectively during sex. In men, this may take the form of **erectile disorder,** the inability to achieve or keep an erection; in women, it often takes the form of **female sexual arousal disorder,** the inability to become sexually excited or to reach orgasm. **Sexual desire disorders** are those in which the person either lacks sexual interest or has an active aversion to sex. People with **orgasmic disorders** experience both desire and arousal but are unable to reach **orgasm.** Other problems that can occur include **premature ejaculation**—the male's inability to inhibit orgasm as

long as desired—and **vaginismus**—involuntary muscle spasms in the outer part of a woman's vagina during sexual excitement that make intercourse impossible.

Paraphilias **Paraphilias** involve the use of unconventional sex objects or situations. These disorders include **fetishism, voyeurism, exhibitionism, frotteurism, transvestic fetishism, sexual sadism,** and **sexual masochism.** One of the most serious paraphilias is **pedophilia,** the desire to have sexual relations with children.

Gender-Identity Disorders **Gender-identity disorders** involve the desire to become, or the insistence that one really is, a member of the other sex. **Gender-identity disorder in children** is characterized by rejection of one's biological gender as well as the clothing and behavior society considers appropriate to that gender during childhood.

Personality Disorders

Personality disorders are enduring, inflexible, and maladaptive ways of thinking and behaving that are so exaggerated and rigid that they cause serious inner distress and/or conflicts with others.

Types of Personality Disorders One group of personality disorders is characterized by odd or eccentric behavior. For example, people who exhibit **schizoid personality disorder** lack the ability or desire to form social relationships and have no warm feelings for other people; those with **paranoid personality disorder** are inappropriately suspicious of others. Another cluster of personality disorders is characterized by anxious or fearful behavior. Examples are **dependent personality disorder** (inability to make decisions or do things independently) and **avoidant personality disorder** (social anxiety leading to isolation). A third cluster of personality disorders is characterized by dramatic, emotional, or erratic behavior. For example, people with **narcissistic personality disorder** display a grandiose sense of self-importance. **Borderline personality disorder** is characterized by a marked instability in self-image, mood, and interpersonal relationships. People with **antisocial personality disorder** lie, steal, cheat, and show little or no sense of responsibility.

Causes of Antisocial Personality Disorder Antisocial personality disorder seems to result from a combination of biological predisposition, adverse psychological experiences, and an unhealthy social environment.

Schizophrenic Disorders

Schizophrenic disorders are severe conditions marked by disordered thoughts and communications, inappropriate emotions, and bizarre behavior that lasts for years. People with schizophrenia are out of touch with reality and usually cannot live anything like a normal life unless they are successfully treated with medication. They often suffer from **hallucinations** (false sensory perceptions) and **delusions** (false beliefs about reality).

Types of Schizophrenic Disorders There are several kinds of schizophrenic disorders, including **disorganized schizophrenia, catatonic schizophrenia, paranoid schizophrenia,** and **undifferentiated schizophrenia.**

Causes of Schizophrenia   Research indicates that a biological predisposition to schizophrenia may be inherited. Part of the problem may lie in excessive amounts of dopamine in the central nervous system; pathology in various structures of the brain may also play a role. The development of schizophrenia may be influenced by environmental factors such as family relationships and social class. According to the systems model, genetic factors predispose some people to schizophrenia, and family interaction and life stress activate the predisposition.

Childhood Disorders

The *DSM-IV-RT* contains a long list of disorders usually first diagnosed in infancy, childhood, or adolescence.

Attention-Deficit/Hyperactivity Disorder   Children diagnosed with **attention-deficit/hyperactivity disorder** (AD/HD) are easily distracted, often fidgety and impulsive, and almost constantly in motion. The most frequent treatment for children with AD/HD is the use of **psychostimulants,** drugs that increase the children's ability to focus their attention.

Autistic Disorder   **Autistic disorder,** a profoundly serious problem identified in the first few years of life, is characterized by a failure to form normal attachments to parents, lack of social instincts, and strange motor behavior.

Gender and Cultural Differences in Psychological Disorders

Gender Differences   Studies have concluded that women have a higher rate of psychological disorders than men do, especially for the mood and anxiety disorders. There is controversy about what accounts for these differences, but it seems both socialization and biology play important roles.

Cultural Differences   Many disorders occur only in particular cultural groups. The prevalence of some disorders among males and females and in children also differs markedly by culture.

key terms

Biological model	487	Hypochondriasis	503	Sexual masochism	509
Psychoanalytic model	488	Body dysmorphic disorder	503	Pedophilia	509
Cognitive-behavioral model	488	Dissociative disorders	504	Gender-identity disorders	509
Diathesis-stress model	489	Dissociative amnesia	504	Gender-identity disorder in children	509
Diathesis	489	Dissociative fugue	504	Personality disorders	510
Systems approach	489	Dissociative identity disorder	505	Schizoid personality disorder	511
Insanity	491	Depersonalization disorder	505	Paranoid personality disorder	511
Mood disorders	492	Sexual dysfunction	507	Dependent personality disorder	511
Depression	492	Erectile disorder or erectile		Avoidant personality disorder	511
Psychotic	493	dysfunction (ED)	507	Narcissistic personality disorder	511
Mania	493	Female sexual arousal disorder	507	Borderline personality disorder	511
Bipolar disorder	493	Sexual desire disorders	507	Antisocial personality disorder	512
Cognitive distortions	495	Orgasm	507	Schizophrenic disorders	514
Anxiety disorders	498	Orgasmic disorders	507	Hallucinations	514
Specific phobia	498	Premature ejaculation	508	Delusions	514
Social phobia	499	Vaginismus	508	Disorganized schizophrenia	515
Agoraphobia	499	Paraphilias	508	Catatonic schizophrenia	515
Panic disorder	499	Fetishism	509	Paranoid schizophrenia	515
Generalized anxiety disorder	499	Voyeurism	509	Undifferentiated schizophrenia	515
Obsessive-compulsive disorder (OCD)	500	Exhibitionism	509	Attention-deficit/hyperactivity disorder	
Psychosomatic disorders	501	Frotteurism	509	(AD/HD)	518
Somatoform disorders	501	Transvestic fetishism	509	Psychostimulants	518
Somatization disorder	502	Sexual sadism	509	Autistic disorder	519
Conversion disorders	502				

Insight Therapies
Psychoanalysis
Client-Centered Therapy
Gestalt Therapy
Recent Developments

Behavior Therapies
Using Classical Conditioning
Techniques
Operant Conditioning
Modeling

Cognitive Therapies
Stress-Inoculation Therapy
Rational-Emotive Therapy
Beck's Cognitive Therapy

Group Therapies
Family Therapy
Couple Therapy
Self-Help Groups

Effectiveness of Psychotherapy
Does Psychotherapy Work?
Which Type of Therapy Is Best
for Which Disorder?

Biological Treatments
Drug Therapies
Electroconvulsive Therapy
Psychosurgery

Institutionalization and Its Alternatives
Deinstitutionalization
Alternative Forms of Treatment
Prevention

Gender and Cultural Differences in Treatments
Gender Differences
Cultural Differences

14

Therapies

•n anxious man lies on a couch in his analyst's office and reveals his innermost dreams and fantasies. During the course of his therapy session, the hostility that he harbored toward his father as a child is unleashed. The analyst, who is seated behind him, remains silent.

• A two-pack-a-day smoker, who is determined to stop, attends weekly behavior therapy sessions. Her therapist provides concrete suggestions to help her learn how to break the smoking habit.

• A 28-year-old computer programmer is disabled by severe depression after the loss of her job. She has convinced herself that she is incompetent, and will never have a successful career. Her therapist helps her to reevaluate her situation more realistically, accepting the loss of her job as a temporary career setback rather than as a statement about her personal worth.

• A young man suffering from bipolar disorder is given a prescription for lithium, a drug that relieves his symptoms. His therapist has tried to treat him with other forms of therapy, but all have failed.

As you can see from these examples, **psychotherapy** takes many forms—literally hundreds of variations practiced by several different types of mental health professionals. Some types of psychotherapy occur outside the therapist's office, as clients confront their fears in real life. Other psychotherapies treat couples or entire families, and still others treat groups of people with similar problems or goals.

In this chapter we will take a close look at the major types of therapy, such as the insight therapies and the newer, shorter-term therapies, including behavioral and cognitive therapies. We will also explore biological or drug therapy, in which a physician attempts to treat the biological basis of the person's symptoms. We will also examine research comparing the effectiveness of different forms of psychotherapies and take an especially close look at the important issues of institutionalization, deinstitutionalization, and prevention.

Our review of individual psychotherapies follows the sequence of their historical development. Insight therapies were developed early in the twentieth century, followed by behavior therapies in the 1960s and 1970s, and more recently by cognitive therapies and biological therapies.

Insight Therapies

What is the common element in all insight therapies? How prevalent is insight therapy today?

While differing in their details, the common goal of various **insight therapies** is to give people a better awareness and understanding of their feelings, motivations, and actions, in the hope that this will lead to better adjustment (Pine, 1998). In this section, we consider three major insight therapies as well as some recent developments in the area.

Psychoanalysis

Psychoanalysis is designed to bring repressed feelings and thoughts to conscious awareness so the person can deal with them more effectively. In Freudian psychoanalysis, the client is instructed to talk about whatever comes to mind, with as little

THINKABOUTIT

You will find the answers to these questions in the chapter:

1. What is the common element in all insight therapies? How prevalent is insight therapy today?

2. How can a therapist "teach" you to overcome a phobia?

3. How can people overcome irrational and self-defeating beliefs about themselves?

4. How does group therapy help the individual members to function more effectively?

5. Is psychotherapy effective?

6. What are the benefits of taking drugs for psychological disorders? What are the possible drawbacks?

7. How can mental illness be prevented?

8. Should therapy for men and women be different?

Psychotherapy The use of psychological techniques to treat personality and behavior disorders.

Insight therapies A variety of individual psychotherapies designed to give people a better awareness and understanding of their feelings, motivations, and actions in the hope that this will help them adjust.

To encourage patients to relax, Freud had them recline on the couch in his study while he sat out of view. You can see this couch if you visit Freud's historic home in Vienna.

editing as possible and without inhibiting or controlling thoughts and fantasies. This process is called **free association.** Freud believed that the resulting "stream of consciousness" would provide insight into the person's unconscious mind. During the early stages of psychoanalysis, the analyst remains impassive, mostly silent, and out of the person's sight. The analyst's silence is a kind of "blank screen" onto which the client eventually projects unconscious thoughts and feelings.

The interview that follows is characteristic of the early stages of psychoanalysis and demonstrates free association. The analyst remains fairly quiet while the client, a 32-year-old male teacher with recurring headaches, talks about whatever occurs to him:

Patient: This is like my last resort. I've been to so many doctors for this headache. But I tell you . . . I don't want . . . I know that there's something wrong with me though. I've known it since I was a kid. Like I started to tell you, when I was 17, I knew there was something wrong with me, that . . . and I told my father that I needed to see a doctor, and he laughed at me and said it was just foolishness, but he agreed to take me to his doctor, Dr. _____ on 125th Street, and I never went in; I chickened out.

Therapist: You chickened out, then. How'd you feel about that chickening out?

Patient: I don't know. I don't feel proud that I wasn't able to talk over these . . . this feeling I had . . . I wouldn't have wanted my father to know about my . . . some of my problems. 'Cause my father, he just . . . you know, I told him, my father, that there was something wrong, that I needed help, and he'd laugh at me and, you know, just to pacify me, you know, he took me to Dr. _____, but I didn't know Dr. _____. He was a friend of my father's, yeah, I don't know if . . . I don't remember thinking about it, but if I had talked to Dr. _____ about my problems like the problems I talk about in here, and my father found out, he might get pretty mad. Yeah.

Therapist: Well, this would be insulting to him? He'd feel it would be a bad reflection on his upbringing of you, if you went to a doctor like this? Would this humiliate him?

Patient: Yeah. I've got . . . My father and I didn't get along too well, and to tell the truth, I was ashamed of my father. He was born in Poland, and he was a self-made man. He went to the University of Warsaw and then Fordham. He was a pharmacist, but he was . . . he didn't care how he dressed. He was all sloppy and dirty, and he was short. He's about five foot one and stoop-shouldered . . . We used to go to restaurants, my mother and him and me, and he would never leave a tip, never leave a tip, never leave a tip. I used to sneak back and I'd throw a few cents that I might have on the table, but he was so stingy, so tight. When we went on a train, when we went somewhere, I would try to pretend I wasn't with them. I'd want . . . I'd go in another . . . I do need some help, and I know I've got to do the talking. That's the hardest part for me, that you won't give me any guidelines, that I have to do everything myself, and you'll analyze me . . . I didn't ever think I'd . . . I didn't want to think I was gonna end up here. I hate to think that this is the problem, but. . . . (Hersher, 1970, pp. 135–139)

Analysis typically proceeds very slowly. After the initial awkwardness wears off, many people enjoy having the chance to talk without interruption and appreciate having someone interested in their problems. Eventually, they may test their analyst by talking about desires and fantasies they have never revealed to anyone else. But the analyst maintains neutrality throughout the process, showing little of his or her own feelings and personality. When people discover that their analyst is not shocked or disgusted by their revelations, they are reassured and project on their

Free association A psychoanalytic technique that encourages the client to talk without inhibition about whatever thoughts or fantasies come to mind.

analyst feelings they have toward authority figures from their childhood—a process known as **transference.** When the client feels good about the analyst, the process is called *positive transference.*

As people continue to expose their innermost feelings, they begin to feel increasingly vulnerable. They want reassurance and affection, but their analyst remains silent. Their anxiety builds. Threatened by their analyst's silence and by their own thoughts, clients may feel cheated and perhaps accuse their analyst of being a money-grabber. Or they may suspect that their analyst is really disgusted by their disclosures or is laughing about them behind their backs. This *negative transference* is thought to be a crucial step in psychoanalysis, for it presumably reveals clients' negative feelings toward authority figures and their resistance to uncovering their repressed emotions.

As therapy progresses, the analyst takes a more active role and begins to *interpret* or suggest alternative meanings for clients' feelings, memories, and actions. The goal of interpretation is to help clients gain **insight**—to become aware of what was formerly outside of their awareness. As what was unconscious becomes conscious, clients may come to see how their childhood experiences have determined how they feel and act now. Analysts encourage clients to confront childhood events and recall them fully. As clients relive their childhood traumas, they become able to resolve conflicts they could not resolve in the past. *Working through* old conflicts is thought to provide people with the chance to review and revise the feelings and beliefs that underlie their problems.

Our description up to this point applies to traditional, or orthodox, psychoanalysis. But only a handful of people who seek therapy go into traditional analysis. As Freud himself recognized, analysis requires great motivation to change and an ability to deal rationally with whatever the analysis uncovers. Moreover, orthodox analysis may take 5 years or longer, and most traditional analysts feel that at least three, and sometimes five, sessions a week are essential. Few people can afford this lengthy treatment. Fewer still possess the verbal and analytical skills necessary to discuss thoughts and feelings in this detailed way. Another disadvantage of this therapy is that it does not give immediate help for immediate problems. Finally, psychoanalysis is not effective with severely disturbed clients. All of these drawbacks led, over the second half of the twentieth century, to the modification of psychoanalytic techniques and the development of less demanding, shorter-term types of therapy. We turn to some of these in the next sections.

Client-Centered Therapy

Carl Rogers, the founder of **client-centered (or person-centered) therapy,** took bits and pieces of the neo-Freudians' views and revised and rearranged them into a radically different approach to therapy. According to Rogers, the goal of therapy is to help people become fully functioning, to open them up to all of their experiences and to all of themselves. Such inner awareness is a form of insight, but for Rogers, it was more important to gain insight into current feelings than into unconscious wishes with roots in the distant past. Rogers called his approach to therapy *client-centered* because he placed the responsibility for change on the person with the problem.

Rogers's ideas about therapy are quite specific. As we saw in Chapter 11, Personality, Rogers believed that people's defensiveness, rigidity, anxiety, and other signs of discomfort stem from their experiences of *conditional positive regard.* They have learned that love and acceptance are contingent on conforming to what other

Transference The client's carrying over to the analyst feelings held toward childhood authority figures.

Insight Awareness of previously unconscious feelings and memories and how they influence present feelings and behavior.

Client-centered (or person-centered) therapy Nondirectional form of therapy developed by Carl Rogers that calls for unconditional positive regard of the client by the therapist with the goal of helping the client become fully functioning.

people want them to be. Therefore, the cardinal rule in person-centered therapy is for the therapist to express *unconditional positive regard*—that is, to show true acceptance of clients no matter what they may say or do. Rogers felt that this was a crucial first step toward getting clients to accept themselves.

Rather than taking an objective approach, Rogerian therapists try to understand things from the clients' point of view. They are also emphatically *nondirective*. They do not suggest reasons why clients feel as they do or how they might better handle a difficult situation. Instead, they try to reflect clients' statements, sometimes asking questions and sometimes hinting at feelings that clients have not put into words. Rogers felt that when therapists provide an atmosphere of openness and genuine respect, clients can find themselves.

The following excerpt conveys the nondirective approach of client-centered therapy. The therapist is far more active and understanding than the traditional analyst, but always follows the client's lead in therapy.

> *Client:* I guess I do have problems at school. . . . You see, I'm chairman of the Science Department, so you can imagine what kind of a department it is.
>
> *Therapist:* You sort of feel that if you're in something that it can't be too good. Is that. . . .
>
> *Client:* Well, it's not that I. . . . It's just that I'm . . . I don't think that I could run it.
>
> *Therapist:* You don't have any confidence in yourself?
>
> *Client:* No confidence, no confidence in myself. I never had any confidence in myself. I—like I told you—like when even when I was a kid I didn't feel I was capable and I always wanted to get back with the intellectual group.
>
> *Therapist:* This has been a long-term thing, then, it's gone on a long time.
>
> *Client:* Yeah, the feeling is—even though I know it isn't, it's the feeling that I have that—that I haven't got it, that—that—that—people will find out that I'm dumb or—or. . . .
>
> *Therapist:* Masquerade. . . .
>
> *Client:* Superficial, I'm just superficial. There's nothing below the surface. Just superficial generalities, that. . . .
>
> *Therapist:* There's nothing really deep and meaningful to you. (Hersher, 1970, pp. 29–32)

Rogers was not interested in comparing his therapy to others, nor was he concerned simply with statistics on outcomes (such as the percentage of clients who recovered). Rather, he wanted to discover what processes or events in client-centered therapy were associated with positive outcomes. Rogers's interest in the process of therapy resulted in important and lasting contributions to the field. For example, it has been found that a therapist's warmth and understanding increase success, no matter what therapeutic approach is used (Frank & Frank, 1991).

Gestalt therapy, which we will discuss next, differs from both classical psychoanalysis and from client-centered therapy in several important ways.

Gestalt Therapy

Gestalt therapy An insight therapy that emphasizes the wholeness of the personality and attempts to reawaken people to their emotions and sensations in the here-and-now.

Gestalt therapy is largely an outgrowth of the work of Frederick (Fritz) Perls at the Esalen Institute in California. Perls began his career as a psychoanalyst but later turned vehemently against Freud and psychoanalytic techniques. He felt that "Freud invented the couch because he could not look people in the eye" (Perls, 1969, p. 118). Gestalt therapy emphasizes the here-and-now and encourages face-to-face confrontations.

Gestalt therapy is designed to help people become more genuine or "real" in their day-to-day interactions. It may be conducted with individuals or with groups ("encounter groups"). The therapist is active and directive, and the emphasis in Gestalt therapy is on the *whole* person, the Gestalt (see Chapter 3, Sensation and Perception). The therapist's role, as Perls describes it, is to "fill in the holes in the personality to make the person whole and complete again" (Perls, 1969, p. 2).

Gestalt therapists try to make people aware of their feelings and to awaken them to sensory information they have been ignoring. They use many techniques to accomplish this. For example, people may be told to "own their feelings" by talking in an active rather than a passive way ("I feel angry when he's around" instead of "He makes me feel angry when he's around"). In this way, Gestalt therapists remind clients that they alone are responsible for their feelings and, ultimately, for their lives. Another method commonly used in Gestalt therapy is the *empty chair technique*. Clients are asked to speak to a part of themselves they imagine to be sitting next to them in an empty chair. The objective is to get clients to become more aware of their conflicting inner feelings and, with this insight, to become more genuine. The empty chair technique and other Gestalt methods are illustrated in the following excerpt.

Therapist: Try to describe just what you are aware of at each moment as fully as possible. For instance, what are you aware of now?

Client: I'm aware of wanting to tell you about my problem, and also a sense of shame—yes, I feel very ashamed right now.

Therapist: Okay. I would like you to develop a dialogue with your feeling of shame. Put your shame in the empty chair over here (indicates chair), and talk to it.

Client: Are you serious? I haven't even told you about my problem yet.

Therapist: That can wait—I'm perfectly serious, and I want to know what you have to say to your shame.

Client: (*awkward and hesitant at first, but then becoming looser and more involved*) Shame, I hate you. I wish you would leave me—you drive me crazy, always reminding me that I have a problem, that I'm perverse, different, shameful—even ugly. Why don't you leave me alone?

Therapist: Okay, now go to the empty chair, take the role of shame, and answer yourself back.

Client: (*moves to the empty chair*) I am your constant companion—and I don't want to leave you. I would feel lonely without you, and I don't hate you. I pity you, and I pity your attempts to shake me loose, because you are doomed to failure.

Therapist: Okay, now go back to your original chair and answer back.

Client: (*once again as himself*) How do you know I'm doomed to failure? (*Spontaneously shifts chairs now, no longer needing direction from the therapist; answers himself back, once again in the role of shame.*) I know that you're doomed to failure because I want you to fail and because I control your life. You can't make a single move without me. For all you know, you were *born* with me. You can hardly remember a single moment when you were without me, totally unafraid that I would spring up and suddenly remind you of your loathsomeness. (Shaffer, 1978, pp. 92–93)

In this way the client becomes more aware of conflicting inner feelings and, with insight, can become more genuine. As we have seen, psychoanalysis, client-centered therapy, and Gestalt therapy differ in their techniques, but all use talk to help people become more aware of their feelings and conflicts, and all involve fairly substantial amounts of time. We turn now to more recent developments in therapy that seek to limit the amount of time people spend in therapy.

Short-term psychodynamic psychotherapy Insight therapy that is time-limited and focused on trying to help people correct the immediate problems in their lives.

Recent Developments

Although Freud, Rogers, and Perls originated the three major forms of insight therapy, other therapists have developed hundreds of variations on those themes. Even among mainstream psychoanalysts, there has been considerable divergence from the traditional form of "couch" psychotherapy. Most present-day insight-oriented therapists are far more active and emotionally engaged with their clients than traditional orthodox psychoanalysts thought fit. And in recent years, virtual therapy, a controversial development, has taken hold (see *On the Cutting Edge: Virtual Therapy*).

Another general trend in recent years is toward shorter-term "dynamic therapy" for most people—usually occurring once a week for a fixed period. In fact, **short-term psychodynamic psychotherapy** is increasingly popular among both clients

ON THE CUTTING EDGE

VIRTUAL THERAPY

For a hundred years or so, people who wanted to see a therapist have literally gone to *see* a therapist—they have taken the time and trouble to visit the therapist's office, plunked themselves down on a couch or chair, and talked through their problems, receiving, if all went well, the benefits of the therapeutic relationship. In recent years, some people who were forced to travel away from home to see a therapist have been able to connect with their therapists by telephone. Today, some people even visit their therapists via cyberspace. The delivery of health care over the Internet, or through other electronic means such as a telephone, is part of a rapidly expanding field known as *telehealth.*

There are some obvious benefits to on-line psychotherapy or counseling. First, some people literally do not want to be *seen* by their therapist or group members—think of a self-help group for people with cleft palates, or a person with an eating disorder who is uncomfortable with her appearance (Hamilton, 1999). Since it is well known that a stigma is associated with receiving treatment for a mental health problem, anonymity can be an important virtue.

While most professional therapists believe that on-line therapy is no substitute for the real thing (Almer, 2000; Rabasca, 2000b), some evidence suggests that telehealth may provide new and cost-effective opportunities for the delivery of mental health services. For example, one study (Schopp, Johnstone, & Merrell, 2000) compared satisfaction with neuropsychological assessments performed either in person or on-line. No differences were found between on-line clients and matched in-person controls on ratings of interpersonal factors. Moreover, the cost of the telehealth assessment was significantly lower than in-person costs, and the telehealth clients reported being more willing to repeat their experience.

Telehealth has also been used to provide access to services for people who live in remote areas (Rabasca, 2000c; Stamm et al., 2003). Dr. Stephen Sulzbacher uses a teleconferencing studio at the University of Washington to work with children who live in remote rural areas in Washington State, Wyoming, Alaska, Montana, and Idaho, who would be unable to obtain psychological services without the use of technology. Dr. Sulzbacher holds virtual office hours every Monday afternoon and does approximately 30 video visits each year. He also uses technology, such as videoconferencing, e-mail and fax, to mentor other health-care professionals who work with children in the field. In Kentucky, a university based telehealth system has been established to provide psychological services to school systems in rural communities (Miller et al., 2003). The Federal Bureau of Prisons has asked correctional psychologists to begin using telehealth techniques to provide behavioral interventions for mentally ill inmates (Magaletta, Fagan, & Peyrot, 2000). Telehealth has even been used effectively by the military to help obese soldiers lose weight (James, Folen, & Earles, 2001).

By far the most common use of technology is plain old telephone contact, which is used by approximately 85 percent of psychologists, with the most common use being for client referrals (Williams, 2000). However, almost 70 percent of psychologists who use the telephone also use it for individual psychotherapy. Another survey of 596 practicing psychologists found that while the use of the telephone in the delivery of clinical services was almost universal, about 2 percent had also used the Internet or satellite to deliver clinical services (VandenBox & Williams, 2000). Clearly, this is an area where research is needed to determine under what, if any, circumstances virtual therapy is effective (Krupinski et al., 2002; Rabasca, 2000d). The one thing that is clear so far is that such services will proliferate in the future.

and mental health professionals (Olfson, Marcus, Druss, & Pincus, 2002; Winston & Winston, 2002). Insight remains the goal, but the treatment is usually time-limited—for example, to 25 sessions. With the trend toward shorter therapy, insight therapies have also become more problem- or symptom-oriented. Although therapists do not discount the impact of early childhood experiences, the focus more often is on the person's current life situation and relationships. In addition, most contemporary therapists give clients more direct guidance and feedback, commenting on what they are told rather than just listening to their clients in a neutral manner.

Even more notable than the trend toward shorter-term therapy has been the proliferation of behavior therapies in the past few decades. In the next section of the chapter, we examine several types of behavior therapy.

CHECK YOUR UNDERSTANDING

1. Which of the following is the major goal of working through problems in psycho-analysis?

___a. free association

___b. positive transference

___c. countertransference

___d. insight

2. Insight therapies focus on giving people

___a. skills to change their behavior

___b. clearer understanding of their feelings, motives, and actions

___c. an understanding of perceptual processes

___d. an understanding of biological influences on behavior

3. Match the name in the left-hand column to the type of therapy he founded.

___ Frederick Perls	a. client-centered therapy
___ Sigmund Freud	b. Gestalt therapy
___ Carl Rogers	c. psychoanalysis

Answers: 1.d, 2.b, 3. Frederick Perls—b; Sigmund Freud—c; Carl Rogers—a

Behavior Therapies

How can a therapist "teach" you to overcome a phobia?

Behavior therapies sharply contrast with insight-oriented approaches in several important ways. First, behavior therapists are more active than insight therapists; second, they concentrate on changing people's *behavior* rather than on increasing their insight into their thoughts and feelings; and finally, they typically operate within an even shorter time frame.

Behavior therapies are based on the belief that all behavior, both normal and abnormal, is learned. Hypochondriacs *learn* that they get attention when they are sick; people with paranoid personalities *learn* to be suspicious of others. The therapist does not need to know exactly how or why a client learned to behave abnormally in the first place. The job of the behavior therapist is simply to teach the person new, more satisfying ways of behaving.

Behavior therapies Therapeutic approaches that are based on the belief that all behavior, normal and abnormal, is learned, and that the objective of therapy is to teach people new, more satisfying ways of behaving.

Learning to overcome a fear of flying through desensitization: Relaxing in the cockpit of an airplane that is safely on the ground.

Behavior therapies also differ from insight therapies in that they attempt to apply basic findings from psychological science, particularly research on learning processes (see Chapter 5, Learning), to the treatment of clinical problems (Onken & Blaine, 1997; Tryon, 2000). Thus, many behavior therapy techniques are simply applications of behavioral concepts discussed in earlier chapters of this text, such as classical and operant conditioning and modeling.

Using Classical Conditioning Techniques

As we saw in Chapter 5, Learning, *classical conditioning* involves the repeated pairing of a conditioned stimulus with an unconditioned stimulus. If the conditions are right, the conditioned stimulus will eventually produce a conditioned response on its own. Several variations on the classical conditioning approach have been used to treat psychological problems. We will discuss two major types: desensitization, including extinction and flooding; and aversive conditioning.

Desensitization, Extinction, and Flooding Systematic desensitization, a method for gradually reducing fear and anxiety, is one of the oldest behavior therapy techniques (Wolpe, 1990). The method works by gradually associating a new response (relaxation) with stimuli that have been causing anxiety. For example, an aspiring politician might seek therapy because he is anxious about speaking to crowds. The therapist looks for more details, asking whether the man feels more threatened by an audience of 500 than by an audience of 50, more tense when addressing men than when speaking to both men and women, and so on. The first step is for the therapist and client to develop a *hierarchy of fears*—a list of situations from the least to the most anxiety-provoking for the client. Next, the therapist teaches the person how to relax: to clear his or her mind, to release tense muscles, and to be able to produce this relaxation response readily.

Once the client has mastered the technique of deep relaxation, he or she begins work at the bottom of the hierarchy of fears. The person is told to imagine the least threatening situation on the list and to signal when he feels the least bit tense. At the signal, the therapist tells the person to forget the scene and to concentrate on relaxing. After a short time, the therapist instructs the client to imagine the scene again. This process is repeated until the person feels completely relaxed when imagining that scene. Then the therapist moves on to the next situation in the client's hierarchy of fears and trains the person to be completely relaxed when imagining that situation as well. Therapist and client advance up the hierarchy in this way until finally the person can imagine the most fearful situation at the top of the hierarchy without experiencing any anxiety whatsoever.

Numerous studies indicate that systematic desensitization helps many people overcome their fears and phobias (Wang & Chen, 2000; Wolpe, 1990). Research suggests, however, that the key to desensitization's success may not be the learning of a new conditioned relaxation response but rather the *extinction* of the old fear response through mere exposure: If a person repeatedly imagines a frightening situation without actually encountering danger, the fear or anxiety associated with that situation should gradually decline.

Flooding is a less familiar, and more aggressive, method of desensitization through exposure (O'Leary & Wilson, 1987; Wolpe, 1990). For example, someone with a powerful fear of snakes might be forced immediately to handle dozens of snakes; or someone with an overwhelming fear of spiders might be forced to stroke a tarantula and allow it to crawl up his or her arm.

Aversive Conditioning Another classical conditioning technique aimed at eliminating undesirable behavior patterns is **aversive conditioning,** in which therapists teach clients to associate pain and discomfort with the behavior that they want to

Systematic desensitization A behavioral technique for reducing a person's fear and anxiety by gradually associating a new response (relaxation) with stimuli that have been causing the fear and anxiety.

Aversive conditioning Behavioral therapy techniques aimed at eliminating undesirable behavior patterns by teaching the person to associate them with pain and discomfort.

unlearn. This form of therapy has been used with limited success to treat alcoholism, obesity, smoking, and some psychosexual disorders. Some clinics, for example, treat alcoholism by pairing the taste and smell of alcohol with drug-induced nausea and vomiting. Before long, clients feel sick just seeing a bottle of liquor. A follow-up study of nearly 800 people who completed alcohol-aversion treatment at one clinic in 1978 and 1979 found that 63 percent had maintained continuous abstinence for at least 12 months after treatment (Wiens & Menustik, 1983). Still, the use of aversive conditioning has declined in recent years because of questions about its long-term effectiveness. Moreover, aversive conditioning is a controversial technique because of its unpleasant nature though it is worth considering the life impairment that can be caused by some disorders that are resistant to other forms of therapy.

Operant Conditioning

As we also saw in Chapter 5, Learning, *operant conditioning* techniques are based on the idea that a person learns to behave in different ways when new behaviors are reinforced and old ones ignored or punished. In one form of operant conditioning, **behavior contracting,** the therapist and the client agree on behavioral goals and on the reinforcement that the client will receive when the goals are reached. This agreement often takes the form of a written contract that specifies the behaviors to be followed, the penalties for not following them, and any privileges to be earned. One such contract might be: "For each day that I smoke fewer than 20 cigarettes, I will earn 30 minutes of time to go bowling. For each day that I smoke more than 20 cigarettes, I will lose 30 minutes from the time that I have accumulated." Behavior contracting has also been used effectively in the school system to assist children with emotional and behavior difficulties. Here the contracts specify which negative behaviors (such as aggressiveness or disruptiveness) will be followed by penalities, and which positive behaviors (such as completing class work on time, or classroom participation) will be followed by reward (Ruth, 1996).

Another form of operant conditioning is called the **token economy.** As we mentioned in the chapter on learning, token economies are usually employed in institutions like schools and hospitals, where controlled conditions are most feasible (Comaty, Stasio, & Advokat, 2001; O'Leary & Wilson, 1987). People earn tokens or points for behaviors that are considered appropriate and adaptive; in turn, the tokens or points can be exchanged for desired items and privileges. On the ward of a mental hospital, for example, improved grooming habits might earn points that can be used to purchase special foodstuffs or weekend passes. Token economies have proved effective in modifying the behavior of people who are resistant to other forms of treatment, such as people with chronic schizophrenia (Kopelowicz, Liberman, & Zarate, 2002; Paul, 1982). Although token economies can work in institutions, the positive changes do not always generalize to everyday life outside the hospital or clinic, where adaptive behavior is not always reinforced with tokens and maladaptive behavior is not always ignored or punished.

Modeling

The behavior therapies we have discussed so far rely on classical and operant conditioning principles to change behavior. But as we saw in Chapter 5, Learning, much human behavior is learned by **modeling**—the process of learning a behavior by watching someone else perform it. Modeling can also be used to treat problem behaviors. One experiment tried to help people overcome snake phobia by having them view films in which models confronted snakes and gradually moved closer and closer to them (Bandura, Blanchard, & Ritter, 1969). The researchers reported a

Ads such as this use classical conditioning to link unpleasant stimuli with undesirable behavior.
Source: © 1986 Bonnie Vierthaler/The BADvertising Institute.

Behavior contracting Form of operant conditioning therapy in which the client and therapist set behavioral goals and agree on reinforcements the person will receive upon reaching those goals.

Token economy An operant conditioning therapy in which clients earn tokens (reinforcers) for desired behaviors and exchange them for desired items or privileges.

Modeling A behavior therapy in which the person learns desired behaviors by watching others perform those behaviors.

notable reduction in the observers' fear of snakes. Similar techniques have succeeded in reducing such common phobias as fear of dental work (Melamed, Hawes, Heiby, & Glick, 1975). Moreover, a combination of modeling and positive reinforcement was successful in helping people with schizophrenia learn and use appropriate behavior both inside and outside the hospital (Bellack, Hersen, & Turner, 1976). Modeling has also been used extensively to teach people with mental retardation job skills and independent living skills (LaGreca, Stone, & Bell, 1983; Matson, Smalls, Hampff, Smiroldo, & Anderson, 1998; Sundel, 1991).

CHECK YOUR UNDERSTANDING

1. Behavior therapies are based on the belief that all behavior is

___a. biological

___b. physiological

___c. learned

___d. instinctive

2. Confronting your fears while in a relaxed state is called _____.

___a. behavior contracting

___b. flooding

___c. systemic desensitization

___d. modeling

3. Which technique aims to eliminate undesirable behavior by associating it with pain and discomfort?

___a. operant conditioning

___b. aversive conditioning

___c. empty chair

___d. desensitization

Answers: 1.c, 2.c, 3.b

Cognitive Therapies

How can people overcome irrational and self-defeating beliefs about themselves?

In modeling, people learn a behavior simply by watching others perform it. Thus, the people with snake phobia learned how to confront snakes by watching a film of others moving closer and closer to the snakes. Cognitive psychologists would point out that in addition to learning a *behavior*, these people also learned from watching the film that snakes are not necessarily dangerous and that one can endure contact with them without suffering ill effects. It might be said that in addition to changing their behavior, these people changed their way of thinking about snakes, and that their new way of thinking should lead to more adaptive behavior in the future. This simple idea—that a person's ideas about the world can be changed, and that such a change will have a beneficial effect on subsequent behavior—is at the heart of the **cognitive therapies.**

Cognitive therapies Psychotherapies that emphasize changing people's perceptions of their life situation as a way of modifying their behavior.

Cognitive therapists believe that their clients suffer from misconceptions about themselves and the world; it is these misconceptions that cause them psychological problems. The task facing cognitive therapists is to identify the erroneous ways of thinking and to correct them. This focus on learning new ways of thinking shares many similarities with behavior therapy; in fact, many professionals consider themselves to be *cognitive behavior therapists*, therapists who combine both cognitive and behavior therapies (Brewin, 1996). Let's examine some of the more popular forms of cognitive therapy.

Stress-Inoculation Therapy

As we go about our lives, we talk to ourselves constantly—we propose courses of action to ourselves, comment on our performance, express wishes, and so on. **Stress-inoculation therapy** is a type of cognitive therapy that makes use of this self-talk process to help people cope with stressful situations (Meichenbaum & Cameron, 1982). Once the stressful situation is identified, the client is taught to suppress any negative, anxiety-evoking thoughts and to replace them with positive, "coping" thoughts. Take a student with exam anxiety who faces every test telling herself: "Oh, another test. I'm so nervous and I'm sure I won't be able to think calmly enough to remember the answers. If only I'd studied more! If I don't get through this course, I'll never graduate!" This pattern of thought is highly dysfunctional because it will only make her anxiety worse. With the help of a cognitive therapist, the student learns a new pattern of self-talk: "I studied hard for this exam and I know the material well. I looked at the textbook last night and reviewed my notes. I should be able to do well. If some questions are hard, they won't all be, and even if it's tough, my whole grade doesn't depend on just one test." Then the person tries out the new strategy in a real situation, ideally one of only moderate stress (like a short quiz). Finally, the person is ready to use the strategy in a more stressful situation (like a final exam). Stress-inoculation therapy works by turning the client's own thought patterns into a kind of vaccine against stress-induced anxiety. This technique, as you might guess, is particularly effective with anxiety disorders.

Rational-Emotive Therapy

Another type of cognitive therapy, one that includes a more elaborate set of assumptions, is known as **rational-emotive therapy (RET)**. According to Albert Ellis (1973), the founder of RET, most people in need of therapy hold a set of irrational and self-defeating beliefs. These include such notions as: they should be competent at everything and liked by everyone; life should always be fair; quick solutions to problems should be available; and their lives should turn out a certain way. The core problem with such beliefs is that they involve absolutes—"musts" and "shoulds" that allow for no exceptions, no room for making mistakes. When people with such irrational beliefs come up against real-life struggles, they often experience excessive psychological distress. For example, when a college student who believes he must be liked by everyone isn't invited to join a fraternity, he may view the rejection as a catastrophe and become deeply depressed, rather than feeling simply sad and disappointed.

In rational-emotive therapy, therapists confront such dysfunctional beliefs vigorously, using a variety of techniques, including persuasion, challenge, commands, and theoretical arguments (Ellis & MacLaren, 1998). Studies have shown that RET techniques often do enable people to *reinterpret* their negative beliefs and experiences in a more positive light, decreasing the likelihood of becoming depressed (Blatt, Zuroff, Quinlan, & Pilkonis, 1996; Bruder et al., 1997).

Stress-inoculation therapy A type of cognitive therapy that trains people to cope with stressful situations by learning a more useful pattern of self-talk.

Rational-emotive therapy (RET) A directive cognitive therapy based on the idea that people's psychological distress is caused by irrational and self-defeating beliefs and that the therapist's job is to challenge such dysfunctional beliefs.

Cognitive therapy Therapy that depends on identifying and changing inappropriately negative and self-critical patterns of thought.

Beck's Cognitive Therapy

Aaron Beck (1967) developed one of the most important and promising forms of cognitive therapy for the treatment of depression. It is usually known simply as **cognitive therapy,** but is sometimes referred to as "Beck's cognitive therapy" to avoid confusion with the broader category of cognitive therapies.

Beck believes that depression results from negative patterns of thought that people develop about themselves. Principally, depressed people interpret events in a distorted way, one that is strongly and inappropriately self-critical. Such people hold unrealistic expectations, magnify their failures, make sweeping negative generalizations about themselves from little evidence, notice only negative feedback from the outside world, and interpret anything less than total success as failure. Take the case of a salesman who reacts to losing an important account with severe, disabling depression. Why? Because the account loss set off a pattern of negative thoughts in his mind: He is not really a good salesman, he will never find any customers as good as the one he just lost, and he will probably now go bankrupt from lack of income. From there his negative thoughts continue to spiral into more general areas of his life, and he may conclude that his life is worthless. According to Beck, this downward spiral of negative thoughts and cognitive distortions is at the heart of depression.

Beck's assumptions about the cause of depression are very similar to the assumptions underlying RET, but the style of treatment differs considerably. Cognitive therapists are much less challenging and confrontational than rational-emotive therapists. Instead, they try to help clients examine each dysfunctional thought in a supportive but objectively scientific manner ("Are you *sure* you'll never find any more good customers? What is your evidence for that?"). Like RET, Beck's cognitive therapy aims to lead the person to more realistic and flexible ways of thinking.

CHECK YOUR UNDERSTANDING

1. Changing a person's ideas about the world and themselves is at the heart of

____ a. stress-inoculation therapy

____ b. rational-emotive therapy

____ c. Gestalt therapy

____ d. cognitive therapy

2. Which therapy uses self-talk?

____ a. stress-inoculation therapy

____ b. rational-emotive therapy

____ c. Beck's cognitive therapy

____ d. couples therapy

3. According to rational-emotive therapy, which of the following is an irrational belief?

____ a. I must be good at whatever I do.

____ b. Everyone should like me.

____ c. Life should be fair.

____ d. All of the above.

Answers: 1.d, 2.a, 3.d

Group Therapies

How does group therapy help the individual members to function more effectively?

The therapies we have been discussing thus far involve only two people, a client and a therapist. Some psychologists think that this sort of therapy is less than ideal, for many of the problems that cause people to go into therapy are interpersonal. They believe that the treatment of several people simultaneously, or **group therapy,** is preferable to individual therapy. Group therapy allows both client and therapist to see how the person acts around others. If a person is painfully anxious and tongue-tied, or chronically self-critical and self-denigrating, or hostile and aggressive toward the opposite sex, these tendencies will show up quickly in a group setting.

Groups have other advantages. A good group offers a client social support, a feeling that he or she is not the only person in the world with emotional problems. The group can also help the person learn useful new behaviors (how to express feelings, how to disagree without antagonizing others). Interactions with other group members may push the person toward insights into his or her own behavior (seeing how annoying another person's constant complaints are, or how helpful his or her words of encouragement are, can lead the person toward useful behavior change). Finally, group therapy is less expensive for each participant than is individual therapy (Fejr, 2003; Yalom, 1995).

There are many kinds of group therapy. Some groups follow the general outlines of the therapies we've already mentioned. Others are oriented toward a specific goal, such as stopping smoking, drinking, or overeating. And some have more open-ended goals—for example, a happier marriage.

Family Therapy

Family therapy is one form of group therapy (Lebow & Gurman, 1995; Molineux, 1985). Family therapists believe that it is a mistake to treat a client in a vacuum, making no attempt to meet the person's parents, spouse, and children, for if one person in the family is having problems, it is often a signal that the entire family needs assistance. The primary goals of family therapy are improving family communication, encouraging family members to become more empathetic, getting members to share responsibilities, and reducing intrafamily conflict. To achieve these goals, all family members must see that they will benefit from changes in their behavior. Family therapists concentrate on changing the ways in which family members satisfy their needs rather than on trying to change those needs or the individual members' personalities (Gurman & Kniskern, 1991).

Family therapy is especially appropriate when there are problems between husband and wife, parents and children, or other family members. It is also called for when a person's progress in individual therapy is slowed by the family for some reason (often because other family members have trouble adjusting to a person's improvement). Unfortunately, not all families benefit from family therapy. Sometimes the problems are too entrenched; in other cases, important family members may be absent or unwilling to cooperate; in still others, one family member monopolizes the sessions. In all these cases, a different therapeutic approach is warranted.

Group therapy Type of psychotherapy in which people meet regularly to interact and help one another achieve insight into their feelings and behavior.

Family therapy A form of group therapy that sees the family as at least partly responsible for the individual's problems and that seeks to change all family members' behaviors to the benefit of the family unit as well as the troubled individual.

Group therapy can help to identify problems that a person has interacting with other people. The group also offers social support, helping people to feel less alone with their problems.

Couple therapy A form of group therapy intended to help troubled partners improve their problems of communication and interaction.

Couple Therapy

Another form of group therapy is **couple therapy,** which is designed to assist partners who are having difficulties with their relationship. In the past, this therapy was generally called *marital therapy*, but the term *couple therapy* is considered more appropriate today because it captures the broad range of partners who may seek help together (Oltmanns & Emery, 2001).

Most couple therapists concentrate on improving the patterns of communication and mutual expectations between the participants. In *empathy training*, for example, each member of the couple is taught to share inner feelings and to listen to and understand the partner's feelings before responding to them. The empathy technique focuses the couple's attention on feelings and requires that the partners spend more time listening and less time in rebuttal.

Other couple therapists employ behavioral techniques. For example, a couple might be helped to develop a schedule for exchanging specific caring actions, such as helping with chores around the house, making time to share a special meal together, or remembering special occasions with a gift or card, on the theory that scheduled exchanges of benefits can result in the learning of behavior that benefits both partners. It isn't terribly romantic, but its supporters point out that any strategy that breaks the cycle of dissatisfaction and hostility in a relationship is an important step in the right direction (Margolin, 1987).

Cognitive therapy can help partners recognize the ways they have been misinterpreting each other's communications (Beck, 1989). For example, when one partner says "How's your work going?" the other partner may take this to mean "I wish you would get a better job" or "I hate the way you're always working late at the office." Or an innocent question about helping around the house can be taken as criticism by the other partner. Misinterpretations like these can turn harmless or friendly remarks into criticism or nagging, and evoke unnecessary conflict. Cognitive therapy in the family setting aims at uncovering and undoing such destructive cognitive distortions.

Whatever form of therapy a couple chooses, research indicates that couple therapy for both partners is generally more effective than therapy for only one of them (Dunn & Schwebel, 1995; Johnson, 2003). One study, for example, found that when two married partners underwent therapy together, 56 percent were still married 5 years later; among those couples who underwent therapy separately, only 29 percent remained married (Cookerly, 1980).

Couple and family therapy are being increasingly used when only one family member has a clear psychological disorder, such as schizophrenia, agoraphobia, a sexual disorder, or, in some cases, depression (Christensen & Heavey, 1999; Lebow & Gurman, 1995). The goal of treatment in these circumstances is to help the mentally healthy members of the family cope more effectively with the effects of the disorder on the family unit. The improved coping of the well-adjusted family members may, in turn, help the troubled person compensate for or overcome his or her problems.

Self-Help Groups

This chapter emphasizes the kinds of therapy provided by trained professionals. But there are not enough mental health professionals to treat everyone who needs or wants therapy. At any given time, about 40 million Americans suffer from some form of psychological disorder (Narrow, Rae, Robins, & Regier, 2001). Mental health professionals can serve only a fraction of those people.

Because of this gap in the mental health system (as well as the high cost of many forms of professional treatment), more and more people faced with life crises are turning to low-cost self-help groups for support and help.

What are self-help groups and how do they work? Most such groups are small, local gatherings of people who share a common problem and who provide mutual assistance at a very low cost. Alcoholics Anonymous is perhaps the best-known self-help group, but self-help groups are available for virtually every conceivable life problem.

Do these self-help groups work? In many cases, apparently they do. Alcoholics Anonymous has developed an enviable reputation for helping people cope with alcoholism. Research confirms that most group members express strong support for their groups (Riordan & Beggs, 1987), and studies that have directly measured the effectiveness of self-help groups have demonstrated that they can indeed be effective (Galanter, 1984; McKellar, Stewart, & Humphreys, 2003; Ouimette et al., 2001; Pisani, Fawcett, Clark, & McGuire, 1993).

Such groups help to prevent psychological disorders by reaching out to people near the limits of their ability to cope with life stresses. The social support they provide is particularly important in an age when divorce, geographic mobility, and other factors have reduced the ability of the family to comfort people. By increasing their members' coping skills through information and advice, self-help groups may significantly reduce the likelihood that people will develop more serious psychological problems and require professional treatment.

CHECK YOUR UNDERSTANDING

1. Which of the following is an advantage of group therapy?

____ a. It often reveals a client's problem more quickly than individual therapy.

____ b. It costs less than individual therapy.

____ c. It offers social support.

____ d. All of the above.

2. Match the name of the technique used in couple therapy with its description.

____ empathy training

____ behavioral training

____ cognitive therapy

a. schedules for caring actions are created

b. attention is directed to feelings, not rebuttal

c. correctly interpreting each other's communications is the focus

3. Which is the best-known self-help group?

____ a. Overeaters Anonymous

____ b. Alcoholics Anonymous

____ c. Gamblers Anonymous

Answers: 1. d, 2. empathy training—b; behavioral training—a; cognitive therapy—c, 3. b

Effectiveness of Psychotherapy

Is psychotherapy effective?

The various therapies we have discussed so far all share one characteristic: All are *psychotherapies*—that is, they use psychological methods to treat disorders. But is psychotherapy *effective*? Is it any better than no treatment at all? And if it is, how much better is it?

Does Psychotherapy Work?

One of the first investigators to raise questions about the effectiveness of psychotherapy was the British psychologist Hans Eysenck (1952). After surveying 19 published reports covering more than 7,000 cases, Eysenck concluded that therapy significantly helped about two out of every three people. However, he also concluded that "Roughly two-thirds of a group of neurotic patients will recover or improve to a marked extent within about two years of the onset of their illness whether they are treated by means of psychotherapy or not" (p. 322). Eysenck's conclusion that individual psychotherapy was no more effective in treating neurotic disorders than no therapy at all caused a storm of controversy in the psychological community and stimulated considerable research.

Ironically, an important but often overlooked aspect of the subsequent debate has little to do with the effectiveness of therapy but rather with the effectiveness of *no* therapy. Many researchers then and today agree with Eysenck that therapy helps about two-thirds of the people who undergo it. More controversial is the question of what happens to people with psychological problems who do not receive formal therapy—is it really true that two-thirds will improve anyway? Bergin and Lambert (1978) questioned the "spontaneous recovery" rate of the control subjects in the studies Eysenck surveyed. They concluded that only about one out of every three people improves without treatment (not the two out of three cited by Eysenck). Since twice as many people improve with formal therapy, therapy is indeed more effective than no treatment at all (Borkovec & Costello, 1993; Lambert, Shapiro, & Bergin, 1986). Furthermore, these researchers noted that many people who do *not* receive formal therapy get some therapeutic help from friends, clergy, physicians, and teachers; thus, it is possible that the recovery rate for people who receive no therapeutic help at all is even less than one-third.

Other attempts to study the effectiveness of psychotherapy have averaged the results of a large number of individual studies. The general consensus among these studies is also that psychotherapy is effective (Leichsenring & Leibing, 2003; Lipsey & Wilson, 1993; Shapiro & Shapiro, 1982; Wampold et al., 1997), although its value appears to be related to a number of other factors. For instance, psychotherapy works best for relatively mild compared to more severe disorders (Kopta, Howard, Lowry, & Beutler, 1994) and seems to provide the greatest benefits to people who really *want* to change (Orlinsky & Howard, 1995).

Finally, one very extensive study designed to evaluate the effectiveness of psychotherapy was reported by *Consumer Reports* (1995). Largely under the direction of psychologist Martin E. P. Seligman, this investigation surveyed 180,000 *Consumer Reports* subscribers on everything from automobiles to mental health. Approximately 7,000 people from the total sample responded to the mental health section of the questionnaire that assessed satisfaction and improvement in people who had received psychotherapy.

According to Seligman (1995), the survey showed that the vast majority of respondents reported significant overall improvement following therapy. Second, there was no difference in the overall improvement score for people who had received therapy alone and those who had combined psychotherapy with medication. Third, no differences were found between the various forms of psychotherapy. Fourth, no differences in effectiveness were indicated between psychologists, psychiatrists, and social workers, although marriage counselors were seen as less effective. And fifth, people who had received long-term therapy reported more improvement than those who had received short-term therapy. This last result, one of the most striking findings of the study, is illustrated in Figure 14–1.

The *Consumer Reports* study lacked the scientific rigor of more traditional investigations designed to assess psychotherapeutic efficacy (Jacobson & Christensen,

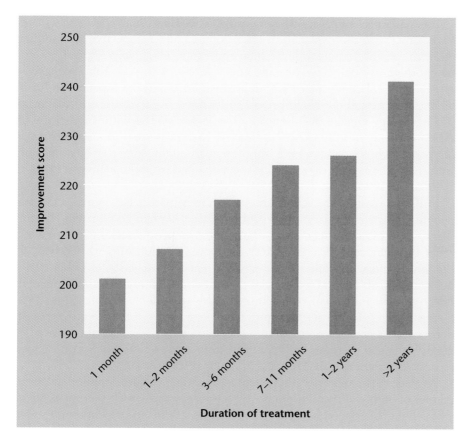

Figure 14–1
Duration of therapy and improvement.
One of the most dramatic results of the *Consumer Reports* (1995) study on the effectiveness of psychotherapy was the strong relationship between reported improvement and the duration of therapy.
Source: Adapted from Seligman, M. E. P. (1995). The effectiveness of psychotherapy: The *Consumer Reports* study. *American Psychologist, 50,* 965–974. Copyright © 1995 by the American Psychological Association. Adapted with permission.

1996; Seligman, 1995, 1996). For example, it did not use a control group to assess change in people who did not receive therapy. Nevertheless, it provides broad support for the idea that psychotherapy does work. Exactly why no differences were found between the various forms of psychotherapy is the topic of the next section. (See *Thinking Critically: Survey Results.*)

Which Type of Therapy Is Best for Which Disorder?

We have seen that researchers generally agree that psychotherapy is usually effective. This raises a second question: Is any particular form of psychotherapy more effective than the others? In general, the answer seems to be "not much." Most of the benefit of treatment seems to come from being in some kind of therapy, regardless of the particular type (Garfield, 1983; Michelson, 1985; Smith, Glass, & Miller, 1980; Wampold et al., 1997).

How can such different forms of psychotherapy be equally effective? To answer this question, some psychologists have focused their attention on what the various forms of psychotherapy have in *common*, rather than emphasizing their differences (Barker, Funk, & Houston, 1988; Roberts, Kewman, Mercer, & Hovell, 1993).

THINKING CRITICALLY

Survey Results

The text states that the *Consumer Reports* study lacked the scientific rigor of more traditional investigations. Think about the following questions:

- How were the respondents selected? How does that compare to the way in which scientific surveys select respondents (see Chapter 1, The Science of Psychology)?

- How did the study determine whether the respondents had improved?

- How would a psychologist conduct a more scientific study of the effectiveness of psychotherapy? What variables would need to be defined? How would the participants be chosen? What ethical issues might need to be considered?

Eclecticism Psychotherapeutic approach that recognizes the value of a broad treatment package over a rigid commitment to one particular form of therapy.

First, all forms of psychotherapy provide people with an *explanation for their problems*. Along with this explanation often comes a new perspective, providing the people with specific actions to help them cope more effectively. Second, most forms of psychotherapy offer *hope*. Because most people who seek therapy have low self-esteem and feel demoralized and depressed, hope and the expectation for improvement increases their feelings of self-worth. And third, all major types of psychotherapy engage the client in a *therapeutic alliance* with the therapist. Despite differing therapeutic approaches, effective therapists are warm, empathetic, and caring people who understand the importance of establishing a strong emotional bond with their clients built on mutual respect and understanding (Blatt, Zuroff, Quinlan, & Pilkonis, 1996).

Still, some kinds of psychotherapy seem to be particularly appropriate for certain people and for certain types of problems (see Nathan & Gorman, 1998). Insight therapy, for example, seems to be best suited to people seeking self-understanding, relief of inner conflict and anxiety, or better relationships with others. Behavior therapy is most appropriate for treating specific anxieties or other well-defined behavioral problems such as sexual dysfunctions. Family therapy is generally more effective than individual counseling for the treatment of drug abuse (Stanton & Shadish, 1997). Cognitive therapies have been shown to be effective treatments for depression (Kopta, Lueger, Saunders, & Howard, 1999; Merrill, Tolbert, & Wade, 2003; Robinson, Berman, & Neimeyer, 1990) and seem to hold promise for treating anxiety disorders as well (Dugas et al., 2003; Howard, 1999).

As you will see later in this chapter, the race, culture, ethnic background, and gender of both client and therapist can also influence which therapy is effective.

In light of the research evidence, the trend in psychotherapy is toward **eclecticism**—that is, moving away from commitment to a single form of therapy and toward a broad package of potential treatments from which the therapist selects the best treatment for a particular problem with a particular client. The majority of therapists now claim to use an eclectic approach (Kopta, Lueger, Saunders, & Howard, 1999; Slife & Reber, 2001). (See *Applying Psychology: How to Find Help* for suggestions on seeking psychological help.)

CHECK YOUR UNDERSTANDING

1. Most researchers agree that psychotherapy helps about _____ of people treated.

___a. one-third

___b. two-thirds

___c. one-fourth

___d. one-half

2. The trend among psychotherapists toward using a broad package of potential treatments is called

___a. eclecticism

___b. Beck's cognitive therapy

___c. free association

___d. transference

Answers: 1.b, 2.a

APPLYING PSYCHOLOGY

HOW TO FIND HELP

The notion that seeking help for your problems is a sign of weakness or mental illness is hard to dispel. But the fact is that hundreds of thousands of people are helped by psychological counseling and therapy every year. These people include business executives, artists, sports heroes, celebrities—and students. Therapy is a common, useful aid in coping with daily living.

College is a time of stress and anxiety for many people. The pressure of work, the competition for grades, the exposure to many different kinds of people with unfamiliar views, the tension of relating to peers—all these factors can add up to considerable emotional and physical stress, especially for students away from home for the first time. Most colleges and universities have their own counseling services, and many of them are as sophisticated as the best clinics in the country. Most communities also have mental health programs. As an aid to a potential search for the right counseling service, we include here a list of some of the other available resources for people who would like the advice of a mental health professional. Many of these services have national offices that will provide you with local branches and the appropriate people to contact in your area.

For Alcohol and Drug Abuse
National Clearinghouse for Alcohol and Drug Information
P.O. Box 2345
Rockville, MD 20847-2345
(301) 468-2600

General Service Board
Alcoholics Anonymous, Inc.
P.O. Box 459, Grand Central Station
New York, NY 10163
(212) 870-3400

For Those with a Friend or Relative Who Has an Alcohol Problem
Al-Anon Family Groups
1600 Corporate Landing Parkway
Virginia Beach, VA 23454
(888) 4ALANON (meeting information)
(757) 563-1600 (personal assistance)

National Association for Children of Alcoholics
11426 Rockville Pike
Rockville, MD 20852
(301) 468-0985

For Depression and Suicide
Mental Health Counseling Hotline
33 East End Avenue
New York, NY 10028
(212) 734-5876

Heartbeat (for survivors of suicides)
2015 Devon Street
Colorado Springs, CO 80909
(719) 596-2575

For Sexual and Sex-Related Problems
Sex Information and Education Council of the United States (SIECUS)
130 W. 42nd Street, Suite 350
New York, NY 10036-7802
(212) 819-9770

National Organization for Women
Legislative Office
1000 16th Street, N.W.
Washington, DC 20036
(202) 331-0066

National Clearinghouse on Marital and Date Rape
2325 Oak Street
Berkeley, CA 94708
(510) 524-1582 (fee required)

For Physical Abuse
Child Abuse Listening and Mediation (CALM)
P.O. Box 90754
Santa Barbara, CA 93190-0754
(805) 965-2376
(805) 692-4011 (help line)

For Help in Selecting a Therapist
National Mental Health Consumer Self-Help Clearinghouse
(215) 751-1810

For General Information on Mental Health and Counseling
The National Alliance for the Mentally Ill
200 N. Glebe Road, Suite 1015
Arlington, VA 22203
(703) 524-7600

The National Mental Health Association
1021 Prince Street
Alexandria, VA 22314
(703) 684-7722

The American Psychiatric Association
1400 K Street. N.W.
Washington, DC 20005
(703) 907-7300

The American Psychological Association
750 1st Street, N.E.
Washington, DC 20002
(202) 336-5500

The National Institute of Mental Health
5600 Fishers Lane
Rockville, MD 20857
(301) 443-4513

To learn more about finding help, visit our web site at www.prenhall.com/morris.

Biological treatments A group of approaches, including medication, electroconvulsive therapy, and psychosurgery, that are sometimes used to treat psychological disorders in conjunction with, or instead of, psychotherapy.

Antipsychotic drugs Drugs used to treat very severe psychological disorders, particularly schizophrenia.

Biological Treatments

What are the benefits of taking drugs for psychological disorders? What are the possible drawbacks?

Biological treatments—a group of approaches including medication, electroconvulsive therapy, and psychosurgery—may be used to treat psychological disorders in addition to, or instead of, psychotherapy. Clients and therapists select biological treatments for several reasons. First, therapists sometimes find that they cannot help people with any of the psychotherapies because they are extremely agitated, disoriented, or totally unresponsive. Second, biological treatment is virtually always used for disorders that have a strong biological component. Third, biological treatment is often used for people who are dangerous to themselves and to others.

The only mental health professionals licensed to offer biological treatments are psychiatrists, who are physicians, but therapists who are not medical doctors often work with physicians who can prescribe medication for their clients if it is needed. Scientists have developed many new medications to treat psychological disorders, and there are many ways of combining biological treatments with psychotherapy. Some recent research has shown that, in the long run, psychotherapy may be more cost-effective than medication (for a review, see Clay, 2000). We will highlight a few of the most widely used biological treatments.

Drug Therapies

Medication is frequently and effectively used to treat a number of different psychological problems (see Table 14–1). In fact, *Prozac*, a drug used to treat depression, is today one of the best-selling of all prescribed medications.

Two major reasons for the widespread use of drug therapy are the recent development of effective drugs and the fact that in some cases drug therapies cost less than psychotherapy. But critics have suggested there is another reason for the widespread use of drug therapy: our society's "pill mentality" (take a medicine to fix any problem).

Antipsychotic Drugs   Before the mid-1950s, drugs were not used widely in therapy for psychological disorders because the only available psychoactive drugs were sedatives that induced sleep as well as calm. Then the major tranquilizers *reserpine* and the *phenothiazines* were introduced. In addition to alleviating anxiety and aggressive behavior, both drugs reduce psychotic symptoms, such as hallucinations and delusions. Thus, they are called **antipsychotic drugs.** Antipsychotic drugs are used primarily for very severe psychological disorders, particularly schizophrenia. They are very effective for treating the "positive symptoms" (such as hallucinations) of this incapacitating disorder, but they are less effective with the "negative symptoms" (such as social withdrawal).

How do antipsychotic drugs work? Research with animals indicates that the effectiveness of antipsychotic medications is directly proportional to their ability to block dopamine receptors (Oltmanns & Emery, 1998). *Dopamine*, you will recall, is a neurotransmitter; the effectiveness of antipsychotic drugs supports the notion that schizophrenia is linked in some way to an excess of this neurotransmitter in the brain (see Chapter 13, Psychological Disorders).

Although their benefits can be dramatic, antipsychotic drugs can also produce a number of undesirable side effects (Kane & Lieberman, 1992; McKim, 1997). Another problem is that while antipsychotic drugs allow many people with schizophrenia to leave the hospital, the drugs by themselves are of little value in treating

table 14-1 MAJOR TYPES OF PSYCHOACTIVE MEDICATIONS

Therapeutic Use	Chemical Structure*	Trade Name(s)*
Antipsychotics	Phenothiazines	Therazine, Thorazine
Antidepressants	Tricyclics	Elavil
	MAO inhibitors	Nardil
	SSRIs	Prozac, Paxil, Zoloft, Effexor
Psychostimulants	Amphetamines	Dexedrine
	Other	Ritalin
Antimanic	Carbamazepine	Tegretol
Antianxiety	Benzodiazepines	Valium
Sedatives	Barbiturates	
Antipanic	Tricyclics	Tofranil
Antiobsessional	Tricyclics	Anafranil

*The chemical structures and especially the trade names listed in this table are often just one example of the many kinds of medications available for the specific therapeutic use.

Source: G. L. Klerman et al. (1994). "Medication and Psychotherapy." In A. E. Bergin and S. L. Garfield (eds.), *Handbook of Psychotherapy and Behavior Change*, 4th ed., pp. 734–782. Copyright © 1994 by John Wiley & Sons, Inc. This material is used by permission of John Wiley & Sons, Inc.

the social incapacity and other difficulties these people encounter when trying to adjust to life outside the institution. And because many discharged clients fail to take their medications, relapse is common unless drug therapy is effectively combined with psychotherapy.

Antidepressant Drugs A second group of drugs, known as antidepressants, is used to combat depression. Until the end of the 1980s, there were only two main types of antidepressant drugs: *monoamine oxidase inhibitors (MAO inhibitors)* and *tricyclics* (named for their chemical properties). Both drugs work by increasing the concentration of the neurotransmitters serotonin and norepinephrine in the brain (McKim, 1997). Both are effective for most people with serious depression, but both produce a number of serious and troublesome side effects.

In 1988, Prozac (fluoxetine) came onto the market. This drug works by reducing the uptake of serotonin in the nervous system, thus increasing the amount of serotonin active in the brain at any given moment (see Figure 14–2). For this reason, Prozac is part of a group of psychoactive drugs known as *selective serotonin reuptake inhibitors (SSRIs)* (see Chapter 2, The Biological Basis of Behavior). Today a number of second generation SSRI's are available to treat depression including *Paxil* (paroxetine), *Zoloft* (sertraline) and *Effexor* (venlafaxine HCl). In addition to increasing serotonin, the last drug in this list, *Effexor* also raises the levels of norepinephrine in the brain so it is technically known as an *SNRI* (serotonin and norepinephrine reuptake inhibitor). For many patients correcting the imbalance in these chemicals in the brain reduces their symptoms of depression and also relieves the associated symptoms of anxiety. Moreover, because these drugs have fewer side effects than MAO inhibitors or tricyclics (Nemeroff & Schatzberg, 2002) they have been heralded in the popular media as "wonder drugs" for the treatment of depression.

Today, antidepressant drugs are not only used to treat depression, but also have shown promise in treating generalized anxiety disorder, panic disorder, obsessive-compulsive disorder, social phobia, and post-traumatic stress disorder (Bourin,

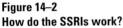

Figure 14–2
How do the SSRIs work?
Antidepressants like Prozac, Paxil, Zoloft and Effexor belong to a class of drugs called SSRIs (Selective Serotonin Reuptake Inhibitors). These drugs reduce the symptoms of depression by blocking the reabsorption (or reuptake) of serotonin in the synaptic space. The increased availability of serotonin to bind to receptor sites on the receiving neuron is thought to be responsible for the ability of these drugs to relieve the symptoms of depression.

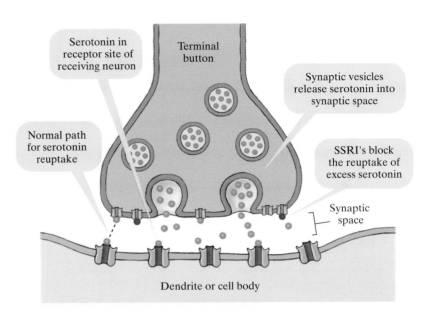

2003; Donnelly, 2003; Shelton & Hollon, 2000). However, antidepressant drugs like the SSRI's do not work for everyone. At least a quarter of the patients with major depressive disorder do not respond to antidepressant drugs (Shelton & Hollon, 2000). Moreover, for some patients these drugs produce unpleasant side effects including nausea, insomnia, headaches, anxiety, and impaired sexual functioning. They can also cause severe withdrawal symptoms in patients who abruptly stop taking them (Balon, 2002; Clayton, McGarvey, Abouesh, & Pinkerton, 2001).

Lithium Bipolar disorder, or manic depression, is frequently treated with lithium carbonate. Lithium is a naturally occurring salt that helps control the wild and unpredictable mood swings of manic depression. Although it is effective in approximately 75 percent of cases (Gnanadesikan, Freeman, & Gelenberg, 2003), lithium is often prescribed along with antidepressants because it is slow to take effect (Solomon, Keitner, Miller, Shea, & Keller, 1995). Unfortunately, some people with bipolar disorder, against the advice of their physicians, stop taking lithium when their symptoms improve, leading to a relatively high relapse rate (Gershon & Soares, 1997; Pope & Scott, 2003). We do not know exactly how lithium works (Oltmanns & Emery, 1998), but studies with mice indicate that it may act to stabilize the levels of specific neurotransmitters in the brain (Dixon & Hokin, 1998).

Source: © 2001 Jack Ziegler from cartoonbank.com. All Rights Reserved.

Other Medications Several other medications can be used to alleviate the symptoms of various psychological problems (see Table 14–1). *Psychostimulants* heighten alertness and arousal. Some psychostimulants, such as *Ritalin*, are commonly used to treat children with attention-deficit/hyperactivity disorder (Adesman, 2000); strangely, in these cases, these drugs have a calming rather than a stimulating effect. However there is increasing concern that psychostimulants are being overused—especially with young children (Rey and Sawyer, 2003). The White House drew attention to this issue in March 2000, citing research that showed the number of children between 2 and 4 years of age taking stimulants and antidepressants has more than doubled in recent years (Zito et al., 2000). (See Figure 14–3 and "Thinking Critically: AD/HD" in Chapter 13 for more information.)

Antianxiety medications (for example, Valium) quickly produce a sense of calm and mild euphoria; they are often used to reduce general tension and anxiety, though their addictive potential limits their current use. *Sedatives* produce both calm and drowsiness; they are used to treat agitation or to induce sleep. These drugs, too, can become addictive.

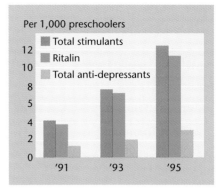

Figure 14–3
Use of psychiatric medications among preschoolers.
A study of 151,675 preschoolers in one Midwestern Medicaid group found that the use of psychiatric medications, particularly stimulants such as Ritalin, increased greatly in recent years.
Source: Data from *Journal of the American Medical Association,* figure by Associated Press as found in *The Charlotte Observer,* Feb. 23, 2000. Reprinted with permission.

ENDURING ISSUES   mindbody

Combining Drugs and Psychotherapy

As we have seen, for some disorders a combination of drugs and psychotherapy works better than either approach used alone. This underscores the fact that the relationship between mind and body is highly complex. The causes of depression have not yet been fully determined, but they will probably be found to include a mixture of genetic predisposition, chemical changes in the brain, and life situation (see Chapter 13, Psychological Disorders).

Electroconvulsive Therapy

Electroconvulsive therapy (ECT) is most often used for cases of prolonged and severe depression that do not respond to other forms of therapy (Birkenhaeger, Pluijms, & Lucius, 2003; Olfson, Marcus, Sackeim, Thompson, & Pincus, 1998). The technique involves briefly passing a mild electric current through the brain or, more recently, through only one hemisphere of the brain (Thomas & Kellner, 2003). The side-effects of ECT include some brief confusion as well as disorientation and memory impairment though research evidence suggests that unilateral ECT produces fewer side effects and is only slightly less effective than the traditional method (Diaz, 1997; Khan, 1993).

No one knows exactly why ECT works, but evidence clearly demonstrates its effectiveness. In addition, the fatality rate for ECT is markedly lower than for people taking antidepressant drugs (Henry, Alexander, & Sener, 1995). Still, ECT has many critics and its use remains controversial (Krystal, Holsinger, Weiner, & Coffey, 2000). In view of the side effects, ECT is usually considered a "last resort" treatment when all other methods have failed.

Psychosurgery

Psychosurgery refers to brain surgery performed to change a person's behavior and emotional state. This is a drastic step, especially because it is irreversible and its effects are difficult to predict. In a *prefrontal lobotomy*, the frontal lobes of the brain are severed from the deeper centers beneath them. The assumption is that in extremely disturbed people the frontal lobes intensify emotional impulses from the lower brain centers (chiefly the thalamus and hypothalamus). Unfortunately, lobotomies can work with one person and fail completely with another—possibly producing permanent undesirable side effects, such as inability to inhibit impulses or a near-total absence of feeling.

Prefrontal lobotomies are rarely performed today. In fact, very few psychosurgical procedures are done nowadays except as desperate measures to control such conditions as intractable psychoses, epilepsy that does not respond to other treatments, Parkinson's disease, severe obsessive-compulsive disorders, and pain in a terminal illness (Baer, Rauch, & Ballantine, 1995; Weingarten & Cummings, 2001).

Electroconvulsive therapy (ECT) Biological therapy in which a mild electrical current is passed through the brain for a short period, often producing convulsions and temporary coma; used to treat severe, prolonged depression.

Psychosurgery Brain surgery performed to change a person's behavior and emotional state; a biological therapy rarely used today.

The Summary Table provides an overview of the goals and techniques of all the treatment methods we have discussed in this chapter.

summarytable MAJOR PERSPECTIVES ON THERAPY

Type of Therapy	Cause of Disorder	Goal	Techniques
Insight Therapies			
Psychoanalysis	Unconscious conflicts and motives; repressed problems from childhood.	To bring unconscious thoughts and feelings to consciousness; to gain insight.	Free association, dream analysis, interpretation, transference.
Client-Centered Therapy	Experiences of conditional positive regard.	To help people become fully functioning by opening them up to all of their experiences.	Regarding clients with unconditional positive regard.
Gestalt Therapy	Lack of wholeness in the personality.	To get people to "own their feelings" and to awaken to sensory experience in order to become whole.	Active rather than passive talk; empty chair techniques; encounter groups.
Behavior Therapies			
	Reinforcement for maladaptive behavior.	To learn new and more adaptive behavior patterns.	Classical conditioning (systematic desensitization, extinction, flooding); aversive conditioning; operant conditioning (behavior contracting, token economies); modeling.
Cognitive Therapies			
	Misconceptions; negative, self-defeating thinking.	To identify erroneous ways of thinking and to correct them.	Rational-emotive therapy (rationally examining negative thought patterns); self-inoculation therapy (consciously replacing negative thoughts with positive, coping thoughts); Beck's cognitive therapy.
Group Therapies			
	Personal problems are often interpersonal problems.	To develop insight into one's personality and behavior by interacting with others in the group.	Group interaction and mutual support; family therapy; couple therapy; self-help groups.
Biological Treatments			
	Physiological imbalance or malfunction.	Eliminate symptoms; prevent recurrence.	Electroconvulsive therapy, drugs, psychosurgery.

CHECK YOUR UNDERSTANDING

1. Most antipsychotic drugs work by

___a. increasing acetylcholine in the brain

___b. increasing serotonin in the brain

___c. inhibiting the function of the hypothalamus

___d. blocking dopamine receptors in the brain

2. Which of the following is true of psychosurgery?

___a. It never produces undesirable side effects.

___b. It is useless in controlling pain.

___c. It is widely used.

___d. Its effects are hard to predict.

3. Match the following medications with the neurotransmitters(s) that each is believed to influence. Some medications influence more than one neurotransmitter.

___ monoamine oxidase inhibitors   a. norepinephrine

___ tricyclics   b. serotonin

___ Prozac   c. epinephrine

Answers: 1.d, 2.d, 3. monoamine oxidase inhibitors—a and b; tricyclics—a and b; Prozac—b

Institutionalization and Its Alternatives

How can mental illness be prevented?

For the severely mentally ill, hospitalization has been the treatment of choice in the United States for the past 150 years. Although various kinds of hospitals offer care to the mentally ill, when most people think of "mental hospitals" it is the large state institutions that come to mind. These public hospitals, many with beds for thousands of patients, were often built in rural areas in the nineteenth century, the idea being that a country setting would calm patients and help restore their mental health. Whatever the good intentions behind the establishment of these hospitals, for most of their history they have not provided adequate care or therapy for their residents. Perpetually underfunded and understaffed, state hospitals have often been little more than warehouses for victims of serious mental illness who were unwanted by their families.

Starting in the 1950s, the development of effective drug therapies led to a number of changes in state hospitals (Shorter, 1997). For one thing, patients who were agitated or violent could now be sedated with drugs. Although the drugs often produced lethargy, this was considered an improvement over the use of physical restraints. The second major, and more lasting, result of the new drug therapies was wholesale discharge of patients. As we shall see, however, this created new problems, both for patients and for society.

Deinstitutionalization

The advent of antipsychotic drugs in the 1950s created a favorable climate for the policy of **deinstitutionalization**—releasing patients with severe psychological disorders back into the community. The idea of deinstitutionalization gained strength in 1963, when Congress passed legislation establishing a network of community mental health centers around the nation. The practice of placing patients in smaller, more humane facilities or returning them under medication to care within the community intensified during the 1960s and 1970s. By 1975, 600 regional mental health centers accounted for 1.6 million cases of outpatient care.

In recent years, however, deinstitutionalization has created serious problems. Discharged patients today often find poorly funded community mental health

Deinstitutionalization Policy of treating people with severe psychological disorders in the larger community, or in small residential centers such as halfway houses, rather than in large public hospitals.

Beginning in the 1950s and 1960s, the policy of deinstitutionalization led to the release of many individuals, who, without proper follow-up care, ended up living on the streets.

centers—or none at all. Many of these ex-patients are poorly prepared to live in the community, and they receive little guidance in coping with the mechanics of daily life. Those who return home can become a burden to their families, especially when they don't get adequate follow-up care. Residential centers, such as halfway houses, vary in quality, but many provide poor medical and psychological care and minimal contact with the outside world. In any case, there is not enough sheltered housing, forcing many former patients into nonpsychiatric facilities—often rooming houses located in dirty, unsafe, isolated neighborhoods. Perhaps the largest single obstacle to their rehabilitation is the social stigma attached to mental illness. Moreover, although outpatient care is presumed to be a well-established national policy objective in mental health, health insurance typically covers inpatient care completely (or nearly so) but discourages outpatient care by requiring substantial co-payments and limiting the number of treatment visits.

The full effects of deinstitutionalization are unknown. Few follow-up studies have been done on discharged patients, who are difficult to keep track of for long periods. Still, it is obvious that, though a worthy ideal, deinstitutionalization in practice has had dire effects on patients and society. Many released patients, unable to obtain follow-up care or to find housing, and incapable of looking after their own needs, have ended up on the streets. Without supervision, they have stopped taking the drugs that made their release possible in the first place and have again become psychotic. Perhaps one of the most tragic outcomes of the deinstitutionalization movement is the increase in the suicide rate among deinstitutionalized patients (Goldney, 2003). Every major U.S. city now has a population of homeless mentally ill men and women living in makeshift shelters or sleeping in doorways, bus stations, parks, and other public spaces (see Drury, 2003). Surveys indicate that nearly 40 percent of homeless people are mentally ill (Burt et al., 1999).

This situation is tragic for the mentally ill homeless, who, often incoherent, are easy prey for criminals. It is also contributing to the coarsening of our society, as the general public, finding the constant presence of "crazies" among them unpleasant, has begun to lose compassion for both the homeless and the mentally ill and to pressure public officials to "get them off the street." Most mental health professionals now agree that many chronically ill patients should not be released to live "in the community" without better planning, more funding, more community support, and readily available short-term rehospitalization for those who require it.

Alternative Forms of Treatment

Deinstitutionalization assumes that institutionalization occurs in the first place. But for several decades Charles Kiesler argued for a shift from the focus on institutionalization to forms of treatment that avoid hospitalization altogether (Kiesler, 1982b; Kiesler & Sibulkin, 1987; Kiesler & Simpkins, 1993). Kiesler (1982a) examined ten controlled studies in which seriously disturbed people were randomly assigned either to hospitals or to an alternative program. The alternative programs took many forms: people living at home who were trained to cope with daily activities; a small homelike facility in which staff and residents shared responsibility for residential life; hostels offering therapy and crisis intervention; family crisis therapy;

day-care treatment; visits from public-health nurses combined with medication; and intensive outpatient counseling combined with medication.

All these alternatives involved daily professional contact and skillful preparation of the community to receive the patients. Even though the hospitals to which some people in these studies were assigned provided very good patient care—probably substantially above average for institutions in the United States—nine out of the ten studies found that the outcome was more positive for alternative treatments than for hospitalization. (It is worth noting that hospitalization costs 40 percent more than the alternative programs.) Moreover, the people who received alternative care were less likely to undergo hospitalization later—which suggests that hospitalizing mental patients is a self-perpetuating process. Many such people "could be treated in alternative settings more effectively and less expensively," Kiesler concluded (1982a, p. 358).

Prevention

Yet another approach to mental illness endeavors to prevent its onset in the first place. **Prevention** refers to reducing the incidence of mental disorders in society (Reppucci, Woolard, & Fried, 1999). This requires finding and eliminating the conditions that cause or contribute to mental disorders and substituting conditions that foster well-being. Prevention takes three forms: primary, secondary, and tertiary.

Primary prevention refers to efforts to improve the overall environment so that new cases of mental disorders do not develop. Family planning and genetic counseling are two examples of primary prevention programs. They assist prospective parents to think through such questions as how many children to have and when. They also provide testing to diagnose genetic defects in embryo, and direct parents to treatments, including fetal surgery, that may be able to alleviate defects before the baby is born. Other primary prevention programs aim at increasing personal and social competencies in a wide variety of groups. For example, some programs are designed to help mothers encourage the development of problem-solving skills in their children; other programs have the goal of enhancing competence and adjustment among the elderly. Current campaigns to educate young people about the consequences of drugs, alcohol abuse, violence, and date rape are other examples of primary prevention (Avery-Leaf, Cano, Cascardi, & O'Leary, 1995; Foxcroft, Ireland, Lister, Lowe, & Breen, 2003; Reppucci, Woolard, & Fried, 1999).

Secondary prevention requires the identification of groups that are at high risk for mental disorders—for example, abused children, people who have recently divorced, and those who have been laid off from their jobs. The main thrust of secondary prevention is *intervention* with such high-risk groups—that is, detecting maladaptive behavior early and treating it promptly. One form of intervention is *crisis intervention*, which includes such programs as suicide hot lines. Another is the establishment of short-term crisis facilities at which a therapist can provide face-to-face counseling and support for high-risk individuals and families.

The main objective of **tertiary prevention** is to help people adjust to community life after release from a mental hospital. For example, hospitals often grant passes to encourage patients to leave the institution for short periods of time prior to their release. Other tertiary prevention measures are halfway houses, where patients find support and skills training during the period of transition between hospitalization and full integration into the larger community, and nighttime and outpatient programs that provide supportive therapy while people live at home and hold down a full-time job. Tertiary prevention also includes efforts to educate the community the person will reenter.

In sum, prevention is clearly cost-effective compared to therapy, but preventive efforts are constrained by several factors: It is very difficult to bring about social

Prevention Strategies for reducing the incidence of emotional disturbance by eliminating conditions that cause or contribute to mental disorders and substituting conditions that foster mental well-being.

Primary prevention Techniques and programs to improve the social environment so that new cases of mental disorders do not develop.

Secondary prevention Programs to identify groups that are at high risk for mental disorders and to detect maladaptive behavior in these groups and treat it promptly.

Tertiary prevention Programs to help people adjust to community life after release from a mental hospital.

Suicide hotlines and other crisis intervention programs are secondary prevention measures designed to serve individuals and groups at high risk for mental disorders.

change; our scientific knowledge about the causes of psychological disorders is far from complete; it is very hard to prove conclusively that prevention works; and there are legitimate concerns about forcing people to accept treatments before their problems are manifest.

CHECK YOUR UNDERSTANDING

1. Match the following technique with the appropriate form of prevention.

___ halfway houses	a. primary prevention
___ educational TV spots	b. secondary prevention
___ hotlines	c. tertiary prevention
___ crisis intervention	
___ genetic counseling	

2. Which of the following were factors that helped promote deinstitutionalization?

___a. the development of effective antipsychotic drugs

___b. the establishment of a network of community mental health centers

___c. federal budget cuts in the 1960s

___d. a and b

Answers: 1. halfway houses—c; educational TV spots—a; hotlines—b; crisis intervention—b; genetic counseling—a, 2. d

Gender and Cultural Differences in Treatments

Should therapy for men and women be different?

In the previous chapter, we saw that there are some significant gender and cultural differences in the prevalence of many psychological disorders. Are there significant differences in treatment as well? In this section, we explore the answer to this question.

THINKING CRITICALLY

Access to Mental Health Care

A friend is exhibiting symptoms of depression and feels overwhelmed by sadness and has lost interest in most activities. He comes to you for advice. How likely would you be to suggest that your friend seek psychotherapy or drug treatment? Think about the following questions:

- Would you seek therapy yourself in a similar situation?

- What would you think of a friend who you knew was seeing a therapist?

- Would your friend be able to obtain therapy services? Would he be able to afford these kinds of services?

- Do you think that mental illness and physical illness are equivalent and should be treated the same by insurance companies?

Gender Differences

First, women are more likely than men to be in psychotherapy. One national survey found that 60 percent of those seeing psychologists and psychiatrists were women (Williams, 1987). In part, this is because women traditionally have been more willing than men to admit they have psychological problems and need help to solve them (Cochran & Rabinowitz, 2003). Moreover, to some extent psychotherapy has been more socially accepted for women than for men (Williams, 1987). However, in recent years, the number of males willing to seek psychotherapy and counseling has increased (Pollack & Levant, 1998). The researchers attribute this increase to the changing roles of men in today's society: Men are increasingly expected to provide emotional as well as financial support for their families.

The treatment given women, in most respects, is the same as that given men. This fact has become somewhat controversial in recent years (Enns, 1993; Ogrodniczuk & Staats, 2002). Because most therapists are male, and most vocational and rehabilitation programs are male-oriented, some critics of "equal treatment" have claimed that women in therapy are often encouraged to adopt traditional, male-oriented views of what is "normal" or "appropriate"; that male therapists tend to urge women to adapt, adjust, or conform to their surroundings passively; and that male therapists are insufficiently sensitive to the fact that much of the stress women experience comes from trying to cope with a world in which they are not treated equally (Brown & Ballou, 1992). For all these reasons, there has been an increase recently in the number of "feminist therapists," who attempt to help their female clients become aware of the extent to which their problems derive from external controls and inappropriate sex roles, become more conscious of and attentive to their own needs and goals, and develop a sense of pride in their womanhood rather than passively accepting or identifying with the status quo.

Cultural Differences

ENDURING ISSUES **diversity**universality

On Being Culture Bound

Imagine the following scenario: As a Native American is interviewed by a psychologist, he stares at the floor. He answers questions politely, but during the entire consultation looks away continually, never meeting the doctor's eye. This body language might lead the psychologist to suppose that the man is depressed or has low self-esteem. Unless, that is, the psychologist knows that in the person's culture, avoiding eye contact is a sign of respect.

This example shows how culture bound are our ideas of what constitutes normal behavior. When psychotherapist and client come from different cultures, misunderstandings of speech, body language, and customs are almost inevitable (see Cardemil & Battle, 2003; Helms & Cook, 1999). Even when client and therapist are of the same nationality and speak the same language, there can be striking differences if they belong to different racial and ethnic groups (Casas, 1995). Some black people, for example, are wary of confiding in a white therapist—so much so that their wariness is sometimes mistaken for paranoia. For this reason, many black people seek out a black therapist, a tendency that has become more common as larger members of black middle-class people have entered therapy (Williams, 1989).

One of the challenges for U.S. therapists in recent years has been to treat refugees from foreign countries, many of whom have fled such horrifying circumstances at home that they arrive in the United States exhibiting post-traumatic stress disorder (Paunovic & Oest, 2001). Not only must these refugees overcome the effects of trauma and flight from it, but they also face the new stresses of settling in a strange country, which often include separation from their families, ignorance of the English language, and inability to practice their traditional occupations.

Therapists in such circumstances must learn something of their clients' culture. Often, they have to conduct interviews through an interpreter—hardly an ideal circumstance for therapy.

These therapists also need to recognize that some disorders that afflict people from other cultures may not exist in Western culture at all. For example, *Taijin Kyofusho* (roughly translated as "fear of people") involves a morbid fear that one's body or actions may be offensive to others. Because this disorder is rarely seen outside of Japan, American therapists require specialized training to identify it.

In August 1990, the American Psychological Association approved a document titled "Guidelines for Psychological Practice with Ethnic and Culturally Diverse Populations." In it, the APA reminds practitioners that different groups may perform differently on psychological tests, express symptoms in different ways, and relate differently to family members and outsiders than members of the dominant population (Moses, 1990). As a result, psychologists today recognize that sensitivity and understanding of cultural diversity will assist them in treating individuals from diverse cultural backgrounds (Gibson & Mitchell, 2003; Pedersen & Carey, 2003; Sue, 1998).

In 1991, following practitioners' observations that in other countries the "standard" dosages of medication are quite different than in the United States, the National Institutes of Health began a study to measure the responses of different ethnic groups to several psychiatric medications (DeAngelis, 1991b). And indeed there is now evidence that the dosages of many medications, such as lithium and some antidepressants, may need to be adjusted for individuals of different racial or cultural backgrounds (for a review, see Lin, Poland, & Nakasaki, 1993).

Ultimately, however, the best solution to the difficulties of serving a multicultural population is to train therapists of many different backgrounds so that members of ethnic, cultural, and racial minorities can choose therapists of their own group if they wish to do so (Bernal & Castro, 1994). Indeed, research has shown that psychotherapy is more likely to be effective when the client and the therapist share a similar cultural background (Sue, Zane, & Young, 1994).

Similarly, efforts aimed at preventing mental illness in society must also be sensitive to cultural diversity. Many intervention programs have proved unsuccessful because they failed to take into account the appropriate cultural norms and values of the group being served (Reppucci, Woolard, & Fried, 1999). To be effective, treatment approaches must reflect the beliefs and cultural practices of the person's ethnic group.

CHECK YOUR UNDERSTANDING

1. Research has shown that psychotherapy is more effective under which conditions?

___a. the client and therapist share similar cultural background

___b. the client and therapist are from different cultural backgrounds

___c. cultural backgrounds make no difference to treatment

2. _____ are more likely to be in therapy than _____.

___a. Men/women

___b. Women/men

___c. Neither. The genders are equal in the amount of treatment received.

Answers: 1.a, 2.b

This chapter presents some of the main types of **psychotherapy,** the use of psychological techniques to treat mental disorders. It also discusses biological therapies as well as institutionalization and its alternatives.

Insight Therapies

The main goal of **insight therapies** is to give people a better awareness and understanding of their feelings, motivations, and actions in the hope that this will lead to better adjustment.

Psychoanalysis   Psychoanalysis is a therapy based on the belief that psychological problems stem from inner conflicts dating back to childhood. Psychoanalysis is designed to bring hidden feelings to conscious awareness. One way of doing so is through **free association,** a process in which the client discloses whatever thoughts or fantasies come to mind without editing or otherwise inhibiting them. In classical psychoanalysis, the client comes to transfer feelings held toward authority figures from childhood to the analyst, a process known as **transference.** The goal of psychoanalysis is **insight,** or awareness of feelings, memories, and actions from the past that were unconscious but were exerting a strong influence on the person's present feelings and behavior.

Client-Centered Therapy   **Client-centered** (or **person-centered**) **therapy,** founded by Carl Rogers, is built on the idea that therapy should be based on the client's view of the world rather than the therapist's and on the client's responsibility for change. The therapist's most important task is to provide unconditional positive regard for clients—that is, to show true acceptance no matter what they may say or do—so that they will learn to accept themselves. The therapist takes a nondirective approach, always following the client's lead.

Gestalt Therapy   **Gestalt therapy** grew out of the work of Fritz Perls and is designed to help people become more aware of their feelings and more genuine in their day-to-day interactions. The emphasis in therapy is on making the person whole and complete.

Recent Developments   Contemporary insight therapists are more active than traditional psychoanalysts, giving clients direct guidance and feedback. They are also more focused on people's immediate problems than on their childhood traumas. An especially significant development is the trend to **short-term psychodynamic psychotherapy,** which recognizes that most people can be successfully treated within a time-limited framework.

Behavior Therapies

Behavior therapies are based on the belief that all behavior, normal and abnormal, is learned, and that the objective of therapy is to teach people more satisfying ways of behaving.

Using Classical Conditioning Techniques   Classical conditioning therapies attempt to evoke a new conditioned response to old stimuli. For example, **systematic desensitization** is a method for gradually reducing irrational fears by imagining—or confronting in real life—increasingly fearful situations while maintaining a relaxed state. Eventually, relaxation replaces fear as a response, perhaps as a result of extinction. Flooding, which subjects the person to feared situations at full intensity and for a prolonged time, is a somewhat harsh but highly effective method of desensitization. **Aversive conditioning** has the opposite goal: It conditions a negative rather than a positive response to a stimulus such as the sight or taste of alcohol. Its purpose is to eliminate undesirable behaviors by associating them with pain and discomfort.

Operant Conditioning   Operant conditioning techniques work by reinforcing new behaviors and ignoring or punishing old ones. In one such technique, called **behavior contracting,** client and therapist agree on certain behavioral goals and on the reinforcement the person will receive upon reaching those goals. In another technique, called the **token economy,** tokens that can be cashed in for desired items are used to positively reinforce many different kinds of desired behavior.

Modeling   In **modeling,** a person learns new behaviors by watching others perform those behaviors.

Cognitive Therapies

Cognitive therapies aim at changing people's maladaptive ways of thinking about themselves and the world.

Stress-Inoculation Therapy   **Stress-inoculation therapy** teaches people new and positive patterns of self-talk they can use to support themselves through stressful situations.

Rational-Emotive Therapy   **Rational-emotive therapy (RET)** is based on the idea that people's emotional problems derive from a set of irrational and self-defeating beliefs they hold about themselves and the world. The therapist vigorously challenges these beliefs until the client comes to see just how irrational and dysfunctional they are.

Beck's Cognitive Therapy   Aaron Beck believes that depression results from negative patterns of thought that are strongly and inappropriately self-critical. His **cognitive therapy** tries to lead the person to more realistic and flexible ways of thinking.

Group Therapies

Group therapy is based on the idea that psychological problems are at least partly interpersonal and are therefore best approached in an interpersonal setting. Group therapy provides social support and is less costly than individual therapy.

Family Therapy   **Family therapy** is based on the idea that an individual's psychological problems are to some extent family problems. Therefore, the therapist treats the family unit rather than the isolated individual, with the goal of improving communication and empathy among family members and reducing intrafamily conflict.

Couple Therapy   **Couple therapy** concentrates on improving patterns of communication and interaction between couples. Forms of couple therapy include empathy training and cognitive marital therapy.

Self-Help Groups   Self-help groups are small, local gatherings of people who share a common problem and provide mutual assistance at a very low cost. They provide social support and increase their members' coping skills through information and advice.

Effectiveness of Psychotherapy

Does Psychotherapy Work?   Most researchers agree that psychotherapy helps about two-thirds of the people treated.

Which Type of Therapy Is Best for Which Disorder?   Most kinds of therapy are more effective than no treatment at all, but researchers have found few major differences in the effectiveness of various forms of therapy. The general trend in psychotherapy is toward **eclecticism,** the use of a broad treatment package rather than one single form of therapy.

Biological Treatments

Biological treatments, including medication, electroconvulsive therapy, and psychosurgery, are sometimes used when psychotherapy does not work or when a person has a disorder for which biological treatment is known to be safe and effective. Medication, especially, is very often used in conjunction with psychotherapy.

Drug Therapies   Drugs are the most common biological therapies. **Antipsychotic drugs** are valuable in the treatment of schizophrenia; they do not cure the disorder, but they do reduce its symptoms. Side effects can be severe, however.

Antidepressant drugs alleviate depression, though some have serious side effects. Often, the effectiveness of antidepressants such as Prozac seems to be due to the person's belief that the drug will work (the placebo effect).

Many other types of medication are used to treat psychological disorders, including lithium (used to treat bipolar disorder), antianxiety drugs, sedatives, and psychostimulants (for children with attention-deficit/hyperactivity disorder).

Electroconvulsive Therapy   **Electroconvulsive therapy (ECT)** is used for cases of severe depression that do not respond to other treatments. An electric current briefly passed through the brain of the patient produces convulsions and temporary coma.

Psychosurgery   **Psychosurgery** is brain surgery performed to change a person's behavior and emotional state. It is rarely done today, and then only as a last desperate measure on patients with intractable psychoses.

Institutionalization and Its Alternatives

Large mental hospitals offer people with severe mental disorders shelter and a degree of care, but a number of problems are linked with institutionalization.

Deinstitutionalization   With the advent of antipsychotic drugs in the 1950s, many patients were released from large public hospitals to be cared for in a community setting, a policy known as **deinstitutionalization.** But community mental health centers and other support services proved inadequate to the task. As a result, many former patients stopped taking their medication, became homeless, and ended up suffering from psychosis and living on the street.

Alternative Forms of Treatment   Alternatives to hospitalization include living at home, with training to cope with daily activities; hostels offering therapy and crisis intervention; day-care treatment; visits from public-health nurses combined with medication; and intensive outpatient counseling combined with medication. Most alternative treatments involve daily professional contact and skillful preparation of the family/community. The majority of studies have found more positive outcomes for alternative treatments than for hospitalization.

Prevention   **Prevention** refers to efforts to reduce the incidence of mental disorder. **Primary prevention** refers to improving the overall environment so that new cases of mental disorders do not develop. **Secondary prevention** refers to identifying high-risk groups and directing services to them. The object of **tertiary prevention** is to help hospitalized patients return to the community.

Gender and Cultural Differences in Treatments

Gender Differences   Women are more likely than men to be in psychotherapy in part because women traditionally have been more willing than men to admit they have psychological problems and seek help. Traditional male-oriented therapy often requires women to conform to gender stereotypes in order to be pronounced "well," so many women have turned to feminist therapists.

Cultural Differences   When client and therapist come from different cultural backgrounds or belong to different racial or ethnic groups, misunderstandings can arise in therapy. The APA has issued guidelines to help psychologists deal more effectively with ethnically and culturally diverse populations.

Psychotherapy	527	
Insight therapies	527	
Free association	528	
Transference	529	
Insight	529	
Client-centered (or person-centered) therapy	529	
Gestalt therapy	530	
Short-term psychodynamic psychotherapy	532	
Behavior therapies	533	

Systematic desensitization	534
Aversive conditioning	534
Behavior contracting	535
Token economy	535
Modeling	535
Cognitive therapies	536
Stress-inoculation therapy	537
Rational-emotive therapy (RET)	537
Cognitive therapy	538
Group therapy	539
Family therapy	539

Couple therapy	540
Eclecticism	544
Antipsychotic drugs	546
Biological treatments	546
Electroconvulsive therapy (ECT)	549
Psychosurgery	549
Deinstitutionalization	551
Prevention	553
Primary prevention	553
Secondary prevention	553
Tertiary prevention	553

key terms

OVERVIEW

Social Cognition
Impression Formation
Attribution
Interpersonal Attraction

Attitudes
The Nature of Attitudes
Prejudice and DiscriminationAttitude Change

Social Influence
Cultural Influence

Cultural Assimilators
Conformity
Compliance
Obedience

Social Action
Deindividuation
Helping Behavior
Group Decision Making
Leadership

Social
Psychology

15

n 1939, when the Germans occupied Warsaw, Poland, the Nazi army segregated the city's Jews in a ghetto surrounded by barbed wire. Deeply concerned about the fate of her Jewish friends, a 16-year-old Catholic girl named Stefania Podgórska made secret expeditions into the ghetto with gifts of food, clothing, and medicine. When the Jewish son of her former landlord made a desperate flight from the ghetto to avoid being deported to a concentration camp, Stefania agreed to hide him in her apartment. At one point, Stefania and her sister sheltered 13 Jews in their attic at the same time that two German soldiers were bivouacked in their small apartment.

In May 1991, the "hidden children" of the Holocaust gathered with their friends and relatives to pay tribute to 22 Christian rescuers who literally saved their lives during World War II.

- Gustave Collet, one of the people honored, was a Belgian soldier during World War II who helped hundreds of Jewish children by hiding them in the sanctuary of a Catholic church. According to Gustave, "We are all the sons of the same Father, and there is no reason there should be differences."
- Gisela Sohnlein, a student during World War II and a member of the Dutch underground, helped save thousands of Jewish children. In 1943 she was arrested by Nazi soldiers and spent one and a half years in a concentration camp. According to Gisela, "We didn't feel like rescuers at all. We were just ordinary students doing what we had to do."
- Wanda Kwiatkowska-Biernacka was 20 when she falsely claimed that a 1-month-old Jewish baby was her illegitimate child. (Lipman, 1991)

Are these people heroes, or, as Gisela Sohnlein stated, were they simply doing what had to be done? Why did they do what so many millions of other people failed to do? What caused people to acquiesce in the murder of millions of innocent people? Were they following orders? What brought about such hatred? Social psychologists address questions like these. **Social psychology** is the scientific study of the ways in which the thoughts, feelings, and behaviors of one individual are influenced by the real, imagined, or inferred behavior or characteristics of other people.

We begin this chapter with social cognition, how people think about other people. Next we consider the ways in which others can shape or change our attitudes and behaviors. Finally, we discuss relationships among people in small groups and large organizations. Throughout the chapter we will examine the impact of culture on social behavior.

Social Cognition

Are first impressions of other people usually accurate?

In everyday life, we interact with many other people. Some encounters are fleeting (sitting next to another passenger on a bus), some brief (asking a police officer for directions), some casual (chatting with a classmate as you leave a lecture hall or greeting a neighbor you bump into on the street), and some more critical (arguing or "making up" with a friend, lover, boss, or enemy). But even in fleeting encounters we form impressions and seek to understand why people act as they do. Is the

Social psychology The scientific study of the ways in which the thoughts, feelings, and behaviors of one individual are influenced by the real, imagined, or inferred behavior or characteristics of other people.

Primacy effect The theory that early information about someone weighs more heavily than later information in influencing one's impression of that person.

person walking toward you on the street friendly, menacing, or simply indifferent? In intimate relationships, we wonder, why am I attracted to this person? Is he or she "right" for me? The study of social perception focuses on how we judge or evaluate other people.

Impression Formation

A significant body of research supports the commonsense belief that first impressions matter. For the critical thinker, the question is, Why?

Schemata   When we meet someone for the first time, we notice a number of surface characteristics—clothes, gestures, manner of speaking, tone of voice, appearance, and so on. Then, drawing on these cues, we assign the person a ready-made *category*. Associated with each category is a *schema* (plural: *schemata*), which, as we saw in Chapter 6 (Memory), is a set of beliefs or expectations about something (in this case, people) that is based on past experience and is presumed to apply to all members of that category (Fiske & Taylor, 1991). For example, if a woman is wearing a white lab coat and has a stethoscope around her neck, we might reasonably categorize her as a doctor. Based on our schema of a doctor, we conclude that she is a highly trained professional, knowledgeable about diseases and their cures, qualified to prescribe medication, and so on.

Schemata serve a number of important functions (Gilbert, 1998). First, they allow us to make inferences about other people. We assume, for example, that a friendly person is likely to be good-natured, to accept a social invitation from us, or to do us a small favor.

Second, schemata play a crucial role in how we interpret and remember information (see Chapter 6, Memory). For example, in one study, half of the participants were told that they would be receiving information about friendly, sociable men, whereas the other half were informed that they would be learning about intellectual men. Both groups were then given the same information about a set of 50 men and asked to say how many of the men were friendly and how many were intellectual. The participants who had expected to hear about friendly men dramatically overestimated the number of friendly men in the set, and those who had expected to hear about intellectual men vastly overestimated the number of intellectual men in the set. Moreover, each group of participants forgot many of the details they received about the men that were inconsistent with their expectations (Rothbart, Evans, & Fulero, 1979). In short, the participants tended to hear and remember what they expected to.

Schemata can also lure us into "remembering" things about people that we never actually observed. Most of us associate the traits of shyness, quietness, and preoccupation with one's own thoughts with the schema *introvert*. If we notice that Melissa is shy, we are likely to categorize her as an introvert. Later, we may "remember" that she also seemed preoccupied with her own thoughts. This kind of thinking can easily lead to errors if we attribute to Melissa qualities that belong to the schema but not to her.

Over time, as we continue to interact with people, we add new information about them to our mental files. However, our later experiences generally do not influence us nearly so much as our earliest impressions. This is known as the **primacy effect.** Susan Fiske and Shelley Taylor (1991) point out that human thinkers are "cognitive misers." Instead of exerting ourselves to interpret every detail we learn about a person, we are stingy with our mental efforts. Once we have

If you were to hail this taxi in New York City, based on your assumptions about cab drivers you might never guess that this man from the Middle East holds an advanced degree in biology and is looking for a job at a university. Schemas can be useful, but they can also keep us from finding out what lies beneath the surface.

formed an impression about someone, we tend to keep it, even if our first impressions were formed by jumping to conclusions or through prejudice (Fiske, 1995). Thus, if you already like a new acquaintance, you may excuse a flaw or vice you discover later on. Conversely, if someone has made an early bad impression on you, you may refuse to believe subsequent evidence of that person's good qualities.

Moreover, first impressions can lead to a **self-fulfilling prophecy.** In one study, pairs of participants played a competitive game (Snyder & Swann, 1978). The researchers told one member of each pair that his or her partner was either hostile or friendly. Players who were led to believe their partner was hostile behaved differently toward the partner than players led to believe their partner was friendly. In turn, those treated as hostile actually began to display hostility. In fact, these people continued to show hostility later on, when they were paired with new players who had no expectations about them at all. The expectation of hostility, it seems, produced actual aggressiveness, and this behavior persisted.

Considerable scientific research has demonstrated the self-fulfilling prophecy. In a classic experiment, Rosenthal and Jacobsen (1968) gave all the children in a California elementary school a test at the beginning of the school year, and then gave teachers a list of children whom the test had identified as "bloomers": children who would demonstrate significant intellectual growth in the coming year. In fact, the "bloomers" were chosen at random. Nevertheless, the "bloomers" made greater gains in test scores and were rated as better students than a control group who had not been identified as bloomers. Why? Apparently teachers were warmer and friendlier to high-expectancy children, provided them with more positive feedback, and assigned them more challenging tasks, which enabled them to demonstrate competence. This finding has been named the *Pygmalion effect* after the mythical sculptor who created the statue of a woman and then brought it to life. Other studies have also shown that teacher expectations influence student performance in the classroom (Cooper, 1993; Harris & Rosenthal, 1985; Osborne, 1997; Rosenthal, 2002; Weinstein, Madison, & Kuklinski, 1995).

If people are specifically warned to beware of first impressions, or if they are encouraged to interpret information about others slowly and carefully, the primacy effect can be weakened or even nullified (Luchins, 1957; Stewart, 1965). One study, for example, compared the performance of "at-risk" ninth-grade students who had been assigned either to regular classrooms or to experimental classrooms that received a year-long intervention aimed at increasing teacher's expectations. After one year, the students in the experimental classrooms had higher grades in English and history compared to the students who were not in the intervention classrooms. Two years later, the experimental students were also found to be less likely to drop out of high school (Weinstein et al., 1991).

Stereotypes A **stereotype** is a set of characteristics believed to be shared by all members of a social category. A stereotype is a special kind of schema that may be based on almost any distinguishing feature, but is most often applied to sex, race, occupation, physical appearance, place of residence, and membership in a group or organization (Hilton & Von Hipple, 1996). When our first impressions of people are governed by a stereotype, we tend to infer things about them solely on the basis of their social category and to ignore facts about individual traits that are inconsistent with the stereotype. As a result, we may remember things about them selectively or inaccurately, thereby perpetuating our initial stereotype. For example, with a quick glance at almost anyone, you can classify that person as male or female. Once you

Self-fulfilling prophecy The process in which a person's expectation about another elicits behavior from the second person that confirms the expectation.

Stereotype A set of characteristics presumed to be shared by all members of a social category.

Suppose you are a new teacher entering this classroom on the first day of school in September. Do you have any expectations about children of any ethnic or racial groups that might lead to a self-fulfilling prophecy?

What is going on here? Would you want to stop and find out? If you held stereotypes about motorcyclists, you would probably want to speed away from this scene. In fact, though, these bikers were preparing for their annual Motorcycle Charity Run, a benefit for a local children's hospital.

have so categorized the person, you may rely more on your stereotype of that gender than on your own perceptions during further interactions with the person.

Stereotypes can easily become the basis for self-fulfilling prophecies. One study paired college-aged men and women who were strangers and arranged for each pair to talk by phone (Snyder, Tanke, & Berscheid, 1977). Before the call, each male was given a snapshot, presumably of the woman whom he was about to call. In fact, the snapshot was a randomly selected photo of either an attractive or unattractive woman. Attractiveness carries with it a stereotype that includes sociability and social adeptness. The men who believed they were talking to an attractive woman were warm, friendly, and animated; in response, the women acted in a friendly, animated way. The other men spoke to their partners in a cold, reserved manner. In response, the women reacted in a cool, distant manner. Thus, the stereotype took on a life of its own as the perceptions of the men determined their behavior, which in turn subtly forced the women to conform to the stereotype.

Recent studies (Macrae & Bodenhausen, 2000) indicate that sorting people into categories is not automatic or inevitable. People are more likely to apply stereotyped schemata in a chance encounter than in a structured, task-oriented situation (such as a classroom or the office); more likely to pay attention to individual signals than to stereotypes when they are pursuing a goal; and consciously or unconsciously suppress stereotypes that violate social norms. For example, a man who has operated according to stereotyped schemata may expect women in gender-typed roles, such as a nurse, a secretary, or his wife, to be warm and gentle, but not hold these expectations toward women he meets in his work life or in their professional roles (as lawyer, executive, or telephone repair person).

ENDURING ISSUES   **person**situation

Interpreting Behavior

The study of attribution, or how people explain their own and other people's behavior, focuses on when and why people interpret behavior as reflecting personal traits or social situations. Suppose you run into a friend at the supermarket. You greet him warmly, but he barely acknowledges you, mumbles "Hi," and walks away. You feel snubbed and try to figure out why he acted like that. Did he behave that way because of something in the situation? Perhaps you did something that offended him; perhaps he was having no luck finding the groceries he wanted; or perhaps someone had just blocked his way by leaving a cart in the middle of an aisle. Or did something within him, some personal trait such as moodiness or arrogance, prompt him to behave that way?

Attribution

Attribution theory The theory that addresses the question of how people make judgments about the causes of behavior.

Explaining Behavior Social interaction is filled with occasions that invite us to make judgments about the causes of behavior. Social psychologists have discovered that we go about this process of assessment in predictable ways. Their findings and the principles derived from them form the basis of **attribution theory.**

An early attribution theorist, Fritz Heider (1958) argued that a simple or "naíve" explanation for a given behavior attributes that behavior to either internal or external causes, but not both. Thus, you might say a classmate's lateness was caused by his laziness (a personal factor—an internal attribution) or by traffic congestion (a situational factor—an external attribution).

How do we decide whether to attribute a given behavior to causes inside or outside a person? According to another influential attribution theorist, Harold Kelley (1967), we rely on three kinds of information about behavior in determining its cause: distinctiveness, consistency, and consensus. For example, if your instructor asks you to stay briefly after class so she can talk with you, you will probably try to figure out what lies behind her request by asking yourself three questions.

First, how *distinctive* is the instructor's request? Does she often ask other students to stay and talk (low distinctiveness), or is such a request unusual (high distinctiveness)? If she often asks students to speak with her, you will probably conclude that she has personal internal reasons for talking with you. But if her request is highly distinctive, you will probably conclude that something about you, not her, underlies her request.

Second, how *consistent* is the instructor's behavior? Does she regularly ask you to stay and talk (high consistency), or is this a first for you (low consistency)? If she has consistently made this request of you before, you will probably guess that this occasion is like those others. But if her request is inconsistent with past behavior, you will probably wonder whether some passing event—perhaps something you said in class—motivated her to request a private conference.

Finally, what is the *consensus* of others' similar behavior? Do your other instructors ask you to stay and talk with them (high consensus), or is this instructor unique in making such a request (low consensus)? If it is common for your instructors to ask to speak with you, this instructor's request is probably due to some external factor. But if she is the only instructor ever to ask to speak privately with you, it is probably something about this particular person—an internal motive or concern—that accounts for her behavior (Iacobucci & McGill, 1990).

Biases in Attributions When making an attribution, you are guessing about the true causes of a particular action. Research shows that these guesses are vulnerable to a number of biases. For instance, imagine that you are at a party and you see an acquaintance, Ted, walk across the room carrying several plates of food and a drink. As he approaches his chair, Ted spills food on himself. You may attribute the spill to Ted's personal characteristics—he is clumsy. However, Ted is likely to make a very different attribution for the event. He will likely attribute the spill to an external factor—he was carrying too many other things. Your explanation for this behavior reflects the **fundamental attribution error**—the tendency to attribute the behavior of others to causes within themselves (Aronson, Wilson, & Akert, 1999; Gilbert & Malone, 1995; Ross & Nisbett, 1991).

More generally, the fundamental attribution error is part of the *actor-observer effect*—the tendency to explain the behavior of others as caused by internal factors and the corresponding tendency to attribute one's own behavior to external forces (Fiske & Taylor, 1991). Thus, Ted, the actor, attributed his own behavior to an external source, whereas you, the observer, attributed the behavior to an internal source.

Recall the examples used to introduce this chapter—people who risked their own safety to help others in Nazi Germany. As observers, we tend to attribute this behavior to personal qualities. Indeed, Robert Goodkind, chairman of the foundation that honored the rescuers, called for parents to "inculcate in our children the values of altruism and moral courage as exemplified by the rescuers." Clearly, Goodkind was making an internal attribution for the heroic behavior. However, the

Fundamental attribution error The tendency of people to overemphasize personal causes for other people's behavior and to underemphasize personal causes for their own behavior.

Defensive attribution The tendency to attribute our successes to our own efforts or qualities and our failures to external factors.

Just-world hypothesis Attribution error based on the assumption that bad things happen to bad people and good things happen to good people.

rescuers themselves attributed their actions to external factors: "We were only ordinary students who did what we had to do."

A related class of biases is called **defensive attribution.** These types of attributions occur when we are motivated to present ourselves well, either to impress others or to feel good about ourselves (Agostinelli, Sherman, Presson, & Chassin, 1992). One example is the *self-serving bias*, which is a tendency to attribute personal failure to external factors and personal success to internal factors (Schlenker & Weigold, 1992; Sedikides, Campbell, Reeder, & Elliot, 1998). For example, students tend to regard exams on which they do well as representing their true abilities and exams on which they do poorly as misrepresenting their abilities (Davis & Stephan, 1980). Similarly, teachers are more likely to assume responsibility for students' successes than for their failures (Arkin, Cooper, & Kolditz, 1980).

A second type of defensive attribution comes from thinking that people get what they deserve: Bad things happen to bad people, and good things happen to good people. This is called the **just-world hypothesis** (Lerner, 1980). When misfortune strikes someone, we often jump to the conclusion that the person deserved it, rather than giving full weight to situational factors that may have been responsible. Why do we do this? One reason is that it gives us the comforting illusion that such a thing could never happen to us. By reassigning the blame for a terrible crime from a chance event (something that could happen to us) to the victim's own negligence (a trait that we, of course, do not share), we delude ourselves into believing that we could never suffer such a misfortune.

Live psych **15.1**

Attribution Across Cultures   Historically, most of the research on attribution theory has been conducted in Western cultures. Do the basic principles of attribution apply to people in other cultures as well? The answer appears to be "not always." In general, East Asians are more likely to attribute both their own and other people's behavior to external, situational factors than to internal dispositions (Choi, Nisbett, & Norenzayan, 1999). For example, in one study, Japanese students studying in the United States usually explained failure as a lack of effort (an internal attribution) and attributed their successes to the assistance they received from others (an external attribution) (Kashima & Triandis, 1986). Research data also suggest that the fundamental attribution error may not be as pervasive as once believed. Researchers are finding that in some other cultures people are much less likely to attribute behavior to internal personal characteristics; they place more emphasis on the role of external, situational factors in explaining both their own behavior and that of others (Cousins, 1989; Markus & Kitayama, 1991; Menon, Morris, Chiu, & Hong, 1998; J. Miller, 1984). In contrast, recent research has shown that the self-serving bias is not just present in people of Western individualistic cultures like America, but is also observed in Eastern collectivist cultures like Japan (Sedikides, Gaertner, & Toguchi, 2003).

Interpersonal Attraction

So far, we have seen how people form impressions of one another and judge the causes of their own and others' behavior. But, when people meet, what determines whether they will like each other? This is the subject of much speculation and even mystification, with popular explanations running the gamut from fate to compatible astrological signs. Romantics believe that irresistible forces propel them toward an inevitable meeting with their beloved, but social psychologists take a more hard-

Attraction and liking are closely linked to such factors as proximity, similar interests and attitudes, and rewarding behavior.

ON THE CUTTING EDGE

BEAUTY AND PRIVILEGE

Poets and philosophers have been fascinated by beauty for centuries. With rare exceptions, the heroes and heroines of ancient myths and contemporary Hollywood fables are physically attractive—and the villains homely and deformed. Yet our culture includes age-old maxims that hold beauty either is not, or should not be, a significant factor in our judgments of, and behavior toward, other people. Judith Langlois and her colleagues (2000) conducted an extensive review and meta-analysis of scientific studies relevant to three of our proverbs.

"Never judge a book by its cover."

Countless studies have found that evaluations and treatment of attractive people are significantly more favorable than evaluations and treatment of unattractive people (see

Hosoda, Stone, & Coats, 2003; Langlois et al., 2000). Moreover, these judgments are not confined to first impressions: People who know an individual well attribute more positive traits to cute children and beautiful or handsome adults.

"Beauty is only skin-deep."

Here again, the scientific evidence contradicts the proverb. Compared with unattractive children, attractive children are more positive toward other people, better adjusted, and display greater intelligence. And so it is for adults: attractive men and women tend to have other positive traits as well, such as occupational success, being liked, enjoying better health, being self-confident, and even being slightly more intelligent (Jackson, Hunter, & Hodge, 1995; Langlois et al., 2000).

"Beauty is in the eye of the beholder."

In other words, judgments of attractiveness are subjective and variable; different people have different ideas about who is or is not beautiful. Langlois and her colleagues found that this, too, is a myth. In general, people agree when rating the attractiveness of others. People who are seen by others as handsome or pretty know they are viewed as being nice-looking (Marcus & Miller, 2003). In addition, people from different cultures and ethnic groups generally agree as to who is or is not beautiful. Even young infants prefer the same faces as adults (Rubenstein, Kalakanis, & Langlois, 1999). This cross-cultural, cross-ethnic agreement suggests the possibility of a universal standard of beauty.

What kind of face do people see as beautiful? Researchers have found that, across cultures, both sexes prefer "ultra-feminine" female faces with a soft, somewhat girlish look (Perret et al., 1998; also see Angier, 1998), and both sexes also preferred feminine-looking men!

Scientific studies have not resolved the mysteries of beauty and perhaps never will. But the evidence does indicate that our culture's maxims are myths: "Beauty is more than just in the eye of the beholder; people do judge and treat others with whom they interact based on attractiveness; and, perhaps most surprisingly, beauty is more than just skin-deep" (Langlois et al., 2000, p. 404).

Proximity How close two people live to each other.

headed view of the matter. They have found that attraction and the tendency to like someone else are closely linked to such factors as *proximity*, *physical attractiveness*, *similarity*, *exchange*, and *intimacy*.

Proximity   **Proximity** is usually the most important factor in determining attraction (Berscheid & Reis, 1998; Brehm, 2002). The closer two people live to each other, the more likely they are to interact; the more frequent their interaction, the more they will tend to like each other. Conversely, two people separated by considerable geographic distance are not likely to run into each other, and thus have little chance to develop a mutual attraction. The proximity effect apparently has less to do with simple convenience than with the security and comfort we feel with people and things that have become familiar. Familiar people are predictable and safe—thus more likable (Bornstein, 1989).

Physical Attractiveness   Physical attractiveness can powerfully influence the conclusions that we reach about a person's character. We generally give attractive people credit for more than their beauty. We presume them to be more intelligent, interesting, happy, kind, sensitive, moral, and successful than people who are not perceived as attractive. They are also thought to make better spouses and to be more sexually responsive (Dion, 1972; Feingold, 1992; Zuckerman, Miyake, & Elkin, 1995). Not surprisingly, we also tend to like them more than we do less attractive people (Baron & Byrne, 1991; Kernis & Wheeler, 1981). But attractiveness isn't everything. In the abstract, people might prefer extremely attractive individuals, but in reality they usually chose friends and partners who are close to their own level of attractiveness (Harvey & Pauwells, 1999).

Our preoccupation with physical attractiveness has material consequences. Research has found that mothers of more attractive infants tend to show them more affection and play with them more often than mothers of unattractive infants (Langlois, Ritter, Casey, & Sawin, 1995). Even in hospitals, premature infants rated as more attractive by attending nurses thrived better and gained weight faster than those judged as less attractive, presumably because they receive more nurturing (Badr & Abdallah, 2001). Attractive children are more likely to be treated leniently by teachers (McCall, 1997), and attractive adults are generally judged to be more productive by their employers (Hosoda, Stone, & Coats, 2003). In general, we give good-looking people the benefit of the doubt: If they don't live up to our expectations during the first encounter, we give them a second chance, ask for or accept a second date, or seek further opportunities for interaction. These reactions can give attractive people substantial advantages in life, becoming a self-fulfilling prophecy. Physically attractive people may come to think of themselves as good or lovable because they are continually treated as if they are (see *On the Cutting Edge: Beauty and Privilege*).

Similarity   Similarity of attitudes, interests, values, backgrounds, and beliefs underlies much interpersonal attractiveness (AhYun, 2002; Buss, 1985; Sano, 2002; Tan & Singh, 1995). When we know that someone shares our attitudes and interests, we tend to have more positive feelings toward that person. For example, voters are more attracted to and are more likely to vote for a candidate with whom they share similar attitudes (Quist & Crano, 2003). In addition, the higher the proportion of attitudes that two people share, the stronger the attraction between them (Byrne & Nelson, 1965). We value similarity because it is important to us to have others agree with our choices and beliefs. By comparing our opinions with those of other people, we clarify our understanding of and reduce our uncertainty about social situations. Finding that others agree with us strengthens our convictions and boosts our self-esteem (Suls & Fletcher, 1983).

If similarity is such a critical determinant of attraction, what about the notion that opposites attract? Extensive research has failed to confirm this notion. In long-term relationships, people overwhelmingly prefer to associate with other people who are similar to them (Buss, 1985). Where it seems that is not the case, research suggests that usually their dissimilarities are not opposites but complements. *Complementary traits* are needs or skills that complete or balance each other (Dryer & Horowitz, 1997). For example, a person who likes to care for and fuss over others will be most compatible with a mate who enjoys receiving such attention. These people are not really opposites, but their abilities and desires complement each other to their mutual satisfaction. Complementarity almost always occurs between people who already share similar goals and values and are willing to adapt to each other. True opposites are unlikely even to meet each other, much less interact long enough to achieve such compatibility.

Exchange According to the *reward theory of attraction*, we tend to like people who make us feel rewarded and appreciated. But the relationship between attraction and rewardingness is subtle and complex. For example, Aronson's (1994) gain-loss theory of attraction suggests that increases in rewarding behavior influence attractiveness more than constant rewarding behavior does. Say you were to meet and talk with a young man at three successive parties, and during these conversations that person's behavior toward you changed from polite indifference to overt flattery. You would be inclined to like this person more than if he had immediately started to praise you during the first conversation and kept up the stream of praise each time you met. The reverse also holds true: We tend to dislike people whose opinion of us changes from good to bad even more than we dislike those who consistently display a low opinion of us from our first encounter with them.

The reward theory of attraction is based on the concept of **exchange.** In social interactions, two people exchange various goods and resources with each other. For example, you may agree to help a friend paint his apartment in exchange for his preparing dinner for you. Every exchange involves both rewards (you get a free dinner, he gets his apartment painted) and costs (you have to paint, he has to cook you dinner). As long as both parties find their interactions more rewarding than costly, and as long as what one person "gets out of it" is roughly equal to what the other gets, their exchanges are likely to continue (Lott & Lott, 1974; Takeuchi, 2000; Van Yperen & Buunk, 1990; Walster, Walster, & Berscheid, 1978).

Intimacy When does liking someone become something more? **Intimacy** is the quality of genuine closeness and trust in another person. People become closer and stay closer through a continuing reciprocal pattern of each person trying to know the other and allowing the other to know him or her (Harvey & Pauwells, 1999). When you are first getting to know someone, you are likely to communicate about "safe," superficial topics such as the weather, sports, or shared activities. As you get to know each other better over time, your conversation progresses to more personal subjects: your personal experiences, memories, hopes and

Exchange The concept that relationships are based on trading rewards among partners.

Intimacy The quality of genuine closeness and trust achieved in communication with another person.

Self-disclosure—revealing personal experiences and opinions—is essential to all close relationships.

THINKING CRITICALLY

Intimacy and the Internet

Many of the studies of interpersonal attraction were conducted before e-mail swept the country.

- What impact (if any) has e-mail had on close relationships?

- Does e-mail make it easier to maintain long-distance relationships? Influence attributions? Encourage self-disclosure with intimates and/or strangers? Subtly shape social cognition in other ways?

- Suppose you were conducting a survey to collect data on these questions. What would you ask your participants? How might you determine whether their self-reports are accurate?

fears, goals, and failures. Because self-disclosure is only possible when you trust the listener, you will seek—and usually receive—a reciprocal disclosure to keep the conversation balanced. For example, after telling your roommate about something that embarrassed you, you may expect him or her to reveal a similar episode; you might even ask directly, "Has anything like that ever happened to you?" Such reciprocal intimacy keeps you "even" and makes your relationship more emotionally satisfying (Collins & Miller, 1994). The pacing of disclosure is important. If you "jump levels" by revealing too much too soon—or to someone who is not ready to make a reciprocal personal response—the other person will probably retreat and communication will go no further.

CHECK YOUR UNDERSTANDING

1. _____ are the sets of beliefs and expectations based on past experience that we apply to all members of a certain category.

___a. Self-fulfilling prophecies

___b. Schemata

___c. Stereotypes

2. Match the following biases in attributing causes to behavior with the appropriate definition.

___ fundamental attribution error

    a. attributing the behavior of others to internal causes and one's own behavior to external causes

___ actor-observer bias

    b. attributing our success to ourselves and our failures to factors beyond our control

___ self-serving bias

    c. assuming that people must deserve the bad things that happen to them

___ just-world hypothesis

    d. the tendency to attribute the behavior of others to personal characteristics

3. Which of the following is a basis for interpersonal attraction? (There can be more than one correct answer.)

___a. proximity

___b. similarity

___c. exchange

___d. attraction of opposites

___e. all of the above

4. According to Fritz Heider, we usually attribute behavior to

___a. internal and external causes both at the same time

___b. either internal or external causes, but not both at the same time

___c. external causes only

___d. internal causes only

Answers: 1.b, 2. fundamental attribution error—d; actor-observer bias—a; self-serving bias—b; just-world hypothesis—c, 3.a, b, and c, 4.b

Attitudes

Is a person's behavior a reflection of his or her attitudes?

The phrase "I don't like his attitude" is a telling one. People are often told to "change your attitude" or make an "attitude adjustment." What does this mean? Just what are attitudes? How are they formed? How can they be changed?

The Nature of Attitudes

An **attitude** is a relatively stable organization of *evaluative beliefs* about the object, *feelings* about the object, and *behavior tendencies* toward the object. Beliefs include facts, opinions, and our general knowledge about the object. Feelings encompass love, hate, like, dislike, and similar sentiments. Behavior tendencies refer to our inclinations to act in certain ways toward the object—to approach it, avoid it, and so on. For example, our attitude toward a political candidate includes our beliefs about the candidate's qualifications and positions on crucial issues and our expectations about how the candidate will vote on those issues. We also have feelings about the candidate—like or dislike, trust or mistrust. And because of these beliefs and feelings, we are inclined to behave in certain ways toward the candidate—to vote for or against the candidate, to contribute time or money to the candidate's campaign, and so forth.

As we will see shortly, these three aspects of an attitude are very often consistent with one another. For example, if we have positive feelings toward something, we tend to have positive beliefs about it and to behave positively toward it. This does not mean, however, that our every action will accurately reflect our attitudes. For example, our feelings about going to dentists are all too often negative, yet most of us make an annual visit anyway. Let's look more closely at the relationship between attitudes and behavior.

Attitudes and Behaviors The relationship between attitudes and behavior is not always straightforward (Andrich & Styles, 1998). Variables such as the strength of the attitude, how easily it comes to mind, how salient a particular attitude is in a given situation, and how relevant the attitude is to the behavior help determine whether a person will act in accordance with his or her attitude (Eagly, 1992; Eagly & Chaiken, 1998; Kraus, 1995).

Personality traits are also important. Some people consistently match their actions to their attitudes (Norman, 1975). Others have a tendency to override their own attitudes in order to behave properly in a given situation. As a result, attitudes predict behavior better for some people than others (Snyder & Tanke, 1976). People who rate highly on **self-monitoring** are especially likely to override their attitudes to behave in accordance with others' expectations. Before speaking or acting, *high self-monitors* observe the situation for cues about how they should react. Then they try to meet those "demands" rather than behave according to their own beliefs or sentiments. In contrast, *low self-monitors* express and act on their attitudes with great consistency, showing little regard for situational clues or constraints. Thus, a high self-monitor who disagrees with the politics of a fellow dinner guest may keep her thoughts to herself in an effort to be polite and agreeable, whereas a low self-monitor who disagrees might dispute the speaker openly, even though doing so might disrupt the social occasion (Snyder, 1987).

Attitude Development How do we acquire our attitudes? Where do they come from? Many of our most basic attitudes derive from early, direct personal

Attitude Relatively stable organization of beliefs, feelings, and behavior tendencies directed toward something or someone—the attitude object.

Self-monitoring The tendency for an individual to observe the situation for cues about how to react.

Attitudes develop early, often through imitation. Can you recall learning positive or negative attitudes by observing or listening to your parents?

experience. Children are rewarded with smiles and encouragement when they please their parents, and are punished through disapproval when they displease them. These early experiences give children enduring positive and negative attitudes (Oskamp, 1991). Attitudes are also formed by imitation. Children mimic the behavior of their parents and peers, acquiring attitudes even when no one is deliberately trying to influence their beliefs.

But parents are not the only source of attitudes. Teachers, friends, and even famous people are also important in shaping our attitudes. New fraternity or sorority members, for example, may model their behavior and attitudes on upper-class members. A student who idolizes a teacher may adopt many of the teacher's attitudes toward controversial subjects, even if they run counter to attitudes of parents or friends.

The mass media, particularly television, also have a great impact on the formation of attitudes in our society. Television bombards us with messages—not merely through its news and entertainment programs but also through commercials. Without experience of their own against which to measure the merit of these messages, children are particularly susceptible to television as an influence on their social attitudes.

Prejudice and Discrimination

Often used interchangeably, the terms *prejudice* and *discrimination* actually refer to different concepts. **Prejudice**—an attitude—is an intolerant, unfavorable, and rigid view of a group of people. People are prejudiced when they assume that all members of a certain group share certain negative qualities; when they are unable to see members of that group as individuals; and when they ignore information that disproves their beliefs. **Discrimination**—a behavior—is an act or a series of acts that denies opportunities and social esteem to an entire group of people or individual members of that group. To discriminate is to treat an entire class of people as less than equal.

ENDURING ISSUES   **person**situation

Does Discrimination Reflect Prejudice?

Prejudice and discrimination do not always occur together. It is possible to be prejudiced against a particular group without openly behaving in a hostile or discriminatory manner toward its members. A prejudiced storeowner may smile at an African American customer, for example, to disguise opinions that could hurt his business. Likewise, many institutional practices can be discriminatory even though they are not based on prejudice. For example, regulations establishing a minimum height requirement for police officers may discriminate against women and certain ethnic groups whose average height falls below the arbitrary standard, even though the regulations do not stem from sexist or racist attitudes.

Prejudice An intolerant, unfavorable, and rigid attitude toward a group of people.

Discrimination An act or series of acts that denies opportunities and social esteem to an entire group of people or individual members of that group.

Prejudice   Like attitudes in general, prejudice has three components: beliefs, feelings, and behavior tendencies. Prejudicial beliefs are negative stereotypes. When a prejudiced employer interviews an African American, for example, the employer may attribute to the job candidate all the traits associated with the African American stereotype, ignoring or dismissing individual qualities of the individual that do not match the stereotype. For example, the employer may belittle the candidate's hard-earned college degree by thinking, "He must have been admitted to college under an affirmative action program." This attribution is known as the *ultimate attribution error*: the tendency for a person with stereotyped beliefs about a particular group of people to make internal attributions for their shortcomings and external attributions for their successes. Notice that in the example above the employer is making an external attribution (affirmative action) for the college success of the African American job seeker. The other side of the ultimate attribution error is to make internal attributions for the failures of people who belong to groups we dislike. For instance, many white Americans believe that differences in income levels between white and black Americans are due to lack of ability or low motivation on the part of African Americans, not to lack of opportunity (Kluegel, 1990).

Along with stereotyped beliefs, prejudice is usually associated with strong emotions, such as dislike, fear, hatred, or loathing. For example, on learning that a person they like is a homosexual, heterosexuals may suddenly view the person as undesirable, sick, a sinner, or a pervert (see Herek, 2000). In Eastern Europe, many people both fear and look down on the traditionally nomadic Roma or "Gypsies."

Sources of Prejudice   Many theories attempt to sort out the causes and sources of prejudice. According to the **frustration-aggression theory,** prejudice is the result of the frustrations experienced by the prejudiced group (Allport, 1954). As we saw in Chapter 9, Motivation and Emotion, under some circumstances frustration can spill over into anger and hostility. People who feel exploited and oppressed often cannot vent their anger against an identifiable or proper target, so they displace their hostility onto those even "lower" on the social scale than themselves in the form of prejudicial attitudes and discriminatory behavior. The people who are the victims of this displaced aggression become scapegoats and are blamed for the problems of the times. African Americans in the United States have been scapegoats for the economic frustrations of some lower-income white Americans who feel powerless to improve their own condition. Latinos, Asian Americans, Jews, and women are also scapegoated—at times by African Americans. Like kindness, greed, and all other human qualities, prejudice is not restricted to a particular racial or ethnic group.

Another theory locates the source of prejudice in a bigoted or **authoritarian personality.** Adorno and his colleagues (1950) linked prejudice to a complex cluster of personality traits called *authoritarianism*. Authoritarian individuals tend to be rigidly conventional, favoring following the rules and abiding by tradition, and exhibiting hostility to those who defy those norms (Stone, Lederer, & Christie, 1993). They respect and submit to authority and are preoccupied with power and toughness. Looking at the world through a lens of rigid categories, they are cynical about human nature, fearing, suspecting, and rejecting all groups other than those to which they belong. Prejudice is only one expression of their suspicious, mistrusting approach to life.

There are also cognitive sources of prejudice. As we saw earlier, people are "cognitive misers" who try to simplify and organize their social thinking as much as possible. Too much simplification—oversimplification—leads to stereotypes, prejudice, and discrimination. For example, a stereotyped view of women as indecisive or weak will prejudice an employer against hiring a qualified woman as a manager. Belief in a just world—where people get what they deserve and deserve what they get—oversimplifies one's view of the victims of prejudice as somehow "deserving" their plight (Fiske & Neuberg, 1990).

Frustration-aggression theory The theory that under certain circumstances people who are frustrated in their goals turn their anger away from the proper, powerful target toward another, less powerful target that is safer to attack.

Authoritarian personality A personality pattern characterized by rigid conventionality, exaggerated respect for authority, and hostility toward those who defy society's norms.

Racism Prejudice and discrimination directed at a particular racial group.

Scenes like this were common in the South before the civil rights movement.

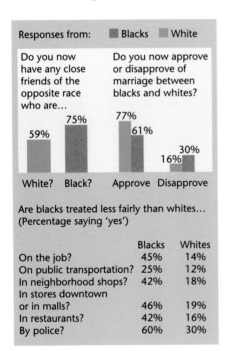

Figure 15–1
Racial attitudes in the United States.
As the figure illustrates, blacks and whites have different views of how blacks are treated in this country.
Source: Gelles, R. J., & Levine, A. (1999). *Sociology: An Introduction,* 6th Edition, fig. 9-7, p. 338; data from *USA Today,* June 11, 1997, p. 9a.

In addition, social psychologists point out that prejudice and discrimination may have their roots in people's attempts to conform in society. If we associate with people who express clear prejudices, we are more likely to go along with their ideas than to resist them. The pressures of social conformity help explain why children quickly absorb the prejudices of their parents and playmates long before they have formed their own beliefs and opinions on the basis of experience. Peer pressure often makes it "cool" or acceptable to express certain biases rather than to behave tolerantly toward members of other social groups.

Racism is the belief that members of certain racial or ethnic groups are *innately* inferior. Racists believe that intelligence, industry, morality, and other valued traits are biologically determined and therefore cannot be changed. Racism leads to either/or thinking: Either you are one of "us" or you are one of "them." An *in-group* is any group of people who feel a sense of solidarity and exclusivity in relation to nonmembers. An *out-group*, in contrast, is a group of people who are outside this boundary and viewed as competitors, enemies, or different and unworthy of respect. These terms can be applied to opposing sports teams, rival gangs, and political parties, or to entire nations, regions, religions, and ethnic or racial groups. According to the *in-group bias*, members see themselves not just as different but also as superior to members of out-groups. In extreme cases, members of an in-group may see members of an out-group as less than human and hatred may lead to violence, civil war, and even genocide.

The most blatant forms of racism in the United States have declined in the last several decades. For example, nine out of ten whites say they would vote for a black president. But racism still exists in subtle forms. For example, many whites say they approve of interracial marriage, but would be "uncomfortable" if someone in their family married an African American. Many whites also support racial integration of schools, but become "uneasy" if the percentage of black students in their child's class or school increases significantly (Jaynes & Williams, 1989). Thus, it is not surprising that blacks and whites have different views of how blacks are treated in our society. In a 1997 survey, two out of three whites agreed with the statement, "Blacks have as good a chance as white people . . . to get any job they are qualified for"; about the same proportion of blacks disagreed (see Figure 15–1 for other differences from the same survey).

Strategies for Reducing Prejudice and Discrimination How can we use our knowledge of prejudice, stereotypes, and discrimination to reduce prejudice and its expression? Three strategies appear promising: *recategorization, controlled processing,* and *improving contact between groups.* (See *Applying Psychology: Understanding Ethnic Conflict and Violence* for a discussion of how these strategies can be used to reduce ethnic conflict.)

- When we *recategorize,* we try to expand our schema for a particular group, say by viewing people from different races or genders as sharing similar qualities. These more inclusive schemata become superordinate categories. For instance, Catholics and Protestants in the United States view themselves as "Christians" or as "Americans" rather than as separate competing groups (as in Northern Ireland). There is considerable evidence that if people can create superordinate categories, they can reduce stereotypes and prejudice (Dovidio & Gaertner, 1999; Hewstone, Islam, & Judd, 1993).

- Research also suggests that we can train ourselves to be more "mindful" of people who differ from us through *controlled processing.* For example, a group of sixth graders was taught to be more understanding of the handicapped by having them view slides and think about their situation by answering such questions as "how might a handicapped person drive a car?" The students were

APPLYING PSYCHOLOGY

UNDERSTANDING ETHNIC CONFLICT AND VIOLENCE

With the end of the Cold War, the dominant form of war has become interethnic conflict (Mays, Bullock, Rosenzweig, & Wessells, 1998; Rouhana & Bar-Tal, 1998). Bosnia, Croatia, East Timor, Russia, Turkey, Iraq, Ireland, Israel, Sri Lanka . . . the list of countries torn by ethnic conflict goes on and on and the deaths of civilians continue to increase by the tens of thousands. As US armed forces entered Iraq in 2003, they had to cope with eruptions of interethnic violence between the Arabs and the Kurds, Turkomans, and Assyrians. In Iraq alone, ethnic violence during the previous decade was responsible for tens of thousands of civilian deaths (Human Rights Watch, 2003). Why does such conflict arise? And why is it so difficult to resolve?

Ethnic conflict has no single cause. Ethnic conflict ". . . is often rooted in histories of colonialism, ethnocentrism, racism, political oppression, human rights abuses, social injustice, poverty, and environmental degradation" (Mays et al., 1998, p. 737; also see Toft, 2003). But these structural problems are only part of the story, determining primarily who fights whom. The rest of the story is to be found in psychological processes such as intense group loyalty, personal and social identity, shared memories, polarization and deep-rooted prejudice, and societal beliefs (Cairns & Darby, 1998; Mays et al., 1998; Rouhana & Bar-Tal, 1998). In other words, structural problems don't have the same effect if people are not prepared to hate and fear others. This hate and fear largely determines the extent to which ethnic conflict becomes violent (Des Forges, 1995; Ross, 1993; D. N. Smith, 1998).

> *"Hate and fear largely determine the extent to which ethnic conflict becomes violent."*

Looking more closely at some of the psychological forces at work, *propaganda* often plays a significant role by painting opponents in the most negative fashion possible, thus perpetuating racism, prejudice, and stereotypes. In Rwanda, for example, Tutsis (who were almost exterminated by the resulting violence with Hutus) for years were accused in the mass media of having committed horrible crimes and of plotting the mass murder of Hutus, none of which was true (Smith, 1998). When ethnic violence is protracted, *shared collective memories* become filled with instances of violence, hostility, and victimization. Prejudices are thus reinforced, and people increasingly come to view the conflict as inevitable and their differences as irreconcilable (Rouhana & Bar-Tal, 1998).

Personal and social identity can also contribute to ethnic conflict. Because group memberships contribute to self-image, if the groups to which you belong are maligned or threatened, then to some extent you are personally maligned and threatened. If you are unable to leave those groups, it is important to defend them in order to enhance your own feelings of self-esteem (Cairns & Darby, 1998). In this way, what starts out as ethnic conflict quickly becomes a highly personal threat.

Finally, widespread *societal beliefs* about the conflict and the parties to the conflict also play a role in prolonged ethnic conflicts. Four especially important societal beliefs are "Our goals are just," "The opponent has no legitimacy," "We can do no wrong," and "We are the victims" (Rouhana & Bar-Tal, 1998). These societal beliefs ". . . provide a common social prism through which society members view the conflict. Once formed, they become incorporated into an ethos and are reflected in the group's language, stereotypes, images, myths, and collective memories . . . " (Rouhana & Bar-Tal, 1998, p. 765). The result is a form of "cognitive freezing" in which people selectively seek out and process information in a way that perpetuates the societal beliefs. This cognitive freezing heightens fear, anger, and hatred—the emotions that are the basis of ethnic violence.

Episodes of ethnic violence kill thousands of people worldwide every year.

It follows that attempts to build peace cannot address only structural problems. Attempts to redistribute resources more equitably, to reduce oppression and victimization, and to increase social justice are essential, but they will succeed only if attention is also given to important psychological processes. Concerted efforts must be made to increase tolerance and improve intergroup relations while also developing new, nonviolent means for resolving conflicts (Mays et al., 1998; Smith, 1998). The strategies of recategorization, controlled processing, and

(continued)

APPLYING PSYCHOLOGY

UNDERSTANDING ETHNIC CONFLICT AND VIOLENCE *(CONT.)*

contact between groups discussed earlier in this chapter have helped reduce the level of ethnic conflict in some countries (Smith, 1998). But cognitive changes must also be made: Societal beliefs must be changed, and new beliefs must be developed that are more consistent with conflict resolution and peaceful relationships. In addition, multidisciplinary techniques will need to be developed if programs are to be fully effective in addressing conflicts in different cultures. As one group of experts put it, "It is both risky and ethnocentric to assume that methods developed in Western contexts can be applied directly in different cultures and contexts. Research on different cultural beliefs and practices and their implications for ethno political conflict analysis and prevention is essential if the field of psychology is going to be successful in its contributions" (Mays et al., 1998, p. 739).

encouraged to see handicapped people as having both strengths and weaknesses. The group showed far less prejudice toward handicapped people after this procedure than before it (Langer, Bashner, & Chanowitz, 1985). Such an approach suggests that tolerance can be taught. Some researchers have suggested that the primary difference between someone who is prejudiced and someone who is not is the ability to suppress prejudiced beliefs. They argue that we all learn the stereotypes in our culture, but some people also learn tolerance and the ability for controlled processing (Devine, 1989; Devine, Monteith, Zuwerink, & Elliot, 1991).

- Finally, we can reduce prejudice and tensions by *improving contact between groups* (Pettigrew, 1998). This was one of the intentions of the famous 1954 U.S. Supreme Court's decision in *Brown v. Board of Education of Topeka, Kansas*, mandating that public schools become racially integrated. However, the evidence from school desegregation has shown us that contact alone is not enough (Taylor & Moghaddam, 1994). Contact between members of two groups can work to undermine prejudicial attitudes, but only if certain conditions are met:

1. **Group members must have equal status.** When blacks and whites were first integrated in the army and in public housing projects, they had relatively equal status, and as a result prejudice between them was greatly reduced (Pettigrew, 1969). School desegregation has been less successful in part because the structure of our school system tends to reward the economic and academic advantages of white children, giving them an edge over black schoolchildren (Cohen, 1984).

2. **People need to have one-on-one contact with members of another group.** Simply putting students together in class does not change attitudes. Personal contact such as that which occurs between friends at lunch and after school is more effective.

3. **Contact between groups improves relations when the groups come together to cooperate rather than compete.** Perhaps because it provides the kind of personal contact just mentioned, as well as a sort of common ground and equal status, working together to achieve a common goal helps break down prejudice. Integrated sports teams are one example of this sort of contact. Cooperative learning techniques have also proved to be effective in overcoming prejudice in schools (Johnson, Johnson, & Maruyama, 1984; Madden & Slavin, 1983).

 15.2

4. **The social norms should encourage contact.** In many cases, school desegregation took place in a highly charged atmosphere. Busloads of children arrived at their new schools only to face the protests of angry parents. These conditions clearly did

not promote contact. In situations where contact is encouraged by the social norms or by those in authority, prejudicial attitudes are less likely to persist.

In all of these suggestions, the primary focus is on changing behavior, not on changing attitudes directly. But changing behavior is often a first step toward changing attitudes as we will see in the following section where we examine some of the major findings in the psychological research on attitude change.

Attitude Change

A man watching TV on Sunday afternoon ignores scores of beer commercials but makes a note when a friend recommends a particular imported beer. A political speech convinces one woman to change her vote in favor of the candidate who made it but leaves her next-door neighbor determined to vote against the candidate. Why would a personal recommendation have greater persuasive power than an expensively produced television commercial? How can two people with similar views derive completely different messages from the same speech? What makes one attempt to change attitudes fail and another succeed? More generally, how and why do attitudes change, and how can we successfully resist attitude changes we do not want?

The answers to these questions depend to some extent on the technique used to influence our attitudes. We will look first at attempts to change attitudes through various kinds of persuasive messages.

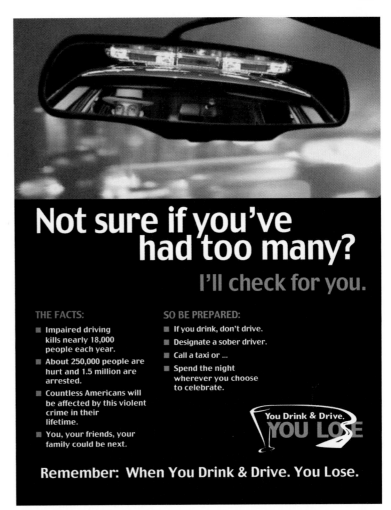

THE FACTS:

■ Impaired driving kills nearly 18,000 people each year.

■ About 250,000 people are hurt and 1.5 million are arrested.

■ Countless Americans will be affected by this violent crime in their lifetime.

■ You, your friends, your family could be next.

SO BE PREPARED:

■ If you drink, don't drive.

■ Designate a sober driver.

■ Call a taxi or ...

■ Spend the night wherever you choose to celebrate.

Remember: When You Drink & Drive. You Lose.

For an ad to affect our behavior, it must first attract our attention.
Source: National Highway Safety Commission.

The Process of Persuasion   To be persuaded, you must first pay attention to the message; then you must comprehend it; finally, you must accept it as convincing (Perloff, 2003). Consider how advertising accomplishes each of these steps.

The first step in persuasion is to seize and retain the audience's attention (Albarracin, 2002). As the competition has stiffened, advertisers have become increasingly creative in seizing your attention. For example, ads that arouse emotions, especially feelings you want to act on, can be memorable and thus persuasive (DeSteno & Braverman, 2002; Engel, Black, & Miniard, 1986). Humor, too, is an effective way to keep you watching or reading an entire ad you would otherwise ignore (Conway & Dube, 2002; Scott, Klein, & Bryant, 1990).

Once a persuasive message grabs your attention, other techniques encourage you to "stay tuned" long enough to comprehend and accept its message. For example, more and more ads "hook" the audience by involving them in a narrative. A commercial might open with a dramatic scene or situation—for example, two people seemingly "meant" for each other but not yet making eye contact—and the viewer stays tuned to find out what happens. Some commercials even feature recurring characters and story lines so that each new commercial in the series is really the latest installment in a soap opera.

With so many clever strategies focused on seizing and holding your attention, how can you shield yourself from unwanted influences and resist persuasive appeals? One strategy for resisting persuasion is to analyze persuasive messages to identify which attention-getting strategies are at work. Make a game of deciphering the advertiser's "code" instead of falling for the ad's appeal. And raise your standards for the kinds of messages that are worthy of your attention and commitment.

The Communication Model   The second and third steps in persuasion—comprehending and then accepting the message—are influenced by both the message itself and the way it is presented. The *communication model* of persuasion spotlights four key elements to achieve these goals: the source, the message itself, the medium of communication, and the characteristics of the audience. Once they have seized your attention, persuaders manipulate each of these factors in the hope of changing your attitudes. Let us take each factor in turn as we consider what is known about effective persuasion.

The effectiveness of a persuasive message first depends on its *source*, the author or communicator who appeals to the audience to accept the message. Here credibility makes a big difference (Ito, 2002; Jain & Posavac, 2001). For example, we are less likely to change our attitude about the oil industry's antipollution efforts if the president of a major refining company tells us about them than if we hear the same information from an impartial commission appointed to study the situation.

Research indicates that the credibility of the source is most important when we are not inclined to pay attention to the *message* itself (Cooper & Croyle, 1984; Petty & Cacioppo, 1981, 1986a). But in cases where we have some interest in the message, it is the message that plays the greater role in determining whether we change our attitudes (Petty & Cacioppo, 1986b). Researchers have discovered that we frequently tune out messages that simply contradict our own point of view. And the more effective you are at generating counter arguments, the less likely you are to be persuaded by new arguments (Jacks & Cameron, 2003). Thus, messages are generally more successful when they present both sides of an argument and when they present novel arguments rather than rehashes of old standbys heard many times before.

Research has shown that fear sometimes works well, especially in convincing people to get tetanus shots (Dabbs & Leventhal, 1966), to drive safely (Leventhal & Niles, 1965), and to take care of their teeth (Evans, Rozelle, Lasater, Dembroski, & Allen, 1970). But if the message generates too much fear, it will have little persuasive effect (Worchel, Cooper, & Goethals, 1991).

When it comes to a choice of *medium*, writing is best suited to making people understand complex arguments, whereas videotaped or live media presentations are more effective with an audience that already grasps the gist of an argument (Chaiken & Eagly, 1976). Most effective, however, are face-to-face appeals or the lessons of our own experience.

The most critical factors in changing attitudes—and the most difficult to control—have to do with *audience*. Attitudes are most resistant to change if (1) the audience has a strong commitment to its present attitudes, (2) those attitudes are shared by others, and (3) the attitudes were instilled during early childhood by such pivotal groups as the family. The discrepancy between the contents of the message and the present attitudes of the audience also affects how well the message will be received. Up to a point, the greater the difference between the two, the greater the likelihood of attitude change. However, if the discrepancy is too great, the audience may reject the new information altogether. The expertise of the communicator is very important in this context: Influence increases with the size of the discrepancy only when the speaker is considered an expert.

Finally, certain personal characteristics make some people more susceptible to attitude change than others. People with low self-esteem are more easily influenced, especially when the message is complex and hard to understand. Highly intelligent people tend to resist persuasion because they can think of counterarguments more easily.

Cognitive Dissonance Theory   One of the most fascinating approaches to understanding the process of attitude change is the theory of **cognitive dissonance** developed by Leon Festinger (1957). Cognitive dissonance exists whenever a person has two contradictory cognitions, or beliefs, at the same time. "I am a considerate and loyal friend" is one cognition; so is "Yesterday I repeated some juicy gossip I heard about my friend Chris." These two cognitions are dissonant—each one implies the opposite of the other. According to Festinger, cognitive dissonance creates unpleasant psychological tension, and this tension motivates the individual to try to resolve the dissonance in some way.

Sometimes changing one's attitude is the easiest way to reduce the discomfort of dissonance. I cannot easily change the fact that I have repeated gossip about a friend. Therefore, it is easier to change my attitude toward my friend. If I conclude that Chris is not really a friend but simply an acquaintance, then my new attitude now fits my behavior—spreading gossip about someone who is not a friend does not contradict the fact that I am loyal and considerate to those who are my friends. Similarly, one way to reduce the discomfort or guilt associated with cheating in school is to show approval of, or support for other students who engage in academic dishonesty (Storch & Storch, 2003).

Discrepant behavior that contradicts an attitude does not necessarily bring about attitude change, however, because there are other ways a person can reduce cognitive dissonance. One alternative is to increase the number of consonant elements—that is, the thoughts that support one or the other dissonant cognitions. For example, I might note that the gossip I repeated was pretty interesting, that anyone who had heard it would be concerned and surprised about Chris, and that it would be only natural to discuss it with others in an effort to determine whether it was true. Now my action is less at odds with my attitude toward Chris as a friend. Another option is to reduce the importance of one or both cognitive elements. "The person I repeated the gossip to was Terry, who doesn't really know Chris very well. Terry doesn't care and won't repeat it. It was no big deal and Chris shouldn't be upset about it." By reducing the significance of my behavior, I reduce the dissonance that I experience and so make it less necessary to change my attitude toward Chris.

Our discussion so far has ignored an important question: Why would someone engage in behavior that goes against an attitude in the first place? One answer is that cognitive dissonance is a natural part of everyday life. For example, simply choosing between two or more desirable alternatives leads inevitably to dissonance. Suppose you are in the market for a computer but can't decide between a Dell and a Macintosh. If you choose one, all of its bad features and all the good aspects of the other contribute to dissonance. After you have bought one of the computers, you can reduce the dissonance by changing your attitude: You might decide that the keyboard on the other computer wasn't "quite right" and that some of the "bad" features of the computer you bought are actually desirable.

You may also engage in behavior at odds with an attitude because you are enticed to do so. Perhaps someone offers you a small bribe or reward: "I will pay you 25 cents just to try my product." Curiously, the larger the reward, the smaller the change in attitude that is likely to result. When rewards are large, dissonance is at a minimum, and attitude change is small, if it happens at all. Apparently, when people are convinced that there is a good reason to do something that goes against their beliefs ("I'll try almost anything in exchange for a large cash

Cognitive dissonance Perceived inconsistency between two cognitions.

THINKING CRITICALLY

Attitudes Toward Smoking

Numerous studies show that most adolescents and young adults are well aware of the dangers of smoking cigarettes. Nonetheless a significant number of those same people smoke regularly. Based on what you have read concerning attitude change, how would you go about changing people's attitudes toward smoking? For each technique you would use, explain why you think it would be effective. How would you demonstrate whether your program was having the desired effect?

incentive"), they experience little dissonance and their attitudes are not likely to shift, even though their behavior may change for a time. However, if the reward is small, just barely enough to induce behavior that conflicts with one's attitude, dissonance will be great, maximizing the chances for attitude change: "I only got 25 cents to try this product, so it couldn't have been the money that attracted me. I must really like this product after all." The trick is to induce the behavior that goes against an attitude while leaving people feeling personally responsible for the dissonant act. That way they are more likely to change their attitudes than if they feel they were forced or blatantly induced to act in a way that contradicts their beliefs.

In the final analysis, the most effective means of changing attitudes—especially important attitudes, behaviors, or lifestyle choices—may be *self-persuasion* (Aronson, 1999). In contrast with traditional, direct techniques of persuasion, people are put in situations where they are motivated to persuade themselves to change their attitudes or behavior. For example, many educators hoped that school integration—by itself—would reduce racial prejudices. But often the reverse proved true: although they attended the same schools and classes, black and white children tended to "self-segregate." When children were assigned to small, culturally diverse study groups, in which they were forced to cooperate, attitudes changed—albeit slowly. Insults and put downs, often ethnically based, decreased. Having learned to both teach and listen to "others," students emerged from the experience with fewer group stereotypes and greater appreciation of individual differences. And this, in turn, made them less likely to stereotype others. In a nutshell, working with diverse individuals who did not fit preconceived notions made it difficult to maintain prejudice because of cognitive dissonance.

CHECK YOUR UNDERSTANDING

1. A(n) _____ is a fairly stable organization of beliefs, feelings, and behavior tendencies toward something or someone.

___a. impression

___b. attribution

___c. attitude

2. Prejudice is to _____ as discrimination is to _____.

___a. attitude; behavior

___b. tolerance; oppression

___c. behavior; attitude

___d. oppression; tolerance

3. Which of the following can be an effective way to reduce prejudice?

___a. equal status contact

___b. one-on-one contact

___c. cooperative group projects

___d. social norms that encourage contact

___e. all of the above

4. _____ is when a person holds two contradictory beliefs at the same time.

___a. Prejudice

___b. Cognitive dissonance

___c. Self-serving bias

___d. Just-world bias

Answers: 1.c, 2.a, 3.e, 4.b

Social Influence

Is conformity a sign that a person lacks self-confidence?

In social psychology, **social influence** refers to the process by which others—individually or collectively—affect our perceptions, attitudes, and actions (Nowak, Vallacher, & Miller, 2003; Petty, Wegener, & Fabrigar, 1997). In the previous section, we examined one form of social influence: attitude change. Next, we'll focus on how the presence or actions of others can control behavior without regard to underlying attitudes.

Cultural Influence

As we saw in Chapter 1, The Science of Psychology, *culture* refers to people's shared ideas, beliefs, values, technologies, and criteria for evaluating what natural events, human actions, and life itself means. Culture exerts an enormous influence on our attitudes and behaviors. We refrain from playing our stereo at full volume when our neighbors are sleeping, comply with jury notices that we receive in the mail, and obey traffic signals even when no one is on the road to enforce the social norms that dictate these actions. Consider for a moment a few other aspects of day-to-day living that are derived from culture:

- Your culture dictates how you dress. A Saudi woman covers her entire body before venturing outside her home; a North American woman freely displays her face, arms, and legs; and women in other societies go about bare-breasted or completely naked.

- Culture specifies what you eat—and what you do not eat. Americans do not eat dog meat, Chinese eat no cheese, and Hindus refuse to eat beef. Culture further guides how you eat: with a fork, chopsticks, or your bare hands.

- People from different cultures seek different amounts of personal space. This is the bubble of space one maintains in one's interactions with others. Latin Americans, French people, and Arabs get closer to each other in most face-to-face interactions than do Americans, English people, or Swedes.

To some extent, culture influences us through formal instruction. For example, your parents may have reminded you from time to time that certain actions are considered "normal" or the "right way" to behave. But more often we learn cultural lessons through modeling and imitation. One result of such learning is the unquestioning acceptance of **cultural truisms**—beliefs or values that most members of a society accept as self-evident (Aronson, 1994; Maio & Olson, 1998).

We also learn cultural lessons through conditioning. We are rewarded (reinforced) for doing as our companions and fellow citizens do in most situations—for going along with the crowd. This learning process is one of the chief mechanisms by which a culture transmits its central lessons and values. In the course of comparing and adapting our own behavior to that of others, we learn the norms of our culture.

Cultural Assimilators

A **norm** is a shared idea or expectation about how to behave or not to behave (Cialdini & Trost, 1998). Norms are often steeped in tradition and strengthened by habit. Thus, cultures seem strange to us if their norms are very different from our own. It is tempting to conclude that *different* means "wrong," simply because unfamiliar patterns of behavior can make us feel uncomfortable. To transcend our

---

Social influence The process by which others individually or collectively affect one's perceptions, attitudes, and actions.

Cultural truisms Beliefs that most members of a society accept as self-evidently true.

Norm A shared idea or expectation about how to behave.

Conformity Voluntarily yielding to social norms, even at the expense of one's own preferences.

differences and get along better with people from other cultures, we must find ways to overcome such discomfort.

One technique for understanding other cultures is the *cultural assimilator*, a strategy for perceiving the norms and values of another group (Baron, Graziano, & Stangor, 1991; Brislin, Cushner, Cherries, & Yong, 1986). This technique teaches by example, asking students to explain why a member of another cultural or social group has behaved in a particular manner. For example, why do the members of a Japanese grade school class silently follow their teacher single file through a park on a lovely spring day? Are they afraid of being punished for disorderly conduct if they do otherwise? Are they naturally placid and compliant? Once you understand that Japanese children are raised to value the needs and feelings of others over their own selfish concerns, their orderly, obedient behavior seems not mindless but disciplined and considerate.

Cultural assimilators encourage us to remain open-minded about others' norms and values by challenging such cultural truisms as "My country is always the best" or "Our way is the only right way."

Conformity

Without norms, social life would be chaotic. With them, the behavior of other people becomes fairly predictable despite great differences in underlying attitudes and preferences. Thus, a certain amount of **conformity** is necessary if social groups are to function effectively. To an extent, people must voluntarily set aside their own preferences or beliefs and abide by the norms or expectations of a larger group.

Since the early 1950s, when Solomon Asch conducted the first systematic study of the subject, conformity has been a major topic of research in social psychology. Asch demonstrated in a series of experiments that under some circumstances people will conform to group pressures even if this forces them to deny obvious physical evidence. His studies ostensibly tested visual judgment by asking people in a small group to choose from a card with several lines of differing lengths the line most similar to the line on a comparison card (see Figure 15–2). The lines were deliberately drawn so that the comparison was obvious and the correct choice was clear. All but one of the people in the group were actually confederates of the experimenter. From time to time these confederates deliberately gave the same, incorrect answer. This put the lone real participant on the spot: Should he conform to what he knew to be a wrong decision and agree with the group, thereby denying the evidence of his own senses? Or should he disagree with the group, thereby risking the social consequences of nonconformity?

Surprisingly, Asch found that participants conformed with the clearly incorrect judgments about one-third of the time. There were large individual differences, however, and in subsequent research, experimenters discovered that two sets of factors influence the likelihood that a person will conform: characteristics of the situation and characteristics of the individual.

The *size* of the group is one situational variable that has been studied extensively. Asch (1951) found that the likelihood of conformity increased with expansion of group size until four confederates were present. After that point, adding more confederates did not increase the likelihood that the participants would ignore the evidence of their own eyes.

Another important situational factor is the degree of *unanimity* in the group. If just one confederate broke the perfect agreement of the

Why do Japanese schoolchildren behave in such an orderly way? How does your answer compare with the discussion of cultural influences?

majority by giving the correct answer, conformity fell to about 25 percent (Asch, 1956). Apparently, having just one "ally" eases the pressure to conform. The ally does not even have to share the participant's viewpoint—just breaking the unanimity of the majority is enough to reduce conformity (Allen & Levine, 1971).

The *nature of the task* is still another situational variable that affects conformity. For instance, conformity has been shown to vary with the difficulty and the ambiguity of a task. When the task is difficult or poorly defined, conformity tends to be higher (Blake, Helson, & Mouton, 1956). In an ambiguous situation, individuals are less sure of their own opinion and more willing to conform to the majority view.

Personal characteristics also influence conforming behavior. The more an individual is attracted to the group, expects to interact with its members in the future, holds a position of relatively low status in the group, and does not feel completely accepted by the group, the more that person tends to conform.

Conformity Across Cultures   A Chinese proverb states that "if one finger is sore, the whole hand will hurt." In a collectivist culture such as China, community and harmony are very important. Although members of all societies show a tendency to conform, one might expect members of collectivist cultures to conform more frequently to the will of a group than members of noncollectivist cultures. And in fact, researchers have found that the levels of conformity in collectivist cultures are often higher than conformity in individualist cultures. (See Chapter 9, Motivation and Emotion, for a discussion of individualist and collectivist cultures.) In collectivist societies as diverse as Fiji, Zaire, Hong Kong, Lebanon, Zimbabwe, Kuwait, Japan, and Brazil, conformity rates ranged from 25 percent among Japanese students to 51 percent among students in Zimbabwe (Smith & Bond, 1994). In a novel extension of this approach, Berry (1967) demonstrated that conformity was greater in farming societies (where members are more dependent on one another for long-term group survival) than in hunting and gathering societies (where people must exercise a good deal of independence to survive).

Not all the research data support the existence of a simple link between collectivism and conformity, however. Although Williams and Sogon (1984) reported that Japanese participants showed a high tendency to conform when they were among friends, Frager (1970) found evidence of nonconformity among Japanese participants when the confederates in the Asch situation were strangers. (In fact, in this situation, Japanese participants often deliberately gave the wrong response even when the majority opinion was correct.)

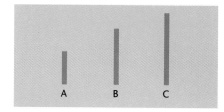

Figure 15–2
Asch's experiment on conformity.
In Asch's experiment on *conformity*, participants were shown a comparison card like the top one and asked to indicate which of the three lines on the bottom card was the most similar.

 15.3

ENDURING ISSUES   **individuality**universality

Social Influence Across Cultures

Given these somewhat conflicting data, what conclusion can we reach about the universality of social influence? The fact that rates of conformity in the Asch situation were relatively high across a variety of cultures suggests that there may be some kind of universal conformity norm. But the fact that conformity was often especially high within collectivist societies suggests that the tendency toward conformity is heightened or lessened by a specific cultural context. As psychologists gain a better understanding of the differences among cultures, the answers to the questions "What is universal about social influence?" and "What is culturally determined?" should become clearer.

Compliance Change of behavior in response to an explicit request from another person or group.

Obedience Change of behavior in response to a command from another person, typically an authority figure.

Compliance

Conformity is a response to pressure exerted by norms that are generally left unstated. In contrast, **compliance** is a change of behavior in response to an explicit request (Cialdini & Trost, 1998). Social psychologists have studied several techniques by which people can induce others to comply with their requests. One procedure is based on the so-called *foot-in-the-door effect* (Cialdini, 1995). Every salesperson knows that the moment a prospect allows the sales pitch to begin, the chances of making a sale improve greatly. The same effect operates in other areas of life: Once people have granted a small request, they are more likely to comply with a larger one.

In the most famous study of this phenomenon, Freedman and Fraser (1966) approached certain residents of Palo Alto, California, posing as members of a Committee for Safe Driving. They asked residents to place a large, ugly sign reading "Drive Carefully" in their front yards. Only 17 percent agreed to do so. Other residents were asked to sign a petition calling for more safe-driving laws. When these same people were later asked to place the ugly "Drive Carefully" sign in their yards, an amazing 55 percent agreed to do so. Compliance with the first small request more than tripled the rate of compliance with the larger request.

Why does the foot-in-the-door technique work so well? One possible explanation is that agreeing to the token act (signing the petition) realigns the participant's self-perception slightly to that of someone who favors the cause. When presented with the larger request, the participant then feels obligated to comply (Cialdini & Trost, 1998).

Another strategy commonly used by salespeople is the *lowball procedure* (Cialdini, Cacioppo, Bassett, & Miller, 1978; Cialdini & Trost, 1998). The first step is to induce a person to agree to do something. The second step is to raise the cost of compliance. Among new-car dealers, lowballing works like this: The dealer persuades the customer to buy a new car by reducing the price well below that offered by competitors. Once the customer has agreed to buy the car, however, the terms of the sale shift abruptly (e.g., the trade-in value promised by the used-car manager is cut), so that in the end the car is more costly than it would be at other dealerships. Despite the added costs, many customers follow through on their commitment to buy. Although the original inducement was the low price (the "lowball" the salesperson originally pitched), once committed, the buyer remains committed to the now-pricier vehicle.

Under certain circumstances, a person who has refused to comply with one request may be more likely to comply with a second. For example, if saying no to the first request made you feel guilty, you may say yes to something else. This phenomenon has been dubbed the *door-in-the-face effect* (Cialdini, 1995; Cialdini et al., 1975). In one study, researchers approached students and asked them to make an unreasonably large commitment: Would they counsel delinquent youths at a detention center for 2 years? Nearly everyone declined, thus effectively "slamming the door" in the face of the researcher making the request. On then being asked to make a much smaller commitment—supervising children during a trip to the zoo—many of the same students quickly agreed. The door-in-the-face effect may work because participants interpret the smaller request as a concession by the experimenter and feel pressured to comply in return.

Obedience

Compliance is agreement to change behavior in response to a request. **Obedience** is compliance with a demand. Like compliance, it is a response to an explicit message; but in this case, the message is a direct order, generally from a person in authority, such as a police officer, principal, or parent, who can back up the command with some sort of force if necessary. Obedience embodies social influence in its most direct and powerful form.

Several studies by Stanley Milgram, discussed in Chapter 1, The Science of Psychology, showed how far many people will go to obey someone in authority (Milgram, 1963). Recall from that chapter that people who agreed to participate in what they believed was a learning experiment administered what they thought were severe electrical shocks to the "learners." More recently, Milgram's research has been replicated in different cultures and with both male and female participants (Smith & Bond, 1999). What factors influence the degree to which people will do what they are told? Studies in which people were asked to put a dime in a parking meter by people wearing uniforms shows that one important factor is the amount of power vested in the person giving the orders. People obeyed a guard whose uniform looked like that of a police officer more often than they obeyed a man dressed either as a milkman or as a civilian. Another factor is surveillance. If we are ordered to do something and then left alone, we are less likely to obey than if we are being watched. This seems to be true especially when the order involves an unethical act. Most of the participants still put a dime in the meter when the police impersonator was out of sight, but Milgram found that his "teachers" were less willing to give severe shocks when the experimenter was out of the room.

Milgram's experiments revealed other factors that influence a person's willingness to follow orders. When the victim was in the same room as the "teacher," obedience dropped sharply. When another "teacher" was present who refused to give shocks, obedience also dropped. But when responsibility for an act was shared, so that the person was only one of many doing it, the degree of obedience was much greater.

Why do people willingly obey an authority figure, even if it means violating their own principles? Milgram (1974) suggested that people come to see themselves as the agents of another person's wishes and therefore not responsible for their own actions or the consequences. Once this shift in self-perception has occurred, obedience follows, because in their own minds, they have relinquished control of their actions. An alternative explanation is that obedient participants do not succumb to situational forces but rather fail to perceive the situation correctly (Nissani, 1990). Thus, in Milgram's study, the participants began with the belief that the experiment would be safe and the experimenter would be trustworthy. The real emotional struggle for the obedient participants, Nissani argues, may not have been in deciding whether to obey malevolent orders, but rather in recognizing that a trusted authority figure proved to be treacherous.

CHECK YOUR UNDERSTANDING

1. Match the following terms with the appropriate definition.

___ social influence	a. voluntarily yielding to social norms, even at the expense of one's own preferences
___ compliance	b. a change of behavior in response to a command from another person
___ obedience	c. a change of behavior in response to an explicit request from another person or from a group
___ conformity	d. any actions performed by one or more persons to change the attitudes, behavior, or feelings of others

2. Which of the following are factors that influence the likelihood that a person will conform? (There can be more than one correct answer.)

___a. the degree of unanimity in the group

___b. the difficulty or ambiguity of the task that the group faces

___c. strong attachment to the group

___d. the group's gender makeup

3. One result of learning about our own culture through modeling and imitation is

___a. rejecting cultural norms

___b. accepting cultural norms

___c. accepting cultural truisms

___d. rejecting cultural truisms

Answers: 1.social influence—d; compliance—c; obedience—b; conformity—a. 2.a, b, and c. 3.c

Social Action

In making decisions, are "two heads better than one"? Or do "too many cooks spoil the broth"?

The various kinds of social influence we have just discussed may take place between two people, in groups of three or more, or even when no one else is physically present. We now turn our attention to processes that do depend on the presence of other people. Specifically, we will examine processes that occur when people interact one-on-one and in groups. The social actions we consider next are *deindividuation, helping behavior, group decision making,* and *organizational behavior.*

Deindividuation

We have seen several cases of social influence in which people act differently in the presence of others than they would if they were alone. The most striking and frightening instance of this phenomenon is *mob behavior.* Some well-known violent examples of mob behavior are the beatings and lynchings of African Americans, the looting that sometimes accompanies urban rioting, and the wanton destruction of property that mars otherwise peaceful protests and demonstrations.

One reason for mob behavior is that people can lose their personal sense of responsibility in a group, especially in a group subjected to intense pressures and anxiety. This process is called **deindividuation,** because people respond not as individuals, but as anonymous parts of a larger group. In general, the more anonymous people feel in a group, the less responsible they feel as individuals (Aronson, Wilson, & Akert, 2002).

But deindividuation only partly explains mob behavior. Another contributing factor is that, in a group, one dominant and persuasive person can convince people to act through a *snowball effect:* If the persuader convinces just a few people, those few will convince others, who will convince still others, and the group becomes an

Deindividuation A loss of personal sense of responsibility in a group.

unthinking mob. Moreover, large groups provide *protection*. Anonymity makes it difficult to press charges. If 2, or even 10, people start smashing windows, they will probably be arrested. If a thousand people do it, very few of them will be caught or punished.

Research on deindividuation seems to support the unfortunate notion that when people get together they become more destructive and irresponsible than they would be individually. But human society depends on people's willingness to work together and help one another. In fact, instances of cooperation and mutual assistance are just as abundant as examples of human conflict and hostility. One need only recall the behavior of people all over the country in the aftermath of the September 11, 2001, terrorist attacks on the World Trade Center and the Pentagon to find hundreds of examples of people working together and helping each other. If, as we saw in Chapter 9, Motivation and Emotion, our willingness to harm others is influenced by social forces, so is our willingness to help others as we will see in the next section of the chapter.

Helping Behavior

What are some of the social forces that can promote helping behavior? One is perceived self-interest. We offer our boss a ride home from the office because we know that our next promotion depends on how much he or she likes us. We volunteer to feed a neighbor's cat while he is away because we want him to do the same for us. But when helpful actions are not linked to such personal gain, it is considered to be **altruistic behavior** (Batson & Powell, 2003). A person who acts in an altruistic way does not expect any recognition or reward in return, except perhaps the good feeling that comes from helping someone in need.

Under what conditions is helping behavior most likely to occur? Like other sociopsychological phenomena, helping is influenced by two sets of variables: those inherent in the situation and those grounded in the individual.

Situational Variables   The most important situational variable is the *presence of other people*. In a phenomenon called the **bystander effect,** as the number of passive bystanders increases, the likelihood that any one of them will help someone in

Altruistic behavior Helping behavior that is not linked to personal gain.

Bystander effect The tendency for an individual's helpfulness in an emergency to decrease as the number of bystanders increases.

After the attacks on the World Trade Center and the Pentagon on September 11, 2001, strangers reached out to help each other with physical and financial support.

trouble decreases (Clarkson, 1996; Chekroun & Brauer, 2002). In one experiment, participants completing a questionnaire heard a taped "emergency" in the next room, complete with a crash and screams. Of those who were alone, 70 percent offered help to the unseen female victim, but of those who waited with a companion—a stranger who did nothing to help—only 7 percent offered help (Latané & Rodin, 1969).

Another key aspect of the situation is its *ambiguity*. Any factors that make it harder for others to recognize a genuine emergency reduce the probability of altruistic actions. One experiment had a "workman" carry a ladder and a venetian blind past a waiting room in which participants were sitting (Clark & Word, 1974). A loud crash soon followed. In this ambiguous situation, the fewer the bystanders, the more likely the workman was to receive help. When he clarified matters by calling out that he was hurt, however, all participants without exception rushed to his aid.

Personal Characteristics The *personal characteristics* of bystanders also affect helping behavior. Not all bystanders are equally likely to help a stranger. Increasing the amount of personal responsibility that one person feels for another boosts the likelihood that help will be extended. In an experiment, participants were more likely to try to stop the theft of a stranger's property if they had promised to watch the property while the stranger was away than if they had had no contact with the stranger (Moriarty, 1975). The amount of empathy that we feel toward another person also affects our willingness to act in a helpful way. One study found that when participants felt that their values and personalities were similar to a victim's, they were more likely to help, even if that meant jeopardizing their own safety (Krebs, 1975).

Mood also makes a difference. A person in a good mood is more likely to help another in need than is someone who is in a neutral or bad mood (Salovey, Mayer, & Rosenhan, 1991). Researchers demonstrated this by leaving a dime in the scoop of a pay phone to put the finder in a good mood (Isen & Levin, 1972). Participants finding the dime were much more likely than other participants to help a confederate who dropped a folder full of papers on the sidewalk near the phone booth. Other research indicates that individuals who fear embarrassment are less likely to help (McGovern, 1976). Mistakenly offering help to someone who does not really need it can be highly embarrassing. Finally, when others are watching, people who score high on the need for approval are more likely to help than are low scorers (Satow, 1975).

Altruism and the Holocaust—In Search of the Altruistic Personality This chapter began with the story of a 16-year-old Catholic girl and others who hid Jewish children from the Nazis during World War II. Throughout Nazi-occupied Europe, only a few thousand non-Jews risked their lives to rescue Jews from persecution, deportation,

THINKING CRITICALLY

Helping Someone in Distress

As we have seen, whether people will help others depends in part on the situation (such as the presence of other people and the ambiguity of the situation) and in part on the characteristics of the potential helpers. Consider the following case: On August 18, 1999, Kevin Heisinger, a 24-year-old, was on his way home to Illinois from the University of Michigan. In the bathroom of a bus station, he was attacked and beaten to death. Several people were within earshot and heard his cries for help, but none of them went to his aid and none of them called the police. One person saw him lying on the floor in a pool of blood but he did nothing. Another person saw him struggling to breathe, but he also walked away. Eventually, a 12-year-old boy called for help. The police arrived in less than 20 seconds but it was too late to save Kevin's life.

- What factors in the situation do you think might have contributed to the unwillingness of people to help Kevin while he was being beaten and afterward?

- One commentator writing for *The Detroit News* said, "Have our souls been this coarsened, this deadened, by the daily barrage of real and imaginary violence? Or have some of us become like a couple of the contestants on that summer television hit, *Survivor*, so consumed with winning our own pot of gold that we really don't care how we treat others?" (DeRamus, 2000). To what extent do you think the failure of bystanders to help was due to personal characteristics?

- Do your answers to the questions above shed light on the question of why a 12-year-old was the only person to call for help?

and death. Why did they do what so many others failed to do? What qualities enabled them to behave so altruistically, bravely, and competently?

In 1981, several researchers set out to find answers to questions like these and combined their efforts 2 years later in the Altruistic Personality Project. By 1985, the project had published findings based on interviews with 25 rescuers and 50 survivors, as well as historical documents about the activities of others (Fogelman & Wiener, 1985). The people with whom the researchers spoke came from several countries and differed widely in education and vocation. The rescuers did, however, share one characteristic: They preferred not to see themselves as heroes but instead considered their behavior to be natural.

Although no single personality characteristic emerged, researchers could identify some common threads. For example, rescuers tended to fall into one of two groups: those who were motivated by deeply rooted moral values and felt ethically bound to rescue victims, and those who were attached personally to the victims and sometimes identified with them emotionally. These findings support the contention of social psychologist Carol Gilligan (1982) that there are fundamentally two forms of moral reasoning: one based on a sense of justice, the other based on a sense of responsibility and caring.

Morally motivated rescuers often harbored intense anti-Nazi attitudes; for some, religious belief played a paramount role in their lives. Those rescuers also tended to help victims regardless of whether they liked or disliked them. On the other hand, emotionally motivated rescuers frequently had strong personal attachments to the people whom they helped—neighbors, for instance. Some helped people whom they scarcely knew but with whom they identified. In certain cases, the empathy sprang from the rescuer's belief that he or she was also vulnerable to persecution. "It is easy to understand what the Jews felt," explained one Ukrainian rescuer, "because Jews and the Ukrainians were in similar positions everywhere" (Fogelman & Wiener, 1985, p. 63).

Despite their varied motivations, the rescuers shared a number of characteristics. Many of them belonged to families with traditions of concern for others outside the family, and many stated that their behavior was strongly guided by their parents' values. Most rescuers had uncommon capacities for perseverance and unusually strong beliefs in their own competence to risk and survive danger.

Helping Behavior Across Cultures   As we have seen, it is unlikely there is a "helping personality," or a single personality trait that determines who is helpful and who is not. Instead, several conditions, both individual and situational, combine to determine when help will be offered. Similarly, it's doubtful that there is such a thing as a "helpful culture"—that is, a society, nation, or group whose members are invariably "more helpful" than those of other groups. Psychologists have instead focused on the cultural factors that make helping more or less likely to take place.

Individualism/collectivism is an important dimension in this area: It seems plausible that members of individualistic cultures would feel less obligated to help other people than would members of collectivist cultures. A study using Indian and American participants investigated this intuitive conclusion (Miller, Bersoff, & Harwood, 1990). Participants were presented with scenarios that involved helping a stranger, a friend, or a close relative whose need was minor, moderate, or extreme. Interestingly, there were no cultural differences in cases of extreme need; members of both groups reported being equally willing to help. But the two groups did differ in cases of minor need; almost three times as many Indians (collectivist culture) as Americans (individualist culture) felt obligated to help in a scenario involving a close friend or a stranger asking for minor assistance.

Risky shift Greater willingness to take risks in decision making in a group than as independent individuals.

Polarization Shift in attitudes by members of a group toward more extreme positions than the ones held before group discussion.

Even within collectivist cultures, however, the prediction of when help will be offered can be problematic (Triandis, 1994). Some members of collectivist societies are reluctant to offer help to anyone outside of their in-group; they are therefore less likely to help strangers. Other cultures treat a stranger as a member of their group until that person's exact status can be determined.

Group Decision Making

Our society tends to turn important decisions over to groups. In the business world, key decisions are often made around a conference table rather than behind one person's desk. In politics, major policy decisions are seldom vested in just one person; groups of advisers, cabinet officers, committee members, or aides meet to deliberate and forge a course of action. In the courts, a defendant may request a trial by jury, and for some serious crimes, a jury trial is required by law. And, of course, the nine-member U.S. Supreme Court renders group decisions on legal issues affecting the entire nation.

Group Polarization   Why are so many decisions entrusted to groups rather than to individuals? For one thing, we assume that an individual acting alone is more likely to take risks than a group considering the same issue. The assumption that groups make more conservative decisions than individuals remained unchallenged until the early 1960s. At that time, James Stoner (1961) designed an experiment to test this idea. He asked participants individually to counsel imaginary people who had to choose between a risky but potentially rewarding course of action and a conservative and less rewarding alternative. Next, the advisers met in small groups to discuss each decision until they reached unanimous agreement. Stoner and many other social psychologists were surprised to find that the groups consistently proposed a riskier course of action than that counseled by the group members working alone. This phenomenon is known as the **risky shift.**

Subsequent research has shown that the risky shift is simply one aspect of a more general group phenomenon called **polarization**—the tendency for individuals to become more extreme in their attitudes as a result of group discussion. Groups that begin deliberations on a fairly risky note will move further in that direction during discussion than groups inclining to be cautious as they consider an issue.

What causes polarization in decision-making groups? First, people discover during discussion that the other group members share their views to a greater degree than they realized. Then, in an effort to be seen in a positive light by the others, at least some group members become strong advocates for what is shaping up to be the dominant sentiment in the group. Arguments leaning toward one extreme or the other not only reassure people that their initial attitudes are correct but also intensify those attitudes so that the group as a whole becomes more extreme in its position (Liu & Latane, 1998). If you refer a problem to a group to ensure that it will be resolved in a cautious, conservative direction, you should make sure that the members of the group hold cautious and conservative views in the first place.

The Effectiveness of the Group   Another reason for assigning so many important problems to groups is the assumption that the members of the group will pool their skills and expertise, and therefore solve the problem more effectively than would any individual member working alone. The adage that "Two heads are better than one" reflects this way of thinking.

In fact, groups are more effective than individuals only under specific circumstances. According to Steiner (1972), the effectiveness of a group depends on three factors: (1) the nature of the task, (2) the resources of the group members, and (3) the interaction among group members. There are many different kinds of tasks, each of which demands specific kinds of skills. If the requirements of the task match the skills of the group members, the group is likely to be more effective than any single individual.

Even if task and personnel are perfectly matched, however, the ways in which the people *interact* in the group may reduce the group's efficiency. For example, high-status individuals tend to exert more influence in groups, regardless of their problem-solving abilities (Torrance, 1954). If high-status members favor an incorrect position or solution, the group is likely to be less effective than would otherwise be the case.

Another factor is group *size*. The larger the group, the more likely it is to include someone who has the skills needed to solve a difficult problem. On the other hand, it is much harder to coordinate the activities of a large group than those of a small group. Large groups may be more likely to encourage **social loafing,** the tendency of people to exert less effort than they would when working individually on the assumption that others in the group will do the work. (Karau & Williams, 1993; Miller, 2002).

Still another variable is the *cohesiveness* of a group. When the people in the group like one another and feel committed to the goals of the group, cohesiveness is high. Under these conditions, members may work hard for the group, spurred on by high morale. But cohesiveness can undermine the quality of group decision making. If the group succumbs to *groupthink*, according to Irving Janis (1982, 1989), strong pressure to conform prevents people in a cohesive group from expressing critical ideas of the emerging consensus. In such a group, amiability and morale supercede judgment. Members with doubts may hesitate to express them. The result may be disastrous decisions—such as the Bay of Pigs invasion, the Watergate burglary and cover-up, or the Challenger and Columbia space flights (Kruglanski, 1986; Raven, 1998; Vaughn, 1996).

Leadership

Every group has a leader, but how do group leaders come to the fore? For many years the predominant answer to this question was the **great person theory,** which states that leaders are extraordinary people who assume positions of influence and then shape events around them. In this view, individuals like George Washington, Winston Churchill, and Nelson Mandela were "born leaders" who would have led any nation at any time in history.

Most historians and psychologists now regard this theory as naive because it ignores social and economic factors. An alternative theory holds that leadership emerges when the right person is in the right place at the right time. For instance, in the later 1950s and early 1960s, Dr. Martin Luther King, Jr., rose to lead the black civil rights movement. Dr. King was clearly a "great person"—intelligent, dynamic, eloquent, and highly motivated. Yet had the times not been right, according to this theory, it is doubtful that he would have been as successful as he was.

Recently, social scientists have argued that there is more to leadership than either the great person theory or the right-place-at-the-right-time theory implies. Rather, the leader's traits, certain aspects of the situation in which the group finds itself, and the response of the group and the leader to each other are all important considerations. Fred Fiedler's *contingency theory* of leader effectiveness is based on such a transactional view of leadership (Fiedler, 1993, 2002).

Social loafing The tendency of people to exert less effort on a task when working in a group than when working individually.

Great person theory The theory that leadership is a result of personal qualities and traits that qualify one to lead others.

One theory of leadership holds that the particularly effective leader is the right person in the right place at the right time. For the American civil rights movement, Martin Luther King, Jr., was such a leader.

According to Fiedler's theory, personal characteristics are important to the success of a leader. One kind of leader is *task-oriented*, concerned with doing the task well even at the expense of worsening relationships among group members. Other leaders are *relationship-oriented*, concerned with maintaining group cohesiveness and harmony. Which style is most effective depends on three sets of situational factors. One is the nature of the task: whether it is clearly structured or ambiguous. The second consideration is the relationship between leader and group: whether the leader has good or bad personal relations with the group members. The third consideration is the leader's ability to exercise great or little power over the group.

Fiedler has shown that if conditions are either very favorable (good leader-member relations, structured tasks, high leader power) or very unfavorable (poor leader-member relations, unstructured task, low leader power) for the leader, the most effective leader is the one who is task-oriented. However, when conditions within the group are only moderately favorable for the leader, the most effective leader is one who is concerned about maintaining good interpersonal relations.

The contingency view of leadership, which has received a great deal of support from research conducted in the laboratory as well as in real-life settings, clearly indicates that there is no such thing as an ideal leader for all situations (Ayman et al., 1998; Graen & Hui, 2001; Hughes, Ginnett, & Curphy, 1998). "Except perhaps for the unusual case," Fiedler states, "it is simply not meaningful to speak of an effective or of an ineffective leader; we can only speak of a leader who tends to be effective in one situation and ineffective in another" (Fiedler, 1967, p. 261).

Leadership Across Cultures   Some leaders are primarily task-oriented, whereas others are more relationship-oriented. This distinction seems to be a main operating principle in most work groups in the United States: Someone explicitly appointed manager is charged with making sure the job gets done, whereas someone else usually emerges informally to act as the relationship-oriented specialist who remembers everyone's birthday, smoothes disputes, and generally maintains morale. In the Western world, this division of leadership is often the primary operating mode of both formal work groups and less formal social groups. In a collectivist culture that values cooperation among group members, one member may be named "the manager," but there is less need for individuals to have clearly defined roles because the emphasis is always on the group's goals.

Leadership in American businesses has undergone a transformation during the past two decades through the introduction of a management style that proved successful in Japan and other Eastern collectivist cultures (Dean & Evans, 1994; McFarland, Senn, & Childress, 1993). This approach emphasizes input from all group members regarding decision making, small work teams that promote close cooperation among members, and a style of leadership in which managers receive much the same treatment as any other employee. In the West, it is not uncommon for executives to have their own parking spaces, dining facilities, fitness and social clubs, as well as separate offices and independent schedules. Most Japanese executives consider this privileged style of management very strange. In many Eastern cultures, managers and executives share the same facilities as their workers, hunt for parking spaces like everyone else, and eat and work side by side with their employees. Interestingly, the Japanese model has effectively combined the two leadership approaches—task-oriented and relationship-oriented—into a single overall style. By being a part of the group, the leader can simultaneously work toward and direct the group's goals, while also contributing to the group's morale and social climate. Combining these roles is an effective strategy for Japanese leaders in such diverse workplaces as banks, bus companies, shipyards, coal mines, and government offices (Misumi, 1985).

Women in Leadership Positions   Just as leadership styles differ across cultures, research has shown that the leadership styles of men and women can also vary considerably. For instance, one 5-year study of 2,482 managers in more than 400 organizations found that female and male coworkers say that women make better managers than men (Kass, 1999). The reason seems to be that female managers have added such traditionally "masculine" task-oriented traits as decisiveness, planning, and setting standards to such "feminine" relationship-oriented assets as communication, feedback, and empowering other employees, whereas male managers still rely on an autocratic style that emphasizes individual competition and achievement. Indeed, one review concluded that in contrast to the directive and task oriented leadership style common among men, women tend to have a more democratic, collaborative, and interpersonally oriented style of managing employees (O'Leary & Flanagan, 2001).

Another large scale review of 45 studies on gender and leadership found the styles of leadership adopted by women are generally more effective than traditional male leadership styles (Eagly, Johannesen-Schmidt, & van-Engen, 2003). This study found that female leaders are generally more effective than male leaders at winning acceptance for their ideas, and instilling self-confidence in their employees (Lips, 2002). Results like these have prompted some experts to call for specialized women-only leadership training programs, to assist women develop their full feminine leadership potential independent of the male influence (Vinnicombe & Singh, 2003).

Organizational Behavior

The places where we work and the various organizations to which we belong shape much of our behavior. **Industrial/organizational (I/O) psychology** spotlights the influence on human interaction of large, complex organizational settings, with special emphasis on behavior in the workplace.

Productivity   I/O psychologists focus on practical problems such as how to reduce employee turnover, improve worker morale, and increase productivity. One of the first studies of the relationship between productivity and working conditions was conducted in the late 1920s by Elton Mayo and his colleagues, who gradually increased the lighting in the Western Electric Hawthorne plant in Cicero, Illinois. The researchers were testing the hypothesis that better lighting would boost worker output. But their results showed something else entirely: Productivity increased with better lighting, too much lighting, and too little lighting. In what has become known as the **Hawthorne effect,** the workers' behavior changed merely because of the researcher's attention, not as a function of any specific manipulations of workplace conditions.

The methods of Mayo's team have since come under criticism (Parsons, 1974, 1992), but their study was one of the first to highlight the importance of psychological and social factors on behavior in the workplace. Since the 1930s, I/O psychologists have attempted to analyze that relationship in more specific terms. For example, workers whose jobs call for a greater variety of skills are more likely to think of their jobs as meaningful and to exhibit increased motivation and satisfaction; and workers whose jobs entail more autonomous activity generally perceive their jobs as responsible and produce work of a higher quality (Melamed, Ben-Avi, Luz, & Green, 1995). Thus, motivation, satisfaction, and productivity in the workplace can all be improved by making the right changes in job components.

Industrial/organizational (I/O) psychology The area of psychology concerned with the application of psychological principles to the problems of human organizations, especially work organizations.

Hawthorne effect The principle that people will alter their behavior because of researchers' attention and not necessarily because of any treatment condition.

Research by I/O psychologists has also found that small, cohesive work groups are more productive than large, impersonal ones (Craig, 2002). Putting this idea into practice, managers of assembly-line workers have developed the *autonomous work group*, replacing the massive assembly line with small groups of workers who produce an entire unit (a whole car, for instance) and periodically alternate their tasks. Additional benefits derived from this approach include greater worker satisfaction, higher-quality output, and decreased absenteeism and turnover (Pearson, 1992).

Communication and Responsibility   The way communications are handled within an organization also has an impact on organizational efficiency and the attitudes of its members (Parker, Axtell, & Turner, 2001). In organizations where members communicate with just one person in authority, for instance, the communications system becomes centralized. This type of communications scheme typically works well in solving simple problems; complex problems, on the other hand, are better handled in a decentralized way, with group members freely communicating with one another (Porter & Roberts, 1976).

I/O psychologists have also examined the issue of assigning responsibility for key decisions to work groups. Although some groups make better decisions than others, it turns out that group decision making in general enhances membership satisfaction (Cotton, 1993). If individuals believe that they had an input into the decision, they are more satisfied with the outcome and their membership in the group. However, the evidence also shows that increasing the number of people who participate in the decision-making process does *not* lead to increased productivity.

Increasingly, corporations are turning to I/O psychologists for advice on issues ranging from helping employees balance work and family to teaching employees at all levels communications skills and building communications networks (Murray, 1999) (see Appendix B).

CHECK YOUR UNDERSTANDING

1. Which is most important in determining who will lead a group?

___a. the personal characteristics of potential leaders

___b. the situation in which the group finds itself

___c. both personal traits and situational factors

2. The process in which people lose their personal sense of responsibility in a group is called

___a. deindividuation

___b. altruism

___c. bystander effect

3. The likelihood that someone will come to the aid of a person in trouble _____ as the number of bystanders _____.

___a. increases/increases

___b. decreases/increases

___c. decreases/decreases

4. The phenomenon known as the "risky shift" is one aspect of a more general phenomenon called

___a. altruism

___b. polarization

___c. the Hawthorne effect

5. According to research by I/O psychologists, small work groups are _____ _____
   _____ large ones.

___a. more productive than

___b. less productive than

___c. as productive as

summary

Social psychology is the scientific study of how the thoughts, feelings, and behaviors of one individual are influenced by the real, imagined, or inferred behavior or characteristics of other people. Research in social psychology has concentrated on four topics: social cognition, attitudes, social influence, and social action.

Social Cognition

The study of social perception or cognition focuses on how we judge or evaluate other people.

Impression Formation   When forming impressions of others, we rely on schemata, sets of expectations and beliefs about different categories of people. Impressions are also affected by the order in which information is acquired. According to the **primacy effect,** first impressions are the strongest. As "cognitive misers," we avoid wasting thought and judge people according to simplistic concepts. One such concept is the **stereotype,** a set of characteristics we presume is shared by all members of a social category or group. Biased treatment of others can bring about the very behavior one expects through the effects of the **self-fulfilling prophecy.**

Attribution   **Attribution theory** holds that people seek to understand one another by making judgments about the causes of behavior. These attributions can be either internal or external. One theorist maintains that attributions are made by analyzing the distinctiveness, consistency, and consensus of a particular behavior pattern. Biases in perception can lead to the **fundamental attribution error,** in which personal (internal) forces are overemphasized as influences on other people's behavior and situational (external factors) are given far more weight in accounting for our own behavior. **Defensive attribution** motivates us to explain our own actions in ways that protect our self-esteem: We tend to attribute our successes to internal factors and our failures to external factors. The **just-world hypothesis** may lead us to blame the victim when bad things happen to other people. These principles of attribution do not appear to apply equally to people in all cultures.

Interpersonal Attraction   People are more attracted to each other when **proximity** brings them into frequent contact. We also like people because of physical attractiveness; similarity of attitudes,

interests, and values; and rewarding **exchanges** that are based on equity. Love is an experience based on such factors as **intimacy,** the quality of genuine closeness and trust achieved in communication with another person.

Attitudes

An **attitude** is a relatively stable organization of one's thoughts, feelings, and behavior tendencies toward something or someone—the attitude object.

The Nature of Attitudes   Attitudes can't always predict behavior, especially if one's actions and expressions are influenced by other factors like **self-monitoring.** Attitudes are acquired through learning and developed through experience.

Prejudice and Discrimination   **Prejudice** is an intolerant, unfavorable, and rigid view of a group of people; **discrimination** is behavior based on prejudice. Prejudiced beliefs often cause us to make the ultimate attribution error about others, attributing failure to internal factors and success to external factors. One explanation of the roots of prejudice is the **frustration-aggression theory,** which states that people who feel exploited and oppressed displace their hostility toward the powerful onto people who are "lower" on the social scale than they are. Another theory links prejudice to the **authoritarian personality,** a rigidly conventional and bigoted personality type marked by exaggerated respect for authority. A third theory proposes a cognitive source of prejudice—oversimplified thinking about classes of people and the world. Finally, conformity to the prejudices of one's social group or society explains much individual prejudice. **Racism** is prejudice and discrimination directed at a particular racial group. Although many people believe that racial prejudice is a thing of the past, racism still exists in subtle forms.

Strategies for reducing prejudice and discrimination include recategorization (expanding our schema for a particular group), controlled processing (training ourselves to be more mindful of people who differ from us), and improving contact between groups.

Attitude Change   Attitudes are sometimes changed in response to new experiences and persuasive efforts. The first step in the persuasive process is to get the audience's attention. Then, the task is to get the audience to comprehend and accept the message. According to the communication model, persuasion is a function of the source, the message itself, the medium of communication, and the characteristics of the audience. According to the theory of cognitive dissonance, attitudes may also be changed when new actions contradict preexisting attitudes, creating **cognitive dissonance.** The most effective means of changing attitudes—especially important attitudes, behaviors, or lifestyle choices—may be *self-persuasion.*

Social Influence

Social influence refers to the idea that the presence and actions of others can control our perceptions, attitudes, and actions.

Cultural Influence   The culture in which we are immersed teaches us what to value and how to behave. Culture dictates differences in dress, diet, and personal space. In adapting our behavior to that of others, we learn the **norms** of our culture. We accept **cultural truisms** without questioning their validity.

Cultural Assimilators   Cultures may seem strange to us if their norms are different from ours. Through such techniques as the cultural assimilator, however, we can learn to understand and accept the perspective of people from different cultures.

Conformity   Yielding one's own preferences or beliefs to the norms of a larger group is called **conformity.** Research by Solomon Asch and others has shown that characteristics of the situation and characteristics of the individual influence the likelihood of conformity. The level of conformity tends to be higher in collectivist cultures.

Compliance   **Compliance** is a change in behavior in response to an explicit request from another person or group. Some techniques used to get others to comply are the foot-in-the-door effect, the lowball procedure, and the door-in-the-face effect.

Obedience   Classic studies by Stanley Milgram showed that many participants were willing to obey orders to administer harmful shocks to other people. This **obedience** was more in evidence when the authority figure was physically close and apparently legitimate, and when the victim was distant and thus easier to punish. According to Milgram, obedience is brought on by the constraints of the situation, but another interpretation holds that participants fail to perceive the situation correctly.

Social Action

Social actions depend on the presence of other people as either recipients or sources of influence.

Deindividuation   Immersion in a group may lead to **deindividuation,** the loss of a sense of personal responsibility that makes possible violent, irresponsible behavior. Mob behavior also gains momentum from the snowball effect and from the protection of anonymity in a group.

Helping Behavior   Help without expectation of reward is considered **altruistic behavior.** Helping is constrained by situational factors such as the presence of passive bystanders, a phenomenon known as the **bystander effect,** and the ambiguity of a situation. Personal characteristics that induce helping are empathy with the victim and good mood.

Group Decision Making   Groups are often entrusted with problem solving in the expectation that they will be more careful and responsible than lone individuals. Research on the **risky shift** and the broader phenomenon of **polarization** shows that group deliberation actually enhances members' tendencies toward extreme solutions. Group effectiveness depends on such factors as the nature of the task, the group's resources, and how members interact. The tendency of people to exert less effort when working in a group than when working on their own is known as **social loafing.** Group cohesiveness can lead to groupthink, a pattern of thought characterized by self-deception and the manufacture of consent through conformity to group values.

Leadership   According to the **great person theory,** leadership is a function of personal traits that qualify one to lead others. An alternative theory attributes leadership to being in the right place at the right time. According to the transactional view, traits of the leader and traits of the group interact with certain aspects of the situation to determine what kind of leader will come to the fore. Fred Fiedler focused on two contrasting leadership styles: task-oriented and relationship-oriented. The effectiveness of each one depends on the nature of the task, the relationship of the leader with group members, and the leader's power over the group.

The task-oriented leadership style typical of American businesses is being transformed through the introduction of a management style that emphasizes small work teams and input from all members of the group. Recent research indicates that women in leadership positions tend to have a more democratic, collaborative and interpersonally oriented style of managing employees than do men in similar positions.

Organizational Behavior   **Industrial/organizational (I/O) psychology** studies behavior in organizational environments such as the workplace. Studies of productivity have revealed that worker output increases as a result of researchers' attention, a phenomenon called the **Hawthorne effect.** I/O findings have also led organizations to establish autonomous work groups to replace less efficient assembly-line arrangements. Productivity and morale may also be improved by increasing worker responsibility and facilitating communication in the workplace.

key terms

Social psychology	561	Stereotype	563	Defensive attribution	566
Primacy effect	562	Attribution theory	564	Just-world hypothesis	566
Self-fulfilling prophecy	563	Fundamental attribution error	565	Proximity	568

Exchange	569	Cognitive dissonance	579	Bystander effect	587
Intimacy	569	Social influence	581	Risky shift	590
Attitude	571	Cultural truisms	581	Polarization	590
Self-monitoring	571	Norm	581	Social loafing	591
Prejudice	572	Conformity	582	Great person theory	591
Discrimination	572	Compliance	584	Industrial/organizational (I/O)	
Frustration-aggression theory	573	Obedience	584	psychology	593
Authoritarian personality	573	Deindividuation	586	Hawthorne effect	593
Racism	574	Altruistic behavior	587		

APPENDIX A

OVERVIEW

Scales of Measurement   598

Measurements of Central
    Tendency   599
Differences Among the Mean,
    Median, and Mode   599

The Normal Curve   602
Skewed Distributions   602
Bimodal Distributions   603

Measures of Variation   603
Range   603
The Standard Deviation   604

Measures of Correlation   605

Using Statistics to Make
    Predictions   607
Probability   607

Using Meta-Analysis in
    Psychological Research   607

Measurement and Statistical Methods

Most of the experiments described in this book involve measuring one or more variables and then analyzing the data statistically. The design and scoring of all the tests we have discussed are also based on statistical methods. **Statistics** is a branch of mathematics that provides techniques for sorting out quantitative facts and ways of drawing conclusions from them. Statistics let us organize and describe data quickly, guide the conclusions we draw, and help us make inferences.

Statistical analysis is essential to conducting an experiment or designing a test, but statistics can only handle numbers—groups of them. To use statistics, the psychologist first must measure things—count and express them in quantities.

Scales of Measurement

No matter what we are measuring—height, noise, intelligence, attitudes—we have to use a scale. The data we want to collect determine the scale we will use and, in turn, the scale we use helps determine the conclusions we can draw from our data.

Nominal Scales   A **nominal scale** is a set of arbitrarily named or numbered categories. If we decide to classify a group of people by the color of their eyes, we are using a nominal scale. We can count how many people have blue eyes, how many have green eyes, how many have brown eyes, and so on, but we cannot say that one group has more or less eye color than the other. The colors are simply different. Since a nominal scale is more of a way of classifying than of measuring, it is the least informative kind of scale. If we want to compare our data more precisely, we will have to use a scale that tells us more.

Ordinal Scales   If we list horses in the order in which they finish a race, we are using an ordinal scale. On an **ordinal scale**, data are ranked from first to last according to some criterion. An ordinal scale tells the order, but nothing about the distances between what is ranked first and second or ninth and tenth. It does not tell us how much faster the winning horse ran than the horses that placed or showed. If a person ranks her preferences for various kinds of soup—pea soup first, then tomato, then onion, and so on—we know what soup she likes most and what soup she likes least, but we have no idea how much better she likes tomato than onion, or if pea soup is far more favored than either one of them.

Since we do not know the distances between the items ranked on an ordinal scale, we cannot add or subtract ordinal data. If mathematical operations are necessary, we need a still more informative scale.

Interval Scales   An **interval scale** is often compared to a ruler that has been broken off at the bottom—it only goes from, say, 5½ to 12. The intervals between 6 and 7, 7 and 8, 8 and 9, and so forth are equal, but there is no zero. A thermometer is an interval scale—even though a certain degree registered on a Fahrenheit or Centigrade thermometer specifies a certain state of cold or heat, there is no such thing as no temperature at all. One day is never twice as hot as another; it is only so many equal degrees hotter.

An interval scale tells us how many equal-size units one thing lies above or below another thing of the same kind, but it does not tell us how many times bigger, smaller, taller, or fatter one thing is than another. An intelligence test cannot tell us that one person is three times as intelligent as another, only that he or she scored so many points above or below someone else.

Ratio Scales   We can only say that a measurement is two times as long as another or three times as high when we use a **ratio scale,** one that has a true zero. For instance, if we measure the snowfall in a certain area over several winters, we can say that six times as much snow fell during the winter in which we measured a total of 12 feet as during a winter in which only 2 feet fell. This scale has a zero—there can be no snow.

Measurements of Central Tendency

Usually, when we measure a number of instances of anything—from the popularity of TV shows to the weights of 8-year-old boys to the number of times a person's optic nerve fires in response to electrical stimulation—we get a distribution of measurements that range from smallest to largest or lowest to highest. The measurements will usually cluster around some value near the middle. This value is the **central tendency** of the distribution of the measurements.

Suppose, for example, you want to keep 10 children busy tossing rings around a bottle. You give them three rings to toss each turn, the game has six rounds, and each player scores one point every time he or she gets the ring around the neck of the bottle. The highest possible score is 18. The distribution of scores might end up like this: 11, 8, 13, 6, 12, 10, 16, 9, 12, 3.

What could you quickly say about the ring-tossing talent of the group? First, you could arrange the scores from lowest to highest: 3, 6, 8, 9, 10, 11, 12, 12, 13, and 16. In this order, the central tendency of the distribution of scores becomes clear. Many of the scores cluster around the values between 8 and 12. There are three ways to describe the central tendency of a distribution. We usually refer to all three as the *average.*

The arithmetical average is called the **mean**—the sum of all the scores in the group divided by the number of scores. If you add up all the scores and divide by 10, the total number of scores in this group of ring tossers, you find that the mean for the group is 10.

The **median** is the point that divides a distribution in half—50 percent of the scores fall above the median, and 50 percent fall below. In the ring-tossing scores, five scores fall at 10 or below, five at 11 or above. The median is thus halfway between 10 and 11 which is 10.5.

The point at which the largest number of scores occurs is called the **mode.** In our example, the mode is 12. More people scored 12 than any other.

Differences Among the Mean, Median, and Mode

If we take many measurements of anything, we are likely to get a distribution of scores in which the mean, median, and mode are all about the same—the score that occurs most often (the mode) will also be the point that half the scores are below and half above (the median). And the same point will be the arithmetical average (the mean). This is not always true, of course, and small samples rarely come out so symmetrically. In these cases, we often have to decide which of the three measures of central tendency—the mean, the median, or mode—will tell us what we want to know.

For example, a shopkeeper wants to know the general incomes of passersby so he can stock the right merchandise. He might conduct a rough survey by standing outside his store for a few days from 12:00 to 2:00 and asking every tenth person who walks by to check a card showing the general range of his or her income. Suppose most of the people checked the ranges between $25,000 and $60,000 a year.

Statistics   A branch of mathematics that psychologists use to organize and analyze data.

Nominal scale   A set of categories for classifying objects.

Ordinal scale   Scale indicating order or relative position of items according to some criterion.

Interval scale   Scale with equal distances between the points or values, but without a true zero.

Ratio scale   Scale with equal distances between the points or values and with a true zero.

Central tendency   Tendency of scores to congregate around some middle value.

Mean   Arithmetical average calculated by dividing a sum of values by the total number of cases.

Median   Point that divides a set of scores in half.

Mode   Point at which the largest number of scores occurs.

Frequency distribution A count of the number of scores that fall within each of a series of intervals.

However, a couple of the people made a lot of money—one checked $100,000–$150,000 and the other checked the $250,000-or-above box. The mean for the set of income figures would be pushed higher by those two large figures and would not really tell the shopkeeper what he wants to know about his potential customers. In this case, he would be wiser to use the median or the mode.

Suppose instead of meeting two people whose incomes were so great, he noticed that people from two distinct income groups walked by his store—several people checked the box for $25,000–$35,000, and several others checked $50,000–$60,000. The shopkeeper would find that his distribution was bimodal. It has two modes—$30,000 and $55,000. This might be more useful to him than the mean, which could lead him to think his customers were a unit with an average income of about $40,000.

Another way of approaching a set of scores is to arrange them into a **frequency distribution**—that is, to select a set of intervals and count how many scores fall into each interval. A frequency distribution is useful for large groups of numbers; it puts the number of individual scores into more manageable groups.

Suppose a psychologist tests memory. She asks 50 college students to learn 18 nonsense syllables, then records how many syllables each student can recall 2 hours later. She arranges her raw scores from lowest to highest in a rank distribution:

2	6	8	10	11	14
3	7	9	10	12	14
4	7	9	10	12	15
4	7	9	10	12	16
5	7	9	10	13	17
5	7	9	11	13	
6	8	9	11	13	
6	8	9	11	13	
6	8	10	11	13	

The scores range from 2 to 17, but 50 individual scores are too cumbersome to work with. So she chooses a set of two-point intervals and tallies the number of scores in each interval:

Interval	Tally	Frequency
1–2	|	1
3–4	|||	3
5–6	⊬⊬ |	6
7–8	⊬⊬ ||||	9
9–10	⊬⊬ ⊬⊬ |||	13
11–12	⊬⊬ |||	8
13–14	⊬⊬ ||	7
15–16	||	2
17–18	|	1

Now she can tell at a glance what the results of her experiment were. Most of the students had scores near the middle of the range, and very few had scores in the

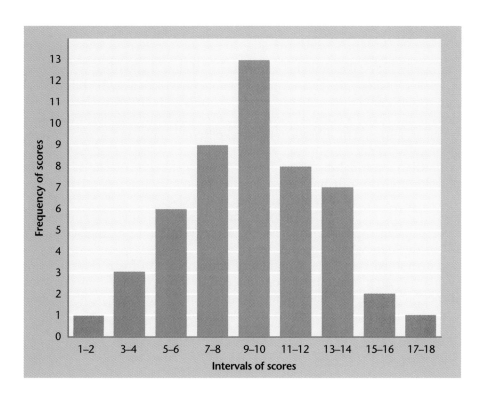

Figure A–1
A frequency histogram for a memory experiment.
The bars indicate the frequency of scores within each interval.

high or low intervals. She can see these results even better if she uses the frequency distribution to construct a bar graph—a **frequency histogram.** Marking the intervals along the horizontal axis and the frequencies along the vertical axis would give her the graph shown in Figure A–1. Another way is to construct a **frequency polygon,** a line graph. A frequency polygon drawn from the same set of data is shown in Figure A–2. Note that the figure is not a smooth curve, since the points are connected by straight lines. With many scores, however, and with small intervals, the angles would smooth out, and the figure would resemble a rounded curve.

Frequency histogram   Type of bar graph that shows frequency distributions.

Frequency polygon   Type of line graph that shows frequency distributions.

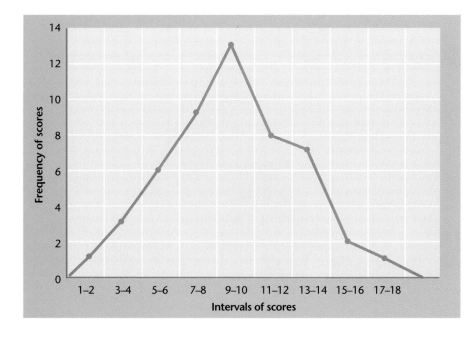

Figure A–2
A frequency polygon drawn from data used in Figure A–1.
The dots, representing the frequency of scores in each interval, are connected by straight lines.

Normal curve   Hypothetical bell-shaped distribution curve that occurs when a normal distribution is plotted as a frequency polygon.

The Normal Curve

Ordinarily, if we take enough measurements of almost anything, we get a *normal distribution*. Tossing coins is a favorite example of statisticians. If you tossed 10 coins into the air 1,000 times and recorded the heads and tails on each toss, your tabulations would reveal a normal distribution. Five heads and five tails would be the most frequent, followed by 4 heads/6 tails and 6 heads/4 tails, and so on down to the rare all heads or all tails.

Plotting a normal distribution on a graph yields a particular kind of frequency polygon, called a **normal curve**. Figure A–3 shows data on the heights of 1,000 men. Superimposed over the bars that reflect the actual data is an "ideal" normal curve for the same data. Note that the curve is absolutely symmetrical—the left slope parallels the right slope exactly. Moreover, the mean, median, and mode all fall on the highest point on the curve.

The normal curve is a hypothetical entity. No set of real measurements shows such a smooth gradation from one interval to the next, or so purely symmetrical a shape. But because so many things do approximate the normal curve so closely, the curve is a useful model for much that we measure.

Skewed Distributions

If a frequency distribution is asymmetrical—if most of the scores are gathered at either the high end or the low end—the frequency polygon will be skewed. The hump will sit to one side or the other, and one of the curve's tails will be disproportionately long.

If a high school mathematics instructor, for example, gives her students a sixth-grade arithmetic test, we would expect nearly all the scores to be quite high. The frequency polygon would probably look like the one in Figure A–4. But if a sixth-grade class were asked to do advanced algebra, the scores would probably be quite low. The frequency polygon would be very similar to the one shown in Figure A–5.

Note, too, that the mean, median, and mode fall at different points in a skewed distribution, unlike in the normal curve, where they coincide. Usually, if you know that the mean is greater than the median of a distribution, you can predict that the

Figure A–3
A normal curve.
This curve is based on measurements of the heights of 1,000 adult males.
Source: From Hill, 1966.

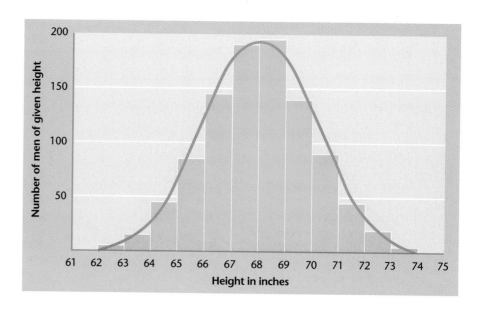

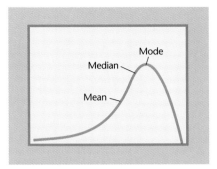

Figure A–4
A skewed distribution.
Most of the scores are gathered at the high end of the distribution, causing the hump to shift to the right. Since the tail on the left is longer, we say that the curve is skewed to the left. Note that the *mean, median,* and *mode* are different.

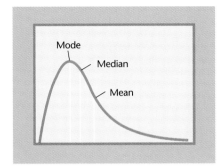

Figure A–5
In this distribution, most of the scores are gathered at the low end, so the curve is skewed to the right. The *mean, median,* and *mode* do not coincide.

frequency polygon will be skewed to the right. If the median is greater than the mean, the curve will be skewed to the left.

Bimodal Distributions

We have already mentioned a bimodal distribution in our description of the shopkeeper's survey of his customers' incomes. The frequency polygon for a bimodal distribution has two humps—one for each mode. The mean and the median may be the same (Figure A–6) or different (Figure A–7).

Measures of Variation

Sometimes it is not enough to know the distribution of a set of data and what their mean, median, and mode are. Suppose an automotive safety expert feels that too much damage occurs in tail-end accidents because automobile bumpers are not all the same height. It is not enough to know what the average height of an automobile bumper is. The safety expert also wants to know about the variation in bumper heights: How much higher is the highest bumper than the mean? How do bumpers of all cars vary from the mean? Are the latest bumpers closer to the same height?

Range

The simplest measure of variation is the **range**—the difference between the largest and smallest measurements. Perhaps the safety expert measured the bumpers of 1,000 cars 2 years ago and found that the highest bumper was 18 inches from the ground, the lowest only 12 inches from the ground. The range was thus 6 inches—18 minus 12. This year the highest bumper is still 18 inches high, the lowest still 12 inches from the ground. The range is still 6 inches. Moreover, our safety expert finds that the means of the two distributions are the same—15 inches off the ground. But look at the two frequency polygons in Figure A–8—there is still something the expert needs to know, since the measurements cluster around the mean in drastically different ways. To find out how the measurements are distributed around

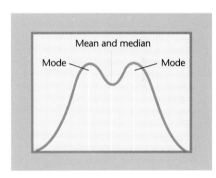

Figure A–6
A bimodal distribution in which the *mean* and the *median* are the same.

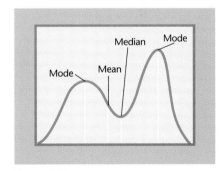

Figure A–7
In this bimodal distribution, the *mean* and the *median* are different.

Range Difference between the largest and smallest measurements in a distribution.

Figure A–8
Frequency polygons for two sets of measurements of automobile bumper heights. Both are normal curves, and in each distribution the *mean, median,* and *mode* are 15. But the variation from the mean is different, causing one curve to be flattened and the other to be much more sharply peaked.

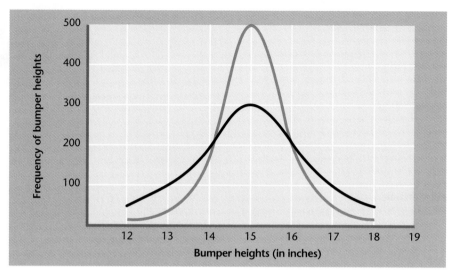

the mean, our safety expert has to turn to a slightly more complicated measure of variation—the standard deviation.

The Standard Deviation

The **standard deviation,** in a single number, tells us much about how the scores in any frequency distribution are dispersed around the mean. Calculating the standard deviation is one of the most useful and widely employed statistical tools.

To find the standard deviation of a set of scores, we first find the mean. Then we take the first score in the distribution, subtract it from the mean, square the difference, and jot it down in a column to be added up later. We do the same for all the scores in the distribution. Then we add up the column of squared differences, divide the total by the number of scores in the distribution, and find the square root of that number. Figure A–9 shows the calculation of the standard deviation for a small distribution of scores.

In a normal distribution, however peaked or flattened the curve, about 68 percent of the scores fall between one standard deviation above the mean and one standard deviation below the mean (see Figure A–10). Another 27 percent fall between one standard deviation and two standard deviations on either side of the mean, and 4 percent more between the second and third standard deviations on either side. Overall, then, more than 99 percent of the scores fall between three standard deviations above and three standard deviations below the mean. This makes the standard deviation useful for comparing two different normal distributions.

Now let us see what the standard deviation can tell our automotive safety expert about the variations from the mean in the two sets of data. The standard deviation for the cars measured 2 years ago is about 1.4. A car with a bumper height of 16.4 is one standard deviation above the mean of 15; one with a bumper height of 13.6 is one standard deviation below the mean. Since the engineer knows that the data fall into a normal distribution, he can figure that about 68 percent of the 1,000 cars he measured will fall somewhere between these two heights: 680 cars will have bumpers between 13.6 and 16.4 inches high. For the more recent set of data, the standard deviation is just slightly less than 1. A car with a bumper height of about 14 inches is one standard deviation below the mean; a car with a bumper height of about 16 is one standard deviation above the mean. Thus, in this distribution, 680 cars have bumpers between 14 and 16 inches high. This tells the safety expert that car bumpers are becoming more similar, although the range of heights is still the same (6 inches), and the mean height of bumpers is still 15.

Standard deviation Statistical measure of variability in a group of scores or other values.

Number of Scores = 10		Mean = 7
Scores	Difference from mean	Difference squared
4	$7 - 4 = 3$	$3^2 = 9$
5	$7 - 5 = 2$	$2^2 = 4$
6	$7 - 6 = 1$	$1^2 = 1$
6	$7 - 6 = 1$	$1^2 = 1$
7	$7 - 7 = 0$	$0^2 = 0$
7	$7 - 7 = 0$	$0^2 = 0$
8	$7 - 8 = -1$	$-1^2 = 1$
8	$7 - 8 = -1$	$-1^2 = 1$
9	$7 - 9 = -2$	$-2^2 = 4$
10	$7 - 10 = -3$	$-3^2 = 9$

$$\text{Sum of squares} = 30$$
$$\div$$
$$\text{Number of scores} = 10$$
$$\text{Variance} = 3$$
$$\text{Standard deviation} = \sqrt{3} = 1.73$$

Figure A–9
Step-by-step calculation of the *standard deviation* for a group of 10 scores with a mean of 7.

Measures of Correlation

Measures of central tendency and measures of variation can be used to describe a single set of measurements—like the children's ring-tossing scores—or to compare two or more sets of measurements—like the two sets of bumper heights. Sometimes, however, we need to know if two sets of measurements are in any way associated with each other—if they are correlated. Is parental IQ related to children's IQ? Does the need for achievement relate to the need for power? Is watching violence on TV related to aggressive behavior?

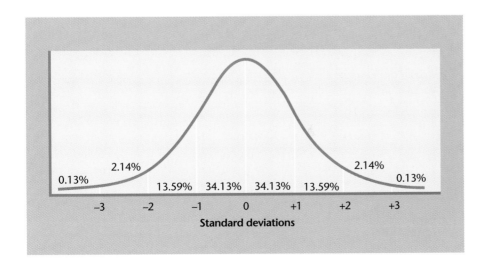

Figure A–10
A normal curve, divided to show the percentage of scores that fall within each *standard deviation* from the *mean.*

Scatter plot Diagram showing the association between scores on two variables.

Correlation coefficient Statistical measure of the strength of association between two variables.

One fast way to determine whether two variables are correlated is to draw a **scatter plot.** We assign one variable (X) to the horizontal axis of a graph, the other variable (Y) to the vertical axis. Then we plot a person's score on one characteristic along the horizontal axis and his or her score on the second characteristic along the vertical axis. Where the two scores intersect, we draw a dot. When several scores have been plotted in this way, the pattern of dots tells whether the two characteristics are in any way correlated with each other.

If the dots on a scatter plot form a straight line running between the lower-left-hand corner and the upper-right-hand corner, as they do in Figure A–11a, we have a perfect positive correlation—a high score on one of the characteristics is always associated with a high score on the other one. A straight line running between the upper-left-hand corner and the lower-right-hand corner, as in Figure A–11b, is the sign of a perfect negative correlation—a high score on one of the characteristics is always associated with a low score on the other one. If the pattern formed by the dots is cigar shaped in either of these directions, as in Figures A–11c and d, we have a modest correlation—the two characteristics are related but not highly correlated. If the dots spread out over the whole graph, forming a circle or a random pattern, as they do in Figure A–11e, there is no correlation between the two characteristics.

A scatter plot can give us a general idea if a correlation exists and how strong it is. To describe the relation between two variables more precisely, we need a **correlation coefficient**—a statistical measure of the degree to which two variables are associated. The correlation coefficient tells us the degree of association between two sets of matched scores—that is, to what extent high or low scores on one variable tend to be associated with high or low scores on another variable. It also provides an estimate of how well we can predict from a person's score on one characteristic how high he or she will score on another characteristic. If we know, for example, that a test of mechanical ability is highly correlated with success in engineering courses, we could predict that success on the test would also mean success as an engineering major.

Correlation coefficients can run from +1.0 to −1.0. The highest possible value (+1.0) indicates a perfect positive correlation—high scores on one variable are always and systematically related to high scores on a second variable. The lowest possible value (−1.0) means a perfect negative correlation—high scores on one

Figure A–11
Scatter plots provide a picture of the strength and direction of a correlation.

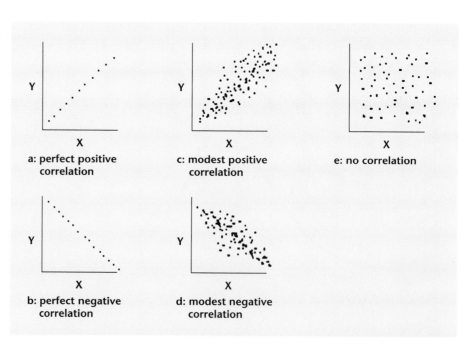

a: perfect positive correlation

c: modest positive correlation

e: no correlation

b: perfect negative correlation

d: modest negative correlation

variable are always and regularly related to low scores on the second variable. In life, most things are far from perfect, so most correlation coefficients fall somewhere between +1.0 and −1.0. A correlation smaller than ±.20 is considered very low, from ±.20 to ±.40 is low, from ±.40 to ±.60 is moderate, from ±.60 to ±.80 is high, and from ±.80 to ±1.0 is very high. A correlation of zero indicates that there is no correlation between two sets of scores—no regular relation between them at all.

Correlation tells us nothing about causality. If we found a high positive correlation between participation in elections and income levels, for example, we still could not say that being wealthy made people vote or that voting made people wealthy. We would still not know which came first, or whether some third variable explained both income levels and voting behavior. Correlation only tells us that we have found some association between scores on two specified characteristics.

Using Statistics To Make Predictions

Behind the use of statistics is the hope that we can generalize from our results and use them to predict behavior. We hope, for example, that we can use the record of how well a group of rats run through a maze today to predict how another group of rats will do tomorrow, that we can use a person's scores on a sales aptitude test to predict how well he or she will sell life insurance, that we can measure the attitudes of a relatively small group of people about pollution control to indicate what the attitudes of the whole country are.

First we have to determine whether our measurements are representative and whether we can have confidence in them. In Chapter 1, The Science of Psychology, we discussed this problem when we considered the problem of proper sampling.

Probability

Errors based on inadequate sampling procedures are somebody's fault. Other kinds of errors occur randomly. In the simplest kind of experiment, a psychologist will gather a representative sample, split it randomly into two groups, and then apply some experimental manipulation to one of the groups. Afterward, the psychologist will measure both groups and determine whether the experimental group's score is now different from the score of the control group. But even if there is a large difference between the scores of the two groups, it may still be wrong to attribute the difference to the manipulation. Random effects might influence the results and introduce error.

Statistics give the psychologist many ways to determine precisely whether the difference between the two groups is really significant, whether something other than chance produced the results, and whether the same results would be obtained with different subjects. These probabilities are expressed as measures of **significance.** If the psychologist computes the significance level for the results as .05, he or she knows that there are 19 chances out of 20 that the results are not due to chance. But there is still 1 chance in 20—or a .05 likelihood—that the results are due to chance. A .01 significance level would mean that there is only 1 chance in 100 that the results are due to chance.

Using Meta-Analysis in Psychological Research

In several places in this text, we have presented findings from reviews of psychological research in which a research team has summarized a wide selection of literature on a topic in order to reach some conclusions on that topic. There are several

Significance Probability that results obtained were due to chance.

Meta-analysis   A statistical procedure for combining the results of several studies so the strength, consistency, and direction of the effect can be estimated.

crucial decisions to be made in such a process: Which research reports should be included? How should the information be summarized? What questions might be answered after all the available information is gathered?

Traditionally, psychologists reviewing the literature in a particular area relied on the box-score method to reach conclusions. That is, after collecting all the relevant research reports, the researcher simply counted the number supporting one conclusion or the other, much like keeping track of the scoring in nine innings of a baseball game (hence the term *box score*). For example, if there were 200 studies of gender differences in aggressive behavior, researchers might find that 120 of them showed that males were more aggressive than females, 40 showed the opposite pattern, and 40 showed no evidence of gender differences. On the basis of these box scores, the reviewer might conclude that males are more likely than females to act aggressively.

Today researchers tend to rely on a more sophisticated strategy known as **meta-analysis.** Meta-analysis provides a way of statistically combining the results of individual research studies to reach an overall conclusion. In a single experiment, each participant contributes data to help the researcher reach a conclusion. In a meta-analysis, each published study contributes data to help the reviewer reach a conclusion, as Figure A–12 illustrates. Rather than relying on the raw data of individual participants, meta-analysis treats the results of entire studies as its raw data. Meta-analysts begin by collecting all available research reports that are relevant to the question at hand. Next they statistically transform these results into a common scale for comparison. That way differences in sample size (one study might have used 50 participants, another 500), in the magnitude of an effect (one study might have

Figure A–12
Meta-analysis.
Meta-analysis enables researchers to combine the results of individual studies to reach an overall conclusion.

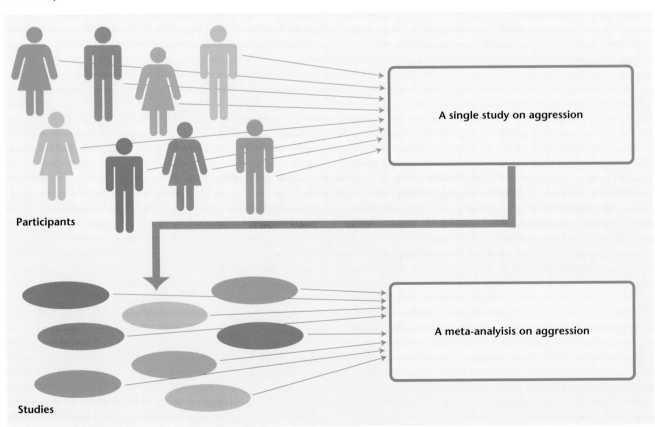

Participants

Studies

found a small difference, another a more substantial one), and in experimental procedures (which might vary from study to study) can be examined using the same methods. The key element in this process is its statistical basis. Rather than keeping a tally of "yeas" and "nays," meta-analysis allows the reviewer to determine both the strength and the consistency of a research conclusion. For example, instead of simply concluding that there were more studies that found a particular gender difference, the reviewer might determine that the genders differ by six-tenths of a percentage point, or that across all the studies the findings are highly variable.

Meta-analysis has proved to be a valuable tool for psychologists interested in reaching conclusions about a particular research topic. By systematically examining patterns of evidence across individual studies that vary in their conclusions, psychologists are able to gain a clearer understanding of the findings and their implications.

VERVIEW

Overview of I/O Psychology 610

Personnel Psychology 610
Job Analysis 611
Recruitment 611
Selection Interview 612
Selection Tests 612
Training 613
Performance Evaluation 613

Organizational Psychology 614
Work Motivation 614
Job Satisfaction 616
Work Teams: An Experiment 616
Leadership 617

Human Factors Psychology 617

Industrial/Organizational Psychology

Throughout this book, we have seen how psychology can be applied to a variety of settings. The purpose of this appendix is to focus on industrial/organizational psychology, a division of psychology concerned with the application of psychological principles to the problems of human organizations. Of particular concern to organizational psychologists is how organizations can best use and develop the talent, skill, and motivation of their employees.

Overview Of I/O Psychology

In this appendix, we will first provide an overview of the field and then examine its three main areas: personnel psychology, organizational psychology, and human factors.

Personnel psychology focuses on selecting, training, and evaluating people in an organization. Personnel psychologists are concerned with finding the "right" worker for the job—that is, someone who has both the necessary skills and the personal attributes for the job. To do this, they may develop and administer tests and become involved in the interview process.

Organizational psychology focuses on how workers adapt to the social environment of complex human organizations. This area deals with questions about work motivation, job satisfaction, group issues, and leadership.

Human factors psychology deals with the arrangement and design of work tasks to promote a safer and healthier as well as more efficient work environment. Primary emphasis is given to designing work environments, technology, and equipment to fit the needs and capabilities of workers.

Personnel Psychology

Matching the attributes of workers with the requirements of jobs is the key challenge for the personnel psychologist. In deciding whether an applicant is qualified for a job, employers often consider a variety of factors, including the worker's knowledge, skill, personality, and motivation. Employers then determine the relative importance of each of these factors for the particular job when making the final hiring decision. For example, in hiring a machinist, knowledge and skill factors might be more important than personality attributes. However, for a sales position, personality and motivational qualities would probably weigh more heavily in the selection process.

Another issue affecting the hiring process is the number of people applying for the position who are qualified. The more qualified applicants there are, the more selective employers can be in deciding whom to hire. Where there are more qualified applicants than jobs, employers might ask a personnel psychologist to develop a specific test battery that will identify the best applicants. Those who make the "cut-off" are then included in the pool of applicants to be interviewed; those who don't are rejected for the position. An alternative approach would be to use the initial interview to identify the more qualified applicants and administer the test battery only to those people.

There are times when an employer will be unable to find any qualified applicant for a position. Consequently, employers will have to provide training for applicants who have the potential to develop such skills. Personnel psychologists can contribute to this process by designing ways to help employers identify applicants with the potential to benefit from training.

Job Analysis

As described above, personnel psychologists attempt to help predict job success among a group of applicants. But job success is not always easy to define or measure. For this reason, industrial psychologists are often called on to help organizations define their jobs in behavioral terms. This process is called **job analysis.** It involves breaking down a job into its basic components to identify the most important ones and thus the most important skills and abilities needed to perform the job successfully.

There are several ways to carry out a job analysis. People can be observed or interviewed on the job, their supervisors can be interviewed, or questionnaires can be developed to assess the opinions of a variety of people about the content of the job and the skills it requires.

Each method can provide useful information about jobs and how they are performed, but each has limitations. It is important to choose a method of job analysis that is appropriate for the type of job being analyzed. For example, observing people on the job works best with jobs that require more physical than mental activity. Also, the act of observing workers sometimes affects performance. (This principle was referred to in Chapter 15, Social Psychology, as the *Hawthorne effect.*)

The limitations of naturalistic observation discussed in the first chapter and the chapter on personality apply here as well: The observer may be biased, may interpret as a common occurrence one that in fact is a rare event, and may be confused by the fluidity of the situation.

The interview approach to job analysis can provide information that might not be attainable through either observation or questionnaires. Interviews provide the personnel psychologist with an opportunity to explore issues in more detail with the individual worker. However, this method should only be used with skilled interviewers who are able to establish trust and confidence with the person whose job is being studied. As we saw in Chapter 3, Sensation and Perception, people's perceptions can be influenced by a variety of factors, including preconceptions about what they are supposed to believe, cognitive style, and cultural background. These factors can influence how workers perceive and understand the purpose of the job analysis, which in turn could affect how much trust and confidence they place in the interviewer. Workers may also portray their work as more important than it really is if they believe that doing so will increase their pay and status.

Recruitment

One of the best ways to match people to jobs is to recruit them. Organizations use a variety of strategies to find employees, including hiring from within, newspaper ads, employment agencies, and employee referrals. One of the key issues in recruitment concerns how to portray the job clearly to potential applicants. One technique, known as the **realistic job preview** (Wanous, 1980), is designed to give applicants a sense of what a typical day at work would be like rather than a rosy view that can eventually result in disappointment and frustration for the job holder.

An interesting application of this approach was reported in a study done with the U.S. Army (Meglino, DeNisi, Youngblood, & Williams, 1988). In an effort to reduce turnover among basic trainees, various kinds of realistic job previews were given, and the results were compared to a control condition with no previews. The study showed that those trainees given previews had less voluntary turnover than those in the control condition. Moreover, the type of realistic job preview used made a difference: Previews that are too negative can result in increased turnover.

Personnel psychology Area of industrial/organizational psychology that focuses on the selection, training, and evaluation of people in an organization.

Organizational psychology Area of industrial/organizational psychology that focuses on how workers adapt to the social environment of complex human organizations.

Human factors psychology Area of industrial/organizational psychology that deals with the arrangement and design of work tasks to promote a safer, healthier, and more efficient work environment.

Job analysis Breaking down a job into its basic components to identify the most important components and thus the most important skills and abilities needed to perform the job.

Realistic job preview A recruitment technique designed to give job applicants a sense of the typical workday on the job.

Selection Interview

Once job candidates have been identified, attention turns to selecting the best person for the job. Many organizations use interviews as part of the selection process. Typically, an applicant meets with several people in the organization, who then pool their impressions and make a decision. How accurately do interviews predict success on the job? Studies have shown that despite their popularity, interviews are not very good predictors (Muchinsky, 1997).

One problem is the sorts of social cognitions and attitudes that, as we saw in the chapter on social psychology, go into impression formation and stereotypes. Interviewers tend to make an accept-reject decision early in the interview rather than waiting until all the information is in. This early bias toward or against the applicant is heavily influenced by first impressions, and it serves to color the remainder of the interview. Also, interviewers often have a stereotype of a good employee that they use to evaluate applicants; like all stereotypes, these models are often inaccurate or oversimplified, and therefore can result in bad decisions. Moreover, while comparing candidates against these stereotypes, interviewers may focus on deviant characteristics and thus give more weight to negative rather than positive factors in the applicant's background.

As we saw in the personality chapter, *structured interviews* can avoid some of these problems. Research shows that interviewer judgment is more consistent and accurate when the interviewer follows a detailed form that lists topics to be covered and provides space for recording the answers. There is some risk, however, that a highly structured interview may not turn up some information that would be important in evaluating a particular candidate. For this reason, some organizations have found it useful to combine a structured interview with a more freewheeling interview later.

Selection Tests

Organizations also use written tests to select people for jobs. During World War I, the army used intelligence tests to screen recruits, and shortly thereafter, employers started using psychological tests and questionnaires to select workers. As we saw in Chapter 8, Intelligence and Mental Abilities, there has been furious debate over the fair and proper use of intelligence tests. A similar debate surrounds the use of personnel selection tests. In fact, legal rulings have restricted their use.

What makes a good test? As discussed in the chapter on intelligence, a good test is both reliable and valid. *Reliability* means that test scores are stable and consistent. *Validity* means that the test measures what it claims to measure. Thus, a good personnel selection test must measure the knowledge, skills, abilities, and personal attributes necessary for good job performance, and it must do so in a way that provides relatively stable, consistent scores.

How do we know if a test is reliable and valid? The answer is to perform research on the test. Two methods for determining test reliability are *test-retest* and *split-half* (see Chapter 8, Intelligence and Mental Abilities). The validity of a test can be determined in a variety of ways. For example, let's assume the XYZ Company has a new test called the Management Abilities Test (MAT), and it wants to find out if the test is valid—whether it does, in fact, accurately measure management ability. One strategy is to use interviews to hire as many management trainees as are needed and then give the MAT test to all those who have been hired. After a period of time (say 6 to 12 months), their performance can be evaluated and compared with their test scores. If the people who scored high on the MAT turn out to be better managers than those who scored low, this would indicate that the test is a valid predictor of job success.

Another strategy for assessing the validity of the MAT would be to give the test to managers already working in the organization and see if the test discriminates between effective and less effective managers.

A third way to assess the validity of the MAT is to examine the content of the test. If the test requires applicants to perform a wide variety of tasks managers actually do in the job—a so-called *work sample test*—we could have some confidence that the test is measuring some management ability.

Training

Personnel psychologists also spend considerable time training people who are already employed by the company. The objective of training is to raise the workers' level of performance by changing their skills and possibly their attitudes. Today's workplace is placing ever-greater demands on workers to produce quality products and services. Moreover, the rapid pace of technological change requires that workers learn new skills. Training can be an effective way to confront these issues. When training is carefully planned, designed, and evaluated, it gives individuals opportunities to perform new functions, to advance in their careers, and, if their existing job is unsatisfactory, to reenter the job market with needed skills.

Training begins by determining the gap between actual and desired performance—that is, the extent to which knowledge and skill are below expected levels. Information from job analyses and performance evaluations (to be discussed in the next section), as well as requests from managers, are typical ways in which training needs are identified.

The next step is to design the training program. Most training programs use a blend of the learning principles discussed in Chapter 5, Learning, and a variety of media, depending on the nature of the training. Today many mechanics are trained using videotaped demonstrations. These are coupled with written training materials that break down the various tasks into carefully defined steps. Afterward the training is evaluated to determine whether it has been effective. This feedback is also useful for modifying the training program to make it more effective with future trainees.

Performance Evaluation

Personnel psychologists also work with managers to develop various methods to evaluate employee performance. Here the objective is to determine how well job performance matches performance expectations. Usually, the specific aspects of job performance to be measured and evaluated are identified through a job analysis.

One procedure is simply to count the number of products of a person's job performance. This approach can work reasonably well in jobs where a quantifiable measure makes sense (e.g., number of cars assembled per day). However, for some jobs it is difficult, if not misleading, to rely on quantity as a measure of success. Consider an employment counselor who helps unemployed people find jobs. How do you measure the counselor's job performance? Should it be based strictly on how many people find jobs? But that measure may not accurately reflect the quality of the counselor's work. For example, the counselor may have helped an individual enroll in a training program that could improve his or her prospects for finding a better-paying job in the future, but that individual would not show up as a "success" on the counselor's record until he or she finds a job. Factors beyond the control of the counselor, such as the state of the economy, may also affect employment opportunities and thus job-placement success rates.

In cases such as this, a more useful procedure is simply to observe the person performing the required job tasks. In many organizations, supervisors are usually the

Performance rating system   A method of performance evaluation in which a numerical rating is given for performance in each key area of the job.

Performance appraisal interview Meeting between the employee and the supervisor in which they discuss the supervisor's evaluation of the employee's job performance.

ones who carry out this function. This approach can work if the supervisor has the time to adequately observe the worker over a long enough period to form a true picture of the worker's job performance and if the supervisor observes important, not trivial, aspects of the job.

A third approach is known as the **performance rating system.** Here a supervisor may be asked to consider the behavior of an employee in certain key areas of the job. The supervisor then assigns a numerical rating that represents how well or poorly the employee performs in these areas. This approach can be effective if the supervisor has a clear understanding of the employee's job and has had ample opportunity to observe the employee's work performance. But even under these conditions, supervisory ratings are often imperfect. For example, ratings can be influenced by such factors as the tendency of the supervisor to be lenient and the extent to which the supervisor likes the employee. Another common error is the *halo effect*, which is the tendency of supervisors to allow their overall impressions of an employee to determine how they rate the employee on each of the dimensions of a rating form (Landy & Farr, 1980). Thus, an employee who is liked may receive excellent ratings on every aspect of the job, even though the employee is not doing excellent work in all areas. Some supervisors also have a tendency to cluster their ratings toward the middle of the scale. This, too, limits the usefulness of the evaluation process, particularly with high- and low-performing employees, since everyone ends up with fairly mediocre overall ratings.

No matter which method of performance evaluation is used, certain guidelines should be followed. First, measures of job performance should be related to the actual content of the worker's job and not to irrelevant factors. Second, employees should be given the opportunity to meet with their supervisors to discuss the evaluation. This meeting is often referred to as a **performance appraisal interview.** For the interview to be effective, supervisors should encourage two-way communication. That is, in addition to discussing the subordinate's job performance, the supervisor should also ask for feedback through such questions as "Are there ways in which I can help you do your job better?" Questions like these can reduce the inevitable tension surrounding performance evaluation, improve communication, and support the goal of performance improvement.

Organizational Psychology

We have seen that personnel psychology concerns itself with the selection, training, and evaluation of individual employees. But work is also a social activity. Organizational psychology focuses on the ways in which groups, leaders, and the culture of the organization influence workers. In this section, we discuss four topics that are central to organizational psychology: work motivation, job satisfaction, group dynamics, and leadership.

Work Motivation

In Chapter 9, Motivation and Emotion, we saw that motivation energizes and directs behavior toward a particular goal. As you might expect, motivation is of great interest to managers. For example, some workers work hard, whereas others appear lazy and uninvolved. Some workers take the initiative and support the goals of the organization, whereas others appear uncooperative and need to be closely supervised.

Why do people differ in their motivation to work? One answer is that people differ in such things as achievement and affiliation motives (see Chapter 9, Motivation and Emotion). Each of these motives can have a powerful effect on work-related behaviors. A worker with a strong achievement motive is likely to prefer challenging tasks and the opportunity to learn and master new skills. Someone with a strong affiliation motive is likely to have a strong desire to be part of a work team. Someone with a strong power motive is likely to seek the recognition, status, and control that come with climbing the corporate ladder.

Work motivation is also affected by the ways in which individuals think about and make choices and decisions regarding their work situation. For example, workers are likely to seek a balanced or fair relationship between what they invest in their work (such as education, skills, experience, and time and effort) and the rewards they receive for that investment (money, promotion, recognition, job satisfaction). Employees often compare themselves to others when making judgments about the equity or fairness of the relationship between what they put in and what they get out of their jobs.

For example, let's consider the hypothetical case of Susan Richards and Carol Hanley who work for XYZ Company. Richards has been with the company for 10 years and has had excellent performance evaluations, but was recently denied a promotion in favor of Hanley, who also has had excellent performance evaluations but has only been with the company for 5 years. Richards feels her situation to be inequitable or unfair and, consequently, is motivated to do something to correct the imbalance.

Susan Richards can reduce the inequity she perceives in a variety of ways. She can meet with her boss to explore another promotional opportunity or possibly a pay raise (thus increasing her rewards). Or she can decide to work less hard (decreasing her investment). Or she can change her perception of the situation—for example, she might realize that Hanley has some special qualifications for the position, or she might decide that the promotion was not really desirable (these are both ways to reduce cognitive dissonance, as we saw in Chapter 15, Social Psychology). If none of these strategies works—that is, if Richards is unable to restore perceived equity—she might quit her job and seek a more equitable situation elsewhere or she might file a lawsuit alleging discrimination.

Expectancies also have a significant effect on work motivation. Employees will be motivated to work if they expect to receive a reward that they value (Porter & Lawler, 1968). Suppose you are a sales representative for a medical supply company. You work hard because you expect to be assigned to a new product line that will provide you with the opportunity to learn more about medical sales and enhance your chances for advancement. Unfortunately, you receive a cash bonus instead. Although you are pleased to get the cash, you are disappointed that the new job assignment did not come through. Since the cash bonus was not very important to you, your willingness to work hard and put forth a lot of effort to sell the same medical products will not increase very much—it might even decrease, contrary to what management expected.

To avoid surprises of this sort, it is helpful, first, to provide workers with clear and attainable performance standards. Second, to the extent possible, rewards for hard work and outstanding performance should take a form that is important to each individual worker. Third, employees should be able to see a clear relationship between obtaining those valued rewards and achieving a high level of performance.

Finally, work motivation is also affected by *goals*. Research studies suggest that goals help to direct employees' attention, focus their efforts, increase their persistence, and foster action plans (Locke, Shaw, Saari, & Latham, 1981). These same studies suggest that managers are more likely to motivate their employees if they set goals that are specific, attainable, and moderately difficult. Moreover, goals should be the product of discussions between a manager and worker in which they reach

Management by objectives (MBO)   A goal-setting process that takes place throughout the organization, with goals for each division and individual linked to the overall goals of the organization.

Job enrichment   Redesigning jobs to provide workers with more meaningful tasks, increased decision-making authority, and opportunities for feedback.

Autonomous work group   A small team of workers that is responsible for an entire product or service.

Self-managed work team   An autonomous work group that has the authority to make decisions in such managerial areas as planning, scheduling, and even hiring.

agreement on what the goals are and how these goals will be used to measure the employee's performance. However, these goals should not be set in concrete; they should be flexible enough to accommodate new developments.

One popular approach to goal setting is **management by objectives (MBO),** in which goal setting takes place throughout the organization. The process often starts at the top of the organizational hierarchy, which develops goals for the company. Then goals are set for the next lower level, and so on down through the organization. At each level, the goals for various divisions and for individuals within divisions are linked to the overall goals of the company. Although MBO can be effective, several types of problems can occur with this technique (Kondrasuk, 1981). For example, MBO often requires time-consuming reports to higher management; it can lead to an overemphasis on short-term goals at the expense of more important long-term goals; and it often requires close coordination among managers.

Job Satisfaction

Organizational psychologists are also concerned with how employees feel about their jobs and the company they work for. Job satisfaction is one of the most frequently studied topics in organizational psychology, in part because job satisfaction is linked to such practical concerns as absenteeism, turnover, and productivity. For example, studies have shown that job satisfaction and absenteeism are related, although the relationship is not a strong one (Hackett & Guion, 1985). Other studies have shown a stronger relationship between job satisfaction and the rate at which people voluntarily quit their jobs to seek employment elsewhere (Cotton & Tuttle, 1986). However, despite the commonsense notion that a happy worker is a productive one, research has shown only a slight connection between satisfaction and job performance (Iaffaldano & Muchinsky, 1985). But job satisfaction does affect an individual's quality of work life and overall health. For example, research studies have shown that job dissatisfaction is related to feelings of stress and poor health among workers (Ivancevich & Matteson, 1980). One way to increase job satisfaction is **job enrichment.** Basically, a job is redesigned to provide workers with more meaningful tasks, increased decision-making authority, and opportunities for feedback. Some organizations are linking this motivational strategy with new technologies that are changing the way workers do their job, an issue that will be covered in the section on Human Factors Psychology.

Work Teams: An Experiment

Much of the research on groups discussed in Chapter 15, Social Psychology, has been useful to industrial/organizational psychologists. For example, the idea of work teams has received a great deal of attention recently. Driven by the need to compete more effectively in the global economy (and to improve the quality of their products and services), organizations have been experimenting with such teams to increase the level of commitment and productivity among their employees. One innovation, mentioned in the chapter on social psychology, is the **autonomous work group** where a small team of workers is responsible for an entire product or service. These teams tend to be cohesive, with members sharing a sense of belonging and unity. As their name implies, autonomous work groups are also designed to give workers significant authority to make decisions in such areas as planning, scheduling, and even hiring. When given this type of managerial authority, they become **self-managed work teams.** In effect, employees in these unique work groups act as their own supervisor.

To date, self-managed teams have not progressed much beyond the experimental stage in the United States. According to one survey, only 7 percent of the largest industrial companies in the United States reported using self-managed work teams. However, half of the firms expected to adopt the technique in the coming years (Dumaine, 1990).

How effective are self-managed teams? One review of research showed that self-managed teams have a positive impact on productivity and specific attitudes related to responsibility and control but no significant impact on overall job satisfaction, absenteeism, or turnover (Goodman, Devadas, & Griffith Hughson, 1988). Moreover, self-managed teams are not without their problems. Not all workers are capable or willing to be part of a self-managed team—some prefer more traditional work arrangements where managerial and nonmanagerial roles are clearly defined. Moreover, workers need to be adequately trained before they can handle the authority and responsibility that exist in a team setting. For example, members of work teams are often asked to learn not only their own job but also the jobs of other team members. In addition, they may need training in such areas as interpersonal communication skills.

Leadership

Organizational psychologists are also interested in understanding the process of leadership, since leadership is an important ingredient of success in any organization. The topic of leadership is discussed in depth in Chapter 15, Social Psychology, and indeed many I/O psychologists consider themselves to be social psychologists as well.

In this and the previous section, we've looked at personnel psychology and organizational psychology. Personnel psychologists are concerned with the selection and evaluation of employees and with developing adequate measures and descriptions of particular jobs. Organizational psychologists are primarily concerned with human relations on the job and the organization's effect on employees. They focus on relations among employees, leadership styles (relations between employees and their supervisors), and ways that organizations can encourage employees' motivation and job satisfaction. In the next section, we turn our attention to a third area of I/O psychology, human factors or engineering psychology.

Human Factors Psychology

Technological advances such as computers and robotics are changing the way we work. Human factors psychologists are interested in the relationship between worker and machine. They are also referred to as *human engineering psychologists* because they design work environments and equipment to match the capabilities of the people who use them. Human factors psychologists have been especially involved in two areas: making machines safer to use, and avoiding or reducing the stress that can result among workers when new technologies are introduced.

Human factors psychology can play a significant role in the prevention of accidents through the design of safer work environments. For example, the way in which dials and controls are displayed in airplanes and nuclear plants can have a significant impact on accident prevention. By designing equipment that yields immediate and clear information that is accessible and compatible with the operator's abilities, the human factors specialist can help minimize the opportunity for human error.

In addition to safety issues, human factors specialists deal with ways of reducing job stress. A key source of job stress is the nature of the job itself: Some jobs are inherently more stressful than others. For example, the job of air traffic controller is stressful because of the enormous pressure of being responsible for the safety of airline passengers. Any lapse in vigilance, the slightest error in instructions, or the pushing of the wrong button can mean disaster. Control room operators in nuclear plants experience similar pressures. In situations such as these, human factors specialists attempt to redesign the job so that it is more compatible with the worker's ability to carry it out. By arriving at a better balance among workload, time pressures, and responsibility, human factors psychologists can reduce performance errors and health-related problems among workers in stressful jobs (Ivancevich & Matteson, 1980).

Another issue of interest to human factors specialists is the effect of rotating shifts on workers. Some jobs require people to rotate from one shift to another at relatively short intervals. As we saw in Chapter 4, States of Consciousness, research has shown that these changes can upset workers' biological clocks (Jamal, 1981). Human factors research can help organizations plan and design work-shift schedules that are less stressful for the individual as well as more efficient for the organization—a guiding principle for the I/O psychologist.

Advances in technology present another challenge for the human factors psychologist (Turnage, 1990). For example, some companies use computers to monitor their employees. This electronic form of supervision designed to provide "objective" measures of employee performance has been used in a variety of work settings, from the telephone industry to the airlines to the post office. Approximately 6 million workers in the United States perform their jobs under some kind of electronic supervision (Turnage, 1990). Human factors specialists are interested in how this technology affects workers. For example, critics of computer monitoring have suggested that it can invade the privacy of workers, lower their motivation, and reduce the amount of control they have over their work performance (Turnage, 1990). Yet, if designed and managed properly, this technology has the potential to produce positive outcomes for both the organization and worker. For example, it can be used in a nonthreatening way to give employees accurate feedback, help them set goals, and improve their performance. It can also make managers' expectations more realistic.

The issue of technology and its impact on the workplace presents opportunities and challenges for the I/O psychologist. Each of the three branches of I/O psychology—personnel, organizational, and human factors—offers a perspective and a set of methods that can improve our understanding of this complex topic. Personnel psychologists can design training programs that will help workers learn new skills, become more productive, and advance in their careers. Organizational psychologists can examine how leadership styles and different kinds of group structures and rewards affect the motivation and productivity of workers. And human factors psychologists can focus on ways to create a more compatible match between technology and the capabilities of the worker. In a larger sense, all three can help improve the productivity and quality of work life of our organizations.

GLOSSARY

Absolute refractory period A period after firing when a neuron will not fire again no matter how strong the incoming messages may be.

Absolute threshold The least amount of energy that can be detected as a stimulation 50 percent of the time.

Achievement motive The need to excel, to overcome obstacles.

Actualizing tendency According to Rogers, the drive of every organism to fulfill its biological potential and become what it is inherently capable of becoming.

Adaptation An adjustment of the senses to the level of stimulation they are receiving.

Additive color mixing The process of mixing lights of different wavelengths to create new hues.

Adjustment Any effort to cope with stress.

Adoption studies Research carried out on children, adopted at birth by parents not related to them, to determine the relative influence of heredity and environment on human behavior

Adrenal glands Two endocrine glands located just above the kidneys.

Aerial perspective Monocular cue to distance and depth based on the fact that more distant objects are likely to appear hazy and blurred.

Affiliation motive The need to be with others.

Afterimage Sense experience that occurs after a visual stimulus has been removed.

Aggression Behavior aimed at doing harm to others; also the motive to behave aggressively.

Agoraphobia An anxiety disorder that involves multiple, intense fear of crowds, public places, and other situations that require separation from a source of security such as the home.

Alcohol Depressant that is the intoxicating ingredient in whiskey, beer, wine, and other fermented or distilled liquors.

Algorithm A step-by-step method of problem solving that guarantees a correct solution.

All-or-none law Principle that the action potential in a neuron does not vary in strength; the neuron either fires at full strength or it does not fire at

Altered state of consciousness Mental state that differs noticeably from normal waking consciousness.

Altruistic behavior Helping behavior that is not linked to personal gain.

Alzheimer's disease A neurological disorder, most commonly found in late adulthood, characterized by progressive losses in memory and cognition and changes in personality.

Amphetamines Stimulant drugs that initially produce "rushes" of euphoria often followed by sudden "crashes" and, sometimes, severe depression.

Amplitude The magnitude of a wave; in sound, the primary determinant of loudness.

Anal stage Second stage in Freud's theory of personality development, in which a child's erotic feelings center on the anus and on elimination.

Analytical intelligence According to Sternberg, the ability to acquire new knowledge and solve problems effectively.

Anima According to Jung, the female archetype as it is expressed in the male personality.

Animus According to Jung, the male archetype as it is expressed in the female personality.

Anorexia nervosa A serious eating disorder that is associated with an intense fear of weight gain and a distorted body image.

Antipsychotic drugs Drugs used to treat very severe psychological disorders, particularly schizophrenia.

Antisocial personality disorder Personality disorder that involves a pattern of violent, criminal, or unethical and exploitative behavior and an inability to feel affection for others.

Anxiety disorders Disorders in which anxiety is a characteristic feature or the avoidance of anxiety seems to motivate abnormal behavior.

Anxiety In Horney's theory, the individual's reaction to real or imagined threats.

Apnea Sleep disorder characterized by breathing difficulty during the night and feelings of exhaustion during the day.

Approach/approach conflict According to Lewin, the result of simultaneous attraction to two appealing possibilities, neither of which has any negative qualities.

Approach/avoidance conflict According to Lewin, the result of being simultaneously attracted to and repelled by the same goal.

Archetypes In Jung's theory of personality, thought forms common to all human beings, stored in the collective unconscious.

Arousal theory Theory of motivation that propose organisms seek an optimal level of arousal.

Association areas Areas of the cerebral cortex where incoming messages from the separate senses are combined into meaningful impressions and outgoing messages from the motor areas are integrated.

Attachment Emotional bond that develops in the first year of life that makes human babies cling to their caregivers for safety and comfort.

Attention The selection of some incoming information for further processing.

Attention-deficit/hyperactivity disorder (AD/HD) A childhood disorder characterized by inattention, impulsiveness, and hyperactivity.

Attitude Relatively stable organization of beliefs, feelings, and behavior tendencies directed toward something or someone—the attitude object.

Attribution theory The theory that addresses the question of how people make judgments about the causes of behavior.

Authoritarian personality A personality pattern characterized by rigid conventionality, exaggerated respect for authority, and hostility toward those who defy society's norms.

Autistic disorder A childhood disorder characterized by a lack of social instincts and strange motor behavior.

Autokinetic illusion The perception that a stationary object is actually moving.

Autonomic nervous system The part of the peripheral nervous system that carries messages between the central nervous system and the internal organs.

Autonomous work group A small team of workers that is responsible for an entire product or service.

Autonomy Sense of independence; a desire not to be controlled by others.

Availability A heuristic by which a judgment or decision is based on information that is most easily retrieved from memory.

Aversive conditioning Behavioral therapy techniques aimed at eliminating undesirable behavior patterns by teaching the person to associate them with pain and discomfort.

Avoidance training Learning a desirable behavior to prevent the occurrence of something unpleasant such as punishment.

Avoidance/avoidance conflict According to Lewin, the result of facing a choice between two undesirable possibilities, neither of which has any positive qualities.

Avoidant personality disorder Personality disorder in which the person's fears of rejection by others leads to social isolation.

Axon Single long fiber extending from the cell body; it carries outgoing messages.

Babbling A baby's vocalizations, consisting of repetition of consonant-vowel combinations.

Barbiturates Potentially deadly depressants, first used for their sedative and anticonvulsant properties, now used only to treat such conditions as epilepsy and arthritis.

Basilar membrane Vibrating membrane in the cochlea of the inner ear; it contains sense receptors for sound.

Behavior contracting Form of operant conditioning therapy in which the client and therapist set behavioral goals and agree on reinforcements the person will receive upon reaching those goals.

Behavior genetics Study of the relationship between heredity and behavior.

Behavior therapies Therapeutic approaches that are based on the belief that all behavior, normal and abnormal, is learned, and that the objective of therapy is to teach people new, more satisfying ways of behaving.

Behaviorism School of psychology that studies only observable and measurable behavior.

Big Five Five traits or basic dimensions currently thought to be of central importance in describing personality.

Binaural cue Cue to sound location that involves both ears working together.

Binet-Simon Scale The first test of intelligence, developed for testing children.

Binocular cues Visual cues requiring the use of both eyes.

Biofeedback A technique that uses monitoring devices to provide precise information about internal physiological processes, such as heart rate or blood pressure, to teach people to gain voluntary control over these functions.

Biographical (or retrospective) study A method of studying developmental changes by reconstructing people's past through interviews and inferring the effects of past events on current behaviors.

Biological model View that psychological disorders have a biochemical or physiological basis.

Biological treatments A group of approaches, including medication, electroconvulsive therapy, and psychosurgery, that are sometimes used to treat psychological disorders in conjunction with, or instead of, psychotherapy.

Biopsychosocial theory The theory that the interaction of biological, psychological, and cultural factors influence the intensity and duration of pain.

Bipolar cells Neurons that have only one axon and one dendrite; in the eye, these neurons connect the receptors on the retina to the ganglion cells.

Bipolar disorder A mood disorder in which periods of mania and depression alternate, sometimes with periods of normal mood intervening.

Blind spot The place on the retina where the axons of all the ganglion cells leave the eye and where there are no receptors.

Blocking A process whereby prior conditioning prevents conditioning to a second stimulus even when the two stimuli are presented simultaneously.

Body dysmorphic disorder A somatoform disorder in which a person becomes so preoccupied with his or her imagined ugliness that normal life is impossible.

Borderline personality disorder Personality disorder characterized by marked instability in self-image, mood, and interpersonal relationships.

Brainstorming A problem-solving strategy in which an individual or a group produces numerous ideas and evaluates them only after all ideas have been collected.

Brightness The nearness of a color to white as opposed to black.

Bulimia nervosa An eating disorder characterized by binges of eating followed by self-induced vomiting.

Bystander effect The tendency for an individual's helpfulness in an emergency to decrease as the number of bystanders increases.

Cannon-Bard theory States that the experience of emotion occurs simultaneously with biological changes.

Case study Intensive description and analysis of a single individual or just a few individuals.

Catatonic schizophrenia Schizophrenic disorder in which disturbed motor behavior is prominent.

Central nervous system Division of the nervous system that consists of the brain and spinal cord.

Central tendency Tendency of scores to congregate around some middle value.

Cerebellum Structure in the hindbrain that controls certain reflexes and coordinates the body's movements.

Cerebral cortex The outer surface of the two cerebral hemispheres that regulates most complex behavior.

Childhood amnesia The difficulty adults have remembering experiences from their first two years of life.

Chromosomes Pairs of threadlike bodies within the cell nucleus that contain the genes.

Chunking The grouping of information into meaningful units for easier handling by short-term memory.

Circadian rhythm a regular biological rhythm with approximately a 24 hour period.

Classical (or Pavlovian) conditioning The type of learning in which a response naturally elicited by one stimulus comes to be elicited by a different, formerly neutral stimulus.

Client-centered (or person-centered) therapy Nondirectional form of therapy developed by Carl Rogers that calls for unconditional positive regard of the client by the therapist with the goal of helping the client become fully functioning.

Cliques Groups of adolescents with similar interests and strong mutual attachment.

Cocaine Drug derived from the coca plant that, while producing a sense of euphoria by stimulating the sympathetic nervous system, also leads to anxiety, depression, and addictive cravings.

Cochlea Part of the inner ear containing fluid that vibrates, which in turn causes the basilar membrane to vibrate.

Cognition The processes whereby we acquire and use knowledge.

Cognitive dissonance Perceived inconsistency between two cognitions.

Cognitive distortions An illogical and maladaptive response to early negative life events that leads to feelings of incompetence and unworthiness that are reactivated whenever a new situation arises that resembles the original events.

Cognitive learning Learning that depends on mental processes that are not directly observable.

Cognitive map A learned mental image of a spatial environment that may be called on to solve problems when stimuli in the environment change.

Cognitive psychology School of psychology devoted to the study of mental processes in the broadest sense.

Cognitive theory States that emotional experience depends on one's perception or judgment of the situation one is in.

Cognitive therapies Psychotherapies that emphasize changing people's perceptions of their life situation as a way of modifying their behavior.

Cognitive therapy Therapy that depends on identifying and changing inappropriately negative and self-critical patterns of thought.

Cognitive-behavioral model View that psychological disorders result from learning maladaptive ways of thinking and behaving.

Cognitive–social learning theories Personality theories that view behavior as the product of the interaction of cognitions, learning and past experiences, and the immediate environment.

Cohort A group of people born during the same period in historical time.

Collective unconscious In Jung's theory of personality, the level of the unconscious that is inherited and common to all members of a species.

Color blindness Partial or total inability to perceive hues.

Color constancy An inclination to perceive familiar objects as retaining their color despite changes in sensory information.

Compensation According to Adler, the person's effort to overcome imagined or real personal weaknesses.

Compensatory model A rational decision-making model in which choices are systematically evaluated on various criteria.

Compliance Change of behavior in response to an explicit request from another person or group.

Compromise Deciding on a more realistic solution or goal when an ideal solution or goal is not practical.

Concept A mental category for classifying objects, people, or experiences.

Concrete-operational stage In Piaget's theory, the stage of cognitive development between 7 and 11 years of age in which the individual can attend to more than one thing at a time and understand someone else's point of view, though thinking is limited to concrete matters.

Conditional positive regard In Rogers's theory, acceptance and love that are dependent on behaving in certain ways and fulfilling certain conditions.

Conditioned food (or taste) aversion Conditioned avoidance of certain foods even if there is only one pairing of conditioned and unconditioned stimuli.

Conditioned response (CR) After conditioning, the response an organism produces when only a conditioned stimulus is presented.

Conditioned stimulus (CS) An originally neutral stimulus that is paired with an unconditioned stimulus and eventually produces the desired response in an organism when presented alone.

Conditioning The acquisition of specific patterns of behavior in the presence of well-defined stimuli.

Cones Receptor cells in the retina responsible for color vision.

Confirmation bias The tendency to look for evidence in support of a belief and to ignore evidence that would disprove a belief.

Conflict Simultaneous existence of incompatible demands, opportunities, needs, or goals.

Conformity Voluntarily yielding to social norms, even at the expense of one's own preferences.

Confrontation Acknowledging a stressful situation directly and attempting to find a solution to the problem or attain the difficult goal.

Consciousness Our awareness of various cognitive processes, such as sleeping, dreaming, concentrating, and making decisions.

Content validity Refers to a test's having an adequate sample of questions measuring the skills or knowledge it is supposed to measure.

Contingency A reliable "if-then" relationship between two events such as a CS and a US.

Control group In a controlled experiment, the group not subjected to a change in the independent variable; used for comparison with the experimental group.

Convergence A visual depth cue that comes from muscles controlling eye movement as the eyes turn inward to view a nearby stimulus.

Conversion disorders Somatoform disorders in which a dramatic specific disability has no physical cause but instead seems related to psychological problems.

Cooperative play Two or more children engaged in play that requires interaction.

Cope Make cognitive and behavioral efforts to manage psychological stress.

Cornea The transparent protective coating over the front part of the eye.

Corpus callosum A thick band of nerve fibers connecting the left and right cerebral cortex.

Correlation coefficient Statistical measure of the strength of association between two variables.

Correlational research Research technique based on the naturally occurring relationship between two or more variables.

Counterfactual thinking Thinking about alternative realities and things that never happened.

Couple therapy A form of group therapy intended to help troubled partners improve their problems of communication and interaction.

Creative intelligence Sternberg's term for the ability to adapt creatively in new situations, to use insight.

Creativity The ability to produce novel and socially valued ideas or objects.

Criterion-related validity Validity of a test as measured by a comparison of the test score and independent measures of what the test is designed to measure.

Critical period A time when certain internal and external influences have a major effect on development; at other periods, the same influences will have little or no effect.

Cross-sectional study A method of studying developmental changes by comparing people of different ages at about the same time.

Cultural truism The belief that most members of a society accept as self-evidently true.

Culture The tangible goods and the values, attitudes, behaviors, and beliefs that are passed from one generation to another.

Culture-fair tests Intelligence tests designed to reduce cultural bias by minimizing skills and values that vary from one culture to another.

Dark adaptation Increased sensitivity of rods and cones in darkness.

Daydreams Apparently effortless shifts in attention away from the here-and-now into a private world of make-believe.

Decay theory A theory that argues that the passage of time causes forgetting.

Decibel Unit of measurement for the loudness of sounds.

Deep structure The underlying meaning of a sentence.

Defense mechanisms Self-deceptive techniques for reducing anxiety and guilt, including denial, repression, projection, identification, regression, intellectualization, reac-

tion formation, displacement, and sublimation.

Defensive attribution The tendency to attribute our successes to our own efforts or qualities and our failures to external factors.

Deindividuation A loss of personal sense of responsibility in a group.

Deinstitutionalization Policy of treating people with severe psychological disorders in the larger community, or in small residential centers such as halfway houses, rather than in large public hospitals.

Delusions False beliefs about reality that have no basis in fact.

Dendrites Short fibers that branch out from the cell body and pick up incoming messages.

Denial Refusal to acknowledge a painful or threatening reality.

Deoxyribonucleic acid (DNA) Complex molecule in a double-helix configuration that is the main ingredient of chromosomes and genes and forms the code for all genetic information.

Dependent personality disorder Personality disorder in which the person is unable to make choices and decisions independently and cannot tolerate being alone.

Dependent variable In an experiment, the variable that is measured to see how it is changed by manipulations in the independent variable.

Depersonalization disorder A dissociative disorder whose essential feature is that the person suddenly feels changed or different in a strange way.

Depressants Chemicals that slow down behavior or cognitive processes.

Depression A mood disorder characterized by overwhelming feelings of sadness, lack of interest in activities, and perhaps excessive guilt or feelings of worthlessness.

Desensitization therapy A conditioning technique designed to gradually reduce anxiety about a particular object or situation.

Developmental norms Ages by which an average child achieves various developmental milestones.

Developmental psychology The study of the changes that occur in people from birth through old age.

Diathesis Biological predisposition.

Diathesis-stress model View that people biologically predisposed to a mental disorder (those with a certain diathesis) will tend to exhibit that disorder when particularly affected by stress.

Dichromats People who are blind to either red-green or yellow-blue.

Difference threshold or just noticeable difference (jnd) The smallest

change in stimulation that can be detected 50 percent of the time.

Discrimination An act or series of acts that denies opportunities and social esteem to an entire group of people or individual members of that group.

Disorganized schizophrenia Schizophrenic disorder in which bizarre and childlike behaviors are common.

Displacement Shifting repressed motives and emotions from an original object to a substitute object.

Display rules Culture-specific rules that govern how, when, and why expressions of emotion are appropriate.

Dissociative amnesia A dissociative disorder characterized by loss of memory for past events without organic cause.

Dissociative disorders Disorders in which some aspect of the personality seems separated from the rest.

Dissociative fugue A dissociative disorder that involves flight from home and the assumption of a new identity, with amnesia for past identity and events.

Dissociative identity disorder A dissociative disorder in which a person has several distinct personalities that emerge at different times.

Dominant gene Member of a gene pair that controls the appearance of a certain trait.

Dreams Vivid visual and auditory experiences that occur primarily during REM periods of sleep.

Drive State of tension or arousal that motivates behavior.

Drive-reduction theory Theory that motivated behavior is aimed at reducing a state of bodily tension or arousal and returning the organism to homeostasis.

Eclecticism Psychotherapeutic approach that recognizes the value of a broad treatment package over a rigid commitment to one particular form of therapy.

Ego Freud's term for the part of the personality that mediates between environmental demands (reality), conscience (superego), and instinctual needs (id); now often used as a synonym for "self."

Ego ideal The part of the superego that consists of standards of what one would like to be.

Egocentric Describes the inability to see things from another's point of view.

Eidetic imagery The ability to reproduce unusually sharp and detailed images of something one has seen.

Elaborative rehearsal The linking of new information in short-term memory to familiar material stored in long-term memory.

Electroconvulsive therapy (ECT) Biological therapy in which a mild electrical current is passed through the brain for a short period, often producing convulsions and temporary coma; used to treat severe, prolonged depression.

Embryo A developing human between 2 weeks and 3 months after conception.

Emotion Feeling, such as fear, joy, or surprise, that underlies behavior.

Emotional intelligence According to Goleman, a form of intelligence that refers to how effectively people perceive and understand their own emotions and the emotions of others, and can manage their emotional behavior.

Emotional memory Learned emotional responses to various stimuli.

Empirical evidence Information derived from systematic, objective observation.

Endocrine glands Glands of the endocrine system that release hormones into the bloodstream.

Episodic memory The portion of long-term memory that stores personally experienced events.

Erectile disorder or erectile dysfunction (ED) The inability of a man to achieve or maintain an erection.

Ethnicity A common cultural heritage—including religion, language, or ancestry—that is shared by a group of individuals.

Evolutionary psychology An approach to, and subfield of, psychology that is concerned with the evolutionary origins of behaviors and mental processes, their adaptive value, and the purposes they continue to serve.

Exchange The concept that relationships are based on trading rewards among partners.

Exhibitionism Compulsion to expose one's genitals in public to achieve sexual arousal.

Expectancies In Bandura's view, what a person anticipates in a situation or as a result of behaving in certain ways.

Experimental group In a controlled experiment, the group subjected to a change in the independent variable.

Experimental method A research technique in which an investigator deliberately manipulates selected events or circumstances and then measures the effects of those manipulations on subsequent behavior

Experimenter bias Expectations by the experimenter that might influence the results of an experiment or its interpretation.

Explicit memory Memory for information that we can readily express in words and are aware of having; these memories can be intentionally retrieved from memory.

Extinction A decrease in the strength or frequency of a learned response because of failure to continue pairing the US and CS (classical conditioning) or withholding of reinforcement (operant conditioning).

Extrinsic motivation A desire to perform a behavior to obtain an external reward or avoid punishment.

Extrovert According to Jung, a person who usually focuses on social life and the external world instead of on his or her internal experience.

Factor analysis A statistical technique that identifies groups of related objects; used by Cattell to identify trait clusters.

Family studies Studies of heritability in humans based on the assumption that if genes influence a certain trait, close relatives should be more similar on that trait than distant relatives.

Family therapy A form of group therapy that sees the family as at least partly responsible for the individual's problems and that seeks to change all family members' behaviors to the benefit of the family unit as well as the troubled individual.

Feature detectors Specialized brain cells that only respond to particular elements in the visual field such as movement or lines of specific orientation.

Female sexual arousal disorder The inability of a woman to become sexually aroused or to reach orgasm.

Feminist theory Feminist theories offer a wide variety of views on the social roles of women and men, the problems and rewards of those roles, and the prescriptions for changing them.

Fetal alcohol syndrome (FAS) A disorder that occurs in children of women who drink alcohol during pregnancy that is characterized by facial deformities, heart defects, stunted growth, and cognitive impairments.

Fetishism A paraphilia in which a nonhuman object is the preferred or exclusive method of achieving sexual excitement.

Fetus A developing human between 3 months after conception and birth.

Figure Entity perceived to stand apart from the background.

Fixation According to Freud, a partial or complete halt at some point

in the individual's psychosexual development.

Fixed-interval schedule A reinforcement schedule in which the correct response is reinforced after a fixed length of time since the last reinforcement.

Fixed-ratio schedule A reinforcement schedule in which the correct response is reinforced after a fixed number of correct responses.

Flashbulb memory A vivid memory of a certain event and the incidents surrounding it even after a long time has passed.

Formal-operational stage In Piaget's theory, the stage of cognitive development between 11 and 15 years of age in which the individual becomes capable of abstract thought.

Fovea The area of the retina that is the center of the visual field.

Framing The perspective or phrasing of information that is used to make a decision.

Fraternal twins Twins developed from two separate fertilized ova and therefore different in genetic makeup.

Free association A psychoanalytic technique that encourages the client to talk without inhibition about whatever thoughts or fantasies come to mind.

Frequency distribution A count of the number of scores that fall within each of a series of intervals.

Frequency histogram Type of bar graph that shows frequency distributions.

Frequency polygon Type of line graph that shows frequency distributions.

Frequency The number of cycles per second in a wave; in sound, the primary determinant of pitch.

Frequency theory Theory that pitch is determined by the frequency with which hair cells in the cochlea fire.

Frontal lobe Part of the cerebral cortex that is responsible for voluntary movement; it is also important for attention, goal-directed behavior, and appropriate emotional experiences.

Frotteurism Compulsion to achieve sexual arousal by touching or rubbing against a nonconsenting person in public situations.

Frustration The feeling that occurs when a person is prevented from reaching a goal.

Frustration-aggression theory The theory that under certain circumstances people who are frustrated in their goals turn their anger away from the proper, powerful target toward another, less powerful target that is safer to attack.

Fully functioning person According to Rogers, an individual whose self-concept closely resembles his or her inborn capacities or potentials.

Functional fixedness The tendency to perceive only a limited number of uses for an object, thus interfering with the process of problem solving.

Functionalist theory Theory of mental life and behavior that is concerned with how an organism uses its perceptual abilities to function in its environment.

Fundamental attribution error The tendency of people to overemphasize personal causes for other people's behavior and to underemphasize personal causes for their own behavior.

Ganglion cells Neurons that connect the bipolar cells in the eyes to the brain.

Gate control theory The theory that a "neurological gate" in the spinal cord controls the transmission of pain messages to the brain.

Gender constancy The realization that gender does not change with age.

Gender identity A little girl's knowledge that she is a girl, and a little boy's knowledge that he is a boy.

Gender roles Behaviors that we expect each gender to engage in.

Gender stereotypes General beliefs about characteristics that men and women are presumed to have.

Gender stereotypes General beliefs about characteristics that are presumed to be typical of each sex.

Gender The psychological and social meanings attached to being biologically male or female. Often used interchangeably with one's biological makeup or sex.

Gender-identity disorder in children Rejection of one's biological gender in childhood, along with the clothing and behavior society considers appropriate to that gender.

Gender-identity disorders Disorders that involve the desire to become, or the insistence that one really is, a member of the other biological sex.

Gender-role awareness Knowledge of what behavior is appropriate for each gender.

General adaptation syndrome (GAS) According to Selye, the three stages the body passes through as it adapts to stress: alarm reaction, resistance, and exhaustion.

Generalized anxiety disorder An anxiety disorder characterized by prolonged vague but intense fears that are not attached to any particular object or circumstance.

Genes Elements that control the transmission of traits; they are found on the chromosomes.

Genetics Study of how traits are transmitted from one generation to the next.

Genital stage In Freud's theory of personality development, the final stage of normal adult sexual development, which is usually marked by mature sexuality.

Gestalt psychology School of psychology that studies how people perceive and experience objects as whole patterns.

Gestalt therapy An insight therapy that emphasizes the wholeness of the personality and attempts to reawaken people to their emotions and sensations in the here-and-now.

Giftedness Refers to superior IQ combined with demonstrated or potential ability in such areas as academic aptitude, creativity, and leadership.

Glial cells (or glia) Cells that form the myelin sheath; they insulate and support neurons by holding them together, removing waste products, and preventing harmful substances from passing from the bloodstream into the brain.

Golgi tendon organs Receptors that sense movement of the tendons, which connect muscle to bone.

Gonads The reproductive glands, testes in males and ovaries in females.

Graded potential A shift in the electrical charge in a tiny area of a neuron.

Grammar The language rules that determine how sounds and words can be combined and used to communicate meaning within a language.

Grasping reflex The reflex that causes newborn babies to close their fists around anything that is put in their hands.

Great person theory The theory that leadership is a result of personal qualities and traits that qualify one to lead others.

Ground Background against which a figure appears.

Group tests Intelligence tests administered by one examiner to many people at one time.

Group therapy Type of psychotherapy in which people meet regularly to interact and help one another achieve insight into their feelings and behavior.

Growth spurt A rapid increase in height and weight that occurs during adolescence.

Hallucinations Sensory experiences in the absence of external stimulation.

Hallucinogens Any of a number of drugs, such as LSD and mescaline, that distort visual and auditory perception.

Hammer, anvil, stirrup The three small bones in the middle ear that relay vibrations of the eardrum to the inner ear.

Hawthorne effect The principle that people will alter their behavior because of researchers' attention and not necessarily because of any treatment condition.

Health psychology A subfield of psychology concerned with the relationship between psychological factors and physical health and illness.

Hertz (Hz) Cycles per second; unit of measurement for the frequency of sound waves.

Heuristics Rules of thumb that help in simplifying and solving problems, although they do not guarantee a correct solution.

Higher-order conditioning Conditioning based on previous learning; the conditioned stimulus serves as an unconditioned stimulus for further training.

Hill climbing A heuristic problem-solving strategy in which each step moves you progressively closer to the final goal.

Hindbrain Area containing the medulla, pons, and cerebellum.

Hindsight bias The tendency to view outcomes as inevitable and predictable after we know the outcome.

Holophrases One-word sentences commonly used by children under 2 years of age.

Homeostasis State of balance and stability in which the organism functions effectively.

Hormones Chemical substances released by the endocrine glands; they help regulate bodily activities.

Hue The aspect of color that corresponds to names such as red, green, and blue.

Human factors psychology Area of industrial/organizational psychology that deals with the arrangement and design of work tasks to promote a safer, healthier, and more efficient work environment.

Human genome The full complement of genes within a human cell.

Humanistic personality theory Any personality theory that asserts the fundamental goodness of people and their striving toward higher levels of functioning.

Humanistic psychology School of psychology that emphasizes nonverbal experience and altered states of consciousness as a means of realizing one's full human potential.

Hypnosis Trancelike state in which a person responds readily to suggestions.

Hypochondriasis A somatoform disorder in which a person interprets insignificant symptoms as signs of serious illness in the absence of any organic evidence of such illness.

Hypothalamus Forebrain region that governs motivation and emotional responses.

Hypotheses Specific, testable predictions derived from a theory.

Id In Freud's theory of personality, the collection of unconscious urges and desires that continually seek expression.

Identical twins Twins developed from a single fertilized ovum and therefore identical in genetic makeup at the time of conception.

Identification Taking on the characteristics of someone else to avoid feeling incompetent.

Identity crisis A period of intense self-examination and decision making; part of the process of identity formation.

Identity formation Erikson's term for the development of a stable sense of self necessary to make the transition from dependence on others to dependence on oneself.

Image A nonverbal mental representation of a sensory experience.

Imaginary audience Elkind's term for adolescents' delusion that they are constantly being observed by others.

Implicit memory Memory for information that we cannot readily express in words and may not be aware of having; these memories cannot be intentionally retrieved from memory.

Imprinting The tendency in certain species to follow the first moving thing (usually its mother) it sees after it is born or hatched.

Incentive External stimulus that prompts goal-directed behavior.

Independent variable In an experiment, the variable that is manipulated to test its effects on the other, dependent variables.

Industrial/organizational (I/O) psychology The area of psychology concerned with the application of psychological principles to the problems of human organizations, especially work organizations.

Inferiority complex In Adler's theory, the fixation on feelings of personal inferiority that results in emotional and social paralysis.

Information-processing model A computerlike model used to describe the way humans encode, store, and retrieve information.

Insanity Legal term for mentally disturbed people who are not considered responsible for their criminal actions.

Insight Awareness of previously unconscious feelings and memories and how they influence present feelings and behavior.

Insight Learning that occurs rapidly as a result of understanding all the elements of a problem.

Insight therapies A variety of individual psychotherapies designed to give people a better awareness and understanding of their feelings, motivations, and actions in the hope that this will help them adjust.

Insomnia Sleep disorder characterized by difficulty in falling asleep or remaining asleep throughout the night.

Instinct Inborn, inflexible, goal-directed behavior that is characteristic of an entire species.

Intellectualization Thinking abstractly about stressful problems as a way of detaching oneself from them.

Intelligence A general term referring to the ability or abilities involved in learning and adaptive behavior.

Intelligence quotient (IQ) A numerical value given to intelligence that is determined from the scores on an intelligence test; the average IQ is arbitrarily set at 100.

Intelligence tests Tests designed to measure a person's general mental abilities.

Intermittent pairing Pairing the conditioned stimulus and the unconditioned stimulus on only a portion of the learning trials.

Interneurons (or association neurons) Neurons that carry messages from one neuron to another.

Interval scale Scale with equal distances between the points or values, but without a true zero.

Intimacy The quality of genuine closeness and trust achieved in communication with another person.

Intrinsic motivation A desire to perform a behavior that stems from the behavior performed.

Introvert According to Jung, a person who usually focuses on his or her own thoughts and feelings.

Ions Electrically charged particles found both inside and outside the neuron.

Iris The colored part of the eye.

Irrational individuals According to Jung, people who base their actions on perceptions, either through the senses (sensation) or through unconscious processes (intuition).

James-Lange theory States that stimuli cause physiological changes in our bodies, and emotions result from those physiological changes.

Job analysis Breaking down a job into its basic components to identify the most important components and thus the most important skills and abilities needed to perform the job.

Job enrichment Redesigning jobs to provide workers with more meaningful tasks, increased decision-making authority, and opportunities for feedback.

Just-world hypothesis Attribution error based on the assumption that bad things happen to bad people and good things happen to good people.

Kinesthetic senses Senses of muscle movement, posture, and strain on muscles and joints.

Language A flexible system of communication that uses sounds, rules, gestures, or symbols to convey information.

Language acquisition device A hypothetical neural mechanism for acquiring language that is presumed to be "wired into" all humans.

Latency period In Freud's theory of personality, a period in which the child appears to have no interest in the other sex; occurs after the phallic stage.

Latent learning Learning that is not immediately reflected in a behavior change.

Law of effect Thorndike's theory that behavior consistently rewarded will be "stamped in" as learned behavior, and behavior that brings about discomfort will be "stamped out" (also known as the principle of reinforcement).

Learned helplessness Failure to take steps to avoid or escape from an unpleasant or aversive stimulus that occurs as a result of previous exposure to unavoidable painful stimuli.

Learning set The ability to become increasingly more effective in solving problems as more problems are solved.

Learning The process by which experience or practice results in a relatively permanent change in behavior or potential behavior.

Lens The transparent part of the eye inside the pupil that focuses light onto the retina.

Libido According to Freud, the energy generated by the sexual instinct.

Light adaptation Decreased sensitivity of rods and cones in bright light.

Light The small segment of the electromagnetic spectrum to which our eyes are sensitive.

Limbic system Ring of structures that play a role in learning and emotional behavior.

Linear perspective Monocular cue to distance and depth based on the fact that two parallel lines seem to come together at the horizon.

Linguistic determinism The idea that patterns of thinking are determined by the specific language one speaks.

Locus of control According to Rotter, an expectancy about whether reinforcement is under internal or external control.

Longitudinal study A method of studying developmental changes by evaluating the same people at different points in their lives.

Long-term memory (LTM) The portion of memory that is more or less permanent, corresponding to everything we "know."

Long-Term Potentiation (LTP) A long-lasting change in the structure or function of a synapse that increases the efficiency of neural transmission, and is thought to be related to how information is stored by neurons.

Lysergic acid diethylamide (LSD) Hallucinogenic or "psychedelic" drug that produces hallucinations and delusions similar to those occurring in a psychotic state.

Management by objectives (MBO) A goal-setting process that takes place throughout the organization, with goals for each division and individual linked to the overall goals of the organization.

Mania A mood disorder characterized by euphoric states, extreme physical activity, excessive talkativeness, distractedness, and sometimes grandiosity.

Marijuana A mild hallucinogen that produces a "high" often characterized by feelings of euphoria, a sense of well-being, and swings in mood from gaiety to relaxation; may also cause feelings of anxiety and paranoia.

Maturation An automatic biological unfolding of development in an organism as a function of the passage of time.

Mean Arithmetical average calculated by dividing a sum of values by the total number of cases.

Means-end analysis A heuristic strategy that aims to reduce the discrepancy between the current situation and the desired goal at a number of intermediate points.

Median Point that divides a set of scores in half.

Meditation Any of the various methods of concentration, reflection, or focusing of thoughts undertaken to suppress the activity of the sympathetic nervous

Memory The ability to remember the things that we have experienced, imagined, and learned.

Menarche First menstrual period.

Menopause The time in a woman's life when menstruation ceases.

Mental representations Mental images or symbols (such as words) used to think about or remember an object, a person, or an event.

Mental retardation Condition of significantly subaverage intelligence combined with deficiencies in adaptive behavior.

Mental set The tendency to perceive and approach problems in certain ways.

Meta-analysis A statistical procedure for combining the results of several studies so the strength, consistency, and direction of the effect can be estimated.

Midbrain Region between the hindbrain and the forebrain; it is important for hearing and sight, and it is one of several places in the brain where pain is registered.

Midlife crisis A time when adults discover they no longer feel fulfilled in their jobs or personal lives and attempt to make a decisive shift in career or lifestyle.

Midlife transition According to Levinson, a process whereby adults assess the past and formulate new goals for the future.

Minnesota Multiphasic Personality Inventory (MMPI-2) The most widely used objective personality test, originally intended for psychiatric diagnosis.

Mnemonics Techniques that make material easier to remember.

Mnemonist Someone with highly developed memory skills.

Mode Point at which the largest number of scores occurs.

Modeling A behavior therapy in which the person learns desired behaviors by watching others perform those behaviors.

Monaural cue Cue to sound location that requires just one ear.

Monochromats People who are totally color-blind.

Monocular cues Visual cues requiring the use of one eye.

Mood disorders Disturbances in mood or prolonged emotional state.

Morphemes The smallest meaningful units of speech, such as simple words, prefixes, and suffixes.

Motion parallax Monocular distance cue in which objects closer than the point of visual focus seem to move in the direction opposite to the viewer's moving head, and objects beyond the focus point appear to move in the same direction as the viewer's head.

Motive Specific need or desire, such as hunger, thirst, or achievement, that prompts goal-directed behavior.

Motor (or efferent) neurons Neurons that carry messages from the spinal cord or brain to the muscles and glands.

Myelin sheath White fatty covering found on some axons.

Narcissistic personality disorder Personality disorder in which the person has an exaggerated sense of self-importance and needs constant admiration.

Narcolepsy Hereditary sleep disorder characterized by sudden nodding off during the day and sudden loss of muscle tone following moments of emotional excitement.

Natural selection The mechanism proposed by Darwin in his theory of evolution, which states that organisms best adapted to their environment tend to survive, transmitting their genetic characteristics to succeeding generations, whereas organisms with less adaptive characteristics tend to vanish from the earth.

Naturalistic observation Research method involving the systematic study of animal or human behavior in natural settings rather than in the laboratory.

Negative reinforcer Any event whose reduction or termination increases the likelihood that ongoing behavior will recur.

Neonates Newborn babies.

NEO-PI-R An objective personality test designed to assess the Big Five personality traits.

Nerve (or tract) Group of axons bundled together.

Neural impulse (or action potential) The firing of a nerve cell.

Neural Plasticity The ability of the brain to change in response to experience.

Neurofeedback A biofeedback technique that monitors brain waves using an EEG to teach people to gain voluntary control over their brain wave activity.

Neurogenesis The growth of new neurons.

Neurons Individual cells that are the smallest units of the nervous system.

Neuroscience The study of the brain and the nervous system.

Neurotic trends Horney's term for irrational strategies for coping with emotional problems and minimizing anxiety.

Neurotransmitters Chemicals released by the synaptic vesicles that travel across the synaptic space and affect adjacent neurons.

Night terrors Frightening, often terrifying dreams that occur during NREM sleep from which a person is difficult to awaken and doesn't remember the content.

Nightmares Frightening dreams that occur during REM sleep and are remembered.

Nominal scale A set of categories for classifying objects.

Non-REM (NREM) sleep Non-rapid-eye-movement stages of sleep that alternate with REM stages during the sleep cycle.

Nonshared environment The unique aspects of the environment that are experienced differently by siblings even though they are reared in the same family.

Norm A shared idea or expectation about how to behave.

Normal curve Hypothetical bell-shaped distribution curve that occurs when a normal distribution is plotted as a frequency polygon.

Obedience Change of behavior in response to a command from another person, typically an authority figure.

Object permanence The concept that things continue to exist even when they are out of sight.

Objective tests Personality tests that are administered and scored in a standard way.

Observational (or vicarious) learning Learning by observing other people's behavior.

Observer bias Expectations or biases of the observer that might distort or influence his or her interpretation of what was actually observed.

Obsessive-compulsive disorder (OCD) An anxiety disorder in which a person feels driven to think disturbing thoughts and/or to perform senseless rit

Occipital lobe Part of the cerebral hemisphere that receives and interprets visual information.

Oedipus complex and Electra complex According to Freud, a child's sexual attachment to the parent of the opposite sex and jealousy toward the parent of the same sex; generally occurs in the phallic stage.

Olfactory bulb The smell center in the brain.

Olfactory epithelium Nasal membranes containing receptor cells sensitive to odors.

Operant behavior Behavior designed to operate on the environment in a way that will gain something desired or avoid something unpleasant.

Operant or instrumental conditioning The type of learning in which behaviors are emitted (in the presence of specific stimuli) to earn rewards or avoid punishments.

Opiates Drugs, such as opium and heroin, derived from the opium poppy, that dull the senses and induce feelings of euphoria, well-

being, and relaxation. Synthetic drugs resembling opium derivatives are also classified as opiates.

Opponent-process theory Theory of color vision that holds that three sets of color receptors (yellow-blue, red-green, black-white) respond to determine the color you experience.

Optic chiasm The point near the base of the brain where some fibers in the optic nerve from each eye cross to the other side of the brain.

Optic nerve The bundle of axons of ganglion cells that carries neural messages from each eye to the brain.

Oral stage First stage in Freud's theory of personality development, in which the infant's erotic feelings center on the mouth, lips, and tongue.

Ordinal scale Scale indicating order or relative position of items according to some criterion.

Organ of Corti Structure on the surface of the basilar membrane that contains the receptor cells for hearing.

Organizational psychology Area of industrial/organizational psychology that focuses on how workers adapt to the social environment of complex human organizations.

Orgasm Peaking of sexual pleasure and release of sexual tension.

Orgasmic disorders Inability to reach orgasm in a person able to experience sexual desire and maintain arousal.

Oval window Membrane across the opening between the middle ear and inner ear that conducts vibrations to the cochlea.

Overtones Tones that result from sound waves that are multiples of the basic tone; primary determinant of timbre.

Pancreas Organ lying between the stomach and small intestine; it secretes insulin and glucagon to regulate blood-sugar levels.

Panic disorder An anxiety disorder characterized by recurrent panic attacks in which the person suddenly experiences intense fear or terror without any reasonable cause.

Papillae Small bumps on the tongue that contain taste buds.

Parallel play Two children playing side by side at similar activities but paying little or no attention to each other; the earliest kind of social interaction between toddlers.

Paranoid personality disorder Personality disorder in which the person is inappropriately suspicious and mistrustful of others.

Paranoid schizophrenia Schizophrenic disorder marked by extreme suspiciousness and complex, bizarre delusions.

Paraphilias Sexual disorders in which unconventional objects or situations cause sexual arousal.

Parasympathetic division Branch of the autonomic nervous system; it calms and relaxes the body.

Parathyroids Four tiny glands embedded in the thyroid; they secrete parathormone.

Parietal lobe Part of the cerebral cortex that receives sensory information from throughout the body.

Participants Individuals whose reactions or responses are observed in an experiment.

Pedophilia Desire to have sexual relations with children as the preferred or exclusive method of achieving sexual excitement.

Peer group A network of same-aged friends and acquaintances who give one another emotional and social support.

Perception The process of creating meaningful patterns from raw sensory information.

Perceptual constancy A tendency to perceive objects as stable and unchanging despite changes in sensory stimulation.

Perceptual illusion Illusion due to misleading cues in stimuli that give rise to inaccurate or impossible perceptions.

Performance appraisal interview Meeting between the employee and the supervisor in which they discuss the supervisor's evaluation of the employee's job performance.

Performance rating system A method of performance evaluation in which a numerical rating is given for performance in each key area of the job.

Performance standards In Bandura's theory, standards that people develop to rate the adequacy of their own behavior in a variety of situations.

Performance tests Intelligence tests that minimize the use of language.

Peripheral nervous system Division of the nervous system that connects the central nervous system to the rest of the body.

Persona According to Jung, our public self, the mask we put on to represent ourselves to others.

Personal fable Elkind's term for adolescents' delusion that they are unique, very important, and invulnerable.

Personal unconscious In Jung's theory of personality, one of the two levels of the unconscious; it contains the individual's repressed thoughts, forgotten experiences, and undeveloped ideas.

Personality An individual's unique pattern of thoughts, feelings, and

behaviors that persists over time and across situations.

Personality disorders Disorders in which inflexible and maladaptive ways of thinking and behaving learned early in life cause distress to the person and/or conflicts with others.

Personality traits Dimensions or characteristics on or in which people differ in distinctive ways.

Personnel psychology Area of industrial/organizational psychology that focuses on the selection, training, and evaluation of people in an organization.

Phallic stage Third stage in Freud's theory of personality development, in which erotic feelings center on the genitals.

Pheromones Chemical molecules that communicate information to other members of a species, and influence their behavior.

Phi phenomenon Apparent movement caused by flashing lights in sequence, as on theater marquees.

Phonemes The basic sound units of a language that indicate changes in meaning.

Pineal gland A gland located roughly in the center of the brain that appears to regulate activity levels over the course of a day.

Pitch Auditory experience corresponding primarily to frequency of sound vibrations, resulting in a higher or lower tone.

Pituitary gland Gland located on the underside of the brain; it produces the largest number of the body's hormones.

Place theory Theory that pitch is determined by the location of greatest vibration on the basilar membrane.

Placebo Chemically inactive substance used for comparison with active drugs in experiments on the effects of drugs.

Placebo effect Pain relief that occurs when a person believes a pill or procedure will reduce pain. The actual cause of the relief seems to come from endorphins.

Placenta The organ by which an embryo or fetus is attached to its mother's uterus and that nourishes it during prenatal development.

Pleasure principle According to Freud, the way in which the id seeks immediate gratification of an instinct.

Polarization Shift in attitudes by members of a group toward more extreme positions than the ones held before group discussion.

Polarization The condition of a neuron when the inside is negatively charged relative to the outside; for example, when the neuron is at rest.

Polygenic inheritance Process by which several genes interact to produce a certain trait; responsible for our most important traits.

Positive psychology An emerging field of psychology that focuses on positive experiences, including subjective well-being, self-determination, the relationship between positive emotions and physical health, and the factors that allow individuals, communities, and societies to flourish.

Positive reinforcer Any event whose presence increases the likelihood that ongoing behavior will recur.

Post-traumatic stress disorder (PTSD) Psychological disorder characterized by episodes of anxiety, sleeplessness, and nightmares resulting from some disturbing event in the past.

Practical intelligence According to Sternberg, the ability to select contexts in which you can excel, to shape the environment to fit your strengths and to solve practical problems.

Prejudice An intolerant, unfavorable, and rigid attitude toward a group of people.

Premature ejaculation Inability of man to inhibit orgasm as long as desired.

Prenatal development Development from conception to birth.

Preoperational stage In Piaget's theory, the stage of cognitive development between 2 and 7 years of age in which the individual becomes able to use mental representations and language to describe, remember, and reason about the world, though only in an egocentric fashion.

Pressure A feeling that one must speed up, intensify, or change the direction of one's behavior or live up to a higher standard of performance.

Prevention Strategies for reducing the incidence of emotional disturbance by eliminating conditions that cause or contribute to mental disorders and substituting conditions that foster mental well-being.

Primacy effect The theory that early information about someone weighs more heavily than later information in influencing one's impression of that person.

Primary drive An unlearned drive, such as hunger, that is based on a physiological state.

Primary motor cortex The section of the frontal lobe responsible for voluntary movement.

Primary prevention Techniques and programs to improve the social environment so that new cases of mental disorders do not develop.

Primary reinforcer A reinforcer that is rewarding in itself, such as food, water, and sex.

Primary somatosensory cortex Area of the parietal lobe where messages from the sense receptors are registered.

Principle of conservation The concept that the quantity of a substance is not altered by reversible changes in its appearance.

Proactive interference The process by which information already in memory interferes with new information.

Problem representation The first step in solving a problem: defining the problem.

Procedural memory The portion of long-term memory that stores information relating to skills, habits, and other perceptual-motor tasks.

Projection Attributing one's own repressed motives, feelings, or wishes to others.

Projective tests Personality tests, such as the Rorschach inkblot test, consisting of ambiguous or unstructured material.

Prototype According to Rosch, a mental model containing the most typical features of a concept.

Proximity How close two people live to each other.

Psychoactive drugs Chemical substances that change moods and perceptions.

Psychoanalysis The theory of personality Freud developed as well as the form of therapy he invented.

Psychoanalytic model View that psychological disorders result from unconscious internal conflicts.

Psychobiology The area of psychology that focuses on the biological foundations of behavior and mental processes.

Psychodynamic theories Personality theories contending that behavior results from psychological forces that interact within the individual, often outside conscious awareness.

Psychology The scientific study of behavior and mental processes.

Psychoneuroimmunology (PNI) A field that studies the interaction between stress on the one hand and immune, endocrine, and nervous system activity on the other.

Psychosomatic disorders Disorders in which there is real physical illness that is largely caused by psychological factors such as stress and anxiety.

Psychostimulants Drugs that increase ability to focus attention in children with AD/HD.

Psychosurgery Brain surgery performed to change a person's behavior and emotional state; a biological therapy rarely used today.

Psychotherapy The use of psychological techniques to treat personality and behavior disorders.

Psychotic Marked by defective or lost contact with reality.

Puberty The onset of sexual maturation, with accompanying physical development.

Punisher A stimulus that follows a behavior and decreases the likelihood that the behavior will be repeated.

Punishment Any event whose presence decreases the likelihood that ongoing behavior will recur.

Pupil A small opening in the iris through which light enters the eye.

Race A subpopulation of a species, defined according to an identifiable characteristic (e.g., geographic location, skin color, hair texture, genes, facial features).

Racism Prejudice and discrimination directed at a particular racial group.

Random sample Sample in which each potential participant has an equal chance of being selected.

Range Difference between the largest and smallest measurements in a distribution.

Ratio scale Scale with equal distances between the points or values and with a true zero.

Rational individuals According to Jung, people who regulate their actions by the psychological functions of thinking and feeling.

Rational-emotive therapy (RET) A directive cognitive therapy based on the idea that people's psychological distress is caused by irrational and self-defeating beliefs and that the therapist's job is to challenge such dysfunctional beliefs.

Reaction formation Expression of exaggerated ideas and emotions that are the opposite of one's repressed beliefs or feelings.

Realistic job preview A recruitment technique designed to give job applicants a sense of the typical workday on the job.

Reality principle According to Freud, the way in which the ego seeks to satisfy instinctual demands safely and effectively in the real world.

Receptor cell A specialized cell that responds to a particular type of energy.

Receptor site A location on a receptor neuron into which a specific neurotransmitter fits like a key into a lock.

Recessive gene Member of a gene pair that can control the appearance of a certain trait only if it is paired with another recessive gene.

Regression Reverting to childlike behavior and defenses.

Reinforcer A stimulus that follows a behavior and increases the likelihood that the behavior will be repeated.

Relative refractory period A period after firing when a neuron is returning to its normal polarized state and will fire again only if the incoming message is much stronger than usual.

Reliability Ability of a test to produce consistent and stable scores.

REM (paradoxical) sleep Sleep stage characterized by rapid eye movements and increased dreaming.

Representative sample Sample carefully chosen so that the characteristics of the participants correspond closely to the characteristics of the larger population.

Representativeness A heuristic by which a new situation is judged on the basis of its resemblance to a stereotypical model.

Repression Excluding uncomfortable thoughts, feelings, and desires from consciousness.

Response acquisition The "building phase" of conditioning during which the likelihood or strength of the desired response increases.

Response generalization Giving a response that is somewhat different from the response originally learned to that stimulus.

Resting potential Electrical charge across a neuron membrane due to excess positive ions concentrated on the outside and excess negative ions on the inside.

Reticular formation (RF) Network of neurons in the hindbrain, the midbrain, and part of the forebrain whose primary function is to alert and arouse the higher parts of the brain.

Retina The lining of the eye containing receptor cells that are sensitive to light.

Retinal disparity Binocular distance cue based on the difference between the images cast on the two retinas when both eyes are focused on the same object.

Retroactive interference The process by which new information interferes with information already in memory.

Retrograde amnesia The inability to recall events preceding an accident or injury, but without loss of earlier memory.

Risky shift Greater willingness to take risks in decision making in a group than as independent individuals.

Rods Receptor cells in the retina responsible for night vision and perception of brightness.

Rooting reflex The reflex that causes a newborn baby to turn its head toward something that touches its cheek and to grope around with its mouth.

Rorschach test A projective test composed of ambiguous inkblots; the way people interpret the blots is thought to reveal aspects of their personality.

Rote rehearsal Retaining information in memory simply by repeating it over and over.

Sample Selection of cases from a larger population.

Saturation The vividness or richness of a hue.

Scatter plot Diagram showing the association between scores on two variables.

Schedule of reinforcement In operant conditioning, the rule for determining when and how often reinforcers will be delivered.

Schema (plural: schemata) A set of beliefs or expectations about something that is based on past experience.

Schizoid personality disorder Personality disorder in which a person is withdrawn and lacks feelings for others.

Schizophrenic disorders Severe disorders in which there are disturbances of thoughts, communications, and emotions, including delusions and hallucinations.

Scientific method An approach to knowledge that relies on collecting data, generating a theory to explain the data, producing testable hypotheses based on the theory, and testing those hypotheses empirically.

Secondary drive A learned drive, such as ambition, that is not based on a physiological state.

Secondary prevention Programs to identify groups that are at high risk for mental disorders and to detect maladaptive behavior in these groups and treat it promptly.

Secondary reinforcer A reinforcer whose value is acquired through association with other primary or secondary reinforcers.

Selection studies Studies that estimate the heritability of a trait by breeding animals with other animals that have the same trait.

Self-actualizing tendency According to Rogers, the drive of human beings to fulfill their self-concepts, or the images they have of themselves.

Self-efficacy According to Bandura, the expectancy that one's efforts will be successful.

Self-fulfilling prophecy The process in which a person's expectation about another elicits behavior from the second person that confirms the expectation.

Self-managed work team An autonomous work group that has the authority to make decisions in such managerial areas as planning, scheduling, and even hiring.

Self-monitoring The tendency for an individual to observe the situation for cues about how to react.

Semantic memory The portion of long-term memory that stores general facts and information.

Semantics The criteria for assigning meaning to the morphemes in a language.

Sensation The experience of sensory stimulation.

Sensory (or afferent) neurons Neurons that carry messages from sense organs to the spinal cord or brain.

Sensory registers Entry points for raw information from the senses.

Sensory-motor stage In Piaget's theory, the stage of cognitive development between birth and 2 years of age in which the individual develops object permanence and acquires the ability to form mental representations.

Serial position effect The finding that when asked to recall a list of unrelated items, performance is better for the items at the beginning and end of the list.

Sex-typed behavior Socially prescribed ways of behaving that differ for boys and girls.

Sexual desire disorders Disorders in which the person lacks sexual interest or has an active distaste for sex.

Sexual dysfunction Loss or impairment of the ordinary physical responses of sexual function.

Sexual masochism Inability to enjoy sex without accompanying emotional or physical pain.

Sexual orientation Refers to the direction of one's sexual interest toward members of the same sex, the other sex, or both sexes.

Sexual sadism Obtaining sexual gratification from humiliating or physically harming a sex partner.

Shape constancy A tendency to see an object as the same shape no matter what angle it is viewed from.

Shaping Reinforcing successive approximations to a desired behavior.

Short-term memory (STM) Working memory; briefly stores and processes selected information from the sensory registers.

Short-term psychodynamic psychotherapy Insight therapy that is time-limited and focused on trying to help people correct the immediate problems in their lives.

Significance Probability that results obtained were due to chance.

Signs Stereotyped communications about an animal's current state.

Sixteen Personality Factor Questionnaire Objective personality test created by Cattell that provides scores on the 16 traits he identified.

Size constancy The perception of an object as the same size regardless of the distance from which it is viewed.

Skinner box A box often used in operant conditioning of animals, which limits the available response and thus increases the likelihood that the desired response will occur.

Social influence The process by which others individually or collectively affect one's perceptions, attitudes, and actions.

Social learning theory A view of learning that emphasizes the ability to learn by observing a model or receiving instructions, without firsthand experience

Social loafing The tendency of people to exert less effort on a task when working in a group than when working individually.

Social phobia An anxiety disorder characterized by excessive, inappropriate fears connected with social situations or performances in front of other people.

Social psychology The scientific study of the ways in which the thoughts, feelings, and behaviors of one individual are influenced by the real, imagined, or inferred behavior or characteristics of other people.

Socialization Process by which children learn the behaviors and attitudes appropriate to their family and culture.

Solitary play A child engaged in a recreational activity alone; the earliest form of play.

Somatic nervous system The part of the peripheral nervous system that carries messages from the senses to the central nervous system and between the central nervous system and the skeletal muscles.

Somatization disorder A somatoform disorder characterized by recurrent vague somatic complaints without a physical cause.

Somatoform disorders Disorders in which there is an apparent physical illness for which there is no organic basis.

Sound A psychological experience created by the brain in response to changes in air pressure that are received by the auditory system.

Sound waves Changes in pressure caused when molecules of air or fluid collide with one another and then move apart again.

Specific phobia Anxiety disorder characterized by intense, paralyzing fear of something.

Spinal cord Complex cable of neurons that runs down the spine, connecting the brain to most of the rest of the body.

Split-half reliability A method of determining test reliability by dividing the test into two parts and checking the agreement of scores on both parts.

Spontaneous recovery The reappearance of an extinguished response after the passage of time, without further training.

Standard deviation Statistical measure of variability in a group of scores or other values.

Stanford-Binet Intelligence Scale Terman's adaptation of the Binet-Simon Scale.

Statistics A branch of mathematics that psychologists use to organize and analyze data.

Stepping reflex The reflex that causes newborn babies to make little stepping motions if they are held upright with their feet just touching a surface.

Stereoscopic vision Combination of two retinal images to give a three-dimensional perceptual experience.

Stereotype A set of characteristics presumed to be shared by all members of a social category.

Stimulants Drugs, including amphetamines and cocaine, that stimulate the sympathetic nervous system and produce feelings of optimism and boundless energy.

Stimulus discrimination Learning to respond to only one stimulus and to inhibit the response to all other stimuli.

Stimulus generalization The transfer of a learned response to different but similar stimuli.

Stimulus motive Unlearned motive, such as curiosity or contact, that prompts us to explore or change the world around us.

Strain studies Studies of the heritability of behavioral traits using animals that have been inbred to produce strains that are genetically similar to one another.

Stress A state of psychological tension or strain.

Stress-inoculation therapy A type of cognitive therapy that trains people to cope with stressful situations by learning a more useful pattern of self-talk.

Stressors The events or circumstances that trigger stress.

Stretch receptors Receptors that sense muscle stretch and contraction.

Stroboscopic motion Apparent movement that results from flashing a series of still pictures in rapid succession, as in a motion picture.

Structuralism School of psychology that stressed the basic units of experience and the combinations in which they occur.

Subgoals Intermediate, more manageable goals used in one heuristic strategy to make it easier to reach the final goal.

Sublimation Redirecting repressed motives and feelings into more socially acceptable channels.

Substance abuse A pattern of drug use that diminishes the ability to fulfill responsibilities at home or at work or school, that results in repeated use of a drug in dangerous situations, or that leads to legal difficulties related to drug use.

Substance dependence A pattern of compulsive drug taking that results in tolerance, withdrawal symptoms, or other specific symptoms for at least a year.

Subtractive color mixing The process of mixing pigments, each of which absorbs some wavelengths of light and reflects others.

Sucking reflex The newborn baby's tendency to suck on objects placed in the mouth.

Superego According to Freud, the social and parental standards the individual has internalized; the conscience and the ego ideal.

Suprachiasmatic nucleus (SCN) A cluster of neurons in the hypothalamus that receives input from the retina regarding light and dark cycles and is involved in regulating the biological clock.

Surface structure The particular words and phrases used to make up a sentence.

Survey research Research technique in which questionnaires or interviews are administered to a selected group of people.

Swallowing reflex The reflex that enables the newborn baby to swallow liquids without choking.

Sympathetic division Branch of the autonomic nervous system; it prepares the body for quick action in an emergency.

Synapse Area composed of the axon terminal of one neuron, the synaptic space, and the dendrite or cell body of the next neuron.

Synaptic space (or synaptic cleft) Tiny gap between the axon terminal of one neuron and the dendrites or cell body of the next neuron.

Synaptic vesicles Tiny sacs in a terminal button that release chemicals into the synapse.

Syntax The rules for arranging words into grammatical phrases and sentences.

Systematic desensitization A behavioral technique for reducing a person's fear and anxiety by gradually associating a new response (relaxation) with stimuli that have been causing the fear and anxiety.

Systems approach to psychological disorders View that biological, psychological, and social risk factors combine to produce psychological disorders.

Taste buds Structures on the tongue that contain the receptor cells for taste.

Telegraphic speech An early speech stage of one- and two-year-olds that omits words that are not essential to the meaning of a phrase.

Temperament Characteristic patterns of emotional reactions and emotional self-regulation.

Temporal lobe Part of the cerebral hemisphere that helps regulate hearing, balance and equilibrium, and certain emotions and motivations.

Teratogens Toxic substances such as alcohol or nicotine that cross the placenta and may result in birth defects.

Terminal button (or synaptic knob) Structure at the end of an axon terminal branch.

Tertiary prevention Programs to help people adjust to community life after release from a mental hospital.

Testosterone The primary male sex hormone.

Texture gradient Monocular cue to distance and depth based on the fact that objects seen at greater distances appear to be smoother and less textured.

Thalamus Forebrain region that relays and translates incoming messages from the sense receptors, except those for smell.

Thematic Apperception Test (TAT) A projective test composed of ambiguous pictures about which a person is asked to write a complete story.

Theory of multiple intelligences Howard Gardner's theory that there is not one intelligence, but rather many intelligences, each of which is relatively independent of the others.

Theory Systematic explanation of a phenomenon; it organizes known facts, allows us to predict new facts, and permits us to exercise a degree of control over the phenomenon.

Threshold of excitation The level an impulse must exceed to cause a neuron to fire.

Thyroid gland Endocrine gland located below the voice box; it produces the hormone thyroxin.

Timbre The quality or texture of sound; caused by overtones.

Tip-of-the-tongue phenomenon Knowing a word, but not being able to immediately recall it.

Token economy An operant conditioning therapy in which clients earn tokens (reinforcers) for desired behaviors and exchange them for desired items or privileges.

Tolerance Phenomenon whereby higher doses of a drug are required to produce its original effects or to prevent withdrawal symptoms.

Transference The client's carrying over to the analyst feelings held toward childhood authority figures.

Transvestic fetishism Wearing the clothes of the opposite sex to achieve sexual gratification.

Triarchic theory of intelligence Sternberg's theory that intelligence involves mental skills (analytical aspect), insight and creative adaptability (creative aspect), and environmental responsiveness (practical aspect).

Trichromatic theory The theory of color vision that holds that all color perception derives from three different color receptors in the retina (usually red, green, and blue receptors).

Trichromats People who have normal color vision.

Twin studies Studies of identical and fraternal twins to determine the relative influence of heredity and environment on human behavior.

Unconditional positive regard In Rogers's theory, the full acceptance and love of another person regardless of our behavior.

Unconditioned response (UR) A response that takes place in an organism whenever an unconditioned stimulus occurs.

Unconditioned stimulus (US) A stimulus that invariably causes an organism to respond in a specific way.

Unconscious In Freud's theory, all the ideas, thoughts, and feelings of which we are not and normally cannot become aware.

Undifferentiated schizophrenia Schizophrenic disorder in which there are clear schizophrenic symptoms that don't meet the criteria for another subtype of the disorder.

Vaginismus Involuntary muscle spasms in the outer part of the vagina that make intercourse impossible.

Validity Ability of a test to measure what it has been designed to measure.

Variable-interval schedule A reinforcement schedule in which the correct response is reinforced after varying lengths of time following the last reinforcement.

Variable-ratio schedule A reinforcement schedule in which a varying number of correct responses must occur before reinforcement is presented.

Vestibular sacs Sacs in the inner ear that sense gravitation and forward, backward, and vertical movement.

Vestibular senses The senses of equilibrium and body position in space.

Vicarious reinforcement and vicarious punishment Reinforcement or punishment experienced by models that affects the willingness of others to perform the behaviors they learned by observing those models.

Visual acuity The ability to distinguish fine details visually.

Volley principle Refinement of frequency theory; it suggests that receptors in the ear fire in sequence, with one group responding, then a second, then a third, and so on, so that the complete pattern of firing corresponds to the frequency of the sound wave.

Vomeronasal organ (VNO) Location of receptors for pheromones in the roof of the nasal cavity.

Voyeurism Desire to watch others having sexual relations or to spy on nude people.

Waking consciousness Mental state that encompasses the thoughts, feelings, and perceptions that occur when we are awake and reasonably alert.

Weber's law The principle that the jnd for any given sense is a constant fraction or proportion of the stimulation being judged.

Wechsler Adult Intelligence Scale–Third Edition (WAIS–III) An individual intelligence test developed especially for adults; it yields verbal, performance, and full scale IQ scores.

Wechsler Intelligence Scale for Children–Third Edition (WISC–III) An individual intelligence test developed especially for school-aged children; it yields verbal, performance, and full scale IQ scores.

Withdrawal Avoiding a situation when other forms of coping are not practical.

Withdrawal symptoms Unpleasant physical or psychological effects that follow the discontinuance of a dependence-producing substance.

Working backward A heuristic strategy in which one works backward from the desired goal to the given conditions.

Yerkes-Dodson law States that there is an optimal level of arousal for the best performance of any task; the more complex the task, the lower the level of arousal that can be tolerated before performance deteriorates.

REFERENCES

A

Abdel, H. T. K. (2003). Exercise and diet in obesity treatment: An integrative system dynamics perspective. *Medicine and Science in Sports and Exercise, 35,* 400–413.

Abramov, I., & Gordon, J. (1994). Color appearance: On seeing red or yellow, or green, or blue. *Annual Review of Psychology, 45,* 451–485.

Acebo, C., & Carskadon, M. A. (2002). Influence of irregular sleep patterns on waking behavior. In M. A. Carskadon (Ed.) *Adolescent sleep patterns: Biological, social and psychological influences* (pp. 220–235). New York: Cambridge University Press.

Achter, J. A., Lubinski, D., & Benbow, C. P. (1996). Multipotentiality among intellectually gifted: "It was never there and already it's vanishing." *Journal of Counseling Psychology, 43,* 65–76.

Ackerman, D. (1995). *A natural history of the senses.* New York: Vintage.

Acredolo, L. P., & Hake, J. L. (1982). Infant perception. In B. B. Wolman (Ed.), *Handbook of developmental psychology* (pp. 244–283). Englewood Cliffs, NJ: Prentice Hall.

Adams, D. B., Gold, A. R., & Burt, A. D. (1978). Rise in female-initiated sexual activity at ovulation and its suppression by oral contraceptives. *New England Journal of Medicine, 299,* 1145–1150.

Adams, G. R., & Gullota, T. (1983). *Adolescent life experiences.* Monterey, CA: Brooks/Cole.

Adams, J. L. (1980). *Conceptual blockbusting: A guide to better ideas* (2nd ed.). New York: Norton.

Adams, K., & Johnson-Greene, D. (1995, August). *PET and neuropsychological performance among chronic alcoholics.* Paper presented at the annual meeting of the American Psychological Association, New York.

Adelson, R. (2002). Figure this: Deciding what's figure, what's ground. *Monitor on Psychology, 33,* 44–45.

Ader, R., & Cohen, N. (1975). Behavioral conditioned immunosuppression. *Psychosomatic Medicine, 37,* 333–340.

Ader, R., & Cohen, N. (1993). Psychoneuroimmunology: Conditioning and stress. *Annual Review of Psychology, 44,* 53–85.

Adesman, A. (2000, April). Does my child need Ritalin? *Newsweek,* p. 81.

Adler, N., Boyce, T., Chesney, M. A., Cohen, S., Folkman, S., Kahn, R. I., & Syme, S. L. (1994). Socioeconomic status and health. The challenge of the gradient. *American Psychologist, 49,* 15–24.

Adler, T. (1990, January). PMS diagnosis draws fire from researchers. *APA Monitor,* p. 12.

Adler, T. (1993a, July). Men and women affected by stress, but differently. *APA Monitor,* pp. 8–9.

Adler, T. (1993b, May). Raising the cigarette tax can lower smoking rates. *APA Monitor,* p. 15.

Adolphs, R., Tranel, D., & Damasio, A. (1998). The human amygdala in social judgment. *Nature, 393,* 470–474.

Adolphs, R., Tranel, D., Damasio, H., & Damasio, A. (1994). Impaired recognition of emotion in facial expressions following bilateral damage to the human amygdala. *Nature, 372,* 669–672.

Adorno, T. W., Frenkel-Brunswick, E., Levinson, D. J., & Sanford, R. N. (1950). *The authoritarian personality.* New York: Harper & Row.

Aeschleman, S. R., Rosen, C. C., & Williams, M. R. (2003). The effect of non-contingent negative and positive reinforcement operations on the acquisition of superstitious behaviors. *Behavioural Processes, 61,* 37–45.

Agostinelli, G., Sherman, S. J., Presson, C. C., & Chassin, L. (1992). Self-protection and self-enhancement biases in estimates of population prevalence. *Personality and Social Psychology Bulletin, 18,* 631–642.

AhYun, K. (2002). Similarity and attraction. In M. Allen & R. W. Raymond (Eds.), *Interpersonal communication research: Advances through meta-analysis. LEA's communication series* (pp. 145–167). Mahwah, NJ: Lawrence Earlbaum Associates, Publishers.

Aiken, L. R. (1988). *Psychological testing and assessment* (6th ed.). Boston: Allyn & Bacon.

Ainsworth, M. D. (1977). Attachment theory and its utility in cross-cultural research. In P. H. Leiderman, S. R. Tulkin, & A. Rosenfields (Eds.), *Culture and infancy: Variation in the human experience* (pp. 49–67). New York: Academic Press.

Ainsworth, M. D. (1989). Attachments beyond infancy. *American Psychologist, 44,* 709–716.

Ainsworth, M. D., Blehar, M. C., Waters, E., & Wall, S. (1978). *Patterns of attachment.* New York: Halstead Press.

Akil, H., & Watson, S. J. (1980). The role of endogenous opiates in pain control. In H. W. Kosterlitz & L. Y. Terenius (Eds.), *Pain and society.* Weinheim: Verlag Chemie.

Akiskal, H. S. (1994). The temperamental borders of affective disorders. *Acta Psychiatrica Scandinavica, 89*(Suppl. 379), 32–37.

Al Dawi, S., Dorvlo, A. S. S., Burke, D. T., Al, B. S., Martin, R. G., & Al Ismaily, S. (2002). Presence and severity of anorexia and bulimia among male and female Omani and non-Omani adolescents. *Journal of the American Academy of Child and Adolescent Psychiatry, 41,* 1124–1130.

Albarracin, D. (2002). Cognition in persuasion: An analysis of information processing in response to persuasive communications. In M. P. Zanna (Ed.), *Advances in experimental social psychology,* (Vol. 34, pp. 61–130). San Diego, CA: Academic Press, Inc.

Albus, M. (1989). Cholecystokinin. *Progress in Neuro-Psychopharmacology and Biological Psychiatry, 12*(Suppl.), 5–21.

Alexander, C. N., Robinson, P., & Rainforth, N. (1994). Treating and preventing alcohol, nicotine, and drug abuse through Transcendental Meditation: A review and statistical meta-analysis. *Alcoholism Treatment Quarterly* [Special Issue], *11*(1–2), 13–87.

Allen, L. S., & Gorski, R. A. (1992). Sexual orientation and size of the anterior commissure in the human brain. *Proceedings of the National Academy of Sciences, 89,* 7199–7202.

Allen, V. L., & Levine, J. M. (1971). Social support and conformity: The role of independent assessment of reality. *Journal of Experimental Social Psychology, 7,* 48–58.

Allgood-Merten, B., Lewinsohn, P. M., & Hops, H. (1990). Sex differences and adolescent depression. *Journal of Abnormal Psychology, 99,* 55–63.

Alloy, L. B., Abramson, L. Y., & Francis, E. L. (1999). Do negative cognitive styles confer vulnerability to depression? *Current Directions in Psychological Science, 8,* 128–132

Alloy, L. B., Abramson, L. Y., Whitehouse, W. G., Hogan, M. E., Tashman, N. A., Steinberg, D. L., Rose, D. T., & Donovan, P. (1999). Depressogenic cognitive styles: Predictive validity, information processing and personality characteristics, and developmental origins. *Behaviour Research and Therapy, 37,* 503–531.

Allport, G. W. (1954). *The nature of prejudice.* New York: Anchor.

Allport, G. W., & Odbert, H. S. (1936). Trait-names: A psycholexical study. *Psychological Monographs, 47* (1, Whole No. 211).

Almagor, M., Tellegen, A., & Waller, N. G. (1995). The big seven model: A cross-cultural replication and further explorations of the basic dimensions of natural language descriptors. *Journal of Personality and Social Psychology, 69,* 300–307.

Almer, E. (2000, April 22). On-line therapy: An arm's-length approach. *New York Times,* pp. A1, A11.

Almgren, G., Guest, A., Immerwahr, G., & Spittel, M. (2002). Joblessness, family disruption, and violent death in Chicago, 1970–90. *Social Forces, 76,* 1465–1493.

Altabe, M. N., & Thompson, J. K. (1994). Body image. In V. S. Ramachandran (Ed.), *Encyclopedia of human behavior* (Vol. 1, pp. 407–414). San Diego, CA: Academic Press.

Altman, L. K. (1995, April 18). Research dispels myth that brain in adults is unable to renew itself. *New York Times,* p. B9.

Aluja-Fabregat, A., & Torrubia-Beltri, R. (1998). Viewing mass media violence, perception of violence, personality and academic achievement. *Personality and Individual Differences, 25,* 973–989.

Amabile, T. M. (1983). The social psychology of creativity: A comparative conceptualization. *Journal of Personality and Social Psychology, 45,* 357–376.

America's Children: Key National Indicators of Well-Being. (2000). A report from the National Maternal and Child Health Clearinghouse. Retrieved November 10, 2000, from the World Wide Web: http://childstats.gov

American Academy of Pediatrics. (1999, August 2). *AAP discourages television for very young children.* Press release.

American Psychiatric Association (2000). *Diagnostic and statistical manual of mental disorders (4th ed. TR).* Washington, DC: American Psychiatric Press.

American Psychiatric Association (APA). (1994). *Diagnostic and statistical manual of mental disorders* (4th ed.). Washington, DC: Author.

American Psychiatric Association. (2000). *Diagnostic and statistical manual of mental disorders* (4th ed., Rev.). Washington, DC: Author.

American Psychological Association (APA). (1953). *Ethical standards of psychologists.* Washington, DC: Author.

American Psychological Association (APA). (1990). *Task force on women's depression (Final Report).* Washington, DC: Author.

American Psychological Association (APA). (1992). *Big world, small screen.* Washington, DC: Author.

Anastasi, A., & Urbina, S. (1997). *Psychological testing* (7th ed.). Upper Saddle River, NJ: Prentice Hall.

Anch, A. M., Browman, C. P., Mitler, M. M., & Walsh, J. K. (1988). *Sleep: A scientific perspective.* Englewood Cliffs, NJ: Prentice Hall.

Andersen, B. L., Kiecolt-Glaser, J. K., & Glaser, R. (1994). A biobehavioral model of cancer stress and disease course. *American Psychologist, 49,* 389–404.

Anderson, C. A. (1997). Effects of violent movies and trait hostility on hostile feelings and aggressive thoughts. *Aggressive Behavior, 23,* 161–178.

Anderson, D. R. (1998). Educational television is not an oxymoron. *Annals of Public Policy Research, 557,* 24–38.

Anderson, D. R., Huston, A. C., Wright, J. C., & Collins, P. A. (1998). Initial findings on the long term impact of Sesame Street and educational television for children: The Recontact Study. In R. Noll & M. Price (Eds.), *A communications cornucopia: Markle Foundation essays on information policy* (pp. 279–296). Washington, DC: Brookings Institution.

Anderson, L. L., Prouty, R. W., & Lakin, K. C. (1999). Closure of large state facilities and reductions of resident populations. *Mental Retardation, 37,* 509–510.

Anderson, S. W., Bechara, A., Damasio, H., Tranel, D., & Damasio, A. R. (1999). Impairment of social and moral behavior related to early damage in human prefrontal cortex. *Nature Neuroscience, 2,* 1032–1037.

Andreasen, N. C. (1997, March 14). Linking mind and brain in the study of mental illnesses: A project for a scientific psychopathology. *Science, 275,* 1586–1593.

Andrews, J. A., & Lewinsohn, P. M. (1992). Suicidal attempts among older adolescents: Prevalence and co-occurrence with psychiatric disorders. *Journal of the American Academy of Child and Adolescent Psychiatry, 31,* 655–662.

Andrich, D., & Styles, I. M. (1998). The structural relationship between attitude and behavior statements from the unfolding perspective. *Psychological Methods, 3,* 454–469.

Ang, R. P., & Woo, A. (2003). Influence of sensation seeking boys' psychosocial adjustment. *North American Journal of Psychology, 5,* 121–136.

Angier, N. (1992? May 20). Is there a male menopause? Jury is still out. *New York Times,* p. A1.

Angier, N. (1995, June 20). Does testosterone equal aggression? Maybe not. *New York Times,* p. 1.

Angier, N. (1998, September 1). Nothing becomes a man more than a woman's face. *New York Times,* p. B9.

Anshel, M. H., Porter, A., & Quek, J-J. (1998). Coping with acute stress in sports as a function of gender: An exploratory study. *Journal of Sport Behavior, 21,* 363–376.

Anthony, J. C., & Helzer, J. E. (2002). Epidemiology of drug dependence. In M. T. Tsuang & M. Tohen (Eds.), *Textbook in psychiatric epidemiology* (2nd ed., pp. 479–561). New York, NY: Wiley-Lis.

APA Practice (2003). New Mexico Governor Signs Landmark Law on Prescription Privileges for Psychologists. Retrieved March 20, 2003, from the World Wide Web: http://www.apa.org/practice/nm_rxp.html

APA's Task Force on Diversity. (1998, August). Integrating aging into introductory psychology. *APA Monitor,* p. 46.

Archer, J. (1996). Sex differences in social behavior: Are the social role and evolutionary explanations compatible? *American Psychologist, 51,* 909–917.

Arias, C., Curet, C. A., Moyano, H. F., Joekes, S., & Blanch, N. (1993). Echolocation: A study of auditory functioning in blind and sighted subjects. *Journal of Visual Impairment and Blindness, 87,* 73–77.

Arkin, R. M., Cooper, H., & Kolditz, T. (1980). A statistical review of literature concerning the self-serving attribution bias in interpersonal influence situations. *Journal of Personality, 48,* 435–448.

Armstrong, T. (1995). *The myth of the A.D.D. child.* New York: Dutton.

Arndt, J., Greenberg, J., Pyszczynski, T., & Solomon, S. (1997). Subliminal exposure to death-related stimuli increases defense of the cultural worldview. *Psychological Science, 8,* 379–385.

Arnett, J. (1991, April). *Sensation seeking and egocentrism as factors in reckless behaviors among a college-age sample.* Paper presented at the meeting of the Society for Research in Child Development, Seattle, WA.

Arnett, J. J. (1999). Adolescent storm and stress, reconsidered. *American Psychologist, 54,* 317–326.

Arnett, J. J. (2000). Emerging adulthood: A theory of development from the late teens through the twenties. *American Psychologist, 55,* 469–480.

Aronson, E. (1994). *The social animal* (7th ed.). New York: Freeman.

Aronson, E. (1999). The power of self-persuasion. *American Psychologist, 54,* 875–884.

Aronson, E., Wilson, T. D., & Akert, R. (1999). *Social psychology* (3rd. ed.) New York: Addison Wesley Longman.

Aronson, E., Wilson, T. D., & Akert, R. M. (2002). *Social Psychology* (4th ed.). Upper Saddle River, NJ: Prentice Hall.

Arrigo, J. M., & Pezdek, K. (1997). Lessons from the study of psychogenic amnesia. *Current Directions in Psychological Science, 6,* 148–152.

Ary, D. V., Duncan, T. E., Duncan, S. C., & Hops, H. (1999). Adolescent problem behavior: The influence of parents and peers. *Behaviour Research and Therapy, 37,* 217–230.

Asch, S. E. (1951). Effects of group pressure upon the modification and distortion of judgments. In H. Guetzkow (Ed.), *Groups, leadership, and men* (pp. 177–190). Pittsburgh: Carnegie Press.

Asch, S. E. (1956). Studies of independence and conformity: I. A minority of one against a unanimous majority. *Psychological Monographs, 70* (9, Whole No. 416).

Ashley, R. (1975, October 17). The other side of LSD. *New York Times Magazine,* pp. 40ff.

Aslin, R. N., & Smith, L. B. (1988). Perceptual development. *Annual Review of Psychology, 39,* 435–473.

Aspinwall, L. G., & Taylor, S. E. (1997). A stitch in time: Self-regulation and proactive coping. *Psychological Bulletin, 121,* 417–436.

Aston, R. (1972). Barbiturates, alcohol and tranquilizers. In S. J. Mule & H. Brill (Eds.), *The chemical and biological aspects of drug dependence.* Cleveland, OH: CRC Press.

Astur, R. S., Taylor, L. B., Marnelak, A. N., Philpott, L., & Sutherland, R. J. (2002). Humans with hippocampus damage display severe spatial memory impairments in a virtual Morris water task. *Behavioural Brain Research, 132,* 77–84.

Atchley, R. C. (1982). Retirement as a social institution. *Annual Review of Sociology, 8,* 263–287.

Auvergne, R., Lere, C., El-Bahh, B., Arthaud, S., Lespinet, V., Rougier, A., & Le-Gal-La-Salle, G. (2002). Delayed kindling epileptogenesis and increased neurogenesis in adult rats housed in an enriched environment. *Brain Research, 954,* 277–285.

Aved, B. M., Irwin, M. M., Cummings, L. S., & Findeisen, N. (1993). Barriers to prenatal care for low-income women. *Western Journal of Medicine, 158,* 493–498.

Avery-Leaf, S., Cano, A., Cascardi, M., & O'Leary, K. D. (1995, July). *Evaluation of a dating violence prevention program.* Paper presented at the 4th Annual International Family Violence Research Conference, Durham, New Hampshire.

Ayas, N. T., White, D. P., Manson, J. E., Stampfer, M. J., Speizer, F. E., Malhotra, A., & Hu, F. B. (2003). A prospective study of sleep duration and coronary heart disease in women. *Archives of Internal Medicine, 163,* 205–209.

Ayman, R., Chemers, M. M., Fiedler, F., Romano, R., Vecchio, R. P. & Zaccaro, S. J. (1998). Contingency model. In F. Dansereau & F. J. Yammarino (Eds.). *Leadership: The multiple-level approaches: Classical and new wave Monographs in organizational behavior and industrial relations* (Vol. 24, pp. 73–143). Stamford, CT: JAI Press, Inc.

Azar, B. (1997, December). Maternal emotions may influence fetal behaviors. *APA Monitor,* p. 17.

Azar, B. (1999a, March). "Decade of Behavior" moves forward. *APA Monitor,* p. 16.

Azar, B. (1999b, May). Decision researchers split, but prolific. *APA Monitor,* p. 14.

B

Baars, B. J. (1998). Metaphors of consciousness and attention in the brain. *Trends in Neuroscience, 21,* 58–62.

Baars, B. J., & McGovern, K. (1994). Consciousness. In V. S. Ramachandran (Ed.), *Encyclopedia of human behavior* (Vol. 1, pp. 687–699). San Diego, CA: Academic Press.

Babkoff, H., Caspy, T., Mikulincer, M., & Sing, H. C. (1991). Monotonic and rhythmic influences: A challenge for sleep deprivation research. *Psychological Bulletin, 109,* 411–428.

Bachtold, L. M., & Werner, E. E. (1973). Personality characteristics of creative women. *Perceptual and Motor Skills, 36,* 311–319.

Baddeley, A. D. (1986). *Working memory.* Oxford: Clarendon Press.

Baddeley, A. D. (1987). Amnesia. In R. L. Gregory (Ed.), *The Oxford companion to the mind* (pp. 20–22). Oxford: Oxford University Press.

Baddeley, A. D. (1994). The magical number seven: Still magic after all these years? *Psychological Review, 101,* 353–356.

Baddeley, A. D. (2002). Is working memory still working? *European Psychologist, 7,* 85–97.

Baddeley, A. D., & Hitch, G. J. (1994). Developments in the concept of working memory. *Neuropsychology, 6,* 485–493.

Badner, J. A. (2003). The genetics of bipolar disorder. In B. Geller & M. DelBello (Eds.), *Bipolar disorder in childhood and early adolescence (pp. 247–254).* New York, NY: Guilford Press.

Badr, L. K., & Abdallah, B. (2001). Physical attractiveness of premature infants affects outcome at discharge from NICU. *Infant Behavior and Development, 24,* 129–133.

Baer, L., Rauch, S. L., & Ballantine, T. (1995). Cingulotomy for intractable obsessive-compulsive disorder: Prospective long-term follow-up of 18 patients. *Archives of General Psychiatry, 52,* 384–392.

Bagemihl, B. (2000). *Biological exuberance: Animal homosexuality and natural diversity.* New York: St. Martin's Press.

Bahrick, H. P. (1984). Semantic memory in permastore: Fifty years of memory for Spanish learned in school. *Journal of Experimental Psychology: General, 113,* 1–31.

Bahrick, H. P., & Hall, L. K. (1991). Lifetime maintenance of high school mathematics content. *Journal of Experimental Psychology: General, 120,* 20–33.

Bahrick, H. P., Bahrick, P. O., & Wittlinger, R. P. (1974, December). Those unforgettable high school days. *Psychology Today,* pp. 50–56.

Bailey, A., Le Couteur, A., Gottesman, I., Bolton, P., Simonoff, E., Yuzda, E., & Rutter, M. (1995). Autism as a strongly genetic disorder: Evidence from a British twin study. *Psychological Medicine, 25,* 63–77.

Baillargeon, R. (1994). How do infants learn about the physical world? *Current Directions in Psychological Science, 3,* 133–140.

Balaguer, A., & Markman, H. (1994). Mate selection. In V. S. Ramachandran (Ed.), *Encyclopedia of human behavior* (Vol. 3, pp. 127–135). San Diego, CA: Academic Press.

Balch, W. R., & Lewis, B. S. (1996). Music-dependent memory: The roles of tempo change and mood mediation. *Journal of Experimental Psychology: Learning, Memory and Cognition, 22,* 1354–1363.

Baldwin, A. Y. (1985). Programs for the gifted and talented: Issues concerning minority populations. In F. D. Horowitz & M. O'Brien (Eds.), *The gifted and talented: Developmental perspectives* (pp. 223–249). Washington, DC: American Psychological Association.

Ball, J. D., Archer, R. P., & Imhof, E. A. (1994). Time requirements of psychological testing: A survey of practitioners. *Journal of Personality Assessment, 63,* 239–249.

Ballie, R. (2001). Teen drinking more dangerous than previously thought. *Monitor on Psychology, 32,* 12.

Balon, R. (2002). Emotional blunting, sexual dysfunction and SSRIs. *International Journal of Neuropsychopharmacology, 5,* 415–416.

Banaji, M. R., & Hardin, C. D. (1996). Automatic stereotyping. *Psychological Science, 7,* 136–141.

Bandura, A. (1962). Social learning through imitation. In M. R. Jones (Ed.), *Nebraska Symposium on Motivation: Vol. 10* (pp. 211–269). Lincoln: University of Nebraska Press.

Bandura, A. (1965). Influence of models' reinforcement contingencies on the acquisition of imitative responses. *Journal of Personality and Social Psychology, 1,* 589–595.

Bandura, A. (1973). *Aggression: A social learning analysis.* Englewood Cliffs, NJ: Prentice Hall.

Bandura, A. (1977). *Social learning theory.* Englewood Cliffs, NJ: Prentice Hall.

Bandura, A. (1986). *Social foundations of thought and action: A social cognitive theory.* Englewood Cliffs, NJ: Prentice Hall.

Bandura, A. (1997). *Self-efficacy: The exercise of control.* New York: Freeman.

Bandura, A., & Locke, E. A. (2003). Negative self-efficacy and goal effects revisited. *Journal of Applied Psychology, 8,* 87–99.

Bandura, A., Blanchard, E. B., & Ritter, B. (1969). Relative efficacy of desensitization and modeling approaches for inducing behavioral, affective, and attitudinal changes. *Journal of Personality and Social Psychology, 13,* 173–199.

Banich, M. T. (1998). Integration of information between the cerebral hemispheres. *Current Directions in Psychological Science, 7,* 32–37.

Bar, M., & Biederman, I. (1998). Subliminal visual priming. *Psychological Science, 9,* 464–469.

Barbaree, H. E., & Seto, M. C. (1997). Pedophilia: Assessment and treatment. In D. R. Laws & W. T. O'Donohue (Eds.), *Handbook of sexual deviance: Theory and application* (pp. 175–193). New York: Guilford.

Barber, B. L., & Eccles, J. E. (1992). Long-term influence of divorce and single parenting on adolescent family- and work-related values, behaviors and aspirations. *Psychological Bulletin, 111,* 108–126.

Barbur, J. L., Harlow, A. J., & Weiskrantz, L. (1994). Spatial and temporal response properties of residual vision in a case of hemianopia. *Philosophical Transactions of the Royal Society of London, B, 43,* 157–160.

Barglow, P., Vaughn, B. E., & Molitor, N. (1987). Effects of maternal absence due to employment on the quality of infant-mother attachment in a low-risk sample. *Child Development, 58,* 945–954.

Barinaga, M. (2000, March 3). Asilomar revisited: Lessons for today. *Science, 287,* 1584–1585.

Barker, S. L., Funk, S. C., & Houston, B. K. (1988). Psychological treatment versus nonspecific factors: A meta-analysis of conditions that engender comparable expectations for improvement. *Clinical Psychology Review, 8,* 579–594.

Barkley, R. A. (1990). *Hyperactive children: A handbook for diagnosis and treatment* (2nd ed.). New York: Guilford.

Barnett, R. C., Brennan, R. T., & Marshall, N. L. (1994). Gender and the relationship between parent role quality and psychological distress: A study of men and women in dual-earner couples. *Journal of Family Issues, 15,* 229–252.

Barnett, W. S. (1998). Long-term effects on cognitive development and school success. In W. S. Barnett & S. S. Boocock (Eds.), *Early care and education for children in poverty* (pp. 11–44). Albany, NY: State University of New York Press.

Baron, R. A., & Byrne, D. (1991). *Social psychology: Understanding human interaction* (6th ed.). Boston: Allyn & Bacon.

Baron, R. M., Graziano, W. G., & Stangor, C. (1991). *Social psychology.* Fort Worth: Holt, Rinehart & Winston.

Barret, G. V., & Depinet, R. L. (1991). A reconsideration of testing for competence rather than for intelligence. *American Psychologist, 46,* 1012–1024.

Barron, F. (1963). *Creativity and psychological health.* Princeton, NJ: Van Nostrand.

Barron, F., & Harrington, D. M. (1981). Creativity, intelligence, and personality. *Annual Review of Psychology, 32,* 439–476.

Bartlett, F. C. (1932). *Remembering: A study in experimental and social psychology.* New York: Macmillan.

Bartoshuk, L. M. (1993). The biological basis of food perception and acceptance. *Food Quality and Preference, 4,* 21–32.

Bartoshuk, L. M., & Beauchamp, G. K. (1994). Chemical senses. *Annual Review of Psychology, 45,* 419–449.

Baruch, F., & Barnett, R. (1986). Role quality, multiple role involvement, and psychological well-being in mid-life women. *Journal of Personality and Social Psychology, 51,* 578–585.

Basow, S. A. (1986). *Gender stereotypes: Traditions and alternatives* (2nd ed.). Pacific Grove, CA: Brooks/Cole.

Bassetti, C., & Aldrich, M. S. (1996). Narcolepsy. *Neurological Clinics, 14,* 545–571.

Bat-Chava, Y. (1994). Group identification and self-esteem of deaf adults. *Personality and Social Psychology Bulletin, 20,* 494–502.

Bateson, G. (1982). Totemic knowledge in New Guinea. In U. Neisser (Ed.), *Memory observed: Remembering in natural contexts.* San Francisco: Freeman.

Batson, C. D., & Powell, A. A. (2003). Altruism and prosocial behahavior. In T. Millon, & M. J. Lerner (Eds.), *Handbook of psychology: Personality and social psychology* (Vol. 5, pp. 463–484). New York, NY: John Wiley & Sons, Inc.

Baumeister, A. A., & Baumeister, A. A. (2000). Mental retardation: Causes and effects. In M. Hersen & R. T. Ammerman (Eds.). *Advanced abnormal child psychology (2nd ed.)* (pp. 327–355). Mahwah, NJ: Lawrence Erlbaum Associates.

Baumeister, R. F., & Leary, M. R. (1995). The need to belong: Desire for interpersonal attachments as a fundamental human motivation. *Psychological Bulletin, 117,* 497–529.

Baumrind, D. (1972). Socialization and instrumental competence in young children. In W. W. Hartup (Ed.), *The young child: Reviews of research* (Vol. 2, pp. 202–224). Washington, DC: National Association for the Education of Young Children.

Baumrind, D. (1985). Research using intentional deception. *American Psychologist, 40,* 165–174.

Baumrind, D. (1991). Parenting styles and adolescent development. In J. Brooks-Gunn, R. Lerner & A. C. Petersen (Eds.) *The encyclopedia of adolescence* (Vol. 2, pp. 746–758). New York, NY: Garland.

Baumrind, D. (1996). The discipline controversy revisited. *Family Relations: Journal of Applied Family and Child Studies, 45,* 405–414.

Baxter, D. W., & Olszewski, J. (1960). Congenital insensitivity to pain. *Brain, 83,* 381.

Bayley, N. (1993). *Bayley Scales of Infant Development Second Edition: Manual.* San Antonio, TX: Psychological Corporation.

Beasley, M., Thompson, T., & Davidson, J. (2003). Resilience in response to life stress: The effects of coping style and cognitive hardiness. *Personality and Individual Differences, 34,* 77–95.

Beatty, S. E., & Hawkins, D. I. (1989). Subliminal stimulation: Some new data and interpretation. *Journal of Advertising, 18,* 4–8.

Beauducel, A., Brocke, B., & Liepmann, D. (2001). Perspectives on fluid and crystallized intelligence: Facets for verbal, numerical and figural intelligence. *Personality and Individual Differences, 30,* 977–994.

Beck, A. T. (1967). *Depression: Clinical, experimental and theoretical aspects.* New York: Harper (Hoeber).

Beck, A. T. (1976). *Cognitive therapy and emotional disorders.* New York: International Universities Press.

Beck, A. T. (1984). Cognition and therapy. *Archives of General Psychiatry, 41,* 1112–1114.

Beck, A. T. (1989). *Love is never enough.* New York: Harper & Row.

Beck, A. T. (2002). Cognitive models of depression. In R. L. Leahy & T. E. Dowd (Eds.), *Clinical advances in cognitive psychotherapy: Theory and Application* (pp. 29–61). New York, NY: Springer Publishing Co.

Beck, J. G. (1995). Hypoactive sexual desire disorder: An overview. *Journal of Consulting and Clinical Psychology, 63,* 919–927.

Beck, R. (1983). *Motivation: Theories and principles* (2nd ed.). Englewood Cliffs, NJ: Prentice Hall.

Bédard, J., & Chi, M. T. H. (1992). Expertise. *Current Directions in Psychological Science, 1,* 135–139.

Beecher, H. K. (1972). The placebo effect as a nonspecific force surrounding disease and the treatment of disease. In R. Jansen, W. D. Kerdel, A. Herz, C. Steichele, J. P. Payne, & R. A. P. Burt (Eds.), *Pain, basic principles, pharmacology, and therapy.* Stuttgart: Thieme.

Beier, E. G. (1974, October). Nonverbal communication: How we send emotional messages. *Psychology Today,* pp. 53–56.

Beirne-Smith, M., Patton, J., & Ittenbach, R. (1994). *Mental retardation* (4th ed.). New York: Macmillan.

Bellack, A. S., Hersen, M., & Turner, S. M. (1976). Generalization effects of social skills training in chronic schizophrenics: An experimental analysis. *Behavior Research and Therapy, 14,* 391–398.

Bellman, S., Forster, N., Still, L., & Cooper, C. L. (2003). Gender differences in the use of social support as a moderator of occupational stress. *Stress and Health: Journal of the International Society for the Investigation of Stress, 19,* 45–58.

Belsky, J., & Rovine, M. (1988). Nonmaternal care in the first year of life and infant parent attachment security. *Child Development, 59,* 157–167.

Bem, D. J., & Honorton, C. (1994). Does psi exist? Replicable evidence for an anomalous process of information transfer. *Psychological Bulletin, 115,* 4–18.

Bem, S. L. (1989). Genital knowledge and gender constancy in preschool children. *Child Development, 60,* 649–662.

Beniczky, S., Keri, S., Voeroes, E., Ungurean, A., Benedek, G., Janka, Z., & Vecsei, L. (2002). Complex hallucinations following occipital lobe damage. *European Journal of Neurology, 9,* 175–176.

Benin, M. H., & Agostinelli, J. (1988). Husbands' and wives' satisfaction with the division of labor. *Journal of Marriage and the Family, 50,* 349–361.

Benjamin, L. T., Jr. (2000). The psychology laboratory at the turn of the 20th century. *American Psychologist, 55,* 318–321.

Bennett, D. A., & Knopman, D. S. (1994). Alzheimer's disease: A comprehensive approach to patient management. *Geriatrics, 49(8),* 20–26.

Bennett, W., & Gurin, J. (1982). *The dieter's dilemma: Eating less and weighing more.* New York: Basic Books.

Benotsch, E. G., Brailey, K, Vasterling, J. J., Uddo, M., Constans, J. I., & Sutker, P. B. (2000). War zone stress, personal and environmental resources, and PTSD symptoms in Gulf War Veterans: A longitudinal perspective. *Journal of Abnormal Psychology, 109,* 205–213.

Benson, E. (2002). Pheromones, in context. *Monitor on Psychology, 33,* 46–48.

Benson, H. (1975). *The relaxation response.* New York: William Morrow.

Benson, H., & Klipper, M. Z. (2000). *The relaxation response.* New York: William Morrow.

Benton, D., & Roberts, G. (1988). Effect of vitamin and mineral supplementation on intelligence of a sample of schoolchildren. *Lancet, 1,* 14–144.

BenTovim, D. I. (2003). Eating disorders: Outcome, prevention and treatment of eating disorders. *Current Opinion in Psychiatry, 16,* 65–69.

Berg, S. J., & Wynne-Edwards, K. E. (2001). Changes in testosterone, cortisol, estradiol levels in men becoming fathers. *Mayo Clinic Proceedings, 76,* 582–592.

Bergin, A. E., & Lambert, M. J. (1978). The evaluation of therapeutic outcomes. In S. L. Garfield & A. E. Bergin (Eds.), *Handbook of psychotherapy and behavior change: An empirical analysis* (pp. 139–189). New York: Wiley.

Berkowitz, M. W., & Gibbs, J. C. (1983). Measuring the developmental features of moral discussion. *Merrill-Palmer Quarterly, 29,* 399–410.

Bernal, M. E., & Castro, F. G. (1994). Are clinical psychologists prepared for service and research with ethnic minorities? *American Psychologist, 49,* 797–805.

Bernhard, F., & Penton-Voak, I. (2002). The evolutionary psychology of facial attractiveness. *Current Directions in Psychological Science, 11,* 154–158.

Bernstein, A., & Lennard, H. L. (1973). The American way of drugging. *Society, 10(4),* 14–25.

Berr, C. (2002). Oxidative stress and cognitive impairment in the elderly. *Journal of Nutrition, Health and Aging, 6,* 261–266.

Berreby, D. (1998, June 19). Studies explore love and the sweaty T-shirt. *New York Times,* p. B4.

Berry, J. W. (1967). Independence and conformity in subsistence level societies. *Journal of Personality and Social Psychology, 7,* 415–518.

Berscheid, E., & Reis, H. T. (1998). Attraction and close relationships. In D. Gilbert, S. T. Fiske, & G. Lindzey (Eds.), *Handbook of social psychology* (4th ed., Vol. 2, pp. 193–381). New York: McGraw-Hill.

Bersoff, D. N. (1981). Testing and the law. *American Psychologist, 36,* 1047–1056.

Bertenthal, B. I., Campos, J. J., & Kermoian, R. (1994). An epigenetic perspective on the development of self-produced locomotion and its consequences. *Current Directions in Psychological Science, 3,* 140–145.

Bertolini, M. (2001). Central masturbatory fantasy, fetish and transitional phenomenon. In M. Bertolini & A. Giannakoulas (Eds.), *Squiggles and spaces: Revisiting the work of D. W. Winnicott (Vol. 1)* (pp. 210–217). London, England: Whurr Publishers, Ltd.

Betancourt, H., & López, S. R. (1993). The study of culture, ethnicity, and race in American psychology. *American Psychologist, 48,* 629–637.

Biddle, S. (2000). Exercise, emotions, and mental health. In Y. Hanin (Ed.), *Emotions in sport* (pp. 267–291). Champaign, IL: Human Kinetics.

Birchler, G. R., & Fals-Stewart, W. S. (1994). Marital dysfunction. In V. S. Ramachandran (Ed.), *Encyclopedia of human behavior* (Vol. 3, pp. 103–113). San Diego: Academic Press.

Birkenhaeger, T. K., Pluijms, E. M., & Lucius, S. A. P. (2003). ECT response in delusional versus non-delusional depressed inpatients. *Journal of Affective Disorders, 74,* 191–195.

Birren, J. E. (1983). Aging in America: Role for psychology. *American Psychologist, 38,* 298–299.

Birren, J. E., & Fisher, L. M. (1995). Aging and speed of behavior: Possible consequences for psychological functioning. *Annual Review of Psychology, 46,* 329–353.

Bjorklund, D. F. (1989). *Children's thinking, developmental function and individual differences.* Pacific Grove, CA: Brooks/Cole.

Bjornson, C. R. R., Rietze, R. L., Reynolds, B. A., Magli, M. C., & Vescovi, A. L. (1999, January 22). Turning brain into blood: A hematopoietic fate adopted by adult neural stem cells in vivo. *Science, 283,* 534–537.

Blackmore, S. (1999). *The meme machine.* Oxford: Oxford University Press.

Blagrove, M., & Akehurst, L. (2000). Effects of sleep loss on confidence-accuracy relationships for reasoning and eyewitness memory. *Journal of Experimental Psychology: Applied, 6,* 59–73.

Blagrove, M., & Akehurst, L. (2001). Personality and the modulation of effects of sleep loss on mood and cognition. *Personality and Individual Differences, 30,* 819–828.

Blake, R. R., Helson, H., & Mouton, J. (1956). The generality of conformity behavior as a function of factual anchorage, difficulty of task and amount of social pressure. *Journal of Personality, 25,* 294–305.

Blakemore, S. J., Wolpert, D. M., & Frith, C. D. (1998). Central cancellation of self-produced tickle sensation. *Nature: Neuroscience, 1,* 635–640.

Blanchard, E. B., Appelbaum, K. A., Radnitz, C. L., Morrill, B., Michultka, D., Kirsch, C., Guarnier, P., Hillhouse, J., Evans, D. D., & Jaccard, J. (1990). A controlled evaluation of thermal biofeedback and thermal biofeedback combined with cognitive therapy in the treatment of vascular headache. *Journal of Consulting & Clinical Psychology, 58,* 216–224.

Blanck, D. C., Bellack, A. S., Rosnow, R. L., Rotheram-Borus, M. J., & Schooler, N. R. (1992). Scientific rewards and conflicts of ethical choices in human subjects research. *American Psychologist, 47,* 959–965.

Blatt, S. J., Zuroff, D. C., Quinlan, D. M., & Pilkonis, P. (1996). Interpersonal factors in brief treatment of depression: Further analysis of the NIMH Treatment of Depression Collaborative Research Program. *Journal of Consulting and Clinical Psychology, 64,* 162–171.

Bliss, T. V., & Collingridge, G. L. (1993). A synaptic model of memory: Long-term potentiation in the hippocampus. *Nature, 361,* 31–39.

Bliwise, D. L. (1996). Chronologic age, physiologic age and mortality in sleep apnea. *Sleep, 19,* 277–282.

Bloom, L. (1970). *Language development: Form and function in emerging grammar.* Cambridge, MA: MIT Press.

Blouin, J. L., Dombroski, B. A., Nath, S. K., Lasseter, V. K., Wolyniec, P. S., Nestadt, G., Thornquist, M., Ullrich, G., McGrath, J., Kasch, L., Lamacz, M., Thomas, M. G., Gehrig, C., Radhakrishnan, U., Snyder, S. E., Balk, K. G., Neufeld, K., Swartz, K. L., DeMarchi, N., Papadimitriou, G. N., Dikeos, D. G., Stefanis, C. N., Chakravarti, A., Childs, B., Pulver, A. E. (1998). Schizophrenia susceptibility loci on chromosomes 13q32 and 8p21. *Nature Genetics, 20,* 70–73.

Blum, J. M. (1979). *Pseudoscience and mental ability: The origins and fallacies of the IQ controversy.* New York: Monthly Review Press.

Blumberg, M. S., & Wasserman, E. A. (1995). Animal mind and the argument from design. *American Psychologist, 50,* 133–144.

Blumenthal, A. L. (1975). A reappraisal of Wilhelm Wundt. *American Psychologist, 30,* 1081–1088.

Blundell, J. E., & Halford, J. C. G. (1998). Serotonin and appetite regulation: Implications for the pharmacological treatment of obesity. *CNS Drugs, 9,* 473–495.

Bodlund, O., & Kullgren, G. (1996). Transsexualism—General outcome and prognostic factors: A five-year follow-up study of nineteen transsexuals in the process of changing sex. *Archives of Sexual Behavior, 25,* 303–317.

Boelte, S., Uhlig, N., & Poustka, F. (2002). The savant syndrome: A review. *Zeitschrift fuer Klinische Psychologie und Psycholtherapie: Forschung und Praxis, 31,* 291–297.

Bohart, A. C., & Greening, T. (2001). Humanistic Psychology and Positive Psychology. *American Psychologist, 56,* 81–82.

Bolles, R. C. (1972). Reinforcement, expectancy, and learning. *Psychological Review, 79,* 394–409.

Bolos, A. M., Dean, M., Lucas-Derse, S., Ramsburg, M., Brown, G. L., & Goldman, D. (1990). Population and pedigree studies reveal a lack of association between the dopamine D2 receptor gene and alcoholism. *Journal of the American Medical Association, 264,* 3156–3160.

Bonanno, G. A., & Kaltman, S. (1999). Toward an integrative perspective on bereavement. *Psychological Bulletin, 125,* 760–776.

Bonvillian, J. D., & Patterson, F. G. P. (1997). Sign language acquisition and the development of meaning in a lowland gorilla. In C. Mandell & A. McCabe (Eds.), *The problem of meaning: Behavioral and Cognitive Perspectives* (pp. 181–219). Amsterdam, Netherlands: North-Holland/Elsevier Science Publishers.

Boomsma, D. I., Koopmans, J. R., Van Doornen, L. J. P., & Orlebeke, J. M. (1994). Genetic and social influences on starting to smoke: A study of Dutch adolescent twins and their parents. *Addiction, 89,* 219–226.

Booth-Kewley, S., & Friedman, H. S. (1987). Psychological predictors of heart disease: A quantitative review. *Psychological Bulletin, 101,* 343–362.

Borkenau, P., & Ostendorf, F. (1998). The big five as states: How useful is the five-factor model to describe intraindividual variations over time? *Journal of Research in Personality, 32,* 202–221.

Borkovec, T. D., & Costello, E. (1993). Efficacy of applied relaxation and cognitive-behavioral therapy in the treatment of generalized anxiety disorder. *Journal of Consulting and Clinical Psychology, 61,* 611–619.

Bornstein, R. F. (1989). Exposure and affect: Overview and meta-analysis of research, 1968–1987. *Psychological Reports, 106,* 265–289.

Bornstein, R. F., & Masling, J. M. (Eds.). (1998). *Empirical studies of the therapeutic hour. Empirical studies of psychoanalytic theories* (Vol. 8). Washington, DC: American Psychological Association.

Bosma, H., vanBoxtel, M. P. J., Ponds, R. W. H. M., Houx, P. J. H., & Jolles, J. (2003). Education and age-related cognitive decline: The contribution of mental workload. *Educational Gerontology, 29,* 165–173.

Bosworth, R. G., & Dobkins, K. R. (1999). Left-hemisphere dominance for motion processing in deaf signers. *Psychological Science, 10,* 256–262.

Botwin, M. D., & Buss, D. M. (1989). The structure of act report data: Is the five factor model of personality recaptured? *Journal of Personality and Social Psychology, 56,* 988–1001.

Bouchard, T. J., Jr. (1984). Twins reared together and apart: What they tell us about human diversity. In S. W. Fox (Ed.), *Individuality and determinism* (pp. 147–178). New York: Plenum.

Bouchard, T. J., Jr. (1996). IQ similarity in twins reared apart: Findings and responses to critics. In R. J. Sternberg & E. Grigorenko (Eds.), *Intelligence: Heredity and environment* (pp 126–160). New York: Cambridge University Press.

Bouchard, T. J., Jr., Lykken, D. T., McGue, M., Segal, N. L., & Tellegren, A. (1990, October 12). Sources of human psychological differences: The Minnesota study of twins reared apart. *Science, 250,* 223–228.

Bourgois, P. (1999). *Participant observation study of indirect paraphernalia sharing/HIV risk in a network of heroin injectors.* Retrieved September 17, 2000, from the World Wide Web: http://165.112.78.61/CEWG/ethno.html

Bourin, M. (2003). Use of paroxetine for the treatment of depression and anxiety disorders in the elderly: A review. *Human Psychopharmacology, 18,* 185–190.

Bourne, L. E., Dominowski, R. L., Loftus, E. F., & Healy, A. F. (1986). *Cognitive processes* (2nd ed.). Englewood Cliffs, NJ: Prentice Hall.

Bouton, M. E. (1993). Context, time and memory retrieval in the interference paradigms of Pavlovian conditioning. *Psychological Bulletin, 114,* 80–99.

Bouton, M. E. (1994). Context, ambiguity and classical conditioning. *Current Directions in Psychological Science, 3,* 49–52.

Bouton, M. E. (2002). Context, ambiguity, and unlearning: Sources of relapse after behavioral extinction. *Biological Psychiatry, 51,* 976–986.

Bower, G. H., & Mann, T. (1992). Improving recall by recoding interfering material at the time of recall. *Journal of Experimental Psychology: Learning, Memory, and Cognition, 18,* 1310–1320.

Bower, G. H., & Sivers, H. (1998). Cognitive impact of traumatic events. *Development & Psychopathology, 10,* 625–653.

Boysen, S. T., & Himes, G. T. (1999). Current issues and emerging theories in animal cognition. *Annual Review of Psychology, 50,* 683–705.

Bradley, C. (1997). Generativity-stagnation: Development of a status model. *Developmental Review, 17,* 262–290.

Brainerd, C. J. (1978). The stage question in cognitive-developmental theory. *Behavioral and Brain Sciences, 2,* 172–213.

Brandon, T. H. (1994). Negative affect as motivation to smoke. *Current Directions in Psychological Science, 3,* 33–37.

Brannon, E. M., & Terrace, H. S. (1998, October 23). Ordering of the numerosities 1–9 by monkeys. *Science, 282,* 746–749.

Braun, A. R., Balkin, T. J., Wesensten, N. J., Gwadry, F., Varga, M., Baldwin, P., Carson, R. E., Belenky, G., & Herscovitch, P. (1998, January 2). Dissociated pattern of activity in visual cortices and their projections during human rapid eye movement sleep. *Science, 279,* 91–95.

Braveman, N. S., & Bornstein, P. (Eds.). (1985). *Annals of the New York Academy of Sciences: Vol. 443. Experimental assessments and clinical applications of conditioned food aversions.* New York: New York Academy of Sciences.

Breetvelt, I. S., & VanDam, F. S. A. M. (1991). Underreporting by cancer patients: The case of response-shift. *Social Science and Medicine, 32,* 981–987.

Brehm, S. S. (2002). *Intimate relationships* (3rd ed.). New York: McGraw-Hill.

Bremner, J. D., & Marmar, C. R. (Eds.). (1998). *Trauma, memory and dissociation.* Washington, DC: American Psychiatric Press.

Brenner, M. H. (1973). *Mental illness and the economy.* Cambridge, MA: Harvard University Press.

Brenner, M. H. (1979). Influence of the social environment on psychopathology: The historical perspective. In J. E. Barrett, R. M. Rose, & G. L. Klerman (Eds.), *Stress and mental disorder* (pp. 8–24). New York: Raven Press.

Brewer, J. B., Zhao, Z., Desmond, J. E., Glover, G. H., & Gabriel, J. D. E. (1998, August 21). Making memories: Brain activity that predicts how well visual experience will be remembered. *Science, 281,* 1185–1187.

Brewin, C. R. (1996). Theoretical foundations of cognitive-behavior therapy for anxiety and depression. *Annual Review of Psychology, 47,* 33–57.

Brickman, P., Coates, D., & Janoff-Bulman, R. (1978). Lottery winners and accident victims: Is happiness relative? *Journal of Personality and Social Psychology, 36,* 917–927.

Brim, O. (1999). *The McArthur Foundation study of midlife development.* Vero Beach, FL: The McArthur Foundation.

Brislin, R. W., Cushner, K., Cherries, C., & Yong, M. (1986). *Intercultural interactions: A practical guide.* Beverly Hills, CA: Sage.

Broadbent, D. E. (1958). *Perception and communication.* New York: Pergamon.

Brobert, A. G., Wessels, H., Lamb, M. E., & Hwang, C. P. (1997). Effects of day care on the development of cognitive abilities in 8-year-olds: A longitudinal study. *Developmental Psychology, 33,* 62–69.

Bröder, A. (1998). Deception can be acceptable. *American Psychologist, 53,* 805–806.

Brodsky, S. L. (1999). *The expert expert witness: More maxims and guidelines for testifying in court.* Washington, DC: American Psychological Association.

Brody, L. (1985). Gender differences in emotional development: A review of theories and research. In A. J. Stewart & M. B. Lykes (Eds.), *Gender and personality: Current perspectives on theory and research* (pp. 14–61). Durham, NC: Duke University Press.

Brody, N. (2000). Intelligence. In A. Kazdin (Ed.), *Encyclopedia of psychology.* Washington, DC: American Psychological Association.

Bronfenbrenner, U. (1986). Ecology of the family as a context for human development: Research perspectives. *Developmental Psychology, 22,* 723–742.

Brooks, D. C., Bowker, J. L., Anderson, J. E., & Palmatier, M. I. (2003). Impact of brief or extended extinction of a taste aversion on inhibitory associations: Evidence from summation, retardation and preference tests. *Learning and Behavior, 31,* 69–84.

Brooks-Gunn, J. (1993). *Adolescence.* Paper presented at the meeting of the Society for Research in Child Development, Kansas City, MO.

Brooks-Gunn, J., & Lewis, M. (1984). The development of early visual self-recognition. *Developmental Review, 4,* 215–239.

Brown, B., & Grotberg, J. J. (1981). *Head Start: A successful experiment.* Courrier. Paris: International Children's Centre.

Brown, D. E. (1991). *Human universals.* New York: McGraw-Hill.

Brown, L. S., & Ballou, M. (1992). *Personality and psychopathology: Feminist reappraisals.* New York: Guilford.

Brown, P. L., & Jenkins, H. M. (1968). Autoshaping of the pigeon's key peck. *Journal of Experimental and Analytical Behavior, 11,* 1–8.

Brown, R. (1958). *Words and things.* New York: Free Press/Macmillan.

Brown, R. W., & Lenneberg, E. H. (1954). A study in language and cognition. *Journal of Abnormal and Social Psychology, 49,* 454–462.

Brown, R., & McNeill, D. (1966). The "tip of the tongue phenomenon."

Journal of Verbal Learning and Verbal Behavior, 8, 325–337.

Bruch, C. B. (1971). Modification of procedures for identification of the disadvantaged gifted. *Gifted Child Quarterly, 15,* 267–272.

Bruch, H. (1980). *The golden cage: The enigma of anorexia nervosa.* New York: Random House.

Bruder, G. E., Stewart, M. W., Mercier, M. A., Agosti, V., Leite, P., Donovan, S., & Quitkin, F. M. (1997). Outcome of cognitive-behavioral therapy for depression: Relation to hemispheric dominance for verbal processing. *Journal of Abnormal Psychology, 106,* 138–144.

Brunner, H. G., Nelen, M., Breakefield, X. O., Ropers, H. H., & Van Oost, B. A. (1993, October). Abnormal behavior associated with a point mutation in the structural gene for monoamine oxidase A. *Science, 262,* 578–580.

Bryant, R. A., & Harvey, A. G. (2003). Gender differences in the relationship between acute stress disorder and posttraumatic stress disorder following motor vehicle accidents. *Australian and New Zealand Journal of Psychiatry, 37,* 226–229.

Buist, C. M. (2002). Reducing essential hypertension in the elderly using biofeedback assisted self-regulatory training. *Dissertation Abstracts International: Section B: The Sciences and Engineering, 63,* 516.

Bulik, C. M., Sullivan, P. F., & Kendler, K. S. (2003). Genetic and environmental contributions to obesity and binge eating. *International Journal of Eating Disorders, 33,* 293–298.

Bursik, K. (1998). Moving beyond gender differences: Gender role comparisons of manifest dream content. *Sex Roles, 38,* 203–214.

Burt, M. R., Aron, L. Y., Douglas, T., Valente, J., Lee, E., & Iwen, B. (1999). Homelessness: Programs and the people they serve. Retrieved September 18, 2003, http://www.urban.org/UploadedPDF/homelessness.pdf.

Bushman, B. J. (1993). Human aggression while under the influence of alcohol and other drugs: An integrative research review. *Current Directions in Psychological Science, 2,* 148–152.

Bushman, B. J., & Cooper, H. M. (1990). Effects of alcohol on human aggression: An integrative research review. *Psychological Bulletin, 107,* 341–354.

Bushman, B. J., Baumeister, R. F., & Stack, A. D. (1999). Catharsis, aggression, and persuasive influence: Self-fulfilling or self-defeating prophecies? *Journal of Personality & Social Psychology, 76,* 367–376.

Buss, D. M. (1985). Human mate selection. *American Scientist, 73,* 47–51.

Buss, D. M. (1989). Sex differences in human mate preferences: Evolution-ary hypotheses tested in 37 cultures. *Behavioral and Brain Sciences, 12,* 1–49.

Buss, D. M. (1990). The evolution of anxiety and social exclusion. *Journal of Social and Clinical Psychology, 9,* 196–210.

Buss, D. M. (1991). Evolutionary personality psychology. *Annual Review of Psychology, 42,* 459–491.

Buss, D. M., & Malamuth, N. M. (Eds.). (1996). *Sex, power, conflict: Evolutionary and feminist perspectives.* New York: Oxford University Press.

Buss, D. M., & Shackelford, T. K. (1997). Human aggression in evolutionary perspective. *Clinical Psychology Review, 17,* 605–619.

Butler, R. N., & Lewis, M. I. (1982). *Aging and mental health: Positive psychological and biomedical approaches.* St. Louis, MO: Mosby.

Byne, W. (1994). The biological evidence challenged. *Scientific American, 270*(5), 50–55.

Byrne, D., & Nelson, D. (1965). Attraction as a linear function of properties of positive reinforcements. *Journal of Personality and Social Psychology, 1,* 659–663.

Byrne, R. W., (2002) *Evolutionary psychology and primate cognition.* Cambridge, Mass: MIT Press.

C

Cabeza, R., & Nyberg, L. (2000). Imaging cognition II: An empirical review of 275 PET and fMRI studies. *Journal of Cognitive Neuroscience, 12,* 1–47.

Cacioppo, J. T., Hawkley, L. C., Berntson, G. G., Ernst, J. M., Gibbs, A. C., Strickgold, R., & Hobson, A. (2002). Do lonely days invade the nights? Potential social modulation of sleep efficiency. *Psychological Science, 13,* 384–387.

Cahill, L., & McGaugh, J. L. (1998). Mechanisms of emotional arousal and lasting declarative memory. *Trends in Neurosciences, 21,* 294–299.

Cain, D. J. (2002). Defining characteristics, history, and evolution of humanistic psychotherapies. In D. J. Cain (Ed.), *Humanistic psychotherapies: Handbook of research and practice* (pp. 3–54). Washington, DC: American Psychological Association.

Cain, W. S. (1981, July). Educating your nose. *Psychology Today,* pp. 48–56.

Cain, W. S. (1982). Odor identification by males and females: Predictions versus performance. *Chemical Senses, 7,* 129–142.

Cairns, E., & Darby, J. (1998). The conflict in Northern Ireland: Causes, consequences, and controls. *American Psychologist, 53,* 754–760.

Calhoun, L. G., & Tedeschi, R. G. (2001). Posttraumatic growth: The positive lessons of loss. In R. A. Neimeyer (Ed.), *Meaning reconstruction & the experience of loss* (pp. 157–172).

Washington, DC: American Psychological Association.

Califano, J. A., Jr. (1999, August 24). White-Line Fever: What an older and wiser George W. should do. *Washington Post,* p. A17.

Callahan, R. (2000, January 13). Tall Polish men have tall kids, study says. *Charlotte Observer,* p. 12A.

Callicott, J. H. (2003). An expanded role for functional neuroimaging in schizophrenia. *Current Opinions in Neurobiology, 13,* 256–260.

Calvert, S., & Cocking, R. (1992). Health promotion through mass media. *Journal of Applied Developmental Psychology, 13,* 143–149.

Campos, J. L., Langer, A., & Krowitz, A. (1970, October 9). Cardiac responses on the visual cliff in prelocomotor human infants. *Science, 170,* 196–197.

Cannon, W. B. (1929). *Bodily changes in pain, hunger, fear and rage.* New York: Appleton.

Caporael, L. R. (2001). Evolutionary psychology: Toward a unifying theory and a hybrid science. *Annual Review of Psychology, 52,* 607–628.

Capron, C., & Duyme, M. (1989). Assessment of effects of socio-economic status on IQ in a full cross-fostering study. *Nature (London), 340,* 552–554.

Cardemil, E. V., & Battle, C. L. (2003). Guess who's coming to therapy? Getting comfortable with conversations about race and ethnicity in psychotherapy. *Professional Psychology: Research and Practice, 34,* 278–286.

Cardena, E., Butler, L. D., & Spiegel, D. (2003). Stress disorders. In G. Stricker & T. A. Widiger (Eds.), *Handbook of psychology: Clinical psychology, Vol. 8* (pp. 229–249). New York: John Wiley & Sons, Inc.

Carlson, N. R. (2000). *Physiology of behavior* (7th ed.). Boston: Allyn & Bacon.

Carmona, F. J., Sanz, L. J., & Marin, D. (2002). Type-A behaviour pattern and coronary heart disease. *Psiquis: Revista de Psiquiatria, Psicologia Medica y Psicosomatica, 23,* 22–30.

Carpenter, S. (2001). Research confirms the virtue of 'sleeping on it'. *Monitor on Psychology, 32,* 49–51.

Carr, M., Borkowski, J. G., & Maxwell, S. E. (1991). Motivational components of underachievement. *Developmental Psychology, 27,* 108–118.

Carskadon, M. A. (2002). Risks of driving while sleepy in adolescents and young adults. In M. A. Carskadon (Ed.) *Adolescent sleep patterns: Biological, social, and psychological influences* (pp. 148–158). New York: Cambridge University Press.

Carskadon, M. A., & Dement, W. C. (1982). Nocturnal determinants of daytime sleepiness. *Sleep, 5*(Suppl. 2), 73–81.

Carson, R. C., & Butcher, J. N. (1992). *Abnormal psychology and modern life* (9th ed.). New York: HarperCollins.

Carson, R. C., Butcher, J. N., & Coleman, J. C. (1988). *Abnormal psychology and modern life* (8th ed.). Glenview, IL: Scott, Foresman.

Carstensen, L. (1995). Evidence for a life-span theory of socioemotional selectivity. *Current Directions in Psychological Science, 4,* 151–156.

Carter, R. (1998). *Mapping the mind.* Berkeley: University of California Press.

Carter, T., Hardy, C. A., & Hardy, J. C. (2001). Latin vocabulary acquisition: An experiment using information processing techniques of chunking and imagery. *Journal of Instructional Psychology, 28,* 225–228.

Cartwright, R. D. (1996). Dreams and adaptation to divorce. In D. Barrett (Ed.), *Trauma and dreams* (pp. 179–185). Cambridge, MA: Harvard University Press.

Caruso, J. C. (2001). Reliable component analysis of the Stanford-Binet: Fourth Edition for 2- to 6-year olds. *Psychological Assessment, 13,* 261–266.

Casas, J. M. (1995). Counseling and psychotherapy with racial/ethnic minority groups in theory and practice. In B. Bongar & L. E. Beutler (Eds.), *Comprehensive handbook of psychotherapy* (pp. 311–335). New York: Oxford University Press.

Caspi, A., & Elder, G. H., Jr. (1986). Life satisfaction in old age: Linking social psychology and history. *Journal of Psychology and Aging, 1,* 18–26.

Caspi, A., Moffitt, T., Newman, D. L., & Silva, P. (1996). Behavioral observations at age 3 years predict adult psychiatric disorders. *Archives of General Psychiatry, 53,* 1033–1039.

Cassaday, H. J., & Rawlins, J. N. (1997). The hippocampus, objects, and their contexts. *Behavioral Neuroscience, 111,* 1228–1244.

Cassidy, J. P. (2002). The Stockholm Syndrome, battered woman syndrome and the cult personality: An integrative approach. *Dissertation Abstracts International: Section B: the Sciences and Engineering, 62,* 5366.

Cattell, R. B. (1965). *The scientific analysis of personality.* Baltimore: Penguin.

Cattell, R. B. (1971). *Abilities: Their structure, growth, and action.* Boston: Houghton Mifflin.

Cattell, R. B., & Kline, P. (1977). *The specific analysis of personality and motivation.* New York: Academic Press.

Cavanaugh, J. C. (1990). *Adult development and aging.* Belmont, CA: Wadsworth.

Ceci, S. J., & Williams, W. M. (1997). Schooling, intelligence, and income. *American Psychologist, 52,* 1051–1058.

Celis, W. (1994, June 8). More college women drinking to get drunk. *New York Times,* p. B8

Cemalcilar, Z., Canbeyli, R., & Sunar, D. (2003). Learned helplessness, therapy, and personality traits: An experimental study. *Journal of Social Psychology*, *143*, 65–81.

Centers for Disease Control and Prevention. (1999). *Suicide deaths and rates per 100,000*. Available on-line at: www.cdc.gov/ncipe/data/us9794/suic.htm

Cervone, D., & Shoda, Y. (1999). Beyond traits in the study of personality coherence. *Current Directions in Psychological Science*, *8*, 27–32.

Chaiken, S., & Eagly, A. H. (1976). Communication modality as a determinant of message persuasiveness and message comprehensibility. *Journal of Personality and Social Psychology*, *34*, 605–614.

Chait, L. D., & Pierri, J. (1992). Effects of smoked marijuana on human performance: A critical review. In L. Murphy & A. Bartke (Eds.), *Marijuana/cannabinoids: Neurobiology and neurophysiology* (pp. 387–424). Boca Raton, FL: CRC Press.

Chance, P. (1992). The rewards of learning. *Phi Delta Kappan*, *73*, 200–207.

Chance, S. A., Esiri, M. M., & Timothy, J. C. (2003). Ventricular enlargement in schizophrenia: A primary change in the temporal lobe? *Schizophrenia Research*, *62*, 123–131.

Chang, E. C., & Sanna, L. J. (2003). Experience of life hassles and psychological adjustment among adolescents: Does it make a difference if one is optimistic or pessimistic? *Personality and Individual Differences*, *34*, 867–879.

Chassin, L., Pitts, S. C., DeLucia, C., & Todd, M. (1999). A longitudinal study of children of alcoholics: Predicting young adult substance use disorders, anxiety, and depression. *Journal of Abnormal Psychology*, *108*, 106–119.

Chaudhari, N., Landin, A. M., & Roper, S. D. (2000). A metabotropic glutamate receptor variant functions as a taste receptor. *Nature: Neuroscience*, *3*, 113–119.

Chekroun, P., & Brauer, M. (2002). The bystander effect and social control behavior: the effect of the presence of others on people's reactions to norm violations. *European Journal of Social Psychology*, *32*, 853–866.

Chen, P., Goldberg, D. E., Kolb, B., Lanser, M., & Benowitz, L. I. (2002). Inosine induces axonal rewiring and improves behavioral outcome after stroke, *Proceedings of the National Academy of Sciences USA*, *99*, 9031–9036.

Cheour, M., Ceponiene, R., Lehtokoski, A., Luuk, A., Allik, J., Alho, K., & Näätänen, R. (1998). Development of language-specific phoneme representations in the infant brain. *Nature Neuroscience*, *1*, 351–353.

Cherlin, A. (1992). *Marriage, divorce, remarriage*. Boston, MA: Harvard University Press.

Cherry, C. (1966). *On human communication: A review, a survey, and a criticism* (2nd ed.). Cambridge, MA: MIT Press.

Chervin, R. D., Killion, J. E., Archbold, K. H., & Ruzicka, D. L. (2003). Conduct problems and symptoms of sleep disorders in children. *Journal of the American Academy of Child and Adolescent Psychiatry*, *42*, 201–208.

Chester, J. A., Lumeng, L., Li, T. K., & Grahame, N. J. (2003). High and low alcohol preferring mice show differences in conditioned taste aversion to alcohol. *Alcoholism: Clinical and Experimental Research*, *27*, 12–18.

Choi, I., Nisbett, R. E., & Norenzayan, A. (1999). Casual attribution across cultures: Variation and universality. *Psychological Bulletin*, *125*, 47–63.

Choi, J., & Silverman, I. (2003). Processes underlying sex differences in route-learning strategies in children and adolescents. *Personality and Individual Differences*, *34*, 113–1166.

Choi, W. S., Pierce, J. P., Gilpin, E. A., Farkas, A. J., & Berry, C. C. (1997). Which adolescent experimenters progress to established smoking in the United States? *American Journal of Preventive Medicine*, *13*, 385–391.

Chomsky, N. (1957). *Syntactic structures*. The Hague: Mouton.

Chomsky, N. (1965). *Aspects of the theory of syntax*. Cambridge, MA: MIT Press.

Chomsky, N. (1986). *Knowledge of language: Its nature, origins and use*. New York: Praeger.

Chomsky, N., Place, U., & Schoneberger, T. (2000). The Chomsky-Place correspondence 1993–1994. *Analysis of Verbal Behavior*, *17*, 7–38.

Christensen, A., & Heavey, C. L. (1999). Interventions for couples. *Annual Review of Psychology*, *50*, 165–190.

Christensen, F. (1986). *Pornography: The other side*. Unpublished manuscript, University of Alberta.

Christie, C. (2003). *Gender and language: Towards a feminist pragmatics*. Edinburgh, Scotland: Edinburgh University Press.

Chua, S. C., Chung, W. K., Wu-Peng, X. S., Zhang, Y., Liu, S. M., Tartaglia, L., & Leibel, R. L. (1996, February 16). Phenotypes of mouse diabetes and rat fatty due to mutations in OB (leptin) receptor. *Science*, *271*, 994–996.

Chwalisz, K., Diener, E., & Gallagher, D. (1988). Autonomic arousal feedback and emotional experience: Evidence from the spinal cord injured. *Journal of Personality and Social Psychology*, *54*, 820–828.

Cialdini, R. B. (1995). Principles and techniques of social influence. In A. Tesser (Ed.), *Advanced social psychology* (pp. 257–282). New York: McGraw-Hill.

Cialdini, R. B., & Trost, M. (1998). Social influence: Social norms, conformity, and compliance. In D. Gilbert, S. T. Fiske, & G. Lindzey (Eds.), *Handbook of social psychology* (4th ed., Vol. 2, pp. 151–192). Boston: McGraw-Hill.

Cialdini, R. B., Cacioppo, J. T., Bassett, R., & Miller, J. A. (1978). Lowball procedure for producing compliance: Commitment then cost. *Journal of Personality and Social Psychology*, *36*, 463–476.

Cialdini, R. B., Vincent, J. E., Lewis, S. K., Catalan, J., Wheeler, D., & Darby, B. L. (1975). A reciprocal concessions procedure for inducing compliance: The door-in-the-face technique. *Journal of Personality and Social Psychology*, *21*, 206–215.

Cicchetti, D., & Toth, S. L. (1998). The development of depression in children and adolescents. *American Psychologist*, *53*, 221–241.

Clark, G. M. (1998). Research advances for cochlear implants. *Auris Nasus Larynx*, *25*, 73–87.

Clark, J. E. (1994). Motor development. In V. S. Ramachandran (Ed.), *Encyclopedia of human behavior* (Vol. 3, pp. 245–255). San Diego, CA: Academic Press.

Clark, R. D., & Word, L. E. (1974). Where is the apathetic bystander? Situational characteristics of the emergency. *Journal of Personality and Social Psychology*, *29*, 279–287.

Clarkson, P. (1996). *To act or not to act: That is the question*. London: Whurr.

Clausen, J. A. (1975). The social meaning of differential physical and sexual maturation. In S. E. Dragastin & G. H. Elder, Jr. (Eds.), *Adolescence in the life cycle: Psychological change and social context* (pp. 25–47). New York: Wiley.

Clauss, E., & Caroline, C. C. (2003). Promoting ecologic health resilience for minority youth: Enhancing health care access through the school health center. *Psychology in the Schools*, *40*, 265–278.

Clay, R. (1997, July). Do hearing devices impair deaf children? *APA Monitor*, p. 1.

Clay, R. A. (2000, January). Psychotherapy is cost-effective. *Monitor on Psychology*, pp. 40–41.

Clayton, A. H., McGarvey, E. L., Abouesch, A. L., & Pinkerton, R. C. (2001). Substitution of an SSRI with bupropion sustained release following SSRI-induced sexual dysfunction. *Journal of Clinical Psychiatry*, *62*, 185–190.

Clements, M. (1996, March). Sex after 65. *Parade Magazine*, 4–5, 7.

Cloninger, S. C. (1993). *Theories of personality: Understanding persons*. Englewood Cliffs, NJ: Prentice Hall.

Cocchini, G., Logie, R. H., Sala, S. D., MacPherson, S. E., & Baddeley, A. D. (2002). Concurrent performance of two memory tasks: Evidence for domain-specific working memory systems. *Memory and Cognition*, *30*, 1086–1095.

Cochran, S. V., & Rabinowitz, F. E. (2003). Gender-sensitive recommendations for assessment and treatment of depression in men. *Professional Psychology: Research and Practice*, *34*, 132–140.

Cohen, A., & Raffal, R. D. (1991). Attention and feature integration: Illusory conjunctions in a patient with a parietal lobe lesion. *Psychological Science*, *2*, 106–110.

Cohen, E. G. (1984). The desegregated school: Problems in status, power and interethnic climate. In N. Miller & M. B. Brewer (Eds.), *Groups in contact: The psychology of desegregation* (pp. 77–96). New York: Academic Press.

Cohen, L. J., & Galynker, I. I. (2002). Clinical features of pedophilia and implications for treatment. *Journal of Psychiatric Practice*, *8*, 276–289.

Cohen, S., & Herbert, T. B. (1996). Health psychology: Psychological factors and physical disease from the perspective of human psychoneuroimmunology. *Annual Review of Psychology*, *47*, 113–142.

Cohen, S., & Williamson, G. M. (1988). Stress and infectious disease in humans. *Psychological Bulletin*, *109*, 5–24.

Cohen, S., Frank, E., Doyle, W. J., Skoner, D. P., Rabin, B. S., & Gwaltney, J. M., Jr. (1998). Types of stressors that increase susceptibility to the common cold in healthy adults. *Health Psychology*, *17*, 214–223.

Cohn, L. D. (1991). Sex differences in the course of personality development: A meta-analysis. *Psychological Bulletin*, *109*, 252–266.

Cole, J. D. (1995). *Pride and a daily marathon runner*. Cambridge, MA: MIT Press.

Coleman, J., Glaros, A., & Morris, C. G. (1987). *Contemporary psychology and effective behavior* (6th ed.). Glenview, IL: Scott, Foresman.

Coley, R. L., & Chase-Lansdale, L. (1998). Adolescent pregnancy and parenthood: Recent evidence and future directions. *American Psychologist*, *53*, 152–166.

Collaer, M. L., & Hines, M. (1995). Human behavioral sex differences: A role for gonadal hormones during early development? *Psychological Bulletin*, *118*, 55–107.

Collett, T. (2000). Measuring beelines to food. *Science*, *287*, 817–818.

Collins, N. L., & Miller, L. C. (1994). Self-disclosure and liking: A meta-analytic review. *Psychological Bulletin*, *116*, 457–475.

Collins, R. C. (1993). Head Start: Steps toward a two-generation program strategy. *Young Children*, *48(2)*, 25–73.

Collins, W. A., Maccoby, E. E., Steinberg, L., Hetherington, E. M., & Bornstein, M. H. (2000). Contemporary research on parenting: The case for nature and nurture. *American Psychologist, 55,* 218–232.

Collins, W.A., Maccoby, E.E., Steinberg, L., Hetherington, E. M., & Bornstein, M. H. (2001). Toward nature WITH nurture. *American Psychologist, 56,* 171–172.

Comaty, J. E., Stasio, M., & Advokat, C. (2001). Analysis of outcome variables of a token economy system in a state psychiatric hospital: A program evaluation. *Research in Developmental Disabilities, 22,* 233–253.

Compas, B. E., Hinden, B. R., & Gerhardt, C. A. (1995). Adolescent development: Pathways and processes of risk and resilience. *Annual Review of Psychology, 46,* 265–293.

Comstock, G., & Scharrer, E. (1999). *Television: What's on, who's watching, and what it means.* San Diego, CA: Academic Press.

Confino, A., & Fritzsche, P. (2002). *The work of memory: New directions in the study of German society and culture.* Champaign, IL: University of Illinois Press.

Conger, J. J., & Petersen, A. C. (1991). *Adolescence and youth* (4th ed.). New York: HarperCollins.

Connelly, B., Johnston, D., Brown, I. D., Mackay, S., & Blackstock, E. G. (1993). The prevalence of depression in a high school population. *Adolescence, 28,* 149–158.

Conroy, J. W. (1996). The small ICF/MR program: Dimensions of quality and cost. *Mental Retardation, 34,* 13–26.

Consumer Reports. (1995, November). Mental health: Does therapy help? pp. 734–739.

Conte, J. J., & Jacobs, R. R. (2003). Validity evidence linking polychronicity and Big Five personality dimensions to absence, lateness and supervisory performance ratings. *Human Performance, 16,* 107–129.

Contreras, D., Destexhe, A., Sejnowski, T. J., & Steriade, M. (1996, November 1). Control of spatiotemporal coherence of a thalamic oscillation by corticothalamic feedback. *Science, 274,* 771–774.

Conway, A. R. A., Cowan, N., & Bunting, M. F. (2001). The cocktail party phenomenon revisited: The importance of working memory capacity. *Psychonomic Bulletin and Review, 8,* 331–335.

Conway, M. A. (1996). Failures of autobiographical remembering. In D. Hermann, C. McEvoy, C. Hertzog, P. Hertel, & M. K. Johnson (Eds.), *Basic and applied memory research: Theory in context* (pp. 295–315). Mahwah, NJ: Erlbaum.

Conway, M., & Dube, L. (2002). Humor in persuasion on threatening topics: Effectiveness is a function of audience sex role orientation. *Personality and Social Psychology Bulletin, 28,* 863–873.

Cook, E. H., Courchesne, R. Y., Cox, N. J., Lord, C., Gonen, D., Guter, S. J., Lincoln, A., Nix, K., Haas, R., Leventhal, B. L., & Courchesne, E. (1998). Linkage-disequilibrium mapping of autistic disorder, with 15q11–13 markers. *American Journal of Human Genetics, 62,* 1077–1083.

Cookerly, J. R. (1980). Does marital therapy do any lasting good? *Journal of Marital and Family Therapy, 6,* 393–397.

Cooper, H. (1993). In search of a social fact. A commentary on the study of interpersonal expectations. In P. Blanck (Ed.), *Interpersonal expectations: Theory, research, and application* (pp. 218–226). Paris, France: Cambridge University Press.

Cooper, J., & Croyle, R. T. (1984). Attitudes and attitude change. *Annual Review of Psychology, 35,* 395–426.

Cooper, R., & Zubek, J. (1958). Effects of enriched and restricted early environments on the learning ability of bright and dull rats. *Canadian Journal of Psychology, 12,* 159–164.

Corder, B., Saunders, A. M., Strittmatter, W. J., Schmechel, D. E., Gaskell, P. C., Small, G. W., Roses, A. D., Haines, J. L., & Pericak-Vance, M. A. (1993, August 13). Gene dose of apolipoprotein E type 4 allele and the risk of Alzheimer's disease in late onset families. *Science, 261,* 921–923.

Coren, S., Porac, C., & Ward, L. M. (1984). *Sensation and perception* (2nd ed.). Orlando, FL: Academic Press.

Coren, S., Ward, L. M., & Enns, J. T. (1994). *Sensation and perception* (4th ed.). Orlando, FL: Harcourt Brace.

Cornelius, R. R. (1996). *The science of emotion: Research and tradition in the psychology of emotions.* Upper Saddle River, NJ: Prentice Hall.

Cosmides, L., & Tooby, J. (2000). Evolutionary psychology and the emotions. In M. Lewis & J .M. Haviland-Jones (Eds.), *Handbook of Emotions* (2nd ed.). New York: Guilford.

Cosmides, L., Tooby, J., & Barkow, J. (1992). *The adapted mind: Evolutionary psychology and the generation of culture.* New York: Oxford.

Costa, A., Peppe, A., Dell'Agnello, G., Carlesimo, G., Murri, L., Bonuccelli, U., & Caltagirone, C. (2003). Dopaminergic modulation of visual-spatial working memory in Parkinson's disease. *Dementia and Geriatric Cognitive Disorders, 15,* 55–66.

Costa, P. T., & McCrae, R. R. (1992). *Revised NEO Personality Inventory (NEO PI-R) and NEO Five-Factor Inventory (NEO-FFI): Professional manual.* Odessa, FL: Psychological Assessment Resources.

Costa, P. T., & McCrae, R. R. (1995). Domains and facets: Hierarchical personality assessment using the Revised NEO Personality Inventory. *Journal of Personality Assessment, 64,* 21–50.

Cotton, J. L. (1993). *Employee involvement: Methods for improving performance and work attitudes.* Newbury Park, CA: Sage.

Cotton, J. L., & Tuttle, J. M. (1986). Employee turnover: A meta-analysis and review with implications for research. *Academy of Management Review, 11,* 55–70.

Council, J. R. (1993). Context effects in personality research. *Current Directions in Psychological Science, 2,* 31–34.

Cousins, N. (1981). *Anatomy of an illness as perceived by the patient.* New York: Bantam.

Cousins, S. (1989). Culture and self-perception in Japan and in the United States. *Journal of Personality and Social Psychology, 56,* 124–131.

Cowan, N. (1988). Evolving conceptions of memory storage, selective attention, and their mutual constraints within the human information-processing system. *Psychological Bulletin, 104,* 163–191.

Coyle, J. T. (1987). Alzheimer's disease. In G. Adelman (Ed.), *Encyclopedia of neuroscience* (pp. 29–31). Boston: Birkhauser.

Coyne, J. C., & Whiffen, V. E. (1995). Issues in personality as diathesis for depression: The case of sociotropy-dependency and autonomy-self-criticism. *Psychological Bulletin, 118,* 358–378.

Craig, A. D., & Bushnell, M. C. (1994, July 8). The thermal grill illusion: Unmasking the burn of cold pain. *Science, 265,* 252–255.

Craig, C. D. (2002). Ripples: Group work in different settings. *Social Work with Groups, 25,* 94–97.

Craig, J. C., & Rollman, G. B. (1999). Somesthesis. *Annual Review of Psychology, 50,* 305–331.

Craighead, L. (1990). Supervised exercise in behavioral treatment for moderate obesity. *Behavior Therapy, 20,* 49–59.

Craik, F. I. M. (1994). Memory changes in normal aging. *Current Directions in Psychological Science, 3,* 155–158.

Craik, F. I. M. (2002). Levels of processing: Past, present . . . and future? *Memory, 10,* 305–318.

Craik, F. I. M., & Lockhart, R. S. (1972). Levels of processing: A framework for memory research. *Journal of Verbal Learning and Verbal Behavior, 11,* 671–684.

Craik, F. I. M., & Watkins, M. J. (1973). The role of rehearsal in short-term memory. *Journal of Verbal Learning and Verbal Behavior, 12,* 599–607.

Craik, F. I. M., Moroz, T. M., Moscovitch, M., Stuss, D. T., Winocur, G., Tulving, E., & Kapur, S. (1999). In search of the self: A positron emission tomography study. *Psychological Science, 10,* 26–34.

Cramer, P. (2000). Defense mechanisms in psychology today: Further processes for adaptation. *American Psychologist, 55,* 637–646.

Crandall, C. S. (1994). Prejudice against fat people: Ideology and self-interest. *Journal of Personality and Social Psychology, 66,* 882–894.

Cronan, T. A., Walen, H. R., & Cruz, S. G. (1994). The effects of community-based literacy training on Head Start parents. *Journal of Community Psychology, 22,* 248–258.

Cronbach, L. J. (1990). *Essentials of psychological testing* (5th ed.). New York: HarperCollins.

Crook, T., & Eliot, J. (1980). Parental death during childhood and adult depression: A critical review of the literature. *Psychological Bulletin, 87,* 252–259.

Crooks, R., & Bauer, K. (2002). *Our sexuality* (8th ed.). Belmont, CA: Wadsworth.

Crovitz, H. F., & Schiffman, H. (1974). Frequency of episodic memories as a function of their age. *Bulletin of the Psychonomic Society, 4,* 517–518.

Cruz, A., & Green, B. G. (2000). Thermal stimulation of taste. *Nature, 403,* 889–892.

Crystal, D. S., Chen, C., Fuligini, A. J., Stevenson, H., Hus, C., Ko, H., Kitamura, S., & Kimura, S. (1994). Psychological maladjustments and academic achievement: A cross-cultural study of Japanese, Chinese, and American high school students. *Child Development, 65,* 738–753.

Csikszentmihalyi, M., Rathunde, K., & Whalen, S. (1993). *Talented teenagers: The roots of success and failure.* New York: Cambridge University Press.

Culbertson, F. M. (1997). Depression and gender: An international review. *American Psychologist, 52,* 25–31.

Cunningham, J. E. C. (2003). Neuropsychology, genetic liability, and psychotic symptoms in those at high risk of schizophrenia. *Journal of Abnormal Psychology, 112,* 38–48.

Curle, C. E., & Williams, C. (1996). Post-traumatic stress reactions in children: Gender differences in the incidence of trauma reactions at two years and examination of factors influencing adjustment. *British Journal of Clinical Psychology, 35,* 297–309.

Cutler, D. M. (2001). The reduction in disability among the elderly. *Proceedings of the National Academy of Sciences, USA, 98,* 6546–6547.

Cutler, W. B., Friedmann, E., & McCoy, N. L. (1998). Pheromonal influences on sociosexual behavior in men. *Archives of Sexual Behavior, 27,* 1–13.

Czeisler, C. A., Duffy, J. F., & Shanahan, T. L. (1999, June 25). Stability, precision, and near-24-hour period of human circadian pacemaker. *Science, 284*, 2177–2181.

D

D'Azevedo, W. A. (1982). Tribal history in Liberia. In U. Neisser (Ed.), *Memory observed: Remembering in natural contexts* (pp. 258–268). San Francisco: Freeman.

D'Esposito, M., Zarahn, E., & Aguirre, G. K. (1999). Event-related functional MRI: Implications for cognitive psychology. *Psychological Bulletin, 125*, 155–164.

D'Silva, M. U., Grant-Harrington, N., Palmgreen, P., Donohew, L., & Pugzles-Lorch, E. (2001). Drug use prevention for the high sensation seeker: The role of alternative activities. *Substance Use and Misuse, 36*, 373–385.

Dabbs, J. M., Jr., & Leventhal, H. (1966). Effects of varying the recommendations in a fear-arousing communication. *Journal of Personality and Social Psychology, 4*, 525–531.

Dabbs, J. M., Jr., & Morris, R. (1990). Testosterone, social class, and antisocial behavior in a sample of 4,462 men. *Psychological Science, 1*, 209–211.

Dabbs, J. M., Jr., Carr, T. S., Frady, R. L., & Riad, J. K. (1995). Testosterone, crime, and misbehavior among 692 male prison inmates. *Personality and Individual Differences, 19*, 627–633.

Daehler, M. W. (1994). Cognitive development. In *Encyclopedia of human behavior* (Vol. 1 pp. 627–637). San Diego, CA: Academic Press.

Dae-Shik, K., Duong, T. Q., & Seong-Gi, K. (2000). High-resolution mapping of iso-orientation columns by fMRI. *Nature: Neuroscience, 3*, 164–169.

Dahl, E. K. (1996). The concept of penis envy revisited: A child analyst listens to adult women. *Psychoanalytic Study of the Child, 51*, 303–325.

Dahlström, W. G. (1993). Tests: Small samples, large consequences. *American Psychologist, 48*, 393–399.

Dalton, P., Doolittle, N., & Breslin, P. A. S. (2002). Gender-specific induction of enhanced sensitivity to odors. *Nature Neuroscience, 5*, 199–200.

Damas, A. (2002). A factorial invariance analysis of intellectual abilities in children across different age and cultural groups using the Wechsler Intelligence Scale for Children. *Dissertation Abstracts International: Section B: The Sciences and Engineering, 62*, 4832.

Damasio, A. (2003). *Looking for Spinoza: Joy, sorrow, and the feeling brain.* NY: Harcourt.

Damasio, A. R. (1999). *The feeling of what happens: Body and emotion in the making of consciousness.* New York: Harcourt Brace.

Damasio, H., Grabowski, T. J., Tranel, D., Hichawa, R. D., & Damasio, A. R. (1996). A neural basis for lexical retrieval. *Nature, 380*, 499–505.

Daniell, H. W. (1971). Smokers' wrinkles: A study in the epidemiology of "Crow's feet." *Annals of Internal Medicine, 75*, 873–880.

Danielle, D. M., Rose, R. J., Viken, R. J., & Kaprio, J. (2000). Pubertal timing and substance use: Associations between and within families across late adolescence. *Developmental Psychology, 36*, 180–189.

Darwin, C. R. (1859). *The origin of species.* London.

Davidson, P. S. R., & Glisky, E. L. (2002). Is flashbulb memory a special instance of source memory? Evidence from older adults. *Memory, 10*, 99–111.

Davidson, R. J. (1992). Emotion and affective style: Hemispheric substrates. *Psychological Science, 3*, 39–43.

Davidson, R. J., Jackson, D. C., & Kalin, N. H. (2000). Emotion, plasticity, context, and regulation: Perspectives from affective neuroscience. *Psychological Bulletin, 126*, 890–909.

Davidson, R. J., Putnam, K. M., & Larson, C. L. (2000, July 28). Dysfunction in the neural circuitry of emotion regulation–A possible prelude to violence. *Science, 289*, 591–594.

Davies, M., Stankov, L., & Roberts, R. D. (1998). Emotional intelligence: In search of an elusive construct. *Journal of Personality and Social Psychology, 75*, 989–1015.

Davies, P. T., & Cummings, E. M. (1994). Marital conflict and child adjustment: An emotional security hypothesis. *Psychological Bulletin, 166*, 387–411.

Davis, C. G., Wortman, C. B., Lehman, D. R., & Silver, R. C. (2000). Searching for meaning in loss: Are clinical assumptions correct? *Death Studies, 24*, 497–540.

Davis, J. R., Vanderploeg, J. M., Santy, P. A., Jennings, R. T., & Stewart, D. F. (1988). Space motion sickness during 24 flights of the space shuttle. *Aviation, Space, and Environmental Medicine, 59*, 1185–1189.

Davis, M. H., & Stephan, W. G. (1980). Attributions for exam performance. *Journal of Applied Social Psychology, 10*, 235–248.

Davis, S. (2000). Testosterone and sexual desire in women. *Journal of Sex Education & Therapy, 25*, 25–32.

Daw, J. (2002). New Mexico becomes first state to gain Rx privileges. *Monitor on Psychology, 33*, 24–25.

Dawes, R. M. (1994). *House of cards: The collapse of modern psychotherapy.* New York: Free Press.

De la Fuente, M. (2002). Effects of antioxidants on the immune system aging. *European Journal of Clinical Nutrition. 56*, (Supplement 3:S5–8)

de Raad, B., & Szirmak, Z. (1994). The search for the "Big Five" in a non-Indo-European language: The Hungarian trait structure and its relationship to the EQP and the PTS. *Revue Européenne de Psychologie Appliqué, 44*, 17–24.

De Waal, F. (1989). *Peacemaking among primates.* Cambridge, MA: Harvard University Press.

De Waal, F. B. M. (1999). The end of nature versus nurture. *Scientific American, 281*(6), 94–99.

Dean, J. W., Jr., & Evans, J. R. (1994). *Total quality: Management, organization, and strategy.* St. Paul, MN: West.

DeAngelis, T. (1991, June). Hearing pinpoints gaps in research on women. *APA Monitor*, p. 8.

Deci, E. L., Koestner, R, & Ryan, R. M. (2001). Extrinsic rewards and intrinsic motivation in education: Reconsidered once again. *Review of Educational Research, 71*, 1–27.

Deci, E. L., Koestner, R., & Ryan, R. M. (1999). A meta-analytic review of experiments examining the effects of extrinsic rewards on intrinsic motivation. *Psychological Bulletin, 125*, 627–668.

Dehaene, S., Spelke, E., Stanescu, R., Pinel, P., & Tsivkin, S. (1999, May 7). Sources of mathematical thinking: Behavioral and brain-imaging evidence. *Science, 284*, 970–974.

Deikman, A. J. (1973). Deautomatization and the mystic experience. In R. W. Ornstein (Ed.), *The nature of human consciousness* (pp. 216–233). San Francisco: Freeman.

DeKay, W. T., & Buss, D. M. (1992). Human nature, individual differences and the importance of context: Perspectives from evolutionary psychology. *Current Directions in Psychological Science, 1*, 184–189.

de-l'Etoile, S. K. (2002). The effect of musical mood induction procedure on mood state-dependent word retrieval. *Journal of Music Therapy, 39*, 145–160.

Dement, W. C. (1965). An essay on dreams: The role of physiology in understanding their nature. In F. Barron (Ed.), *New directions in psychology* (Vol. 2). New York: Holt, Rinehart & Winston.

Dement, W. C. (1974). *Some must watch while some must sleep.* San Francisco: Freeman.

DeNeve, K. M., & Cooper, H. (1998). The happy personality: A meta-analysis of 137 personality traits and subjective well-being. *Psychological Bulletin, 124*, 197–229.

Dennerstein, L., & Burrows, G. D. (1982). Hormone replacement therapy and sexuality in women. *Clinics in Endocrinology and Metabolism, 11*, 661–679.

Dennerstein, L., Dudley, E., & Guthrie, J. (2002). Empty nest or revolving door? A prospective study of women's quality of life in midlife during the phase of children leaving and re-entering the home. *Psychological Medicine, 32*, 545–550.

DePaulo, B. M., & Pfeifer, R. L. (1986). On-the-job experience and skill detecting deception. *Journal of Applied Social Psychology, 16*, 249–267.

DeRamus, B. (2000, August 26). Lax reaction to killing shows how numb many have become. *Detroit News.* Available on-line at: detnews.com/2000/features/0008/26/c01–110895.htm

Derry, F. A., Dinsmore, W. W., Fraser, M., Gardner, B. P., Glass, C. A., Maytom, M. C., & Smith, M. D. (1998). Efficacy and safety of oral sildenafil (Viagra) in men with erectile dysfunction caused by spinal cord injury. *Neurology, 51*, 1629–1633.

Des Forges, A. L. (1995). The ideology of genocide. *Issue: A Journal of Opinion, 23*(2), 44–47.

DeSteno, D., & Braverman, J. (2002). Emotion and persuasion: Thoughts on the role of emotional intelligence. In L. F. Barrett & P. Salovey, *The wisdom in feeling: Psychological processes in emotional intelligence* (pp. 191–210). New York, NY: Guilford Press.

Detweiler, J. B., Bedell, B. T., Salovey, P., Pronin, E., & Rothman, A. J. (1999). Message framing and sunscreen use: Gain-framed messages motivate beach-goers. *Health Psychology, 18*, 189–196.

Devine, P. G. (1989). Stereotypes and prejudice: Their automatic and controlled components. *Journal of Personality & Social Psychology, 56*, 5–18.

Devine, P. G., Monteith, M. J., Zuwerink, J. R., & Elliot, A. J. (1991). Prejudice with and without compunction. *Journal of Personality & Social Psychology, 60*, 817–830.

DeZazzo, J., & Tully, T. (1995). Dissection of memory formulation from behavioral pharmacology to molecular genetics. *Trends in Neuroscience, 18*, 212–218.

Diamond, J. (1994, November). Race without color. *Discover*, pp. 82–92.

Diaz, J. (1997). *How drugs influence behavior: Neuro-behavioral approach.* Upper Saddle River, NJ: Prentice Hall.

Diener, E. (2000). Subjective well-being: The science of happiness and a proposal for a national index. *American Psychologist, 55*, 34–43.

Diener, E., & Suh, E. (1998). Age and subjective well-being: An international analysis. *Annual Review of Gerontology and Geriatrics, 17*, 304–324.

Diener, E., Suh, E. M., Lucas, R. E., & Smith, H. L. (1999). Subjective well-being: Three decades of progress. *Psychological Bulletin, 125*, 276–302.

DiFranza, J. R., & Lew, R. A. (1995). Effect of maternal cigarette smoking on pregnancy complications and sudden infant death syndrome. *Journal of Family Practice, 40,* 385–394.

DiGiovanna, A. G. (1994). *Human aging: Biological perspectives.* New York: McGraw-Hill.

Digman, J. M., & Takemoto-Chock, N. K. (1981). Factors in the natural language of personality: Re-analysis, comparison, and interpretation of six major studies. *Multivariate Behavioral Research, 16,* 149–170.

Dill, S. (1994, July). Baby's grunts may mean more than parents think. *American Weekend,* p.10C.

DiMatteo, M. R., & Friedman, H. S. (1982). *Social psychology and medicine.* Cambridge, MA: Oelgeschlager, Gunn, & Hain.

Dinsmore, W. W., Hodges, M., Hargreaves, C., Osterloh, I. H., Smith, M. D., & Rosen, R. C. (1999). Sildenafil citrate (Viagra) in erectile dysfunction: Near normalization in men with broad-spectrum erectile dysfunction compared with age-matched healthy control subjects. *Urology, 53,* 800–805.

Dion, K. K. (1972). Physical attractiveness and evaluations of children's transgressions. *Journal of Personality and Social Psychology, 24,* 285–290.

DiPietro, J. A., Hodgson, D. M., Costigan, K. A., & Johnson, T. R. (1996). Fetal antecedents of infant temperament. *Child Development, 67,* 2568–2583.

Dixon, J. F., & Hokin, L. E. (1998). Lithium acutely inhibits and chronically up-regulates and stabilizes glutamate uptake by presynaptic nerve endings in mouse cerebral cortex. *Proceedings of the National Academy of Sciences, 95,* 8363–8368.

Domhoff, G. W. (1996). *Finding meaning in dreams: A quantitative approach.* New York: Plenum.

Domjan, M. (1987). Animal learning comes of age. *American Psychologist, 42,* 556–564.

Domjan, M., & Purdy, J. E. (1995). Animal research in psychology: More than meets the eye of the general psychology student. *American Psychologist, 50,* 496–503.

Donatelle, R. J., & Davis, L. G. (1993). *Access to health* (2nd ed.). Englewood Cliffs, NJ: Prentice Hall.

Donnelly, C. L. (2003). Pharmacologic treatment approaches for children and adolescents with posttraumatic stress disorder. *Child and Adolescent Psychiatric Clinics of North America, 12,* 251–269.

Dorfman, W. I., & Leonard, S. (2001). The Minnesota Multiphasic Personality Inventory-2 (MMPI-2). In W. I. Dorfman & M. Hersen (Ed.), *Understanding psychological assessment: Perspectives on Individual Differences* (pp. 145–171). Dordrecht, Netherlands: Kluwer Academic Publishers.

Doty, R. L. (1989). Influence of age and age-related diseases on olfactory function. *Annals of the New York Academy of Sciences, 561,* 76–86.

Doty, R. L. (2001). Olfaction. *Annual Review of Psychology, 52,* 423–452.

Doty, R. L., Shaman, P., Applebaum, S. L., Giberson, R., Sikorski, L., & Rosenberg, L. (1984). Smell identification ability: Changes with age. *Science, 226,* 1441–1443.

Douglas, H. M., Moffitt, T. E., Dar, R., McGee, R., & Silva, P. (1995). Obsessive-compulsive disorder in a birth cohort of 18-year-olds: Prevalence and predictors. *Journal of the American Academy of Child and Adolescent Psychiatry, 34,* 1424–1429.

Dovidio, J. F., & Gaertner, S. I. (1999). Reducing prejudice: Combating intergroup biases. *Current Directions in Psychological Science, 8,* 101–105.

Downs, H. (1994, August 21). Must we age? *Parade Magazine,* pp. 3, 5, 7.

Doyle, R. (2000). By the numbers: Women and the professions. *Scientific American, 282*(4), 30–32

Drury, L. J. (2003). Community care for people who are homeless and mentally ill. *Journal of Health Care for the Poor and Underserved, 14,* 194–207.

Dryer, D. C., & Horowitz, L. M. (1997). When do opposites attract? Interpersonal complementary versus similarity. *Journal of Personality and Social Psychology 72,* 592–603.

Dryer, D. C., & Horowitz, L. M. (1997). When do opposites attract?: Interpersonal complementarity versus similarity. *Journal of Personality and Social Psychology, 72,* 592–603.

Du, L., Faludi, G., Palkovits, M., Demeter, E., Bakish, D., Lapierre, Y. D., Sotonyi, P., & Hrdina, P. D. (1999). Frequency of long allele in serotonin transporter gene is increased in depressed suicide victims. *Biological Psychiatry, 46,* 196–201.

Dubner, R., & Gold, M. (1998, December). *The neurobiology of pain.* Paper presented at the National Academy of Sciences colloquium, Irvine, CA.

Dugas, M. J., Ladouceur, R., Leger, E., Freeston, M. H., Langolis, F., Provencher, M. D., & Boisvert, J. M. (2003). Group cognitive behavioral therapy for generalized anxiety disorder: Treatment outcome and long-term follow-up. *Journal of Consulting and Clinical Psychology, 71,* 821–825.

Dumaine, B. (1990, Mary 7). Who needs a boss? *Fortune,* pp. 52–55, 58, 60.

Duncan, J., Seitz, R. J., Kolodny, J., Bor, D., Herzog, H., Ahmed, A., Newell, F. N., & Emslie, H. (2000, July 21). A neural basis for general intelligence. *Science, 285,* 457–460.

Dunkle, T. (1982, April). The sound of silence. *Science, 82,* pp. 30–33.

Dunn, R. L., & Schwebel, A. I. (1995). Meta-analytic review of marital therapy outcome research. *Journal of Family Psychology, 9,* 58–68.

E

Eacott, M. J. (1999). Memory for the events of early childhood. *Current Directions in Psychological Science, 8,* 46–48.

Eagly, A. H. (1992). Uneven progress: Social psychology and the study of attitudes. *Journal of Personality and Social Psychology, 63,* 693–710.

Eagly, A. H., & Chaiken, S. (1998). Attitude structure and function. In D. Gilbert, S. T. Fiske, & G. Lindzey (Eds.), *Handbook of Social Psychology* (4th ed., Vol. 2, pp. 269–322). New York: McGraw-Hill.

Eagly, A. H., & Steffen, V. J. (1986). Gender and aggressive behavior: A meta-analytic review of the social psychological literature. *Psychological Bulletin, 100,* 309–330.

Eagly, A. H., & Wood, W. (1999). The origins of sex differences in human behavior: Evolved dispositions versus social roles. *American Psychologist, 54,* 408–423.

Eagly, A. H., Johannesen-Schmidt, & van-Engen, M. L. (2003). Transformational, transactional, and laissez-faire leadership styles: A meta analysis comparing women and men. *Psychological Bulletin, 129,* 569–591.

Eaves, L. J., Heath, A. C., Neale, M. C., Hewitt, J. K., & Martin, N. G. (1993). *Sex differences and non-additivity in the effects of genes on personality.* Unpublished manuscript, cited in F. S. Mayer & K. Sutton. (1996). *Personality: An integrative approach.* Upper Saddle River, NJ: Prentice Hall.

Eccles, J., Midgley, C., Wigfield, A., Buchanan, C. M., Reuman, D., Flanagan, C., & MacIver, D. (1993). Development during adolescence: The impact of stage-environment fit on young adolescents' experiences in school and families. *American Psychologist: Special Issue: Adolescence, 48,* 90–101.

Eccleston, C., & Crombez, G. (1999). Pain demands attention: A cognitive-affective model of the interruptive function of pain. *Psychological Bulletin, 125,* 356–366.

Eckerman, C. O., Davis, C. C., & Didow, S. M. (1989). Toddlers' emerging ways of achieving social coordinations with a peer. *Child Development, 60,* 440–453.

Edelman, S., Lemon, J., Bell, D. R., & Kidman, A. D. (1999). Effects of group CBT on the survival time of patients with metastatic breast cancer. *Psycho-Oncology, 8,* 474–481.

Edwards, W. J. (1996). A sociological analysis of an in/visible minority group: Male adolescent homosexuals. *Youth and Society, 27,* 334–355.

Efklides, A., Niemivirta, M., & Yamauchi, H. (2002). Introduction:

Some issues on self-regulation to consider. *Psychologia: An International Journal of Psychology in the Orient, 45,* 207–210.

Egeth, H., & Lamy, D. (2003). Attention. In A. F. Healy & R. W. Proctor (Eds.), *Handbook of Psychology: Experimental Psychology, Vol. 4* (pp. 269–292). New York: John Wiley & Sons.

Eich, E., Macaulay, D., Loewenstein, R. J., & Dihle, P. H. (1997). Memory, amnesia, and dissociative identity disorder. *Psychological Science, 8,* 417–422.

Eich, J. E., Weingartner, H., Stillman, R. C., & Gillin, J. C. (1975). State dependent accessibility of retrieval cues in the retention of a categorized list. *Journal of Verbal Learning and Verbal Behavior, 14,* 408–417.

Eichenbaum, H. (1997). Declarative memory: Insights from cognitive neurobiology. *Annual Review of Psychology, 48,* 547–572.

Eimas, P. D., & Tartter, V. C. (1979). On the development of speech perception: Mechanisms and analogies. In H. W. Reese & L. P. Lipsitt (Eds.), *Advances in child development and behavior* (Vol. 13, pp. 155–193). New York: Academic Press.

Eisenberg, N., & Lennon, R. (1983). Sex differences in empathy and related capacities. *Psychological Bulletin, 94,* 100–131.

Eisenberger, R., & Cameron, J. (1996). Detrimental effects of reward. *American Psychologist, 51,* 1153–1166.

Eisenberger, R., & Rhoades, L. (2001). Incremental effects of reward on creativity. *Journal of Personality and Social Psychology, 81,* 728–741.

Eisenman, R. (1994). Birth order, effect on personality and behavior. In V. S. Ramachandran (Ed.), *Encyclopedia of human behavior* (Vol. 1, pp. 401–405). San Diego, CA: Academic Press.

Ekman, P. (1992). An argument for basic emotions. *Cognition and Emotion, 6,* 169–200.

Ekman, P. (1994). Strong evidence for universals in facial expressions: A reply to Russell's mistaken critique. *Psychological Bulletin, 115,* 268–287.

Ekman, P., & Friesen, W. V. (1971). Constants across cultures in the face and emotion. *Journal of Personality and Social Psychology, 17,* 124–129.

Ekman, P., & Friesen, W. V. (1975). *Unmasking the face.* Englewood Cliffs, NJ: Prentice Hall.

Ekman, P., & O'Sullivan, M. (1991). Who can catch a liar? *American Psychologist, 46,* 913–920.

Ekman, P., Friesen, W. V., & Ellsworth, P. (1972). *Emotion in the human face.* Elmsford, NY: Pergamon.

Ekman, P., Friesen, W. V., O'Sullivan, M., Chan, A., Diacoyanni-Tarlatzis, I., Heider, K., Krause, R., LeCompte, W. A., Pitcairn, T., Ricci-Bitti, P. E., Scherer, K., Tomita, M., & Tzavaras, A. (1987). Universals and cultural differences in the judgments of facial expressions of emotion. *Journal of Personality and Social Psychology, 53,* 712–717.

Ekman, P., Sorenson, E. R., & Friesen, W. V. (1969). Pancultural elements in facial displays of emotion. *Science, 164,* 86–88.

Elbert, T., Pantev, C., Wienbruch, C., Rockstroh, B., & Taub, E. (1995, October 13). Increased cortical representation of the fingers of the left hand in string players. *Science, 270,* 305–307.

Eley, T. C., & Stevenson, J. (1999). Exploring the covariation between anxiety and depression symptoms: A genetic analysis of the effects of age and sex. *Journal of Child Psychology & Psychiatry & Allied Disciplines, 40,* 1273–1282.

Eley, T. C., Bishop, D. V. M., Dale, P. S., Oliver, B., Petrill, S. A., Price, T. S., Saudino, K. J., Simonoff, E., Stevenson, J., Plomin, R., & Purcell, S. (1999). Genetic and environmental origins of verbal and performance components of cognitive delay in 2-year olds. *Developmental Psychology, 35,* 1122–1131.

Eley, T. C., Lichenstein, P., & Stevenson, J. (1999). Sex differences in the etiology of aggressive and nonaggressive antisocial behavior: Results from two twin studies. *Child Development, 70,* 155–168.

Elkind, D. (1968). Cognitive development in adolescence. In J. F. Adams (Ed.), *Understanding adolescence.* Boston: Allyn & Bacon.

Elkind, D. (1969). Egocentrism in adolescence. In R. W. Grinder (Ed.), *Studies in adolescence* (2nd ed.). New York: Macmillan.

Ellens, J. H. (2002). Psychological legitimization of violence by religious archetypes. In C. E. Stout (Ed.), *The psychology of terrorism: Theoretical understandings and perspectives, Vol. III. Psychological dimensions to war and peace* (pp. 149–162). Westport, CT: Praeger Publishers/Greenwood Publishing Group, Inc.

Ellis, A., & Harper, R. A. (1975). *A new guide to rational living.* North Hollywood, CA: Wilshire Book Co.

Ellis, A., & MacLaren, C. (1998). *Rational emotive behavior therapy: A therapist's guide.* San Luis Obispo, CA: Impact.

Ellis, L., & Coontz, P. D. (1990). Androgens, brain functioning, and criminality: The neurohormonal foundations of antisociality. In L. Ellis & H. Hoffman (Eds.), *Crime in biological, social, and moral contexts* (pp. 36–49). New York: Praeger Press.

Elloy, D. F., & Mackie, B. (2002). Overload and work-family conflict among Australian dual-career families: Moderating effects of support. *Psychological Reports, 91,* 907–913.

Ellsworth, P. C. (2002). Appraisal processes in emotion. In R. R. David-son, K. R. Scherer & H. H. Goldsmith (Eds.), *Handbook of affective science.* New York, NY: Oxford University Press.

Elzinga, B. M., & Bremner, J. D. (2002). Are the neural substrates of memory the final common pathway in post-traumatic stress disorder (PTSD)? *Journal of Affective Disorders, 70,* 1–17.

Emmorey, K. (1994). Sign language. In V. S. Ramachandran (Ed.), *Encyclopedia of human behavior* (Vol. 4, pp. 193–204). San Diego, CA: Academic Press.

Enard, W., Przeworski, M., Fisher, S. E., Lai, C. S. L., Wiebe, V., Kitano, T., Monaco, A., & Paeaebo, S. (2002). Molecular evolution of FOXP2, a gene involved in speech and language. *Nature, 418,* 869–872.

Engel, J. F., Black, R. D., & Miniard, P. C. (1986). *Consumer behavior.* Chicago: Dryden Press.

Engel, S., Zhang, X., & Wandell, B. (1997). Colour tuning in human visual cortex measured with functional magnetic resonance imaging. *Nature, 388,* 68–71.

Engen, T. (1982). *The perception of odors.* New York: Academic Press.

Enns, C. Z. (1993). Twenty years of feminist counseling and therapy: From naming biases to implementing multifaceted practice. *Counseling Psychologist, 21,* 3–87.

Epstein, A. N., Fitzsimmons, J. T., & Simmons, B. (1969). Drinking caused by the intracranial injection of angiotensin into the rat. *Journal of Physiology, 200,* 98–100.

Epstein, R., Kirshnit, C. E., Lanza, R. P., & Rubin, L. C. (1984). "Insight" in the pigeon: Antecedents and determinants of an intelligent performance. *Nature (London), 308,* 61–62.

Epstein, S. (1962). The measurement of drive and conflict in humans: Theory and experiment. In M. R. Jones (Ed.), *Nebraska Symposium on Motivation: Vol. 10* (pp. 127–209). Lincoln: University of Nebraska Press.

Erdley, C. A., & D'Agostino, P. R. (1988). Cognitive and affective components of automatic priming effects. *Journal of Personality and Social Psychology, 54,* 741–747.

Erickson, D. (1990). Electronic earful: Cochlear implants sound better all the time. *Scientific American, 263* (5), 132, 134.

Ericsson, K. A., & Charness, N. (1994). Expert performance. *American Psychologist, 49,* 725–747.

Ericsson, K. A., & Chase, W. G. (1982). Exceptional memory. *American Scientist, 70,* 607–615.

Erikson, E. H. (1968). *Identity: Youth and crisis.* New York: Norton.

Eriksson, P. S., Perfilieva, E., Björk-Eriksson, T., Alborn, A. M., Nordborg, C., Peterson, D. A., & Gage, F. H. (1998). Neurogenesis in the adult human hippocampus. *Nature Medicine, 4,* 1313–1317.

Eron, L. D. (1982). Parent-child interaction, television violence, and aggression of children. *American Psychologist, 37,* 197–211.

Esposito, M. D., Zarahn, E., & Aguirre, G. K. (1999). Event-related functional MRI: Implications for Cognitive Psychology. *Psychological Bulletin, 125,* 155–164.

Esterson, A. (1993). *Seductive mirage: An exploration of the work of Sigmund Freud.* Chicago: Open Court.

Esterson, A. (1998). Jeffrey Masson and Freud's seduction theory: A new fable based on old myths. *History of the Human Sciences, 11,* 1–21.

Esterson, A. (2002). The myth of Freud's ostracism by the medical community in 1896–1905: Jeffrey Masson's assault on truth. *History of Psychology, 5,* 115–134.

Evans, G. W., & English, K. (2002). The environment of poverty: Multiple stressor exposure, psychophysiological stress, and socioemotional adjustment. *Child Development, 73,* 1238–1248.

Evans, L. I., Rozelle, R. M., Lasater, T. M., Dembroski, R. M., & Allen, B. P. (1970). Fear arousal, persuasion and actual vs. implied behavioral change: New perspective utilizing a real-life dental hygiene program. *Journal of Personality and Social Psychology, 16,* 220–227.

Evans, R. B. (1999, December). A century of psychology. *APA Monitor,* pp. 14–30.

Exner, J. E. (1996). A comment on "the comprehensive system for the Rorschach: A critical examination." *Psychological Science, 7,* 11–13.

Eyer, J. (1977). Prosperity as a cause of death. *International Journal of Health Services, 7,* 125–150.

Eysenck, H. J. (1947). *Dimensions of personality.* London: Routledge & Kegan Paul.

Eysenck, H. J. (1952). The effects of psychotherapy: An evaluation. *Journal of Consulting and Clinical Psychology, 16,* 319–324.

Eysenck, H. J. (1970). *The structure of human personality* (3rd ed.). London: Methuen.

Eysenck, H. J. (1976). *The measurement of personality.* Baltimore, MD: University Park Press.

Eysenck, H. J. (1992). Four ways five factors are not basic. *Personality and Individual Differences, 13,* 667–673.

Eysenck, H. J. (1993). Commentary on Goldberg. *American Psychologist, 48,* 1299–1300.

F
- -

Fagiolini, M., & Hensch, T. K. (2000). Inhibitory threshold for critical-period activation in primary visual cortex. *Nature, 404,* 183–186.

Fagot, B. I. (1994). Parenting. In V. S. Ramachandran (Ed.), *Encyclopedia of human behavior* (Vol. 3, pp. 411–419). San Diego, CA: Academic Press.

Fairburn, C. G., & Brownell, K. D. (2002). *Eating disorders and obesity: A comprehensive handbook (2nd ed.).* London: Guildford Press.

Fairburn, C. G., & Wilson, G. T. (Eds.). (1993). *Binge eating: Nature, assessment and treatment.* New York: Guilford Press.

Fairburn, C. G., Cooper, Z., & Shafran, R. (2003). Cognitive behaviour therapy for eating disorders: A transdiagnostic theory and treatment. *Behaviour Research and Therapy, 41,* 509–528.

Fallon, A., & Rozin, P. (1985). Sex differences in perceptions of desirable body states. *Journal of Abnormal Psychology, 84,* 102–105.

Fantz, R. L., Fagan, J. F., & Miranda, S. B. (1975). Early visual selectivity. In L. B. Cohen & P. Salapatek (Eds.), *Infant perception: From sensation to cognition* (Vol. 1, pp. 249–346). New York: Academic Press.

Farber, S. (1981, January). Telltale behavior of twins. *Psychology Today,* pp. 58–62, 79–80.

Farthing, C. W. (1992). *The psychology of consciousness.* Englewood Cliffs, NJ: Prentice Hall.

Fausto-Sterling, A. (1993, March/April). The five sexes. *The Sciences,* pp. 20–25.

Fausto-Sterling, A. (2000a). *Sexing the body.* New York: Basic Books.

Fausto-Sterling, A. (2000b, July/August). The five sexes, revisited. *The Sciences,* pp. 18–23.

Featherstone, R. E., Fleming, A. S., & Ivy, G. O. (2000). Plasticity in the maternal circuit: Effects of experience and partum condition on brain astrocycte number in female rats. *Behavioral Neuroscience, 114,* 158–172.

Fehr, B. (1994). Prototype-based assessment of laypeople's views of love. *Personal Relationships, 1,* 309–331.

Feinauer, L., Hilton, H. G., & Callahan, E. H. (2003). Hardiness as a moderator of shame associated with childhood sexual abuse. *American Journal of Family Therapy, 31,* 65–78.

Feingold, A. (1992). Good-looking people are not what we think. *Psychological Bulletin, 111,* 304–341.

Feinson, M. C. (1986). Aging widows and widowers: Are there mental health differences? *International Journal of Aging and Human Development, 23,* 244–255.

Fejr, S. S. (2003). *Introduction to group therapy: A practical guide* (2nd ed.). New York, NY: Haworth Press, Inc.

Feldhusen, J. F., & Goh, B. E. (1995). Assessing and accessing creativity: An integrative review of theory, research, and development. *Creativity Research Journal, 8,* 231–247.

Feldman, R. S., Salzinger, S., Rosario, M., Alvarado, L., Caraballo, L., & Hammer, M. (1995). Parent, teacher, and peer ratings of physically abused and nonmaltreated children's behavior. *Journal of Abnormal Child Psychology*, *23*, 317–334.

Feng, A. S., & Ratnam, R. (2000). Neural basis of hearing in real-world situations. *Annual Review of Psychology*, *51*, 699–725.

Ferguson, C. A., & Macken, M. A. (1983). The role of play in phonological development. In K. E. Nelson (Ed.), *Children's language* (Vol. 4). Hillsdale, NJ: Erlbaum.

Fernandez, G., Klaver, P., Fell, J., Grunwald, T., & Elger, C. E. (2002). Human declarative memory formation: Segregating rhinal and hippocampal contributions. *Hippocampus*, *12*, 514–519.

Festinger, L. (1957). *A theory of cognitive dissonance*. Evanston, IL: Row, Peterson.

Fibiger, H. C., Murray, C. L., & Phillips, A. G. (1983). Lesions of the nucleus basalis magoncellularis impair long-term memory in rats. *Society for Neuroscience Abstracts*, *9*, 332.

Fiedler, F. E. (1967). *A theory of leadership effectiveness*. New York: McGraw-Hill.

Fiedler, F. E. (1993). The leadership situation and the black box contingency theories. In M. Chemers & R. Ayman (Eds.), *Leadership theory and research: Perspective and directions* (pp. 1–28). San Diego, CA: Academic Press.

Fiedler, F. E. (2002). The curious role of cognitive resources in leadership. In R. E. Riggio & S. E. Murphy (Eds.), *Multiple intelligences and leadership. LEA's organization and management series* (pp. 91–104). Mahwah, NJ, Lawrence Erlbaum Associates, Publishers.

Field, T. M. (1986). Interventions for premature infants. *Journal of Pediatrics*, *109*, 183–191.

Filipek, P. A., Accardo, P. J., Ashwal, S., Baranek, G. T., Cook, E. H., Dawson, G., Gordon, B., Gravel, U. S., Johnson, C. P., Kallen, R. J., Levy, S. E., Minshew, N. J., Ozonoff, S., Prizant, B. M., Rapin, I., Rogers, S. J., Stone, W. L., Teplin, S. W., Tuchman, R. F., & Volkmar, F. R. (2000). Practice parameter: Screening and diagnosis of autism. *Neurology*, *55*, 468–479.

Filipek, P. A., Semrund-Clikeman, M., Steingard, R. J., Renshaw, P. R., Kennedy, D. N., & Biederman, J. (1997). Volumetric MRI analysis comparing subjects having attention-deficit hyperactivity disorder with normal controls. *Neurology*, *48*, 589–601.

Finkelhor, D., Hotaling, G., Lewis, I. A., & Smith, C. (1990). Sexual abuse in a national sample of adult men and women: Prevalence, characteristics, and risk factors. *Child Abuse and Neglect*, *14*, 19–28.

Finkenauer, C., Luminet, O., Gisle, L., El-Ahmadi, A., Van der Linden, M., &

Philippot, P. (1998). Flashbulb memories and the underlying mechanisms of their formation: Toward an emotional-integrative model. *Memory & Cognition*, *26*, 516–531.

Finn, P. R., Sharkansky, E. J., Brandt, K. M., & Turcotte, N. (2000). The effects of familial risk, personality, and expectancies on alcohol use and abuse. *Journal of Abnormal Psychology*, *109*, 122–133.

Fischhoff, B. (1975). Hindsight & foresight: The effect of outcome knowledge on the judgment under uncertainty. *Journal of Experimental Psychology: Human Perception and Performance*, *1*, 288–299.

Fischhoff, B., & Downs, J. (1997). Accentuate the relevant. *Psychological Science*, *8*, 154–158.

Fischman, J. (1985, September). Mapping the mind. *Psychology Today*, pp. 18–19.

Fisher, S., & Greenberg, R. (1996). *Freud scientifically appraised*. New York: Wiley.

Fisher, S., & Greenberg, R. P. (1985). *The scientific credibility of Freud's theories and therapy*. New York: Columbia University Press.

Fiske, S. (1995). Social cognition. In A. Tesser (Ed.), *Advanced social psychology* (pp. 149–194). New York: McGraw-Hill.

Fiske, S. T., & Neuberg, S. L. (1990). A continuum of impression formation, from category-based to individuating processes: Influence of information and motivation on attention and interpretation. In M. P. Zanna (Ed.), *Advances in experimental social psychology* (Vol. 23, pp. 399–427). New York: Academic Press.

Fiske, S. T., & Taylor, S. E. (1991). *Social cognition* (2nd ed.). New York: McGraw-Hill.

Fitzgerald, S. (1999, October 11). "Brain exercise" under scrutiny to aid attention deficit. *Charlotte Observer*, p. 12E.

Flannery, R. B. (2002). Treating learned helplessness in the elderly dementia patient: Preliminary inquiry. *American Journal of Alzheimer's Disease and Other Dementias*, *17*, 345–349.

Flavell, J. F. (1986). The development of children's knowledge about the appearance-reality distinction. *American Psychologist*, *41*, 418–425.

Flavell, J. H. (1999). Cognitive development: Children's knowledge about the mind. *Annual Review of Psychology*, *50*, 21–45.

Flavell, J. H., Miller, P. H., & Miller, S. A. (2002). *Cognitive development* (4th ed.). Upper Saddle River, NJ: Prentice Hall.

Fleeson, W. (1998, July). Across-time within-person structures of personality: Common and individual traits. In G. V. Caprara & D. Cervone (Chairs), *Personality and social cognition*. Symposium conducted at the 9th European

Conference on Personality, Guildford, United Kingdom.

Flieller, A. (1999). Comparison of the development of formal thought in adolescent cohorts aged 10–15 years. *Developmental Psychology*, *35*, 1048–1058.

Flier, J. S., & Maratos-Flier, E. (1998). Obesity and the hypothalamus: Novel peptides for new pathways. *Cell*, *92*, 437–440.

Flor, H., Elbert, T., Knecht, S., Wienbruch, C., & Pantev, C. (1995). Phantom-limb pain as a perceptual correlate of cortical reorganization following arm amputation. *Nature*, *375*, 482–484.

Flynn, J. R. (1984). The mean IQ of Americans: Massive gains 1932 to 1978. *Psychological Bulletin*, *95*, 29–51.

Flynn, J. R. (1987). Massive IQ gains in 14 nations: What IQ tests really measure. *Psychological Bulletin*, *101*, 171–191.

Flynn, J. R. (1999). Searching for justice: The discovery of IQ gains over time. *American Psychologist*, *54*, 5–20.

Flynn, P. M., Luckey, J. W., Brown, B. S., Hoffman, J. A., Dunteman, G. H., Theisen, A. C., Hubbard, R. L., Needle, R., Schneider, S. J., Koman, J. J., Atef-Vahid, M., Karson, S., Palsgrove, G. L., & Yates, B. T. (1995). Relationship between drug preference and indicators of psychiatric impairment. *American Journal of Drug and Alcohol Abuse*, *21*, 153–166.

Fogelman, E., & Wiener, V. L. (1985, August). The few, the brave, the noble. *Psychology Today*, pp. 60–65.

Folkman, S., & Moskowitz, S. T. (2000). Positive affect and the other side of coping. *American Psychologist*, *55*, 647–654.

Folkman, S., Chesney, M. A., & Christopher-Richards, A. (1994). Stress and coping in partners of men with AIDS. *Psychiatric Clinics of North America*, *17*, 33–55.

Ford, B. D. (1993). Emergenesis: An alternative and a confound. *American Psychologist*, *48*, 1294.

Ford, W. C. L., North, K., Taylor, H., Farrow, A., Hull, M. G. R., & Golding, J. (2000). Increasing paternal age is associated with delayed conception in a large population of fertile couples: Evidence for declining fecundity in older men. *Human Reproduction*, *15*, 1703–1708.

Ford-Mitchell, D. (1997, November 12). Daydream your way to better health. *Ann Arbor News*, p. C3.

Forgatch, M. S., & DeGarmo, D. S. (1999). Parenting through change: An effective prevention program for single mothers. *Journal of Consulting and Clinical psychology*, *67*, 711–724.

Foulkes, D. (1999). Childrens dreaming and the development of consciousness. Cambridge, MA: Harvard University Press.

Fouts, R. (with S. T. Mills). (1997). *Next of kin: What chimpanzees have taught me about who we are*. New York: William Morrow.

Fouts, R. S. (1973). Acquisition and testing of gestural signs in four young chimpanzees. *Science*, *180*, 978–980.

Fowles, D. C. (1992). Schizophrenia: Diathesis-stress revisited. *Annual Review of Psychology*, *43*, 303–336.

Foxcroft, D. R., Ireland, D., Lister, S. D. J., Lowe, G., & Breen, R. (2003). Longer-term primary prevention for alcohol misuse in young people: a systematic review. *Addiction*, *98*, 397–411.

Frager, R. (1970). Conformity and anticonformity in Japan. *Journal of Personality and Social Psychology*, *15*, 203–210.

Frank, J. D., & Frank, J. B. (1991). *Persuasion and healing* (3rd ed.). Baltimore: Johns Hopkins University Press.

Freedman, J. L., & Fraser, S. C. (1966). Compliance without pressure: The foot-in-the-door technique. *Journal of Personality and Social Psychology*, *4*, 195–202.

Freeman, W., Brebner, K., Lynch, W., Patel, K., Robertson, D., Roberts, D. C., & Vrana, K. E. (2002). *Molecular Brain Research*, *104*, 11–20.

Freud, S. (1900). The interpretation of dreams. In J. Strachey (Ed. and Trans.), *The standard edition of the complete psychological works of Sigmund Freud* (Vol. 4, pp. 1–331). London: Hogarth Press.

Freudenberger, H. J. (1983). Hazards of psychotherapeutic practice. *Psychotherapy in Private Practice*, *1*, 83–89.

Frezza, M., di Padova, C., Pozzato, G., Terpin, M., Baraona, E., & Lieber, C. S. (1990). High blood alcohol levels in women: The role of decreased gastric alcohol dehydrogenase activity and first-pass metabolism. *New England Journal of Medicine*, *322*, 95–99.

Friedman, H. S. (2002). *Health Psychology* (2nd ed.). Upper Saddle River NJ: Prentice Hall.

Friedman, M. J., Schnurr, P. P., & McDonagh-Coyle, A. (1994). Posttraumatic stress disorder in the military veteran. *Psychiatric Clinics of North America*, *17*, 265–277.

Friedman, M., & Rosenman, R. H. (1959). Association of specific overt behavior patterns with blood and cardiovascular findings: Blood cholesterol level, blood clotting time, incidence of arcus senilis and clinical coronary artery disease. *Journal of the American Medical Association*, *169*, 1286–1296.

Friedman, M., Breall, W. S., Goodwin, M. L., Sparagon, B. J., Ghandour, G., & Fleischmann, N. (1996). Effect of Type A behavioral counseling on frequency of episodes of silent myocardial ischemia in coronary patients. *American Heart Journal*, *132*, 933–937.

Friman, P. C., Allen, K. D., Kerwin, M. L. E., & Larzelere, R. (1993). Changes in modern psychology. *American Psychology, 48,* 658–664.

Froelich, L., & Hoyer, S. (2002). The etiological and pathogenetic heterogeneity of Alzheimer's disease. *Nervenarzi, 73,* 422–427.

Fu, Q., Heath, A. C., Bucholz, K. K., Nelson, E., Goldberg, J., Lyons, M. J., True, W. R., Jacob, T., Tsuang, M. T., & Eisen, S. A. (2002). Shared genetic risk of major depression, alcohol dependence, and marijuana dependence: Contribution of antisocial personality disorder in men. *Archives of General Psychiatry, 59,* 1125–1132.

Fu, Q., Heath, A. C., Bucholz, K. K., Nelson, E., Goldberg, J., Lyons, M. J., True, W. R., Jacob, T., Tsuang, M. T., & Eisen, S. A. (2002). Shared genetic risk of major depression, alcohol dependence, and marijuana dependence: Contributions of antisocial personality disorder in men. *Archives of General Psychiatry, 59,* 1125–1132.

Fuchs, T., Birbaumer, N., Lutzenberger, W., Gruzelier, J. H., & Kaiser, J. (2003). Neurofeedback treatment for attention-deficit/hyperactivity disorder in children: A comparison with methylphenidate. *Applied Psychophysiology and Biofeedback, 28,* 1–12.

Fultz, D. E. (2002). Behaviorism and neurofeedback: Still married. *Journal of Neurotherapy, 6,* 67–74.

Funder, D. C. (1991). Global traits: A neo-Allportian approach to personality. *Psychological Science, 2,* 31–39.

Funder, D. C. (1995). On the accuracy of personality judgment: A realistic approach. *Psychological Review, 102,* 652–670.

Furstenberg, F. F., Jr., Brooks-Gunn, J., & Chase-Lansdale, L. (1989). Teenaged pregnancy and childbearing. *American Psychologist, 44,* 313–320.

Furumoto, L. (1980). Mary Whiton Calkins (1863–1930). *Psychology of Women Quarterly, 5,* 55–68.

Furumoto, L., & Scarborough, E. (1986). Placing women in the history of psychology: The first American women psychologists. *American Psychologist, 41,* 35–42.

Fuster, J. M. (1997). The prefrontal cortex. New York: Raven Press.

G

Gable, M., Wilkens, H. T., Harris, L., & Feinberg, R. (1987). An evaluation of subliminally embedded sexual stimuli in graphics. *Journal of Advertising, 16,* 25–31.

Gabrieli, J. D. E. (1998). Cognitive neuroscience of human memory. *Annual Review of Psychology, 49,* 87–115.

Gabrieli, J. D., Desmond, J. E., Bemb, J. B., Wagner, A. D., Stone, M. V., Vaidya, C. J., & Glover, G. H. (1996). Functional magnetic resonance imaging of semantic memory processes in the frontal lobes. *Psychological Science, 7,* 278–283.

Gage, F. H. (2000, February 25). Mammalian neural stem cells. *Science, 287,* 1433–1438.

Galambos, N. L., & Leadbeater, B. J. (2002). Transitions in adolescent research. In W. W. Hartup & R. K. Silbereisen (Eds.), *Growing points in developmental science: An introduction* (pp. 287–306). Philadelphia, PA: Psychology Press.

Galanter, M. (1984). Self-help large-group therapy for alcoholism: A controlled study. *Alcoholism, Clinical and Experimental Research, 8,* 16–23.

Galef, B. G. (1993). Functions of social learning about food: A causal analysis of effects of diet novelty on preference transmission. *Animal Behaviour, 46,* 257–261.

Gallistel, C. R. (1981). Bell, Magendie, and the proposals to restrict the use of animals in neurobehavioral research. *American Psychologist, 36,* 357–360.

Gallup, G. G., Jr. (1985). Do minds exist in species other than our own? *Neuroscience and Biobehavioral Reviews, 9,* 631–641.

Gallup, G. G., Jr. (1998). Self-awareness and the evolution of social intelligence. *Behavioural Processes, 42,* 239–247.

Gandhi, N., Depauw, K. P., Dolny, D. G., & Freson, T. (2002). Effect of an exercise program on quality of life of women with fibromyalgia. *Women and Therapy, 25,* 91–103.

Garb, H. N., Florio, C. M., & Grove, W. M. (1998). The validity of the Rorschach and the Minnesota Multiphasic Personality Inventory: Results from meta-analysis. *Psychological Science, 9,* 402–404.

Garber, H., & Heber, R. (1982). Modification of predicted cognitive development in high risk children through early intervention. In D. K. Detterman & R. J. Sternberg (Eds.), *How and how much can intelligence be increased?* (pp. 121–137). Norwood, NJ: Ablex.

Garcia, J., & Koelling, R. A. (1966). Relation of cue to consequence in avoidance learning. *Psychonomic Science, 4,* 123–124.

Garcia, J., Kimeldorf, D. J., Hunt, E. L., & Davies, B. P. (1956). Food and water consumption of rats during exposure to gamma radiation. *Radiation Research, 4,* 33–41.

Gardner, H. (1983). *Frames of mind: The theory of multiple intelligences.* New York: Basic Books.

Gardner, H. (1993). *Multiple intelligences: The theory in practice.* New York: Basic Books.

Gardner, H. (1998). A multiplicity of intelligences. *Scientific American, 9*(4), 19–22.

Gardner, H. (1999). *Intelligence reframed: Multiple intelligences for the 21st century.* New York: Basic Books, Inc.

Gardner, R. A., & Gardner, B. T. (1969). Teaching sign language to a chimpanzee. *Science, 165,* 664–672.

Gardner, R. A., & Gardner, B. T. (1975). Evidence for sentence constituents in the early utterances of child and chimpanzee. *Journal of Experimental Psychology: General, 3,* 244–267.

Gardner, R. A., & Gardner, B. T. (1977). Comparative psychology and language acquisition. In K. Salzinger & R. Denmark (Eds.), *Psychology: The state of the art* (pp. 37–76). New York: New York Academy of Sciences.

Garfield, S. L. (Ed.). (1983). Special section: Meta-analysis and psychotherapy. *Journal of Consulting and Clinical Psychology, 51,* 3–75.

Garnets, L. K. (2002). Sexual orientation in perspective. *Cultural Diversity and Ethnic Minority Psychology, 8,* 115–129.

Garry, M., & Polaschek, D. L. L. (2000). Imagination and memory. *Current Directions in Psychological Science, 9,* 6–10.

Gartstein, M. A., & Rothbart, M. K. (2003). Studying infant temperament via the revised infant behavior questionnaire. *Infant Behavior and Development, 26,* 64–86.

Gathchel, R. J., & Oordt, M. S. (2003). Insomnia. In R. J. Gathchel & M. S. Oordt (Eds.) *Clinical health psychology and primary care: Practical advice and clinical guidance for successful collaboration* (pp. 135–148). Washington, D.C.: American Psychological Association.

Gazzaniga, M. S., Fendrich, R., & Wessiner, C. M. (1994). Blindsight reconsidered. *Current Directions in Psychological Science, 3,* 93–96.

Gécz, J., & Mulley, J. (2000). Genes for cognitive function: Developments on the X. *Genome Research, 10,* 157–163.

Geen, R. G. (1998). Aggression and antisocial behavior. In D. Gilbert, S. T. Fiske, & G. Lindzey (Eds.), *Handbook of social psychology* (4th ed., Vol. 2, pp. 317–356). Boston: McGraw-Hill.

Geldard, F. A. (1972). *The human senses* (2nd ed.). New York: Wiley.

Gelles, R. J., & Levine, A. (1999). *Sociology: An Introduction,* (6th Ed.), Figure 9–7, p. 338. data from *USA Today.* June 11, 1997, p. 9a.

Gelman, D. (1990, October 29). A fresh take on Freud. *Newsweek,* pp. 84–86.

Gelman, D. (1994, June 13). Reliving the painful past. *Newsweek,* pp. 20–22.

George, L. K. (2001). The social psychology of health. In R. H. Binstock & L. K. George (Eds.), *Handbook of the psychology of aging* (5th ed.). San Diego: Academic Press.

Gerber, D. J., Hall, D., Miyakawa, T., Demars, S., Gogos, J. A., Karayiorgou, M., & Tonegawa, S. (2003). Evidence for association of schizophrenia with genetic variation in 8p21.3 gene, PPP3ccc, encoding the calcineurin gamma subunit. *Proceedings of the National Academy of Sciences, 100,* 8993–8998.

Gergen, K. J. (1973). The codification of research ethics—views of a Doubting Thomas. *American Psychologist, 28,* 907–912.

Gernsbacher, M. A., & Kaschak, M. P. (2003). Neuroimaging studies of language production and comprehension. *Annual Review of Psychology, 54,* 91–114.

Gershoff, E. T. (2002). Corporal punishment by parents and associated child behaviors and experiences: A meta-analytic and theoretical review. *Psychological Bulletin, 128,* 539–579.

Gershon, E. S. (1990). Genetics. In F. K. Goodwin & K. R. Jamison (Eds.), *Manic depressive illness* (pp. 373–401). New York: Oxford University Press.

Gershon, S., & Soares, J. C. (1997). Current therapeutic profile of lithium. *Archives of General Psychiatry, 54,* 16–20.

Getzels, J. W. (1975). Problem finding and the inventiveness of solutions. *Journal of Creative Behavior, 9,* 12–18.

Gfeller, J. D. (1994). Hypnotizability enhancement: Clinical implications of empirical findings. *American Journal of Clinical Hypnosis, 37,* 107–116.

Gibson, R. L., & Mitchell, M. (2003). *Introduction to counseling and guidance* (6th Ed.). Upper Saddle River, NJ: Prentice Hall.

Giese-Davis, J., Koopman, C., Butler, L. D., Classen, C., Cordova, M., Fobair, P., Benson, J., Draemer, H. C., & Spiegel, D. (2002). Change in emotion-regulation strategy for women with metastic breast cancer following supportive-expressive group therapy. *Journal of Consulting and Clinical Psychology, 70,* 916–925.

Gilbert, D. (1998). Ordinary personology. In D. Gilbert, S. T. Fiske, & G. Lindzey (Eds.), *Handbook of social psychology* (4th ed., Vol. 2, pp. 89–150). New York: McGraw-Hill.

Gilbert, D. T., & Malone, P. S. (1995). The correspondence bias. *Psychological Bulletin, 117,* 21–38.

Gilbert, L. A. (1994). Current perspectives on dual-career families. *Current Directions in Psychological Science, 3,* 101–105.

Gilligan, C. (1982). *In a different voice: Psychological theory and women's development.* Cambridge, MA: Harvard University Press.

Gilligan, C. (1992, August). *Joining the resistance: Girls' development in adolescence.* Paper presented at the meeting of the American Psychological Association, Montreal.

Gilman, S. L. (2001). Karen Horney, M. D., 1885–1952. *American Journal of Psychiatry, 158,* 1205.

Gilovich, T. (1991). *How we know what isn't so: The fallibility of human reason in everyday life.* New York: Free Press.

Ginsberg, H. (1972). *The myth of the deprived child.* Englewood Cliffs, NJ: Prentice Hall.

Glassman, A. H., & Koob, G. F. (1996). Neuropharmacology—Psychoactive smoke. *Nature, 379,* 677–678.

Gnanadesikan, M., Freeman, M. P., & Gelenberg, A. J. (2003). Alternatives to lithium and divalproex in the maintenance treatment of bipolar disorder. *Bipolar Disorders, 5,* 203–216.

Gobet, F. L., Peter, C. R., Croker, S., Cheng, P., Jones, G., Oliver, I., & Pine, J. M. (2001). Chunking mechanisms in human learning. *Trends in Cognitive Sciences, 5,* 236–243.

Godden, D. R., & Baddeley, A. D. (1975). Context-dependent memory in two natural environments: On land and underwater. *British Journal of Psychology, 66,* 325–331.

Goerge, R. M., & Lee, B. J. (1997). Abuse and neglect of the children. In R. A. Maynard (Ed.), *Kids having kids: Economic costs and social consequences of teen pregnancy* (pp. 205–230). Washington, DC: Urban Institute Press.

Gold, M. S. (1994). The epidemiology, attitudes, and pharmacology of LSD use in the 1990s. *Psychiatric Annals, 24,* 124–126.

Goldberg, L. R. (1993). The structure of phenotypic personality traits. *American Psychologist, 48,* 26–34.

Goldman, W., McCulloch, J., Cuffel, B., Zarin, D., Suarez, A., & Burns, B. (1998). Outpatient utilization patterns of integrated and split psychotherapy and pharmacotherapy for depression. *Psychiatric Services, 49,* 477–482.

Goldney, R. D. (2003). Deinstitutionalization and suicide. *Crisis, 24,* 39–40.

Goldsmith, H. H. (2002). Genetics of emotional development. In R. J. Davidson, K. R., Scherer, & H. H. Goldsmith (Eds.), *Handbook of affective sciences.* New York, NY: Oxford University Press.

Goldsmith, H. H., & Harman, C. (1994). Temperament and attachment: Individuals and relationships. *Current Directions in Psychological Sciences, 3,* 53–57.

Goldstein, E. B. (1999). *Sensation and perception* (5th ed.). Pacific Grove, CA: Brooks-Cole.

Goldstein, I., Lue, T. F., Padma-Nathan, H., Rosen, R. C., Steers, W. D., & Wicker, P. A. (1998). Oral sildenafil in the treatment of erectile dysfunction. Sildenafil study group. *New England Journal of Medicine, 338,* 1397–1404.

Goleman, D. (1996, February 26). Studies suggest older minds are stronger than expected. *New York Times,* p. A1.

Goleman, D. (1997). *Emotional intelligence.* New York: Bantam Books.

Goleman, D., Boyatzis, R., & McKee, A. (2002). *Primal leadership: Realizing the power of emotional intelligence.* Boston, MA: Harvard Business School Press.

Golomb, J., Kluger, A., de Leon, M. J., Ferris, S. H., Convit, A., Mittelman, M. S., Cohen, J., Rusinek, H., DeSanti, S., & George, A. E. (1994). Hippocampal formation size in normal human aging: A correlate of delayed secondary memory performance. *Learning & Memory, 1,* 45–54.

Goodall, J. (1971). *In the shadow of man.* New York: Dell.

Goode, E. (1992, December 7). Spiritual questing. *U. S. News & World Report,* pp. 64–71.

Goodman, P. S., Devadas, R., & Griffith (Hughson), T. L. (1988). Groups and productivity: Analyzing the effectiveness of self-managing teams. In J. P. Campbell, R. J. Campbell, & Associates (Eds.), *Productivity in organizations: New perspectives from industrial and organizational psychology* (pp. 295–325). San Francisco, CA: Jossey-Bass.

Goodwin, P. J., Leszcz, M., Ennis, M., Koopmans, J., Vincent, L., Guther, H., Drysdale, E., Hundleby, M., Chochinov, H. M., Navarro, M., Speca, M., & Hunter, J. (2001). The effect of group psychosocial support on survival in metastatic breast cancer. *New England Journal of Medicine, 345,* 1719–1726.

Gopnik, A., Meltzoff, A. N., & Kuhl, P. (1999). *The scientist in the crib: Minds, brains and how children learn.* New York: William Morrow.

Gordis, E. (1996). Alcohol research: At the cutting edge. *Archives of General Psychiatry, 53,* 199–201.

Gosling, S. D., & John, O. P. (1999). Personality dimensions in nonhuman animals: A cross-species review. *Current Directions in Psychological Science, 8,* 69–75.

Gotesdam, K. G., & Agras, W. S. (1995). General population based epidemiological survey of eating disorders in Norway. *International Journal of Eating Disorders, 18,* 119–126.

Gottesman, I. I. (1991). *Schizophrenia genesis: The origins of madness.* New York: Freeman.

Gouzoulis-Mayfrank, E., Daumann, J., Tuchtenhagen, F., Pelz, S., Becker, S., Kunert, H. J., Fimm, B., & Sass, H. (2000). Impaired cognitive performance in drug free users of recreational ecstasy (MDMA). *Journal of Neurology, Neurosurgery and Psychiatry, 68,* 719–725.

Graen, G. B, & Hui, C. (2001). Approaches to leadership: Toward a complete contingency model of face-to-face leadership. In M. Erez & U. Kleinbeck (Eds.). *Work motivation in the context of a globalizing economy* (pp. 211–225). Mahwah, NJ: Lawrence Erlbaum Associates, Publishers.

Grafton, S. T., Mazziotta, J. C., Presty, S., Friston, K. J., Frackowiak, R. S. J., & Phelps, M. E. (1992). Functional anatomy of human procedural learning determined with regional cerebral

blood flow and PET. *Journal of Neuroscience, 12,* 2542–2548.

Graham, K. (1997). *Personal history.* New York: Knopf.

Grandey, A. A. (2000). Emotional regulation in the workplace: A new way to conceptualize emotional labor. *Journal of Occupational Health Psychology, 5,* 95–110.

Grant, J. E., Kim, S. W., & Eckert, E. D. (2002). Body dysmorphic disorder in patients with anorexia nervosa: Prevalence, clinical features and delusionality of body image. *International Journal of Eating Disorders, 32,* 291–300.

Gray, P. B., Kahlenberg, S. M., Barrett, E. S., Lipson, S. F., & Ellison, P. T. (2002). Marriage and fatherhood are associated with lower testosterone in males. *Evolution and Human Behavior, 23,* 193–201.

Green, J. P., & Lynn, S. J. (2000). Hypnosis and suggestion-based approaches to smoking cessation: An examination of the evidence. *International Journal of Clinical & Experimental Hypnosis [Special Issue: The Status of Hypnosis as an Empirically Validated Clinical Intervention], 48,* 195–224.

Green, J. T., & Woodruff-Pak, D. S. (2000). Eyeblink classical conditioning: Hippocampal formation is for neutral stimulus associations as cerebellum is for association-response. *Psychological Bulletin, 126,* 138–158.

Greene, J., & Haidt, J. (2002). How (and where) does moral judgment work? *Trends in Cognitive Sciences, 6,* 517–523.

Greene, R. L. (1987). Effects of maintenance rehearsal on human memory. *Psychological Bulletin, 102,* 403–413.

Greenfield, P. M. (1997). You can't take it with you: Why ability assessments don't cross cultures. *American Psychologist, 52,* 1115–1124.

Greenfield, P. M. (1998). The cultural evolution of IQ. In U. Neisser (Ed.), *The rising curve: Long-term gains in IQ and related measures* (pp. 81–123). Washington, DC: American Psychological Association.

Greenfield, P.M., & Smith, J. H. (1976). *The structure of communication in early language development.* New York: Academic Press.

Greenstein, T. H. (1993). Maternal employment and child behavioral outcomes. *Journal of Family Issues, 14,* 323–354.

Greenwald, A. G. (1992). New Look 3: Unconscious cognition reclaimed. *American Psychologist, 47,* 766–779.

Greenwald, A. G., & Banaji, M. R. (1995). Implicit social cognition: Attitudes, self-esteem, and stereotypes. *Psychological Review, 102,* 4–27.

Greenwald, A. G., Spangenberg, E. R., Pratkanis, A. R., & Eskenazi, J. (1991). Double-blind tests of subliminal self-

help audiotapes. *Psychological Science, 2,* 119–122.

Griffiths, R. A., & Channon-Little, L. D. (1995). Dissociation, dieting disorders and hypnosis: A review. *European Eating Disorders Review [Special Issue: Dissociation and the Eating Disorders], 3,* 148–159.

Gruber, H. E., & Wallace, D. B. (2001). Creative work: The case of Charles Darwin. *American Psychologist, 56,* 346–349.

Guenther, V. K., Schaefer, P., Holzner, B. J., & Kemmler, G. W. (2003). Long-term improvements in cognitive performance through computer-assisted cognitive training: A pilot study in a residential home for older people. *Aging and Mental Health, 7,* 200–206.

Guérin, D. (1994, August). *Fussy infants at risk.* Paper presented at the meeting of the American Psychological Association, Los Angeles.

Gunderson, J. G. (1984). *Borderline personality disorder.* Washington, DC: American Psychiatric Press.

Gunderson, J. G. (1994). Building structure for the borderline construct. *Acta Psychiatrica Scandinavica, 89*(Suppl. 379), 12–18.

Gunne, L. M., & Anggard, E. (1972). *Pharmical kinetic studies with amphetamines—relationship to neuropsychiatric disorders.* International Symposium on Pharmical Kinetics, Washington, DC.

Gurman, A. S., & Kniskern, D. P. (1991). *Handbook of family therapy* (Vol. 2). Philadelphia, PA: Brunner/ Mazel, Inc.

Gurvits, T. V., Gilbertson, M. W., Lasko, N. B., Orr, S. P., & Pitman, R. K. (1997). Neurological status of combat veterans and adult survivors of sexual abuse PTSD. *Annals of the New York Academy of Sciences, 821,* 468–471.

Gurwitch, R. H., Sitterle, K. A., Young, B. H., & Pfefferbaum, B. (2002). The aftermath of terrorism. In A. M. La Greca & W. K. Silverman (Eds.), *Helping children cope with disasters and terrorism* (pp. 327–357). Washington, DC: American Psychological Association.

Guthrie, R. (1976). *Even the rat was white.* New York: Harper & Row.

Guzder, J., Paris, J., Zelkowitz, P., & Marchessault, K. (1996). Risk factors for borderline personality in children. *Journal of the American Academy of Child and Adolescent Psychiatry, 35,* 26–33.

H

Haber, R. N. (1969). Eidetic images. *Scientific American, 220*(4), 36–44.

Haberlandt, K. (1997). *Cognitive psychology.* Boston: Allyn & Bacon.

Hack, M., Breslau, N., Weissman, B., Aram, D., Klein, N., & Borawski, E. (1991). Effect of very low birth weight and subnormal head size on cognitive abilities at school age. *New England Journal of Medicine, 325,* 231–237.

Hackett, R. D., & Guion, R. M. (1985). A reevaluation of the absenteeism-job satisfaction relationship. *Organizational Behavior and Human Decision Processes, 35,* 340–381.

Hackman, J. R., & Morris, C. G. (1975). Group tasks, group interaction process, and group performance outcomes. In L. Berkowitz (Ed.), *Advances in experimental social psychology* (Vol. 9, pp. 45–99). New York: Academic Press.

Hage, J. J. (1995). Medical requirements and consequences of sex reassignment surgery. *Medicine, Science and the Law, 35,* 17–24.

Hagerman, R. J., & Hagerman, P. J. (2002). Fragile-X syndrome. In P. Howlin & O. Udwin (Eds.), *Outcomes in neurodevelopmental and genetic disorders. Cambridge child and adolescent psychiatry* (pp. 198–219). New York, NY: Cambridge University Press.

Haier, R. J. (1993). Cerebral glucose metabolism and intelligence. In P. A. Vernon (Ed.), *Biological approaches to the study of human intelligence* (pp. 317–332). Norwood, NJ: Ablex.

Haier, R. J. (2003). Brain imaging studies of intelligence: Individual differences and neurobiology. In R. J. Sternberg & J. Lautrey (Eds.), *Models of intelligence: International perspectives* (pp. 18–193). Washington, DC: American Psychological Association.

Hall, C. C. I. (1997). Cultural malpractice: The growing obsolescence of psychology with the changing U.S. population. *American Psychologist, 52,* 642–651.

Hall, G. S. (1904). *Adolescence: Its psychology and its relations to physiology, anthropology, sex, crime, religion and education* (Vol. 1). New York: Appleton-Century-Crofts.

Hall, J. A. (1984). *Nonverbal sex differences: Communication accuracy and expressive style.* Baltimore: Johns Hopkins University Press.

Hall, W. G., Arnold, H. M., & Myers, K. P. (2000). The acquisition of an appetite. *Psychological Science, 11,* 101–105.

Halpern, D. F. (1992). *Sex differences in cognitive abilities* (2nd ed.). Hillsdale, NJ: Erlbaum.

Halpern, D. F. (1997). Sex differences in intelligence: Implications for education. *American Psychologist, 52,* 1091–1102.

Hamann, S. B., Ely, T. D., Hoffman, J. M., & Kilts, C. D. (2002). Ecstasy and agony: Activation of the human amygdale in positive and negative emotion. *Psychological Science, 13,* 135–141.

Hamberger, M. J., & Seidel, W. T. (2003). Auditory and visual naming tests: Normative and patient data for accuracy, response time, and tip-of-

the-tongue. *Journal of the International Neuropsychological Society, 9,* 479–489.

Hameroff, S. R., Kaszniak, A. W., & Scott, A. C. (Eds.). (1996). *Toward a science of consciousness: The first Tucson discussions and debates.* Cambridge, MA: MIT Press.

Hamilton, A. (1999, May 24). On the virtual couch. *Time,* p. 71.

Hammack, S. E. (2002). The role of corticotrophin releasing hormone in learned helplessness. *Dissertation Abstracts International: Section B: The Sciences and Engineering, 62,* 4965.

Hammen, C. L. (1985). Predicting depression: A cognitive-behavioral perspective. In P. Kendall (Ed.), *Advances in cognitive-behavioral research and therapy* (Vol. 4, pp. 29–71). New York: Academic Press.

Hammen, C., Gitlin, M., & Altshuler, L. (2000). Predictors of work adjustment in bipolar I patients. A naturalistic longitudinal follow-up. *Journal of Consulting & Clinical Psychology, 68,* 220–225.

Hampson, E., & Kimura, D. (1992). Sexual differentiation and hormonal influences on cognitive function in humans. In J. B. Becker, S. M. Breedlove, & D. Crews (Eds.), *Behavioral endocrinology* (pp. 357–398). Cambridge, MA: MIT Press.

Hampson, J., & Nelson, K. (1993). The relation of maternal language to variation in rate and style of language acquisition. *Journal of Child Language, 20,* 313–342.

Hansel, C. E. (1969). ESP: Deficiencies of experimental method. *Nature, 221,* 1171–1172.

Harburg, E., DiFranceisco, W., Webster, D. W., Gleiberman, L., & Schork, A. (1990). Familial transmission of alcohol use: II. Imitation of and aversion to parent drinking (1960) by adult offspring (1977)—Tecumseh, Michigan. *Journal of Studies on Alcohol, 51,* 245–256.

Harburg, E., Gleiberman, L., DiFranceisco, W., Schork, A., & Weissfeld, L. A. (1990). Familial transmission of alcohol use: III. Impact of imitation/non-imitation of parent alcohol use (1960) on the sensible/problem drinking of their offspring (1977). *British Journal of Addiction, 85,* 1141–1155.

Hardaway, R. A. (1991). Subliminally activated symbiotic fantasies: Facts and artifacts. *Psychological Bulletin, 107,* 177–195.

Hare, R. D. (1983). Diagnosis of antisocial personality disorder in two prison populations. *American Journal of Psychiatry, 140,* 887–890.

Hare, R. D. (1993). *Without conscience: The disturbing world of the psychopaths among us.* New York: Pocket Books.

Harley, H. E., Roitblat, H. L., & Nachtigall, P. E. (1996). Object representation in the bottlenose dolphin (Tursiops truncatus): Integration of visual and echoic information. *Journal of*

Experimental Psychology and Animal Behavior Process, 22, 164–174.

Harlow, H. F. (1949). The formation of learning sets. *Psychological Review, 56,* 51–65.

Harlow, H. F. (1958). The nature of love. *American Psychologist, 13,* 673–685.

Harlow, H. F., & Zimmerman, R. R. (1959, August). Affectional responses in the infant monkey. *Science, 130,* 421–432.

Harrell, R. F., Woodyard, E., & Gates, A. I. (1955). *The effect of mother's diet on the intelligence of the offspring.* New York: Teacher's College, Columbia Bureau of Publications.

Harris, J. A., Gorissen, M. C., Bailey, G. K., & Westbrook R. F. (2000). Motivational state regulates the content of learned flavor preferences. *Journal of Experimental Psychology: Animal Behavior Processes, 26,* 15–30.

Harris, J. C. (2003). Pinel delivering the insane. *Archives of General Psychiatry, 60,* 552.

Harris, J. R. (1998). *The nurture assumption: Why children turn out the way they do.* New York: Free Press.

Harris, J. R., & Liebert, R. M. (1991). *The child: A contemporary view of development* (3rd ed.). Englewood Cliffs, NJ: Prentice Hall.

Harris, M., & Rosenthal, R. (1985). Mediation of the interpersonal expectancy effect: A taxonomy of expectancy situations. In P. Blanck (Ed.), *Interpersonal expectations: Theory, research, and application* (pp. 350–378). Paris, France: Cambridge University Press.

Hart, B., & Risley, T. R. (1995). *Meaningful differences in the everyday experience of young American children.* Baltimore: Brookes.

Hart, N. (1985). *The sociology of health and illness.* London: Causeway Books.

Hartung, C. M., & Widiger, T. A. (1998). Gender differences in the diagnosis of mental disorders: Conclusions and controversies of DSM-IV. *Psychological Bulletin, 123,* 260–278.

Hartup, W. W., & Stevens, N. (1999). Friendships and adaptation across the lifespan. *Current Directions in Psychological Science, 8,* 76–79.

Harvey, E. (1999). Short-term and long-term effects of early parental employment on children of the National Longitudinal Survey of Youth. *Developmental Psychology, 35,* 445–459.

Harvey, J. H., & Miller, E. D. (1998). Toward a psychology of loss. *Psychological Science, 9,* 429–434.

Harvey, J. H., & Pauwells, B. G. (1999). Recent developments in close-relationships theory. *Current Directions in Psychological Science, 8,* 93–95.

Hashimoto, T., Volk, D. W., Eggan, S. M., Mirnics, K., Pierri, J. N., Sun, Z., Sampson, A. R., & Lewis, D. A. (2003). Gene expression deficits in a

subclass of GABA neurons in the prefrontal cortex of subjects with schizophrenia. *Journal of Neuroscience, 16,* 6315–6326.

Hasselmo, M. E., & Bower, J. M. (1993). Acetylcholine and memory. *Trends in Neurosciences, 6,* 218–222.

Hasselmo, M. E., Schnell, E., & Barkai, E. (1995). Dynamics of learning and recall at excitatory recurrent synapses and cholinergic modulation in rat hippocampal region CA3. *Journal of Neuroscience, 15,* 5249–5262.

Hathaway, S. R., & McKinley, J. C. (1942). A multiphasic personality schedule (Minnesota): III. The measurement of symptomatic depression. *Journal of Psychology, 14,* 73–84.

Hauri, P. (1982). *Sleep disorders.* Kalamazoo, MI: Upjohn.

Hay, M. S., & Ellig, T. W. (1999). The 1995 Department of Defense sexual harassment survey: Overview and methodology. *Military Psychology [Special Issue: Sexual harassment], 11,* 233–242.

Hayden, T., & Mischel, W. (1976). Maintaining trait consistency in the resolution of behavioral inconsistency: The wolf in sheep's clothing? *Journal of Personality, 44,* 109–132.

Hayes, C., & Hayes, K. (1951). The intellectual development of a home-raised chimpanzee. *Proceedings of the American Philosophical Society, 95,* 105–109.

He, L. (1987). Involvement of endogenous opioid peptides in acupuncture analgesia. *Pain, 31,* 99–122.

Heath, A. C., & Martin, N. G. (1993). Genetic models for the natural history of smoking: Evidence for a genetic influence on smoking persistence. *Addictive Behavior, 18,* 19–34.

Heath, A. C., Cloninger, C. R., & Martin, N. G. (1994). Testing a model for the genetic structure of personality: A comparison of the personality systems of Cloninger and Eysenck. *Journal of Personality and Social Psychology, 66,* 762–775.

Heath, R. C. (1972). Pleasure and brain activity in man. *Journal of Nervous and Mental Disease, 154,* 3–18.

Hebb, D. O. (1949). *The organization of behavior: A neuropsychological theory.* New York: Wiley.

Heber, R., Garber, H., Harrington, S., & Hoffman, C. (1972). *Rehabilitation of families at risk for mental retardation.* Madison: University of Wisconsin, Rehabilitation Research and Training Center in Mental Retardation.

Hechtman, L. (1989). Teenage mothers and their children: Risks and problems: A review. *Canadian Journal of Psychology, 34,* 569–575.

Hedges, L. V., & Nowell, A. (1995, July 7). Sex differences in mental test scores, variability, and numbers of high-scoring individuals. *Science, 269,* 41–45.

Heider, E. R., & Oliver, D. C. (1972). The structure of the color space in naming and memory in two languages. *Cognitive Psychology, 3,* 337–354.

Heider, F. (1958). *The psychology of interpersonal relations.* New York: Wiley.

Heinz, A., Hermann, D., Smolka, M. N., Rieks, M., Graef, K. J., Poehlau, D., Kuhn, W., & Bauer, M. (2003). Effects of acute psychological stress on adhesion molecules interleukins and sex hormones: Implications for coronary heart disease. *Psychopharmacology, 165,* 111–117

Helgesen, S. (1998). *Everyday revolutionaries: Working women and the transformation of American life.* New York: Doubleday.

Hellige, J. B. (1990). Hemispheric asymmetry. *Annual Review of Psychology, 41,* 55–80.

Hellige, J. B. (1993). *Hemispheric asymmetry: What's right and what's left.* Cambridge, MA: Harvard University Press.

Helmreich, R., & Spence, J. (1978). The Work and Family Orientation Questionnaire: An objective instrument to assess components of achievement motivation and scientific attainment. *Personality and Social Psychology Bulletin, 4,* 222–226.

Helms, J. E. (1992). Why is there no study of cultural equivalence in standardized cognitive ability testing? *American Psychologist, 47,* 1083–1101.

Helms, J. E., & Cook, D. A. (1999). *Using race and culture in counseling and psychotherapy: Theory and process.* Needham Heights, MA: Allyn & Bacon.

Helson, R. (1971). Women mathematicians and the creative personality. *Journal of Consulting and Clinical Psychology, 36,* 210–220.

Hendrick, C. & Hendrick, S. S. (2003). Romantic love: Measuring cupid's arrow. In S. J. Lopez & C. R. Snyder (Eds.), *Positive psychological assessment: A handbook of models and measures* (pp 235–249). Washington, DC: American Psychological Association.

Henkel, L. A., Franklin, N., & Johnson, M. K. (2000). Cross-modal source monitoring confusions between perceived and imagined events. *Journal of Experimental Psychology: Learning, Memory, & Cognition, 26,* 321–335.

Henriques, J. B., & Davidson, R. J. (1990). Regional brain electrical asymmetries discriminate between previously depressed and healthy control subjects. *Journal of Abnormal Psychology, 99,* 22–31.

Henry, J. A., Alexander, C. A., & Sener, E. K. (1995). Relative mortality from overdose of antidepressants. *British Medical Journal, 310,* 221–224.

Henry, S. (1996, March 7). Keep your brain fit for life. *Parade Magazine,* pp. 8–11.

Herberman, R. B. (2002). Stress, natural killer cells, and cancer. In H. G. Koenig & H. J. Cohen (Eds.), *The link between religion and health: Psychoneuroimmunology and faith factor* (pp.

69–83). London: Oxford University Press.

Herek, G. M. (2000). The psychology of sexual prejudice. *Current Directions in Psychological Science, 9,* 19–22.

Hergenhahn, B. R., & Olson, M. H. (1993). *An introduction to theories of learning* (4th ed.). Englewood Cliffs, NJ: Prentice Hall.

Herman, L. M., Richards, D. G., & Wolz, J. P. (1984). Comprehension of sentences by bottlenosed dolphins. *Cognition, 16,* 1–90.

Hermann, C., & Blanchard, E. B. (2002). Biofeedback in the treatment of headache and other childhood pain. *Applied Psychophysiology and Biofeedback, 27,* 143–162.

Herrnstein, R. J., & Murray, C. (1994). *The bell curve.* New York: Free Press.

Hersher, L. (Ed.). (1970). *Four psychotherapies.* New York: Appleton-Century-Crofts.

Herz, R. S. (1997). The effects of cue distinctiveness on odor-based context-dependent memory. *Memory & Cognition, 25,* 375–380.

Herzog, H. A. (1995). Has public interest in animal rights peaked? *American Psychologist, 50,* 945–947.

Herzog, T. A. (1999). Effects of alcohol intoxication on social inferences. *Experimental & Clinical Psychopharmacology, 7,* 448–453.

Heston, L. L. (1966). Psychiatric disorders in foster-home-reared children of schizophrenic mothers. *British Journal of Psychiatry, 112,* 819–825.

Hetherington, E. M., Bridges, M., & Insabella, G. M. (1998). What matters? What does not? Five perspectives on the association between marital transitions and children's adjustment. *American Psychologist, 53,* 167–184.

Hewstone, M., Islam, M. R., & Judd, C. M. (1993). Models of cross categorization and intergroup relations. *Journal of Personality and Social Psychology, 64,* 779–793.

Heyes, C. M., Jaldow, E., & Dawson, G. R. (1993). Observational extinction: Observation of nonreinforced responding reduces resistance to extinction in rats. *Animal Learning & Behavior, 21,* 221–225.

Hibbard, S. R., Farmer, L., Wells, C., Difillipo, E., & Barry, W. (1994). Validation of Cramer's defense mechanism manual for the TAT. *Journal of Personality Assessment, 63,* 197–210.

Hilgard, E. R., Hilgard, J. R., & Kaufmann, W. (1983). *Hypnosis in the relief of pain* (2nd ed.). Los Altos, CA: Kaufmann.

Hill, C. E., Zack, J. S., Wonnell, T. L., Hoffman, M. A., Rochlen, A. B., Goldberg, J. L., Nakayama, E. Y., Heaton, K. J., Kelly, F. A., Eiche, K., Tomlinson, M. J., & Hess, S. (2000). Structured brief therapy with a focus on dreams or loss for clients with troubling dreams and recent loss.

Journal of Counseling Psychology, 47, 90–101.

Hill, J. (2003). Early identification of individuals at risk for antisocial personality disorder. *British Journal of Psychiatry, 182* (Suppl 44).

Hillier, L., Hewitt, K. L., & Morrongiello, B. A. (1992). Infants' perception of illusions in sound locations: Responding to sounds in the dark. *Journal of Experimental Child Psychology, 53,* 159–179.

Hilton, J., & von Hipple, W. (1996). Stereotypes. *Annual Review of Psychology, 47,* 237–271.

Hobfoll, S. E., Cameron, R. P., Chapman, H. A., & Gallagher, R. W. (1996). Social support and social coping in couples. In G. R. Pierce, B. R. Sarason, & I. G. Sarason (Eds.), *The handbook of social support and the family* (pp. 413–433). New York: Plenum.

Hobson, J. (1988). *The dreaming brain.* New York: Basic Books.

Hobson, J. A. (1994). *The chemistry of conscious states: How the brain changes its mind.* Boston: Little, Brown.

Hochschild, A. R. (1983). *The managed heart.* Berkeley: University of California Press.

Hochschild, A., & Machung, A. (1989). *The second shift: Working parents and the revolution at home.* New York: Viking.

Hoffman, H. S., & DePaulo, P. (1977). Behavioral control by an imprinting stimulus. *American Scientist, 65,* 58–66.

Hoffman, L. (1989). Effects of maternal employment in the two-parent family. *American Psychologist, 44,* 283–292.

Hoffman, M. (1991, May 24). Unraveling the genetics of fragile X syndrome. *Science, 252,* 1070.

Hoffrage, U., Hertwig, R., & Gigerenzer, G. (2000). Hindsight bias: A byproduct of knowledge updating? *Journal of Experimental Psychology: Learning, Memory & Cognition, 26,* 566–581.

Hogan, R., Hogan, J., & Roberts, B. W. (1996). Personality measurement and employment decisions: Questions and answers. *American Psychologist, 51,* 469–477.

Holland, C. A., & Rabbitt, P. M. A. (1990). Aging memory: Use versus impairment. *British Journal of Psychology, 82,* 29–38.

Hollis, K. L. (1997). Contemporary research on Pavlovian conditioning: A "new" functional analysis. *American Psychologist, 52,* 956–965.

Hollister, L. E. (1986). Health aspects of cannibis. *Pharmacological Reviews, 38,* 1–20.

Holmbeck, G. N. (1994). Adolescence. In V. S. Ramachandran (Ed.), *Encyclopedia of human behavior* (Vol. 1, pp. 17–28). San Diego, CA: Academic Press.

Holmes, D. S. (1976). Debriefing after psychological experiments. II. Effectiveness of spot experimental desensi-

tizing. *American Psychologist, 31,* 868–875.

Holmes, T. H., & Rahe, R. H. (1967). The social readjustment rating scale. *Journal of Psychosomatic Research, 11,* 213–218.

Holtkamp, K., Hebeband, J., Mika, C., Grzella, I., Heer, M., Heussen, N., & Herpertz, D. B. (2003). The effect of therapeutically induced weight gain on plasma leptin levels in patients with anorexia nervosa. *Journal of Psychiatric Research, 37,* 165–169.

Honeybourne, C., Matchett, G., & Davey, G. C. (1993). Expectancy models of laboratory preparedness effects: A UCS-expectancy bias in phylogenetic and ontogenetic fear-relevant stimuli. *Behavior Therapy, 24,* 253–264.

Hood, B. M., Willen, J. D., & Driver, J. (1998). Adult's eyes trigger shifts of visual attention in human infants. *Psychological Science, 9,* 131–134.

Hood, D. C. (1998). Lower-level visual processing and models of light adaptation. *Annual Review of Psychology, 49,* 503–535.

Hopkins, B., & Westra, T. (1990). Motor development, maternal expectation, and the role of handling. *Infants Behavior and Development, 13,* 117–122.

Hoptman, M. J., & Davidson, R. J. (1994). How and why do the two cerebral hemispheres interact? *Psychological Bulletin, 116,* 195–219.

Horn, J. (1983). The Texas Adoption Project: Adopted children and their intellectual resemblance to biological and adoptive parents. *Child Development, 54,* 268–275.

Horney, K. (1937). *The neurotic personality of our time.* New York: Norton.

Hosoda, M., Stone, R. E., & Coats, G. (2003). The effects of physical attractiveness on job-related outcomes: A meta-analysis of experimental studies. *Personnel Psychology, 56,* 431–462.

House, J. S., Landis, K. R., & Umberson, D. (1988, July 29). Social relationships and health. *Science, 241,* 540–545.

Howard, R. C. (1999). Treatment of anxiety disorders: Does specialty training help? *Professional Psychology: Research & Practice, 30,* 470–473.

Hoyert, D. L., Kochanek, K. D., & Murphy, S. L. (1999). Deaths: Final data for 1997. *National Vital Statistics Reports, 47*(19), 1–104. Hyattsville, MD: National Center for Health Statistics.

Hsu, L. K. (1996). Epidemiology of the eating disorder. *Psychiatric Clinics of North America, 19,* 681–700.

Huang, T. (1998, February 3). Weathering the storms. *Charlotte Observer,* pp. 1–2E.

Hubel, D. H., & Livingstone, M. S. (1990). Color and contrast sensitivity in the lateral geniculate body and primary visual cortex of the macaque monkey. *Journal of Neuroscience, 10,* 2223–2237.

Hubel, D. H., & Wiesel, T. N. (1959). Receptive fields of single neurons in the cat's striate cortex. *Journal of Physiology (London), 148,* 574–591.

Hubel, D. H., & Wiesel, T. N. (1979). Brain mechanisms of vision. *Scientific American, 241*(3), 150–162.

Hudson, J. A., & Sheffield, E. G. (1998). Deja vu all over again: Effects of reenactment on toddlers' event memory. *Child Development, 69,* 51–67.

Hudspeth, A. J. (1997). How hearing happens. *Neuron, 19,* 947–950.

Huebner, A. M., Garrod, A., & Snarey, J. (1990). *Moral development in Tibetan Buddhist monks: A cross-cultural study of adolescents and young adults in Nepal.* Paper presented at the meeting of the Society for Research in Adolescence, Atlanta, GA.

Huesmann, L. R., Moise, T. J., Podolski, C. L., & Eron, L. D. (2003). Longitudinal relations between children's exposure to TV violence and their aggressive and violent behavior in young adulthood. *Developmental Psychology, 39,* 201–221.

Huffman, C. J., Matthews, T. D., & Gagne, P. E. (2001). The role of part-set cuing in the recall of chess positions: Influence of chunking in memory. *North American Journal of Psychology, 3,* 535–542.

Hughes, R. L., Ginnett, R. C., & Curphy, G. J. (1998). Contingency theories of leadership. In G. R. Hickman (Ed.), *Leading organizations: Perspectives for a new era* (pp. 141–157). Thousand Oaks, CA: Sage Publications, Inc.

Huizink, A. C., Robles, de M., Pascale, G., Mulder, E. J. H., Visser, G. H. A., & Buitelaar, J. K. (2002). Psychological measures of prenatal stress as predictors of infant temperament. *Journal of the American Academy of Child and Adolescent Psychiatry, 41,* 1078–1085.

Human Rights Watch (2003). *Iraq: Impending inter-ethnic violence in Kirkuk.* New York, NY. Accessed September 6, 2003 at: http://www.hrw.org/press/2003/03/iraq032703.htm.

Humphreys, L. G. (1992). Commentary: What both critics and users of ability tests need to know. *Psychological Science, 3,* 271–274.

Hunt, E., Streissguth, A. P., Kerr, B., & Olson, H. C. (1995). Mothers' alcohol consumption during pregnancy: Effects on spatial-visual reasoning in 14-year-old children. *Psychological Science, 6,* 339–342.

Huston, A. C., Watkins, B. A., & Kunkel, D. (1989). Public policy and children's television. *American Psychologist, 44,* 424–433.

Hutschemaekers, G. J. M., & van de Vijver, F. J. R. (1989). Economic recessions and neurotic problems: The

Netherlands 1930–1985. In R. Veenhoven & A. Hagenaars (Eds.), *Did the crisis really hurt? Effects of the 1980–1982 economic recessions on satisfaction, mental health and mortality.* Rotterdam: Universitaire Pers Rotterdam.

Huttenlocher, J., Smiley, P., & Charney, R. (1983). Emergence of action categories in the child: Evidence from verb meanings. *Psychological Review, 90,* 72–93.

Hyde, J. S. (1982). *Understanding human sexuality* (2nd ed.). New York: McGraw-Hill.

Hyde, J. S. (1984a). Children's understanding of sexist language. *Developmental Psychology, 20,* 697–706.

Hyde, J. S. (1984b). How large are gender differences in aggression? A developmental meta-analysis. *Developmental Psychology, 20,* 722–736.

Hyde, J. S., & Linn, M. C. (1988). Gender differences in verbal ability: A meta-analysis. *Psychological Bulletin, 104,* 53–69.

Hyde, J. S., & Mezulis, A. H. (2002). Gender differences research: Issues and critique. In J. Worrell (Ed.), *Encyclopedia of women and gender.* San Diego: Academic Press.

Hyde, J. S., Fennema, E., & Lamon, S. J. (1990). Gender differences in mathematics performance: A meta-analysis. *Psychological Bulletin, 107,* 139–155.

Hyman, I. E., Husband, T. H., & Billings, F. J. (1995). False memories of childhood experiences. *Applied Cognitive Psychology, 9,* 181–197.

I

Iacobucci, D., & McGill, A. L. (1990). Analysis of attribution data: Theory testing and effects estimation. *Journal of Personality and Social Psychology, 59,* 426–441.

Iaffaldano, M. T., & Muchinsky, P. M. (1985). Job satisfaction and job performance: A meta-analysis. *Psychological Bulletin, 97,* 251–273.

Inciardi, J. A., & Harrison, L. D. (1998). *Heroin in the age of crack cocaine.* Thousand Oaks, CA: Sage.

Inciardi, J. A., Surratt, H. L., & Saum, C. A. (1997). *Cocaine-exposed infants: Social, legal, and public health issues.* Thousand Oaks, CA: Sage.

Irwin, M. (2002). Psychoneuroimmunology of depression: clinical implications. *Brain, Behavior and Immunity, 16,* 1–16.

Irwin, R. J., & Whitehead, P. R. (1991). Towards an objective psychophysics of pain. *Psychological Science, 2,* 230–235.

Isen, A. M., & Levin, P. F. (1972). The effect of feeling good on helping: Cookies and kindness. *Journal of Personality and Social Psychology, 21,* 384–388.

Ito, K. (2002). Additivity of heuristic and systematic processing persuasion: Effects of source credibility, argument

quality, and issue involvement. *Japanese Journal of Experimental Social Psychology, 41,* 137–146.

Ito, T. A., Miller, N., & Pollock, V. (1996). Alcohol and aggression: A meta-analysis on the moderating effects of inhibitory cues, triggering events, and self-focused attention. *Psychological Bulletin, 120,* 60–82.

Ivancevich, J. M., & Matteson, M. T. (1980). Stress and work: A managerial perspective. In J. C. Quick, R. S. Bhagat, J. E. Dalton, & J. D. Quick (eds.), *Work stress: Health care systems in the workplace* (pp. 27–49). New York: Praeger.

Iwamasa, G. Y., & Smith, S. K. (1996). Ethnic diversity in behavioral psychology: A review of the literature. *Behavioral Modification, 20,* 45–59.

Izard, C. E. (1971). *The face of emotion.* New York: Appleton-Century-Crofts.

Izard, C. E. (1980). Cross-cultural perspectives on emotion and emotion communication. In H. C. Triandis & W. J. Lonner (Eds.), *Handbook of cross-cultural psychology* (Vol. 3, 185–222). Boston: Allyn & Bacon.

Izard, C. E. (1992). Basic emotions, relations among emotions, and emotion-cognition relations. *Psychological Review, 99,* 561–565.

Izard, C. E. (1994). Innate and universal facial expressions: Evidence from developmental and cross-cultural research. *Psychological Bulletin, 115,* 288–299.

J

Jacks, J. Z., & Cameron, K. A. (2003). Strategies for resisting persuasion. *Basic and Applied Social Psychology, 25,* 145–161.

Jackson, L. A., Hunter, J. E., & Hodge, C. N. (1995). Physical attractiveness and intellectual competence: A meta-analytic review. *Social Psychology Quarterly, 58,* 108–122.

Jackson, P. A., Kesner, R. P., & Amann, K. (1998). Memory for duration: Role of hippocampus and medial prefrontal cortex. *Neurobiology Learning and Memory, 70,* 328–348.

Jacobs, G. H. (1993). The distribution and nature of color vision among the mammals. *Biological Review of the Cambridge Philosophical Society, 68,* 413–471.

Jacobs, W. J., & Nadel, L. (1997). Neurobiology of reconstructed memory. *Psychology, Public Policy, & Law, 4,* 1110–1134.

Jacobsen, P. B., Bovbjerg, D. H., Schwartz, M. D., & Andrykowski, M. A. (1994). Formation of food aversions in patients receiving repeated infusions of chemotherapy. *Behaviour Research & Therapy, 38,* 739–748.

Jacobson, K. (1999, November). *In search of a "normal" student: Six months in a British classroom.* Paper presented at the annual meeting of the American

Anthropological Association, Chicago, IL.

Jacobson, N. S., & Christensen, A. (1996). Studying the effectiveness of psychotherapy: How well can clinical trials do the job? *American Psychologist, 51,* 1031–1039.

Jain, S., & Posavac, S. S. (2001). Prepurchase attribute verifiability, source credibility, and persuasion. *Journal of Consumer Psychology, 11,* 169–180.

Jamal, M. (1981). Shift work related to job attitudes social participation and withdraw behavior: A study of nurses and industrial workers. *Personnel Psychology, 34,* 535–547.

James, L. C., Folen, R. A., & Earles, J. (2001). Behavioral telehealth applications in the treatment of obese soldiers. A feasibility project and a report on preliminary findings. *Military Psychology, 13,* 177–186.

James, L., & Nahl, D. (2000). *Road rage and aggressive driving: Steering clear of highway warfare.* Amherst, NY: Prometheus.

James, W. (1884). What is an emotion? *Mind, 19,* 188–205.

James, W. (1890). *The principles of psychology.* New York: Holt.

Jang, K. L., Livesley, W. J., & Vernon, P. A. (1996). Heritability of the Big Five personality dimensions and their facets: A twin study. *Journal of Personality, 64,* 577–591.

Jang, K. L., Livesley, W. J., Angleitner, A., Riemann, R., & Vernon, P. A. (2002). Genetic and environmental influences on the convariance of facets defining the domains of the five-factor model of personality. *Personality and Individual Differences, 33,* 83–101.

Jang, K. L., Livesley, W. J., McCrae, R. R., Angleitner, A., & Riemann, R. (1998). Heritability of facet-level traits in a cross-cultural twin sample: Support for a hierarchical model of personality. *Journal of Personality and Social Psychology, 74,* 1556–1565.

Janis, I. (1982). *Groupthink: Psychological studies of policy decisions and fiascoes* (2nd ed.). Boston: Houghton Mifflin.

Janis, I. L. (1989). *Crucial decisions: Leadership in policymaking and crisis management.* New York, NY: Free Press.

Janis, I. L., Mahl, G. G., & Holt, R. R. (1969). *Personality: Dynamics, development and assessment.* New York: Harcourt Brace Jovanovich.

Janofsky, M. (1994, December 13). Survey reports more drug use by teenagers. *New York Times,* p. A1.

Janos, P. M., & Robinson, N. M. (1985). Psychosocial development in intellectually gifted children. In F. D. Horowitz & M. O'Brien (Eds.), *Gifted and talented: Developmental perspectives* (pp. 149–195). Washington, DC: American Psychological Association.

Jaycox, L. H., Zoellner, L., & Foa, E. B. (2002). Cognitive-behavior therapy for PTSD in rape survivors. *Journal of Clinical Psychology, 58,* 891–906.

Jaynes, G. D., & Williams, R. M. (Eds). (1989). *Common destiny: Blacks and American society*. Washington, DC: National Academy Press.

Jaynes, J. H., & Wlodkowski, R. J. (1990). *Eager to learn: Helping children become motivated and love learning*. San Francisco: Jossey-Bass.

Jemmott, J. B., III, Jemmott, L. S., Fong, G. T., & McCaffree, K. (2002). Reducing HIV risk-associated sexual behavior among African American adolescents: Testing the generality of intervention effects. *American Journal of Community Psychology, 27*, 161–187.

Jenkins, L. (2000). *Biolinguistics*. Cambridge, England: Cambridge University Press.

Jensen, A. R. (1969). How much can we boost IQ and scholastic achievement? *Harvard Educational Review, 39*, 1–123.

Jensen, A. R. (1992). Commentary: Vehicles of g. *Psychological Science, 3*, 275–278.

Jensen, M. P., & Karoly, P. (1991). Motivation and expectancy factors in symptom perception: A laboratory study of the placebo effect. *Psychosomatic Medicine, 53*, 144–152.

Johansson, M., & Arlinger, S. D. (2003). Prevalence of hearing impairment in a population in Sweden. *International Journal of Audiology, 42*, 18–28.

Johnsen, B. H., Laberg, J. C., Eid, J., & Hugdahl, K. (2002). Dichotic listening and sleep deprivation: Vigilance effects. *Scandinavian Journal of Psychology, 43*, 413–417.

Johnson, A. (2003). Procedural memory and skill acquisition. In A. F. Healy & R. W. Proctor (Eds.), *Handbook of psychology: Experimental psychology, Vol. 4* (pp. 499–523). New York: John Wiley & Sons, Inc.

Johnson, C. (2002). Obesity, weight management, and self-esteem. In T. A. Wadden & A. J. Stunkard, *Handbook of obesity treatment* (pp. 480–493). New York, NY: Guilford Press.

Johnson, D. (1990). Can psychology ever be the same again after the human genome is mapped? *Psychological Science, 1*, 331–332.

Johnson, D. M., & Erneling, C. A. (Eds.). (1997). *The future of the cognitive revolution*. New York: Oxford University Press.

Johnson, D. W., Johnson, R. T., & Maruyama, G. (1984). Effects of cooperative learning: A meta-analysis. In N. Miller & M. B. Brewer (Eds.), *Groups in contact: The psychology of desegregation* (pp. 187–212). New York: Academic Press.

Johnson, E. S., Levine, A., & Doolittle, F. (1999). *Fathers' fair share: Helping poor men manage child support and fatherhood*. New York: Russell Sage.

Johnson, G. (1995, June 6). Chimp talk debate: Is it really language? *New York Times*, p. C1.

Johnson, P. J. (2003). Obesity is America's greatest threat, Surgeon General says. *The Orlando Sentinel: Knight Ridder News Features*. Available on-line at: http://www.defeatdiabetes.org/Articles/obesity2030123.htm (last accessed June 6, 2003).

Johnson, S. M. (2003). Couples therapy research: Status and directions. In G. P. Sholevar (Ed.), *Textbook of family and couples therapy: Clinical applications* (pp. 797–814). Washington, DC: American Psychiatric Publishing, Inc.

Johnson-Greene, D., Adams, K. M., Gilman, S., Kluin, K. J., Junck, L., Martorello, S., & Heumann, M. (1997). Impaired upper limb coordination in alcoholic cerebellar degeneration. *Archives of Neurology, 54*, 436–439.

Johnston, L. D., O'Malley, P. M., & Bachman, J. G. (2003). *The Monitoring the Future national survey results on adolescent drug use: Overview of key findings, 2002* (NIH Publication No. 03–5374). Bethesda, MD: National Institute on Drug Abuse.

Jones, C. J., & Meredith, W. (2000). Developmental paths of psychological health from early adolescence to later adulthood. *Psychology & Aging, 15*, 351–360.

Jones, C. P., & Adamson, L. B. (1987). Language use and mother-child-sibling interactions. *Child Development, 58*, 356–366.

Jones, F. D., & Koshes, R. J. (1995). Homosexuality and the military. *American Journal of Psychiatry, 152*, 16–21.

Jones, L. W., Sinclair, R. C., & Courneya, K. S. (2003). The effects of source credibility and message framing on exercise intentions, behaviors and attitudes: An integration of the elaboration likelihood model and prospect theory. *Journal of Applied Social Psychology, 33*, 179–196.

Jones, M. C. (1924). Elimination of children's fears. *Journal of Experimental Psychology, 7*, 381–390.

Jorge, J. M. N., Habr, G. A., & Wexner, S. D. (2003). Biofeedback therapy in the colon and rectal practice. *Applied Psychophysiology and Biofeedback, 28*, 47–61.

Julius, M., Harburg, E., Cottington, E. M., & Johnson, E. H. (1986). Anger-coping types, blood pressure, and all-cause mortality: A follow-up in Tecumseh, Michigan (1971–1983). *American Journal of Epidemiology, 124*, 220–233.

Junginger, J. (1997). Fetishism. In D. R. Laws & W. T. O'Donohue (Eds.), *Handbook of sexual deviance: Theory and application* (pp. 92–110). New York: Guilford.

K

Kadotani, H., Kadotani, T., Young, T., Peppard, P. E., Finn, L., Colrain, I. M., Murphy, G. M., & Mignot, E., (2001). Association between apolipoprotein EC4 and sleep-disordered breathing in adults. *Journal of the American Medical Association, 285*, 2888–2890.

Kagan, J. (1989). Temperamental contributions to social behavior. *American Psychologist, 44*, 668–674.

Kagan, J. (1994, October 5). The realistic view of biology and behavior. *Chronicle of Higher Education*, p. A64.

Kagan, J., & Snidman, N. (1991). Infant predictors of inhibited and uninhibited profiles. *Psychological Science, 2*, 40–44.

Kagan, J., Arcus, D., & Snidman, N. (1993). The idea of temperament: Where do we go from here? In R. Plomin & G. E. McClearn (Eds.), *Nature, nurture, and psychology*, pp. 197–210. Washington, DC: American Psychological Association.

Kagan, J., Reznick, J. S., Snidman, N., Gibbons, J., & Johnson, M. O. (1988). Childhood derivatives of inhibition and lack of inhibition to the unfamiliar. *Child Development, 59*, 1580–1589.

Kagan, J., Snidman, N., & Arcus, D. M. (1992). Initial reactions to unfamiliarity. *Current Directions, 1*, 171–174.

Kagitcibasi, C. (1997). Individualism and collectivism. In J. W. Berry, Y. H. Poortinga, & J. Kirpatrick (Eds.), *Person, self, and experience: Exploring pacific ethnopsychologies* (pp. 3–32). Berkeley: University of California Press.

Kahneman, D., & Tversky, A. (1996). On the reality of cognitive illusions. *Psychological Review, 103*, 582–591.

Kalat, J. W. (1988). *Biological psychology* (3rd ed.). Belmont, CA: Wadsworth.

Kamin, L. J. (1969). Selective association and conditioning. In N. J. Mackintosh & W. K. Honig (Eds.), *Fundamental issues in associative learning* (pp. 42–64). Halifax: Dalhousie University Press.

Kaminski, M. (1999). *The team concept: A worker-centered alternative to lean production*. APA Public Interest Directorate. Available on-line at: www.apa.org/pi/wpo/niosh/abstract22 html

Kane, J., & Lieberman, J. (1992). *Adverse effects of psychotropic drugs*. New York: Guilford Press.

Kantrowitz, B., Rosenberg, D., Rogers, P., Beachy, L., & Holmes, S. (1993, November 1). Heroin makes an ominous comeback. *Newsweek*, p. 53.

Kaplan, W. S., & Novorr, M. J. (1994). Age and season of birth in sudden infant death syndrome in North Carolina, 1982–1987: No interaction. *American Journal of Epidemiology, 140*, 56–58.

Karau, S. J., & Williams, K. D. (1993). Social loafing: A meta-analytic review and theoretical integration. *Journal of Personality and Social Psychology, 65*, 681–706.

Karmiloff-Smith, A. (2002). Elementary, my dear Watson, the clue is in the genes. Or is it? *Psychologist, 15*, 608–611.

Kashdan, T. B., & Fincham, F. D. (2002). "Facilitating creativity by regulating curiosity": Comment. *American Psychologist, 57*, 373–374.

Kashima, Y., & Triandis, H. C. (1986). The self-serving bias in attributions as a coping strategy: A cross-cultural study. *Journal of Cross-Cultural Psychology, 17*, 83–98.

Kass, S. (1999, September). Employees perceive women as better managers than men, finds five-year study. *APA Monitor*, p. 6.

Kassebaum, N. L. (1994). Head Start: Only the best for America's children. *American Psychologist, 49*, 123–126.

Kassin, S. M., Tubb, V. A., Hosch, H. M., & Memon, A. (2001). Cases of wrongful conviction often contain erroneous testimony by eyewitnesses. Experts agree that the current state of the literature strongly supports 7 conclusions about the accuracy of eyewitness identification. *American Psychologist, 56*, 405–416.

Kathuria, S., Gaetani, S., Fegley, D., Valino, F., Duranti, A., Tontini, A., Mor, M. Tarzia, G., La Rana, G., Calignano, A., Giustino, A., Tattoli, M., Palmery, M., Cuomo, V., & Piomelli, D. (2003). Modulation of anxiety through blockade of anandamide hydrolysis. *Nature Medicine, 9*, 76–81.

Kato, T. (2001). Molecular genetics of bipolar disorder. *Neuroscience Research, 40*, 105–113.

Katz, R., & McGuffin, P. (1993). The genetics of affective disorders. In D. Fowles (Ed.), *Progress in experimental personality and psychopathology research*. New York: Springer.

Kavale, K. A. (2002). Mainstreaming to full inclusion: From orthogenesis to pathogenesis of an idea. *International Journal of Disability, Development and Education, 49*, 201–214.

Kavanagh, D. J. (1992). Recent developments in expressed emotion and schizophrenia. *British Journal of Psychiatry, 160*, 601–620.

Kawai, N., & Matsuzawa, T. (2000). Cognition: Numerical memory span in a chimpanzee. *Nature, 403*, 39–40.

Keane, G., & Shaughnessy, M. F. (2002). An interview with Robert J. Sternberg about educational psychology: The current "state of the art." *Educational Psychology Review, 14*, 313–330.

Keefe, F. J., & France, C. R. (1999). Pain: Biopsychosocial mechanisms and management. *Current Directions in Psychological Science, 8*, 137–140.

Kelemen, W. L., & Creeley, C. E. (2003). State-dependent memory effects using caffeine and placebo do not extend to metamemory. *Journal of General Psychology, 130*, 70–86.

Keller, H. (1948). From a letter to Dr. J. Kerr Love, March 31, 1910, from the souvenir program commemorating Helen Keller's visit to Queensland

Adult Deaf and Dumb Mission in 1948.

Kelley, H. H. (1967). Attribution theory in social psychology. In D. Levine (Ed.), *Nebraska Symposium on Motivation: Vol. 15* (pp 192–238). Lincoln: University of Nebraska Press.

Kellogg, W. N. (1968). Communication and language in the home-raised chimpanzee. *Science, 162,* 423–427.

Kelly, J. B. (1982). Divorce: The adult perspective. In B. B. Wolman (Ed.), *Handbook of developmental psychology* (pp. 734–750). Englewood Cliffs, NJ: Prentice Hall.

Kelly, K., & Dawson, L. (1994). Sexual orientation. In V. S. Ramachandran (Ed.), *Encyclopedia of human behavior* (Vol. 4, pp. 183–192). San Diego: Academic Press.

Kendler, K. S., Myers, J. M., O'Neill, F. A., Martin, R., Murphy, B., MacLean, C. J., Walsh, D., & Straub, R. E. (2000). Clinical features of schizophrenia and linkage to chromosomes 5q, 6p, 8p, and 10p in the Irish study of high-density schizophrenia families. *American Journal of Psychiatry, 157:* 402–408.

Kendler, K. S., Neale, M. C., Kessler, R. C., Heath, A. C., & Eaves, L. J. (1992). Generalized anxiety disorder in women: A population-based twin study. *Archives of General Psychiatry, 49,* 267–272.

Keppel, B. (2002). Kenneth B. Clark in patterns of American culture. *American Psychologist, 57,* 29–37.

Kernis, M. H., & Wheeler, L. (1981). Beautiful friends and ugly strangers: Radiation and contrast effects in perception of same-sex pairs. *Personality and Social Psychology Bulletin, 7,* 617–620.

Kessler, R. C., McGonagle, K. A., Zhao, S., Nelson, C. R., Highes, M., Eshleman, S., Wittchen, H., & Kendler, K. S. (1994). Lifetime and 12-month prevalence of DSM-III-R psychiatric disorders in the United States: Results from the National Comorbidity Survey. *Archives of General Psychiatry, 51,* 8–19.

Kessler, R. C., Price, R. H., & Wortman, C. B. (1985). Social factors in psychopathology: Stress, social support, and coping processes. *Annual Review of Psychology, 36,* 531–572.

Kessler, R. C., Sonnega, A., Bromet, E., Hughes, M., & Nelson, C. B. (1995). Post-traumatic stress disorder in the national Comorbidity Survey. *Archives of General Psychiatry, 52,* 1057.

Keverne, E. B. (1999, October 22). The vomeronasal organ. *Science, 286,* 716–720.

Khan, A., Mirolo, M. H., Hughes, D., & Bierut, L. (1993). Electroconvulsive therapy. *Psychiatric Clinics of North America, 16,* 497–513.

Kiecolt-Glaser, J. K., & Glaser, R. (2002). Depression and immune function: Central pathways to morbidity and mortality. *Journal of Psychosomatic Research, 53,* 873–876.

Kiecolt-Glaser, J. K., Bane, C., Glaser, R., & Malarkey, W. B. (2003). Love, marriage, and divorce: Newlyweds' stress hormones foreshadow relationship changes. *Journal of Consulting and Clinical Psychology, 71,* 176–188.

Kiecolt-Glaser, J. K., Malarkey, W. B., Chee, M., Newton, T., & Cacioppo, J. T. (1993). Negative behavior during marital conflict is associated with immunological down-regulation. *Psychosomatic Medicine, 55,* 395–409.

Kiesler, C. A. (1982a). Mental hospitals and alternative care: Noninstitutionalization as a potential public policy for mental patients. *American Psychologist, 37,* 349–360.

Kiesler, C. A. (1982b). Public and professional myths about mental hospitalization: An empirical reassessment of policy-related beliefs. *American Psychologist, 37,* 1323–1339.

Kiesler, C. A., & Sibulkin, A. E. (1987). Alternative treatment: Noninstitutionalization. In C. A. Kiesler & A. E. Sibulkin (Eds.), *Mental hospitalization: Myths and facts about a national crisis* (pp. 152–180). Newbury Park, California: Sage Publications, Inc.

Kiesler, C. A., & Simpkins, C. G. (1993). *The unnoticed majority in psychiatric inpatient care.* New York: Plenum.

Kihlström, J. F. (1998). Dissociations and dissociation theory in hypnosis: Comment on Kirsch and Lynn (1998). *Psychological Bulletin, 123,* 186–191.

Kihlström, J. F. (1999). The psychological unconscious. In L. A. Pervin & O. P. John (Eds.), *Handbook of personality: Theory and research* (2nd ed., pp. 424–442). New York: Guilford.

Kihlström, J. F., & Harackiewicz, J. M. (1982). The earliest recollection: A new survey. *Journal of Personality, 50,* 134–148.

Kileny, P. R., Zwolan, T.A., & Ashbaugh, C. (2001). The influence of age at implantation on performance with a cochlear implant in children. *Otology and Neurotology, 22,* 42–46.

Kilpatrick, D. G., Acierno, R., Saunders, B., Resnick, H. S., Best, C. L., & Schnurr, P. P. (2000). Risk factors for adolescent substance abuse and dependence: Data from a national sample. *Journal of Consulting & Clinical Psychology, 68,* 19–30.

Kim, K. H. S., Relkin, N. R., Lee, K., & Hirsch, J. (1997). Distinct cortical areas associated with native and second languages. *Nature, 388,* 171–174.

Kimberg, D. Y., D'Esposito, M. D., & Farah, M. J. (1997). Cognitive functions in the prefrontal cortex–working memory and executive control. *Current Directions in Psychological Science, 6,* 185–192.

Kimmel, D. C. (1974). *Adulthood and aging.* New York: Wiley.

Kimura, D., & Hampson, E. (1994). Cognitive pattern in men and women is influenced by fluctuations in sex hormones. *Current Directions in Psychological Science, 3,* 57–61.

Kingstone, A., Enns, J. T., Mangun, G. R., & Gazzaniga, M. S. (1995). Right-hemisphere memory superiority: Studies of a split-brain patient. *Psychological Science, 6,* 118–121.

Kinsey, A. C., Pomeroy, W. B., & Martin, C. E. (1948). *Sexual behavior in the human male.* Philadelphia: Saunders.

Kinsey, A. C., Pomeroy, W. B., Martin, C. E., & Gebhard, P. H. (1953). *Sexual behavior in the human female.* Philadelphia: Saunders.

Kirsch, I. (Ed.). (1999). *How expectancies shape experience.* Washington, DC: American Psychological Association.

Kirsch, I., & Braffman, W. (2001). Imaginative suggestibility and hypnotizability. *Current Directions in Psychological Science, 10,* 57–60.

Kirsch, I., & Lynn, S. J. (1998). Dissociating the wheat from the chaff in theories of hypnosis: Reply to Kihlström (1998) and Woody and Sadler (1998). *Psychological Bulletin, 123,* 198–202.

Kirsch, I., Montgomery, G., & Saperstein, G. (1995). Hypnosis as an adjunct to cognitive behavioral psychotherapy: A meta analysis. *Journal of Consulting and Clinical Psychology, 63,* 214–220.

Kish, S. J., Furukawa, Y., Ang, L., Vorce, S. P., & Kalasinsky, K. S. (2000). Striatal serotonin is depleted in brain of a human MDMA (Ecstasy) user. *Neurology, 55,* 294–296.

Kissane, D. W., Bloch, S., Miach, P., Smith, G. C., Seddon, A., & Keks, N. (1997). Cognitive-existential group therapy for patients with primary breast cancer—techniques and themes. *Psychooncology, 6,* 25–33.

Kite, M. E., Russo, N. F., Brehm, S. S., Fouad, N. A., Hall, C. C., Hyde, J. S., & Keita, G. P. (2001). Women psychologists in academe. *American Psychologist, 56,* 1080–1098.

Klatzky, R. L. (1980). *Human memory: Structures and processes* (2nd ed.). San Francisco: Freeman.

Kleim, J. A., Vij, K., Ballard, D. H., & Greenough, W. T. (1997). Learning-dependent synaptic modifications in the cerebellar cortex of the adult rat persist for at least four weeks. *Journal of Neuroscience, 17,* 717–721.

Klein, G. (1997). Developing expertise in decision making. *Thinking & Reasoning [Special Issue: Expert thinking], 3,* 337–352.

Klein, G. S. (1951). The personal world through perception. In R. R. Blake & G. V. Ramsey (Eds.), *Perception: An approach to personality* (pp. 352–355). New York: Ronald Press.

Klein, G., Wolf, S., Militello, L., & Zsambok, C. (1995). Characteristics of skilled option generation in chess. *Organizational Behavior & Human Decision Processes, 62,* 63–69.

Kleinfield, N. R. (2001, Sept. 12). U.S. Attacked; Hijacked jets destroy twin towers and hit Pentagon in day of terror. *New York Times,* pp. A7.

Kleinmuntz, D. N. (1991). Decision making for professional decision makers. *Psychological Science, 2,* 135, 138–141.

Kling, K. C., Hyde, J. S., Showers, C. J., & Buswell, B. N. (1999). Gender differences in self-esteem: A meta-analysis. *Psychological Bulletin, 125,* 470–500.

Klingenspor, B. (1994). Gender identity and bulimic eating behavior. *Sex Roles, 31,* 407–432.

Kluckhohn, C. (1949). *Mirror for man: The relation of anthropology to modern life.* New York: Whittlesey House.

Kluckhohn, C., Murray, H. A., & Schneider, D. M. (Eds.). (1961). *Personality in nature, society, and culture.* New York: Knopf.

Kluegel, J. R. (1990). Trends in whites' explanations of the black-white gap in socioeconomic status, 1977–1989. *American Sociological Review, 55,* 512–525.

Kluger, J. (1998, March 23). Following our noses. *Time.*

Klump, K. L., McGue, M., & Iacono, W. G. (2002). Genetic relationships between personality and eating attitudes and behaviors. *Journal of Abnormal Psychology, 111,* 380–389.

Knapp, C. (1999, May 9). The glass half empty. *New York Times Magazine,* 19–20.

Knight, G. P., Fabes, R. A., & Higgins, D. A. (1996). Concerns about drawing causal inferences from meta-analyses: An example in the study of gender differences in aggression. *Psychological Bulletin, 119,* 410–421.

Knight, J. A. (2002). The biochemistry of aging. *Advances in Clinical Chemistry, 35,* 1–62.

Kobasa, S. C. (1979). Stressful life events, personality, and health: An inquiry into hardiness. *Journal of Personality and Social Psychology, 37,* 1–11.

Koenig, H. G. (1997). *Is religion good for your health? The effects of religion on physical and mental health.* Binghamton, NY: Haworth Press.

Koenig, H. G., Cohen, H. J., George, L. K., Hays, J. C., Larson, D. B., & Blazer, D. G. (1997). Attendance at religious services, interleukin-6 and other biological parameters of immune function in older adults. *International Journal of Psychiatry in Medicine, 27,* 242–256.

Koh, P. O., Bergson, C., Undie, A., S., Goldman, R., Patricia, S., & Lidow, M. S. (2003). Up regulation of D1 dopamine receptor interacting protein, calcyon, in patients with schizophrenia. *Archives of General Psychiatry, 60,* 311–319.

Kohlberg, L. (1969). Stage and sequence: The cognitive-developmental approach to socialization. In D. A.

Goslin (Ed.), *Handbook of socialization theory and research* (pp. 347–480). Chicago: Rand McNally.

Kohlberg, L. (1979). *The meaning and measurement of moral development* (Clark Lectures). Worcester, MA: Clark University.

Kohlberg, L. (1981). *The philosophy of moral development* (Vol. 1). San Francisco: Harper & Row.

Kolb, H. (2003). How the retina works. *American Scientist, 91,* 28–35.

Kolchakian, M. R., & Hill, C. E. (2002). Dream interpretation with heterosexual dating couples. *Dreaming: Journal of the Association For the Study of Dreams, 12,* 1–16.

Komatsu, L. K. (1992). Recent views of conceptual structure. *Psychological Bulletin, 112,* 500–526.

Komiya, N., Good, G. E., & Sherrod, N. B. (2000). Emotional openness as a predictor of college students' attitudes toward seeking psychological help. *Journal of Counseling Psychology, 47,* 138–143.

Kondrasuk, J. N. (1981). Studies in MBO effectiveness. *Academy of Management Review, 6,* 419–430.

Kopelowicz, A., Liberman, R. P., & Zarate, R. (2002). Psychosocial treatments for schizophrenia. In P. E. Nathan & J. M. Gorman (Eds.), *A guide to treatments that work* (2nd ed.) (pp. 201–228). London: Oxford University Press.

Kopta, S. M., Howard, K. I., Lowry, J. L., & Beutler, L. E. (1994). Patterns of symptomatic recovery in psychotherapy. *Journal of Consulting and Clinical Psychology, 62,* 1009–1016.

Kopta, S. M., Lueger, R. J., Saunders, S. M., & Howard, K. I. (1999). Individual psychotherapy outcome and process research: Challenges leading to greater turmoil or a positive transition? *Annual Review of Psychology, 50,* 441–469.

Koriat, A., Goldsmith, M., & Pansky, A. (2000). Toward a psychology of memory accuracy. *Annual Review of Psychology, 51,* 481–537.

Korn, J. H. (1998). The reality of deception. *American Psychologist, 53,* 805.

Koss, M. P. (1990). Violence against women. *American Psychologist, 45,* 374–380.

Kosslyn, S. M. (1980). *Image and mind.* Cambridge, MA: Harvard University Press.

Kosslyn, S. M. (1987). Seeing and imaging in the cerebral hemispheres: A computational approach. *Psychological Review, 94,* 148–175.

Kosslyn, S. M. (1994). *Image and brain.* Cambridge, MA: MIT Press.

Kosslyn, S. M., & Sussman, A. L. (1995). Roles of imagery in perception: Or, there is no such thing as immaculate perception. In Michael S. Gazzaniga (Ed.), *The cognitive neurosciences* (pp. 1035–1041). Cambridge, MA: MIT Press.

Koukounas, E., & Over, R. (1997). Male sexual arousal elicited by film and fantasy matched in content. *Australian Journal of Psychology, 49,* 1–5.

Krasne, F. B., & Glanzman, D. L. (1995). What we can learn from invertebrate learning. *Annual Review of Psychology, 46,* 585–624.

Kraus, S. J. (1995). Attitudes and the prediction of behavior: A meta-analysis of the empirical literature. *Personality and Social Psychology Bulletin, 21,* 58–75.

Krebs, D. (1975). Empathy and altruism. *Journal of Personality and Social Psychology, 32,* 1134–1140.

Kringlen, E. (1981). *Stress and coronary heart disease. Twin research 3: Epidemiological and clinical studies.* New York: Alan R. Liss.

Kroger, R. O., & Wood, L. A. (1993). Reification, "faking" and the Big Five. *American Psychologist, 48,* 1297–1298.

Kropp, P., Sinatchkin, M., & Gerber, W. D. (2002). On the pathophysiology of migraine: Links for "empirically based treatment" with neurofeedback. *Applied Psychophysiology and Biofeedback, 27,* 203–213.

Krosnick, J. A. (1999). Survey research. *Annual Review of Psychology, 50,* 537–567.

Krueger, R. F., & Markon, K. E. (2002). Behavior genetic perspectives on clinical personality assessment. In J. N. Butcher (Ed.), *Clinical personality assessment: Practical approaches* (2nd ed.). *Oxford textbooks in clinical psychology, Vol. 2* (pp. 40–55). London: Oxford University Press.

Kruglanski, A. W. (1986, August). Freeze-think and the Challenger. *Psychology Today,* pp. 48–49.

Krupinski, E., Nypaver, M., Poropatich, R., Ellis, D., Safwat, R., & Sapci, H. (2002). Clinical applications in telemedicine/telehealth. *Telemedicine Journal and eHealth, 8,* 13–34.

Krystal, A. D., Holsinger, T., Weiner, R. D., & Coffey, C. E. (2000). Prediction of the utility of a switch from unilateral to bilateral ECT in the elderly using treatment 2 ictal EEG indices. *Journal of ECT, 16,* 327–337.

Kübler-Ross, E. (1969). *On death and dying.* New York: Macmillan.

Kübler-Ross, E. (1975). *Death: The final stage of growth.* Englewood Cliffs, NJ: Prentice Hall.

Kuhl, P. K., Williams, K. A., & Lacerda, F. (1992, January 31). Linguistic experience alters phonetic perception in infants by 6 months of age. *Science, 255,* 606–608.

Kuhn, P. K., Williams, K. A., & Lacerda, F. (1992). Linguistic experience alters phonetic perception in infants by 6 months of age. *Science, 255,* 606–608.

Kulik, J., & Brown, R. (1979). Frustration, attribution of blame, and aggression. *Journal of Experimental Social Psychology, 15,* 183–194.

Kunkel, D., Wilson, B. J., Linz, D., Potter, J., Donnerstein, E., Smith, S. L., Blumenthal, E., & Gray, T. (1996). *The national television violence study.* Studio City, CA: Mediascope.

Kunst-Wilson, W. R., & Zajonc, R. B. (1980). Affective discrimination of stimuli that cannot be recognized. *Science, 207,* 557–558.

Kupfermann, I. (1991). Hypothalamus and limbic system motivation. In E. R. Kandel, J. H. Schwartz, & T. M. Jessel (Eds.), *Principles of neural science* (3rd ed., pp. 750–760). New York: Elsevier.

Kurdek, L. A. (1991). Correlates of relationship satisfaction in cohabiting gay and lesbian couples: Integration of contextual, investment, and problem-solving models. *Journal of Personality & Social Psychology, 61,* 910–922.

Kurdek, L. A. (1992). Assumptions versus standards: The validity of two relationship cognitions in heterosexual and homosexual couples. *Journal of Family Psychology, 6,* 164–170.

Kurdek, L. A., Fine, M. A., & Sinclair, R. J. (1995). School adjustment in sixth graders: Parenting transitions, family climate, and peer norm effects. *Child Development, 66,* 430–445.

Kwon, S. M., & Oei, T. P. S. (2003). Cognitive change processes in a group cognitive behavior therapy of depression. *Journal of Behavior Therapy and Experimental Psychiatry, 34,* 73–85.

L

Laan, E., Everaerd, W., & Evers, A. (1995). Assessment of female sexual arousal: Response specificity and construct validity. *Psychophysiology, 32,* 476–485.

Laan, E., Everaerd, W., van Berlo, R., & Rijs, L. (1995). Mood and sexual arousal in women. *Behavior Research Therapy, 33,* 441–443.

Labouvie-Vief, G. (1986). Modes of knowledge and the organization of development. In M. L. Commons, L. Kohlberg, F. A. Richards, & J. Sinnott (Eds.), *Beyond formal operations: 2. Models and methods in the study of adult and adolescent thoughts.* New York: Praeger.

Lachman, S. J. (1984, August). *Processes in visual misperception: Illusions for highly structured stimulus material.* Paper presented at the 92nd annual convention of the American Psychological Association, Toronto, Canada.

Lachman, S. J. (1996). Processes in perception: Psychological transformations of highly structured stimulus material. *Perceptual and Motor Skills, 83,* 411–418.

LaGreca, A. M., Stone, W. L., & Bell, C. R., III. (1983). Facilitating the vocational-interpersonal skills of mentally retarded individuals. *American Journal of Mental Deficiency, 88,* 270–278.

Laird, J. (2003). Lesbian and gay families. In F. Walsh (Ed.), *Normal family processes: Growing diversity and complexity* (3rd ed., pp. 176–209). New York, NY: Guilford Press.

Lal, S. (2002). Giving children security. *American Psychologist, 57,* 20–28.

Lamb, J. A., Moore, J., Bailey, A., & Monaco, A. P. (2000). Autism: Recent molecular genetic advances. *Human Molecular Genetics, 9,* 861–868.

Lamberg, L. (1998). New drug for erectile dysfunction boon for many, "viagravation" for some. *JAMA: Medical News & Perspectives, 280,* 867–871.

Lambert, M. J., Shapiro, D. A., & Bergin, A. E. (1986). The effectiveness of psychotherapy. In S. L. Garfield & A. E. Bergin (Eds.), *Handbook of psychotherapy and behavior change* (3rd ed., pp. 157–212). New York: Wiley.

Lambert, W. W., Solomon, R. L., & Watson, P. D. (1949). Reinforcement and extinction as factors in size estimation. *Journal of Experimental Psychology, 39,* 637–641.

Lampl, M., Veldhuis, J. D., & Johnson, M. L. (1992, October 30). Saltation and stasis: A model of human growth. *Science, 258,* 801–803.

Landesman, S., & Butterfield, E. C. (1987). Normalization and deinstitution of mentally retarded individuals: Controversy and facts. *American Psychologist, 42,* 809–816.

Landy, F. L., & Farr, J. L. (1980). Performance rating. *Psychological Bulletin, 87,* 72–107.

Lang, E. V., Benotsch, E. G., Fick, L. J., Lutgendorf, S., Berbaum, M. L., Berbaum, K. S., Logan, H., & Spiegel, D. (2000). Adjunctive non-pharmacological analgesia for invasive medical procedures: A randomised trial. *Lancet, 355,* 1486–1490.

Lange, K., Williams, L. M., Young, A. W., Bullmore, E. T., Brammer, M. J., Williams, S. C. R., Gray, J. A., & Philips, M. L. (2003). Task instructions modulate neural responses to fearful facial expressions. *Biological Psychiatry, 53,* 226–232.

Langer, E. J., Bashner, R. S., & Chanowitz, B. (1985). Decreasing prejudice by increasing discrimination. *Journal of Personality and Social Psychology, 49,* 113–120.

Langlois, J. H., Kalakanis, L., Rubinstein, A. J., Larson, A., Hallam, M., & Smoot, M. (2000). Maxims of myths of beauty? A meta-analytic and theoretical review. *Psychological Bulletin, 126,* 390–423.

Langlois, J. H., Ritter, J. M., Casey, R. J., & Sawin, D. B. (1995). Infant attractiveness predicts maternal behaviors and attitudes. *Developmental Psychology, 31,* 464–472.

Lantz, M. S., Buchalter, E. N., & McBee, L. (1997). The wellness group: A novel intervention for coping with disruptive behavior in elderly nursing home residents. *Gerontologist, 37*, 551–556.

Larimer, M. E., Lydum, A. R., Anderson, B. K., & Turner, A. P. (1999). Male and female recipients of unwanted sexual contact in a college student sample: Prevalence rates, alcohol use, and depression symptoms. *Sex Roles, 40*, 295–308.

Lashley, K. S. (1950). In search of the engram. *Symposia of the Society for Experimental Biology, 4*, 454–482.

Latané, B., & Rodin, J. (1969). A lady in distress: Inhibiting effects of friends and strangers on bystander intervention. *Journal of Experimental Social Psychology, 5*, 189–202.

Laumann, E. O., Gagnon, J. H., Michael, R. T., & Michaels, S. (1994). *The social organization of sexuality: Sexual practices in the United States.* Chicago: University of Chicago Press.

Lavie, P. (2001). Sleep-wake as a biological rhythm. *Annual Review of Psychology, 52*, 277–303.

Layton, B., & Krikorian, R. (2002). Memory mechanisms in posttraumatic stress disorder. *Journal of Neuropsychiatry and Clinical Neurosciences, 14*, 254–261.

Lazarus, R. S. (1981, July). Little hassles can be hazardous to health. *Psychology Today*, pp. 58–62.

Lazarus, R. S. (1982). Thoughts on the relations between emotion and cognition. *American Psychologist, 37*, 1019–1024.

Lazarus, R. S. (1991a). Cognition and motivation in emotion. *American Psychologist, 46*, 352–367.

Lazarus, R. S. (1991b). Progress on a cognitive-motivational-relational theory of emotion. *American Psychologist, 46*, 819–834.

Lazarus, R. S. (1991c). *Emotion and adaptation.* New York: Oxford University Press.

Lazarus, R. S. (1993). From psychological stress to the emotions: A history of changing outlooks. *Annual Review of Psychology, 44*, 1–21.

Leary, W. E. (1990, January 25). Risk of hearing loss is growing, panel says. *New York Times*, Sec. B.

LeBoeuf, R. A., & Shafir, E. (2003). Deep thoughts and shallow frames on the susceptibility to framing effects. *Journal of Behavioral Decision Making, 16*, 77–92.

Leborgne, L., Maziere, J. C., & Andrejak, M. (2002). Oxidative stress, atherogenesis and cardiovascular risk factors. *Arch Mal Coeur Vaiss, 95*, 805–814.

Lebow, J. L., & Gurman, A. S. (1995). Research assessing couple and family therapy. *Annual Review of Psychology, 46*, 27–57.

Leccese, A. P. (1991). *Drugs and society.* Englewood Cliffs, NJ: Prentice Hall.

LeDoux, J. E. (1994). Emotion, memory and the brain. *Scientific American, 270*(6), 50–57.

LeDoux, J. E. (1996). *The emotional brain.* New York: Simon and Schuster.

Lee, S., Chan, Y. Y. L., & Hsu, L. K. G. (2003). The intermediate term outcome of Chinese patients with anorexia nervosa in Hong Kong. *American Journal of Psychiatry, 160*, 967–972.

Lees-Haley, P. R., Iverson, G. L., Lange, R. T., Fox, D. D., & Allen, L. M. III (2002). Malingering in forensic neuropsychology: Daubert and the MMPI-2. *Journal of Forensic Neuropsychology, 3*, 167–203.

Lehman, D. R., Lempert, R. O., Nisbett, R. E. (1988). The effects of graduate training on reasoning: Formal discipline and thinking about everyday-life events. *American Psychologist, 43*, 431–442.

Leibowitz, H. W., & Owens, D. A. (1977). Nighttime driving accidents and selective visual degradation. *Science, 197*, 422–423.

Leichsenring, F., & Leibing, E. (2003). The effectiveness of psychodynamic therapy and cognitive behavior therapy in the treatment of personality disorders: A meta-analysis. *American Journal of Psychiatry, 160*, 1223–1232.

Leigh, R. J. (1994). Human vestibular cortex. *Annals of Neurology, 35*, 383–384.

Leit, R. A., Gray, J. J., & Pope, H. G. (2002). The media's representation of the ideal male body: A cause for muscle dysmorphia? *International Journal of Eating Disorders, 31*, 334–338.

Leitenberg, H., & Henning, K. (1995). Sexual fantasy. *Psychological Bulletin, 117*, 469–496.

Lemish, D., & Rice, M. L. (1986). Television as a talking picture book: A prop for language acquisition. *Journal of Child Language, 13*, 251–274.

Lerman, C., Caporaso, N. D., Audrain, J., Main, D., Bowman, E. D., Lockshin, B., Boyd, N. R., & Shields, P. G. (1999). Evidence suggesting the role of specific genetic factors in cigarette smoking. *Health Psychology, 18*, 14–20.

Lerman, H. (1996). *Gender bias in the diagnostic classification of mental disorders.* New York: Basic Books.

Lerner, M. J. (1980). *The belief in a just world: A fundamental delusion.* New York: Plenum.

Leroy, P., Dessolin, S., Villageois, P., Moon, B. C., Friedman, J. M., Ailhaud, G., & Dani, C. (1996). Expression of ob gene in adipose cells. Regulation by insulin. *Journal of Biological Chemistry, 271*, 2365–2368.

Leschied, A. W., & Cummings, A. L. (2002). Youth violence: An overview of predictors, counseling interventions, and future directions. *Canadian Journal of Counseling, 36*, 256–264.

Leshner, A. I. (1996). Understanding drug addiction: Implications for treatment. *Hospital Practice, 31*, 7–54.

Lev, M. (1991, May). No hidden meaning here: Survey sees subliminal ads. *New York Times*, Sec. C.

LeVay, S. (1991, August). A difference in hypothalamic structure between heterosexual and homosexual men. *Science, 253*, 1034–1038.

LeVay, S. (2000). Brain invaders. *Scientific American, 282*(3), 27.

LeVay, S., & Hamer, D. H. (1994). Evidence for a biological influence in male homosexuality. *Scientific American, 270*(5), 44–49.

Levenson, M. R., & Aldwin, C. M. (1994). Aging, personality, and adaptation. In V. S. Ramachandran (Ed.), *Encyclopedia of human behavior* (Vol. 1, pp. 47–55). San Diego, CA: Academic Press.

Levenson, R. W. (1992). Autonomic nervous system differences among emotions. *Psychological Science, 3*, 23–27.

Leventhal, H., & Niles, P. (1965). Persistence of influence for varying duration of exposure to threat stimuli. *Psychological Reports, 16*, 223–233.

Levin, J. S., & Vanderpool, H.Y. (1989). Is religion therapeutically significant for hypertension? *Social Science and Medicine, 29*, 69–78.

Levine, S., Johnson, D. F., & Gonzales, C. A. (1985). Behavioral and hormonal responses to separation in infant rhesus monkeys and mothers. *Behavioral Neuroscience, 99*, 399–410.

Levinson, D. J. (1978). *The seasons of a man's life.* New York: Knopf.

Levinson, D. J. (1986). A conception of adult development. *American Psychologist, 41*, 3–13.

Levinson, D. J. (1987). *The seasons of a woman's life.* New York: Knopf.

Lewin, K. A. (1935). *A dynamic theory of personality* (K. E. Zener & D. K. Adams, Trans.). New York: McGraw-Hill.

Lewin, T. (1994a, May 18). Boys are more comfortable with sex than girls are, survey finds. *New York Times*, p. A10.

Lewin, T. (1994b, October 7). Sex in America: Faithfulness thrives after all. *New York Times*, p. A1.

Lewin, T. (1995, May 30). The decay of families is global study says. *New York Times*, p. A5.

Lewin, T. (1996, March 27). Americans are firmly attached to traditional roles for sexes, poll finds. *New York Times*, p. A12.

Lewy, A. J., Ahmed, S., Latham, J. J., & Sack, R. (1992). Melatonin shifts human circadian rhythms according to a phase-response curve. *Chronobiology International 9*, 380–392.

Li, Y. J., & Low, W. C. (1997). Intraretrosplenial cortical grafts of fetal cholinergic neurons and the restoration of spatial memory function. *Cell Transplant, 6*, 85–93.

Lichstein, K. L., Wilson, N. M., & Johnson, C. T. (2000). Psychological treatment of secondary insomnia. *Psychology & Aging, 15*, 232–240.

Lichtenstein, E. (1999). Nicotine Anonymous: Community resource and research implications. *Psychology of Addictive Behaviors, 13*, 60–68.

Lichtenstein, P., Holm, N. V., Verkasalo, P. K., Iliadou, A., Kaprio, J., Koskenvuo, M., Pukkala, E., Skytthe, A., & Hemminki, K. (2000). Environmental and heritable factors in the causation of cancer—Analyses of cohorts of twins from Sweden, Denmark, and Finland. *New England Journal of Medicine, 343*, 78–85.

Liggett, D. R. (2000). *Sport hypnosis.* Champaign, IL: Human Kinetics.

Lightdale, J. R., & Prentice, D. A. (1994). Rethinking sex differences in aggression: Aggressive behavior in the absence of social roles. *Personality and Social Psychology Bulletin, 20*, 34–44.

Lilienfeld, S. O., & Lynn, S. J. (2003). Dissociative identity disorder: Multiple personalities, multiple controversies. In S. O. Lilienfeld & S. J. Lynn (Eds.), *Science and pseudoscience in clinical psychology* (pp. 109–142). New York, NY: Guilford Press.

Limber, J. (1977). Language in child and chimp. *American Psychologist, 32*, 280–295.

Lin, L., Umahara, M., York, D. A., & Bray, G. A. (1998). Beta-casomophins stimulate and enterostatin inhibits the intake of dietary fat in rats. *Peptids, 19*, 325–331.

Lin, M., Poland, R., & Nakasaki, G. (1993). *Psychopharmacology and psychobiology of ethnicity.* Washington, DC: American Psychiatric Association Press.

Lindberg, N., Virkkunen, M., Tani, P., Appleber, B., Virkkala, J., Rimon, R., & Porkka-Heiskanen, T. (2002). Effects of a single dose of olanzapine on sleep in healthy females and males. *International Clinical Psychopharmacology, 17*, 177–184.

Lindsay, D. S. (1993). Eyewitness suggestibility. *Current Directions in Psychological Science, 2*, 86–89.

Lindsay, D. S., & Johnson, M. K. (1989). The eyewitness suggestibility effect and memory for source. *Memory & Cognition, 17*, 349–358.

Lindsay, P. H., & Norman, D. A. (1977). *Human information processing* (2nd ed.). New York: Academic Press.

Linn, R. L. (1982). Admissions testing on trial. *American Psychologist, 37*, 279–291.

Lipman, S. (1991). *Laughter in Hell: The use of humor during the Holocaust.* Northvale, NJ: J. Aronson.

Lips, H. M. (2002). *A new psychology of women: Gender, culture, and ethnicity* (2nd ed.). New York, NY: McGraw-Hill.

Lipsey, M., & Wilson, D. (1993). The efficacy of psychological, educational, and behavioral treatment: Confirmation from meta-analysis. *American Psychologist, 48,* 1181–1209.

Lipsky, D. K., & Gartner, A. (1996). Inclusive education and school restructuring. In W. Stainback & S. Stainback (Eds.), *Controversial issues confronting special education: Divergent perspectives* (pp. 3–15). Baltimore: Brookes.

Little, K. Y., Krowlewski, D. M., Zhang, L., & Cassin, B. J. (2003). Loss of striatal vesicular monoamine transporter protein (VMAT2) in human cocaine users. *American Journal of Psychiatry, 160,* 47–55.

Liu, C., Weaver, D. R., Jin, X., Shearman, I. P., Pieschl, R. I., Gribkoff, V. K., & Reppert, S. M. (1997). Molecular dissection of two distinct actions of melatonin on the suprachiasmatic circadian clock. *Neuron, 19,* 99–102.

Liu, J. H., & Latane, B. (1998). Extremitization of attitudes: Does thought- and discussion-induced polarization cumulate? *Basic and Applied Social Psychology, 20,* 103–110.

Livesley, W. J., Jang, K. L., & Vernon P. A. (2003). Genetic basis of personality structure. In T. Millon & M. J. Lerner, (Eds.), *Handbook of psychology: Personality and social psychology, Vol. 5* (pp. 59–83). New York, NY: John Wiley & Sons, Inc.

Livingstone, M. S., & Hubel, D. H. (1988b, May 6). Segregation of form, color, movement, and depth: Anatomy, physiology, and perception. *Science, 340,* 740–749.

Llinás, R. (1996). *The mind-brain continuum.* Proceedings of a meeting held in Madrid, 1995. Cambridge, MA: MIT Press.

Locke, E. A., Shaw, K. N., Saari, L. M., & Latham, G. P. (1981). Goal setting and task performance: 1969–1980. *Psychological Bulletin, 90,* 125–152.

Loeb, L. A. (1985). Apurinic sites as mutagenic intermediates. *Cell, 40,* 483–484.

Loehlin, J. C. (1989). Partitioning environmental and genetic contributions to behavioral development. *American Psychologist, 44,* 1285–1292.

Loehlin, J. C., Horn, J. M., & Willerman, L. (1997). Heredity, environment, and IQ in the Texas adoption study. In R. J. Sternberg & E. Grigorenko (Eds.), *Intelligence: Heredity and environment* (pp. 105–125). New York: Cambridge University Press.

Loehlin, J. C., McCrae, R. R., Costa, P. T., & John, O. P. (1998). Heritability of common and measure-specific components of the Big Five personality traits. *Journal of Research in Personality, 32,* 431–453.

Loehlin, J. C., Willerman, L., & Horn, J. M. (1988). Human behavior genetics. *Annual Review of Psychology, 39,* 101–133.

Loewenstein, G. (1994). The psychology of curiosity: A review and reinter-

pretation. *Psychological Bulletin, 116,* 75–98.

Loewenstein, G., & Frederick, S. (1998). Hedonic adaptation: From the bright side to the dark side. In D. Kahneman, E. Diener, & N. Schwarz (Eds.), *Well-being: The foundations of hedonic psychology* (pp. 302–329). New York: Russell Sage.

Loftus, E. F., & Palmer, J. C. (1974). Reconstruction of automobile destruction: An example of the interaction between language and memory. *Journal of Verbal Learning and Verbal Behavior, 13,* 585–589.

Loftus, E. F., & Pickrell, J. E. (1995). The formation of false memories. *Psychiatric Annals, 25,* 720–725.

Loftus, E. F., Coan, J. A., & Pickrell, J. E. (1996). Manufacturing false memories using bits of reality. In L. Reder (Ed.), *Implicit memory and metacognition* (pp. 195–220). Mahwah, NJ: Erlbaum.

Logue, A. W., Ophir, I., & Strauss, K. E. (1981). The acquisition of taste aversions in humans. *Behavior Research and Therapy, 19,* 319–333.

López, S. R., & Guarnaccia, P. J. J. (2000). Cultural psychopathology: Uncovering the social world of mental illness. *Annual Review of Psychology, 51,* 571–598.

Lorenz, K. (1935). Der Kumpan inder Umwelt des Vogels. *Journal of Ornithology, 83,* 137–213, 289–413.

Lorenz, K. (1968). *On aggression.* New York: Harcourt.

Lott, A. J., & Lott, B. E. (1974). The role of reward in the formation of positive interpersonal attitudes. In T. L. Huston (Ed.), *Foundations of interpersonal attraction* (pp. 171–192). New York: Academic Press.

Louie, T. A., Curren, M. T., & Harich, K. R. (2000). "I knew we could win": Hindsight bias for favorable and unfavorable decision outcomes. *Journal of Applied Psychology, 85,* 264–272.

Lovibond, P. F., Siddle, D. A., & Bond, N. W. (1993). Resistance to extinction of fear-relevant stimuli: Preparedness or selective sensitization? *Journal of Experimental Psychology: General, 122,* 449–461.

Lubinski, D. (2000). Scientific and social significance of assessing individual differences: "Sinking shafts at a few critical points." *Annual Review of Psychology, 51,* 405–444.

Lubinski, D., & Benbow, C. P. (2000). States of excellence. *American Psychologist, 55,* 137–150.

Luchins, A. (1957). Primacy-recency in impression formation. In C. Hovland, W. Mandell, E. Campbell, T. Brock, A. Luchins, A. Cohen, W. McGuire, I. Janis, R. Feierabend, & N. Anderson (Eds.), *The order of presentation in persuasion* (pp. 33–40, 55–61). New Haven, CT: Yale University Press.

Luine, V., Villegas, M., Martinez, C., & McEwen, B. S. (1994). Repeated stress

causes reversible impairments of spatial memory performance. *Brain Research, 639,* 167–170.

Luria, A. R. (1968). *The mind of a mnemonist* (L. Solotaroff, Trans.). New York: Basic Books.

Luria, A. R., & Solotaroff, L. (1987). *The mind of a mnemonist: A little book about a vast memory.* Cambridge, MA: Harvard University Press.

Lyness, S. A. (1993). Predictors of differences between Type A and B individuals in heart rate and blood pressure reactivity. *Psychological Bulletin, 114,* 266–295.

Lynn, R. (1989). Positive correlation between height, head size and IQ: A nutrition theory of the secular increases in intelligence. *British Journal of Educational Psychology, 59,* 372–377.

Lyons, M. J., True, W. R., Eisen, S. A., Goldberg, J., Meyer, J. M., Faraone, S. V., Eaves, L. J., & Tsuang, M. T. (1995). Differential heritability of adult and juvenile antisocial traits. *Archives of General Psychiatry, 52,* 906–915.

Lyubomirsky, S., & Ross, L. (1999). Changes in attractiveness of elected, rejected and precluded alternatives: A comparison of happy and unhappy individuals. *Journal of Personality and Social Psychology, 76,* 988–1007.

M

Maas, J. (1998). *Power sleep: The revolutionary program that prepares your mind for peak performance.* New York: Villard.

Maccoby, E. E. (1998). *The two sexes: Growing up apart, coming together.* Cambridge, MA: Belknap Press.

Maccoby, E. E. (2000). Parenting and its effects on children: On reading and misreading behavior genetics. *Annual Review of Psychology, 51,* 1–27.

MacDonald, T. K., Fong, G. T., Zanna, M. P., & Martineau, A. M. (2000). Alcohol myopia and condom use: Can alcohol intoxication be associated with more prudent behavior. *Journal of Personality & Social Psychology, 78,* 605–619.

MacDonald, T. K., MacDonald, G., Zanna, M. P., & Fong, G. (2000). Alcohol, sexual arousal and intentions to use condoms in young men: Applying alcohol myopia theory to risky sexual behavior. *Health Psychology, 19,* 290–298.

Macionis, J. J. (1993). *Sociology* (4th ed.). Englewood Cliffs, NJ: Prentice Hall.

Mackavey, W. R., Malley, J. E., & Stewart, A. J. (1991). Remembering autobiographically consequential experiences: Content analysis of psychologists' accounts of their lives. *Psychology and Aging, 6,* 50–59.

MacLean, P. D. (1970). The limbic brain in relation to the psychoses. In P. Black (Ed.), *Physiological correlates of*

emotion (pp. 129–146). New York: Academic Press.

MacLeod, D. I. A. (1978). Visual sensitivity. *Annual Review of Psychology, 29,* 613–645.

Macrae, C. N., & Bodenhausen, G. V. (2000). Social cognition: Thinking categorically about others. *Annual Review of Psychology, 51,* 93–120.

MacWhinney, B. (1999). *The emergence of language.* Mahwah, NJ: Erlbaum.

Madden, N. A., & Slavin, R. E. (1983). Effects of cooperative learning on the social acceptance of mainstreamed academically handicapped students. *Journal of Special Education, 17,* 171–182.

Maddi, S. R. (1989). *Personality theories: A comparative approach* (5th ed.). Homewood, IL: Dorsey.

Magaletta, P. R., Fagan, T. J., & Peyrot, M. F. (2000). Telehealth in the federal bureau of prisons: Inmates' perceptions. *Professional Psychology: Research & Practice, 31,* 497–502.

Maier, S. F., & Seligman, M. E. (1976). Learned helplessness: Theory and evidence. *Journal of Experimental Psychology: General, 105,* 3–46.

Maio, G. R., & Olson, J. M. (1998). Values as truisms: Evidence and implications. *Journal of Personality and Social Psychology, 74,* 294–311.

Maisto, A. A., & German, M. L. (1986). Reliability, predictive validity and interrelationships of early assessment indices used with developmentally delayed infants and children. *Journal of Clinical Child Psychology, 15,* 327–332.

Maisto, A. A., & Hughes, E. (1995). Adaptation to group home living for adults with mental retardation as a function of previous residential placement. *Journal of Intellectual Disability Research, 39,* 15–18.

Maj, M. (2003). The effect of lithium in bipolar disorder: A review of recent research evidence. *Bipolar Disorders, 5,* 180–188.

Mandel, D. R., & Lehman, D. R. (1996). Counterfactual thinking and ascriptions of cause and preventability. *Journal of Personality and Social Psychology, 71,* 450–463.

Mandel, D. R., Jusczyk, P. W., & Pisoni, D. B. (1995). Infants' recognition of the sound patterns of their own names. *Psychological Science, 6,* 314–317.

Manfredi, M., Bini, G., Cruccu, G., Accornero, N., Beradelli, A., & Medolago, L. (1981). Congenital absence of pain. *Archives of Neurology (Chicago), 38,* 507–511.

Manton, K. G., & Gu, X. (2001). Changes in the prevalence of chronic disability in the United States black and nonblack population above age 65 from 1982 to 1999. *Proceedings of the National Academy of Sciences, USA, 98,* 6354–6359.

Maquet, P., Laureys, S., Peigneus, P., Fuchs, S., Petiau, C., Phips, C., Aerts, J., Fiore, G. D., Degueldre, C., Meulemans, T., Luxen, A., Franck, G., VanDerLinden, M., Smith, C., & Axel, C. (2000). Experience-dependent changes in cerebral activation during human REM sleep. *Nature: Neuroscience, 3,* 831–836.

Marano, H. E. (1997, July 1). Puberty may start at 6 as hormones surge. *New York Times,* pp. C1, C6.

Marcia, J. E. (1976). Identity six years after: A follow-up study. *Journal of Youth and Adolescence, 5,* 145–160.

Marcia, J. E. (1980). Identity in adolescence. In J. Adelson (Ed.), *Handbook of adolescent psychology* (pp. 159–187). New York: Wiley.

Marcia, J. E. (1994). The empirical study of ego identity. In H. A. Bosna, T. L. G. Graafsma., H. D. Grotevant, & D. J. de Levita (Eds.), *Identity and development: An interdisciplinary approach* (pp. 67–80). Thousand Oaks, CA: Sage.

Marcus, D. K., & Miller, R. S. (2003). Sex differences in judgments of physical attractiveness: A social relations analysis. *Personality and Social Psychology Bulletin, 29,* 325–335.

Marcus, G. F. (1996). Why do children say "breaked"? *American Psychological Society, 5,* 81–85.

Margolin, G. (1987). Marital therapy: A cognitive-behavioral-affective approach. In N. S. Jacobson (Ed.), *Psychotherapists in clinical practice* (pp. 232–285). New York: Guilford.

Markon, K. E., Krueger, R. F., Bouchard, T. J. Jr., & Gottesman, I. I. (2002). Normal and abnormal personality traits: Evidence for genetic and environmental relationships in the Minnesota Study of Twins Reared Apart. *Journal of Personality, 70,* 661–693.

Markovic, B. M., Dimitrijevic, M., & Jankovic, B. D. (1993). Immunomodulation by conditioning: Recent developments. *International Journal of Neuroscience, 71,* 231–249.

Marks, I. M., & Nesse, R. M. (1994). Fear and fitness: An evolutionary analysis of anxiety disorders. *Ethology and Sociobiology, 15,* 247–261.

Marks, L. S., Duda, C., Dorey, F. J., Macairan, M. L., & Santos, P. B. (1999). Treatment of erectile dysfunction with sildenafil. *Urology, 53,* 19–24.

Markus, H. R., & Kitayama, S. (1991). Culture and self: Implications for cognition, emotion, and motivation. *Psychological Review, 98,* 224–253.

Marr, D. (1982). *Vision.* San Francisco: Freeman.

Martin, R. L., Roberts, W. V., & Clayton, P. J. (1980). Psychiatric status after a one-year prospective follow-up. *Journal of the American Medical Association, 244,* 350–353.

Martin, S., (2001). Substance abuse is nation's No. 1 health problem, but there is hope. *Monitor on Psychology, 32,* 10.

Martinez, J. L., Barea-Rodriguez, E. J., & Derrick, B. E. (1998). Long-term potentiation, long-term depression, and learning. In J. L. Martinez & R. P. Kesner (Eds.), *Neurobiology of learning and memory* (pp. 211–246). San Diego, CA: Academic Press.

Martino, A. (1995, February 5). Mid-life usually brings positive change, not crisis. *Ann Arbor News.*

Maslach, C., & Leiter, M. P. (1997). *The truth about burnout.* San Francisco: Jossey-Bass.

Masling, J. (2002). How do I score thee? Let me count the ways. Or some different methods of categorizing Rorschach responses. *Journal of Personality Assessment, 79,* 399–421.

Maslow, A. H. (1954). *Motivation and personality.* New York: Harper & Row.

Mason, F. L. (1997). Fetishism: Psychopathology and theory. In D. R. Laws & W. T. O'Donohue (Eds.), *Handbook of sexual deviance: Theory and application.* New York: Guilford.

Massaro, D. W., & Cowan, N. (1993). Information processing models: Microscopes of the mind. *Annual Review of Psychology, 44,* 383–425.

Masson, J. M. (1984). *The assault on truth: Freud's suppression of the seduction theory.* New York: Farrar, Strauss, & Giroux.

Masters, W. H., & Johnson, V. E. (1970). *Human sexual inadequacy.* Boston: Little, Brown.

Masters, W. H., & Johnson, V. E. (1966). *Human sexual response.* London: J. & A. Churchill.

Mateo, J. M., & Johnston, R. E. (2000). Kin recognition and the "armpit effect": Evidence of self-referent phenotype matching. *Proceedings of the Royal Society: Biological Sciences, 267,* 695–700.

Mather, M., Shafir, E., & Johnson, M. (2000). Misremembrance of options past: Source monitoring and choice. *Psychological Science, 11,* 132–138.

Matlin, M. W., (1989). *Cognition* (2nd ed.). Fort Worth, TX: Holt, Rinehart & Winston.

Matson, J. L., Smalls, Y., Hampff, A., Smiroldo, B. B., & Anderson, S. J. (1998). A comparison of behavioral techniques to teach functional independent-living skills to individuals with severe and profound mental retardation. *Behavior Modification, 22,* 298–306.

Matsumoto, D. (1995). *People: Psychology from a cultural perspective.* Pacific Grove, CA: Brooks/Cole.

Matsumoto, D. (1996). *Culture and psychology.* Pacific Grove, CA: Brooks/Cole.

Matsumoto, D., & Kupperbusch, C. (2001). Idiocentric and allocentric differences in emotional expression, experience and the coherence between expression and experience. *Asian Journal of Social Psychology, 4,* 113–131.

Matsumoto, D., Kudoh, T., Scherer, K., & Wallbott, H. G. (1988). Emotion antecedents and reactions in the U. S. and Japan. *Journal of Cross-Cultural Psychology, 19,* 267–286.

Matta, M. A. (2002). Parental corporal punishment as a predictor of child maladjustment: Race and parental responsiveness as potential moderators. *Dissertation Abstracts International: Section B: The Sciences and Engineering, 63,* 2091.

Matthews, D. B., Best, P. J., White, A. M., Vandergriff, J. L., & Simson, P. E. (1996). Ethanol impairs spatial cognitive processing: New behavioral and electrophysiological findings. *Current Directions in Psychological Science, 5,* 111–115.

Matthews, G., Zeidner, M., & Roberts, R. D. (2002). *Emotional intelligence: Science and myth.* Cambridge, MA: MIT Press.

Mattson, S. N., Riley, E. P., Gramling, L., Delis, D. C., & Jones, K. L. (1998). Neuropsychological comparison of alcohol-exposed children with or without physical features of fetal alcohol syndrome. *Neuropsychology, 12,* 146–153.

Maugh, T. H., II. (1999, September 1). Smarter mice set the stage for raising human IQs. *Charlotte Observer,* p. 1A.

Maunsell, E., Brisson, J., Mondor, M., Verreault, R., & Deschenes, L. (2001). Stressful life events and survival after breast cancer. *Psychosomatic Medicine, 63,* 306–315.

Maurer, D., & Maurer, C. (1988). *The world of the newborn.* New York: Basic Books.

May, J., & Kline, P. (1987). Measuring the effects upon cognitive abilities of sleep loss during continuous operations. *British Journal of Psychology, 78*(Pt 4), 443–455.

Mayer, D. J., & Watkins, L. R. (1984). Multiple endogenous opiate and nonopiate analgesia systems. In L. Kruger & J. C. Liebeskind (Eds.), *Neural mechanisms of pain* (pp. 253–276). New York: Raven Press.

Mayer, J. D., & Geher, G. (1996). Emotional intelligence and the identification of emotion. *Intelligence, 22,* 89–113.

Mays, V. M., Bullock, M., Rosenzweig, M. R., & Wessells, M. (1998). Ethnic conflict: Global challenges and psychological perspectives. *American Psychologist, 53,* 737–742.

Mazur, J. E. (1994). *Learning and behavior* (3rd ed.). Englewood Cliffs, NJ: Prentice Hall.

Mazzoni, G. A. L., Lombardo, P., Malvagia, S., & Loftus, E. F. (1999). Dream interpretation and false beliefs. *Professional Psychology: Research & Practice, 30,* 45–50.

McBurney, D. H., & Collings, V. B. (1984). *Introduction to sensation/perception* (2nd ed.). Englewood Cliffs, NJ: Prentice Hall.

McCabe, P. M., Schneiderman, N., Field, T., & Wellens, A. R. (2000). *Stress, coping, and cardiovascular disease.* Mahwah, NJ: Erlbaum.

McCall, M. (1997). Physical attractiveness and access to alcohol: What is beautiful does not get carded. *Journal of Applied Social Psychology, 27,* 453–462.

McCall, R. B. (1979). *Infants.* Cambridge, MA: Harvard University Press.

McCann, I. L., & Holmes, D. S. (1984). Influence of aerobic exercise on depression. *Journal of Personality and Social Psychology, 46,* 1142–1147.

McCann, U. D., Slate, S. O., & Ricaurte, G. A. (1996). Adverse reactions with 3,4-methylene dioxymethamphetamine (MDMA; "ecstasy"). *Drug Safety, 15,* 107–115.

McCann, U. D., Szabo, Z., Scheffel, U., Dannals, R. F., & Ricaurte, G. A. (1998). Positron emission tomographic evidence of toxic effect of MDMA ("Ecstasy") on brain serotonin neurons in human beings. *Lancet, 352,* 1443–1437.

McClearn, G. E., Plomin, R., Gora-Maslak, G., & Crabbe, J. C. (1991). The gene chase in behavioral science. *Psychological Science, 2,* 222–229.

McClelland, D. C. (1973). Testing for competence rather than for "intelligence." *American Psychologist, 28,* 1–14.

McClelland, D. C., & Atkinson, J. W. (1948). The projective expression of needs: I. The effect of different intensities of the hunger drive on perception. *Journal of Psychology, 25,* 205–222.

McClintock, M. K. (1971). Menstrual synchrony and suppression. *Nature (London), 229,* 244–245.

McClintock, M. K. (1978). Estrous synchrony and its mediation by airborne chemical communication (Rattus norvegicus). *Hormones & Behavior, 10,* 264–276.

McClintock, M. K. (1999). Reproductive biology: Pheromones and regulation of ovulation. *Nature, 401,* 232–233.

McClintock, M. K., & Herdt, G. (1996). Rethinking puberty: The development of sexual attraction. *Current Directions in Psychological Science, 5,* 178–183.

McClure, E. B. (2000). A meta-analytic review of sex differences in facial expression processing and their development in infants, children, and adolescents. *Psychological Bulletin, 126,* 424–453.

McConnell, R. A. (1969). ESP and credibility in science. *American Psychologist, 24,* 531–538.

McCrae, R. R., & Costa, P. T., Jr. (1985). Updating Norman's "adequate taxonomy": Intelligence and personality dimensions in natural language and in questionnaires. *Journal of Personality and Social Psychology, 49,* 710–721.

McCrae, R. R., & Costa, P. T., Jr. (1987). Validation of the five-factor model of personality across instruments and observers. *Journal of Personality and Social Psychology, 52,* 81–90.

McCrae, R. R., & Costa, P. T., Jr. (1989). More reasons to adopt the five-factor model. *American Psychologist, 44,* 451–452.

McCrae, R. R., & Costa, P. T., Jr. (1994). The stability of personality: Observations and evaluations. *Current Directions in Psychological Science, 3,* 173–175.

McCrae, R. R., & Costa, P. T., Jr. (1996). Toward a new generation of personality theories: Theoretical contexts for the five-factor model. In J. S. Wiggins (Ed.), *The five-factor model of personality: Theoretical perspectives* (pp. 51–87). New York: Guilford Press.

McCrae, R. R., & Costa, P. T., Jr. (1997). Personality trait structure as a human universal. *American Psychologist, 52,* 509–516.

McDaniel, M. A., Waddill, P. J., & Shakesby, P. S. (1996). Study strategies, interest, and learning from text: The application of material appropriate processing. In D. Herrmann, C. McEvoy, C. Hertzog, P. Hertel, & M. K. Johnson (Eds.), *Basic and applied memory research: Theory in context* (pp. 385–397). Mahwah, NJ: Erlbaum.

McDonald, J. W. (1999). Repairing the damaged spinal cord. *Scientific American, 281*(3), 65–73.

McElhatton, P. R., Bateman, D. N., Evans, C., Pughe, K. R., & Thomas, S. H. L. (1999). Congenital anomalies after prenatal ecstasy exposure. *Lancet, 354,* 1441–1442.

McFarland, L. J., Senn, L. E., & Childress, J. R. (1993). *21st century leadership: Dialogues with 100 top leaders.* Los Angeles: The Leadership Press.

McGaugh, J. L. (1983). Preserving the presence of the past: Hormonal influences on memory storage. *American Psychologist, 38,* 161–174.

McGaugh, J. L. (1990). Significance and remembrance: The role of neuromodulatory systems. *Psychological Science, 1,* 15–25.

McGeer, P. L., & McGeer, E. G. (1980). Chemistry of mood and emotion. *Annual Review of Psychology, 31,* 273–307.

McGinnis, M. (1994). The role of behavioral research in national health policy. In S. Blumenthal, K. Matthews, & S. Weiss (Eds.), *New research frontiers in behavioral medicine: Proceeding of the National Conference.* Washington, DC: NIH Publications.

McGovern, L. P. (1976). Dispositional social anxiety and helping behavior under three conditions of threat. *Journal of Personality, 44,* 84–97.

McGue, M. (1993). From proteins to cognitions: The behavioral genetics of alcoholism. In R. Plomin & G. E. McClearn (Eds.), *Nature, nurture & psychology* (pp. 245–268). Washington, DC: American Psychological Association.

McGue, M. (1999). The behavioral genetics of alcoholism. *Current Directions in Psychological Science, 8,* 109–115.

McGuffin, P., Katz, R., Watkins, S., & Rutherford, J. (1996). A hospital-based twin register of the heritability of DSM-IV unipolar depression. *Archives of General Psychiatry, 53,* 129–136.

McGuire, M. T., Wing, R. R., Klem, M. L., Lang, W., & Hill, J. O. (1999). What predicts weight regain in a group of successful weight losers? *Journal of Consulting & Clinical Psychology, 67,* 177–185.

McGuire, P. A. (1999, June 6). Psychology and medicine connecting in the war over cancer. *APA Monitor,* pp. 8–9.

McGuire, P. A. (2000, February). New hope for people with schizophrenia. *Monitor on Psychology,* pp. 24–28.

McIntyre, C. K., Marriott, L. K., & Gold, P. E. (2003). Cooperation between memory systems: Acetylcholine release in the amygdale correlates positively with performance on a hippocampus-dependent task. *Behavioral Neuroscience, 117,* 320–326.

McKay, R. (1997, April 4). Stem cells in the nervous system. *Science, 276,* 66–71.

McKellar, J., Stewart, E., & Humphreys, K. (2003). Alcoholics anonymous involvement and positive alcohol-related outcomes: Cause, consequence, or just a correlate? A prospective 2-year study of 2,319 alcohol-dependent men. *Journal of Consulting and Clinical Psychology 71,* 302–308.

McKenna, M. C., Zevon, M. A., Corn, B., & Rounds, J. (1999). Psychosocial factors and the development of breast cancer: A meta-analysis. *Health Psychology, 18,* 520–531.

McKim, W. A. (1997). *Drugs and behavior* (3rd ed.). Upper Saddle River, NJ: Prentice Hall.

McLoyd, V. (1998). Socioeconomic disadvantage and child development. *American Psychologist, 53,* 185–204.

McMillan, T. M., Robertson, I. H., & Wilson, B. A. (1999). Neurogenesis after brain injury: Implications for neurorehabilitation. *Neuropsychological Rehabilitation, 9,* 129–133.

McMurray, G. A. (1950). Experimental study of a case of insensitivity to pain. *Archives of Neurology and Psychiatry, 64,* 650.

McNally, R. J. (2003). Experimental approaches to the recovered memory controversy. In M. F. Lenzenweger & J. M. Hooley (Eds.), *Principles of experimental psychopathology: Essays in honor of Brendan A. Maher* (pp. 269–277).

Washington, DC: American Psychological Association.

McNamara, H. J., Long, J. B., & Wike, E. L. (1956). Learning without response under two conditions of external cues. *Journal of Comparative and Physiological Psychology, 49,* 477–480.

McNeil, B. J., Pauker, S. G., Sox, H. C., Jr., & Tversky, A. (1982). On the elicitation of preferences for alternative therapies. *New England Journal of Medicine, 306,* 1259–1262.

Mead, M. (1935). *Sex and temperament in three primitive societies.* New York: Morrow.

Mednick, S. A. (1962). The associative basis of creativity. *Psychological Review, 69,* 220–232.

Mednick, S. C., Nakayama, K., Cantero, J. L., Atienza, M., Levin, A. A., Pathak, N., & Stickgold, R. (2002). The restorative effect of naps on perceptual deterioration. *Nature Neuroscience, 5,* 677–681.

Meglino, B. M., DeNisi, A. S., Youngblood, S. A., & Williams, K. J. (1988). Effects of realistic job previews: A comparison using an enhancement and a reduction preview. *Journal of Applied Psychology, 73,* 259–266.

Meichenbaum, D., & Cameron, R. (1982). Cognitive-behavior therapy. In G. T. Wilson & C. M. Franks (Eds.), *Contemporary behavior therapy: Conceptual and empirical foundations* (pp. 310–338). New York: Guilford.

Melamed, B. G., Hawes, R. R., Heiby, E., & Glick, J. (1975). Use of filmed modeling to reduce uncooperative behavior of children during dental treatment. *Journal of Dental Research, 54,* 797–801.

Melamed, S., Ben-Avi, I., Luz, J., & Green, M. (1995). Objective and subjective work monotony: Effects on job satisfaction, psychological distress, and absenteeism in blue-collar workers. *Journal of Applied Psychology, 80,* 29–42.

Mellers, B. A., Schwartz, A., & Cooke, A. D. J. (1998). Judgment and decision making. *Annual Review of Psychology, 49,* 447–47.

Meltzoff, A. N., & Gopnik, A. (1997). *Words, thoughts and theories.* Boston, MA: MIT Press.

Meltzoff, A. N., & Moore, M. K. (1989). Imitation in newborn infants: Exploring the range of gestures imitated and the underlying mechanisms. *Developmental Psychology, 25,* 954–962.

Melzack, R., & Wall, P. D. (1965). Pain mechanisms: A new theory. *Science, 150,* 971–979.

Mendez, B., & Martha, M. (2001). Changes in parental sense of competence and attitudes in low-income Head Start parents as a result of participation in a Parent Education Workshop. *Dissertation Abstracts International: Section B: The Sciences and Engineering, 62,* 2976.

Menon, T., Morris, M. W., Chiu, C. Y., & Hong, Y. Y. (1998). *Culture and the perceived autonomy of individuals and groups: American attributions to personal dispositions and Confucian attributions to group.* Unpublished manuscript, Stanford University.

Menzel, E. W. (1974). A group of young chimpanzees in a one-acre field. In A. M. Schrier & F. Stollnitz (Eds.), *Behavior of nonhuman primates* (Vol. 5, pp. 83–153). New York: Academic Press.

Mercer, T. B., & Lewis, J. G. (1978). Using the system of multicultural assessment (SOMPA) to identify the gifted minority child. In A. Y. Baldwin, G. H. Gear, & L. J. Lucito (Eds.), *Educational planning for the gifted: Overcoming cultural, geographic, and socioeconomic barriers.* Reston, VA: Council for Exceptional Children.

Merikangas, K. R., Angst, J., Eaton, W., Canino, G., Rubio-Stepic, M., Wacker, H., Wittchen, H.-U., Andrade, E. C., Whitaker, A., Kraemer, H., Robins, L. N., & Kupfer, D. J. (1996). Comorbidity and boundaries of affective disorders with anxiety disorders and substance misuse: Results of an International Task Force. *British Journal of Psychiatry, 168*(Suppl. 30), 58–67.

Merrill, K. A., Tolbert, V. E., & Wade, W. A. (2003). Effectiveness of cognitive therapy for depression in a community mental health center: A benchmarking study. *Journal of Consulting and Clinical Psychology, 71,* 404–409.

Mershon, B., & Gorsuch, R. L. (1988). Number of factors in the personality sphere: Does increase in factors increase predictability of real-life criteria? *Journal of Personality and Social Psychology, 55,* 675–680.

Mersky, H. (1992). The manufacture of personalities: The production of multiple personality disorder. *British Journal of Psychiatry, 160,* 327–340.

Merzer, M. (1998, January 12). Asleep in the cockpit. *Newsweek.*

Meston, C. M., & Frohlich, M. A. (2000). The neurobiology of sexual function. *Archives of General Psychiatry, 57,* 1012–1030.

Metcalfe, J., Funnell, M., & Gazzaniga, M. S. (1995). Guided visual search is a left-hemisphere process in split-brain patient. *Psychological Science, 6,* 157–173.

Meyer, G. J., Finn, S. E., Eyde, L. D., Kay, G. G., Moreland, K. L., Dies, R. R., Eisman, E. J., Kubiszyn, T. W., & Reed, G. M. (2001). Psychological testing and psychological assessment: A review of evidence and issues. *American Psychologist, 56,* 128–165.

Michael, R. T., Gagnon, J. H., Laumann, E. O., & Kolata, G. (1994). *Sex in America.* Boston, MA: Little, Brown.

Michelson, L. (Ed.). (1985). Meta-analysis and clinical psychology [Special issue]. *Clinical Psychology Review, 5.*

Migliaccio, E., Giorgio, M., Mele, S., Pelicci, G., Reboldi, P., Pandolfi, P. P., Lanfrancone, L., & Pelicci, P. G. (1999). The p66shu adaptor protein controls oxidative stress response and life span in mammals. *Nature, 402,* 309–313.

Milgram, S. (1963). Behavioral study of obedience. *Journal of Abnormal and Social Psychology, 67,* 371–378.

Milgram, S. (1974). *Obedience to authority: An experimental view.* New York: Harper & Row.

Miller, A. I. (1992). Scientific creativity: A comparative study of Henri Poincare and Albert Einstein. *Creativity Research Journal, 5,* 385–418.

Miller, G. A. (1999). On knowing a word. *Annual Review of Psychology, 50,* 1–19.

Miller, G. E., & Cohen, S. (2001). Psychological interventions and the immune system: A meta-analytic review and critique. *Health Psychology, 20,* 47–63.

Miller, J. (1984). Culture and the development of everyday social explanation. *Journal of Personality and Social Psychology, 46,* 961–978.

Miller, J. A. (2002). Individual motivation loss in group settings: An exploratory study of the social-loafing phenomenon. *Dissertation Abstracts International Section A: Humanities and Social Sciences, 62,* 2972.

Miller, J. G., Bersoff, D. M., & Harwood, R. L. (1990). Perceptions of social responsibilities in India and the United States: Moral imperatives or personal decisions? *Journal of Personality and Social Psychology, 58,* 33–47.

Miller, L. K. (1999). The savant syndrome: Intellectual impairment and exceptional skill. *Psychological Bulletin, 125,* 31–46.

Miller, P. A., Kliewer, W., & Burkeman, D. (1993, March). *Effects of maternal socialization on children's learning to cope with divorce.* Paper presented at the biennial meeting of the Society for Research in Child Development, New Orleans, LA.

Miller, T. Q., Smith, T. W., Turner, C. W., Guijarro, M. L., & Hallet, A. J. (1996). A meta-analytic review of research on hostility and physical health. *Psychological Bulletin, 119,* 322–348.

Miller, T. Q., Turner, C. W., Tindale, R. S., Posavac, E. J., & Dugoni, B. L. (1991). Reasons for the trend toward null findings in research on Type A behavior. *Psychological Bulletin, 110,* 469–485.

Miller, T. W., Miller, J. M., Kraus, R. F., Kaak, O., Sprang, R., & Veltkamp, L. J. (2003). Telehealth: A clinical application model for rural consultation. *Consulting Psychology Journal: Practice and Research, 55,* 119–127.

Miller, W. R., & Brown, S. A. (1997). Why psychologists should treat alcohol and drug problems. *American Psychologist, 52,* 1269–1279.

Millis, R. M. (1998). Smoking. In H. S. Friedman (Ed.). *Encyclopedia of mental health* (Vol. 3). San Diego: Academic Press.

Milner, B., Corkin, S., & Teuber, H. H. (1968). Further analysis of the hippocampal amnesic syndrome: 14-year follow-up study of H. M. *Neuropsychologia, 6,* 215–234.

Milton, J., & Wiseman, R. (1999). Does psi exist? Lack of replication of an anomalous process of information transfer. *Psychological Bulletin, 125,* 387–391.

Mineka, S., & Oehman, A. (2002). Phobias and preparedness: The selective, autonomic, and encapsulated nature of fear. *Biological Psychiatry, 51,* 927–937.

Mineka, S., Watson, D., & Clark, L. A. (1998). Comorbidity of anxiety and unipolar mood disorders. *Annual Review of Psychology, 49,* 377–412.

Minor, T. R., & Hunter, A. M. (2002). Stressor controllability and learned helplessness research in the United States: Sensitization and fatigue processes. *Integrative Physiological and Behavioral Science, 37,* 44–58.

Minton, H. L. (2002). Psychology and gender at the turn of the century. *American Psychologist, 55,* 613–615.

Minton, H. L., & Schneider, F. W. (1980). *Differential psychology.* Monterey, CA: Brooks/Cole.

Mirsky, S. (1995). The noses have it. *Scientific American, 273*(6), 20.

Mischel, W. (2003). Challenging the traditional personality psychology paradigm. In R. J. Sternberg (Ed.), *Psychologists defying the crowd: Stories of those who battled the establishment and won* (pp. 139–156). Washington, DC: American Psychological Association.

Mischel, W., & Shoda, Y. (1995). A cognitive-affective system theory of personality: Reconceptualizing situations, dispositions, dynamics, and invariance in personality structure. *Psychological Review, 102,* 246–268.

Mischel, W., & Shoda, Y. (1998). Reconciling processing dynamics and personality dispositions. *Annual Review of Psychology, 49,* 229–258.

Mistry, J., & Rogoff, B. (1994). Remembering in cultural context. In W. W. Lonner & R. Malpass (Eds.), *Psychology and culture* (pp. 139–144). Boston: Allyn & Bacon.

Misumi, J. (1985). *The behavioral science of leadership: An interdisciplinary Japanese leadership program.* Ann Arbor: University of Michigan Press.

Mitchell, R. W., Thompson, N. S., & Miles, H. L. (1997). *Anthropomorphism, anecdotes, and animals.* Albany: State University of New York Press.

Mitchell, S. H., Laurent, C. L., & de Wit, H. (1996). Interaction of expectancy and the pharmacological effects of d-amphetamine: Subjective effects and self-administration. *Psychopharmacology, 125,* 371–378.

Mittleman, M. (2000, March). *Association between marijuana use and cardiovascular disease.* Paper presented at the conference of the American Heart Association, San Diego.

Moen, P., Kim, J., & Hofmeister, H. (2001). Couples' work/retirement transitions, gender, and marital quality. *Social Psychology Quarterly, 64,* 55–71.

Moffitt, T. W. (1993). Adolescence-limited and life-course-persistent antisocial behavior: A developmental taxonomy. *Psychological Review, 100,* 674–701.

Moghaddam, F. M., Taylor, D. M., & Wright, S. C. (1993). *Social psychology in cross-cultural perspective.* New York: Freeman.

Molineux, J. B. (1985). *Family therapy: A practical manual.* Springfield, IL: Charles C Thomas.

Mollica, R. F. (2000). Invisible wounds. *Scientific American, 282*(6), 54–57.

Monahan, J. L., Murphy, S. T., & Zajonc, R. B. (2000). Subliminal mere exposure: Specific, general and diffuse effects. *Psychological Science, 11,* 462–466.

Monastra, V. J., Monastra, D. M., & George, S. (2002). The effects of stimulant therapy, EEG biofeedback, and parenting style on the primary symptoms of attention-deficit/hyperactivity disorder. *Applied Psychophysiology and Biofeedback, 27,* 231–249.

Moncrieff, R. W. (1951). *The chemical senses.* London: Leonard Hill.

Monroe, S. M., & Simons, A. D. (1991). Diathesis-stress theories in the context of life stress research: Implications for the depressive disorders. *Psychological Bulletin, 110,* 406–425.

Montgomery, G. H., DuHamel, K. N., & Redd, W. H. (2000). A meta-analysis of hypnotically induced analgesia: How effective is hypnosis? *International Journal of Clinical & Experimental Hypnosis [Special Issue: The Status of Hypnosis as an Empirically Validated Clinical Intervention], 48,* 138–153.

Moore, K. A., Morrison, D. R., & Greene, A. D. (1997). Effects on the children born to adolescent mothers. In R. A. Maynard (Ed.), *Kids having kids: Economic costs and social consequences of teen pregnancy* (pp. 145–180). Washington, DC: Urban Institute Press.

Moore, R. Y. (1999, June 25). A clock for the ages. *Science, 284,* 2102–2103.

Morgan, W. G. (2002). Origin and history of the earliest thematic apperception test pictures. *Journal of Personality Assessment, 79,* 422–445.

Moriarty, T. (1975). Crime, commitment and the responsive bystander: Two field experiments. *Journal of Personality and Social Psychology, 31,* 370–376.

Morin, C. M., Bastien, C. H., Brink, D., & Brown, T. R. (2003). Adverse effects of temazepam in older adults with chronic insomnia. *Human Psychopharmacology Clinical and Experimental, 18,* 75–82.

Morin, C. M., Stone, J., McDonald, K., & Jones, S. (1994). Psychological management of insomnia: A clinical replication series with 100 patients. *Behavior Therapy, 25,* 291–309.

Morris, C. G. (1990). *Contemporary psychology and effective behavior* (7th ed.). Glenview, IL: Scott, Foresman.

Mortensen, E. L., Michaelsen, K. F., Sanders, S. A., & Reinisch, J. M. (2002). The association between duration of breastfeeding and adult intelligence. *Journal of the American Medical Association, 287,* 2365–2371.

Moses, S. (1990, December). Sensitivity to culture may be hard to teach. *APA Monitor,* p. 39.

Moyers, F. (1996). Oklahoma City bombing: Exacerbation of symptoms in veterans with PTSD. *Archives of Psychiatric Nursing, 10,* 55–59.

Mroczek, D. K., & Kolarz, C. M. (1998). The effect of age on positive and negative affect: A developmental perspective on happiness. *Journal of Personality & Social Psychology, 75,* 1333–1349.

Muchinsky, P. M. (1997). *Psychology applied to work: An introduction to industrial and organizational psychology* (5th ed.). Pacific Grove, CA: Brooks/Cole.

Muir, D. W. (1985). The development of infants' auditory spatial sensitivity. In S. Trehub & B. Schneider (Eds.), *Auditory development in infancy.* New York: Plenum.

Mumford, M. D., & Gustafson, S. B. (1988). Creativity syndrome: Integration, application, and innovation. *Psychological Bulletin, 103,* 27–43.

Muris, P., Merchelbach, H., Gadet, B., & Moulaert, V. (2000). Fears, worries, and scary dreams in 4- to 12-year-old children: Their content, developmental pattern, and origins. *Journal of Clinical Child Psychology, 29,* 43–52.

Murray, B. (1999, October). Psychologists can boost the corporate bottom line. *APA Monitor,* p. 17.

Murray, B. (2002). More students blend business and psychology. *Monitor on Psychology, 33,* 34–35.

Murray, H. A. (1938). *Explorations in personality.* New York: Oxford University Press.

Murray, H. G., & Denny, J. P. (1969). Interaction of ability level and interpolated activity in human problem solving. *Psychological Reports, 24,* 271–276.

Mustanski, B. S., Viken, R. J., Kaprio, J., & Rose, R. J. (2003). Genetic influences on the association between personality risk factors and alcohol use and abuse. *Journal of Abnormal Psychology, 112*, 282–289.

Myers, D. G. (1996). *Social psychology* (5th ed.). New York: McGraw-Hill.

N

Naglieri, J. A., & Kaufman, J. C. (2001). Understanding intelligence, giftedness and creativity using PASS theory. *Roeper Review, 23*, 151–156.

Nair, L., Deb, S., & Mandal, J. (1993). A study on repression-sensitization, personality characteristics and early childhood experiences of male cancer patients. *Journal of Personality and Clinical Studies, 9*, 87–94.

Nairne, J. S. (2003). Sensory and working memory. In A. F. Healy & R. W. Proctor (Eds.), *Handbook of Psychology: Experimental Psychology, Vol. 4* (pp. 423–444). New York: John Wiley & Sons.

Narayanan, L., Shanker, M., & Spector, P. E. (1999). Stress in the workplace: A comparison of gender and occupations. *Journal of Organizational Behavior, 20*, 63–73.

Narrow, W. E., Rae, D. S., Robins, L. N., & Regier D. A. (2001). Revised prevalence estimates of mental disorders in the United States: Using a clinical significance criterion to reconcile 2 survey estimates. *Archives of General Psychiatry, 59*, 115–123.

Nash, M. R. (2001, July). The truth and the hype of hypnosis. *Scientific American*, p. 47–54.

Nathan, P. E., & Gorman, J. M. (1998). *A guide to treatments that work.* New York: Oxford University Press.

Nathan, P. E., & Langenbucher, J. W. (1999). Psychopathology: Description and classification. *Annual Review of Psychology, 50*, 79–107.

National Adolescent Health Information Center. (2003). *Fact sheet on suicide: Adolescents and young adults.* Retrieved June 21, 2003 from http://youth.ucsf.edu/nahic/img/Suicide.pdf

National Advisory Mental Health Council. (1995). Basic behavioral science research for mental health: A national investment emotion and motivation. *American Psychologist, 50*, 838–845.

National Clearing House on Child Abuse and Neglect, (2003). *Summary of Key Findings.* U. S. Department of Health and Human Services, Child Maltreatment 2001. Available online at: http://www.calib.com/nccanch/pubs/factsheets/canstats.cfm#backnotetwo. Last accessed June 7, 2003.

National Household Survey on Drug Abuse. (1998). *Summary of findings from the 1998 National Household Survey on Drug Abuse.* Retrieved September 16, 2000, from the World Wide Web: http://www.samhsa.gov/oas/nhsda/pe1996/rtst1013.htm#E8E26

National Institute of Mental Health (2000). *Suicide facts.* Washington, DC.

Accessed July 16, 2003 at: http://www.nimh.nih.gov/research/suifact.cfm

National Institute of Neurological Disorders and Stroke (2003). Brain Basics: Understanding Sleep. Available on-line at: http://www.ninds.nih.gov/health_and_medical/pubs/understanding_sleep_brain_basic_.htm.

National Institute on Alcohol Abuse and Alcoholism. (2000c). *Tenth Special Report to the U.S. Congress on Alcohol and Health.* Retrieved September 12, 2000, from the World Wide Web: http://silk.nih.gov/silk/niaaa1/publication/10report/10-order.htm

National Institute on Drug Abuse. (1998). *Marijuana: Facts parents need to know.* Retrieved September 12, 2000, from the World Wide Web: http://165.112.78.61/MarijBroch/Marijparentstxt.html

National Institute on Drug Abuse. (1999). *The economic costs of alcohol and drug abuse in the United States–1992.* Retrieved September 13, 2000, from the World Wide Web: http://www.nida.nih.gov/EconomicCosts/Chapter1.html

National Institute on Drug Abuse. (2000a). *Marijuana.* Retrieved September 9, 2000, from the World Wide Web: http://165.112 78.61/Infofax/marijuana.html

National Institute on Drug Abuse. (2000b). *Methamphetamine.* Retrieved September 14, 2000, from the World Wide Web: http://165.112.78.61/Infofax/methamphetamine.html

National Institute on Drug Abuse. (2000c). *Origins and pathways to drug abuse: Research findings (from 9/98).* Retrieved September 13, 2000, from the World Wide Web: http://165.112.78.61/ICAW/origins/originsfindings998.html

Neal, A., & Turner, S. M. (1991). Anxiety disorders research with African Americans: Current status. *Psychological Bulletin, 109*, 400–410.

Neale, J. M., & Oltmanns, T. F. (1980). *Schizophrenia.* New York: Wiley.

Neath, I. (1993). Contextual and distinctive processes and the serial position function. *Journal of Memory and Language, 32*, 820–840.

Neher, A. (1991). Maslow's theory of motivation: A critique. *Journal of Humanistic Psychology, 31*, 89–112.

Neher, A. (1996). Jung's theory of archetypes: A critique. *Journal of Humanistic Psychology, 36*, 61–91.

Nehlig, A., Daval, J. L., & Debry, G. (1992). Caffeine and the central nervous system: Mechanisms of action, biochemical, metabolic and psychostimulant effects. *Brain Research Reviews, 17*, 139–170.

Neisser, U. (1982). *Memory observed: Remembering in natural contexts.* San Francisco: Freeman.

Neisser, U. (1998). Introduction: Rising test scores and what they mean. In U. Neisser (Ed.), *The rising curve: Long-*

term gains in IQ and related measures (pp. 3–22). Washington, DC: American Psychological Association.

Neisser, U., Boodoo, G., Bouchard, T. J., Jr., Boykin, A. W., Brody, N., Ceci, S. J., Halpern, D. F., Loehlin, J. C., Perloff, R., Sternberg, R. J., & Urbina, S. (1996). Intelligence: Knowns and unknowns. *American Psychologist, 51*, 77–101.

Neitz, J., Geist, T., & Jacobs, G. H. (1989). Color vision in the dog. *Visual Neuroscience, 3*, 119–125.

Neitz, J., Neitz, M., & Jacobs, G. H. (1993). More than three cone pigments among people with normal color vision. *Vision Research, 33*, 117–122.

Nelson, C. A. (1999). Neural plasticity and human development. *Current Directions in Psychological Science, 8*, 42–45.

Nelson, C. A., Monk, C. S., Lin, J., Carver, L. C., Thomas, K. M., & Truwit, C. L. (2000). Functional neuroanatomy of spatial working memory in children. *Developmental Psychology, 36*, 109–116.

Nemeroff, C. B., & Schatzberg, A. F. (2002). Pharmacological treatments for unipolar depression. In P. Nathan & J. M. Gorman (Eds.), *A guide to treatments that work* (2nd ed.) (pp. 212–225). New York, NY: Oxford University Press.

Ness, R. B., Grisso, J. A., Hirschinger, N., Markovic, N., Shaw, L. M., Kay, N. L., & Kline, J. (1999). Cocaine and tobacco use and the risk of spontaneous abortion. *New England Journal of Medicine, 340*, 333–339.

Nesse, R. M. (1998). Emotional disorders in evolutionary perspective. *British Journal of Medical Psychology [Special Issue: Evolutionary Approaches to Psychopathology], 71*, 397–415.

Nesse, R. M. (2000). Is depression an adaptation? *Archives of General Psychiatry, 57*, 14–20.

Netting, J. (1999). Wink of an eye. *Scientific American*, 26–27.

Neubauer, A. C. (2000). Physiological approaches to human intelligence: A review. *Psychologische Beitrage, 42*, 161–173.

Neugarten, B. L. (1977). Personality and aging. In I. Birren & K. W. Schaie (Eds.), *Handbook of the psychology of aging* (pp. 626–649). New York: Van Nostrand.

Newcombe, N. S., Drummey, A. B., Fox, N. A., Lie, E., & Ottinger-Alberts, W. O. (2000). Remembering early childhood: How much, how, and why (or why not). *Current Directions in Psychological Science, 9*, 55–58.

Niccols, A., & Latchman, A. (2002). Stability of the Bayley Mental Scale of Infant Development with high risk infants. *British Journal of Developmental Disabilities, 48*, 3–13.

NICHD Early Child Care Research Network. (1997). The effects of infant child care on infant-mother attach-

ment security: Results of the NICHD study of early child care. *Child Development, 68*, 860–879.

Nickerson, R. S., & Adams, M. J. (1979). Long-term memory for a common object. *Cognitive Psychology, 11*, 287–307.

Nisbett, R. E., & Norenzayan, A. (2002). Culture and cognition. In H. Pashler & D. Medin (Eds.), *Steven's handbook of experimental psychology (3rd Ed.), Vol. 2 Memory and cognitive processes* (pp. 561–597). New York: John Wiley & Sons, Inc.

Nisbett, R. E., Fong, G. T., Lehman, D. R., & Cheng, P. W. (1987, October 30). Teaching reasoning. *Science, 238*, 625–631.

Nisbett, R. E., Peng, K., Choi, I., & Norenzayan, A. (2001). Culture and systems of thought: Holistic versus analytic cognition. *Psychological Review, 108*, 291–310.

Nishimura, Y., Nishimura, T., Hattori, H., Hattori, C., Yonekura, A., & Suzuki, K. (2003). Obesity and obstructive sleep apnea syndrome. *Acta Oto Laryngologica, 123*, 22–24

Nissani, M. (1990). A cognitive reinterpretation of Stanley Milgram's observations on obedience to authority. *American Psychologist, 45*, 1384–1385.

Nixon, S. J. (1999). Neurocognitive performance in alcoholics: Is polysubstance abuse important? *Psychological Science, 10*, 181–185.

Noga, J. T., Bartley, A. J., Jones, D. W., Torrey, E. F., & Weinberger, D. R. (1996). Cortical gyral anatomy and gross brain dimensions in monozygotic twins discordant for schizophrenia. *Schizophrenia Research, 22*, 27–40.

Noice, T., & Noice, H. (2002). The expertise of professional actors: A review of recent research. *High Ability Studies, 13*, 7–20.

Nolen-Hoeksema, S. (1999, October). Men and women handle negative situations differently, study suggests. *APA Monitor.*

Nolen-Hoeksema, S., Girgus, J. S., & Seligman, M. E. P. (1986). Learned helplessness in children: A longitudinal study of depression, achievement, and explanatory style. *Journal of Personality and Social Psychology, 51*, 435–442.

Norman, R. (1975). Affective-cognitive consistency, attitudes, conformity, and behavior. *Journal of Personality and Social Psychology, 32*, 83–91.

Norris, F. H., & Murrell, S. A. (1990). Social support, life events, and stress as modifiers of adjustment to bereavement by older adults. *Psychology and Aging, 45*, 267–275.

Novak, C. M., & Albers, H. E. (2002). N-Methyl-D-aspartate microinjected into the suprachiasmatic nucleus mimics the phase-shifting effects of light in the diurnal Nile grass rat. *Brain Research, 951*, 255–263.

Novak, K. (1999). Amyloid-beta vaccine for Alzheimer disease. *Nature Medicine, 5,* 870.

Novak, M. A. (1991, July). "Psychologists care deeply" about animals. *APA Monitor,* p. 4.

Novick, L. R., & Sherman, S. J. (2003). On the nature of insight solutions: Evidence from skill differences in anagram solution. *Quarterly Journal of Experimental Psychology: Human Experimental Psychology, 56A,* 351–382.

Novick, L. R., & Sherman, S. J. (2003). On the nature of insight solutions: Evidence from skill differences in anagram solution. *Quarterly Journal of Experimental Psychology: Human Experimental Psychology, 56A,* 351–382.

Nowak, A., Vallacher, R. R., & Miller, M. E. (2003). Social influence and group dynamics. In T. Millon & M. J. Lerner (Ed.), *Handbook of psychology: Personality and social psychology* (Vol. 5, pp. 383–417). New York, NY: John Wiley & Sons, Inc.

Nucci, L. P. (2002). The development of moral reasoning. In U. Goswami (Ed.) *Blackwell handbook of childhood cognitive development* (pp. 303–325). Malden, MA: Blackwell Publishers.

Nurmi, E. L., Amin, T., Olson, L. M., Jacobs, M. M., McCauley, J. L., Lam, A. Y., Organ, E. L., Folstein, S. E., Haines, J. L., & Sutcliffe, J. S. (2003). Dense linkage disequilibrium mapping in the 15q11-q13 maternal expression domain yields evidence for association in autism. *Molecular Psychiatry, 8,* 624–634.

Nuttall, J. (2002). Archetypes and architecture: The coniunction of Carnary Wharf. *Psychodynamic Practice: Individuals, Groups and Organizations, 8,* 33–53.

Nyberg, L., Marklund, P., Persson, J., Cabeza, R., Forkstarn, C., Petersson, K. M., & Ingvar, M. (2003). Common prefrontal activations during working memory, episodic memory, and semantic memory. *Neuropsychologia, 41,* 371–377.

O

O'Brien, K. M., & Vincent, N. K. (2003). Psychiatric comorbidity in anorexia and bulimia nervosa: Nature, prevalence and causal relationships. *Clinical Psychology Review, 23,* 57–74.

O'Callahan, M., Andrews, A. M., & Krantz, D. S. (2003). Coronary heart disease and hypertension. In A. M. Nezu, & C. M. Nezu (Eds.). *Handbook of psychology: Health psychology, Vol. 9* (pp. 339–364). New York, NY: John Wiley & Sons, Inc.

O'Connell, A., & Russo, N. (Eds.). (1990). *Women in psychology: A bibliographic sourcebook.* Westport, CT: Greenwood Press.

O'Connor, N., & Hermelin, B. (1987). Visual memory and motor programmes: Their use by idiot savant

artists and controls. *British Journal of Psychology, 78,* 307–323.

O'Connor, T. G., McGuire, S., Reiss, D., Hetherington, E. M., & Plomin, R. (1998). Co-occurrence of depressive symptoms and antisocial behavior in adolescence: A common genetic liability. *Journal of Abnormal Psychology, 107,* 27–37.

O'Leary, A. (1990). Stress, emotion, and human immune function. *Psychological Bulletin, 108,* 363–382.

O'Leary, K. D., & Wilson, G. T. (1987). *Behavior therapy: Application and outcome.* Englewood Cliffs, NJ: Prentice Hall.

O'Leary, S. G. (1995). Parental discipline mistakes. *Current Directions in Psychological Science, 4,* 11–14.

O'Leary, V. E., & Flanagan, E. H. (2001). Leadership. In J. W. Worell (Ed.) *Encyclopedia of gender and women.* San Diego: Academic Press.

O'Leary, V. E., & Smith, D. (1988, August). *Sex makes a difference: Attributions for emotional cause.* Paper presented at the meeting of the American Psychological Association, Atlanta, GA.

Offer, D., Ostrov, E., Howard, K. I., & Atkinson, R. (1988). *The teenage world: Adolescents' self-image in ten countries.* New York: NY: Plenum Press.

Ogawa, S., Lubahn, D., Korach, K., & Pfaff, D. (1997). Behavioral effects of estrogen receptor gene disruption in male mice. *Proceedings of the National Academy of Sciences of the U. S. A., 94,* 1476.

Ogrodniczuk, J., & Staats, H. (2002). Psychotherapy and gender: Do men and women require different treatments? *Zeitschrift fuer Psychosomatische Medizin und Psychotherapie, 48,* 270–285.

Öhman, A. (1996). Preferential preattentive processing of threat in anxiety: Preparedness and attentional biases. In R. M. Rapee (Ed.), *Current controversies in the anxiety disorders* (pp. 252–290). New York: Guilford.

Ojemann, G., Ojemann, J., Lettich, E., & Berger, M. (1989). Cortical language localization in left, dominant hemisphere: An electrical stimulation mapping investigation in 117 patients. *Journal of Neurosurgery, 71,* 316–326.

Olds, M. E., & Forbes, J. L. (1981). The central basis of motivation: Intracranial self-stimulation studies. *Annual Review of Psychology, 32,* 523–574.

Olfson, M., Marcus, S. C., Druss, B., & Pincus, H. A. (2002). National trends in the use of outpatient psychotherapy. *American Journal of Psychiatry, 19,* 1914–1920.

Olfson, M., Marcus, S., Sackeim, H. A., Thompson, J., & Pincus, H. A. (1998). Use of ECT for the inpatient treatment of recurrent major depression. *American Journal of Psychiatry, 155,* 22–29.

Olson, C. B. (1988). *The influence of context on gender differences in performance attribution: Further evidence of a "feminine modesty effect."* Paper presented at the annual meeting of the Western Psychological Association, San Francisco.

Olson, M.V., & Varki, A. (2003). Sequencing the chimpanzee genome: insights into human evolution and disease. *Nature Review Genetics, 4,* 20–8.

Oltmanns, T. F., & Emery, R. E. (1998). *Abnormal psychology* (2nd ed.). Upper Saddle River, NJ: Prentice Hall.

Oltmanns, T. F., & Emery, R. E. (2001). *Abnormal psychology.* Upper Saddle River, NJ: Prentice Hall.

Oltmanns, T. F., & Emery, R. E. (2001). *Abnormal psychology* (3rd ed.). Upper Saddle River, NJ: Prentice Hall.

Oltmanns, T. F., & Emery, R. E. (2001). *Abnormal psychology* (3rd ed.). Upper Saddle River, NJ: Prentice-Hall.

Olton, D. S., & Noonberg, A. R. (1980). *Biofeedback: Clinical applications in behavioral science.* Englewood Cliffs, NJ: Prentice Hall.

Olzewski-Kubilius, P. (2003). Gifted education programs and procedures. In W. M. Reynolds & G. E. Miller (Eds.), *Handbook of psychology: Educational psychology (Vol. 7),* (pp. 487–510). New York, NY: John Wiley & Sons, Inc.

Omi, M., & Winant, H. (1994). *Racial formation in the United States: From the 1960s to the 1990s* (2nd ed) New York: Routledge.

Ommundsen, Y. (2003). Implicit theories of ability and self-regulation strategies in physical education classes. *Educational Psychology, 23,* 141–157.

Ones, D. S., Viswesvaran, C., & Schmidt, F. L. (1993). Comprehensive meta-analysis of integrity test validation: Findings and implications for personnel selection and theories of job performance. *Journal of Applied Psychology, 78,* 679–703.

Onken, L. S., & Blaine, J. D. (1997). Behavioral therapy development and psychological science: Reinforcing the bond. *Psychological Science, 8,* 143–144.

Onyskiw, J. E. (2000). Processes underlying children's responses to witnessing physical aggression in their families. *Dissertation Abstracts International: Section B: The Sciences and Engineering, 61,* 1620.

Orbuch, T. L., House, J. S., Mero, R. P., & Webster, P. S. (1996). Marital quality over the life course. *Social Psychology Quarterly, 59,* 162–171.

Orlinsky, D. E., & Howard, K. I. (1995). Unity and diversity among psychotherapies: A comparative perspective. In L. E. Beutler & B. Bongar (Eds.), *Comprehensive textbook of psychotherapy: Theory, and practice* (pp. 3–23). Oxford: Oxford University Press.

Orlofsky, J. L. (1978). Identity formation, n achievement, and fear of success in college men and women. *Journal of Youth and Adolescence, 7,* 49–62.

Orlofsky, J. L. (1993). Intimacy status: Theory and research. In J. E. Marcia, A. S. Waterman, D. R. Matteson, S. L. Archer, & J. L. Orlofsky (Eds.), *Ego identity: A handbook for psychosocial research.* New York: Springer-Verlag.

Orlofsky, J. L., Marcia, J. E., & Lesser, I. M. (1973). Ego identity status and the intimacy versus isolation crisis of young adulthood. *Journal of Personality and Social Psychology, 27,* 211–219.

Ortar, G. (1963). Is a verbal test cross-cultural? *Scripta Hierosolymitana, 13,* 219–235.

Ortmann, A., & Hertwig, R. (1997). Is deception acceptable? *American Psychologist, 52,* 746–747.

Ortmann, A., & Hertwig, R. (1998). The question remains: Is deception acceptable? *American Psychologist, 53,* 806–807.

Osborne, J. W. (1997). Race and academic disidentification. *Journal of Educational Psychology, 89,* 728–735.

Oskamp, S. (1991). *Attitudes and opinions* (2nd ed.). Englewood Cliffs, NJ: Prentice Hall.

Ouimette, P., Humphreys, K., Moos, R. H., Finney, J. W., Cronkite, R., & Federman, B. (2001). Self-help group participation among substance use disorder patients with posttraumatic stress disorder. *Journal of Substance Abuse Treatment, 20,* 25–32.

Overmier, J. B. (2002). On learned helplessness. *Integrative Physiological and Behavioral Science, 37,* 4–8.

Ozer, D. J., & Reise, S. P. (1994). Personality assessment. *Annual Review of Psychology, 45,* 357–388.

P

Pace, R. (1994, July 28). Christy Henrich, 22, gymnast plagued by eating disorders. *New York Times,* p. A12.

Paikoff, R. L., & Brooks-Gunn, J. (1991). Do parent-child relationships change during puberty? *Psychological Bulletin, 110,* 47–66.

Paivio, A. (1986). *Mental representations: A dual coding approach.* New York: Oxford University Press.

Panksepp, J. (1986). The neurochemistry of behavior. *Annual Review of Psychology, 37,* 77–107.

Panksepp, J. (1998). Attention deficit hyperactivity disorders, psychostimulants, and intolerance of childhood playfulness: A tragedy in the making? *Current Directions in Psychological Science, 7,* 91–98.

Panksepp, J., Siviy, S., & Normansell, L. A. (1984). The psychology of play: Theoretical and methodological perspectives. *Neuroscience and Biobehavioral Reviews, 8,* 465–492.

Papassotiropoulos, A., Luetjohann, D., Bagli, M., Locatelli, S., Jessen, F., Buschfort, R., Ptok, U., Bjoerkhem, I., von Bergmann, K., & Heun, R. (2002). 24S-hydroxycholesterol in cerebrospinal fluid is elevated in early stages of dementia. *Journal of Psychiatric Research, 36,* 27–32.

Pare, D., Collins, D. R., & Guillaume, P. J. (2002). Amygdala oscillations and the consolidation of emotional memories. *Trends in Cognitive Sciences, 6,* 306–314.

Paris, S. G., & Weissberg, J. A. (1986). Young children's remembering in different contexts: A reinterpretation of Istomina's study. *Child Development, 57,* 1123–1129.

Park, D. C. (1998). Aging and memory: Mechanisms underlying age difference in performance. *Australasian Journal on Aging: Supplement, 17,* 69–72.

Park, D. C., Cherry, K., Smith, A. D., & Frieske, D. (1997). Pictorial rehearsal effects in young and older adults. *Aging, Neuropsychology, and Cognition, 4,* 113–125.

Parke, R. D., & O'Neil, R. (1999). Social relationships across contexts: Family-peer linkages. In A. W. Collins & B. Laursen (Eds.), *Relationships as developmental contexts. The Minnesota symposia on child psychology* (Vol. 30, pp. 211–239). Mahwah, NJ: Lawrence Erlbaum.

Parker, K. C. H., Hanson, R. K., & Hunsley, J. (1988). MMPI, Rorschach, and WAIS: A meta-analytic comparison of reliability, stability, and validity. *Psychological Bulletin, 103,* 367–373.

Parker, S. K., Axtell, C. M., & Turner, N. (2001). Designing a safer workplace: Importance of job autonomy, communication quality, and supportive supervisors. *Journal of Occupational Health Psychology, 6,* 211–228.

Parnetti, L., Senin, U., & Mecocci, P. (1997). Cognitive enhancement therapy for Alzheimer's disease: The way forward. *Drugs, 53,* 752–768.

Parsons, H. M. (1974, March 8). What happened at Hawthorne? *Science, 183,* 922–932.

Parsons, M. (1992). Hawthorne: An early OBM experiment. *Journal of Organizational Behavior Management, 12,* 27–43.

Patenaude, A. F., Guttmacher, A. E., & Collins, F. S. (2002). Genetic testing and psychology: New roles, new responsibilities. *American Psychologist, 5,* 271–282.

Patrick, C. J. (1994). Emotion and psychopathy: Startling new insights. *Psychophysiology, 31,* 319–330.

Patterson, C. J. (2000). Family relationships of lesbians and gay men. *Journal of Marriage and the Family, 62,* 1052–1069.

Patterson, D. R., & Ptacek, J. T. (1997). Baseline pain as a moderator of hypnotic analgesia for burn injury treatment. *Journal of Consulting & Clinical Psychology, 65,* 60–67.

Patterson, F. G. (1978). The gestures of a gorilla: Language acquisition in another pongid. *Brain and Language, 5,* 72–97.

Patterson, F. G. (1980). Innovative uses of language by a gorilla: A case study. In K. E. Nelson (Ed.), *Children's language* (Vol. 2, pp. 497–561). New York: Gardner Press.

Patterson, F. G. (1981). *The education of Koko.* New York: Holt, Rinehart & Winston.

Patterson, F. G., & Cohn, R. H. (1990). Language acquisition by a lowland gorilla: Koko's first ten years of vocabulary development. *Word, 41,* 97–143.

Patterson, G. R, & Bank, L. (1989). Some amplifying mechanisms for pathologic processes in families. In M. R. Gunnar & E. Thelen (Eds.), *Systems and development: The Minnesota Symposia on Child Psychology* (Vol. 22, pp. 167–209). Hillsdale, NJ: Erlbaum.

Patterson, G. R., DeBaryshe, B. D., & Ramsey, E. (1989). A developmental perspective on antisocial behavior. *American Psychologist, 44,* 329–335.

Paul, G. L. (1982). *The development of a "transportable" system of behavioral assessment for chronic patients.* Invited address, University of Minnesota, Minneapolis.

Paunovic, N., & Oest, L. G. (2001). Cognitive behavior therapy vs. exposure therapy in the treatment of PTSD in refugees. *Behaviour Research and Therapy, 39,* 1183–1197.

Pavlov, I. P. (1927). *Conditional reflexes* (G. V. Anrep, Trans.). London: Oxford University Press.

Peabody, D., & Goldberg, L. R. (1989). Some determinants of factor structures from personality-trait descriptors. *Journal of Personality and Social Psychology, 57,* 552–567.

Pearson, C. A. L. (1992). Autonomous workgroups: An evaluation at an industrial site. *Human Relations, 9,* 905–936.

Pedersen, P. B., & Carey, J. C. (2003). *Multicultural counseling in schools* (2nd Ed.). Boston: Allyn & Bacon.

Pedlow, R., Sanson, A., Prior, M., & Oberklaid, F. (1993). Stability of maternally reported temperament from infancy to 8 years. *Developmental Psychology, 29,* 998–1007.

Pellegrini, A. D., & Galda, L. (1994). Play. In V. S. Ramachandran (Ed.), *Encyclopedia of human behavior* (Vol. 3, pp. 535–543). San Diego: Academic Press.

Pellegrini, R. J., Roundtree, T., Camagna, T. F., & Queirolo, S. S. (2000). On the epidemiology of violent juvenile crime in America: A total arrest-referenced approach. *Psychological Reports, 86,* 1171–1186.

Peng, K., & Nisbett, R. E. (1999). Culture, dialectics, and reasoning about contradiction. *American Psychologist, 54,* 741–754.

Pennisi, E. (1999, October 22). Enzymes point way to potential Alzheimer's therapies. *Science, 286,* 650–651.

Peplau, L. A., & Cochran, S. D. (1990). A relationship perspective on homosexuality. In D. P. McWhirter, S. A. Sanders, & J. M. Reinisch (Eds.), *Homosexuality/heterosexuality: The Kinsey scale and current research* (pp. 321–349). New York: Oxford University Press.

Pepperberg, I. M. (2000). *The Alex studies: Cognitive and communicative abilities of gray parrots.* Cambridge, MA: Harvard University Press.

Pepperberg, I. M. (2002). Cognitive and communicative abilities of grey parrots. In M. Bekoff & C. Allen (Eds.), *The cognitive animal: Empirical and theoretical perspectives on animal cognition* (pp. 247–253). Cambridge, MA: MIT Press.

Perloff, R. M. (2003). *The dynamics of persuasion: Communication and attitudes in the 21st century* (2nd ed.). Mahwah, NJ: Lawrence Erlbaum Associates, Publishers.

Perls, F. S. (1969). *Gestalt theory verbatim.* Lafayette, CA: People Press.

Perret, D. I., Lee, K. J., Penton-Voak, I., Rowland, D., Yoshikawa, S., Burt, D. M., Henzi, S. P., Castles, D. L., & Akamatsu, S. (1998). Effects of sexual dimorphism on facial attractiveness. *Nature, 394,* 884.

Perry, D. G., Perry, L. C., & Weiss, R. J. (1989). Sex differences in the consequences that children anticipate for aggression. *Developmental Psychology, 25,* 312–319.

Persky, H. (1983). Psychosexual effects of hormones. *Medical Aspects of Human Sexuality, 17,* 74–101.

Persson-Blennow, I., & McNeil, T. F. (1988). Frequencies and stability of temperament types in childhood. *Journal of the American Academy of Child and Adolescent Psychiatry, 27,* 619–622.

Peterson, C. (2000). The future of optimism. *American Psychologist, 55,* 44–55.

Peterson, C., Maier, S. F., & Seligman, M. E. P. (1993b). *Learned helplessness: A theory for the age of personal control.* New York: Oxford University Press.

Peterson, C., Vaillant, G. E., & Seligman, M. E. P. (1988). Explanatory style as a risk factor for illness. *Cognitive Therapy and Research, 12,* 119–132.

Peterson, L. R., & Peterson, M. J. (1959). Short-term retention of individual verbal items. *Journal of Experimental Psychology, 58,* 193–198.

Petitto, L. A., & Marentette, P. F. (1991, March 22). Babbling in the manual mode: Evidence for the ontogeny of language. *Science, 251,* 1493–1496.

Pettigrew, T. F. (1969). Racially separate or together? *Journal of Social Issues, 25,* 43–69.

Pettigrew, T. F. (1998). Intergroup contact theory. *Annual Review of Psychology, 49,* 65–85.

Petty, R. E., & Cacioppo, J. T. (1981). *Attitudes and persuasion: Classic and contemporary approaches.* Dubuque, IA: Wm. C. Brown.

Petty, R. E., & Cacioppo, J. T. (1986a). The elaboration likelihood model of persuasion. In L. Berkowitz (Ed.), *Advances in experimental social psychology* (Vol. 19, pp. 123–205). Orlando, FL: Academic Press.

Petty, R. E., & Cacioppo, J. T. (1986b). *Communication and persuasion: Central and peripheral routes to attitude change.* New York: Springer-Verlag.

Petty, R. E., Wegener, D. T., & Fabrigar, L. R. (1997). Attitudes and attitude change. *Annual Review of Psychology, 48,* 609–647.

Phelps, J. A., Davis, J. O., & Schartz, K. M. (1997). Nature, nurture, and twin research strategies. *Current Directions in Psychological Science, 6,* 117–121.

Phelps, L., & Bajorek, E. (1991). Eating disorders of the adolescent: Current issues in etiology, assessment, and treatment. *School Psychology Review, 20,* 9–22.

Phinney, J. S. (1996). When we talk about American ethnic groups, what do we mean? *American Psychologist, 51,* 918–927.

Piaget, J. (1967). *Six psychological studies.* New York: Random House.

Piaget, J. (1969). The intellectual development of the adolescent. In G. Caplan & S. Lebovici (Eds.), *Adolescence: Psychosocial perspectives.* New York: Basic Books.

Pine, F. (1998). *Diversity and direction in psychoanalytic techniques.* New Haven, CT: Yale University Press.

Pinker, S. (1994). *The language instinct: How the mind creates language.* New York: HarperCollins.

Pinker, S. (1997). *How the mind works.* New York: Norton.

Pinker, S. (1999). *Words and rules: The ingredients of language.* New York: Basic Books.

Pinker, S. (2002). *The blank slate: The modern denial of human nature.* NY, NY: Viking Press.

Pinker, S. (2002). *The blank slate: The modern denial of human nature.* New York, NY: Viking.

Piomelli, D. (2001). Cannabinoid activity curtails cocaine craving. *Nature Medicine, 7,* 1099–1100.

Pion, G. M., Mednick, M. T., Astin, H. S., Hall, C. C. I., Kenkel, M. B., Keita, G. P., Kohout, J. L., & Kelleher, J. C. (1996). The shifting gender composition of psychology: Trends and implications for the discipline. *American Psychologist, 15,* 509–528.

Piotrowski, C. (1998). Assessment of pain: A survey of practicing clinicians. *Perceptual and Motor Skills, 86,* 181–182.

Pisani, V. D., Fawcett, J., Clark, D. C., & McGuire, M. (1993). The relative contributions of medication adherence and AA meeting attendance to abstinent outcome for chronic alcoholics. *Journal of Studies on Alcohol, 54,* 115–119.

Pitman, G. E. (2003). Evolution, but no revolution. The "tend and befriend" theory of stress and coping. *Psychology of Women Quarterly, 27,* 194–195.

Platt, J. J. (1997). *Cocaine addiction: Theory, research, and treatment.* Cambridge, MA: Harvard University Press.

Plomin, R. (1994). *Genetics and experience: The interplay between nature and nurture.* Thousand Oaks, CA: Sage.

Plomin, R. (1997). Identifying genes for cognitive abilities and disabilities. In R. J. Sternberg & E. Grigorenko (Eds.), *Intelligence: Heredity and environment* (pp. 89–104). New York: Cambridge University Press.

Plomin, R. (1998). A quantitative trait locus associated with cognitive ability. *Psychological Science, 9,* 159–166.

Plomin, R., & Crabbe, J. (2000). DNA. *Psychological Bulletin, 126,* 806–828.

Plomin, R., & Rende, R. (1991). Human behavioral genetics. *Annual Review of Psychology, 42,* 161–190.

Plomin, R., Corley, R., DeFries, J. C., & Fulker, D. W. (1990). Individual differences in television watching in early childhood: Nature as well as nurture. *Psychological Science 1,* 371–377.

Plomin, R., DeFries, J. C., & McClearn, G. E. (1990). *Behavioral genetics: A primer* (2nd ed.). New York: Freeman.

Plomin, R., Defries, J. C., Craig, I. W., & McGuffin, P. (2003). Behavioral genomics. In R. Plomin & J. C. Defries (Eds.) *Behavioral genetics in the postgenomic era,* (pp. 531–540). Washington, DC: American Psychological Association.

Plomin, R., McClearn, G. E., Smith, D. L., Vignetti, S., Chorney, M. J., Chorney, K., Venditti, C. P., Kasarda, S., Thompson, L. A., Detterman, D. K., Daniels, J., Owen, M. J., & McGuffin, P. (1994). DNA markers associated with high versus low IQ: The IQ quantitative trait loci (QTL) Project. *Behavior Genetics, 24,* 107–119.

Plous, S. (1996). Attitudes toward the use of animals in psychology research and education: Results from a national survey of psychologists. *American Psychologist, 51,* 1167–1180.

Plutchik, R. (1980). *Emotion: A psychoevolutionary synthesis.* New York: Harper & Row.

Plutchik, R. (1994). *The psychology and biology of emotion.* New York: HarperCollins.

Pogarsky, G., & Piquero, A. R. (2003). Can punishment encourage offending? Investigating the "resetting" effect. *Journal of Research in Crime and Delinquency, 40,* 95–120.

Pohl, R. F., Schwarz, S., Sczesny, S., & Stahlberg, D. (2003). Hindsight bias in gustatory judgements. *Experimental Psychology, 50,* 107–115.

Poikolainen, K. (1993). Does fear of war impair mental health among psychi-

atric patients? *Nordic Journal of Psychiatry, 47,* 455–457.

Pollack, A. (2000, May 30). Neural cells, grown in labs, raise hopes on brain disease. *New York Times,* pp. F1, F6.

Pollack, W. S., & Levant, R. F. (1998). *New psychotherapy for men.* New York: Wiley.

Pollatasek, A., Rayner, K., & Lee, H. W. (2000). Phonological coding in word perception and reading. In A. Kennedy & R. Radach (Eds.), *Reading as a perceptual process* (pp. 399–425). Amsterdam, Netherlands: North-Holland/Elsevier Science Publishers.

Pomerleau, C. S. (1997). Co-factors for smoking and evolutionary psychobiology. *Addiction, 92,* 397–408.

Pontieri, F. E., Tanda, G., Orzi, F., & DiChiara, G. (1996). Effects of nicotine on the nucleus accumbens and similarity to those of addictive drugs. *Nature, 382,* 255–257.

Pope, H. (2000). *The Adonis complex: The secret crisis of male obsession.* New York: Free Press.

Pope, M., & Scott, J. (2003). Do clinicians understand why individuals stop taking lithium? *Journal of Affective Disorders, 74,* 287–291.

Porkka-Heiskanen, T., Strecker, R. E., Thakkar, M., Bjørkum, A. A., Greene, R. W., & McCarley, R. W. (1997, May 23). Adenosine: A mediator of the sleep-inducing effects of prolonged wakefulness. *Science, 276,* 1265–1268.

Porter, L. S., & Stone, A. A. (1995). Are there really gender differences in coping? A reconsideration of previous results from a daily study. *Journal of Social and Clinical Psychology, 14,* 184–202.

Porter, L. W., & Roberts, K. H. (1976). Communication in organizations. In M. D. Dunnette (Ed.), *Handbook of industrial and organizational psychology* (pp. 1553–1589). Chicago: Rand McNally.

Porter, L., & Lawler, E. (1968). *Managerial attitudes and performance.* Homewood, IL: Irwin.

Porter, R. H., Balogh, R. D., Cernoch, J. M., & Franchi, C. (1986). Recognition of kin through characteristic body odors. *Chemical Senses, 11,* 389–395.

Porter, R. H., Cernich, J. M., & McLaughlin, F. J. (1983). Maternal recognition of neonates through olfactory cues. *Physiology & Behavior, 30,* 151–154.

Postman, L. (1975). Verbal learning and memory. *Annual Review of Psychology, 26,* 291–335.

Pothier, P. K. T. (2002). Effect of relaxation on neuro-immune responses of persons undergoing chemotherapy. *Dissertation Abstracts International: Section B: The Sciences and Engineering, 62,* 4471.

Powell, D. H., & Driscoll, P. F. (1973). Middle class professionals face unemployment. *Society, 10(2),* 18–26.

Powell, N. B., Schechtman, K. B., Riley, R. W., Li, K., Troell, R., & Guilleminault, C., (2001). The road to danger:

The comparative risks of driving while sleepy. *Laryngoscope, 111,* 887–893.

Powell, S., Rosner, R., Butollo, W., Tedeschi, R. G., & Calhoun, L. G. (2003). Postraumatic growth after a war: A study with former refugees and displaced people in Sarajevo. *Journal of Clinical Psychology, 59,* 71–83.

Power, F. C. (1994). Moral development. In V. S. Ramachandran (Ed.), *Encyclopedia of human behavior* (Vol. 3, pp. 203–212). San Diego, CA: Academic Press.

Powers, S. I, Hauser, S. T., & Kilner, L. A. (1989). Adolescent mental health. *American Psychologist, 44,* 200–208.

Premack, D. (1971, May 21). Language in chimpanzee? *Science, 172,* 808–822.

Premack, D. (1976). *Intelligence in ape and man.* Hillsdale, NJ: Erlbaum.

Preti, G., Cutler, W. B., Garcia, C. R., Huggins, G. R., & Lawley, J. J. (1986). Human auxiliary secretions influence women's menstrual cycles: The role of donor extract from females. *Hormones & Behavior, 20,* 474–482.

Prior, M., Smart, D., Sanson, A., & Obeklaid, F. (1993). Sex differences in psychological adjustment from infancy to 8 years. *Journal of the American Academy of Child and Adolescent Psychiatry, 32,* 291–304.

Pruneti, C. A., L'Abbate, A., & Steptoe, A. (1993). Personality and behavioral changes in patients after myocardial infarction. *Research Communication in Psychology, Psychiatry and Behavior, 18,* 37–51.

Ptacek, J. T., Smith R. E., & Dodge, K. L. (1994). Gender differences in coping with stress: When stressor and appraisals do not differ. *Personality and Social Psychology Bulletin, 20,* 421–430.

Puca, A. A., Daly, M. J., Brewster, S. J., Matise, T. C., Barrett, J., Shea-Drinkwater, M., Kang, S., Joyce, E., Nicoli, J., Benson, E., Kunkel, L. M., & Peris, T. (2001). A genome-wide scan for linkages to human exceptional longevity identifies a locus on chromosome 4. *Proceedings of the National Academy of Sciences, USA, 98,* 10505–10508.

Putnam, F. W. (1984). The psychophysiological investigation of multiple personality: A review. *Psychiatric Clinics of North America, 7,* 31–39.

Putnam, F. W., Guroff, J. J., Silberman, E. D., Barban, L., & Post, R. M. (1986). The clinical phenomenology of multiple personality disorder: Review of 100 recent cases. *Journal of Clinical Psychology, 47,* 285–293.

Q

Quadagno, D. M. (1987). Pheromones and human sexuality. *Medical Aspects of Human Sexuality, 21,* 149–154.

Quadrel, M. J., Prouadrel, Fischoff, B., & Davis, W. (1993). Adolescent (In)vulnerability. *American Psychologist, 2,* 102–116.

Quan, N., Zhang, Z. B., Demetrikopoulos, M. K., Kitson, R. P., Chambers, W. H., Goldfarb, R. H., & Weiss, J. M. (1999). Evidence for involvement of B lymphocytes in the surveillance of lung metastases in the rat. *Cancer Research, 59,* 1080–1089.

Quesnel, C., Savard, J., Simard, S., Ivers, H., & Morin, C. M. (2003). Efficacy of cognitive-behavioral therapy for insomnia in women treated for nonmetastatic breast cancer. *Journal of Consulting and Clinical Psychology, 71,* 189–200.

Quill, T. E. (1985). Somatization disorder: One of medicine's blind spots. *Journal of the American Medical Association, 254,* 3075–3079.

Quinn, P. C., Bhatt, R. S., Brush, D., Grimes, A., & Sharpnack, H. (2002). Development of form similarity as a gestalt grouping principle in infancy. *Psychological Science, 13,* 320–328.

Quist, R. M., & Crano, W. D. (2003). Assumed policy similarity and voter preference. *Journal of Social Psychology, 143,* 149–162.

R

Rabasca, L. (1999a, June). Improving life for the survivors of cancer. *APA Monitor,* pp. 28–29.

Rabasca, L. (1999b, November). Is it depression? Or could it be a mild traumatic brain injury? *APA Monitor,* pp. 27–28.

Rabasca, L. (1999d, February). Women addicts vulnerable to trauma. *APA Monitor,* p. 32.

Rabasca, L. (2000a, March). Lessons in diversity [and] Helping American Indians earn psychology degrees. *Monitor on Psychology,* 50–53.

Rabasca, L. (2000b, April). Self-help sites: A blessing or a bane? *Monitor on Psychology,* pp. 28–30.

Rabasca, L. (2000c, April). Taking telehealth to the next step. *Monitor on Psychology,* pp. 36–37.

Rabasca, L. (2000d, April). Taking time and space out of service delivery. *Monitor on Psychology,* pp. 40–41.

Rabin, B. S., & Koenig, H. G. (2002). Immune, neuroendocrine, and religious measures. *The link between religion and health: Psychoneuroimmunology and the faith factor* (pp. 197–249). London: Oxford University Press.

Rainer, G., & Miller, E. K. (2002). Timecourse of object-related neural activity in the primate prefrontal cortex during a short-term memory task. *European Journal of Neuroscience, 15,* 1244–1254.

Ramey, C. T., Ramey, S. L., & Lanzi, R. G. (2001). Intelligence and experience, In R. J. Sternberg & E. L. Grigorenko (Eds.), *Environmental effects on cognitive abilities.* Mahwah, NJ: Erlbaum.

Ramey, S. L. (1999). Head Start and preschool education: Toward continued improvement. *American Psychologist, 54,* 344–346.

Ramus, F., Hauser, M. D., Miller, C., Morris, D., & Mehler, J. (2000, April 14). Language discrimination by human newborns and by cotton-top Tamarin monkeys. *Science, 288,* 349–351.

Rao, S. C., Rainer, G., Miller, E. K. (1997, May 2). Integration of what and where in the primate prefrontal cortex. *Science, 276,* 821–824.

Rapoport, M. J., McCullagh, S., Streiner, D., & Feinstein, A. (2003). The clinical significance of major depression following mild traumatic brain injury. *Psychosomatics: Journal of Consultation Liaison Psychiatry, 44,* 31–37.

Rasika, S., Alvarez-Buylla, A., & Nottebohm, F. (1999). BDNF mediates the effects of testosterone on the survival of new neurons in an adult brain. *Neuron, 22,* 53–62.

Rau, H., Buehrer, M., & Weitkunat, R. (2003). Biofeedback of R-wave-to-pulse interval normalizes blood pressure. *Applied Psychophysiology and Biofeedback, 28,* 37–46.

Raven, B. H. (1998). Groupthink: Bay of Pigs and Watergate reconsidered. *Organizational Behavior and Human Decision Processes, 73,* 352–361.

Ravussin, E., Pratley, R. E., Maffei, M., Wang, H., Friedman, J. M., Bennett, P. H., & Bogardus, C. (1997). Relatively low plasma leptin concentrations precede weight gain in Pima Indians. *Nature Medicine 3,* 238–240.

Rayman, P., & Bluestone, B. (1982). *The private and social response to job loss: A metropolitan study.* Final report of research sponsored by the Center for Work and Mental Health, National Institute of Mental Health.

Ree, M. J., & Earles, J. A. (1992). Intelligence is the best predictor of job performance. *Current Directions in Psychological Science, 1,* 86–89.

Reed, S. K. (1996). *Cognition: Theory and applications* (4th ed.). Pacific Grove, CA: BrooksCole.

Reinisch, J. M., & Sanders, S. A. (1982). Early barbiturate exposure: The brain, sexually dimorphic behavior and learning. *Neuroscience and Biobehavioral Reviews, 6,* 311–319.

Reinisch, J. M., Ziemba-Davis, M., & Sanders, S. A. (1991). Hormonal contributions to sexually dimorphic behavioral development in humans. *Psychoneuroendocrinology, 16,* 213–278.

Reis, S. M. (1989). Reflections on policy affecting the education of gifted and talented students, past and future perspectives. *American Psychologist, 44,* 399–408.

Rende, R., & Plomin, R. (1992). Diathesis-stress models of psychopathology: A quantitative genetic perspective. *Applied & Preventive Psychology, 1,* 177–182.

Renner, M. J., & Mackin, R. S. (1998). A life stress instrument for classroom use. *Teaching of Psychology, 25,* 46–48.

Renner, M. J., & Mackin, R. S. (2002). A life stress instrument for classroom use. In R. A. Griggs (Ed.), *Handbook for teaching introductory psychology: Vol 3,* (pp. 236–238). Mahwah, NJ: Lawrence Erlbaum Associates.

Renzulli, J. S. (1978). What makes giftedness? Reexamining a definition. *Phi Delta Kappan, 60,* 180–184, 216.

Reppucci, N. D., Woolard, J. L., & Fried, C. S. (1999). Social, community and preventive interventions. *Annual Review of Psychology 50,* 387–418.

Rescorla, R. A. (1966). Predictability and number of pairings in Pavlovian fear conditioning. *Psychonomic Science, 4,* 383–384.

Rescorla, R. A. (1967). Pavlovian conditioning and its proper control procedures. *Psychological Review, 74,* 71–80.

Rescorla, R. A. (1988). Pavlovian conditioning: It's not what you think. *American Psychologist, 43,* 151–160.

Rescorla, R. A., & Solomon, R. L. (1967). Two-process learning theory: Relationships between Pavlovian conditioning and instrumental learning. *Psychological Review, 74,* 151–182.

Resing, W. C., & Nijland, M. I. (2002). Are children becoming more intelligent? Twenty-five years' research using the Leiden Diagnostic Test. *Kind-en-Adolescent, 23,* 42–49.

Reuter-Lorenz, P. A., & Miller, A. C. (November 1998). The cognitive neuroscience of human laterality: Lessons from the bisected brain. *Current Directions in Psychological Science, 7,* 15–20.

Rey, J. M., & Sawyer, M. G. (2003). Are psychostimulant drugs being used appropriately to treat child and adolescent disorders? *British Journal of Psychiatry, 182,* 284–286.

Reyna, V. F., & Titcomb, A. L. (1997). Constraints on the suggestibility of eyewitness testimony: A fuzzy-trace theory analysis. In D. G. Payne & F. G. Conrad (Eds.), *Intersections in basic and applied memory research* (pp. 27–55). Mahwah, NJ: Erlbaum.

Rhue, J. W., Lynn, S. J., & Kirsch, I. (1993). *Handbook of clinical hypnosis.* Washington, DC: American Psychological Association.

Rice, B. (1979, September). Brave new world of intelligence testing. *Psychology Today,* pp. 27–38.

Rice, B. J. (1997). Effects of aerobic exercise on stress and depression. *Dissertation Abstracts International: Section B: The Sciences and Engineering, 58,* 2697.

Richardson, G. S., Miner, J. D., & Czeisler, C. A. (1989–1990). Impaired driving performance in shiftworkers: The role of the circadian system in a multifactorial model. *Alcohol, Drugs & Driving, 5/6,* 265–273.

Ricurte, G. A., Yuan, J., Hatzidimitriou, G., Cord, B. J., & McCann, U. D. (2002). Severe dopaminergic neurotoxicity in primates after a common recreational dose regimen of MDMA ("ecstasy"). *Science, 297,* 2260–2263.

Rieber, R. W. (1998, August). *Hypnosis, false memory and multiple personality: A trinity of affinity.* Paper presented at the annual meeting of the American Psychological Association, San Francisco, CA.

Riley, E. P., Guerri, C., Calhoun, F., Charness, M. E., Foroud, T. M., Li, T. K., Mattson, S. N., May, P. A., & Warren, K. R. (2003). Prenatal alcohol exposure: Advancing knowledge through international collaborations. *Alcoholism: Clinical and Experimental Research, 27,* 118–135.

Riley, V. (1981). Psychoneuroendocrine influences on immunocompetence and neoplasia. *Science, 212,* 1100–1109.

Rilling, M. (2000). John Watson's paradoxical struggle to explain Freud. *American Psychologist, 55,* 301–312.

Rini, C. K., Dunkel-Schetter, C., Wadhwa, P. D., & Sandman, C. A. (1999). Psychological adaptation and birth outcomes: The role of personal resources, stress, and sociocultural context in pregnancy. *Health Psychology, 18,* 333–345.

Riordan, R. J., & Beggs, M. S. (1987). Counselors and self-help groups. *Journal of Counseling and Development, 65,* 427–429.

Ripple, C. H., Gilliam, W. S., Chanana, N., & Zigler, E. (1999). Will fifty cooks spoil the broth? The debate over entrusting head start to the states. *American Psychologist, 54,* 327–343.

Roberson, D., Davies, I., & Jules, D. (2000). Color categories are not universal: Replications and new evidence from a stone-age culture. *Journal of Experimental Psychology: General, 129,* 369–398.

Roberts, A. H., Kewman, D. G., Mercer, L., & Hovell, M. (1993). The power of nonspecific effects in healing: Implications for psychosocial and biological treatments. *Clinical Psychology Review, 13,* 375–391.

Robertson, R. G., Rolls, E. T., Georges-Francois, P. (1998). Spatial view cells in the primate hippocampus: Effects of removal of view details. *Journal of Neurophysiology, 79,* 1145–1156.

Robins, L. N., & Regier, D. A. (1991). *Psychiatric disorders in America: The Epidemiologic Catchment Area Study.* New York: Free Press.

Robins, L. N., Schoenberg, S. P., Holmes, S. J., Ratcliff, K. S., Benham, A., & Works, J. (1985). Early home environment and retrospective recall: A test for concordance between siblings with and without psychiatric disorders. *American Journal of Orthopsychiatry, 55,* 27–41.

Robins, R. W., Gosling, S. D., & Craik, K. H. (1999). An empirical analysis of trends in psychology. *American Psychologist, 54,* 117–128.

Robinson, A., & Clinkenbeard, P. R. (1998). Giftedness: An exceptionality examined. *Annual Review of Psychology, 49,* 117–139.

Robinson, L. A., Berman, J. S., & Neimeyer, R. A. (1990). Psychotherapy for the treatment of depression: A comprehensive review of controlled outcome research. *Psychological Bulletin, 108,* 30–49.

Rodier, P. M. (2000). The early origins of autism. *Scientific American, 282*(2), 56–63.

Rodin, J. (1985). Insulin levels, hunger, and food intake: An example of feedback loops in body weight regulation. *Health Psychology, 4,* 1–24.

Rodriguez, M. (1994). Influence of sex and family history of alcoholism on cognitive functioning in heroin users. *European Journal of Psychology, 8,* 29–36.

Roese, N. J. (1997). Counterfactual thinking. *Psychological Bulletin, 121,* 133–148.

Rofe, Y. (1984). Stress and affiliation: A utility theory. *Psychological Review, 91,* 251–268.

Rofe, Y., Hoffman, M., & Lewin, I. (1985). Patient affiliation in major illness. *Psychological Medicine, 15,* 895–896.

Rogers, C. R. (1961). *On becoming a person: A therapist's view of psychotherapy.* Boston: Houghton Mifflin.

Rogers, D. (1980). *The adult years: An introduction to aging.* Englewood Cliffs, NJ: Prentice Hall.

Rogoff, B., & Chavajay, P. (1995). What's become of research on the cultural basis of cognitive development. *American Psychologist, 50,* 859–877.

Roitbak, A. I. (1993). *Glia and its role in nervous activity.* Saint Petersburg, Russia: Nauka.

Roitblat, H. L., Penner, R. H., & Nachtigall, P. E. (1990). Matching-to-sample by an echolocating dolphin (Tursiops truncatus). *Journal of Experimental Psychology: Animal Behavior Processes, 16,* 85–95.

Rolls, E. T. (1996). A theory of hippocampus function in memory. *Hippocampus, 6,* 601–620.

Rolls, E. T. (2000). Memory systems in the brain. *Annual Review of Psychology, 51,* 599–630.

Rolls, E. T., Tovee, M. J., & Panzeri, S. (1999). The neurophysiology of backward visual masking: Information analysis. *Journal of Cognitive Neuroscience, 11,* 335–346.

Roper, R., & Shewan, D. (2002). Compliance and eyewitness testimony: Do eyewitnesses comply with misleading 'expert pressure' during investigative interviewing? *Legal and Criminological Psychology, 7,* 155–163.

Rosch, E. (1998). Principles of categorization. In A. M. Collens & E. E. Smith (Eds.), *Readings in cognitive science: A perspective from psychology and artificial intelligence* (pp. 312–322), San Mateo, CA: Morgan Kaufman, Inc.

Rosch, E. (2002). Principles of categorization. In D. J. Levitin (Ed.) *Foundations of cognitive psychology: Core Readings* (pp. 251–270). Cambridge, MA: MIT Press.

Rosch, E. H. (1973). Natural categories. *Cognitive Psychology, 4,* 328–350.

Rosch, E. H. (1978). Principles of categorization. In E. H. Rosch & B. B. Lloyd (Eds.), *Cognition and categorization* (pp. 27–48). Hillsdale, NJ: Erlbaum.

Rosen, R. C., & Rosen, L. (1981). *Human sexuality.* New York: Knopf.

Rosenbaum, M. (1999). The role of leptin in human physiology. *New England Journal of Medicine, 341,* 913–915.

Rosenthal, D. (1970). *Genetic theory and abnormal behavior.* New York: Mc-Graw-Hill.

Rosenthal, R. (2002). The Pygmalion effect and its mediating mechanisms. In J. Aronson (Ed.), *Improving academic achievement: Impact of psychological factors on education* (pp.25–36). San Diego, CA: Academic Press.

Rosenthal, R., & Jacobsen, L. (1968). *Pygmalion in the classroom: Teacher expectations and pupils' intellectual development.* New York: Holt, Rinehart and Winston.

Rosenvinge, J. H., Borgen, J. S., & Boerresen, R. (1999). The prevalence and psychological correlates of anorexia nervosa, bulimia nervosa and binge eating among 15-year-old students: A controlled epidemiological study. *European Eating Disorders Review, 7,* 382–391.

Rosenzweig, M. R. (1984). Experience, memory, and the brain. *American Psychologist, 39,* 365–376.

Rosenzweig, M. R. (1996). Aspects of the search for neural mechanisms of memory. *Annual Review of Psychology, 47,* 1–32.

Rosenzweig, M. R., & Bennett, E. L. (1976). *Enriched environments: Facts, factors, and fantasies.* In L. Petrinovich & J. L. McGaugh (Eds.), *Knowing, thinking, believing* (pp. 179–214). New York: Plenum.

Rosenzweig, M. R., & Leiman, A. L. (1982). *Physiological psychology.* Lexington, MA: D. C. Heath.

Ross, C. A., Norton, G. R., & Wozney, K. (1989). Multiple personality disorder: An analysis of 236 cases. *Canadian Journal of Psychiatry, 34,* 413–418.

Ross, G. W., Abbott, R. D., Petrovitch, H., Morens, D. M., Grandinetti, A., Tung, K. H., Tanner, C. M., Masaki, K. H., Blanchette, P. L., Curb, J. D., Popper, J. S., & White, L. R. (2000). Association of coffee and caffeine intake with the risk of Parkinson disease. *Journal of the American Medical Association, 283,* 2674–2679.

Ross, L., & Nisbett, R. E. (1991). *The person and the situation.* New York: Mc-Graw-Hill.

Ross, M. H. (1993). *The culture of conflict.* New Haven, CT: Yale University Press.

Rossiter, T. (2002). Neurofeedback for AD/HD: A ratio feedback case study and tutorial. *Journal of Neurotherapy, 6,* 9–35.

Roth, D., & Rehm, L. P. (1980). Relationships among self-monitoring processes, memory, and depression. *Cognitive Therapy and Research, 4,* 149–157.

Rothbart, M. K., Derryberry, D., & Hershey, K. (2000). Stability of temperament in childhood: Laboratory infant assessment to parent report at seven years. In V. J. Molfese & D. L. Molfese (Eds.), *Temperament and personality development across the life span* (pp. 85–119). Mahwah, NJ: Lawrence Erlbaum Associates.

Rothbart, M., Evans, M., & Fulero, S. (1979). Recall for confirming events: Memory processes and the maintenance of social stereotypes. *Journal of Experimental Social Psychology, 15,* 343–355.

Rothblum, E. D, Brand, P. A., Miller, C. T., & Oetjen, H. A. (1990). The relationship between obesity, employment discrimination, and employment-related victimization. *Journal of Vocational Behavior, 37,* 251–266.

Rottenstreich, Y., & Tversky, A. (1997). Unpacking, repacking, and anchoring: Advances in support theory. *Psychological Review, 104,* 406–415.

Rotter, J. B. (1954). *Social learning and clinical psychology.* Englewood Cliffs, NJ: Prentice Hall.

Rouhana, N. N., & Bar-Tal, D. (1998). Psychological dynamics of intractable ethnonational conflicts: The Israeli-Palestinian case. *American Psychologist, 53,* 761–770.

Roussy, J. M. (2000). How poverty shapes women's experiences of health during pregnancy: A grounded theory study. *Dissertation Abstracts International: Section B: The Sciences and Engineering, 60,* 3205.

Rovner, S. (1990, December 25). The empty nest myth. *Ann Arbor News,* p. D3.

Rowan, A., & Shapiro, K. J. (1996). Animal rights, a bitten apple. *American Psychologist, 51,* 1183–1184.

Rowe, D. C., & Rodgers, J. L. (2002). Expanding variance and the case of historical changes in IQ means: a critique of Dickens and Flynn (2001). *Psychological Review, 109,* 79–763.

Rowland, N. E. (2002). Thirst and water-salt appetite. In H. Pashler & R. Gallistel (Eds.), *Steven's handbook of experimental psychology (3rd ed.) (Vol. 3): Learning, motivation and emotion* (pp. 669–707). New York, NY: John Wiley & Sons, Inc.

Roy, T. S., Seidler, F. J., & Slotkin, T. A. (2002). Prenatal nicotine exposure evokes alterations of cell structure in hippocampus and somatosensory cor-

tex. *Journal of Pharmacology and Experimental Therapeutics, 300,* 124–133.

Rubenstein, A. J., Kalakanis, L., & Langlois, J. H. (1999). Infant preferences for attractive faces: A cognitive explanation. *Developmental Psychology, 35,* 848–855.

Rubin, K. H., Coplan, R. J., Chen, X., & McKinnon, J. E. (1994). Peer relationships and influences in childhood. In V. S. Ramachandran (Ed.), *Encyclopedia of human behavior* (Vol. 3, pp. 431–439). San Diego, CA: Academic Press.

Ruble, D. N., Fleming, A. S., Hackel, L. S., & Stangor, C. (1988). Changes in the marital relationship during the transition to first time motherhood: Effects of violated expectations concerning division of household labor. *Journal of Personality and Social Psychology, 55,* 78–87.

Rugulies, R. (2002). Depression as a predictor for coronary heart disease: A review and meta-analysis. *American Journal of Preventive Medicine, 23,* 51–61.

Rule, R. R. (2001). Modulation of the orienting response by prefrontal cortex. *Dissertation Abstracts International: Section B: The Sciences and Engineering, 61,* 3894.

Rumbaugh, D. M. (1977). *Language learning by a chimpanzee.* New York: Academic Press.

Rumbaugh, D. M. (1990). Comparative psychology and the great apes: Their competence in learning, language, and numbers. *Psychological Record, 40,* 15–39.

Rumbaugh, D. M., & Savage-Rumbaugh, E. S. (1978). Chimpanzee language research: Status and potential. *Behavior Research Methods and Instrumentation, 10,* 119–131.

Rumbaugh, D. M., von Glaserfeld, E., Warner, H., Pisani, P., & Gill, T. V. (1974). Lana (chimpanzee) learning language: A progress report. *Brain and Language, 1,* 205–212.

Russell, D. E. H. (1986). The incidence and prevalence of intrafamilial and extrafamilial sexual abuse of female children. *Child Abuse and Neglect, 7,* 133–146.

Russell, J. A. (1991). Culture and the categorization of emotions. *Psychological Bulletin, 110,* 426–450.

Russell, T. G., Rowe, W., & Smouse, A. D. (1991). Subliminal self-help tapes and academic achievement: An evaluation. *Journal of Counseling and Development, 69,* 359–362.

Russo, N. F. (1990). Overview: Forging research priorities for women's mental health. *American Psychologist, 45,* 368–373.

Russo, N. F., & Denmark, F. L. (1987). Contributions of women to psychology. *Annual Review of Psychology, 38,* 279–298.

Russo, N. F., & Sobel, S. B. (1981). Sex differences in the utilization of mental

health facilities. *Professional Psychology, 12,* 7–19.

Ruth, W. (1996). Goal setting and behavior contracting for students with emotional and behavioral difficulties: Analysis of daily, weekly, and total goal attainment. *Psychology in the Schools, 33,* 153–158.

Rutter, M. L. (1997). Nature-nurture integration: An example of antisocial behavior. *American Psychologist, 52,* 390–398.

Ryan, R. M., & Deci, E. L. (2000). Self-determination theory and the facilitation of intrinsic motivation, social development, and well-being. *American Psychologist, 55,* 68–78.

Rymer, J., Wilson, R., & Ballard, K. (2003). Making decisions about hormone replacement therapy. *British Medical Journal, 326,* 322–326.

S

Saade, S., Balleine, B., W., & Minor, T. R. (2003). The L-type calcium channel blocker nimodipine mitigates "learned helplessness" in rats. *Pharmacology, Biochemistry and Behavior, 74,* 269–278.

Sack, R. L., Brandes, R. W., Kendall, A. R., & Lewy, A. J. (2001). Entrainment of free-running circadian rhythms by melatonin in blind people. *The New England Journal of Medicine, 343,* 1070–1077.

Sacks, O. (2000). *Seeing voices: A journey into the world of the deaf.* New York: Vintage.

Saczynski, J. S., Willis, S. L., & Schaie, K. W. (2002). Strategy use in reasoning training with older adults. *Aging, Neuropsychology, and Cognition, 9,* 48–60.

Sadeh, A., Raviv, A., & Gruber, R. (2000). Sleep patterns and sleep disruptions in school-age children. *Developmental Psychology, 36,* 291–301.

Sadoski, M., & Paivio, A. (2001). *Imagery and text: A dual coding theory of reading and writing.* Mahwah, NJ: Lawrence Erlbaum Assoc.

Safdar, S., & Lay, C. H. (2003). The relations of immigrant-specific and immigrant-nonspecific daily hassles to distress controlling for psychological adjustment and cultural competence. *Journal of Applied Social Psychology, 33,* 299–320.

Salgado, J. F., Moscoso, S., & Lado, M. (2003). Evidence of cross-cultural invariance of the Big Five personality dimensions in work settings. *European Journal of Personality, 17* (Supplement 1): S67–S76.

Salovey, P., Mayer, J. D., & Rosenhan, D. L. (1991). Mood behavior. In M. S. Clark (Ed.), *Review of personality and social psychology: Prosocial behavior* (Vol. 12, pp. 215–237). Newbury Park, CA: Sage.

Salovey, P., Mayer, J. D., Caruso, D., & Lopes, P. N. (2003). Measuring emotional intelligence as a set of abilities with the Mayer-Salovey-Caruso Emotional Intelligence test. In S. J. Lopez & C. R. Snyder (Eds.), *Positive psychological assessment: A handbook of models and measures* (pp. 251–265). Washington, DC: American Psychological Association.

Salovey, P., Rothman, A. J., Detweiler, J. B., & Steward, W. T. (2000). Emotional states and physical health. *American Psychologist, 55*, 110–121.

Salthouse, T. A. (1991). Mediation of adult age differences in cognition by reductions in working memory and speed of processing. *Psychological Science, 2*, 179–183.

Sampson, G. (1999). *Educating Eve: The "language instinct" debate.* London, England: Cassell Academic.

Sanderson, C., & Clarkin, J. F. (2002). Further use of the NEO-PI-R personality dimensions in differential treatment planning. In P. T. Costa, Jr. & T. A. Widiger (Eds.), *Personality disorders and the five-factor model of personality* (2nd ed.) (pp.351–375). Washington, DC: American Psychological Association.

Sanford, R. N. (1937). The effects of abstinence from food upon imaginal processes: A further experiment. *Journal of Psychology, 3*, 145–159.

Sano, D. L. (2002). Attitude similarity and marital satisfaction in long-term African American and Caucasian marriages. *Dissertation Abstracts International Section A: Humanities and Social Sciences, 62*, 289.

Saporta, I., & Halpern, J. J. (2002). Being different can hurt: Effects of deviation from physical norms on lawyers' salaries. *Industrial Relations: A Journal of Economy and Society, 41*, 442–466.

Sarason, I. G., & Sarason, B. R. (1987). *Abnormal psychology: The problem of maladaptive behavior* (5th ed.). Englewood Cliffs, NJ: Prentice Hall.

Sarason, I. G., & Sarason, B. R. (1999). *Abnormal psychology: The problem of maladaptive behavior.* Upper Saddle River, NJ: Prentice Hall.

Sarbin, T. R. (1997). On the futility of psychiatric diagnostic manuals (DSMs) and the return of personal agency. *Applied and Preventive Psychology, 6*, 233–243.

Sarter, M., Berntson, G. G., & Cacioppo, J. T. (1996). Brain imaging and cognitive neuroscience: Toward strong inference in attributing function to structure. *American Psychologist, 51*, 13–21.

Satcher, D. (1999, October). A report of the surgeon general–executive summary. *APA Monitor*, p. 16.

Satow, K. K. (1975). Social approval and helping. *Journal of Experimental Social Psychology, 11*, 501–509.

Sattler, J. M. (1992). *Assessment of children* (3rd ed.). San Diego: Jerome M. Sattler.

Sattler, J. M. (2002). *Assessment of children: Behavioral and clinical applications* (4th ed.). La Mesa, CA: Jerome M. Sattler, Publisher, Inc.

Savage-Rumbaugh, E. S., & Fields, W. M. (2000). Linguistic, cultural and cognitive capacities of bonobos (Pan paniscus). *Culture and Psychology, 6*, 131–153.

Savage-Rumbaugh, S., & Lewin, R. (1994). *Kanzi: The ape at the brink of the human mind.* New York: Wiley.

Savic, I., Berglund, H., Gulyas, B., & Roland, P. (2001). Smelling of odorous sex hormone-like compounds causes sex differentiated hypothalamic activations in humans. *Neuron, 31*, 661–668.

Scarr, S. (1995). Inheritance, intelligence and achievement. *Planning for Higher Education, 23*, 1–9.

Scarr, S. (1999). Freedom of choice for poor families. *American Psychologist, 54*, 144–145.

Scarr, S., & McCartney, K. (1983). How people make their own environments: A theory of genotype-environment effects. *Child Development, 54*, 424–435.

Scarr, S., & Weinberg, R. (1983). The Minnesota Adoption Study: Genetic differences and malleability. *Child Development, 54*, 260–267.

Schaal, B. (1986). Presumed olfactory exchanges between mother and neonate in humans. In J. L. Camus & J. Conler (Eds.), *Ethology and psychology.* Toulouse: Private IEC.

Schaal, B., Marlier, L., & Soussignan, R. (1998). Olfactory function in the human fetus: Evidence from selective neonatal responsiveness to the odor of amniotic fluid. *Behavioral Neuroscience, 112*, 1438–1449.

Schab, F. R. (1990). Odors and the remembrance of things past. *Journal of Experimental Psychology: Learning, Memory, & Cognition, 16*, 648–655.

Schachter, S., & Singer, J. (1962). Cognitive, social, and physiological determinants of emotional state. *Psychological Review, 69*, 379–399.

Schachter, S., & Singer, J. E. (2001). Cognitive, social, and psychological determinants of emotional state. In G. W. Parrott (Ed.), *Emotions in social psychology: Essential readings* (pp. 76–93). Philadelphia, PA: Psychology Press.

Schacter, D. L. (1999). The seven sins of memory: Insights from psychology and cognitive neuroscience. *American Psychologist, 54*, 182–203.

Schacter, D. L., Norman, K. A., & Koutstaal, W. (1998). The cognitive neuroscience of constructive memory. *Annual Review of Psychology, 49*, 289–318.

Schafe, G. E., & LeDoux, J. E. (2002). *Steven's handbook of experimental psychology (3rd ed.), Vol. 3 Learning, motivation, and emotion* (pp. 535–561). New York, NY: John Wiley & Sons, Inc.

Schaie, K. W. (1983). Consistency and changes in cognitive functioning of the young-old and old-old. In M. Bergner, U. Lehr, E. Lang & R. Schmidt-Scherzer (Eds.), *Aging in the eighties and beyond.* New York, NY: Springer.

Schaie, K. W. (1984). Midlife influences upon intellectual functioning in old age. *International Journal of Behavioral Development, 7*, 463–478.

Schaie, K. W. (1994). The course of adult intellectual development. *American Psychologist, 4*, 304–313.

Schaie, K. W. (1996). *Intellectual development in adulthood: The Seattle Longitudinal Study.* New York, NY: Cambridge University Press.

Schaie, K. W., & Willis, S. L. (2001). *Adult development and aging* (5th ed.). Upper Saddle River, NJ: Prentice Hall.

Schatzman, E. L. (1992). *L'outil theorie.* Paris: Eshel.

Schiffman, H. R. (1982). *Sensation and perception: An integrated approach* (2nd ed.). New York: Wiley.

Schiffman, S. S. (1997). Taste and smell losses in normal aging and disease. *Journal of the American Medical Association, 278*, 1357–1352.

Schleidt, M., & Genzel, C. (1990). The significance of mother's perfume for infants in the first weeks of their life. *Ethology & Sociobiology, 11*, 145–154.

Schlenker, B. R., & Weigold, M. F. (1992). Interpersonal processes involving impression regulation and management. *Annual Review of Psychology, 43*, 133–168.

Schmolck, H., Buffalo, E. A., & Squire, L. R. (2000). Memory distortions develop over time: Recollections of the O. J. Simpson trial verdict after 15 months and 32 months. *Psychological Science, 11*, 29–45.

Schoenthaler, S. J., Amos, S. P., Eysenck, H. J., Peritz, E., & Yudkin, J. (1991). Controlled trial of vitamin-mineral supplementation: Effects on intelligence and performance. *Personality and Individual Differences, 12*, 251–362.

Scholey, A. B., Bosworth, J. A. J., & Dimitrakaki, V. (1999). The effects of exposure to human pheromones on mood and attraction. *Proceedings of the British Psychological Society, 7(1)*, 77.

Schooler, C. (1998). Environmental complexity and the Flynn effect. In U. Neisser (Ed.), *The rising curve: Long-term gains in IQ and related measures* (pp. 67–79). Washington, DC: American Psychological Association.

Schopp, L., Johnstone, B., & Merrell, D. (2000). Telehealth and neuropsychological assessment: New opportunities for psychologists. *Professional Psychology: Research & Practice, 13*, 179–183.

Schroeder, S. R., Schroeder, C. S., & Landesman, S. (1987). Psychological services in educational setting to persons with mental retardation. *American Psychologist, 42*, 805–808.

Schulz, D. A. (1984). *Human sexuality* (2nd ed.). Englewood Cliffs, NJ: Prentice Hall.

Schwartz, B. (1989). *Psychology of learning and behavior* (3rd ed.). New York: Norton.

Schwartz, B. (2000). Self-determination: The tyranny of freedom. *American Psychologist, 55*, 79–88.

Schwartz, B. L. (2002). *Tip-of-the-tongue states: Phenomenology, mechanism, and lexical retrieval.* Mahwah, NJ: Lawrence Erlbaum Assoc.

Schwartz, C. E., Christopher, I. W., Shin, L. M. Kagan, J., & Rauch, S. L. (2003a). Inhibited and uninhibited infants "grown up": Adult amygdalar response to novelty. *Science, 300*, 1952–1953.

Schwartz, C. E., Wright, C. I., Shin, L. M., Kagan, J., Whalen, P. J., McMullin, K. G., & Rauch, S. L. (2003b). Differential amygdalar response to novel versus newly familiar neutral faces: A functional MRI probe developed for studying inhibited temperament. *Biological Psychiatry, 53*, 854–862.

Schwartz, G. E. (1974, April). TM relaxes some people and makes them feel better. *Psychology Today*, pp. 39–44.

Schwartz, P. (1994, November 17). Some people with multiple roles are blessedly stressed. *New York Times.*

Schwartzman, J. B., & Glaus, K. D. (2000). Depression and coronary heart disease in women: Implications for clinical practice and research. *Professional Psychology: Research & Practice, 31*, 48–57.

Schweinhart, L. J., Barnes, H. V., & Weikart, D. P. (1993). *Significant benefits: The High/Scope Perry Study through age 27* (Monographs of the High/Scope Educational Research Foundation, No. 10). Ypsilanti, MI: High/Scope Press.

Scott, C., Klein, D. M., & Bryant, J. (1990). Consumer response to humor in advertising: A series of field studies using behavioral observation. *Journal of Consumer Research, 16*, 498–501.

Scully, J. A., Tosi, H., & Banning, K. (2000). Life event checklists: Revisiting the Social Readjustment Rating Scale after 30 years. *Educational and Psychological Measurement, 60*, 864–876.

Scupin, R. (1995). *Cultural anthropology* (2nd ed.). Englewood Cliffs, NJ: Prentice Hall.

Seamon, J. G., & Kenrick, D. T. (1992). *Psychology.* Englewood Cliffs, NJ: Prentice Hall.

Sears, D. O. (1994). On separating church and lab. *Psychological Science, 5*, 237–239.

Sedikides, C., Campbell, W. K., Reeder, G. D., & Elliot, A. J. (1998). The self-serving bias in relational context.

Journal of Personality and Social Psychology, 74, 378–386.

Sedikides, C., Gaertner, L., & Toguchi, Y. (2003). Pancultural self-enhancement. *Journal of Personality and Social Psychology, 84,* 60–79.

Seeley, R. J., & Schwartz, J. C. (1997). The regulation of energy balance: Peripheral hormonal signals and hypothalamic neuropeptides. *Current Directions in Psychological Science, 6,* 39–44.

Segall, M. H., Lonner, W. J., & Berry, J. W. (1998). Cross-cultural psychology as a scholarly discipline: On the flowering of culture in behavioral research. *American Psychologist, 53,* 1011–1110.

Segura, S., & McCloy, R. (2003). Counterfactual thinking in everyday life situations: Temporal order effects and social norms. *Psicologica, 24,* 1–15.

Seligman, J., Rogers, P., & Annin, P. (1994, May 2). The pressure to lose. *Newsweek,* pp. 60, 62.

Seligman, M. E. P. (1971). Phobias and preparedness. *Behavior Therapy, 2,* 307–320.

Seligman, M. E. P. (1995). The effectiveness of psychotherapy: The Consumer Reports study. *American Psychologist, 50,* 965–974.

Seligman, M. E. P. (1996). Science as an ally of practice. *American Psychologist, 51,* 1072–1079.

Seligman, M. E. P. (2003). Positive psychology: Fundamental assumptions. *Psychologist, 16,* 126–127.

Seligman, M. E. P., & Csikzentmihalyi, M. (2000). Positive psychology. *American Psychologist, 55,* 5–14.

Seligman, M. E., & Maier, S. F. (1967). Failure to escape traumatic shock. *Journal of Experimental Psychology, 74,* 1–9.

Seligmann, J. (1992, February 3). The new age of Aquarius. *Newsweek,* p. 65.

Sell, R. L., Wells, J. A., & Wypij, D. (1995). The prevalence of homosexual behavior and attraction in the United States, the United Kingdom and France: Results of national population-based samples. *Archives of Sexual Behavior, 24,* 235–238.

Selman, R. (1981). The child as friendship philosopher. In S. R. Asher & J. M. Gottman (Eds.), *The development of children's friendships* (pp. 242–272). New York: Cambridge University Press.

Selye, H. (1956). *The stress of life* New York: McGraw-Hill.

Selye, H. (1976). *The stress of life* (rev. ed.). New York: McGraw-Hill.

Semenza, C., & Zettin, M. (1989). Evidence from aphasia for the role of proper names as pure referring expressions. *Nature, 342,* 678–679.

Semrud-Clikeman, M., & Hynd, G. W. (1990). Right hemispheric dysfunction in nonverbal learning disabilities: Social, academic, and adaptive functioning in adults and children. *Psychological Bulletin, 107,* 196–209.

Sengpiel, F., Stawinski, P., & Bonhoeffer, T. (1999). Influence of experience on orientation maps in cat visual cortex. *Nature: Neuroscience, 2,* 727–732.

Seppa, N. (1997, June). Children's TV remains steeped in violence. *APA Monitor,* p. 36.

Shaffer, D. R., (1999). *Developmental psychology: Childhood and adolescence* Pacific Grove, CA: Brooks/Cole.

Shaffer, J. B. P. (1978). *Humanistic psychology* Englewood Cliffs, NJ: Prentice Hall.

Shalev, A., & Munitz, H. (1986). Conversion without hysteria: A case report and review of the literature. *British Journal of Psychiatry, 148,* 198–203.

Shapiro, D., & Shapiro, D. (1982). Meta-analysis of comparative therapy outcome studies: A replication and refinement. *Psychological Bulletin, 92,* 581–604.

Shapiro, K. (1991, July). Use morality as basis for animal treatment. *APA Monitor,* p. 5.

Shapiro, T. F. (2002). Suggestibility in children's eyewitness testimony: Cognitive and social influences. *Dissertation Abstracts International: Section B: The Sciences and Engineering, 63,* 2086.

Shaw, P. J., Cirelli, C., Greenspan, R. J., & Tononi, G. (2000, March 10). Correlates of sleep and waking in drosophila melanogaster. *Science, 287,* 1834–1837.

Shaywitz, S. E., Shaywitz, B. A., Pugh, K. R., Fulbright, R. K., Constable, R. T., Mencl, W. E., Shankweiler, D. P., Liberman, A. M., Skudlarski, P., Fletcher, J. M., Katz, L., Marchione, K. E., Lacadie, C., Gatenb, C., & Gore, J. C. (1998). Functional disruption in the organization of the brain for reading in dyslexia. *Neurobiology, 95,* 2636–2641.

Sheldon, K. M., & King, L. (2001). Why positive psychology is necessary. *American Psychologist, 56,* 216–217.

Shelton R. C., & Hollon, S. D. (2000). Antidepressants. In A. Kazdin (Ed.), *Encyclopedia of psychology.* Washington, DC: American Psychological Association.

Shepard, R. N, & Metzler, J. (1971, February 19). Mental rotation of three-dimensional objects. *Science, 171,* 701–703.

Shepard, R. N. (1978). Externalization of mental images and the act of creation. In B. S. Randhawa & W. E. Coffman (Eds.), *Visual learning, thinking, and communication* (pp. 138–189). New York: Academic Press.

Sherin, J. E., Shiromani, P. J., McCarley, R. W., & Saper, C. B. (1996, January 12). Activation of ventrolateral preoptic neurons during sleep. *Science, 271,* 216–219.

Sherman, R. A. (1996). *Unraveling the mysteries of phantom limb sensations* New York: Plenum Press.

Shettleworth, S. J. (1975). Reinforcement and the organization of behavior in golden hamsters: Hunger, environment, and food reinforcement. *Journal of Experimental Psychology: Animal Behavior Processes, 1,* 56–87.

Shimamura, A. P., & Prinzmetal, W. (1999). The mystery spot illusion and its relation to other visual illusions. *Psychological Science, 10,* 501–507.

Shimamura, A. P., Berry, J. M., Mangels, J. A., Rusting, C. L., & Jurica, P. J. (1995). Memory and cognitive abilities in university professors: Evidence for successful aging. *Psychological Science, 6,* 271–277.

Shneidman, E. (1989). The Indian summer of life: A preliminary study of septuagenarians. *American Psychologist, 44,* 684–694.

Shorter, E. (1997). *A history of psychiatry: From the era of the asylum to the age of Prozac* New York: Wiley.

Shriver, M. D., & Piersel, W. (1994). The long-term effects of intrauterine drug exposure: Review of recent research and implications for early childhood special education. *Topics in Early Childhood Special Education, 14,* 161–183.

Siegel, K., Anderman, S. J., & Schrimshaw, E. W. (2001). Religion and coping with health stress. *Psychology and Health, 16,* 631–653.

Siegel, L. (1993). Amazing new discovery: Piaget was wrong. *Canadian Psychology, 34,* 239–245.

Siegert, R., & Ward, T. (2002). Evolutionary psychology: Origins and criticisms. *Australian Psychologist, 37,* 20–29.

Simon, H. A. (1974, February 8). How big is a chunk? *Science, 165,* 482–488.

Singer, J. L., & Singer, D. G. (1983). Psychologists look at television: Cognitive, developmental, personality, and social policy implications. *American Psychologist, 38,* 826–834.

Singer, P. (1998). *Ethics into action: Henry Spira and the animal rights movement.* Lanham, MD: Rowman & Littlefield.

Singh, G. K., & Yu, S. M. (1995). Infant mortality in the United States: Trends, differentials, and projections, 1950 through 2010. *American Journal of Public Health, 85,* 957–964.

Singular, S. (1982, October). A memory for all seasonings. *Psychology Today,* pp. 54–63.

Sinha, P. (1996). I think I know that face . . . *Nature, 384,* 404.

Sinnott, J. D. (1994). Sex roles. In V. S. Ramachandran (Ed.), *Encyclopedia of human behavior* (Vol. 4, pp. 151–158). San Diego, CA: Academic Press.

Skaalvik, E. M., & Rankin, R. J. (1994). Gender differences in mathematics and verbal achievement, self-perception and motivation. *British Journal of Educational Psychology, 64,* 419–428.

Skeels, H. M. (1938). Mental development of children in foster homes.

Journal of Consulting Psychology, 2, 33–43.

Skeels, H. M. (1942). The study of the effects of differential stimulation on mentally retarded children: A follow-up report. *American Journal of Mental Deficiencies, 46,* 340–350.

Skeels, H. M. (1966). Adult status of children with contrasting early life experiences. *Monographs of the Society for Research in Child Development, 31(3),* 1–65.

Skinner, B. F. (1938). *The behavior of organisms* New York: Appleton-Century-Crofts.

Skinner, B. F. (1948). *Science and human behavior* New York: Macmillan.

Skinner, B. F. (1953). Some contributions of an experimental analysis of behavior to psychology as a whole. *American Psychologist, 8,* 69–78.

Skinner, B. F. (1957). *Verbal behavior* Englewood Cliffs, NJ: Prentice Hall.

Skinner, B. F. (1987). Whatever happened to psychology as the science of behavior? *American Psychologist, 42,* 780–786.

Skinner, B. F. (1989). The origins of cognitive thought. *American Psychologist, 44,* 13–18.

Skinner, B. F. (1990). Can psychology be a science of mind? *American Psychologist, 45,* 1206–1210.

Skre, I., Onstad, S., Torgersen, S., & Lygren, S. (1993). A twin study of DSM-III-R anxiety disorders. *Acta Psychiatrica Scandinavica, 88,* 85–92.

Slater, A. (2000). Visual perception in the young infant. Early organization and rapid learning. In D. Muir & A. Slater (Eds.), *Infant development: Essential readings in developmental psychology* (pp. 9–116). Malden, MA: Blackwell Publishers.

Sleek, S. (1998, May). Older vets just now feeling pain of war. *APA Monitor,* pp. 1, 28.

Sleek, S. (1999, February). Programs aim to attract minorities to psychology. *APA Monitor,* p. 47.

Slife, B. D., & Reber, J. S. (2001). Eclecticism in psychotherapy: Is it really the best substitute for traditional theories? In B. D. Slife & R. N. Williams, (Eds.), *Critical issues in psychotherapy: Translating new ideas into practice* (pp. 213–233). Thousand Oaks, CA: Sage Publications, Inc.

Sloan, R. P., Bagiella, E., & Powell, T. (1999). Religion, spirituality, and medicine. *The Lancet, 353,* 664–667.

Slovic, P. (1995). The construction of preference. *American Psychologist, 50,* 364–371.

Smith, B. W. (2000). Noah revisited: Religious coping by church members and the impact of the 1993 Midwest flood. *Journal of Community Psychology, 28,* 169–186.

Smith, C. T. (1985). Sleep states and learning: A review of the animal literature. *Neuroscience & Biobehavioral Reviews, 9,* 157–168.

Smith, C. T., & Kelly, G. (1988). Paradoxical sleep deprivation applied two days after end of training retards learning. *Physiology & Behavior, 43*, 213–216.

Smith, C. T., & Lapp, L. (1986). Prolonged increase in both PS and number of REMS following a shuttle avoidance task. *Physiology & Behavior, 36*, 1053–1057.

Smith, D. (2001). Impairment on the job. *Monitor on Psychology, 32*, 52–53.

Smith, D. E., Roberts, J., Gage, F. H., & Tuszynski, M. H. (1999). Age-associated neuronal atrophy occurs in the primate brain and is reversible by growth factor gene therapy. *Proceedings of the National Academy of Sciences, 96*, 10893–10898.

Smith, D. N. (1998). The psychocultural roots of genocide: Legitimacy and crisis in Rwanda. *American Psychologist, 53*, 743–753.

Smith, D. V., & Margolskee, R. F. (2001). Making sense of taste. *Scientific American, 284 (3)*, 32–39.

Smith, K. H., & Rogers, M. (1994). Effectiveness of subliminal messages in television commercials: Two experiments. *Journal of Applied Psychology, 79*, 866–874.

Smith, M. L., Glass, G. V., & Miller, T. I. (1980). *The benefits of psychotherapy*. Baltimore: Johns Hopkins University Press.

Smith, P. B., & Bond, M. H. (1994). *Social psychology across cultures: Analysis and perspectives* Boston: Allyn & Bacon.

Smith, P. B., & Bond, M. H. (1999). *Social psychology across cultures: Analysis and perspectives* (2nd ed.). Boston: Allyn & Bacon.

Smith, S. M., Gleaves, D. H., Pierce, B. H., Williams, T. L., Gilliland, T. R., & Gerkens, D. R. (2003). Eliciting and comparing false and recovered memories: An experimental approach. *Applied Cognitive Psychology, 17*, 251–279.

Smith, S. M., Glenberg, A. M., & Bjork, R. A. (1978). Environmental context and human memory. *Memory & Cognition, 6*, 342–355.

Smollar, J., & Youniss, J. (1989). Transformations in adolescents' perceptions of parents. *International Journal of Behavioral Development, 12*, 71–84.

Snodgrass, S. E. (1992). Further effects of role versus gender on interpersonal sensitivity. *Journal of Personality and Social Psychology, 62*, 154–158.

Snyder, M. (1987). *Public appearances/private realities: The psychology of self-monitoring* New York: Freeman.

Snyder, M., & Swann, W. B., Jr. (1978). Behavioral confirmation in social interaction: From social perception to social reality. *Journal of Experimental Social Psychology, 14*, 148–162.

Snyder, M., & Tanke, E. D. (1976). Behavior and attitude: Some people are more consistent than others. *Journal of Personality, 44*, 501–517.

Snyder, M., Tanke, E. D., & Berscheid, E. (1977). Social perception and interpersonal behavior: On the self-fulfilling nature of social stereotypes. *Journal of Personality & Social Psychology, 35*, 656–666.

Snyder, S. H. (1977). Opiate receptors and internal opiates. *Scientific American, 236(3)*, 44–56.

Snyderman, M., & Rothman, S. (1987). Survey of expert opinion on intelligence and aptitude testing. *American Psychologist, 42*, 137–144.

Solomon, D. A., Keitner, G. I., Miller, I. W., Shea, M. T., & Keller, M. B. (1995). Course of illness and maintenance treatments for patients with bipolar disorder. *Journal of Clinical Psychiatry, 56*, 5–13.

Somer, E. (2002). Maladaptive daydreaming: A qualitative inquiry. *Journal of Contemporary Psychotherapy, 32*, 197–212.

Sommers-Flanagan, R., Sommers-Flanagan, J., & Davis, B. (1993). What's happening on music television? A gender role content analysis. *Sex Roles, 28*, 745–754.

Sonstroem, R. J. (1997). Physical activity and self-esteem. In W. P. Morgan (Ed.), *Physical activity and mental health* (pp. 127–143). Philadelphia, PA: Taylor & Francis.

Sotres, J. F. C., Velasquez, C. B., & Cruz, M. L. V. (2002). Profile of emotional intelligence: Construction, validity and reliability. *Salud Mental, 25*, 50–60.

Soussignan, R. (2002). Duchenne smile, emotional experience, and autonomic reactivity: A test of the facial feedback hypothesis. *Emotion, 2*, 52–74.

South, N. (Ed.). (1999). Debating drugs and everyday life: Normalisation, prohibition and "otherness." In N. South (Ed.), *Drugs: Culture, controls & everyday life* (pp. 1–16). Thousand Oaks, CA: Sage.

Southern, S., & Gayle, R. (1982). A cognitive behavioral model of hypoactive sexual desire. *Behavioral Counselor, 2*, 31–48.

Soyguet, G., & Tuerkcapar, H. (2001). Assessment of interpersonal schema patterns in antisocial personality disorder: A cognitive interpersonal perspective. *Turk Psikoloji Dergisi, 16*, 55–69.

Spanos, N. P. (1996). *Multiple identities and false memories*. Washington, DC: American Psychological Association.

Spanos, N. P., Burgess, C. A., Burgess, M. F., Samuels, C., & Blois, W. O. (1997). *Creating false memories of infancy with hypnotic and non-hypnotic procedures*. Unpublished manuscript, Carlton University, Ottawa, Canada.

Sperling, G. (1960). The information available in brief visual presentations. *Psychological Monographs, 74*, 1–29.

Sperry, R. W. (1964). The great cerebral commissure. *Scientific American, 210(1)*, 42–52.

Sperry, R. W. (1968). Hemisphere disconnection and unity in conscious awareness. *American Psychologist, 23*, 723–733.

Sperry, R. W. (1970). Perception in the absence of neocortical commissures. *Research Publications of the Association for Research in Nervous and Mental Diseases 48*, 123–138.

Sperry, R. W. (1988). Psychology's mentalists paradigm and the religion/science tension. *American Psychologist, 43*, 607–613.

Sperry, R. W. (1995). The future of psychology. *American Psychologist, 5*, 505–506.

Spettle, C. M., & Liebert, R. M. (1986). Training for safety in automated person-machine systems. *American Psychologist, 41*, 545–550.

Spiegel, D. (1995). Essentials of psychotherapeutic intervention for cancer patients. *Support Care Cancer, 3*, 252–256.

Spiegel, D., & Moore, R. (1997). Imagery and hypnosis in the treatment of cancer patients. *Oncology, 11*, 1179–1189.

Spiesman, J. C. (1965). Autonomic monitoring of ego defense process. In N. S. Greenfield & W. C. Lewis (Eds.), *Psychoanalysis and current biological thought*. Madison: University of Wisconsin Press.

Spiesman, J. C., Lazarus, R. S., Mordkoff, A., & Davison, L. (1964). Experimental reduction of stress based on ego-defense theory. *Journal of Abnormal & Social Psychology, 68*, 367–380.

Spinhoven, P., Nijenhuis, E. R. S., & Van Dyck, R. (1999). Can experimental memory research adequately explain memory for trauma? *Psychotherapy, 36*, 257–267.

Spitzer, R. L., Skodal, A. E., Gibbon, M., & Williams, J. B. W. (1981). *DSM-III case book*. Washington, DC: American Psychiatric Association.

Spoendlin, H. H., & Schrott, A. (1989). Analysis of the human auditory nerve. *Hearing Research, 43*, 25–38.

Squier, L. H., & Domhoff, G. W. (1998). The presentation of dreaming and dreams in introductory psychology textbooks: A critical examination with suggestions for textbook authors and course instructors. *Dreaming: Journal of the Association for the Study of Dreams, 8*, 149–168.

Squire, L. R., & Kandel, E. R. (1999). *Memory: From mind to molecules*. New York: Scientific American Library.

Squire, L. R., Knowlton, B., & Musen, G. (1993). The structure and organization of memory. *Annual Review of Psychology, 44*, 453–495.

Squire, L. R., Slater, P. C., & Chace, P. M. (1975, January). Retrograde amnesia: Temporal gradient in very long term memory following electroconvulsive therapy. *Science, 187*, 77–79.

Squire, S. (1983). *The slender balance: Causes and cures for bulimia, anorexia, and the weight loss/weight gain seesaw*. New York: Putnam.

Sridhar, K. S., Ruab, W. A., & Weatherby, N. L. (1994). Possible role of marijuana smoking as a carcinogen in development of lung cancer at a young age. *Journal of Psychoactive Drugs, 26*, 285–288.

Srinivasan, M. V., Zhang, S., Altwein, M., & Tautz, J. (2000, February 4). Honeybee navigation: Nature and calibration of the "odometer." *Science, 287*, 851–853.

Stack, S. (1994). Divorce. In V. S. Ramachandran (Ed.), *Encyclopedia of human behavior* (Vol. 2, pp. 153–163). San Diego, CA: Academic Press.

Stamm, B. H. (2003). Bridging the rural-urban divide with telehealth and telemedicine. In B. H. Stamm (Ed.), *Rural behavioral health care: An interdisciplinary guide* (pp. 145–155). Washington, DC: American Psychological Association.

Stancliffe, R. J. (1997). Community residence size, staff presence and choice. *Mental Retardation, 35*, 1–9.

Stanton, C., Spirito, A., Donaldson, D., & Doergers, J. (2003). Risk taking behavior and adolescent suicide attempts. *Suicide and Life Threatening Behavior, 33*, 74–79.

Stanton, M. D., & Shadish, W. R. (1997). Outcome, attrition, and family-couples treatment for drug abuse: A meta-analysis and review of the controlled, comparative studies. *Psychological Bulletin, 122*, 170–191.

Steele, C. M., & Josephs, R. A. (1990). Alcohol myopia: Its prized and dangerous effects. *American Psychologist, 45*, 921–933.

Steiger, H., Gauvin, L., Jabalpurwala, S., Seguin, J. R., & Stotland, S. (1999). Hypersensitivity to social interactions in bulimic syndromes: Relationships to binge eating. *Journal of Consulting & Clinical Psychology, 67*, 765–775.

Stein, J. (2002, November 4). The new politics of pot. *Time*, pp. 56–66.

Steiner, J. A. (1972). A questionnaire study of risk-taking in psychiatric patients. *British Journal of Medical Psychology, 45*, 365–374.

Steiner, J. E. (1979). Facial expressions in response to taste and smell stimulation. In H. W. Reese & L. P. Lipsitt (Eds.), *Advances in child development and behavior* (Vol. 13). New York: Academic Press.

Steinhauer, J. (1997, July 6). Living together without marriage or apologies. *New York Times*, p. A9.

Steinmetz, J. E. (1998). The localization of a simple type of learning and memory: The cerebellum and classical eyeblink conditioning. *Current Directions in Psychological Science, 7*, 72–76.

Stelmack, R. M., Knott, V., & Beauchamp, C. M. (2003). Intelligence and neural transmission time: A brain stem auditory evoked potential analysis. *Personality and Individual Differences, 34*, 97–107.

Stern, L. (1985). *The structures and strategies of human memory.* Homewood, IL: Dorsey Press.

Stern, P., & Marx, J. (1999, October 22). Making sense of scents. *Science, 286*, 703–704.

Stern, R. M., & Koch, K. L. (1996). Motion sickness and differential susceptibility. *Current Directions in Psychological Science, 5*, 115–120.

Sternberg, R. J. (1982, April). Who's intelligent? *Psychology Today*, pp. 30–39.

Sternberg, R. J. (1986). *Intelligence applied.* Orlando, FL: Harcourt Brace Jovanovich.

Sternberg, R. J. (1993). *Sternberg Triarchic Abilities Test.* Unpublished test.

Sternberg, R. J. (1997). Educating intelligence: Infusing the triarchic theory into school instruction. In R. J. Sternberg & E. Grigorenko (Eds.), *Intelligence: Heredity and environment* (pp. 343–362). New York: Cambridge University Press.

Sternberg, R. J. (2001). What is the common thread of creativity? Its dialectical relation to intelligence and wisdom. *American Psychologist, 56*, 360–362.

Sternberg, R. J. (2003). Intelligence. In D. K. Freedheim (Ed.), *Handbook of psychology: History of psychology, Vol. 1* (pp. 135–156). New York, NY: John Wiley & Sons, Inc.

Sternberg, R. J. (2003). Intelligence: The triarchic theory of intelligence. In. J. W. Gutherie (Ed.), *Encyclopedia of education (2nd ed.).* New York: Macmillan.

Sternberg, R. J., & Davidson, J. E. (1985). Cognitive development in the gifted and talented. In F. D. Horowitz & M. O'Brien (Eds.), *The gifted and talented: Developmental perspectives* (pp. 5–35). Washington, DC: American Psychological Association.

Sternberg, R. J., & Kaufman, J. C. (1998). Human abilities. *Annual Review of Psychology, 49*, 479–502.

Sternberg, R. J., Castejon, J. L., Prieto, M. D., Hautamaeki, J., & Grigorenko, E. L. (2001). Confirmatory factor analysis of the Sternberg Triarchic Abilities Test in three international samples. An empirical test of the triarchic theory of intelligence. *European Journal of Psychological Assessment, 17*, 1–16.

Sternberg, R. J., Conway, B. E., Ketron, J. L., & Bernstein, M. (1981). People's conceptions of intelligence. *Journal of Personal and Social Psychology, 41*, 37–55.

Stevens, G., & Gardner, S. (1982). *Women of psychology: Expansion and refinement* (Vol. 1). Cambridge, MA: Schenkman.

Stevenson, H. W. (1992). Learning from Asian schools. *Scientific American, 267* (6), 70–76.

Stevenson, H. W. (1993). Why Asian students still outdistance Americans. *Educational Leadership, 50*, 63–65.

Stevenson, H. W., Chen, C., & Lee, S.-Y. (1993, January 1). Mathematics achievement of Chinese, Japanese, and American children: Ten years later. *Science, 259*, 53–58.

Stevenson, H. W., Lee, S., & Mu, X. (2000). Successful achievement in mathematics: China and the United States. In F. M. van Lieshout & P. G. Heymans (Eds.), *Developing talent across the life span* (pp. 167–183). Philadelphia, PA: Psychology Press.

Stevenson, H. W., Lee, S.-Y., & Stigler, J. W. (1986, February 14). Mathematics achievement of Chinese, Japanese, and American children. *Science, 231*, 693–697.

Stewart, R. H. (1965). Effect of continuous responding on the order effect in personality impression formation. *Journal of Personality and Social Psychology, 1*, 161–165.

Stickgold, R., Rittenhouse, C. D., & Hobson, J. A. (1994). Dream splicing: A new technique for assessing thematic coherence in subjective reports of mental activity. *Consciousness and Cognition, 3*, 114–128.

Stiles, W. B., Shapiro, D. A., & Elliott, R. (1986). Are all psychotherapies equivalent? *American Psychologist, 41*, 165–180.

Stock, M. B., & Smythe, P. M. (1963). Does undernutrition during infancy inhibit brain growth and subsequent intellectual development? *Archives of Disorders in Childhood, 38*, 546–552.

Stodghill, R. (1998, June 15). Where'd you learn that? *Time*, 52–59.

Stone, J. S., Oesterle, E. C., & Rubel, E. W. (1998). Recent insights into regeneration of auditory and vestibular hair cells. *Current Opinion in Neurology, 11*, 17–24.

Stone, W. F., Lederer, G., & Christie, R. (1993). Introduction: Strength and weakness. In W. F. Stone, G. Lederer, & R. Christie (Eds.), *The authoritarian personality today: Strength and weakness* (pp. 285–325). New York: Springer-Verlag.

Stoner, J. A. F. (1961). *A comparison of individual and group decisions involving risk.* Unpublished master's thesis, School of Industrial Management, MIT, Cambridge MA.

Storch, E. A., & Storch, J. B. (2003). Academic dishonesty and attitudes towards academic dishonest acts: Support for cognitive dissonance theory. *Psychological Reports, 92*, 174–176.

Storm, L., & Ertel, S. (2001). Does Psi exist? Comments on Milton and Wiseman's (1999) meta-analysis of Ganzfeld research. *Psychological Bulletin, 12*, 424–433.

Stowell, J. R., McGuire, L., Robles, T., Glaser, R., & Kiecolt-Glaser, J. K. (2003). Psychoneuroimmunology. In A. M. Nezu & C. M. Nezu (Eds.).

Handbook of psychology: Health psychology, Vol. 9 (pp. 75–95). New York, NY: John Wiley & Sons, Inc.

Strausbaugh, H. J., Paul, G. G., Lo, E., Tangemann, K., Reichling, D. B., Rosen, S. D., & Levine, J. D. (1999). Painful stimulation suppresses joint inflammation by inducing shedding of L-selectin from neutrophils. *Nature: Medicine, 5*, 1057–1061.

Strecker, R. R., Moriarty, S., Thakkar, M. M., Porkka-Heiskanen, T., Basheer, R., Dauphin, L. J., Rainnie, D. G., Portas, C. M., Greene, R. W., & McCarley, R. W. (2002). Adenosinergic modulation of basal forebrain and preoptic/anterior hypothalamic neuronal activity in the control of behavioral state. *Behavioural Brain Research, 115*, 183–204.

Strickland, B. R. (2000). Misassumptions, misadventures, and the misuse of psychology. *American Psychologist, 55*, 331–338.

Stromswold, K. (1995). The cognitive and neural bases of language acquisition. In M. S. Gazzaniga (Ed.), *The cognitive neurosciences* (pp. 855–870). Cambridge, MA: MIT Press.

Studer, J. R. (2000). Adolescent suicide: Aggression turned inward. In D. S. Sandhu & C. B. Aspy (Eds.), *Violence in American schools: A practical guide for counselors* (pp. 269–284). Alexandria, VA: American Counseling Association.

Stumpf, H., & Stanley, J. C. (1998). Stability and change in gender-related differences on the college board advanced placement and achievement tests. *Current Directions in Psychological Research, 7*, 192–196.

Stylianou, D. A. (2002). On the interaction of visualization and analysis: The negotiation of a visual representation in expert problem solving. *Journal of Mathematical Behavior, 21*, 303–317.

Subotnik, K. L., Goldstein, M. J., Nuechterlein, K. H., Woo, S. M., & Mintz, J. (2002). Are communication deviance and expressed emotion related to family history of psychiatric disorders in schizophrenia. *Schizophrenia Bulletin, 28*, 719–729.

Subotnik, R. F., & Arnold, K. D. (1994). *Beyond Terman: Contemporary longitudinal studies of giftedness and talent.* Norwood, NJ: Ablex.

Sue, S. (1998). In search of cultural competence in psychotherapy and counseling. *American Psychologist, 53*, 440–448.

Sue, S., Zane, N., & Young, K. (1994). Research on psychotherapy with culturally diverse populations. In A. E. Bergin & S. L. Garfield (Eds.), *Handbook of psychotherapy and behavior change* (4th ed., pp. 783–820). New York: Wiley.

Suga, N. (1990). Bisonar and neural computation in bats. *Scientific American, 262*(6), 60–68.

Suhr, J. A. (2002). Malingering, coaching, and the serial position effect.

Archives of Clinical Neuropsychology, 17, 69–77.

Suls, J., & Fletcher, B. (1983). Social comparison in the social and physical sciences: An archival study. *Journal of Personality and Social Psychology, 44*, 575–580.

Sumova, A., Sladek, M., Jac, M., & Illnervoa, H. (2002). The circadian rhythm of Perl gene product in rat's suprachiasmatic nucleus and its modulation by seasonal changes in daylight. *Brain Research, 947*, 260–270.

Sundel, S. S. (1991). The effects of videotaped modeling on the acquisition, performance, and generalization of job-related social skills in adults with mental retardation living in group homes. *Dissertation Abstracts International, 51*, 2522.

Swaab, D. F., & Hoffman, M. A. (1995). Sexual differentiation of the human hypothalamus in relation to gender and sexual orientation. *Trends in Neuroscience, 18*, 264–270.

Swan, N. (1998). Brain scans open window to view cocaine's effects on the brain. *NIDA Notes, 13*, 12.

Symons, C. S., & Johnson, B. T. (1997). The self-reference effect in memory: A meta-analysis. *Psychological Bulletin, 121*, 371–394.

Szatkowska, I., Grabowska, A., & Szymanska, O. (2001). Evidence for involvement of ventro-medial prefrontal cortex in a short-term storage of visual images. *Neuroreport: for Rapid Communication of Neuroscience Research, 12*, 1187–1190.

Szobiova, E. (2001). Relationship of creativity and intelligence: Coincidence, similarities, and differences. *Ceskoslovenska Psychologie, 45*, 323–337.

T

Tagano, D. W., Moran, D. J., III, & Sawyers, J. K. (1991). *Creativity in early childhood classrooms.* Washington, DC: National Education Association.

Takaki, A., Nagai, K., Takaki, S., & Yanaihara, N. (1990). Satiety function of neurons containing CCKK-like substance in the dorsal parabrachial nucleus. *Physiology & Behavior, 48*, 865–871.

Takami, S., Getchell, M. L., Chen, Y., Monti-Bloch, L., & Berliner, D. L. (1993). Vomeronasal epithelial cells of the adult human express neuron-specific molecules. *Neuroreport, 4*, 374–378.

Takeuchi, S. A. (2000). If I don't look good, you don't look good? Toward a new matching theory of interpersonal attraction based on the behavioral and the social exchange principles. *Dissertation Abstracts International Section A: Humanities and Social Sciences, 60*, 4198.

Tan, D. T. Y., & Singh, R. (1995). Attitudes and attraction: A developmental study of the similarity-attraction and dissimilarity-repulsion hypotheses. *Personality and Social Psychology Bulletin, 21,* 975–986.

Tang, Y.-P., Shimizu, E., Dube, G. R., Rampon, C., Kerchner, G. A., Zhuo, M., Liu, G., & Tsien, Z. T. (1999). Genetic enhancement of learning and memory in mice. *Nature, 401,* 63–69.

Tanner, J. M. (1978). *Foetus into man: Physical growth from conception to maturity.* Cambridge, MA: Harvard University Press.

Tanofsky, M. B., Wilfley, D. E., Spurrell, E. B., Welch, R., & Brownell, K. D. (1997). Comparison of men and women with binge eating disorder. *International Journal of Eating Disorders, 21,* 49–54.

Tavris, C. (1992). *The mismeasure of woman.* New York: Simon & Schuster.

Taylor, D. M., & Moghaddam, F. M. (1994). *Theories of intergroup relations: International social psychological perspectives.* Westport, CT: Praeger.

Taylor, S. E. (1986). *Health psychology.* New York: Random House.

Taylor, S. E. (2003). *Health Psychology* (5th ed.). New York, NY: McGraw Hill.

Taylor, S. E., & Repetti, R. L. (1997). Health psychology: What is an unhealthy environment and how does it get under the skin? *Annual Review of Psychology, 48,* 411–447.

Taylor, S. E., Kemeny, M. E., Reed, G. H., Bower, J. E., & Gruenwald, T. L. (2000). Psychological resources, positive illusions, and health. *American Psychologist, 55,* 99–109.

Taylor, S. E., Peplau, L. A., & Sears, D. O. (1994). *Social psychology.* Englewood Cliffs, NJ: Prentice Hall.

Taylor, S. E., Pham, L. B., Rivkin, I. D., & Armor, D. A. (1998). Harnessing the imagination: Mental simulation, self-regulation, and coping. *American Psychologist, 53,* 429–439.

Terman, L. M. (1925). *Mental and physical traits of a thousand gifted children: Genetic studies of genius* (Vol. 1). Stanford, CA: Stanford University Press.

Terrace, H. S. (1979). *Nim: A chimpanzee who learned sign language.* New York: Knopf.

Terrace, H. S. (1985). On the nature of animal thinking. *Neuroscience and Biobehavioral Reviews, 9,* 643–652.

Terrace, H. S., Son, L. K., & Brannon, E. M. (2003). Serial expertise of rhesus macaques. *Psychological Science, 14,* 66–73.

Testa, M., Livingston, J. A., & Collins, R. L. (2000). The role of women's alcohol consumption in evaluation of vulnerability to sexual aggression. *Experimental & Clinical Psychopharmacology, 8,* 185–191.

Thelen, E. (1994). Three-month-old infants can learn task-specific patterns of interlimb coordination. *Psychological Science, 5,* 280–288.

Thelen, E. (1995). Motor development: A new synthesis. *American Psychologist, 50,* 79–95.

Thiffault, P., & Bergeron, J. (2003). Fatigue and individual differences in monotonous simulated driving. *Personality and Individual Differences, 34,* 159–176.

Thomas, A., & Chess, S. (1977). *Temperament and development.* New York: Brunner/Mazel.

Thomas, S. G., & Kellner, C. H. (2003). Remission of major depression and obsessive-compulsive disorder after a single unilateral ECT. *Journal of ECT, 19,* 50–51.

Thompson, J. K., & Thompson, C. M. (1986). Body size distortion and self-esteem in asymptomatic, normal weight males and females. *International Journal of Eating Disorders, 5,* 1061–1068.

Thompson, P. M., Hayashi, K. M., Zubicaray, G. D., Janke, A. L., Rose, S. E., Semple, J., Herman, D., Hong, M. S., Dittmer, S. S., Doddrell, D. M., & Toga, A. W. (2003). Dynamics of gray matter loss in Alzheimer's disease. *The Journal of Neuroscience, 23,* 994.

Thorndike, E. L. (1898). Animal intelligence. *Psychological Review Monograph, 2*(4, Whole No. 8).

Thorne, F., Neave, N., Scholey, A., Moss, M., & Fink, B. (2002). Effects of putative male pheromones on female ratings of male attractiveness: influence of oral contraceptives and the menstrual cycle. *Neuroendocrinology Letters, 23,* 291–297.

Thorne, F., Scholey, A. B., & Neave, N. (2000). Love is in the air? Effects of pheromones, oral contraceptive use and menstrual cycle phase on attraction. *Proceeding of the British Psychological Society, 8*(2), 49.

Thornhill, R., & Gangestad, S. W. (1999). The scent of symmetry: A human sex pheromone that signals fitness. *Evolution and Human Behavior, 20,* 175–201.

Thune, L. E., & Underwood, B. J. (1943). Retroactive inhibition as a function of degree of interpolated learning. *Journal of Experimental Psychology, 32,* 185–200.

Thurber, J. G. (1942). The secret life of Walter Mitty. In J. G. Thurber (Ed.), *My world and welcome to it.* New York: Harcourt, Brace.

Thurstone, L. L. (1938). Primary mental abilities. *Psychometric Monographs, 1.*

Tincoff, R., & Jusczyk, P. W. (1999). Some beginnings of word comprehension in 6-month-olds. *Psychological Science, 10,* 172–176.

Tobler, I. (1997). What do we know about the evolution of sleep—when it arose and why?. Available on-line at: www.sciam.com/askexpert/biology/biology24.html

Toft, M. D. (2003). *The geography of ethnic violence: Identity, interests, and the indivisibility of territory.* Princeton, NJ: Princeton University Press.

Tolman, E. C., & Honzik, C. H. (1930). Introduction and removal of reward, and maze performance in rates. *University of California Publications in Psychology, 4,* 257–275.

Tomarken, A. J., Davidson, R. J., & Henriques, J. B. (1990). Resting frontal brain asymmetry predicts affective responses to films. *Journal of Personality and Social Psychology, 59,* 791–801.

Tomkins, S. S. (1962). *Affect, imagery, consciousness: The positive affects* (Vol. 1). New York: Springer.

Tooby, J., & Cosmides, L. (1990). The past explains the present: Emotional adaptations and the structure of ancestral environments. *Ethology and Sociobiology, 10,* 29–50.

Torgersen, S. (1983). Genetic factors in anxiety disorders. *Archives of General Psychiatry, 40,* 1085–1089.

Torrance, E. P. (1954). Leadership training to improve air-crew group performance. *USAF ATC Instructor's Journal, 5,* 25–35.

Torrey, E. F., Bowler, A. E., Taylor, E. H., & Gottesman, I. I. (1994). *Schizophrenia and manic-depressive disorder: The biological roots of mental illness as revealed by the landmark study of identical twins.* New York: Basic Books.

Treaster, J. B. (1994, February 1). Survey finds marijuana use is up in high schools. *New York Times,* p. A1.

Treisman, A. M. (1960). Contextual cues in selective listening. *Quarterly Journal of Experimental Psychology, 12,* 242–248.

Treisman, A. M. (1964). Verbal cues, language and meaning in selective attention. *American Journal of Psychology, 77,* 206–219.

Treisman, A. M. (1986). Features and objects in visual processing. *Scientific American, 255*(5), 114–125.

Treisman, A. M., Cavanagh, P., Fischer, B., Ramachandran, V. S., & von der Heydt, R. (1990). Form perception and attention: Striate cortex and beyond. In L. Spillman & J. S. Werner (Eds.), *Visual perception* (pp. 273–316). San Diego, CA: Academic Press.

Triandis, H. C. (1994). *Culture and social behavior.* New York: McGraw-Hill.

Trice, A. D. (1986). Ethical variables? *American Psychologist, 41,* 482–483.

Trichopoulou, A., Costacou, T., Bamia, C., & Trichopoulos, D. (2003). Adherence to a Mediterranean diet and survival in a Greek population. *The New England Journal of Medicine, 348,* 2599–2608.

Trotter, R. J. (1983, August). Baby face. *Psychology Today,* pp. 12–20.

Tryon, R. C. (1940). Genetic differences in maze-learning abilities in rats. In *39th Yearbook: Part I. National Society for the Study of Education* (pp. 111–119). Chicago: University of Chicago Press.

Tryon, W. W. (2000). Behavior therapy as applied learning theory. *Behavior Therapist, 23,* 131–133.

Tsien, J. Z. (2000). Building a brainier mouse. *Scientific American, 282*(4), 62–68.

Tucker, C. M., & Herman, K. C. (2002). Using culturally sensitive theories and research to meet the academic needs of low-income African American children. *American Psychologist, 57,* 762–773.

Tulving, E. (1985). How many memory systems are there? *American Psychologist, 40,* 385–398.

Tulving, E., Kapur, S., Markowitsch, H. J., Craik, F. I. M., Habib, R., & Houle, S. (1994). Neuroanatomical correlates of retrieval in episodic memory: Auditory sentence recognition. *Proceedings of the National Academy of Sciences of the U. S. A., 91,* 2012–2015.

Tupes, E. C., & Christal, R. W. (1961). *Recurrent personality factors based on trait ratings.* USAF ASD Technical Report, No. 61–97.

Turkheimer, E. (1991). Individual and group differences in adoption studies of IQ. *Psychological Bulletin, 110,* 392–405.

Turkheimer, E., & Waldron, M. (2000). Nonshared environment: A theoretical, methodological, and quantitative review. *Psychological Bulletin, 126,* 78–108.

Turnage, J. J. (1990). The challenge of new workplace technology for psychology. *American Psychologist [Special Issue: Organizational Psychology], 45,* 171–178.

Turnbull, C. M. (1961). Observations. *American Journal of Psychology, 1,* 304–308.

Turnbull, S., Ward, A., Treasure, J., Jick, H., & Derby, L. (1996). The demand for eating disorder care. An epidemiological study using the general practice research database. *British Journal of Psychiatry, 169,* 705–712.

Tversky, A., & Kahneman, D. (1973). Availability: A heuristic for judging frequency and probability. *Cognitive Psychology, 5,* 207–232.

Tyrer, P. (1994). What are the borders of borderline personality disorder? *Acta Psychiatrica Scandinavica, 89*(Suppl. 379), 38–44.

U

Uchino, B. N., Cacioppo, J. T., & Kiecolt-Glaser, J. K. (1996). The relationship between social support and physiological processes: A review with emphasis on underlying mechanisms and implications for health. *Psychological Bulletin, 119,* 488–531.

Uchino, B. N., Uno, D., & Holt-Lunstad, J. (1999). Social support, psychological processes, and health. *Current Directions in Psychological Science, 8,* 145–148.

Uhl, G. R., Sora, I., & Wang, Z. (1999, December). *The u opiate receptor as a* candidate gene for pain: Polymorphisms, variations in expression, nociception, and opiate responses. Paper presented at the National Academy of Sciences Colloquium, Irvine, CA.

Uhl, G., Blum, K., Nobel, E. P., & Smith, S. (1993). Substance abuse vulnerability and D2 dopamine receptor gene and severe alcoholism. *Trends in Neuroscience, 16*, 83–88.

Ulf, E. (1999). Neurobiology: Turning a corner in vision research. *Nature, 399*, 641–644.

Ulrich, R., & Azrin, N. (1962). Reflexive fighting in response to aversive stimulation. *Journal of Experimental Analysis of Behavior, 5*, 511–520.

Underwood, G. (1994). Subliminal perception on TV. *Nature, 370*, 103.

U.S. Bureau of the Census (2002a). *United States Department of Commerce News*. Washington, DC. Accessed August 23, 2003 at: http://www.census.gov/Press-Release/www/2002/cb02-19.html.

U.S. Bureau of the Census, (2002b). *Median Age at First Marriage*. Washington, DC. Accessed August 23, 2003 at: http://www.infoplease.com/ipa/A0005061.html.

V

Vaidya, C. J., Austin, G., Kirkorian, G., Ridlehuber, H. W., Desmond, J. E., Glover, G. H., & Gabrieli, J. D. E. (1998). Selective effects of methylphenidate in attention deficit hyperactivity disorder: A functional magnetic resonance study. *Proceedings of the National Academy of Sciences, U.S.A., 96*, 8301–8306.

Vaillant, G. E. (1977). *Adaptation to life*. Boston: Little, Brown.

Vaillant, G. E. (2000). Adaptive mental mechanisms: Their role in positive psychology. *American Psychologist, 55*, 89–98.

Vaisse, C., Halaas, J. L., Horvath, C. M., Darnell, J. E., Stoffell, M., & Friedman, J. M. (1996). Leptin activation of Stat3 in the hypothalamus of wild-type and ob/ob mice but not db/db mice. *Nature Genetics, 14*, 95–97.

Valian, V. (1998). *Why so slow?: The advancement of women*. Cambridge, MA: MIT Press.

Valkenburg, P. M., & van der Voort, T. H. A. (1994). Influence of TV on daydreaming and creative imagination: A review of research. *Psychological Bulletin, 116*, 316–339.

van Elst, L. T., & Trimble, M. R. (2003). Amygdala pathology in schizophrenia and psychosis of epilepsy. *Current Opinion in Psychiatry, 16*, 321–326.

Van Natta, P., Malin, H., Bertolucci, D., & Kaelber, C. (1985). The influence of alcohol abuse as a hidden contributor to mortality. *Alcohol, 2*, 535–539.

Van Praag, H., & Gage, F. H. (2002). Stem cell research, part 1: New neurons in the adult brain. *Journal of the*

American Academy of Child and Adolescent Psychiatry, 41, 354–356.

Van Yperen, N. W., & Buunk, B. P. (1990). A longitudinal study of equity and satisfaction in intimate relationships. *European Journal of Social Psychology, 54*, 287–309.

VandenBox, G., & Williams, S. (2000). The Internet versus the telephone: What is telehealth anyway? *Professional Psychology: Research & Practice, 31*, 490–492.

Vanderschuren, L. J., Niesink, R. J., & Van Ree, J. M. (1997). The neurobiology of social play behavior in rats. *Neuroscience and Biobehavioral Reviews, 21*, 309–326.

Van-Hoff, J. C., & Golden, S. (2002). Validation of an event-related potential memory assessment procedure: Intentional learning as opposed to simple repetition. *Journal of Psychophysiology, 16*, 12–22.

Vauclair, J. (1996). *Animal cognition: An introduction to modern comparative psychology*. Cambridge, MA: Harvard University Press.

Vaughn, B. E., Azria, M. R., Krzysik, L., Caya, L. R., Bost, K. K., Newell, W., & Kazura, K. L. (2000). Friendship and social competence in a sample of preschool children attending Head Start. *Developmental Psychology, 36*, 326–338.

Vaughn, D. (1996). *The Challenger launch decision: Risky technology, culture, and deviance at NASA*. Chicago, Ill: University of Chicago Press.

Vaughn, M. (1993, July 22). Divorce revisited. *Ann Arbor News*, p. C4.

Vazdarjanova, A., & McGaugh, J. L. (1999). Basolateral amygdala is involved in modulating consolidation of memory for classical fear conditioning. *Journal of Neuroscience, 19*, 6615–6622.

Vecera, S. P., Vogel, E. K., & Woodman, G. F. (2002). Lower region: A new cue for figure-ground assignment. *Journal of Experimental Psychology: General, 131*, 194–205.

Vermetten, E., & Bremner, J. D. (2002). Circuits and systems in stress: II. Applications to neurobiology and treatment in posttraumatic stress disorder. *Depression and Anxiety, 16*, 14–38.

Vermetten, E., & Bremner, J. D. (2003). Olfaction as a traumatic reminder in posttraumatic stress disorder: Case reports and review. *Journal of Clinical Psychiatry, 64*, 202–207.

Vernon, D., Egner, T., Cooper, N., Compton, T., Neilands, C., Sheri, A., & Gruzelier, J. (2003). The effect of training distinct neurofeedback protocols on aspects of cognitive performance. *International Journal of Psychophysiology, 47*, 75–85.

Vernon, P. A. (2000). Biological theories. In A. E. Kazdin (Ed.), *Encyclopedia of psychology* (Vol. 5, pp. 145–147). Washington, DC: American Psychological Association and New York: Oxford University Press.

Vernon, P. A. (Ed.). (1993). *Biological approaches to the study of human intelligence*. Norwood, NJ: Ablex.

Vgontzas, A. N., & Kales, A. (1999). Sleep and its disorders. *Annual Review of Medicine, 50*, 387–400.

Viers, D., & Prouty, A. M. (2001). We've come a long way? An overview of research of dual-career couples' stressors and strengths. *Journal of Feminist Family Therapy, 13*, 169–190.

Viglione, D. J., & Taylor, N. (2003). Empirical support for interrater reliability of Rorschach comprehensive system coding. *Journal of Clinical Psychology, 59*, 111–121.

Vingerhoets, G., Berckmoes, C., & Stroobant, N. (2003). Cerebral hemodynamics during discrimination of prosodic and semantic emotion in speech studied by transcranial Doppler ultrasonography. *Neuropsychology, 17*, 93–99.

Vinnicombe, S., & Singh, V. (2003). Women-only management training: An essential part of women's leadership development. *Journal of Change Management, 3*, 294–306.

Violani, C., & Lombardo, C. (2003). Peripheral temperature changes during rest and gender differences in thermal biofeedback. *Journal of Psychosomatic Research, 54*, 391–397.

Virkkunen, M. (1983). Insulin secretion during the glucose tolerance test in antisocial personality. *British Journal of Psychiatry, 142*, 598–604.

Vogel, G. (2000, February 25). Can old cells learn new tricks? *Science, 287*, 1418–1419.

von Frisch, K. (1974). Decoding the language of the bee. *Science, 185*, 663–668.

von Hippel, W., Hawkins, C., & Narayan, S. (1994). Personality and perceptual expertise: Individual differences in perceptual identification. *Psychological Science, 5*, 401–406.

von Hofsten, C., & Fazel-Zandy, S. (1984). Development of visually guided hand orientation in reaching. *Journal of Experimental Child Psychology, 38*, 208–219.

Vossel, G. & Rossman, R. (1986). Classical conditioning of electodermal activity and Maltzman's conception of voluntary orienting responses: A successful replication. *Zeitschrift fuer Experimentelle und Angewandte Psychologie, 33*, 312–328.

Voydanoff, P., & Donnelly, B. W. (1999). Risk and protective factors for psychological adjustment and grades among adolescents. *Journal of Family Issues, 20*, 328–349.

Voyer, D., Voyer, S., & Bryden, M. P. (1995). Magnitude of sex differences in spatial abilities: A meta-analysis and consideration of critical variables. *Psychological Bulletin, 117*, 250–270.

Vygotsky, L. S. (1979). *Mind in society: The development of higher mental*

processes. Cambridge, MA: Harvard University Press. (Original works published in 1930, 1933, and 1935.)

W

Wadden, T. S., Vogt, R. A., Anderson, R. E., Bartlett, S. F., Foster, G. D., Kuebnel, R. H., Wilk, F., Weinstock, R., Buckenmeyer, P., Berkowitz, R. I., & Steen, S. N. (1997). Exercise in the treatment of obesity: Effects of four interventions on body composition, resting energy expenditure, appetite and mood. *Journal of Consulting and Clinical Psychology, 65*, 269–277.

Waddington, K. D., Nelson, C. M., & Page, R. E. (1998). Effects of pollen quality and genotype on the dance of foraging honey bees. *Animal Behaviour, 5*, 35–39.

Wade, T. D., Bulik, C. M., Neale, M., & Kendler, K. S. (2000). Anorexia nervosa and major depression: Shared genetic and environmental risk factors. *American Journal of Psychiatry, 157*, 469–471.

Wagner, B. M. (1997). Family risk factors for child and adolescent suicidal behavior. *Psychological Bulletin, 121*, 246–298.

Wagner, R. K., & Sternberg, R. J. (1986). Tacit knowledge and intelligence in the everyday world. In R. J. Sternberg & R. K. Wagner (Eds.), *Practical intelligence* (pp. 51–83). New York: Cambridge University Press.

Wahlsten, D. (1999). Single-gene influences on brain and behavior. *Annual Review of Psychology, 50*, 599–624.

Waite, P. O. (1995). Exploring preadolescent attitudes towards obesity. *Dissertation Abstracts International: Section B: The Sciences and Engineering, 56*, 3509.

Walchle, S. B., & Landman, J. (2003). Effects of counterfactual thought on postpurchase consumer affect. *Psychology and Marketing, 20*, 23–46.

Walcutt, D. L. (2001). The efficacy of neurofeedback on migrainous neuralgia. *Dissertation Abstracts International: Section B: The Sciences and Engineering, 62*, 568.

Walk, R. D., & Gibson, E. J. (1961). A comparative and analytical study of visual depth perception. *Psychological Monographs, No. 75*.

Walker, E. F., & Diforio, D. (1997). Schizophrenia: A neural diathesis-stress model. *Psychological Review, 104*, 667–685.

Wall, P. D., & Melzack, R. (1996). *The Challenge of Pain* (2nd ed.). Harmondworth, UK: Penguin.

Wallerstein, J. S., Blakeslee, S., & Lewis, J. (2000). *The unexpected legacy of divorce: Twenty-five year landmark study*. New York: Hyperion.

Walster, E., Walster, G. W., & Berscheid, E. (1978). *Equity: Theory and research*. Boston: Allyn & Bacon.

Walters, E. E., & Kendler, K. S. (1995). Anorexia nervosa and anorexic-like syndromes in a population-based female twin sample. *American Journal of Psychiatry, 152,* 64–67.

Walton, G. E., & Bower, T. G. R. (1993). Newborns form "prototypes" in less than 1 minute. *Psychological Science, 4,* 203–206.

Walton, G. E., Bower, N. J. A., & Bower, T. G. R. (1992). Recognition of familiar faces by newborns. *Infant Behavior and Development, 15,* 265–269.

Waltz, J. A., Knowlton, B. J., Holyoak, K. J., Boone, K. B., Mishkin, F. S., Santos, M. M., Thomas, C. R., & Miller, B. L. (1999). A system for relational reasoning in human prefrontal cortex. *Psychological Science, 10,* 119–125.

Wampold, B. E., Mondin, G. W., Moody, M., Stich, F., Benson, K., & Ahn, H. (1997). A meta-analysis of outcome studies comparing bona fide psychotherapies: Empirically, "all must have prizes." *Psychological Bulletin, 122,* 203–215.

Wang, C., & Chen, W. (2000). The efficacy of behavior therapy in 9 patients with phobia. *Chinese Mental Health Journal, 14,* 351–352.

Wang, Q. (2003). Infantile amnesia reconsidered: A cross-cultural analysis. *Memory, 11,* 65–80.

Wanous, J. P. (1980). *Organizational entry: Recruitment, selection, and socialization of newcomers.* Reading, MA: Addison-Wesley.

Warr, P., & Perry, G. (1982). Paid employment and women's psychological well-being. *Psychological Bulletin, 91,* 498–516.

Warrington, E. K., & Weiskrantz, L. (1970). Amnesic syndrome: Consolidation or retrieval? *Nature, 228,* 628–630.

Washburn, M. F. (1916). *Movement and mental imagery: Outlines of a motor theory of the complexer mental processes.* Boston: Houghton Mifflin.

Wass, T. S., Simmons, R. W., Thomas, J. D., & Riley, E. P. (2002). Timing accuracy and variability in children with prenatal exposure to alcohol. *Alcoholism: Clinical and Experimental Research, 26,* 1887–1896.

Waterman, C. K., Bleubel, M. E., & Waterman, A. S. (1970). Relationship between resolution of the identity crisis and outcomes of previous psychosocial crises. *Proceedings of the Annual Convention of the American Psychological Association, 5*(Pt. I), 467–468.

Waters, A. J., Gobet, F., & Leyden, G. (2002). Visuospatial abilities of chess players. *British Journal of Psychology, 93,* 557–565.

Watkins, C. E., Campbell, V. L., Nieberding, R., & Hallmark, R. (1995). Contemporary practice of psychological assessment by clinical psychologists. *Professional Psychological Research & Practice, 26,* 54–60.

Watkins, P. C., Vache, K., Verney, S. P., Mathews, A., & Muller, S. (1996). Unconscious mood-congruent memory bias in depression. *Journal of Abnormal Psychology, 105,* 34–31.

Watson, D. L., & Tharp, R. G. (1997). *Self-directed behavior: Self-modification for personal adjustment* (7th ed.). Pacific Grove, CA: Brooks/Cole.

Watson, J. B. (1913). Psychology as the behaviorist views it. *Psychological Review, 20,* 158–177.

Watson, J. B. (1924). *Behaviorism.* Chicago: University of Chicago Press.

Watson, J. B., & Rayner, R. (1920). Conditioned emotional reactions. *Journal of Experimental Psychology, 3,* 1–14.

Waugh, N., & Norman, D. A. (1960). Primary memory. *Psychological Review, 72,* 89–104.

Wauters, M., Mertens, I. K., Chagnon, M., Rankinen, T., Considine, R. V., Chagnon, Y. C., Van Gaal, L. F., & Bouchard, C. (2001). Polymorphisms in the leptin receptor gene, body composition, and fat distribution in overweight and obese women. *International Journal of Obesity and Related Metabolic Disorders, 25,* 714–720.

Webb, W. B., & Levy, C. M. (1984). Effects of spaced and repeated total sleep deprivation. *Ergonomics, 27,* 45–58.

Wechsler, H., Dowdall, G. W., Davenport, A. & DeJong, W. (2000). Binge drinking on college campuses: Results of a national study. Available on-line at: www.hsph.harvard.edu/cas.

Wedeking, C., Seebeck, T., Bettens, F., & Paepke, A. J. (1995). MHC-dependent mate preferences in humans. *Proceedings of the Royal Society of London, B, 260,* 245–249.

Wehr, T. A., Giesen, H. A., Moul, D. E., Turner, E. H., & Schwartz, P. J. (1995). Suppression of men's responses to seasonal changes in day length by modern artificial lighting. *American Journal of Physiology, 269,* 173–178.

Weinberg, M. K., Tronick, E. Z., Cohn, J. F., & Olson, K. L. (1999). Gender differences in emotional expressivity and self-regulation during early infancy. *Developmental Psychology, 35,* 175–188.

Weinberg, R. S., & Gould, D. (1999). *Foundations of sport and exercise psychology* (2nd ed.). Champaign, IL: Human Kinetics.

Weinberger, D. R. (1997). The biological basis of schizophrenia: New directions. *Journal of Clinical Psychiatry, 58*(Suppl. 10), 22–27.

Weiner, I. B. (1996). Some observations on the validity of the Rorschach Inkblot Method. *Psychological Assessment, 8,* 206–213.

Weiner, I. B. (1997). Current status of the Rorschach Inkblot Method. *Journal of Personality Assessment, 68,* 5–19.

Weingarten, S. M., & Cummings, J. L. (2001). Psychosurgery of frontal-subcortical circuits. In D. G. Lichter, & J. L. Cummings (Eds.), *Frontal-subcortical circuits in psychiatric and neurological disorders* (pp. 421–435). New York, NY: Guilford Press.

Weinstein, R. S., Madison, W., & Kuklinski, M. (1995). Raising expectations in schooling: Obstacles and opportunities for change. *American Educational Research Journal, 32,* 121–160.

Weinstein, R. S., Soule, C. R., Collins, F., Cone, J., Melhorn, M., & Simantocci, K. (1991). Expectations and high school change: Teacher-researcher collaboration to prevent school failure. *American Journal of Community Psychology, 19,* 333–402.

Weinstein, S. (1968). Intensive and extensive aspects of tactile sensitivity as a function of body part, sex, and laterality. In D. R. Kenshalo (Ed.), *The skin senses* (pp. 195–222). Springfield, IL: Charles C Thomas.

Weiskrantz, L. (1995). Blindsight–Not an island unto itself. *Current Directions in Psychological Science, 4,* 146–151.

Weiskrantz, L. Barbur, J. L., & Sahraie, A. (1995). Parameters affecting conscious versus unconscious visual discrimination with damage to the visual cortex (VI). *Proceedings of the National Academy of Science, U. S. A., 92,* 6122–6126.

Weissman, M. M. (1993). The epidemiology of personality disorders: A 1990 update. *Journal of Personality Disorders* (Suppl.), 44–62.

Weissman, M. M., & Olfson, M. (1995, August 11). Depression in women: Implications for health care research. *Science, 269,* 799–801.

Weisz, J. R., McCarty, C. A., Eastman, K. L., Chaiyasit, W., & Suwanlert, S. (1997). Developmental psychopathology and culture: Ten lessons from Thailand. In S. S. Luthar, J. A. Burack, D. Cicchetti, & J. R. Weisz (Eds.), *Developmental psychopathology: Perspectives on adjustment, risk, and disorder* (pp. 568–592). Cambridge: Cambridge University Press.

Wells, G. L. (1993). What do we know about eyewitness identification? *American Psychologist, 48,* 553–571.

Wells, G. L., & Olsen, E. A. (2003). Eyewitness testimony. *Annual Review of Psychology, 54,* 277–295.

Werker, F. J., & Desjardins, R. N. (1995). Listening to speech in the 1st year of life: Experiential influences on phoneme perception. *Current Directions in Psychological Science, 4,* 76–81.

Werker, J. F. (1989). Becoming a native listener. *American Scientist, 77,* 54–59.

Werner, E. E. (1995). Resilience in development. *Current Directions in Psychological Science, 4,* 81–84.

Werner, E. E. (1996). Vulnerable but invincible: High risk children from birth to adulthood. *European Child & Adolescent Psychiatry, 5*(Suppl. 1), 47–51.

Weschler, H., Dowdall, G. W., Davenport, A., & DeJong, W. (2000). *Binge drinking on college campuses: Results of a national study.* Available on-line at: www.hsph.havard.edu/cas

Wheeler, M. A., Stuss, D. T., & Tulving, E. (1997). Toward a theory of episodic memory: The frontal lobes and autonoetic consciousness. *Psychological Bulletin, 121,* 331–354.

Whisman, M. A., & Kwon, P. (1993). Life stress and dysphoria: The role of self-esteem and hopelessness. *Journal of Personality and Social Psychology, 65,* 1054–1060.

Whitbourne, S. K. (1998). Physical changes in the aging individual: Clinical implications. In I. H. Nordhus, G. R. VandenBos, S. Berg, & P. Fromholt (Eds.), *Clinical geropsychology* (pp. 79–108). Washington, DC: American Psychological Association.

White, K. K., & Abrams, L. (2002). Does priming specific syllables during tip-of-the-tongue states facilitate word retrieval in older adults? *Psychology and Aging, 17,* 226–235.

White, M. A., Kohlmaier, J. R., Varnado, S. P., & Williamson, D. A. (2003). Racial/ethnic differences in weight concerns: Protective and risk factors for the development of eating disorders and obesity among adolescent females. *Eating and Weight Disorders, 8,* 20–25.

Whorf, B. L. (1956). *Language, thought, and reality.* New York: MIT Press-Wiley.

Widiger, T. A., & Sankis, L. M. (2000). Adult psychopathology: Issues and controversies. *Annual Review of Psychology, 51,* 377–404.

Wielkiewicz, R. M., & Calvert, C. R. X. (1989). *Training and habilitating developmentally disabled people: An introduction.* Newbury Park, CA: Sage.

Wiens, A. N., & Menustik, C. E. (1983). Treatment outcome and patient characteristics in an aversion therapy program for alcoholism. *American Psychologist, 38,* 1089–1096.

Wierzbicki, M. (1993). *Issues in clinical psychology: Subjective versus objective approaches.* Boston: Allyn & Bacon.

Wiggins, J. S. (Ed.). (1996). *The five-factor model of personality: Theoretical perspectives.* New York: Guilford Press.

Wilcoxon, H. C., Dragoin, W. B., & Kral, P. A. (1971). Illness-induced aversions in rat and quail: Relative salience of visual and gustatory cues. *Science, 171,* 826–828.

Wilder, B. J., & Bruni, J. (1981). *Seizure disorders: A pharmacological approach to treatment.* New York: Raven Press.

Wilding, J., & Valentine, E. (1997). *Superior memory.* Hove, England: Psychology Press/Erlbaum.

Wiley, J. (1998). Expertise as mental set: The effects of domain knowledge in creative problem solving. *Memory and Cognition, 26,* 716–730.

Wilke, R. R. (2001). The effect of active learning on college students' achievement, motivation, and self-efficacy in a human physiology course for non-majors. *Dissertation Abstracts International Section A: Humanities and Social Sciences, 61*, 4329.

Will, G. (1993, April 6). How do we turn children off to the violence caused by TV? Wise up parents. *Philadelphia Inquirer*, p. A1.

Williams, J. C., Paton, C. C., Siegler, I. C., Eigenbrodt, M. L., Nieto, F. J., & Tyroles, H. A. (2000). Anger proneness predicts coronary heart disease risk: Prospective analysis from the atherosclerosis risk in communities (ARIC) study. *Circulation, 101*, 2034–2039.

Williams, J. E., Satterwhite, R. C., & Saiz, J. L. (1998). *The importance of psychological traits: A cross-cultural study.* New York: Plenum.

Williams, J. H. (1987). *Psychology of women: Behavior in a biosocial context* (3rd ed.). New York: Norton.

Williams, L. (1989, November 22). Psychotherapy gaining favor among blacks. *New York Times.*

Williams, N. M., Rees, M. I., Holmans, P., Norton, N., Cardno, A. G., Jones, L. A., Murphy, K. C., Sanders, R. D., McCarthy, G., Gray, M. Y., Fenton, I., McGuffin, P., & Owen, M. J. (1999). A two-stage genome scan for schizophrenia susceptibility genes in 196 affected sibling pairs. *Human Molecular Genetics, 8*, 1729–1739.

Williams, R. A., Hagerty, B. M., Cimprich, B., Therrien, B., Bay, E., & Oe, H. (2000). Changes in directed attention and short-term memory in attention. *Journal of Psychiatric Research, 34*, 227–238.

Williams, R. B. (2001). Hostility and other psychological risk factors: Effects on health and the potential for successful behavioral approaches to prevention and treatment. In A. Baum, T. A. Revenson, & J. E. Singer (Eds.), *Handbook of health psychology.* Mahwah, NJ: Erlbaum.

Williams, R. B., Barefoot, J. C., Califf, R. M., Haney, T. L., Saunders, W. B., Pryor, D. B., Hatky, M. A., Siegler, I. C., & Mark, D. B. (1992). Prognostic importance of social and economic resources among medically treated patients with angiographically documented coronary artery disease. *Journal of the American Medical Association, 267*, 520–524.

Williams, S. (2000, April). How is telehealth being incorporated into psychology practice? *Monitor on Psychology*, p. 15.

Williams, T. P., & Sogon, S. (1984). Group composition and conforming behavior in Japanese students. *Japanese Psychological Research, 26*, 231–234.

Williams, W. M. (1999). Peering into the nature-nurture debate. *Contemporary Psychology, 44*, 267–269.

Willis, S. L., & Schaie, K. W. (1986). Training the elderly on the ability factors of spatial orientation and inductive reasoning. *Psychology and Aging, 1*, 239–247.

Willis, S. L., & Schaie, K. W. (1999). Intellectual functioning in midlife. In S. L. Willis & J. D. Reid (Eds.), *Life in the middle: Psychological and social development in middle age* (pp. 233–247). San Diego, CA: Academic Press.

Wilson, G. D. (1987). An ethological approach to sexual deviation. In G. D. Wilson (Ed.), *Variant sexuality: Research and theory* (pp. 84–115). London: Croom Helm.

Wincze, P., Hoon, E. F., & Hoon, P. W. (1978). Multiple measure analysis of women experiencing low sexual arousal. Behavior *Research and Therapy, 16*, 43–49.

Wing, H. (1969). *Conceptual learning and generalization.* Baltimore, MD: Johns Hopkins University.

Winn, P. (1995). The lateral hypothalamus and motivated behavior: An old syndrome reassessed and a new perspective gained. *Current Directions in Psychological Science, 4*, 182–187.

Winner, E. (1998). *Psychological aspects of giftedness.* New York: Basic Books.

Winner, E. (2000). The origins and ends of giftedness. *American Psychologist, 55*, 159–169.

Winson, J. (1990). The meaning of dreams. *Scientific American, 263(5)*, 94–96.

Winston, A., & Winston, B. (2002). *Handbook of integrated short-term psychotherapy.* Washington, DC: American Psychiatric Association.

Witelson, S. F., Kigar, D. L., & Harvey, T. (1999). The exceptional brain of Albert Einstein. *Lancet, 353*, 2149–2153.

Witkin, A. H., Dyk, R. B., Faterson, H. F., Goodenough, D. R., & Karp, S. A. (1962). *Psychological differentiation.* New York: Wiley.

Wolf, S. S., & Weinberger, D. R. (1996). Schizophrenia: A new frontier in developmental neurobiology. *Israel Journal of Medical Science, 32*, 51–55.

Wolfson, C., Wolfson, D. B., Asgharian, M., M'Lan, C. E., Ostbye, T., Rockwood, K., & Hogan, D. B. (2001). Reevaluation of the duration of survival after the onset of dementia. *The New England Journal of Medicine, 344*, 1111–1116.

Wolpe, J. (1973). *The practice of behavior therapy* (2nd ed.). New York: Pergamon.

Wolpe, J. (1982). *The practice of behavior therapy* (3rd ed.). New York: Pergamon.

Wolpe, J., & Plaud, J. J. (1997). Pavlov's contributions to behavior therapy: The obvious and the not so obvious. *American Psychologist, 52*, 966–972.

Wolpe, P. R. (1990). The holistic heresy: Strategies of ideological challenge in the medical profession. *Social Science & Medicine, 31*, 913–923.

Wolsko, C., Park, B., Judd, C. M., & Wittenbrink, B. (2000). Framing interethnic ideology: Effects of multicultural and color-blind perspectives on judgments of groups and individuals. *Journal of Personality & Social Psychology, 78*, 635–654.

Wood, F., Taylor, B., Penny, R., & Stump, B. A. (1980). Regional cerebral blood flow response to recognition memory versus semantic classification tasks. *Brain & Language, 9*, 113–122.

Wood, J., Foy, D. W., Goguen, C. A., Pynoos, R., & James, C. B. (2002). Violence exposure and PTSD among delinquent girls. In R. Greenwald (Ed.), *Trauma and juvenile delinquency: Theory, research, and interventions* (pp. 109–126). Binghamton, NY: Haworth Maltreatment and Trauma Press/The Haworth Press, Inc.

Wood, N. L., & Cowan, N. (1995). The cocktail party phenomenon revisited: Attention and memory in the classic selective listening procedure of Cherry (1953). *Journal of Experimental Psychology: General, 124*, 243–262.

Wood, W., Wong, F. Y., & Chachere, J. G. (1991). Effects of media violence on viewers' aggression in unconstrained social interaction. *Psychological Bulletin, 109*, 371–383.

Woodruff-Pak, D. S. (2001a). Eyeblink classical conditioning differentiates normal aging from Alzheimer's disease. *Integrative Physiological and Behavioral Science, 36*, 87–108.

Woodruff-Pak, D. S. (2001b). Insights about learning in Alzheimer's disease from the animal model. In M. E. Carrol & B. J. Overmier (Eds.) *Animal Research and Human Health: Advancing Human Welfare Through Behavioral Science* (pp. 385–406). Washington, DC: American Psychological Association.

Woodruff-Pak, D. S., Green, J. T., Heifets, B., & Pak, M. H. (2002). The effect of scopolamine in older rabbits tested in the 750ms delay eyeblink classical conditioning procedure. *Integrative Physiological and Behavioral Science, 37*, 103–113.

Woods, S. C., Schwartz, M. W., Baskin, D. G., & Seeley, R. J. (2000). Food intake and the regulation of body weight. *Annual Review of Psychology, 51*, 255–277.

Woods, S. C., Seeley, R. J., Porte, D., Jr., & Schwartz, M. W. (1998, May 29). Signals that regulate food intake and energy homeostasis. *Science, 280*, 1378–1383.

Woodward, K. L., & Springen, K. (1992, August 22). Better than a gold watch. *Newsweek*, p. 71.

Woody, E., & Sadler, P. (1998). On reintegrating dissociated theories: Comment on Kirsch and Lynn (1998). *Psychological Bulletin, 123*, 192–197.

Worchel, S., Cooper, J., & Goethals, G. R. (1991). *Understanding social psychology* (5th ed.). Pacific Grove, CA: Brooks/Cole.

Wortman, C. B., & Silver, R. C. (1989). The myths of coping with loss. *Journal of Consulting & Clinical Psychology, 57*, 349–357.

Wright, A. A. (1998). Auditory list memory in rhesus monkeys. *Psychological Science, 9*, 91–98.

Wright, J. C., Anderson, D. R., Huston, A. C., Collins, P. A., Schmitt, K. L., & Linebarger, D. L. (1999). Early viewing of educational television programs: The short- and long-term effects on schooling. *Insights, 2*, 5–8.

Wright, R. (1994). *The moral animal: The new science of evolutionary psychology.* New York: Pantheon.

Wyatt, W. J. (1993). Identical twins, emergenesis, and environments. *American Psychologist, 48*, 1294–1295.

Wynn, K. (1995). Infants possess a system of numerical knowledge. *Current Directions in Psychological Science, 4*, 172–177.

Wyrwicka, W. (1988). Imitative behavior: A theoretical view. Pavlovian *Journal of Biological Science, 23*, 125–131.

Wysocki, C. J., & Meredith, M. (1987). *The vomeronasal system.* New York: Wiley.

Y

Yaffe, K., Yung, L. L., Zmuda, J., & Cauley, J. (2002). Sex hormones and cognitive function in older men. *Journal of the American Geriatrics Society, 50*, 707–712.

Yalom, I. D. (1995). *The theory and practice of group psychotherapy* (4th ed.). New York: Basic Books.

Yang, Q., & Chen, F. (2001). Behavior problems in children with simple obesity. *Chinese Journal of Clinical Psychology, 9*, 273–274.

Yanovski, S. Z., & Yanovski, J. A. (2002). Obesity. *New England Journal of Medicine, 346*, 591–602.

Yi, H., Williams, G. D., & Dufour, M. C. (December 2002). Surveillance Report #61: Trends in Alcohol-Related Fatal Traffic Crashes, United States, 1977–2000. Rockville, MD: National Institute on Alcohol Abuse and Alcoholism, Division of Biometry and Epidemiology.

York, J. L., & Welte, J. W. (1994). Gender comparisons of alcohol consumption in alcoholic and nonalcoholic populations. *Journal of Studies on Alcohol, 55*, 743–750.

Yotsutsuji, T., Saitoh, O., Suzuki, M., Hagino, H., Mori, K., Takahashi, T., Kurokawa, K., Matsui, M., Seto, H., & Kurachi, M. (2003). Quantification of lateral ventricular subdivisions in schizophrenia by high-resolution three-dimensional magnetic resonance imaging. *Psychiatry Research: Neuroimaging, 122*, 1–12.

Young, Q. W., Hellawell, D. J., Wan de Wal, C., & Johnson, M. (1996). Facial expression processing after amygdalotomy. *Neuropsychologia, 34*, 31–39.

Z

Zadra, A., & Donderi, D. C. (2000). Nightmares and bad dreams: Their prevalence and relationship to well-being. *Journal of Abnormal Psychology, 109,* 273–281.

Zajonc, R. B. (1980). Feeling and thinking: Preferences need no inferences. *American Psychologist, 35,* 151–175.

Zajonc, R. B. (1984). On the primacy of affect. *American Psychologist, 39,* 117–129.

Zajonc, R. B., Murphy, S. T., & Inglehart, M. (1989). Feeling and facial efference: Implications of the vascular theory of emotion. *Psychological Review, 96,* 395–416.

Zaragoza, M. S., & Mitchell, K. J. (1996). Repeated exposure to suggestion and the creation of false memories. *Psychological Science, 7,* 294–300.

Zaragoza, M. S., Lane, S. M., Ackil, J. K., & Chambers, K. L. (1997). Confusing real and suggested memories: Source monitoring and eyewitness suggestibility. In N. L. Stein, P. A. Ornstein, B. Tversky, & C. Brainerd (Eds.), *Memory for everyday and emotional events* (pp. 401–425). Mahwah, NJ: Erlbaum.

Zehr, D. (2001). Portrayals of Wundt and Titchener in introductory psychology texts: A content analysis. *Teaching of Psychology, 27,* 122–123.

Zeki, S. (1992). The visual image in mind and brain. *Scientific American, 267*(3), 68–76.

Zeki, S. (1993). *A vision of the brain.* London: Blackwell.

Zigler, E. (1998). By what goals should Head Start be assessed? *Children's Services: Social Policy, Research, and Practice, 1,* 5–18.

Zigler, E. (2003). What would draw a basic scientist into Head Start (and why would he never leave)? In R. J. Sternberg (Ed.), *Psychologists defying the crowd: Stories of those who battled the establishment and won* (pp. 273–282). Washington, DC: American Psychological Association.

Zigler, E. F., Finn-Stevenson, M., & Hall, N. W. (2002). *The first three years & beyond: Brain development and social policy.* New Haven, CT: Yale University Press.

Zigler, E., & Muenchow, S. (1992). *Head Start: The inside story of America's most successful educational experiment.* New York: Basic Books.

Zigler, E., & Styfco, S. J. (1994). Head Start: Criticisms in a constructive context. *American Psychologist, 49,* 127–132.

Zigler, E., & Styfco, S. J. (2001). Extended childhood intervention prepares children for school and beyond. *Journal of the American Medical Association, 285,* 2378–2380.

Zigler, E., & Styfco, S. J. (Eds.). (1993). *Head Start and beyond.* New Haven, CT: Yale University Press.

Zipursky, R. B., Lambe, E. K., Kapur, S., & Mikulis, D. J. (1998). Cerebral gray matter volume deficits in first episode psychosis. *Archives of General Psychiatry, 55,* 540–546.

Zisapel, N. (2001). Circadian rhythm sleep disorders: Pathophysiology and potential approaches to management. *CNS Drugs, 15,* 311–328.

Zito, J. M., Safer, D. J., dosReis, S., Gardner, J. F., Boles, M., & Lynch, F. (2000). Trends in the prescribing of psychotropic medications to preschoolers. *Journal of the American Medical Association, 283,* 1025–1030.

Zubieta, J., Heitzeg, M. M., Smith, Y. R., Bueller, J. A., Yanjun Xu, K. X., Koeppe, R. A., Stohler, C. S., & Goldman, D. (2003, February 21). COMT val[158]met genotype affects μ-Opioid neurotransmitter responses to a pain stressor. *Science, 299,* 1240–1243.

Zucker, R. A., & Gomberg, E. S. L. (1990). Etiology of alcoholism reconsidered: The case for a biopsychosocial process. *American Psychologist, 41,* 783–793.

Zuckerman, M. (1979). *Sensation seeking: Beyond the optimal level of arousal.* Hillsdale, NJ: Erlbaum.

Zuckerman, M. (1994). *Behavioral expressions and biosocial bases of sensation seeking.* NY: Cambridge University Press.

Zuckerman, M. (2000). Sensation seeking. In A. Kazdin (Ed.), *Encyclopedia of Psychology.* Washington, DC: American Psychological Association.

Zuckerman, M. (2002). Genetics of sensation seeking. In J. Benjamin & R. P. Ebstein (Eds.), *Molecular enetics and the human personality* (pp. 193–210). Washington, DC: American Psychiatric Publishing, Inc.

Zuckerman, M., Miyake, K., & Elkin, C. S. (1995). Effects of attractiveness and maturity of face and voice on interpersonal impression. *Journal of Research in Personality, 29,* 253–272.

Zuger, A. (1998, July 28). A fistful of aggression is found among women. *New York Times,* p. B8.

Zwislocki, J. J. (1981). Sound analysis in the ear: A history of discoveries. *American Scientist, 245,* 184–192.

PHOTO CREDITS

CHAPTER 1

Opener: Chuck Savage/Corbis/Bettman; p. 3: Ellen Senisi/The Image Works; p. 5: (top) Ellen Senisi/The Image Works (bottom) Scott Camazine/Photo Researchers, Inc.; p. 10: B. Daemmrich/The Image Works; p. 12: Picture Desk, Inc./Kobal Collection; p. 15: Bildarchiv der Oesterreichische National-bibliothek; p. 17: (top) G. Paul Bishop, Photographer (bottom) Chris J. Johnson/Stock Boston; p. 20: (left) Peter Johnson/Corbis/Bettman (right) The Image Works; p. 22: (top) Archives of the History of American Psychology/The University of Akron (bottom) Corbis/Bettman; p. 24: (far left) Travelpix/Getty Images, Inc.-Taxi (left) Robert Caputo/Stock Boston (middle) Arvind Garg/Getty Images, Inc.-Liason (right) B. Gerard/Getty Images, Inc.-Liason (far right) Frank Siteman/Index Stock Imagery, Inc.; p. 25: (top) Jerry Bauer/Carol Gillian (bottom left) Philippe Brylak/Getty Images, Inc.-Liaison (bottom right) Cary Wolinsky/Stock Boston; p. 27: Bob Daemmrich/Stock Boston; p. 28: UPI/Corbis/Bettman; p. 29: Catherine Karnow/Corbis/Bettman; p. 31: (top) Breese/Getty Images Inc.-Liaison (bottom) Jeff Greenberg/Index Stock Imagery, Inc.; p. 32: Bill Anderson/Photo Researchers, Inc.; p. 33: (top) R. Lord/The Image Works; (bottom left) T. Kitamona/Agence France-Presse AFP (bottom right) Lee Snider/The Image Works; p. 37: Alexandra Milgram p. 41: Roby Bettolini/Granata/The Image Works.

CHAPTER 2

Opener: Sally E. Shaywitz, M.D./Yale Medical School; p. 47: Rick Browne/Stock Boston; p. 53: E. R. Lewis, Y. Y. Zeevi, T. E. Everhart/Edwin R. Lewis; p. 54: Rick Browne/Stock Boston; p. 57: Brad Markel/Getty Images, Inc.-Liaison; p. 62: Dan McCoy/Rainbow; p. 64: Library of Congress; p. 68: Mazziotta Et/Photo Researchers, Inc.; p. 69: Richard T. Nowitz/Photo Researchers, Inc.; p. 70: (top) Catherine Pouedras/Science Photo Library/Photo Researchers, Inc. (middle) Howard Sochurek/Woodfin Camp & Associates (bottom) Dan McCoyRainbow; p. 75: Bruce Herman/Getty Images Inc.-Stone Allstock; p. 79: (top) CNRI/Science Photo Library/Science Source/Photo Researchers, Inc. (bottom) CNRI/Science Photo Library/Photo Researchers, Inc.; p. 80: Jean Claude Revy/Phototake NYC; p. 81: Renate Hiller; p. 82: (top)B. Daemmrich/The Image Works (bottom) Mike Mazzachi/Stock Boston.

CHAPTER 3

Opener: Owen Franken/Corbis/Bettman; p. 93 Gianni Giansanti/Corbis/Sygma; p. 94: Dr. Michael E. Phelps; p. 96: Bob Daemmrich/The Image Works; p. 101: Don Wong/Science Source/Photo Researchers, Inc.; p. 102: E. R. Lewis, Y. Y. Zeevi, F. S. Werblin. Scanning elec-tron microscopy of vertebrate receptors, Brain Research 15 (1969): 559–562; p. 105 Pearson Education/PH College; p. 111: AP/Wide World Photos; p. 115: Dorothy Littell Greco/The Image Works; p. 120: Gianni Giansanti/Corbis/Sygma; p. 121: Nik Kleinberg/Stock Boston; p. 123: Fujifotos/The Image Works; p. 125 Signac, Paul (1863-1935). Saint-Tropez, in a thunderstorm. Musee de l'Annonciade, St. Tropez, France. Reunion des Musees Nationaux/Art Resource, NY; p. 126: (top) USDA/APHIS/Animal and Plant Health Inspection Service (middle) John R. MacGregor/Peter Arnold, Inc. (bottom) ©The New Yorker Collection 2000 John O'Brien from cartoonbank.com All Rights Reserved; p. 127: (top) M.C. Escher's "Circle Limit IV", © 2003 Cordon Art B.V.—Baarn—Holland. All rights reserved (bottom) Kaiser Porcelain Ltd.; p. 131: (top) Pawan Sinha and Tomaso Poggio, Photo © Dirck Halstead/Gamma Liaison/Getty Images, Inc. (bottom) Paul Griffin/Stock Boston; p. 133: Elizabeth Marshall/Getty Images, Inc.-Liaison; p. 134: Fred Charles/Getty Images Inc.-Stone Allstock; p. 136: M. C. Escher Heirs/Cordon Art B.V.; p. 138: Michele Burgess/Stock Boston.

CHAPTER 4

Opener: Tibor Hirsch/Photo Researchers, Inc.; p. 145: Corbis Royalty Free; p. 146: Lisa Peardon/Getty Images, Inc.-Taxi; p. 150: Michael Newman/PhotoEdit; p. 151: Alvis Upitis/Getty Images Inc.-Image Bank; p. 153: Will & Deni McIntyre/Photo Researchers, Inc.; p. 160: Marc Chagall (1887–1985), Russian, "Above the City." Tretyakov Gal-lery, Moscow, Russia. SuperStock, Inc./©Artists Rights Society (ARS), New York; p. 162: The Granger Collection; p. 167: (top) William Hogarth (1697-1765), "Gin Lane." The Metro-politan Museum of Art, Harris Brisbane Dick Fund, 1932. [32.35(124)] (bottom) The Image Works; p. 170: The Granger Collection; p. 173: Kal Muller/Woodfin Camp & Associates; p. 179: (top) Carl Frank/Photo Researchers, Inc. (bottom) John Ficara/Woodfin Camp & Associates.

CHAPTER 5

Opener: Digital Vision/Getty Images; p. 185: William R. Sallaz/Duomo Photography Incor-porated; p. 188: Corbis/Bettmann; p. 189: Ira Wyman/Corbis/Sygma; p. 190: Joe Sohm/The Image Works; p. 192: Gregory K. Scott/Photo Researchers, Inc.; p. 195: The Granger Collec-tion; p. 197: Charles Gupton/Corbis/Bettmann; p. 198: Marian and Robert Bailey/Eclectic Science Productions; p. 202: (top)Walter Dawn/Photo Researchers, Inc. (bottom) Dubrowsky/Getty Images, Inc.-Hulton Archive Photos; p. 203: William R. Sallaz/Duomo Photography Incorporated; p. 205: Carroll Seghers/Photo Researchers, Inc. p. 206: Andre Nadeau/

A

Abbott, R.D., 171
Abdallah, B., 568
Abdel, H.T.K, 338
Abramov, I., 107
Abrams, L., 238
Abramson, L.Y., 495, 496
Accardo, P.J., 519
Acebo, C., 150
Achter, J.A., 321
Acierno, R., 177
Ackerman, D., 93, 99, 107, 108, 115
Acredolo, L.P., 372
Adams, D.B., 78
Adams, G.R., 395, 397
Adams, K.M., 166
Adamson, L.B., 382
Adelson, R., 126
Ader, R., 190
Adesman, A., 548
Adler, N., 462
Adler, T., 462, 490
Adolphs, R., 357, 397
Adorno, T.W., 573
Aeschleman, S.R., 198
Agostinelli, G., 566
Agostinelli, J., 403
Agras, W.S., 336
Ahmed, S., 152
AhYun, K., 568
Aiken, L.R., 307
Ainsworth, M.D., 348, 384
Akehurst, L., 150
Akil, H., 123
Albarracin, D., 577
Albers, H.E., 151
Albus, M., 334
Al Dawi, S., 336
Aldrich, M.S., 156
Aldwin, C.M., 408
Alexander, C.A., 549
Alexander, C.N., 179
Allen, K.D., 21
Allen, L.S., 343
Allen, V.L., 583
Allgood-Merten, B., 397
Alloy, L.B., 495, 496
Allport, G.W., 434, 573
Almagor, M., 437
Almer, E., 532
Almgren, G., 475

Altabe, M.N., 397
Altman, L.K., 56
Aluja-Fabregat, A., 390
Alvarez-Buylla, A., 57
Amabile, T.M., 278, 323
American Academy of Pediatrics, 390
American Psychiatric Association (APA), 164, 319, 336, 489, 502, 506, 509
American Psychological Association (APA), 22, 23, 38, 40, 511, 521
America's Children: Key National Indicators of Well-Being, 388
Amin, T., 488
Amos, S.P., 311
Anastasi, A., 295, 302, 307, 445
Anch, A.M., 152, 159
Anderman, S.J., 470
Andersen, B.L., 469
Anderson, C.A., 346
Anderson, D.R., 390
Anderson, L.L., 320
Anderson, S.W., 488, 512
Andreasen, N.C., 488
Andrews, J.A., 397, 398
Andrich, D., 571
Ang, R.P., 332
Anggard, E., 172
Angier, N., 77, 406, 567
Angst, J., 164
Anshel, M.H., 462
Anthony, J.C., 164
Appelbaum, K.A., 179
Archer, J., 20, 86
Archer, R.P., 446
Arcus, D., 371
Arias, C., 133
Arkin, R.M., 566
Arlinger, S.D., 114
Armstrong, T., 518
Arndt, J., 97
Arnett, J.J., 394, 403
Arnold, H.M., 339
Arnold, K.D., 517
Aron, L.Y., 552
Aronson, E., 565, 569, 580, 581, 586
Arrigo, J.M., 254
Ary, D.V., 177, 387
Asch, S.E., 582, 583
Ashissar, M., 126
Ashley, R., 173

Aslin, R.N., 372
Aspinwall, L.G., 470
Aston, R., 169
Atchley, R.C., 409
Atkinson, J.W., 137
Austin, G., 71, 518
Auvergne, R., 57
Aved, B.M., 369
Avery-Leaf, S., 553
Axtell, C.M., 594
Ayas, N.T., 156
Ayman, R., 592
Azar, B., 115, 285, 371, 467, 468
Azria, M.R., 313
Azrin, N., 345

B

Baars, B.J., 147, 148
Babkoff, H., 150
Bachtold, L.M., 323
Baddeley, A.D., 229, 230, 231, 243, 245
Badner, J.A., 495
Badr, L.K., 568
Baer, L., 549
Bagemihl, B., 342
Bagiella, E., 470
Bahrick, H.P., 232, 248
Bahrick, P.O., 232
Bailey, A., 519
Baillargeon, R., 378
Bajorek, E., 337
Balaguer, A., 399
Balch, W.R., 245
Baldwin, A.Y., 321
Balkin, T.J., 160
Ball, J.D., 446
Balleine, B., 199
Ballie, R., 166
Ballou, M., 555
Balogh, R.D., 118
Balon, R., 548
Banaji, M.R., 266
Bandura, A., 216, 218, 219, 345, 438, 535
Bane, C., 470
Banich, M.T., 65
Bank, L., 371
Bar, M., 97
Barbaree, H.E., 509
Barber, B.L., 403
Barbur, J.L., 104

Barea-Rodriguez, E.J., 56
Barglow, P., 388
Barinaga, M., 57, 88
Barker, S.L., 543
Barkley, R.A., 518
Barnes, H.V., 313
Barnett, R.C., 403, 462
Barnett, W.S., 313
Baron, R.A., 568
Baron, R.M., 582
Barret, G.V., 307, 309
Barron, F., 323, 479
Bar-Tal, D., 575
Bartlett, F.C., 246, 255
Bartley, A.J., 516
Bartoshuk, L.M., 117
Baruch, F., 403
Bashner, R.S., 576
Basow, S.A., 520
Bassetti, C., 156
Bastien, C.H., 156
Bat-Chava, Y., 114
Bateman, D.N., 172
Bateson, G., 255
Batson, C.D., 587
Battle, C.L., 555
Bauer, K., 406
Baumeister, A.A., 320
Baumeister, R.F., 345, 348
Baumrind, D., 39, 385
Baxter, D.W., 122
Bayley, N., 303, 374
Beasley, M., 458
Beatty, S.E., 97
Beauchamp, G.K., 117
Beauducel, A., 296
Bechara, A., 488, 512
Beck, A.T., 459, 495, 538, 540
Beck, J.G., 507
Beck, R., 345
Bedard, J., 251, 280
Bedell, B.T., 284
Beecher, H.K., 123
Beggs, M.S., 541
Beier, E.G., 356
Beirne-Smith, M., 320
Bellack, A.S., 39, 536
Bellman, S., 462
Belsky, J., 388
Bem, D.J., 98
Bem, S.L., 388
Ben-Avi, I., 593
Benbow, C.P., 321
Beniczky, S., 64
Benin, M.H., 403
Benjamin Jr., L.T., 13, 14
Bennett, D.A., 243, 410
Bennett, E.L., 56, 312
Bennett, W., 338
Benotsch, E.G., 123, 477

Benson, E., 117
Benson, H., 178
Benton, D., 311
BenTovim, D.I., 337
Berg, S.J., 77
Bergeron, J., 331
Bergin, A.E., 542, 547
Berglund, H., 118
Bergson, C., 515
Berkowitz, M.W., 513
Berman, J.S., 544
Bernal, M.E., 556
Bernhard, F., 20
Bernstein, A., 177
Berntson, G.G., 71
Berreby, D., 118
Berry, J.M., 134
Berry, J.W., 583
Berscheid, E., 568
Bersoff, D.N., 308, 589
Bertenthal, B.I., 372, 375
Bertolini, M., 509
Best, D.L., 389
Best, P.J., 167
Betancourt, H., 27
Bhatt, R.S., 126
Biddle, S., 469
Biederman, I., 97
Bini, G., 122
Birbaumer, N., 199
Birchler, G.R., 400
Birkenhaeger, T.K., 549
Birren, J.E., 408, 409
Bishop, D.V.M., 82
Bjorklund, D.F., 370
Bjornson, C.R.R., 57
Black, R.D., 577
Blackmore, S., 216
Blagrove, M., 150
Blaine, J.D., 534
Blake, R.R., 583
Blakemore, S.J., 121
Blakeslee, S., 475
Blanchard, E.B., 75, 179, 535
Blanck, D.C., 39
Blatt, S.J., 537, 544
Blehar, M.C., 384
Bleubel, M.E., 430
Bliss, T.V., 56
Bliwise, D.L., 150
Bloch, S., 468
Blouin, J.L., 84
Bluestone, B., 475
Blum, J.M., 307, 309
Blum, K., 84
Blumberg, M.S., 269, 272
Blumenthal, A.L., 14
Blundell, J.E., 334
Bodenhausen, G.V., 564
Bodlund, O., 510

Boelte, S., 319
Bohart, A.C., 18
Bolles, R.C., 332
Bolos, A.M., 176
Bonanno, G.A., 476
Bond, M.H., 346, 583, 585
Bonvillian, J.D., 270
Boodoo, G., 314
Boomsma, D.I., 83
Booth-Kewley, S., 467
Borgen, J.S., 336
Boring, E.G., 130, 133
Borkenau, P., 436
Borkovec, T.D., 542
Borkowski, J.G., 348
Bornstein, P., 191
Bornstein, R.F., 215, 568
Bosma, H., 409
Bosworth, J.A.J., 118
Bosworth, R.G., 56
Botwin, M.D., 434
Bourgois, P., 170
Bourin, M., 547
Bourne, L.E., 232, 260, 276, 277
Bouton, M.E., 203
Bovbjerg, D.H., 192
Bower, G.H., 237, 245
Bower, J.M., 243
Bower, N.J.A., 372
Bower, T.G.R., 372
Bowker, J.L., 191
Bowler, A.E., 516
Boyatzis, R., 298, 350
Boyce, T., 462
Boysen, S.T., 219, 268, 269
Bradley, C., 427
Braffman, W., 179
Brailey, K., 477
Brainerd, C.J., 378
Brand, P.A., 339
Brand, R.J., 467
Brandes, R.W., 152
Brandon, T.H., 171
Brannon, E.M., 269
Brauer, M., 588
Braun, A.R., 160
Braveman, N.S., 191
Braverman, J., 577
Breall, W.S., 467
Brebner, K., 55
Breetvelt, I.S., 352
Brehm, S.S., 568
Bremner, J.D., 237, 239, 246
Brennan, R.T., 462
Brenner, M.H., 475
Breslau, N., 311
Brewer, J.B., 240
Brewin, C.R., 537
Brickman, P., 352

Bridges, M., 403
Brim, O., 405
Brisson, J., 468
Broadbent, D.E., 227
Brobert, A.G., 388
Brocke, B., 296
Broder, A., 39
Brodsky, S.L., 252
Brody, L., 359, 387
Brody, N., 316
Bronfenbrenner, U., 394
Brooks, D.C., 191
Brooks-Gunn, J., 337, 377, 392, 397
Browman, C.P., 152, 159
Brown, B., 313
Brown, D.E., 507
Brown, L.S., 555
Brown, P.L., 212
Brown, R.W., 238, 265, 345, 382
Brown, S.A., 176
Brownell, K.D., 338
Bruch, H., 337
Bruder, G.E., 537
Bruni, J., 169
Brunner, H.G., 80
Bryant, R.A., 462
Buchalter, E.N., 179
Buffalo, E.A., 252
Buist, C.M., 75
Bulik, C.M., 337, 338
Bullock, M., 575, 576
Burrows, G.D., 78
Burt, M.R., 552
Bushman, B.J., 167, 345
Bushnell, M.C., 121
Buss, D.M., 20, 86, 347, 348, 434, 568, 569
Butcher, J.N., 500, 505
Butler, L.D., 237
Butler, R.N., 408, 411
Butterfield, E.C., 320
Buunk, B.P., 569
Byne, W., 343
Byrne, D., 568
Byrne, R.W., 20

C
Cabeza, R., 71
Cacioppo, J.T., 156, 469, 470, 578, 584
Cahill, L., 241
Cain, D.J., 426
Cairns, E., 575
Calhoun, L.G., 478
Califano Jr., J.A., 172
Callahan, R., 86
Callicott, J.H., 488

Calvert, C.R.X., 319
Calvert, S., 390
Cameron, J., 195
Cameron, K.A., 578
Cameron, R.P., 470, 537
Campbell, V.L., 446
Campos, J.L., 372, 375
Canbeyli, R., 199
Cannon, W.B., 464
Cano, A., 553
Caporaso, N.D., 83, 176
Capron, C., 312
Cardemil, E.V., 555
Cardena, E., 237
Carey, J.C., 556
Carlson, N.R., 152
Carmona, F.J., 467
Caroline, C.C., 459
Carpenter, S., 160
Carr, M., 348
Carr, T.S., 77
Carskadon, M.A., 150, 151
Carson, R.C., 500, 505
Carstensen, L., 408
Carter, R., 359
Carter, T., 230
Cartwright, R.D., 160
Caruso, J.C., 300
Casas, J.M., 555
Caspi, A., 408, 430
Caspy, T., 150
Cassaday, H.J., 241
Cassidy, J.P., 422
Castejon, J.L., 299
Castro, F.G., 556
Cattell, R.B., 296, 323, 432, 434
Cavanagh, P., 129
Cavanaugh, J.C., 395, 404, 407
Ceci, S.J., 309
Celis, W., 169
Cemalcilar, Z., 199
Centers for Disease Control and Prevention, 397, 497
Ceponiene, R., 380
Cernich, J.M., 118
Cervone, D., 436
Chaiken, S., 571, 578
Chait, L.D., 174, 175
Chan, Y.Y.L., 337
Chance, P., 333
Chance, S.A., 488
Chang, E.C., 453
Channon-Little, L., 180
Charness, N., 251
Chase, W.G., 251
Chase-Lansdale,L., 392
Chassin, L., 177
Chaudhari, N., 117
Chavajay, P., 266

Chekroun, P., 588
Chemers, M.M., 592
Chen, F., 339
Chen, P., 57
Chen, W., 534
Cheour, M., 380
Cherlin, A., 475
Cherry, C., 228
Cherry, K., 305
Chervin, R.D., 156
Chesney, M.A., 470
Chess, S., 370
Chester, J.A., 191
Chi, M.T.H., 251, 280
Chimbidis, M.E., 323
Choi, I., 566
Choi, J., 316
Chomsky, N., 261, 382, 383
Christal, R.W., 434
Christensen, A., 540, 542
Christensen, F., 341
Christie, C., 266
Christopher, I.W., 371
Chua, S.C., 334
Chung, W.K., 334
Chwalisz, K., 353
Cialdini, R.B., 581, 584
Cicchetti, D., 493
Cirelli, C., 149
Clark, G.M., 113
Clark, J.E., 374, 375
Clark, R.D., 588
Clarkin, J.F., 443
Clarkson, P., 588
Clausen, J.A., 392
Clauss, E., 459
Clay, R.A., 114, 545
Clayton, A.H., 548
Clements, M., 409
Clinkenbeard, P.R., 320, 321
Cloninger, C.R., 83
Cloninger, S.C., 430, 431
Coan, J.A., 253
Cocchini, G., 230
Cochran, S.D., 399
Cochran, S.V., 554
Cocking, R., 390
Cohen, A., 64
Cohen, E.G., 576
Cohen, H.J., 470
Cohen, L.J., 509
Cohen, N., 190
Cohen, S., 190, 462, 467
Cohn, L.D., 380
Cohn, R.H., 271
Cole, J.D., 119
Coleman, J., 423, 475
Coley, R.L., 392
Collaer, M.L., 389
Collett, T., 129

Collingridge, G.L., 56
Collings, V.B., 95
Collins, D.R., 242
Collins, N.L., 570
Collins, R.C., 313
Collins, W.A., 83, 386, 387, 389, 403
Comaty, J.E., 535
Compas, B.E., 395
Comstock, G., 218
Confino, A., 254
Conger, J.J., 379, 391, 392
Connelly, B., 398
Conroy, J.W., 320
Consumer Reports, 542
Conte, J.J., 435
Contreras, D., 147
Conway, A.R.A., 228
Conway, B.E., 295, 322
Conway, M.A., 249, 577
Cook, D.A., 555
Cook, E.H., 579
Cook, R.G., 269
Cookerly, J.R., 540
Coontz, P.D., 346
Cooper, H.M., 167, 352, 563, 566
Cooper, J., 578
Cooper, R., 312
Cooper, Z., 337
Coplan, R.J., 387
Corder, B., 84
Coren, S., 105, 123
Corkin, S., 234
Cornelius, R.R., 350, 351, 352
Costa, A., 52
Costa, P.T., 435, 443
Costacou, T., 472
Costa Jr., P.T., 434, 435
Costello, E., 542
Cotton, J.L., 594, 616
Council, J.R., 443
Courchesne, R.Y., 579
Cousins, N., 471
Cousins, S., 566
Cowan, N., 225, 226, 227, 228, 231, 232
Coyle, J.T., 243
Coyne, J.C., 496
Crabbe, J., 84
Craig, A.D., 121
Craig, C.D., 594
Craig, J.C., 121
Craik, F.I.M., 71, 233, 409
Cramer, P., 423, 460
Crandall, C.S., 337
Crano, W.D., 568
Creeley, C.E., 245
Crombez, G., 121
Cronan, T.A., 313

Cronbach, L.J., 301
Crook, T., 496
Crooks, R., 406
Crovitz, H.F., 249
Croyle, R.T., 578
Cruz, A., 119
Crystal, D.S., 395
Csikzentmihalyi, M., 20, 320
Culbertson, F.M., 496, 520, 522
Cummings, A.L., 398
Cummings, E.M., 403
Cummings, J.L., 549
Cunningham, J.E.C., 80
Curet, C.A., 133
Curle, C.E., 478
Curren, M.T., 285
Cushner, K., 582
Cutler, D.M., 407
Cutler, W.B., 118
Czeisler, C.A., 151, 152

D

Dabbs Jr., J.M., 77, 578
Daehler, M.W., 378
Dae-Shik, K., 129
D'Agostino, P.R., 97
Dahl, E.K., 424
Dahlstrom, W.G., 308
Dalton, P., 116
Daly, M.J., 407
Damas, A., 308
Damasio, A.R., 48
Damasio, H., 240, 241
Daniell, H.W., 171
Danielle, D.M., 391
Darwin, C.R., 84, 383
Daumann, J., 172
Daval, J.L., 55
Davidson, J.E., 321
Davidson, R.J., 62, 65, 67, 353, 357
Davies, I., 265
Davies, M., 298
Davies, P.T., 403
Davis, C.C., 387
Davis, C.G., 475
Davis, J.O., 83
Davis, J.R., 120
Davis, L.G., 174
Davis, M.H., 566
Davis, S., 78
Daw, J., 42
Dawes, R.M., 446
Dawson, L., 343
D'Azevedo, W.A., 255
Dean, M., 176
DeAngelis, T., 556
Dean Jr., J.W., 592

Deb, S., 443
DeBaryshe, B.D., 513
Deci, E.L., 21, 332, 333, 457
DeFries, J.C., 80, 82, 83, 84, 88
DeGarmo, D.S., 403
Dehaene, S., 71
Deikman, A.J., 178
DeKay, W.T., 20
De la Fuente, M., 408
de-l'Etoile, S.K., 245
Dement, W.C., 151, 161
DeNeve, K.M., 352
DeNisi, A.S., 611
Denmark, F.L., 22
Dennerstein, L., 78, 402
DePaulo, B.M., 358
DePaulo, P., 384
Depauw, K.P., 473
de Raad, B., 435
DeRamus, B., 588
Derry, F.A., 507
Derryberry, D., 371
Des Forges, A.L., 575
Desjardins, R.N., 373
Desmond, J.E., 70
D'Esposito, M., 19
Dessolin, S., 334
DeSteno, D., 577
Destexhe, A., 147
Detweiler, J.B., 284
Devenas, R., 617
Devine, P.G., 576
De Waal, F.B.M., 87, 270
DeZazzo, J., 243
Diamond, J., 27
Diaz, J., 549
Diener, E., 352, 353
Diforio, D., 489
DiFranceisco, W., 177
DiFranza, J.R., 369
DiGiovanna, A.G., 407
Digman, J.M., 434
Dill, S., 380
DiMatteo, M.R., 123
Dimitrijevic, M., 190
Dion, K.K., 568
di Padova, C., 168
DiPietro, J.A., 371
Dixon, J.F., 548
Dobkins, K.R., 56
Dombroski, B.A., 84
Domhoff, G.W., 159, 160, 161
Dominowski, R.L., 232, 260, 276, 277
Domjan, M., 39, 214
Donatelle, R.J., 174
Donderi, D.C., 155
Donnelly, B.W., 387
Donnelly, C.L., 548
Doolittle, N., 116

Dorfman, W.I., 443
Dorvlo, A.S.S., 336
Doty, R.L., 116, 117
Douglas, H.M., 520
Dovidio, J.F., 574
Dowdall, G.W., 168
Downs, H., 406
Downs, J., 283
Doyle, R., 403, 404
Dragoin, W.B., 192
Driscoll, P.F., 475
Drummey, A.B., 250
Drury, L.J., 552
Dryer, D.C., 569
D'Silva, M.U., 331
Du, L., 84
Dube, L., 577
Dubner, R., 122
Duda, C., 507
Dudley, E., 402
Duffy, J.F., 152
Dugas, M.J., 544
DuHamel, K.N., 179
Dumaine, B., 617
Duncan, J., 64
Duncan, T.E., 177, 387
Dunkel-Schetter, C., 369
Dunkle, T., 110, 114
Dunn, R.L., 539
Duong, T.Q., 129
Duyme, M., 312
Dyk, R.B., 137

E

Eacott, M.J., 250
Eagly, A.H., 346, 437, 463, 571, 578, 593
Earles, J.A., 309
Eaves, L.J., 437
Eccles, J.E., 394, 397, 403
Eccleston, C., 121
Eckerman, C.O., 387
Edelman, S., 468
Efklides, A., 217
Egeth, H., 227
Egner, T., 200
Eich, E., 505
Eich, J.E., 245
Eichenbaum, H., 241
Eimas, P.D., 373
Eisenberg, N., 358
Eisenberger, R., 195
Eisenman, R., 387
Ekman, P., 350, 351, 356, 358, 361
Elbert, T., 56, 122
Elder Jr., G.H., 408
Eley, T.C., 82
Eliot, J., 496

Elkind, D., 394
Ellens, J.H., 425
Ellig, T.W., 32
Ellis, A., 459, 537
Ellis, L., 346
Elloy, D.F., 403
Ellsworth, P.C., 353
Ely, T.D., 62
Elzinga, B.M., 237
Emery, R.E., 453, 468, 478, 489, 500, 506, 511, 540, 546, 548
Emmorey, K., 114
Engel, J.F., 577
Engel, S., 107
Engen, T., 115
English, K., 462
Enns, C.Z., 555
Enns, J.T., 67
Epstein, A.N., 339
Epstein, R., 215
Epstein, S., 452
Erdley, C.A., 97
Erickson, D., 113
Ericsson, K.A., 251
Erikson, E.H., 395
Eriksson, P.S., 58
Eron, L.D., 390
Ertel, S., 98
Esiri, M.M., 488
Esposito, M.D., 71
Esterson, A., 15, 430
Evans, G.W., 462
Evans, J.R., 592
Evans, L.I., 578
Evans, M., 562
Evans, R.B., 14, 17, 22
Everaerd, W., 340, 341
Exner, J.E., 446
Eyer, J., 475
Eysenck, H.J., 436, 437, 501, 542

F

Fabes, R.A., 10, 346
Fagan, J.F., 372
Fagan, T.J., 532
Fagiolini, M., 126, 129
Fairburn, C.G., 336, 337, 338
Fallon, A., 337
Faludi, G., 84
Fantz, R.L., 372
Farber, S., 82
Farmer, L., 446
Farr, J.L., 614
Farthing, C.W., 160, 179
Fausto-Sterling, A., 510
Fawcett, J., 541
Fazel-Zandy, S., 375

Featherstone, R.E., 50
Fehr, B., 351
Feinauer, L., 458
Feingold, A., 568
Feinson, M.C., 411
Fejr, S.S., 539
Feldhusen, J.F., 324
Feldman, R.S., 346
Fendrich, R., 104
Feng, A.S., 112
Fennema, E., 316
Ferguson, C.A., 380
Festinger, L., 579
Fibiger, H.C., 243
Fiedler, F.E., 591, 592
Field, T.M., 121, 344
Fields, W., 270
Fincham, F.D., 344
Fine, M.A., 403
Finkelhor, D., 509
Finkenauer, C., 252
Finn, P.R., 175, 177
Finn, S.E., 305
Finn-Stevenson, M., 313
Fischhoff, B., 283, 285
Fischman, J., 70
Fisher, L.M., 409
Fisher, S., 430
Fiske, S.T., 562, 563, 573
Fitzgerald, S., 199
Fitzsimmons, J.T., 339
Flannery, R.B., 199
Flavell, J.F., 377
Flavell, J.H., 393
Fleeson, W., 436
Fleming, A.S., 50, 400
Fletcher, B., 569
Flieller, A., 314
Flier, J.S., 334
Florio, C.M., 446
Flynn, J.R., 314, 315
Flynn, P.M., 164
Fogelman, E., 589
Folen, R.A., 532
Folkman, S., 457, 470
Fong, G.T., 13
Forbes, J.L., 62
Ford, B.D., 83
Ford, W.C.L., 406
Ford-Mitchell, D., 148
Forgatch, M.S., 403
Forster, N., 462
Foulkes, D., 159
Fouts, R.S., 268, 270
Fowles, D., 489
Foxcroft, D.R., 553
Foy, D.W., 478
Frager, R., 583
France, C.R., 121, 122
Frank, E., 467

Frank, J.B., 530
Frank, J.D., 530
Franklin, N., 253
Fraser, S.C., 584
Frederick, S., 352
Freedman, J.L., 584
Freeman, M.P., 548
Freeman, W., 55
Frenkel-Brunswick, E., 573
Freud, S., 159, 419
Freudenberger, H.J., 465
Frezza, M., 168
Friedman, H.S., 123, 467, 472
Friedman, M.J., 466, 467, 478
Friedmann, E., 118
Friesen, W.V., 351, 361
Friman, P.C., 21
Froelich, L., 52
Frohlich, M.A., 507
Fu, Q., 437, 512
Fuchs, T., 199
Fultz, D.E., 200
Funder, D.C., 434, 436, 443
Funk, S.C., 543
Funnell, M., 67
Furstenberg Jr., F.F., 392
Furukawa, Y., 172
Furumoto, L., 21, 22
Fuster, J.M., 240

G ----------------------

Gable, M., 97
Gabrieli, J.D.E., 70, 240
Gaertner, L., 566
Gaertner, S.I., 574
Gaetani, S., 175
Gage, F.H., 57
Gagnon, J.H., 341, 342
Galambos, N.L., 394
Galanter, M., 541
Galda, L., 386
Galef, B.G., 218
Gallistel, C.R., 39
Gallup Jr., G.G., 39, 269
Gandhi, N., 473
Gangestad, S.W., 340
Garb, H.N., 446
Garber, H., 313
Garcia, J., 191
Gardner, B.T., 270
Gardner, H., 270, 297, 299
Gardner, S., 22
Garfield, S.L., 543
Garnets, L.K., 343
Garrod, A., 380
Garry, M., 253
Gartner, A., 320
Gartstein, M.A., 370
Gathchel, R.J., 156, 157

Gauvin, L., 337
Gayle, R., 507
Gazzaniga, M.S., 104
Gecz, J., 84
Geen, R.G., 347
Geher, G., 298
Geist, T., 107
Geldard, F.A., 121
Gelles, R.J., 574
Gelman, D., 424, 477
Genzel, C., 118
George, L.K., 408
Gerber, D.J., 488
Gergen, K.J., 39
German, M.L., 303
Gernsbacher, M.A., 68
Gershoff, E.T., 195, 196
Gershon, E.S., 495
Gershon, S., 548
Getchell, M.L., 117
Getzels, J.W., 323
Gibbs, J.C., 513
Gibson, E.J., 372
Gibson, R.L., 556
Giese-Davis, J., 468
Giesen, H.A., 152
Gilbert, D.T., 562, 563
Gilbert, L.A., 403
Gilbertson, M.W., 478
Gilliam, W.S., 313
Gilligan, C., 589
Gilman, S.L., 427
Gilovich, T., 283
Ginnett, R.C., 592
Ginsberg, H., 307
Giorgio, M., 84
Girgus, J.S., 439
Gitlin, M., 30
Glanzman, D.L., 187
Glass, G.V., 543
Glassman, A.H., 164, 171
Glaus, K.D., 467
Gleaves, D.H., 253
Gleiberman, L., 177
Glenberg, A.M., 245
Glenberg, A.M., 245
Glenberg, T.H., 388
Gnanadesikan, M., 548
Gobet, F.L., 230, 280
Godden, D.R., 245
Goerge, R.M., 392
Goh, B.E., 324
Gold, A.R., 78
Gold, M.S., 122, 174
Goldberg, D.E., 57
Goldberg, L.R., 434, 436
Golden, S., 233
Goldman, W., 42
Goldney, R.D., 552
Goldsmith, H.H., 356, 370
Goldsmith, M., 249
Goldstein, E.B., 113, 126

Goldstein, I., 507
Goleman, D., 297, 298, 350, 409
Golomb, J., 243
Good, G.E., 358
Goodall, J., 270
Goode, E., 20, 265, 425, 463
Goodman, P.S., 617
Goodwin, P.J., 468
Gopnik, A., 370, 378
Gordis, E., 176, 177
Gordon, J., 107
Gorissen, M.C., 335
Gorman, J.M., 544
Gorski, R.A., 343
Gorsuch, R.L., 437
Gosling, S.D., 18, 19, 435
Gotesdam, K.G., 336
Gottesman, I.I., 82, 83, 515, 517
Gould, D., 473
Gouzoulis-Mayfrank, E., 172
Grabowska, A., 240
Grabowski, T.J., 240, 241
Grafton, S.T., 240
Graen, G.B., 592
Graham, K., 365
Grandey, A.A., 298
Grant, J.E., 336
Gray, J.J., 336
Gray, P.B., 77
Graziano, W.G., 582
Green, B.G., 119
Green, J.P., 180
Green, J.T., 189
Greenberg, J., 97
Greene, J., 64
Greene, R.L., 231, 233
Greenfield, P.M., 304, 307, 315, 380
Greening, T., 18
Greenstein, T.H., 388
Griffiths, R.A., 180
Grisso, J.A., 163, 369
Grotberg, J.J., 313
Gu, X., 407
Guarnaccia, P.J.J., 521
Guenther, V.K., 409
Guerin, D., 371
Guerri, C., 368
Guest, A., 475
Guion, R.M., 616
Gullota, T., 395, 397
Gunderson, J.G., 511
Gunne, L.M., 172
Gurin, J., 338
Gurman, A.S., 539, 540
Guroff, J.J., 505
Gurvits, T.V., 478
Gurwitch, R.H., 477

Gustafson, S.B., 322
Guthrie, R., 24
Guttmacher, A.E., 88
Guzder, J., 511

H ----------------------

Haber, R.N., 250
Haberlandt, K., 251, 275
Hack, M., 311
Hackett, R.D., 616
Hackman, J.R., 279
Hage, J.J., 509
Hagerman, P.J., 320
Hagerman, R.J., 320
Hagerty, B.M., 493
Haidt, J., 64, 231, 233
Haier, R.J., 71, 302
Hake, J.L., 372
Halaas, J.L., 334
Halford, J.C.G., 334
Hall, C.C.I., 29
Hall, D., 488
Hall, G.S., 394
Hall, J.A., 359
Hall, L.K., 248
Hall, W.G., 339
Halpern, D.F., 316, 317
Halpern, J.J., 339
Hamann, S.B., 62
Hamberger, M.J., 238
Hamer, D.H., 27, 342
Hamilton, A., 532
Hammack, S.E., 199
Hammen, C.L., 30, 496
Hampson, E., 78
Hampson, J., 381
Hansel, C.E., 98
Hanson, R.K., 307
Harackiewicz, J.M., 250
Harburg, E., 177, 359
Hardaway, R.A., 97
Hardin, C.D., 266
Hardy, C.A., 230
Hare, R.D., 512
Harley, H.E., 269
Harlow, A.J., 104
Harlow, H.F., 215, 344
Harman, C., 370
Harper, R.A., 459
Harrell, R.F., 311
Harrington, D.M., 323
Harris, J.A., 335
Harris, J.C., 487
Harris, J.R., 177, 385, 386, 388, 394, 403
Harris, M., 563
Harrison, L.D., 170
Hart, B., 312

Hart, N., 475
Hartung, C.M., 520
Hartup, W.W., 470
Harvey, E., 388
Harvey, J.H., 476, 568, 569
Hashimoto, T., 488
Hasselmo, M.E., 243
Hathaway, S.R., 443
Hauri, P., 156
Hauser, M.D., 383
Hauser, S.T., 391
Hawes, R.R., 536
Hawkins, C., 138
Hawkins, D.I., 97
Hawkley, L.C., 156
Hay, M.S., 32
Hayashi, K.M., 70
Hayden, T., 440
Hayes, C., 270
Hayes, K., 270
He, L., 123
Heath, A.C., 83, 437, 512
Heath, R.C., 340
Heavey, C.L., 540
Hebb, D.O., 85, 331
Hebeband, J., 334
Heber, R., 313
Hechtman, L., 392
Hedges, L.V., 316
Heider, E.R., 265
Heinz, A., 466
Heitzeg, M.M., 123
Helgesen, S., 409
Hellawell, D.J., 242
Hellige, J.B., 65, 67
Helmreich, R., 347
Helms, J.E., 308, 555
Helson, H., 583
Helson, R., 323
Helzer, J.E., 164
Hendrick, C., 351
Hendrick, S.S., 351
Henkel, L.A., 253
Henning, K., 340
Henriques, J.B., 67
Henry, J.A., 549
Henry, S., 410
Hensch, T.K., 126, 129
Herberman, R.B., 468
Herbert, T.B., 467
Herek, G.M., 573
Hergenhahn, B.R., 185
Herman, K.C.
Herman, L.M., 269
Hermann, C., 75
Hermann, D., 466
Hermelin, B., 319
Herrnstein, R.J., 308, 314
Hersen, M., 536
Hersher, L., 528, 530

Hertwig, R., 39, 285
Herz, R.S., 245
Herzog, T.A., 167
Heston, L.L., 83
Hetherington, E.M., 403
Hewitt, K.L., 373
Hewstone, M., 574
Heyes, C.M., 218
Hibbard, S.R., 446
Hilgard, E.R., 180
Hill, C.E., 159, 160
Hill, J., 513
Hillier, L., 373
Hilton, H.G., 458
Hilton, J., 563
Himes, G.T., 219, 268, 269
Hinden, B.R., 395
Hines, M., 389
Hitch, G.J., 229, 230
Hobfoll, S.E., 470
Hobson, J.A., 155, 160
Hochman, J.S., 26
Hochschild, A.R., 360
Hodges, M., 507
Hodgson, D.M., 371
Hoffman, H.S., 384
Hoffman, L., 520
Hoffman, M.A., 27, 320, 343, 348
Hoffrage, U., 285
Hogan, J., 435
Hogan, R., 435
Hokin, L.E., 548
Holland, C.A., 250
Hollis, K.L., 190
Hollister, L.E., 175
Hollon, S.D., 548
Holm, N.V., 466
Holmbeck, G.N., 395, 397
Holmes, D.S., 39, 473
Holmes, T.H., 453
Holsinger, T., 549
Holtkamp, K., 334
Honeybourne, C., 191
Hood, B.M., 372
Hood, D.C., 96, 100
Hoon, E.F., 507
Hopkins, B., 374
Hoptman, M.J., 65, 67
Horn, J.M., 83, 311
Horney, K., 426
Horowitz, L.M., 569
Hosoda, M., 567, 568
Hotaling, G., 509
House, J.S., 402, 470
Howard, K.I., 542
Howard, R.C., 544
Hoyer, S., 52
Hsu, L.K., 337
Huang, T., 458

Hubel, D.H., 100, 102, 103, 129
Hudson, J.A., 250
Hudspeth, A.J., 132
Huebner, A.M., 380
Huesmann, L.R., 390
Huffman, C.J., 280
Hughes, E., 320
Hughes, R.L., 592
Hui, C., 592
Huizink, A.C., 371
Human Rights Watch, 575
Humphreys, K., 541
Humphreys, L.G., 314
Hunt, E., 369
Hunt, M., 7, 15
Hunter, A.M., 199
Hunter, J.E., 567
Husband, T.H., 253
Huston, A.C., 389, 390
Hutschemaekers, G.J.M., 475
Huttenlocher, J., 381
Hyde, J.S., 266, 316, 317, 340, 346, 397
Hyman, E.E., 253
Hynd, G.W., 65, 67

I

Iacobucci, D., 563
Iaffaldano, M.T., 616
Inciardi, J.A., 170, 173
Inoue, M., 453
Ireland, D., 553
Irwin, M.M., 369, 468
Irwin, R.J., 122
Isen, A.M., 588
Islam, M.R., 574
Ito, K., 578
Ito, T.A., 167
Ivancevich, J.M., 616, 618
Iverson, G.L., 443
Iwamasa, G.Y., 28
Izard, C.E., 351, 354, 356, 360

J

Jacks, J.Z., 578
Jackson, D.C., 62
Jackson, L.A., 567
Jackson, P.A., 241, 323
Jacobs, G.H., 107
Jacobs, W.J., 250
Jacobsen, L., 563
Jacobsen, P.B., 192
Jacobson, K., 518
Jacobson, N.S., 542
Jain, S., 578
Jaldow, E., 218
Jamal, M., 618
James, L.C., 455, 532

James, W., 15, 124, 146, 229, 352
Jang, K.L., 435, 437
Janis, I.L., 591
Janofsky, M., 174
Janos, P.M., 321
Jaycox, L.H., 478
Jaynes, G.D., 574
Jemmott, L.S., 474
Jemmott III, J.B., 474
Jenkins, H.M., 212
Jenkins, L., 382
Jensen, A.R., 314
Jensen, M.P., 177
Johannesen-Schmidt, A., 463
Johansson, M., 114
John, O.P., 435
Johnson, A., 235, 337, 540
Johnson, B.T., 247
Johnson, C., 339
Johnson, D.F., 121
Johnson, D.M., 19, 80, 81
Johnson, D.W., 576
Johnson, E.S., 452
Johnson, G., 271
Johnson, M.K., 253
Johnson, R.T., 576
Johnson, V.E., 508
Johnson, V.J., 341, 342
Johnson-Greene, D., 166
Johnston, D., 398
Johnston, L.D., 166, 172, 174
Johnston, R.E., 117
Johnstone, B., 532
Jones, C.J., 405
Jones, C.P., 382
Jones, F.D., 27
Jones, L.W., 284
Jones, M.C., 17, 188
Jorge, J.M.N., 200
Josephs, R.A., 166, 167, 168
Julius, M., 359
Junginger, J., 509
Jusczyk, P.W., 380

K

Kadotani, H., 156
Kadotani, T., 156
Kagan, J., 371
Kagitcibasi, C., 29
Kahlenberg, S.M., 77
Kahneman, D., 282, 283
Kalakanis, L., 567
Kalat, J.W., 77, 340
Kales, A., 156
Kaltman, S., 476
Kaminski, M., 455
Kandel, E.R., 239
Kane, J., 546

Kantrowitz, B., 170
Kaplan, W.S., 400
Kapur, S., 70
Karau, S.J., 591
Karmiloff-Smith, A., 383
Karoly, P., 177
Kaschak, M.P., 68
Kashdan, T.B., 344
Kashima, Y., 566
Kass, S., 593
Kassebaum, N.L., 313
Kassin, S.M., 253
Kaszniak, A.W., 179
Kathuria, S., 175
Kato, T., 495
Katz, R., 495
Kaufman, J.C., 295, 323
Kavale, K.A., 320
Kavanagh, D.J., 517
Kawai, N., 269
Keane, G., 299
Keefe, F.J., 121, 122
Keitner, G.I., 548
Kelemen, W.L., 245
Kelley, H.H., 565
Kellner, C.H., 549
Kellogg, W.N., 270
Kelly, G., 160
Kelly, J.B., 403
Kelly, K., 343
Kemeny, M.E., 471
Kendler, K.S., 84, 337
Keppel, B., 28
Keri, S., 64
Kernis, M.H., 568
Kesner, R.P., 241
Kessler, R.C., 458, 477, 498,
    521
Keverne, E.B., 117
Kewman, D.G., 543
Khan, A., 549
Kiecolt-Glaser, J.K., 469, 470
Kiesler, C.A., 552, 553
Kigar, D.L., 67
Kihlstrom, J.F., 179, 250
Kileny, P.R., 113
Killion, J.E., 156
Kilpatrick, D.G., 177
Kim, J., 409
Kim, K.H.S., 382
Kim, S.W., 336
Kimberg, D.Y., 64
Kimeldorf, D.J., 191
Kimmel, A.J., 39
Kimmel, D.C., 410
Kimura, D., 78
King, L., 20
Kingstone, A., 67
Kinsey, A.C., 342, 506
Kirsch, I., 177, 179

Kirshnit, C.E., 215
Kish, S.J., 172
Kissane, D.W., 468
Kitayama, S., 360
Kite, M.E., 22
Klatzky, R.L., 225
Kleim, J.A., 55
Klein, D.M., 577
Klein, G.S., 138, 280, 284
Klein, L.C., 463
Kleinfield, N.R., 451
Kleinmuntz, D.N., 283
Kliewer, W., 403
Kline, P., 161, 432
Kling, K.C., 397
Klingenspor, B., 337
Kluckhohn, C., 9, 28
Kluegel, J.R., 573
Kluger, A., 243
Kluger, J., 118
Klump, K.L., 437
Knapp, C., 168
Knight, G.P., 10, 346
Kniskern, D.P., 539
Knopman, D.S., 243, 410
Knott, V., 302
Knowlton, B.J., 64
Kobasa, S.C., 457
Koch, K.L., 117
Kochanek, K.D., 397, 497
Koelling, R.A., 191
Koenig, H.G., 470
Koestner, R., 332, 333
Koh, P.O., 515
Kohlberg, L., 378
Kohlmaier, J.R., 336, 338
Kolarz, C.M., 408
Kolata, G., 283, 407
Kolb, H., 102, 103
Kolchakian, M.R., 159
Komatsu, L.K., 262
Komiya, N., 358
Kondrasuk, J.N., 616
Koob, G.F., 164, 171
Koopman, C., 468
Koopmans, J.R., 83
Kopelowicz, A., 535
Kopta, S.M., 542, 544
Korn, J.H., 39
Koshes, R.J., 27
Koss, M.P., 520
Kosslyn, S.M., 129, 262
Koukounas, E., 341
Krasne, F.B., 187
Kraus, S.J., 571
Krebs, D., 588
Krikorian, R., 237
Kringlen, E., 466
Kroger, R.O., 436
Kropp, P., 200

Krosnick, J.A., 32
Krowlewski, D.M., 173
Krueger, R.F., 434, 437
Krupinski, E., 532
Krystal, A.D., 549
Kubler-Ross, E., 410, 411
Kudoh, T., 360
Kuhl, P.K., 380, 382
Kulik, J., 345
Kullgren, G., 510
Kunkel, D., 390
Kunst-Wilson, W.R., 97
Kupfermann, I., 62
Kupperbusch, C., 361
Kurdek, L.A., 400, 403
Kwon, P., 453
Kwon, S.M., 496

L

Laan, E., 340, 341
L'Abbate, A., 443
Labouvie-Vief, G., 404
Lachman, S.J., 137
Ladouceur, R., 544
LaGreca, A.M., 530
Laird, J., 400
Lal, S., 28
Lamb, J.A., 488, 519
Lambe, E.K., 516
Lamberg, L., 507
Lambert, W.W., 137
Lampl, M., 374
Lamy, D., 227
Landesman, S., 320
Landin, A.M., 117
Landis, K.R., 470
Landman, J., 285
Landy, F.J., 210
Landy, F.L., 614
Lane, S.M., 253
Lang, E.V., 123
Lange, K., 62
Langenbucher, J.W., 489
Langer, A., 372
Langer, E.J., 576
Langfeld, H.S., 130, 133
Langlois, J.H., 567, 568
Lantz, M.S., 179
Lapp, L., 160
Larimer, M.E., 32
Lashley, K.S., 240
Latane, B., 588, 590
Latchman, A., 303
Laumann, E.O., 342
Laurent, C.L., 177
Laureys, S., 160
Lavie, P., 152
Lawler, E., 615

Lay, C.H., 453
Layton, B., 237
Lazarus, R.S., 350, 353, 354,
    453, 460
Leadbeater, B.J., 394
Leary, W.E., 113
LeBoeuf, R.A., 284
Leborgne, L., 408
Lebow, J.L., 539, 540
Leccese, A.P., 172, 175
Le Couteur, A., 519
Lederer, G., 573
LeDoux, J.E., 240, 357
Lee, B.J., 392
Lee, K.J., 567
Lee, S., 317, 337
Lees-Haley, P.R., 443
Lehman, D.R., 13, 286
Leibing, E., 542
Leibowitz, H.W., 102
Leichsenring, F., 542
Leigh, R.J., 120
Leiman, A.L., 107
Leit, R.A., 336
Leitenberg, H., 340
Leiter, M.P., 465
Lemish, D., 390
Lemon, J., 468
Lempert, R.O., 13
Lennard, H.L., 177
Lenneberg, E.H., 265
Lennon, R., 358
Lere, C., 57
Lerman, C., 83, 176
Lerman, H., 520
Lerner, M.J., 566
Leroy, P., 334
Leschied, A.W., 398
Leshner, A.I., 164
Leszcz, M., 468
Lev, M., 32, 97
Levant, R.F., 555
LeVay, S., 27, 113, 342, 343
Levenson, M.R., 408
Levenson, R.W., 353
Leventhal, H., 578
Levin, J.S., 470
Levin, P.F., 588
Levine, A., 452, 574
Levine, J.M., 583
Levine, S., 121
Levinson, D.J., 405
Levy, C.M., 150
Lew, R.A., 369
Lewin, K.A., 456
Lewin, R., 271
Lewin, T., 341, 388, 392, 402
Lewinsohn, P.M., 397, 398
Lewis, B.S., 245
Lewis, J.G., 321

Lewis, M.I., 408, 411
Lewy, A.J., 152
Li, Y.J., 243
Liberman, R.P., 535
Lichenstein, P., 82
Lichstein, K.L., 156
Lichtenstein, E., 176
Lichtenstein, P., 466
Lieberman, J., 546
Liebert, R.M., 284, 385, 388, 394, 403
Liggett, D.R., 180
Lightdale, J.R., 11
Lilienfeld, S.O., 505
Limber, J., 271
Lin, L., 334
Lin, M., 556
Lindberg, N., 151
Lindsay, D.S., 253
Lindsay, P.H., 265
Linn, R.L., 307
Lipman, S., 561
Lips, H.M., 593
Lipsey, M., 542
Lipsky, D.K., 320
Little, K.Y., 173
Liu, C., 152
Liu, J.H., 590
Livesley, W.J., 435, 437
Livingston, J.A., 168
Livingstone, M.S., 102
Llinas, R., 147
Locke, E.A., 438, 615
Lockhart, R.S., 233
Loeb, L.A., 113
Loehlin, J.C., 80, 311, 437
Loewenstein, G., 344, 352
Loftus, E.F., 252, 253, 254
Logie, R.H., 230
Logue, A.W., 192
Lombardo, C., 199
Lombardo, P., 160
Long, J.B., 214
Lonner, W.J., 28
Lopez, S.R., 27, 521
Lorenz, K., 345, 385
Lott, B.E., 569
Louie, T.A., 285
Lovibond, P.F., 191
Low, W.C., 243
Lubahn, D., 77
Lubinski, D., 295, 321, 437
Luchins, A., 563
Luckey, J.W., 164
Lue, T.F., 507
Lueger, R.J., 542
Luetjohann, D., 84
Luine, V., 240
Lumeng, L., 191
Luminet, O., 252

Luria, A.R., 251
Lydum, A.R., 32
Lykken, D.T., 82
Lyness, S.A., 467
Lynn, R., 315
Lynn, S.J., 179, 180, 505
Lyons, M.J., 512
Lyubomirsky, S., 246

M

Maas, J., 150
Macaulay, D., 505
Maccoby, E.E., 83, 371, 386, 387, 389, 403
MacDonald, G., 168
MacDonald, T.K., 168
Macionis, J.J., 27
Mackavey, W.R., 250
Macken, M.A., 380
Mackie, B., 403
Mackin, R.S., 453, 454
MacLaren, C., 537
MacLean, P.D., 62
MacLeod, D.I.A., 100
Macrae, C.N., 564
MacWhinney, B., 383
Madden, N.A., 576
Maddi, S.R., 432
Madison, S.M., 563
Madsen, P.L., 149
Magaletta, P.R., 532
Maier, S.F., 198, 458
Maio, G.R., 581
Maisto, A.A., 303, 320
Maj, M., 495
Malarkey, W.B., 470
Malenka, R.C., 56
Malin, H., 166
Malley, J.E., 250
Malone, P.S., 563
Mandel, D.R., 286, 380
Manfredi, M., 122
Mann, T., 245
Manton, K.G., 407
Maquet, P., 160
Marano, H.E., 391
Maratos-Flier, E., 334
Marcia, J.E., 395, 427, 430
Marcus, D.K., 567
Marcus, S.C., 533, 549
Marentette, P.F., 380
Margolin, G., 540
Margolskee, R.F., 117
Markes, L.S., 507
Marklund, P., 240
Markman, H., 399
Markon, K.E., 434, 437
Markovic, B.M., 190
Marks, I.M., 500

Markus, H.R., 360
Marlier, L., 118
Marmar, C.R., 246
Marr, D., 129
Marriott, L.K., 243
Martha, M., 313
Martin, N.G., 83
Martin, R.L., 78
Martin, S., 164
Martinez, J.L., 56
Martino, A., 405
Maslach, C., 465
Masling, J.M., 215, 446
Maslow, A.H., 348, 349, 480
Mason, F.L., 509
Massaro, D.W., 225
Masters, W.H., 341, 342, 508
Matchett, G., 191
Mateo, J.M., 117
Mather, M., 246
Matsumoto, D., 266, 267, 360, 361
Matsuzawa, T., 269
Matta, M.A., 196
Matteson, M.T., 616, 618
Matthews, D.B., 167
Matthews, G., 298
Matthews, T.D., 280
Mattson, S.N., 369
Maugh II, T.H., 85
Maunsell, E., 468
Maurer, C., 372
Maurer, D., 372
May, J., 161
Mayer, D.J., 123
Mayer, J.D., 298, 588
Mayers, J.D., 298
Mays, V.M., 575, 576
Maziere, J.C., 408
Mazur, J.E., 192
Mazziotta, J.C., 240
Mazzoni, G.A.L., 160
McBurney, D.H., 95
McCabe, P.M., 467
McCall, R.B., 370
McCann, I.L., 473
McCann, U.D., 172
McCartney, K., 83
McCarty, C.A., 521, 522
McClearn, G.E., 80, 84
McClelland, D.C., 137, 309
McCloy, R., 285
McClure, E.B., 359
McConnell, R.A., 98
McCrae, R.R., 434, 435, 437, 443
McCullagh, S., 493
McCulloch, J., 42
McDaniel, M.A., 248
McElhatton, P.R., 172

McFarland, L.J., 592
McGarvey, E.L., 548
McGaugh, J.L., 239, 241
McGeer, E.G., 353
McGeer, P.L., 353
McGill, A.L., 563
McGinnis, M., 466
McGonagle, K.A., 498, 521
McGovern, K., 148
McGovern, L.P., 588
McGue, M., 84, 437
McGuffin, P., 495
McGuire, L., 467
McGuire, M.T., 338
McGuire, P.A., 468, 514
McGuire, S., 82
McIntyre, C.K., 243
McKay, R., 57
McKellar, J., 541
McKenna, M.C., 468
McKim, W.A., 168, 169, 174, 546, 547
McKinley, J.C., 443
McLoyd, V., 314
McMillan, T.M., 57
McMurray, G.A., 122
McNally, R.J., 253
McNamara, H.J., 214
McNeil, B.J., 284
McNeil, T.F., 371
McNeill, D., 238
Mead, M., 29
Mednick, M.T., 22
Mednick, S.A., 323
Meglino, B.M., 611
Meichenbaum, D., 537
Melamed, B.G., 536
Melamed, S., 593
Mellers, B.A., 282
Meltzoff, A.N., 378
Melzack, R., 122, 123
Mendez, B., 313
Menon, T., 566
Menustik, C.E., 535
Menzel, E.W., 270
Mercer, T.B., 321
Merchelbach, H., 155
Meredith, M., 117
Merikangas, K.R., 164
Merrill, K.A., 544
Mershon, B., 437
Mersky, H., 505
Mertens, I.K., 334
Merzer, M., 145
Meston, C.M., 507
Metcalfe, J., 67
Metzler, J., 262, 263
Meyer, G.J., 305
Mezulis, A.H., 317
Michael, R.T., 341

Michaelsen, K.F., 311
Michelson, L., 543
Migliaccio, E., 84
Milgram, S., 38, 585
Miller, A.C., 67
Miller, A.I., 262
Miller, E.D., 476
Miller, E.K., 226, 240
Miller, G.A., 383
Miller, G.E., 190
Miller, J.G., 566, 589
Miller, J.M., 532
Miller, L.K., 319
Miller, N., 167
Miller, P.A., 403
Miller, P.H., 393
Miller, R.S., 567
Miller, T.Q., 46
Miller, T.W., 532
Miller, W.R., 176
Millis, R.M., 473
Milner, B., 31, 234
Milton, J., 98
Miner, J.D., 152
Minor, T.R., 199
Minton, H.L., 22, 26, 320
Mirsky, S., 118
Mischel, W., 436, 440
Mistry, J., 254
Mitchell, K.J., 253
Mitchell, M., 556
Mitchell, R.W., 268
Mitchell, S.H., 177
Mittleman, M., 174
Moen, P., 409
Moffitt, T.W., 512
Moghaddam, F.M., 346
Moise, T.J., 390
Molineux, J.B., 539
Mollica, R.F., 476, 477
Monahan, J.L., .97
Monastra, D.M., 75
Monastra, V.J., 75
Moncrieff, R.W., 115
Mondin, G.W., 542, 543
Monroe, S.M., 496
Monteith, M.J., 576
Montgomery, G.H., 179
Moore, J., 488, 519
Moore, K.A., 392
Moore, M.K., 370
Moore, R.Y., 151, 468
Moore-Ede, M.C., 151
Morairty, S., 151
Moran III, D.J., 195
Morgan, W.G., 446
Moriarty, T., 588
Morin, C.M., 156, 157
Moroz, T.M., 71
Morris, C.G., 279, 452, 453,

455, 460, 476, 480
Morris, M.W., 566
Morrison, D.R., 392
Mortensen, E.L., 311
Moscicki, E.K., 497
Moscoso, S., 435
Moses, S., 556
Moskowitz, S.T., 457
Moyers, F., 477
Mroczek, D.K., 408
Muchinsky, P.M., 612, 616
Muenchow, S., 313
Muir, D.W., 373
Mumford, M.D., 322
Munitz, H., 503
Muris, P., 155
Murphy, S.T., 97, 354
Murray, B., 41, 594
Murray, C.L., 243, 308, 314
Murray, H.A., 9, 347
Murray, H.G., 278
Murrell, S.A., 411
Mustanski, B.S., 437
Myers, D.G., 283, 352
Myers, J.M., 84

N

Nadel, L., 250
Nagai, K., 334
Naglieri, J.A., 323
Nahl, D., 455
Nair, L., 443
Nairne, J.S., 229
Nakayama, K., 151
Narayanan, L., 462
Narrow, W.E., 491, 540
Nash, M.R., 179, 180
Nathan, P.E., 489, 544
National Adolescent Health
    Information Center, 397
National Advisory Mental
    Health Council, 350
National Center for Health
    Statistics, 369
National Clearing House on
    Child Abuse and Neglect,
    345
National Household Survey on
    Drug Abuse, 171
National Institute of Mental
    Health, 496
National Institute of
    Neurological Disorders and
    Stroke, 156
National Institute on Alcohol
    Abuse and Alcoholism, 168
National Institute on Drug
    Abuse, 166, 170, 172, 175,
    176

Neal, A., 501
Neath, I., 233
Neave, N., 118
Neher, A., 349, 425
Nehlig, A., 55
Neisser, U., 225, 252, 314, 315
Neitz, J., 107
Neitz, M., 107
Nelson, C.A., 55, 71
Nelson, C.M., 270
Nelson, D., 568
Nelson, K., 381
Nemeroff, C.B., 547
Ness, R.B., 163, 369
Nesse, R.M., 86, 493, 500
Netting, J., 149
Neubauer, A.C., 302
Neuberg, S.L., 573
Neugarten, B.L., 405
Newcombe, N.S., 250
Niccols, A., 303
Nicoll, R.A., 56
Niesink, R.J., 518
Nijenhuis, E.R.S., 237
Niles, P., 578
Nishimura, T., 337
Nishimura, Y., 337
Nissani, M., 585
Noga, J.T., 516
Noice, H., 248
Noice, T., 248
Nolen-Hoeksema, S., 439, 462
Noonberg, A.R., 200
Norman, D.A., 229, 265
Norman, K.A., 246
Norman, R., 571
Norris, F.H., 411
North, K., 406
Norton, G.R., 505
Novak, C.M., 151
Novak, K., 410
Novak, M.A., 39
Novick, L.R., 215, 278
Novorr, M.J., 400
Nowak, A., 581
Nowell, A., 316
Nucci, L.P., 380
Nurmi, E.L., 488
Nuttall, J., 425
Nypaver, M., 532

O

O'Brien, K.M., 336
O'Connell, A., 22
O'Connor, N., 319
O'Connor, T.G., 82
Odbert, H.S., 434

Oehman, A., 191
Oei, T.P.S., 496
Oest, L.G., 555
Oesterle, E.C., 113
Offer, D., 394
Ogawa, S., 77
Ogrodniczuk, J., 555
Ohman, A., 500
Ojemann, G., 64
Ojemann, J., 64
Olds, M.E., 62
O'Leary, A., 350, 468
O'Leary, K.D., 534, 535
O'Leary, V.E., 358, 593
Olfson, M., 496, 533, 549
Oliver, D.C., 265
Olsen, E.A., 252
Olson, C.B., 26
Olson, J.M., 581
Olson, M.H., 185
Olson, M.V., 81
Oltmanns, T.F., 453, 468, 478,
    489, 500, 506, 511, 540,
    546, 548
Olton, D.S., 200
Olzewski-Kubilius, P., 321
O'Malley, P.M., 166, 172, 174
Omi, M., 27
Ommundsen, Y., 217
O'Neil, R., 387
Ones, D.S., 435
Onken, L.S., 534
Onstad, S., 501
Onyskiw, J.E., 346
Oordt, M.S., 156, 157
Ophir, I., 192
Orbuch, T.L., 402
Orlinsky, D.E., 542
Orlofsky, J.L., 427, 430
Ortar, G., 308
Ortmann, A., 39
Osborne, J.W., 563
Oskamp, S., 572
Ostendorf, F., 436
Ostrov, E., 394
O'Sullivan, M., 358
Ouimette, P., 541
Over, R., 341
Overnier, J.B., 198
Ozer, D.J., 436

P

Pace, R., 335
Paikoff, R.L., 397
Paivio, A., 231
Palmer, J.C., 252
Panksepp, J., 52, 518
Pantev, C., 56
Papassotiropoulos, A., 84

Pare, D., 242
Paris, J., 511
Paris, S.G., 378
Park, B., 284
Park, D.C., 305
Parke, R.D., 387
Parker, K.C.H., 307
Parker, S.K., 594
Parnetti, L., 243
Parsons, H.M., 593
Parsons, M., 593
Patenaude, A.F., 88
Paton, C.C., 467
Patrick, C.J., 512
Patterson, C.J., 343
Patterson, F.G.P., 270, 271
Patterson, G.R., 371, 513
Pauker, S.G., 284
Paul, G.G., 121
Paul, G.L., 535
Paunovic, N., 555
Pauwells, B.G., 568, 569
Peabody, D., 434
Pearson, C.A.L., 594
Pedersen, P.B., 556
Pedlow, R., 371
Pedroarena, C., 147
Pellegrini, A.D., 386
Pellegrini, R.J., 398
Peng, K., 267
Penner, R.H., 269
Penton-Voak, I., 20
Peplau, L.A., 359, 399
Peppe, A., 52
Pepperberg, I.M., 269
Perfilieva, E., 58
Perls, F.S., 530, 531
Perret, D.I., 567
Perry, D.G., 347
Perry, L.C., 347
Persky, H., 340
Pert, C.B., 53
Peter, C.R., 230
Petersen, A.C., 379, 391, 392
Peterson, C., 198, 439, 458
Peterson, L.R., 243
Peterson, M.J., 243
Petitto, L.A., 380
Pettigrew, T.F., 576
Petty, R.E., 578, 581
Pezdek, K., 254
Pfeifer, R.L., 358
Pham, L.B., 253
Phelps, J.A., 83
Phelps, L., 337
Phinney, J.S., 24
Piaget, J., 394
Pierce, J.P., 473
Pierri, J., 174, 175
Piersel, W., 369
Pine, F., 215, 527

Pinker, S., 85, 87, 148, 382, 383
Piomelli, D., 175
Piotrowski, C., 122
Piquero, A.R., 196
Pisani, V.D., 541
Pitman, G.E., 463
Pitts, S.C., 177
Place, U., 261
Platt, J.J., 162
Plaud, J.J., 190
Plomin, R., 80, 82, 83, 84, 87, 88, 320, 387, 388, 437, 489
Plous, S., 39
Plutchik, R., 350, 351
Pogarsky, G., 196
Pohl, R.F., 285
Poland, R., 556
Polaschek, D.L.L., 253
Pollack, A., 57
Pollack, W.S., 555
Pollatasek, A., 231
Pomerleau, C.S., 164
Pomeroy, W.B., 342, 506
Pontieri, F.E., 171
Pope, H., 336
Pope, M., 548
Porac, C., 105
Porkka-Heiskanen, T., 151
Porter, A., 462
Porter, L.S., 462, 615
Porter, L.W., 594
Porter, R.H., 118
Posavac, S.S., 578
Postman, L., 233
Pothier, P.K.T., 469
Powell, A.A., 587
Powell, D.H., 475
Powell, N.B., 150
Power, F.C., 380
Powers, S.I., 391
Pratley, R.E., 334
Premack, D., 269
Prentice, D.A., 11
Preti, G., 118
Price, R.H., 458
Prouadrel, F.B., 392
Prouty, A.M., 403
Prouty, R.W., 320
Pruneti, C.A., 443
Przeworski, M., 86, 838
Ptacek, J.T., 180, 462
Puca, A.A., 407
Purdy, J.E., 39
Putnam, F.W., 505
Putnam, K.M., 357

Q ----------------------

Quadagno, D.M., 118
Quadrel, M.J., 392

Quan, N., 468
Quesnel, C., 468
Quill, T.E., 502
Quinn, P.C., 126
Quist, R.M., 568

R ----------------------

Rabasca, L., 18, 28, 451, 468, 478, 493, 532
Rabbitt, P.M.A., 250
Rabin, B.S., 470
Rabinowitz, F.E., 554
Rae, D.S., 491, 540
Raffal, R.D., 64
Rahe, R.H., 453
Rainer, G., 226, 240
Ramey, C.T., 320
Ramey, S.L., 313
Ramus, F., 383
Rankin, R.J., 317
Rao, S.C., 240
Rapoport, M.J., 493
Rasika, S., 57
Rathunde, K., 320
Ratnam, R., 112
Rau, H., 200
Rauch, S.L., 549
Raven, B.H., 591
Raviv, A., 154
Ravussin, E., 334
Rawlins, J.N., 241
Rayman, P., 475
Rayner, R., 17, 188
Regier, D.A., 82
Rehm, L.P., 496
Reinish, J.M., 347
Reis, H.T., 568
Reis, S.M., 321
Reise, S.P., 436
Relkin, N.R., 382
Rende, R., 80, 84, 388, 489
Renner, M.J., 453, 454
Renzulli, J.S., 321
Repetti, R.L., 462
Reuter-Lorenz, P.A., 67
Rey, J.M., 548
Reyna, V.F., 253
Reznick, J.S., 371
Rhoades, L., 195
Rhue, J.W., 180
Rice, B., 309
Rice, J., 488
Rice, M.L., 390
Richards, D.G., 269
Richardson, G.S., 152
Ricurte, G.A., 172
Rieber, R.W., 505
Rietze, R.L., 57
Riley, E.P., 368, 369
Riley, V., 468

Rilling, M., 16, 17
Rini, C.K., 369
Riordan, R.J., 541
Ripple, C.H., 313
Rittenhouse, C.D., 154
Ritter, J.M., 568
Roberson, D., 265
Roberts, A.H., 543
Roberts, G., 311
Roberts, K.H., 594
Roberts, W.V., 78
Robertson, I.H., 57
Robertson, R.G., 241
Robins, L.N., 82, 249
Robins, R.W., 18, 19
Robinson, A., 320, 321
Robinson, L.A., 544
Robinson, N.M., 321
Robinson, P., 179
Robles, de M., 371
Rodgers, J.L.
Rodier, P.M., 519
Rodin, J., 334, 588
Rodriguez, M., 443
Roese, N.J., 285
Rofe, Y., 348
Rogers, C.R., 432
Rogers, D., 410
Rogers, M., 97
Rogers, P., 336
Rogoff, B., 254, 266
Roitbak, A.I., 50
Roitblat, H.L., 269
Rollman, G.B., 121
Rolls, E.T., 240, 241
Roper, R., 253
Rosch, E.H., 264, 265
Rose, R.J., 391
Rosen, C.C., 198
Rosen, L., 508
Rosen, R.C., 508
Rosenberg, D., 170
Rosenman, R.H., 466, 467
Rosenthal, D., 489
Rosenthal, R., 563
Rosenvinge, J.H., 336
Rosenzweig, M.R., 55, 56, 107, 312
Rosner, R., 478
Ross, C.A., 505
Ross, G.W., 171
Ross, L., 246, 565
Rossiter, T., 199
Rossman, R., 212
Roth, D., 496
Rothblum, E.D., 339
Rothman, A.J., 471
Rothman, S., 295
Rottenstreich, Y., 283
Rotter, J.B., 439
Rouhana, N.N., 575

Roundtree, T., 398
Roussy, J.M., 369
Rovner, S., 402
Rowan, A., 39
Rowe, D.C., 315
Rowe, W., 97
Rowland, N.E., 339
Roy, T.S., 368
Rozelle, R.M., 578
Rozin, P., 337
Ruab, W.A., 174
Rubenstein, A.J., 567
Rubin, K.H., 387
Ruble, D.N., 400
Ruffin, C.L., 453
Rugulies, R., 467
Rule, R.R., 64
Rumbaugh, D.M., 269, 271
Russell, J.A., 351
Russell, T.G., 97
Russo, N.F., 22, 520, 521
Ruth, W., 535
Rutter, M.L., 88
Ryan, R.M., 21, 457
Rymer, J., 405

S

Saade, S., 199
Sack, R.L., 152
Sacks, O., 259
Saczynski, J.S., 409
Sadeh, A., 154
Sadler, P., 179
Sadoski, M., 231
Safdar, S., 453
Safer, D.J.
Saitoh, O., 488, 516
Salgado, J.F., 435
Salovey, P., 298, 471, 588
Salthouse, T.A., 409
Salzinger, S., 346
Sampson, G., 383
Sanderson, C., 443
Sanford, R.N, .137
Sankis, L.M., 488
Sanna, L.J., 453
Sano, D.L., 568
Sanson, A., 371
Saporta, I., 339
Sarason, B.R., 488, 501
Sarason, I.G., 488, 501
Sarbin, T.R., 490
Sarter, M., 71
Satcher, D., 464
Satow, K.K., 588
Satterwhite, R.C., 389
Sattler, J.M., 307, 321
Saunders, A.M., 84
Savage-Rumbaugh, E.S., 270, 271

Savage-Rumbaugh, S., 271
Savard, J., 468
Savic, I., 118
Sawyer, M.G., 548
Scab, F.R., 245
Scarr, S., 20, 383, 388
Schaal, B., 118
Schachter, S., 354
Schacter, D.L., 19, 246
Schaefer, P., 409
Schafe, G.E., 357
Schaie, K.W., 404, 405, 409
Scharrer, E., 218
Schatzberg, A.F., 547
Schatzman, E.L., 430
Schechtman, K.B., 150
Schiffman, H.R., 122, 249
Schiffman, S.S., 116
Schleidt, M., 118
Schlenker, B.R., 566
Schmolck, H., 252
Schneiderman, N., 467
Schnell, E., 243
Schnurr, P.P., 478
Schoenberg, S.P., 249
Schoenthaler, S.J., 311
Scholey, A.B., 118
Schooler, C., 315
Schopp, L., 532
Schroeder, C.S., 320
Schrott, A., 111
Schulz, D.A., 341
Schwartz, A., 282
Schwartz, B.L., 21, 196, 201, 238
Schwartz, G.E., 178
Schwartz, J.C., 334
Schwartz, M.W., 335
Schwartz, P., 404
Schwartzman, J.B., 467
Schwarz, S., 285
Schweinhart, L.J., 313
Scott, C., 577
Scott, J., 548
Scully, J.A., 453
Scupin, R., 335
Sedikides, C., 566
Seebeck, T., 118, 340
Segura, S., 285
Seidler, F.J., 368
Seitz, R.J., 64
Seligman, J., 336
Seligman, M.E.P., 20, 190, 198, 352, 542, 543
Seligmann, J., 174
Sell, R.L., 342
Selman, R., 387
Selye, H., 464
Semenza, C., 240
Semrud-Clikeman, M., 65, 67, 518

Sengpiel, F., 126, 129
Senin, U., 243
Senn, L.E., 592
Seppa, N., 390
Seto, M.C., 509
Shackelford, T.K., 20, 347
Shadish, W.R., 544
Shaffer, D.R., 369
Shafir, E., 246, 284
Shalev, A., 503
Shaman, P., 116
Shanker, M., 462
Shapiro, D.A., 430, 542
Shapiro, K.J., 39
Shapiro, T.F., 253
Sharkansky, E.J., 175, 177
Shaughnessy, M.F., 299
Shaw, K.N., 615
Shaw, P.J., 149
Sheffield, E.G., 250
Sheldon, K.M., 20
Shelton, R.C., 548
Shepard, R.N., 262, 263
Sherin, J.E., 156
Sherman, R.A., 122
Sherman, S.J., 566
Shettleworth, S.J., 197
Shewan, D., 253
Shimamura, A.P., 134, 409
Shimizu, E., 85
Shneidman, E., 409
Shoda, Y., 436, 440
Shorter, E., 551
Shriver, M.D., 369
Sibulkin, A.E., 552
Siddle, D.A., 191
Siegel, K., 470
Siegel, L., 378
Siegert, R.J., 20, 86
Silver, R.C., 475
Silverman, I., 316
Simmons, R.W., 368
Simons, A.D., 496
Simpkins, C.G., 552
Sinatchkin, M., 200
Singer, D.G., 390
Singer, J.E., 354
Singer, J.L., 390
Singer, P., 39
Singh, R., 568
Singh, V., 593
Sinnott, J.D., 388
Sitterle, K.A., 477
Sivers, H., 237
Siviy, S., 518
Skaalvik, E.M., 317
Skeels, H.M., 312
Skinner, B.F., 17, 196, 198, 381
Skodal, A.E., 493, 503, 504, 515
Skre, I., 501

Sladek, M., 151
Slater, A., 372
Slater, P.C., 239
Slavin, R.E., 576
Sleek, S., 28
Slife, B.D., 544
Sloan, R.P., 470
Smalls, Y., 536
Smart, D., 389
Smiley, P., 381
Smith, B.W., 470
Smith, C.T., 160
Smith, D.E., 164, 243
Smith, D.N., 575, 576
Smith, D.V., 117
Smith, J.H., 380
Smith, K.H., 97
Smith, L.B., 372
Smith, M.L., 543
Smith, P.B., 346, 583, 585
Smith, R.E., 462
Smith, S.K., 28
Smith, S.M., 245, 253
Smith, T.W., 467
Smollar, J., 396
Smythe, P.M., 311
Snidman, N., 371
Snodgrass, S.E., 359
Snyder, M., 563, 564, 571
Snyder, S.H., 53
Snyderman, M., 295
Sogon, S., 583
Solomon, D.A., 548
Solomon, R.L., 137, 332
Solotaroff, L., 251
Somer, E., 148
Sommers-Flanagan, J., 347
Sommers-Flanagan, R., 347
Son, L.K., 269
Sonnega, A., 477
Sonstroem, R.J., 469
Sora, I., 122
Sorenson, E.R., 361
Soule, C.R., 563
Soussignan, R., 354
South, N., 177
Southern, S., 507
Soyguet, G., 513
Spangenberg, E.R., 97, 98
Spanos, N.P., 254
Speisman, J.C., 354
Spence, J., 347
Sperling, G., 226, 231
Sperry, R.W., 19, 66
Spettle, C.M., 284
Spiegel, D., 468
Spirito, A., 398
Springen, K., 409
Squire, L.R., 236, 239
Squire, S., 336
Sridhar, K.S., 174

Srinivasan, M.V., 129
Staats, H., 555
Stack, S., 403
Stamm, B.H., 532
Stancliffe, R.J., 320
Stankov, L., 298
Stanley, J.C., 316
Stanton, C., 398
Stanton, M.D., 544
Stawinski, P., 126, 129
Steele, C.M., 166, 167, 168
Steffen, V.J., 346
Steiger, H., 337
Stein, J., 175
Steiner, J.E., 590
Steinhauer, J., 399
Steinmetz, J.E., 189
Stelmack, R.M., 302
Stern, L., 229
Stern, P., 117
Sternberg, R.J., 295, 296, 297, 299, 314, 321, 322
Stevens, G., 22
Stevens, N., 470
Stevenson, H.W., 317, 318
Stevenson, J., 82
Stewart, E., 541
Stewart, R.H., 563
Stickgold, R., 154
Stiles, W.B., 430
Stock, M.B., 311
Stodghill, R., 392
Stone, A.A., 462
Stone, J.S., 113, 157
Stone, R.E., 567, 568
Stone, W.F., 573
Stone, W.L., 530
Stoner, J.A.F., 590
Storch, E.A., 579
Storch, J.B., 579
Storm, L., 98
Stowell, J.R., 467
Strausbaugh, H.J., 121
Strecker, R.E., 151
Strecker, R.R., 151
Streissguth, A.P., 369
Strickland, B.R., 24, 28
Stuss, D.T., 233, 240, 250
Styfco, S.J., 313
Styles, I.M., 571
Stylianou, D.A., 262
Subotnik, K.L., 517
Sue, S., 556
Suga, N., 109
Suh, E.M., 352
Suhr, J.A., 233
Sullivan, P.F., 338
Suls, J., 569
Sumova, A., 151
Sundel, S.S., 536

Surratt, H.L., 170
Sussman, A.L., 262
Swaab, D.F., 27, 343
Swan, N., 173
Swann Jr., W.B., 563
Symons, C.S., 247
Szabo, Z., 172
Szatkowska, I., 240
Szobiova, E., 322

T

Tagano, D.W., 195
Takaki, A., 334
Takami, S., 117
Takemoto-Chock, N., 434
Takeuchi, S.A., 569
Tamis, J.E., 26
Tan, D.T.Y., 568
Tang, Y.P., 85
Tanner, J.M., 391
Tanofsky, M.B., 336
Tartter, V.C., 373
Tavris, C., 26
Taylor, B., 240
Taylor, D.M., 346, 576
Taylor, N., 446
Taylor, S.E., 253, 359, 457, 458, 462, 463, 470, 471, 562, 563
Tedeschi, R.G., 478
Tellegen, A., 437
Terman, L.M., 320
Terrace, H.S., 269, 271
Testa, M., 168
Tharp, R.G., 204
Thelen, E., 375
Thiffault, P., 331
Thomas, A., 370
Thomas, S.G., 549
Thompson, C.M., 337
Thompson, J.K., 337, 397
Thompson, N.S., 268
Thompson, P.M., 70
Thompson, T., 458
Thorne, F., 118
Thornhill, R., 340
Thune, L.E., 244
Thurber, J.G., 148
Thurstone, L.L., 296
Tincoff, R., 380
Titcomb, A.L., 253
Tobler, I., 149
Toft, M.D., 575
Tomarken, A.J., 67
Tomkins, S.S., 354
Tooby, J., 20, 332, 356
Torgerson, S., 501
Torrance, E.P., 591
Torrey, E.F., 516

Torrubia-Beltri, R., 390
Tosi, H., 453
Toth, S.L., 493
Tovee, M.J., 240
Tranel, D., 357, 397
Treaster, J.B., 174
Treisman, A.M., 129, 228
Triandis, H.C., 346, 566, 590
Trice, A.D., 39
Trichopoulou, A., 472
Trimble, M.R., 516
Tronick, E.Z., 359
Trost, M., 581, 584
Trotter, R.J., 354
True, W.R., 512
Tryon, R.C., 310
Tryon, W.W., 534
Tsien, J.Z., 85, 86
Tubb, V.A., 253
Tucker, C.M., 24
Tully, T., 243
Tulving, E., 70, 235
Tupes, E.C., 434
Turkheimer, E., 314, 388
Turnage, J.J., 618
Turnbull, S., 126, 336
Turner, C.W., 467
Turner, S.M., 501
Tuttle, J.M., 616
Tversky, A., 282, 283
Tyrer, P., 511

U

Uchino, B.N., 469, 470
Uhl, G.R., 84, 122
Uhlig, N., 319
Ulf, E., 129
Ulrich, R., 345
Umahara, M., 334
Underwood, B.J., 244
Underwood, G., 97
Uno, D., 470
Urbina, S., 295, 302, 307, 445
U.S. Bureau of the Census, 399, 403
USA Today, 508

V

Vache, K., 496
Vaidya, C.J., 71, 518
Vaillant, G.E., 405, 439, 470, 471
Vaisse, C., 334
Valentine, E., 225, 251
Valian, V., 403
Vallacher, R.R., 581
vanBoxtel, M.P.J., 409
VandenBox, G., 532

Vanderploeg, J.M., 120
Vanderpool, H.Y., 470
Vanderschuren, L.J., 518
van der Voort, T.H.A., 147
van de Vijver, F.J.R., 475
van Elst, L.T., 516
Van-Hoff, J.C., 233
Van Natta, P., 166
Van Praag, H., 57
Van Yperen, N.W., 569
Varki, A., 81
Vauclair, J., 269
Vaughn, B.E., 313, 388
Vaughn, D., 591
Vazdarjanova, A., 241
Vecera, S.P., 126
Veldhuis, J.D., 374
Vermetten, E., 237, 239
Vernon, D., 200
Vernon, P.A., 302
Vgontzas, A.N., 156
Viers, D., 403
Viglione, D.J., 446
Vij, K., 55
Viken, R.J., 437
Villegas, M., 240
Vincent, N.K., 336
Vinnicombe, S., 593
Violani, C., 199
Viswesvaran, C., 435
Vogel, E.K., 126
Vogt, R.A., 338
von Frisch, K., 270
von Glaserfeld, E., 271
von Hippel, W., 138
von Hofsten, C., 375
Vossel, G., 212
Voydanoff, P., 387
Voyer, D., 316
Voyer, S., 316
Vygotsky, L.S., 378

W

Wadden, T.S., 338
Waddill, P.J., 248
Waddington, K.D., 270
Wade, T.D., 337
Wagner, B.M., 398
Wagner, R.K., 296
Wahlsten, D., 80, 81
Waite, P.O., 339
Walchle, S.B., 285
Waldron, M., 388
Walen, H.R., 313
Walk, R.D., 372
Walker, E.F., 489
Wall, P.D., 122, 123
Wallerstein, J.S., 475
Walster, E., 569

Walster, G.W., 569
Walters, E.E., 337
Walton, G.E., 372
Waltz, J.A., 64
Wampold, B.E., 542, 543
Wang, C., 534
Wang, Q., 250
Wanous, J.P., 611
Ward, A., 126, 336
Ward, L.M., 123
Ward, T., 20, 86
Warrington, E.K., 237
Washburn, M.F., 22
Wass, T.S., 368
Waterman, C.K., 430
Waters, A.J., 280
Watkins, B.A., 389
Watkins, C.E., 446
Watkins, L.R., 123
Watkins, M.J., 233
Watkins, P.C., 496
Watson, D., 495, 500
Watson, D.L., 204
Watson, J.B., 16, 17, 147, 188
Watson, S.J., 123
Waugh, N., 229
Wauters, M., 334
Weaver, D.R., 152
Webb, W.B., 150
Wechsler, H., 168
Wedeking, C., 118, 340
Wehr, T.A., 152
Weinberg, M.K., 359
Weinberg, R.S., 473
Weinberger, D.R., 516
Weiner, I.B., 446
Weingarten, S.M., 563
Weingartner, H., 245
Weingold, M.F., 566
Weinstein, R.S., 563
Weinstein, S., 121
Weiskrantz, L., 104, 237
Weissman, M.M., 496
Weisz, J.R., 521, 522
Wells, G.L., 252, 253
Welte, J.W., 168
Werker, F.J., 373

Werker, J.F., 373
Werner, E.E., 323, 395, 458
Wessels, H., 388
Westen, D., 161, 237, 418
Westra, T., 374
Wheeler, L., 568
Wheeler, M.A., 233, 240, 250
Whiffen, V.E., 496
Whisman, M.A., 453
Whitbourne, S.K., 407
White, D.P., 156
White, K.K., 238
White, M.A., 336, 338
Whitehead, P.R., 122
Whorf, B.L., 265
Widiger, T.A., 488, 520
Wielkiewicz, R.M., 319
Wiener, V.L., 589
Wiens, A.N., 535
Wierzbicki, M., 446
Wiesel, T.N., 103, 129
Wiggins, J.S., 434
Wilcoxon, H.C., 192
Wilder, B.J., 169
Wilding, J., 225, 251
Wiley, J., 280
Wilfley, D.E., 336
Wilke, R.R., 248
Wilkens, H.T., 97
Will, G., 390
Willen, J.D., 372
Willerman, L., 80, 311
Williams, J.C., 467
Williams, J.E., 389, 435
Williams, J.H., 520, 554
Williams, K.A., 380, 382
Williams, K.D., 591
Williams, L., 555
Williams, L.M., 62
Williams, R.A., 493
Williams, R.M., 574
Williams, S., 532
Williams, T.P., 583
Williams, W.M., 309, 387
Willis, S.L., 404, 409
Wilson, B.J., 390
Wilson, D., 542

Wilson, G.D., 509
Wilson, G.T., 336
Wilson, N.M., 156
Wilson, R., 405
Wilson, T.D., 565, 586
Wincze, P., 507
Wing, H., 323
Wing, R.R., 338
Winn, P., 61, 334
Winner, E., 321
Winston, A., 533
Winston, B., 533
Wiseman, R., 98
Witelson, S.F., 67
Witkin, A.H., 137
Wolf, S.S., 280, 516
Wolfson, C., 410
Wolfson, D.B., 410
Wolpe, J., 190
Wolpe, P.R., 534
Wolpert, D.M., 121
Wolsko, C., 284
Wong, F.Y., 346
Woo, A., 332
Wood, F., 240
Wood, J., 478
Wood, L.A., 436
Wood, N.L., 228
Wood, W., 346, 463
Woodruff-Pak, D.S., 189
Woods, S.C., 334, 335
Woodward, K.L., 409
Woody, E., 179
Woodyard, E., 311
Woolard, J.L., 553, 556
Worchel, S., 578
Word, L.E., 588
Wortman, C.B., 475
Wright, A.A., 233
Wright, C.I., 371
Wright, J.C., 390
Wright, R., 10, 20
Wyatt, W.J., 83
Wynn, K., 378
Wyrwicka, W., 370
Wysocki, C.J., 117

Y

Yaffe, K., 78
Yahiro, K., 453
Yalom, I.D., 539
Yamamoto, K., 323
Yang, Z., 339
Yanovski, J.A., 338
Yanovski, S.Z., 338
York, J.L., 168
Yotsutsuji, T., 488, 516
Young, Q.W., 242
Youniss, J., 396
Yu, S.M., 369
Yuan, J., 172
Yung, L.L., 78

Z

Zack, J.S., 160
Zadra, A., 155
Zajonc, R.B., 97, 354
Zaragoza, M.S., 253
Zehr, D., 14
Zeidner, M., 298
Zeki, S., 104
Zettin, M., 240
Zevon, M.A., 468
Zhang, S., 129
Zhang, X., 107
Zhang, Z.B., 468
Zhao, Z., 240
Ziemba-Davis, M., 347
Zigler, E., 313
Zimmerman, R.R., 344
Zipursky, R.B., 516
Zisapel, N., 151
Zito, J.M., 548
Zoellner, L., 478
Zubek, J., 312
Zubieta, J., 123
Zuroff, D.C., 537, 544
Zwolan, T.A., 113

SUBJECT INDEX

A

Ability, 294, 295
Abnormal behavior, 485
Absolute refractory period, 51
Absolute threshold, 95
Academic and applied psychology, 41
Acetylcholine (ACh), 52, 54
Achievement motive, 347–348
Activation-synthesis theory, 160
Actor-observer effect, 565
Actualizing tendency, 432
Acute stress disorder, 500
Adaptation, 96
   visual, 101–102
Addiction, 164, 176
Additive color mixing, 106
Adjustment, 452
Adolescence, 391–399
   cognitive changes, 394
   identity formation, 396–397
   personality and social development, 394–395
   physical changes, 392–393
   problems of, 397–399
Adolescent psychologists, 4
Adoption studies, 83–84
Adrenal cortex, 78
Adrenal glands, 78
Adrenaline, 464
Adrenal medulla, 78
Adrenocorticotropic hormone (ACTH), 78
Adulthood, 399–406
   cognitive changes, 404–405
   love, partnerships, and parenting, 399–400
   parenthood, 400–402
   personality changes, 405–406
   relationship, ending, 402–403
   work, 403–404
Aerial perspective, 130
Affect, 492
Affiliation motive, 348
Afterimages, 102
   color, 107
Aggression, 345–347
   and culture, 345, 346
   and gender, 346–347
Agoraphobia, 499

Alarm reaction, 464
Alcohol, 166–169
   binge drinking, 168–169
   women, 168
Alcoholics Anonymous, 541
Alcohol myopia, 167
Algorithms, 276
All-or-none law, 50
Alpha waves, 70, 153
Altered states of consciousness, 145
Altruism, 20
   Holocaust, 588–589
Altruistic behavior, 587
Altruistic Personality Project, 589
Alzheimer's disease, 243, 409–410
American Psychological Association (APA), 22, 43
   code of ethics, 38
   divisions in, 4, 6–7
   guidelines, 39
Amniocentesis, 88
Amphetamine psychosis, 516
Amphetamines, 171–172
Amplitude, 109
Amygdala, 62
Anal stage, 423
Analytical intelligence, 297
Analytic psychology, 424
Androgen, 77
Anima/animus, 425
Animal cognition, 268–270
Animal Welfare Act, 40
Anorexia nervosa, 335
Anosmia, 116
Anthropocentrism, 268
Anthropomorphism, 268
Antianxiety medication, 549
Antidepressant drugs, 548–549
Antigens, 467
Antipsychotic drugs, 546–547
Antisocial personality disorder, 512
   causes of, 512–513
Anvil, 111, 113
Anxiety, 420, 426
Anxiety disorders, 498–501
   causes of, 500–501
   generalized anxiety disorder, 499
   obsessive-compulsive disorder (OCD), 500

panic disorder, 499
   specific phobias, 498–499
Apnea, 155–156
Apparent movement, 134
Approach/approach conflict, 456
Approach/avoidance conflict, 456
Aptitude, 294, 295
Archetypes, 424
Arousal theory, 330–332
Association areas
   brain, 63
Ataque de nervios, 521
Attachment
   development of, 384
Attention, 227–229
Attention deficit disorder (ADD), 199
Attention deficit/hyperactivity disorder (ADHD), 71, 518
Attitude change, 577–580
   cognitive dissonance theory, 579–580
   communication model, 578
   persuasion, process of, 577–578
Attitudes, 571–580
   change, 577–580
   development, 571–572
   discrimination, 572–577
   nature of, 571–572
   prejudice, 572–577
Attribution, 564–566
   behavior, explaining, 564–565
   biases in, 565–566
   cultures, across, 566
Attribution theory, 564
Auditory registers, 226–227
Authoritarianism, 573
Authoritarian personality, 573
Autistic disorder519
Autobiographical memory, 249–250
Autoganzfeld, 98
Autoimmune disorders, 190
Autokinetic illusion, 134
Automaticity, 283
Autonomic nervous system, 59, 73–75
Autonomous work group, 616
Autonomy, in infants, 384

Availability, 283
Average, 599
Averse conditioning, 534–535
Avoidance/avoidance conflict, 456
Avoidance training, 197
Avoidant personality disorder, 511
Axons, 48, 51

B

Babbling, 380
Backward conditioning, 208
Barbiturates, 169–170
Basic trust, 384
Basilar membrane, 111
Bayley Scales of Infant Development, 303
Beck's cognitive therapy, 538
Behavior
    abnormal, 485
    altruistic, 587
    helping, 587–590
    interpreting, 564
    modification of own, 204
    operant, 193
    organizational, 593–594
    sex-typed, 389
    sexual, 341–342
    study of, 16–17
    superstitious, 198
Behavior contracting, 535
Behavior genetics, 79, 80–84
    adoption studies, 83–84
    animal, 81–82
    human, 82–83
    molecular, 84
Behaviorial geneticists, 5
Behaviorism, 16–17
Behavior therapies, 533–536
    classical conditioning, 534–535
    modeling, 535–536
    operant conditioning, 535
Beta waves, 70
Big Five, 434–436
Bilingualism, 382
Bimodal distributions, 603
Binaural cue, 132
Binet-Simon Scale, 300
Binocular cues, 130, 131
Biofeedback, 75, 200
Biographical study, 366
Biological clock, 151
Biological model
    psychological disorders, 487
Biological treatments, 546–551
    definition of, 546
    drug therapies, 546–549

electroconvulsive therapy (ECT), 549
    psychosurgery, 549
Biopsychosocial model, 489
Biopsychosocial theory, 122
Bipolar cells, 100
Bipolar disorder, 30, 493–495
Blackouts, 167
Blindsight, 104
Blind spot, 100
Blocking, 208
Body dysmorphic disorder, 503
Body language, 356–357
Borderline personality disorder, 511
Box score, 608
Brain, 59–65
    central core, 59–61
    cerebral cortex, 62–65
    limbic system, 62
    parts and functions, 61
    tools for studying, 68
Brainstorming, 278
Brightness, 105
Bulimia nervosa, 335–336
Bystander effect, 587

C

Caffeine, 170–171
Cannon-Bard theory, 353, 355
Careers, 40–43
Case study, 31, 36
Catatonic schizophrenia, 515
Central nervous system, 58–72
    brain, 59–65
    brain study, tools for, 68–71
    hemispheric specialization, 65–68
    organization of, 58–59
    spinal cord, 71–72
    studying, tools for, 69
Central tendency, 599
    measures of, 599–601
    differences among, 599–601
Cerebellum, 60
Cerebral cortex, 62–65, 94
Cerebrum, 62
Childhood amnesia, 250
Childhood disorders, 518–519
    Attention deficit/hyperactivity disorder (ADHD), 518
    autistic disorder, 519
Child psychologists, 4
Chorionic villus sampling, 88
Christensen-Guilford Test, 323
Chromosomes, 79
Chronic anger and hostility, 467

Chronic stress, 468
Chunking, 230
Circadian rhythms, 151
Clairvoyance, 98
Classical conditioning, 186–193, 534
    elements of, 186–187
    in humans, 187–190
    and immune system, 190
    selective, 190–193
Classical eyeblink conditioning, 189
Client-centered therapy, 529–530; see also
    Person–centered therapy
Clinical and counseling psychology, 7
Clinical depression, 493
Clinical psychologists, 7
    prescription privileges for, 42
Cliques, 395
Closure, 128
Cocaine, 172–173
Cochlea, 111
Cocktail-party phenomenon, 228
Cognition, 259
    animal, 268–270
    nonhuman, 270
    social, 561–570
Cognitive-behavioral model
    psychological disorders, 488
Cognitive changes
    in adolescence, 394
    in adulthood, 404–405
    in late adulthood, 409–410
Cognitive development
    in infants and children, 376–378
Cognitive dissonance, 579–580
Cognitive distortions, 495
Cognitive learning, 185, 213–219
    insight and learning sets, 214–216
    latent learning and cognitive maps, 213–214
    in nonhumans, 218–219
    observation, 216–218
Cognitive maps, 213–214
Cognitive psychology
    development of, 18–19
    rise of, 18–19
Cognitive revolution, 19
Cognitive-social learning theories, 438–441
    evaluating, 440–441
    expectancies, 438–440
    Jaylene Smith's view, 440

locus of control, 438–440
    self-efficacy, 438–440
Cognitive style, 137–138
Cognitive theory, 354
    challenges to, 354
Cognitive therapies, 536–538
    Beck's, 538
    rational-emotive therapy (RET), 537, 538
    stress-inoculation, 537
Cohort, 366
Cohort difference, 366
Collective unconscious, 424
Color
    properties of, 105
Color blindness, 106
Color constancy, 128
Color vision, 104–105
    in other species, 107
    theories of, 105–107
Communication, 594
Communication model, 578
Community psychology, 8
Compensation, 425
Compensatory model, 282
Competency, 491
Competitiveness, 347
Complementary traits, 569
Compliance, 584
Compromise, 460–461
Compulsions, 500
Computerized axial tomography (CAT or CT) scanning, 70
Concepts, 262–264
Concrete-operational stage, 377–378
Conditional positive regard, 432, 529
Conditioned food (or taste) aversion, 191
Conditioned response (CR), 186
Conditioned stimulus, 186
Conditioning, 16, 185
    backward, 208
    classical, 186193
    comparison of classical and operant, 201–213
    operant, 193–200
    Pavlovian, 186
Confirmation bias, 283
Conflict, 455–457
Conflict resolution
    in intimate relationships, 401
Conformity, 582–583
    cultures, across, 583
Confrontation, 460

Conscious experience, 146–149
  waking consciousness
    definition of, 146
    explanation of, 147–148
Consciousness, 145
  adaptation, 147–148
  altered states of, 145
  drug-altered, 162–178
  waking, 145
Contact, 344
Content validity, 306
Contingencies
  in classical and operant conditioning, 208–211
Contingency theory, 591
Continuity, 128
Continuous reinforcement, 209
Control group, 35
Conventional level, 379
Convergence, 131
Conversion disorders, 502
Convolutions, 62
Cooperative play, 387
Cope, 460
Coping strategies, 461–462
Cornea, 100
Coronary heart disease (CHD), 466, 467
Corpus callosum, 65, 66
Correlation, measures of, 605–607
Correlational research, 32, 36
Correlation coefficient, 305, 606
Cortical blindness, 104
Counseling psychologists, 7
Counterfactual thinking, 285
Couple therapy, 540
Creative intelligence, 297
Creativity, 322–324
  origin, 278–279
  tests, 323–324
Crisis intervention, 553
Criterion-related validity, 305–306
Critical period, 368
Cross-sectional study, 366
Crystalized intelligence, 296
Cue-dependent forgetting, 245
Cultural assimilators, 581–582
Cultural influence, 581
Cultural truisms, 581
Culture, 138, 581
  cognition, 267–268
  collectivist, 29
  definition of, 28–29
  emotion, 360–361
  individualistic, 29
  and memory, 255
  mental abilities, 317–318

Culture-Fair Intelligence Test, 303
Curiosity, 344

D ----------------------

Dark adaptation, 101
Daydreams, 147, 148
Day terrors, 451
Deaf culture, 114
Death, facing
  in late adulthood, 410–411
Decay theory, 242
Decibels, 109
Decibel scale, 110
Decision making, 281–286
  explaining, 286–287
  framing, 284
  heuristics, 282–283
  logical, 282
  under pressure, 284–285
Decision-making heuristics, 282–283
Declarative memory, 236
Deep structure, 261
Defense mechanisms, 420, 421
Defensive attribution, 566
Defensive coping, 461–462
Deindividuation, 586–587
Deinstitutionalization, 487, 551–552
Delta waves, 70, 153
Delusions, 514
Dendrites, 48, 51
Denial, 420–421
Deoxyribonucleic acid (DNA), 80
Dependent personality disorder, 511
Depersonalization disorder, 505–506
Depolarization, 50
Depressants, 165–170
  alcohol, 165–170
  barbiturates, 165–170
  opiates, 165–170
Depression, 86, 467, 492–493
  in adolescence, 397–398
  recognizing, 494
Depth perception, 129–133
  in newborns, 372
Desensitization, 17, 534
  therapy, 190
Desynchronization, 152
Developmental norms, 374
Developmental psychology, 4–5, 365
  methods, 366–368
Diabetes mellitus, 77
Diathesis, 489
Diathesis-stress model

psychological disorders, 488–489
Dichromats, 106
Difference threshold, 96
Direct coping, 460–461
Discrimination
  in classical and operant conditioning, 206–207
Disorganized schizophrenia, 515
Displacement, 422
Display rules, 361
Dissociation, 504
Dissociative amnesia, 504
Dissociative disorders, 504–506
  causes of, 506
  depersonalization disorder, 505–506
  dissociative amnesia, 504
  dissociative identity disorder, 505
Dissociative fugue, 504
Dissociative identity disorder, 505
Distance perception, 129–133
Distractor studies, 242
Diversity
  mental abilities, 315–318
  psychology and human, 24–29
Dominant gene, 80
Door-in-the-face effect, 584
Dopamine, 52, 54, 515, 546
Down syndrome, 320
Dreams, 158–162
  content of, 159
  information processing, 160
  necessity of, 161
  neural activity, 160–161
  reason for, 159–161
  as unconsious wishes, 159–160
  waking life, 161
Drive, 330
Drive-reduction theory, 330
Drosophila, 149
Drug abuse
  biological factors, 175–176
  explanation, 175–178
  psychological, social, cultural factors, 177–178
Drugs
  altered consciousness, 162–178
  antidepressant, 548–549
  antipsychotic, 546–547
  characteristics and effects of, 165
  depressants, 164, 165–170
  hallucinogens, 164, 173–174

lithium, 548
marijuana, 174–175
stimulants, 164
substance use, abuse, dependence, 163–165
Drug therapies, 546–549
  antidepressant, 548–549
  antipsychotic, 546–547
  lithium, 548
  other medications, 548–549
Dual coding, 231
Dying, acceptance of in stages, 410–411
Dysthymia, 493

E ----------------------

Ear, 111–112
  neural connections, 111–112
Eating disorders, 335–337
Echo, 227
Eclecticism, 544
Ecstasy, 172
Ego, 419, 420
Egocentric, 377
Ego ideal, 420
Eidetic imagery, 250
Eight stages of life, 429
Elaborative rehearsal, 235, 283–234
Electra complex, 423, 430
Electroconvulsive therapy (ECT), 549
Electroencephalograph (EEG), 70, 152, 199
Embryo, 368
Emotion, 329
  culture, 360–361
  expressed, 517
  gender, 358–360
  nonverbal communication of, 356–358
Emotional experiences, storing, 237
Emotional intelligence, 297–298
  five traits of, 298
Emotional labor, 360
Emotional memories, 236
Emotions, 350–355
  basic, 350–352
  theories of, 352–355
Empathy training, 540
Empirical evidence, 30
Empty chair technique, 531
Endocrine glands, 76
Endocrine system, 76–78
Endorphins, 53, 54
Environmental psychology, 8
Epinephrine, 78
Episodic memories, 235

Erectile disorder, 507
Erectile dysfunction (ED), 507
Esprit de corps, 348
Estrogen, 77
Ethnic conflict, understanding, 575–576
Ethnicity
 definition of, 27–28
Evolutionary biologists, 85
Evolutionary psychologists, 85
Evolutionary psychology, 19–20, 79, 84–87
Exchange, 569
Exhaustion, 465
Exhibitionism, 509
Expectancies, 438, 615
Expectations, 137
Experimental group, 35
Experimental method, 34
Experimental psychology, 5
Experimental research, 34–35, 36
Experimenter bias, 35
Explicit acts, 357–358
Explicit memory, 236–237
Exploration, 344
Expressed emotion, 517
External locus, 439
Extinction, 203, 534
Extraordinary memory, 250–251
Extrasensory perception (ESP), 98–99
Extreme stress, 474–479
 sources, 474–476
Extrinsic motivation, 332–333
Extroverts, 425
Eyewitness testimony, 252–253

F

Facial expressions, 356
Factor analysis, 434
Family studies, 82, 83
Family therapy, 539
Fantasy, 148–149
Fantasy play, 377
Fears
 evolutionary basis of, 191
 hierarchy of, 534
Feature detectors, 103
Female sexual arousal disorder, 507
Feminist psychology, 26
Feminist theory, 26
Fetal alcohol syndrome (FAS), 369
Fetal stage, 368
Fetishism, 509
Fetus, 368

Fight-or-flight response, 73, 170, 464, 466
Figures, 125
Five-factor model, 434
Fixation, 423
Fixed-interval schedule, 209
Fixed-ratio schedule, 209
Flashbacks, 174
Flashbulb memories, 251–252
Flavor, 117
Flooding, 534
Fluid intelligence, 296
Flynn Effect, 314, 315
Foot-in-the-door effect, 584
Forensic psychology, 8
Forgetting, 242–249
 biology of, 242–243
 experience, 243–246
 interference, 244–245
 reconstructive process, 245–246
 reduction of, 246–249
 situational factors, 245
 state-dependent memory, 245
Formal-operational stage, 378
Fragile X syndrome, 320
Framing, 284
Free association, 528
Free radical theory, 408
Frequency, 109
Frequency distribution, 600
Frequency histogram, 601
Frequency polygon, 601
Frequency theory, 113
Frontal lobe, 64
Frotteurism, 509
Frustration, 455
Frustration-aggression therapy, 573
Fully functioning person, 432
Functional fixedness, 277
Functional imaging, 70–71
Functionalism, 14–15
Functional magnetic resonance imaging (fMRI), 71
Fundamental attribution error, 565

G

GABA (Gamma aminobutyric acid), 54
Ganglion cells, 102
Gate control theory, 122
Gender
 constancy, 388
 definition of, 25
 emotion, 358–360
 identity, 388
 mental abilities, 315–317

roles, 26
 stereotypes, 25–26, 388
Gender-identity disorders, 509–510
 in children, 509
Gender-role awareness, 388
General adaptation syndrome (GAS), 464
Generalization, 17
 in classical and operant conditioning, 206–207
Generalized anxiety disorder, 499
Genes, 79
 dominant, 80
 recessive, 80
Genetics, 79–80
Genital stage, 424
Genome, 81
Gestalt psychologists, 125
Gestalt psychology, 18
Gestalt therapy, 530–531
Giftedness, 320–321
Glacagon, 77
Glia, 50
Glial cells, 50
Glucose, 334
Glutamate, 54
Glycene, 54
Goals, 615
Golgi tendon organs, 119
Gonads, 77
Goodenough-Harris Drawing Test, 303
Grasping reflex, 370
Great person theory, 591
Ground, 125
Group decision making, 590–591
 effectiveness of, 590–591
 polarization, 590
Group tests, 302
Group therapies, 539–541
 couple, 540
 family, 539
 self-help groups, 540–541
Growth spurt, 392

H

Hallucinations, 514
Hallucinogens, 173–174
Halo effect, 614
Hammer, 111, 113
Hardiness, 457–459
Hawthorne effect, 593, 611
Head Start, 313
Health psychology, 452
Hearing, 108–114
 disorders, 113–114
 ear, 111–112

sound, 109–110
 theories of, 112–113
Helping behavior, 587–590
 cultures, across, 589–590
Hemispherectomies, 47
Hemispheric specialization, 65–69
Hertz (Hz), 109
Heuristics, 276
 decision-making, 282–283
Higher-order conditioning, 207
Hill climbing, 276
Hindbrain, 59
Hindsight bias, 285
Hippocampus, 62
Holophrases, 381
Homeostasis, 330
Hormones, 76
Hues, 105
Human engineering psychologists, 617
Human factors psychology, 610, 617–618
Human genome, 80
Human Genome Project, 84
Humanistic personality theories, 431–433
Humanistic psychology, 18
Humanistic theories
 Evaluating, 433
Humanistic view
 Jaylene Smith, 432–433
Humor, 471
Hunger, 333–339
 biological factors, 333–335
 cultural and environmental factors, 335
 eating disorders and obesity, 335–339
Hunger drive, 334–335
Hypnosis, 179–180
 clinical applications of, 180
Hypnotic suggestions, 179–180
Hypochondriasis, 503
Hypoglycemia, 77
Hypothalamus, 61
Hypotheses, 10

I

Id, 419
Ideal selves, 433
Identification, 422
Identity crisis, 395
Identity diffusion, 395
Identity formation
 in adolescence, 395
Images, 261–262
Imaginary audience, 394

Immune system
  stress, 467–469
Implicit memory, 236–237
Impression formation, 562–564
Imprinting, 384
Incentives, 332
Inclusion, 320
Industrial/organizational (I/O)
    psychology, 8, 41, 593,
    610–618
  overview of, 610
Infallible clue, 357
Infancy and childhood,
    373–391
  cognitive development,
    376–378
  language development,
    380–382
  moral development, 378–380
  motor development, 374–375
  physical development, 374
  sex-role development,
    388–389
  social development, 382–388
  television, 389–391
Infantile amnesia, 250; *see also*
    Childhood amnesia
Inferiority complex, 425
Influence
  cultural, 581
  social, 581–586
Information-processing model,
    225
Information retrieval, 276
Insanity, 491
Insight, 214–216, 529
  human, 215
Insight therapies, 527–533
  client-centered, 529–530
  Gestalt, 530–531
  psychoanalysis, 527–529
  recent developments,
    532–533
Insomnia, 155–156
  occasional, coping with, 157
Instincts, 330
Institutionalization, 551–554
Instrumental conditioning, 17,
    193; *see also* Operant con-
    ditioning
Insulin, 77
Intellectualizaiton, 422
Intelligence, 294, 295
  analytical, 297
  comparison of theories,
    298–300
  creative, 297
  creativity and, 322–324
  crystalized, 296
  determining, 310–315
  emotional, 297–298

environment, 311–314
  extremes of, 319–322
  fluid, 296
  giftedness, 320–321
  heredity, 310–311
  heredity versus environment,
    314–315
  multiple, 297
  practical, 297
  theories of, 295–300
  triarchic theory of, 297
Intelligence quotient (IQ), 300
Intelligence tests, 295, 300–304
  criticisms of, 307–309
  group, 302
  IQ and success, 309–310
  performance and culture-fair,
    303–304
  reliability, 304–305
  Stanford-Binet Intelligence
    Scale, 300–301
  test content and score,
    307–308
  use of, 308
  validity, 306–307
  Wechsler Intelligence Scales,
    301–302
Interference, 203
Intermittent pairing, 201
Intermittent reinforcement,
    209
Internal cues, 245
Internal locus, 439
Interpersonal attraction,
    566–570
  exchange, 569
  intimacy, 569–570
  physical attractiveness, 568
  proximity, 568
  similarity, 568–569
Interval scales, 598
Intervention, 553
Intervention programs, 313
Interview, personal, 442
Intimacy, 569–570
  internet and, 569–570
Intonation, 380
Intrinsic motivation, 332–333
Introverts, 425, 562
Ions, 50
IQ tests, 87
Iris, 100
Irrational individuals, 425

J

James-Lange theory, 352–353,
    355
Job analysis, 611
Job enrichment, 616
Job satisfaction, 616

Just noticeable difference (jnd),
    96
Just-world hypothesis, 566

K

Kinesthetic senses, 119–120
Korsakoff's syndrome, 243

L

Language, 260
  cognition, 265–266
  control center in brain,
    67–68
  male-domination, question
    of, 266
  question of, 270–273
Language, structure of,
    260–261
  grammar, 260–261
  semantics, 261
  sound and meaning, 260
Language acquisition device,
    382
Language development
  in infants and children,
    380–382
  theories of, 381–382
Late adulthood, 406–411
  cognitive changes, 409–410
  death, facing, 410–411
  physical changes, 407–408
  social development, 408–409
Latency period, 423
Latent content, 159
Latent learning, 213–214
Lateral hypothalamus, 333
Laudanum, 162
Law of effect, 194
Leadership, 591–593, 617
  cultures, across, 592–593
  women in, 593
Lean production, 453
Learned helplessness, 198–199
Learning, 185
  cognitive, 185, 213–219
Learning sets, 214–216
Learning theorists, 216
Lens, 100
Libido, 423
Life changes
  and stress, 453
Life functioning, 485
Life-span psychologists, 4
Life style, healthy, 472–474
Light, 100
Light adaptation, 101
Limbic system, 62
Linear perspective, 130
Linguistic determinism, 265
Lithium, 548

Locus of control, 439, 457
Logical decision making, 282
Longitudinal study, 366
Long-term memory, 232–239
  capacity of, 232
  definition of, 232
  encoding in, 232
  maintaining, 233–235
  serial position effect,
    232–233
  types of, 235–239
Long-term potentiation (LTP),
    56, 85, 239
Love, in adulthood,
    399–400
Lowball procedure, 584
Lysergic acid diethylamide
    (LSD), 173, 174

M

Macroelectrode techniques, 68,
    70
Magnetic resonance imaging
    (MRI), 70
Magnetic source imaging
    (MSI), 70
Magnetoencephalography
    (MEG), 70
Mainstreaming, 320
Maintenance rehearsal, 231; *see
    also* Rote rehearsal
Major depressive disorder, 493
Male menopause, 406
Management Abilities Test
    (MAT), 612, 613
Management by objectives
    (MBO), 616
Mania, 493–495
Manipulation, 344
Marijuana, 174–175
Marital therapy, 540; *see also*
    Couple therapy
Masking, 227
Mastery, 347
Maturation, 375
Mean, 599
Means-end analysis, 277
Measurement, scales of,
    598–599
Measurement and statistical
    methods, 598–609
Measurements of central
    tendency, 599–601
Median, 599
Media violence
  aggressive behavior, connec-
    tions, 218
Meditation, 178–179
Medulla, 59
Melatonin, 76
Memories

emotional, 236
episodic, 235
procedural, 235
semantic, 235
Memory, 225
  autobiographical, 249–250
  biology of, 239–242
  childhood amnesia, 250
  cultural influence on,
      254–255
  declarative, 236
  explicit, 236
  extraordinary, 250–251
  eyewitness testimony,
      252–253
  flashbulb, 251–252
  formation of, 239
  implicit, 236
  improving, 248
  as information-processing
      system, 235
  long-term, 232–239
  recovered, 253–254
  short-term, 229–231
  storage of, 240–242
  types of, 236, 237
Menarche, 392
Menopause, 405
Mental abilities
  culture, 317–318
  gender, 315–317
Mental disorders
  causes of, 489
Mental illness and law, 491
Mental representation, 376
Mental retardation, 319–320
  causes, 320
Mental set, 277
Mesmerism, 179; see also
      Hypnotism
Meta-analysis, 607–609
Methamphetamine, 172
Microelectrode techniques, 68
Midbrain, 60
Midlife crisis, 405
Midlife transition, 405
Mild traumatic brain injury
      (MTBI), 493
Minnesota Multiphasic
      Personality Inventory
      (MMPI-2), 443, 445
Mirage, 137
Mnemonics, 246
Mnemonists, 251
Mob behavior, 586
Modeling, 535–536
Model-punished condition,
      217
Model-rewarded condition,
      217
Molecular genetics, 84

Monaural cue, 132
Monoamine oxidase inhibitors
      (MAO inhibitors), 547
Monochromats, 106
Monocular cues, 130
Monocular distance cues, 132
Mood, 587
Mood disorders, 492–498
  causes of, 495–496
  depression, 492–493
  mania and bipolar disorder,
      493–495
  suicide, 496–498
Moral development
  in infants and children,
      378–380
Morphemes, 260
Mortality frame, 284
Motherese, 380
Mothers Against Drunk
      Driving (MADD), 470
Motion, sensations of, 120
Motion parallax, 131
Motion sickness, 120
Motivation, 137
  arousal theory, 330–332
  drive-reduction theory, 330
  instincts, 330
  intrinsic and extrinsic,
      332–333
  perspectives on, 330–333
Motives, 329, 343–350
  achievement, 347–348
  affiliation, 348
  aggression, 345–347
  contact, 344
  curiosity, 344
  exploration, 344
  hierarchy of, 348–350
  manipulation, 344
  stimulus, 343
Motor development
  in infants and children,
      374–375
Movement perception,
      133–134
Multimethod research, 35
Multiple intelligences, theory
      of, 297, 298
Multiple personality, 505
Muscle dysmorphia, 336
Myelin sheath, 49

N

Narcissism, 511
Narcissistic personality disor-
      der, 511
Narcolepsy insomnia, 155–156
National Association of the
      Deaf, 114

National Institutes of Health
      (NIH), 40
Naturalistic observation, 30,
      32, 36
Natural selection, 84
Nature versus nurture issue, 8,
      79
Negative reinforcers, 194
Neonates, 369
NEO-PI-R, 443
Nerve, 48
Nervous system
  ability to repair itself, 57
Neural activity
  dreams, 160
Neural connections
  ear, 111–112
Neural impulse, 50–51
Neural plasticity, 55–59
  definition of, 55
Neurofeedback, 200
Neurogenesis, 55–59, 113
  definition of, 56
Neurons, 48–50
  afferent, 50
  association, 50
  efferent, 50
  inter-, 50, 72, 102
  motor, 50
  sensory, 50
Neuropsychologists, 47
Neuroscience, 47
  and psychological psycholo-
      gy, 5
  revolution, 488
Neurotic trends, 426
Neurotransmitters, 52–54
  effects of, 54
Newborn baby, 369–373
  perceptual abilities, 371–373
  reflexes, 370
  temperament, 370–371
Nicotine, 171
Nightmares, 155, 451
Night terrors, 155
Night vision, 100
NMDA receptors, 85
No-consequences condition,
      217
Nominal scales, 598
Nonconditional positive
      regard, 530
Nonconscious, 147
Non-REM (NREM), 154, 158
Nonshared environment, 387
Nonverbal communication
  body language, 356–357
  explicit acts, 357–358
  facial expression, 356
  personal space, 357
  voice quality, 356

Norepinephrine, 78, 464
Norm, 581
Normal curve, 602–603
  bimodal distributions, 603
  skewed distributions,
      602–603
Normal distribution, 602

O

Obedience, 584–586
Obesity, 337–339
Objective tests, 442–445
Object permanence, 376
Observation
  learning by, 216–218
  naturalistic, 30, 32, 36
Observational (or vicarious)
      learning, 216
Observer bias, 30
Obsessions, 500
Obsessive-compulsive disorder
      (OCD), 500
Occipital lobe, 64
Odorant binding protein
      (OBP), 116
Oedipus complex, 423, 430
Olfactory bulb, 116
Olfactory epithelium, 116
Omnivores, 117
Operant behavior, 193
Operant conditioning,
      193–200, 535
  behaviorial change, 199–200
  elements of, 193–194
  formation of, 17
  learned helplessness,
      198–199
  punishment, 195–197
  reinforcement, types of,
      194–195
  selective, 197–198
  superstitious behavior,
      198
Opiates, 53, 54, 170
Opponent-process theory, 107
Optic chiasm, 103, 104
Optic nerves, 102
Optimism, 457
Oral stage, 423
Ordinal scales, 598
Organizational behavior,
      593–594
Organizational psychology,
      610, 614–617
  job satisfaction, 616
  leadership, 617
  work motivation, 614–616
  work teams, 616–617
Organ of Corti, 111, 113
Orgasm, 507
Orgasmic disorders, 507

Oval window, 111
Ovaries, 77
Overtones, 109

P

Pain, 121–124
Pancreas, 77
Panic attack, 499
Panic disorder, 499
Papillae, 117
Paradoxical heat, 121
Paradoxical sleep, 154
Parallel play, 386
Paranoid personality disorder, 511
Paranoid schizophrenia, 515
Paraphilias, 508–509
Parapsychology, 98
Parasympathetic division, 75
Parathyroids, 76
Paraventricular nucleus, 334
Parenthood, 400–402
Parietal lobe, 64
Participants, 34
Partnerships
  in adulthood, 399–400
Pavlovian conditioning, 186;
  see also Classical conditioning
Peace psychology, 8
Pedophilia, 509
Peer group, 387
Perception, 93, 124–139
  constancies, 126–129
  distance and depth, 129–133
  ethnicity, influence of, 136–137
  extrasensory, 98–99
  movement, 133–134
  observer characteristics, 135–139
  organization, 125–126
  subliminal, 97–98
  visual illusions, 134–135
Perceptual abilities, in newborns, 371–373
  depth perception, 372
  senses, 372–373
  vision, 372
Perceptual constancies, 126–129
Perceptual experience, 139
Perceptual familiarization, 137
Perceptual generalization, 137
Perceptual illusions, 134
Perceptual organization, 125–126
Performance
  appraisal interview, 614
  evaluation, 613–614

rating system, 614
  standards, 438
  tests, 302
Peripheral nervous system, 59, 73–75
  autonomic, 73–75
  definition of, 73
  somatic, 73
Persona, 425
Personal discomfort, 485
Personal fable, 394
Personality, 138, 418
  assessment, 441–446
    direct observation, 442
    interview, 442
    objective tests, 442–445
    projective tests, 445–446
  authoritarian, 573
  changes, in adulthood, 405–406
  development of, 423–424
  disorders, 510–513
    types of, 511–512
  environment, interacting with, 439–440
  evaluating, 444
  heredity, 434
  psychology, 5–7
  and social development
    in adolescence, 394–397
  structure of, 419–420
  traits, 433
  type, 426
Personal space, 357
Personal unconscious, 424
Person-centered therapy, 529–530; *see also*
  Client–centered therapy
Personnel psychology, 610–614
  job analysis, 611
  performance evaluation, 613–614
  recruitment, 611
  selection interview, 612
  selection tests, 612–613
  training, 613
Persuasion, process of, 577–578
Pessimism, 457
Phallic stage, 423
Phantom limb phenomenon, 122
Phenothiazines, 546
Phenylketonuria (PKU), 320
Pheromones, 116–117, 118, 340
Phi phenomenon, 134
Phobias, 35
  social, 499
Phonemes, 260
Physical attractiveness, 568

Physical changes
  in adolescence, 392–393
  in late adulthood, 407–408
Physical development
  in infants and children, 374
Physiological psychologists, 5
Pineal gland, 76
Pitch, 109
Pituitary gland, 77
Placebo, 123, 177
Placebo effect, 123
Placenta, 368
Place theory, 112
Plasticity, 47
Pleasure principle, 419
Polarization, 50, 590
Pons, 59
Porteus Maze, 303, 306
Positive psychology, 20–21
Positive reappraisal, 471
Positive reinforcement, 196
Positive reinforcers, 194
Positron emission tomography (PET), 71
Postconventional level, 379
Posthypnotic command, 180
Posttraumatic growth, 478
Post-traumatic stress disorder (PTSD), 476–478, 500
Potential
  action, 50, 51
  graded, 50
  resting, 50, 51
Practical intelligence, 297
Practice effect, 305
Precognition, 98
Preconventional level, 379
Prefrontal lobotomy, 549
Prejudice, 572–577
  sources of, 573–574
  strategies for reducing, 574–577
Premature ejaculation, 508
Premenstrual dysphoric disorder, 490
Prenatal development, 368–369
Preoperational stage, 377
Pressure, 453–454
Prevention, 553–554
Primacy effect, 232, 562
Primary appraisal, 457
Primary drives, 330
Primary gain, 503
Primary motor cortex, 64
Primary prevention, 553
Primary reinforcers, 207
Primary somatosensory cortex, 64
Priming, 237–238
Principle of reinforcement, 194

Principles of conservation, 377
Proactive coping, 470
Proactive interference, 244
Probability, 607
Problem representation, 274
Problems
  in adolescence
    depression, 397–398
    self-esteem, decline in, 397
    suicide, 397–398
    youth violence, 398
  interpretation of, 274–275
Problem solving, 273–281
  experience and expertise, 280–281
  improving, 279
  interpretation of problems, 274–275
  obstacles, 277–280
  strategies, producing and evaluating, 275–277
Procedural memories, 235
Productivity, 593–594
Progressive Matrices, 303, 306
Projection, 421–422
Projective tests, 445–446
Prototype, 264
Proximity, 128, 568
Prozac, 546
Psychiatrists, definition of, 43
Psychoactive drugs, 162
Psychoanalysis, 419, 428, 527–529
Psychoanalysts, 15
  definition of, 43
Psychoanalytic model
  psychological disorders, 488
Psychobiology, 47
Psychodynamic psychology, 15–16
Psychodynamics, 418
Psychodynamic theories, 418–431
  evaluating, 428–431
Psychodynamic theory, 15
Psychodynamic view (Jaylene Smith), 428
Psycholneuroimmunology (PNI), 467
Psychological disorders
  classifying, 489–490
  gender and cultural differences in, 520–522
  historical views of, 486–487
  mental illness and law, 491–492
  perspectives on, 485–492
  prevalence of, 490–491
  theories of nature, causes, and treatments of, 487–489

Psychological research
  meta-analysis, using,
    607–609
Psychologists for the Ethical
  Treatment of Animals
  (PsyETA), 39
Psychology
  benefits of studying, 12–13
  careers in, 40–43
  cognitive, 18–19
  community, 8
  definition of, 4
  enduring issues in, 8–9
  evolutionary, 19–20, 79
  feminist, 26
  fields of, 4–9
  forensic, 8
  Gestalt, 18
  growth of, 13–23
  health, 452
  human diversity and, 24–25
  human factors, 610, 617–618
  humanistic, 18
  multiple perspectives of, 21
  organizational, 610, 614–617
  peace, 8
  personnel, 610–614
  positive, 20–21
  psychodynamic, 15–16
  racial and ethnic minorities
    in, 28
  research methods, 30–40
  as science, 9–11
  social, 561
  sports, 8
  women in, 21–23
Psychoneuroimmunologists,
  468
Psychopharmacology, 54–55
Psychosomatic disorders, 502
Psychostimulants, 518, 548
Psychosurgery, 549
Psychotherapy, 41, 527
  effectiveness of, 541–544
Psychotic, 493
Puberty, 392
Punishers, 193
Punishment, 195–197
  definition of, 197
Pupil, 100
Pygmalion effect, 563

R

Race, definition of, 27–28
Racism, 574
Range, 603
Rapid eye movement (REM)
  sleep, 154, 158, 160, 161
Rational-emotive therapy
  (RET), 537, 538

Rational individuals, 425
Ratio scales, 599
Realistic job preview, 611
Reality principle, 420
Real movement, 133
Recency effect, 232
Receptor cells, 94, 100–101
Receptor sites, 52, 122
Recessive gene, 80
Reconstructive process,
  245–246
Recovered memories, 253–254
Recovering alcoholic, 176
Recreational drugs, 163
Recruitment, 611
Reflexes, in newborns, 370
Regression, 422
Rehabilitation psychology, 8
Rehearsal
  elaborative, 234, 283
  rote, 283
Reinforced concrete, 194
Reinforcement, 194–195
  examples of, 210
  negative, 194
  positive, 194
  schedules of, 209–211
Reinforcers, 193
Relationship, ending, 402–403
Relative refractory period, 51
Relaxation training, 469
Reliability, 304, 489, 612
  of intelligence tests, 304–305
Remote Associates Test (RAT),
  323
REM rebound, 161
Renewal effect, 203
Representatives, 282
Repression, 421
Research
  ethics in, 37–40
    on humans, 37–39
    on nonhumans, 39–40
  media accounts, 87
  methods, 30–40
    case studies, 31
    correlational, 32–34
    ethics, 37–40
    experimental, 34–35
    multimethod, 35
    sampling, importance of,
      35–37
    surveys, 31–32
Reserpine, 546
Resilience, 457–459
Resistance, 465
Response acquisition, 201–202
  classical conditioning, 201
  operant conditioning,
    201–202
Response generalization, 206

Responsibility, 594
Reticular formation (RF), 61
Retina, 100
Retinal disparity, 131
Retirement, 408–409
Retroactive interference, 244
Retrograde amnesia, 243
Retrospective study, 366
Reward theory of attribution,
  569
Risky shift, 590
Ritalin, 548
Road rage, 455, 456
Rods, 100
Rooting reflex, 370
Rorschach test, 446
Rote rehearsal, 231; *see also*
  Maintenance rehearsal

S

Sample, 35
  random, 36
  representative, 37
Sampling, importance of,
  35–37
Saturation, 105
Savant performance, 319
Scales
  interval, 598–599
  nominal, 598
  ordinal, 598
  ratio, 599
Scatter plot, 606
Schedule of reinforcement, 209
Schemata, 234–235, 562
Schizoid personality disorder,
  511
Schizophrenic disorders,
  514–517
  causes of, 515–517
  types of, 515
Science, psychology as, 9–11
Scientific method, 9, 10
Secondary appraisal, 457
Secondary drives, 330
Secondary gain, 503
Secondary prevention, 553
Secondary reinforcers, 207
  in operant conditioning,
    207–208
Sedatives, 549
Seguin Form Board, 303
Selection interview, 612
Selection studies, 81
Selection tests, 612–613
Selective serotonin reuptake
  inhibitors (SSRIs), 547
Self-actualizing tendency, 432
Self-concepts, 432
Self-deception, 461

Self-efficacy, 438
Self-fulfilling prophecy, 563
Self-help groups, 532, 540–541
Self-hypnosis, 180
Self-imposed stress, 459
Self-managed work teams, 616
Self-monitoring, 571
Self-persuasion, 580
Semantic memories, 235
Sensation
  basic process, 94–95
  definition of, 93
  nature of, 93–99
  thresholds, 95–97
Sensation seeking, 331
Sense of self, 269
Senses, 115–124
  kinesthetic and vestibular,
    119–120
  of newborns, 372–373
  other, 114–124
  pain, 121–124
  sensations of motion, 120
  skin, 120–121
  smell, 115–117
  taste, 117, 119
Sensorimotor feedback, 354
Sensory-motor stage, 376
Sensory registers, 226–229
  attention, 227–229
  definition of, 226
  visual and auditory, 226–227
Sensory thresholds, 95–97
Serial position effect,
  232–233
Serotonin, 53, 54
Sex, 340–343
  behavior, 341–342
  motivation, 340–341
  orientation, 342–343
Sex drive, 340
Sex-role development
  in infants and children,
    388–389
Sex-typed behavior, 389
Sexual behavior, 341–342
  in late adulthood, 409
Sexual desire disorders, 507
Sexual development
  in adolescence, 392
Sexual disorders, 506–509
  paraphilias, 508–509
  sexual dysfunction, 507–508
Sexual dysfunction, 507–508
Sexual masochism, 509
Sexual motivation, 340–341
Sexual orientation, 26–27,
  342–343
  bisexual, 342
  heterosexual, 342
  homosexual, 342

Sexual reassignment surgery, 509
Sexual response cycle, 341
Sexual sadism, 509
Shape constancy, 128, 130
Shaping, 202
Short-term memory (STM), 229–231
  capacity of, 229–230
  definition of, 229
  encoding in, 231
  maintaining, 231
Short-term psychodynamic psychotherapy, 532
Sibling, 85
Significance, 607
Similarity, 128, 568–569
Sine wave, 109
Single photon emission computed tomography (SPECT), 71
Sixteen Personality Factor Questionnaire, 443
Size constancy, 127
Skewed distributions, 602–603
Skinner box, 202
Skin senses, 120–121
Sleep, 149–158
  circadian cycles, 151–152
  disorders, 154–158
  drug-altered consciousness, 162–178
  rhythms of, 152–154
  waves, 153
Sleep disorders, 154–158
  apnea, 155–156
  insomnia, 155–156
  narcolepsy insomnia, 155–156
  night terrors, 155
  sleeptalking, 155
  sleepwalking, 155
Sleep rhythms, 152–154
Sleep spindles, 153
Sleeptalking, 155
Sleepwalking, 155
Snowball effect, 586
Social action, 586–594
  deindividuation, 586–587
  group decision making, 590–591
  helping behavior, 587–590
  leadership, 591–593
  organizational behavior, 593–594
Social cognition, 561–570
  attribution, 564–566
  impression formation, 562–564
  interpersonal attraction, 566–570

Social cognitive theory, 217
Social development
  in infants and children, 382–388
  in late adulthood, 408–409
Social influence, 581–586
  compliance, 584
  conformity, 582–583
  cultural, 581
  cultural assimilators, 581–582
  obedience, 584–586
Socialization, 386
Social learning theory, 216
Social phobia, 499
Social psychology, 7–8, 561
Social Readjustment Rating Scale (SRRS), 453
Social support, 469
Solitary play, 386
Somatic nervous system, 59, 73
Somatization disorder, 502
Somatoform disorders, 502–503
  causes of, 503–504
Sound, 109–110
Sound waves, 109
Source error, 252
Spatial ability, 316
Specific phobias, 498–499
Spinal cord, 71–72
Split-half reliability, 305
Spontaneous recovery
  classical conditioning, 202–203
  and extinction, 202–206
  operant conditioning, 203–206
Sports psychology, 8
Standard deviation, 604
Stanford-Binet Intelligence Scale, 300–301, 306, 316
State-dependent memory, 245
Statistics
  prediction, using to make, 607
  probability, 607
Stepping reflex, 370
Stereoscopic vision, 131
Stereotypes, 563
Stimulants, 170–173
  amphetamines, 171–172
  caffeine, 170–171
  cocaine, 172–173
  nicotine, 171
Stimulus discrimination, 206
Stimulus generalization, 206
Stimulus motives, 343
Stirrup, 111, 113
Stoboscopic motion, 134
Strain studies, 81
Stream of consciousness, 147

Stress, 452
  biology of, 464–467
  body and brain, effects on, 239–240
  coping with, 460–464
    defensive, 461–462
    direct, 460–461
    socioeconomic and gender differences, 462–464
  extreme, 474–479
  and health, 464–469
  heart disease, 466–467
  immune system, 467–469
  on individuals, 457–459
  physical illness, 465
  reduction, 469–472
  sources of, 452–459
    everyday hassles, 453–459
    life changes, 453
Stress-inoculation therapy, 537
Stressors, 452
Stretch receptors, 119
Structual imaging, 70
Structuralism, 13–14
Structured interviews, 612
Style of life, 426
Subgoals, 276
Subjective well-being (SWB), 352
Sublimation, 422–423
Subliminal perception, 97–98
Substance abuse, 163
  and mental illness, 163
Substance dependence, 164
  signs of, 164
Subtractive color mixing, 106
Sucking reflex, 370
Suicide, 496–498
  in adolescence, 397–398
Superego, 419, 420
Superstitious behavior, 198
Suprachiasmatic nucleus (SCN), 151
Surface structure, 261
Survey research, 31, 36
Survival frame, 284
Swallowing reflex, 370
Symbolic gestures, 377
Sympathetic division, 74
Synapse, 51–55
  definition of, 52
Synaptic cleft, 51
Synaptic knob, 52
Synaptic space, 51
Synaptic transmission, 53
Synaptic vesicles, 52
Syntax grammar, 260
Systematic desensitization, 534
System of Multicultural Pluralistic Assessment (SOMPA), 309

Systems approach to psychological disorders, 489

T

Tabula rasa, 16
Taijin kyofusho, 521, 556
Taste, 117, 119
Taste buds, 117, 119
Teenage pregnancy, 393
Telegraphic speech, 270
Telehealth, 532
Telepathy, 98
Television and children, 389–391
  effects on, 390
Telomeres, 408
Temperament, in newborns, 370–371
Temporal disintegration, 175
Temporal lobe, 64
Tend and befriend, 463
Teratogens, 368
Terminal button, 49, 52
Tertiary prevention, 553
Testes, 77
Testing, school, 303
Testosterone, 77, 340
Tetrahydrocannabinol (THC), 174
Texture gradient, 130
Thalamus, 60
Thematic Apperception Test (TAT), 446
Theory, 10
Therapeutic alliance, 544
Therapies
  Beck's, 538
  behavior, 533–536
  client-centered, 529–530
  cognitive, 536–538
  couple, 540
  drug, 546–549
  electroconvulsive, 549
  family, 539
  frustration-aggression theory, 573
  Gestalt, 530–531
  insight, 527–533
  perspectives on, 550
  rational-emotive (RET), 537, 538
  self-help groups, 540–541
  stress-inoculation, 537
  virtual, 532
Thirst, 333–339, 339
Thought, 260–264
  concepts, 262–264
  images, 261–262
  language, 260
  structure of, 260–261

Threshold of excitation, 50
Threshold theory, 323
Thyroid gland, 76
Thyroxin, 76
Timbre, 110
Tinnitus, 114
Tip-of-the-iceberg, 147
Tip-of-the-tongue phenomenon (TOT), 238
Token economy, 535
Tolerance, 164
Torrance Test of Creative Thinking, 323
Tract, 48
Training, 613
Trait theories, 433–438
    development of, 433–434
    evaluating, 436–438
Trait theorists, 433
Trait view (Jaylene Smith), 437
Transference, 529
    negative, 529
    positive, 529
Transvestic fetishism, 509
Treatment
    alternative forms, 552–553
    cultural differences, 555–556
    gender differences, 554–555
Trial, 201
Trial and error, 275
Triarchic theory of intelligence, 297
Trichromatic theory, 106
Trichromats, 106

Tricyclics, 547
Twins
    fraternal, 82
    identical, 82
Twin studies, 82, 83
Two-Factor Theory of Emotion, 354
Type A personality, 466

U

Ultimate aggression error, 573
Umami, 117
Unconditional positive regard, 432
Unconditioned response, 186
Unconditioned stimulus (US), 186
Unconscious, 419
Undifferentiated schizophrenia, 515

V

Vaginismus, 508
Validity, 612
    of intelligence tests, 306–307
Values, 137
Variable
    dependent, 34
    independent, 34
Variable-interval schedule, 209
Variable-ratio schedule, 209
Variation, measures of, 603–604

range, 603–604
    standard deviation, 604
Ventromedial hypothalamus, 334
Vestibular sacs, 120
Vestibular senses, 119–120
Vicarious punishment, 217
Vicarious reinforcement, 217
Virtual therapy, 532
Vision, 99–108
    color, 104–105
        theories of, 105–108
    in newborns, 372
    night, 100
    system, 100–104
Visual acuity, 101
Visual cliff, 372
Visual field, 103
Visual illusions, 134–135
Visual registers, 226–227
Visual system, 100–104
Voice quality, 356
Volley principle, 113
Voluntarism, 13–14
Vomeronasal organ (VNO), 117
Voyeurism, 509

W

Waking consciousness, 145
Wallach and Kogan Creative Battery, 323
Weber's law, 96

Wechsler Adult Intelligence Scale-Third Edition (WAIS-III), 301, 306, 317
Wechsler Intelligence Scale for Children-Third Edition (WISC-III), 302, 306
Wechsler Intelligence Scales, 301–302
Well-adjusted person, 479–480
Widowhood, 411
Wish fulfillment, 419
Withdrawal, 461
Withdrawal symptoms, 164
Work, in adulthood, 403–404
Work and Family Orientation scale (WOFO), 347
Working backward, 277
Working memory, 229; see also Short-term memory
Work motivation, 614–616
Work orientation, 347
Work sample test, 613
Work teams, 616–617

Y

Yerkes-Dodson law, 331
Youth violence, 398

Z

Zygote, 79